# CIVIL PROCEDURE AND LITIGATION

# CIVIL PROCEDURE AND LITIGATION

Jack S. Emery, J.D.

Linda L. Edwards, J.D.

J. Stanley Edwards, J.D.

Africa • Australia • Canada • Denmark • Japan • Mexico • New Zealand • Philippines
Puerto Rico • Singapore • Spain • United Kingdom • United States

**West Legal Studies Staff:**

Business Unit Director: Susan Simpfenderfer
Executive Editor: Marlene McHugh Pratt
Acquisitions Editor: Joan Gill
Developmental Editor: Rhonda Dearborn
Editorial Assistant: Lisa Flatley
Executive Marketing Manager: Donna Lewis
Executive Production Manager: Wendy Troeger
Production Editor: Laurie Boyce
Cover Design: Susan Mathews, Stillwater Studio
Cover Image: Michael Dzaman

Printed in the United States of America
6 7 8 9 10 XXX 05

For more information, contact:
Delmar, 5 Maxwell Drive, PO Box 8007, Clifton Park, NY, 12065-8007;
or find us on the World Wide Web at http://www.westlegalstudies.com

**Library of Congress Cataloging-in-Publication Data**

Emery, Jack S.
    Civil procedure and litigation: a practical approach / Jack S. Emery, Linda L. Edwards,
 J. Stanley Edwards.
        p. cm.
    Includes bibliographical references and index.
    ISBN 0-314-12636-8
        1. Civil procedure—United States. 2. Legal assistants—United States—Handbooks,
 manuals, etc. I. Edwards, Linda L. II. Edwards, J. Stanley. III. Title.

KF8841 .E54 2000
347.73'5—dc21
                                                                    99-057371

# PREFACE

This book is directed to paralegal students striving to understand the civil litigation process and the rules that guide that process. It is broad enough in scope and detailed enough in coverage to be used as either an introductory civil procedures text or as a more advanced civil litigation text. Enough material is contained in this book to fuel a two-semester course, but it is organized in such a manner that it could be used in a one-semester course. Because workshops can be used or omitted at the discretion of the instructor and the chapters themselves can be used as either a review or as an overview of the litigation process, the text can be adapted to the needs of the class and the instructor.

## REASON FOR THE DEVELOPMENT OF THIS TEXT

The impetus behind the creation of this text was the desire to provide students with the tools they would need when they began their work in the paralegal field. Practicing paralegals are expected to have a working knowledge of the procedural rules and customs in their jurisdiction. Unfortunately, students are often poorly equipped to engage in the practical realities of paralegal practice when they graduate. Having been thoroughly indoctrinated in legal philosophy, principle, and terminology, they are typically bereft of any hands-on experience in the preparation of legal documents or the handling of legal paperwork. This book is designed to remedy that deficiency.

Another problem inherent in the writing of legal procedures texts is that every jurisdiction has its own set of procedural rules. Even those states that have adopted the Federal Rules of Civil Procedure have modified those rules to some extent and have adopted their own formatting and organizational requirements as well as other customs that dictate how documents are to be prepared and filed and how legal processes are to be conducted. Instead of simply adhering to the Federal Rules (which most texts do), we use the Federal Rules as a model and then provide prompts throughout the text, reminding the instructor to talk about the applicable local rules and norms. Space is allocated throughout the text so students can write in those rules and easily reference them in the future.

Preliminary reviews by faculty and responses from students who have used parts of the text attest to its uniqueness and usefulness. Students who have used the workshops to assist them in fulfilling assignments have consistently commented that they wished all their books provided them with such fail-safe instructions. The degree of student experience does not seem to matter. Both beginning and advanced students have benefited from using the workshops.

## ORGANIZATION OF THIS TEXT

This text is organized in a unique fashion. The first eight chapters are devoted to a sweeping overview of the civil litigation process. Terminology is introduced and basic concepts are explained. Following the chapters are nineteen workshops, each of which is dedicated to an in-depth exploration of a specific subject, such as the preparation of a motion, the drafting of a complaint, the serving of court papers, or the drafting of a response to a request for discovery. Each workshop contains a set of step-by-step instructions guiding the student through the task and explaining the reason for each step. These universal instructions are then applied to a specific fact situation, allowing the student to experience each step in the context of a concrete fact pattern. Each workshop closes with a "Learning by Doing" exercise that challenges the student to follow the step-by-step instructions using different facts.

Flexibility is the credo of this text. In that vein, the workshops can be used in any order and in any fashion that meets the needs of the class and the instructor. Some instructors may prefer to go through all eight chapters, providing students with a general knowledge of the litigation process as a whole, before delving into the workshops. Those who are using the text in a more advanced litigation class may want to use the chapters for review only and focus on the workshops for the bulk of the class. If time is limited, only selected workshops may be used, allowing students to develop skills in performing particular tasks and omitting other tasks for future classes. As an aid to instructors, "Workshop Alerts" are provided at the end of most chapters, letting instructors know which workshops most closely correlate with each chapter. Additionally, the Instructor's Manual has a suggested lecture outline for each chapter; this outline indicates at what point in the chapter the instructor may want to introduce a particular workshop.

## UNIQUE FEATURES

In addition to its distinctive overall design, this text has many other unique features designed to help students assimilate and apply information:

- Intriguing hypothetical situation that links each chapter (beginning with Chapter 3) with the other chapters and helps put the subject matter of each chapter in a factual context
- Local Notes that prompt instructor and students to consider the relevant rules and customs in their jurisdiction
- Ethical Etiquette features at the end of each chapter that highlight specific ethical considerations that students are likely to encounter on the job
- Practice Pointers at the end of each chapter and workshop that provide students with practical tips they will find advantageous when they enter the work world
- Techno Tips at the end of each chapter and workshop that inform students about technological tools and alert them to technical considerations related to law practice
- Putting It into Practice questions sprinkled throughout the chapters that challenge students to apply the information they have just read
- Litigation Lingo exercises in the form of crossword puzzles, word scrambles, and other game-like formats that allow students to practice their recollection and spelling of key terms
- Litigation Logistics that require students to look up the procedural rules in their jurisdiction governing hypothetical situations
- Procedural Ponderables that challenge students to apply the concepts they have learned to various fact patterns and then to go beyond the text and consider policy questions
- Answers to the Practice Exam, Litigation Lingo, and Litigation Logistics sections in Appendix A, allowing students immediate feedback
- A glossary and a copy of the most recent Federal Rules of Civil Procedure in Appendix B

In addition, the customary features of chapter objectives, summary, key terms, review questions, and a practice exam are provided for each chapter.

# HOW TO USE THIS TEXT

Because this text is designed to be as flexible as possible, instructors can use it in a number of different ways. We offer you four options:

### OPTION ONE

Cover the material in each chapter sequentially without reference to the workshops. In each chapter the students can:

* \*\* Respond to the Putting It into Practice questions found throughout each chapter
* \*\* Answer the Review Questions to test knowledge of basic concepts
* \*\* Take the Practice Exam (consisting of multiple choice, fill-in-the-blank, and true–false questions)
* \*\* Do the Litigation Lingo and Litigation Logistics exercises to practice vocabulary and apply the procedural rules
* \*\* Write out responses to the Procedural Ponderables to apply chapter content and to explore questions unanswered in the chapter

After going over all the chapters, work with the workshops on a discretionary basis. Students using this approach will have a basic understanding of the whole process before delving into the details of specific tasks. They will, in other words, have the big picture before being asked to master the details. Unless the class is a two-semester course, however, they will not realistically be able to cover all of the workshops.

### OPTION TWO

Have the students read all of the chapters as a review. To ensure that they have mastered the major concepts and basic vocabulary, have them answer the review questions, do the Litigation Lingo, and take the Practice Exam. They can compare their answers with those in Appendix A. Class time can then be spent going over each of the workshops in depth. Although the workshops can be completed in any order, their order of presentation in the book correlates with the typical sequencing of the litigation process.

This option works best with advanced students who have already had classes in civil procedures and are now ready to develop their practical skills in document preparation and management.

### OPTION THREE

Intersperse coverage of the workshops with the chapters. The workshops are designed to be able to be used independently or in conjunction with the chapters but if they are used concurrently, they correlate as follows:

CHAPTER ONE   INTRODUCTION
    No Workshops

CHAPTER TWO   COURTS AND FILINGS
    No Workshops

CHAPTER THREE   PREFILING PREPARATION AND PLEADINGS
    Workshop 1   Claims and Their Elements
    Workshop 2   Choosing a Court: Jurisdiction, Venue, and Choice of Law
    Workshop 3   Working Up a Case for Suit
    Workshop 4   Court Papers
    Workshop 5   Drafting Pleadings: Complaints
    Workshop 6   Serving the Complaint
    Workshop 7   Paper Flow in a Litigation Office: Service, Docketing, and Deadlines
    Workshop  8   Drafting Pleadings: Responsive Pleadings
    Workshop 19   Ethics in Litigation

This option allows students to develop their practical skills as they are learning the basic legal concepts and vocabulary. Instead of simply reading about pleadings, for example, they have the experience of preparing a complaint and an answer. The concept of service of process becomes more real as they learn to prepare a summons and calculate the time during which service must be completed. Doing all of the chapters and workshops will require at least two semesters.

**OPTION FOUR**

Intersperse the chapters with the workshops but use only certain workshops. This allows students to combine their assimilation of legal concepts and vocabulary with a practical application of those concepts. Choosing specific workshops allows instructors to adapt the text to limited timelines.

## ANCILLARY MATERIALS

The Instructor's Manual includes these elements:

- Suggested lecture outlines, which indicate specific points in the chapters to insert the appropriate workshops
- Classroom activities
- Answers to the review questions, Procedural Ponderables, and Learning by Doing exercises in the workshops
- Transparency masters that correlate with the chapters and workshops are also included
- Test bank

In addition, the following support material is available:

- PowerPoint slides are provided on CD-ROM
- *Computerized test bank.* The test bank found in the Instructor's Manual is also offered in a computerized format on CD-ROM. The platforms supported include Windows 3.1 and 95, Windows NT, and Macintosh
- *Web page.* Come visit this book's specific web page at www.westlegal studies.com where you will find sample materials, hot links, and text-

book updates as well as much more information on many other West Legal Studies products

- *Westlaw.* West's on-line computerized legal research system offers students hands-on experience with a system commonly used in law offices. Qualified adopters can receive 10 free hours of Westlaw. A modem is required

- *West's paralegal video library.* Adopters of 1–99 paralegal texts may select one video. Adopters of 100–199 paralegal texts may select two videos. Adopters of 200–299 texts may select three videos

- *"The Drama of the Law II" paralegal issues video.* Five separate dramatizations intended to stimulate classroom discussion about issues and problems faced by paralegals on the job. Dramatizations cover intake interviews, client confidentiality, UPL, etc

- *"The Making of a Case" video.* A case is followed from the court system to the law library shelf. Provides introduction to significant aspects of our legal system

- *"Arguments to the U.S. Supreme Court" video.* Accomplished lawyers, professors and judges play various roles as the case of the *F.T.C. v. The American Tobacco Company* is argued before a mock U.S. Supreme Court

## ACKNOWLEDGMENTS

We gratefully acknowledge the feedback we have received from the hundreds of students we have had the privilege of working with over the years. This text reflects our understanding of the learning process as they have demonstrated it to us.

Writing this text has at times been an intimidating task. Having launched into uncharted waters from an organizational and design standpoint, we have sometimes found reason to defer this project to other tasks with which we felt more comfortable. We owe thanks to Rhonda Dearborn, developmental editor, for her tenacious support. Were it not for her persistent "nipping at our heels" this book might never have become a reality. We are also grateful to Joan Gill, editor, for her enthusiastic support of this somewhat unprecedented approach to teaching civil procedures and litigation.

Finally, we very much relied on the feedback and insights from our unsung assistants, the reviewers. Their candor and eagerness to offer suggestions helped make this book as conducive as possible to clear and efficient learning. We acknowledge them now individually:

C. Suzanne Bailey, Western Illinois University, IL
Jeptha Clemens, Northwest Mississippi Community College, MS
Frances Coles, CSU
Richard J. Dimanin, Madonna University, MI
Paula D. Emmons, Watterson College, CA
Mary Kubicheck, Casper College, WY
Marion MacIntyre, Harrisburg Area Community College, PA
Kathryn L. Myers, Saint Mary-of-the-Woods College, IN
Larry Nordick, Moorehead State University, MN

## FEEDBACK

We would very much like to receive your comments, suggestions, and questions in reference to the text, especially in regards to its unique approach to presenting the material. Please feel free to contact us.

# ABOUT THE AUTHORS

**JACK S. EMERY, J.D.** Jack Emery practiced as a litigation attorney in Phoenix, Arizona for nearly twenty years before taking up a second career as a community college professor. He graduated first in his class from the Arizona State University College of Law. He has a bachelor's degree in civil engineering and a master's degree in biomedical engineering in addition to his law degree. Jack is a licensed patent attorney. Currently, he lives in the mountains of southeastern Arizona and teaches computer programming at Cochise College.

**J. STANLEY EDWARDS, J.D.** Stan has been a sole practitioner for over 22 years after a brief stint as associate patent counsel for Honeywell, Inc. He has offices in Cave Creek and Springerville, Arizona. Stan's initial career was as a digital design engineer with a bachelor's degree in electrical engineering. He has a general litigation practice and has tried more than 20 cases to juries. Stan is a *judge pro tempore* for the Maricopa County Superior Court and a certified arbitrator for the U.S. District Court for Arizona. Stan has twice been named volunteer lawyer of the month by the Maricopa County Bar Association.

**LINDA L. EDWARDS, J.D., Ph.D.** The author of two other books with ITP, *Tort Law for Legal Assistants* and *Practical Case Analysis,* Dr. Edwards is an attorney in Phoenix, Arizona. She has been an instructor in the Justice and Legal Studies Department at Phoenix College for 24 years. She has served as both program director of the Legal Assisting Program and as chairperson of the department. During her tenure as program director she was involved in getting the Legal Assisting program approved by the ABA. She is responsible for creating dozens of new classes in both legal assisting and criminal justice and is known for her innovations in the field of education. An individual of many interests, she has a bachelor's degree in chemistry, a master's degree in criminal justice, and a Ph.D. in holistic healing; she is also a certified homeopath, Bowen therapist, and Edu-K practitioner.

## DEDICATION

I dedicate this book to my wife Neble and son Jack, from whom were stolen the hours necessary to write it.

Jack Emery

We dedicate this book to our family members, Bill, Ester, Audrey, and Louis, without whose support and patience we could not have completed this project.

Stan and Linda Edwards

# CONTENTS

## CHAPTER 8

### ROAD MAP OF A LAWSUIT: JUDGMENT COLLECTION AND APPEAL   **193**

# WORKSHOPS

## WORKSHOP 1

### CLAIMS AND THEIR ELEMENTS   **221**

## WORKSHOP 2

### CHOOSING A COURT: JURISDICTION, VENUE, AND CHOICE OF LAW   **235**

## WORKSHOP 3

### WORKING UP A CASE FOR SUIT   **253**

## WORKSHOP 4

### COURT PAPERS   **273**

## WORKSHOP 10

### WRITTEN DISCOVERY                                  385

## WORKSHOP 11

### RESPONDING TO DISCOVERY REQUESTS  409

## WORKSHOP 12

### DISCLOSURE RULES AND LIMITATIONS
### ON DISCOVERY                                       435

## WORKSHOP 13

### DEPOSITIONS AND WORKING
### WITH WITNESSES                                     459

## WORKSHOP 19

### ETHICS IN LITIGATION                                                605

## APPENDIX A

### ANSWERS TO PRACTICE EXAMS AND LITIGATION LINGO AND LITIGATION LOGISTICS FEATURES                                           619

## APPENDIX B

### FEDERAL RULES OF PROCEDURE FOR THE UNITED STATES DISTRICT COURTS                             633

### GLOSSARY   725

### INDEX   733

# CIVIL PROCEDURE
## AND LITIGATION

# CHAPTER 1

# INTRODUCTION

## OBJECTIVES

**In this chapter you will learn:**

- What civil procedure is

- Why procedural law is important

- What the main steps in a lawsuit are

- What common lawsuit terminology means

*A drunk driver sideswipes your new sports car, which is parked at the time. It will cost thousands to repair. The drunk driver has no money, and his insurance company refuses to pay.*

*You decide to supplement your income by using some of your savings as a down payment on a house, which you can rent out at a profit. Your tenant loses her job, and stops paying rent. She refuses to move out.*

*Your cousin is starting up a new restaurant. Since his budget is limited, you agree to work part-time for free until the business is up and running, with the understanding that you will be rewarded appropriately at that time. Six months later, you have worked hundreds of hours in the restaurant, neglecting your studies, but the business is a success. Your cousin thanks you profusely and hands you a check for $1,000; he calls your suggestion that you are entitled to a percentage of the business "ridiculous."*

*You enroll in a karate class at your favorite health club. An instructor, disobeying the rules, launches a flying side kick toward your face, miscalculates, and breaks your nose. You feel that the health club should pay your medical bills. The health club's insurance company denies coverage—it claims that the instructor was a volunteer, not an employee of the health club.*

*You hire a contractor to install a new roof on your house. The job is finished and you pay for it. Two weeks later you return from an out-of-town trip to find that (1) it has rained; (2) the roof still leaks in a number of places; and (3) the ceilings, carpets, and several pieces of antique furniture have been destroyed by water damage. When you confront the contractor about his shoddy work, his reply is, "Yeah? What are you going to do about it?"*

Good question. What *can* you do about it when someone refuses to do what the law requires of them? What can you do when there is a genuine dispute about what the law requires? How can you force other people to carry out their legal obligations to you, even when they may prefer not to?

These questions are the central themes of civil procedure and of this text.

# BACKGROUND

In less civilized times and places, one way to resolve a dispute might have been to use direct physical force against one's opponent. In other societies, the king or the church might be asked to intercede. Outcomes tended to favor the powerful or the well connected; justice, if any, was often coincidental.

In modern America, most people believe that it is best to let the government resolve disputes between citizens, using its system of courts and police. In America, if you wish to force someone else to do something that they do not want to do, you must first go to court and persuade a judge or jury that you are entitled to what you are asking for. In other words, you sue them. If you win, the court can use the police powers of the government to force your opponent to obey the court's decision.

How do you sue someone? Do you just show up at the courthouse and ask to see a judge? What if your opponent does not wish to go to court and refuses to cooperate? What procedures must you follow to have your case heard and decided by the court? If your opponent refuses to accept the court's decision, what do you do then?

# WHAT IS CIVIL PROCEDURE AND WHY SHOULD YOU STUDY IT?

The study of civil procedure is the study of lawsuits and the rules that govern them. Its focus is not on legal rights themselves, but rather on what you can do about it when someone violates your rights. Civil procedure is the branch of law that tells you how to sue someone.

Why, you may wonder, does it take an entire branch of the law to give instructions on how to sue someone? All you want is to present your case to the court and get a final decision—surely that is not very complicated?

In small claims cases, procedures are often quite simple: You fill out a form stating what you are suing for, a court date is set, and the judge listens to each side and makes a decision.

In a typical full-blown lawsuit, however, a great deal of preparation must take place before the case can be presented for final decision. You and your opponent may not agree on what laws apply to the case. There may be disputes about what evidence will be allowed, or about what instructions should be given to the jury, or even whether the case should be decided by a jury. Your opponent may be holding documents or other evidence that you need access to. To prepare for trial, you will somehow need to find out what evidence and testimony your opponent intends to present. These are but a few examples of the "mini-disputes" that the court must resolve before a case can be tried and a final decision rendered on the main dispute. Before the judge rules on each issue, both sides will want to research the applicable law and present arguments. Each of these pretrial events has the potential to strengthen or weaken your case, or sometimes even to win or lose the case then and there.

## THE IMPORTANCE OF PROCEDURE

The difference between good and bad handling of procedure can make the difference between winning and losing. Remember, your opponent is likely to be doing everything possible to reduce your chances of winning. Most lawsuits are defended with sufficient vigor to make the outcome far less than a certainty, even in cases where the parties' rights may seem very clear.

You might reasonably ask how such a thing can be. How, for example, can you lose a suit against a drunk driver who sideswipes your car while it is parked? Surely even the most inept of lawyers should be able to win such a case? This question brings into focus the main reason for studying civil procedure and learning it well: It is not enough to have a good case that rests "on its merits"—you must also choose the right procedural steps and carry them out as well as or better than your opponent does. If you do not believe this, visit any law library and choose any volume of reported cases at random. You will find that it contains a significant number, perhaps even a majority, of cases that were either won by some clever procedural strategy or lost by a procedural mistake. To win consistently, you must be able to weave a carefully chosen series of procedural steps into a winning strategy, while surviving the attacks of your opponent and avoiding making any fatal blunders yourself.

The first step in learning how to put together a winning strategy is a thorough understanding of the rules that govern the conduct of lawsuits. In the chapters that follow, we will study those rules in considerable detail. In procedural law, perhaps more than in any other branch of the law, the details are important. Lawsuits are literally won or lost over such seeming minutiae as whether holidays are counted when computing a deadline or whether a particular paper was delivered to someone in the right way.

**S I D E B A R**

## Substance vs. Procedure

*Much of the law is devoted to making rules that regulate people's behavior in various specific situations. Tort law, for example, lays down rules that make it wrongful for a drunk driver to destroy your car or for a fellow student to break your nose. Contract law requires your tenant to pay rent as agreed and may make a roofing contractor liable for the damage caused by his poor workmanship. All of these are examples of rules of **substantive law**, and most people would agree that organized society could not survive and prosper without these and many other similar rules of conduct.*

*These substantive rules are, however, rather empty unless there is some way of enforcing them. It does little good to have a law requiring roofing contractors to perform their contracts in a workman-like manner if homeowners have no way to extract payment from contractors who fail to do the job properly. It will be of little help to you that the law prohibits drunk driving if the law does not also give you some way to force the drunk driver or his insurance company to pay for your car. Rights are meaningless without remedies. **Procedural law** is the law of remedies.*

To make the material in this text as meaningful as possible, we begin by defining common terminology, presenting some background ideas, and giving a quick overview of the main steps, or phases, in a lawsuit. In Chapter 2, we will study how court systems are organized. Then, in Chapter 3, we will offer a more detailed road map of the territory to which the remainder of the course will be devoted in the form of a step-by-step look at the procedural maneuvering in a typical lawsuit.

# TERMINOLOGY

In any academic subject, it is essential to use words accurately and to have a clear understanding of their meaning. Words encapsulate ideas; you cannot understand the ideas if you do not know the meanings of the words. In your career as a paralegal, your employer will expect you to be familiar with the common vocabulary of the law office.

Moreover, words take on a special significance in the law: Laws themselves are essentially just complex definitions of words. For example, if you sue the drunk driver who sideswiped your car, the judge will instruct the jury on the meaning of the word *negligence*. Whether you win or lose will depend on whether the members of the jury think the drunk driver's conduct fits that definition.

This book will stress correct use of terminology, and each chapter highlights definitions of terms pertinent to the subject of that chapter, with examples illustrating their meanings. You may also wish to refer to a law dictionary for additional guidance.

**Civil procedure,** as already noted, is the body of law that deals with the rules for conducting civil lawsuits. A civil lawsuit, or a **civil action,** is a process by which a person who believes that someone else has wronged her can ask a court to order her adversary to repair the wrong. A lawsuit is called *civil* to distinguish it from prosecutions under the criminal law (see sidebar). Criminal actions must be initiated by the government, and they

## SIDEBAR

# Remedies: Criminal vs. Civil

*The American legal system uses two main weapons to enforce its rules of behavior: criminal punishment and the civil lawsuit. Criminal punishment is intended to deal with offenses that damage society as a whole. Whatever you may think of its effectiveness for that purpose, the criminal justice system is of little use in, for example, getting a shoddy roofing contractor to pay for your ruined furniture. Only the government can bring a criminal prosecution—you can neither start criminal proceedings against your roofing contractor nor control the proceedings once begun. Worse, the criminal law's focus is on punishing or rehabilitating the wrongdoer and only incidentally, if at all, on compensating the victim. Even if you manage to persuade the government prosecutor that a crime has been committed—and breaching a contract, like most garden-variety misdeeds, is usually not a crime—getting the contractor punished will not replace your furniture or fix your ceilings.*

*In the examples given at the beginning of the chapter, the civil lawsuit fits your needs considerably better, though not perfectly. In most cases (but not all, as we will see), you can decide on your own whether, when, and for what to sue—you do not have to persuade a prosecutor or other government agency to act first. Nor will your strategy and timetable be dictated by the caseload and budgetary limitations of a prosecuting agency. You will be free to pursue your civil remedies in whatever way you deem best or can afford to pay for. And therein lies one of the disadvantages: Civil lawsuits, unlike criminal prosecutions, are not free of cost to the aggrieved party; in fact, they can be extraordinarily expensive for the person suing and for the person sued.*

seek to punish the accused. Civil actions can be filed by anyone (filing does not, of course, guarantee winning).

Usually, the remedy given by courts in civil actions is an award of **damages,** which refers to an amount of money determined by the court. In certain special situations, the court may order someone to do some particular thing (such as turn over title to property) or to refrain from doing something. Such an order is called an **injunction.** Or the court may enter a judgment for **specific performance** of a contract, ordering a party to do some particular thing that the party has contracted to do.

To **litigate** means to conduct or defend a lawsuit. A person who begins a lawsuit is called a **plaintiff.** A person who is sued is called a **defendant.** There can be more than one of each. The people who are suing or being sued are referred to as the **parties** to the suit. A plaintiff is a party, and so is a defendant. The lawyers are not parties, nor is the judge. The parties to a lawsuit are also sometimes called **litigants.** Do not confuse this with the word *litigator;* a **litigator** is an attorney who specializes in handling lawsuits.

Must a plaintiff or defendant be what the law calls a **natural person**—that is, a live human being? No; **entities**—artificial "persons" or organizations, such as corporations, partnerships, and limited liability companies—can be parties, and so can the estates of deceased persons. **Political subdivisions,** such as cities and counties, and government agencies at all levels can be parties in certain cases. The rules for deciding what kinds of entities are permitted to sue and be sued are not the same in every case or in every court.

Parties to lawsuits are usually represented by **attorneys.** The requirements to be licensed as an attorney vary from state to state but typically include graduation from an accredited law school, passing of a bar examination,

*Putting It
Into Practice:*

*Why might civil procedure arguably be one of the most important subjects for a paralegal to master?*

and a character investigation. Parties can usually handle their own lawsuits if they wish (although it may be imprudent to do so without proper training), but only attorneys may represent other people in a lawsuit.

We will often speak of the parties taking a particular action in a case—for example, we may say that Jane Doe has filed her complaint against Ajax Roofing Company—but this is really just a shorthand way of saying that Jane Doe's attorney prepared a complaint, signed it on her behalf, and had a messenger deliver it to the clerk of the court. In a lawsuit, for most purposes, when a party's attorney does a particular thing, it is the same as if the party had done it.

Lawsuits are conducted in courts. A **court** is an agency of the government that has the power to **adjudicate** (decide) particular kinds of disputes and render a **judgment** (a formal decision) that the government will enforce, through the use of its police power, if necessary. Various branches of the government have established courts; the federal government has courts, and so do the states, and the counties of most states. The governments of many cities have their own courts.

In general, each court has limitations on the kinds of cases it can decide. If a court has the power to adjudicate a particular kind of case, we say that the court has **jurisdiction** over that kind of case. For example, the federal courts have jurisdiction over disputes that involve questions of federal law. It may surprise you that state courts also, typically, have jurisdiction over disputes involving questions of federal law; in this respect, the federal and state courts are said to have **concurrent jurisdiction.** Thus, a plaintiff may have the opportunity to choose which court to sue in from among two or more courts that have jurisdiction. Deciding which court to sue in can be complicated, and we will discuss the issue in detail in a later chapter.

**Venue** is a concept related to jurisdiction; venue rules place further limitations on a plaintiff's choice of where to file suit and are intended to require suits to be brought at a place that is least inconvenient for the parties and witnesses. You may have heard of defendants in criminal cases asking for a change of venue in order, for example, to move the case to a location where it will be easier to find jurors who have not already been exposed to the facts of the case as told in the news media. In civil suits, however, venue transfers are more likely to depend on such questions as whether the defendant is a resident of the county in which the plaintiff brought suit, or whether the events that led to the dispute occurred in that county.

Each court is presided over by one or more **judges.** A judge is a government official, usually required to be a lawyer, who is appointed or elected to preside over cases. The judge's job is to control the adjudication of the cases assigned to him or her. The judge may or may not decide who wins and who loses in a particular case; often that decision is made by a jury, or, increasingly, by an **arbitrator,** or by the parties themselves when they reach a settlement. An arbitration may be required to hear a claim due to contract requirements, statutes, or rules of court. An arbitrator is a disinterested third party who may be chosen by the parties or appointed by the court. The method of selecting the arbitrator may also be contractual. In some courts, each case is assigned to a single judge, who is responsible for all aspects of the case from beginning to end. In other courts, judges are assigned to particular tasks, so that a number of judges may preside over various aspects of the case as it wends its way through the system.

Much of the activity in a lawsuit consists of written documents, prepared by the parties or their lawyers, which are **filed** with the court. Papers are filed by delivering them to the office of the clerk of the court, where they are added to the court's permanent file of the lawsuit. You will often hear people refer to court papers generically as **pleadings,** although, technically, the term *pleadings* includes only certain papers such as the complaint and answer. In this

---

*Putting It Into Practice:*

*Why is it important to know the jurisdictional powers of each court?*

## SIDEBAR

### Common Words, Uncommon Meanings

*What does the word party mean? Do you know? Are you sure?*

*We use this "trick" question to illustrate a very important point: The law often "borrows" commonplace English words to use as technical terms, giving them new and precise meanings that you would never guess at from their commonplace definitions. In ordinary English, for example,* party *is more or less synonymous with* person. *But in procedural law, as we have seen, a* party *is a person or other entity who is a plaintiff or defendant in a lawsuit. When a procedural rule refers to* any party, *it does not mean* any person*—it means anyone who is a plaintiff or defendant in the lawsuit in question. If you skimmed over the definition of* party, *assuming that you already knew what the word meant, you would find it impossible to make sense out of future material that depends on the distinction between parties and nonparties.*

*So be warned! When you see a word in* bold type *in this book, pay attention to the definition—do not assume its legal meaning is the same as its everyday meaning.*

text, we will use the term **court papers** to mean any papers generated in the lawsuit that are required by the rules to be filed with the court or to be delivered to an opposing party.

As you would expect, court rules typically require a party filing any papers with the court to deliver copies to the other parties to the suit. Delivery of a copy to the assigned judge may also be required. Delivering copies of a court paper to a person is often called **service.** Thus, if we say that Jane Doe's complaint was **served** on Ajax Roofing Company, we mean that a copy of the complaint prepared by Jane's lawyer was delivered to Ajax in some way that complies with the court's rules. There are detailed rules, which we will analyze in a later chapter, that specify how delivery must be made under various circumstances.

Lawsuits are made up of issues. An issue is simply a question about which the litigants disagree. A distinction that comes up a great deal in procedural law is that between **issues of fact** and **issues of law.** Issues of fact arise when the litigants disagree about what happened. For example, was the karate instructor who broke your nose an employee of the health club or not? That is a question of fact. Does the law require a health club owner to compensate someone injured by a volunteer instructor? That is a question of law. In an actual lawsuit, both issues would likely be disputed, but they would be decided in quite different ways.

Deciding issues of fact requires evidence. Evidence is any information that tends to establish the facts. The most common kinds of evidence in civil suits are **testimonial evidence** and **documentary evidence. Testimony** consists of a witness **testifying**—telling what he or she knows about the case after swearing an oath to tell the truth. Documentary evidence is written or recorded information—contracts, payroll records, computer printouts, and tape recordings are all examples of documentary evidence.

Issues of fact are ordinarily decided in a **trial.** A trial is a formal proceeding in which each side presents its evidence and argument. The purpose of a trial is to reach a verdict. A **verdict** is a formal, written decision indicating what was decided at the trial. Who does the deciding in a trial?: the **trier of fact.** In a jury trial, the trier of fact is the jury. In cases in which there is no right

## SIDEBAR

# Common Law Pleading

*Modern American procedural rules may seem arbitrary and exacting, but our system of civil courts has evolved a great deal from its ancestor, the English law courts of past centuries.*

*In all legal systems there is a constant tension between two competing goals. On one hand, we want the system to be flexible—we consider it unjust for someone to lose his case because he failed to follow some trivial bureaucratic rule. On the other hand, we want justice to be uniform and predictable; we do not want the outcome of a case to depend on the whim of the judge who happens to decide it.*

*Prior to the late fourteenth century, English civil procedure leaned toward flexibility. Nearly all procedural matters were handled orally, so the judge was free to fashion a solution to fit the situation at hand.*

*Beginning in the fifteenth century, the pendulum swung decisively in the opposite direction with the invention of what is today referred to as* common law pleading. *Suing someone consisted of convincing the court to issue a* writ—*a highly formalized document that had to conform to very specific rules. There was a writ for each type of case; if your grievance did not happen to fit one of the existing writs, you were out of luck. If you mistakenly chose a writ that did not fit your case, you lost, even if you would have been entitled to win had you used some other writ. You did not dare make any factual mistakes, because you were required to prove each and every fact set out in the writ, whether or not necessary to your case.*

*Over the ensuing centuries, the English civil court system spawned ever more complicated and arbitrary procedural rules. By the nineteenth century, civil cases could drone on for decades, and the court system was fodder for Dickensian satire. English litigants turned increasingly to the church for adjudication of civil disputes, taking advantage of the power of the chancellor—the head of the church—to jail anyone who disobeyed him. Modern injunction practice evolved from the practice of petitioning the English chancellor to order an opponent to do something.*

*In the twentieth century, reformers, seeking to make court procedure less arbitrary and complex, gained the upper hand in America. The Federal Rules of Civil Procedure, adopted in 1938, enormously simplified lawsuit procedure in federal courts, and most states followed suit in the next few decades.*

*The current explosion of litigation may be eroding this hard-won simplicity. Court systems find it efficient to create new divisions that specialize in particular kinds of cases, but each new specialty creates its own set of procedural rules. This promotes uniformity, allowing courts—and law offices—to create an efficient, "production line" operation. But it also makes the system less flexible and harder for nonspecialists to understand.*

to a jury trial, or in which the parties waive a jury, the judge acts as the trier of fact. The function of the trier of fact is, as the term indicates, to decide all of the issues of fact—in other words, to decide what really happened when the litigants do not agree on what happened.

Issues of law are always decided by the judge. Even if the parties disagree about what the law means, it is the judge, not the jury, who decides the issue. There is no need for evidence when deciding issues of law, which makes it possible for the judge to decide such issues at any convenient time, not just during the trial. Usually, the judge decides issues of law in response to a **motion** by one of the litigants. A motion is simply a formal request asking the court to decide some issue about which the litigants disagree.

# THE MAIN PHASES OF A LAWSUIT

What are the main events in a typical lawsuit? We can answer the question only by arbitrarily choosing what is "typical"—the rules of procedure offer great scope for creativity and variation. A lawsuit is a little like a car trip from Los Angeles to New York: The starting point and destination are fixed, but there are many possible routes. With that warning, we find it convenient to think of a lawsuit as consisting of several phases, as diagrammed in Figure 1–1.

---

**Figure 1–1   Phases of a Lawsuit**

| Phase | Tasks |
|---|---|
| Pre-suit | Investigate; form strategies; assemble evidence; explore settlement; choose forum |
| Preparation | Pleadings; discovery; motion practice; pretrial practice |
| Trial | Presentation of evidence; verdict; post-verdict motions; judgment |
| Post-Judgment | Appeals; collection procedures |

---

## PRE-SUIT PHASE

The real work of a lawsuit begins well before any papers are filed with the court. During what we will call the pre-suit preparation phase, attorneys for both sides may conduct investigations and attempt to negotiate settlements. It is also important for the attorneys to think through their strategies before filing suit; options will be more limited once the suit has begun and each side has stated its position in writing.

## PREPARATION PHASE

The lawsuit itself begins when the plaintiff files a complaint with the court. Plaintiff's goal is usually to obtain a favorable judgment, which usually requires getting the case to trial; defendant's goal is usually to have the case dismissed as early as possible. A number of things must, under typical rules of procedure, occur before a trial can take place. We categorize these as pleading, discovery, motion practice, and pretrial practice. These categories are arbitrary. We will call them *tasks* rather than *phases*, to emphasize that they do not necessarily take place in sequence—all four can be going on at the same time.

**Pleadings**—The complaint is part of what we will call the pleadings task, in which each party to the suit is required to state what the dispute is about and what it is that he wants the court to do. The goal of the pleadings is to define exactly what issues the court is being asked to decide.

*Putting It Into Practice:*

*A plaintiff is injured on a hike sponsored by the resort at which she is a guest. Who will decide whether the resort had any legal obligation to warn the plaintiff about the possible risks of going on the hike?*

**Discovery—** **Discovery** refers to the procedures used to locate evidence and prepare it for trial. In modern litigation, it is often necessary to obtain records and information from an opponent, and discovery procedures provide ways to do this. There are also procedures for obtaining documents or testimony from third parties—that is, people who are not directly involved in the suit. Naturally, not everyone cooperates, so procedures exist for forcing people to testify or turn over evidence. In a typical lawsuit, discovery goes on more or less continuously and accounts for a great deal of the time and effort expended prior to trial.

**Motion Practice—Motion practice** is the process by which the parties can ask the judge to decide preliminary matters. The parties almost always disagree about what questions should be decided at the trial and what lines of evidence should be allowed. It is most efficient for the judge to decide such things well in advance. Otherwise, the lawyers would have to waste time preparing for presentations they might not be allowed to make. Disputes also arise about discovery procedures and pleadings. At times, a party may refuse to do something—turn over evidence, for example—that the other party believes is required. In general, any time the parties are in disagreement about some procedure, one or the other can file a **motion** asking the judge to decide who is right.

**Pretrial Practice** —The task that we will call pretrial practice consists of accomplishing the necessary procedures and paperwork to get the case set for trial and allow the trial to begin. You might expect this to be a simple task, but the overwhelming case loads in many urban court systems have led to rules specifying various procedures that must be followed before a trial setting will be granted, and additional procedures may be required before trial can begin. These are intended to ensure that, in every case that actually goes to trial, the parties are fully prepared, have focused on the issues so that the court's time will not be wasted with unnecessary matters, and, in an increasing number of court systems, have made a reasonable effort to reach a settlement.

## TRIAL PHASE

Trials, like all other phases of a lawsuit, are governed by rules of procedure. These dictate such things as the order in which evidence and arguments are presented, and whether a jury will be used and if so what instructions it will be given. There are also procedures—motions for directed verdict and the like—that allow the judge to cut the trial short if one party or the other fails to offer enough evidence to support a decision in his or her favor. The trial typically ends in a verdict for one side. After the trial, the rules allow a short period of time for the parties to present motions seeking to have the verdict overturned or asking for the case to be retried. Then, the court will enter judgment.

## POST-JUDGMENT PHASE

**Putting It
Into Practice:**

*Identify all the points at which a party could lose a case.*

You might imagine that when the court enters judgment, the dispute is resolved and the lawsuit is over. In the American civil court system, however, entry of judgment often merely marks the beginning of a new phase of the battle. First, it is a rare case in which a party who is not satisfied with the court's decision cannot find at least some plausible grounds for appeal. Appeals may delay the final resolution of the dispute for several years even if the trial court's decision is ultimately upheld; if the appeals court disagrees with the trial court's decision, the case may have to be rescheduled for a new trial.

But suppose the trial court's judgment is not appealed—surely, now, the dispute is over? Far from it: A judgment is not self-executing. In most cases, a civil judgment is merely a declaration by the court that one party owes money to the other. It is entirely up to the winning party to figure out how actually to collect the money. There are procedures designed to help that allow the winning party to obtain information about what assets the loser has and where they are located; impose and foreclose liens on those assets; and obtain the assistance of the police or sheriff in seizing and selling assets.

# ALTERNATIVE PATHS

Lawsuits involve complicated procedures, cost enormous amounts of money, and sometimes take years to resolve. Surely, you might ask, there must be better ways of resolving disputes?

In fact, many court systems now actively encourage various forms of ADR—**alternative dispute resolution.** To reduce the caseloads of judges, courts can require that cases be decided by a volunteer arbitrator if the amount of money in dispute is small. An arbitrator is someone who is appointed by the court or selected by the parties to decide a case. Many courts actively promote settlement of cases by requiring parties to meet with a judge for a formal settlement conference. Another approach is to enlist the help of a **mediator**—someone who, instead of choosing a winner, will conduct negotiations to try to reach a compromise. We will revisit the subject of ADR in detail in a later chapter, because it clearly represents the emergence of a strong trend in litigation.

# ROLE OF THE PARALEGAL

It may already be obvious to the reader that the aspects of litigation that must be conducted by a licensed attorney—court appearances, mainly—represent only a small part of the process. In modern litigation firms, paralegals are actively involved at every stage of a lawsuit. Particularly when cases are factually complex, the assistance of paralegals in assembling, indexing, organizing, and analyzing documents can be indispensable. Paralegals are often given the tasks of preparing pleadings and writing motions, and are often assigned to prepare and respond to discovery requests. Even at trial, it is not uncommon for attorneys to be assisted by one or more paralegals, whose detailed familiarity with the facts of the case and ability to locate particular items of evidence quickly may confer a competitive advantage. In short, litigation is a field in which the scope for paralegal involvement is nearly unlimited, and an ambitious and well-trained paralegal can advance to a high level of challenge and responsibility.

*Putting It Into Practice:*

*Why might litigation be a good choice for a paralegal who likes diversity and thrives on stress?*

# ETHICAL ETIQUETTE

Because the legal assisting field is relatively new, legal assistants are still carving out their niche, defining for themselves, attorneys, and the public in general the parameters of their role. While unable to perform tasks specifically reserved for lawyers, they are members of a professional team and share the prestige and responsibilities of being part of such a team. Although not classified as professionals (because they are not self-regulating and are not bound by a code of ethics), they, like dental hygienists, nurse practitioners, and others in the allied health field, are considered paraprofessionals.

As paraprofessionals they are not obligated to adhere to the code of conduct that binds attorneys. They cannot, for example, be disbarred (lose a license to practice) for unprofessional

*continued*

## ETHICAL ETIQUETTE *continued*

conduct because they are not licensed to begin with. If legal assistants are to enhance their status as paraprofessionals, however, and if they want to expand their role within the legal profession, they must not only adhere to the ethical code of attorneys but must also forge a code of professional conduct for themselves.

The subject of professionalism is a hot topic in the legal assisting field. One of the professionalism issues that is currently being debated is whether legal assistants should be licensed, thereby requiring them to meet prescribed educational and character requirements and to pass an examination. We will not engage in this debate in this text, but we will point out in the Ethical Etiquette section of each chapter critical ethical issues of which you should be aware. Even if you have covered ethics in another course, please take the time to at least refresh your memory. Beyond being scrupulously honest with your colleagues, clients, and court personnel, you must learn to avoid the ethical land mines that await you when you enter the field of legal assisting.

 **PRACTICE POINTERS**

The diversity of tasks a litigation paralegal performs is astounding. They include, but are not limited to:

- Drafting correspondence,
- Reviewing and organizing documents,
- Investigating facts,
- Setting up case files,
- Interviewing witnesses,
- Conducting research,
- Indexing files,
- Drafting responses to discovery requests,
- Preparing internal memoranda,
- Summarizing depositions,
- Setting up tickler systems,
- Creating trial notebooks,
- Preparing trial exhibits,
- Communicating with clients,
- Identifying potential experts,
- Working with witnesses,
- Working with court staff,
- Handling details attorneys forget or shun, and
- Billing time.

A quick review of these tasks reveals that legal assistants must not only possess knowledge of substantive law, procedural rules, and computer technology, but must also be able to communicate effectively and clearly with a wide variety of personalities. Furthermore, because of the time pressures created by hectic litigation schedules, they must have excellent organizational and time management skills.

The Practice Pointers sections in each chapter are dedicated to helping you cultivate these latter skills. They will show you how to be efficient, orderly, and highly effective even under the most stressful circumstances.

## TECHNO TIP

A basic requirement of any legal assistant is a working knowledge of word processing and associated programs dealing with spreadsheets and databases. The most popular word processing program in the legal community is WordPerfect®. Microsoft's Word® is also a popular program and with the advent of the Office suite of programs is gaining ground in the legal environment. A legal assistant should be able to type competently, format text, insert graphics, and utilize the program's bells and whistles, such as the spelling and grammar checkers and the thesaurus. An added skill, which is becoming more of a requirement, is the ability to use higher level program functions that, for instance, can automatically generate a table of contents and a table of authorities that includes a listing of all cases cited.

Spreadsheet programs, such as Lotus 1-2-3® and Excel®, provide more than enough functionality to meet the needs of most any legal assistant. Database managers such as Access® and dBase® round out the "trio" of program types with which you should be familiar.

Due to the special needs of the legal community, specialized programs for law office applications, incorporating spreadsheets and database management, have been created. They will be discussed in a later Techno Tip.

## SUMMARY

Civil procedure is the study of lawsuits and the laws that govern them; it is the law of remedies. How litigants deal with the details dictated by the rules of civil procedure may determine the outcome of a case.

Plaintiffs in civil actions are seeking damages, injunctions, or specific performance. Plaintiffs may be either natural persons, entities, estates, or political subdivisions. To adjudicate a matter, a court must have proper jurisdiction. Lawsuits are initiated when plaintiffs file pleadings with the clerk of the court and serve the defendant with a complaint. Lawsuits revolve around issues of fact (which are resolved by the trier of fact) and issues of law (which are resolved by judges). Issues of fact require the introduction of testimonial and documentary evidence at trial, whereas issues of law are usually brought to the court's attention when one of the parties files a motion.

During the pre-suit phase prior to a lawsuit being filed the attorneys conduct investigations, attempt negotiations, and prepare their strategies. The lawsuit begins officially when a complaint is filed. Discovery, which consumes most of the time and effort expended in preparing for trial, occurs subsequent to the filing of pleadings and is the time in which evidence is located. To resolve the inevitable disputes that arise in reference to what evidence should be introduced at trial, what discovery should be allowed, and what issues should be presented at trial, attorneys file motions with the judge. Prior to trial the parties must follow pretrial procedures that help ensure the parties are prepared to go to trial, that the issues are refined, and that some efforts at settlement have been attempted. Procedural rules also dictate the admission of evidence at trial, the presentation of arguments, the appropriateness of making motions, and the offering of jury instructions. After a verdict is entered the parties are given an opportunity to request that the verdict be overturned or that the case be re-tried. The parties may then appeal the court's judgment. Because judgments are not self-executing, the prevailing party must follow the procedures required to ascertain, locate, and seize the assets of the defendant.

As an alternative to the litigation process, parties may opt for some form of alternative dispute resolution, involving the use of an arbitrator or mediator. ADR is used frequently today as a means of reducing the caseloads of courts.

## KEY TERMS

| | | |
|---|---|---|
| Adjudicate | Injunction | Pleading |
| Alternative dispute resolution | Issue of fact | Political subdivision |
| Arbitrator | Issue of law | Procedural law |
| Attorney | Judge | Served |
| Civil action | Judgment | Service |
| Civil procedure | Jurisdiction | Specific performance |
| Concurrent jurisdiction | Litigant | Substantive law |
| Court | Litigate | Testifying |
| Court paper | Litigator | Testimonial evidence |
| Damages | Mediator | (testimony) |
| Defendant | Motion | Trial |
| Discovery | Motion practice | Trier of fact |
| Documentary evidence | Natural person | Venue |
| Entity | Party | Verdict |
| Filed | Plaintiff | |

## REVIEW QUESTIONS

1. Why is it important to study civil procedure?

2. What is the difference between procedural law and substantive law?

3. How does a civil suit differ from a criminal case?

4. Explain what is meant by the following:
   a. Judgment
   b. Jurisdiction
   c. Venue
   d. Pleadings
   e. Service
   f. Trier of fact
   g. Discovery
   h. Motion practice
   i. Alternative dispute resolution
   j. Arbitrator

5. How does an issue of fact differ from an issue of law?

6. What are two of the most common types of evidence in a civil suit?

7. How do the two goals of flexibility and uniformity cause tension in the legal system? How has that tension affected the evolution of pleadings in England and the United States?

8. What are the four phases of a lawsuit? Describe what happens at each phase.

9. Use the following groups of words in a single sentence:
   a. Litigate; plaintiff; defendant; damages
   b. Concurrent jurisdiction; judgment; venue; adjudicate
   c. Parties; pleadings; jurisdiction; filed
   d. Issue of fact; documentary evidence; trier of fact; verdict

## PRACTICE EXAM

*(Answers in Appendix A)*          **MULTIPLE CHOICE**

1. Learning the procedural rules is important because
   a. knowing the rules could make the difference between winning and losing a lawsuit.
   b. meritorious cases can be lost if the right procedural steps are not followed.
   c. your opponent will use the procedural rules to try to defeat you.
   d. all of the above.

2. Procedural rules
   a. are the rules that set forth people's rights.
   b. include the rules of tort law and contract law.
   c. constitute the law of remedies.
   d. are the rules that govern the conduct of lawsuits.
   e. c and d.

3. The civil system
   a. deal with offenses that damage society as a whole.
   b. focuses on compensating the victim.
   c. depends on the decisions of a prosecutor.
   d. must be initiated by the government.

4. A plaintiff in a civil suit may seek
   a. damages.
   b. injunction.
   c. specific performance.
   d. all of the above.

5. Pleadings include
   a. complaints.
   b. answers.

   c. discovery documents.
   d. only a and b.

6. Motion practice
   a. takes place primarily during a trial.
   b. facilitates the resolution of disputes that arise between parties.
   c. is a procedure used to locate evidence before trial.
   d. goes on between the parties but does not involve a judge.

7. Pretrial practice
   a. is relatively simple in most cases.
   b. helps ensure that parties are prepared for trial.
   c. encourages parties to make a reasonable effort toward settlement.
   d. b and c.

8. Once a judgment is entered
   a. the lawsuit is over.
   b. the prevailing party can immediately recover damages.
   c. the prevailing party must figure out how to locate the loser's assets.

9. Alternative dispute resolution
   a. can save money.
   b. reduces the time necessary to resolve disputes.
   c. reduces the caseload of judges.
   d. all of the above.

**FILL IN THE BLANKS**

10. ___Civil litigation___ is the study of lawsuits and the rules that govern them.

11. ___Substantive___ are the rules that regulate people's behavior and include the rules set forth in tort law and contract law.

12. A ___Civil Action___ is initiated by an individual seeking damages to right a wrong she has suffered.

13. A plaintiff may seek an ___Injunction___ to force a defendant to refrain from engaging in a particular activity.

14. A ___Judgment___ is a formal decision rendered by a court and enforced by the government.

15. A court can adjudicate a case only if it has ___Jurisdiction___ over that case.

16. The rules of ___Venue___ require plaintiffs to bring suit in places that are least inconvenient for the parties and witnesses.

17. An ___Arbitrator___ is a disinterested third party chosen by the parties or appointed by the court to render a decision in a case.

**18.** The delivery of court papers to a person is called _____*Service*_____ .

**19.** Technically the term _____*Pleading*_____ refers to the complaint and answer.

**20.** An _____*Issue*_____ is a question that litigants disagree about in reference to what happened.

**21.** The two most common types of evidence are _____*Documentary*_____ evidence and _____*Testimony*_____ evidence.

**22.** A formal proceeding at which parties present evidence and arguments is a _____*Trial*_____ ; the formal, written decision at the end of this proceeding is called a _____*Verdict*_____ .

**23.** The goal of _____*pleading*_____ is to set forth the issues the court is being asked to decide.

**24.** _____*Discovery*_____ refers to the procedures used to locate evidence and prepare it for trial.

**25.** The use of arbitrators and mediators exemplifies an alternative to the court system, called _____*ADR*_____ .

**26.** An _____ is someone selected by the parties or appointed by the court to decide a case, whereas a _____ is someone who helps the parties negotiate a compromise.

## TRUE OR FALSE

**27.** Only natural persons can file lawsuits.    T    F

**28.** Procedural rules rarely affect the outcomes of cases.    T    F

**29.** The emphasis of criminal law is on compensating victims.    T    F

**30.** An injunction requires a party to do something the party has contracted to do.    T    F

**31.** Political subdivisions can never be parties in civil cases.    T    F

**32.** State courts and federal courts can have concurrent jurisdiction.    T    F

**33.** Arbitration is sometimes required by contract, statute, or the rules of court.    T    F

**34.** The term *party* for purposes of the law refers to a plaintiff or defendant.    T    F

**35.** Issues of law are decided by the trier of fact.    T    F

**36.** Issues of law are decided at trial, whereas issues of fact are decided before the trial.    T    F

**37.** Issues of fact are usually decided in response to motions.    T    F

**38.** Discovery accounts for a great deal of the time and money expended before trial.    T    F

**39.** If the defendant refuses to turn over evidence, the plaintiff may file a motion with the court requesting that the evidence be turned over.    T    F

**40.** Once parties have completed the discovery process, nothing more is required before the case will be set for trial.    T    F

**41.** A judge cannot cut a trial short under any circumstances.    T    F

**42.** After trial the losing party can move to have a verdict overturned or the case retried.    T    F

**43.** A judgment is self-executing.    T    F

**44.** Appeals can delay the final resolution of a case for years.    T    F

**45.** Settlement conferences are a form of alternative dispute resolution that courts use to promote the settlement of cases.    T    F

## LITIGATION LINGO

*(Answers in Appendix A)* **CROSSWORD PUZZLE**

**DOWN**

1. To conduct or defend a lawsuit
3. Requirement that lawsuits be brought in place least inconvenient for parties and witnesses
4. Agency of the government that has the power to adjudicate
5. Information that tends to establish facts
8. Power of court to adjudicate particular kind of case
9. Disinterested third party chosen by parties or appointed by court to decide outcome of case
10. Order by court to refrain from doing something

**ACROSS**

2. Delivery of copies of court papers
6. Question about which litigants disagree
7. Complaint and answer
8. Formal decision rendered by court and enforced by government
9. Decide outcome of case
11. Law of remedies
12. Formal request asking court to resolve issue over which parties disagree
13. Someone who helps parties negotiate a compromise
14. Acronym for alternative to court system
15. What federal and state courts share

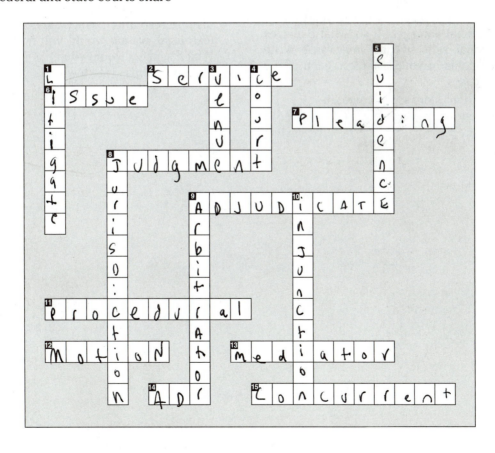

## LITIGATION LOGISTICS

*(Answers in Appendix A)*

***Using the hypothetical at the beginning of the chapter involving the drunk driver sideswiping your car, answer the following questions:***

1. What is a substantive law issue that is likely to arise in this case?

2. What is a procedural law issue that is likely to arise in this case?

3. What factors would you consider in deciding which court to sue in?

4. What would you have to do to initiate suit?

5. Give an example of an issue of fact that would likely have to be resolved in this case.

6. Give an example of an issue of law that would likely arise in this case.

7. Give an example of documentary evidence you would probably want to produce.

8. Give an example of an issue that might be resolved by filing a motion with the court.

9. If the jury returned a verdict in your favor, what would you have to do to collect damages from the defendant? What might happen that would prevent you from collecting damages from the defendant immediately?

10. What kind of ADR is likely to be used in this case?

## PROCEDURAL PONDERABLES

1. Five potential lawsuits are described at the beginning of this chapter. Assume that you are the plaintiff in each case. What type of resolution would you consider acceptable? In other words, would you be satisfied with being compensated for your losses or would you want to seek additional damages? If so, what damages or additional relief would you want? Write down the goals of your lawsuit in each of the following cases:

   a. Drunk driver sideswipes your car.
   b. Tenant stops paying rent and refuses to move out.
   c. Cousin refuses to pay you a percentage of his business.
   d. Karate instructor breaks your nose.
   e. Contractor does shoddy work on house.

2. If you had the power to create a new system for dispute resolution, which aspects of the American legal system would you adopt and why? Which aspects would you change and why? Explain how your system would operate.

# CHAPTER 2

# COURTS AND FILINGS

## OBJECTIVES

**In this chapter you will learn:**

- What a court is and where its power comes from

- What kinds of courts there are

- A few procedural tools and concepts that apply to all courts

- How to find out what procedures are followed in a given court

*Your firm's client received minor injuries in an automobile collision. Your supervising attorney hands you a file containing a traffic accident report and a completed client questionnaire in which she has written down the information related by the client. The file also includes a rough draft of the main body of the complaint which she has prepared. She tells you to prepare a lawsuit for filing.*

\* \* \* \* \*

*A friend of yours enters into a contract to buy a house. The bank turns down his credit application, and he is unable to complete the purchase. The seller sues him for damages. You introduce him to an attorney in your firm. After reviewing the complaint against your friend and obtaining the necessary information, the attorney assigns you to prepare an answer to the suit.*

\* \* \* \* \*

*Your supervising attorney agreed to defend a lawsuit in which his client's answer must be filed today. He hurriedly prepares the necessary documents. It is now 4:15 P.M. and he hands them to you, telling you to be sure they are filed at the court and stamped with today's date. "Take these papers down to the court. . . ."*

# INTRODUCTION

Most of us have a general idea of what a court is—it is a place where judges preside over trials. If you want to sue someone, however, you need to know a bit more than that. How do you find the right court? How many different ones are there, anyway? How are they organized? Having found the right court, how do you figure out what to do there? How do you find the rules that apply to that particular court? Do your court papers have to be in some special format in order to be accepted for filing?

The answers to these questions vary from place to place. We begin with a number of general principles that apply everywhere. In keeping with our goal of making this text practical and relevant to the needs of working paralegals, however, we do not stop there: We offer specific information on how and where to find the details for your particular state and city, and we provide space in this chapter and throughout this text for you to write in the details for your area as you obtain them or as your instructor provides them. We strongly encourage you to supplement your text with local notes in this way; you will find it quite valuable later to have this information available in an organized, easily accessible way.

# WHAT ARE COURTS AND WHERE DO THEY COME FROM?

The ultimate law of the land in America is the United States Constitution. The Constitution controls all other laws. Similarly, each state has a constitution, which is the highest law in that state. The United States Constitution, as well as each of the constitutions of the fifty states, follows the doctrine of "separation of powers." To prevent any one part of the government from becoming too powerful, the functions of government are divided among the legislative, judicial, and executive branches. Congress and the state legislatures make the laws; the executive branch, consisting of the president and the cabinet de-

## SIDEBAR

## Where Do All of These Rules Come From, Anyway?

*The study of civil procedure is the study of rules. There are rules for everything: who can sue, how to sue, who can be sued, how trials are conducted, even what kind of paper must be used for court filings.*

*As you may have learned in other classes, most legal rules in America come either from statutes—laws passed by Congress or a state legislature—or case law, which consists of rules created by judges in deciding previous cases. Federal statutes, the laws passed by Congress, are assembled in a multivolume set of books called the United States Code. Another set, called United States Code Annotated, contains each federal statute followed by a summary of all court decisions interpreting that statute. State statutes are similarly available as sets of books containing all of the statutes for a given state.*

*Your Local Notes*
*The set of statutes for your state is:*

_____

_____

*Because legislatures are continually adding new laws and amending and repealing old ones, sets of statutes are supplemented, usually once a year. Statute research is never complete until you have checked the supplements! Statutes are also available on-line or in the form of CD-ROM.*

*Case law—reported opinions of judges in actual lawsuits—is found in huge sets of books called reporters. There are reporter sets for each state, for the federal courts, and for each major region of the country. These, too, are also available on-line and as CD-ROM sets.*

*Certainly, some procedural law comes from statutes and case law. The primary source of procedural law in the federal courts and in the courts of most states, however, is court rules. Judges, often with the help of committees of attorneys and scholars, adopt their own rules for the conduct of cases in their own courts. The U.S. Supreme Court made the Federal Rules of Civil Procedure, which prescribe the procedure in all federal courts. Each lower federal court also has its own rules for any situations not covered by the Federal Rules of Civil Procedure that the local judges consider important enough to need a rule.*

*Similarly, in most states, the highest court prescribes general rules of procedure that apply to all courts in the state (in a few states, notably California, procedural rules are established by statute). Lower courts then adopt "local rules" of their own.*

partments, carries them out. Courts—the judicial branch—apply them to individual cases, interpret them when disputes arise, and enforce them. Thus courts in our system are rooted directly in Article III of the Constitution itself.

The Constitution does not, however, dictate exactly what kinds of courts there are to be; neither, in general, do the constitutions of the fifty states. It is up to Congress and the state legislatures to invent the details of the court system. Congress and the legislatures decide which courts should hear which kinds of cases and supply all of the administrative bureaucracy necessary to keep a court system running. As for civil procedure, in most states, the courts themselves make the rules under authority delegated by the legislature or the state constitution (see sidebar).

> *Your Local Notes*
>
> *The general rules of civil procedure in your state are:*
>
> _____
>
> _____

Naturally, the details vary considerably from state to state, and they are in a constant state of change as legislatures and court rules committees seek to improve the system and deal with the increasing volume of litigation.

## FEDERAL COURTS

We begin with the federal courts, because these are present in every state, and many state court systems model their procedures after the federal courts. **Federal courts** are, of course, those belonging to the federal government, in contrast to the **state courts,** which derive their power from state governments (although they are often actually administered by county governments). In the federal system and in most states, there are three main "levels" of courts, as diagrammed in Figure 2–1. First, there is a **trial court** of general jurisdiction, in which almost all lawsuits must begin. The trial court is responsible for the case from the time it begins until a judgment is rendered. Any proceedings to collect the judgment also take place in the trial court.

**Figure 2–1   Federal Judicial System and Flow of Cases to United States Supreme Court**

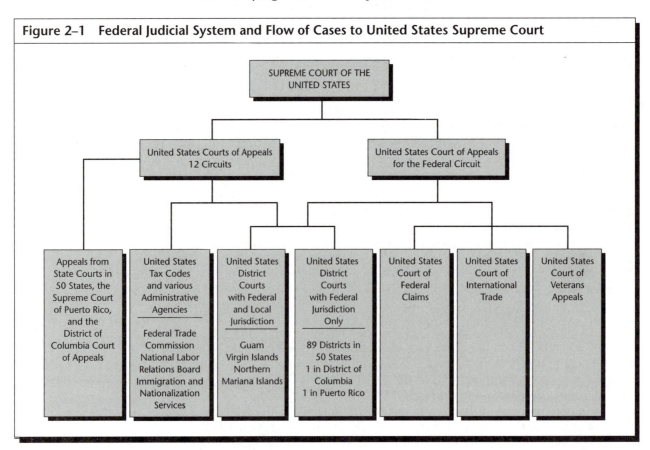

*Source:* United States Administrative Office of Courts.

In the federal system, the trial court is the U.S. **district court.** As the name implies, there is a U.S. district court for each federal district; each state has at least one district, and some of the more populous states have two or three. Each U.S. district court has a number of judges, who are appointed by the president and serve for life unless impeached for improper behavior. If you file a lawsuit in federal court, a U.S. district judge will preside over the case and conduct the trial. Ordinarily, lawsuits in U.S. district court are heard by a single judge; in certain special situations, a panel of three judges may preside.

The second level of courts is responsible for appeals. An **appeal** is a formal request in which a party asks a higher court to review the decision of a lower court and change it in some way. Courts that decide appeals are called **appellate courts.**

In the federal system, this second level of courts is called the U.S. Court of Appeals. The U.S. Court of Appeals is divided into eleven geographical regions, called **circuits.** Each circuit is responsible for the appeals from all U.S. district courts within its region (Figure 2–2). (The regions are called *circuits* because in times past appellate court judges had to travel from district to district to hear appeals. Today, they usually stay in one place and make litigants come to them.) In addition, there is a separate Circuit Court of Appeals for the District of Columbia, since government activities there produce a great deal of litigation and there is a federal circuit that hears specialized cases from all across the country. If you are dissatisfied with the judgment of a U.S. district court, your appeal will ordinarily be to the Court of Appeals for the circuit in which your state is included. Lawyers often refer to U.S. Courts of Appeals simply as a "Circuit"; for example, the U.S Court of Appeals for the Second Circuit, which hears appeals from districts in New York and several northeastern states, is referred to in lawyer jargon as "the Second Circuit."

The highest court in the federal system is, of course, the U.S. Supreme Court. The main function of the U.S Supreme Court is to offer a final level of appeal. If you lose your appeal in the U.S. Court of Appeals, you can ask the U.S. Supreme Court to review the case. In most situations, review by the U.S. Supreme Court is **discretionary;** this means that it is up to the Court whether or not to hear the appeal. In practice, the U.S. Supreme Court chooses carefully from among the thousands of cases it is asked to review, and accepts only a tiny fraction. This is in contrast to appeals to the U.S. Court of Appeals, which are normally not discretionary; because the U.S. Court of Appeals represents the first level of appeal, the court must ordinarily hear all appeals. (The U.S. Court of Appeals can, however, impose penalties on litigants who waste its time with "frivolous" appeals that are clearly without merit.)

## PROCEDURE IN APPELLATE COURTS

This book is devoted to trial court procedure. Procedure in appellate courts is quite different—in general, appellate courts do not hear testimony or receive evidence, because appellate courts decide only issues of law. Appellate courts may review lower court decisions on issues of fact, but only to the extent of determining whether the decision was reasonable based on the evidence received in the trial court. Thus, if the appellate court decides that the trial judge was wrong on some issue of law, the appellate court can change the decision accordingly; but if the error involved an issue of fact, usually the case must be returned to the trial court and retried.

Appellate courts are not equipped to take testimony, receive evidence, or conduct trials; they make their decisions by reviewing the record, hearing argument, and researching the law. In the U.S. Court of Appeals and most state appellate courts, appeals are heard and decided by panels of several judges.

*Putting It Into Practice:*

*Does every state have a district court? A circuit court? Where is the district court in your state? Is there a circuit court in your state? Where is the circuit court for your jurisdiction located?*

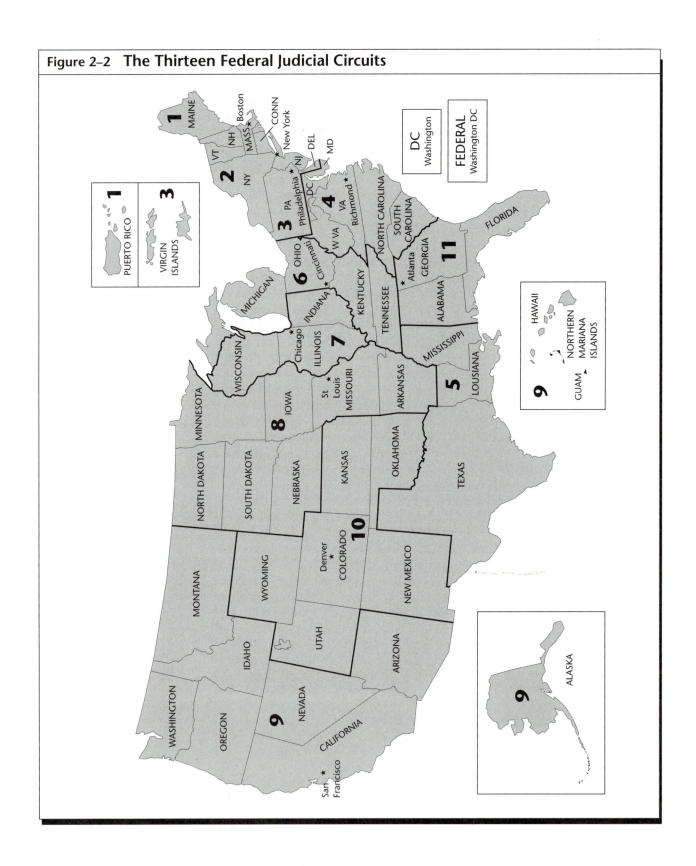

**Figure 2–2  The Thirteen Federal Judicial Circuits**

The party who began the **appeal**—the **appellant**—furnishes to the court a written argument, called a **brief,** detailing the reasons why appellant thinks the trial court decision was in error. The other party—the **appellee**—prepares a brief in response. The court of appeals may schedule an argument, at which attorneys for each party are given a short time (usually less than an hour) to explain their arguments and answer any questions that the judges may have. Or, the court may decide the appeal on the briefs submitted, without hearing argument. Naturally, there are detailed rules specifying all of these procedures, which we leave for another text.

The decision by the court of appeals usually consists either of affirming or reversing the trial court's decision. If the trial court's decision is **affirmed,** it is left unchanged. If it is **reversed,** the court of appeals will order the trial court either to change its judgment or to redo the trial. Do not confuse the term *reverse* with the term **overrule.** *Reverse* means to change the trial court's decision *in the case now on appeal.* When an appellate court *overrules* a decision, it means the court has decided not to follow the rules laid down in some earlier decision. (Recall that in the American system courts rely on earlier published decisions as a source of case law.)

## STATE COURTS

In most states, the courts responsible for general civil lawsuits are organized in three levels in a manner similar to the federal courts, that is, a trial court of general jurisdiction, an appeals court, and a supreme court.

In most states, the trial court is called the superior court. (Exceptions include New York, where the general civil trial court is called the supreme court, and Louisiana, whose court system is derived from French law and is based on a different philosophy entirely.) Throughout this text, to avoid cumbersome repetition, we will use the term *superior court* to mean the general civil trial court of the state, even though it is not called that in a few states. Superior courts are state courts in the sense that they are created by state law, but there is usually one for each county, and they are usually funded and administered by county governments.

Appeals from the decisions of state civil courts are taken to the state court of appeals (in New York, the appellate division of the state supreme court). Procedure is similar to that already described for the U.S. Court of Appeals. State courts of appeals are headquartered in the state's capital city, and may have branches in a few other cities in the state.

Each state has a state supreme court (except New York, where the highest court is called the Court of Appeals) whose function is to hear appeals whose issues it considers important. State supreme courts are located in the capital cities of each state.

Each state typically has many superior courts (one for each county) but only one court of appeals (which may have several divisions or departments) and one supreme court (Figure 2–3).

## ADMINISTRATION

There is a great deal more to a court system than just judges conducting trials. Someone has to keep track of the cases, assign them to judges, schedule the trials and hearings, maintain custody of evidence, make sure that all the papers filed with the court can be found when needed, and manage all of the other administrative tasks without which the system would come to an immediate standstill. When you consider that a typical urban court system disposes of

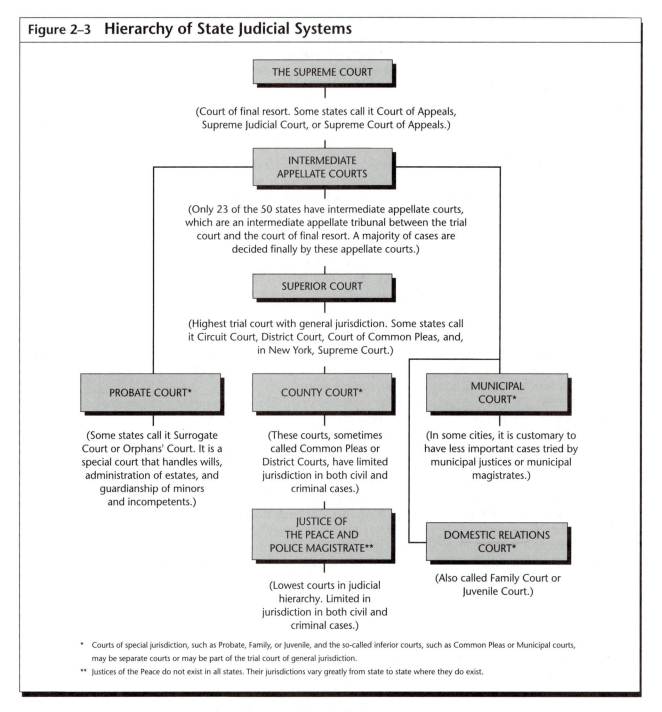

**Figure 2–3  Hierarchy of State Judicial Systems**

THE SUPREME COURT

(Court of final resort. Some states call it Court of Appeals, Supreme Judicial Court, or Supreme Court of Appeals.)

INTERMEDIATE APPELLATE COURTS

(Only 23 of the 50 states have intermediate appellate courts, which are an intermediate appellate tribunal between the trial court and the court of final resort. A majority of cases are decided finally by these appellate courts.)

SUPERIOR COURT

(Highest trial court with general jurisdiction. Some states call it Circuit Court, District Court, Court of Common Pleas, and, in New York, Supreme Court.)

PROBATE COURT*

(Some states call it Surrogate Court or Orphans' Court. It is a special court that handles wills, administration of estates, and guardianship of minors and incompetents.)

COUNTY COURT*

(These courts, sometimes called Common Pleas or District Courts, have limited jurisdiction in both civil and criminal cases.)

MUNICIPAL COURT*

(In some cities, it is customary to have less important cases tried by municipal justices or municipal magistrates.)

JUSTICE OF THE PEACE AND POLICE MAGISTRATE**

(Lowest courts in judicial hierarchy. Limited in jurisdiction in both civil and criminal cases.)

DOMESTIC RELATIONS COURT*

(Also called Family Court or Juvenile Court.)

\*   Courts of special jurisdiction, such as Probate, Family, or Juvenile, and the so-called inferior courts, such as Common Pleas or Municipal courts, may be separate courts or may be part of the trial court of general jurisdiction.

\*\*  Justices of the Peace do not exist in all states. Their jurisdictions vary greatly from state to state where they do exist.

*Source: Law and the Courts,* 20 (American Bar Association, 1974).

tens of thousands of cases in a year, and receives millions of pages of filings, it is obvious that the task of administering the system is a major function in itself.

If the administrative functions of the court system seem uninteresting, consider this: To have a case decided in your client's favor, you first have to get it accepted. Keeping cases moving through the system is an important function of paralegals. Often, understanding the administrative functioning of the court system and knowing how to get a case scheduled for a particular action at the desired time can make a significant difference in the overall outcome.

The administrative functions of courts are typically divided among several entities, including the office of the clerk of the court, the office of the presiding judge, the secretaries and staff of the individual judges, and in many court systems, a court administrator.

The function of the clerk of the court is to deal with paperwork. Every step in a lawsuit generates paper, all of which must be filed and kept available for future proceedings. All papers pertaining to all cases flow through the clerk's office. A separate chronological file is kept for each case. The clerk's office also has the power to issue routine court orders such as summonses and subpoenas, thus freeing judges from such mundane tasks.

The presiding judge has overall responsibility for the smooth running of the court system. The presiding judge makes policy decisions about how the workload is divided among all the judges in the court, which judges are assigned to which specialty divisions, and other matters involving the work of

## SIDEBAR

### Filing

*A great deal of the activity in a lawsuit involves the submission of written material to the court for inclusion in the permanent record of the case; this is referred to as* filing. *Papers are filed in a case by delivering them to the office of the clerk of the court. The clerk of the court is a government official who is appointed or elected to accept and keep track of the enormous volume of paper that flows into a typical court system. In most urban court systems, the clerk's office is staffed by a number of deputy clerks, and often resembles a bank lobby with its counters and windows for handling transactions with the public. The clerk will accept for filing only papers that are in proper form. Local court rules typically specify formal requirements such as paper size, line spacing, and captions. A filing fee will also be required for many types of filings.*

*The clerk of the court keeps a separate file for each lawsuit. Papers filed by the litigants are added to the file in chronological order and usually indexed. These files are public records and can be inspected and copied by anyone, unless a judge orders particular papers to be sealed. Whenever there is a hearing before a judge in the case, or when the judge is asked to rule on an issue, the file may be sent to the judge so that he can quickly become informed about what the case is about and what rulings have already been made. If there is an appeal, the file can be sent to the appellate court, providing the appeals judges with a complete record of everything that happened in the case.*

*You may be curious about who actually goes and stands in line at the clerk's office to file the court papers. Busy law offices usually have many papers to file with the clerk of the court each day, so they employ messenger services or process service firms to take filings to the clerk's office. Occasionally, however, situations will arise in which a lawyer is working feverishly to complete some required filing prior to a deadline, and a paralegal will be sent rushing to the clerk's office at closing time to file the paper. We recommend that you file papers at the clerk's office yourself occasionally, so as to become familiar with the process and the requirements. This knowledge will help you avoid common mistakes that can cause the clerk to reject a filing. You can also place yourself in a position to be very useful to your employer if you make a few friends at the clerk's office, so that you have someone you can call and ask when some obscure question arises about an office procedure. For example, merely knowing how to get a paper filed after closing time can be extremely valuable information when your employer is facing a deadline.*

the judges. In some court systems, each case is assigned to one judge, who conducts all proceedings in that case. The benefit of this approach is that it allows the judge to become familiar with the facts of the case as it progresses. In other courts, cases are not permanently assigned to one judge; instead, judges are assigned by function, so that motions will be heard by a motions judge, discovery disputes by a discovery judge or referee, and trials assigned to trial judges at the time a case is ready for trial. This system is thought to promote efficiency by allowing judges to become specialized and ensuring an uninterrupted flow of work to each judge. In court systems that have court administrators, the work of assigning cases to judges and maintaining and scheduling the case flow is done by the court administrator's office.

Each judge has his or her own office and staff, typically consisting at least of a secretary, a bailiff, a court reporter, and one or more administrative clerks. Federal judges and state court appellate judges also have one or more law clerks on staff, typically recent law graduates who are hired to do legal research and help write opinions.

The judge's secretary and clerical staff are important people in litigation, because they are responsible for keeping the judge's calendar and scheduling most routine activity in the case. Also, rules of ethics prohibit lawyers (and paralegals!) from engaging in *ex parte* communications with the judge about a pending lawsuit—that is, speaking to the judge without the opposing attorney having an opportunity to participate. Therefore, if you need to know whether the judge has made a ruling on a particular issue, or whether a particular paper has been received, or if you need to have a hearing scheduled, or if you have general questions about preferred practices in this judge's court, it is the judge's secretary or clerk to whom you inquire.

*Putting It Into Practice:*

*Why is it important to establish a good working relationship with the judge's secretary and office staff?*

## SPECIALTY COURTS

In addition to the normal three levels of courts—one general trial court and two levels of appellate courts—the federal government and many states have established other courts to hear particular types of cases. These include, on the federal level, the U.S. Court of Claims, which hears cases involving claims against the government; the U.S. Tax Court, which, as the name implies, hears tax cases; and the U.S. Court of Appeals for the Federal Circuit, which hears appeals in patent and trademark cases. Another major specialty court is the U.S. Bankruptcy Court, which hears bankruptcy matters. Many states have also created specialty courts, particularly for tax cases. What specialty courts has your state created?

| *Your Local Notes* |
|---|
| |
| |

The hope is that by specializing in a single type of case, these courts can make more informed decisions and process cases more efficiently. One side effect of this specialization is, of course, that procedure in these courts also becomes specialized. Procedure in specialty courts, though often similar to that in general civil suits, is beyond the scope of this text.

Even where separate specialty courts have not been established, the trend is to organize existing courts in "divisions" devoted to particular types of cases. On the civil side, state trial courts often have separate divisions for, say, divorce and probate cases.

We have said little so far about criminal cases. Because this text is devoted to civil suits, we limit ourselves to the observation that procedure in criminal cases, whether heard in the same court as civil cases or in a separate court or division devoted exclusively to them, is completely different from that in civil cases. An entirely separate set of rules governs criminal procedure, and many of the rules involve difficult constitutional issues pertaining to the rights of accused criminals and prisoners. We make no pretense of addressing the subject here.

## CITY AND SMALL CLAIMS COURTS

In most metropolitan areas, the volume of civil litigation has increased so rapidly that the superior courts simply cannot keep up with the caseload. One way to try to keep the system moving is to separate the smaller cases and send them elsewhere. Usually the smallest cases—those in which the amount in dispute is a few thousand dollars or less, the precise amount varying with the locality—are not eligible for filing in superior court. Such small claims cases are required to go to another court, such as a small claims court, justice of the peace court, or city court, depending on the locality. These courts typically offer streamlined procedures designed to adjudicate such cases quickly and cheaply, often without the involvement of lawyers.

*Putting It Into Practice:*

*Prepare a diagram showing the identities of all the courts in your jurisdiction and their relationships to one another. Where are each of these courts located?*

# WHICH COURT DO I SUE IN?

Out of all of these courts, how do you decide which one to file your lawsuit in? At a minimum, you will fall within the geographic area of one federal district court and one state court. If the suit involves people who live in different states, or if the acts or events you are suing about happened in another state or in more than one state, more possibilities may exist.

In general, you are free to file suit in any court that has jurisdiction. Jurisdiction, you may recall, is the power to decide a particular case. There are rules, which we will cover in detail in Chapter 4, for deciding whether a particular court has jurisdiction of a given case. In general, the answer depends on such questions as whether one of the parties resides in the state in which the court is located (called the **forum state**); how much money is in dispute; whether the dispute involves acts or events that happened in the forum state; and whether the dispute should be decided under federal law, the state law of the forum state, or the state law of some other state. The goal of jurisdictional rules is to try to send cases to the court best equipped to resolve them—it would not be very efficient to ask a New York state court to resolve a dispute between California residents involving federal law, for example.

The garden-variety lawsuit is a state law dispute between people who reside in the same state; then the proper choice of forum is the local superior court. Complications arise when, for example, one of the parties is a resident of another state; this can occur when a vacationing motorist is involved in an auto accident. Similarly, business disputes often arise in transactions that cross state lines, and may also depend on federal law or the laws of more than one state. It is possible, and indeed not uncommon, for more than one court to have jurisdiction over such suits. In that case, strategy enters the picture, and it is necessary to decide which of the possible choices is likely to lead to the most favorable outcome for your client. This is sometimes referred to as **forum shopping.**

# HOW DO I FIND OUT WHAT PROCEDURES APPLY?

In this text, you will learn considerable detail about the rules of procedure that govern civil cases in federal court. The basic procedural concepts you will learn are valid in all American courts, and the details are valid in all federal district courts and, with minor modifications, in the state courts of a majority of the states.

Thus, the broad foundation for your knowledge of procedural law will be the **Federal Rules of Civil Procedure.** Future references to the Federal Rules of Civil Procedure will be in the form of **FRCP,** Rule _____ . In federal court cases, you will go directly to the federal rules for your answers to procedural questions. In many situations, you may find that, although there is a federal rule that pertains to your particular question, it does not offer enough detail. Then you resort to secondary sources to help you interpret the rules.

## GENERAL QUESTIONS OF FEDERAL PROCEDURE

If you have a federal procedure question requiring more detail than the rules provide, a good place to start is a multivolume treatise such as *Federal Practice and Procedure* by Wright and Miller. This is like an "encyclopedia" of federal procedure law and is available in most law libraries. It has a detailed index, and it covers each of the federal rules in numerical order so that you can proceed directly to the volume you need if you know which rule applies.

As with many law books, Wright and Miller's book has *pocket parts*—a pamphlet inserted into a pocket inside the cover of the book. The pocket parts are the publisher's way of keeping the set up to date without having to publish entirely new volumes every year. The pocket parts contain any new information and cases that appeared after the original volume was published. When you research, always check the pocket parts; otherwise, you may be relying on information that is no longer valid.

Another good place to go for more detail on federal rules questions is the *United States Code Annotated* (U.S.C.A.). The Federal Rules of Civil Procedure appear in full after Title 28; the text of each rule is given, followed by the comments of the committee that advised the court when the rule was adopted. After each rule, there is a complete, indexed listing of summaries of all cases in which the rule was interpreted. You can review these summaries (which are usually called **annotations**), pick from them the cases that seem to address your question, and look up the full text of those cases using the citations given in the annotations. (A **citation** is simply a short reference giving the name of the case, which reporter series it can be found in, and the volume and page number. (See Sidebar on page 32.) Finding a case from its citation is not difficult, but it is properly the subject of a course on legal research, so we will not cover it in detail here. The law librarian can show you how to find a case from the citation if you need help.) When you check the annotations in USCA, remember to check the pocket parts.

If you follow this systematic approach, you can be reasonably sure that you have covered all of the case law available up to the publication date of the pocket parts. In many situations, that is not good enough, though, because pocket parts may be up to a year old. For absolutely up to the minute research, you need to consult an on-line database such as Westlaw®.

## STATE LAW PROCEDURE QUESTIONS

Each state (except California, which has a procedure code) has adopted rules of procedure for state courts. These are typically called the (*name of state*) Rules of Civil Procedure, and are found in the court rules volume(s) of the annotated statutes of the state in question.

When you encounter state law procedure issues, you should first consult the state rules of procedure and the annotations that follow each rule. Again, do not forget to check the pocket parts. Where are your state rules of procedure found?

*Your Local Notes*

A majority of states have adopted the Federal Rules of Civil Procedure, or some modified version, for use in state courts. The state version is published separately, of course, and you should always use the state version when researching state court procedure issues. However, particularly in smaller states, many procedure issues will not have been ruled on yet by state courts, so there may not be any state court cases to find. In states that use the federal rules as a benchmark for their own rules of procedure, one solution to this problem is to research the question under the federal rules. Usually trial courts in such states will accept cases interpreting the federal rules as authority for how similar state court rules should be interpreted. Even in states whose rules are not derived from the federal rules, you can often use cases interpreting similar or analogous federal rules as a part of your argument.

Another good source of state law procedural information is state bar association publications such as handbooks and continuing legal education course materials. These are available in the law library, and often give "nuts and bolts" information about how to accomplish various procedural tasks.

## ADMINISTRATIVE DETAIL

Neither the Federal Rules of Civil Procedure nor typical state rules of procedure cover the mundane details of clerk's office requirements. Does this mean there are no rules and you can do whatever you want? Sorry, but no. Each court adopts local rules of procedure, which dictate such things as the size and type of paper to be used for court filings; the proper format of court papers; limitations on how many pages can be submitted; and a great many other such details that, if ignored, will result in the clerk's office instantly rejecting your filing. If, as often occurs, you are trying to get a paper filed shortly before a deadline, this can cause considerable consternation! These rules can seem incredibly arbitrary at times, but—trust us—arguing with the clerk about it will get you nowhere. So, get a copy of the local rules for each court in which you will be litigating, read them, and follow them.

Where do you obtain local rules? The best place is directly from the clerk or court administrator of the court in question—that way you will be sure your copy is up to date. Local rules can sometimes be found in law libraries, but if you rely on this source, be sure to double-check whether there have been any revisions. What are your local rules of procedure called? Where are they found?

*Putting It Into Practice:*

*You want to depose a witness to an accident. How would you determine if you have a right, in your state trial court, to depose this individual?*

*Your Local Notes*

_____

_____

# SIDEBAR

## Citations

*All citations to cases follow this format:*

| Name of Case | Volume Number | Name of Reporter | Page Number | Court Name | Date |
|---|---|---|---|---|---|

*As an example, consider the following citation:*

<u>May v. West</u>*, 695 F.2d 43 (1st Cir. 1998).*

*This citation tells us that the case of* <u>May v. West</u>*, (note that case names are always underlined) can be found in Volume 695 of the Federal Reporter (2d series) on page 43; it is a First Circuit case and was published in 1998. All cases published in the circuit courts are found in the Federal Reporter. The reporter has a first and second series. After publishing a designated numbers of volumes, the publisher (West) began a second series (indicated by the "2d" in the citation).*

*Another example is found in the Federal Supplement, which contains all cases published by the district courts.*

<u>Ritter v. Sanchez</u>*, 895 F. Supp. 95 (S.D. N.J. 1997).*

*This case (*<u>Ritter v. Sanchez</u>*,) is found in Volume 895 of the Federal Supplement on page 95. The decision was rendered in the Southern District of New Jersey in 1997.*

*U.S. Supreme Court decisions are published in three reporters: the U.S. Reports (the only official reporter), the Supreme Court Reporter (an unofficial reporter published by West), and Lawyer's Edition (published by the former Lawyers' Cooperative). Official reporters (which are published by governmental agencies) contain only the written decision, whereas unofficial reporters contain research aids that assist the researcher.*

*Reported cases for the states follow the same format:*

<u>Nocturne v. Chuang</u>*, 642 P.2d 136 (Ariz. 1996).*

*This case is found in Volume 642 of the Pacific Reporter (second) on page 136. It is an Arizona case that was decided in 1996; because the level of the court is not indicated, we know that the Arizona Supreme Court rendered this decision. If the decision had come out of the Arizona Court of Appeals, "Ariz. Ct. App." would have been indicated in the parentheses.*

<u>Nocturne v. Chuang</u>*, 642 P.2d 136 (Ariz. Ct. App. 1996).*

*The other regional reporters are:*

> *Atlantic Reporter*
>
> *Northeast Reporter*
>
> *Northwest Reporter*
>
> *Southern Reporter*
>
> *Southeast Reporter*
>
> *Southwest Reporter*

---

**Figure 2–4   Courts in Your Locality**

---

Here is a checklist of things you will need to know about the court systems in your area. Space is also left for any facts your instructor may have about each court.

*Federal Court*
Name of U.S. District Court having jurisdiction over this geographical area:
Location of courthouse:
Location of clerk's office in courthouse:
Instructor's comments:


Name of U.S. Circuit Court of Appeals for this area:
Location:
Instructor's comments:


*State Court*
Name of trial court of general jurisdiction for your area:
Location of courthouse:
Location of clerk's office in courthouse:
Instructor's comments:


Name of appellate court to which first appeal is taken:
Location:
Instructor's comments:


Name of state's highest court:
Location:
Instructor's comments:


*Other Courts*
Name of court in which small cases would be filed:
Location:
Instructor's comments:

---

Figure 2–4 provides a place to keep track of pertinent information about your local courts.

## SPECIALTY CASES

Another subject often addressed in local rules is the procedure in specialty cases such as domestic relations and probate. Such cases often involve specialized court papers designed to promote efficient processing of that kind of case; these specialized requirements will be found in the local rules.

---

*Your Local Notes*

_____

_____

---

## ROLE OF THE PARALEGAL

**Putting It Into Practice:**

*Why is it important for paralegals to have good management and "people skills" as well as a good command of legal procedures and principles?*

Interaction with the court system is a fundamental part of litigation. Communications with the judge will normally be handled by the lawyer responsible for a case (although some jurisdictions are experimenting with rules allowing paralegals to make certain types of court appearances). Paralegals are often given rather wide responsibility for administrative interactions with court system staff: scheduling hearings, maintaining calendars, making sure required filings are made on time, determining why a case has "gotten stuck" in the system and figuring out what to do to get it moving again, and so forth. The importance of these functions cannot

## ETHICAL ETIQUETTE

*T*he *Model Code of Professional Responsibility* was published by the American Bar Association (ABA) in 1969 and serves as a model set of rules designed to govern the conduct of lawyers. The model code contains:

■ Canons, statements of general principles;

■ Disciplinary rules, rules that are mandatory; and

■ Ethical considerations, aspirational comments that assist in interpreting the disciplinary rules.

This code was modified by the ABA in 1983 and was retitled the *Model Rules of Professional Conduct.* The new model rules are formatted differently than the model code and no longer distinguish between mandatory and aspirational rules although they do contain interpretative commentary. Most states have patterned their ethical rules after the new model rules; some have retained the old model code; California has its own code based on neither the model code nor the model rules.

Because legal assistants are not attorneys, they are not bound by the ethical rules promulgated by the states. They are, however, liable for negligent or intentional conduct that causes injury to clients. Furthermore, some states have adopted guidelines designed to assist attorneys in their use of legal assistants and the ABA has developed *Model Guidelines for the Utilization of Legal Assistant Services* that states are encouraged to look to when drafting their own guidelines. The professional organization for legal assistants, the National Association of Legal Assistants (NALA), has also adopted *Model Standards and Guidelines for the Utilization of Legal Assistants.* Both it and the other major paralegal professional association, the National Federation of Paralegal Associations (NFPA), have created codes of ethics to guide the actions of their members.

Check with your local bar association to see if a committee has been established to deal with legal assistants. Has this committee established guidelines for attorneys working with legal assistants? Does this committee recommend that legal assistants become certified (a voluntary form of recognition of competence in certain designated areas of practice)? Has this committee considered the licensing of legal assistants (a mandatory form of regulation controlled by the government)?

*Your Local Notes*

_____

_____

be overstated; it does no good to have the city's most brilliant trial lawyer ready to try a case if the trial setting has been cancelled because of some scheduling glitch in the court system. Top litigation firms expect their paralegals to work proactively with the court system staff to anticipate administrative problems and keep cases moving through the system in the most advantageous possible way.

# PRACTICE POINTERS
## *To Do Lists*

One of the most challenging tasks legal assistants face is organizing their time. In many firms, they report to several attorneys and must interact with other legal assistants and legal secretaries. In the course of one day, they can be assigned numerous tasks by a number of attorneys and need to delegate or discuss responsibilities with many different people. Details can be overlooked in the process and deadlines can be easily overlooked or confused.

To facilitate the organization of each day, we encourage you to prepare "to do" lists that enumerate each task that needs to be accomplished, its projected date of completion, and its actual date of completion. Using this list can help you budget your time and can also help keep you on task so that you do not get distracted by the many demands on your time. Checking off each task as you complete it provides a feeling of accomplishment and reduces the sense of frustration you are likely to feel when everything seems to interfere with your anticipated work plan. The tasks that you do not complete can be rolled over to the next day, thereby eliminating the risk of forgetting prior assignments when new ones are given. By recording both projected and actual dates of completion, you can begin to assess your efficiency and how realistically you budget time.

To better evaluate how effectively you are managing your workload, consider adding a column that records the causes of delays. Over time you may realize that certain people in your office are frequently the cause of your not being able to accomplish your assignments within your allocated time frame. By realizing this you can then plan accordingly in the future or come up with ways to gently and subtly alter the obstructing individual's behavior. If an attorney, for example, consistently fails to respond to you within an agreed on time limit, thereby precluding you from completing your work in a timely manner, consider gentle (and, if possible, humorous) reminders presented in such a fashion that she cannot possibly avoid seeing them. Doing this not only makes you look more efficient and reliable to your supervisor but also better serves your client.

## TECHNO TIP

Today many courts have automated their systems and allow for access (but not modification) of the court's files electronically. Some provide access only to the docket—the names and dates on which document were filed or orders and minute entries entered. Others allow the documents to be viewed, usually as a graphics file. Many also show scheduled appearances such as oral arguments and trial dates. Access to the court's database may be free or a charge may be made to the viewer. The Maricopa County Superior Court in Arizona has automated its system (individual documents cannot be viewed). Visit www.supcourt.maricopa.gov/esp/public.html to see the types of court information available on the Internet. Note that attorney calendar information is available only to the individual attorney, and even then he must first obtain his own password. The U.S. Bankruptcy Court also has its own computer access system called PACER. PACER costs $0.60 per minute for access and requires that you set up an account prior to obtaining a password for access.

## SUMMARY

The United States Constitution is the highest law of the land just as the constitution in each state is the highest law of that state. The courts were created by the constitution, but the administrative bureaucracy necessary to run the courts is created by the legislative branch. The highest court of each state is responsible for creating state procedural rules while the U.S. Supreme Court wrote the Federal Rules of Civil Procedure.

The federal court system consists of district courts (trial courts), circuit courts (courts of appeal), and the U.S. Supreme Court. There are eleven circuit courts plus a Circuit Court of Appeals for the District of Columbia and a federal circuit court for specialized cases. The appeal process ends with the U.S Supreme Court, which accepts only a small fraction of the cases it is asked to review. Federal specialty courts include the bankruptcy and tax courts, the U.S. Court of Claims, and the U.S. Court of Appeals for the Federal Circuit.

Appellate courts review the trial court record, hear oral arguments, and research the law to arrive at their decisions to either affirm or reverse the decision of the trial court. They focus on issues of law and can review issues of fact only to the extent they decide that the trial court's decision was reasonably based on the evidence presented at trial. Appellants and appellees may present briefs but can only make oral arguments if the court allows them. Most states mirror the federal system with trial courts (usually called superior courts), courts of appeal, and a supreme court (except in New York where the highest court is the court of appeals). Claims below an established threshold amount are often tried in small claims, justice of the peace, or city courts.

The administrative function of the courts is a vital aspect of the system that is essential to the efficient management of thousands of cases. The court clerk is responsible for dealing with all of the paperwork generated by cases, has the authority to issue summonses and subpoenas, and is the official with whom all court documents are filed. The presiding judge decides how the workload will be distributed among judges, and the court administrator assigns judges to cases and maintains the case flow. The judge's clerical staff maintains the judge's calendar and answers questions from parties so that they do not interact *ex parte* with the judge.

A plaintiff can sue in any court that has jurisdiction. Jurisdiction is dependent on the residence of the parties, how much money is in dispute, whether the dispute involved acts or events in the forum state, and whether the dispute should be decided under federal or state law. Looking for the court that will provide the optimum results is called forum shopping.

More detail about the federal rules can be found in *Federal Practice and Procedure* by Wright and Miller or in the United States Code Annotated (U.S.C.A.). The state procedural rules can be found in their Rules of Civil Procedure publication as well as the court rules volume of the annotated state statutes. All of these resources can be updated by looking at the pocket parts. Compliance with the local rules, which dictate such things as paper size and format for court filings, can prevent the rejection of these filings by the court clerk's office.

## KEY TERMS

| | | |
|---|---|---|
| **Affirm** | **Circuit** | **Filing** |
| **Annotation** | **Citation** | **Forum shopping** |
| **Appeal** | **Discretionary** | **Forum state** |
| **Appellant** | **District court** | **Overrule** |
| **Appellate court** | **Federal court** | **Reverse** |
| **Appellee** | **Federal Rules of Civil** | **State court** |
| **Brief** | **Procedure (FRCP)** | **Trial court** |

## REVIEW QUESTIONS

1. Who creates the details of the court system? Who creates the procedural rules that govern the courts?

2. What are the three levels of courts in the federal system?
   a. What is a *circuit*?
   b. How does a district court differ from a circuit court?
   c. Are appeals before a U.S. Circuit Court of Appeals typically discretionary? What about appeals before the U.S. Supreme Court?

3. How do the three levels of state courts compare with the three levels of federal courts? Is the organization of court systems uniform from state to state?

4. How is an appellate judge's treatment of questions of law different from her treatment of questions of fact?

5. What is the difference between "reversing" a decision and "overruling" a decision?

6. Why is it important for paralegals to understand the administrative functioning of the court system?

7. What is the function of each of the following:
   a. Clerk of the court
   b. Presiding judge
   c. Judicial secretary
   d. Specialty court
   e. Small claims court

8. How are court papers filed?
   a. Are court files public records?
   b. Why is it important for paralegals to know their way around the court clerk's office?

9. What is the goal of jurisdictional rules?
   a. Give examples of the factors that go into determining what the appropriate jurisdiction is.
   b. What is the *forum state*?
   c. What is *forum shopping*?

10. What source would you consult first to answer a federal procedural question?
    a. If you cannot find the answer there, what sources might you next consult?
    b. What source would you consult first to answer a state procedural question?
    c. Where can you get a copy of the rules that govern the court clerk's office?

11. Why are the paralegal's administrative interactions with the court system so important?

## PRACTICE EXAM

*(Answers in Appendix A)*    **MULTIPLE CHOICE**

1. The courts
   a. were created by the legislative branch.
   b. interpret the laws created by the legislative branch.
   c. are independent of the other two branches of government.
   d. none of the above.

2. Federal statutes
   a. can be found in the *United States Code*.
   b. must be continually updated.
   c. are available on-line.
   d. all of the above.

3. In the federal system
   a. all cases begin in the circuit courts.
   b. there are district courts.
   c. district court judges serve for life.
   d. all appeals heard by the circuit courts are discretionary.

4. Appellate courts
   a. focus on resolving issues of fact by receiving evidence and hearing testimony.
   b. must return cases to the trial court to be re-tried if they determine that an error was made regarding an issue of fact.
   c. are comprised of panels of judges.
   d. make decisions by reviewing the record and hearing arguments.
   e. c and d.

5. The administration of a court system
   a. oftentimes involves the handling of tens of thousands of cases.
   b. is one thing a legal assistant need not know anything about.
   c. deals only with the scheduling of trials and the assigning of cases to judges.
   d. is a relatively minor aspect of the court system.

6. The court clerk
   a. handles all the papers pertaining to a case.
   b. can issue subpoenas and summonses.
   c. is the one with whom all court documents are filed.
   d. all of the above.

7. The presiding judge
   a. is always responsible for assigning judges to cases.
   b. decides how the workload is to be divided among judges.
   c. assigns judges to specialty divisions.
   d. all of the above.
   e. b and c.

8. Examples of specialty courts include
   a. bankruptcy courts.
   b. U.S. Court of Claims.
   c. U.S. Court of Appeals for the Federal Circuit.
   d. U.S. Court of Appeals.
   e. a, b, and c.

9. Small claims cases
   a. can be tried in justice of the peace or city courts.
   b. are usually eligible for filing in superior court.
   c. involve procedures that often complicate the process.
   d. none of the above.

10. Jurisdiction is dependent on
    a. which laws will be used to decide the case.
    b. where the acts or events involved in the dispute occurred.
    c. where the parties reside.
    d. all of the above.

### FILL IN THE BLANKS

11. The ultimate law of the land in the United States is the _____ .

12. Under the doctrine of _____ , the functions of the judicial, legislative, and executive branches of government are divided.

13. The _____ Court created the Federal Rules of Civil Procedure.

14. All cases must begin in a _____ court while all appeals must be heard by a _____ court.

15. The trial court in the federal system is called a _____ court; the appellate court is called _____ .

16. Each _____ court is responsible for all of the appeals from all of the district courts in its region.

17. At the appellate level, the _____ , who is beginning the appeal, must file a _____ with the court, detailing the reasons why it believes the trial court was in

error, and must allow the _____ to respond.

**18.** An appellate court that changes a trial court's decision is said to have _Reverse_ that decision but an appellate court that decides not to follow the rules laid down in a previous decision is said to have _____ that decision.

**19.** The function of the _____ is to handle paperwork.

**20.** The overall responsibility of the _____ is to make sure the court system runs smoothly.

**21.** It is the judge's _____ who is responsible for maintaining the judge's calendar and the person to whom attorneys should direct questions regarding the status of a judge's ruling.

**22.** An attorney is prohibited from having _____ communications with a judge, that is, discussing a case with a judge outside the presence of opposing counsel.

**23.** The state in which the court is located is referred to as the _____ state; shopping for a court that will lead to the most favorable results for the plaintiff is called _____ .

**24.** To find out some detail about a federal rule you could consult _____ or in the _____ ; to update your research in this treatise you would need to look at the _____ .

**25.** In the U.S.C.A. you find _____ , which is a collection of summaries of cases following each procedural rule; you can find those cases using _____ , which are short references, giving the name of the case and the reporter in which it is found.

**26.** The _____ rules of procedure dictate the proper format of court papers, the size and type of paper to be used, and other details relating to requirements set forth by the court clerk's office.

## TRUE OR FALSE

**27.** The U.S. Constitution controls all other laws.      **T  F**

**28.** The executive branch of government carries out the laws created by the legislative branch.      **T  F**

**29.** The state legislatures and Congress must decide which cases the courts will hear.      **T  F**

**30.** Case law can be found in the *United States Code* or the *United States Code Annotated.*      **T  F**

**31.** The primary source of federal procedural law is court rules.      **T  F**

**32.** Most state procedural rules are created by the highest court in the state.      **T  F**

**33.** The U.S. Court of Appeals is divided into thirteen circuits.      **T  F**

**34.** Most appeals to the U.S. Supreme Court are discretionary.      **T  F**

**35.** The U.S. Supreme Court accepts almost all of the cases that are presented to it for review.      **T  F**

**36.** Appellate courts focus on issues of law.  **T  F**

**37.** An appellate court must allow parties to present oral arguments.      **T  F**

**38.** In all states the trial court is called the superior court and the highest court is called the supreme court.      **T  F**

**39.** Superior courts are usually created by state law but funded and administered by county governments.      **T  F**

**40.** The court administrator is responsible for handling all of the administrative functions of the courts.      **T  F**

**41.** The benefit of assigning one judge to a case is that the judge becomes familiar with the facts of the case as it progresses.      **T  F**

**42.** Assigning judges by function rather than by case arguably promotes efficiency in the court system.      **T  F**

**43.** Papers filed with the court clerk's office are considered public records.      **T  F**

**44.** Legal assistants rarely need to file papers with the court clerk so having a working knowledge of the court clerk's office is not important.      **T  F**

**45.** Electronic access to court files is prohibited by case law.                                    **T   F**

**46.** The procedures in specialty courts may differ somewhat from the procedures employed in other civil courts.                         **T   F**

**47.** The goal of jurisdictional rules is to send cases to courts that are most convenient for the parties.                                   **T   F**

**48.** When researching state procedural issues, consult the state version of the procedural rules before looking at the Federal Rules of Civil Procedure.                                    **T   F**

**49.** The Federal Rules of Civil Procedure are irrelevant to any procedural issue at the state level.                                    **T   F**

**50.** Failure to comply with the local rules of procedure can result in the court clerk rejecting your filing.                                    **T   F**

**51.** The local rules are not written down anywhere.                                    **T   F**

## LITIGATION LINGO

*(Answers in Appendix A)*
**Read the description and provide the word that matches that description.**
### WHAT'S MY NAME?

1.  I help you locate cases in law reporters.

2.  I am the trial court at the federal level.

3.  I am a written argument prepared for the appellate court.

4.  I am the person who has to respond to number 3.

5.  I am the summaries of cases found in the U.S.C.A.

6.  I am the state in which the court is located that is hearing a case.

7.  I am the judge who is responsible for the smooth running of the courts.

8.  I am the person who is most likely to reject your court filing.

9.  I am the court where cases involving relatively small amounts of money are heard.

10. I am one of the eleven geographical regions into which the U.S. Court of Appeals is divided.

11. I am what an appellate court judge does when she changes the trial court's decision in a case up on appeal.

12. I am one of the rules that dictates the required format for a document that is about to be filed.

13. I am a type of appeal that a court can decide to hear or not to hear.

14. I am responsible for maintaining the orderly flow of cases and for assigning cases to judges.

15. I am the one you contact if you have a question about whether the judge has received a particular document or if you want to know how the judge prefers to set up exhibits during trial.

16. I am a treatise you could consult if you wanted to find out more about a particular federal rule.

17. I am where you would look if you wanted to update the rule you looked up in number 16.

## LITIGATION LOGISTICS

*(Answers in Appendix A)*

***For each question give the rule of civil procedure in your jurisdiction that applies and then answer the question.***

1. Suppose the drunk driver that sideswiped your car (hypothetical situation at the beginning of Chapter 1) was an undercover police officer whose residence was in another jurisdiction and whose act of hitting you constituted a tort under the Federal Tort Claims Act. What courts could you possibly sue in? What would you have to know to make your decision about where to sue?

2. You have just been hired at a personal injury firm. As part of its orientation the firm takes you down to the court clerk's office. What kinds of questions will you ask of the deputy court clerk?

3. Your supervising attorney asks you to research a federal rule in reference to discovery. Where will you look?

## PROCEDURAL PONDERABLES

1. Consider the hypothetical situations given at the beginning of Chapter 1. Can you think of any reason you might choose to sue in federal court in any of those situations? If you opted to sue in state court, what factors would determine whether you sued in a small claims court or trial court?
   a. Drunk driver sideswipes your car.
   b. Tenant stops paying rent and refuses to move out.
   c. Cousin refuses to pay you a percentage of his business.
   d. Karate instructor breaks your nose.
   e. Contractor does shoddy work on house.

2. Visit the federal court, state court, city court, and small claims court in your jurisdiction. Locate the court clerk's office and ask for a copy of the local rules.

# CHAPTER 3

# ROAD MAP OF A LAWSUIT: PREFILING PREPARATION AND PLEADINGS

## OBJECTIVES

**In this chapter you will learn:**

■ What happens in the beginning stages of a typical lawsuit

■ What tasks need to be completed before suit is filed

■ How a lawsuit is started

■ What pleadings are and what goes into them

■ What paralegals do in the early stages of lawsuits

The discussion of the next few chapters will draw examples from the following narrative. The people, places, and occurrences described are entirely fictitious. We have chosen to place these events in particular named states because the alternative of inventing fictitious states would make the narrative awkward. In describing the litigation that might result from this hypothetical situation (or "hypo," in the jargon of law students everywhere) we will refer to the courts of the states named; the procedure we describe, however, is that of a generic federal district court or of a generic state court in a federal rules state. It is a composite of common procedural practices taken from various courts. For details applicable to a specific court, you should refer to that court's rules.

### Shannon's Ordeal

*S*hannon was not sure, afterward, what had awakened her. It might have been the muted swish of the solid hotel room door opening over the thick carpet, or the rustle of the curtains as the light summer breeze wafted momentarily through the open window, or perhaps it was the change in pitch of the traffic sounds from the nearby freeway. Shannon shifted restlessly under the single sheet, and blinked as she struggled to make out the luminous digits of her designer wristwatch—one-fifteen in the morning. She groaned quietly, willing herself to go back to sleep, needing to be sharp for her sales presentation at nine o'clock tomorrow morning—no, she corrected herself, this morning.

Suddenly, Shannon was seized with the certainty that she was not alone in the room. Afraid of making noise and alarming the intruder, she silently opened her eyes. Her breath caught in her throat as she observed the tall man standing at the foot of the bed, his back to her, removing first his trousers, then his boxer-style underwear.

She had to do something—quickly, now, think! Where had she left her purse? In the bathroom . . . no! There it was, on the bedside table, a few feet away. Silently, silently, feigning sleep, she edged to her right, toward the bedside table, reaching for the purse. . . . Miraculously, the intruder still had his back turned, taking his time . . . a few seconds more . . . quietly opening the flap of the purse. . . .

Then, everything happened in a blur. Shannon withdrew the cheap "Saturday Night Special" 0.22-caliber revolver from her purse as the intruder turned toward the bed. Shannon aimed at the intruder's chest and pulled the trigger. The hammer fell with a harmless click. The intruder, startled, froze for a moment. Shannon pulled the trigger again, pulling the shot low and to the right, this time striking the tall man in the side. The intruder yelled in pain, threw himself on top of Shannon before she could fire again, and wrenched the gun from her hand. Shannon screamed as her forefinger, caught in the trigger guard, broke with an audible snap.

Shannon's mind had already begun shutting out the reality of the inevitable violation, so it took a moment for the intruder's words to register. "What the devil is the matter with you, you . . . crazy. . . ." Then, bleeding profusely from his gunshot wound, the tall man collapsed on top of her, unconscious.

Crazy with fear, Shannon wriggled out from under her attacker. She ran from the room and, bypassing the elevators as too slow, raced down the fire stairs to the lobby.

Arnie Trevayne, stuck with the graveyard shift at the front desk this week, knew he was in deep trouble the minute he saw Shannon burst hysterically from the stairwell in her nightgown. The tall man, Dr. Art Collins, here in Las

*Vegas for a medical convention, had returned from a late dinner, stopped at the desk, and asked Arnie for his room key. The elevator doors were closing behind Dr. Collins when Arnie realized his mistake. Arnie thought of rushing after the doctor, but he really shouldn't leave the desk—there were no other hotel employees around at that time of night. Anyway, the man would certainly return when the key failed to open his door.*

*Except it wasn't Dr. Collins who was now running toward him, it was that sales executive lady from the room next to Dr. Collins—the room whose key Arnie had mistakenly given to Dr. Collins. She was screaming incoherently, something about calling the police.*

*Quickly weighing his options, Arnie dialed 911.*

*Then he calmly palmed the key to Dr. Collins's room—the correct key this time—took the service elevator to the fourth floor, entered Shannon's room, and quickly spotted the room key laying on the dresser.*

*Arnie didn't hesitate. He switched the keys, left the room, and was back at the registration desk before the police arrived.*

# THE PHASES OF A LAWSUIT

Most of us have a general idea what it means to sue someone. The aggrieved party goes to a lawyer and "files suit"; two or three commercials later, there is a trial, in which two lawyers extract the real truth from a few witnesses by clever questioning, then deliver impassioned and eloquent arguments to a jury. The jury returns a verdict, there is a winner and a loser, and the suit is over.

There is, as you would expect, a great deal more to litigation than that. Trials make exciting television, but most of the important activity in a lawsuit—meaning the activity that determines who wins or loses—happens long before the trial begins, some of it even before suit is filed.

Lawsuits come in all shapes and sizes; some end quickly, others drag on for years or even decades. It may surprise you that very few end in a jury verdict; many more are settled somewhere along the way. Outcomes are rarely as satisfyingly decisive as depicted by Hollywood. To a determined litigant, an adverse jury verdict merely marks the beginning of another phase of the conflict.

Nevertheless, most lawsuits follow a rather predictable path. Many variations are possible, but the broad outlines are dictated by the rules of procedural law. We now tour some of the main landmarks along that path, using as a point of departure the "hypo" related at the beginning of this chapter.

Our exploration generally follows along the route laid out by the descriptions of the phases of a lawsuit from Chapter 1 (see Figure 1–1). We reiterate that you should not attach too much importance to the sequence of events; in most lawsuits, many tasks occur simultaneously, rather than in sequence.

*As Shannon entered the Phoenix law offices of Simon and Porter, the first thing she noticed was the statue of the blindfolded goddess holding the scales of justice, prominently displayed on a pedestal in the reception area. Perhaps it was a good omen, she reflected bitterly—she certainly hadn't seen much justice so far, in the two weeks that had passed since what she had come to think of as The Ordeal.*

*Physically, Shannon was a wreck. Each night, around two in the morning, overcome by exhaustion and lulled by the sound of the television that she now left on continuously for company, she would drift into a troubled and restless sleep, only to be jerked bolt upright minutes later, heart pounding in terror, gripped by the vivid image of the tall man as he threw himself on top of her yet again in her imagination. Her broken finger throbbed with pain, but the pain pills seemed to intensify the panic attacks, so she avoided taking them.*

*Shannon tried earnestly to continue her demanding schedule of sales meetings and product demonstrations without interruption. But when, for the second time, she burst spontaneously into fits of weeping in the midst of her presentation, Shannon's sales manager gently but firmly insisted that she take a leave of absence, to "get some rest, get yourself back together"—which only made the situation all the more unbearable. Her job had provided at least some distraction, some escape from the endless mental replays, and, worse, without the continual infusion of sales commissions from new accounts, Shannon's income would quickly dwindle.*

*The police investigation, far from being a source of satisfaction and comfort, had merely added another dimension to Shannon's distress. She had cooperated fully when the first police officers arrived at the hotel, expecting sympathetic treatment. The officer's words still echoed in Shannon's memory: "Shannon Martin, you are under arrest for aggravated assault and battery and illegal discharge of a firearm. . . . You have the right to remain silent. . . ."*

*"But I'm the victim!" she had wanted to scream. They had waited for a woman officer, who drove her in a police car to the hospital to have her broken finger set. Then she had sat for what seemed like hours in a locked room at the police station.*

*Finally, with the sun's first rays penetrating the room's grimy barred window, a well-dressed woman appeared. "I'm Detective Sergeant Marnell, with the Las Vegas Police Department. . . ." Something about an investigation. "You're free to go, but please stay in touch." Shannon had a thousand questions, but the impulse to escape, to get out of there as fast as possible, was so intense that she mutely collected her belongings, rushed outside, and flagged down a cab to the airport, where, after waiting two hours, she was first in line to board the 8:00 A.M. flight back to Phoenix.*

*Since then, she had called every day, persisting in the face of Detective Marnell's thinly veiled impatience. Had her attacker been arrested? Did they need her to file charges? "These things take time. . . ."*

*Finally, today, as Shannon sat in her kitchen, her thoughts drifting from the mindless babble emanating from the television, something snapped. With sudden resolve, she opened the yellow pages, chose a number, and dialed.*

*Now, a few hours later, Shannon strode resolutely up to the receptionist's desk. "My name is Shannon Martin. I have an appointment with Allen Porter."*

# PREFILING PHASE

Meeting Shannon for the first time, Allen Porter will have little or no idea why she has decided to see a litigator. The first step is to interview his prospective client and get enough of the facts to allow him to decide whether there is a potential lawsuit lurking amid the confusion, and, if so, whether it is one that he should undertake. If any of Shannon's claims might create conflicts of interest with other clients of his firm, or if her case presents too many issues outside his area of expertise, he will decline the representation and offer to refer her to another attorney.

If he accepts the case, the next task is to obtain whatever pertinent information Shannon herself can provide. Often, there will be important gaps in the client's knowledge of the facts. Shannon, for example, can tell her lawyer volumes about what happened to her and how it has affected her life, but she simply does not know many of the facts that will be needed to prepare a lawsuit—she probably does not even know who she should sue.

One of Allen Porter's first duties, therefore, will be to obtain more detailed facts from other sources. With the facts in hand, he will be better equipped to make strategic decisions about how best to carry out the suit, as well as to attempt settlement if feasible.

*Allen Porter looked up from his notepad as Shannon finished speaking and smiled reassuringly. "It certainly sounds as though you ought to sue someone—I'm just not sure who, at this point." He paused, waiting for Shannon to make eye contact. "Why don't we see if Detective—Marnell, right?—Detective Marnell is in, maybe she can fill in some of the blanks." He looked at his notepad again, then reached for the telephone.*

## INVESTIGATION AND FACT GATHERING

How much does the lawyer or paralegal need to know about the facts of a case before filing suit? How much investigation is necessary to do?

First, a certain minimum level of factual information is necessary merely to be able to draft a complaint. You need to know the names and residences of the people you are suing. You need to have a clear idea of "who did what to whom," so that you can draft the part of the complaint that describes what the dispute is about. Ethical rules and FRCP, Rule 11(b), require that a lawyer signing a complaint have a reasonable basis for believing that the claims made are well grounded, both factually and legally.

---

*Your Local Notes*

_____

_____

---

You are probably thinking that it would not be very difficult to obtain this minimal information, and you are right. In garden-variety auto accident cases, the information needed to draft a complaint can often be obtained from the police report. There are often good reasons to do considerably more investigating before suing, however.

Modern courts generally take a somewhat active role in moving cases through the system. Lawyers are expected to prepare cases for trial diligently once suit is filed, and most courts require particular tasks in the preparation of the case to be completed within specified time periods after suit is begun. Many courts have adopted rules requiring each party to give written disclosure, within the first few months after suit is filed, spelling out in detail exactly what each party's claims are, what written evidence exists, what witnesses might be called, and what information each witness has about the case. At this stage, lack of preparedness can carry a heavy penalty: Parties may be barred from using evidence that is not promptly disclosed.

---

*Your Local Notes*

_____

_____

---

The point is that once suit is filed, there will be a great deal of pressure to meet various deadlines, so it is an advantage to prepare as much material beforehand as possible. Ideally, plaintiff's attorney would prefer to delay filing until she is fully familiar with the case, has reviewed all the evidence, has planned a strategy, and can easily meet the court-imposed disclosure and other deadlines with a minimum of last minute scrambling. Other considerations often preclude an ideal level of prefiling preparation, but, in general, an early and thorough factual investigation may give one contestant a nearly unbeatable edge, whereas a poor or careless one may create an insurmountable handicap.

> *Shannon waited expectantly as Allen Porter thanked Detective Marnell and hung up the telephone.*
>
> *"Okay, I think the picture is becoming a bit clearer now. It seems that Dr. Collins—the man in your room—thought he was going into his own room. He picked up his key from the front desk when he came in, and he swears he used it to open your door. You were in 407, he was in 409, right next door. He's recovering, by the way—it looks as though he'll get out of the hospital in another week or two."*
>
> *Shannon interrupted, "Are they going to arrest him? They wouldn't tell me."*
>
> *"They don't think that they have any grounds for arrest. They believe Dr. Collins, that it was a mistake. He's a prominent physician in Dallas, a family man, nothing at all in his background to suggest this kind of thing. The big question is, how did he get into your room? The Banbury Park Hotel people are apparently saying that you must have left the door ajar and forgotten to lock it."*
>
> *Shannon exploded. "That's a lie. I checked it twice before I went to bed. I'm practically paranoid about that. Why do you think I bought a gun?"*

**Putting It Into Practice:**

*Why might Allen Porter have reservations about suing at this point? Are there any ethical considerations for him to ponder?*

## STRATEGIC DECISION MAKING

A number of strategic decisions must be made before suit is filed, and these, too, require a thorough knowledge of the facts of the case.

Who, for example, should Shannon sue, and what claims should she make? Should she sue Dr. Collins? For battery? For negligence? Is he liable, even if he entered Shannon's room by mistake? Should she also sue the hotel? How *would* you sue the hotel? Is Banbury Park a corporation, or a partnership, or what? Does she sue its partners or shareholders too? If the hotel turns out to be a locally owned franchise, can she sue the parent company? Should she sue Arnie Trevayne, the desk clerk? On what grounds?

And what about the less obvious targets? (How many can you think of?) Should Shannon consider suing her employer? Her supervisor? The Las Vegas Police Department? The officers that arrested her? The insurance companies that insure the various potential defendants? The medical group that employs Dr. Collins? Dr. Collins's wife (Texas is a community property state)? Can Shannon sue the Phoenix pawnshop that sold her the misfiring handgun? The manufacturer of the handgun?

In what court should suit be filed? Depending on the facts, Shannon may have the option of suing in federal court or in the state courts of two or more states. (We will see why this is so in Chapter 5.)

What relief should Shannon ask for? Her medical expenses? Psychiatrist bills? Damages for pain and suffering? Punitive damages? Can she claim damages for the commissions on the sales she would have made had she continued working without interruption? For the slight but permanent stiffness in her finger after it heals?

These questions involve mainly issues that are substantive, not procedural, but they need to be answered before a complaint can be properly drafted. Shannon's complaint must, among other things, state who she is suing and what she is asking the court for. Each question will require factual investigation and legal research before a dependable answer can be given.

We do not mean to imply that these decisions are forever carved in stone and unchangeable after suit is filed. Within limits, complaints can be amended, parties and claims can be added and deleted. It is sometimes necessary to file suit quickly and fill in the gaps later. Amending the complaint usually requires the opponent's acquiescence or the judge's permission. Agreement to amend from the defendant will be hard to come by if the changes benefit the plaintiff, so it is far better to get it right the first time if possible.

## PREREQUISITES TO SUIT

Injured parties are not always free to fire off a lawsuit as their first offensive move. There is a category of suits, usually involving situations that come under the regulation of some government agency, in which the aggrieved party must first "exhaust administrative remedies." Injured employees covered by workers' compensation laws, for example, are usually prohibited from suing their employer; they must instead apply for compensation from the workers' compensation fund. Resort to the courts is possible only after the applicable state agency has made its decision. Claims involving illegal discrimination often must first be brought to the Equal Employment Opportunity Commission or other administrative agency having jurisdiction; the agency in question must investigate and give permission before the aggrieved party can sue.

Suits against government agencies and departments are particularly demanding of careful pre-suit planning. Historically, the government was immune from suit altogether. Although this absolute **sovereign immunity** no longer applies, vestiges remain in the form of statutes that require anyone intending to sue an agency of the government to give notice of his or her claim before filing suit. Prerequisites for suit against the federal government are found in the Federal Tort Claims Act. State, county, and city requirements, if any, vary from place to place. Notices of claims must be in the correct form and delivered to the correct government official within the allowed time period, which is typically short. Often, even a seemingly trivial defect in the notice will cause the suit to be dismissed, perhaps forever. If Shannon sues the Las Vegas Police Department for false arrest, her lawyer will need to comply carefully with any notice of claim requirement.

> *Your Local Notes*
> _____
> _____

These examples are intended as a small sample of the kinds of prerequisites to suit that may exist. Obviously, it is impossible to provide an exhaustive list, because each case presents its own factual problems. But the attorneys defending the suit will be combing the facts in search of any basis on which to get the case dismissed quickly, so the prudent plaintiff's attorney will do everything possible to avoid giving the defense any ammunition.

*Putting It Into Practice:*

*Why might a commercial litigator find it difficult to represent an employee alleging discrimination?*

## POSITIONING THE CASE

The pre-suit phase also represents an opportunity for the attorneys on each side to try to "engineer" the factual development of the case. Once an attorney knows an opposing party is represented by an attorney, ethical rules prohibit direct contact. (It is, of course, also unethical for an attorney to have a paralegal do something that the attorney could not ethically do.) Before suit is filed, however, the attorney or paralegal can usually contact others involved in the dispute, obtain statements, and ask for information. In accident cases where one of the drivers is insured, it is commonplace for insurance company representatives to take statements from all drivers and witnesses. The purpose is not merely to determine the facts, but also to record important observations in a way that precludes one's opponents from inventing more convenient versions later.

> *"Hi, I'm Chuck Fletcher. I have a reservation."*
>
> *The desk clerk handed him a card. "Here, fill this out."*
>
> *"I heard you had some excitement here a couple weeks ago."*
>
> *"Yeah, some woman left her room door open, and this other guy, it's late at night, he goes in there by accident, and the crazy bimbo shoots him."*
>
> *"No kidding! She left her door open? In the middle of the night? Strange!"*
>
> *"Yeah, well, you know, this is an old hotel, some of the doors, they don't always close all the way by themselves. She probably didn't realize."*
>
> *Chuck Fletcher accepted the proffered key from Arnie Trevayne. As he walked toward the elevators, he made detailed notes of the conversation.*

## SETTLEMENT NEGOTIATIONS

A reasonable settlement is almost always better than a lawsuit, even for the winner of the lawsuit. Litigation is expensive and time consuming and distracts the litigants from their regular pursuits, and the emotional toll can be devastating. Filing a lawsuit tends to cause a degree of polarization of the parties that may make settlement more difficult; hence, if any possibility of settlement exists, it should be explored before suit is filed unless there are strong strategic reasons not to. Even if settlement is not feasible, it may be to the benefit of both parties to consider some form of alternative dispute resolution, such as arbitration or mediation.

One way of initiating settlement negotiations is through the use of a demand letter. Pre-suit demand letters are routinely used in auto accident cases and other tort suits where insurance companies will be calling the shots on the defense side.

In multiparty disputes, pre-suit settlement takes on another dimension: Parties may find it advantageous to settle with one potentially adverse party, so as to be able to join forces against a third. This is particularly common among codefendants. For example, even though Banbury Park Hotel has a potential claim against its negligent employee, Arnie Trevayne, the hotel's lawyers will certainly reach some accommodation with Arnie. Otherwise, he might decide to settle separately with Shannon, and testify in her favor. For this reason, employees who subject their employers to lawsuits often enjoy great job security—at least until the suit is over!

## OTHER CONSIDERATIONS

Proper technical preparation is not, of course, an excuse for procrastination. In most cases, the need for pre-suit preparation must be balanced against the need to maintain momentum. An opponent who carries out each task decisively and

---

*Putting It
Into Practice:*

*Would this be an appropriate time for Shannon to offer to settle with the hotel?*

without delay will likely be taken as a more credible threat than one who is long on talk but short on action. Another possible reason for speed in filing is to pre-empt action by the other party. With many disputes, suit could be brought by either party. In our hypothetical situation, we have been assuming that Shannon would file suit first. But it is equally likely that some other party—Dr. Collins, for example—may get to the courthouse ahead of Shannon, if for no other reason than to seize the initiative in deciding which court to litigate in.

## ROLE OF THE PARALEGAL

Attorneys often rely heavily on the assistance of paralegals in managing pre-suit preparation. Merely having access to a complete and well-organized set of pertinent documents can be an enormous advantage. In offices that concentrate on particular types of cases, such as automobile accident or debt collection practices, a case management system will often be in place, with established procedures and checklists to ensure that routine pre-suit requirements are completed in each case. In practices involving a greater variety of cases, or cases of greater procedural complexity (such as our hypo!), considerably more individualized judgment and planning may be required. In either situation, paralegals can make an important contribution, not merely by performing assigned tasks, but also by seeking to identify requirements that may have been overlooked, and by paying close attention to the progress of each task, so that filing of suit will not be unnecessarily delayed by some item that has "fallen through a crack."

In practices involving a high volume of individual clients, such as personal injury and divorce practices, a good deal of the pre-suit factual workup and case screening may be assigned to paralegals. Paralegals may be assigned to interview clients and prospective clients, often with the aid of an information checklist or questionnaire, for the purpose of obtaining the factual data necessary to prepare the suit for filing, and perhaps to help decide which cases to accept.

> *"Shannon, thank you for coming in. I think we're about ready to file, but I wanted to go over everything with you and make sure that you understand what we're doing and why. You've met our paralegal, Chuck Fletcher, of course—Chuck will be drafting up the papers to get the lawsuit going."*
>
> *"Sure. Hi, Chuck."*
>
> *Allen Porter continued. "Let me just summarize where we are. First, Dr. Collins. This is all very puzzling. I spoke to Dr. Collins's lawyer in Dallas and, frankly, I find it very hard to believe he intended to attack you."*
>
> *"I locked my room. I locked my room. If you don't believe me, I—"*
>
> *Chuck Fletcher interrupted. "Of course we believe you. But just ask yourself, how did the man get in? Did he use lockpicks? Did he have a master key? The police didn't find anything like that, and he was still in your bed, unconscious, when the police arrived, remember."*
>
> *Shannon had no response.*
>
> *Allen Porter resumed, "The point is, we're obviously still missing some facts. We need to get the suit filed so we can take some discovery and see what we can pry loose. Clearly, we have enough to support a claim against Dr. Collins, for negligence, at least. After all, he was in your room, not his own. You just need to understand that if we sue him, he will certainly countersue—you shot him, don't forget—yes, I know, you thought you were defending yourself, I'm just telling you what his lawyer will do. And, thanks to Chuck's investigating—great job, Chuck—I think we have a pretty good negligence claim against the hotel. We have the desk clerk's admission that the doors don't always close securely. We*

**Putting It Into Practice:**

On what grounds could Dr. Collins sue? What damages could he allege?

**Putting It Into Practice:**

If you worked as a paralegal for Allen Porter, how could you assist at this stage of Shannon's case?

**Putting It
Into Practice:**

*With the facts as you now
know them, what
potential claims exist in
this case? Evaluate the
pros and cons of each
claim.*

*have your testimony that you checked the door, twice. There isn't any other plau-
sible explanation for how Dr. Collins got into your room."*

*Shannon considered the lawyer's words in silence. Porter summed up:
"So, bottom line, my advice is to go ahead and file suit against Dr. Collins and
the hotel. We can do that in federal court here in Phoenix."*

# SUIT PREPARATION PHASE: PLEADINGS

The first formal activity in a lawsuit consists of a process called pleading,
which is intended to force all parties to specify, on the written record, exactly
what the dispute is about. This is done in turns: Plaintiff files a complaint, each
defendant files an answer to the complaint, and finally plaintiff files a reply to
any new claims (called counterclaims) made by any defendant against plaintiff. Defendants are also given an opportunity to make claims against each
other and against others who are not yet parties; see FRCP, Rules 7–11. When
complete, the pleadings frame the issues for the entire lawsuit; no party is allowed to delve into issues that are outside the scope of the pleadings.

> *Your Local Notes*
>
> _____
>
> _____

## COMPLAINT

A civil lawsuit is begun by the plaintiff filing a **complaint** with an appropriate
court. The plaintiff is the party who starts the suit; the defendant is the party
being sued. The complaint is a formal, written statement in which the plaintiff
describes, in summary fashion, what the dispute is about, and what plaintiff
wants the court to do.

The statements in a pleading in which a party lays out his version of what
happened to cause the dispute are called **allegations.** It is customary for the allegations of a complaint to be organized in numbered paragraphs so that they
can be easily referred to in the answer and in other court papers. The complaint
ends with a **prayer for relief,** a concluding section stating specifically what
plaintiff wants the court to do (typically, award a money judgment for damages). The complaint is signed by plaintiff's attorney; see FRCP, Rule 11(a).
There can be more than one plaintiff in a lawsuit, but only one complaint.

How do you decide what allegations to put into a complaint, how to organize them, and how to express them? Good complaint drafting is an art; we
will consider it in detail in Workshop 5. For now, it suffices to say that the allegations must be sufficient to **state a claim.** To state a claim, the allegations
must include each of the **elements** of the **cause of action** for which plaintiff is
suing. Meaning what, exactly? (See sidebar.)

## FILING AND SERVICE OF PROCESS

After Shannon's complaint has been prepared and signed, it must be filed with
the clerk of the court—in other words, it is presented to a deputy clerk with
the required filing fee. Many jurisdictions also require a completed *information*

---

**SIDEBAR**

## Elements of a Cause of Action

*What is a cause of action? The law does not impose liability for every offense. You can win a lawsuit against someone only if you prove that they did something that the law recognizes as an **actionable wrong**—that is, they did something that falls into one of the established categories of offenses for which lawsuits are allowed.*

*How can you tell if a particular set of facts comprises one of the recognized causes of action? By checking to see whether each of the elements of that cause of action is satisfied. The elements of a cause of action are the specific things that you must prove in order to win a lawsuit based on it. For example, the cause of action for negligence has four elements: duty, breach of duty, causation, and damages. Thus, to state a cause of action for negligence against Banbury Park Hotel, Shannon's complaint might allege that (1) the hotel had a duty to provide safe accommodations for guests; (2) the hotel breached that duty by knowingly allowing the room doors to fall into a poor state of repair so that they do not close properly; (3) the hotel's failure to maintain the doors properly caused Shannon to be injured; and (4) Shannon was injured and lost money as a result. If Shannon fails to prove each of those four things at trial, she loses as to the negligence claim. Of course, if the facts can support claims based on other causes of action, she can include those in her complaint too—each cause of action is considered separately.*

*Being able to think of lawsuits as made up of separate claims or causes of action, and of causes of action as being broken down into specific required elements, is a fundamental skill in litigation. Where do the elements of causes of action come from? Mainly from case law: Appellate courts decide what is required. For a concise summary of the elements of the various tort causes of actions, a good place to start is the Restatement of Torts, which you can find in any law library.*

---

**Putting It Into Practice:**

*What facts can Shannon use to support her cause of action?*

---

*sheet* or *cover sheet* to be filed with the complaint; this is typically a printed form listing the names and addresses of the parties and their attorneys, telephone numbers, and other information needed by the clerk's office. Other papers, such as statements of whether the case is subject to compulsory arbitration, may also be required.

The clerk of the court keeps the original, signed complaint to be placed in the court's file. The person filing the complaint has brought additional copies, which the clerk stamps and returns; these are for the plaintiff's lawyer's file and for delivery to each defendant. The clerk also issues summonses addressed to each defendant. A **summons** is a court order, usually a one-page printed form completed by the plaintiff that the clerk signs and stamps, requiring each defendant to appear before the court and defend the suit; see FRCP, Rule 4(a–c).

Court papers are supplied to the involved parties via the **service** process. A copy of the summons and complaint is served on each defendant. To serve a paper on another party means to deliver it to them in a formal manner prescribed by the rules. As you can readily imagine, it is very important that each defendant be notified that he has been sued, and it is equally important that plaintiff be able to prove that each defendant was notified. The rules of procedure include detailed instructions on how process is to be served under a variety of common circumstances. One method used in many courts is to have

## SIDEBAR

### Captions

*One format requirement found in all courts is the **caption**. The complaint, and all other papers filed with the court, must begin with a caption, which is a kind of title block that includes the name of the court, the names of the plaintiff and defendant, and the case number. The caption also identifies what the paper is: complaint, answer, motion to dismiss, etc. The clerk's office uses the caption to ensure that the paper goes to the right file. Each court has rules specifying caption format, spacing, and content. The caption of Shannon's complaint might look like this:*

**IN THE UNITED STATES DISTRICT COURT OF ARIZONA**

| | | |
|---|---|---|
| SHANNON MARTIN, a single woman, | ) | |
| | ) | |
| | ) | NO. _____ |
| Plaintiff, | ) | |
| | ) | COMPLAINT |
| v. | ) | |
| | ) | |
| ARTHUR COLLINS and JANE DOE | ) | |
| COLLINS, husband and wife; PARK | ) | |
| HOTELS GROUP, INC., a Delaware | ) | |
| corporation; DOES I through X; | ) | |
| BLACK CORPORATIONS I through V; | ) | |
| | ) | |
| | ) | |
| Defendants. | ) | |
| _____ | ) | |

*(Why the "John Does" and the "Black Corporations"? See Workshop 5.)*

someone locate each defendant and hand deliver the summons and complaint in person; this is called **personal service.** (Personal service is not the only possible way to serve the summons and complaint; we will take up others in Chapter 4; see FRCP, Rule 4). The person who serves the summons and complaint may be a sheriff or other government official, or, in many courts, the job is done by a private **process server,** who makes a profession of locating parties and witnesses and serving court papers on them. Courts that allow private process servers often require them to be trained and licensed. However, see FRCP, Rule 4(c)(2), which allows service by a noninterested party at least 18 years of age. After serving a copy of the summons and complaint on each defendant, the sheriff or process server signs and files an affidavit of service with the court, which serves as proof that delivery was actually made. [In some jurisdictions, this affidavit may be called a **return of service,** and the specific form and contents of the paper may vary, but the purpose is to establish the fact of delivery in the court record; see FRCP, Rule 4(l).]

*Your Local Notes*

_____

_____

## SIDEBAR

### Court Papers

*The complaint is the first of many papers that will be filed with the court during the course of a lawsuit. (Papers filed with the court are sometimes referred to generically as pleadings, although, strictly speaking, the term pleadings includes only the complaint, answer, and replies to counterclaims or cross-claims, if any.) Each court has rules on the format of papers to be filed with the court, and the clerk of the court will refuse to accept papers that are not in the proper format. These rules may at times seem arbitrary, but when you remember that the clerk's office in a busy urban court system is responsible for keeping track of literally millions of pages of new filings each year, you can appreciate the need for uniformity.*

*How do you find out what format is required in a particular court? Check the local rules for that court.*

*Putting It Into Practice:*

*What format would Shannon be required to conform to if she filed suit in your state?*

It sometimes happens that defendant already knows that plaintiff is filing suit and is willing to waive formal service of process. Usually, this is perfectly permissible as long as both parties agree, but plaintiff must take care to follow the rules of the particular court in filing the appropriate documents to establish the waiver. Many courts have established procedures for voluntary acceptance of service that must be followed if you are to be able to claim the

*Putting It Into Practice:*

*If Allen Porter asked you to file Shannon's complaint and serve Dr. Collins, how would you do it in your state?*

## SIDEBAR

### Affidavits

*Often in the course of a lawsuit, you will find that you need a formal way to establish some fact, without going to the expense and difficulty of scheduling a hearing or a deposition and having a witness appear and give live testimony. For example, the fact that the summons and complaint were served on each defendant must be established in the court record, but it would be impractical to hold hearings and force judges to waste their time listening to process servers testify that they delivered the required papers.*

*The solution is to use an **affidavit**. An affidavit is simply the sworn testimony of a witness, which has been written down and signed in the presence of a notary public. It can be filed with the clerk of the court as a substitute for actual, live testimony of a witness in many routine situations. The rules of procedure specify under what circumstances affidavits may be used. For example, after the process server serves Shannon's complaint on Dr. Collins, she will prepare an **affidavit of service** and file it with the court, sending a copy to Shannon's attorney. The affidavit of service is a court paper, bearing the caption of the case. Below the caption, the affidavit will state the facts to be established—for example, that the process server has delivered a copy of the summons and complaint to Dr. Collins, in person, and specifying the time and place that this was done, together with other important details. The process server must sign the affidavit "under oath"; as a practical matter, this is done by having the signature notarized. Just as the laws against perjury prohibit a witness from lying under oath in a courtroom proceeding, giving false testimony in a notarized affidavit is a criminal offense.*

*Putting It Into Practice:*

*If Dr. Collins claims he was not served, how would you verify service?*

costs of service at the conclusion of the lawsuit [should the opposing party refuse to voluntarily accept service; see FRCP, Rule 4 (d).]

```
┌─────────────────────────────────────────────────────────────────────┐
│ Your Local Notes                                                      │
│                                                                       │
│ _____   │
│                                                                       │
│ _____   │
│                                                                       │
└─────────────────────────────────────────────────────────────────────┘
```

## ANSWER

Each defendant receives a copy of the summons and complaint. Under the federal rules and in many state courts, the summons orders a defendant who is personally served to "appear and defend" within twenty days; see FRCP, Rule 12. The time period may be longer if the defendant was served in a different state than the one in which suit was brought.

What does it mean to "appear and defend"? The phrase is perhaps somewhat misleading, and people with little experience in the legal arena often, after being served with a summons, show up at the courthouse on the twentieth day and ask where they are supposed to appear!

The term *appear* is one of those ordinary words that has a legal meaning different from its everyday meaning. As used in the summons, **appear** means to submit formally to the jurisdiction of the court. Ordinarily, this is done by filing an **answer** to the complaint. (A motion to dismiss is another possibility, but we will reserve that level of complexity for a later chapter.)

An answer is a pleading, similar in appearance and content to the complaint, in which the defendant gives his side of the story. In the answer, the defendant must admit or deny the allegations of the complaint, and may add any factual allegations that defendant thinks plaintiff has omitted. Usually, this is done by responding to each of the numbered paragraphs of the complaint. We will take a detailed look at how answers are constructed in Workshop 8.

```
┌─────────────────────────────────────────────────────────────────────┐
│ Your Local Notes                                                      │
│                                                                       │
│ _____   │
│                                                                       │
│ _____   │
│                                                                       │
└─────────────────────────────────────────────────────────────────────┘
```

Defendant must also raise in the answer any affirmative defenses. An **affirmative defense** is one in which, instead of denying plaintiff's allegations, defendant offers some independent reason why defendant cannot be found liable. For example, when Shannon sues Banbury Park Hotel for negligence claiming that the hotel failed to maintain its doors and locks in a safe condition, the hotel will counter with the allegation that Shannon was also negligent in failing to check that the door was securely locked. That is an affirmative defense and the hotel must state it in its answer. If you are not sure how to tell whether a defense qualifies as an affirmative defense, do not worry—there is a rule to help, and we will examine it in Workshop 8; see FRCP, Rule 8(c).

```
┌─────────────────────────────────────────────────────────────────────┐
│ Your Local Notes                                                      │
│                                                                       │
│ _____   │
│                                                                       │
│ _____   │
│                                                                       │
└─────────────────────────────────────────────────────────────────────┘
```

The answer is also the place where the defendant can raise any claims against the plaintiff or against third parties. Often, the best defense is a good offense; it is an unusual dispute in which the defendant cannot think of some reason why the plaintiff is really the one at fault. Any defendant may include **counterclaims** in her answer; a counterclaim is, in effect, a lawsuit by the defendant against the plaintiff. The allegations of a counterclaim are written in the same way as if the defendant were preparing a complaint against the plaintiff. The answer may also include **cross-claims**—claims by one defendant against another defendant. In our hypo, for example, Dr. Collins will counterclaim against Shannon for battery and crossclaim against the hotel for negligence; see FRCP, Rule 13.

If the defendant believes that there is someone whom plaintiff has not sued who should be involved, defendant may also bring **third-party claims,** which are the equivalent of defendant suing someone else. Suppose, for example that Shannon sued Dr. Collins but did not include the hotel as a defendant in the suit. Dr. Collins could bring the hotel into the suit and make his claims against the hotel via a third-party claim. Typically, he would do this by filing and serving (on the hotel) a **third-party complaint,** following rules similar to those that apply to plaintiff's complaint; see FRCP, Rule 4.

> *Putting It Into Practice:*
>
> Might the hotel have any potential counterclaims? Any cross-claims? If Shannon sued the hotel only, what response would you anticipate from the hotel?

---

**Your Local Notes**

_____

_____

---

To the extent that they involve similar issues, all of these counterclaims, cross-claims, and third-party claims will be decided in a single lawsuit. The judge can **sever,** or split off for separate decision, claims that are not sufficiently related to the original suit; see FRCP, Rule 42.

## FILING AND SERVICE OF ANSWER

Having prepared an answer to the complaint, what exactly is the defendant required to do with it? He must file it and serve a copy on plaintiff. At this point, and from now on in this lawsuit, formal service of papers via a process server is generally not necessary. Formal service of the complaint is required because the United States Supreme Court has ruled that anyone being sued is entitled to be notified of that fact by the best means possible in the circumstances. Once the complaint has been served, however, all parties are at least aware that a suit is pending, and can check the court file or simply contact opposing counsel if in doubt about whether a particular paper has been filed. Therefore, the rules provide that all papers after the complaint can be served simply by mailing or delivering a copy to the opposing party's attorney; see FRCP, Rule 5.

Each defendant must answer the complaint within the prescribed time period, which is typically twenty days, but other periods may apply depending on how and where the complaint was served. The last day to file the answer is the first of many deadlines in a lawsuit. Each time a party files some paper with the court, there will usually be a deadline by which the opposing party must respond. Such deadlines are often shifted, either with the agreement of the opposing lawyer or by asking the court for more time.

> *Putting It Into Practice:*
>
> If you were responsible for filing Dr. Collins's answer to Shannon's complaint, how would you do it in your state? How would your handling of Shannon's complaint differ from your handling of Dr. Collins's answer?

> *Putting It Into Practice:*
>
> If you wanted to determine the deadline for Dr. Collins's answer, where would you look?

---

**Your Local Notes**

_____

_____

---

## SIDEBAR

### Forms

*Where do court papers come from? Usually, the lawyers or paralegals in the case write them, and they are typed and printed by a secretary or word processing clerk.*

*In your work as a paralegal, you will often hear lawyers speak of using a "form" complaint or other pleading or court paper. When we speak of "forms" in a law office, we usually do not mean preprinted forms in the sense of, for example, IRS tax forms, in which we simply fill in the blanks. Generally, the complaint, answer, and other court papers are prepared by the parties or their lawyers "from scratch" and preprinted forms are not used. There are exceptions: Printed forms are often used in small claims courts; in certain highly systematized practices such as debt collection; and in most offices for certain routine, one-page clerical items such as subpoenas, praecipes (instructions to the court clerk) and summonses.*

*When a lawyer speaks of, for example, a "form" complaint, she is usually referring to a copy of a complaint that was filed in some other, similar case. Parts of the "form" may be cut and pasted into the rough draft of the current project; other parts may be modified or merely used as a guide. In a modern computerized office, many "form" documents are kept in word processing files so that they can be easily modified without retyping the entire document. Thus, when Chuck Fletcher drafts Shannon's complaint, he will likely begin with a "form" complaint from some other tort case in the office and modify the language to fit Shannon's situation. This prevents lawyers from having to reinvent the wheel at their clients' expense and also serves as a kind of checklist to reduce the chance that some important allegation may be forgotten.*

*A good, complete form file is a valuable tool for a litigator and for a litigation paralegal. Even if your employer maintains an office form file, as most do, we strongly recommend that you build and maintain your own as well. When you draft a new type of document or when you see a well-drafted one prepared by someone else (even an opponent!) make a copy, and add it to your file.*

---

**Putting It Into Practice:**

*What are the possible consequences of incorrectly calculating a filing date and filing papers after the legally required time?*

What happens if the defendant fails or refuses to file an answer on time? In theory, plaintiff wins—a **default judgment** will be entered in plaintiff's favor. This is not automatic. There are, as you have undoubtedly guessed, some procedural steps to be taken—papers to be filed, perhaps hearings to be held— before the court will actually sign a default judgment. Unless the default was deliberate (can you think of a reason why a party might deliberately default?), defendant's attorney will be doing everything possible to derail the process. In practice, the defendant must usually be given notice of the impending default and will somehow manage to scramble out of it, but defaults do occasionally stick, and even where they are eventually set aside, they cause the lawyer (or paralegal!) responsible great embarrassment and poor sleep quality in the meantime; see FRCP, Rule 55.

| Your Local Notes |
|---|
| _____ |
| _____ |

## REPLY

Because any defendant's answer can include counterclaims against the plaintiff, there has to be a mechanism whereby plaintiff can respond to the allegations in the counterclaims. That mechanism is the **reply.** A reply is exactly like an answer, except that it is made by plaintiff in response to a defendant's counterclaims. You might suppose that the defendant would then respond to what plaintiff says in the reply, but modern practice cuts off the exchange of allegations and counterallegations with the reply, mainly because otherwise the pleading phase might never end! See FRCP, Rules 7 and 12.

## CHOICE OF FORUM

More often than you might expect, the outcome of a lawsuit will depend on who ultimately decides it. Judges and juries are people, and they have as many biases and preconceived ideas as the rest of us. Different courts have different procedural rules. Simply moving a case to the courts of another state may also result in quite different substantive law being applied. Case backlogs can differ greatly; a plaintiff will usually prefer a court in which cases reach trial quickly (say, a year), whereas a defendant will often prefer a court in which the caseload is so great that several years may pass before trial.

The particular court that a case proceeds in is called the **forum** for deciding that case. Initially, plaintiff chooses the forum by choosing the court in which to file the complaint. As you might guess, however, there are procedural moves a defendant can make to try to move the case to a different forum, hopefully one more favorable to defendant.

If, for example, the case is filed in state court, and the circumstances are such that it could have been filed in federal court, defendant may have the right to **remove** the case to federal court. If the defendant can convince the current court that it lacks jurisdiction or that venue is improper, or that the case is really more closely connected with some other state and ought to be decided there, the court may dismiss the case, forcing plaintiff to file elsewhere. We take up these subjects in detail in Workshop 2.

> *"Okay, what is it, Chuck?" Allen Porter asked after Shannon left. "I can tell there's something bothering you about this."*
>
> *"Well, as a matter of fact—I didn't want to bring it up in front of the client, but—you told her we could file suit in federal court here in Phoenix. And—," Chuck paused, thinking, "I just don't see how you can get personal jurisdiction over Dr. Collins in Arizona. Doesn't this case have to be filed in Nevada?"*
>
> *"That's quick thinking!" Porter replied. "I was wondering whether you'd pick up on that. You're right, of course. We can sue the Park Hotels Group here in Arizona, because they do business here—they own the Montezuma Park Hotel in Scottsdale—but there is no basis for personal jurisdiction over Dr. Collins, as far as I know."*
>
> *"So—"*
>
> *"I raised the matter with Dr. Collins's attorney in Dallas, and he decided that he would just as soon litigate this in Arizona as in Nevada, so they're willing to consent to jurisdiction here."*

## JOINDER OF ISSUE

In a simple case, there may be a single plaintiff suing one or a few defendants. The only pleadings may be the complaint and an answer filed by all defendants jointly. In more complex cases, there may be several plaintiffs who join in suing

**Putting It Into Practice:**

Who might file a reply in Shannon's case?

**Putting It Into Practice:**

What court in your state would be most favorable for Shannon to file in?

***Putting It Into Practice:***

*If Allen Porter is a busy litigator, why might he be relieved to experience a delay in having the issue joined?*

several defendants, each of whom countersues plaintiffs, makes cross-claims against each other, and brings third-party claims against others whom plaintiff did not sue. In such cases, there is still only one complaint, but there may be a number of separate answers, followed by replies to counterclaims, answers to cross-claims, and answers to third-party claims.

Regardless of the number of parties and the complexity of the claims, there comes a point at which all permissible pleadings have been filed. At this point, we say that "**issue has been joined.**" To oversimplify only a little, this somewhat archaic and mysterious sounding term merely means that the pleading task is complete.

Why do we care when issue is joined? In most courts, you cannot ask for a trial setting until the pleadings are complete.

---

*Your Local Notes*

_____

_____

---

***Putting It Into Practice:***

*If you were Allen Porter's paralegal, what would you include in Shannon's file at this point?*

## ROLE OF THE PARALEGAL

Drafting of routine pleadings is a common assignment for litigation paralegals. In offices that handle a large volume of cases in a particular area of specialization, such as personal injury, insurance defense, or debt collection, complaint drafting generally involves making straightforward modifications to form complaints. Paralegals are handed a file and expected to produce a finished complaint, ready to sign and file with the court. In cases of greater complexity or those that present difficult substantive issues, complaint drafting requires a detailed analysis of the issues based on appropriate legal research. Here, research-qualified paralegals may be asked to prepare a draft for review and editing, but the responsible attorney will participate more actively in the pleading process.

Another important task often performed by paralegals is the administrative job of making sure that pleadings are filed on time and that responses are received when due. Failure to file an answer by the due date can lead to a default judgment against the client and a malpractice suit against the unfortunate lawyer responsible. On the plaintiff's side, it is essential to keep track of the due date so that a notice of default can be filed the instant the answer time has expired and to ensure that any replies are filed by the due date. It is also necessary to work with the process server to ensure that the complaint is served on all defendants within a reasonable time.

***Putting It Into Practice:***

*Would it be ethically proper for Shannon to sue Dr. Collins based on the facts as she understands them at the time she goes to see Allen Porter?*

## ETHICAL ETIQUETTE

Although lawyers should consider all possible claims when preparing a complaint, they are forbidden to bring "frivolous" or unmeritorious claims. Such claims can arise if an attorney brings an action simply to generate fees or fails to confirm information supplied by a client and prepares a complaint based on erroneous information. An attorney who assists a party in bringing a lawsuit in order to maliciously harm, harass, or intimidate his opponent violates various ethical rules. Attorneys are also prohibited from preparing claims that are unwarranted under existing law unless they can make a good faith argument that the law should be changed.

## ETHICAL ETIQUETTE *continued*

In addition to being censured for committing ethical violations, attorneys who bring frivolous suits can be sanctioned under FRCP, Rule 11. Rule 11 requires that complaints be "well grounded in fact" and "warranted by existing law or a good faith argument for the extension, modification, or reversal of existing law" and that they not be filed for any "improper purpose, such as to harass or to cause unnecessary delay or needless increase in the cost of litigation." Violation of this rule may result in being ordered to pay the attorney's fees and expenses of the opponent or in having the complaint dismissed with prejudice. In some cases attorneys or their clients or both have also been required to pay fines. Rule 11 applies to all pleadings, motions, and documents filed with the court. Legal assistants can help prevent attorneys from violating Rule 11 by carefully conducting thorough factual investigations and by checking out all details in preparation for drafting a complaint.

# PRACTICE POINTERS
## *Obtaining Documentary Evidence*

Documents are critical to establishing the factual elements of a case and the responsibility for obtaining these documents is often relegated to legal assistants. Most documentary evidence can be obtained by sending a letter requesting the document. These letters are fairly straightforward (identifying the need for the document and what specific documents are needed), but be careful to phrase your request with sufficient specificity that the individual holding the document will understand what is being requested. With medical doctors, for example, you need to specify whether you need the doctor's notes or her narrative report outlining the patient's treatment and prognosis.

Because medical and employment records are confidential, you need the client to sign a written authorization before the doctor's office or employer will release any records. Although most firms have standard release forms, check the form before using it to make sure it provides everything that you need. Having clients sign several authorization forms in advance prevents them from having to return to the office every time an authorization is needed. Because some institutions require authorizations to be notarized, you may save time by having them all notarized at once.

Before requesting records from any institution, contact them first to see what procedures they require. Find out, for example, if any fees are charged and if those fees must be paid before the records can be released. Many doctors charge nominal fees for their notes and several hundred dollars for their narrative reports.

Once you receive records, review them immediately to ensure that you can read any handwritten entries and that you understand any abbreviations or shorthand notations. Clarifying any ambiguities in advance may save time later, prevent misunderstandings, or open up new avenues of investigation. Treat each new document you receive as a potential "smoking gun" that is critical in winning the case. With this attitude you will be less tempted to procrastinate in your review of records.

## TECHNO TIP

When preparing a complaint or other pleading from your forms file do not merely copy it to a new file. Paste the entire document to your clipboard, create a new document with your word processor, and then copy the pleading into the new document. When you use the "save as" or similar function to reproduce a document, any glitches with the old document are recreated in the new one. This is especially important if you are using a form created with an older version of your word processor or if you are converting from one word processor to another (such as creating a new Word document with a form that was created in WordPerfect).

# SUMMARY

During the initial interview the attorney attempts to get enough information to assess whether a potential lawsuit exists, whether any conflicts of interest prevent him from taking the case, and whether the case falls within the range of his expertise. Having decided to take the case, the attorney does as much investigation as possible before filing suit. Doing so ensures that the attorney has a reasonable basis for believing that the claims made are factually and legally well grounded and minimizes the pressure to meet disclosure and other procedural deadlines after the suit has been filed. On the other hand, the prompt filing of suit can give the plaintiff more credibility as a viable threat and can preempt action by the opponent. When preparing to file a suit, the attorney must decide whom to sue, what claims to allege, which court to sue in, and what relief to request. Although most of these decisions can be amended at a later date, the plaintiff benefits from making the optimal decision up front.

Plaintiffs filing suit against administrative agencies must first exhaust their administrative remedies. Before filing suit against a governmental entity the plaintiff must check to make sure that the entity is not protected by sovereign immunity and that any prerequisites to filing suit have been satisfied. Attorneys should contact others involved in a dispute before suit is filed in order to obtain statements and get information because once the complaint is filed attorneys are precluded from making direct contact with opposing parties.

Reaching a settlement agreement is almost always better than filing a lawsuit because of the time and expense entailed in a lawsuit and because of the emotional toll litigation exacts on its participants. Because filing suit often further polarizes parties, settlement should be attempted before suit is filed. Settlement negotiations include the use of demand letters and, when multiple parties are involved, settlement with only one of the parties.

Legal assistants assist in the pretrial phase of litigation by interviewing prospective clients, by ensuring that all tasks germane to filing suit are completed, and by making sure that no details are overlooked.

A lawsuit begins with the filing of pleadings, which include the complaint filed by the plaintiff, the answer filed by the defendant, and the reply filed by the plaintiff. Parties are not allowed to explore issues outside the framework of the pleadings. The allegations of the complaint must state a claim by establishing all elements of the cause of action. To prevail, the plaintiff must prove each of these elements. In addition to allegations, the complaint must begin with a caption and end with a prayer for relief. Many jurisdictions require the complaint to be accompanied by a cover or information sheet. The clerk of the court keeps the original complaint, stamps the copy that is sent to the defendant, and issues a summons to the defendant. The complaint and summons is then served on the defendant by the process server or sheriff, who is required to file an affidavit of return of service with the court after delivery is completed. Parties can agree to waive formal service of process.

Under the federal rules, defendants typically must file an answer within twenty days of having received service. In the answer the defendant can either admit or deny allegations made by the plaintiff, add factual allegations, raise affirmative defenses, or include counterclaims or cross-claims. Defendants can also bring third-party claims against defendants whom the plaintiff has not sued. Judges who believe that any claim is not sufficiently related to the remainder of the suit have the option of severing that claim. Plaintiffs have the opportunity to reply to counterclaims. All court papers other than the complaint can be mailed or delivered to the opposing party; they do not require formal service. If the defendant fails to answer, a default judgment may be entered in the plaintiff's favor. Trial cannot be set until the issues are joined.

Plaintiffs choose their forum based on several considerations: the procedural rules and substantive law that are applied in that court, the backlog, and the predispositions of the judges in that court. Defendants have an opportunity to remove cases to another court if they can prove that the court chosen by the plaintiff lacks jurisdiction, if venue is improper, or there is some other compelling reason another court should hear the case.

## KEY TERMS

| | | |
|---|---|---|
| Actionable wrong | Cross-claim | Return of service |
| Affidavit | Default judgment | Service |
| Affidavit of service | Element | Sever |
| Affirmative defense | Forum | Sovereign immunity |
| Allegation | Issue has been joined | State a claim |
| Answer | Personal service | Summons |
| Appear | Praecipe | Third-party claim |
| Caption | Prayer for relief | Third-party complaint |
| Cause of action | Process server | |
| Complaint | Removal | |
| Counterclaim | Reply | |

## Workshop Alert

*The following workshops correlate well with this chapter and you would be well advised to work with them.*

| | |
|---|---|
| Workshop 1 | Claims and Their Elements |
| Workshop 2 | Choosing a Court |
| Workshop 3 | Working Up a Case for Suit |
| Workshop 4 | Court Papers |
| Workshop 5 | Drafting Pleadings: Complaints |
| Workshop 6 | Serving the Complaint |
| Workshop 7 | Paper Flow in a Litigation Office |
| Workshop 8 | Drafting Pleadings: Responsive Pleadings |

## REVIEW QUESTIONS

1. What type of information does an attorney try to elicit from a potential client during the initial interview?

2. What minimal information is necessary to draft a complaint?

3. Why is it important to investigate a case substantially before filing suit? On the other hand, why should a party avoid procrastinating when filing suit?

4. What types of strategic decisions must be made when filing suit?

5. In what situations is a party required to "exhaust administrative remedies"?

6. What special considerations must be contemplated when suing a government agency?

7. In what way does an attorney try to "engineer" the facts before filing suit?

8. Why should settlement usually be considered before filing suit? What types of steps are typically taken as part of pre-suit settlement?

9. What role does a paralegal play in pre-suit preparation?

10. Identify the following pleadings:
    a. Complaint
    b. Answer
    c. Reply

11. What must a complaint contain? What are the elements of a cause of action?

12. By what process is a defendant notified of a suit that has been filed against her?
    a. How is personal service carried out?
    b. What is an "affidavit of service"?

13. How does a defendant "appear and defend"?
    a. What is usually contained in an answer?
    b. What is the difference between a counterclaim, a cross-claim, and a third-party claim?

14. How does filing an answer differ from filing a complaint?

15. What are the consequences of a defendant failing to file an answer in a timely manner?

16. What is contained in a reply?

17. Who chooses the forum for a case? How can a defendant affect that decision?

18. What is meant by the declaration "the issue has been joined"?

19. How does a paralegal participate in the pleading process?

20. Use the following sets of words in a single sentence:
    a. Complaint; affidavit of service; personal service; summons
    b. Answer; affirmative defense; third-party claims; sever
    c. Pleading; prayer for relief; allegations; counterclaim

## PRACTICE EXAM

*(Answers in Appendix A)*   **MULTIPLE CHOICE**

1. During an initial interview with a client the attorney must determine
   a. if any conflicts of interest exist.
   b. if he will win the case.
   c. if he likes the client.
   d. none of the above.

2. Attorneys usually carefully investigate cases before filing complaints because
   a. once suit is filed they will be pressured to meet several deadlines.
   b. many times they must disclose the evidence on which their claim is based within a few months after suit is filed.
   c. they may be barred from using evidence they do not promptly disclose.
   d. all of the above.

3. Some of the strategic decisions attorneys face in drafting complaints are
   a. deciding what court to sue in.
   b. deciding what kind of relief to request.
   c. deciding whom to sue.
   d. all of the above.

4. The advantage in filing suit quickly is that
   a. you can preempt a suit being filed by your opponent.
   b. you may intimidate your opponent.

*(Answers in Appendix A)*                    **MULTIPLE CHOICE**

    c. a and b.

    d. There is no advantage to filing suit quickly.

**5.** Pleadings include

    a. replies.

    b. answers.

    c. complaints.

    d. all of the above.

**6.** A defendant has the option of

    a. filing cross-claims but not third-party claims.

    b. raising affirmative defenses and moving to dismiss.

    c. admitting or denying allegations but not adding allegations.

    d. filing counterclaims against other defendants.

**7.** Formal service is required for the serving of

    a. complaints.

    b. answers.

    c. counterclaims.

    d. all of the above.

**8.** Plaintiffs choose their forum based on

    a. court backlogs.

    b. procedural rules and substantive law the court will apply.

    c. biases and prejudices of the judges.

    d. all of the above.

**9.** Defendants can ask for the removal of cases based on

    a. jurisdictional and venue issues.

    b. having closer connections with another court.

    c. a and b.

    d. Defendants cannot ask for the removal of cases.

**FILL IN THE BLANKS**

**10.** Governmental agencies can sometimes protect themselves from suit by claiming _____ .

**11.** Sending a _____ letter is one way of initiating settlement negotiations.

**12.** _____ force parties to specify in writing what the dispute is about; the first of these is prepared by the plaintiff and is referred to as a _____ . The response prepared by the defendant is called an _____ .

**13.** A complaint is organized in numbered paragraphs called _____ , opens with a title block called the _____ , and ends with a _____ .

**14.** Many jurisdictions require a _____ to be filed along with the complaint; this sheet lists the names, phone numbers, and addresses of the parties and their attorneys.

**15.** A _____ is a court order served on a defendant requiring her to appear before the court and defend the suit.

**16.** After a private _____ serves a summons and complaint on a defendant, he must file an _____ with the court, attesting to the fact that he delivered the documents.

**17.** An _____ is a sworn, notarized statement that can serve as a substitute for live testimony of a witness in some situations.

**18.** The term _____ in a summons means the defendant must formally submit to the jurisdiction of the court; this is done by filing an _____ to the complaint.

**19.** An _____ defense is raised by the defendant in the answer as an independent reason why the defendant cannot be found liable.

20. A defendant can take the offensive with the plaintiff by including _____ in his answer or can make claims against fellow defendants by including _____ .

21. A defendant can bring a new defendant into a lawsuit by filing a _____ claim; if the judge determines that the latter is not sufficiently related to the remainder of the suit, she has the option of _____ that claim.

22. If a defendant fails to answer a plaintiff's complaint, the plaintiff may win by seeking to have a _____ entered in his favor.

23. A plaintiff can respond to a defendant's counterclaims by filing a _____ .

24. The court that a case proceeds in is called the _____ for deciding that case; if the defendant wants to have another court hear the case, she can ask for _____ .

25. Once all the permissible pleadings have been filed, the _____ and the trial can be set.

## TRUE OR FALSE

26. The federal rules of civil procedure require only that an attorney have some basis, however minimal, for believing that the claims being made are well grounded.   T   F

27. A good attorney gets as little information as possible before filing a lawsuit.   T   F

28. Complaints cannot be amended once they are filed.   T   F

29. If a plaintiff wants to file suit against an administrative agency, she must first exhaust her administrative remedies.   T   F

30. A claim against a governmental agency can be dismissed if it is not in the correct form or if it is delivered to the wrong government official.   T   F

31. An attorney always has the right to make direct contact with the opposing party.   T   F

32. Attorneys should try to contact opposing parties in a suit before suit is filed.   T   F

33. Insurance companies usually get statements from all parties and witnesses before suit is filed.   T   F

34. When multiple parties are involved, the plaintiff may find it advantageous to settle with one of the defendants before filing suit.   T   F

35. The first party to file suit has the advantage of being able to choose the forum in which to sue.   T   F

36. Legal assistants have very little involvement in the pretrial phase of litigation.   T   F

37. Parties cannot go into issues that are not included in the pleadings.   T   F

38. The allegations in a complaint must be sufficient to state a claim.   T   F

39. To win a lawsuit, a plaintiff must prove each element of her cause of action.   T   F

40. The elements of a tort cause of action are best determined by consulting the appropriate statutes.   T   F

41. The plaintiff keeps the original of the complaint after filing it with the court clerk.   T   F

42. To determine the format required for court papers, one should consult the local rules for the court in question.   T   F

43. Personal service is required for all complaints.   T   F

44. Only process servers can serve a summons and complaint.   T   F

45. Parties cannot waive formal service of process.   T   F

46. A defendant that has been summoned to "appear and defend" must appear at the courthouse within the time specified on the summons.   T   F

**47.** In an answer to a complaint a defendant may admit or deny allegations but may not add factual allegations. **T  F**

**48.** A defendant can raise cross-claims against the plaintiff. **T  F**

**49.** Third-party claims allow the defendant to bring new defendants into a lawsuit. **T  F**

**50.** Plaintiffs rarely win by obtaining a default judgment in their favor. **T  F**

**51.** Defendants have an opportunity to respond to the plaintiff's reply. **T  F**

**52.** The choice of forum usually has little effect on the outcome of a case. **T  F**

**53.** The plaintiff has absolute control over the choice of forum. **T  F**

**54.** In most courts the trial cannot be set until the issue has been joined. **T  F**

**55.** Drafting of routine pleadings is a common task for litigation legal assistants. **T  F**

**56.** In many firms that handle a large volume of specialized cases, complaint drafting consists of making modifications to form complaints. **T  F**

**57.** The task of ensuring that pleadings are filed on time and responses are received when due usually falls to the attorney rather than the legal assistant because of the critical nature of meeting deadlines. **T  F**

## LITIGATION LINGO

*(Answers in Appendix A)*
**Unscramble the letters to form the word described.**

| | | |
|---|---|---|
| **1.** | TINMOCPAL | Formal statement by plaintiff of what dispute is about |
| **2.** | TULAFED | What will happen if defendant fails to file answer |
| **3.** | PYLER | Plaintiff's response to defendant's counterclaim |
| **4.** | SAGELTNLOAI | Numbered paragraphs in a complaint |
| **5.** | TONCIPA | Title block in a complaint |
| **6.** | EVICRES | Delivery of complaint |
| **7.** | VEROMLA | Change of court |
| **8.** | DITAFIFVA | Signed, sworn statement |
| **9.** | NGOSREVIE | _____ immunity |
| **10.** | ADNMED | Letter initiating settlement |
| **11.** | NIJODE | When the issue is _____ , trial can be set |
| **12.** | SROCS | Type of claim filed against other defendants |
| **13.** | EFRIMFAVITA | Type of defense |
| **14.** | UMROF | Court where case is heard |
| **15.** | YRERAP | Complaint ends with this |
| **16.** | LEMTENES | Plaintiff must prove each of these |
| **17.** | REWNSA | Defendant's response to complaint |
| **18.** | PEAPAR | Submitting to jurisdiction of court |
| **19.** | LIAMCNTREOCU | Defendant's allegation against plaintiff |
| **20.** | MUSSONM | Court order requiring defendant to appear |

## LITIGATION LOGISTICS

*(Answers in Appendix A)*

### For each question give the rule of civil procedure in your jurisdiction that applies and then answer the question.

1. Suppose you decide to sue the drunk driver who sideswiped your car. If you had the choice, would you choose to sue in federal or state court in your jurisdiction? How would you go about making this determination?
   a. What would the defendant have to do to get the case removed to another court?
   b. Suppose you decide to sue in your state court. What do your local rules dictate as far as the format of your complaint? Would you have to file a cover sheet with your complaint? Or something indicating that your case was or was not subject to compulsory arbitration?
   c. Suppose the drunk driver turns out to be a federal agent. How would you determine whether you could sue him for your damages under the Federal Tort Claims Act?
   d. If you decided to send a demand letter before suing, what would you demand in order to settle the case?

2. Suppose you decide to sue your karate instructor for negligence. What would you have to prove, that is, what would be the elements of your cause of action? How would you go about determining this?
   a. What will you be required to do to serve your complaint in your state court? How long will you have to serve the complaint?
   b. What options will you have other than personal service?
   c. What must you do if the karate instructor agrees to waive formal service?
   d. What is required of the person who serves the complaint and summons?

3. Suppose you have filed suit in your state court against your cousin who has refused to pay you. In how many days must your cousin file an answer?
   a. Must he formally serve his answer?
   b. Suppose your cousin fails to file a timely answer. What must you do to secure a default judgment?
   c. What kind of affirmative defenses could your cousin raise?
   d. What kind of counterclaims might your cousin make? What format is required for a counterclaim?
   e. How long would you have to respond to these counterclaims?

4. Suppose you have sued the contractor who did the shoddy work on your house. What kind of third-party claims might he make?
   a. Would he need permission of the court to make these third-party claims?
   b. Would he be required to formally serve these third-party complaints?
   c. How long would these defendants have to respond?
   d. Suppose you sue some of the subcontractors as well. How might the contractor respond in his answer?

5. Suppose you have sued the tenant who stopped paying rent. Then after filing suit you find out in the process of investigating the case that she had paid you but you had misplaced the rent checks. What might be the consequences under FRCP 11? Do you have a procedural rule comparable to FRCP 11 in your state?

## PROCEDURAL PONDERABLES

1. Many people are concerned about the extent of litigation in this country. What, if any, steps do you think litigants should be required to take before being allowed to file suit? Should they, for example, be required to go through some type of preliminary dispute resolution process? What, if any, limitations should be imposed on litigants as far as their right to sue?

2. Consider all of the individuals and legal entities you think should be sued in each of the following cases (taken from the hypos at the beginning of Chapter 1). What steps would you take prior to filing suit?
   a. Drunk driver sideswipes your car.
   b. Tenant stops paying rent and refuses to move out.
   c. Cousin refuses to pay you a percentage of his business.
   d. Karate instructor breaks your nose.
   e. Contractor does shoddy work on house.

3. What do you think will be the essence of the complaint in each of the following cases? What do you anticipate will be found in the answers of the defendants? What possible counter-claims, cross-claims, and third-party claims might be filed?
   a. Drunk driver sideswipes your car.
   b. Tenant stops paying rent and refuses to move out.
   c. Cousin refuses to pay you a percentage of his business.
   d. Karate instructor breaks your nose.
   e. Contractor does shoddy work on house.

# CHAPTER 4

# ROAD MAP OF A LAWSUIT: DISCOVERY

## OBJECTIVES

**In this chapter you will learn:**

- What discovery is and how litigators gather evidence

- What a deposition is

- What interrogatories, requests for admission, and requests for production of documents and things are

- How experts are used in litigation

- What an I.M.E. is

- How discovery is limited and how discovery rules are enforced

hypothetical

**_Shannon's Ordeal,_** _continued_

"*Chuck was going over Dr. Collins's statement to the police, and he had what I think might be a brilliant flash of insight. But first, we need to ask you, when you checked to be sure the door was locked, how did you do it?"*

*"As I said," Shannon began impatiently, "I checked it before I went to bed, then a few minutes later, I got up and checked it again. It was locked. What else can I say?"*

*"But how did you check it? What did you do? Did you turn the knob? Did you pull on it? Shake it? What, exactly?"*

*"Both. I turned the knob, it wouldn't turn, and I pulled on it. Believe me, it was locked."*

*"What about the chain?"*

*"I didn't use it. I read somewhere that they're dangerous if there's a fire and you need to get out in a hurry, and they aren't strong enough to keep anyone out."*

*Chuck spoke up: "Dr. Collins told the police he picked up his key from the desk clerk, and used it to open the door. The only way that could be true is if the door were not closed all the way—in which case it wouldn't matter whether the key turned the lock—or else if the key the clerk gave Dr. Collins actually fit your door. So if the door was completely closed, that would mean either the same key fit both your door and Dr. Collins's door, or else the clerk gave Dr. Collins the key to your room. Either way, it would sure put the hotel on the hook."*

*Shannon was doubtful. "It still wasn't his room. I don't see why you have to make it so complicated—the man took off his clothes and attacked me, he broke my finger. . . . Anyway, how could you ever prove what key they gave him?"*

*"Discovery," Porter responded confidently. "We take Dr. Collins's deposition and nail down the details, then we subpoena the keys from the police and try them on the doors. I'm betting that the key they gave Dr. Collins fits the lock on your room—it's the only logical explanation."*

## THE INVISIBLE MIDDLE

We now turn to the phase during which the real work of litigation is done, and in which most cases are won or lost. This phase begins soon after the complaint is filed, and ends as the parties are gearing up in earnest for trial. This "middle" phase may not be glamorous, but it is here—via discovery and motions—that the strengths and weaknesses of each party's case will become apparent, so much so that experienced litigators can usually make a reasonably accurate guess about the outcome of the suit well before the trial actually begins.

As we said in the preceding chapter, the first task in a typical lawsuit is the pleadings. Completing the pleading phase usually takes at least a few weeks and can take as much as several months. Delays may arise from difficulty in serving process on all defendants; also, defense attorneys commonly ask for additional time in which to file an answer, and plaintiff's attorneys, who also occasionally need to ask for extensions of deadlines, routinely grant such requests. In most lawsuits, as a practical matter, not much happens during these first few weeks or months, although this is not always the case, as we shall see.

After the pleading task has been completed, activity takes place more or less simultaneously on two main battlefields. The first is the discovery process, which is the means by which each party seeks to develop the factual aspects of the case by obtaining evidence and getting it into the record in a form that can be used at trial. The second involves pretrial motions. Any party can, by filing a motion, ask the judge to settle pertinent questions about the substantive law that applies to the case; to decide procedural disputes; or, in appropriate situations, to render a final decision disposing of all or part of the case. After these two activities are well under way, the litigants begin to carry out the necessary procedures to get an actual trial date scheduled on the court's trial calendar, a task that we will leave for Chapter 5.

## DISCOVERY

Ultimately, trials are decided on the basis of evidence. **Evidence** is the factual information about the dispute that is presented to the judge or jury. In civil suits, evidence consists mainly of two things: The first is the testimony of witnesses, who appear in person and answer questions about what they have seen or done. The second is documentary evidence—papers. These are presented as exhibits, shown to the jury, and made a part of the trial record. Complex rules (which we do not present here since they are properly the subject of a separate course on evidence) are applied to decide what documents and testimony will be "admitted in evidence." When we say that evidence has been **admitted,** we mean that the judge has ruled that it may be made a part of the record and considered in reaching a decision in the case. The judge will **exclude**—reject—evidence that is not admissible under the rules of evidence. The judge—not the jury—makes all decisions about what evidence will be admitted.

---

*Your Local Notes*

_____

_____

---

Where does all this evidence come from? You might suppose that plaintiff would be required to have his evidence ready before filing suit—people should not be allowed to bring lawsuits based on evidence they do not have, should they?

In practice, things are rarely that simple, as our hypo illustrates. The problem is that, by the time a dispute blossoms into a lawsuit, each side has possession of some of the evidence or information that is critical to the other side's case. Few suits could go forward without some means of prying evidence away from opposing parties. Then, there is the problem of obtaining evidence from third parties (like Arnie Trevayne, our hypothetical hotel clerk) who may not wish to cooperate.

In our hypo, for example, defense attorneys for the hotel and Dr. Collins will certainly need access to Shannon's medical records—the amount of Shannon's damages will be in dispute, and the defense attorneys will want to verify the extent of her injuries and seek their own doctor's opinions about them. Shannon will need to obtain information and records from the hotel about the maintenance of the doors and locks. These are but a few examples—in practice, the attorneys for all three parties will likely spend many hours on discovery involving scores if not hundreds of factual issues and subissues.

And what does a party do about the opposing party's evidence? Does each party go to trial "blind," without any knowledge of what evidence the other party will present? Would you want to cross-examine, say, Arnie Trevayne, at trial, in front of the jury, with your entire case possibly riding on his testimony, without having any idea what he may say? How would you prepare?

In fact, at "common law"—lawyer shorthand for the way American and English courts worked in past centuries—litigants pretty much came to trial with whatever evidence they had and took their chances. Nowadays, however, a number of mechanisms are used whereby parties can obtain almost any information pertinent to their dispute, under compulsion of a court order, if necessary. These mechanisms are collectively called **discovery,** and their use is governed by—you guessed it—the rules of procedure. How much information can a party to a lawsuit be forced to disclose? In general, the limits are broad indeed: Under the federal rules (see FRCP, Rule 26), any information that is "reasonably calculated to lead to admissible evidence" and not "privileged"—that is, does not belong to one of the "taboo" categories such as discussions between lawyer and client, doctor and patient, or priest and penitent—is fair game. If you participate in litigation, whether you sue someone or someone sues you, you can expect to be forced to turn over plenty of information that you would probably think of as private.

Here we briefly summarize the main tools available for obtaining evidence; we will cover specific discovery procedures in detail in later chapters. Before we begin, it is worth mentioning that discovery is an evolving area of procedural law in which the rules are still undergoing development and change. For several decades beginning in the 1940s and 1950s, discovery was entirely an adversary process, in which the party seeking evidence had to take affirmative steps to demand specific information from the opposing party. Nowadays, although the adversary procedures remain in place to be used when necessary, many courts are experimenting with mandatory disclosure rules, under which a party in possession of evidence is required to disclose it to the opposing party, even without being asked to. These disclosure rules have created still another arena for procedural maneuvering, one in which the details are not yet settled. We address mandatory disclosure rules in detail in Workshop 11, because they appear to represent an important trend.

The principal discovery mechanisms authorized by the rules of procedure are depositions of witnesses (see FRCP, Rules 27, 28, 30, and 31), written interrogatories to parties (see FRCP, Rule 33), requests for production or inspection of documents and things (see FRCP, Rule 34), requests for medical examinations of a party whose medical condition is an issue in the suit (see FRCP, Rule 35), and requests for admissions of facts (see FRCP, Rule 36).

**Putting It Into Practice:**

*What do you think should happen when a party knows of evidence that is damaging to her own case and of which the opposing party is not aware? Should disclosure be required?*

## DEPOSITIONS

Much of the evidence at a trial is presented in the form of live testimony: Witnesses are called to the stand and **examined,** or questioned, by the lawyers for both sides. For the lawyer preparing for trial, it would be handy to be able to question the opposing party's witnesses ahead of time. It would be especially useful to be able to have the witnesses' answers recorded, so as to make it more difficult for the witness to change his story later. How can this be accomplished?

The rules of civil procedure allow any party to a lawsuit to take depositions (see FRCP, Rule 30). A **deposition** is a discovery procedure in which a witness is required to appear at a specified place and time (usually long before trial) to answer questions. Most often, a deposition is held in a conference room at the office of the lawyer who will do the questioning. Lawyers for the opposing parties also appear, and can make objections; see FRCP, Rule 30(c). A **court reporter** is present to administer the oath to the witness and to take down in shorthand (typically using a computerized shorthand machine) every word that is said—questions, answers, and objections. The court reporter will later prepare a written **transcript** of the testimony, which is a printed or typewritten booklet containing every word said by anyone during the deposition. The judge is not present; any disputes or objections requiring the attention of the judge can be ruled on later, based on the written transcript.

---

*Your Local Notes*

_____

_____

---

The deposition transcript is useful in two important ways. First, it helps the trial lawyers prepare by giving them an idea about what to expect from each **deponent** (one who is deposed) when they testify as a witness. Second, under appropriate circumstances, the transcript itself—the written record of what the witness said at the deposition—can be used as evidence at the trial. This is routinely done when a witness gives an answer at the trial that is different from the answer the witness gave in a deposition. Trial lawyers love to **impeach** (discredit) opposing party's witnesses by catching them trying to "change their story"; the lawyer will, on occasion, walk dramatically over to the counsel table, pick up a deposition transcript, turn back to the witness, read the question and the witness's previous answer from it, and ask, "Isn't it a fact that you gave that response [a different answer] to the same question at your deposition?"

As you might expect, witnesses do not always want to appear for depositions, just as they do not always want to appear and give testimony in a trial. In both situations, the court will issue a subpoena; a **subpoena** is an order of the court directing the witness to appear at a specified time and place and give testimony. A subpoena is like any other court order: The judge can punish a disobedient witness with fines or even jail. A subpoena is another of those routine orders that the clerk of the court issues without having to consult a judge, so, as a practical matter, lawyers for either side can subpoena anyone they care to. We provide more detailed instructions on how to obtain a subpoena in Workshop 8; see FRCP, Rule 45.

Who decides what witnesses will be deposed in a case? In general, the lawyers do. Under the rules as they existed in most jurisdictions until the late 1990s, lawyers were free to take as many depositions as they wished in a case, the only limitation being that an opposing party could protest to the

**Putting It
Into Practice:**

*Whom do you think Allen
Porter should depose and
why?*

judge if the number of depositions became extremely unreasonable. Lawyers tended to depose every witness who might possibly know something about the case. In the hands of the less scrupulous, excessive deposition-taking (and other excessive and burdensome discovery) became a weapon for delaying trials and for deterring legitimate claims by making litigation unnecessarily expensive.

Increasingly, as a way of trying to reduce the cost of litigation, court rules are being amended to place limits on discovery. The federal rules currently require court permission or a written stipulation to take more than ten depositions; see FRCP, Rule 30(a)(2)(A). Another common approach is to allow parties to take depositions of any opposing parties, but to require advance permission from the judge before witnesses who are not parties can be deposed. Many courts also place time limits on depositions. Expert witnesses—witnesses hired by a party to give an opinion on some scientific or technical question—can also usually be deposed without a need for permission from the judge.

---

**Your Local Notes**

_____

_____

---

*Arnie Trevayne had obviously been well coached before the deposition. That was expected—Allen Porter habitually did the same with his own clients, going over possible questions, listening to the answers, instructing them over and over, "listen to the question, answer it, and stop—don't volunteer information."*

*So far, Arnie hadn't given away much. Porter looked around the conference room, and glanced at the court reporter who was waiting expectantly, fingers poised over her shorthand machine, then at Gail Stoddard, the lawyer representing the hotel. Finally he looked at Arnie, waiting for him to make eye contact, then resumed the questioning.*

*"Dr. Collins testified at his deposition that he took the key you gave him, inserted it in the lock of Room 407, turned the key, and opened the door. Do you have any idea how that could be?"*

*"Beats me."*

*"Did you give him a key to Room 407?"*

*"407? Of course not."*

*"What key did you give him?"*

*"The key to his room, 409."*

*"Is there any way you can think of that the key to 409 could have opened the door to Room 407?"*

*"Sure—if she left the door unlocked."*

*"Isn't it true that the doors are old, and they don't always close all the way?"*

*"Not that I know of."*

*"Have you ever told anyone that the doors are old and they don't always close all the way?"*

*Arnie frowned, as if in deep thought, then answered. "No."*

*"Didn't you tell Chuck Fletcher, who is seated here to my left, that the doors are old and they don't close all the way?"*

*"Not that I remember."*

**Putting It
Into Practice:**

*How far do you think
lawyers should be allowed
to go in advising clients
about how to answer
deposition questions?
What is the penalty for a
witness who lies in a
deposition? For a lawyer
who allows a client to do
so? What should the
penalty be?*

## WRITTEN INTERROGATORIES

Written **interrogatories** are written questions directed to one of the other parties. Instead of requiring an in-person appearance to answer questions orally, the questions are submitted in writing. It is customary to prepare interrogatories in the form of a court paper, with a caption, and (traditionally) leaving space after each question for the answer to be written or typed. The interrogatories are served on the party whose answers are desired, usually by mailing or delivering them to the party's attorney. The process of preparing written interrogatories and submitting them to another party to be answered is called **propounding** interrogatories; the party who is asking the questions is the **propounding party** and the party who is required to answer them is the **responding party.**

The responding party has a limited time, normally thirty or forty days [thirty days in federal court; (see FRCP, Rule 30(b)] in which to answer the questions in writing and serve the answers on the propounding party. (As with most discovery procedures, voluntary extensions of time are commonplace.)

> *Your Local Notes*
> _____
> _____

One important difference between interrogatories and depositions is that any witness may be deposed, but only parties to the suit can be made to answer interrogatories. In other words, if a witness is not a plaintiff or defendant in the lawsuit, you cannot submit written interrogatories to him.

Why do we need written interrogatories? Can we not take the deposition of the responding party instead? Certainly—parties may be deposed and almost always are. But each procedure has its own strengths and weaknesses. Depositions allow great flexibility. The lawyer conducting the questioning can follow any unexpected threads wherever they may lead, and can deal with evasive or ambiguous answers simply by persisting until the witness gives a clear answer. On the other hand, depositions are expensive, and usually each witness may be deposed only once. Sending out interrogatories is cheaper and can be done as often as needed. [Although many courts place limits on the total number of interrogatories that may be propounded without court permission. Twenty-five is the limit in federal court; see FRCP, Rule 33(a).] Experienced litigators often begin with interrogatories, which they use to locate documents, identify potential witnesses, and pin other parties down as to the general outlines of their stories; then depositions are taken to zero in on the details.

> *Your Local Notes*
> _____
> _____

*Putting It Into Practice:*

*How might Allen Porter use interrogatories in Shannon's case?*

## REQUESTS FOR PRODUCTION OF DOCUMENTS AND THINGS

Depositions and interrogatories are very useful for obtaining discovery about testimonial evidence, but what about documents? Not enough information is gained merely by asking questions about a document—lawyers often need to see the document itself. Two procedures are available for compelling someone to turn over documents.

The first is called a **request for production of documents and things** (often abbreviated to simply "request for production"). A request for production is a court paper, prepared by the requesting party and served on the responding party, which is the party from whom the documents are requested. The request for production will specify a time and place at which the responding party must appear and produce documents, and will include a list of the documents being asked for. In practice, the responding party usually does not actually show up at the appointed hour with documents in hand; instead, copies are mailed or delivered. The responding party must also file a written response—another court paper—stating what items have been produced, which items are not in her control, and objecting to any parts of the request that may call for items that the requesting party is not entitled to discover.

Requests for production can only be used to obtain documents from other *parties* to the suit. What happens if you need documents from someone who is not a party? You can obtain them using a **subpoena *duces tecum*.** A subpoena *duces tecum* is a subpoena that, in addition to ordering a witness to appear, also orders the witness to "bring with you" (*duces tecum* in Latin) specific listed documents or things. Again, in practice, the usual way to comply with a subpoena *duces tecum* is to mail or deliver copies.

Both requests for production and subpoenas *duces tecum* can also be used to obtain physical objects other than documents when necessary. A closely related procedure—the **request for entry upon land for inspection**—is used to obtain entry to a location (an accident site, for example) that is under another party's control.

---

**Putting It Into Practice:**

*How might Allen Porter use a request for production in Shannon's case?*

---

> **Your Local Notes**
>
> _____
>
> _____

---

*"Kind of blows a hole in my theory, doesn't it," lamented Chuck Fletcher. Allen Porter had just returned from Las Vegas, where he had taken the depositions of two of the investigating officers from the Las Vegas Police Department. In response to his subpoena duces tecum, the Police Department had produced the two room keys found at the scene. One was for Room 407, one for 409. The Polaroid photos that Porter had taken showed the cuts on the two keys, and they were obviously different.*

*"Hmmm." Allen Porter stared out the window of his twentieth floor office, idly watching an airliner on final approach to the nearby airport. After a moment, he turned: "Trouble is, it doesn't make sense. Remember Dr. Collins's deposition? He was very definite that the key turned in the lock. I don't think he was lying, and the man is a surgeon, he's trained to observe details."*

*"Then how can you explain the two keys? I thought you were going to file a Rule 34 request for entry so that you could try the keys out in the actual doors."*

*"I did. We tried it. The Room 409 key wouldn't turn in the lock for Room 407. The key fit in the keyway, but it wouldn't turn."*

*"Any chance they could have changed the locks since then?"*

*"They claimed not, but let's not take their word for it—better ask for the lock maintenance records for that floor in our next request for production of documents."*

*Chuck thought for a moment. "So then, how do you explain Dr. Collins's testimony that the key turned in the lock?"*

*"I think you were right the first time. Dr. Collins had a key to 407."*

*"But you just said that the keys—"*

*"What if somebody switched them?"*

*"But they've been in police custody, right? Surely the police wouldn't have any reason. . . ."*

*"Not the police. How about one of the hotel people, covering up a mistake?"*

## REQUESTS FOR ADMISSIONS

When we finally get to present our case to a jury, we would like to concentrate on the most compelling parts of our case and not waste time on tedious side issues that the jurors will find uninteresting. Unfortunately, a typical lawsuit involves a great many items of proof, some of which are unexciting but nevertheless important. In our hypo, for example, one of the elements of damages will be Shannon's medical bills. Before he will be allowed to argue to the jury that, for example, "my client incurred over $20,000 of medical bills as a result of this incident," Shannon's attorney will first have to prove that each one of the medical bills is genuine, that each related to treatment for the injuries that she is suing about and not some unrelated medical problem, that each of the bills was for treatment that was medically necessary, and that amounts of all the separate bills, if added together, add up to the amount Shannon is claiming for that item. Must we really spend trial time going through clerical minutiae capable of rendering a tax accountant comatose with boredom?

One way in which we can short-cut some of the tedium is to take the facts that the opposing party does not seriously dispute and get him to admit them in advance of trial—if our opponent has already admitted a fact, we no longer need to take up trial time proving it. FRCP, Rule 36, provides a procedure for obtaining such admissions of fact: the **request for admissions.** A request for admissions is a court paper, similar in appearance to a set of interrogatories, that lists facts that we want to establish and asks the opposing party to admit or deny them.

---

*Your Local Notes*

_____

_____

---

Why would someone whom we are suing want to help us by admitting facts that we need in order to prove our case? Why would our opponent not simply deny everything and make us prove each fact on our own? The rules impose a penalty on litigants who refuse to admit facts that are not genuinely in dispute. Returning to our hypo, suppose Allen Porter serves a request for admissions asking Park Hotels and Dr. Collins to admit that the medical bills in question are genuine, medically necessary, and related to Shannon's broken finger, and that they total to a specified sum of money. If Park Hotels and Dr. Collins refuse to admit these facts, and Allen Porter goes on and proves them the hard way, FRCP, Rule 37(c)(2), allows Shannon to ask the judge to assess the reasonable expenses of making that proof—including her attorney's fees—against Park Hotels and Dr. Collins. The judge would be required by Rule 37 to grant Shannon's request unless he or she finds that the facts in question were reasonably in dispute or that there were other legitimate reasons for denying the request for admissions.

Requests for admissions can sometimes be used to nail down substantive issues as well as technical or clerical ones. For example, Shannon could conceivably try to establish the causation element of her claim for battery against Dr. Collins by requesting that both defendants admit that her injuries were caused by Dr. Collins' physical contact. As a practical matter, however, admissions of this kind are usually not very helpful, since they relate to facts that will be obvious when the main witnesses tell their stories.

> *Your Local Notes*
>
> _____
>
> _____

## DISCOVERY OF EXPERT OPINION

Most of the witnesses who testify in a trial are "fact" witnesses—people who describe some event that they personally observed. Another category of witnesses is becoming more and more important as society becomes more and more dominated by complex technologies: expert witnesses. Expert witnesses are employed to give opinions on specialized subjects that ordinary jurors might not be able to grasp on their own. **Expert witnesses** are people who can be proven to have training and experience in some specialized field involved in the suit, say, some branch of medicine. Usually, each party locates, hires, and pays her own expert witnesses; university faculties are a fruitful source of experts on almost everything imaginable. Although expert witnesses are theoretically impartial in their opinions, lawyers naturally try to find experts whose "impartial" opinions will most help their cases; thus there is often a certain element of advocacy in expert testimony.

Expert testimony may play a decisive role in the outcome of some lawsuits. In our hypo, there will certainly be medical testimony (of which we will say more later). There will also quite likely be testimony from experts on doors and locks as all parties try to prove whether Shannon's door could have closed incompletely or whether a particular key could have opened the lock.

It goes without saying that each party will want to find out, well before trial, who the opposing party's experts are, what their opinions are, and how those opinions were arrived at. Because expert testimony represents a substantial investment of work and money by the party who hires the expert, there are special limitations on discovery of experts.

## INDEPENDENT MEDICAL EXAMINATIONS

Lawsuits often involve physical injuries, and the amount of money to be won or lost depends on how severe and how permanent the injuries are. Proof usually requires testimony by doctors. In our hypo, for example, Shannon's doctor will be asked to testify about Shannon's broken finger—how it was treated, how much the treatment cost, whether any future treatment will be needed—and to give an opinion about whether there is any permanent impairment.

Naturally, the hotel's lawyers are not about to take Shannon's doctor's word for these things. They will want a doctor of their own choosing to conduct an examination and give an opinion. Can they do this? Yes, the rules of procedure (see FRCP, Rule 35) allow a party to file and serve a **Notice of Independent Medical Examination** (often called an **IME**) on another party whose medical condition is a legitimate issue in the suit. This notice, which is usually a single page court paper, simply instructs the person to be examined to appear at the specified doctor's office at the date and time stated.

*Putting It
Into Practice:*

*Suppose Shannon claims ongoing anxiety attacks as a result of her confrontation with Dr. Collins. How will the hotel likely test the validity of her claims?*

| Your Local Notes |
| --- |
| |
| |

*"I don't get it. You just let him talk and talk. You didn't ask him anything about giving Dr. Collins my room key, or about switching the keys. He didn't admit anything at all." Shannon had just finished reading the completed transcript of the deposition of Arnie Trevayne, the desk clerk.*

*Allen Porter smiled. "This isn't L.A. Law. People don't usually break down and confess at depositions. Even if he had wanted to, his lawyer would have stopped him. Anyway, that isn't the purpose of depositions."*

*Shannon was not satisfied. "Then what is the purpose?"*

*Porter leaned back in his executive chair and took a sip of coffee before answering. "There were several purposes. One is to get his story on the record so he can't change it later. The more he talks, the better, it just gives us more ammunition to use at trial. That's why I always begin a deposition by encouraging the witness to tell his story in his own words. Another purpose is to get a chance to see what kind of witness he'll make. I thought he seemed kind of easily provoked, didn't you, Chuck? I might try pushing his buttons a little at trial, if this thing doesn't settle before then."*

*Chuck nodded in agreement. Porter looked at Shannon and continued, "Also, you notice he lied about saying that the doors didn't close right, as the hotel's lawyers will be finding out right about now—we mailed out our mandatory disclosure statement yesterday, and we had to disclose the conversation with Chuck, of course. We'll have some fun watching them try to scramble out of that one."*

## MANDATORY DISCLOSURE STATEMENTS AND LIMITATIONS ON DISCOVERY

Discovery, like everything else in a lawsuit, is an adversarial process. It can be used to obtain evidence, but it can also easily be used to make the litigation expensive for the opposing party. Any experienced litigator can dictate, in an hour, interrogatories that will take many hours and cost thousands of dollars to answer. Disputes over discovery, each requiring a motion, a response, and perhaps a hearing before the judge, bring additional cost and delay.

Courts have begun responding to the growing perception of wastefulness and gamesmanship in the discovery process by creating new rules intended to reduce the use of discovery as a tactical weapon and to minimize the time spent by judges in refereeing discovery squabbles. Initially, this response took the form of limitations; for example, requiring court permission to submit more than twenty-five interrogatories, or limiting depositions to no more than four hours. Such limitations are now becoming widespread. They may take the form of changes in the discovery rules themselves, but often such limitations come from local rules, so it is wise to check.

More recently, some courts have been experimenting with an entirely new way of conducting discovery: Instead of putting the burden on the party seeking information to ask for it, **mandatory disclosure rules** require the party who has information to turn it over to opposing parties without being asked! Such rules list the categories of information that must be produced, and typically require exchange of relevant documents, disclosure of the names and addresses of witnesses, and computations of damages, to give just a few examples. The federal courts (see FRCP, Rule 26) have now joined the ranks of jurisdictions

*Putting It
Into Practice:*

*Suppose Arnie Trevayne
admits to the hotel
lawyers that he gave Dr.
Collins the wrong key.
Under the discovery rules
in your state, must the
lawyer disclose this
information? Is the lawyer
ethically obligated to
disclose this information?*

with mandatory disclosure requirements; as with most federal rules changes, most of the state courts will sooner or later follow suit.

> **Your Local Notes**
>
> _____
>
> _____

In most cases, any competent litigator (or litigation paralegal!) would have propounded interrogatories asking for all the same categories of information as those called for by the mandatory disclosure rules, so the rules do not change the end result very much. Mandatory disclosure can, however, create some knotty ethical dilemmas, pitting a lawyer's duty to disclose against the client's expectation that information given to the lawyer will be held in confidence and kept private. Mandatory disclosure rules also lend some potentially new strategic dimensions, since the punishment for failing to disclose can be severe, especially if shown to have been deliberate. We will take up mandatory disclosure and its various ramifications in detail in Workshop 12.

## ENFORCEMENT

The motivations underlying the discovery process are simple: Each party tries to find out about any "good evidence" that will help win the case and prefers that any "bad evidence" remain hidden. Thus it is not uncommon, for example, to receive answers to interrogatories in which some of the crucial questions are "inadvertently" skipped or answered evasively or incompletely. Parties may fail to show up for depositions. Responses to requests for production of documents may omit a few documents that the requesting party knows should exist—or the responding party may deliver a huge quantity of documents, making it difficult to find the ones actually requested. Parties may even answer discovery requests untruthfully.

The discovery rules must have "teeth" if the process is to work, and they do. If a party fails to respond to a discovery request, or responds incompletely or evasively, the requesting party can ask the judge to intervene via an appropriate discovery motion. We take up the subject of discovery motions in the next chapter; see FRCP, Rule 37.

## INFORMAL GATHERING OF EVIDENCE

*Putting It
Into Practice:*

*Can you think of any
evidence that might exist
in Shannon's case that
could be obtained outside
of the discovery process?*

Underlying the discovery rules is the supposition that the evidence we are trying to obtain would not be given voluntarily. There is, of course, nothing whatever to prevent attorneys from gathering evidence by other means to the extent they can lawfully do so. There is no need, for example, to take depositions of cooperative witnesses (except to preserve testimony if there is a risk that the witness cannot be produced at trial). It may be better, cheaper, and less revealing to your opponent if you simply talk to a witness informally or take a tape-recorded statement. Many documents can be obtained from sources other than an opposing party. Private investigators and paralegals can be employed to ferret out some kinds of information.

Do not become so immersed in the discovery rules that you overlook these informal ways of obtaining evidence. One thing you can be sure of is that any piece of evidence that shows up in a discovery response has been thought about, thoroughly massaged, and defanged if possible, long before it gets to you. Thinking up ways to get important bits of evidence without the opposing party having to be involved is a great way for paralegals to be noticed (always with the responsible attorney's permission, of course).

## ROLE OF THE PARALEGAL

Preparation of discovery requests and responses probably accounts for more growth in paralegal employment than any other task in litigation. Although preparation of discovery requests may be quite routine, responding to them is a time-consuming job that can be delegated only to someone with thorough training and good judgment. The trick is to comply fully with the rules without giving the opposing side any unnecessary advantages, and errors can be expensive. Assembling and organizing the required documents and information often involves considerable client contact, so many paralegals find this aspect of discovery quite rewarding.

Another paralegal task is to analyze the information received from the opposing party in response to discovery. In document-intensive litigation (securities and antitrust cases are prime examples) it is not at all unusual to be confronted with a room full of file boxes that must be gone through, page by page, evaluated, indexed, and, increasingly, incorporated into a litigation support computer database. This is paralegal work—having it all done by attorneys is too expensive, and clerks and secretaries lack the training and legal judgment necessary to recognize the evidentiary nuggets hiding in the mountains of irrelevant paper.

*Putting It Into Practice:*

*What do you imagine you would be doing if you were assigned to help with the discovery in Shannon's case?*

## ETHICAL ETIQUETTE

Attorneys are obligated to "zealously" represent their clients. In an effort to uphold this standard of representation, some attorneys forget that the adversary process is, ideally at least, a search for truth. In their desire to vigorously and wholeheartedly advocate on behalf of their client, they lose sight of their role as officers of the court and their ethical obligation to carry out their duties with integrity and honesty.

Overzealousness manifests itself in the discovery process in several ways. It can be seen in the serving of voluminous interrogatories whose relevance is at best questionable and that serve more to inundate and discourage the opponent than to garner useful information. It can be seen in repeated unfounded objections to discovery requests and other tactics designed to obfuscate and delay the truth-finding process. It is suspected in the case of the attorney who provides many more documents than requested in an apparent effort to hide the "smoking gun."

Such abusive practices violate both the Model Rules and Model Code. Model Rule 3.4(d) specifically prohibits frivolous discovery requests and failure to comply with appropriate discovery requests. In addition to requesting sanctions against a party that manipulates discovery for illegitimate purposes, any party that falls victim to inappropriate discovery practices can sue for abuse of process, a tort claim that imposes liability on those who misuse the legal process.

Keep in mind that zealous advocacy does not entail withholding evidence that the rules of discovery require be disclosed or concealing or destroying evidence that is adverse to a client [the latter being prohibited by Model Rule 3.4(a)]. Representation of a client's interests is to be carried out within the confines of the ethical rules requiring attorneys to be honest and candid in their dealings with the court and opposing parties.

# PRACTICE POINTERS
## *Working File*

A working file is similar to a trial notebook, but it is prepared for your own reference. You should take it with you to every meeting and to every out-of-the-office assignment relating to the referenced case. Begin assembling this file as soon as the client is accepted. Some of the items this file should contain include the following:

- Personal notes from client and witness interviews and investigative research
- Witness directory (names, phone numbers, and addresses of witnesses along with notes)
- Case memorandum (information about client, facts, causes of action, legal issues, and discovery plan)
- Central index (see Practice Pointer in Chapter 5)
- Pleadings index (listing pleadings and relevant dates)
- Discovery index (listing documents and relevant dates)
- Deposition schedule (identifying who has been deposed, who the court reporter was, and whether the transcript is available and has been summarized)
- Chronology of events (listing key events in chronological order and referencing key documents and testimony)
- Case calendar (showing all the events leading up to trial)
- Trial exhibit log (listing exhibits by number along with description of exhibit and witness who introduced it)

This file can be used at trial if you are allowed to accompany the attorney to the courtroom, assisting you as you take notes and monitor the evidence being introduced. Because this is probably the single most important file you will work from throughout a case, make a backup diskette in case you lose the file.

## TECHNO TIP

When preparing your pleadings files, keep the forms for each type of case separate. Contract cases, for example, generally require that the same types of documents be requested. Tort cases have a separate attachment describing the documents to be produced. If you are consistent in preparing the forms, after creating a new document (as suggested in Chapter 3), in most cases you can use the find (search) and replace mechanism of your word processor to change the names of the plaintiffs and defendants.

Be very careful when using prior documents as a base to create new ones. More often than you would like to know, the "old" case number creeps into the new document, which can cause misfiling of the document by the court clerk. Be alert to the need to change not only the names, but the gender. You will look foolish if you refer to the plaintiff, John Smith, as "her."

## SUMMARY

Once the pleadings have been completed, the discovery motion process can begin. Litigants use discovery to ferret out the facts of their opponent's case as well as to prepare their own. Under the federal rules any nonprivileged information that is "reasonably calculated to lead to admissible evidence" must be disclosed. The primary mechanisms of discovery are depositions, interrogatories, requests for admission, requests for production of documents and things, and requests for medical examination.

By deposing witnesses, attorneys can question opposing witnesses in advance of trial and record their answers so that witnesses are less able to change their answers at trial. Any party to a lawsuit is allowed to take depositions. Opposing counsel is allowed to make objections to questions asked, and a court reporter is present to prepare a transcript. Such transcripts not only help attorneys prepare for trial but they can also be introduced as evidence at trial. Court clerks or judges issue the subpoenas that require witnesses to appear at depositions. Although in the past attorneys were allowed to depose as many witnesses as they wanted, today most jurisdictions limit the number of depositions by requiring attorneys to receive court permission before deposing nonparties. Under the federal rules, parties must have court permission to conduct more than ten depositions.

Interrogatories are written questions directed toward the opposing party. Responding parties have limited time to serve the answers to the propounding party and propounding parties are often limited in the number of interrogatories they can propound without receiving court permission. Interrogatories are cheaper than depositions and can be used to locate documents and potential witnesses, but they are less flexible than depositions, can be used only on parties (not witnesses), and are less effective in pinning down parties to specific details.

Requests for production of documents and things and subpoenas *duces tecum* are used to obtain documents or physical objects. The former is used with parties to a lawsuit and the latter with nonparties. The responding party complies by either mailing or delivering copies of the documents. Permission to enter a location may be obtained by filing a request for entry upon land for inspection.

Expert witnesses often play an important role in litigation. Their experience and training in a specialized field allow them to offer opinions that can be critical to a case. Although opposing parties want to be able to examine expert witnesses before trial, the procedural rules limit the discovery of experts.

When a party's medical condition is at issue, the opposing party may serve a Notice of Independent Medical Examination, requiring that person to be examined by a specified doctor at a specified time and place.

Limitations have been imposed on discovery to reduce the costs and delay caused by abusive discovery practices. More recently mandatory disclosure rules have been imposed, requiring parties to disclose information even without being asked to do so. Typically these rules require the disclosure of names and addresses of witnesses, the computation of damages, the exchange of documents, and the production of certain categories of information. These rules can create ethical dilemmas for litigators when their obligation to disclose conflicts with their duty to preserve the confidentiality of their client. If a party fails to comply with these rules, the opposing party may file a discovery motion with the court.

Legal assistants play a key role in the discovery process. They can conduct investigations as well as assemble, organize, and analyze documents and other information. Their training allows them to carry out detailed and painstaking tasks that would be too expensive for an attorney to perform and that are beyond the expertise of clerks and legal secretaries.

## KEY TERMS

| | | |
|---|---|---|
| Admit | Impeach | Request for entry upon land |
| Court reporter | Interrogatory |   for inspection |
| Deponent | Mandatory disclosure rules | Request for production of docu- |
| Deposition | Notice of Independent Medical |   ments and things |
| Discovery |   Examination (IME) | Responding party |
| Evidence | Propounding | Subpoena |
| Examine | Propounding party | Subpoena duces tecum |
| Exclude | Request for admissions | Transcript |
| Expert witness | | |

## Workshop Alert

*The following workshops correlate well with this chapter and you would be well advised to work with them.*

Introduction to Discovery Workshops

Workshop 9            Document Discovery

Workshop 10          Written Discovery

Workshop 11          Responding to Discovery Requests

Workshop 12          Disclosure Rules and Limitations on Discovery

Workshop 13          Depositions and Working with Witnesses

## REVIEW QUESTIONS

1. What are the two types of evidence that can be admitted at trial? Who decides what evidence will be excluded?

2. What is the purpose of discovery? What are the primary tools of discovery?

3. What transpires at a deposition?
   a. What two purposes does a deposition transcript serve?
   b. Can witnesses be compelled to attend a deposition? How?
   c. What types of limitations are currently being imposed in reference to depositions?

4. What is meant by the phrase *propounding interrogatories*?
   a. What is the advantage of using interrogatories rather than deposing someone?
   b. What is the advantage of deposing someone rather than using interrogatories?
   c. Can any witness be required to answer interrogatories?

5. What are two procedures that can be used to compel someone to turn over documents?

What is the difference between the two procedures?

6. What are expert witnesses and why do attorneys use them?

7. What is the purpose of serving a Notice of Independent Medical Examination?

8. Why have courts been limiting the discovery process in recent times? Give some examples of recent changes in the rules surrounding discovery.

9. What is the purpose of a motion to compel discovery? What are the possible consequences of failure to comply with a motion to compel?

10. What are two ways in which paralegals can assist in the discovery process?

11. Use the following groups of words in one sentence:
    a. Examined; transcript; court reporter; subpoena
    b. Expert witness; subpoena duces tecum; motion to compel discovery; IME

## PRACTICE EXAM

*(Answers in Appendix A)*    **MULTIPLE CHOICE**

1. Discovery involves
    a. obtaining evidence.
    b. preparing a record that can be used at trial.
    c. establishing facts.
    d. all of the above.

2. A pretrial motion
    a. cannot result in a final disposition to a case.
    b. can resolve a procedural dispute.
    c. is prepared by the judge.
    d. is written to another party.

3. Under the federal rules information must be disclosed
    a. even if it is privileged.
    b. only if a party can prove definitively that it will be admissible at trial.
    c. if it is reasonably calculated to lead to admissible evidence.
    d. if it is helpful to the party seeking it.

4. The purpose of a deposition is
    a. to record witnesses' answers so they are less able to change their answers at trial.
    b. to allow attorneys to question opposing witnesses before trial.
    c. to make it easier to examine witnesses at trial.
    d. all of the above.

5. In reference to how many depositions may be conducted
    a. some jurisdictions require court permission before allowing attorneys to depose non-parties.
    b. some jurisdictions require court permission if an attorney wants to take more than ten depositions.

    c. the procedural rules used to allow attorneys to take as many depositions as they wanted to take.
    d. all of the above.

6. In contrasting depositions with interrogatories
    a. interrogatories allow greater flexibility.
    b. interrogatories are used to hone in on details.
    c. interrogatories are better used to locate documents and potential witnesses.
    d. depositions can be used only with parties.

7. Responding parties to requests for production
    a. must actually show up and deliver the requested documents.
    b. must file a written response indicating what documents have been produced.
    c. must indicate why they object to requests they believe the opposing party is not entitled to.
    d. b and c.
    e. all of the above.

8. Mandatory disclosure rules
    a. create ethical dilemmas for litigators.
    b. almost always require competent attorneys to disclose much more than they would have under the old rules of discovery.
    c. have not been adopted by the federal courts.
    d. require disclosure only if the opposing party requests it.

9. A party may file a discovery motion if
    a. an opposing party fails to respond to a discovery request.
    b. an opposing party responds evasively to a discovery request.
    c. a party fails to show up for a deposition.
    d. if any of the above occur.

### FILL IN THE BLANKS

10. To get an answer to a pertinent legal question from a judge one can file a _____ .

11. Evidence at a civil trial consists primarily of _____ and _____ evidence.

12. Evidence that is prohibited from being heard at trial is said to be _____ , whereas evidence that can be heard is said to be _____ .

13. Under the _____ disclosure rules a party must disclose evidence even without being asked to do so.

14. A _____ is a procedure in which a witness is required to appear at a specified time and place to answer questions.

15. Court reporters prepare _____ of depositions often using a computerized shorthand machine.

16. A _____ is an order of the court directing a witness to appear at a specified time and place and give testimony.

17. Under the federal rules attorneys must have court permission to take more than _____ depositions.

18. An _____ witness is hired to give an opinion on a scientific or technical question.

19. The party that prepares _____ , which are written questions directed to the opposing party, is called the _____ party; the party supplying the answers is called the _____ party.

20. Two procedures used to compel someone to turn over documents are _____ (which is used to obtain documents from parties to a suit) and _____ (which is used to obtain documents from nonparties).

21. To obtain permission to inspect an accident site, a party should file a _____ .

22. If the medical condition of a party is at issue, the opposing party may request an _____ .

## TRUE OR FALSE

23. The jury decides what evidence will be excluded at trial.                               **T   F**

24. Under the common law parties came to trial with whatever evidence they had at the time.                               **T   F**

25. Only parties to a lawsuit are allowed to take depositions.                               **T   F**

26. Only the attorney conducting the questioning is allowed to be present during a deposition.                               **T   F**

27. Transcripts are made only of testimony given at trial.                               **T   F**

28. Judges are not present at depositions so objections must be ruled on later.                               **T   F**

29. A witness who fails to appear at a deposition can be fined or jailed.                               **T   F**

30. Only judges can issue subpoenas.          **T   F**

31. Some courts place time limits on depositions.                               **T   F**

32. Expert witnesses can usually be deposed without receiving permission from the judge. **T   F**

33. Any witness in a lawsuit can be made to answer interrogatories.                               **T   F**

34. Interrogatories are served on the party whose answers are desired.                               **T   F**

35. Many courts place limits on the number of interrogatories that can be propounded without seeking court permission.                               **T   F**

36. Responding parties have a limited time to serve the answers to interrogatories.                               **T   F**

37. Requests for production and subpoenas duces tecum serve identical purposes.                               **T   F**

38. A discovery procedure other than requests for production must be used to obtain physical objects.                               **T   F**

39. Expert witnesses are treated like any other witness for purposes of discovery.          **T   F**

40. Experts are rarely used in civil litigation today.                               **T   F**

41. A personal injury plaintiff should not be surprised if defense counsel requests an IME.                               **T   F**

42. Mandatory disclosure rules were enacted in response to the gamesmanship and wastefulness of abusive discovery practices.          **T   F**

43. Legal assistants can assist in the discovery process by coming up with ways to acquire evidence without involving the opposing party.                               **T   F**

44. A critical role of legal assistants in discovery is the assembling, organizing, and analyzing of large volumes of documents.          **T   F**

## LITIGATION LINGO

*(Answers in Appendix A)*

**Fill in the missing letters.**

| | | |
|---|---|---|
| 1. | _ _ P _ _ I _ _ _ _ | A time and a place for an attorney to ask questions of a witness |
| 2. | _ R _ _ _ _ R _ _ _ | A record prepared by a court reporter |
| 3. | _ _ P _ _ _ H | To discredit |
| 4. | _ _ C _ _ _ _ C _ _ | Bring with you |
| 5. | _ X _ _ _ _ E | To question |
| 6. | _ _ O _ O _ _ _ | To send interrogatories |
| 7. | _ X _ _ _ _ | Someone with specialized knowledge |
| 8. | _ _ T _ R _ _ _ _ _ _ R _ | Written question directed at another party |
| 9. | _ R _ _ C _ _ _ _ | Request for _____ |
| 10. | _ O _ _ _ _ OF _ _ _ | Order requiring plaintiff to be examined by a medical doctor |
| 11. | _ _ S _ _ O _ _ _ _ | Mandatory rule requiring party to turn over information without being asked to do so |
| 12. | _ X _ _ _ D _ | To reject evidence |
| 13. | _ D _ _ _ | To allow evidence |
| 14. | _ D _ _ S _ _ _ _ | Discovery mechanism that asks party to admit or deny |
| 15. | _ _ P _ _ _ _ T | Person being deposed |
| 16. | _ _ _ C _ _ _ R _ | Process of obtaining information from the other side during a lawsuit |
| 17. | _ _ B _ _ E _ _ | Court order directing a witness to appear to testify |
| 18. | _ _ _ P _ _ T _ _ _ | Request for entry upon land for _____ |

## LITIGATION LOGISTICS

*(Answers in Appendix A)*

**For each question give the rule of civil procedure in your jurisdiction that applies and then answer the question.**

1. Suppose the drunk driver that struck your car lives out of state.
   a. Can you depose him?
   b. What must you do in order to depose him? Is there a time limit during which you must depose him?
   c. Suppose he is critically ill and says he is not able to travel. What can you do?
   d. Suppose you want to depose the driver plus five other witnesses. Can you depose all of them or are you limited in how many people you can depose?
   e. Suppose you find out that the opposing party will be calling a toxicologist to testify on his behalf. What must you do to depose the toxicologist?

2. Suppose you decide to send interrogatories to the tenant who has stopped paying rent.
   a. Will you be limited in the number of interrogatories you can send?
   b. Can you expand on the number of questions you can ask by dividing each interrogatory into subparts?
   c. If the tenant is a business owned by several partners, how many interrogatories can you send to each partner? To whom should you send the interrogatories?
   d. What format do your local rules require for interrogatories?
   e. On what grounds could the tenant object to specific interrogatories?
   f. How long will the tenant have to respond to the interrogatories?

## LITIGATION LOGISTICS *continued*

*(Answers in Appendix A)*

***For each question give the rule of civil procedure in your jurisdiction that applies and then answer the question.***

3. Suppose you want to obtain your cousin's financial records for his business in your suit against him for monies he has refused to pay you.
   a. How would you go about obtaining them?
   b. How would you obtain accounting statements from his accountant?
   c. Suppose the business is an apartment complex and you would like to be able to see what the current condition of the complex is but your cousin refuses to let you on the premises. How would you get court permission to inspect the premises? How long will your cousin have to respond to this motion?
   d. Suppose your cousin's attorney claims that some papers you have requested in your discovery requests are privileged. How would you go about determining if this claim is valid?

4. Suppose you sue your contractor for the problems you are now experiencing with your new home.
   a. Under the rules of your state is there any evidence he will be obligated to disclose to you without you asking for it? If so, what is that evidence?
   b. You intend to have a contractor testify about the standard of care expected in the construction industry. Will the defendant be able to determine in advance what the nature of this testimony will be? Will there be any limitations on what the defendant will be able to discover about this testimony?
   c. Is there any limit in your jurisdiction to the number of requests for admission you will be able to make?

## PROCEDURAL PONDERABLES

1. What types of discovery do you envision occurring in each of the following cases? Who would you depose? What types of discovery do you anticipate the defense will use?
   a. Drunk driver sideswipes your car.
   b. Tenant stops paying rent and refuses to move out.
   c. Cousin refuses to pay you a percentage of his business.
   d. Karate instructor breaks your nose.
   e. Contractor does shoddy work on house.

# CHAPTER 5

# ROAD MAP OF A LAWSUIT: MOTIONS

## OBJECTIVES

**In this chapter you will learn:**

- What motions are and how they are presented and decided

- The various types of motions, both on the merits and those relating to discovery

- Tactical reasons for preparing and presenting motions

hypothetical

**Shannon's Ordeal,** *continued*

"*L*ook, Allen, you ought to seriously consider this. Your client's real beef isn't against the hotel—we didn't barge into her room in the middle of the night, we're not the ones who broke her finger. This way she gets some money in her pocket, we're out of it, which will make your case a lot less complicated, and you can go after Collins for whatever you think you can win.*"

*"Well, Gail, I appreciate the offer, I really do, and of course I will discuss it with my client and call you back. But I have to tell you, in all candor, I don't see it quite the same way—this case isn't just about a broken finger. Shannon's career is in ruins, her health is shot. . . . And you and I both know that if your client is found negligent, which I don't think will be that hard to prove here, you'll be looking at a much bigger number than $20,000."*

*"You could also be looking at zero. You have to win the case to get anything, and I think I have a pretty good shot at getting rid of the whole thing on a motion for summary judgment."*

## MOTION PRACTICE

Motions are simply formal requests for the judge to do something—usually, to enter an order or make a ruling of some kind. Because litigation is a contest between adversaries, it is crucial to be sure that judges hear from both sides before making important rulings. As a practical matter, in modern court systems, this is accomplished by requiring essentially all communication with the judge to be by motion, coupled with ethical rules prohibiting either attorney from contacting the judge without the opposing attorney's knowledge.

### HOW MOTIONS ARE PRESENTED

Except during trial, motions are submitted in writing. Written motions are court papers, beginning with a caption, then stating briefly what the moving party is asking the judge to do. It is also customary to state on the face of the motion which rule of civil procedure authorizes the type of motion being made. All motions except the very simplest are accompanied by a written legal argument, called a **memorandum of points and authorities,** usually at least several pages long, laying out in detail all of the reasons why the judge should do as the moving party is asking. The format and layout is quite standard (see Figure 5–1 for an example) and applies to all written motions, but stylistic variations exist from one court system to another. It is a good idea to imitate the format and style used by established lawyers in the particular court in which a motion is to be filed—stylistic inventiveness tends to be interpreted as a sign of inexperience; see FRCP, Rule 7(b).

| Your Local Notes |
| --- |
|  |
|  |

**Figure 5–1  What Motions Look Like**

**IN THE UNITED STATES DISTRICT COURT**
**DISTRICT OF ARIZONA**

SHANNON MARTIN, a single woman,   )
    )
    )   NO. 95-770 PHX-JML
    Plaintiff,   )
    )   MOTION FOR PARTIAL
    v.   )   SUMMARY JUDGMENT
    )
ARTHUR COLLINS, et ux., et al.,   )
    )
    Defendants.   )
_____ )

    Plaintiff respectfully moves pursuant to Rule 56, Federal Rules of Civil Procedure, for partial summary judgment in favor of plaintiff and against defendant Park Hotels Group, Inc. on the issue of liability.

    This motion is based upon the affidavit of Shannon Martin and upon the accompanying Memorandum of Points and Authorities.

    RESPECTFULLY SUBMITTED this _____ day of _____ , 19_____ .

SIMON & PORTER

_____

Allen Porter
Attorneys for plaintiff

(Memorandum of points and authorities giving detailed legal argument follows)

---

How many kinds of motions are there? As many as there are things that you could ask the judge to do. Some kinds of motions are appropriate to almost every case, and have commonly accepted names: Motions for summary judgment (FRCP, Rule 56), motions to dismiss [FRCP, Rule 12(b)], and motions to compel discovery (FRCP, Rule 37). You are not limited to these standard categories, however—here, inventiveness is entirely appropriate and often indispensable. If you need to ask the court for something that does not fit one of the garden-variety motions that you know about, then create one! Simply change the title as needed.

When you have written your motion and the supporting memorandum, the next step (as with all court papers) is to file it with the clerk of the court and serve copies on all other parties. Local rules may also require delivering a copy to the assigned judge. The opposing party is then given some period of time in which to file and serve a written response. The **response** is a court paper similar to the motion, and is likewise supported by a memorandum of points and authorities, this time giving all of the opposing party's reasons why the judge should *not* do what the motion is asking; see FRCP, Rule 56.

**Putting It**
**Into Practice:**

*Under your local rules what would you have to do to file a motion in Shannon's case?*

**Your Local Notes**

_____

_____

**Putting It Into Practice:**

*In your state how much time would Dr. Collins have to respond to a motion for summary judgment filed by Allen Porter?*

How does the responding party know when the response will be due? The answer depends on the court. Some courts set a briefing schedule and notify the attorneys. In others, rules of procedure or local rules establish a set number of days for response. It is important to know how the system works in each court in which you will be litigating, because missing response deadlines is hazardous. Many judges simply dispose of unresponded-to motions summarily—that is, they grant the motion immediately unless there is some obvious reason not to. Note, however, that recent case law has, in many states, required the court to review the entire record prior to granting a motion for the sole reason that a response has not been filed.

---

*Your Local Notes*

_____

_____

---

After the opposing party responds, the moving party is allowed to file a written reply. The format is the familiar one, a court paper accompanied by a short memorandum, this time rebutting the arguments made in the response. Notice the three-stage sequence: Party A makes an argument, party B makes a response, and party A replies to the response. This pattern of argument occurs over and over in litigation—motions, jury summations, appellate briefs. Almost always, the sequence is argument, then response, then reply.

Motions, responses, replies, and the accompanying memoranda are referred to generically as **motion papers.**

## HOW MOTIONS ARE DECIDED

After all the motion papers have been filed and served, the most important motions will be decided after a **hearing** before the judge. A hearing is a proceeding at the courthouse in which the judge listens to **oral argument**—that is, spoken presentations—from each of the opposing attorneys and has an opportunity to ask them questions. Depending on the court and the judge, hearings can be very formal affairs, held in the courtroom with a bailiff and court reporter present and the attorneys standing at a lectern to deliver argument. Or they can be quite informal, held in the judge's **chambers** (the judge's private office), with the judge and the attorneys seated comfortably around the judge's desk, usually with a court reporter present.

---

*Your Local Notes*

_____

_____

---

In theory, oral argument follows the three-stage sequence with the moving attorney speaking first, the opposing attorney second, and the moving attorney then giving a brief reply. In practice, most judges feel free to interrupt with questions at any time, and some do not enforce the idea of the attorneys taking turns—in some courts arguments on motions can descend into a kind of free-for-all of interruptions and counter-interruptions.

Not all motions are scheduled for hearings. Given their increasingly impossible caseloads, many judges prefer not to spend time listening to attorneys give speeches repeating the same arguments that they have made (or should have made!) in their written memoranda. In many courts, hearings are scheduled only if specifically requested, and even then the judge is always free to cancel the hearing and issue a decision based on the written memoranda alone. The lesson should be clear: Always write a legal memorandum as if it will be the only argument on your side that the judge will see. Never assume that you can patch any holes at the hearing, because there may not be one; see FRCP, Rule 78.

---

*Your Local Notes*

_____

_____

---

How do the parties learn of the judge's decision? Sometimes, the judge will announce a decision at the conclusion of the hearing. More commonly, though, the judge will take the motion **under advisement** (also called **under submission**), meaning that she will issue a decision later. This gives the judge time to reflect on the arguments and to reread the memoranda if desired. It also lets the judge avoid the potentially awkward task of giving the loser the bad news face to face. The judge's **order** (a written decision either denying or granting the motion), whenever it is arrived at, will be formally communicated to the parties via a **minute entry** (see Figure 5–2). The term is another of those throwbacks to the courts of yore, where the clerk kept the "minutes," entering everything that happened in court meticulously in a minute book. In modern courts, each of the rulings of the judge is typed on a printed form, with one copy mailed to each of the attorneys involved in the case to which the ruling pertains, one copy placed in the court file for that case, and one copy added to a file in which all of the minutes of that judge are kept in chronological order. A word of caution: Don't waste valuable relationships by constantly calling the judge's secretary to find out if a decision has been made!

> "Gail Stoddard speaking."
>
> "Hi, Gail, this is Allen Porter. I just wanted to let you know I did discuss your settlement offer with my client, and, frankly, $20,000 just isn't the ballpark that we're playing in."

*Putting It Into Practice:*

*Suppose Dr. Collins files a motion for summary judgment. How will that motion be decided? How will he be notified of the outcome?*

---

**Figure 5–2  Sample Minute Entry**

**UNITED STATES DISTRICT COURT
FOR THE DISTRICT OF ARIZONA**

February 10, 1998

Minute Order

Case No. 2:97-cv-00551

Title: Johnson v. USA

**DOCKET ENTRY**

MINUTE ORDER: per Arbitrator Edwards' letter dated Feb. 5, 1998, counsel/parties are advised that the arbitration hearing is set for 10:00 AM on May 28, 1998 to be held at the Law Office of Harry L. Howe, 10505 No. 69th St, Suite 1300, Scottsdale, Arizona (cc: all counsel/Edwards) [14-2]

**CASE ASSIGNED TO:**

Hon. Stephen M McNamee, Judge

*"Do you have a counteroffer?"*

*"No, not really—our original settlement demand was for $400,000, as you'll recall, and if you want to get somewhere up into that range we would probably negotiate, but I really don't see any point in lowering our demand in response to such a low offer."*

*"Well, counselor, you'll be getting my motion for summary judgment."*

*"That's fine, Gail—maybe your clients will take this more seriously after the court denies the motion and they know they can't avoid going to trial."*

---

### SIDEBAR

## Claims

*One of the best ways of analyzing something is to break it up into smaller pieces that can be more easily understood. That is exactly what we do in complicated lawsuits. We think of the suit as being composed of separate claims or causes of action (the terms are interchangeable), and deal with each one individually.*

*To oversimplify only slightly, a claim is a "chunk" of the lawsuit that could be sustained as a separate lawsuit all by itself. For example, our hypo involves a claim by Shannon against the hotel for negligence, another claim by Shannon against Dr. Collins for negligence, a claim by Shannon against Dr. Collins for battery, a claim by Dr. Collins against Shannon for battery, and so forth. Each of these claims could, standing alone, potentially sustain a lawsuit, even if all the others were dropped. Each claim is asserted by at least one party and defended by at least one other party. (Notice that the party defending a claim is not necessarily a defendant—remember, as discussed in Chapter 3, the defendant can bring counterclaims against the plaintiff, and defendants can make cross-claims against each other.)*

---

## MOTIONS ON THE MERITS

Not all motions pertain to procedural minutiae or to discovery disputes. Some, such as motions to dismiss and motions for summary judgment, call for the judge to decide once and for all whether a party's claim or defense is good enough to go forward or so lacking in merit that it should be declared dead on the spot. As you can readily imagine, judges have little enthusiasm for wasting days or weeks of trial time on a case that could never be won in the first place, and these procedures give them plenty of scope to weed out such cases at an early stage.

This culling process is done one claim at a time. (Please take the time to read and understand the sidebar. The concept of a *claim* is important in procedural law.) Each claim stands or falls as a separate entity. The judge can **dismiss** a claim prior to trial—that is, declare it invalid. The judge can also decide in favor of a claim before trial and grant judgment on it. Either way, the lawsuit is over *as to that claim*. The third possible outcome is that the claim does not get weeded out and has to be decided at trial; see FRCP, Rule 56.

**Putting It Into Practice:**

*What would be the consequence for Shannon if the judge dismissed her claim for negligent infliction of emotional distress against the hotel and Dr. Collins?*

---

Your Local Notes

_____

_____

**Motions to Dismiss—Motions to dismiss** are always made by a party who is *defending* a claim. (This is not necessarily the defendant. Remember that there can be counterclaims, cross-claims, and third-party claims. For simplicity, however, the discussion to follow refers to claims made by plaintiff and defended by defendant.) A motion to dismiss asks the judge to find that there is something wrong with a claim as it appears in plaintiff's complaint. The judge does not consider any evidence, or worry about whether there is any proof to support the claim. In deciding a motion to dismiss, the judge must assume that every allegation in plaintiff's complaint is true and can be proven. The claim will be dismissed only if the judge decides that plaintiff must lose even if he proved everything alleged in the complaint.

Suppose, for example, that Shannon's complaint included claims not only against Park Hotels Group, Inc. (the owner and operator of the hotel) but also against several of its shareholders who were not personally involved in corporate management. Such claims are "dead on arrival"—the law does not make shareholders personally liable for torts committed by a corporation. It does not matter whether Shannon has enough evidence to convince a jury that the hotel was negligent; either way, the shareholders are not liable. Because we can dispose of these claims merely by knowing what the law is, without worrying about the facts, we say that the claims are defective **as a matter of law.** The shareholders would move to dismiss the claims against them, and the motion would be granted. The lawsuit would continue against the other defendants, but would be over as far as the shareholders were concerned.

Where a claim is defective because the law simply does not allow that kind of claim, as in the foregoing example, the motion to dismiss is for **failure to state a claim.** There can be other reasons for moving to dismiss. Lack of jurisdiction is a common ground, and FRCP, Rule 12(b), lists several others such as improper venue, insufficiency of process, insufficiency of service of process, failure to state a claim and failure to join a party under FRCP, Rule 19.

> *Your Local Notes*
> 
> _____
> 
> _____

**Motions to Strike—**What if defendant's answer attempts to raise a *defense* that is defective as a matter of law? Can you move to dismiss a defense? No, only *claims* can be dismissed. To eliminate an insufficient defense, the remedy is a **motion to strike.** Suppose the hotel's answer to Shannon's complaint included an allegation that Shannon's negligence claim is barred by the statute of limitations. When we research the law, we find that the statute of limitations requires negligence suits to be brought within two years after the cause of action arises. Because Shannon's suit was filed only a few weeks after her injury, we can easily conclude that the statute of limitations defense is invalid, without knowing anything about the facts of the case. Shannon (through her lawyers, of course) can move to strike the statute of limitations defense from the hotel's answer; see FRCP, Rule 12(f).

> *Your Local Notes*
> 
> _____
> 
> _____

**Motions for Summary Judgment**—A **motion for summary judgment** can be made by either party, and, in contrast to motions to dismiss, the strength of each party's evidence is very much a factor. In fact, the main purpose of motions for summary judgment is to decide claims immediately—"summarily"—when the evidence is so lopsided that a reasonable jury could decide the case in only one way. If the evidence is so strongly in favor of the defendant that a reasonable jury could never find in favor of the plaintiff, then defendant is entitled to summary judgment, and plaintiff loses, then and there. If defendant's evidence is so weak that a reasonable jury must find for plaintiff, then plaintiff should be granted summary judgment. The outcome in both situations is the same as if the case had proceeded to trial in the normal way; the result is simply reached sooner, with no trial and much less expenditure of effort. To grant summary judgment for either party, the judge must first find that there is no "genuine issue of material fact"—that is, that the evidence points to only one reasonable conclusion.

How does the judge evaluate the evidence without holding a trial? Documentary evidence is no problem—it can simply be submitted with the motion. To establish what a cooperative witness would testify to, a party can submit the witness's affidavit. (Recall that an affidavit is a notarized written statement by a witness.) If it is necessary to establish what an adverse party's testimony would be, deposition transcripts or answers to interrogatories can be submitted.

As a practical matter, when a party moves for summary judgment on a claim, the motion will include the evidence that favors the moving party. It is then up to the opposing party to come forward with enough conflicting evidence to convince the judge that there is a genuine issue of fact. The objective in defending against a motion for summary judgment is to persuade the judge that the facts are in dispute—and factual disputes must be left for the jury.

Even if the judge decides that there is conflicting evidence about some factual issue, the judge may grant "partial" summary judgment disposing of the rest of the claim. Suppose, for example, that it is clear that defendant is liable to plaintiff, but there is a genuine dispute about the amount of compensation to which plaintiff is entitled. Plaintiff may then move for partial summary judgment on the issue of liability. If the motion is granted, there will still need to be a trial, but the jury will not decide who wins—its only function will be to decide the amount of damages to be awarded; see FRCP, Rule 56.

---

*Putting It
Into Practice:*

*On what basis might Dr. Collins move for a summary judgment?*

---

Your Local Notes

_____

_____

---

*"All rise."*

*The thirty or more attorneys who were gathered in the gallery of the large courtroom for the court's weekly motions calendar broke off their conversations and got to their feet. The judge emerged from his private entrance behind the bench and ascended to his chair. The bailiff continued, "The United States District Court for the District of Arizona is now in session, the Honorable Jerome Lewis presiding. Be seated."*

*The clerk announced Allen Porter's motion first. "Number 95-770 civil, Martin versus Collins, et al., defendant's motion for summary judgment. Appearances, counsel?" She handed a file up to the judge.*

*A conservatively dressed young woman rose, walked over to the lectern, and leaned over to speak into the microphone. "May it please the Court, Gail Stoddard, of Crandall, Elkins, appearing for defendant Park Hotels Group,*

*Your Honor." She stood to the side to let Allen Porter approach the microphone.*

*"Allen Porter, Simon and Porter, for plaintiff Shannon Martin, Your Honor."*

*"Are you there, Mr. Yarborough?" The judge leaned over toward the speaker telephone on the clerk's bench. "Good. The record will show the appearance of Roger Yarborough, telephonically from Dallas, for defendant Collins."*

*The judge leafed through his file. "I have read your motion papers. As I understand it, your client, Mr. Porter, was asleep in her room at Ms. Stoddard's hotel, when Mr. Yarborough's client turned up in her room, and she thought he was attacking her and she shot him. Is that about it?"*

*"That's exactly right, Your Honor, and of course the reason for the claim against the hotel is that Dr. Collins could not have gotten into the room absent the hotel's negligence."*

*The judge turned to Gail Stoddard. "Ms. Stoddard?"*

*"Thank you, Your Honor. Our motion is very simple—there is no evidence that the hotel was negligent. The key that Dr. Collins had, which has been in police custody the entire time, could not have unlocked plaintiff's door. There is no dispute about that. Therefore, either the door was already unlocked, or plaintiff opened it from the inside. The usual notices were posted on the door, warning guests to keep the doors locked. We sympathize with plaintiff and we certainly regret what happened, but Banbury Park Hotel did not injure her—Dr. Collins did."*

*The judge's expression was impassive. "Mr. Porter?"*

*"Thank you, Your Honor. You have before you my client's affidavit that the door was locked, she checked it twice. We submitted Dr. Collins's deposition testimony that he inserted his key in the lock and turned it. The point is, we don't know how or why Dr. Collins was able to open the door—the evidence is conflicting. Certainly, defendant's expert's affidavit that the key the police have doesn't fit the lock is evidence. But my client's testimony and Dr. Collins's testimony are also evidence. And I would just take issue with Ms. Stoddard's statement about the key being in police custody the entire time—it was only in police custody after the police arrived. Before that, anyone could have had access to it. Whether the hotel gave Dr. Collins a key that fit my client's door is a genuine issue of fact, and it should be left for the jury to decide after hearing all of the evidence."*

*"Thank you, counsel. It will be ordered taking defendant's motion for summary judgment under advisement. Clerk, call the next case please."*

## OTHER TACTICAL MOTIONS

A few other common motion-filing situations occur with sufficient regularity to deserve mention. Perhaps chief among these is the amendment of pleadings. Parties rarely know everything there is to know about their cases at the time suit is filed—that is why we have discovery. Lawyers also make mistakes. Suppose Allen Porter learns during discovery that Banbury Park Hotel, though owned by Park Hotels Group, Inc., is actually operated and managed by another company, Park Management, Inc. The complaint should have named Park Management as a defendant. Or suppose he realizes, after receiving a motion to dismiss, that he has inadvertently forgotten to include in the complaint some fact that is essential to his cause of action. What can he do? He can file a **motion for leave to amend** the complaint, attaching a new complaint, rewritten as desired. In general, courts are liberal in allowing

***Putting It
Into Practice:***

*As a strategic matter, why
is a motion to dismiss
often better than a
motion for a more
definitive statement?*

amendments to pleadings. Naturally, there are some limits; you should not count on being allowed to make some amendment that completely changes the nature of the case a week before the trial, for example. But in general, the rule is "no harm, no foul"; as long as an amendment does not unfairly hinder another party's trial preparation, it will usually be allowed; see FRCP, Rule 15.

You will occasionally be called on to answer a complaint that is so poorly drafted that you cannot tell for sure what the suit is about. One option is to file a **motion for a more definitive statement,** asking the judge to order the plaintiff to be more specific. (As a strategic matter, a motion to dismiss is often a better choice. After all, why educate your opponent about the problems with her case if you can get the case dismissed instead?) See FRCP, Rule 12(e).

---

*Your Local Notes*

_____

_____

---

## DISCOVERY MOTIONS

The area of motion practice that consumes by far the greatest amount of lawyer and paralegal time—and the area disliked by most judges—is discovery. Discovery is an adversarial process. No party wants to turn loose evidence that will help an opponent's case. Disputes arise constantly and must be refereed by the court. Discovery disputes are tedious and time consuming because the judge has to understand the factual details of the case in order to decide what information has to be disclosed.

Discovery responses are rarely complete the first time they are submitted. The first task of the lawyer seeking the discovery—a task often delegated to paralegals—is to analyze the response to determine what is missing. This is often far from easy, because considerable guesswork may be entailed in figuring out exactly what records should exist and what information the opposing party should have available.

In practice, incomplete discovery responses are, if not the norm, at least commonplace. They are generally followed by a series of demand letters and phone calls by the party asking for the discovery, the purpose of which is to create a written record showing that every possible effort has been made to obtain the requested information without bothering the judge. In many courts, the rules make such a showing mandatory—the court will not even hear a motion to compel discovery unless the moving attorney certifies he has personally conferred with opposing counsel and tried to resolve the dispute.

**Motions to Compel Discovery**—The next step is for the propounding party to file a **motion to compel discovery.** This is a formal motion asking the judge to order the responding party to produce the information that has been requested. It is up to the moving party to convince the judge that the information or documents sought have been properly requested using the correct discovery procedure, that the other party's response is deficient, and that the moving party is entitled to the disclosure being asked for. The responding party may defend the motion by attempting to persuade the judge that the information asked for is privileged, or they may be able to find case law supporting an argument that the particular requests are improper for some reason. Or, and unfortunately all too often, the responding party may defend simply by throwing a lot of dust in the air—peppering the argument with large

***Putting It
Into Practice:***

*Why are so-called
"obstructionist" tactics
tolerated in the American
legal system?*

volumes of complicated and extraneous factual issues in the hope that the judge, who has little time to devote to each motion, will be unable to reach a clear understanding of what has really happened; see FRCP, Rule 37.

---

*Your Local Notes*

_____

_____

---

If the judge concludes that the responding party has failed to provide disclosure as required by the rules, the court will order the responding party to turn over the information and will usually set a deadline. The judge also has the power to order the responding party to pay the fees charged by the moving party's attorney for preparing and arguing the motion to compel. As a practical matter, however, most judges rarely assess fees in discovery motions, except in the most egregious cases of deliberate disobedience.

*"Allen, do you remember the request for production of documents that we served on Park Hotels Group? We just got the response; do you want to look at it?"*

*Allen Porter's lack of enthusiasm was apparent as he eyed the four-inch sheaf of photocopies in Chuck Fletcher's hand. "Why don't you just give me a quick rundown."*

*Chuck dropped the pile of documents on Porter's table and sank into a nearby chair. "This is the one where we asked for all those records from the hotel. Maintenance records on the fourth floor locks—they've given us that, along with all the other maintenance records for the whole place for the last six months, which is most of this stack. I haven't waded through all of it, but so far I haven't found any record of the locks being changed on 407 or 409. Of course, there's no way to know if any records are missing, either. Registration cards for all the fourth floor guests that night—remember, we wanted to see if we could find any witnesses—they're still stonewalling on that one, 'objected to as irrelevant and violating the right of hotel guests to privacy.' Ditto on the incoming phone call printout for that night. Trevayne's personnel file, objected to as confidential."*

*Porter shook his head resignedly. "In other words, still nada. Didn't we get danced around on this one once already?"*

*"Yeah, their first response said they were still looking for the records. You sent them a demand letter."*

*"Okay. Well, why don't you draft another letter, pointing out that there's no legal basis for those objections, and demanding a full response within fourteen days. 'Right of hotel guests to privacy' doesn't come under any privilege I ever heard of."*

*"Sure, if that's what you want to do, but, can I ask, why don't you just move to compel?"*

*"The federal court rules say that before I can move to compel I have to personally confer with opposing counsel and make a good faith effort to obtain voluntary compliance, and I have to certify in the motion that I've done it. And as a practical matter, these motions are easier to win if you can attach a series of correspondence to the motion showing that you really tried to work with the other side to get what you need. We'll wait the fourteen days, then I'll call up Gail Stoddard and let her tell me for the third time why she thinks she doesn't have to give me this stuff, and then we'll file the motion to compel.*

*Then the judge will give her a deadline and tell her to file a complete response, and when she files it, it still won't be complete, and we'll do it all again. But if we're persistent, sooner or later we'll get what we need. Then you can start contacting some of the other guests and see if anyone saw anything."*

*"What do I put in the letter about why the phone printout is relevant?"*

*Porter thought for a moment. "Say that it's to confirm the exact time of the desk clerk's 911 call."*

**Motions for Protective Orders**—When you receive a discovery request from an opposing party, one of your first tasks should be to peruse it carefully to determine if each of the items requested is properly discoverable. (We will show you how to do this in Workshop 11). You will find that most discovery requests contain at least a few items that exceed the requesting party's right to inquire.

There are several ways to deal with these "overreaching" requests. If the requested information is not damaging to your case, you may choose to turn it over, even though you are not required to—that may entail less work than getting into a motion battle over it. Another option is to object: In the written response, you state your objection and the grounds for it in lieu of giving an answer. Then it is up to the requesting party to move to compel and to attempt to convince the judge that the objection is without merit.

In some instances, however, you may wish to seize the initiative yourself and get an immediate ruling. This is done via a **motion for protective order.** A motion for protective order asks the judge to rule that your opponent's discovery request is improper, and that you need not comply with it.

Motions for protective orders are rarely used in the case of written discovery. It is much easier to note your objection in the response than to file, brief, and argue a motion. When the dispute involves a deposition, however—particularly if the deposition would have to be taken in another state, at great cost in terms of time and travel—a protective order should be sought. Similarly, if your opponent is attempting to obtain information by subpoena from someone who is not a party to the suit, a motion for protective order may be the only possible remedy. If, for example, privileged medical information is being subpoenaed from your client's doctor, merely objecting will not prevent the doctor from turning over the information; see FRCP, Rule 26(c).

---

*Your Local Notes*

_____

_____

---

**Motions for Sanctions**—Suppose the court hears a motion to compel, orders the responding party to turn over information, and the responding party offers up still another evasive or incomplete answer. What then? Does the lawsuit turn into an endless series of motions to compel, ending only when one party runs out of money or patience and gives up? No, as you would expect, the sanctions become stronger the second time the judge has to get involved in the same discovery dispute. On a **motion for sanctions**—a motion seeking to punish a party who continues to stonewall even after a motion to compel has been made and granted and the court has ordered the party to disclose—the judge has several options. (Please notice that these stronger sanctions are available only where there has already been one motion to compel made, granted, and disobeyed relating to the same subject matter. A motion for sanctions is *not* an appropriate procedure to use on the "first offense.") See FRCP, Rule 37(b).

If the moving party was seeking the information in question for the purpose of trying to prove some particular fact, the judge may simply declare that fact as established. In our hypo, for example, suppose that the hotel refused to turn over the maintenance records on the door locks, even after being ordered to by the judge. Shannon's attorney wants the maintenance records in order to see whether the locks may have been changed—for all he knows, perhaps the Room 409 key *did* fit the Room 407 lock at the time Dr. Collins entered Shannon's room. If the hotel refuses to produce the maintenance records even after being ordered to, the court might simply declare as a fact that the hotel gave Dr. Collins a key that fit Shannon's room. At trial, the judge would then so instruct the jury, and the hotel would be prohibited from offering evidence to the contrary. Obviously, such a finding would blow a serious hole in the hotel's defense.

If the information sought has to do with evidence that favors the disobedient party, the sanction may be an order prohibiting the use of that evidence. In extreme cases, the court can even enter judgment against the disobedient party, at which point that party loses the entire lawsuit, then and there.

If these sanctions seem harsh, keep in mind that they can always be avoided simply by obeying the court's orders. The system cannot work if parties are free to ignore court orders with which they do not agree, so judges tend to come down hard on people who willfully defy them.

> **Your Local Notes**
>
> _____
>
> _____

***Putting It
Into Practice:***

*Suppose Gail Stoddard inundates Allen Porter with hundreds of totally irrelevant interrogatories. How should he respond? Would it be appropriate for him to move for sanctions? Does your state require any prerequisites prior to filing a motion for sanctions?*

# SCHEDULING ORDERS AND DEADLINES

Who decides what motions need to be filed, what discovery needs to be taken, and when these tasks will be done? For many years the answer was clear: The initiative lay with the attorneys for each party. The result was somewhat of a free-for-all, with each side filing motions, noticing depositions, and sending out discovery requests more or less whenever the urge struck.

The traditional approach was not without its drawbacks. Cases tended to drag on and on—attorneys can always think of one more motion to file or one more deposition to take. Discovery tended to multiply, at enormous cost to the parties. Judges wasted valuable time hearing motions for continuances when scheduled trial dates arrived and cases were not ready to be tried.

In the search for greater efficiency, more and more courts have begun taking an active part in scheduling the tasks necessary to prepare a case for trial. Many courts now require the attorneys to appear before the judge for a **scheduling conference** shortly after the pleadings are complete. After discussing the case with the attorneys, the judge issues a scheduling order, specifying, at least in a general way, what motions will be filed, what discovery will be taken, and setting firm deadlines for the completion of each task.

*Putting It
Into Practice:*

*What is a possible
downside of increased
judicial management
of cases?*

Increasingly, courts are enforcing such deadlines. If the scheduling order says that all motions for summary judgment are to be filed by May 15, a motion filed on May 16 is apt to be summarily rejected. Some judges also schedule **status conferences** every few months as the case progresses. The attorneys must appear in court and inform the judge of their progress, and the judge has a chance to ferret out any nascent disagreement and resolve it, thereby nipping a future motion in the bud. The experience so far with this kind of active case management by the judges has been generally positive in the sense that cases get to trial faster and with less wasted motion; see FRCP, Rule 16.

# THE ALL-PURPOSE MOTION: MOTION FOR A PRETRIAL CONFERENCE

The motions we have described thus far in this chapter—motions to dismiss, motions for summary judgment, motions to compel—these are the workhorses of litigation and you will see them in nearly every lawsuit. In using these procedures, you are travelling on the well-trodden main highways of motion practice; the rules are clear, and there will be little need for procedural inventiveness.

Occasionally, however, you will find yourself needing the judge to intervene in some situation that does not fit any of the familiar pigeonholes. Perhaps the parties cannot agree on a schedule for depositions and other discovery, or on deadlines for various motions. Perhaps the case involves a huge volume of documents, to which both sides need access—you need the judge to order the creation of a central document depository. Perhaps the battle of expert witnesses is getting out of control, with each side trying to gain the upper hand by hiring "one more" expert—you need an order placing some limits. Or perhaps the case has simply mired itself in a procedural swamp—progress toward trial is at a standstill and you have no way to get it off dead center without some cooperation from your opponent.

There are no specific rules of procedure covering these situations—is there a remedy? Yes! The court has the power to hold a pretrial conference at any time, at the request of either party or even on the judge's own initiative. The attorneys appear before the judge, in much the same way as hearings on motions are conducted. At a pretrial conference, the judge has the power to make any ruling that will "facilitate the just, speedy, and inexpensive disposition of the action." See FRCP, Rule 16.

## ROLE OF THE PARALEGAL

Though procedurally routine, motions to dismiss and motions for summary judgment usually must be supported by memoranda arguing potentially complex substantive law issues. Preparing such memoranda can be a job for very experienced paralegals who have well-developed research and writing skills, but, in most firms, such assignments are more likely to go to associate attorneys.

Discovery motions, however, are a rich source of work for paralegals. Motions to compel are a natural outgrowth of the task of digesting and analyzing discovery responses, and the additional work required—summarizing the defects in the responses and corresponding with opposing counsel to create a record of your efforts to obtain compliance—is well suited for the skills you are learning in your paralegal training.

*Putting It
Into Practice:*

*Why is the ability to
prepare accurate, concise
deposition summaries an
important skill for
paralegals?*

# ETHICAL ETIQUETTE

*P*rivileged information is protected from discovery. Therefore, it is vitally important that you do everything possible to preserve the attorney–client privilege and thereby avoid challenges that particular communications are discoverable because they were not intended to be confidential. Care should be taken to reserve client communications to those rooms that ensure privacy; avoid conversing in open areas such as hallways and elevators. Calls should not be taken from clients in the presence of other clients or individuals outside the firm. When visitors are in your room make sure that confidential information is not visible on your computer screen or that files are not lying open on your desk. Conversations over speakerphones and intercoms should be limited to nonconfidential matters.

The most common—and potentially most damaging—breach of confidentiality occurs in casual conversations with friends, family, and coworkers. Not only is the client's trust betrayed but these apparently innocent conversations may be overheard or inadvertently repeated to others. Some firms develop sophisticated means of protecting client identity and limiting access to confidential information, but if legal assistants do not honor the code of silence in their everyday conversations, these elaborate protective mechanisms are for naught.

If you become involved in the discovery process, you will be responsible for purging confidential information from documents and other materials before they are disclosed as well as flagging documents that may be protected by a privilege. To handle such tasks responsibly, you must have a clear understanding of the parameters of the attorney–client and work-product privileges. (The work-product privilege protects trial preparation materials, including attorneys' mental impressions, and legal opinions.) Far from being academic issues, privileges are integral to the discovery process and you would do well to explore these concepts in some depth.

# PRACTICE POINTERS
## *Central Index*

A central index is the master index of all indexes. This index lists every file and identifies its contents. Of course, the more comprehensive this file is, the more useful it will be when you are called on to locate a document. This simple organizational tool should allow you to put your fingers on any document within seconds.

This index should contain the following general categories:

- Notes and correspondence
- Pleadings
- Discovery
- Client documents
- Opposition documents
- Witness files
- Trial exhibits

*continued*

# PRACTICE POINTERS
## *Central Index* continued

Because the document files are usually the most extensive and the most frequently worked with, you would be well advised to further subdivide client documents into originals and documents produced to opposition, and to subdivide opposition documents into those produced from investigation, those produced in response to a discovery request, and a working set.

Assign each category of items a separate number; notes and correspondence can begin with 100, pleadings with 200, discovery with 300, and so on. As each new accordion file is added, increase the file number by one. So if three accordion files are created for discovery, the first one will be numbered 300, the second one 301, and the third one 302. Then color code all file labels according to category so that pleadings, discovery, and client documents, for example, all have different colored labels.

## TECHNO TIP

If you have a friend in the legal business in a different city or state you can still share files efficiently (assuming, of course, your supervisor and theirs give permission). You do not need to send paper copies or floppy disks. Instead, use your e-mail and include the desired file as an attachment. It is instantaneous and cheap. If you find a useful pleading in your review of court files of similar cases, make a copy of it. While the authors have never seen a court filing with a copyright notice on it, professional courtesy requires you to contact the author and ask permission to utilize the work. Once that is accomplished, the document can be scanned into your computer and the graphic file that results from the scanning can be run through your OCR (optical character recognition) program to convert the graphics file (a digital picture of the document scanned) into text file that can be utilized in your word processor. OCR programs, operating with today's high-speed processors and lots of computer memory, are surprisingly fast and accurate. Most such programs are also capable of "learning" the vocabulary and format of legal documents.

# SUMMARY

Motions are formal requests for a judge to enter an order or make a ruling. Practically speaking, all communications with judges are through motions. Written motions are accompanied by a memorandum of points and authorities explaining why the judge should do what the moving party is requesting. Motions must be filed with the court clerk and copies must be served on all parties. The opposing parties are then given a time period to file a response explaining why the judge should not do what the moving party is requesting. Failure to file a response in a timely fashion may result in the motion being granted. After a response is filed, the moving party is then allowed to file a reply, which rebuts the arguments made in the response.

Some motions are resolved after a hearing at which oral arguments are held either in the courtroom or in the judge's chambers. Because oral arguments are not always permitted, memoranda should always be written as if they will be the only arguments the judge will receive. Most motions are taken under advisement and are formally communicated via minute entries. A judge has the option of dismissing some claims, granting judgment on others, and allowing others to be heard at trial.

A motion to dismiss will be granted when a claim is defective as a matter of law. Motions to dismiss can be based on failure to state a claim, lack of jurisdiction, and other reasons set forth in FRCP Rule 12(b). To eliminate an insufficient defense, a motion to strike must be filed. If a judge decides that no "genuine issue of material fact" exists, she will grant a motion for summary judgment. To defend against such a motion the opposing party must persuade the judge that a factual dispute exists. A grant of a partial motion for summary judgment allows some issues to be heard at trial while disposing of others. If a party fails to include a fact or party in a complaint, he can file a motion for leave to amend the complaint. On the other hand, if a party cannot answer a complaint because it is so poorly drafted, he has the option of moving for a more definitive statement, which asks the plaintiff to be more specific.

Discovery motions are the most tedious and time-consuming motions with which judges deal. Motions to compel discovery are commonplace and typically follow a series of demand letters and phone calls requesting discovery. These motions must show that the information was properly requested, that the party is entitled to this information, and that the opposing party's response was deficient. If the judge concludes that the responding party failed to conform to the disclosure rules, she may order that party to turn over the information, set a deadline, and/or order the responding party to pay the moving party's fees. If the responding party still fails to comply, the party requesting discovery can file a motion for sanctions. Such sanctions may involve either declaring the questioned fact as established or prohibiting evidence from being used or even entering judgment against the disobedient party. If a discovery request is overreaching, a party may choose to comply anyway, object in writing, or file a motion for a protective order. A motion for a pretrial conference is appropriate when no other procedural option seems to apply. By virtue of this motion a judge can order anything that will "facilitate the just, speedy, and inexpensive disposition" of the case.

To promote greater efficiency and reduce the expense of discovery, judges have begun to take a more active role in scheduling discovery tasks. Some require attorneys to attend a scheduling conference once the pleadings are completed, while others schedule periodic status conferences.

Legal assistants can help in the preparation of motions to compel and other discovery motions by carefully digesting and analyzing discovery responses.

## KEY TERMS

| | | |
|---|---|---|
| As a matter of law | Motion for a pretrial conference | Oral argument |
| Chambers | | Order |
| Dismiss | Motion for leave to amend | Response |
| Failure to state a claim | Motion for protective order | Scheduling conference |
| Hearing | Motion for sanctions | Status conference |
| Memorandum of points and authorities | Motion for summary judgment | Under advisement (under submission) |
| | Motion papers | |
| Minute entry | Motion to compel discovery | |
| Motion for a more definitive statement | Motion to dismiss | |
| | Motion to strike | |

## Workshop Alert

*The following workshops correlate well with this chapter and you would be well advised to work with them.*

| Workshop 14 | How to Present a Motion |
| Workshop 15 | Discovery Motions |
| Workshop 16 | Motions for Summary Judgment, Motions to Dismiss, and other Tactical Motions |

## REVIEW QUESTIONS

1. What purpose does a memorandum of points and authorities serve and where is such a memorandum found?

2. Is it appropriate for an attorney to invent a motion if none of the standard motions accommodates his needs?

3. What is contained in a response to a motion? In a reply?

4. What transpires at a hearing on a motion?
   a. Why is it important to write a memorandum as if it will be the only argument seen by the judge?
   b. What does it mean if a judge says she is taking a matter under advisement? In those circumstances how does the judge convey her decision to the parties?

5. How does a claim relate to a cause of action?

6. How does a judge weed out nonmeritorious claims?
   a. When dealing with a motion to dismiss does a judge consider any evidentiary issues or whether any proof exists to support the claim?
   b. When is a claim considered defective as a matter of law?

7. On what basis does a defendant win a motion to dismiss for failure to state a claim?

8. Can a plaintiff move to dismiss a defense? How is an insufficient defense eliminated?

9. What is the purpose of a motion for summary judgment?
   a. Under what circumstances is such a motion granted?
   b. What type of evidence does a judge evaluate when considering a motion for summary judgment?
   c. What is the goal of the party defending a motion for summary judgment?
   d. Under what circumstances might a judge grant a partial motion for summary judgment?

10. How can an attorney rectify an error in a complaint?

11. Why is filing a motion for a more definitive statement not generally advised strategically?

12. What options are available to a party who has received incomplete discovery responses?
    a. What responses are available to the responding party?
    b. What are the potential consequences to a party that is found to be out of compliance with the discovery rules?

13. How can a party deal with overreaching discovery requests? When is a motion for a protective order appropriate?

14. What is a motion for sanctions and when is it appropriate? What sanctions are available to a court when it grants such a motion?

15. Why do courts today tend to take a more active role in scheduling the activities that precede trial?

16. What can a party do if the discovery process bogs down but no specific procedural rule covers the situation? On what grounds can a pretrial conference be held?

17. What types of motion are paralegals generally well suited to prepare?

18. Use the following groups of words in one sentence:
    a. Motion for summary judgment; claims; memorandum of points and authorities; oral argument
    b. Motion to dismiss; minute entry; chambers; under advisement

## PRACTICE EXAM

*(Answers in Appendix A)*     **MULTIPLE CHOICE**

1. Motions are
   a. always resolved at a hearing.
   b. decided by judges who communicate their decisions via minute entries.
   c. usually decided by judges immediately after oral arguments.
   d. always resolved informally in the judge's chambers.

2. In considering a motion to dismiss a judge must
   a. dismiss some claims and grant judgment on others.
   b. consider the evidence.
   c. consider whether there is any proof to support a claim.
   d. decide whether the plaintiff will win if he proves every allegation in the complaint.

3. Motions to dismiss can be based on
   a. failure to state a claim.
   b. lack of jurisdiction.
   c. lack of sufficient evidence.
   d. a and b.

4. A motion for summary judgment
   a. will be granted if no genuine issue of material fact exists.
   b. should be accompanied by documentary evidence, witness affidavits, deposition transcripts, and interrogatories.
   c. will be denied if a factual dispute exists.
   d. all of the above.

5. Discovery motions
   a. are generally the easiest motions for judges to deal with.
   b. rarely involve motions to compel.
   c. consume a great deal of legal assistants' time.
   d. all of the above.

6. If a judge determines that a responding party has failed to conform to the disclosure rules, he may
   a. order the responding party to turn over the information.
   b. not set a deadline by which the information must be provided.
   c. may not assess fees.
   d. all of the above.

7. If a party receives an overreaching discovery request, the party may
   a. choose to comply.
   b. file a motion for protective order.
   c. object in writing.
   d. all of the above.

8. Under the traditional approach to discovery
   a. cases tended to be resolved relatively quickly.
   b. parties usually encumbered great expenses.
   c. cases were usually ready to go to trial when the time came.
   d. none of the above.

9. In the contemporary approach to discovery
   a. cases usually get to trial faster than under the traditional approach.
   b. judges sometimes schedule status conferences.
   c. greater expense is entailed than under the traditional approach.
   d. a and b.

## FILL IN THE BLANKS

**10.** Written motions are accompanied by a written legal argument called a _Memorandum_ .

**11.** Within a specified period of time the opposing party to a motion must file a written _Response_ ; subsequently the moving party can then file a written _reply_ .

**12.** Motions, responses, and replies are referred to as _Motion Papers_ .

**13.** _Oral arguments_ can either be organized (with the moving attorney speaking first, then the opposing attorney, followed by the moving attorney again) or they can be free flowing.

**14.** Judges often take motions _under advisement_ thereby giving themselves time to reflect on the arguments made.

**15.** A judge communicates her resolution of a motion via a _Minute entry_

**16.** A judge must dismiss a claim that is defective, as a _Matter of law_ .

**17.** To eliminate a defense that is defective as a matter of law, the opposing party should file a _Motion to Strike_

**18.** If a judge decides that no genuine issue of material fact exists, he may grant a motion for _Summary Judgment_ ; but if he decides that some factual issues exist but wants to dispose of other claims he may grant a _Partial Summary Judgment_

**19.** If a plaintiff forgets to include an essential fact in his complaint, he may file a motion _to leave to amend_ the complaint.

**20.** If a defendant finds it difficult to prepare an answer because a complaint is so poorly drafted, she may file a motion _for a more definite statement_ ; for strategic purposes, however, she may be better advised to file a motion _to Dismiss_ .

**21.** A motion _to Compel_ may be necessary if the opposing party provides incomplete responses to discovery requests.

**22.** If your opponent attempts to obtain privileged information from your client's doctor, you should file a motion _to Protective order_

**23.** If you prevail on a motion to compel discovery and your opponent continues to stonewall, you should file a motion _for Sanctions_

**24.** If a case becomes mired in one procedural dispute after another, effectively keeping the case at a standstill, a party has the option of filing a motion _a Motion for PTC_ .

## TRUE OR FALSE

25. Attorneys are prohibited from contacting a judge without knowledge of opposing counsel. **(T)** **F**

26. Written motions are not considered court papers. **T** **(F)**

27. Virtually all communication attorneys have with judges is via motions. **(T)** **F**

28. Motions must be filed with the court clerk, who then sends copies to the parties. **(T)** **F**

29. Only the courts determine the time period during which a response must be filed. **(T)** **F**

30. Failure to respond in a timely fashion to a motion may result in the judge summarily granting the motion. **(T)** **F**

31. Oral arguments are always held in the courtroom. **T** **(F)**

32. Oral arguments are always highly structured affairs. **T** **(F)**

33. Because motions are not always scheduled for hearings, memoranda should be written with the assumption the judge will never receive any additional arguments. **(T)** **F**

34. Judges are required to render decisions on motions immediately but then must follow their verbal pronouncement with a formal minute entry. **T** **(F)**

35. A judge has the option of dismissing one claim in a case and allowing the other claims to stand. **(T)** **F**

36. Motions to dismiss can be based on only one situation: failure to state a claim. **T** **(F)**

37. A plaintiff can move to dismiss a defense that is defective as a matter of law. **T** **(F)**

38. The strength of a party's case is not taken into consideration when deciding a motion for summary judgment. **T** **(F)**

39. Granting a motion for summary judgment simply allows a case to be decided summarily,

thereby eliminating the time and expense of a trial. **(T)** **F**

40. To prevail against a motion for summary judgment, a party must produce evidence that a factual dispute exists because factual disputes must be resolved by a jury. **(T)** **F**

41. Discovery responses are rarely complete the first time they are submitted. **(T)** **F**

42. Some courts will not hear a motion to compel discovery unless the moving attorney certifies that he has tried to resolve the dispute and has personally conferred with opposing counsel. **(T)** **F**

43. Judges commonly assess fees in discovery motions where they have concluded that the responding party failed to follow the disclosure rules. **T** **(F)**

44. Motions for protective order are commonly used by attorneys in reference to written discovery. **T** **(F)**

45. A motion for sanctions is the appropriate recourse when a party fails to respond to a request for discovery. **T** **(F)**

46. A judge can prohibit the use of evidence that favors a party if that party fails to comply with an order to produce that evidence to the moving party. **(T)** **F**

47. Today courts are rarely involved in scheduling the tasks necessary to be completed before trial. **T** **(F)**

48. Today parties are often required to attend a scheduling conference shortly after pleadings have been completed. **(T)** **F**

49. At a pretrial conference a judge has the power to render any decision that will facilitate a speedy and inexpensive disposition of the case. **(T)** **F**

50. Helping prepare discovery motions is a task well suited for legal assistants. **(T)** **F**

## LITIGATION LINGO

*(Answers in Appendix A)*

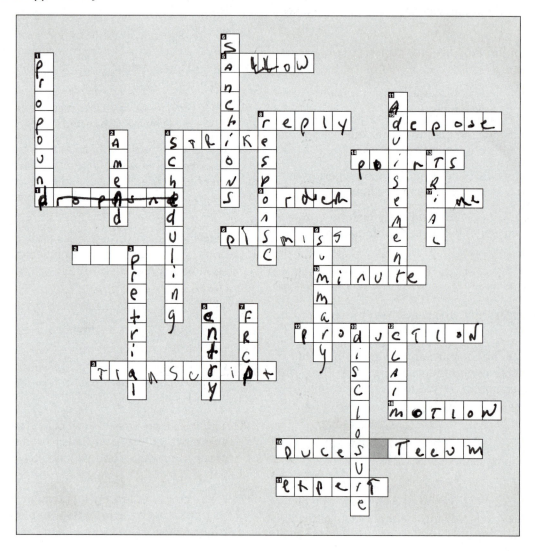

CROSSWORD PUZZLE (This crossword puzzle reviews terminology from both Chapters 4 and 5.)

**DOWN**

1. To submit interrogatories to another to answer

2. When a party errs in drafting a complaint they can move for leave to _____ .

3. An all-purpose motion that can be used when no other procedural mechanism applies is a motion for a _____ conference.

4. A conference some judges require attorneys to appear at after completing their pleadings

5. A judge communicates her decision via a [13 ACROSS] _____ .

6. The "teeth" in the discovery rules

7. Abbreviation for the federal rules

8. A court paper giving all the reasons why the court should not do what the moving party is requesting

9. The type of judgment that can be requested when there is no "genuine issue of material fact"

10. Mandatory _____ rules require parties to turn over evidence without being requested to do so

11. When a judge does not want to render an immediate decision she takes the matter under _____ .

12. A "chunk" of a lawsuit

13. Issues that are not disposed of via a partial summary judgment remain to be resolved at _____ .

**ACROSS**

1. An alternative to a motion to dismiss when dealing a poorly drafted complaint is a motion for a more _____ statement.

2. The type of motion that a party can use against a recalcitrant party that refuses to respond to discovery requests

3. What a court reporter prepares at a deposition

4. A type of motion that serves as a remedy to an insufficient defense

5. To allow evidence into the record

6. A failure to state a claim is an example of this type of motion

8. A court paper rebutting the arguments made in the response

9. A party that feels the opposing party is being unreasonable in its discovery requests can file a motion for a protective _____

10. "Bring with you"

11. Someone who has special scientific or technical knowledge

12. This request is used during discovery to obtain documents from the opposition

13. A judge communicates her decision via a _____ [ 5 DOWN].

14. A memorandum of _____ and authorities must accompany a motion.

15. To require a witness to answer questions at a specific time and place

16. Formal request for a court to do something

17. What is ordered when a party's medical condition is at issue

## LITIGATION LOGISTICS

*(Answers in Appendix A)*

***For each question give the rule of civil procedure in your jurisdiction that applies and then answer the question.***

1. Suppose the drunk driver that hit your car raises the defense of immunity, claiming that he is immune from suit because he is a police officer. How could you eliminate his defense if under the laws of your state he could not claim immunity if he committed a tort that fell outside the scope of his duties as a police officer? How long will he have to respond to your motion?

2. Suppose you decide to send interrogatories to the tenant who has stopped paying rent and he responds "I don't know" to all the interrogatories. What can you do?

   Suppose the tenant files a counterclaim against you but it is so poorly written that you're not sure how to respond. What are two possible motions you could file in response? Is there a time limit during which you must file these motions?

3. Suppose the attorney for the karate instructor that hit you sends you a notice for an IME.

   a. What might be the consequences if you fail to show up for the IME and refuse steadfastly to be examined?

   b. Suppose you discover that the karate school is part of a franchise. What would you have to do to amend the complaint to include the corporate franchisor as a defendant?

4. Suppose you sue your contractor for the problems you are now experiencing with your new home. You decide that no issue exists in reference to the contractor's negligence and that only the issue of damages should have to be decided by a jury. What kind of motion will you have to file and what will you have to show? Will you be entitled to make an oral argument?

   Suppose you and the defendant contractor have just completed your pleadings and are already experiencing conflict in reference to setting up a deposition schedule. Will the court in your jurisdiction be of any help to you in resolving this conflict? If not, is there any kind of motion you could file that would address such a conflict?

## PROCEDURAL PONDERABLES

1. Describe the circumstances under which you might find it appropriate

   a. to file a motion for summary judgment in the drunk driver case.

   b. to file a motion to dismiss against the tenant who stops paying rent.

   c. to file a motion to compel against your cousin, who refuses to pay you a percentage of his business, for copies of his financial records.

   d. to file a motion for a protective order against the karate instructor who broke your nose.

   e. to file a motion for sanctions against the contractor who did shoddy work on your house.

2. What types of discovery do you envision occurring in each of the following cases? Who would you depose? What types of discovery do you anticipate the defense will use?

   a. Drunk driver sideswipes your car.

   b. Tenant stops paying rent and refuses to move out.

   c. Cousin refuses to pay you a percentage of his business.

   d. Karate instructor breaks your nose.

   e. Contractor does shoddy work on house.

# CHAPTER 6

# ALTERNATIVE DISPUTE RESOLUTION

## OBJECTIVES

**In this chapter you will learn:**

- To distinguish among the various types of ADR

- How to determine the most appropriate form of ADR to use

- The advantages and disadvantages of using ADR

- What roles paralegals play in the ADR process

hypothetical

**Shannon's Ordeal,** *continued*

"*S*hannon, now that you have decided you do not want to accept their settlement offer, we will have to go to trial. Litigation is a lengthy and tiring process and you should know up front that you may not get what you want when all is said and done. Are you sure you want to take this case to trial?"

"I'm not sure about anything at this point," lamented Shannon. "Is this really an either/or decision? Aren't there any other alternatives?"

"Of course, there are always alternatives," responded Allen Porter. "You could consider submitting your claim for arbitration or mediation or to a combination of these two approaches called med-arb. We could also agree to a summary jury trial or . . . . "

"OK, OK, I get the point. I wanted alternatives but now you're overwhelming me. Tell me a little about each of these approaches. Which one do you think would give the best results?"

"If you choose to go the arbitration route we would have a hearing before one or more impartial third parties who would listen to the evidence and render a decision. If all of us agreed to binding arbitration, we could not appeal the decision but if we agreed to arbitrate only if it were nonbinding, we could still appeal the decision."

Shannon interrupted, "Arbitration sounds an awful lot like going to trial. What's the advantage?"

"Although arbitration is similar to a trial, the formal rules of evidence are not followed," pointed out Allen. "Also the process tends to go much faster and is much cheaper than a trial."

"If you would rather negotiate directly with the defendants, then you should choose mediation," Allen continued. "A mediator would help you negotiate a settlement but would have no authority to render a decision."

"How does a mediator help with the negotiation? I mean, if I wanted to negotiate a settlement couldn't I do it on my own?"

"Well, you certainly could try but a mediator makes sure the dispute doesn't get worse and that goodwill is preserved among all the disputants. The emphasis of mediation is on compromise rather than winning and so the mediator attempts to find a solution that is acceptable to all concerned."

"So what happens when arbitration and mediation are combined?" asked Shannon.

"If you opted to try med-arb you would first have your claim mediated by a neutral third party. Then if the mediation failed to create resolution, you would have the same neutral third party arbitrate your case," explained Allen.

"Doesn't sound like that third party is too neutral to me. What if this person hears information during the mediation that would not be admissible during the arbitration?" questioned Shannon.

"Good point," responded Allen, "and that's one of the problems with resorting to med-arb. Of course, if you want to have the benefits of having neutral third parties hear your case without the expense of a full-length trial, you could consider having a summary jury trial."

"Does this mean a jury would still hear the evidence?" asked Shannon.

"Yes," replied Allen, "but they would hear a capsulized version of the evidence from me rather than having you and other witnesses testify. Also, the jury's verdict would be advisory rather than binding."

*"What's the point of going to all the trouble of presenting the evidence to a jury if its verdict is not binding?"* questioned Shannon, who was becoming somewhat perplexed by all of these permutations of the trial process.

*"Because someone from each side is present to observe the presentation of the evidence and the jury's deliberation process, the attorneys can get a sense of how an actual jury would come out on the case. This reality check often prompts them to settle. There's another process similar to a summary jury trial called a mini-trial but I'm not sure this would be appropriate in your case."*

*"That's OK; I've heard enough. You've certainly given me something to think about,"* offered Shannon, feeling overwhelmed yet comforted in knowing that she had several options from which to choose. *"Give me a few days to reflect on this and I'll get back to you."*

## WHAT IS ADR?

**Alternative dispute resolution (ADR)** encompasses all those approaches to dispute resolution that allow individuals their "day in court" but save them some of the time, expense, and psychological trauma of going to trial. These are the primary forms of ADR in use in the United States today:

- *Arbitration:* hearing held before a neutral third party, also referred to as a **neutral,** who renders a decision and issues an award.

- *Mediation:* problem-solving process involving a neutral third party who facilitates the parties in reaching a resolution but who has no authority to render a decision.

- *Med-arb:* a mediation conducted by a neutral third party followed by an arbitration using the same neutral third party if the mediation fails to resolve the conflict.

- *Summary jury trial:* an abbreviated trial in which the parties present evidence in summary fashion to a jury, thereby allowing the attorneys to receive an evaluation of their case.

- *Mini-trial:* settlement process in which the parties present their case to a neutral third party who issues an advisory opinion, which the parties use to negotiate a settlement.

Although other variations of ADR exist, these are the most commonly used forms in the United States as of 2000 and will serve to illustrate the nature and scope of ADR. Let us explore each of these variations individually.

---

*Your Local Notes*

_____

_____

---

## HISTORY OF ADR

Although ADR is relatively new to mainstream America, it has been used for years by various segments of our society who preferred to settle disputes without litigation. The Puritans and Quakers, for example, used mediation and arbitration, and resorted to the legal system only when absolutely necessary. In the nineteenth century, Mormons, as well as Chinese and Jewish immigrants, developed their own community dispute resolution mechanisms.

In the 1970s some, including Chief Justice Warren Burger and consumer advocate Ralph Nader, talked about a need for a less expensive and less formal means of resolving disputes. ADR began to be seen as a possible solution to clogged court calendars and general inaccessibility of the judicial system to the poor and even middle-class individuals. By the mid-1980s, the ADR world expanded to include mini-trials used to resolve large corporate disputes, private judging, mediation in divorce proceedings, and mediation and arbitration in medical malpractice disputes.

The message that ADR had been accepted in the federal system became clear when Congress passed the Administrative Dispute Resolution Act of 1996 (ADRA). This bill encouraged the increased use of mediation and arbitration. Like its predecessor passed in 1990, ADRA required each federal agency to adopt an ADR policy, appoint an ADR specialist, develop an ADR training program, and review existing agency agreements for possible incorporation of ADR clauses. ADRA also increased the federal government's use of ADR, eliminated an escape clause that deterred parties from entering into binding arbitration, and prevented delays in the acquisition and hiring of third-party neutrals. Signaling the future of ADR, the 1996 act broadened the scope of its coverage to include a wider range of administrative disputes.

Several district courts have now made ADR mandatory. Not surprisingly, local rules requiring ADR have been challenged on constitutional and statutory grounds as well as on the grounds that they are inconsistent with various provisions of the Federal Rules of Civil Procedure. Most courts, however, have concluded that mandatory ADR procedures are valid. In one such case a local rule required that certain cases involving damage claims for $50,000 or less were to be automatically referred to nonbinding arbitration with the option for a trial *de novo* (new trial) within 20 days after the entry of an award. The appellate court reasoned that this rule did not violate the constitutional right to a jury trial because it created a statutory right coextensive with the Constitution. Also, the court determined the provision was not inconsistent with the Federal Rules of Civil Procedure because it found that ADR greatly enhanced the efficiency of the court system. The court was pleased that ADR allowed litigants to test their claims shortly after filing them and encouraged settlement when arbitration revealed that no viable claim existed.

> **Putting It Into Practice:**
>
> *Why might ADR be more acceptable today than it was 50 years ago?*

## ARBITRATION

One of the first forms of ADR was originally embraced by the business community as a means of resolving labor disputes. **Arbitration** allows parties to enjoy all the benefits of a trial without the inordinate expenditure of time and money. Attorneys still play the role of advocate and a neutral third party still serves as an arbiter. Arbitration's primary advantage lies in its reduction, or in some cases elimination, of the discovery process. Control of the discovery process lies with the arbitrator (the neutral third party who hears the evidence and renders a decision). Many arbitration statutes allow discovery only as a "permissible" process.

Arbitration has been used longer than any other form of ADR in this country and continues to be one of the most popular forms of ADR. Arbitration can be ordered by the court, sometimes one party can demand it, or the parties can enter into it voluntarily. Many states have adopted statutes that compel parties to arbitrate disputes before going to trial.

## FORMS OF ARBITRATION

Arbitration can take a number of different forms. In some cases arbitration is **mandatory,** which means that the parties must try arbitration before being granted a conventional trial. The mandate to arbitrate can come from a statute, a contractual agreement, a court rule, or a custom. Note that the parties cannot usually be forced to settle their dispute under mandatory arbitration but can be required to at least try. In other cases, arbitration is **voluntary,** which means it is used by the parties by choice as a means of attempting to resolve their dispute.

Arbitration can also be either **binding** or **nonbinding.** Binding arbitration is final and generally cannot be appealed. The courts rarely overturn binding arbitration awards. Binding arbitration is usually found in the private sector and is entered into by agreement or custom. Nonbinding arbitration is generally mandated by the courts and can be appealed.

Furthermore, arbitration can be **private,** which is based on a contractual agreement, or **court annexed,** which takes place within the court system and is governed by local rules. Private arbitration typically arises from a contract clause that specifies that the parties must arbitrate any disputes. Real estate agreements and labor union contracts often contain such clauses. Stockbrokers, lawyers, health care organizations, and automobile manufacturers commonly use arbitration clauses in their contracts. The parties choose an arbitrator or go through a private provider, such as the American Arbitration Association, and must pay for the arbitrator's services.

In accordance with court-annexed arbitration the parties are notified after filing their pleadings that they must present their claim to an arbitrator. Often the statutes allow the courts to refer matters to arbitration by their own motion or by motion of a party requesting it. Parties can, however, object to arbitration by showing cause why it should not be attempted. The parties generally do not choose the arbitrators nor the rules of arbitration to be followed. The award, however, is nonbinding and the parties generally do not have to pay for the arbitrator's services. If the parties are satisfied with the arbitrator's award, a judgment is entered, but if either party is dissatisfied, a **trial de novo** is scheduled. Disincentives to appeal exist in the form of fees required to appeal and potential liability for costs and attorney's fees if the appellant fails to improve his position at trial.

Arbitration can be any combination of the above. You can, for example, have binding, voluntary, private arbitration or nonbinding, mandatory, court-annexed arbitration. A dispute involving a contract that contains an arbitration clause will go to private, binding arbitration. The procedure for this arbitration will be governed by the contract. A matter involving a complaint filed in the courts that falls within a statute requiring arbitration (e.g., a federal statute requiring all civil claims involving a disputed amount less than $100,000 in monetary damages to be arbitrated) is considered nonbinding, court-annexed arbitration.

> *Putting It Into Practice:*
>
> *Under what circumstances should Shannon's claim be subject to mandatory arbitration?*

---

*Your Local Notes*

_____

_____

---

## SELECTION OF ARBITRATORS

Under the rules of the American Arbitration Association arbitrators are selected by having each side strike any unacceptable arbitrators from a list of eight to twelve randomly selected names. These names come from a list of approved

> ### SIDEBAR
>
> ## American Arbitration Association (AAA)
>
> *The American Arbitration Association (AAA) is a private, nonprofit organization that provides rules for parties to follow in private arbitrations. It also maintains a list of qualified arbitrators with knowledge in specific areas. Although the AAA does nothing to render or enforce arbitration awards, it will assist in the logistics of arbitration hearings by, among other things, providing meeting places. The AAA's primary office is in New York but it has regional offices around the country.*
>
> *In some cases, contracts will specify the use of AAA rules. In other cases, the parties agree to modify the AAA rules to meet their own needs or they use rules developed by some other organization. Another commonly used private organization that has established arbitration rules and procedures is the Center for Public Resources (CPR).*

arbitrators with expertise in various fields. Potential arbitrators who are friends of either party or who are interested parties are ineligible. The AAA chooses an arbitrator from the list of names that were not stricken by either side. The AAA has the option of removing an arbitrator or filling a vacancy.

Parties who choose to find their own arbitrator rather than using the services of organizations like the AAA or the National Academy of Arbitration (NAA) can use private sources. Legal publications often have advertisements for arbitrators; local bar associations are another good source for initiating the process of securing an arbitrator. Most arbitrators are retired judges, private attorneys, or citizens with expertise in a particular field.

---

*Your Local Notes*

_____

_____

---

## ARBITRATION PROCESS

Voluntary arbitrations are initiated when one of the parties files a motion to refer to arbitration or a demand for arbitration. If the opposing party does want to arbitrate, a jurisdictional battle may ensue. If, for example, a contract clause provides for jurisdiction in advance, the opposing party may dispute the interpretation of this clause. Or if a statute sets forth the grounds for jurisdiction, the dispute may revolve around the interpretation of this statute. In other instances the court itself orders a case to be arbitrated. The statutes allowing courts to do this give judges wide discretion and the presumption is in favor of arbitration.

If an arbitration agreement exists or a demand to arbitrate has been filed, the complaint is contained in the agreement or demand. The respondent is allowed to file an answer. With court-annexed arbitrations the complaint, answer, and other pleadings are usually on file with the court. Motion practice, however, in both types of arbitration may be very limited. While access to discovery tools is not a right under many statutes, arbitrators do have the authority to permit discovery to the extent they deem it reasonable. Because of the informality of the procedures, parties are not as well informed about their opponent's position as they are in litigation. Some complain that this amounts to "playing blind man's bluff" at the hearing. Because the discovery rules vary so much, those engaging in arbitration must consult the arbitration statutes in their jurisdiction before beginning the process.

The arbitrator initiates the hearing by swearing in the parties and witnesses who will testify. The parties then give opening arguments and present both documentary and testimonial evidence. The attorneys are allowed to question witnesses and the arbitrator may ask questions if necessary. Rebuttal questions are also allowed. Although the rules of evidence are not followed, they may be used as guidelines. At the end of questioning, the parties may either present closing arguments or prepare post-hearing briefs. Some arbitrators may not allow both or may require submissions of a brief when the hearing is over.

Arbitration hearings, unlike trials, are not open to the public. Everything discussed in the context of the hearing is confidential and any matters disclosed often are not discoverable in future proceedings.

Arbitrators usually take the matter under advisement after the hearing. By statute, agreement, or organizational rules, they are limited in the amount of time they can consider the matter. Arbitrators are not required to commit the reasons for their decisions in writing. An award that is binding on the parties can be set aside only if the arbitrator engaged in misconduct, refused to hear material testimony or admit material evidence, failed to decide the issues submitted for arbitration, or exceeded the limits of her authority. Courts reviewing arbitration decisions may not retry the issues of the case but are instead limited to deciding whether the award was valid.

*Putting It Into Practice:*

*Why might some attorneys not like the arbitration process? Why might it appeal to others?*

---

**Your Local Notes**

_____

_____

---

## ROLE OF THE PARALEGAL

The paralegal's role in arbitration is similar to that in litigation—preparing the file, preparing witnesses, conducting research, and so on. If the efforts to arbitrate in a court-annexed arbitration fail, the case will go to trial eventually. Therefore, the paralegal must enter into preparations anticipating that a trial is a possible outcome.

Some concerns unique to arbitration may confront the paralegal, including the question of jurisdiction. (Is arbitration appropriate under the governing statute or contract clause?) The paralegal must also ensure that the parties are following the most current rules governing the arbitration. Paralegals are often responsible for drafting the demand for arbitration, the motion for referral, and the responses to such demands and motions.

Assisting in the selection of arbitrators is another task that falls to paralegals. When appropriate they conduct background checks on potential arbitrators and conflict checks to make sure no conflict of interest exists between any member of the firm and potential arbitrators.

During the hearing paralegals must be even more familiar with documents than they are in litigation because of the impromptu nature of arbitration hearings. Being able to "think on your feet" is a particularly important attribute of paralegals in the arbitration field.

Litigation paralegals are not the only paralegals potentially connected to the arbitration process. Paralegals working in the corporate and real estate areas must research jurisdictional arbitration requirements to ensure that the arbitration clauses in their contracts comply with these requirements. This can be particularly tricky in the international arena where arbitration laws vary greatly. Careful drafting of arbitration clauses prevents jurisdictional disputes at a later date.

Paralegals with expertise in a particular field may want to look into becoming an arbitrator. The AAA accepts nonlawyers who are experts in their field and some organizations use nonlawyers as arbitrators. To get experience as an arbitrator, consider consulting the Better Business Bureau, which uses arbitrators on a volunteer basis to preside over consumer disputes.

# MEDIATION

**Mediation** uses a neutral third party to facilitate communication between disputing parties, assisting them in defining key issues, identifying possible options and alternatives, and enabling them to reach a mutually agreeable compromise. Unlike an arbitrator, a mediator cannot force a decision on the parties; therefore, a mediator must rely on effective communication skills to encourage parties to express their feelings and to listen to their opponent's position. For mediation to be effective the parties often must undergo a perceptual shift. Winning at any cost is such a predominant theme in American culture that parties have to understand that mediation is designed to create a "win–win" situation that meets everyone's needs.

Mediation is usually voluntary although participation is sometimes mandated by contract or by the court. Settlement, however, can never be mandated. When settlement is reached, studies show that mediated agreements are more likely to be complied with than decisions imposed by arbitrators or judges. This success may be because the parties take an active role in the decision-making process.

---

*Your Local Notes*

_____

_____

---

## FORMS OF MEDIATION

Several models of mediation exist. Under some models, such as the community model, the mediator takes a very nondirective role, helping the parties brainstorm and keeping the lines of communication open. The mediator does little or nothing to suggest resolution. His primary role is to encourage the parties to express their feelings and explore possible solutions. Although some preliminary research indicates that agreements reached under this approach appear to be longer lasting than those obtained under the direction of a more controlling mediator, this approach can be very time consuming and impractical when time constraints exist.

The approach more likely to be used when attorneys are involved is the model typically used in the business community. Here the mediator participates more actively, suggesting resolutions and urging the parties to accept these resolutions. Under this approach the expertise of the mediator can be helpful in assisting the parties to understand their conflict, evaluate their position, and forge some kind of agreement. This approach seems to result in higher rates of settlement than the nondirective approach described earlier but not necessarily in settlements that are as permanent.

One of the newest approaches to mediation is called **transformative mediation** and is used extensively by the U.S. Postal Service. This approach is even less directive than the community model. No expectation exists that any settlement will necessarily be reached. The primary purpose of this type of mediation is to allow the parties to speak until they have nothing else to say. If at the end of the mediation, the parties have not reached any consensus but have experienced some kind of "transformation" in that they understand the conflict and feel they can live with a lack of resolution, the mediation is considered successful. Very few guidelines limit the parties' conduct and emotional flare-ups are expected and permitted. The rationale is that by fully ventilating pent-up feelings and thoughts, the parties can eventually get to what is at the core of their dispute. This kind of mediation seems to work well in employment disputes and in domestic relations cases.

Attorneys may or may not attend mediation sessions. If, however, one side is represented by counsel, the opposing side most certainly should be represented; nothing is served in mediation if one of the parties feels besieged. Advocates of mediation often recommend that an attorney serving as litigation counsel should not also serve as mediation counsel because the roles are so different. Litigators in particular often find it difficult to switch to a mediator role because they are so geared for combat in the courtroom.

> *Putting It Into Practice:*
>
> *What type of mediation process would be most appropriate in Shannon's case?*

---

**Your Local Notes**

_____

_____

_____

---

## MEDIATION PROCESS

Although the mediation process varies depending on the type of model used, certain general procedures are followed. The mediator sets the date for the mediation and informs the parties of the rules that will be followed during the mediation. Some mediators will meet with the parties separately before the mediation begins so they better understand the dispute. Some mediators also allow the parties to submit position papers outlining their positions and the reasons they have assumed this stance. Other mediators believe that any foreknowledge about the dispute will create preconceived notions that make it more difficult for the mediator to be neutral. They contend that preparing position papers allows the parties to become more deeply entrenched and committed to their positions, thereby inhibiting resolution of their dispute.

At the beginning of the formal mediation, the mediator explains her role, the confidential nature of the proceedings, any ground rules (e.g., no name-calling), the benefits of mediation, and the procedural steps that will be followed (if any). She begins to establish a rapport with the parties, identifies any potential conflicts of interest, encourages the parties to mediate in good faith, solicits their active participation, and asks if they have questions.

During the fact-gathering stage that follows the introduction, the party who brought the dispute to the mediator is usually asked to tell his story first and then the opposing party is given an opportunity to respond. The mediator is not obliged to follow this order, however, and if multiple issues are involved, the parties may prioritize the issues before beginning the mediation. Depending on the level of participation of the mediator, she may assist the parties in practicing good communication skills, may reword judgmental language used by anyone, and may ensure that the parties have equal opportunities to speak. This first phase of mediation can be highly charged if the parties ventilate their feelings and opinions.

After this "venting" the mediator may choose to caucus with the parties separately. This is done if the mediator feels the session is getting out of control or if the mediator needs to clarify an issue outside the hearing of the other party. Caucuses cannot be done without the consent of the other party and nothing discussed during a caucus can be disclosed to the other party without consent of each party.

During the fact-gathering stage, the mediator will begin to define the issues, helping the parties to focus on the issues rather than their positions. At appropriate times the mediator will reinforce points of agreement and conduct "reality checks" whenever necessary. The mediator steers the parties away from past events and focuses them on what they want to see happen in the future. The mediator is responsible for creating an environment in which the parties feel free to brainstorm possible options and to offer solutions without fear of censure. If no suggestions are forthcoming, the mediator may, depending on the style of mediation, offer some suggestions or ask questions that may lead to creative problem solving. In the event of an impasse, the mediator uses all of her skills to circumvent the "obstruction" so that the discussion can continue. As solutions are proposed the mediator must guide the parties in assessing the practicality and reasonableness of their proposals. Doing this often requires focusing the disputants on the consequences of their decisions in terms of potential future litigation, economic and emotional costs, stress on relationships, and other practical concerns.

Once a tentative agreement is reached, the mediator clarifies the terms of the agreement and makes sure all parties understand the terms of this agreement. One way this can be accomplished is by having the parties restate the agreement in their own words. The essence of the agreement is then prepared in writing, although the parties may want to have the agreement reviewed by an attorney before signing a formal agreement. In a court-ordered mediation the parties may be required to appear before a judge to finalize their agreement. Whatever the formal requirements for closure, advocates of mediation recommend some kind of personal closure as well, symbolized by perhaps a handshake or a sharing of coffee.

*Putting It
Into Practice:*

*Would you advise
Shannon to try mediation
to resolve her case?*

---

**Your Local Notes**

_____

_____

---

## ROLE OF THE PARALEGAL

Unlike the field of arbitration, mediation is wide open to paralegals. Mediators are not required, or even necessarily encouraged, to be attorneys. Attorneys tend to view disputes in terms of who is "right" and "wrong," whereas mediators must be nonjudgmental in both attitude and behavior. They must avoid even the appearance of evaluation if they are to preserve their role of neutrality. Accordingly, they must know how to use non–value-laden verbal language and how to exhibit neutral body language.

Mediators must model active and empathic listening. They must be able to discern what is actually being said (which is sometimes different from the

---

### SIDEBAR

## Advocacy in Mediation

*Advocacy in mediation requires different skills from those needed for litigation. Litigators must persuade the trier of fact to accept their position. In opening statements, for example, they must sell their client's story with such persuasiveness that any alternative version seems implausible. Mediators, on the other hand, must sell their client, not their client's story, during opening statements. They must persuade their adversary, more so than the mediator, to be sympathetic to their cause. Because most parties arrive at mediation already distrusting the opposing lawyer, attorneys are wise to use opening statements to set a tone of humility, respect, and humanity rather than to gain a competitive advantage. A persuasive but sympathetic opening addressed to the adverse party and counsel can set the stage for a positive settlement.*

*Likewise, good advocacy in mediation requires being able to understand the other party's perceptions. Indeed, the attorney's motto should be "seek first to understand and then to be understood." Understanding the opponent's perspective allows attorneys to be more flexible if that perspective makes sense, and to persevere for a more favorable settlement if the opponent's perspective makes no sense.*

*Gaining that perspective can take time and for that reason the mediation process is often time consuming. People need time to process information; if not allowed sufficient time to do that, they will cling tenaciously to their original perspective. Consequently, two of the most important qualities of a good advocate in mediation are patience and perseverance.*

*For obvious reasons, attorneys should never threaten or make pejorative statements about their opponents. Settlements are essentially based on trust; by undermining that trust, threats and pejorative statements minimize the chances of settlement. Furthermore, opponents may react to threats and insults by hardening their position and resolving to take the dispute to the courthouse. While ridicule or accusation may serve to discredit or rattle a witness at trial, they are simply not effective negotiating tools.*

words being used). Similarly, they must be able to reframe what a party has said in a nonjudgmental way that reduces the "charge" (sting) on the communication so that the receiving party can respond rather than react. It is this capacity to keep the lines of communication clean that enables mediators to keep parties on track rather than going down emotional "rabbit holes" that jeopardize the possibility of settlement.

In addition to excellent listening skills, paralegals must be flexible enough to adapt to the particular needs of the participants. Some individuals respond better to gentle, restrained intervention, whereas others need more forceful guidance. The interpersonal skills required to be an effective mediator are quite sophisticated. Mediators must know, for example, how and when to steer people through impasses, how to help them save face, and how to stimulate creative problem solving without suggesting the resolution.

In general, successful mediators have patience, a sense of humor, a strong sense of caring, and a desire to help others solve challenging problems. They are able to stay calm in the presence of strong emotions. They express themselves clearly and hear others with minimal distortion. Above all, they genuinely like people and are tolerant of human eccentricities.

**Putting It
Into Practice:**

*What types of people do
you think are best suited
to be mediators?*

Paralegals who want to remain in litigation can still play a role in mediation. The same tasks that must be completed to prepare for litigation are also needed to prepare for mediation. With those matters that do not begin with litigation, investigative research is still necessary to ascertain information about assets, background of the parties, basic information relating to the issues, and so on, to ensure that any negotiations are conducted in good faith and that any settlement reached is as fair as possible. If a matter starts down the litigation path but is referred by the court to mediation, the paralegal may assist in drafting such documents as a motion for referral to mediation. If mediation becomes a reality, the paralegal may help prepare a position paper to educate the mediator about the case and if settlement is reached, the paralegal may prepare a settlement agreement and any related documents.

Nonlitigation paralegals are often responsible for drafting agreement-to-mediate clauses in real estate contracts and other commercial transactions. As with arbitration clauses, preparation of such clauses requires research of the ADR laws in the relevant jurisdiction.

---

*Your Local Notes*

_____

_____

---

# MED-ARB

A hybrid form of ADR created by combining mediation and arbitration is **med-arb.** In this approach mediation is attempted first; if the parties fail to agree to a settlement, the same neutral that facilitated the mediation conducts an arbitration. The obvious problem that arises in this case is that the so-called "neutral" is no longer neutral, having heard information that could influence the arbitration. On the other hand, the med-arb approach is efficient and cost effective in that the parties present their evidence only once.

Some critics of med-arb point out that parties are less likely to fully disclose information to a mediator who may then use that information against their interests in the arbitration. If, for example, a party during mediation admits that it would be willing to accept a settlement of $10,000, the mediator turned arbitrator would then know that it could award $10,000 rather than the $20,000 being demanded by that party. If, on the other hand, the party failed to disclose its bottom line during the mediation for fear of how this information might be used in the event of an arbitration, the mediation process would be compromised and settlement would be less likely. By the same token, an arbitrator who wanted to obtain referrals for future mediations/arbitrations would be reluctant to grant an award based on disclosures made during a mediation for fear of the disclosing party's reaction. Therefore, the integrity of both the mediation and the arbitration can be compromised when the two are combined.

**Putting It
Into Practice:**

*Do you think med-arb
is a viable form of
dispute resolution in
Shannon's case?*

The best use of med-arb seems to be with parties who like the cost savings and efficiency of this approach, who trust the integrity of the mediator/arbitrator being used, and who stand in relatively equal bargaining relationship with each other, thereby minimizing the chances of one party manipulating the process to its advantage. Parties who feel they run the risk of being outmaneuvered in this process are probably better advised to go through mediation and then a separate arbitration using a different neutral.

> *Your Local Notes*
>
> _____
>
> _____

## ROLE OF THE PARALEGAL

Paralegals have the potential to serve the same functions as they would in a traditional mediation or arbitration. Additionally, they may be asked to research the potential uses of med-arb when drafting ADR provisions in contracts.

## SUMMARY JURY TRIAL

The only ADR approach that uses an actual jury is the **summary jury trial.** In this approach the attorneys present an abbreviated version of the evidence; live testimony may not be allowed. The jury is selected from an actual jury pool using a modified *voir dire* process (generally only two peremptory strikes are allowed). After hearing the summarized evidence, with each side being given a short time, usually an hour or two, the jurors are allowed to deliberate and asked to deliver a consensual verdict if possible. If consensus proves impossible, each juror is asked to submit separate and anonymous findings. Although the jury's verdict is nonbinding (which the jurors may or may not be told), the attorneys are encouraged to engage in a round-table discussion with the jurors to gain some insights into how the jurors reached their conclusions.

To participate in this form of ADR, the litigants must have completed discovery and essentially be ready to go to trial. The attorneys must draft proposed jury instructions and submit trial briefs. A few days before the summary trial, the judge hears motions in limine and rules on objections in advance. At trial, objections are kept to an absolute minimum or are not allowed at all.

Summary jury trials seem to work best when only one or two key issues are involved, the financial stakes are high, each party wants to go to trial and is convinced that it will win, and a normal trial would probably take at least one week to complete. After seeing the outcome of a summary jury trial, the litigants are sometimes more willing to settle or to settle for a more reasonable amount. Parties that stubbornly refuse to believe they could lose at trial become less recalcitrant when a verdict is rendered against them or they receive an award that is substantially less than what they anticipated.

Even proponents of this approach, however, point out that summary trials are not for everyone and will definitely not work until the parties are substantially ready to go to trial. Although one of the benefits of summary trials is the reduction of trial costs (since a summary trial is substantially less expensive than a regular trial), the costs can actually increase if the parties refuse to accept the jury's verdict and insist on going to trial. Sometimes, however, even though the parties still go on to a full-length trial, that trial is shortened because the parties agree to limit the issues that must be tried. In short, the benefits of summary jury trials are that they expedite trials, reduce the cost of litigation, and help crystallize the issues that must be resolved.

A major criticism of summary jury trials is that because they present the evidence in such an abbreviated manner, the jurors are left with an incomplete picture and, therefore, their conclusion is inconsistent with the verdict that would have been rendered had they been presented with all the evidence. Similarly, some point out that the jury is being asked to evaluate evidence based on the attorneys' presentation of that evidence, whereas they might decide differently if they were exposed to all of the actual witnesses.

Many states have adopted rules encouraging the use of summary jury trials. At the federal level, proponents maintain that the process is firmly rooted in the Rules of Civil Procedure (particularly FRCP, Rule 16, which gives the judiciary the right to order litigants to attend pretrial conferences). Considerable controversy exists, however, as to whether judges can compel litigants to use summary jury trials. Although most federal courts agree the process can be mandated, those who disagree argue that the drafters of FRCP, Rule 16, intended judges to encourage litigants to explore nonadjudicatory procedures but did not intend to require them.

Beyond the question of whether summary jury trials can be compelled is the question of whether these proceedings are confidential or open to the public. Those who claim they are confidential maintain that this form of ADR is a settlement technique that should enjoy the same protected status as other settlement procedures. In contrast, those who argue against confidentiality point out that civil matters are presumed to be open to the public and that doing so ensures the integrity of the process.

***Putting It Into Practice:***

*Are there any ways Shannon might benefit from having a summary jury trial? Would you advise her to take this route?*

---

*Your Local Notes*

_____

_____

---

# MINI-TRIAL

A process that shares some similarities with the summary jury trial is the **mini-trial.** As with the summary jury trial, the attorneys prepare as if they were going to trial but then present their cases in an abbreviated fashion. Unlike the summary jury trial, their case is put before party representatives who have the authority to settle. Also unlike the summary jury trial, the mini-trial is a voluntary proceeding (not mandated by a judge) and the referee is usually an expert in the matter at hand rather than a judge. Because of this setup the parties have the freedom, as they do in mediation, to create their own solutions.

No exact format for mini-trials exists because the parties are encouraged to create their own format. However, certain steps are taken in every mini-trial. The parties agree in advance to the procedural rules, including the limits on discovery, that will be followed. Live testimony can be presented but often is not and the trial process is abbreviated, usually lasting less than one week. A neutral third party serves as referee but representatives of the party decide how the case will be resolved. If the parties fail to settle, the neutral may advise the parties of the strengths and weaknesses of their case.

As with summary jury trials, mini-trials help the parties focus on the key issues of their case and help reduce the posturing in which parties typically engage. Hence this process reduces the time and cost spent litigating relatively minor issues. Advocates of mini-trials point out that this form of ADR is favored by business executives because it allows them rather than their attorneys to be in control of the dispute. Therefore, mini-trials are most successful when the parties have an ongoing business relationship that they would like to continue. Mini-trials are not recommended when high emotional stakes are involved or when an individual is suing a company. The process works best when equally sophisticated business representatives sit on opposite sides of the issue. Those who object to the sometimes mandatory nature of summary jury trials often find mini-trials acceptable because they are voluntary. They also satisfy some parties' need to have their "day in court." Attorneys find them particularly useful for clients who overestimate the strength or value of their case. Clients who are adamantly opposed to negotiations sometimes soften to the notion of settlement after hearing both sides of the case presented.

---

*Your Local Notes*

_____

_____

---

*Putting It
Into Practice:*

*Are there any ways
Shannon might benefit
from having a mini-trial?
Would you advise her to
take this route?*

## ROLE OF THE PARALEGAL

The role of the paralegal in both mini-trials and summary jury trials is similar. The work done during the prefiling, filing, and discovery phases of such cases is the same as that done in preparing a case for litigation. If the parties decide to have a mini-trial, however, the paralegal may participate in drafting the mini-trial agreement, which will set forth the agreed-on procedures to be followed.

In preparation for the summary presentation of evidence, the paralegal will review all documents and depositions with an eye toward refining and condensing them. Good summation skills are essential to carry out this crucial task because all of the evidence must be crystallized into a form that captures the essence of the case. As part of this process the paralegal may be asked to retrieve selected excerpts from various documents and depositions. Therefore, an intimate knowledge of all relevant documents is critical if this task is to be manageable. As in litigation preparation, the paralegal will be asked to prepare evidentiary displays that can be used during the presentation of evidence. If the case is settled, the paralegal may be allowed to assist in drafting the settlement agreement as well as in organizing any confidential materials that are either to be destroyed or stored. But throughout this process, the paralegal must have in mind that the case may not settle and be prepared to get ready to go to trial.

## OTHER OPTIONS

Other options that exist as alternatives to litigation are private judging, neutral expert fact finding, and the ombudsman. With **private judging** the parties agree to have a neutral, who is usually a retired judge, hear and decide their case. This option gives the parties the power to select their own judge (including one who has expertise in the matter at hand), to schedule an expedited hearing, and to establish their own rules governing the procedure. This process can occur outside the realm of the court's jurisdiction by private agreement between the parties or can occur when a judge or the parties request a private judge. In the latter case, the so-called "rent-a-judge" statutes require that the private judge follow the procedural requirements of a formal trial and apply the law of that jurisdiction. The private judge must then submit his findings of fact to the presiding judge (the judge with whom the case had been filed). The private judge's decision is binding but can be appealed.

**Neutral expert fact finding** can be voluntary (private and outside the court's intervention) or involuntary (court ordered); in both cases it is non-binding. A neutral with expertise in the question at issue is used to make recommendations. This approach is used to resolve complex disagreements in the securities, patent, medical malpractice, and antitrust areas of the law. Such proceedings tend to be very informal and of an investigatory nature. They focus on obtaining impartial feedback from someone whose expertise in the area of question is respected by both parties. This process is sometimes followed by an arbitration, mediation, or litigation.

A nonadjudicatory process that is used involves the use of an **ombudsman,** who is accustomed to hearing disputes or complaints and recommending how they might be resolved. Hospitals, corporations, and educational organizations use ombudsmen to resolve employee as well as customer complaints. These people work for the organization but report to the chief executive of the agency and remain outside of the internal chains of command. Ombudsmen typically engage in a wide range of activities, including mediation, arbitration, fact finding, counseling, problem solving, and information exchange.

### Putting It Into Practice:

*Do you think Shannon might benefit from any of the ADR options described in this section?*

---

*Your Local Notes*

_____

_____

---

# BRIGHT AND DARK SIDE OF ADR

ADR is still in its infancy. As such, little research has been done to date to test its efficacy either as it is used privately or in the court system. However, both proponents and skeptics agree that ADR can potentially save time and money. In light of the alleged litigation explosion, ADR represents a means of resolving disputes more expeditiously and without the inordinate costs of litigation. Businesses in particular, especially those who engage in international commerce, have found ADR to be a viable form of dispute resolution. Furthermore, by relieving some of the congestion in the courts, ADR opens the door for cases that truly demand litigation.

On the other hand, one of the criticisms levied against ADR is that it actually adds time and creates more expense to resolve disputes. This criticism is particularly applicable to court-annexed arbitration that mandates that cases below a certain dollar amount must go to arbitration. The parties must prepare for a hearing, take time off work to attend the hearing, wait for the arbitrator's award, and then notify the court they are dissatisfied with the award before they are allowed a trial *de novo.* Mediation can also require more time to complete than would litigation, particularly if the issue involves several people in a community and has a strong emotional context.

In rebuttal, however, efficiency is not necessarily the best measure of success in cases of this nature. Giving people the time to vent their frustrations and express their feelings may save time in the long run because the solution that is eventually crafted may resolve the problem permanently. A more expeditious resolution, on the other hand, may result in the parties coming back to court at a later date because of their unwillingness or inability to conform to a court's dictate. Furthermore, evidence exists that supports the premise that compliance with the resultant decision is greater with those who are given an opportunity to participate in the decision making than those to whom the outcome is simply dictated. As mentioned earlier, those mediations in which the mediator plays a nondirective role result in greater compliance than those in which the mediator is more directive.

Another benefit of ADR is that the availability of the many varieties of ADR allows parties to enjoy more flexibility than is found in traditional litigation. They can choose from a simplified hearing process or can assert control over the decision-making process through mediation. They can enjoy the privacy and nonbinding nature of some forms of ADR, which allow them to air their grievances simply and efficiently and still fall back on the traditional forms of litigation if they so decide. All the preparation they put toward preparing their case for ADR can be applied to litigation. Even when ADR fails, it can still simplify the litigation process and allow attorneys to prepare cases more efficiently and less expensively. It also helps parties avoid the uncertainty of litigation and provides them with remedies that are more flexible than typically available in the judicial process.

Some are concerned, however, that ADR may force those who cannot afford to litigate to lose some of the rights to which they are entitled in litigation. They point out that inexpensive and expeditious adjudication is not necessarily synonymous with fair and just adjudication. Because parties do not always possess equal power and resources, the concern is that informal processes lacking procedural protection will result in ill-informed decisions. These critics point to family law as one area where ADR may bring about a "second-class" justice. They argue that the rights that women have gained during the 1990s may be lost if domestic relations disputes are pushed into ADR. Although studies show that mediation program participants are often pleased with the process and the results, divorce mediation raises concerns about power imbalances between the mediating parties. Especially where there is a history of domestic violence, the party being abused may feel incapable of negotiating on her own behalf. Critics of ADR believe that disadvantaged individuals benefit most from formal legal processes, that the more intimate ADR processes may actually prejudice weaker individuals, and that even after agreement is reached, judicial oversight may be necessary to protect the weaker parties.

Despite the possibility of not protecting less powerful individuals, ADR often preserves relationships that might otherwise be severed after enduring the travails of litigation. With mediation in particular, parties are able to communicate directly with another. After venting their feelings, they can then focus on a rational cost/benefit analysis of the difference between litigating and settling.

In contrast, however, some point out that some disputes cannot be resolved by mutual agreement and good faith because these disputes reflect sharply contrasting views about fundamental public values that cannot be eliminated by simply encouraging disputants to understand each other. These critics maintain that a potential danger of ADR is that disputants who seek only reconciliation may ignore public values reflected in rules of law established by the legislature. Some controversies, they argue further, should be brought to the public's attention. They feel difficult issues of constitutional or public law and matters that affect large groups, such as pollution and corporate fraud, should be adjudicated to ensure the proper application of public values. Environmental disputes, which they cite as illustrative of this problem, are often settled by mediation. The danger, these critics maintain, is that environmental standards will be created by private groups without the democratic checks of governmental institutions.

One of the strengths of ADR is that it helps people focus on their real needs and overcome perceptual differences. Neutrals who facilitate the ADR process

***Putting It Into Practice:***

*What is your overall assessment of ADR as an option to litigation?*

assist parties in realistically evaluating their case by pointing out its weaknesses. As a result, proposals suggested by these third parties can avoid the knee-jerk negative reactions that might be precipitated by proposals suggested by the other party. Figure 6–1 summarizes the pros and cons of ADR.

**Your Local Notes**

_____

_____

---

**Figure 6–1    Pros and Cons of ADR**

| Pros | Cons |
|---|---|
| Saves time | Can take more time than litigation alone |
| Saves money | In some cases costs more money than litigation alone |
| Relieves court congestion | Requires some parties to take extra steps |
| Increases compliance with decisions rendered | Not always efficient |
| Gives parties more flexibility | Parties do not get their day in court |
| Allows parties to avoid uncertainty of litigation | Denies litigation to those who need it |
| Assists in preparing for litigation | Increases cost of eventual litigation |
| Gives alternative form of dispute resolution to poor | Provides "second-class" justice to poor |
| Helps preserve relationships | Fails to protect weaker parties |
| Allows venting of feelings and opinions | Some disputes cannot be resolved just through understanding |
| Helps people realistically assess their case | Denies procedural protections to some |

---

## SIDEBAR

## Quality Control

*ADR works only if the neutrals are well trained. The question then is "What kind of training should be required?" Some believe that neutrals must have substantive expertise in the field in which the dispute arose, as do most arbitrators, who are experts in their field and certainly more knowledgeable about the issue at hand than the average juror. Others argue that a lack of substantive knowledge is an asset because the neutral will be less likely to prejudge the situation (in an arbitration) or offer options (in a mediation). They point out that those who opt for ADR can select another neutral if they believe the one they have been assigned is unqualified, whereas litigators have little or no choice about the judge they are given.*

*A corollary to the training issue is the question of whether ADR should be regulated and, if so, by whom it should be regulated. Bar associations often see themselves as best equipped to moderate ADR but nonlawyer facilitators often see it differently. Their concern is that the legal profession will make ADR the province of those with legal training and will strip ADR of its unique characteristics by making facilitators become mini-lawyers.*

# LIMITATIONS OF ADR

Even the most ardent supporters of ADR understand that ADR cannot be used to resolve every controversy, ADR is not appropriate, for example, when one party needs a judicial precedent. Without this legal guidance others in similar situations will have no signpost by which to model their conduct. Certainly the state of civil rights law would have been seriously compromised had all race discrimination cases in the 1960s and 1970s been mediated rather than adjudicated. ADR is also inappropriate when there is a need to bind nonparties (e.g., to establish title to property).

Some go one step further and contend that the courts should not be allowed to annex ADR. Putting ADR into the courthouse, they contend, makes both ADR and the court processes more cumbersome. Even parties with cases that ought to be adjudicated are forced into the time, expense, and apparent irrelevancy of ADR.

On a more philosophical note, they argue that reformers of the legal system have confused the purpose of ADR (reaching settlement) and the trial process (vindicating rights, establishing societal norms, and determining fault). These critics urge reformers to channel those disputes where settlement is the goal into ADR and those where fault needs to be assigned or rights/norms established into the court system. Once the parties' interests have been identified, they suggest dispute resolution mechanisms be chosen that do not compromise the parties' interests. Furthermore, they argue that the system should consider the nature of the rights involved in the dispute and determine whether the public has an interest in resolving the dispute. The sidebar below summarizes the questions that still remain unanswered in reference to ADR.

*Putting It Into Practice:*

What do you think the future of ADR is in this country?

> **Your Local Notes**
>
> _____
>
> _____

---

## SIDEBAR

### Questions That Remain to Be Answered About ADR

- *Can ADR programs be adequately staffed and funded over the long term?*
- *Will litigants choose ADR in lieu of litigation or in addition to litigation?*
- *What effect will ADR have on the judicial caseload?*
- *Can we avoid "second-class" justice for the poor and disenfranchised?*
- *How do we ensure that public law questions are resolved appropriately?*
- *What criteria should we use to evaluate ADR programs?*
- *Should neutrals have substantive expertise in the field in which they are facilitating dispute resolution?*
- *Should ADR be mandatory or voluntary?*
- *Should ADR be regulated and by whom?*
- *Is ADR an appropriate means of resolving all kinds of disputes?*

hypothetical

**Shannon's Ordeal,** *continued*

"*S*o have you decided what you want to do?" asked Allen when he called Shannon a few days later.

"Yes, I've decided I want to go to trial. I thought about mediation but I really don't want to have to sit across a table from Collins. I don't think I could stand to look at him. Every time I even think of his face I go through that whole nightmare all over again." Shannon shuddered involuntarily just thinking about the possibility.

"And you've eliminated arbitration as well?" queried Allen.

"Yes. I like the idea of a simpler, cheaper way of getting this whole mess resolved but the bottom line is that I want to have a jury hear my story. I really think a jury would understand what I went through better than some arbitrator and I'd rather take my chances with six to twelve people than one."

"And the summary jury trial. . . . "

"I thought about that too and although I like having a jury I want them to hear the whole story. I don't want to rush through it just so we can get done in a day. Don't take it personally, but I don't want you telling my story. I want to be able to tell it myself. I've seen enough TV shows. I know what the defense attorneys will try to do to me but I don't care. I want my day in court and I don't want to settle for anything else," explained Shannon, emphasizing her last statement.

"And that you shall have," declared Allen. "We will prepare to go to trial. So let's start talking about what you can expect after we get a trial date."

## ETHICAL ETIQUETTE

### ETHICAL RULES FOR MEDIATORS

*T*he American Bar Association (ABA), the American Arbitration Association (AAA), and the Society of Professionals in Dispute Resolution (SPIDR) have developed a set of standards to be used as guidelines in the practice of mediation. These standards are designed to be a first step in the process of assisting practitioners, and the developers of this code recognize that these standards may have to be altered due to statutes or contractual agreements. They are designed, however, to guide mediators, to inform parties, and to enhance public confidence in the mediation process.

The following standards are found in the Standard Code of Conduct (note that we have not reproduced the entire code with its discussions and comments, merely the basic standards):

1. *Self-determination:* A mediator shall recognize that mediation is based on the principle of self-determination by the parties.

2. *Impartiality:* The mediator shall conduct the mediation in an impartial manner.

3. *Conflicts of interest:* A mediator shall disclose all actual and potential conflicts of interest reasonably known to the mediator. After disclosure, the mediator shall decline to mediate unless all parties choose to retain the mediator. The need to protect against conflict of interest also governs conduct that occurs during and after the mediation.

4. *Competence:* A mediator shall mediate only when the mediator has the necessary qualifications to satisfy the reasonable expectations of the parties.

## ETHICAL ETIQUETTE *continued*

5. *Confidentiality:* A mediator shall maintain the reasonable expectations of the parties with regard to confidentiality.

6. *Quality of the process:* A mediator shall conduct the mediation fairly, diligently, and in a manner consistent with the principle of self-determination of the parties.

7. *Advertising and solicitation:* A mediator shall be truthful in advertising and solicitation for mediation.

8. *Fees:* A mediator shall fully disclose and explain the basis of compensation, fees, and charges to the parties.

9. *Obligations to the mediation process:* Mediators have a duty to improve the practice of mediation.

# PRACTICE POINTERS
## *Client Preparation*

Preparing a client for ADR is important and yet is often overlooked by attorneys, some of whom do not really understand ADR processes. If you know what clients must know and understand to more fully participate in the ADR process of their choice, it will be easier for you to assist in preparing them. To begin with, clients must know before entering into any kind of alternative process what they want, what the dispute means to them, and the risks of entering into litigation. Clients must also understand the mechanics and benefits of the ADR process and the role of each person in the process (including their role, the attorney's role, and the role of the neutral).

Clients must be guided in realistically assessing the strengths and weaknesses of their case (something neither attorneys nor clients enjoy doing) and in assessing what their best interests are, as opposed to their legal position. Following this objective evaluation, clients must be made to consider the variety of possibilities that might settle the case and what would constitute a fair settlement under the circumstances.

Although sometimes contrary to the instincts of the litigator, clients must be instructed as to the importance of listening to the opponent with an open mind and being willing to reevaluate their position on hearing their opponent's presentation. Beyond that, clients will benefit from learning the importance (in some forms of ADR, such as mediation) of apology and listening empathetically. At the very least, clients must be instructed not to insult or provoke the opponent or do anything that would unnecessarily jeopardize the possibility of settlement. Furthermore, clients must be forewarned to be patient and allow the negotiation drama (of monetary offers, counteroffers, counter-counteroffers, and so on) to unfold.

Finally, clients must be counseled to consider their best alternative to a negotiated agreement (BATNA) as well as worst alternative to a negotiated agreement (WATNA). Is the best alternative litigation? If so, what are the costs, risks, and burdens associated with litigation? The BATNA drives parties toward offers that are better than the best alternative and away from offers that are worse than the best alternative. By the same token, if the WATNA is highly likely, even slightly better offers are more attractive. The point is that parties are not fully prepared to begin the ADR process until they know their BATNA and WATNA and those of their adversary and are able to express them clearly.

## TECHNO TIP

To find out the latest trends in commercial litigation, as well as to determine what the American Arbitration Association has to offer, go to their web site at www.adr.com.org. The AAA also has a link to the Federal Arbitration Act and the Administrative Dispute Resolution Act of 1996 and they have a listing of all the various state's arbitration statutes. You can also visit the site of the Center for Public Resources (CPR) at www.cpradr.org. The CPR site has a list of more than 700 available arbitrators/mediators for use in resolving disputes using ADR. The National Academy of Arbitration can be found at www.igc.org/naarb.

In addition to the national and international ADR organizations you should not lose site of the services provided by local and state bar associations. Many retired judges and attorneys, as well as active practitioners specializing in ADR, can be located by a call to the bar associations.

## SUMMARY

The primary forms of ADR used in this country are arbitration, mediation, med-arb, summary jury trials, and mini-trials. Although ADR is relatively new to mainstream Americans, it has been used by the Quakers, Puritans, Mormons, and Chinese and Jewish immigrants as a means of avoiding litigation. ADR was first considered as a means of conflict resolution because some thought it might be a solution to overburdened courts and the inaccessibility of the judicial system to the poor and middle class. The status of ADR was strengthened in the federal system by the passage of ADRA, which encouraged the use of ADR by the federal government. Most district courts that have reviewed mandatory ADR provisions have found them to be constitutional.

Arbitration was one of the first forms of ADR to be used. It allows attorneys to present their case to a neutral third party but saves the time and money required to go to trial. Arbitration can be mandatory or voluntary, binding or nonbinding, and private or court annexed. Private arbitration typically arises out of a contract clause requiring the parties to arbitrate disputes, whereas court-annexed arbitration is usually dictated by statute. With private arbitration the award is usually binding and the parties must pay for the arbitrator's services. With court-annexed arbitration the award is usually nonbinding and the parties can request a trial *de novo;* the parties do not have to pay for the arbitrator's services. Appeals are often discouraged, however, by requiring fees or by holding parties liable for costs if they do not improve their position at trial. Disputes involving contracts containing arbitration clauses will go to private, binding arbitration, whereas matters filed in the courts governed by statutes requiring arbitration will go to nonbinding, court-annexed arbitration.

The procedures for private arbitration are set forth in the contract requiring arbitration. Many contracts specify the use of AAA rules. Under these rules arbitrators are selected from a list of names provided by the AAA. The parties strike those names that are unacceptable, allowing the AAA to select an arbitrator from the remaining names. Parties can also choose arbitrators from private sources.

Arbitration can be initiated by one of the parties filing a motion to refer to arbitration or a demand for arbitration, which the opposing party can dispute. Court-annexed arbitration begins after the parties file their pleadings. The arbitrator determines how much latitude will be given in the discovery process but motion practice is generally quite limited. Arbitrations are generally informal procedures in which the rules of evidence are used only as guidelines. Because of the informality of the process and the lack of extensive discovery, some feel that going into an arbitration is like playing "blind man's bluff." Hearings follow the same outline as trials, beginning with opening statements and the presentation of evidence, and ending with closing arguments and/or the presentation of post-hearing briefs. They differ from trials in that they are closed to the public.

Arbitrators usually take the matter under advisement but must render a decision within a specified time period. Binding awards cannot be set aside except for specific misconduct on the part of the arbitrator. Courts reviewing these decisions can decide only whether the award was valid and cannot retry the issues.

Mediation allows parties to find their own way to resolution. The neutral facilitates communication, assists in defining the issues, identifies possible solutions, and generally aids the parties in working toward compromise. The level of directiveness of the neutral depends on the type of mediation being used. The community and transformative models are very nondirective, whereas the business model most often used when attorneys are involved encourages the mediator to be more participatory. Some studies indicate that the latter approach results in a higher rate of settlement but that settlements arising out of the less directive approaches are longer lasting.

Mediation is usually voluntary but can be mandated by contract or by the court. Although attorneys need not be present, if one side is represented by counsel, it is usually best for the opposing side to also be represented. When attorneys participate in the mediation process, they must manifest different skills than those required in litigation. Above all, they must keep in mind that their primary function is to facilitate compromise, not to win.

The mediation process varies. Some mediators like to meet with the parties before the mediation and ask them to prepare position papers. Other mediators believe that any prior knowledge about the dispute makes it more difficult for the mediator to be neutral. Most mediators open the process by establishing the rules, explaining their role and the process, identifying any conflicts of interest, and encouraging the full participation of the parties. During the fact-gathering stage, the parties tell their stories and vent their feelings. The mediator may then choose to caucus with the parties separately. Nothing said during a caucus can be disclosed to the opposing party without consent of each party. The mediator then helps the parties focus on the issues rather than their positions and on what they want rather than what has happened in the past. As the parties offer solutions, the mediator encourages them to assess the practicality and reasonableness of their proposals and if no solutions are proposed may suggest some herself. If an agreement is reached, she clarifies the terms of the agreement, making sure that everyone understands what the agreement is. Once the agreement is formalized, the mediator brings closure to the process.

A hybrid of arbitration and mediation, called med-arb, begins with a mediation, which, if it is unsuccessful, culminates in an arbitration. The same neutral serves as both arbitrator and mediator. One primary criticism of this approach is the tainted neutrality of the facilitator, which can potentially compromise the integrity of both the arbitration and mediation. Efficiency and cost effectiveness are the primary benefits of this process. Med-arb works best when the parties have relatively equal bargaining power and trust the neutral.

Summary jury trials and mini-trials both provide means of presenting evidence in an abbreviated fashion and obtaining feedback from neutral third parties. With summary jury trials the evidence is presented to a jury with whom the attorneys can engage in a round-table discussion after the jury has rendered its verdict, or if no consensus is reached, after individual jurors have submitted their verdicts. With mini-trials the evidence is presented to a neutral who is usually an expert in the question at hand. Summary jury trials work best when only a few key issues are at stake, when a regular trial would last a week or more, and when the financial stakes are high and each party is convinced it would win at trial. They do not work unless the parties are substantially prepared to go to trial, and they may result in a skewed outcome because the jurors do not get to hear all of the evidence and what evidence they do hear is presented by the attorneys rather than the actual witnesses. Some controversy exists over whether judges can mandate summary jury trials and whether the proceedings should be open to the public. Mini-trials also assist the parties to focus on the key issues and to avoid the costs of conventional litigation. Business executives often like this form of ADR because it gives them—rather than their attorneys—control of the dispute. Mini-trials work best when the parties have an ongoing relationship they want to preserve and when no highly emotional issues are at stake. They give parties their "day in court" and often encourage those who are adamantly opposed to negotiations to see the value of settlement.

Other less popular ADR options include private judging, neutral expert fact finding, and the use of an ombudsman. Private judging allows parties to select their own judge, to schedule an expedited hearing, and to establish their own rules to govern the procedure. Neutral expert fact finding is often used when complex issues are involved and is frequently followed by arbitration, mediation, or litigation. Ombudsmen are used by hospitals, corporations, and educational organizations to resolve employee and consumer complaints.

Paralegals must prepare cases going to ADR as if they were going to trial. From the nonlitigation standpoint they may draft contracts with clauses requiring some form of ADR in the event of a dispute. With arbitration, they have an opportunity to assist in the selection of arbitrators and in drafting demands for arbitration and responses to those demands. Although paralegals cannot become arbitrators unless they have expertise in a particular field, they can become mediators. Good mediators must have excellent communication and interpersonal skills, patience, a sense of caring, tolerance for human eccentricities, and a willingness to allow others to express strong emotions. Litigation paralegals also draft referrals to mediation and help prepare position papers and settlement documents. If the parties opt for a summary jury trial or a mini-trial, the paralegal may be asked to prepare a summary presentation of the evidence and must, therefore, have an intimate knowledge of all pertinent documents and depositions.

## KEY TERMS

| | | |
|---|---|---|
| Alternative dispute resolution (ADR) | Mediation | Private judging |
| Arbitration | Mini-trial | Summary jury trial |
| Binding | Neutral | Transformative mediation |
| Court-annexed arbitration | Neutral expert fact finding | Trial *de novo* |
| Mandatory arbitration | Nonbinding | Voluntary arbitration |
| Med-Arb | Ombudsman | |
| | Private arbitration | |

## Workshop Alert

*None of the workshops deal with ADR.*

## REVIEW QUESTIONS

1. How did ADR first appear in this country? How is it being treated by Congress and the federal courts today?

2. Identify the following forms of arbitration:
   a. Private
   b. Court-annexed
   c. Mandatory
   d. Voluntary
   e. Binding
   f. Nonbinding

3. How are arbitrators selected under the AAA rules?

4. Describe the basic arbitration process. Explain how it may be initiated, the precursors to the hearing, the hearing process itself, and the procedures subsequent to the issuing of an award.

5. How does mediation differ from arbitration?

6. What are the various types of mediation?

7. Describe the various stages of a typical mediation.

8. What are the qualities of an attorney advocating well for a client during a mediation?

9. What is the role of the paralegal in arbitration? In mediation?

10. What are the qualities of a good mediator?

11. Describe each of the following:
    a. med-arb
    b. summary jury trial
    c. mini-trial
    d. private judging
    e. neutral expert fact finding
    f. ombudsman

12. What are the advantages and disadvantages of the following:
    a. med-arb
    b. summary jury trial
    c. mini-trial

13. Under what circumstances would you use each of the following:
    a. private judging
    b. neutral expert fact finding
    c. ombudsman

14. Discuss at least four reasons that ADR should be utilized as a means of conflict resolution; then give a counterargument to each of these reasons.

## PRACTICE EXAM

*(Answers in Appendix A)*     **MULTIPLE CHOICE**

1. Alternative dispute resolution includes
   a. arbitration.
   b. mediation.
   c. private judging.
   d. all of the above.

2. ADR was
   a. never used in this country until recently.
   b. strengthened in the federal system by the passage of ADRA.
   c. foreign to people outside of this country.
   d. determined by most district courts to be an unconstitutional violation of the right to a jury trial.

3. Binding arbitration
   a. results in awards that are appealable.
   b. is not allowed in the context of private arbitration.
   c. results in awards that are rarely overturned by the courts.
   d. none of the above.

4. With court-annexed arbitration
   a. the parties are referred to arbitration after filing their pleadings.
   b. parties cannot object to arbitration.
   c. the award is binding.
   d. all of the above.

5. A binding arbitration award can be set aside if
   a. the arbitrator engaged in misconduct.
   b. the arbitrator exceeded the limits of his authority.
   c. the arbitrator refused to hear material evidence.
   d. all of the above.

6. At arbitration hearings
   a. no rebuttal questions are allowed.
   b. the discovery rules vary from jurisdiction to jurisdiction.
   c. no closing arguments are allowed.
   d. the rules of confidentiality do not apply.

7. During the arbitration process, paralegals
   a. have little to do because most of the work falls to the attorney.
   b. do not have to be as familiar with documents as they are in litigation because of the informality of the hearing process.
   c. may assist in the screening of arbitrators.
   d. do not have to be able to "think on their feet" as much as they do during a trial.

8. A mediator
   a. facilitates communication between the disputants.
   b. renders a decision and issues an award.
   c. must do everything possible to steer the parties toward compromise.
   d. tries to get the parties to accept her proposed solution.

9. Mediation
   a. requires a directive approach by the mediator.
   b. exists in a variety of forms.
   c. is usually mandated by the courts.
   d. agreements are less likely to be complied with than decisions rendered by arbitrators.

10. All mediators
    a. require parties to submit position papers.
    b. meet with the parties prior to the mediation.
    c. help the parties identify the key issues.
    d. allow parties to vent without restriction.

11. During the mediation
    a. the party bringing the dispute to the mediator is always allowed to speak first.
    b. the parties are allowed to express their feelings.
    c. the parties can caucus with one another.
    d. an impasse automatically terminates the mediation.

12. Once a tentative agreement is reached
    a. the mediation is over.
    b. the parties must find some way to create closure.
    c. the parties' attorneys negotiate a settlement.

d. the mediator makes sure that each party understands the terms of the agreement.

13. Attorneys who advocate in a mediation
    a. should come across as humble and respectful in their opening statements.
    b. must persuade the mediator that his client is right.
    c. should reserve ridicule and threats until an impasse is reached.
    d. must focus more on making sure that their client is understood than on understanding their opponent's position.

14. Good mediators
    a. are tolerant.
    b. are interested in helping others solve their problems.
    c. know how to help people save face.
    d. all of the above.

15. Med-arb
    a. works best when the parties have unequal bargaining power.
    b. is cost effective but not efficient.
    c. can be problematic because the same neutral is used for the arbitration and mediation.
    d. uses a different arbitrator and mediator.

16. Summary jury trials
    a. work best when the financial stakes are low.
    b. allow attorneys to gain insights from how the jury reached its verdict.
    c. allow parties to go before a mock jury without having to actually prepare for trial.
    d. are open to the public.

17. Mini-trials
    a. allow parties to have their "day in court."
    b. are particularly useful for parties who are adamantly opposed to settlement.
    c. are favored by business executives.
    d. all of the above.

*(Answers in Appendix A)* **MULTIPLE CHOICE**

18. Hospitals, educational organizations, and corporations often resolve customer and employee disputes using
    a. ombudsmen.
    b. neutral expert fact finding.
    c. summary jury trials.
    d. private judging.

19. The strength of ADR is
    a. that it always reduces the cost of resolving disputes.
    b. that it always protects weaker parties.
    c. that it always takes less time than litigation.
    d. relieves court congestion.

20. ADR
    a. is most appropriate when there is a need to establish precedent.
    b. is inappropriate when there is need to bind non-parties.
    c. can effectively be used to resolve every controversy.
    d. is particularly effective when fault needs to be assigned or rights need to be established.

**FILL IN THE BLANKS**

21. _____ involves a third-party neutral who facilitates the resolution of the conflict but who lacks authority to render a decision.

22. _____ involves a third-party neutral who hears the presentation of evidence by the attorneys and who issues an award, whereas _____ involves a third-party neutral who hears presentation of evidence by the attorneys and who issues an advisory opinion that the attorneys can use to negotiate a settlement.

23. _____ uses the same neutral third party to mediate and, if necessary, arbitrate.

24. A _____ requires the use of a jury but the jury's decision is not binding on the parties.

25. _____ arbitration awards cannot be appealed (unless the arbitrator engaged in misconduct), whereas _____ arbitration awards can be set aside and result in a trial _____.

26. Under _____ arbitration the parties must try arbitration before they can go to trial.

27. A _____ arbitration takes place within the court system and is governed by local rules, whereas a _____ arbitration is based on a contractual agreement and is governed by rules agreed on by the parties.

28. Under the rules of the _____ arbitrators are selected from a list from which the parties have stricken any potential arbitrators that are not acceptable to them.

29. A _____ arbitration is initiated by filing a motion to refer to arbitration or a demand for arbitration.

30. In the _____ model of mediation, the mediator encourages the parties to communicate but does little to suggest resolution, whereas in the _____ model of mediation the mediator takes an even less directive approach and does not necessarily expect the parties to reach settlement.

31. A hybrid form of ADR involving both arbitration and mediation is called _____.

32. The only form of ADR that actually uses a jury is called a _____.

33. _____ help parties focus on key issues by having the parties present an abbreviated form of the evidence to representatives of the parties who have the authority to settle.

34. With _____ the parties hire a neutral (usually a retired judge) who hears their case and renders a decision whereas with _____ a neutral with expertise in the matter at hand is used to listen to the evidence and make recommendations.

35. _____ are used by hospitals, corporations, and educational organizations to resolve employee and customer disputes.

## TRUE OR FALSE

**36.** ADR was not used in the United States until the early 1970s. **T F**

**37.** Arbitration was one of the first forms of ADR to be used in this country. **T F**

**38.** ADR was initially perceived as a means of solving the problem of overburdened courts that seemed to be inaccessible to the poor. **T F**

**39.** The 1996 passage of ADRA signaled the demise of ADR in the federal system. **T F**

**40.** Most district courts that have reviewed mandatory ADR provisions have concluded that those provisions do not violate the constitutional right to a jury trial. **T F**

**41.** Arbitration can never be mandated by a court. **T F**

**42.** Private arbitration usually arises out of a contract clause requiring parties to arbitrate any disputes. **T F**

**43.** An award arising out of nonbinding arbitration cannot be appealed. **T F**

**44.** Under mandatory arbitration parties can be forced to settle their dispute. **T F**

**45.** Parties engaged in a court-annexed arbitration can request a trial *de novo* if they are dissatisfied with the arbitrator's award. **T F**

**46.** A contract containing an arbitration clause will go to private, binding arbitration and the contract will dictate the procedures to be followed in the arbitration. **T F**

**47.** A matter filed in the courts that by statute must be arbitrated is considered nonbinding, court-annexed arbitration. **T F**

**48.** Parties involved in binding arbitration do not have to pay for the services of the arbitrator but parties involved in nonbinding arbitration do have to pay for the services of the arbitrator. **T F**

**49.** Some courts have held parties who appeal arbitration awards liable for costs if they fail to improve their position at trial. **T F**

**50.** Under the rules of the AAA parties have no input in the selection of arbitrators. **T F**

**51.** Statutes authorizing judges to order arbitration usually have presumptions favoring arbitration. **T F**

**52.** A complaint must be filed with the court before arbitration can be commenced. **T F**

**53.** Parties have an absolute right to discovery if they agree to arbitration. **T F**

**54.** Some attorneys feel that going into an arbitration hearing is like playing "blind man's bluff." **T F**

**55.** The rules of evidence are usually followed in arbitration hearings. **T F**

**56.** Attorneys who are involved in an arbitration are required to file post-hearing briefs as well as give closing arguments. **T F**

**57.** Arbitration hearings are open to the public. **T F**

**58.** Arbitrators are limited in the amount of time they can take a matter under advisement. **T F**

**59.** Courts reviewing arbitration awards are allowed to basically retry the issues. **T F**

**60.** Paralegals working in real estate and corporate law must learn to draft arbitration clauses that meet jurisdictional requirements. **T F**

**61.** Paralegals cannot serve as arbitrators. **T F**

**62.** Unlike arbitrators, mediators do not impose decisions on the parties. **T F**

**63.** Mediation itself is usually voluntary but settlement is mandatory. **T F**

**64.** The community and transformative models of mediation require a directive approach from the mediator. **T F**

**65.** The business model of mediation results in higher rates of settlement than less directive approaches but those agreements are not as long lasting. **T F**

**66.** The transformative model considers mediation successful if the parties understand the conflict and decide they can live with it even if they do not reach a consensus. **T F**

**67.** Attorneys are not allowed to attend mediation sessions. **T F**

**68.** Litigators sometimes find it difficult to advocate in mediations because their roles are so different. **T F**

69. All mediators require parties to submit position papers before the mediation. **T F**

70. The fact-gathering stage of mediation is usually very quiet because the parties are simply listening to each other. **T F**

71. The mediator has a right to reveal anything disclosed to her during a caucus with the opposing party. **T F**

72. The mediator tries to steer the parties away from past events and focus them on what they want to achieve. **T F**

73. A mediator may never offer suggested solutions. **T F**

74. Mediators help parties assess the practicality and reasonableness of their proposals and assist them in doing "reality checks." **T F**

75. Two of the most important qualities of a good advocate in mediation are patience and perseverance. **T F**

76. Mediators should model passive and reactive listening. **T F**

77. Mediators should develop a technique for mediation and use that same technique with every mediation they conduct. **T F**

78. Paralegals generally make poor mediators because they do not have a law degree. **T F**

79. Once a tentative agreement is reached, the mediator's job is over. **T F**

80. Med-arb can create problems for both the parties and the neutral because the neutrality of the latter can be called into question. **T F**

81. Med-arb works best when the parties are looking for a cost-effective and efficient method of resolving their dispute and feel they have comparable bargaining power. **T F**

82. Parties in med-arb are usually more willing to disclose confidential information than they are in a simple mediation. **T F**

83. With summary jury trials the attorneys often present an abbreviated form of the evidence themselves rather than using "live" testimony. **T F**

84. Mini-trials and summary jury trials work best when the litigants are still involved in the discovery process and not yet prepared to go to trial. **T F**

85. Summary jury trials are the most appropriate form of ADR when the financial stakes are low and several key issues are involved. **T F**

86. Summary jury trials reduce the cost of trial even if the parties refuse to accept the jury's verdict and go to trial. **T F**

87. The conclusion of a summary jury trial can be inconsistent with the verdict that would have been rendered if the jury had been able to hear all of the evidence. **T F**

88. Judges have an undisputed right to mandate summary jury trials and to open them to the public. **T F**

89. The neutral in a mini-trial is usually a retired judge. **T F**

90. Parties are encouraged to create their own format for a mini-trial. **T F**

91. Business executives favor mini-trials because they, not their attorneys, decide how the case will be resolved. **T F**

92. Mini-trials are most appropriate when high emotional stakes are involved and when an individual is suing a company. **T F**

93. Paralegals typically have very little involvement in summary jury trials and mini-trials because the presentation of evidence is so abbreviated. **T F**

94. With private judging parties can select their own judge, schedule their own hearing time, and establish their own procedural rules. **T F**

95. The neutral expert fact-finding process is used most frequently in complex cases because experts in the field in question are used to make recommendations to the parties. **T F**

96. Ombudsmen are successful in resolving disputes for organizations because they are employed outside of those organizations. **T F**

**97.** In some cases ADR can actually add time and create more expense to resolve disputes.          **T   F**

**98.** Allowing people to participate in the decision-making process may actually increase the likelihood of them complying with the resultant decision.          **T   F**

**99.** When ADR fails it further complicates the litigation process.          **T   F**

**100.** In some cases ADR may bring about a "second-class" justice.          **T   F**

**101.** ADR helps preserve relationships that might otherwise be severed in the litigation process.          **T   F**

**102.** A potential danger of ADR is that parties may be content with seeking resolution at the expense of sacrificing public values that should be brought to the public's attention.     **T   F**

**103.** Neutrals are required to have substantive expertise in the field in which they are serving as a neutral.          **T   F**

**104.** ADR is currently regulated by local bar associations.          **T   F**

**105.** ADR is inappropriate when a judicial precedent is needed or when non-parties need to be bound by a decision.          **T   F**

**106.** Some believe that courts should not be allowed to annex ADR.          **T   F**

**107.** Some believe that cases where rights need to be established or fault assigned should be channeled into ADR whereas those cases where settlement is the goal should be channeled into litigation.          **T   F**

## LITIGATION LINGO

*(Answers in Appendix A)*
***Fill in the missing letters.***

| | | |
|---|---|---|
| **1.** __ E __ __ V __ | New trial |
| **2.** __ __ B __ __ S __ A __ | Used to resolve consumer complaints |
| **3.** __ E __ __ R __ | Hybrid form of ADR |
| **4.** __ __ A __ __ F __ __ __ A __ __ __ __ | Very nondirective form of mediation |
| **5.** __ __ N __ __ N __ | Arbitration decision that cannot be appealed |
| **6.** __ __ D __ __ T __ __ | Person who facilitates dispute resolution but who cannot render decisions |
| **7.** __ __ N __ - __ __ I __ __ | Abbreviated trial presented to neutral third party who issues an advisory opinion |
| **8.** __ __ M __ __ __ Y __ __ __ Y | Abbreviated trial presented to jury |
| **9.** __ R __ __ T __ __ T __ __ | Neutral third party who renders decisions and issues awards |
| **10.** __ N __ __ X __ __ | Court arbitration that occurs within the court system |

## LITIGATION LOGISTICS

*(Answers in Appendix A)*

1. Would you suggest using ADR in any of the following cases and, if so, which form of ADR would you suggest and why?

   a. Drunk driver sideswipes your car.

   b. Tenant stops paying rent and refuses to move out.

   c. Karate instructor breaks your nose.

   d. Cousin refuses to pay you a percentage of his business.

   e. Contractor does shoddy work on house.

2. Check the local rules for arbitration in your jurisdiction and answer the following questions:

   a. What cases are eligible for arbitration? Is arbitration required or voluntary in these cases?

   b. What are the requirements to be an arbitrator?

   c. What process is used to select arbitrators?

   d. Where are arbitration hearings held?

   e. Are continuances allowed? If so, under what conditions?

   f. What kind of evidentiary rules are followed?

   g. Is testimony allowed at the hearing?

   h. Are transcripts of the hearing available?

   i. Within what time frame must the arbitrator render a decision?

   j. At what point is the award entered on the docket?

   k. What must a party do to obtain a trial *de novo?*

   l. Is evidence of an arbitration hearing admissible at the trial *de novo?*

   m. Does a party take any risks by requesting a trial *de novo?*

# CHAPTER 7

# ROAD MAP OF A LAWSUIT: PRETRIAL PRACTICE, TRIALS, AND JUDGMENTS

## OBJECTIVES

**In this chapter you will learn:**

- What procedural steps must be taken to obtain a trial setting

- What goes on behind the scenes as the attorneys and judges prepare for trial

- How a civil trial is conducted

- What happens when the trial is over

- What the losing party's options are

- How appeals are taken and decided

- What the winning party must do to collect the winnings

hypothetical

**Shannon's Ordeal,** *continued*

*"This is the time set for trial in the matter of Martin versus Collins, et al., case number 97-770 civil. Is the plaintiff ready?"*

*Allen Porter felt his heartbeat accelerate as he rose from his chair. After twenty years of trying cases, he had long ago conquered his youthful tendency toward stage fright, but, even now, there was something about the beginning of a federal court trial that shot a bolt of adrenaline into his gut. It would pass quickly, though. He smiled reassuringly at Shannon, who was seated beside him at the plaintiff's counsel table—by tradition, the one nearest the jury box.*

*"Plaintiff is ready, your honor."*

*Light years beyond ready, thought Shannon, as she regarded Judge Lewis with a steady gaze. A year of paperwork, depositions, hassling with the hotel's lawyers, assembling evidence, and even then, it had taken another six months of "procedural maneuvering"—Allen Porter's words—to finally drag the defendants into court for trial. What kind of system was this, anyway?*

*Allen Porter had warned her that getting everything ready for trial would not be easy, but, at the time, buoyed by the judge's decision denying the hotel's motion for summary judgment, she had optimistically assumed that the worst was over. "How hard can it be?" she remembered asking Chuck Fletcher. Chuck hadn't answered.*

## GETTING TO TRIAL

How hard can it be? At the risk of repetition, litigation is a contest between adversaries. Once trial begins, it is highly likely that, in a few days or weeks, there is going to be a judgment for one side or the other. In a lawsuit, plaintiff is asking the court to take a positive action—usually, order the defendant to pay plaintiff money. What defendant wants, however, is for the court to do nothing—to leave things the way they are. One way for defendant to achieve this goal is to win the case and get plaintiff's claims dismissed. But often a perfectly acceptable alternative is simply to drag the proceedings out for as long as possible. There can be no judgment for plaintiff as long as there is no judgment! Barring a successful motion for summary judgment, there can be no judgment as long as there is no trial.

### OBTAINING A TRIAL SETTING

What, exactly, *is* a trial setting? What do you have when you have one? The answers to these questions are not as simple as you might suppose.

Superficially, a **trial setting** consists of a minute entry specifying a date, time, and place for trial. Ideally, the date would be firm and unchangeable, and once the trial setting has been issued all parties could depend on going to trial as scheduled. Few if any courts operate that way, however. In practice, courts, like airlines, nearly always "overbook" their reservations, and may schedule as many as a half dozen cases for trial at the same time before the same judge. Otherwise, judges would be sitting around with nothing to do every time a case settled "on the courthouse steps," which occurs more often than not.

Moreover, there are plenty of ways in which a trial setting can be vacated or postponed, even at the last moment. Attorneys, parties, witnesses, or even the judge can get sick or injured. Attorneys can be ordered to trial at the same time in other cases having a higher priority in the court system. Judges can be

**Putting It Into Practice:**

*What would be the advantage of settling "on the courthouse steps" to Shannon? What would be the disadvantages?*

transferred to a different division, or retire, or take vacations. Surprise evidence or witnesses can come to light at the last minute, requiring additional preparation time. The trial that the judge is hearing just before yours can drag on unexpectedly for a few extra days, wiping out your allotted time slot. A defendant can file for bankruptcy, bringing all proceedings in any lawsuits involving that defendant to a standstill. Judges can and do grant continuances and vacate trial dates for all of these reasons and many others. In many courts, it is a rare case that actually makes it to trial on the first setting.

So how does one obtain this minute entry designating a trial date, however firm or unfirm it may be? The court issues it in response to some triggering event, which varies from court to court. Some courts set cases for trial automatically when the filed pleadings or discovery reach a certain stage, or do so early in the case as a part of a scheduling order. In others, the triggering event is the filing of a **motion to set and certificate of readiness** by any party. A motion to set is typically a one- or two-page printed form and informs the court how many trial days are needed, whether a jury trial is demanded, and any other information that the calendar clerk needs in order to schedule the necessary block of time.

> *Putting It*
> *Into Practice:*
>
> *What rules govern the setting of trials in your state?*

---

**Your Local Notes**

_____

_____

---

## PRETRIAL CONFERENCES, STATEMENTS, AND ORDERS

Modern court rules prescribe a series of procedural steps that must be completed before a trial can begin. The necessary steps vary considerably from one jurisdiction to another—a check of the local court rules for the details is indispensable.

These procedures are designed to ensure that the attorneys have fully prepared their cases and honed the issues. The judge does not want to waste trial time listening to attorneys argue about whether one of the exhibits was properly disclosed in discovery or whether some factual issue was fairly raised by the pleadings. More and more, trials are carefully planned and choreographed events, with every step carefully thought out in advance. Most judges have little patience with unprepared attorneys who fumble around trying to "wing it."

The main weapon used to enforce the requisite level of preparedness is, depending on the court, the pretrial order or joint pretrial statement. (In this chapter, we will use *pretrial order* to refer to either or both.) Regardless of whether the rules of the particular court call for a pretrial order (signed by the judge) or a joint pretrial statement (signed by the attorneys), the procedure and content are essentially the same. The finished **pretrial order** or **pretrial statement** is a filed court paper that will set out the exact boundaries of what the attorneys can and cannot present at trial, in effect taking over the job of the pleadings. The rules require the opposing attorneys—the attorneys who will actually conduct the trial, not merely assistants—to meet and confer in good faith and prepare this document together. (In practice, each side usually prepares proposed drafts of their contributions, which they then mark up and pass back and forth by fax until something resembling a finished product emerges.) The deadline for submitting the joint pretrial statement or proposed draft of the pretrial order depends on the court; in some, this document may be required a number of weeks in advance, and in others not until a day or so before trial.

Specifically, how does the pretrial statement or pretrial order set the boundaries of what is allowed at trial? First, it sets out an agreed list of witnesses and documents that can be used at trial. In most courts, the rules require that plaintiff and defendant furnish each other with a list naming every witness that each may attempt to call to testify at trial. The parties must also exchange copies of every document that they may wish to offer in evidence as an exhibit. Typically, the deadline for this exchange of witness and exhibit lists is set weeks or months in advance of trial, so the information necessary to include final lists in the pretrial statement should be readily available—at least in theory.

This pretrial listing of documents saves a good deal of trial time, because the rules require each party to specify in the pretrial statement any known objections to a particular exhibit. If a document is listed and no objections are specified, that document will be admitted at trial without further debate. Often, a document may be technically objectionable—there may not be a witness handy to testify that the signature on a letter is authentic, for example, even though everyone knows that the letter *is* authentic and can be proven authentic by wasting half an hour dragging the person who wrote it as a witness to testify, "Yes, I wrote this." Judges have ways of getting even with attorneys who are determined to stand on ceremony by raising trivial objections, so there is a strong incentive to limit document objections to the important ones.

Next, the pretrial order includes lists of issues of fact and issues of law to be decided at trial. These lists of issues must be written with care, because the pretrial statement supersedes the pleadings at trial; the court may refuse to allow evidence that is outside the scope of the issues listed in the pretrial order. The pretrial order is the end product of all the honing and shaping of issues—all the responsive pleadings, motions for summary judgment, amended pleadings, legal research by both sides, discovery, investigation—it all comes together here.

Naturally, the parties do not always agree on what the issues are, or how they should be worded, or whether a given document is admissible as an exhibit. The pretrial order has separate sections in which each party can stake out his or her own positions on any disputed issues. The rules encourage the attorneys to compromise on such things to the extent reasonable, however, and judges do not appreciate being handed proposed pretrial orders in which each party has insisted on his or her own wording of every issue, however trivial. The goal is for the attorneys to cooperate in defining the issues in such a way that the trial can concentrate on the questions that are seriously in dispute; see FRCP, Rule 16.

**Putting It Into Practice:**

*Who will prepare the pretrial order or statement in Shannon's case? What information will this order or statement contain? What will Allen Porter attempt to achieve as he prepares this order/statement?*

> **Your Local Notes**
>
> _____
>
> _____

## THE COUNTDOWN TO TRIAL

After the pretrial order has been hammered out, signed by the attorneys for both sides, and filed with the court, the attorneys spend the last few days before trial (often including evenings and weekends) pulling all the pieces together. Important direct testimony, that is, the testimony of one's own, friendly witnesses, should be scripted word for word, or nearly so, and rehearsed with the witnesses—far better to be skewered by some surprise answer in the privacy of one's own office, than in open court in front of the jury. Cross-examination of opposing witnesses should be outlined, question by question. Opening and closing arguments should be written out or outlined, rehearsed in the presence of others, and adjusted as needed. It is true that not all lawyers take such great pains in every case—the expense is not always justified—but every well-tried case is, to a great degree, scripted and rehearsed in advance.

Before the trial can begin, several items of unfinished business with the judge must be resolved. These are usually handled on the day the trial is to begin, or a day or two before.

**Motions *in Limine*—**When we think of trials, we inevitably think of lawyers jumping to their feet making an impassioned objection to some bit of evidence. Objections may be high drama, but once a prejudicial question has been asked so that you can object to it, the cat may well be out of the bag. Questions about whether the defendant has insurance, for example, are improper (with a few exceptions), but once plaintiff's lawyer asks the defendant if he has liability insurance, every juror is likely to assume that any verdict is going to come from an insurance company, no matter how much the judge instructs the jury to disregard the question. Believe it or not, the art of "wafting innuendo into the jury box" via the intentional use of improper questions is a skill that many trial lawyers deliberately cultivate, and one that is sometimes taught in seminars on trial practice! Generally, the worst penalty to be expected is a scolding from the judge, which is a small price to pay to get a crucial idea before the jury.

Lawyers preparing for trial can usually anticipate many of the "improper" questions that their opponent will likely try to ask. Usually, all they have to do is imagine which ones they would ask if they were representing their opponent's client. Is there some way of seizing the initiative and, in effect, making the objection before the question is asked, outside the hearing of the jury? Yes; that is the purpose of a **motion *in limine.***

A motion *in limine* asks the judge to rule in advance on the admissibility of evidence. In our hypo, defendant's attorney, Gail Stoddard, knows that Chuck Fletcher took notes of his conversation with Arnie Trevayne in which Arnie said that the hotel room doors are old and do not always close properly. She knows that Arnie denied having said it at his deposition, and that Allen Porter may call Chuck to the stand to have the notes admitted under FRE (Federal Rules of Evidence), Rule 803(1), to make Arnie look like a liar. She can certainly find enough case law to make at least some argument that Chuck's testimony and the notes are inadmissible, but if she waits to object until Porter questions Chuck on the witness stand about the conversation, it will not matter how the judge rules—the damage may already have been done. Instead, she can file a motion *in limine,* asking the judge to rule in advance that Chuck not be permitted to testify or such inquiry to be made. If the judge rules in her favor, he will prohibit Porter from mentioning or referring to the conversation and the notes and will order Porter to instruct his witnesses not to do so either. That is an order that Porter will obey—an attorney who deliberately defies the judge's order *in limine* is inviting a mistrial, jeopardizing his license to practice law, and risking being jailed for contempt of court.

Motions *in limine* can also be used offensively, to confirm that a particular piece of evidence *is* admissible. Suppose Gail Stoddard does not make a motion *in limine* to exclude the evidence, but Allen Porter is afraid the judge may exclude the evidence if he tries to use it—after he sets up Arnie Trevayne for the big bombshell, the judge may take away the bomb, leaving the lawyer looking foolish. He can, if he wishes, file his own motion *in limine* asking the judge for an advance ruling that the evidence is admissible. Then, if the judge denies the motion, he can modify his cross-examination of Arnie accordingly.

> *Your Local Notes*
>
> _____
>
> _____

**Proposed Jury Instructions**—In the American court system, the jury is in charge of deciding what the facts are—i.e., what happened—but it is the judge's job to say what the law is—i.e., what rules apply to the situation. Because it is the jurors who will render the verdict, the judge must somehow communicate to the jurors the legal principles he wants them to apply.

How is this accomplished? Does the judge simply give the jury an off-the-cuff lecture on, say, the law of negligence? Do the jurors get to ask questions or take notes? Is there a textbook? A quiz afterward?

Not exactly. Imperfect though it may seem, the procedure is for the judge to read formal instructions on the law to the jury. Then the jurors are on their own; they do the best they can from the instructions given. In most courts, the judge reads the jury instructions just before the jury retires to deliberate. (Some courts are experimenting with the idea of instructing the jury on undisputed, relevant issues of law at the start of trial, hoping that the jury will then be better able to assess the evidence as it is presented.) The jury instructions specify, in concise terms, the elements of each of the causes of action to be submitted to the jury. (If the concept of causes of action is still a bit fuzzy to you, please reread the sidebar "Elements of a Cause of Action" in Chapter 3.)

The exact wording of jury instructions is very important, for a reason that you might not guess. The reason has nothing to do with the effect on the jury. Many trial lawyers think that jury instructions have rather little influence on the decisions of jurors. If you have not won over the minds of the jurors by the time jury instructions are read, your case is probably in trouble. Rather, the importance of jury instructions is on appeal: If the court of appeals decides that an instruction does not correctly explain the elements of the cause of action to which it pertains, the case will likely be sent back for a new trial.

Trial judges, who are perfectly aware of the importance that courts of appeals place on jury instructions, react by putting the burden on the attorneys to get them right. Both sides are required to submit, in writing (and perhaps also on a diskette to facilitate editing), any instructions they wish the judge to give the jury. A party may not complain to the court of appeals about an instruction that was not given, if it was never requested.

The deadline for requesting jury instructions may be set by local rule or may be up to the trial judge, but it is commonplace to require their submission just prior to the start of trial. This gives the judge and the opposing attorneys a chance to digest the proposals, and to do any last minute legal research required to get the wording exactly right. Then, after each side has put on its case, but (usually) before closing arguments, the judge will hear arguments and decide exactly what instructions will be read to the jury.

Even if the judge does not require jury instructions to be submitted before trial starts, wise trial lawyers nevertheless have them ready at that time. The reason? The jury instructions are the final, definitive statement of the elements of plaintiff's causes of action. Plaintiff's attorney needs to be sure that plaintiff's evidence covers each required element; defendant's attorney needs to evaluate which are the weakest elements, the ones most vulnerable to attack. Once the trial begins in earnest, the lawyers will be too busy to devote much energy to honing their jury instructions.

How do lawyers (or paralegals) come up with jury instructions? As with most paperwork in litigation, they begin with what has already been done in previous cases. In many jurisdictions, you can find a book of recommended jury instructions published by the court, the state bar association, or some other authoritative body, covering the most common causes of action: motor vehicle negligence, breach of contract to pay a debt, and the like. These can be modified as necessary to fit your particular case. For more esoteric causes of action, try searching the Westlaw database using the phrase "jury instruction" and the name of the cause of action (or its digest topic number) as search terms. This will likely turn up appellate opinions quoting and critiquing jury instructions of the kind you are looking for.

**Preparation of Exhibits**—By the time the trial date arrives, the attorneys should know precisely what documents each side may use as exhibits during the trial. Many courts, as already noted, mandate an exchange of exhibits well in advance of the trial date. Even in courts that do not require copies of exhibits to be delivered to opponents as a matter of course, any competent litigator automatically sends out a set of interrogatories and a request for production of documents requiring the opposing party to identify and supply copies of all trial exhibits. (In practice, particularly in cases involving massive quantities of documents, corners tend to be cut in document discovery responses, so it may still be necessary for the attorneys to hash out the final exhibit list at the last minute.)

How are these exhibits readied for use at trial? There are two important considerations. The first is admissibility: The law of evidence imposes various requirements, depending on the type of document and its source. At a minimum, for example, all documents to be used as exhibits must be proven authentic; that is, a witness must testify that the document is what it appears to be and not a forgery. To save time, judges prefer that the attorneys **stipulate** to the admissibility of all documents except those few that they have a serious basis to challenge, and it is common for the pretrial order to include such stipulations. The point is that by the time the trial starts, each attorney (or the paralegal in charge of the exhibits) should have checked off each individual document and made sure that whatever is required to have it admitted in evidence—be it a stipulation or a witness's testimony—is in place and ready to be presented.

The second consideration is the physical handling of the documents themselves. In times past, and even now in rural courts or in small cases, introduction of an exhibit at trial required a time-consuming ritual in which the document would be first handed to the clerk for marking with an exhibit number, then passed around for the opposing lawyer and perhaps the judge to examine, and only then shown to the witness to be identified. In busy metropolitan court systems, where the exhibits in many civil cases may number in the hundreds, judges will likely require the attorneys to bring in their exhibits before the trial starts, so that the clerk can mark them and list them in advance. Either way, all exhibits—the physical documents that will actually be used at trial—must be readied and organized so that each can be located quickly when needed in the hectic atmosphere that may prevail in the courtroom during trial.

---

*Your Local Notes*

_____

_____

---

### Putting It Into Practice:

*What evidentiary exhibits would you expect Allen Porter to introduce at trial? If he asked you to prepare these exhibits for trial, what would you do? What demonstrative evidence might Allen Porter use to build his case?*

So much for the evidentiary exhibits—the documents that will actually constitute a part of the evidence in the case. There remains the question of the assorted charts, diagrams, pictures, and blowups that have become so much a part of the courtroom scene in the era of television. These visual aids—called **demonstrative evidence**—are not really evidence in the same way as the documents that are used to help prove the facts of the case. They are employed to make the facts easier for the jury to understand. Well-designed visual aids can be quite compelling, but they take time to create, and the specialty graphic arts services required are not usually available within the law office. The trial attorney must plan in advance what demonstrative evidence will be needed, and the person responsible for making it happen—often a paralegal—must see that all the pieces come together in time for the start of trial.

---

*Your Local Notes*

_____

_____

---

*"How's it coming?" asked Allen Porter, eyeing the confusion of papers strewn over the large conference room table as he closed the door and removed his jacket. "Are we going to make it?"*

*Chuck Fletcher checked his watch. "We have until 5:00 P.M. to get the joint pretrial statement over to the court. Two more hours. I just got off the phone with Gail Stoddard's secretary, and they're supposed to be faxing their latest version as we speak. The exhibit list is done, that was the hard part. Any word from the court on the trial setting?"*

*"Still looks like a go. The judge is still tied up with that wrongful death case, but they think at most it might drag out an extra day or two. They say we can ride the calendar. Either way, they want the exhibits in and marked by Monday, and we should be able to start trial by Wednesday at the latest. Oh, and the proposed jury instructions—I've marked up your draft. Will you please check them over, have them printed out in final, and make sure they get sent over to the judge? I have to go to Tucson tomorrow for depositions in that divorce case."*

*"No problem. I think we're pretty much on schedule. Hard to believe it's been a year and a half, though."*

## ROLE OF THE PARALEGAL

Many of the tasks involved in trial preparation are ideally suited for the talents of paralegals. Obviously, it is the trial lawyer who will "choreograph" the trial, deciding what evidence will be presented and in what order. But if it is the trial lawyer who writes the script, it is often the paralegal who manages the stage, in the sense of making sure that all the necessary "props" are present at the right time.

This practical side of trial preparation requires well-developed organizational skills: the ability to make checklists and keep track of the myriad details that must all come together at the start of trial.

# TRYING THE CASE

The last week or so before a trial begins is a hectic time for trial lawyers and the paralegals, secretaries, and junior lawyers who work under their direction. Working hours lengthen as the simplest tasks develop unforeseen complications, and at times it seems as though a platoon of lawyers working twenty-four hours a day could not get the job done in time. Not every lawyer—or paralegal—is cut out for the pressures of trial work!

During this time, in addition to preparing the witnesses, rehearsing the arguments, and attending to all paperwork, the opposing lawyers are usually negotiating intensively in an effort to reach a settlement. The reason is simple: It costs a great deal of money to try a civil suit—often in the thousands of dollars per day for attorney fees alone. Better to spend the money on a settlement that makes the case go away forever than to spend it on a trial that you might lose (see sidebar below).

**Putting It Into Practice:**

*Suppose Allen Porter has never used a paralegal's services. You are interviewing with him for a job. Explain how you could assist him in preparing for trial.*

## SIDEBAR

### Meanwhile, Back at the Negotiating Table

*Of all the civil lawsuits filed in federal court in a year, what percentage would you guess eventually reach trial, and how many are settled before trial? The answer for tort cases appears at the end of this sidebar.*

*To **settle** a case means that the parties agree to end their dispute. Usually, the defendant agrees to pay plaintiff an agreed sum of money in return for plaintiff voluntarily dismissing the suit. Parties are free to settle their cases at any time if they can reach an agreement acceptable to all concerned.*

*If it surprises you that so many cases are settled, consider this: How much would you guess that it costs to file an average, garden-variety civil suit, prepare it for trial, and try the case? The answer naturally depends greatly on the complexity of the case, the vigorousness of the defense, and the price of legal talent in your locality, but you can probably buy a new luxury car for less than the cost of even a relatively inexpensive lawsuit.*

*Given the broad factual outlines of a case, experienced litigators can usually estimate fairly accurately the probability of the plaintiff winning or losing and the approximate range of the likely verdict if plaintiff does win. If both sides' attorneys reach similar estimates of the probable outcome, it is far better to take a shortcut to that outcome by settling than to spend huge sums litigating to reach the same end result.*

*Experience teaches that cases most often settle either in the early stages, just after the complaint is filed, or else at the time of trial. It is not a coincidence that the filing of suit and the beginning of trial are the two times when parties are most painfully aware that continuing the dispute is going to put a big dent in both sides' wallets.*

*(Answer: Of 96,284 tort cases filed in federal court in fiscal year 1996–97, only 3,023, or 3 percent, ended in a trial and verdict.)*

On the morning of the first day of trial, the judge begins by holding a conference with the attorneys, probably in chambers. In part, this meeting is to tie up any remaining loose ends, such as checking that all pending motions have been decided, discussing the scheduling and order of presentation of witnesses, going over the pretrial order, perhaps working on jury instructions. Here, too, the judge has an opportunity to express any individual preferences about the way the trial is to be conducted. Increasingly, judges also take advantage of the chance to twist the parties' arms and encourage them to settle.

The formal commencement of trial occurs in the courtroom. A court reporter is present and, using a shorthand machine, will take down every word spoken until the trial is over. The judge or the clerk calls the case by number, and the judge asks first whether the plaintiff is ready; then whether defendant is ready (both had better be!).

---

*Your Local Notes*

_____

_____

---

## JURY SELECTION

The first task in a jury trial is to select a jury. The procedure for accomplishing this varies considerably from one court to another. The details often depend in large part on the preferences of the individual judge, so referring to the local rules of procedure may not yield many answers; it may be necessary to also consult the judge's staff. The broad outlines are these: First, a predetermined number of prospective jurors are sent into the courtroom; the number depends on the local customs and the type of case. These are ordinary citizens who have been drawn at random from voter registration lists, driver's license records, or some other public source, and sent jury summonses ordering them to appear on this date for jury duty. Each prospective juror has filled out a questionnaire; the resulting information, typically including such things as education, occupation, and previous involvement with the court system, is given to the attorneys.

The purported goal of jury selection is to start with a sizable panel of prospective jurors who comprise a broad cross-section of typical citizens, weed out those who the judge or the attorneys think may not be able to act fairly and impartially, and end up with the required number of jurors to decide the case. (How many? Traditionally, there were always twelve, but nowadays, to cut costs and save time, more likely six or eight plus an alternate or two.) The real goal of the attorneys is, of course, somewhat different: A trial attorney wants a jury composed not of the fairest jurors, but of the ones most likely to find in her client's favor.

The first step in the weeding-out process is to ask the prospective jurors questions about their backgrounds and about any feelings or beliefs they have that may interfere with their ability to follow the judge's instructions. This questioning is called **voir dire.** There is considerable variation in *voir dire* customs from one court to another. In some courts, the attorneys must submit all *voir dire* questions beforehand, and the judge addresses the questions to the jurors; in others, attorneys are given great freedom to buttonhole individual jurors and ask them pointed questions about their personal habits and prejudices. Where attorneys are allowed to conduct their own *voir dire,* part of the strategy is to craft *voir dire* questions that are really thinly disguised arguments designed to get a jump start on selling the jury on the merits of their cases: "If the evidence shows that Banbury Park Hotel, by failing to maintain the door locks properly, set in motion the chain of events that led to Shannon Martin being injured, is there any reason why you could not vote to grant her a substantial sum of money to fairly compensate her for those injuries?"

---

*Your Local Notes*

_____

_____

---

Prospective jurors may be excused for any of a number of reasons. These may involve personal problems, such as family duties or illness, making it unreasonably difficult for a juror to attend. (Usually, a fairly compelling story is required, because judges become quite unreceptive to the usual excuses for not serving after hearing them all a few hundred times.) Prospective jurors who are relatives or close friends of any of the parties or attorneys, or who are already familiar with the facts of the case, are also likely to be excused.

Jurors may also be excused "for cause." This occurs when a prospective juror says something, or reveals something about his background, that persuades the judge that the juror may be prone to base a decision on personal beliefs or prejudices rather than on the evidence and the judge's instructions. In our hypo, for example, there may be a prospective juror who has strong religious beliefs against the use of violence (i.e., firearms) even in self-defense. Such a person could not fairly decide the claims at issue between Dr. Collins and Shannon and would be excused for cause.

---

*Your Local Notes*

_____

_____

---

After *voir dire* is completed, each side is allowed a specified number of **peremptory challenges;** that is, each side has a chance to strike some small number of prospective jurors from the panel. Naturally, attorneys will use the allotted strikes to remove the jurors they think are least likely to vote in the desired way. No "cause" is needed when an attorney uses a peremptory challenge to strike a juror—the decision of which jurors to strike is based entirely on the attorney's best guess as to what sorts of people will least improve the chances of winning. This guess may be based on almost anything, from astrology to psychology to personal experience. (There is only one significant restriction: peremptory challenges may not be used to exclude racial minorities from jury panels.) Most attorneys rely mainly on the information furnished by the jurors in their questionnaires and in their responses to *voir dire* questions, and on their instincts about what sorts of people are likely to be receptive to particular kinds of cases.

The end result of all this maneuvering is a panel of the required number of jurors, all of whom have managed to avoid being excused or stricken. These people are sworn in as jurors and seated in the jury box. Jury selection has consumed at least a substantial part of the first day (it can take much longer in highly publicized cases, where it is hard to find jurors who have not already heard all about the case from the news media). With jury selection completed, the judge will take a recess, perhaps until the next day.

## Putting It Into Practice:

*What type of juror will Allen Porter be looking for? What type of juror will Gail Stoddard be looking for?*

*Your Local Notes*

_____

_____

---

**SIDEBAR**

## Trials to the Court

*Not all trials are jury trials. Plaintiff may fail to demand a jury trial in time; both parties may agree that a jury is not needed; or the case may be of a kind for which there is no right to a jury trial (i.e., divorce).*

*In a nonjury trial, the judge takes over the function of the jury and decides both the factual issues and the legal issues. Naturally, there is no need for jury selection. Nor will there be jury instructions. The lack of jury instructions poses a potential problem: Without jury instructions, how will we know what rules of law the judge used to decide the case? More to the point, how will we appeal if the judge applied the wrong rules? The rules of procedure offer a solution: FRCP, Rule 52(a), requires the judge in a nonjury case to make **findings of fact and conclusions of law.** That is, the judge will sign a court paper listing each of the factual and legal findings on which the judge's decision is based. In practice, before announcing a decision, the judge will order both plaintiff and defendant to submit proposed findings. The judge will adopt the proposed findings of the winning party (perhaps with modifications).*

*Judges often relax the formal rules of evidence in nonjury cases. Juries are (supposedly) not allowed even to see or hear evidence that is inadmissible. The judge, however, presumably has the training and impartiality to be able to resist being swayed by improper evidence. In nonjury trials, judges become cranky when attorneys insist on wasting time by constantly jumping to their feet with objections. For similar reasons, it is not uncommon for judges to "encourage" the attorneys to skip making closing arguments in nonjury cases. The judge may ask for a written argument instead.*

*In a jury trial, the verdict is the jury's and is announced immediately after the jury finishes deliberating. In a nonjury trial, the verdict is up to the judge, and it is common for judges to take the matter under advisement and inform the parties of the verdict by minute entry later—sometimes weeks later.*

---

**Putting It
Into Practice:**

*Why do you think Allen Porter opted for a jury trial in Shannon's case?*

---

## OPENING STATEMENTS

Next on the agenda are the **opening statements.** Each attorney makes what amounts to a speech, giving the jury her client's version of the facts. Plaintiff's attorney goes first; defendant's attorney can reply immediately, or wait until it is defendant's turn to start calling witnesses.

This is not a time to present argument. Allen Porter may, in his opening statement, describe the evidence he intends to present; he is free to read to the jury from the complaint or answer; and he may tell the jurors what he will be asking them for at the end of the case. He may *not,* however, launch into impassioned oratory about, say, how dangerous the world is for women traveling alone—that sort of speech-making must be saved for closing argument. Most attorneys use their opening statements simply to tell their client's story—which will hopefully be the same story that the evidence will tell—in the most sympathetic and persuasive way possible.

---

Your Local Notes

_____

_____

---

> *Wednesday morning, 9:30 A.M. Allen Porter sat at the plaintiff's counsel table, immersed in his notes, oblivious to the activity around him. Chuck Fletcher was bantering with Shannon about the Phoenix Suns, keeping her distracted, making sure Allen could concentrate without interruption. At the defendant's table, Gail Stoddard was searching through a pile of documents with one of her paralegals, while at the same time fielding questions from the Park Hotels' vice president who was here to speak for the corporation. The door adjacent to the jury box opened, and the jurors followed the bailiff into the courtroom and found their seats. In the gallery, spectators sat or stood in small groups, conversing quietly.*
>
> *"All rise." Porter reluctantly put down his note pad as the judge entered.*
>
> *The judge settled himself comfortably in his chair; it was going to be a long morning. He turned to the jury. "Good morning, ladies and gentlemen. It is now time for the opening statements. In their opening statements, each of the attorneys will tell you what he or she believes the evidence will show. First, plaintiff's attorney, Mr. Porter, will speak to you; then Ms. Stoddard will speak for defendant Park Hotels Group; finally, Mr. Yarborough will give you the point of view of defendant Dr. Collins. I instruct you that opening statements are not evidence, they are merely the attorneys' explanations of what they expect to prove." The judge turned to Allen Porter. "Mr. Porter, you may begin."*
>
> *"Thank you, Your Honor," Allen Porter said, as he rose, picked up his notepad, and strode confidently over to the lectern. Making eye contact with as many of the jurors as possible, he began. "Ladies and gentlemen, here is what the evidence will show: My client, Shannon Martin whom you see seated here, was in Las Vegas for a series of business meetings. . . ."*

What would you say to the jury in your opening statement if you represented Shannon? If you represented Dr. Collins? The hotel? Although paralegals do not ordinarily get to make opening statements in jury cases, an understanding of what is involved will allow you to help your supervising attorney write, rehearse, and polish the opening statements to be given in the cases on which you are assisting.

## PRESENTATION OF EVIDENCE

Now comes the main event: the presentation of each side's case. This is done in turns, in the familiar, three-step pattern: plaintiff's case is first, defendant's case is second, and finally plaintiff is given a chance to rebut defendant's case. What does a party's "case" consist of? Witnesses. A trial consists of questioning witnesses, one after the other. Documents and other exhibits can of course be used, but they are presented via the testimony of witnesses—the witness identifies, describes, and reads from the document. An example of how documents are introduced appears in the trial transcript excerpt from our hypo presented later in this chapter.

**Plaintiff's Case**—After the opening statements, the judge instructs plaintiff's attorney to call the first witness. The witness comes forward, is asked to

# SIDEBAR

## Links in a Chain

*To understand the parties' procedural objectives in a trial, you may find the following metaphor instructive: Imagine that each of plaintiff's theories of liability is a chain, which plaintiff will use to hoist the huge sum of money that plaintiff hopes to win. To win the lawsuit, plaintiff must construct at least one complete chain sufficiently strong to lift the load. Each chain has one link for each element of that cause of action.*

*Thus, for a cause of action for negligence, there will be four links in the chain: one labeled "duty," one labeled "breach of duty," one labeled "causation," and one labeled "damages." Plaintiff's goal is to have a chain made of those four links at the end of the trial. During plaintiff's part of the trial, plaintiff must make each link by putting on at least some evidence supporting each element. If plaintiff has not done so by the time plaintiff finishes putting on witnesses—that is, if the chain is missing a link—then the judge will grant a motion for a directed verdict, and plaintiff will lose then and there as to the cause of action for negligence.*

*During defendant's part of the trial, defendant will try to cut, or at least weaken, plaintiff's chain. If defendant can present enough evidence to cut even one of the links, and plaintiff is unable to repair the damage, that chain is broken and plaintiff will lose (as to that cause of action—plaintiff may have other chains, of course). After defendant has had a turn, plaintiff gets one more chance to repair any links that defendant has managed to cut or weaken. This is the final phase of trial, called rebuttal. During rebuttal, plaintiff cannot delve into new areas—no new "links" are allowed during rebuttal—but plaintiff can call witnesses to attack or contradict the evidence that defendant put on during defendant's case.*

*If at the end of the trial it is clear that plaintiff's chain has all of its links, the judge will grant a directed verdict for plaintiff; if it is clear that one or more links has been cut, the judge will grant a directed verdict for defendant. Finally, if it is uncertain whether all of the links in plaintiff's chain have held up under defendant's attacks—that is, if reasonable jurors could disagree about whether the evidence supports each of the elements of the cause of action—the judge will submit the cause of action to the jury for decision. In an actual trial, of course, there is usually more than one cause of action. In such a case, the judge will simply test plaintiff's chains one cause of action at a time. For example, the judge may direct a verdict on one cause of action and let another go to the jury for decision.*

*In theory, the jury will test each of the links in the chain, and find for plaintiff if and only if the evidence supporting each link is more than fifty–fifty in plaintiff's favor. In practice, jury deliberations are seldom so analytical; once the case is submitted to the jury, fairness and common sense are likely to play a more important role.*

take the familiar oath to "tell the truth, the whole truth, and nothing but the truth," and takes a seat on the witness stand to the side of the judge's bench. Plaintiff's attorney examines (that is, questions) the witness first. Because plaintiff's attorney is examining a witness that he himself called to the stand, this is **direct examination.** When plaintiff's attorney finishes, defendant's attorney has a turn. This is **cross-examination:** Because defendant's attorney is questioning a witness called by an opponent (and therefore presumed to be antagonistic), different rules apply in cross-examination (see sidebar below). If plaintiff's attorney feels a need to shore up any of the damage inflicted by his opponent's cross-examination, he may conduct a **redirect examination.** It is even possible, though rare, for the judge to allow the questioning to go back and forth several times in a series of redirect and recross examinations; see FRE, Rule 611.

---

### SIDEBAR

## Limitations on Scope

*Scope* refers to the subject matter covered during the examination. In direct examination, an attorney is free to ask about any aspect of the case. In some courts, however, cross-examination questions must be limited to the scope of the direct examination. In other words, the cross-examining attorney may not ask questions on subjects that the direct examination did not get into. Why? If the scope of cross-examination were unlimited, as it is with direct examination, there would be nothing to stop the defendant from putting on his entire case by cross-examining plaintiff's witnesses. The result would be both parties putting on their cases simultaneously, one witness at a time, instead of the intended sequence of plaintiff's case first, defendant's case second.

Not all courts limit the scope of cross-examination. Almost all, however, limit redirect examination to the subjects raised during cross-examination unless there is some compelling reason to do otherwise. Here, the purpose is to force the attorney who calls the witness, to ask all the questions he has for that witness, all at once, rather than piecemeal.

---

Who decides which witnesses to call, and in what order? This part of the trial belongs to plaintiff, so plaintiff's attorney decides. Cooperative witnesses will show up voluntarily; it is up to plaintiff's attorney (or paralegal) to stay in contact with them as the trial progresses and make sure that each witness arrives in time to testify when needed. Plaintiff can also call uncooperative or **hostile witnesses.** To do so, subpoenas are issued and served, ordering them to appear at court. Plaintiff can even call the defendant as a witness; one not uncommon tactic is to call the defendant as the first witness, thereby depriving defendant of the chance to listen to all of plaintiff's witnesses and adjust her story accordingly; see, however, FRE, Rule 611(a).

Before the questioning begins, either side may ask the judge to put witnesses "under the rule." The judge will then order that all witnesses who are not parties to the suit must remain outside the courtroom and must refrain from talking with anyone about the case, except while actually testifying. The purpose is to preclude witnesses from being able to change their testimony in response to what other witnesses are saying. The parties themselves are entitled to remain in the courtroom during the entire trial; parties cannot be put "under the rule." Also, many judges allow each party to select one person, who may also be a witness, to remain in the courtroom to assist the attorney during trial; see FRE, Rule 615.

Plaintiff must, at a minimum, establish a ***prima facie* case** for each theory of liability. A *prima facie* case means that at least some credible evidence has been presented in support of each element of the cause of action in question. (If you have forgotten exactly what the concept of "elements of a cause of action" entails, please reread the sidebar on that subject in Chapter 3.) In terms of the "links in a chain" metaphor (see sidebar), putting on a *prima facie* case

***Putting It Into Practice:***

*How would you as a paralegal assist Allen Porter in working with witnesses in Shannon's case? Why might it be important to educate those witnesses about how to be effective witnesses?*

*Putting It
Into Practice:*

*Why do you think
witnesses are generally
advised to keep their
answers short and to the
point when being
questioned?*

## SIDEBAR

## Cross-Examination and Leading Questions

*In a trial, there are two kinds of witnesses: plaintiff's witnesses and defendant's witnesses. What do we mean when we say that a witness is "plaintiff's" or "defendant's"? Do we have to figure out which party the witness is rooting for to win the case? No, witnesses "belong" to the party who calls them. If plaintiff calls a witness during plaintiff's part of the trial, that person is plaintiff's witness.*

*What difference does it make? In general,* a party may not cross-examine his own witnesses. *An exception is made only if the witness's own answers demonstrate hostility—then the judge may allow the witness to be treated as if belonging to the opposing party. And, of course, if plaintiff calls the defendant as a witness, plaintiff can treat her as adverse, and vice versa.*

*Cross-examination is different from direct examination. In direct examination, leading questions are forbidden. A* **leading question** *is a question that tells the witness what answer the attorney wants to hear. "Didn't you spend last Saturday night at home watching television with your wife?" is a leading question. The same question, rephrased so as not to be leading, would be "What did you do last Saturday night?" In the leading version, it is really the attorney who is telling the story, not the witness.*

*In cross-examination, leading questions are not only allowed, they are often essential. The purpose of direct examination is for the witness to tell his story in his own words. The purpose of cross-examination is to test the witness's credibility and truthfulness—in other words, to poke as many holes in his testimony as possible. This is not done by giving the witness another opportunity to repeat his story; it is best done by asking questions that must be answered with a "yes" or a "no" and making sure that if the witness picks the wrong answer, you have plenty of ammunition to discredit him.*

*A final word about cross-examination: Skillful, well-planned cross-examination can be spectacular and fun to watch, but the thing that wins cases is skillful, well-planned* direct *examination. Usually, you must win your case on the strength of your own story, not the weaknesses in your opponent's story. This is almost always true if you represent the plaintiff, and true more often than not if you represent the defendant.*

means putting on at least some evidence establishing each of the links. That is, the links need not necessarily be very strong to make a *prima facie* case, but no link can be missing entirely.

**"Halftime"**—When plaintiff has called and examined all of her witnesses, plaintiff's attorney will announce to the judge that "plaintiff rests." When a party **rests,** it means that the party is finished putting on witnesses, and now it will be the opposing party's turn. Usually, judges require both sides to indicate in advance what witnesses they will be calling and in what order, so the participants know when to expect plaintiff to rest.

For plaintiff's attorney, resting is a somewhat anxious event, because it means that plaintiff has now taken her best shot, and plaintiff's claims must stand or fall on what has been presented. Once plaintiff rests, plaintiff is through, and defendant is entitled to have the judge decide whether plaintiff has put on at least some evidence supporting each of the elements of each of plaintiff's causes of action—that is, whether plaintiff has made a *prima facie* case for each cause of action. If defendant thinks that plaintiff has missed putting on evidence in support of some element of one of the causes of action for which plaintiff is suing, defendant may make a motion for a directed verdict as to that cause of action. If the judge agrees with defendant, that cause of action will be dismissed, and plaintiff will lose—as to that particular cause of action. Therefore, before resting, a wise plaintiff's attorney reflects carefully to be sure that each of plaintiff's chains has all of its links; see FRCP, Rule 50.

---

**Your Local Notes**

_____

_____

---

**Putting It Into Practice:**

*What should the hotel do if it thinks Shannon has failed to prove that the hotel contributed, in any way, to her injuries? What will be the consequence if the judge grants the defendant's motion for a directed verdict?*

If there are motions to be heard, the jury will leave the room and return when defendant is ready to begin calling witnesses. If not, defendant's case may begin immediately, or the judge may allow a recess to give defendant's attorney a short time to prepare. Some plaintiff's attorneys prefer to rest near the end of the trial day, making it likely that defendant will not be able to begin until the following day; then the jury will have the whole night for plaintiff's case to sink in, with no interference from defendant's evidence. Most lawyers like to time their presentations so that the last thing on the jurors' minds at the end of the day is some strong and favorable bit of evidence.

*Excerpts from the reporter's transcript of the trial in Martin v. Collins:*

*Direct examination of Shannon Martin:*

Q. *(By Mr. Porter) Now, before all of this happened, had you locked the door to your room?*

A. *Yes.*

Q. *When and how did you do that?*

A. *Well, the doorknob was the kind that locks itself as long as you don't turn the button on the inside to unlock it, which I didn't do. And when I got back from dinner, I went into my room, and closed the door, and I also checked to be sure it had locked.*

Q. *How did you do that?*

A. *I tried to turn the knob and it wouldn't turn, and I pulled out on it, and the door wouldn't open. It was locked.*

Q. *Did you open the door at any time after you got back from dinner and before you saw an intruder at the foot of your bed?*

A. *No. Not only that, I checked it again before I went to bed.*

Q. *How did you do that?*

A. *Same way, tried to turn the knob, tried to pull out on the knob. . . .*

———

*Cross-examination of Shannon Martin:*

Q. *(By Ms. Stoddard) Now, you have already testified that you did not set the chain, isn't that right?*

A. *Yes, that's right, because I—*

Q. *Are you aware that there was a printed notice attached to the inside of the hotel room door?*

A. *Yes, I know there are some instructions, I think about putting your valuables in the hotel safe, and—*

Q. *Did you read the notice?*

A. As I recall, you know, I've certainly read those notices before. I don't necessarily read it every time I stay in a hotel. In my job, I was traveling a lot, and—

Q. So you feel you are familiar with what the notice says?

A. Yes.

Q. Doesn't the notice specifically instruct you to set the chain?

A. I'm not sure. Probably.

Q. Doesn't it tell you to do that for your own safety?

A. I guess so.

Q. But you decided to ignore that advice?

A. As I said, I read somewhere that—

Q. Excuse me, Ms. Martin, my question is, you decided to ignore the specific instructions on the notice? Yes or no?

A. Well, I guess, yes. But—

Q. Thank you Ms. Martin. No further questions, Your Honor.

*Direct examination of Dr. Arthur Collins:*

Q. (By Mr. Porter) And then what happened?

A. I got out of the elevator on the fourth floor and went to my room, or what I thought was my room.

Q. Was it your room?

A. No.

Q. Whose room was it?

A. It was Ms. Martin's room.

Q. Did you intend to enter Ms. Martin's room?

A. No, of course not. I thought it was my room. And, of course, the key opened the door.

Q. Now, tell us exactly how you opened the door.

A. I put the key in the lock, turned the key to the right until the knob started to turn, turned it some more to open the latch, then I pushed the door open.

Q. Now, Doctor, this is very important, sir. Did the key turn the lock within the knob, or did it merely turn the lock and the knob together? Do you understand my question?

A. Yes, I think so. And the answer is, the lock turned first, about a quarter turn, and then the whole thing turned. I remember that because the first quarter turn, it turned easily, and then once the knob started to turn, it was a lot harder to turn, as though the bolt was sticking. At that point I had to use my other hand on the knob to get it to turn.

Q. Is it possible that the door was already slightly ajar, and that that's how you were able to open it?

A. No. I'm sure it wasn't. As I said, the knob was hard to turn, and I had to pull in on it and turn with my other hand to get it to open.

Q. Sir, you are aware, I believe, that the key the police found in the room is not capable of turning the lock in the knob?

A. That's what I've been told.

Q. Yet you have testified that the key you had did turn the lock in the knob.

*A. Yes, that's right.*

*Q. Do you have any explanation of how that could be?*

*By Ms. Stoddard: Objection, calls for speculation.*

*Judge: Sustained.*

*Q. Was the key the hotel clerk gave you the same key the police found?*

*By Ms. Stoddard: Objection, lack of foundation. There's been no showing this witness has any firsthand knowledge about the key the police found.*

*Judge: Sustained.*

*Q. If someone switched the key before the police found it, would that explain it?*

*By Ms. Stoddard: Same objection.*

*Judge: Sustained. Move on, Mr. Porter.*

*Cross-examination of Dr. Collins*

*Q. (By Ms. Stoddard) Did you look at the number on the door, or the number on the key?*

*A. Actually, the keys don't have the room number on them, I think they do that in case a key gets stolen, so the thief won't know which room it fits.*

*Q. What about the number on the door?*

*A. I don't recall. If I did, it didn't register.*

*Q. Had you been drinking that night?*

*A. I had a cocktail before dinner, and a glass of wine with dinner.*

*Q. And when you returned to the hotel, at one-fifteen in the morning— having had only one cocktail and one glass of wine—you somehow mistook Miss Martin's room for your own room?*

*A. Yes.*

*Q. Now, you are telling us that you remember specifically whether the key turned the lock in the knob or just the whole knob, isn't that right?*

*A. Yes.*

*Q. A relatively tiny detail in something that happened nearly two years ago.*

*By Mr. Porter: Objection, argumentative.*

*Judge: Sustained.*

*Q. Do you have a good memory, Doctor?*

*A. Yes, I think so.*

*Q. And you are asking this jury to believe that your memory is so good that you can be absolutely sure about whether the key turned the lock in the knob, nearly two years ago?*

*A. I'm sure.*

*Q. Yet, on the night in question, isn't it a fact you remembered your room number wrong, which had been given you that same day?*

*A. Well, I wasn't really going by the number. . . .*

*By Ms. Stoddard: No further questions.*

*Cross-examination of Arnold Trevayne*

———

Q. (By Mr. Porter) Isn't it a fact, Mr. Trevayne, that what really happened was that when Dr. Collins came in around one-fifteen in the morning, you gave him the wrong key, the key to Ms. Martin's room, number 407?

A. No. He had the right key. The key the police found is the right key.

Q. Is that so? Well, let's explore that. Dr. Collins has testified that the key you gave him turned the lock in the door to Ms. Martin's room. Would you agree with me that his testimony and your testimony can't both be true?

A. I don't know if he's lying or what, but I gave him the key to his own room.

Q. Which room was that?

A. 409.

Q. Would you agree with me that, either what he said about the key turning the lock isn't true, or else what you're saying about giving him the right key isn't true? Has to be one or the other, doesn't it?

A. I don't know. Maybe she didn't lock the door all the way. Maybe she let him in.

Q. Maybe she let him in. Is that what you said? I want to be sure the jury heard you right. Maybe she let him in?

A. Well, it could be, or maybe the door wasn't completely closed.

Q. If Ms. Martin let Dr. Collins in, that would mean both she and he are lying, wouldn't it? Is that what you're saying, that you think they're both lying?

By Ms. Stoddard: Objection, argumentative, calls for speculation.

Judge: Sustained.

Q. Are you aware of any facts, of your own personal knowledge, that would show that Ms. Martin intentionally let Dr. Collins into her room?

A. No.

Q. Now, you also said maybe the door wasn't completely closed. The doors are spring-loaded, aren't they, so if you let go of them, they close by themselves?

A. Yes, they're supposed to, but maybe it didn't.

Q. Mr. Trevayne, do you recall me asking you the following question and you giving me the following answer at your deposition: "Question: Isn't it true that the doors are old, and they don't always close all the way? Answer: Not that I know of." Was that your testimony at your deposition?

A. Yes.

Q. Was that testimony true when you gave it?

A. Yes.

Q. Then, Mr. Trevayne, isn't it a fact that you don't have any reason to think that the door wasn't completely closed?

A. I don't know.

Q. Are you aware of any facts, of your own personal knowledge, that would show that the door might not have closed all the way?

A. I don't know.

By Mr. Porter: Your Honor,—

*Judge: That question can be answered yes or no, Mr. Trevayne. Either you know of some facts, or you don't. The witness is instructed to answer the question.*

*A. I forgot the question.*

*Judge: Read back the question.*

*(The pending question is read.)*

*A. No.*

*Q. Ms. Martin has testified that the door to her room was locked, that she checked it twice, tried to turn the knob, tried to pull the door open, and it was locked. If the door hadn't been closed completely, then when she pulled on the knob it would have opened, wouldn't it?*

*A. I guess.*

*Q. We don't want you to guess, Mr. Trevayne. If the door hadn't been closed completely, then when she pulled on the knob it would have opened, wouldn't it?*

*A. It should.*

*Q. Now, Mr. Trevayne, let's talk about what really happened that night: You gave Dr. Collins the wrong key. When Ms. Martin came down to the lobby and asked you to call the police, you realized your mistake. Before the police got there, you went up to Ms. Martin's room and switched the keys to cover up your mistake. Isn't that what really happened, Mr. Trevayne?*

*A. No. No. And if you're going to accuse me—*

*Judge: That will do, Mr. Trevayne. Sit down. Sir, I said sit down.*

*Q. No, that isn't what happened?*

*A. No.*

*Q. At your deposition, you testified that from the time you called 911 until the police arrived, you remained at the front desk. Ms. Martin has testified that right after you called 911, you left the front desk and were gone for several minutes. Is it still your testimony that you remained at the front desk the entire time?*

*A. Yes.*

*By Mr. Porter: Your Honor, may the witness be shown plaintiff's exhibit 24?*

*(Plaintiff's exhibit 24 is shown to the witness.)*

*Q. (By Mr. Porter) Mr. Trevayne, can you identify that document as a computer printout generated by the telephone system at the Banbury Park Hotel?*

*A. Yes.*

*Q. And it shows what telephone calls were placed or received at the hotel between midnight and 6:00 A.M. on the same night as the incident that we've been discussing?*

*A. It appears to.*

*By Mr. Porter: Your Honor, offer plaintiff's exhibit 24.*

*Ms. Stoddard: No objection to its admission, but I reserve objections as to relevance.*

*Judge: Plaintiff's exhibit 24 is admitted in evidence.*

*Q. (By Mr. Porter) Now, Mr. Trevayne, I want you to take a look at that printout, about twelve lines down from the top, the line beginning with "01:15:37," do you see that?*

*A. Yes.*

*Q. That shows your telephone call to 911, at 1:15 A.M. and 37 seconds, does it not?*

*A. It looks like, the—yes.*

*Q. And it shows it being made from your extension at the front desk, doesn't it?*

*A. Yes.*

*Q. And the next line shows an incoming telephone call, doesn't it?*

*A. Yes.*

*Q. About two minutes later, at 1:17 A.M. and 43 seconds, right?*

*A. Yes.*

*Q. And where does the printout show that call going to?*

*A. It looks like, to the voice mail.*

*Q. Isn't it a fact, Mr. Trevayne, that incoming calls at that time of night go first to the front desk, and then if they aren't answered within six rings, they go to the voice mail?*

*A. Yes. Probably I was busy.*

*Q. I see you have anticipated my next question. Probably you were busy, that's why you didn't answer the phone at the front desk, after six rings?*

*A. Well, you know, your client there, was pretty hysterical. . . .*

*Q. You were busy.*

*A. Yeah.*

*Q. You were busy switching the keys, weren't you?*

*A. No.*

**Defendant's Case**—After plaintiff rests, it is defendant's turn to call witnesses. Naturally, plaintiff may cross-examine each witness when defendant finishes asking questions.

Defendant may use either (or both) of two main strategies. The first is a direct attack on some part of plaintiff's evidence. Defendant's task is, in some ways, easier than plaintiff's. Plaintiff must offer evidence establishing every single element of a cause of action; defendant can succeed by knocking out just one element of plaintiff's case. It is not uncommon for defendants to choose the tactic of mounting a strong attack on the weakest link in plaintiff's chain, and letting the rest of plaintiff's case go by without much challenge. Moreover, defendant need not actually *disprove* one element of plaintiff's cause of action—the burden of proof is on plaintiff (see sidebar). Defendant can win merely by casting enough doubt on the evidence supporting one of the elements of plaintiff's case, so that plaintiff's evidence will fall short of a preponderance of the evidence.

Sometimes the burden of proof can be on defendant. If defendant raises an affirmative defense, ordinarily defendant has the burden of establishing the defense by a preponderance of the evidence. Suppose, for example that Shannon proves Dr. Collins intended to throw himself on top of her, but Dr. Collins argues that he did so in self-defense (to prevent her from shooting him again). It happens that, under the substantive law pertaining to battery, self-defense is an affirmative defense. Dr. Collins will have the burden of proving, by a preponderance of the evidence, each of the elements of self-defense.

*Putting It Into Practice:*

*If you were Gail Stoddard, what aspect of Shannon's case would you focus on and why?*

---

### SIDEBAR

## Burden of Proof

*Most people are familiar with the idea that, in a criminal case, the defendant is entitled to be acquitted unless the government proves the defendant guilty "beyond a reasonable doubt." This is an example of the concept of* **burden of proof.** *Notice that there are two dimensions to burden of proof: (1) Who has the burden (in a criminal case, the government has it) and (2)* **how high** *a level of proof is required.*

*In civil lawsuits, plaintiff has the burden of proof to establish all the elements of a cause of action. This is why plaintiff loses if one element is missing. As for the level of proof, for most causes of action, plaintiff must establish each element by a* **preponderance of the evidence.** *The preponderance of the evidence test works like a balance scale. In our hypo, for example, suppose the jury is trying to decide whether Dr. Collins intended to attack Shannon (intent is one element of the cause of action for battery). We place all the evidence that tends to show that Dr. Collins did act with intent on one side of the scale. We place all the evidence that tends to show that Dr. Collins did not intend to attack Shannon on the other side of the scale. If the scale tips, even slightly, in the direction of the evidence showing intent, Shannon has sustained her burden of proof as to the element of intent. If the scale tips the other way, or stays level, Shannon has failed to sustain her burden of proof, and her cause of action for battery fails. To put it another way, "preponderance of the evidence" requires Shannon to put on enough evidence to persuade the jury that it is more probable than not—i.e., there is greater than a fifty–fifty chance—that Dr. Collins acted with intent.*

***Putting It Into Practice:***

*What is one of the reasons Shannon pursued a civil cause of action against Dr. Collins rather than attempt to persuade the state to prosecute him criminally?*

Sometimes a higher burden of proof than "preponderance of the evidence" applies, even in a civil suit. Proof of civil fraud, for example, often carries a burden of clear and convincing evidence, which is greater than a preponderance but less than the criminal standard of beyond a reasonable doubt. The burden for proving the right to punitive damages may also be by clear and convincing evidence.

| *Your Local Notes* |
| --- |
| _____ |
| _____ |

***Putting It Into Practice:***

*How can you tell what the burden of proof is for a given cause of action?*

✗ An alternative strategy is for defendant to raise an affirmative defense. An affirmative defense is some circumstance that allows defendant to win *even after plaintiff has established each element of the cause of action in question.* Often, affirmative defenses involve some legitimate excuse for doing whatever defendant did. In our hypo, for example, Shannon can probably establish each of the elements of a cause of action for battery against Dr. Collins—he intentionally threw himself on top of her. However, self-defense is an affirmative defense to the tort of battery, so if Dr. Collins can establish each of the elements of self-defense, Shannon's cause of action for battery will fail, even though she has established each of the elements of battery. The law recognizes many affirmative defenses. Some of the common ones are listed in FRCP, Rule 8(c). Some, like discharge in bankruptcy, can be raised against almost any cause of action; most, like self-defense, apply only to certain specific theories of liability. Which affirmative defenses apply to which causes of action is a matter of substantive law.

---

*Your Local Notes*

_____

_____

---

**Putting It Into Practice:**

*Why do you think plaintiffs are allowed rebuttal and defendants are not?*

**Rebuttal**—When defendant is through calling witnesses, defendant rests, and plaintiff gets one last turn. This phase is called **rebuttal.** During rebuttal, plaintiff may call witnesses, and defendant may cross-examine each of them.

The scope of the evidence that plaintiff is allowed to present during rebuttal is quite limited: It must directly rebut some item of evidence offered during defendant's part of the case. It would not be fair to allow plaintiff to bring up new matters at this late stage, because defendant's part of the trial is over, and defendant will have no chance to give his side of the story. Naturally, plaintiff's attorneys are sometimes tempted to save some juicy bit of evidence and try to sneak it in during rebuttal, so that defendant will have no chance to offer evidence to disprove it. This practice is referred to as *sandbagging.* Most judges vigorously enforce the restrictions on the scope of rebuttal, however, so it is generally risky to count on getting important evidence in during rebuttal.

**More Motions**—After rebuttal is over, the trial enters another housekeeping phase, again outside the hearing of the jury. Both parties may now make a **motion for a directed verdict.** In principle, the judge is always free to bypass the jury and render an immediate verdict, *for either party,* if the judge is persuaded that the facts are so clear that no reasonable juror could reach a different conclusion. Plaintiff is entitled to a directed verdict on any cause of action if plaintiff has made out a *prima facie* case and defendant has not presented any credible evidence to rebut any of the elements of plaintiff's cause of action. Defendant is entitled to a directed verdict if defendant's evidence so clearly destroys one of the elements of plaintiff's cause of action that no reasonable juror could find otherwise. As a practical matter, directed verdicts at the close of the evidence do not gain very much in terms of efficient use of the court system—at most, some jury deliberating time will be saved. On the other hand, if an appellate court disagrees with the judge, the entire trial will have been wasted and the case will have to be tried again. Therefore, most judges are cautious in the use of their power to grant a directed verdict, and do so only in circumstances where the correct outcome is clear; see FRCP, Rule 50.

---

*Your Local Notes*

_____

_____

---

This is also the time when the judge must make a final decision about what instructions to give the jury, if that has not already been done. The attorneys need to know the exact wording of the jury instructions in order to prepare their closing arguments. Otherwise, attorneys run the risk that they might argue some point, only to have the judge instruct the jury to the contrary a few minutes later. In all but the simplest cases, settling jury instructions usually requires argument, and plenty of it, as the attorneys debate the case law pertaining to the theories of liability involved in the trial. Plaintiff's attorney wants jury instructions that do not require proof of elements for which plaintiff's evidence is weak. Defendant's goal is the opposite—the more elements plaintiff has to prove, the better. The wording of instructions is also a battleground. The party with the best case—which may be either plaintiff or defendant—will prefer instructions that are clearly worded and easy to apply; the opposing party, on the other hand, will be perfectly happy for the judge to give instructions that are confusing and difficult to understand.

---

*Your Local Notes*

_____

_____

---

*Putting It Into Practice:*

*Some courts have instituted written jury instructions that are approved by a special judicial committee. Do you think plaintiff's attorneys or defendant's attorneys would be most supportive of this innovation?*

The exact procedure for settling jury instructions varies from court to court. Generally, by this stage in the trial, each side has already submitted proposed jury instructions, and each side has also submitted written objections to the opponent's proposals, or will at least make verbal objections on the record. It is a general principle in the law that appeals courts are not interested in listening to a party complain about trial court "errors" unless the party doing the complaining pointed the errors out to the trial judge early enough that they could have been corrected. Thus, if you think there is something wrong with one of your opponent's proposed jury instructions, you cannot keep silent about it, hoping to use the defect to get the case reversed on appeal if you lose the trial. If you do not get your objection on the record before the jury retires to deliberate, most courts of appeal will rule that the instruction stands, erroneous or not.

*Putting It Into Practice:*

*Should an error that seriously affects the outcome of the case, but which no one notices until after the jury has decided, be allowed to be objected to on appeal?*

**Closing Arguments**—The **closing argument** is where the attorneys pull all of the pieces of their cases together into, we hope, a coherent and persuasive unit. Until now, most of the trial has been devoted to listening to witnesses, one after the other. This results in a "piecemeal" presentation. Imagine what your favorite movie would be like if the script were rearranged so that each actor appeared only once and spoke all of his or her lines for the whole movie—it would be pretty hard to follow the plot! You would probably have to have someone explain to you, afterward, exactly what was supposed to have happened, and that is exactly what closing argument is for in a trial. Some trial lawyers like to describe the process this way: A trial is like a puzzle. In the evidentiary phase, we lay out all of the pieces, without being able to see exactly how they go together. In the closing argument, we put all the pieces together into a single picture.

Closing arguments are different from opening statements. In an opening statement, the lawyers are limited to saying what the evidence will be. Closing arguments are much less restricted, and attorneys may argue what they think the evidence means. In addition to talking about the testimony presented during the trial, they are free to draw inferences, to talk about common sense, to bring up facts and ideas that everyone knows from experience, to argue about what is good or bad for society, and—especially—to talk about what is the fair and just outcome. In an opening statement, if an attorney begins to "argue"—to stray much beyond the cold facts to be presented—the opposing attorney will object and the judge will remind the offender to stick to the evidence. In a closing argument, objections are considered the equivalent of belching in church, and will be tolerated only if the arguer is clearly misrepresenting the

*Putting It
Into Practice:*

*Do you think jurors are
more persuaded by
opening statements or
closing arguments?*

evidence on an important point. The assumption is that the jury knows that this is argument, not evidence, and if one party's reasoning is flawed, the other is free to point out the flaws when it is her turn to argue.

---

**Your Local Notes**

_____

_____

---

Closing arguments follow the familiar three-step sequence: plaintiff first, then defendant, then plaintiff again. Because plaintiff (generally) has the burden of proof, plaintiff has the right to the first and last word to the jury.

Closing argument is important to you, as a paralegal, in several ways. The most obvious is the need for "props." In modern trial practice, charts, pictures, and "blowups"—poster-sized enlargements of juicy excerpts from document exhibits—are often indispensable as a way of explaining complicated evidence. If an attorney reads a few sentences out of, say, a contract to the jury, few jurors will follow and none will likely remember any of it an hour later. If the attorney instead puts a huge blowup of the few sentences on an easel in front of the jury while arguing (and, with luck, manages to leave the blowup where the jury can still see it while the opposing attorney is arguing!) the point is much more likely to be understood and remembered. Paralegals are often given responsibility for designing these "visuals" and having them made.

*Putting It
Into Practice:*

*What kind of visuals
would you design for use
in Shannon's case?*

The other great significance of closing argument is as a blueprint for the rest of the case. Many trial lawyers believe that trial preparation should start with the closing argument. First, figure out exactly what you want to argue to the jury; then you will know what testimony and documents you need in order to support that argument. (It isn't quite that simple, of course. As you now know, you also have to include enough evidence to avoid a directed verdict, even if you do not intend to argue all of it to the jury.) If you understand how closing arguments work, you will be much better equipped to make effective judgments about the importance of the various bits of evidence that make up the case. Mainly for this reason, even though paralegals generally do not argue before juries, we encourage you to try your hand at arguing, and we include an exercise for this purpose (see Procedural Ponderables 2 at the end of the chapter).

**Reading of Jury Instructions and Submission to Jury**—After both sides have finished their closing arguments, the judge instructs the jury. First, the judge will read a series of **jury instructions** that are given in every civil suit—instructions about how to deliberate, how to select a foreperson, how to reach a verdict, and other housekeeping matters. Second, the judge will read the instructions on the rules of substantive law that the jury is to use in deciding the case; by now, these should have been thoroughly researched and honed to perfection.

In the federal courts, and in a few state courts, the judge is also allowed to comment on the evidence. In practice, most federal judges use this privilege sparingly and carefully. Refraining from commenting on the evidence is safe—the judge is not required to do it, even in federal court, so keeping quiet cannot cause a reversal on appeal. The wrong kinds of comments can result in a reversible error. If the court of appeals perceives the judge's comments as misstating the evidence or as overly argumentative in favor of one side, the court of appeals may send the case back for another trial.

The judge concludes the instructions by submitting the case to the jury for deliberation. The jurors are given verdict forms on which to record their decision, and sent off to the jury room.

"They only deliberated for two hours, so that's bad, isn't it, Allen?" Shannon asked. "When the jury makes a decision quickly, it's usually for the defendant, isn't it? Isn't that what they said in the O. J. Simpson case?"

Allen smiled. "I thought it was the other way around. Anyway, in my experience, you can't really guess what a jury will do. Let's just wait and see what they decided. The bailiff will be bringing them back in a few minutes; then we'll know."

"I don't know. I just have a bad feeling about this. It's all kind of my word against theirs, isn't it? I mean, we didn't really prove that they gave Dr. Collins the wrong key."

"It is your word against theirs, or actually your and Dr. Collins's word against the desk clerk's. But that's what it always comes down to in a trial. That is proof, or at least its the best proof you ever get. Think about it—if we had a photograph of him switching the keys, do you think the hotel would have gone to trial on it? Of course not; they would have paid us off long ago."

"But we did have Chuck's notes—at least that was some proof—"

"Yes. The decision not to use them was a judgment call, and we'll soon see whether it was the right one. The problem with the notes were, in addition to showing Trevayne was a liar, it tended to prove that the door might not have closed. Right or wrong, we made the decision to go on the theory that the clerk switched the keys. If we then put in evidence that the door might not have closed properly, that undercuts our theory of what happened. Alternative theories of liability are okay at the pleading stage, but, in front of a jury, at least in my experience, it's better to pick your best explanation of the facts and stick to it. And I think that making it a "swearing contest" with you and Dr. Collins on one side and Trevayne on the other was a pretty good way to go."

**Deliberation and Verdict**—The jury's first task is to elect a foreperson; then the jurors discuss the case and try to arrive at a decision. In general, the members of the jury decide how to accomplish this. There are very few restrictions, and, as a practical matter, the jurors are free to decide the case in any way they wish, taking as little or as much (within reason) time as they wish, based on whatever reasons seem sufficient to them. In theory, there are a few cardinal sins—using a coin toss or other game of chance to decide the case is one—that, if proven, can lead to a finding of jury misconduct and a mistrial. In practice, if you lost the case because two of the jurors thought your opponent's lawyer had a better tailor, the bottom line is still that you lost the case.

This is definitely not rocket science. Lawyers often find it instructive to talk to the jurors after a case is over, as a way of learning which tactics were persuasive and which ones fell flat. We recommend that you attend such "postmortems" whenever you are given the chance. More often than you might expect, the lesson learned is that there are many factors beside the law and the evidence that influence jurors. The wise lawyer (and paralegal) does not fight this; instead, he learns how to identify and use these other factors. Among other things, experience teaches that many verdicts come down to nothing more complicated than that the jury believed that some important witness was lying to them. Lawyer demeanor is also important; a professional appearance, good grooming, and a likeable, pleasant, and confident attitude are usually helpful (although some lawyers manage to achieve success without them).

*Putting It Into Practice:*

For what reasons do judges make every effort to avoid committing reversible errors?

*Putting It Into Practice:*

Do you agree with Allen Porter's statement that it is best to go to the jury with one consistent theory of what happened, or do you think it would have been better to argue both possibilities—that either the clerk switched the keys or the door didn't close properly—and let the jury choose? Assuming that the decision is to pick one version or the other, which would you pick and why? Based only on the testimony in the trial transcript excerpts, how would you vote if you were on the jury?

In the vast majority of cases, only a **general verdict** will be called for; that is, the jury will be asked merely to find for the plaintiff or defendant and, if the verdict is for the plaintiff, to decide the amount of money to be awarded. If there are multiple parties, there may be a need for separate verdicts as to each; for example, in our hypo, the jury would need to render one verdict on Shannon's claims against the hotel, and another on her claims against Dr. Collins.

The federal rules also provide mechanisms whereby the judge can require the jury to be more specific about what they are deciding. One is the **special verdict,** consisting of written findings on particular issues of fact. In a battery case, for example, the jury might be asked to render separate verdicts on whether defendant made physical contact with the plaintiff; whether defendant acted intentionally; whether plaintiff suffered damages; and whether the damages were caused by defendant's conduct. The judge would then decide whether the specific facts found in the special verdict are enough to support liability, and render judgment accordingly. Another procedure is to submit the case for a **general verdict with written interrogatories** to the jury about specific facts on which the verdict depends. Here, the judge might ask the jury to reach a general verdict, in the usual way, on whether defendant is liable to plaintiff for battery and, in addition, to answer the question, "Did defendant intend to make physical contact with plaintiff?" If the answers to any of the factual questions are inconsistent with the verdict, the judge can send the jury back to try again or order a new trial.

Most judges try to avoid using these procedures, correctly seeing them mainly as a way for one side or the other to plant the seeds of reversible error and set up an appeal. The judge's power to use special verdicts or interrogatories to the jury is **discretionary**—that is, the judge is not required to use them, but may do so if he wishes. Therefore, the court of appeals is very unlikely to send the case back for a new trial just because the judge used a general verdict. If the judge uses special verdicts or jury interrogatories, however, and the jury comes back with the wrong answers—inconsistent findings, for example—the judge may have no choice but to order a new trial; see FRCP, Rules 49 and 58.

What happens if the jurors cannot agree on a verdict? It depends on the situation. In federal court, as well as in many state courts, a unanimous verdict is required, so one determined holdout can cause a **hung jury,** a jury unable to reach a verdict. Judges are never eager to waste time retrying cases, so a deadlocked jury will likely be sent back several times with increasingly adamant exhortations to come to some agreement. In many cases, the jurors can negotiate with each other and reach some compromise—for example, awarding a smaller amount of money in return for the holdout's vote. If the judge becomes convinced that there is no hope of breaking the deadlock, the only option is to order a new trial with a new jury. In courts where the verdict can be by a majority of the jurors, it is still possible to have a hung jury, because the majority required is almost always more than a simple majority. Nevertheless, majority verdicts make hung juries much less likely, which is one of the reasons why some states use them.

When the jurors reach a decision, they send word to the judge. Because no one can predict how long it will take the jury to reach a decision, the judge and the attorneys have likely gone back to their offices and moved on to other work. The judge's secretary notifies the attorneys that the jury has returned, everyone returns to the courtroom, and the judge has the verdict read. Any party then has the right to have the jury polled. **Polling the jury** consists of the judge asking each juror, in open court, whether he or she agreed to the verdict. This is supposed to provide a safeguard against coercion, giving any jurors who feel they were pressured into a decision an opportunity to say so.

*Putting It
Into Practice:*

*If given the opportunity, should Allen Porter request a special verdict?*

The trial is now over, all the participants leave, and the suit enters another phase of procedural maneuvering.

# GETTING FROM VERDICT TO JUDGMENT

*Shannon was elated. Three hundred seventy-five thousand dollars! That would go a long way toward rebuilding her life and getting her shattered career back on track. Of course, Allen Porter would get a third of it, plus all the expenses, but even so. . . .*

*Allen Porter was talking to Gail Stoddard at the defense table; Shannon could not hear what they were saying, but Gail's expression was grim and determined, and she kept shaking her head. After a few moments, Porter returned and led Shannon out of the courtroom.*

*Shannon went straight to the question that was uppermost on her mind: "So, how long before we get the money?"*

*Porter did not reply immediately. As they reached the elevators, he turned to Shannon. "It may be quite a while. We'll have to see. That was a big verdict—Gail's ego is stung right now, and I don't detect much inclination on her part to resolve this. But I'm hoping that after she has a chance to evaluate the situation and go over it with her clients, they'll decide not to drag things out any further."*

*"What does Gail's ego have to do with it? We won—"*

*"We won the trial. We don't have a judgment yet, and, right now, Gail is saying that the verdict is obviously excessive, and that it's inconsistent to find the hotel negligent without also holding Dr. Collins liable, and she'll think of a few other, better arguments in plenty of time for her motion for a new trial. And even when we do have a judgment, they can always appeal. But don't worry, this was a big win for us, and it should at least get them back to the negotiating table. And if it doesn't, we'll just press ahead."*

The path to this point in the case has been long and arduous. We have spent at least a year, and possibly several, in preparation; tens of thousands of dollars in attorney time and costs have gone down the drain. Our client is asking "Are we there yet?"

Not by a long shot. What we have is a verdict—a jury decision. What we need is a final judgment—an order of the court declaring that the opposing party owes our client money. We face several potential hurdles before we can get a judgment, and even then the opposing party may appeal. Remember, too, that judgments are not self-executing. Once we get a judgment, we still have to figure out how to collect the money!

The loser at trial has several possible procedural moves to choose from. The first is a **motion for a new trial.** A motion for a new trial must be based on some error committed during the trial. In effect, it is a way of short-circuiting the appeal process when some mistake has been made that the judge knows will lead the court of appeals to order a new trial. There is no point in wasting everyone's time and money on an appeal whose outcome is a foregone conclusion. It is better and cheaper for the trial judge to bite the bullet, acknowledge the error, and retry the case. As you would expect, motions for a new trial are hard to win. No judge wants to try the same case twice, so if the alleged error is reasonably debatable, the motion will be denied and the losing party can then appeal; see FRCP, Rule 59.

+------------------------------------------------+
| *Your Local Notes*                             |
|                                                |
| _____  |
|                                                |
| _____  |
|                                                |
+------------------------------------------------+

A **motion for a judgment notwithstanding the verdict** (often called **judgment n.o.v.,** where the initials stand for the Latin *non obiter verdictum*) is a request for the judge to disregard the jury's decision completely and enter judgment in favor of the party who lost the trial. Can the judge do this? Yes, if the judge is persuaded that the jury reached a verdict that no "reasonable person" could have arrived at from the evidence by following the judge's jury instructions. You may be wondering how any judge could have the effrontery to declare, in effect, that an entire jury reached a decision that no "reasonable person" could have made! In fact, judges do occasionally grant motions for judgment n.o.v. The typical sequence of events is this: One party moves for a directed verdict after both sides have finished their evidence (that is, before the jury retires to deliberate). The judge may be inclined to grant the directed verdict. But if the judge does so, and the court of appeals disagrees, the whole case will have to be retried. Having already invested days or weeks in a jury trial, it usually makes more sense to go ahead and let the jury render a verdict. If the jury decides in the same way as the judge would have, the judge lets the jury verdict stand. If the jury reaches the "wrong" decision, the judge grants a motion for judgment n.o.v. Then, if the court of appeals decides that the judge should not have taken the decision away from the jury, it can simply reinstate the jury verdict, and a second trial is avoided. It is safer for the judge to deny the motion for directed verdict and grant the motion for judgment n.o.v. after the verdict, than it is to grant the motion for directed verdict, send the jurors home, and risk reversal on appeal.

Notice that motions for a new trial and motions for a judgment notwithstanding the verdict are used in distinct situations: motions for a new trial are used when the *judge* has made some mistake during the trial itself, such as allowing evidence that should have been excluded; motions for judgment n.o.v. are used when the claim is that the *jury* reached the wrong decision; see FRCP, Rule 50.

### Putting It Into Practice:

*On what basis might Gail Stoddard file both a motion for a new trial and a motion for a judgment n.o.v.?*

+------------------------------------------------+
| *Your Local Notes*                             |
|                                                |
| _____  |
|                                                |
| _____  |
|                                                |
+------------------------------------------------+

Still another option available to a losing defendant is to ask for a **remittitur.** Suppose the jury finds in favor of plaintiff and awards an unexpectedly large amount of money for damages. If the defendant can persuade the judge that the award is unreasonable and excessive, the judge has the power to let the verdict stand and reduce the amount of the award. (Plaintiff can appeal, of course.)

All of these procedural maneuvers occur relatively quickly after trial, if at all. The deadline for a motion for judgment notwithstanding the verdict is ten days after the verdict is entered. The deadline for filing a motion for new trial in federal court is ten days after entry of judgment; see FRCP, Rules 50 and 59.

---

*Your Local Notes*

_____

_____

---

**Putting It Into Practice:**

*If Allen Porter asked you to lodge a form of judgment in your jurisdiction, how would you do it?*

The event that formally ends the trial phase of the litigation is the **entry of judgment.** It is important to know exactly when a judgment is entered, because various important deadlines—especially the deadline for filing an appeal—are counted from the entry of judgment. In federal court, judgment is entered when it is signed by the court and recorded in the clerk's docket in accordance with FRCP, Rule 79. In federal court, the clerk or the judge's staff typically prepares the actual piece of paper that the court will sign. In state courts, procedures vary, and it may be up to the winning party to **lodge** a proposed form of judgment with the court. To lodge a **form of judgment** means to prepare and deliver the actual judgment that you want the judge to sign. Your instructor will tell you the appropriate procedure for your locality; see FRCP, Rules 58 and 79.

---

*Your Local Notes*

_____

_____

---

A judgment is a court paper, with the usual caption. Depending on the court and the type of judgment, it is signed either by the judge or by the clerk of the court, not by the attorneys. Simple money judgments are short, typically a page or two long.

Skirmishes can arise over the contents of the judgment. With a garden-variety judgment on a general verdict where there is only an award of money damages, there is typically no basis to argue about the wording of the judgment, and the judge will sign it immediately. Not all judgments are simple, however. If an injunction is involved, or declaratory relief, or if the judgment involves disposition of property as in a divorce case, the exact wording can become quite important. Then there must be a procedure whereby the court can hear argument about the form of judgment. Again, procedures for settling the form of judgment vary with the locality.

Another potential battleground is the assessment of costs. The winning party—plaintiff or defendant—is entitled to have judgment against the loser for taxable court costs. **Taxable costs** do not include all expenses related to the suit; there is a statute (in federal court, 28 U.S.C. 1920) or rule that lists the categories of expenses that can be assessed against the losing party. Typically, the most expensive category of taxable costs is the court reporter fees for depositions; filing fees and process service fees are also taxable. Two of the greatest expenses of litigating are generally *not* taxable: attorney's fees and the fees of expert witnesses, both of which can add up to tens of thousands of dollars even in relatively ordinary cases.

**Putting It Into Practice:**

*Do you think losers in litigation should have to pay their opponent's attorney's fees? Is there such a requirement in your state?*

Should the loser also have to pay the winner's attorney's fees? This is an important question, because it is not at all unusual for the attorney's fees to add up to more than the amount of damages being sued for! In the American system, the general rule is that each party must pay his or her own attorney. There are many exceptions. Because most contracts written by lawyers include an agreement that, in case of a dispute, the loser pays the attorney's fees,

***Putting It Into Practice:***

*Do you agree with the long-standing tradition of having trial testimony manually recorded by a court reporter, limiting courts of appeals to review of the written record? Would it be better if trials were videotaped so that the court of appeals could review "live" testimony?*

attorney's fees are often awarded in breach of contract lawsuits. There are also many statutes of recent vintage that create new causes of action (for such things as consumer fraud, securities fraud, and the like) and that provide for an award of attorney's fees to the winner. In many courts, the judge has the power to award attorney's fees if the judge feels that a party is deliberately abusing the system; filing a frivolous lawsuit merely to harass the opposing party, for example. Some advocates of reform believe that the laws should be changed to require the loser to pay the winner's attorney's fees in all cases. Such proposals are particularly popular with defense lawyers, because they expect (probably correctly) that many fewer plaintiffs would sue if losing meant getting assessed tens of thousands of dollars for the defendant's attorney's fees.

How does the court determine the amount of costs to assess? The procedure varies, but one way is for the winner to file a **statement of costs,** after which the loser can file written objections to any items deemed improper. Attorney's fees are a different matter: Proceedings to determine the amount of attorney's fees to be awarded can become quite complex and drawn out, possibly requiring evidentiary hearings as the parties argue the reasonableness of various charges; see FRCP, Rules 54(d)(1) and (d)(2).

## ETHICAL ETIQUETTE

*I*n preparing for trial you will be talking with opposing parties and witnesses on both sides. Both the Model Rules and Code prohibit attorneys from discussing anything related to the issue being litigated with any opposing party that is represented by counsel without the consent of that counsel unless they are expressly authorized by law. The purpose of this prohibition is to prevent attorneys from disrupting the relationship between client and attorney and thereby gaining an advantage over the opposition. Attorneys may discuss issues unrelated to the matter in controversy. Therefore, if you receive a phone call from an opposing party asking you a question relating to litigation, you must tell them you cannot talk to them without the permission of their attorney.

You may talk with parties who are not represented; however, you should use caution. First, you must avoid giving legal advice (which constitutes the unauthorized practice of law) and thereby avoid committing a serious ethical breach. Second, attorneys must avoid giving legal advice to unrepresented parties if there is a "reasonable possibility of being in conflict with the interest" of their client unless that advice is to secure representation. As an agent of an attorney you are subject to the same prohibition.

Part of your trial preparation tasks will often involve helping prepare witnesses for trial. Witnesses who know the questions they will be asked by the attorney calling them to the stand and who can anticipate the types of questions opposing counsel will ask generally make more effective witnesses. You will want to advise them about how to dress, how to conduct themselves on the stand, and how to respond to certain tactics commonly employed in cross-examination. You may also want to help them prepare by exposing them to a *mock trial,* asking them in advance the questions they are most likely to be asked on the stand. Refrain, however, from doing anything that might encourage them to give false testimony or by overcoaching them to the point that their testimony appears staged and they lose credibility.

# PRACTICE POINTERS

The practice of law is both a profession and a business. As such the generation of profits is essential to the success of any law practice (other than government law offices, such as the county attorney's office or federal district attorney's office). These profits arise out of the hours billed by each attorney and legal assistant on staff. These so-called "billable hours" are the staple of any law practice. Therefore, it is absolutely essential that every attorney and legal assistant maintain an accurate record of the hours they have expended working on each case to which they have been assigned.

Firms use a variety of procedures for recording time spent and many have employed computerized timekeeping procedures. Regardless of the details, however, every procedure requires you to maintain a record of the client for whom you have done the work, the type of work you did (e.g., phone call, document review, preparation of letter, travel, or research), the date you performed the work, and the time you spent doing it. Not all work is considered billable. For example, the time you spend learning how to perform a task that is required to serve a client and that you should be expected to be able to perform as a reasonably competent legal assistant cannot be billed. For this reason inexperienced legal assistants spend more time accomplishing the same goal as a more experienced legal assistant but amass fewer billable hours.

Familiarize yourself immediately with the billing practice of your firm. Some firms have minimum billing practices. Every phone call, for example, may be billed as 0.1 or 0.2 hour even if the client does not answer and even if the conversation actually takes less time. Every letter may be billed at a minimum of 0.5 hour even if it is a form letter that can be completed in a few minutes. Other firms are less rigid in their billing practices but do require legal assistants to log every hour expended and then review these records to determine which hours will actually be billed for.

Learn the details of the billing practice in your firm and then routinely assess your own billing rate. If in an eight-hour day, you are typically billing only four hours, you need to reassess how you are using your time. If you are not filling out your time slip immediately after you complete a task, you may be forgetting the time you expended and may find yourself at the end of the day unable to account for the time you spent.

Beyond the economic necessity of maintaining accurate records, the court in some instances may need to be able to determine the amount of time spent on a case. The awarding of attorney's fees, for example, requires that the court be able to review the amount of time spent in preparing a case to determine if that amount of time falls within the realm of standard practice. Any time attorney's fees become an issue, a law firm must be able to bolster its claims of reasonableness by producing records of the time expended by each staff member. Failure to keep accurate and consistent records may result in a loss of fees to the firm. Furthermore, inability to justify fees to a client can result in a client that not only resents the amount of monies being paid, but harbors such hostility toward the firm that any future relations become impossible.

## TECHNO TIP

The courtroom of the future is now in many jurisdictions. Some of the larger court systems (including many federal courts) have one or more courtrooms set up for digital presentation of evidence. These courtrooms generally have at least five, and sometimes more, large screen computer monitors for viewing by the judge, witness, counsel, and jurors. In addition to exhibit books for the jurors (where allowed) all the participants in the trial (or hearing on a motion) can view the documents as they are being discussed. Important phrases or graphics (including pictures) can be highlighted to focus the attention of the witness and the jury. Instead of fumbling through a stack of exhibits at the clerk's desk a mere press of a keyboard button can bring a contract, an expert's report, a medical record, or a photograph to the screen. Deposition testimony can be read by the jury and witness alike—at the same time. Various programs are on the market to streamline the cataloging of documents and allow indexing and cross-referencing of exhibits. The technologically proficient legal assistant can become a huge asset to her employer and, at the same time, get to spend a good part of her time in court, rather than the office, by developing skills in this area.

Currently the expense of purchasing and preparing equipment for a digital courtroom precludes their use in more mundane (i.e., not high dollar) cases. As the use of scanners and trial preparation software becomes less expensive and easier, the digital courtroom will encompass more and more trials. You will advance your career opportunities considerably by being able to take charge in this area.

## SUMMARY

Trial settings are not firm because judges usually schedule more cases for trial than they can possibly handle, anticipating that most of them will settle before going to trial and that other contingencies will arise that will result in delays. Judges set trial dates after some triggering event. Some courts set dates after the pleadings are filed or after discovery is at a certain stage, whereas others set dates after a motion to set and certificate of readiness is filed. To help ensure that attorneys will be prepared to go to trial, courts prepare a pretrial order or require the attorneys who will actually be going to trial to prepare a joint pretrial statement, which sets forth the boundaries of what can and cannot be presented at trial. The pretrial order or statement contains a list of the witnesses and documents that will be presented at trial as well as a list of the issues of fact and law that must be decided at trial. The rules generally require attorneys to exchange names of witnesses and copies of documents months before trial. Listing the documents saves trial time because any documents to which an attorney does not object in the pretrial statement will be admitted at trial. Judges encourage attorneys to compromise on issues as much as possible so that the trial can focus on the most serious issues in dispute.

Immediately before trial, witnesses are carefully prepared and cross-examination questions as well as opening and closing arguments are outlined. Motions *in limine* must be submitted to the judge, thus establishing the boundaries within which the attorneys must ask their questions. Jury instructions are prepared prior to trial. The exact wording of these instructions is important because of the potential importance this wording may play on appeal. Trial exhibits must be marked by the clerk before or during trial so that they can be located quickly. The authenticity of exhibits must be established, although most pretrial orders contain stipulations of authenticity except for those the attorneys plan to challenge. Demonstrative evidence must be planned for well in advance of trial because the assistance of a graphics service is frequently required. The organizational skills of legal assistants are essential in making sure that all the elements of a trial come together before the "play" begins.

Most cases are settled before trial and on the first day of trial many judges meet with the attorneys in their chambers to, among other things, try once more to convince the attorneys to settle. If the trial moves forward, jurors are selected through the process of *voir dire*. Some courts control the *voir dire* process, while others allow the attorneys to ask the questions. Jurors may be excused for personal reasons or "for cause." The attorneys also have the option of striking jurors by using a specified number of peremptory challenges.

In nonjury trials jury selection and jury instructions are dispensed with, but the judge must make findings of fact and conclusions of law. Typically the judge requires both parties to submit proposed findings before the trial and then adopts the findings of the winning party. In nonjury trials, judges commonly relax the formal rules of evidence and encourage attorneys to waive closing arguments. Parties are usually informed of the judge's verdict by minute entry several days or weeks after the trial.

The trial opens as each side gives opening statements during which they tell their client's story. The plaintiff then presents evidence, followed by the defendant, and concluding with the plaintiff, who is given an opportunity to rebut the defendant's case. This evidence is presented and rebutted through direct examination, during which leading questions are prohibited, and cross-examination, during which leading questions are essential. Attorneys cannot cross-examine their own witnesses unless those witnesses are hostile. Either side can ask that witnesses be placed "under the rule." Some courts limit the scope of cross-examination to areas that were covered on direct examination; all courts limit redirect examination to the scope of cross-examination.

After the plaintiff rests, the defendant can move for a directed verdict on one or more claims if the defendant believes the plaintiff has failed to establish a *prima facie* case for those claims. The judge will allow a claim to go before the jury if reasonable jurors could differ as to whether the evidence supported the plaintiff's claim. Judges are reluctant to enter directed verdicts unless the outcome of the case is very clear.

The defendant then has the choice of attacking the plaintiff's case or raising an affirmative defense. Because the plaintiff has the burden of proving each element of her case by a preponderance of the evidence, the defendant need go after only the weakest link in the plaintiff's case to prevail. The defendant, however, has the burden of proving an affirmative defense. The plaintiff has the opportunity of rebuttal once the defendant has rested, but is restricted to rebutting evidence that was brought in by the defendant. Introducing new evidence at this point is called *sandbagging* and is vigorously opposed by judges. Motions are generally made both when the plaintiff rests and when the defendant rests. At the end of the case jury instructions are once again debated and both parties are careful to get their objections to these instructions on the record so they are preserved on appeal.

Attorneys pull all the pieces of their case together in the closing arguments, where they are allowed to explain the evidence, to draw inferences, and to talk about commonly accepted ideas and general principles, such as fairness and justice. Objections are seldom made during closing arguments. Because closing arguments serve as a blueprint for the case, many trial attorneys believe that trial preparation should begin with the outlining of closing arguments. Legal assistants are often given the responsibility of preparing the visuals used to explain complicated evidence during closing arguments.

Before the jury retires to deliberate, the judge reads them two sets of jury instructions. The first is a set of general instructions that is used in every civil case and the second is a set of specific instructions addressing the substantive law to be applied in the case at hand. In federal courts and some state courts, judges are permitted to comment on the evidence but few do because of the possibility of committing reversible error.

Jurors are allowed to render their decision on almost any basis except a coin toss or other game of chance. Juries usually give a general verdict although judges have it within their discretion to order a special verdict or a general verdict with written interrogatories. If a jury becomes deadlocked, resulting in a hung jury, a judge must order a new trial. Hung juries are less likely to result when a majority verdict is allowed. Once a verdict is entered, attorneys have the option of polling jurors. Attorneys are advised to talk to jurors after trial to learn what entered into their decision-making process.

The loser has the option of filing a motion for a new trial, thereby circumventing the appeal process, or a motion for a judgment notwithstanding the verdict, which allows the judge to disregard a jury decision the judge believes is unreasonable. The defendant can also ask for a remittitur.

The trial phase formally ends with an entry of judgment. In federal courts judgment is entered when it is recorded in the clerk's docket but in some state courts the winning party must lodge a proposed form of judgment with the court. The form of judgment, the assessment of taxable costs, and the determination of attorney's fees are potential sources of further disagreement. Taxable costs, for which the loser is liable, include court reporter, filing, and service fees. Courts sometimes determine the assessable costs by reviewing a statement of costs prepared by the winner. An ongoing philosophical as well as personal debate is whether the loser should have to pay the winner's attorney's fees. Generally each party is required to pay its own fees although exceptions exist in cases involving contractual disputes or where state statutes provide otherwise or where the judge feels that the losing party deliberately abused the legal system.

## KEY TERMS

Burden of proof

Closing argument

Cross-examination

Demonstrative evidence

Direct examination

Discretionary

Entry of judgment

Findings of fact and conclusions of law

Form of judgment

General verdict

General verdict with written interrogatories

Hostile witness

Hung jury

Jury instructions

Leading question

Lodge

Motion for a directed verdict

Motion for a judgment notwithstanding the verdict (judgment n.o.v.)

Motion for a new trial

Motion *in limine*

Motion to set and certificate of readiness

Opening statement

Peremptory challenge

Poll the jury

Preponderance of the evidence

Pretrial order

Pretrial statement

*Prima facie* case

Rebuttal

Redirect examination

Remittitur

Rests

Scope

Settle

Special verdict

Statement of costs

Stipulate

Taxable costs

Trial setting

*Voir dire*

## Workshop Alert

*The following workshop correlates well with this chapter and you would be well advised to work with it.*

Workshop 17          How to Prepare for Trial

## REVIEW QUESTIONS

1. What is a trial setting?
   a. For what reasons are trial settings not concrete?
   b. What prompts the setting of a trial date?

2. What is the purpose of a pretrial order or statement? What is contained in such an order or statement?

3. What is a motion *in limine*? What is the purpose of such a motion?

4. Why do attorneys and judges work so hard at crafting jury instructions? Why do most attorneys prepare jury instructions prior to trial?

5. What are two important things to consider when preparing evidentiary exhibits for trial? What is the purpose of demonstrative evidence?

6. Why do negotiations reach a higher level of intensity immediately before trial?

7. What is the purpose of *voir dire*? What is the difference between a peremptory challenge and a challenge for cause?

8. In what respects is it easier to try a case before a judge than before a jury?

9. What does an attorney try to convey during opening statements? What limitations are placed on opening statements?

10. If a plaintiff's theory of liability is analogized to a chain, what must a plaintiff do to win a case?
    a. What must the defendant do to win the case?
    b. At what point in this chain is a plaintiff determined to have made a *prima facie* case?

11. How does the scope of cross-examination differ from the scope of direct examination? What is a leading question and when is it allowed?

12. What is required of a witness who has been put "under the rule"?

13. What may a defendant do once the plaintiff rests? What happens after the plaintiff rests?

14. What are two strategies a defendant can use in mounting a defense?
    a. Why is the defendant not required to disprove the plaintiff's case?
    b. What is the burden of proof that a plaintiff must meet in a civil case?
    c. Under what circumstances is the burden of proof on the defendant?

15. What is the purpose of rebuttal? What limitations are placed on rebuttal?

16. When is a plaintiff entitled to a directed verdict?
    a. When is a defendant entitled to a directed verdict?
    b. Why are judges generally reluctant to grant directed verdicts after all the evidence has been presented?

17. Why are jury instructions such a battleground for attorneys?

18. What is the purpose of closing arguments?
    a. How do they differ from opening statements?
    b. Why does the plaintiff get to speak twice during closing arguments?
    c. Why do many attorneys write their closing arguments first?

19. Do judges have a right to comment on the evidence?

20. Why do attorneys often find it helpful to talk to jurors after they render a verdict?

21. What is the difference between a general verdict and a special verdict?
    a. What is a general verdict with written interrogatories?
    b. Why do judges usually prefer general verdicts?

22. Why do judges do everything possible to avoid hung juries?

23. Why might a party want to poll a jury?

24. On what basis might a party move for a new trial?
    a. On what basis might a party move for a judgment notwithstanding the verdict?
    b. What is the essential difference between a motion for a new trial and motion for a judgment n.o.v.?

25. On what grounds might a defendant ask for a remittitur?

26. What event formally ends the trial?
    a. Why is it important to know when a judgment is entered?

b. What conflicts can arise over the form of a judgment?

27. What is the winning party entitled to in terms of costs of litigation?
    a. Do taxable costs include the expenses related to suit?
    b. What is typically the most expensive category of taxable costs?
    c. Are attorney's fees and expert witness fees considered taxable costs?
    d. Is the loser in litigation required to pay the winner's attorney's fees?

## PRACTICE EXAM

*(Answers in Appendix A)*    **MULTIPLE CHOICE**

1. Trial settings are usually not firm because
   a. new evidence is discovered and the parties ask for a continuance.
   b. parties or witnesses get sick or judges are moved to other divisions.
   c. judges overschedule cases.
   d. all of the above.

2. A trial date can be set
   a. any time a court feels like setting it.
   b. after some triggering event, such as one of the parties filing a motion to set.
   c. when one of the parties request a date be set.
   d. none of the above.

3. A pretrial order
   a. includes only a list of witnesses and documents that will be used at trial.
   b. includes only a list of issues of fact and law to be decided at trial.
   c. includes a list of witnesses and documents that will be used at trial and a list of issues of fact and law that will be decided at trial.
   d. has nothing to do with any of the above.

4. A motion *in limine*
   a. is appropriate to make only during the trial.
   b. prevents attorneys from getting "improper" questions before a jury.
   c. occurs spontaneously during trial.

   d. cannot be used offensively.

5. Jury instructions
   a. are important because of the influence they have on jurors.
   b. are prepared by attorneys on both sides and jurors are given both sets of instructions.
   c. can be an important basis of appeal.
   d. summarize the facts of the case.

6. Trial exhibits
   a. must be authenticated.
   b. must always be marked by the clerk prior to trial.
   c. only need to be authenticated when there has been a stipulation.
   d. do not need to be brought to the attention of opposing counsel.

7. Jurors are selected from
   a. driver's license records.
   b. voter registration lists.
   c. a source of public records.
   d. all of the above.

8. A juror may be excused or struck
   a. for "cause."
   b. for personal reasons.
   c. because the attorney does not feel the juror will be sympathetic to his client.
   d. all of the above.

*(Answers in Appendix A)*

## MULTIPLE CHOICE

9. A nonjury trial occurs when
    a. the issue being litigated is personal injury.
    b. the plaintiff fails to request a jury in a timely manner.
    c. one of the parties decides that a jury is not needed.
    d. none of the above.

10. During opening statements attorneys typically
    a. tell their client's story.
    b. give impassioned speeches relating to the theme of their case.
    c. describe the evidence that has been presented.
    d. none of the above.

11. At the close of evidence a judge could
    a. direct a verdict for the plaintiff but not for the defendant.
    b. direct a verdict for the defendant if the plaintiff clearly failed to prove her case.
    c. not direct a verdict on one claim and allow the jury to decide another claim.
    d. none of the above.

12. A defendant can prevail
    a. only by proving an affirmative defense using clear and convincing evidence.
    b. by attacking one element of the plaintiff's case.
    c. only if the plaintiff fails to prove each element of his case.
    d. none of the above.

13. In closing arguments the attorneys can
    a. draw inferences.
    b. explain what the evidence means.
    c. talk about fairness and justice.
    d. all of the above.

14. Jurors
    a. are allowed to base their decision on anything, including a coin toss.
    b. must conform to specific restricted guidelines in reaching a decision.
    c. can reach a verdict based on their like or dislike of one of the attorneys.
    d. cannot be questioned by the attorneys after they have rendered their decision.

15. After the jury's verdict is rendered
    a. a plaintiff can move for a judgment n.o.v.
    b. a defendant can move for a directed verdict.
    c. a plaintiff should ask for a remittitur.
    d. none of the above.

16. The entry of judgment
    a. is important only to the clerk's office.
    b. occurs in federal court when the verdict is rendered.
    c. is the formal end of the trial.
    d. determines when a directed verdict can be requested.

17. Taxable costs include
    a. attorney's fees.
    b. expert witness fees.
    c. court reporter fees.
    d. none of the above.

## FILL IN THE BLANKS

18. A _____ is a minute entry specifying the time, date, and place for trial.

19. One way courts help ensure that attorneys are ready to go to trial is to prepare a _____ , which sets forth the limits of what attorneys can and cannot present at trial.

20. A motion to _____ can be filed by any party and informs the court how many trial days will be necessary and whether a jury will be needed.

21. To ensure that opposing counsel will not ask an objectionable question at trial, an attorney can in effect make an objection in advance by filing a motion _____ .

22. _____ are directed toward the jury and specify in concise terms the elements of each cause of action a jury is considering.

23. Visual aids that are used at trial to help jurors understand facts or concepts are called _____ evidence.

24. The purpose of _____ is to weed out prospective jurors whom the attorneys or judge feels may not be able to act impartially.

25. An attorney can use a _____ to strike a juror that she believes will vote against her client.

26. A judge in a nonjury case is required to make _____ and _____ .

27. The trial opens with the plaintiff giving _____ , which is the plaintiff's version of the facts.

28. Failure to establish a _____ case for a claim in a plaintiff's cause of action could result in the judge granting a motion for a _____ on that claim.

29. The examination of one's own witness is called _____ examination; the examination of the opponent's witnesses is called _____-examination.

30. A plaintiff can subpoena a _____ witness who refuses to testify voluntarily.

31. A witness who is placed _____ must remain outside the courtroom when not testifying and must not discuss the case with anyone.

32. _____ questions are not allowed on direct examination but are essential to cross-examination.

33. A plaintiff has the burden of proving each element of his case by a _____ .

34. An attorney that sneaks in new evidence during rebuttal is said to be _____ .

35. All the puzzle pieces of the trial come together when the attorneys give their _____ .

36. Most juries are asked to render a _____ verdict, deciding only whether the plaintiff or defendant prevailed, but in some courts the judge requires the jury to make written findings on particular issues of fact by rendering a _____ verdict.

37. If a judge requires a jury to reach a _____ , the judge can send the case back to the jury if its verdict is inconsistent with its answers to any of the factual questions.

38. A jury that is unable to reach a decision is called a _____ .

39. Attorneys have the right to _____ to find out if each juror agreed to the verdict.

40. The loser at trial can move for a _____ , based on an allegation that an error was committed during the trial, or can move for a _____ , asking the judge to disregard the jury's decision.

41. A defendant that believes an award is excessive can ask for a _____ .

42. The deadline for filing an appeal is counted from the _____ , the formal end of the trial phase of litigation.

43. In state courts the winning party may be required to _____ a proposed form of judgment with the court.

44. The winner of a lawsuit is often asked to file a _____ , from which the court can determine the costs to assess.

## TRUE OR FALSE

**45.** Pretrial statements do not need to be prepared by the attorneys who will actually be going to trial. **T F**

**46.** Pretrial statements are prepared by the court, not the attorneys. **T F**

**47.** Witness and exhibit lists are usually exchanged by attorneys months before trial. **T F**

**48.** Submitting document lists in advance of trial saves time because any document that is not objected to will be admitted at trial. **T F**

**49.** A pretrial order is the end product of all the work that goes into shaping the legal issues of a case. **T F**

**50.** The goal of pretrial statements is to have attorneys stake out each and every issue as to how they would ideally like to have that issue phrased. **T F**

**51.** Attorneys can avoid permitting opposing counsel from planting ideas in the jury's mind through the use of prejudicial questions by filing motions *in limine* during the trial. **T F**

**52.** It is the jury's job to decide what the facts are, but it is the judge's job to say what the law is. **T F**

**53.** Jury instructions are always read at the beginning of the trial. **T F**

**54.** The exact wording of jury instructions is very important. **T F**

**55.** A party may not complain about a jury instruction that was not given if the party did not request the instruction. **T F**

**56.** Jury instructions do not need to be prepared until after trial. **T F**

**57.** Most jurisdictions have a book of recommended jury instructions. **T F**

**58.** Attorneys usually stipulate in pretrial orders to the authenticity of exhibits unless they have a serious basis for challenging that authenticity. **T F**

**59.** The basis for establishing the authenticity of each exhibit to be presented at trial should be determined before trial. **T F**

**60.** In all courts the clerk marks exhibits during trial. **T F**

**61.** Demonstrative evidence is not really evidence in that it is not used to prove the facts of a case. **T F**

**62.** Once the trial date is near, attorneys usually quit engaging in any efforts to negotiate a settlement. **T F**

**63.** Most cases are settled before going to trial. **T F**

**64.** On the first day of trial the attorneys meet in the judge's chambers and the judge often takes advantage of this time to once more encourage the parties to settle. **T F**

**65.** Local rules dictate the details of jury selection. **T F**

**66.** Juries always consists of twelve members. **T F**

**67.** The real goal of jury selection is to find a jury of the fairest jurors. **T F**

**68.** *Voir dire* questions are always asked by the judge. **T F**

**69.** No cause is needed to use a peremptory challenge to strike a prospective juror. **T F**

**70.** Peremptory challenges cannot be used to exclude racial minorities from a jury. **T F**

**71.** Judges still adhere to the formal rules of evidence in nonjury trials. **T F**

**72.** In nonjury trials verdicts are usually rendered immediately following closing arguments. **T F**

**73.** Attorneys present their arguments during an opening statement. **T F**

**74.** In a civil action the plaintiff presents evidence first and then has an opportunity to offer rebuttal evidence after the defendant presents evidence. **T F**

**75.** During rebuttal a plaintiff cannot introduce new evidence. **T F**

**76.** All courts limit the scope of cross-examination to subjects raised during cross-examination. **T F**

**77.** An attorney has the right to cross-examine his own witnesses. **T F**

78. Leading questions are allowed on cross-examination because the purpose of cross-examination is to test the credibility and truthfulness of the witness.     **T   F**

79. Most cases are won on the strength of cross-examination.     **T   F**

80. The defendant cannot move for a directed verdict until the plaintiff has rested.     **T   F**

81. A plaintiff has sustained her burden of proof if she can show there is a fifty–fifty probability each element in her case is supported by the evidence.     **T   F**

82. A defendant has the burden of proving an affirmative defense.     **T   F**

83. Judges are reluctant to grant a directed verdict.     **T   F**

84. The party with the worst case generally prefers clearly worded, easy-to-apply jury instructions.     **T   F**

85. Most appellate courts will allow jury instructions to stand if the party objecting to them does not get its objections on the record before the jury begins to deliberate.     **T   F**

86. Closing arguments are more restricted than opening statements.     **T   F**

87. Judges frequently uphold objections made during closing arguments.     **T   F**

88. The defendant makes the final closing argument.     **T   F**

89. Many trial attorneys believe that trial preparation should begin with the closing arguments.     **T   F**

90. Legal assistants often prepare the visuals used during closing arguments.     **T   F**

91. Judges give two sets of jury instructions: general instructions that are given in every civil suit and specific instructions regarding the substantive law to be applied in the case at hand.     **T   F**

92. Judges can never comment on the evidence.     **T   F**

93. Judges frequently use special verdicts.   **T   F**

94. The decision to submit a special verdict lies within the discretion of the parties.     **T   F**

95. Judges usually make every effort to get deadlocked juries to reach agreement.     **T   F**

96. If a jury is hopelessly deadlocked a judge has no option other than to order a new trial.     **T   F**

97. Hung juries are less likely when a majority vote is allowed.     **T   F**

98. A case is finally over when the verdict is entered.     **T   F**

99. Judgments are self-executing.     **T   F**

100. Granting a motion for a new trial is a judge's way of circumventing the appeal process.     **T   F**

101. Motions for a new trial are hard to win.   **T   F**

102. A judge can grant a motion for judgment n.o.v. only if he decides that no reasonable person could have reached the jury's decision based on the evidence presented.     **T   F**

103. Parties have several months in which to file motions for a new trial and motions for judgment n.o.v.     **T   F**

104. A judgment is entered in federal court when it is recorded in the clerk's docket.     **T   F**

105. Knowing exactly when a judgment has been entered is irrelevant for litigation purposes.     **T   F**

106. Judgments are signed by the attorneys.   **T   F**

107. In some cases the form of judgment is very important.     **T   F**

108. Taxable costs do not include all expenses related to a lawsuit.     **T   F**

109. It is not unusual for the attorney's fees to add up to more than the amount of damages being sued for.     **T   F**

110. In the American legal system each party is required to pay its own attorney's fees.   **T   F**

111. Attorney's fees are determined via the statement of costs.     **T   F**

## LITIGATION LINGO

*Read the description and provide the word that matches that description.*

### WHAT'S MY NAME?

1. The defendant must prove me if he raises me.

2. I am a visual aid and other kinds of evidence that help clarify the facts for the jury.

3. I am what an attorney makes at the beginning of trial to set the stage.

4. I am prepared by the judge and set forth the parameters of what attorneys can and cannot present at trial.

5. I am a motion prepared by the parties that informs the judge about how many days are needed for trial and whether a jury will be needed.

6. I am the plaintiff's response to the defendant's case.

7. I am a pretrial motion that prevents the opposition from asking prejudicial questions at trial.

8. I am the process that is used to weed out undesirable jurors.

9. I am the event that signals the end of the trial phase of litigation.

10. I am a motion the defense can make when the plaintiff rests.

11. I can be used to eliminate an undesirable juror without cause.

12. I allow an attorney to pull all the pieces of the trial together.

13. I am what a judge is required to make when rendering her decision in a nonjury trial.

14. I am what the losing party has to pay, including court reporter, filing, and service fees.

15. I am the process that is used to question opposing witnesses.

16. I am an uncooperative witness.

17. I am the exact wording of a judgment.

18. I am what a plaintiff must establish to avoid a directed verdict.

19. I am what a jury renders if they are asked to make special findings of fact.

20. I am a deadlocked jury.

21. I am a question that tells the witness the answer the attorney wants to hear.

22. I am the amount of proof the plaintiff must establish in a civil suit.

23. I am a motion made by the losing party that wants the judge to disregard the jury's decision because it is unreasonable in light of the evidence presented.

24. I am rendered by the jury when it is asked to make a decision about the outcome of the case as well as answer specific questions in reference to the facts.

25. I am a request by the defendant to reduce an excessive damage award.

26. I am what an attorney does to make sure that each juror agrees with the verdict.

## LITIGATION LOGISTICS

***For each question give the rule of civil procedure in your jurisdiction that applies and then answer the question.***

1. How would you go about setting a trial date if you were planning to sue your cousin who did not pay you what you were owed?
   a. Would you be required to prepare a pretrial statement or a draft of a pretrial order?
      i. When would this document be due?
      ii. What would you have to include in this document?
   b. On what areas of law would you need jury instructions?
      i. When would you have to submit proposed jury instructions to the judge?
      ii. Where would you look to find jury instructions in this case?
   c. Would you be required to provide copies of any exhibits you plan to use at trial?
      i. If so, when would you have to provide these?
      ii. How would you determine how to establish the authenticity of each exhibit?
      iii. Will these documents need to be marked in advance of trial?

2. Suppose you are unable to settle the case involving you and the drunk driver and you end up going to trial.
   a. What kinds of jurors would you like to have?
   b. How many peremptory challenges will you get?
   c. Will the judge conduct *voir dire*?
   d. What types of questions will you be allowed to ask?
   e. Would you prefer to have a trial to the court? If you did opt for a nonjury trial, would the judge be required to prepare a findings of fact and conclusions of law?
   f. Will you be able to get a special verdict?

3. What must the karate instructor do if he wants to move for a directed verdict?
   a. What must he show?
   b. What must he do if he wants a new trial? What time frame does he have to do this?
   c. What must he do if he wants the judge to change the jury's verdict? What time frame does he have to do this?
   d. What must he do if he wants the judge to reduce the damages awarded by the jury?

4. Suppose you prevail in your suit against the shoddy contractor.
   a. What must you do to enter a judgment?
   b. Within what time limit must the defendant file an appeal?
   c. How is the form of judgment determined?
   d. What are the taxable costs for which the contractor will be liable?
   e. How will attorney's fees be determined?

5. Suppose you are preparing a witness to testify in the suit against your tenant. Consult the rules of evidence in your jurisdiction and answer the following:
   a. What is the scope of cross-examination?
   b. What is the scope of redirect examination?
   c. What kinds of questions can the tenant's attorney ask your witness?

## PROCEDURAL PONDERABLES

1. Look at the hypos in Chapter 1. Consider each situation and decide whether you would opt for a jury trial or a trial to the judge and why. If you did opt for a jury, what types of jurors would you be seeking in *voir dire*? Consider what evidence you would present in terms of witnesses and exhibits. Would you want to make any motions *in limine*? What types of jury instructions would you need to research?

   a. Drunk driver sideswipes your car.
   b. Tenant stops paying rent and refuses to move out.
   c. Cousin refuses to pay you a percentage of his business.
   d. Karate instructor breaks your nose.
   e. Contractor does shoddy work on house.

2. Select one of the hypos from Chapter 1 and prepare an outline of your closing arguments. What story would you want to tell? What would be the theme of your presentation? How would you present this theme in your opening statements? How do you anticipate the defendant would attack your case and how would you rebut those arguments? Do you think you could avoid a directed verdict for the defendant?

   a. Drunk driver sideswipes your car.
   b. Tenant stops paying rent and refuses to move out.
   c. Cousin refuses to pay you a percentage of his business.
   d. Karate instructor breaks your nose.
   e. Contractor does shoddy work on house.

3. If you were granted three wishes in reference to the trying of civil cases, how would you use those wishes to change the American trial system? What do you see as the single most important impediment to the search for justice in the courtroom?

# CHAPTER 8

# ROAD MAP OF A LAWSUIT: JUDGMENT COLLECTION AND APPEAL

## OBJECTIVES

**In this chapter you will learn:**

- How to collect on a judgment

- How to determine the assets of a judgment debtor and decide which assets to execute on

- How a judgment debtor can escape paying a judgment

- The procedural rules that must be followed to obtain an appeal

- The process followed by the appellate courts in reviewing appeals

hypothetical

**Shannon's Ordeal, continued**

"*T*hey'll appeal. Gail hasn't given me a definite answer yet, but I know she thinks she can get the judgment reversed." Allen Porter and Chuck Fletcher were discussing the case over a quick lunch at the local deli.

Chuck chewed his pastrami sandwich in silence for a moment. "So there go another two years down the drain, huh? There's nothing we can do?"

"To speed it up? No, two years is about what it'll take. Of course, we get interest on the money, now that there's a judgment. But the sixty-four dollar question is whether they'll really come up with a supersedes bond. I was getting some vibes before that Gail thought we might have trouble finding any money to collect. It's a Delaware corporation, remember, and at this point we haven't a clue whether it has any assets. And you have to wonder what's going on—pretty unusual for a business this size not to have liability insurance. There are three possibilities, it seems to me. One is that they're substantial enough to be self-insured—we hope. But it could also be that they're running on a shoestring and trying to cut corners, or, worse yet, that they think they're judgment proof."

"But surely the hotel must be worth more than the three hundred seventy-five thousand—"

"Sure. But it'll be mortgaged to the hilt, probably. How much did your house cost, a hundred twenty thousand or so? How much would you get if you sold it, after you pay off the mortgage?"

"I see what you mean. I hadn't thought of that. But can't we find out if they have assets?"

"It depends. Up until now, we couldn't—the general rule is you aren't entitled to take discovery on what kind of assets the opposing party has. Now that we have a judgment, we can take asset discovery, unless the other side puts up a supersedes bond, and if they do that, we won't need to, of course."

"Supersedes bond—that's where they put up a bond in the amount of the judgment guaranteeing that if they lose the appeal, the judgment gets paid?"

"Right. And if they do that, the judgment is stayed during the appeal—we can't try to collect until the appeal is over."

"But if they do that, and if they lose the appeal, they won't be able to play 'hide and go seek' with the assets, right?"

"It won't matter—if they try it, we just collect from the bonding company and let the bonding company go after them."

"And if they don't put up the bond—"

"We take asset discovery and start looking for things to seize."

# INTRODUCTION

Entry of judgment marks the end of the trial phase of the lawsuit, but it is by no means the end of the road for the parties to the dispute. The parties' strategies and options depend on who won, and on whether a significant amount of money has been awarded.

The simplest scenario is a judgment for defendant that awards costs but not attorney's fees. Because the costs are typically trivial compared to the amount in dispute, plaintiff's options are simple: Appeal or give up. Often defendant will agree to cancel the judgment for costs if plaintiff will agree not to appeal.

The situation is more complicated when one party has a judgment against the other for a significant amount of money. Notice that this can be either a plaintiff's or defendant's judgment. It may be that plaintiff won the suit and the jury awarded damages. Or it may be that defendant won the suit but was entitled to an award of attorney's fees. We call the party to whom the money is awarded the **judgment creditor.** The party ordered to pay the money is called the **judgment debtor.** Now each of the parties has a potential weapon in hand: The judgment debtor can appeal, and the judgment creditor can try to collect the money awarded in the judgment.

Procedurally, appeal and collection are separate processes, and we will describe them separately. As a matter of strategy, however, they are related: Appealing can be one way for the loser at trial to delay collection of the judgment, but the threat of collection while the appeal is pending can put a serious damper on the loser's enthusiasm for the appeal.

Can the judgment creditor—Shannon in our hypo—begin trying to collect the judgment immediately, or must she wait until the appeal is decided? As a general rule in American courts, a judgment is effective and enforceable as soon as it is entered, and the judgment creditor can begin collection proceedings immediately. There can be some slight delay—in federal court, there is a ten-day waiting period [see FRCP, Rule 62(a)], and in most courts, if a motion for new trial is made, the judge can order the judgment creditor to wait until the motion is decided.

If Park Hotels wants to prevent Shannon from collecting the judgment while the case is on appeal, it must somehow obtain a **stay;** see FRCP, Rule 62. A stay is a court order, issued either by the trial court or the court of appeals, that prohibits the judgment creditor from trying to collect on the judgment while the stay is in effect. One common way to obtain a stay is by posting a supersedes bond (see sidebar). Another is to file for bankruptcy, which will result in an automatic stay of all proceedings against the judgment debtor.

*Putting It Into Practice:*

*Who is the judgment creditor in Shannon's case? Who is the judgment debtor?*

---

## SIDEBAR

### Supersedes Bonds

*Shannon has won a judgment for a large sum of money, and Park Hotels Groups has appealed. Now we have a dilemma. The trial court has determined that, in effect, Park Hotels is holding money that belongs to Shannon. It seems unfair to allow Park Hotels to keep Shannon's money for what may be years while the case is on appeal, especially since Park Hotels may use the time to hide the money or simply lose it in a bad business deal, leaving Shannon with nothing. On the other hand, if we allow Shannon to collect the money, and Park Hotels wins the appeal, how is Park Hotels going to get its money back? By then, Shannon may have spent it! How would you solve the problem?*

*The law's solution is to let Park Hotels keep the money for now, but only if it guarantees that the money will be there when the appeal is over. What kind of guarantee?: a **supersedes bond.** A bond is a promise to pay, accompanied by some form of security. The security can be cash deposited with the court—in effect, the court will hold the money during the appeal—or, more commonly, it will be an insurance contract from an approved insurance company. If it is cash, and Shannon wins the appeal, the court will turn the cash over to her. If the bond is secured by an insurance contract, the court can order the insurance company to pay Shannon.*

*Putting It Into Practice:*

*In your state what does Park Hotels Group have to do to obtain a supersedes bond?*

---

*Your Local Notes*

_____

_____

---

Naturally, the insurance company will make sure that, if it has to pay Shannon, it has some way of getting the money back from Park Hotels. Before an insurance company will issue a supersedes bond, it will insist on getting some security, perhaps a mortgage on the judgment debtor's property or perhaps a written guarantee from a large corporation that is clearly able to pay the amount in question. If Park Hotels has few assets, probably no insurance company will issue a bond, and Park Hotels will be forced to try to dodge Shannon's collection efforts while the appeal proceeds.

## COLLECTING THE JUDGMENT

*Chuck Fletcher was trying to explain the ins and outs of post-trial proceedings to Shannon. It was not going well.*

*"It just seems to me like a dumb way to run a system. I mean, what's the point of suing somebody if they don't have to pay you when you win?"*

*Chuck tried again. "While the case is on appeal, if they post—"*

*"I understood the part about the bond. What I don't understand is, let's say they don't put up a bond—why wouldn't the court make them pay me?"*

*"How?"*

*"I don't know—how about, put them in jail until they turn over the money?"*

*"See, that would be like having a debtor's prison—we don't do that in this country. And, what if the judgment debtor doesn't have the money? Is the judge supposed to let them rot in jail forever? Besides, this is a corporation. Who are you going to put in jail? It just doesn't work, you couldn't do it that way."*

*"Well—how about having the court seize the hotel and sell it, or grab their bank account, something like that?"*

*"That's what we will try to do if it comes to that. But the thing is, the court doesn't do it. Basically, courts don't do anything unless the attorneys prepare everything first. It's up to the judgment creditor to find the assets and arrange for them to be seized and sold. All the court will do is sign the necessary papers—after we prepare them."*

*"So if they manage to hide all their assets, we're out in the cold?"*

*"Pretty much. Of course, with a going business like a hotel, it would be hard for them to hide absolutely everything. They'd have to have an operating bank account, for example, but it probably doesn't have more than a few thousand in it at any given time, so you'd have to keep coming back. What judgment debtors do, sometimes, is just make it so tedious and expensive to collect, that it's easier to give up and settle for a smaller amount of money."*

Winning a final judgment does not automatically result in plaintiff getting paid. You cannot take a judgment down to the bank and deposit it in your account. A judgment merely gives the winner of a lawsuit the right to try to seize the loser's assets. Even this right is limited, as we shall see shortly. The loser can, of course, simply pay the judgment, or the parties can agree to settle the case for some lesser amount. But if the loser refuses to cooperate, the winner must somehow find the loser's property and have it seized and sold to pay the judgment, which may be difficult or impossible. The process of seizing the judgment debtor's property and applying it to pay the judgment is called **execution.**

## THE COLLECTIBILITY CONUNDRUM

One of the most important considerations in deciding whether a lawsuit is worth filing in the first place is the question of whether the person to be sued is **judgment proof,** i.e., has no assets from which a judgment could be collected. Every plaintiff's lawyer regularly turns down great cases that would be fantastic moneymakers—except that the person to be sued has no insurance and no reachable assets.

Like it or not, the importance of collectibility is a central fact of litigation. A case will make a "good" lawsuit only if (1) you can prove liability, (2) there are significant damages, *and* (3) there is some way to collect a judgment. Herein lies one of the great Catch-22's of litigation: As a practical matter, there is often no good way to know whether you can collect a judgment until you have obtained one. Before judgment, the defendant is not required to allow plaintiff to invade his financial privacy.

Does this mean plaintiff is always flying blind on the question of whether a judgment can be collected? Not at all. For one thing, insurance coverage is always discoverable; if defendant has enough insurance to cover the judgment plaintiff is seeking, the collectibility problem evaporates. Also, if the defendant is a large corporation and not visibly teetering on the edge of bankruptcy, it is usually safe to assume that a judgment can be collected. There is also a procedural tactic for getting discovery of the defendant's financial circumstances, which is often tried and occasionally works: Include in the complaint a claim for punitive damages. Punitive damages are awarded to punish unusually reprehensible conduct, and in order to administer punishment at a suitable level of pain, the jury has to know how much money the defendant has to start with. If the trial judge agrees that the conduct in question is reprehensible enough to warrant punitive damages—a big "if"—then plaintiff is entitled to take discovery aimed at finding out how much money defendant has.

In many situations, it is obvious that a judgment could not be collected. The prime example is the automobile collision where the driver at fault has no insurance. As a practical matter, it is difficult or impossible to collect any significant amount of money from an ordinary working person if there is no insurance. You may reasonably wonder how this can be—if the person is working, surely they have a salary, a house, a car? Can we not seize these things and get paid that way?

Not usually. In the American system, we do not allow the winners of lawsuits to strip the losers down to their underwear and leave them to sleep in the street! The law allows a judgment debtor to keep enough money and property to be able to survive. How much money and what kind of property? Each state has so-called "exemption statutes" that list a number of items that any judgment debtor is entitled to keep. These lists have been added to and adjusted upward from time to time, to the point that today, in some states, the "survival" level can be luxurious indeed. A typical middle-class judgment debtor will be able to keep her house, at least one car, some clothes, books, furniture, tools, jewelry—most of the common badges of middle-class existence. As for wages, federal law allows the judgment debtor to keep either three-fourths of her take-home pay or the equivalent of thirty hours at minimum wage, whichever is greater. This leaves, at most, one-fourth of the judgment debtor's take-home pay that can be seized, and even that meager source of payment will likely dry up quickly if targeted. For instance, the judgment debtor can change jobs, move to another state, or simply file for bankruptcy.

**Putting It
Into Practice:**

*What should Allen Porter
have done at the onset of
litigation to ensure that
any judgment against
Park Hotels Group could
be collected?*

(We hasten to add that these exemptions prevent seizure of exempt property by a *judgment* creditor—not by a *secured* creditor. If you decide to quit making your car payment, you can be sure that the lender will repossess your new Porsche in a heartbeat, and no exemption statute will prevent it. That is because, when you bought the car, you signed a contract in which you voluntarily agreed that this specific car would be security for the loan.)

## FINDING ASSETS

Suppose you already have a final judgment. Now can you find out what assets your opponent has? The action is no longer pending, so the normal discovery rules do not apply. The law, however, provides other, equivalent procedures for discovering assets.

Asset discovery begins with a **judgment debtor's examination,** often called a **debtor's exam.** A debtor's exam is, in effect, like a deposition of the judgment debtor, in which the judgment creditor's attorney asks questions about the judgment debtor's assets. The procedure for scheduling a debtor's exam varies; you should consult the statutes or rules for your locality. Some debtor's exams are held at the court, under the supervision of a court officer (who may be called a magistrate or any of several other titles) who is not a judge but is appointed to handle routine matters in the judge's place. The supervising officer does not actually attend the examination—there are too many! He merely swears in the judgment debtor and stands by in case there is a need for a ruling or order of some kind. The judgment creditor's attorney and the judgment debtor are sent into any available conference room to do the questioning. If the judgment debtor is evasive or uncooperative, it is easy to haul her back before the supervising court officer, who will likely administer a dose of reality. The court will force the judgment debtor to answer any reasonable questions about her property, under threat of jail if she refuses. Debtor's exams are also sometimes held at the judgment creditor's attorney's office, in a manner similar to a deposition. A court reporter may or may not be present at the option of the judgment creditor's attorney. Often, it is deemed easier and cheaper simply to take notes.

**Putting It
Into Practice:**

*In your state how would
you schedule a debtor's
examination for Park
Hotels Group?*

The objective of a debtor's exam is to find property or money belonging to the judgment debtor. The modern reality is that most kinds of property have some kind of paperwork associated with them: Real estate has deeds, cars have title certificates, bank accounts have statements, etc. Therefore, it is customary to summon the judgment debtor to the debtor's exam via a subpoena *duces tecum* (or other similar order provided for in the statute or rules dealing with debtor's exams), which includes a long and detailed list of documents for the judgment debtor to bring. The examination will consist of going through these records one by one, noting down the information necessary to find and seize the property in question. Of equal importance, the attorney will question the judgment debtor about the categories of property for which no documents have been produced. There will be questions about the judgment debtor's income and expenses and where any excess money has gone.

When you are going after a bigger fish—say, a corporation that does business in several states—the situation is more complicated. If you schedule a debtor's exam, the corporation will designate some employee to appear and testify. That person will probably claim not to have all of the information you need. Some of the information you need may be in other offices, in other states. Here, tenacity is the key. In principle, the judgment creditor can take whatever discovery is necessary to find out what assets the company has and where they are located. Procedures vary, and a judge's permission may be required at certain stages.

## EXECUTION

Once you have found assets, then what? How can you translate them into money to pay your judgment? It depends on the type of asset. We describe the procedure for three of the main kinds of property: real estate, tangible personal property, and money. These procedures vary from state to state, and you must follow the laws of the state in which the property to be seized is located.

When we seize and sell a particular item of property to pay a judgment, we say that we are *executing on* that item of property. To execute on real estate, the first step in most states is to obtain a judgment lien. A **lien** is a security interest, similar to a mortgage, giving the lienholder the right to have the property sold to pay off a debt. There are many kinds of liens, most of which do not concern us here; a lien that comes from recording a judgment is called a **judgment lien.** In some states, a lien on the judgment debtor's real estate automatically arises when the judgment is entered; in others, it is necessary to record the judgment at the office of the county recorder or docket the judgment with the clerk of the court in the county where the real estate is located.

> *Putting It Into Practice:*
>
> *How would you record a judgment lien against Park Hotels Group if they did business in your state?*

| Your Local Notes |
| --- |
| |
| |

Once the judgment lien is in existence, the judgment debtor can have the property sold and the proceeds applied to pay the judgment. In some states, the judgment creditor must foreclose the judgment lien in the same way that a lender forecloses a delinquent mortgage. In general, this is done by filing a suit for foreclosure in court and obtaining a court order to have the sheriff (or some other court officer) sell the property at auction. Still another lawsuit? Yes; the problem is that, often, the judgment debtor is not the only one with rights to the property. There may be lenders, co-owners, lessees, spouses, partners—everyone who has an interest in the property must be notified and given a chance to salvage what is theirs. If the property is the judgment debtor's house, the situation is even more complicated, because the exemption laws may apply to all or part of the judgment debtor's equity. There may even have to be a trial—and an appeal! In other states, real property can be executed on and sold in a manner similar to that used for personal property (see later discussion).

You will probably be relieved to know that we do not expect you to master the intricacies of foreclosure law here—it is a specialty to which some lawyers devote their entire careers. For our purposes, the message is just this: The judgment creditor should routinely record the judgment in the county recorder's office of every county where the judgment debtor may have real estate, and can then (eventually) get a court order to have any nonexempt real estate sold at auction.

Tangible personal property means *things*. It does not include real estate nor does it include bank accounts, contract rights, or anything else that has no physical existence (such things are not tangible). Examples of tangible personal property are furniture, cars, tools, jewelry—anything that can be physically held or touched. To execute on tangible personal property, we obtain a writ of execution from the clerk of the court. A **writ of execution** is a court order directing the sheriff (or other law enforcement official) to go levy on (seize) specific property and sell it at public auction. The judgment creditor's lawyer prepares the writ of execution, which is a court paper, typically a one- or two-page printed form with an attached list of property to be levied on. The clerk of the court issues it more or less on request, without the judge having to be involved. The procedure to be followed by the sheriff in seizing and selling the property varies considerably from one state to another because each state has statutes that set out the requirements.

As a practical matter, writs of execution on tangible personal property are rarely of much use. There are several reasons: First of all, by the time a judgment is entered and a writ issued, the judgment debtor has had plenty of warning, and any tangible property of any value is likely to be long gone or well hidden. Second, when the deputy sheriff goes out to levy on the property, he cannot enter private property and conduct a search without permission. If the owner of the premises refuses to let the deputy sheriff in, telling him that the property sought is not there, the sheriff will simply return the writ "*nulla bona*"—nothing found. And finally, most of the common kinds of used personal property are unlikely to sell for much money at an auction. Execution on tangible personal property works best when there is some object that is large and difficult to hide—machinery, say—and the judgment creditor knows exactly where it is and can lead the deputy sheriff to it.

**Putting It Into Practice:**

*Would there be any reason to secure a writ of execution in Shannon's case?*

---

*Your Local Notes*

_____

_____

---

The best and easiest assets to execute on are, of course, money and other financial assets. Not cash, of course, because it is too easy to hide. A judgment creditor's best targets are accounts in banks, stockbrokerages, and other financial institutions, because they generate a constant flow of statements and records, all of which can be subpoenaed from the institution if necessary, making the money relatively easy to trace. If the judgment debtor transfers money from a known account trying to make it disappear from the radar screen, the judge can simply order her to transfer it back, under threat of jail.

How do you execute on a bank account? A bank account is actually a debt owed by the bank to the account holder. When you deposit money in a bank account, you are, in effect, lending the money to the bank. What we need, therefore, is a procedure that we can use when we find someone who owes money to the judgment debtor, and force them to pay us the money instead. That procedure is called **garnishment.** When you garnish, say, a bank account, you are simply having the court order the bank to take the money that it owes to the judgment debtor and pay it to the judgment creditor instead. Naturally, the procedure is more complicated than that, and the bank must be given an opportunity to be heard, in case (for example) it disagrees about how much it owes the judgment debtor. But, in principle, any time you can find a debt owed to the judgment debtor, you can, via a writ of garnishment, step in and collect it on behalf of the judgment creditor. A writ of garnishment is a court order directed to the person who owes the judgment debtor money. It is issued by the clerk under procedures that vary from state to state—consult your local garnishment statute.

**Putting It Into Practice:**

*Under the garnishment statutes in your state, what would Allen Porter have to do to garnish Park Hotels Group's bank account?*

---

*Your Local Notes*

_____

_____

The same procedure is used to seize the judgment debtor's wages. Wages are, again, in essence a debt owed by the employer to the employee. Here, however, there are limits imposed by federal law, as already noted: You can never seize more than one-fourth of the employee's take-home pay, or leave the employee with less than thirty hours per week of pay at minimum wage.

There are, of course, many other procedural weapons in the judgment collector's arsenal. Nearly all are creatures of state law, and each state has its own procedures. One of the requirements to use most of these weapons is that you must produce a final judgment that the clerk of the court, county recorder, or other official is willing to recognize. If your judgment comes from a court in the same state, at most you will need to get a certified copy from the clerk of the court that issued it. Federal judgments are entitled to the same treatment as a state court judgment; see 28 U.S.C. 1962.

If you have a judgment from one state and are chasing property in another state, however, the problem becomes more complicated. Although every state must give "full faith and credit" to the judgments of every other state, it may be necessary to go through additional procedures in the target state to have the judgment accepted. In some states, registering an out-of-state judgment is relatively simple: You can file the judgment with the clerk of a court in the target state, together with some additional papers and a filing fee. In others, it is necessary to sue on the judgment; that is, file a whole new lawsuit in the target state based on the debt created by the judgment, and obtain a new judgment in the target state!

## THE JUDGMENT DEBTOR'S OPTIONS

It should be obvious by now that a judgment debtor who is willing to resist collection aggressively and is not afraid to bend the rules can make it extremely tedious and difficult to convert a judgment into actual money! Litigation is an adversarial process, and you cannot necessarily expect a defendant to throw in the towel and pay up merely because you won a judgment.

The very best ways to escape paying judgments require advance planning, which is best done before engaging in any conduct that may lead to lawsuits. Everyone is familiar with the common type of armor against lawsuits: the corporation. One of the main reasons to incorporate a business is the fact that any lawsuit arising from the business goes against the corporation, not the shareholders. Say you have a million dollars in the bank, and you decide to go into the roller blade rental business. Every time one of your customers falls down, you risk losing your million in a lawsuit. But if you form a corporation, of which you are the sole stockholder, and you fund the corporation with a reasonable amount of capital—say, $25,000—your customers are stuck with suing the corporation, and the most they can get is (in theory) $25,000.

Naturally, plaintiffs' lawyers are always chipping away at the corporate shield, and every once in a while they manage to break through and get judgment against the shareholders—no defense is perfect. In the professions of, for example, law and medicine, the corporate shield does not work because ethical rules make the individual lawyer or doctor liable for malpractice even if his practice is incorporated. Does this mean that a doctor can never become judgment proof? Not at all. It just takes more complicated planning, involving (for example) a combination of a limited partnership and a trust created in a suitable foreign country. There are lawyers who specialize in setting up such arrangements, which make it possible for individuals to have essentially unlimited amounts of money without any risk that a successful plaintiff can reach any of it to satisfy a judgment.

What if the judgment debtor did not plan ahead? There are still a number of options, ranging from some that are clearly legal and appropriate to others that are clearly illegal but nonetheless often resorted to.

*Putting It Into Practice:*

If Park Hotels Group did business in your state and Allen Porter had a judgment against Park Hotels Group from another state, what would Mr. Porter have you do to register the judgment in your state?

If the judgment debtor is a natural person—a live human being as opposed to a corporation or other entity—the first line of defense is to take advantage of the exemption statutes. It is perfectly legal for the judgment debtor to take assets that could be seized and convert them into exempt assets, even after the judgment has been entered. A judgment debtor who has $50,000 in the bank may be able to render it unreachable simply by using it to pay down the mortgage on her house. Cash is subject to execution, but the equity in a debtor's personal residence is exempt in most states (at least to a set amount, such as $100,000).

Merely rearranging assets to take advantage of the exemption statutes does not, of course, extinguish the judgment. The instant that the judgment debtor acquires any nonexempt property, the judgment creditor can swoop down and levy on it. And if the judgment creditor wants to "play hardball," there is nothing to prevent him from garnishing each of the judgment debtor's paychecks, even if the amount to be collected that way is limited. Can the judgment debtor do anything to escape this aggravation? Certainly: File for bankruptcy. The bankruptcy court will allow the debtor to keep all exempt property and grant a discharge in bankruptcy that will extinguish the judgment!

Another tactic is for the judgment debtor simply to move to another state with her assets—again, perfectly legal. In theory, the judgment creditor can pursue the assets in the new state, but doing so takes time and money, and will likely require hiring a lawyer in the new state—and if the judgment creditor gets close, the judgment debtor can always move again. And if moving to another state is not enough to seriously dampen the judgment creditor's enthusiasm, moving to another country almost certainly will be. In theory, it is possible to collect judgments in other countries; in practice, except for a few friendly countries like Canada, it is difficult and expensive to the point of futility unless there is a huge amount of money at stake.

**Your Local Notes**

_____

_____

When the judgment is against a business entity, instead of an individual, exemption laws do not apply. Now the bankruptcy laws take on great importance. Chapter 11 of the bankruptcy act allows corporations and other business entities to file for "reorganization" under the bankruptcy laws. The bankruptcy court has the power to approve a "plan" for dealing with creditors that will allow the business to remain viable. Usually, the "plan" will involve paying off debts over a long period of time and at a substantial discount. Reorganization does not usually result in the judgment debtor making a clean getaway—some amount will have to be paid sooner or later—but once a Chapter 11 filing has occurred the judgment creditor is unlikely to see his money any time soon.

Judgment debtors who do not mind breaking the law (and there are surprisingly many of them) can make collection difficult or impossible by the simple expedient of transferring their property to someone else. Consider a simple hypo: Joe Sixpack crashes into your car and breaks your arm, so you sue him and get a judgment for $50,000. Joe has plenty of money. He also has a sister, Jane, whom he trusts completely, and who lives in another state. Before you can execute on your judgment, Joe makes a "gift" to Jane, and all Joe's money winds up in Jane's bank account. Now what? You do not have a judgment against Jane!

Most states have laws against so-called "fraudulent conveyances." In general, a **fraudulent conveyance** is any transfer made by a judgment debtor that leaves him without sufficient assets to pay the judgment. The specifics of fraudulent conveyance laws are quite technical, and not all transfers will be

***Putting It Into Practice:***

*If your dog bit a house guest and you were afraid of losing your limited assets if you were sued, how would you go about protecting those assets from being seized?*

found fraudulent. The real problem for the judgment creditor, however, is this: Once the transfer is made, the assets are in the hands of someone else, against whom there is no judgment. Before you can garnish the money in Jane Six-pack's account, you need a judgment against Jane. The fraudulent conveyance laws probably entitle you to ask for one, but getting it may take the equivalent of another lawsuit! And by the time you get the judgment against Jane, she may have given the money to her cousin Bob. . . .

Perhaps, by now, you are beginning to understand why most lawyers avoid suing individuals unless they have insurance. As a practical matter, individuals (and small business companies) who are sufficiently determined can make judgment collection so difficult as to not be worth the expense.

---

*Your Local Notes*

_____

_____

---

*Putting It
Into Practice:*

*What should Allen Porter anticipate Park Hotels Group might do to avoid collection? What could he do in response?*

## ROLE OF THE PARALEGAL

In personal injury practices, which probably account for a majority of litigators, judgment collection is rarely a problem—the target is always insurance. Normally, personal injury litigators do not file lawsuits in cases where judgment collection problems may arise.

At the other extreme, some lawyers make a specialty of collecting debts. They represent doctors, dentists, hospitals, collection agencies—anyone with a large volume of delinquent bills to collect. In a debt collection practice, obtaining judgments is usually easy and routine, because most delinquent debtors do not contest the suit. Here, judgment collection becomes a large part of the practice. Debt collection practices are high-volume operations, because of the relatively small amounts usually involved in each case. To keep the volume of cases flowing efficiently, the paperwork is usually computerized and highly dependent on the use of forms. Much of this work is perfectly suited for paralegals—the dollar amounts involved are too small to justify much attorney time, yet more legal judgment is needed than an untrained clerk is capable of bringing to bear. The paralegal in such a practice will be given extensive responsibility, and the attorneys may never even review most of the files.

Somewhere in the middle are the litigators who handle commercial litigation, suits involving business disputes. Collection problems often arise in commercial cases, because the targets are often able to pay for a considerable amount of legal planning and maneuvering in their efforts to escape payment. Such cases involve meticulous strategizing by the lawyers, and the paralegal's role is a supportive one, carrying out individual assignments, often involving the discovery aspects of judgment collection.

*Putting It
Into Practice:*

*What would be the benefits of working as a paralegal for an attorney who had primarily a debt collection practice? What would be the downside?*

## APPEAL

*"Well, Chuck, that's how I spell relief," said Allen Porter, hanging up the phone. "S-u-p-e-r-s-e-d-e-s."*

*"They filed the bond?"*

*"Yesterday. I was pretty sure Gail was bluffing about them being judgment proof, just trying to con me into taking their $100,000 settlement offer."*

*"You must have been sweating—if they really hadn't had any assets we could execute on, and you turned down $100,000. . . ."*

*"That's why you always, always, keep the clients informed and let them make the final decision. With proper advice, of course."*

An appeal is a procedure for challenging the decision of the trial court. The court of appeals has the power to *reverse* the trial court's decision—that is, to set it aside—or to *affirm,* and let the trial court's judgment stand as it is. If the court of appeals reverses, the case will ordinarily be sent back to the trial court for a new trial. However, if the court of appeals is able to determine from the record what the trial court decision should have been, it may not be necessary to retry the case. The court of appeals will simply instruct the trial court to enter a different decision.

Appeals are about error. Before the court of appeals will reverse or modify a trial court judgment, the court must be persuaded that **reversible error** was committed in the trial court. Not all error is reversible error. Probably no case makes it all the way to judgment without a few errors along the way, and if the errors are trivial, or if they did not affect the ultimate outcome of the case, they will be branded "harmless error" and the judgment will be affirmed in spite of them. Reversible error comes in many flavors; a few common ones are allowing evidence that should have been excluded, refusing to allow evidence that should have been admitted, or misstating the law in a jury instruction, or refusing to give a jury instruction that should have been given. Reversible error can also come from the judge's rulings on various pretrial motions.

One kind of error that courts of appeals generally never address is error committed by the jury in deciding the facts. The jury had the opportunity to hear the witnesses in person and observe them, while the court of appeals has only the cold, sterile record. The court of appeals will not substitute its judgment for that of the jury. The court of appeals reviews the *process* of a trial, not the *outcome.* The court will reverse if the process was not conducted according to the rules, but will not reverse merely because the members of the court of appeals would have reached a different verdict than the jury did. (Of course, one part of the *process* is the motion for judgment notwithstanding the verdict—if the verdict is so clearly contrary to the evidence that "reasonable minds could not differ," then the trial judge should have granted judgment n.o.v., and the court of appeals can send the case back with an order to do so. In that sense, the court of appeals can review the "outcome" in an extreme case.)

Normally, appeals involve only one or a few specific errors (or claimed errors). The court of appeals does not comb through the whole record looking for mistakes. It is up to the appellant to do that, and to specify exactly what errors appellant is asking the court of appeals to consider. We will discuss the procedures for doing this, but first we need to review some terminology.

The party who starts the appeal is called the *appellant.* All other parties are called *appellees.* Notice that the appellant may be either the plaintiff or the defendant. Usually, the appellant is the party that lost the case, but it is also possible for the winner to appeal. For example, plaintiff may win a substantially smaller amount of money than expected and decide it is worth going through the delay and expense of an appeal in order to get a chance at another shot with a different jury. (Of course, for this tactic to succeed, plaintiff will have to find some reversible error on which to base the appeal.) There can also be **cross-appeals;** in fact, when the loser appeals, it is quite common for the winner to cross-appeal. In our hypo, for example, Park Hotels has appealed. Allen Porter will at least consider a cross-appeal on Shannon's behalf—otherwise, the court of appeals will hear about, and possibly reverse, those of the trial judge's rulings that Park Hotels did not like, but will never hear about whatever erroneous rulings went against Shannon. If the case should be reversed, the rulings adverse to Park Hotels will be changed, and the ones adverse to Shannon would stay the same.

*Putting It Into Practice:*

*If Park Hotels Group appeals and Shannon cross-appeals, who will be the appellant? The appellee?*

> *Your Local Notes*
>
> _____
>
> _____

An appeal can be made only after a final judgment is entered. This rule may not seem to make much sense—after all, if the judge makes some fatal error early in the case, why should you have to waste time and money litigating to a final judgment, only to have the case sent back for a new trial? The reason for prohibiting **interlocutory appeals**—appeals taken before the case is over and judgment entered—is simple expediency. Appellate courts are afraid (probably with good reason) that cases would be appealed "piecemeal," with one attorney or the other running off to the court of appeals every time the trial judge made a decision on some minor motion. There are a few limited ways to get interlocutory review (see sidebar), but, on the whole, the final judgment rule is strictly enforced.

The appeal process begins with the appellant filing a **notice of appeal** with the clerk of the trial court. (The court of appeals is a *different* court, and it has its own clerk and administrative staff.) The notice of appeal is a court paper, typically one page, which simply says that the party filing it is appealing. The notice of appeal sets in motion a chain of events that varies somewhat from court to court. In the federal system, the courts of appeals follow the Federal Rules of Appellate Procedure, which is another set of rules nearly as extensive and complicated as the Federal Rules of Civil Procedure. Each court also has local rules. State appellate courts also operate under a separate set of rules that are applicable only to appeals—typically, the rules of civil procedure that govern the trial courts do not apply, because appeal proceedings are quite different from trials.

After the notice of appeal is filed, several things must happen more or less simultaneously; the exact procedure for doing them is prescribed by the rules. The trial court must transmit the record to the court of appeals. The entire record can be huge. It includes the transcript of the trial, the trial exhibits, the entire court file containing the pleadings and other court papers, and, potentially, various court papers pertaining to discovery, which, under modern practice, may not have been filed with the court. Therefore, there will likely be some procedure whereby the parties can designate the parts of the record that they intend to use in the appeal, so as to avoid having to prepare and transmit unnecessary items. Arrangements must be made for the court reporter to transcribe the shorthand notes and prepare a typed or printed transcript of the testimony. Preparing and transmitting the record typically takes several weeks to several months.

Once the record has been transmitted, the parties will have a short time in which to submit written arguments, called *briefs*. The content of a brief is similar to that in a legal memorandum in support of a motion in the trial court. That is, it consists of an argument, citing **authorities** (statutes and reported appellate cases), giving reasons why the court of appeals should reverse or not reverse the case. Briefs are, however, much more formal documents than trial court motions. Appellate court rules typically require briefs to be bound like a booklet, to include a table of contents, table of cases cited, and other formal niceties, and to conform to quite picky rules of style and layout. (One stylistic matter that all beginning lawyers and paralegals suffer through at first is the requirement that citations of cases and other authorities conform to very finicky rules that say how each source must be abbreviated, what order sources are cited in, and even where the periods, commas, and parentheses go. Appellate briefs reach a much higher level of fastidiousness than typical trial court motions.) There will also be a page limit, and the clerk will refuse to accept briefs that exceed it.

***Putting It Into Practice:***

*Why do you think the rules surrounding briefs are so exacting?*

## SIDEBAR

## Interlocutory Appeals

*As you might expect, attorneys are always looking for ways to get around the final judgment rule. It can be a bitter pill to swallow when the trial judge makes some absurd ruling (yes, this does occasionally happen!) that essentially destroys your case, and you have to waste months or years and spend tens of thousands of dollars of your client's money taking the case to trial, before you have a chance to ask the court of appeals to fix the problem. Or, if you represent a defendant in a suit where plaintiff's claims are essentially frivolous and should be dismissed out of hand, you can become frustrated when the trial court denies your motion for summary judgment. Now your client has to bear the expense of a trial, spending huge sums that she will probably never get back.*

*A few strategies are possible that can be tried in such situations. One involves so-called "extraordinary writs." These are (or evolved from) arcane appellate court petitions with names that reek of history, like "certiorari," or "mandamus," or "quo warranto," that were originally intended for other purposes, and have been bent to the task of giving the court of appeals an excuse for reaching down and fixing a particularly egregious trial court mistake. The procedures involved vary enormously from one court to another, and we will not attempt to elucidate them here. These petitions are often tried and seldom successful.*

*In federal court and in some state courts, the trial judge has the power to "certify" a ruling for immediate appeal. Naturally, the trial judge will do this only if the ruling is important and the judge is in some doubt about its correctness. Also, under FRCP, Rule 54(b), the trial judge can declare a judgment that disposes of part but not all of the lawsuit to be final for appeal purposes; this is often done when, say, the judge grants summary judgment as to some defendants but sets the case for trial as to the others.*

### Putting It Into Practice:

*Suppose in Shannon's case the judge makes a ruling that is critical to Shannon's position and that involves an unsettled area of law in that jurisdiction. What might Allen Porter do if the ruling is adverse to him? What should Allen Porter have done to prepare for such an eventuality prior to the ruling?*

---

*Your Local Notes*

_____

_____

---

Briefs are filed with the clerk of the court of appeals, in the familiar three-stage sequence: appellant's **opening brief,** giving reasons why the court of appeals should reverse the trial court's decision; appellee's **responding brief,** arguing the contrary; and finally, appellant's **reply brief,** typically much shorter than the other two, in which appellant answers any new arguments raised in appellee's responding brief. Appellate court rules provide for time deadlines for filing these briefs that are typically about a month apart. In practice, the opposing lawyers often agree among themselves to extend the deadlines, since it is a major undertaking to do a professional job on an appellate brief, and a few extra weeks spent on the briefs makes little difference in the context of an appeal that will likely drag on for at least another year.

Tedious and slow though it may be to take a case from complaint to verdict, trial courts move at supersonic speed compared to the glacial pace of most appellate courts. After all the briefs have been filed, the appeal is said to be "at issue"; the next step is to wait for the court of appeals to take up the case for decision. This can take anywhere from six months to several years, depending on the court and the level of its backlog.

At some point, the appeal will be assigned to the panel of judges that will decide it. Appeals are heard and decided by panels of (typically) at least three appellate court judges. Often, the judges making up the panel will meet with each other periodically and divide up their pending cases, so that each appeal will be assigned to one judge for a preliminary workup. Each appellate judge has one or more law clerks (clerking for an appellate judge is a sought-after apprenticeship for new lawyers) who will be assigned the work of reading the briefs, researching the legal issues, and making recommendations to the judge.

Appellate cases can be decided either with or without oral argument. In some cases, the parties may decide to waive argument (or not request it) and submit the case for decision on the written briefs. Why? Typically, because it gets the case decided faster! In others, the court of appeals may not wish to hear argument.

When argument is allowed, the attorneys appear at the court of appeal's courtroom at the designated time and present a formal argument. Unlike arguments on trial court motions, appellate arguments are formal affairs, never done in chambers, and each side will be under strict time limits—the court will cut the lawyers off in mid-sentence if they try to keep talking after the time runs out. As a rule, appellate judges tend to be well prepared for argument, and will have read and understood the briefs. Therefore, the attorneys will not be allowed simply to repeat what is in the briefs. Most of the argument time will be spent answering pointed questions from the judges, not only about the case being decided, but also about any cases cited as authorities in the briefs. Skillful appellate lawyers learn to work their best arguments into their answers to the judges' questions.

At some time after hearing argument (or earlier, if the case is not to be orally argued), the panel of judges who will decide the appeal holds a conference, makes a tentative decision, and assigns one of their number to write an opinion. This written opinion will not only decide the case, it will also describe the pertinent facts, indicate what questions the court is deciding, and explain the decision and the reasons underlying it. Other members of the panel may, if they wish, write concurring opinions—opinions agreeing with the result but disagreeing with all or part of the reasoning in the main opinion—or dissenting opinions—opinions disagreeing with the result reached by the majority of the panel. Appellate court opinions like these serve both to inform the parties of the outcome of the appeal and as a part of the common law, furnish rules to be applied in future cases.

Once the opinions have been completed, copies are sent to the attorneys. Several months typically elapse between oral argument and announcement of the decision. At the same time or within some short time period thereafter (prescribed by rules), the court of appeals issues a mandate. A **mandate** is an order telling the trial court what to do next. The appellate court's decision may require a new trial, require the trial court to change the judgment in some way or follow other specific instructions, or simply sustain the trial court's judgment.

For the party who loses the appeal, this is not quite the end of the appellate road: The state supreme court can be asked to review the court of appeals' decision. The procedure for asking for this additional review varies, but it is (almost) always discretionary. The supreme court can, and usually does, refuse to consider the matter, in which case the court of appeals' mandate will stand and little if any additional time will be lost. If the supreme court does decide to review the appeal, the decision process will begin again in the supreme court, and additional months or years will pass before the supreme court issues its own written opinion and mandate.

***Putting It Into Practice:***

*Why do you think attorneys often advise clients not to appeal a judgment?*

> *Your Local Notes*
>
> _____
>
> _____

## ROLE OF THE PARALEGAL

Appellate practice tends to be divided between specialists, who devote all or most of their practice to handling appeals, and general litigators, some of whom prefer to handle the appeals that arise from their own cases. The biggest single task in an appeal, in terms of the time and effort required, is researching and writing the briefs. Most of this research and writing is necessarily done by attorneys, because the legal issues involved are usually somewhat novel or complex. (If they were routine, the answers would be clear and there would be no need for an appeal!) In larger firms, brief writing is often a job for associate attorneys who are recent law school graduates; nevertheless, some paralegals do, with experience, develop the skills and judgment necessary to make a contribution in the research arena.

The other primary consideration in appellate work is meticulous compliance with the detailed requirements of the rules, especially those that impose deadlines for various tasks. There is considerable scope for paralegal involvement in scheduling, docketing, and maintaining the flow of paperwork, and in monitoring the brief-printing process for compliance with format and style rules.

*"Shannon Martin, calling from Seattle."*

*"Put her through."*

*"Hi, Allen, long time no see. I hear you have good news for me."*

*"Yes. I'm glad you got my message. New job going well, I hope?"*

*"Great! So, don't keep me in suspense—what happened?"*

*"I assume you got my letter, telling you that the court of appeals affirmed our judgment. The supreme court has turned down the hotel's petition for review, so that's it. It's over."*

*"Just like that? So, finally, after—what is it, almost four years?—I'm finally going to get some money out of this?"*

*"That's right."*

*"I get paid?"*

*"You get paid."*

*"Are you sure there isn't one more 'procedure' the hotel can take? It seems as though, this civil litigation—you never get to the end."*

*"That's true, in a way. If they were determined to keep litigating, they could always try the U.S. Supreme Court, or file a countersuit in a different state—but those are desperation moves, and they wouldn't stop us from collecting on the bond. And Crandall, Elkins is a reputable firm, they wouldn't be a party to that sort of thing. No, I think we're there—either they pay up or we hit the bond."*

*Shannon was silent for a moment. Four years of litigating. The expense, the hassle, the lost sleep. The aggravation of being raked over the coals by the hotel's lawyers, first in depositions and then on the witness stand at trial. Instead of helping her put her life back together after The Ordeal, the lawsuit had, if anything, added to the stress. She hadn't even gotten the satisfaction of seeing her attacker punished—Dr. Collins had gotten off without punishment. The hotel clerk who had apparently mixed up the keys was just an employee, so he wouldn't be paying anything either. Collecting some money from some anonymous Delaware hotel company just wasn't very satisfying, somehow, although she could certainly use the cash.*

*Now, finally, it was over.*

*Had it all been worth it?*

*Shannon could not say.*

## ETHICAL ETIQUETTE

One of the most important land mines for legal assistants to avoid is the unauthorized practice of law. Because the definition of the "practice of law" defies any reasonably precise characterization, legal assistants can become unwittingly ensnared in this controversial area of ethics if they do not use precaution. Debt collection is one of those areas of legal practice that skirts the edges of unauthorized practice for legal assistants. For that reason, we need to consider how the courts have defined what constitutes the practice of law.

Some unauthorized practice of law cases do attempt to define the practice of law, but most do not; therefore, we shall consult one of the more helpful treatises on ethics, Charles Wolfram's treatise *Modern Legal Ethics* (1986). Wolfram's synthesis of the case law on this subject indicates that most courts rely on one of three tests: (1) whether the activity involves professional judgment, that is, the skills and training unique to lawyers; (2) whether the activity is traditionally performed by lawyers; and (3) whether the activity is essentially legal in nature or is incidental to a business routine (e.g., filling out legal documents related to a real estate transaction and for which no separate fee is charged is not the practice of law). Those activities that clearly constitute the practice of law are representing clients in court, conducting depositions, giving legal advice, and signing pleadings. Those areas that clearly fall within the realm of legal assistant practice include drafting pleadings, preparing standard form documents, serving as a liaison with clients, carrying out legal and factual research, and organizing, summarizing, and analyzing legal documents.

Less clarity is found in classifying other areas of legal activity. Are legal assistants, for example, allowed to represent clients at administrative hearings? Some states authorize representation by legal assistants and other nonlawyers at administrative hearings and others do not. The federal government allows nonlawyers to practice in some of its administrative agencies, such as the Social Security Administration and the Small Business Administration. Some states allow legal assistants to attend real estate closings and the execution of wills without attorney supervision. Freelancing by legal assistants (serving as independent contractors) is becoming more common as some legal assistants have moved beyond offering litigation support services for attorneys and began offering their services directly to the public. In some states this increasing independence of legal assistants has come under criticism by those who perceive this encroachment on the territory of attorneys as a disservice to the public.

Routine debt collection is form-intensive work that is highly structured and computerized and requires little attorney input. For this reason many attorneys who specialize in debt collection rely heavily on legal assistants. But because at least one state (Illinois) has limited the practice of legal assistants in collection agencies, you would be well advised to consult the statutes and case law in your state before engaging in any activities that may be considered the practice of law.

# PRACTICE POINTERS
## *Locating Assets of Judgment Debtors*

Once you have obtained a final judgment against a defendant (or against the plaintiff on a counterclaim or an award for attorney's fees and/or costs) the process of collecting on the judgment begins. Many states have enacted the Uniform Enforcement of Foreign Judgments Act, or some amended version, that allows for the registration of any judgment not entered by that state's courts to be registered, and enforced, as if the judgment was rendered by that state's court.

Usually before, but certainly after registration of the judgment, the county recorder's records should be checked to see if any real property is held in the county by the judgment debtor. The county assessor's records should also be checked for records of certain personal property (such as mobile homes) and to give an idea of the value of the property.

The state's corporation commission should always be reviewed for corporate debtors to make sure they are still lawfully doing business. In many states some "bare-bones" financial records are part of the corporation's annual report. Usually the names of officers and directors, and their addresses, are also available.

Databases can be searched to find out if an individual defendant is a shareholder or officer or director of a corporation or a partner of a partnership or member of an LLC. Many states that mandate disclosure, however, require that only 10 or 20 percent or greater equity owners be listed.

If your state registers LLCs and partnerships at the corporation commission, you can find information on the entity at the commission. Some state's make it the responsibility of the secretary of state to maintain entity information.

Checking the secretary of state's office for UCC (uniform commercial code) filings can help determine if the debtor has borrowed money using personal property as collateral. If the debtor has made secured loans on personal property she should be listed as the secured party on the UCC-1 financing statement. This type of information can be especially helpful if your other efforts turn up empty. You could subpoena the file of the secured creditor to determine what assets were listed by the debtor to obtain the borrowed funds.

As the Internet becomes more sophisticated, new search engines are sure to be developed to assist in locating assets and the current engines refined to be of greater assistance.

## TECHNO TIP

When searching for the assets of debtors, do not forget to search the debtor's and his spouse's (if there is one) names separately. Some search engines (both on the Internet and governmental database engines) often search for the exact search term submitted. If the phrase "John Doe and Jane Doe" is used, many search engines will not list any "Jane Doe" hits that do not have a "John Doe" preceding it. All possible combinations should be used if you are not positive how the search engine functions; that is, "John Doe and Jane Doe," "Jane Doe and John Doe," "John and Jane Doe," "Jane and John Doe," "John Doe," "Jane Doe," "Doe, John," "Doe, Jane," etc.

# SUMMARY

The entry of judgment marks the end of the trial phase of a lawsuit but not necessarily the end of the dispute. If the judgment is in favor of the defendant for costs but not for attorney's fees, the plaintiff has the option of giving up or appealing. The situation is more complicated if the judgment involves a significant amount of money. In that case the judgment creditor may try to collect the monies awarded in the judgment and the judgment debtor may appeal.

A judgment creditor can begin collection proceedings immediately after the judgment is entered unless a motion for a new trial has been filed or a stay has been obtained. A stay can be obtained by posting a supersedes bond or it occurs automatically when a judgment debtor files bankruptcy. In federal court a ten-day waiting period is required before collection proceedings can begin.

Collectibility of a judgment is a key fact of litigation. Prior to filing suit, the plaintiff should take steps to ensure that a judgment can be collected. A judgment can probably be collected against a defendant corporation that appears solvent or a defendant that has sufficient insurance coverage. If a plaintiff can prove that punitive damages are justified, she is warranted in doing discovery that will reveal the defendant's assets. A judgment debtor's property and wages are protected to some extent by exemption statutes but the judgment can be executed through the seizure of any nonexempt property.

A judgment debtor's examination is used to determine the assets of a judgment debtor. These exams may be conducted at the court under the indirect supervision of a court officer or at the office of the attorney representing the judgment creditor. These exams are similar to a deposition; a court reporter may or may not be used. Judgment debtors are often summoned using a subpoena *duces tecum* so that they bring the documents containing the information necessary to locate and seize the debtor's assets. Tenacity is required when dealing with corporations of any size because they often do all they can to stonewall the process.

A judgment lien must be obtained before executing on real estate. This lien arises automatically in some states when the judgment is entered and must be recorded with the county recorder in other states. The judgment creditor can then file a suit for foreclosure, have the property sold, and apply the proceeds to the judgment. This process becomes more complicated if others also have rights to the property or if the property in question is the judgment debtor's home. Judgment creditors are strongly urged to record a judgment in the county recorder's office of every county in which the judgment debtor may own real estate.

To execute on tangible personal property a writ of execution must be obtained from the court clerk. As a practical matter these writs are of little value because by the time they are issued judgment debtors have often hidden or disposed of the property, the judgment debtor can refuse to allow the sheriff to enter his property when the sheriff arrives to levy on the property, and most such property is unlikely to sell for much at an auction.

The best assets to execute on are money and other financial assets that can be easily traced, such as bank accounts. To execute on a bank account, a writ of garnishment must be filed. The same procedure is used to seize a judgment debtor's wages; the procedures for garnishment vary from state to state.

To execute any judgment, a copy of the final judgment must be presented. If the judgment comes from a court in the same state, a certified copy from the court clerk that issued it will suffice. If the judgment comes from a state other than the one in which the judgment creditor is seeking to execute property, the procedures can be more complicated; in some states it is necessary to sue on the judgment by filing another lawsuit.

Judgment debtors can escape paying judgments by converting their assets into exempt assets (which can be done even after a judgment is entered), by filing for bankruptcy, or by moving to another state or foreign country. Doing the latter does not prevent the judgment creditor from pursuing the judgment but makes it more difficult and expensive to do so. Debtors can avoid personal liability by incorporating although the corporate shield does not protect lawyers and doctors from being liable for malpractice. Exemption laws do not apply to businesses and creditors can reach judgment debtors who have declared Chapter 11 bankruptcy but they are delayed in satisfying their judgment. Judgment debtors who are involved in fraudulent conveyances can frustrate judgment creditors (even though such transfers are illegal) by requiring them to get a judgment against the individual to whom the property was given.

Collection of judgments is rarely a problem in personal injury practice because the target of litigation is almost always an insurance company. Collection problems often do arise in commercial litigation, however, because the targets are often able to afford the considerable effort required to escape payment. Attorneys with debt collection practices often rely extensively on legal assistants because of the high volume and routine nature of their cases.

Appellate courts will reverse or modify a trial court's judgment if they believe reversible error has been committed. Reversal usually requires a new trial, although an appeals court may simply instruct the trial court to enter a different decision if the record reveals what the decision should have been. Appellate courts review the *process* followed by the trial court and not the *outcome;* therefore, they will not substitute their judgment for that of the jury. Appellants must specify the errors they believe were committed at the trial level; the appellate court will not comb the record looking for errors. Appellees also have an opportunity to file cross-appeals. Appeals cannot be taken before a final judgment is entered. Interlocutory appeals are prohibited out of a desire to prevent appeals from being made on a piecemeal basis. In the federal courts a trial judge can "certify" a ruling for immediate appeal if the ruling is very important and the judge has some doubt regarding the correctness of her ruling.

To initiate an appeal the appellant must file a notice of appeal with the clerk of the trial court. The trial court must then transmit the trial record to the appellate court. The parties can indicate the parts of the record they intend to use in the appeal so that not all of the record has to be transmitted. The court reporter prepares a transcript of the testimony. Once the record is transmitted, both parties submit written briefs, which must conform to strict stylistic rules and fall within designated page limits. The appellant's opening brief is followed by the appellee's responding brief, which is followed by the appellant's reply brief. Several months or even years may transpire after the appeal is at issue until the appellate court hears the appeal.

Appeals are typically heard by panels of three judges. Each of the judges has one or more law clerks who read the briefs, research the issues, and make recommendations to the judge. Oral arguments, which may be waived by the parties, are formal arguments made within strict time limits during which the attorneys must respond to pointed questions posed by the appellate judges. After oral arguments, the judges meet in conference, make a decision, and assign one of the judges to write an opinion. Other judges may prepare concurring or dissenting opinions. Copies of the opinion are sent to the attorneys and a mandate is issued to the trial court. The party who loses the appeal can try to appeal to the state supreme court although supreme courts usually deny such requests. If the supreme court denies review, the mandate of the court of appeals stands.

## KEY TERMS

Authorities
Cross-appeal
Execution
Fraudulent conveyance
Garnishment
Interlocutory appeal
Judgment creditor
Judgment debtor

Judgment debtor's examination
    (debtor's exam)
Judgment lien
Judgment proof
Lien
Mandate
Notice of appeal
Opening brief

Reply brief
Responding brief
Reversible error
Stay
Supersedes bond
Writ of execution

## Workshop Alert

*The following workshop correlates well with this chapter and you would be well advised to work with it.*

Workshop 18             How to Obtain a Judgment

## REVIEW QUESTIONS

1. What is the relationship between a judgment creditor and judgment debtor?

2. How are appeals and collections connected?

3. Must a judgment creditor wait before an appeal is decided before being able to collect a judgment?
   a. How can a judgment debtor prevent a judgment creditor from collecting a judgment?
   b. How can a judgment debtor obtain a stay?
   c. How does a supersedes bond protect a judgment creditor and assist a judgment debtor?

4. How can a plaintiff determine whether he will be able to collect a judgment against a defendant? Is it reasonable to assume that one can collect on a judgment levied against a defendant who is working? Why or why not?

5. What occurs at a debtor's exam? Why is a subpoena duces tecum often used to summon a judgment debtor to a debtor's exam?

6. What is meant by executing on a piece of real property?
   a. How does one execute on real estate?
   b. How does a judgment lien help a judgment creditor to collect a judgment?
   c. What is the potential problem with judgment liens?

7. How does one execute on tangible personal property?
   a. How does a judgment creditor obtain a writ of execution?
   b. Why are writs of execution on tangible personal property often worthless?

8. What are a judgment creditor's best targets and why?
   a. How does one execute on a bank account?
   b. What does a writ of garnishment provide?

9. Why is it difficult to execute on property in state B if a judgment was obtained in state A?

10. Why is it said that winning a judgment is only half the battle?

11. How does the corporate entity protect individuals from paying judgments?
    a. How can a corporate entity discourage collection efforts by a judgment creditor?
    b. How can an individual protect herself against collection efforts by a judgment creditor?
    c. What is a fraudulent conveyance and how does it relate to collections?

12. Why are paralegals ideally suited for debt collection practice?

13. Does the fact that a trial court erred necessarily result in a reversal? Why or why not?

    a. In general is an error committed by a jury considered reversible error?

    b. Does a court of appeals review the outcome of a trial or the trial process?

14. Is an appellant necessarily a defendant and an appellee necessarily a plaintiff? Explain.

15. What is an interlocutory appeal?

    a. Why are interlocutory appeals usually prohibited?

    b. Under what conditions will a trial court certify a ruling for immediate appeal?

16. When does the appeal process begin?

    a. What happens once a notice of appeal is filed?

    b. What are the three types of briefs and when are they prepared?

17. Do all members of the court of appeals hear each case?

    a. How are appellate arguments organized?

    b. How do appellate court opinions shape the common law?

    c. What is a court of appeals mandate?

18. How likely is a state supreme court to review a court of appeals decision?

19. How does the speed of the appellate process compare with the speed of trial practice?

20. Use the following sets of words in a single sentence:

    a. Judgment creditor; stay; supersedes bond; appeal

    b. Judgment lien; writ of execution; garnishment; fraudulent conveyance

    c. Appellee; reversible error; cross-appeal; mandate

    d. Notice of appeal; appellant's opening brief; interlocutory appeal; harmless error

## PRACTICE EXAM

*(Answers in Appendix A)*     **MULTIPLE CHOICE**

1. Once a judgment is entered

   a. the defendant may agree to cancel a judgment for costs if the plaintiff agrees not to appeal.

   b. the judgment creditor can begin collection proceedings but must wait for at least one month.

   c. the judgment creditor should appeal.

   d. the judgment debtor can file an appeal even if a motion for a new trial is pending.

2. A stay

   a. is a court order that allows a judgment creditor to begin collection proceedings.

   b. can be obtained by posting a supersedes bond.

   c. is terminated when the judgment debtor files for bankruptcy.

   d. all of the above.

3. A supersedes bond

   a. guarantees that the money will be available to the judgment debtor when the appeal is over.

   b. does not require any form of security.

   c. is often an insurance contract from an approved insurance company.

   d. cannot be in the form of cash.

4. To determine a defendant's financial status

   a. a plaintiff should determine the extent of the defendant's insurance coverage.

   b. a plaintiff should allege punitive damages so that he is automatically entitled to review the defendant's financial records.

   c. a plaintiff should conduct extensive discovery into the defendant's property assets and wages.

   d. none of the above.

5. Debtor's exams

   a. can be held only at the courthouse.

   b. are supervised by an officer of the court who personally manages the debtor's examination.

   c. are always transcribed by a court reporter.

   d. consist of questions about the debtor's income and expenses.

*(Answers in Appendix A)* **MULTIPLE CHOICE**

6. A judgment lien
   a. may arise automatically when a judgment is entered.
   b. may not arise until the judgment is recorded at the county recorder's office.
   c. may have to be foreclosed by the judgment creditor.
   d. all of the above.

7. Writs of execution on tangible property
   a. are seldom useful because once they are obtained the judgment debtor has already disposed of or hidden the property.
   b. allow the sheriff to search the judgment debtor's property without the debtor's permission.
   c. must be prepared by a judge.
   d. all of the above.

8. To execute on a judgment
   a. the judgment creditor must first realize that not every state gives "full faith and credit" to judgments of other states.
   b. the judgment creditor must file a whole new lawsuit.
   c. the judgment creditor must be able to produce a final judgment that is recognized by the clerk of the court or the county recorder.
   d. all of the above.

9. Judgment debtors
   a. cannot protect their assets by converting them to exempt assets.
   b. are not protected by the corporate shield if they are doctors or lawyers.
   c. are not allowed to file bankruptcy and thereby escape paying a judgment.
   d. are protected from paying a judgment if they move to another state because judgment creditors cannot pursue assets in another state.

10. An example of reversible error is
    a. failure to give a jury instruction that should have been given or misstating the law in a jury instruction.
    b. error on the part of the jury in rendering its decision.
    c. refusing to allow evidence that should have been admitted or admitting evidence that should not have been admitted.
    d. a and c.

11. Once the appellant files an opening brief
    a. the appellee files a reply brief.
    b. the appellant has no more opportunities to respond to the appellee.
    c. the parties have an opportunity to make oral arguments almost immediately.
    d. none of the above.

## FILL IN THE BLANKS

12. Entry of _____Judgment_____ marks the end of the trial phase of a lawsuit.

13. The party to whom money is awarded in the judgment is called a ___Creditor___ , while the party that is ordered to pay money is called a ___Debtor___ .

14. A ___stay___ is a court order prohibiting the judgment creditor from initiating collection proceedings. It can be obtained by filing a

_____supersedeas_____ bond, which is a promise to pay accompanied by some form of security.

15. Seizing a judgment debtor's property and applying it to pay a judgment is called ___writ of execution___ .

16. The objective of a ___debtor's Exam___ is to find money or property of the judgment debtor.

17. A ___lien___ is a security interest that provides the right to sell property to pay off a debt

and when it comes from recording a judgment it is called a _Judgment lien_

18. A _Writ of Execution_ directs a sheriff to levy on tangible property and sell it at public auction.

19. A _garnishment_ is a court order directed to the person who owes the judgment debtor money; this process is used to execute on bank accounts.

20. A judgment debtor who transfers his assets to someone else, leaving himself with insufficient assets to pay a judgment is said to have carried out a _fraudulent conveyance_

21. An appellate court will reverse a trial court if it commits some kind of _reversible_ error but not it if commits a _harmless_ error.

22. When the loser in a lawsuit files an appeal, the winner frequently will file a _Cross-Appeal_.

23. _Interlocutory_ appeals, which are appeals taken before a final judgment is entered, are generally prohibited.

24. The appellate process begins when the _Appellant_, the party filing the appeal, files a _notice to Appeal_, a one-page paper that says an appeal is being filed. The _Appellee_, the party responding to the appeal, is then on notice that an appeal has been filed.

25. The appellant files an _Opening_ brief, which consists of arguments citing _Authority_ (statutes and case law); in response the appellee files a _responding_ brief, arguing to the contrary; and the appellant then files a _reply_ brief in which she answers any new arguments raised in the appellees' brief.

26. Once the court of appeals completes its opinion, it issues a _mandate._ instructing the trial court what it is to do.

## TRUE OR FALSE

27. Appeals and collections are separate processes although they are related strategically.   **T**  F

28. A judgment creditor can begin collection procedures immediately although in federal court a thirty-day waiting period is required.   T  **F**

29. A judge can require a judgment creditor to wait to begin collection proceedings until a motion for a new trial has been decided.   **T**  F

30. An insurance company will probably not issue a supersedes bond to an entity that has few assets.   **T**  F

31. A supersedes bond allows a judgment debtor to retain its money while pursuing an appeal and guarantees the judgment creditor that the money will be available after the appeal process is completed.   **T**  F

32. Filing for bankruptcy will result in an automatic stay of all proceedings against a judgment debtor.   **T**  F

33. Winning a judgment automatically results in a plaintiff getting paid.   T  **F**

34. Because insurance coverage is discoverable, ascertaining the extent of coverage can be used to help determine if any judgment would be collectible.   **T**  F

35. Exemption statutes allows judgment creditors to strip judgment debtors of all but the necessities of life.   T  **F**

36. Under federal law a judgment creditor can seize at least one-half of a judgment debtor's wages.   T  **F**

37. A subpoena duces tecum is often used to summon the judgment debtor to the debtor's examination.   **T**  F

38. Tenacity is often required in conducting a debtor's examination of a major corporation.   **T**  F

39. Having a judgment lien guarantees the judgment creditor of being paid.    T  **F**

40. In some states a judgment creditor with a judgment lien has to file suit for foreclosure and obtain a court order requiring the sheriff to sell the property at auction.    **T**  F

41. A judgment creditor should record a judgment in the county recorder's office of every county in which the judgment debtor may have real estate.    **T**  F

42. One of the best assets to execute on is bank accounts.    **T**  F

43. A judgment creditor cannot collect on a debt owed to a judgment debtor through the process of garnishment.    T  **F**

44. If a judgment creditor has a judgment from a state other than the one in which the debtor's property is located, the judgment creditor need only produce a certified copy of the judgment to the clerk of the court in the target state in order to execute on the judgment.    T  **F**

45. Not every state gives "full faith and credit" to the judgments of other states.    **T**  F

46. Each state has its own procedures regulating the registration of judgments.    **T**  F

47. One of the main reasons for forming corporations is that in the event of a lawsuit the corporation rather than the shareholders are liable.    **T**  F

48. The corporate shield does not protect lawyers and doctors from being personally liable for malpractice.    **T**  F

49. A judgment debtor cannot take assets that could be seized and convert them into exempt assets after a judgment has been entered.    T  **F**

50. Exemption laws do not apply to business entities.    **T**  F

51. When a judgment debtor files Chapter 11 bankruptcy the judgment creditor finds it easier to get the judgment paid.    T  **F**

52. Judgment debtors can legally escape paying a judgment by "gifting" their assets to a family member.    T  **F**

53. Despite the fraudulent conveyance laws, judgment creditors will often find it expensive and burdensome to seize assets once the judgment debtor has transferred them to someone else.    **T**  F

54. The collection of judgments is frequently a problem in personal injury litigation but rarely a problem in commercial litigation.    T  **F**

55. Legal assistants are utilized extensively by attorneys who specialize in debt collection.    **T**  F

56. If an appellate court reverses a decision of the trial court, the case must be retried.    T  **F**

57. An appellate court will not reverse or modify a trial court's judgment if the trial court committed harmless errors.    **T**  F

58. An appellate court will reverse a trial court decision if it would have reached a different verdict than the jury did.    T  **F**

59. Part of the appellate court's task is to comb through the record looking for errors.    T  **F**

60. Only the losers in lawsuits file appeals.    T  **F**

61. Interlocutory appeals are never allowed.    T  **F**

62. Federal court judges can "certify" a ruling for immediate appeal if they believe the ruling is important and that they may have erred in making that ruling.    **T**  F

63. The procedural rules that control the appellate process are different from but nearly as extensive and complicated as those controlling the trial process.    **T**  F

64. The parties have a right to designate the parts of the record they intend to use on appeal.    **T**  F

65. Preparation of the record is relatively straightforward and often completed in a few days.    T  **F**

66. Briefs are very similar in style and content to trial court motions.    T  **F**

67. Once the appeal is at issue the appellate court will hear oral arguments almost immediately.    T  **F**

68. Appeals are almost always heard by panels of three judges.    **T**  F

69. Appellate judges usually have one or more law clerks who read the briefs, research the issues, and make recommendations to the judges.  **T** F

70. Oral arguments are heard in every case.  **T** **F**

71. Oral arguments are relatively informal affairs in which the judges ask the attorneys to respond to questions they have about their briefs.  **T** **F**

72. After oral arguments the judges meet in conference and assign one of the judges to write the opinion.  **T** F

73. Concurring opinions agree with the reasoning of the majority opinion but disagree with the result.  T **F**

74. The parties are usually informed of the appellate court's decision within days of oral arguments.  T **F**

75. In most cases the state supreme court refuses to consider issues brought before it and the mandate of the court of appeals stands.  **T** F

76. Most briefs are researched and written by attorneys rather than legal assistants.  **T** F

## LITIGATION LINGO

*(Answers in Appendix A)*

**Unscramble the following words:**

1. YOURNITELCTOR — An appeal that is heard before a final judgment is entered
2. YAST — Court order prohibiting judgment creditor from collecting on judgment
3. DESREPUSSE DONB — Promise to pay accompanied by some form of security
4. RAGSHIN — What can be done to a judgment debtor's bank account or wages
5. TENLUARFDU YENEVOCACN — Illegal transfer of property by judgment debtor to avoid paying judgment
6. BELVERIRES — Type of trial court error that will result in appellate court changing trial court judgment
7. EPELPALE — Party responding to appeal
8. LYPER — Brief prepared by appellant
9. DMATENA — Order telling trial court what to do next
10. TOXICENEU — Process of seizing debtor's property and applying it to pay judgment
11. ROFOP — Judgment debtor with no assets is said to be "judgment _____"
12. MAXEAOTININ — Asset discovery begins with this
13. NIEL — Security interest similar to mortgage
14. SETUHROTIAI — Statutes and case law cited in appellate brief

## LITIGATION LOGISTICS

*(Answers in Appendix A)*

***For each question give the rule of civil procedure in your jurisdiction that applies and then answer the question.***

1. After reading this chapter, what would you want to ascertain before suing the drunk driver who damaged your vehicle? Suppose you discover that he is underinsured but that he has just begun working as a salesman for a major computer firm. What would you have to do under the laws of your state to garnish his wages?

2. Suppose you get a judgment against the corporation that owns the karate school employing the karate instructor who negligently hit you. What procedures must the corporation follow if it wants to prevent you from collecting on the judgment immediately?
   a. What must the corporation do to initiate an appeal?
   b. During what time frame must the corporation submit an opening brief?
   c. What are the page limits for each of these briefs?
   d. What format is required for these briefs? Must there, for example, be a table of contents and a table of authorities? Must they be bound?
   e. How many judges will hear your oral arguments (assuming you have oral argument)?

3. Suppose you obtain a judgment against your tenant. What options do you have in collecting on this judgment?
   a. Suppose the tenant owns a vehicle that is considered a collector's item and that is in excellent condition. What procedures would you have to follow to execute on this property?
   b. Would this vehicle be considered exempt in your state?
   c. What procedures would the sheriff have to follow in seizing and selling this vehicle?

d. Suppose the tenant gives this vehicle to his brother shortly after you obtain your judgment against him. Would this be considered a fraudulent conveyance under the laws of your state?

4. Suppose you obtain a judgment against the contractor who built your house and two of the subcontractors and that the contractor files for Chapter 11 bankruptcy. Will you be able to collect anything from the contractor?
   a. What procedures must you follow to collect on this judgment?
   b. What must you do to arrange a debtor's examination of the two subcontractors?
   c. Suppose one of the subcontractors owns the building in which his business is housed.
      i. How would you go about obtaining a judgment lien on this property?
      ii. What would you have to do to foreclose on this judgment lien?

5. Suppose that during the trial involving your dispute with your cousin that the trial judge makes a ruling that is critical to your case and that raises an issue that is novel in your state. You want to appeal this ruling before the trial goes on because a change in this ruling could easily alter the outcome of the case. What would you have to do in order to go forward with this appeal before the end of the trial?

   Suppose your cousin has countersued you on what you believe are totally frivolous grounds. You move to dismiss these claims but the trial judge refuses to dismiss them. Do you have any recourse to the court of appeals or must you simply expend the time and energy defending yourself against claims you know to be nonmeritorious?

## PROCEDURAL PONDERABLES

1. Consider each of the situations represented in the hypos presented in Chapter 1. What potential obstacles to collection can you conceive of in each case? What might you do if you were the defendant in those cases to protect yourself against collection?
   a. Drunk driver sideswipes your car.
   b. Tenant stops paying rent and refuses to move out.

   c. Cousin refuses to pay you a percentage of his business.
   d. Karate instructor breaks your nose.
   e. Contractor does shoddy work on house.

2. What would you do to expedite the appeals process? Would you focus on restricting appeals or streamlining the process?

## INTRODUCTION: THE SUBSTANTIVE BUILDING BLOCKS OF A LAWSUIT

Everyone knows that to win a lawsuit as a plaintiff, you must "prove your case." But what, exactly, is this "case" that you have to prove? Do you simply get the witnesses to tell what happened, and let the jury take it from there? Or are there specific things that you must prove in order to win?

**What a Cause of Action Is**—This workshop provides the answers to these questions. We will see that what the plaintiff must prove is something called a cause of action. Not all of the unpleasant things that people do to each other will support a lawsuit—only those particular categories of wrongful acts that the law recognizes as actionable wrongs will suffice. You might think of a cause of action as a kind of checklist that is used to determine whether the facts of a particular case fall within one of the actionable categories. The individual items on the checklist are called elements of the cause of action.

A simple example may make this clearer. In our hypo, suppose Shannon wants to sue the Las Vegas Police Department for false arrest. Obviously, not everyone arrested by the police is entitled to sue. We do some legal research and find that the law recognizes a tort called false imprisonment. We discover that the elements of false imprisonment are (1) confinement (2) which is intentional, and (3) the person confined is aware of the confinement or harmed by it. Therefore, Shannon would have to prove that she was confined; that the police intended to confine her; and that she was aware of being confined.

If Shannon fails to prove one of these required elements, she loses (as to that cause of action; there can be more than one in the same suit). One of the common ways to defend a case is simply to try to convince the judge (by motion for summary judgment) or jury (at trial) that one of the required elements of the cause of action has not been proved.

Another way for the defendant to win is to prove an affirmative defense. Affirmative defenses work exactly like causes of action: They are made up of elements that you find by researching the substantive law. In our example, one affirmative defense to the tort of false imprisonment is called privilege (or sometimes justification). We research the elements of the defense of privilege and find that a confinement is privileged if it is (1) done by a law enforcement officer (2) for a proper purpose. Therefore, even if Shannon proves all elements of the tort of false imprisonment, the Las Vegas Police Department can escape liability by proving that Sergeant Marnell is a law enforcement officer and that she detained Shannon for a proper purpose (i.e., to investigate the shooting).

**A Lawsuit Is Made Up of Claims**—In a lawsuit, the plaintiff will be trying to prove one or more **claims.** Each claim in the lawsuit represents one distinct cause of action—one combination of circumstances that the law recognizes as actionable. A simple lawsuit may be based on a single claim; a complex one may have a dozen or so. When the facts will arguably support claims based on more than one cause of action, it becomes a matter of strategy whether to limit the case to the best and easiest to prove, or whether to "shotgun" with every cause of action that might conceivably apply.

One or many of the claims and their elements are the building blocks of which the lawsuit is made. They define the specific things that the plaintiff will try to prove and the defendant will try to disprove. The concepts covered here will appear again and again, because the whole purpose of procedural law is to provide an orderly way of proving or disproving claims. An understanding of what claims are is essential at nearly every stage—studying civil procedure without understanding what claims are would be about like trying to study bricklaying without knowing what a brick is!

Figuring out what causes of action might apply to your fact situation, and what the elements of each of those causes of action are, is something that must be done in every lawsuit. Everything else you do during the rest of the lawsuit depends on getting this one thing right. As we will see in later workshops, the complaint must specifically set out each element of each cause of action on which you are suing; the complaint can be dismissed if an element is left out. If the defendant can persuade the court that it is impossible for the plaintiff to prove one of the elements, the court may grant a motion for summary judgment, ending the suit then and there. At trial, failure to prove each element can lead to a directed verdict against the plaintiff. When the case goes to the jury for decision, the jury's function, aided by instructions from the judge, will be to decide whether the plaintiff has proved each of the elements of a cause of action.

## SIDEBAR

### Claims, Causes of Action, and Theories of Liability

*These three terms—claim, cause of action, and **theory of liability**—are often used somewhat interchangeably. All involve a single concept, namely, a way of testing a specific set of facts to see whether it is appropriate for the court to step in and make someone pay.*

*If the defendant's act (or failure to act) is of a kind that the law recognizes as an actionable wrong, then a lawsuit can be sustained. When we say that a particular set of facts is actionable, we mean that there is some cause of action that applies to it and that each of the elements of that cause of action is present. Theory of liability usually refers to the rationale offered by the plaintiff for why the court should hold the defendant liable. As a practical matter, theories of liability that are not based on recognized causes of action do not usually get very far, so the two terms mean essentially the same thing.*

*A claim is an assertion of liability based on a single cause of action and made in an actual lawsuit. Again, because a claim is an assertion of a cause of action, the two terms have similar meanings. Thus, the judge may ask, "What claims has the plaintiff alleged?" or "What causes of action has the plaintiff alleged?" or even "What theories of liability has the plaintiff alleged?"*

**Where Do Causes of Action Come From?**—We have already seen several examples of causes of action: If a defendant has a duty to the plaintiff, and breaches that duty, and the breach causes damages, that is "negligence"; if the defendant confines the plaintiff, and does so intentionally, and the plaintiff is aware of or damaged by the confinement, that is "false imprisonment"; if the defendant touches the plaintiff, and does so in a manner that is offensive or harmful, that is "battery"; and so on. The law recognizes many causes of action—a few dozen commonplace ones and scores of more esoteric or specialized ones.

Where do all these causes of action come from? More importantly, how do you find out about them? Are they all listed in a book somewhere? Who gets to invent new ones?

Unfortunately, there is no "bible" you can go to that lists every cause of action. Causes of action have several sources. One is the courts, via the common law. Many of the more commonplace causes of action were invented in the English law courts and have been around for centuries. Others have been added or modified by American courts, usually at the appellate level. If the highest appellate court in a state (usually the state supreme court) declares that there is a cause of action for, say, putting anchovies on a pepperoni pizza, then, at least in that state, there is one! Because of this power of appellate courts to modify causes of action and invent new ones, the list of what things are actionable is constantly changing.

Legislatures also have the power to create causes of action. Many of the causes of action in technical areas of the law (i.e., securities fraud, commercial law, banking law) have been created by state legislatures or by Congress.

An enormous amount of study and experience is required to become expert in the causes of action that apply to a single area of the law (say, environmental law). Common law torts like battery or false imprisonment are relatively simple to understand and apply, but statutory causes of action in technical areas can be unbelievably complex. Learning what causes of action are applicable in various areas of the law is a great deal of what a law school education is devoted to.

## THE ISSUES OUTLINE

A client comes into your office with some "story" and wants you to file a lawsuit against someone. How do you decide what causes of action might apply?

One way—though not a particularly good way—is simply to listen and see what causes of action jump into your mind. These will doubtless be causes of action whose elements you are quite familiar with and which you can apply from memory. If your entire practice consists of, say, automobile negligence suits, this approach may actually work most of the time.

For more complicated situations, though, you need a more systematic approach—a way of making sure you have not overlooked any potential causes of action, a way of making sure you have checked each element.

## The Issues Outline: Step-by-Step Instructions

Hence, the *issue outline*. The issue outline is an outline of each of the possible causes of action and their elements as applied to the facts of your case, designed to foster a systematic, element-by-element analysis of the case. Do real lawyers

---

**Figure W1–1 The Issues Outline**

Step 1: Make a List of Possible Theories of Liability

Step 2: Determine the Elements of Each Theory of Liability

Step 3: Determine What Defenses May Apply

Step 4: Determine the Elements of Each Defense

Step 5: For Each Element of Each Cause of Action and Each Defense, List Each Fact Supporting It

Step 6: For Each Fact, List Each Item of Evidence Supporting It

---

actually do this? Most emphatically, yes. In complex cases, even very experienced litigators routinely go through the process described in this chapter—the mechanics may vary, some of the steps may be delegated to clerks, but the thought process is essential. In simple cases, experienced litigators may not need the issue outline process in every case, but that is merely because they have already done it in so many similar cases that they can now do it in their heads!

A properly prepared issues outline will yield rich dividends as the case proceeds, and you will revisit it again and again. When you draft the complaint, it will provide a reliable way to be sure that each claim states a valid cause of action, with no elements inadvertently left out. When the defendant moves for summary judgment, you will immediately be able to zero in on the issue and focus your research. The issues outline will make clear exactly what facts you must prove, thus serving as a framework on which to base your discovery plan. Even at the end of the case, when you are drafting jury instructions, the issues outline will tell you what instructions you need and what points need to be covered in each.

Should the defendant make an issues outline? Or can the defendant start with the causes of action alleged in the complaint and ignore anything else that might have applied, thereby avoiding the additional work of analyzing the case from scratch?

Sorry; the defendant should *always* defend on the assumption that the plaintiff will make the best case possible under the circumstances. Complaints can be amended. What if the plaintiff changes lawyers in midstream, the new lawyer takes a fresh look, and suddenly the defendant is facing some new theories? Furthermore, by analyzing the causes of action for herself, the defendant can often identify potential defenses that might otherwise be overlooked.

The issues outline is not a court paper, it will never be filed or seen by anyone outside your own office. Therefore, do not hesitate to modify the format, layout, or organization in whatever way may improve its usefulness for your particular project. In particular, you may want to start each new cause of action on a new page so as to be able to insert additional matter as you research. The steps for creating an issues outline are listed in Figure W1–1 and discussed in more detail next.

**Step 1** *Make a List of Possible Theories of Liability*

We will begin simply by listing every cause of action we can think of that might possibly apply. If we have a "collection" of causes of action in a notebook somewhere (see Figure W1–2), we can go through it one by one to jog our memories. If the facts of the case fall within some recognized branch of the law (i.e., tort, contract, securities law, or commercial law) we may skim through the table of contents of a textbook on the subject so as to pick up any causes of action we may have overlooked.

We list each possible cause of action *against each possible defendant.* To do this, we must consider what people and what entities we might conceivably sue.

At this stage, we do not worry about whether we have the facts to prove a given cause of action, or whether the cause of action may have some element that automatically ruins our case. If a cause of action is somewhere in the ballpark, we list it.

**Step 2** *Determine the Elements of Each Theory of Liability*

Now we take each of the possible causes of action we have listed and do whatever research is necessary to determine what its elements are. For well-established common law torts like battery, this may be as simple as finding an authoritative source (the *Restatement,*

**Figure W1–2   Causes of Action in Tort Cases**

NEGLIGENCE

Duty
Breach of duty
    Reasonableness of conduct
    Causation
    Actual (factual)
        Nature of cause
        Nature of harm
    Proximate
        Foreseeability
        Intervening and superseding causes
        Nature of the plaintiff
        Nature of harm caused

Damages
    Nature of damages
        General
        Special
        Punitive
    Extent of damages
    Calculation of damages
        Pain and suffering
        Medical expenses
        Property damage
        Lost wages
        Loss of consortium
        Impaired earning capacity
        Litigation expenses

DEFENSES TO NEGLIGENCE

Contributory negligence
Comparative negligence
Assumption of risk

INTENTIONAL TORTS

Assault
    Intent
    Apprehension of harm
    Ability to carry out threat
Battery
    Intent
    Harmful contact
    Offensive contract
False imprisonment
    Intent
    Confinement
    Knowledge of confinement
Emotional distress
    Intent
    Outrageous conduct
Nature of emotional distress

Trespass to land
    Intent
    Enter or remain unlawfully
    Contact with land
    Revocation of permission to enter
    Extent of liability
Trespass to chattels
    Intent
    Interference with chattel
    Actual harm
Conversion
    Intent
    Interference with chattel
    Transfer of title
    Extent of harm

DEFENSES TO INTENTIONAL TORTS

Consent
    Capacity to consent
    Scope of consent
    Voluntariness
Defense of person
    Extent of force
    Imminent harm
    Belief of actor
    Necessity of force

Defense of others
    Extent of force
    Imminent harm
    Belief of actor
    Necessity of force
    Belief of person being defended

**Figure W1–2  Causes of Action in Tort Cases,** *continued*

Defense of property
    Extent of force
    Imminent harm
    Belief of actor
    Necessity of force
    Duty to retreat
    Request that intruder stop
Regaining possession of chattel
    Extent of force
    Property wrongfully taken
    Belief of actor
    Fresh pursuit

Reentry on land
    Extent of force
    Belief of actor
    Purpose for entry
    Consent of possessor
Necessity
    Purpose of invasion
    Public or private interest
    Extent of invasion
    Damages

---

**STRICT LIABILITY**

Intent
Liability for animals
    Wild
    Domestic
Abnormally dangerous activities

Defective products
    Sale of product rather than service
    Nature of defect
    Time defect existed
    Causation
    Manufacture or sale by the defendant
    Nature of the plaintiff (who can sue)
    Nature of the defendant (who can be sued)

---

**DEFENSES TO STRICT LIABILITY**

Contributory negligence
Comparative negligence

Assumption of risk
Statute of limitations or repose

---

**MISREPRESENTATION**

Intent
    Intentional
    Negligent
    Innocent
    Inducing reliance on misrepresentation

Plaintiff's justifiable reliance
Nature of relationship between the plaintiff
    and the defendant
Causation
Damages

---

**DEFAMATION**

Harm to the plaintiff's reputation
Intent of the defendant
Status of the plaintiff (public official or public figure)
Interpretation of statement

Publication
Truth or falsity of statement
Damages
Privileged communications

---

**NUISANCE**

Substantial interference
Effect on the plaintiff's use of land
Plaintiff's interest in land

Extent of injury or interference with land
Nature of damages

Derived from the *Restatement 2d, Torts.*

as described in the next section, or an appellate case) and listing them. More complex causes of action, particularly those based on statutes, may require considerable research.

One caveat: For nonfederal causes of action, the elements can differ considerably from state to state. It is not enough to pull a general list of elements out of some textbook without also checking the case law in your state for any important variations.

> *Your Local Notes*
> _____
> _____

How much detail? The answer varies from case to case. One of the reasons why we are making an issues *outline* and not an issues *list* is because issues have subissues, elements have subelements. How do you decide whether the Las Vegas police are liable to Shannon for false imprisonment? You apply the elements of the cause of action for false imprisonment: confinement, intent, knowledge of confinement. But how do you decide whether the element of "confinement" is present? How do you decide whether Shannon was "confined"? Did anyone tell her she could not leave? Was the door locked? What does the term *confinement* mean? If you research the law of false imprisonment, you will find cases that will answer these questions. What you will discover is that just as "false imprisonment" has elements, such as "confinement," "confinement" itself has elements, and perhaps *its* elements have elements. Thus, after doing your research, you will finish with an outline of elements and subelements that may go several levels deep.

**How to Research Causes of Action and Their Elements**—Obviously, this is not the place for a treatise on legal research. We can, however, offer a few general suggestions to help with the issues outline project.

For a litigator or litigation paralegal, it is worthwhile to begin and maintain a collection of causes of action, starting with the most common ones. A notebook is useful for this purpose, with a divider for each cause of action, followed by a summary of its elements, a list of applicable defenses and their elements, and source material such as copies of appellate cases providing more detail on how the elements are applied.

Where can you find the necessary information about causes of action and their elements? Suppose, for example, that you want to determine the elements of the tort of false imprisonment. What sources should you consult?

For this and other tort causes of action, an excellent starting point is the *Restatement of the Law of Torts*. The *Restatement* is an attempt by a committee of academic experts to summarize various tort causes of action and list their elements concisely. We might also consult a tort textbook such as *Prosser on Torts*. Still another place to look is in the appropriate topic (such as "false imprisonment") in a legal encyclopedia such as *American Jurisprudence* or *Corpus Juris Secundum*. From sources such as these, we should be able to obtain enough information to list the main elements of false imprisonment.

Then we refine our research by checking the case law in our own state, for two reasons. One is that substantive law varies from state to state, so we want to be sure we are using the correct elements for our state. The other is that the case law is where we will find the detail necessary to resolve the subissues (such as deciding what "confinement" means). Old fashioned as it may seem, the best way to access the case law for our purposes is via the West Digest system, because it is already organized in a way that lays out the elements of the various causes of action in an outline form. (We will visit this point again later in the chapter.) On-line research can also be used, but cautiously! A computer search does not necessarily ensure that you have found every single element of the cause of action you are researching—most of the cases you find will analyze one element in great detail, rather than listing all the elements.

For other causes of action not based on tort, the approach would be similar, but using sources appropriate to the cause of action and area of law in question.

**Step 3**     *Determine What Defenses May Apply*

As we consult the various research sources to outline each cause of action, we will also be on the lookout for any defenses specific to that cause of action (for example, privilege or justification as a defense to false imprisonment). We list these in our outline under the causes of action to which they apply. As with the causes of action, at this stage we paint with a broad brush, listing any defenses that might conceivably apply without worrying about whether they can be proved or not.

There are also affirmative defenses that may apply to the entire lawsuit, rather than to individual causes of action. FRCP, Rule 8(c), lists some of the common ones. These include defenses that should be considered in every lawsuit, such as statute of limitations. [We will revisit Rule 8(c) in Workshop 8 on drafting responsive pleadings. Your instructor will inform you of any local provisions similar to Federal Rule 8(c) applicable in your state.]

Most of the Rule 8(c) defenses involve technicalities that go beyond the scope of this introductory chapter, so we will leave them for later. Keep in mind, however, that a proper issues outline should list the elements of any applicable affirmative defenses in the same way that we list the elements of the causes of action. If you represent the defendant, you should always run through a checklist of Rule 8(c) defenses to be sure you have considered each one. If you represent the plaintiff, you should do the same because you want to anticipate what defenses your opponent is likely to raise.

In addition to the Rule 8(c) defenses, several procedural defenses should be considered in every lawsuit: jurisdiction of the person, jurisdiction of the subject matter, venue, sufficiency of service of process, and indispensable parties. To some extent, analysis of these defenses will have to await the filing of the lawsuit because they depend in part on where and how it is filed. These defenses involve procedural issues that we have not yet covered, so we will leave them aside for now.

### Step 4 — Determine the Elements of Each Defense

Following the methods described in Step 2, we determine and include in our issues outline the elements of each of the defenses we have listed.

### Step 5 — For Each Element of Each Cause of Action and Each Defense, List Each Fact Supporting It

Now we are ready to start tying the elements to our facts. Under each element of each cause of action, we list every fact that we can think of that tends to prove or *disprove* that element. For example, under the element "confinement" of the cause of action "false imprisonment," we might list on the positive side such facts (if true) as "Shannon tried the door to the interrogation room and it was locked," or "Shannon asked to go to the bathroom and an officer was sent to accompany her" or "The police officer told Shannon she was under arrest." These facts would tend to show that she was not, in fact, free to leave. On the negative side we might list (if true) "While Shannon was at the emergency room, the accompanying officer left and came back an hour later carrying a box of doughnuts."

We list all the facts that we are aware of, regardless of whether we think we can prove them. We also list any important facts that we think *could* have happened, both positive and negative, because we will be using this list to guide our investigation and discovery. By approaching the problem in a systematic way from causes of action to elements to facts supporting the elements, we provide ourselves with a checklist of facts to look for. As often as not, the spectacular piece of evidence that wins the lawsuit—the "smoking gun"—is not discovered by accident, it is discovered because someone realized that this particular piece of evidence could win the suit and went looking to see if it might exist. What, for example, might really nail down the confinement issue? How about, "Emergency room doctor had to ask officer to remove handcuffs?" Did this happen? We do not know, at this stage, but now that we have thought about it, we should certainly try to find out.

### Step 6 — For Each Fact, List Each Item of Evidence Supporting It

How is Step 6 different from Step 5? Facts and evidence are not the same thing. A fact is some event that happened; evidence is something we can use in court to prove that the event happened. "Shannon tried the interrogation room door and it was locked" is a fact. Shannon could testify in court that she tried the door and it was locked—her *testimony* would be evidence. If that were our only evidence, we might be concerned, because all it would take is for a police officer to testify to the contrary—at this stage, we have no idea what the police officer will say—and suddenly our proof of this fact is a long way from a slam dunk. We might look for other evidence: Perhaps the lock on this door is designed so that it is always locked and requires a key to open, in which case we could obtain the manufacturer's specifications for the lock.

At this stage, we have assembled very little actual evidence. We take this opportunity to list, in our outline, under each element of each cause of action, all the evidence that we think we might be able to get, through investigation, discovery, or from the client. For example, under the "damages" issue, we will need to prove the fact that Shannon spent some specific amount of money for her emergency room treatment. As evidence of that fact, we will need copies of the medical bills. We do not have them yet, but we list them so that we will remember to obtain them.

**Conclusion**—Notice that we have still not attempted to make judgments about which of our causes of action will be used. We will do that as we prepare the complaint. At this stage, we are wearing our "creative" hat, in keeping with our purpose of trying to think of every possible approach that might benefit us. Later, we will put on our "judgmental" hat and take a critical look at each cause of action, rejecting any that fail to advance our overall strategy.

## The Issues Outline: Learning by Example

We now offer an example of the issues outline process, based on our Shannon hypo. We limit this example to the potential claims against Dr. Collins, so as to leave the remaining claims for use in exercises for you, the student, to complete.

**Step 1** *Make a List of Possible Theories of Liability*

Against Dr. Collins only, the "obvious" theories of liability are assault and battery. (Assault is one cause of action, battery is another.) What other causes of action might apply? We look through the table of contents of the *Restatement* or of a torts textbook, considering and accepting or rejecting causes of action one by one. Many can be rejected instantly—this is not a libel case or trespass on land—or is it? Maybe we should take a closer look at trespass. Negligence is a real possibility: Dr. Collins was evidently careless about making sure which room he was entering. Outrageous conduct causing mental distress is a cause of action under the *Restatement* and in some states is one worth considering. We may also take a look at the Nevada statutes, since it is always possible that the Nevada legislature may have created some cause of action for, say, sexual assault.

*Your Local Notes*

_____

_____

Why would we care about adding these other, esoteric causes of action when we have something simple like battery? Because the elements of each will be different. We may run into some unexpected problem with some element of our battery cause of action. Also, some causes of action are easier to prove than others. Probably, in this case, we will stick to assault, battery, and perhaps negligence. On the other hand, we might find that there is a Nevada statute entitling any female person who proves (say) that another person entered her hotel room without permission to sue for a civil penalty of $10,000 per offense, regardless of intent—unlikely, but possible. We will never know unless we look.

**Step 2** *Determine the Elements of Each Theory of Liability*

Next we research the elements of each of the causes of action we have listed. The assault and battery causes of action are sufficient for illustration purposes; in a real-life case, we would research the elements of each possible cause of action.

Assault and battery are torts that are created by state law, not federal law. To be entirely sure that we have identified the correct elements, we would need to find a reported decision of an appellate court in the state whose laws will apply to this suit (here, most likely Nevada, since it is the place where the tort occurred). An equally good source, if it exists and can be obtained for the state in question, is the book of recommended jury instructions for the courts of that state. Keep in mind that if you miss one of the required elements of a particular cause of action, you are inviting a motion to dismiss as to that cause of action.

*Your Local Notes*

_____

_____

You will sometimes find that there are no appellate decisions in your state that specify the elements of a given cause of action. Then you will have to use a secondary source such as the American Law Institute's *Restatement of the Law* series. Here is what the *Restatement (2d) of Torts* says about assault and battery:

Section 21. ASSAULT

(1) An actor is subject to liability to another for assault if

(a) he acts intending to cause a harmful or offensive contract with the person of the other or a third person, or an imminent apprehension of such a contact, and

(b) the other is thereby put in such imminent apprehension.

(2) An action which is not done with the intention stated in Subsection (1)(a) does not make the actor liable to the other for an apprehension caused thereby although the act involves an unreasonable risk of causing it and, therefore, would be negligent or reckless if the risk threatened bodily harm.

Section 13. BATTERY: HARMFUL CONTACT

An actor is subject to liability to another for battery if

(a) he acts intending to cause a harmful or offensive contact with the person of the other or a third person, or an imminent apprehension of such a contact, and

(b) a harmful contact with the person of the other directly or indirectly results.

We see from Section 21 that the elements of assault, as applied to our hypo, are (1) an act by Dr. Collins; (2) intent by Dr. Collins to cause harmful or offensive contact, or imminent apprehension of harmful or offensive contact; (3) causing Shannon to feel imminent apprehension of harmful or offensive contact. To this we add: (4) damages proximately caused by Dr. Collins's wrongful conduct.

Analyzing Section 13, the elements of battery are the same as those of assault, except that the third element is now *actual harmful contact* instead of *apprehension of harmful contact.*

When we get to the "intent to cause harmful or offensive contact" element, we realize that we may have a problem—did Dr. Collins "intend to cause a harmful or offensive contact" with Shannon? Presumably he intended to throw himself on top of her, he will say, to keep her from shooting him. Most people would regard having someone suddenly land on top of them as offensive. So does Dr. Collins have the requisite intent because he intended the act and the act is offensive? Or did he *not* have the requisite intent because, whatever the act, his purpose was not to be offensive but to avoid being shot? These are the kinds of distinctions about which appellate courts love to write opinions, and we will need to check the case law in more depth on the "intent" issue.

## Step 3 — Determine What Defenses May Apply

Again referring to the *Restatement,* we find that the defenses to assault and battery include self-defense (*Restatement 2d, Torts,* §63), defense of others (§76), consent (§49), privilege to arrest for a crime (§118), and privilege to use force to prevent a serious crime (§141 *et seq.*), as well as a few obviously inapplicable ones involving such topics as military action and disciplining of children.

Checking FRCP, Rule 8(c), we can quickly eliminate most of the affirmative defenses listed there. We add to our outline for further analysis the defenses of contributory negligence and assumption of risk. We also add headings to our outline for the defenses of personal jurisdiction, subject matter jurisdiction, venue, sufficiency of service of process, and proper joinder of parties but do not

attempt to expand them at this point. If we represent the defendant, they will serve to remind us to review these issues after the complaint is filed. If we represent the plaintiff, it is our responsibility to prepare and file the complaint in such a way as to avoid creating these defenses. The steps we will discuss in Workshops 2 and 3 are designed to help us do this.

## Step 4 — Determine the Elements of Each Defense

In a real lawsuit, we would outline each of the possible defenses, at least to the extent of listing the elements. We would do this even for defenses that seem unlikely to apply (i.e., privilege to arrest for a crime). See the sidebar on analyzing a case.

Here, for brevity, we have shown how this would be done for one defense, that of self-defense. We begin with the *Restatement* formulation, found in *Restatement 2d, Torts,* §63:

§63. Self-Defense by Force Not Threatening Death or Serious Bodily Harm
 (1) An actor is privileged to use reasonable force, not intended or likely to cause death or serious bodily harm, to defend himself against unprivileged harmful or offensive contact or other bodily harm which he reasonably believes that another is about to inflict intentionally upon him.

From this, we can extract the elements of the defense of "self-defense" as applied to our case as follows:

*1.* The force used (here, by Dr. Collins) must have been "reasonable."

*2.* No intent (again by Dr. Collins) to cause death or serious bodily harm.

*3.* The force used must not have been *likely* to cause death or serious harm.

*4.* The purpose must have been to defend against "harmful or offensive contact or other bodily harm."

*5.* The harm defended against must itself have been "unprivileged." (Here, things get a bit complicated: If Shannon acted properly in self-defense in trying to shoot Dr. Collins, then *her* actions would be privileged, in which case Dr. Collins would be unable to establish that he was defending himself against an "unprivileged" harm.)

*6.* Reasonable belief (by Dr. Collins) that another (Shannon) was about to inflict harm on him and do so intentionally.

---

*Your Local Notes*

_____

_____

---

## SIDEBAR

### Analyzing A Case: Top-Down vs. Bottom-Up Approach

*One way—often the obvious or intuitive way—to analyze a case is to think about the fact situation and see what causes of action or defenses jump into your mind to fit those facts. Almost always, a trained lawyer or paralegal will be able to look at a set of facts and say, "Aha! Battery!" or "Aha! Breach of contract!"*

*Unfortunately, that method of analysis is almost certain to overlook other causes of action or defenses that might turn out to be easier to establish. There are many possible paths to liability—at least as many paths as there are causes of action—and the one you want is the easiest and safest, not the most obvious. Perhaps the case does look, superficially, like a case of battery, but maybe there is a big problem with proving, say, intent. If you take that path, eight times out of ten you would lose on a motion for summary judgment on the intent issue. If you instead treated the case as a negligence case, you would not have to prove intent, and you would be almost certain of at least getting to tell your story to a jury.*

*The only possible way to be sure that you have selected the best possible path is to check out all paths. There is no substitute for this. Some paths will lead straight to the edge of a cliff and can be rejected quickly. Others may require some research. But we always at least consider every possible cause of action and defense we can think of, even those that may seem clearly inapplicable at first glance. Remember, we do not have all of the facts yet.*

*One of the most important effects of taking this top-down approach is that it makes us look at the facts in a different way. Instead of trying to find causes of action that fit the facts (the bottom-up approach), now we can look for facts that fit the various causes of action. Instead of reacting to the facts as they are given to us, we can seize the initiative, decide what facts we want, and try to come up with them.*

Whew! Hopefully, you can see from this list of elements why it is impossible to decide whether you have the facts to support a given cause of action or defense without analyzing each one, element by element.

As we did in researching causes of action, we would then check the case law of the state whose law will apply to our lawsuit, to fine-tune our list of elements and be sure we are accurately reflecting local law.

**Step 5**    *For Each Element of Each Cause of Action and Each Defense, List Each Fact Supporting It*

Now that we have our lists of elements, we go through them, one by one, and try to list as many facts as we can, both pro and con. Our example outline shown next demonstrates how this might be done for the cause of action for battery. Naturally, in a real lawsuit, the factual universe is likely to be much broader and the lists correspondingly longer.

**Step 6**    *For Each Fact, List Each Item of Evidence Supporting It*

Similarly, the example outline shows how some of the evidence might be filled in.

**Conclusion**—When completed, our issues outline might look like this (for brevity, we have expanded only the part pertaining to the battery cause of action against Dr. Collins, and we expand the facts and evidence sublevels only in a few selected segments):

ISSUES OUTLINE

I. Causes of Action

  A. Against the hotel

    . . . .

  B. Against Dr. Collins

    1. Negligence

      . . . .

    2. Assault

      . . . .

    3. Battery

      a. a threatening act by Dr. Collins

        i. (fact) entered room at night without permission

          (A) (evidence) testimony of Shannon

          (B) (evidence) testimony of investigating police officer that Dr. Collins was found on bed

   (C) (counterevidence) testimony of investigating police officer that only key found other than Shannon's key was to Dr. Collins's room, raising inference that he could not have entered room unless Shannon let him in

  ii. (fact) Dr. Collins undressed

  iii. (fact) Shannon did not know Dr. Collins

  iv. (contrary fact) no weapon visible

  v. (contrary fact) no threat spoken

 b. intent to cause harmful or offensive contact

  i. (subissue) intent to do act + act is offensive, or intent to produce an offensive result

   . . . .

 c. actual harmful or offensive contact

  . . . .

 d. damages proximately caused

  . . . .

 e. defenses

  i. self-defense

   (A) reasonable force

    . . . .

   (B) no intent to cause serious harm or death

    . . . .

   (C) no likelihood of serious harm or death

    . . . .

   (D) purpose to defend against bodily harm

    . . . .

   (E) harm defended against is unprivileged

    . . . .

   (F) reasonable belief that other was about to intentionally inflict harm

 4. Outrageous conduct causing mental distress

  . . . .

C. Against the police department

 . . . .

D. Against Shannon's employer

 . . . .

II. General Defenses

 A. Jurisdiction

  . . . .

We reiterate that the format, layout, and organization of the issues outline is a matter of individual preference. The objective is to force a systematic analysis of the causes of action and defenses that might apply to the case.

## The Issues Outline: Learning by Doing

Your assignment for this workshop is to prepare an issues outline. For most students, we suggest the following, based on our Shannon hypo:

You are a paralegal in the law office of Roger Yarborough, attorney for Dr. Arthur Collins. Assume that Dr. Collins is a resident of your city, that Banbury Park Hotel is located in another city in your state, and that Roger Yarborough practices in your city. Shannon Martin resides in Arizona, and Park Hotels Group, Inc., is incorporated in Delaware.

  After discussing the case with Allen Porter, Roger Yarborough realizes that Porter is about to file suit on Shannon's behalf, naming Dr. Collins as one of the defendants. Yarborough decides that he would prefer to seize the initiative and file the suit himself. He assigns you to draft a complaint on behalf of Dr. Collins, for filing in the state superior court (or county trial court) having jurisdiction in your locality.

## EXERCISES

In carrying out this assignment, you should follow the step-by-step formula described in this workshop.

***1.*** Following the instructions for Step 1, try to list as many causes of action as you can that Dr. Collins could assert *against* anyone arising from the facts of the hypo. Do not worry about whether he could ultimately prevail on each one—if a cause of action has any reasonable bearing on the situation, list it. (We will decide which of the causes of action seem meritorious when we draft the complaint. See Exercise 4 in Workshop 5.)

***2.*** Prepare an issues outline limited to Dr. Collins's cause of action against Shannon for assault:

 a. Begin with the elements of the cause of action for assault as set out in *Restatement (2d), Torts,* Section 21.

 b. At your instructor's option, research the case law of your own state pertaining to assault and attempt to list the elements of assault based on your state's case law. Cite the cases on which you base your conclusions.

 c. Following Step 5, list, under each element in your outline of "assault," all of the facts you can think of that bear on that element.

Include facts that tend to establish that element *and* also facts that tend to disprove that element.

d. Following Step 6, list, under each fact that you listed, any evidence that you can think of that would tend to either prove or disprove that fact. (In doing this and the preceding step, keep in mind the difference between facts and evidence. Reread the instructions for Steps 5 and 6 if you are unsure.)

3. Prepare an issues outline limited to the issue of self-defense. Assume that you represent Shannon, and that Dr. Collins has sued Shannon for battery (remember, she shot him). One affirmative defense to the tort of battery is self-defense.

a. Determine the elements of the defense of self-defense by consulting the *Restatement,* case law from your state, and/or any other source that your instructor assigns.

b. Following Step 5, list, under each element of "self-defense," all of the facts you can think of that bear on that element. Include facts that tend to establish that element *and* also facts that tend to disprove that element.

c. Following Step 6, list, under each fact that you listed, any evidence that you can think of that would tend to either prove or disprove that fact. (In doing this and the preceding step, keep in mind the difference between facts and evidence. Reread the instructions for Steps 5 and 6 if you are unsure.)

# PRACTICE POINTERS
## *Organizing a Case File*

At the same time you are beginning to prepare court materials, you also need to begin organizing the case file that will contain all documents, notes, court papers, and investigative materials for the case at hand. Having already met with the client at this point, you will need to file your notes from this initial meeting as well as any telephone conversations you may have had with the client.

Having been made aware at that initial interview of some of the potential witnesses in this case, you can also create a witness directory that will list alphabetically all the witnesses of which you are currently aware, their telephone numbers and addresses, and any other identifying information. This directory will assist you in the future to schedule interviews and depositions and to issue subpoenas.

In your computer you will need to prepare a case directory (often entitled by the client's surname). At the beginning of this directory you will put your "to do" list, which will contain tasks that you jotted down during and after your initial interview with the client. The case directory should also contain an inventory document called the "original documents list." This list should include the documents the client brought to the first meeting and should identify the nature of the document and the date it was received. Original documents should not, by the way, be hole-punched or altered in any way because they may be used at trial.

Finally, the case directory should include a letter you have written to the client, thanking her for choosing your firm and acknowledging that she has provided the firm with documentation. Listing the documents provided should be done only with the permission of your supervising attorney.

## TECHNO TIP

The elements of a claim can be found in many sources. If your state follows the *Restatements,* such as *Torts, Contracts,* etc., these treatises are a good place to begin. For claims created by statute, such as state security law issues, non-common law torts, federal law violations, and the like, you can look on the Internet for free access to the applicable jurisdiction's statutes. The *United States Code,* for example, is accessible in searchable form at http://law.house. gov/uscsrch.htm. Another example of free access to a state's statutes is the statutes for the state of Arizona at http://www.azleg.state.az.us/ars/ars.htm. Whenever you find a relevant page on the Internet, whether as a specific resource or as a road map to other sites, keep its address and a brief description of its contents in a separate file. The "bookmarks" kept by your browser may not have the ability to keep as many pages as you may find you need, are generally not as easy to manipulate, and cannot be easily passed on to others not sharing the same server as you, assuming you are on your firm's network.

## FORMS FILE

*When you begin your first job as a legal assistant, you will find it helpful to have documents that you can use as forms to remind you of the proper format and content of the document you are asked to prepare. You will, for example, want to have copies of various types of complaints, motions, memoranda, subpoenas, contracts, wills, and so on. You can easily prepare a forms file by keeping copies of the documents you prepare or that are provided as samples in each class. Purchase a three-hole notebook and a three-hole punch and insert a sample of each document as you discuss it in class. You can use tabs to organize these documents systematically for easy and logical reference.*

*Therefore, at the end of each workshop, we will recommend documents that you may want to include in your forms file that relate to that particular workshop. In this chapter, for example, we suggest you include a section that summarizes the causes of action in each substantive area you study. As you learn about contract law, for example, list the elements of a contract claim under common law, a contract claim under the U.C.C., all of the defenses to contract formation, and so on. You can begin by including the elements of the basic causes of action in tort law, which are set forth in Figure W1–2, in your forms notebook.*

## KEY TERMS

**Claim**                                **Theory of liability**

## INTRODUCTION: WHY THE CHOICE OF FORUM IS IMPORTANT

The United States has many hundreds of courts: federal courts, county courts, city courts, justice of the peace courts, magistrate courts, tax courts, bankruptcy courts, probate courts, equity courts, admiralty courts—the list goes on and on. We refer to the particular court in which a given lawsuit is filed as the forum for that lawsuit.

How do you decide which, out of all of these hundreds of courts, is the right one in which to prosecute your lawsuit? We can use two considerations to narrow the list.

First, we must choose a court that has legal authority to hear our case—the court must have jurisdiction, and venue rules must be satisfied. We must also consider whether there are factors present that may lead the court itself to decide that the case should be brought elsewhere. For instance, even if the court we choose has jurisdiction, the judge may have the power to transfer or dismiss a case if the forum is deemed "inconvenient." We discuss these concepts in detail in this workshop.

Second, out of all the courts in which we could file, we would prefer to choose the one in which we are *most likely to win our case.* All courts are not created equal, nor do all courts apply the same laws. Procedural rules differ greatly from one court to another, and substantive law varies considerably from one state to another. Delay is a major consideration. In some courts a lawsuit can be prosecuted to trial and judgment in as little as a year or two, while in others it may routinely take five years or more. And, as graphically demonstrated by certain recent cases (Rodney King, O. J. Simpson), choice of geographical location implies a choice of jury demographics, which can be enough, by itself, to determine who wins or loses.

## Choosing a Court: Step-by-Step Instructions

**Choice of forum** refers to the process by which we decide which court will hear our case. Who gets to make this important decision? The initial choice belongs to the plaintiff, because the plaintiff decides in which court to file the complaint. However, in certain circumstances, a defendant who disagrees with the plaintiff's choice can get the case transferred to a different court or dismissed in a way that forces the plaintiff to refile in a different court. And, if the defendant knows that a dispute is likely to lead to a lawsuit, the defendant can sometimes seize the initiative and file first (as a plaintiff, of course, naming the "natural" plaintiff as a defendant), thereby cementing a more defense-friendly choice of forum.

Therefore, the defendants as well as the plaintiffs should analyze the forum choices. A further motivation for the defendants is the potential for finding additional defenses (jurisdictional defenses, for example).

As with other potentially complex decisions in the course of a lawsuit, the odds favor those who apply a systematic approach to ensure that promising alternatives are not overlooked. If you always jump up and file in the obvious forum (usually, the local county or superior court), at least some of the time you will be missing the chance to file in some other court in which your case might be more easily won.

Hence, we proceed in our usual step-by-step fashion (see Figure W2–1).

| **Step 1** | *List All Courts Where the Case Might Be Filed* |

Our first task is simply to make a list of every court we can think of in which our case might conceivably be filed.

We begin by weeding out the cases in which the choice of forum is a foregone conclusion. The two main classes of such cases are garden-variety suits for damages between local residents, and specialty cases that have to be filed in a particular court. For such cases, if we apply the step-by-step instructions of this workshop, we would arrive at the result that only one choice of forum is possible. In practice, however, most litigators would not go through a detailed analysis in cases for which the outcome is obvious. With a few simple observations, we can identify many of the routine cases and save ourselves the effort of going through all the steps.

---

**Figure W2–1    Choosing a Court**

**Step 1: List All Courts Where the Case Might be Filed**

    *Easy Choice Type 1: Garden-Variety Suits for Damages between Local Residents*
    *Easy Choice Type 2: Cases for the Specialty Courts*
    *Cases Where the Choice Is Not as Easy: Listing the Possibilities*

**Step 2: Check Each Forum for Jurisdiction of the Subject Matter**

    *State Courts*
    *Federal Courts*
        *Federal Question Jurisdiction*
        *Diversity Jurisdiction*
        *Disputes Over Subject Matter Jurisdiction*

**Step 3: Check for Jurisdiction of the Person of Each Defendant**

    *Personal Jurisdiction the Easy Way*
        *Personal Jurisdiction by Consent*
        *Personal Jurisdiction over State Residents*
        *Personal Jurisdiction over Corporations "Present" in the State*
    *Personal Jurisdiction the Hard Way*
        *Tag Jurisdiction*
        *Long-Arm Statutes*
        *Personal Jurisdiction in Federal Court*
        *In Rem and Quasi-In Rem*

**Step 4: Decide Whether Venue Would Be Proper**

    *State Court*
    *Federal Court*
    *Remedies*

**Step 5: Consider Defendant's Transfer Options**

    *Removal*
    *Forum non Conveniens*
    *Federal Transfer*

**Step 6: Decide Which of the Possible Courts Is Best**

    *Procedural Law*
    *Substantive Law*
        *Federal Law Causes of Action*
        *State Law Causes of Action*
        *State Law Causes of Action in Federal Court*
    *Other Factors In Choosing a Forum*
        *Caseload and Average Time to Trial*
        *Who Decides?—Judges and Jury Demographics*
        *Convenience, Cost, and Attorney Familiarity*

---

**Easy Choice Type 1: Garden-Variety Suits for Damages between Local Residents**—In typical automobile fender-bender cases, routine business disputes, run-of-the-mill debt collection cases, and many other kinds of lawsuits that comprise much of the case flow in a metropolitan court system, the only court that will have jurisdiction is the local county court, and that is where the suit will have to be filed.

Based on the legal principles that we will be studying in this workshop, we can make up a check-list. If we are able to check off *all* of the points on the checklist as true, we will likely conclude that we must file in the local county court, for better or worse. If we cannot confirm every point, then we need to do the step-by-step analysis. After doing so, we may still conclude that our only choice is the county court—being unable to check off all the points does not guarantee that there are other choices; it merely guarantees that we need to analyze the situation in more detail.

Here is the checklist:

- All parties to the lawsuit are now, and were at the time of the events in dispute, residents of the forum county. (We discuss in more detail what it means to be a resident under Step 2.)

- The dispute is over some set of circumstances that occurred entirely within the forum county.

- The case is a suit for money damages.

- The case does not involve any government agencies as plaintiff or defendant.

- The amount of money in question is above the local county court threshold (i.e., not so small as to force the case into small claims court).

- None of the causes of action on which the suit will be based arises from federal law or from the law of some other state or country.

**Easy Choice Type 2: Cases for the Specialty Courts**—In certain situations, the subject matter of the case limits the choice of forum. For example, only the Federal Bankruptcy Court can grant a bankruptcy, so it would be pointless to consider filing a bankruptcy case anywhere else. (It may still be necessary to decide in which district to file.) Where a specialty court exists and where, in addition, the parties and the events in dispute are all local, the choice of forum will often be obvious: A divorce between two local residents probably belongs in the local divorce court. Nevertheless, the existence of a specialty court does not necessarily or in all cases foreclose the possibility of filing in some other forum, especially where the case involves out-of-state parties or disputes that arose partly in some other state.

We will have more to say about specialty courts later when we discuss jurisdiction of the subject matter.

Recognizing which specialty cases require detailed consideration of the choice of forum issues is a skill that comes with experience. Meanwhile we suggest erring on the side of caution: When in doubt, analyze.

**Cases Where the Choice Is Not As Easy: Listing the Possibilities**—For the cases that we cannot weed out as obvious, we proceed to list all the possible forums. As usual, we do not attempt at this stage to evaluate each alternative; our goal is merely to list as many as we can.

What do we mean by a "possible" forum? First, we do not bother to list courts whose jurisdiction is limited in some way that clearly excludes us. For example, if we are filing a lawsuit for damages against a private person, we do not need to list the Tax Court as a possibility. Second, we limit ourselves to

---

> ### SIDEBAR
>
> ## The Importance of Being Connected
>
> *A court will ordinarily hear a case if and only if (1) it has jurisdiction of the subject matter, (2) it has jurisdiction of the person of each defendant, and (3) venue is proper. Rules of jurisdiction and venue can be quite technical and complex, but they will be easier to understand if we realize that they are all designed to achieve one main purpose: to channel lawsuits into the courts that can most conveniently hear them.*
>
> *Courts are usually reluctant to hear cases that have no connection to the locality where the court sits. This is not surprising when you consider that it is the taxpayers of that locality who are paying for the court.*
>
> *What does it mean to be connected to the locality? The precise answer depends on the jurisdictional rules, but here is a useful rule of thumb: At a minimum, at least one of the parties must be a resident of the forum county, or, failing that, part of the events that gave rise to the dispute itself must have happened in the forum county. Certainly, it is possible for cases to sneak under the jurisdictional radar that are even less connected than our rule of thumb would allow, but this does not happen often.*

courts that are connected in some way to the dispute (see sidebar).

At a minimum, in a suit for damages, we should include in our list:

1. Our own local county or superior court;

2. The local county or superior court for any county, in our state or in some other state, in which any defendant is a resident;

3. The local county or superior court for any county, in our state or in some other state, in which any significant part of the events in dispute happened;

4. The federal district court for the district in which we practice;

5. The federal district court for each federal district in which any defendant resides; and

6. The federal district court for each federal district in which any significant part of the events in dispute happened.

In specialty cases, the possibilities will depend on what specialty courts exist in the localities to which the case is connected. Your instructor will inform you of any specialty courts that you need to be aware of in your locality.

```
Your Local Notes
_____
_____
```

## SIDEBAR

### Jurisdiction: Original vs. Appellate

*A further level of complication in deciding which court to choose is knowing in which level to file. Suppose you have decided to file your lawsuit in federal court—which one? District court? Court of appeals? Supreme Court?*

*You probably know instinctively that you could not start your lawsuit in the Court of Appeals or Supreme Court—but why not? Is there anything preventing you from taking your case straight to the Supreme Court?*

*Sorry, you can only originate a lawsuit in a court that has* **original jurisdiction** *over it. For most types of federal cases, the U.S. district court has original jurisdiction and the Court of Appeals and Supreme Court have only* **appellate jurisdiction**—*that is, they have the power to hear only appeals. (There are, however, a few classes of cases—certain disputes between state governments, for example—over which the U.S. Supreme Court has original jurisdiction.)*

**Step 2**    *Check Each Forum for Jurisdiction of the Subject Matter*

Now we go through our list of possible forums one by one and eliminate any that would not have jurisdiction of the subject matter. Recall from Chapter 2 that jurisdiction is the power to hear and decide a case.

Jurisdiction comes in two main flavors: jurisdiction of the subject matter and jurisdiction of the person. **Jurisdiction of the subject matter** is the power to hear and decide cases of a given type and it is important for this reason: Defects in the court's jurisdiction of the subject matter cannot be waived and can be raised at any time, even when the case

is on appeal. If the court finds that it lacks subject matter jurisdiction, it must dismiss the case.

This creates the potential for a nasty trap: Suppose you file your lawsuit in a court that lacks subject matter jurisdiction. Obviously, you would not do this deliberately, but perhaps the jurisdictional defect involves some subtle, technical problem that you overlooked. Suppose your opponent also fails to notice the problem. You litigate the case at great expense, finally winning a jury trial and obtaining judgment. Your opponent appeals. The appeals court notices the jurisdictional problem. What will happen?

Your case will be dismissed. *Subject matter jurisdiction defects can be raised at any time.*

Fortunately, this sort of thing does not happen often, but the possibility should be enough to make you careful about subject matter jurisdiction!

**State Courts**—State trial courts—county or superior courts—are usually courts of **general subject matter jurisdiction.** Originally, this meant that state trial courts had the power to hear all types of cases, so it was unnecessary to worry about subject matter jurisdiction if you were filing your case in state court.

Increasingly, however, there are exceptions to the generality of state court subject matter jurisdiction. Some of the most common include the following:

- Divorce cases, which must, in some but not all localities, be filed in a specialty divorce or family court;

- Probate cases, which must, in some but not all localities, be filed in probate court;

- Small claims cases (i.e., cases in which the amount in dispute is below a certain threshold amount of money, typically on the order of a few thousand dollars), which may have to be filed in a court designated to handle small claims (which may be called a small claims court or something else, depending on the locality);

- State tax cases, for which some states have created specialty tax courts. (Choice of forum in federal tax cases is a complex issue into which we will not delve.); and

- Cases of exclusive federal jurisdiction, which must be filed in federal district court. [Where the cause of action comes from a federal statute, the statute may provide that suit must be brought in federal court. Normally, state courts do have jurisdiction to hear federal causes of action, but Congress can, and occasionally does, specify otherwise. An example: securities fraud cases under Rule 10(b)(5) of the Securities Exchange Commission can be brought only in federal court.]

---

*Your Local Notes*

_____

_____

_____

---

In ordinary lawsuits filed in state court, subject matter jurisdiction is not usually a concern. However, any time you are suing in state court on an unusual cause of action—one based on federal law or one that you have not seen asserted routinely in other state court lawsuits—it is wise to do some research and be sure you are right about the particular case's subject matter jurisdiction.

**Federal Courts**—Federal courts, in contrast to the state courts, are courts of **limited subject matter jurisdiction.** Their jurisdiction extends only to a few specific categories of cases for which Congress has passed laws allowing suits in federal court. With state trial courts, we assume that the court has subject matter jurisdiction over everything, except where there is some law that makes an exception. With federal courts, we must assume that the court does *not* have subject matter jurisdiction unless we can find a federal statute (a law passed by Congress) granting jurisdiction over our specific type of case.

Congress has, in fact, granted jurisdiction to the federal district courts over a number of categories of cases. Many of these involve matters of specific federal concern, such as suits between the governments of two states or suits against foreign powers. Some of the categories can be found in Title 28, Chapter 85, of the *U.S. Code* (28 U.S.C. §1330 *et seq.*) Other grants of subject matter jurisdiction can be found in federal statutes regulating particular classes of activity (taxes, patents, securities, etc.).

For litigators who are not government agency lawyers or practitioners of some esoteric specialty, however, the important categories of federal subject matter jurisdiction can be narrowed down to two: federal question jurisdiction and diversity jurisdiction.

*Federal question jurisdiction:* Federal district courts have subject matter jurisdiction over "all civil actions arising under the Constitution, laws, or treaties of the United States" (28 U.S.C. §1331). This is called **federal question jurisdiction.** In practice, this means that if your cause of action is based on a federal statute, you can sue in federal court. This jurisdiction is not exclusive; you are not *required* to sue in federal court merely because your case is based on a federal statute, and many, perhaps even most, such cases are filed in state court.

But wait—what about lawsuits in which you assert some causes of action based on federal statutes and others based on state law? Does including a state law cause of action in an otherwise federal case deprive the federal court of subject matter jurisdiction?

In general, no. If there is at least one valid federal cause of action, the federal court is said to have **pendent jurisdiction** over the appended state law causes of action. In fact, it is commonplace for lawsuits in federal court to include both federal and state causes of action. Pendent jurisdiction poses one significant hazard, however: If your federal law cause(s) of action were to be dismissed for some reason (i.e., you lose a motion for summary judgment), then there would be no federal claim for the state law causes of action to be appended to. Then they would be dismissed for lack of subject matter jurisdiction and your whole case would be gone.

*Diversity jurisdiction:* The other main category of federal subject matter jurisdiction is **diversity of citizenship jurisdiction.** The idea here is that the federal courts should provide an impartial forum for suits between residents of different states. Presumably, state courts might tend to favor their own residents over others. Whatever may be your view of the logic of that rationale, 28 U.S.C. §1332 gives the federal district courts original jurisdiction over all civil actions between "citizens of different states." Federal district courts are also given jurisdiction over certain civil actions involving citizens of foreign countries.

What does it mean for an action to be between citizens of different states? *Citizenship* as used here means "domicile," a clarification that does not necessarily help us much, since litigators are not shy to engage in disputes over what domicile means. Usually, a person's **domicile** is the state in which the person lives, although the correct legal definition is somewhat more complicated (see sidebar). A corporation is considered to be a citizen of any state in which it is incorporated and also of the state in which its principal place of business is located.

Where a lawsuit is between one plaintiff and one defendant, it is easy to decide whether the action is between citizens of different states, as long as we know what states the plaintiff and the defendant are citizens of. What about more complex disputes in which there may be a number of plaintiffs and defendants? The statute (28 U.S.C. §1332) does not furnish a rule for this situation, so the federal courts have supplied one: For there to be federal diversity jurisdiction, there must be "complete diversity." That is, there can be no defendant who is a resident of the same state as any plaintiff. To see how this works in a given case, try this: Make a plaintiffs' list of all the

## S I D E B A R

### Citizenship, Residence, and Domicile

*How do you tell which state you are a citizen of? Perhaps you were not even aware that you are a citizen of some state—you thought you were a citizen of the United States, or perhaps some other country.*

*Legally, however, for many purposes, each state of the United States is considered a separate sovereign entity, each with its own government and its own citizens.*

*Fortunately (thanks to the U.S. Constitution), we do not have to go through customs or immigration when we move from one state to another. You are a citizen of the state in which you have your domicile, and you are free to choose any domicile you wish and change it as often as you wish. Literally, domicile means "home"; legally, it means any state in which you are physically present with the intention to remain indefinitely. This means that to choose a state as your domicile, you do have to actually go there (physical presence); simply taking a vacation there is not enough (no intent to remain indefinitely). For some people, such as "snowbirds" who winter in the Sun Belt and spend summers in one of the northern states, domicile can be an ambiguous concept.*

*For purposes of procedural law, citizenship of a state and domicile in a state are the same thing. Residence is a less exact term; in this text, we will use it to mean the same as domicile, but in some other contexts (i.e., deciding whether you have to pay out-of-state tuition) it may have other meanings.*

states in which any plaintiff resides, and a defendants' list of all the states in which any defendant resides. (Keep in mind that corporations can have more than one state of residence.) Compare the two lists; if there is any state that appears on both lists, there can be no federal diversity jurisdiction.

There is one other requirement for diversity jurisdiction: the "matter in controversy" must exceed "the sum or value of $75,000." This is referred to as the **jurisdictional amount.** It is determined by how much the plaintiff asks for in the complaint, not by how much is actually won. You do not get thrown out of court for lack of jurisdiction if you ask for $100,000 and the jury awards you only $49,999. But federal judges have ways of getting even with the plaintiffs who inflate their demands in order to

bring penny-ante cases into federal court, and the statute allows the judge to make the plaintiff pay the court costs.

***Disputes over subject matter jurisdiction:*** It takes little imagination to see that much disagreement can arise about whether a given lawsuit qualifies for federal subject matter jurisdiction. Not only that, there are often opportunities for litigators to engineer the situation to their advantage by careful addition or subtraction of parties and causes of action. A plaintiff who is desperate to get into federal court may add an utterly meritless cause of action based on some federal law merely to create federal question jurisdiction. Or a defendant may try to bring in an additional defendant whose state of residence is the same as that of one of the plaintiffs, so as to negate complete diversity. Individuals may move to other states to try to avoid being sued in an unfavorable forum. The possible permutations are endless, and legal research will often be necessary to figure out whether federal jurisdiction exists in a given situation. (A good place to start is Wright and Miller, *Federal Practice and Procedure,* a multivolume encyclopedia of federal procedure. The first volume is devoted to issues of jurisdiction.)

What is the defendant's remedy if the defendant believes that the court lacks subject matter jurisdiction? Most commonly, a motion to dismiss for lack of jurisdiction under FRCP, Rule 12 (b)(1). We will take up the subject of motions to dismiss in detail in Workshop 16.

**Step 3**    *Check for Jurisdiction of the Person of Each Defendant*

In Step 2, we crossed off any of the forums on our list that would not have jurisdiction of the subject matter. Now we consider whether we can obtain jurisdiction of the person of each defendant in each of the forums left.

**Jurisdiction of the person** of a party is the power to render a decision that will be binding *on that party.* The requirement of jurisdiction of the person has its roots in the U.S. Constitution, specifically in the Due Process Clauses of the Fifth and Fourteenth Amendments.

The issue that jurisdiction of the person addresses is this: "Is it fair under these circumstances to force this person to litigate in this state?" The answer depends on two main factors. The first is whether the person in question has a sufficient connection with the forum state to make it fair to force him to litigate there. The second—whether the person has been adequately notified that she has been sued—tends, as a practical matter, to come up in the form of a dispute over the sufficiency of service of process, so we will leave it for Workshop 6.

Because personal jurisdiction issues depend on the relationship of the defendant to the forum state, we can usually analyze federal court personal jurisdiction in exactly the same way that we would analyze the personal jurisdiction of a state court in the same state. For example, if a Nevada state court would have jurisdiction of the person of Dr. Collins, then so would the U.S. District Court for the District of Nevada. (There are, however, a few situations in which we can stretch the jurisdictional reach of federal courts a bit, as we will see.)

Notice that personal jurisdiction issues always occur at the level of states. We do not need to worry about which county we choose within the state (that is a question of venue, not jurisdiction; see Step 4 later).

**Personal Jurisdiction the Easy Way**—There are easy ways to get personal jurisdiction of a defendant, and then there are harder ways. As you might guess, most cases involve the easy ways. These are (1) get consent or (2) sue in the state in which the defendant resides (or, in the case of corporations, is "present").

*Personal jurisdiction by consent:* Recall that with jurisdiction of the subject matter, the court either has it or does not—whether the parties are willing to have the court hear the case has nothing to do with it. Jurisdiction of the person is different: A party can voluntarily submit to the jurisdiction of the court. This is why the court always, automatically, has jurisdiction of the person of the plaintiff who files the suit: by filing suit, the plaintiff consents to be bound by the court's decision.

Similarly, the defendant can consent to the court's jurisdiction of his person. When the plaintiff's choice of forum is reasonable, the defendant will often accept it voluntarily, preferring to avoid unnecessary expense and save ammunition for more important issues. Less adroit defendants also sometimes consent to jurisdiction without intending to—a defendant who makes a general appearance in the case (i.e., files an answer) without properly raising the defense of personal jurisdiction is deemed to have consented.

*Personal jurisdiction over state residents:* What happens when the defendant does not want to consent to litigate in a particular forum? If the defendant is a citizen of the forum state—the state in which the court sits—the court automatically has personal jurisdiction of that defendant. The courts of a state always have personal jurisdiction over the citizens of the state, and so do federal courts located in the same state.

*Personal jurisdiction over corporations "present" in the state:* We have said that corporations are citizens of the state of incorporation and the state in which the corporation's main office is located, for purposes of federal *subject matter jurisdiction* by "diversity of citizenship." *Personal jurisdiction* of corporations is a different issue: Courts of a state (and federal courts sitting within the state) can exercise personal jurisdiction over corporations and other business entities if they are "present" within the state. What does it mean to be "present"? Maintaining a place of business in the state is enough; merely engaging in advertising or mail order business may not be; and in a close case you will have to research the issue.

Many states require out-of-state corporations to file papers with a state agency before doing business in the state, consenting (among other things) to be subject to suit in the state's courts. As a practical matter, therefore, when suing an out-of-state corporation, your first thought should be to call the state corporation commission (or whatever state agency regulates corporations in the state in question) and find out whether the corporation has filed papers qualifying to do business in the state.

**Personal Jurisdiction the Hard Way**—Obviously, the easy way does not work in all cases. Perhaps you are suing someone from another state, and you would prefer to do it in your state's courts rather than his. Or perhaps you are suing several defendants, each from different states—then it is impossible to sue all of them in their states of residence unless you sue each one separately. Now what?

There are two main ways of getting personal jurisdiction of a defendant who refuses to consent to be sued in the state of your choice and does not reside there. One is to serve process on her within the boundaries of the forum state; the other is to take advantage of the so-called "long-arm" statutes.

*Tag jurisdiction:* Courts always have jurisdiction of the person of anyone located within the boundaries of the state, whether the person is a resident of the state or not. This means that if you can manage to catch the defendant in the state in which you want to sue, and get a process server to serve process on him before he leaves the state, the court will have personal jurisdiction. (Personal service of process, as you may recall from Chapter 3, consists of having a process server physically hand the defendant a copy of the summons and complaint. We will cover the procedure for doing this in more detail in Workshop 6). Thus in theory, if Shannon wanted to file suit against Dr. Collins in, say, North Dakota, if she could manage to have a process server drop the papers on him as he rode through the corner of the state on a bus, the North Dakota court would have jurisdiction of his person. (As a practical matter, the North Dakota court might well find other reasons not to take the case—see the later discussion of *forum non conveniens.*)

***Long-arm statutes:*** You are probably not very impressed with tag jurisdiction as a practical way to get jurisdiction over recalcitrant defendants. What you really need is a way to reach out and sue people who are not residents of the state, never intend to go there, and are not about to consent to be sued there.

Can you do this? Yes, but there are limitations. Every state now has a so-called **long-arm statute** authorizing suits against nonresidents in certain situations. The first limitation is that you can sue only nonresidents in the situations specified by the forum state's long-arm statute.

The second limitation is the Constitution's due process requirement. The U.S. Supreme Court has held that it would be fundamentally unfair (and therefore a violation of due process) to allow people to be dragged into lawsuits in other states with which they have no minimum contacts. An example may help to clarify this: Suppose Sam Snowbird from Duluth, Minnesota, is driving through Albuquerque, New Mexico, when he is involved in a collision with Larry Local, a New Mexico resident. It seems perfectly reasonable to allow Larry to sue Sam in New Mexico—after all, it was Sam's choice to drive there. On the other hand, it would be fundamentally unfair to allow Sam to sue Larry in Duluth—Larry has not done anything to subject himself to the authority of the government of Minnesota.

In practice, constitutional issues rarely arise nowadays. This is because most state long-arm statutes have been designed with the constitutional limits in mind, and have by now been challenged on constitutional grounds and upheld by the courts. Therefore, litigators usually assume that if they have complied with the forum state's long-arm statute, personal jurisdiction is assured.

Most state long-arm statutes have been carefully drafted to extend the reach of the state's courts as far as the Constitution allows. The most common formulation allows suits against any person, including a nonresident, if that person (1) caused an act or event to occur within the forum state and (2) the cause of action which the plaintiff is suing on arises from that act or event. These two factors comprise the U.S. Supreme Court's definition of the **minimum contacts** required to satisfy constitutional due process.

There remains the problem of giving notice. Due process requires *both* minimum contacts *and* that the defendant be given notice of the lawsuit. (Obviously, it would be fundamentally unfair to allow suits in which the defendant never finds out she has

## Personal Jurisdiction Cases

*To get a feel for the concept of minimum contacts, the following are brief summaries of two leading federal cases:*

*World-Wide Volkswagen Corp. v. Woodson, 444 U.S. 286, 100 S. Ct. 559 (1980)—Involved a suit in an Oklahoma court by New York plaintiffs against a New York car distributor and a dealership that sold plaintiffs a car that burned up in Oklahoma injuring the plaintiffs. Neither of the defendants conducted any business in Oklahoma and did not regularly sell to Oklahoma buyers.* **HELD: Defendants had insufficient contacts with Oklahoma to allow assertion of jurisdiction; foreseeability of injury alone is an insufficient basis for asserting personal jurisdiction.**

*Burger King Corp. v. Rudzewicz, 471 U.S. 462, 105 S. Ct. 2174 (1985)—Florida corporation sued Michigan residents in federal court in Florida (based on diversity) for breach of a franchise agreement. Defendants alleged breach occurred in Michigan, not Florida, and Florida court did not have jurisdiction over them. Florida's long-arm statute provided that it had jurisdiction over any breech of contract to be performed in Florida (the franchisees' payments were made to plaintiff in Florida).* **HELD: Defendants had sufficient contacts with Florida to allow assertion of jurisdiction.**

*An example of a state court's analysis of its "long-arm" statute is:*

*Hoskins v. California, 168 Ariz. 250, 812 P.2d 1068 (1990), review denied, 168 Ariz. 177, 812 P.2d 1034 (1991)—California parolee killed an Arizona resident in Arizona. Plaintiff alleged that the state of California failed to control the killer in California. Plaintiff also alleged that the state of California was doing business in Arizona for purposes of general jurisdiction.* **HELD: Defendant state of California had insufficient contacts with Arizona to allow assertion of jurisdiction (also discussed sovereignty issues).**

been sued until it is too late to defend!) In practice, the constitutional notice requirement is satisfied by having process served in accordance with the applicable rule or statute. We will leave the details of service of process for Workshop 6.

It is important not to confuse personal jurisdiction with service of process requirements. Service of process is *necessary* to obtain personal jurisdiction, but not always *sufficient.* Without valid service of process, the court will not have personal jurisdiction over the defendant who was not properly served. However, the best service of process in the world will not give the court jurisdiction over a defendant who is not a resident of the forum state, not served within the forum state, and does not have minimum contacts with the forum state. You may find it helpful to think of personal jurisdiction as centering on the question, "Is it possible to sue this defendant in this place?" Then service of process involves the question, "Have we taken the right steps to *obtain* personal jurisdiction in these circumstances?"

**Personal Jurisdiction in Federal Court**—In general, the jurisdictional reach of federal district courts is the same as that of state courts in the same state. See FRCP, Rule 4(k)(1)(A), which grants personal jurisdiction over any person "who could be subjected to the jurisdiction of a court of general jurisdiction in the state in which the district court is located." There is no federal long-arm statute; to sue people who are not residents of the forum state, you refer to the long-arm statute *of the state in which the district court sits.* The long-arm jurisdiction of the federal courts is determined by state law, not federal law.

The personal jurisdiction of federal courts is slightly greater than that of a state court in two ways. The first is that federal courts can take jurisdiction over any person who can be served inside the United States and within 100 miles of the courthouse where the district court sits. This may be useful to litigators who practice in metropolitan areas that straddle a state border.

The second is that, by federal statute, in cases under the federal antitrust laws or the federal securities laws, federal courts have nationwide personal jurisdiction. Thus, in an antitrust suit or a securities fraud suit, you can sue in any federal district court and obtain personal jurisdiction over anyone who can be served anywhere inside the United States.

A final warning: Service of process in federal court, unlike questions of personal jurisdiction, is governed by the federal rules, specifically FRCP, Rule 4. In some instances, Rule 4 allows process to be served in the same manner as in state court; in others, it imposes its own requirements.

**In Rem and Quasi-In Rem**—We have said that personal jurisdiction is the power to render a decision that will be binding on the persons who are sued. Rare situations may arise, however, in which you do not need the decision to be binding on the

defendants. What if the lawsuit concerns, for example, conflicting claims to ownership of a particular item of property? If the court can obtain jurisdiction over the item of property itself, then we may not care whether there is jurisdiction of the persons of the disputing claimants.

The intricacies of *in rem* and quasi-*in rem* jurisdiction are beyond the scope of this introductory text. You may find it useful, however, to bear in mind that a court may have the power to make orders concerning specific property under its jurisdiction, even when the people claiming the property are beyond its reach.

---

*Your Local Notes*

_____

_____

_____

---

**Step 4** | *Decide Whether Venue Would Be Proper*

We have seen that the concept of jurisdiction allows us to answer the question, "Would a court in this state have the power to render a binding decision in this case?" Jurisdiction does not, however, answer an important related question: "Is this court a *reasonable and convenient* place in which to litigate this case?"

**Venue** is a further limitation on the place of suit, based on convenience. Even if a given court has jurisdiction over our suit, we cannot proceed there if venue is not proper.

In theory, the venue rules are designed to channel each lawsuit into the court that can hear it most efficiently, preferably without making the parties and witnesses travel great distances. In practice, venue rules are made by legislatures and, at times, tend to be arbitrary and illogical. Attempting to psychoanalyze them will make you crazy, so it is probably best to regard venue as simply another hoop to be jumped through on the way to filing a lawsuit.

**State Court**—Jurisdictional considerations allow us to decide whether we can proceed in a given state. But which county should we file the suit in? Are we free to pick any county we wish? Perhaps we should encourage the defendant to settle by choosing a county that will be expensive for him to litigate in? No; venue rules limit our choice.

Under the venue rules of most states, we are always free to choose a county in which any defendant resides. Depending on the state and the circumstances of the case, other permissible choices may include the plaintiff's county of residence, or the county in which the events in dispute occurred.

In routine cases, venue issues rarely arise—quite commonly, the parties, the attorneys, and the dispute are all tied to one county, and that is where the suit is filed. In the rare case in which there is some compelling reason to file in a county in which venue is not obvious, it is necessary to read the venue statute for the forum state to decide whether the case can proceed there.

**Federal Court**—Venue in federal court is governed by a federal statute, 28 U.S.C. §1391. (There are a few extra venue options in certain special cases, such as copyright and shareholder suits, but in general, 28 U.S.C. §1391 is the place to look when you have a federal venue question. Also, be warned that Congress completely rewrote 28 U.S.C. §1391 in 1990, so court opinions from before 1990 may not reflect current law.)

In state court, as we have seen, venue applies at the county level. Venue rules tell us whether we can file in a particular county. In federal court, venue applies at the district level. In many states, there is only one federal district, so the district boundaries and the state boundaries are the same. Populous states have more than one district—New York, California, and Texas each have four, and a number of states have three. In these states, federal venue rules may limit us to a particular district within the state.

The federal venue statute, 28 U.S.C. §1391, gives us three main venue choices. The first two are the same in all federal cases; the details of the third choice depend, for reasons understood by no one, on whether the case is based on diversity jurisdiction or not.

Choice 1 is a district where any defendant resides, but there is a catch: We can use choice 1 only if all the defendants reside in the same state. (Notice that venue depends on which state the defendants are *residents* of, not which state they are *citizens* of. Do the two terms mean the same thing? The courts have not given a definitive answer.)

Choice 2 is a district in which "a substantial part of the events or omissions giving rise to the claim occurred."

In cases in which the federal court's subject matter jurisdiction is based *solely* on diversity of citizenship, choice 3 is any district in which personal jurisdiction over all the defendants can be obtained. In practice, this means that if we can get long-arm jurisdiction over all the defendants, venue will be proper.

In cases in which any basis for subject matter jurisdiction besides diversity exists (i.e., if there is *any* federal question involved in the case), then choice 3 is "any district in which any defendant may be found," but there is another catch: In a nondi-versity case, we can use choice 3 only if the action could be brought in no other district.

Clear? No? As we said, you will be disappointed if you expect venue rules always to make sense. The best approach is to analyze each case based on its own facts.

**Remedies**—What happens if we file suit in a court for which venue is not proper? The outcome is partly up to the defendant. Venue rules, unlike subject matter jurisdiction, can be waived, and if the defendant is satisfied with the plaintiff's choice of forum, she can simply keep quiet about any venue defect and the case will likely proceed. Or the defendant can move to dismiss the case on the grounds of improper venue. The defendant must raise a venue defense promptly [in federal court, in the first responsive pleading; see FRCP, Rule 12(h)] or it will be waived.

If venue is improper and the defendant objects in time, the court can dismiss the case. This is not necessarily the disaster for the plaintiff that it might seem, since the plaintiff will usually be free to refile in some other court, as long as the statute of limitations has not run out.

In federal court, as well as in the courts of some states, there is one other option: The judge can order the case transferred. Federal courts can, in fact, order cases transferred to some other district even when venue is proper, as we are about to see.

**Step 5** *Consider Defendant's Transfer Options*

After Steps 2, 3, and 4 we should be left with a list of courts in which we can file our suit without inviting motions to dismiss due to jurisdictional or venue problems. Can we then be confident that the case will be heard in the court we select?

Not necessarily. Depending on the plaintiff's choice of forum, the defendant may have a counter-move or two to make. Before making a final decision, the plaintiff must take into account the risk that the defendant can interfere with the choice made.

**Removal**—Suppose the plaintiff could have filed the case in either federal district court or state court, but chose state court. Is the defendant stuck with the choice? Not usually. In most cases that would qualify for federal subject matter jurisdiction, the defendant has a right of removal—the defendant can have the case transferred to federal court. 28 U.S.C. §1441 is the general statute on removal; other removal provisions exist in certain specialized types of cases.

The procedure for removal is laid out in 28 U.S.C. §1446. The defendant initiates the process by filing a notice of removal in the federal district court in the same state in which the plaintiff filed the state court action. The defendant must do this within thirty days after receiving the complaint or the right is lost. There are procedures by which the plaintiff can contest the removal if the plaintiff thinks the case does not qualify to be removed. If the removal is successful, the case then proceeds in federal court as if the plaintiff had filed it there in the first place.

Why remove? A common situation is the suit in state court against an out-of-state motorist: Sam Snowbird from Minnesota runs over Larry Local while vacationing in Albuquerque, New Mexico. Larry sues in New Mexico state court. Does the state court have jurisdiction? Yes, under the long-arm statute, since the accident occurred in New Mexico. Would the federal court have jurisdiction? Yes, because of diversity of citizenship, assuming Larry is suing for more than $50,000. Would Sam prefer to be in federal court? Quite likely—whether justified or not, many people have a perception that federal courts are less likely to administer a nasty dose of local justice to the outsider. (Have you ever gotten a speeding ticket while driving through another state? Did you get the same treatment as a local would have?)

**Forum non Conveniens**—Suppose the plaintiff decides to file in a state court that has jurisdiction and in which venue is proper, but the place chosen has little or no connection with the parties or the events in dispute. (Why would the plaintiff do this? One reason might be to make things expensive and difficult for the defendant. Remember, litigation is a contest between adversaries, not a church social.)

In such cases the court has the power to tell the plaintiff to go elsewhere. The defendant can move to dismiss based on the doctrine of **forum non conveniens** (Latin for "the forum is not convenient"). In practice, such motions are seldom successful, because it is normally the plaintiff's privilege to decide where to file. To get a case dismissed on *forum non conveniens* grounds, the defendant will have to convince the court that it would be very burdensome to proceed at the plaintiff's chosen location, because, for example, most of the witnesses and evidence are located in some other distant state. Even then, the case will probably stay where the plaintiff filed it if the plaintiff can point to some legitimate reason for the choice of forum.

**Federal Transfer**—In federal court, the defendants chances of successfully arguing *forum non conveniens* are somewhat better. By statute (28 U.S.C. §1404), a federal district court can transfer the case to some other more appropriate district instead of dismissing it. In practice, federal judges typically feel free to grant a transfer if it appears that some other district has a significantly greater connection with the dispute.

## Step 6   *Decide Which of the Possible Courts Is Best*

Finally, we come to the whole reason for all of this laborious evaluating of possible forums: We want to file in the place that gives our client the best possible shot at winning. The choice of forum will automatically have a huge impact on what procedure will be followed, what rules of substantive law will be applied, and how the case will be decided. Why do we care? It is entirely possible, even likely, that a given lawsuit would succeed in state A and fail in state B merely due to differences in the laws of the two states.

**Procedural Law**—Every court applies its own procedural law. (Recall that procedural law gives us the rules on how to conduct a lawsuit; substantive law gives us the rules by which the court will measure the defendant's conduct and decide who wins or loses. If you are unsure of the distinction between substance and procedure, this would be a good time to reread the sidebar "Substance v. Procedure" in Chapter 1.)

In the federal courts, the source of procedural law is the Federal Rules of Civil Procedure. Thus, procedural law is theoretically uniform in all federal district courts, whether the court is sitting in Alaska or Washington, D.C. In practice, there are minor variations, in part due to local rules, in part because some of the discovery rules allow districts to choose which of several options to follow, and in part because the U.S. Court of Appeals is divided geographically into thirteen circuits, each of which may interpret the rules differently.

In state courts, procedure is determined by state law. In most states, the highest court issues rules of procedure, which are often patterned after the Federal Rules of Civil Procedure. In a few states, the legislature prescribes court procedure by statute. In all states, the interpretation of procedural rules is up to the appellate courts of the state.

As a practical matter, procedure under the federal rules is sufficiently uniform that most attorneys who have experience litigating in federal court in one district feel perfectly comfortable litigating in another district. Local rules usually allow out-of-state attorneys to be admitted to practice before any federal district court for the purpose of handling a single case (although a local attorney must often be retained as local counsel to assist).

In state court, the situation is entirely different. Although the general principles are the same everywhere, the details of state court procedure are extremely variable from state to state, and it is the details that will get you sued for malpractice. Few competent attorneys would even dream of handling suits in the state courts of some other state without having a license to practice there and a thorough familiarity with the court system. It is nearly always preferable to refer the case to a litigator in the state in which the suit will proceed.

**Substantive Law**—A given cause of action may be based on federal substantive law or state substantive law—it is up to the plaintiff to decide under which substantive laws to sue. For example, if you sue someone for violating the federal securities laws, your cause of action will be based on federal substantive law. If you sue someone for the tort of battery, your cause of action will be based on the state substantive law of battery.

*Federal law causes of action:* With federal causes of action, it is relatively easy to decide what substantive law will apply. Almost always, the cause of action will be based on some federal statute. Assuming personal jurisdiction can be obtained, the suit can be filed in any U.S. district court in any state, or in the state courts of any state, and the substantive law applied will always be the same.

*State law causes of action:* You might suppose that state law rules of substantive law would also be the same everywhere in the country—that is, that what "negligence" is in California would be "negligence" in New York. It turns out that nothing could be further from the truth. Each state has its own legislators and appellate judges, each with their own opinions about what the law should be, and each free to legislate accordingly.

You might also suppose that each state would always apply its own substantive law. In general, you would be right, but there is a complication: A part of the substantive law of each state consists of "choice of law" laws, which may require a given case to be decided under the substantive laws of some other state! Thus, for example, if Dr. Collins sues Shannon in Texas (assuming personal jurisdiction could be obtained), the Texas "choice of law" laws might well require the Texas court to decide the case according to Nevada law of battery, since Nevada is the place where the battery occurred. To make matters even more complicated, the "choice of law" laws vary from state to state, and several intricate constitutional issues are involved. Law schools offer entire courses devoted to "choice of law" laws; this is not a simple subject, and cases with connections to more than one state often require careful research of the choice of law issues.

*State law causes of action in federal court:* Are you confused yet? If not, consider what happens when the plaintiff sues in *federal* district court on a cause of action based on *state* substantive law. (Can this happen? Certainly; by definition, federal diversity jurisdiction cases involve causes of action based on state substantive law; otherwise they would be federal question cases.)

Now a further complication sets in: In diversity cases, federal courts apply federal *procedural* law (the federal rules as interpreted by the federal courts), but the *substantive* law is the law of the state in which the court sits, including state appellate court case law. In other words, a federal district court sitting in state X should, in theory, determine substantive law issues exactly as if it were a state court in state X, deferring to state X appellate court decisions exactly as a state trial court would do. (For some historical flavor on this, see the sidebar.)

That seems easy enough, until you realize that the line between procedure and substance is not always very clear. For example, states have statutes of limitations that require lawsuits to be filed within a certain number of years after the cause of action arises. Are these procedural or substantive? (Substantive, according to the U.S. Supreme Court.) Fortunately, in modern practice, such questions seldom arise. As a practical matter, in federal district court, we can generalize and say that except in rare instances:

1. Any issue covered by the Federal Rules of Civil Procedure is procedural, and the rules control.

2. Any cause of action involving a federal statute is a federal question, and federal substantive law (including federal appellate court interpretations) controls.

3. On any other issues, state law controls, as interpreted by the state appellate courts of the state in which the district court sits.

**Other Factors in Choosing a Forum**—In deciding which of several possible forums offers the best chance of winning, the law to be applied is one important consideration. A number of other factors are important, which we mention only briefly.

*Caseload and average time to trial:* Crowded dockets are a modern-day fact of life. In some forums, it may take an average of as much as five years to get a case to trial; in others, it may be possible to be in front of a jury telling your story in as little as a year after filing the complaint. Long delays usually favor the defendants, since the defendants ordinarily prefer to delay the possibility of having to pay the plaintiff anything for as long as possible.

*Who decides?—Judges and jury demographics:* It goes without saying that the judge to whom a lawsuit is assigned may have a very great influence on the outcome. Judges are people, with the usual array of biases and prejudices. Intellectual

## SIDEBAR

### Swift, Erie, and the Rules of Decision Act

*Historically, the idea of federal district courts deferring to state appellate courts in their interpretations of state law was a matter of considerable controversy. (This issue, known as the Erie doctrine after the leading Supreme Court case, is a cherished icon among law professors and tends to be elaborated in bewildering detail in procedure textbooks; we will try to restrain ourselves, since the matter has now been settled law for some sixty years and, quite frankly, none of us has seen a single Erie issue in more than fifty combined years of litigation practice.)*

*The controversy surrounded a 1789 act of Congress called the Rules of Decision Act. The act still exists, essentially unchanged from its 1789 incarnation. You can find it at 28 U.S.C. §1652, and it says:*

The laws of the several states, except where the Constitution or treaties of the United States or Acts of Congress otherwise require or provide, shall be regarded as rules of decision in civil actions in the courts of the United States, in cases where they apply.

*Remember that in lawsuits, the substantive law we are dealing with often does not come from statutes. Instead, it comes from the common law—that is, the decisions of appellate courts as explained in published opinions. When the Rules of Decision Act refers to "the laws of the several states," does it mean only the statutes of the states, or does it mean the state common law as well?*

*In 1842, the U.S. Supreme Court decided the case Swift v. Tyson, 16 Pet. 1, 10 L.Ed.865 (1842). The issue was whether the suit would be decided under New York state common law of negotiable instruments, or whether the federal courts were free to devise their own federal common law. Justice Story, writing for the Court, held that federal courts should devise their own common law, so that the common law applied in federal courts would be uniform throughout the whole country.*

*Legal scholars spent the next hundred years debating the issue. Finally, in 1938, in a case whose particulars every first-year law student can recite in his or her sleep—Erie Railroad Co. v. Tompkins, 304 U.S. 64 (1938)—the U.S. Supreme Court overruled its earlier decision in Swift v. Tyson and held that there is no federal common law, that it would be an unconstitutional invasion of states' rights to create one, and that federal courts would henceforth defer to the common law as established by the state appellate courts of the state in which the district court is sitting.*

---

abilities vary, as do judges' levels of interest in particular areas of the law. Most urban courts have a number of judges, and cases are assigned at random, so usually you will not have the opportunity to select a particular judge for your case. However, it seems that the bench (meaning all the judges taken together) of a particular court often develops its own personality, enough so that there may be a discernibly higher probability of getting your particular lawsuit assigned to a "good" judge (defined as one more likely to decide important issues in your favor) if you file in, say, U.S. district court than if you file in your state's state court (or vice versa).

Another important variable is the way in which judges are assigned. In some courts, once a judge is assigned to your case, you are stuck with the assignment. In others, there is a procedure by which you can "strike" a judge and have a different one assigned. Some courts take the type of case into account in assigning cases to judges, so that judges can develop "specialty" expertise; in other courts, case assignments are totally random. What are your court's rules for changing a judge? Do you have to have "cause" to get a new judge?

| *Your Local Notes* |
| ------------------ |
| _____ |
| _____ |

Still another factor to consider is the effect of a forum choice on the demographics of the eventual jury pool. Trial lawyers usually have very definite ideas about the kinds of jurors they would prefer in a particular case; choosing a forum in which the desired kinds of people are prevalent in the local population is one easy way to gain an advantage in jury selection.

***Convenience, cost, and attorney familiarity:*** All other things being equal, attorneys usually prefer to litigate in their home state. The procedure and the court systems are familiar, and the judges and the local substantive law are known quantities. Filing in another state, whether in federal or state court, will usually require bringing in a local lawyer in the forum state to share the responsibility, and necessitate travel back and forth to the forum state, all of which add to the costs.

# Choosing a Court: Learning by Example

Now we will apply our step-by-step analysis to the problem of deciding where Allen Porter might file suit on Shannon's behalf. To keep the example reasonably simple, we assume that she will sue only Dr. Collins and the hotel.

### Step 1 — List All Courts Where the Case Might Be Filed

To list the possible forums, we first need to know what states the parties are citizens of. We know that Shannon is a resident of Arizona and Dr. Collins is a resident of Texas. What about the hotel? After investigating, we find that Banbury Park Hotel is owned and operated by Park Hotels Group, a Delaware corporation with its main office in New Jersey and hotels in a number of states including Nevada, Texas, and Arizona.

Our list of forums therefore includes these possibilities:

1. Arizona state court (Because of the advantages of convenience, familiarity, and cost effectiveness, the attorney's local state and federal courts should always be on the list);

2. U.S. District Court for the District of Arizona;

3. Nevada state court (The place where most of the events happened should always be on the list);

4. U.S. District Court for the District of Nevada;

5. Texas state court (A defendant can always be sued in the state in which he or she resides); and

6. U.S. District Court for the _____ District of Texas.

These are the main alternatives; we could also list as more remote possibilities:

7. Delaware federal and state courts (Park Hotels' place of incorporation);

8. New Jersey federal and state courts (Park Hotels' main office); and

9. Any other state in which Park Hotels does business.

### Step 2 — Check Each Forum for Jurisdiction of the Subject Matter

State trial courts have general subject matter jurisdiction, and garden-variety tort suits are unlikely to involve any esoteric subject matter jurisdiction is-sues. We will assume for now that any of the state courts would have subject matter jurisdiction, subject perhaps to rechecking the issue if we should narrow the list down to a state court with which we are unfamiliar.

There does not seem to be any federal question involved, so federal court jurisdiction, if any, would have to be based on diversity of citizenship. Does it exist? The plaintiff's citizenship is Arizona; the defendants' are Texas, and Delaware and New Jersey. No defendant has the same citizenship as the plaintiff, so there would be diversity jurisdiction as long as the amount in controversy is greater than the jurisdictional limit of $75,000. Therefore, any of the federal courts would have subject matter jurisdiction.

### Step 3 — Check for Jurisdiction of the Person of Each Defendant

Now we come to a factor that will reduce the size of our list. First of all, we can quickly reject Delaware and New Jersey. Because Dr. Collins has not caused an act or event to occur in either of those states in connection with this dispute, we could not get long-arm jurisdiction over him there. Although we might conceivably get tag jurisdiction if we followed him around and he entered one of those states, a New Jersey or Delaware court would most likely dismiss under the *forum non conveniens* doctrine if we did so, since the case has no real connection to either of those states.

In Nevada, we could clearly get jurisdiction of the person of Park Hotels Group, Inc., since it is doing business there and our claim arises from that business. We could likely get long-arm jurisdiction of Dr. Collins because he caused an act or event to occur in Nevada.

In Texas, we could get personal jurisdiction of Dr. Collins since he is a citizen of Texas. Texas courts should have jurisdiction over Park Hotels Group, Inc., since it operates a hotel in Texas and is therefore "present" there.

In Arizona, the courts would have jurisdiction over Park Hotels Group, Inc., since it operates a hotel in Arizona. Dr. Collins presents a difficult problem, which Allen Porter solved in our hypo by convincing Dr. Collins's attorney to consent to suit in Arizona. Had Dr. Collins not consented, the only remaining possibility would have been to catch him inside Arizona and serve process on him, an uncertain strategy at best.

| Step 4 | *Decide Whether Venue Would Be Proper* |
|---|---|

State court venue rules vary from state to state. To decide in which counties in Texas, Arizona, or Nevada Shannon could file suit, we would have to consult each state's venue statute. Often, venue statutes allow suit in any county in which any defendant resides, or failing that, in which the plaintiff resides.

Two of our federal court possibilities, Arizona and Nevada, are states that have only one federal district, so venue issues do not arise—there is only one possible venue. Texas has four districts, and, under the federal venue statute, 28 U.S.C. §1391, venue is proper in any district in which personal jurisdiction over all defendants can be obtained. In theory, this means we could sue in any Texas district; in practice, a choice other than the Northern District (which includes Dallas) would invite a transfer motion.

| Step 5 | *Consider Defendant's Transfer Options* |
|---|---|

We have already seen that the federal courts of Arizona, Nevada, and Texas would have jurisdiction over Shannon's suit. Therefore, if Shannon files suit in the state courts of any of those states, either Park Hotels Group or Dr. Collins could petition to remove the case to the federal court of the same state.

If Shannon files in Arizona federal court, there is some possibility that Park Hotels Group could persuade the judge to order the case transferred to another district (probably Nevada). The argument would be that because the important events occurred in Nevada, most of the witnesses are likely to be there.

| Step 6 | *Decide Which of the Possible Courts Is Best* |
|---|---|

In our hypo, Allen Porter chose to file suit in federal district court in Arizona. Why Arizona? First of all, the other choices are Texas and Nevada, the home states of the two defendants. Do juries tend to favor their own state residents in suits brought by outsiders, especially where (in Nevada) the suit involves a major state industry (hotels and tourism)? Is there such a thing as a "home court advantage" in litigation? In our opinion, probably so.

Another reason for choosing Arizona is that that is where Allen Porter practices. Choosing Nevada or Texas would mean having to employ local counsel to assist (an expense); having to travel back and forth to attend hearings (another expense); and having to become familiar with new judges and procedural details (time consuming and a risk of making mistakes arises). If Porter had concluded that the case should be filed in Nevada, he might well have decided simply to refer the case to a Nevada attorney.

Why federal court? The choice between federal and state court is a judgment call. In our hypo, we can surmise that one of the out-of-state defendants would have petitioned to remove to federal court, had Shannon filed suit in Arizona state court. Better, then, to save time and expense and file in federal court in the first place.

## Choosing a Court: Learning by Doing

Your assignment for this workshop is to analyze the jurisdictional and choice-of-forum issues from the standpoint of Dr. Collins. Assume the following:

> You are a paralegal in the law office of Roger Yarborough, attorney for Dr. Arthur Collins. Assume that Dr. Collins is a resident of your city, and that Roger Yarborough practices in your city. Assume that Park Hotels Group, Inc., operates a hotel in your city, and assume that Shannon Martin often comes to your city to make sales presentations. The remaining facts are as described in the hypo.
>
> After discussing the case with Allen Porter, Roger Yarborough realizes that Porter is about to file suit on Shannon's behalf, naming Dr. Collins as one of the defendants. Yarborough decides that he would prefer to seize the initiative and file the suit himself. He assigns you to prepare a memo listing the possible places where Dr. Collins might file suit, and the issues and problems that would arise in connection with each choice.

### EXERCISES

In carrying out this assignment, you should follow the step-by-step formula described in this workshop.

*1.* List all of the courts in which Dr. Collins's suit might conceivably be filed.

*2.* For each of the courts you listed, give your conclusion about whether the court would have subject matter jurisdiction, and the reasons for it.

*3.* For the state and federal courts of your state only, locate the applicable long-arm statute and read it. In a suit by Dr. Collins against Shannon and Park Hotels Group, could you obtain personal jurisdiction over both defendants? List each possible basis for doing so, and indicate what problems each might entail.

4. For the state and federal courts of your state only, locate the applicable venue statute and read it. In a suit by Dr. Collins against Shannon and Park Hotels Group in your state's state court, in which county or counties would venue lie? In federal court, in which district would venue lie?

5. Look up the removal statute and the federal transfer statute and read them. Assume that Dr. Collins sues Shannon and Park Hotels Group in the state courts of your state, and Park Hotels Group does not like that choice of forum. List all the possible strategies that Park Hotels Group might try in order to get the case into some other forum, and discuss whether you think each strategy would work and why. Suppose Park Hotels Group would prefer to litigate in Nevada—can you think of any way in which they can achieve that result?

6. Suppose you could file Dr. Collins's suit against Shannon and Park Hotels Group either in federal or state court in your state. Which would you choose and why? List all the factors you can think of that might influence the choice.

# PRACTICE POINTERS
## *Document Management*

One of the crucial tasks a litigation legal assistant performs is document management. This includes the production, organization, review, and analysis of documents. Documents are extremely important in any case and are the most common "smoking gun" around which many a legal drama revolves. What makes legal assistants particularly valuable in reference to document management is that attorneys generally dislike anything having to do with the reading or organizing of documents.

How documents are managed can make or break a case. A paper trail is often times a more effective witness to a chain of events than is a human. The human memory can falter or fill in the blanks, but documents do not fabricate. Documents can either substantiate or discredit a witness's story, thereby enhancing a witness's credibility or destroying it. Documents can also illustrate relationships between parties and establish a chronology of events. They can be used to refresh a witness's memory or to impeach a witness. They are extremely powerful tools in the hands of an astute litigator and the wise legal assistant learns how to masterfully manage them.

Therefore, you must carefully review, analyze, and organize every document you receive. Merely skimming over documents will not afford you the opportunity to pick up the kind of detail that attorneys are looking for in proving their cases. You must read them in the context of the primary legal questions raised in the case and, relying on your logic and understanding of the law, seek those facts that are especially pertinent to proving your client's position and discrediting your opponent.

You must then organize each document in such a manner that it is easily accessible by you and anyone else who seeks it. Attorneys are notorious for popping their heads in the door and demanding that you immediately retrieve a document they need. You must be so familiar with each document and the overall organization of all of the documents that you can literally lay your hand on whatever you need within minutes.

Furthermore, as the custodian of all original documents, you must ensure that documents are never misfiled or lost. No matter who has access to the files, it is the responsibility of the legal assistant to make sure all documents are correctly filed.

## TECHNO TIP

One way of finding out about your judge in the federal district court is to review his opinions. Most rulings by district court judges are not published but are memorandum opinions that cannot be cited as precedent. They can, however, be cited to establish the law of the case, *res judicata* or collateral estoppel. Westlaw® does maintain a database on some of the memorandum opinions. You may want to go to the local district court to see if an index of each judge's cases is maintained to see if he has had prior, similar cases to yours.

Most state trial courts do not have such an index. The state's trial court opinions are not published (except as they may be quoted from in an appellate decision). You can, however, search the reported case database to find out from which cases a particular judge was appealed. From a cursory review of these cases you can determine the judge's appellate record (percentage of reversals v. those affirmed) and hopefully get a glimpse of her judicial philosophy. For example, does the judge grant motions for summary judgment on a regular basis? If so, is she affirmed on appeal more often than not? Is the judge inclined to grant a new trial, enter judgment n.o.v., or direct a verdict?

Today many, if not most, state appellate courts have their own web sites and post their decisions as soon as they are filed. Although the database is usually quite limited (only the current year's decisions to date or the past few years), many are searchable—and all are free. You may also want to contact the person in charge of the court's web site. By asking just a few questions you may find out what new "bells and whistles" may soon be available. You might also be able to find a central web site with links to all the other states or other useful databases.

## FORMS FILE

*For your forms notebook we suggest you prepare a list of all the jurisdictional elements you need to consider when deciding in which court to sue. Although you think you will never forget this information after you have been tested over it, you will find that this is precisely the kind of information that fades away after you have studied it. Although jurisdictional issues are typically dealt with by attorneys, you will benefit from having a quick reference you can use to refresh your memory.*

## KEY TERMS

Appellate jurisdiction
Choice of forum
Diversity of citizenship
   jurisdiction
Domicile
Federal question jurisdiction
*Forum non conveniens*
General subject matter
   jurisdiction

Jurisdiction of the person
Jurisdiction of the subject
   matter
Jurisdictional amount
Limited subject matter
   jurisdiction
Long-arm statute
Minimum contacts

Original jurisdiction
Pendent jurisdiction
Venue

## INTRODUCTION: CASE WORKUP

In litigation as in most other human endeavors, the odds favor those who prepare diligently. Preparation of your case should begin at the moment of first contact with the prospective client. Whether you represent plaintiff or defendant, you can do a great deal during the early stages that will improve your chances of winning.

In this workshop, we present a systematic approach for pre-suit case preparation, consisting of a series of steps that will merit consideration in most if not all cases. The steps suggested are intended as a guide, not as a rote formula to be mechanically applied. We stress that each case is unique, and you will doubtless find yourself adding or subtracting steps as circumstances dictate.

If you represent a plaintiff, these preparation steps should normally be well under way, if not actually completed, before you file a complaint with the court. If you are defending, you may not have the luxury of pre-suit preparation, because your client may not contact you until he or she has actually been sued. What then? You do as much as you can, as early as you can, preferably before filing an answer.

**On the Care and Feeding of Clients**—Much of the information you need to get started will come from your client. Lawyers often rely on paralegals to do the detail work in preparing a case for filing, and this often brings paralegals in direct and frequent contact with clients.

Keeping the clients happy is job number one at every law firm, large or small. For the paralegal, an offended client is the quickest of all tickets to the unemployment line. In large part, maintaining good client relations is a matter of common courtesy and consideration, the same qualities that enhance any interpersonal relationship. (If you feel a need to improve your general client relationship skills, the classic book by Dale Carnegie, *How to Win Friends and Influence People,* is well worth a read.)

Of the various ways of making clients extremely unhappy, a few recurring themes are worth mentioning.

*Client confidentiality:* First—and the importance of this principle cannot be overstated— lawyers have a duty to keep their clients' business confidential. (See also Workshop 19 on the ethics of litigation.) This duty extends to everyone in the firm, including paralegals. Client business is not a proper subject for casual gossip, even with other employees of the firm and most especially with outsiders. You may not talk about the business of the firm's clients to your friends or even to your spouse.

In real life, clients expect more than just confidentiality. They expect, and are entitled to, absolute privacy. Even if the particular facts that you are talking about happen to be (technically) public information (i.e., described in some paper that has been filed with the court), trust us, the client will not appreciate it when he finds out you have been talking about the case to others. Similarly, when you are out having lunch with one of your paralegal friends, even if you both work for the same firm, find something else to talk about; if your conversation is overheard and reported, unpleasant consequences are almost a certainty.

*Keeping your promises:* Clients have a right to expect you to keep your promises. In our experience, broken promises are probably the foremost cause of clients becoming angry with their lawyers. When you tell a client that you will have a document ready for filing on Friday, do it! Avoid overpromising. If it cannot be done by Friday, don't tell your client that it will be. And on the (hopefully) rare occasions when you miscalculate, call the client *before* the promised deadline and explain. On a related theme, be scrupulous about being on time for appointments with clients.

*Communications with clients:* Clients rightly expect their lawyers to keep them apprised of what is going on in their cases and to answer their questions promptly. As a litigation paralegal, it is very important that you have a clear understanding with your supervising attorney about the scope of your role in furnishing information to clients. Ask your supervising attorney how you should respond when clients ask you questions, particularly those that might be interpreted as asking for legal advice. Find out what kinds of information you are authorized to give clients. Many attorneys find it worthwhile to send copies of all correspondence and court papers to the client automatically. Find out what your firm's policy is and follow it. Often, supervising attorneys will want to review your correspondence with clients before it is sent; be sure you know what is expected of you.

---

**Figure W3–1  Client Interviewing and Case Workup Steps**

Step 1:   *Determine Who the Adverse Parties Are*
Step 2:   *Determine What the Dispute Is About*
Step 3:   *Determine What Damages Are Involved*
Step 4:   *Determine When the Dispute Arose*
Step 5:   *Determine Where to Get More Information*
Step 6:   *Get Needed Administrative Information*
Step 7:   *Inform the Client*
Step 8:   *Properly Document the Outcome*
Step 9:   *Research Causes of Action and Defenses*
Step 10:  *Assemble Available Documents*
Step 11:  *Interview Main Witnesses*
Step 12:  *Determine to Whom Demand Should Be Directed*
Step 13:  *Describe Facts of Dispute*
Step 14:  *Estimate Probability of Prevailing*
Step 15:  *Calculate Damages*
Step 16:  *Make a Specific Demand*

---

# Case Workup:
# Step-by-Step Instructions

Figure W3–1 shows the steps we will cover in our discussion of case workups, which is broken down into three sections: (1) client interviewing, (2) investigation, and (3) settlement demands.

## CLIENT INTERVIEWING STEPS

It goes without saying that the kinds of information to be obtained from prospective clients vary from one case to another. This workshop is intended to familiarize you with some of the basic information that will be required in nearly every case. As you gain experience, you will want to add new categories, tailored to the types of cases on which you are working.

The role of paralegals in client interviewing varies widely. In some firms, paralegals conduct all or most initial client interviews; in others, especially those devoted to more complex litigation, attorneys do the client interviewing, perhaps with a paralegal assisting. We describe the steps in this workshop as if you, the paralegal, were performing each of the tasks. (Note, that the same principles apply if an attorney is conducting the interview.)

At some point, a decision will have to be made about whether to accept the case. This decision must be made by the attorneys (not the paralegal) and will depend on a number of factors. We mention many of these in the discussion to follow, since we assume that you are interested in knowing how attorneys decide which cases to accept. If you work in a law firm in which paralegals participate in client interviewing, your supervising attorney will tell you precisely when and how you are to interact with her regarding acceptance of cases.

**Preparation**—Checklists or questionnaires are an invaluable tool to ensure that important facts are not missed. If you work in a firm whose practice is devoted mainly to a specialized type of case (e.g., automobile accidents), your employer will undoubtedly be using them already. If not, you will want to begin creating your own. A good checklist is always a work in progress. As usual with litigation forms, whenever you see a good interview checklist, try to get a copy, add it to your form file, and use it to improve your own.

As useful as checklists and questionnaires are, however, they are not a substitute for good judgment. Before conducting an interview (and during the interview, too!) take some time to think about what you are trying to accomplish. Your ultimate goal is not just to collect information; it is to win a lawsuit. What kinds of facts would help do that? What things can your client tell you that will help you find the facts that you need?

## SIDEBAR

# An Interview Checklist

*Although an interview checklist is a flexible document, certain basic information is almost always necessary. You may want to fashion a separate checklist for each type of case your firm accepts, such as personal injury, other torts, contracts, securities, and bankruptcy. An example of a "basic" personal injury checklist follows. Remember that you do not want to appear to be interrogating your client. If possible, you may want to send her home with a copy of your firm's standard personal injury interrogatories to be answered at her leisure. If your court has adopted a set of standard interrogatories, they might be used, either separately or together, with your firm's. If the answers are not relevant or necessary to your representation of the client, do not ask them.*

Name:

Address:

Spouse:

Children:

Employer:

Title:

Other Employment Information:

*Note—do not ask for salary or other income information unless needed. If the case does not warrant a lost wage claim, you have no reason to ask a person's income.*

Social Security No.:

Prior Marriages:

*Note—only if relevant to the case.*

Prior Litigation Experiences:

Date, Time, Place of Incident:

Detailed Narrative of Incident:

*Find out who the potential defendants are. Let the client ramble as much as she will. Afterwards direct her to areas that may have been overlooked, such as, witnesses, speeds, other vehicles involved, passengers, lighting conditions, colors, traffic control devices, etc.*

Investigation:

*Was incident investigated? If so, by whom? Was a report made? If so, does the client have a copy?*

Medical Information:

*Paramedics at scene? Was client treated at the scene? Was an ambulance called? Was client transported? Which hospital? Emergency room care? Postaccident treatment; with family doctor or specialist(s)? You need to get the names and addresses of all treating health care providers (such as doctors and chiropractors). Obtain all funeral expenses if a death occurred.*

Current Health Status:

Prior Medical Treatment:

*Note—we would be ashamed to have to admit how many times prior treatment to a client, often for similar symptoms, was discovered by the opposing side from a review of our client's medical records. Be very, very thorough in eliciting the client's prior medical history. Ask specific questions about possible prior treatment for similar injuries or symptoms to those claimed to have been caused by the incident.*

Medical Insurance Coverage:

*Does the client have medical coverage? Are her medical bills from the incident being billed to the carrier? Who is the carrier and what type of plan is it? Note—some medical plans have the right to seek reimbursement for any medical payments made due to the act of a third party; most employer-provided plans are ERISA plans that allow for reimbursement and are governed by federal, not state, law. If there is no insurance, or insurance will pay for the incident or the health care professional, did the client give a lien to the provider to insure payment? If so, make sure you get a copy of the lien!*

Automobile Insurance Coverage:

*Does the client have insurance to cover any property damage that occurred (collision)? Is uninsured and underinsured motorist coverage available? Did she carry any medical payments coverage? Is there any "bells and whistles" coverage that might be applicable, such as accidental death and dismemberment or disability coverage.*

---

## SIDEBAR

## An Interview Checklist *continued*

*Other Insurance Coverage:*

*Is there nonautomobile disability coverage, accidental death or dismemberment coverage, credit card coverage, mortgage coverage, and the like? Many people do not know what insurance coverage is provided and/or when it is applicable. You will be doing your client a disservice by not thoroughly checking for any source of compensation that might be due them, even though your firm will not share in the proceeds!*

*Post-Interview Follow-Up:*

*After you have taken the initial information you will need to obtain the medical, police, and insurance records of the client. Review them carefully with your outline. Discrepancies almost always can be found. Bring the client back to the office to review the materials with you and explain any new issues you have found. If you sent the client interrogatories, review them with her as well.*

---

Your Local Notes

_____

_____

**The Interview**—Clients expect lawyers and paralegals to conduct themselves as professionals. Most clients are not experts on litigation, so they are not equipped to judge the quality of your work on its merits. Instead, they will judge you mainly by the way in which you relate to them. Always try to set a professional, business-like tone when dealing with clients; do not use slang or profanity, do not joke about the case, do not wear inappropriate attire. Take the case seriously; you can be sure your client does.

In the interview, listen carefully and take notes. In fact, we recommend that you get in the habit of taking notes whenever you are talking about a case to anyone, whether it is your client, a witness, or (especially) your supervising attorney. In our experience, the failure of inexperienced paralegals to take notes when receiving instructions is one of the chief gripes of supervising attorneys. Invariably, it leads to a return visit to clarify something that the paralegal should have written down in the first place.

**Step 1**  *Determine Who the Adverse Parties Are*

The first task in interviewing a new client is to find out who else may be involved in the dispute. The purpose is obvious: An attorney cannot ethically represent a client if he already represents one of the adverse parties.

This information must be obtained before you get into the facts of the dispute. A simple hypo will

illustrate this: Suppose you are assigned to interview a new client, Joe Jogger, who was injured when a delivery truck hit him while he was crossing the street. You introduce yourself, and Joe immediately starts telling you all about what happened; being polite, you do not interrupt. Finally, Joe runs down a bit, and you ask him who the truck belonged to. Bad news: Joe was run over by Steve's Trucking Company, which happens to be your senior partner's oldest and most lucrative client.

Obviously, you cannot accept the case, because your senior partner is not about to sue his best client. But now you have a worse problem: You have obtained confidential information from Joe, which means that your firm cannot ethically represent Steve's Trucking Company in this case, either. Your senior partner will have to refer Steve to some other lawyer, at least for this case—an outcome not likely to improve the career of the paralegal who caused it.

A further problem is that not all fact situations are as simple as the Joe vs. Steve hypo. Prospective clients usually know, or think they know, whom they want to sue. But often, after hearing the facts and evaluating the client's position, you will find that the best claim is against someone whom the client never thought of suing. Therefore, when you ask the prospective client who the adverse parties are, cast your net wide, and try to identify every person, every corporation or other entity, and every insurance company that may be involved in the dispute, however peripherally. And do this *before* you get into the facts of the dispute itself.

Once you have the names of all the potentially adverse parties, how do you find out whether your firm represents any of them? Most law firms maintain a conflict database of some kind. In a very small office this may consist of nothing more than a card file of all of the firm's clients. In larger firms, the conflict database will be computerized, often under the control of a single employee who is responsible for maintaining it and to whom you would submit your list of names for checking. If it appears that your new client's case may involve someone whom the firm has represented in the past, the firm's attorneys will have to make a decision about whether to accept the representation.

### Step 2 — Determine What the Dispute Is About

Once you have determined that the case would not create a conflict of interest with other clients of the firm, it is time to start digging out the facts of the dispute. We recommend that you begin by letting your client tell her story, while you listen carefully, without interrupting, and take accurate notes. In part, this is simply good public relations: Clients are usually anxious to talk, to be listened to, and to be taken seriously. More importantly, you are likely to find out more if you listen to the whole story before launching into your checklist of questions.

One reason why you need the facts of the dispute is so that you can give your supervising attorney enough information that he can decide whether to accept the case. Several factors will play a part in the decision: Does the case fit within the firm's area of practice? Does the firm have the necessary resources to devote to the case at this time? Is it in the client's best interests to pursue the case, or are the chances of success too small to merit the effort and expense that would be required (see Step 3)?

Eventually, if your firm accepts the case, it will be necessary to write a complaint or respond to one. (You will practice doing both in Workshops 5 and 8). One of the most time-consuming tasks in drafting a complaint or answer is looking up all of the factual details that have to be included—names, dates, places. Your complete and accurate notes of your client's description of the facts will save you a great deal of effort, not to mention embarrassing phone calls to the client to obtain details that you were told but have forgotten.

### Step 3 — Determine What Damages Are Involved

Another important issue is whether the case makes financial sense, both to the client and to the attorney. In almost all civil litigation, the plaintiff's goal is to win money, and the defendant's goal is to avoid paying money. Thus, for the client, the overriding question should be "Does the value of the expected outcome, taking into account the chances of losing, exceed the expected cost of litigating?"

From the law firm's standpoint, the issue is whether the case is one on which the firm can make money. Like it or not, a law firm is a business, and its continued existence depends on making a profit. (Pro bono, or charity, cases may sometimes be accepted, but most attorneys prefer to know in advance when they are doing so!) Financial considerations loom especially large in contingent fee plaintiff's litigation, in which the attorney's fee is a percentage of the client's winnings, and the expenses will be borne by the attorney—perhaps for years—until the case is over. Then the decision to accept or reject a case will depend greatly on the chances of winning and the amount available to be won. Even with hourly rate work, it is poor business to accept cases that are likely to cost the client more than the desired result is worth. Therefore, in deciding whether or not to take a case, one of the things an attorney ordinarily does is to make some judgment about the strength of the case and the amount of money likely to be won or lost. To do so, some preliminary fact gathering is required.

Litigators think of the claims in a lawsuit as being composed of two main parts: (1) liability, *whether* plaintiff should win; and (2) damages, the *amount* plaintiff hopes to win. Leaving aside complications such as comparative negligence statutes and jurors who do not follow instructions, these are entirely separate issues. Whether Joe Jogger wins or loses his suit against Steve's Trucking does not depend on how badly Joe was injured—it depends on the evidence of what Steve did. For example, how many credible witnesses can Joe produce who will testify that Steve's truck ran a red light? Joe may be merely scratched up, or every bone in his body may be broken—it does not matter. Joe's injuries have (in theory) nothing to do with the issue of *whether* Joe wins.

Conversely, the *amount* Joe will win does not depend on how strong his case is—it depends *only* on the dollar value of Joe's provable injuries and losses. Thus (again, in theory) Joe's evidence that Steve ran the red light may be barely enough to convince the jury, or it may consist of a busload of priests who all saw the red light—either way, the *amount* that Joe wins should be the same.

To estimate the value of a claim (see sidebar), you need to be able to make an educated guess about both (1) plaintiff's chances of winning and (2) the amount plaintiff might win. To estimate the amount plaintiff might win, we need to gather information about the extent of plaintiff's injuries and losses.

We begin by trying to think of all of the ways in which plaintiff may have been damaged. For example, in an injury case, we want to know such things as

## The Value of a Claim

*The usual rule of thumb for assessing the value of a claim works like this: First, estimate the probable verdict range, that is, the maximum and minimum amounts that a jury would likely award if the decision is in favor of plaintiff. Then, average the two. Next, estimate what percentage of the time you would expect plaintiff to win, based on everything you know about the strength of both parties' cases. That is, if the case were tried a hundred times before a hundred different juries, how many of those hundred times would you expect plaintiff to win? Finally, multiply the estimated average verdict by the percentage probability of plaintiff winning; the result is an estimate of the value of plaintiff's claim.*

*An example may help make the concept clearer. Suppose Sam Sideswipe is driving down Main Street and decides to change lanes. Sam does not notice Kathy Klutz driving obliviously along in his blind spot. Kathy might have been able to avoid a collision had she reacted quickly, but she was busy changing the CD in her CD player, so she did not notice Sam changing lanes until it was too late. Kathy sues Sam for the damage to her car, her medical bills, and her lost time from work. Approximately how much is Kathy's claim worth?*

*There are two variables: (1) How much is Kathy likely to win, if she wins? (2) How likely is she to win? Neither question can be answered with any scientific exactitude, and both require judgments of the goodness of Kathy's case, based on experience. You evaluate Kathy's damages, and estimate that if she wins, the award should be between $8,000 and $12,000—an average of $10,000. Because a jury might find that the accident was mostly Kathy's fault, this is not a "slam dunk" (few cases are); you estimate that if the case were tried ten times, Kathy would win six out of the ten, or 60 percent. The approximate value of the claim is $10,000 times 60 percent, which is equal to $6,000.*

(1) how much plaintiff's medical bills add up to; (2) how much income plaintiff lost by missing work; (3) whether future medical treatment will be needed, and how much it will cost; and (4) whether any of plaintiff's injuries will be permanent, and, if so, what sort of value a jury might place on a permanent injury of that kind. Each case is different, and no checklist can possibly anticipate every possible kind of damages. It is up to the lawyer (or paralegal) to apply her skill and judgment to be sure that no items of damages are overlooked.

At the initial interview stage, of course, we will not be able to obtain a complete breakdown of plaintiff's damages. In fact, plaintiff's damages may not all have happened yet—plaintiff may still be undergoing medical treatment, for example. Therefore, our goals at this early stage are twofold: first, to get enough facts to allow us to at least make an estimate of the value of the claim; and second, to get as much information as we can that will help us pull together the details later (i.e., names and addresses of doctors, hospitals, employers, etc.). A good checklist is invaluable here.

When we have estimated the value of the claim, do we then have enough information to allow us to decide whether the case is worth pursuing? Not quite; remember, not all judgments can be collected. From the plaintiff's standpoint, it is usually pointless to sue unless either (1) there is insurance or (2) defendant has enough nonexempt assets that a judgment could be executed. Does collectibility really become a significant issue in deciding whether to accept a case? Yes, more often than you might imagine. As a practical matter, judgments against ordinary (i.e., not wealthy) individuals are essentially worthless unless there is insurance from which the judgment can be collected. (For more detail on why this is so, see Chapter 8). Therefore, a final essential task in evaluating a claim is to get information about any insurance coverage that may apply and about the extent of defendant's assets.

Obviously, your client is unlikely to have all of the damages information you need at the time of the first interview. Follow-up will be required (see Step 5 later).

## Step 4 — Determine When the Dispute Arose

Time limits apply to the filing of lawsuits. Usually (but not always), these arise from **statutes of limitations.** A statute of limitations is a statute that requires suit to be filed on a particular type of claim within a specified length of time after the claim arises. For example, the statute of limitations for negligence claims may provide that all claims for negligence must be sued on within two years after the claim arises.

When does a claim arise? It depends on the situation, and, as with most issues in litigation, there may be a dispute about what date the claim arose on. This elementary text will not make you an expert on the intricacies of statutes of limitations (but see the sidebar for some general concepts). Fortunately,

## SIDEBAR

## Fun with Statutes of Limitations

*Statutes of limitations are statutes that place a time limit on the right to file a lawsuit. Different causes of action may have different **limitations periods**. For example, many states require suit to be filed on a cause of action for negligence within two years after the cause of action accrues. On a cause of action for, say, breach of contract, the limitations period is often longer—perhaps as much as six years. When a cause of action can no longer be sued on because the limitations period has run out, we say that the cause of action is **time-barred**.*

*When does a cause of action accrue? Courts often say that a cause of action accrues on the date by which all of the elements of the cause of action have happened. Often, the date will be obvious—in an automobile negligence case, for example, all four elements of the cause of action for negligence (duty, breach of duty, causation, and damages) are established at the moment of impact.*

*You are probably wondering how something as simple as a time limit can be made complicated. One reason is that statute of limitations law is riddled with exceptions. For example, the statutes of limitations*

*clock is typically stopped whenever plaintiff is under a disability. **Disability** is another of those common words that has a special meaning in the law: In the context of statutes of limitations, it means some situation, recognized by the statute, that tends to prevent plaintiff from being able to sue. Commonly recognized disabilities are when plaintiff is insane, or under the age of majority, or in prison.*

*Another common exception is when the cause of action is concealed in some way so that plaintiff does not find out about it until long after it has already accrued. (How could that happen? Suppose defendant embezzles funds from plaintiff, and plaintiff does not discover the embezzlement until there is an audit.) In many states, some version of the discovery rule applies; that is, the clock may not start running until plaintiff has a reasonable chance to discover the facts supporting the cause of action.*

*One further complication: A lawsuit may involve several different causes of action, and different limitations periods may apply to each one. Thus it is possible in a given lawsuit for some of the causes of action to be time-barred and others not.*

in most cases, there will be some date that we can easily identify as the earliest possible date on which the claim could have arisen, and we will be safe if we get the lawsuit filed within the prescribed period of time after that date. In an auto accident case, for example, we can safely assume that the date of the accident is the earliest date on which the claim could have arisen; we will be safe if we count from that date in deciding when the statute of limitations will run. There may be arguments we could make in favor of some later date (and we may make them if we are forced to, such as in cases where the client waited too long before seeing a lawyer) but usually our wisest course is to err on the side of caution.

Whenever you talk to a prospective client about a possible lawsuit for the first time, it is extremely important that you nail down the relevant dates. You will need them in drafting the complaint or answer, of course, but, more importantly, you need them in order to be sure that you can get the suit filed before any applicable statute of limitations runs. To fail to do this is to invite a malpractice suit when it turns out that the client contacted you two days before the statute expired and you assumed you had plenty of time.

Which dates are the relevant ones? It depends on the circumstances. As a paralegal, it will not be your job to make judgment calls on statute of limitations questions; your job, if you are assigned to interview prospective clients, is to collect the facts. Therefore, try to obtain dates for every occurrence that your client tells you about.

What are the pertinent dates? For statute of limitations purposes, the important date is (for example) the date the accident actually happened, not the date your client mistakenly remembered. Do not take your client's word for the date—check the documentation (for example, the police accident report).

What are the relevant statutes of limitation in your state?

| Your Local Notes |
| --- |
| _____ |
| _____ |

## SIDEBAR

### Other Time Issues to Watch For

*Statutes of limitations are the most common source of time limits on lawsuits, but they are not the only ones. Here are a few others (but be warned that this is not a complete list!):*

1. *Laches. Traditionally, statutes of limitations do not apply to equity causes of action (typically, those in which the relief sought is an injunction or court order instead of money damages). Instead, the court may use the doctrine of laches to throw out the suit if the court finds that plaintiff has delayed too long in pursuing his rights. How long a delay is too long? The answer is up to each court.*

2. *Administrative remedies. The law requires some types of disputes (such as labor claims) to be taken first to a designated government agency. Suit can be filed only after the government agency has had a chance to try to resolve the problem. Often, the government agency has strict time limits; as a practical matter, if these are not complied with, suit can never be filed, since the prerequisite—agency action—will never occur. The lesson here is that specialty claims involving disputes that fall within the purview of government agencies are not for amateurs.*

3. *Arbitration. Certain types of contracts provide that any dispute under the contract must be arbitrated, rather than taken to court. Usually, such contracts specify time limits for commencing arbitration.*

---

### Step 5  —  *Determine Where to Get More Information*

One of the most important purposes of an initial interview is to obtain leads to all of the information that your client does not have. As you completed Steps 1 through 4, you undoubtedly noticed gaps in your information; this is the time to think about how you are going to fill them, and what information you can get from your client that will help you do so.

Inevitably, you will eventually need to obtain every document having any bearing on the case. Inevitably, your client does not have all of them. Find out what documents are likely to exist and who has them. Get names, addresses, telephone numbers, and specific descriptions of any documents known to exist—you will need them when you send out subpoenas. Do not neglect the damages portion of your case—you will need bills, statements, estimates, appraisals, whatever it takes to establish the amount of plaintiff's losses. In personal injury cases, you will need copies of medical records; to get them, you need to know where and by whom plaintiff has been treated and you need to complete a medical release authorization (Figure W3–2). In accident cases, you will need police investigation reports; to get them, you need the date, time, location of the accident, and the identities of the drivers. In business disputes, you need copies of any contracts involved in the suit, as well as copies of all of the written correspondence between the parties.

To the extent that your client has brought pertinent documents, make copies of them now. To the extent that your client has pertinent documents but has not brought them, make definite arrangements now to obtain copies. Experience teaches that the best time to get a copy of a document is at the first opportunity.

Sooner or later, it will be necessary to prepare a complete list of the names, addresses, and telephone numbers of every potential witness in the case—that is, every person having any knowledge or information about any of the facts in dispute. This includes experts such as treating physicians and police investigating officers. Start the list now, fill in as much as your client knows, and start making plans to obtain the rest. We recommend that you keep an ongoing witness list in the file, updating it whenever you obtain new information. Such a list will be useful when you respond to your opponent's discovery requests, and it will also help you plan your own evidence-gathering work.

### Step 6  —  *Get Needed Administrative Information*

Before concluding the interview, be sure you have obtained all of the mundane data you will need in processing the case. Use your checklist. Be sure you know where your client wants mail sent and when and where you can contact your client by phone. Get Social Security numbers of everyone involved if you can.

---

**Figure W3–2  Sample Medical Release Authorization**

### MEDICAL AUTHORIZATION RELEASE

**TO WHOM IT MAY CONCERN:**

Please be advised that my attorney, Allen Porter, is hereby authorized to request, and to receive, all medical information which you may have in your possession concerning me.

You are hereby authorized to allow my attorney complete access to any and all of my medical records, including x-rays, results of other procedures and all billing statements, which are or may later be in your possession or in any way reflect anything concerning me. I hereby waive, in favor of my attorney, any and all confidential relationships.

I hereby authorize the use of a copy of this release as though it were an original.

_____

**Client**

**Social Security No.** _____

**Date:** _____, 2000

---

## Step 7 — *Inform the Client*

As a paralegal, you should avoid making statements to clients that could be construed as giving legal advice. Undoubtedly, your client will have questions; with experience and guidance from your supervising attorney, you will learn which ones you can safely answer and which you should refer to an attorney. Typically, questions about what happens next are fairly safe, if you know the answer. Questions about "How much am I going to win?" or "What are my chances of winning?" are hazardous to the careers of paralegals.

Most attorneys have some standard instructions to be given to clients at the beginning of a case. These instructions vary depending on the type of case. For example, it is usually wise to ask clients to save any receipts for expenses related to their claims and to keep a diary of any important events. Some attorneys routinely ask clients to write a narrative describing the events involved in the suit, so as to get the facts recorded while they are fresh in the client's mind. If you are assigned client interviewing duties, your supervising attorney will tell you what instructions should be given.

## Step 8 — *Properly Document the Outcome*

In modern litigation practices, it is (or should be) an ironclad rule that every contact with a prospective client must be followed up with a letter documenting what, if anything, the attorney agreed to do.

If the firm is not accepting the case, the letter must say so, in the clearest possible terms. To do otherwise is to invite a malpractice suit or a bar In modern litigation practices, it is (or should be) an ironclad rule that every contact with a prospective client must be followed up with a letter documenting what, if anything, the attorney agreed to do.

If the firm is not accepting the case, the letter must say so, in the clearest possible terms. To do otherwise is to invite a malpractice suit or a bar complaint, when the client later claims that she believed you were accepting the case. Many attorneys also consider it wise to include in the letter a recital of the dates of events as related by the client, and a suggestion to see another lawyer promptly or before a specified date. Does a lawyer who rejects a case have a duty to advise the client to see another lawyer and have suit filed before the statute of limitations runs? Trust us, this is not an issue that you want to litigate!

If the firm does accept the case, a written engagement letter or fee agreement should be prepared and signed by the lawyer and the client. The ethics rules of some jurisdictions require this, particularly in contingent fee cases. Even where rules do not require one, a written agreement is cheap insurance against a future misunderstanding. As a paralegal, you may be assigned to prepare a fee agreement for a particular case, usually based on a form agreement from the firm's form file. An attorney must sign the agreement.

## INVESTIGATION STEPS

Evidence in a lawsuit is like pieces of a jigsaw puzzle which must be put together, piece by piece, into a complete picture that can be presented to the judge or jury. The client has provided some of the pieces; the attorney, assisted by the paralegal, must find and assemble the rest.

**The Requirements of Rule 11**—How much of this work must be done before suit is filed and how much can be left for later? The bare minimum is the level of preparation required by FRCP, Rule 11(a), which states:

> The signature of an attorney . . . constitutes a certificate by the signer that the signer has read the pleading . . . [and] that to the best of the signer's knowledge, information, and belief formed after reasonable inquiry it is well grounded in fact and is warranted by existing law or a good faith argument for the extension, modification, or reversal of existing law. . . .

Rule 11 tells us that, before filing a complaint or answer, we must make enough of a "reasonable inquiry" to assure ourselves that whatever we say is "well grounded in fact." Furthermore, we must have an understanding of the causes of action that we intend to raise, sufficient that we can certify to the court that our legal theories are "warranted."

Steps 9 through 11 involve tasks that will be ongoing throughout the entire lawsuit. How far should we take them before filing suit? Once we have done enough to satisfy Rule 11, should we go ahead and file a complaint? Or should we aim for a higher target?

Ideally, it would be nice to have our entire case prepared, with all our strategies thought out in advance, because once suit is filed, we will have a judge scrutinizing everything we do, and an opponent taking shots at our case while we are preparing it. Can we achieve this ideal? Almost never. A number of forces are at work that will compel us to file suit without too much delay. If we wait, we run the risk that potential defendants will die or disappear; statutes of limitations or other deadlines may pass; someone else may file suit first and preempt our choice of forum; momentum and credibility will be lost. Moreover, informal investigation can go only so far; for some of our evidence gathering, we will need the subpoena powers of the court. Therefore, in most cases, the preparation process is not far along when suit is filed.

### Step 9   *Research Causes of Action and Defenses*

As we will see in Workshop 5, we cannot draft a complaint or answer without knowing at least the basic elements of the causes of action that we will be alleging. Rule 11 requires us to have a reasonable basis for whatever legal theories we assert. Perhaps a more compelling motivation is that if we allege a cause of action incorrectly, our opponent will try to use our mistake to get the claim dismissed. In Workshop 1, we outlined a basic approach for researching the causes of action and defenses in a case. To the extent possible, this task should be completed before suit is filed.

### Step 10   *Assemble Available Documents*

In most lawsuits, the evidence ultimately presented to the court will consist of two things: (1) testimony of witnesses and (2) documents. In most cases, you will assemble many more documents than will actually be presented to the court. The best strategy is to try to assemble the entire universe of all documents that may have anything to do with your case; then you can pick and choose the ones that best support your client's position.

The document-gathering task will continue throughout the suit, and, as a paralegal, you will likely be heavily involved in it. Document gathering takes time, and the earlier you begin, the better.

Before suit is filed, you will not be able to use the tools of discovery (such as subpoenas) to pry documents from uncooperative sources. You can, however, begin the process of ordering any documents that your client has a right to obtain (i.e., his own medical records) and any records that are open to the public (i.e., police reports, court records, recorded documents).

The procedure for obtaining documents varies with the source. Often, you can request records by letter; to do so, you need to know to whom to write, whether there is a charge for copies, and what information you must provide so that the documents you want can be located. You may need to spend some time on the telephone to find out these things. Do not hesitate to make a phone call and ask. Offices that keep records often seem to delight in inventing new hoops for you to jump through in obtaining copies, and no one can anticipate all of them. When you send out written requests for documents, be sure to make a note on your calendar so that you will remember to follow up if you do not receive a response within a reasonable time.

How do you know what documents to look for? Document gathering is a skill that comes with experience. In Workshop 9 (Document Discovery), we will develop a systematic way of attacking the problem. For now, in the pre-suit stage, concentrate on

## S I D E B A R

# Some Ethical Traps to Watch For

*One type of involved witness requires special mention: employees of an opposing party. If we are suing a company, and we know the company has a lawyer, can we contact employees of the company and ask them questions about the matters in dispute? This common situation raises potentially complex questions of ethics and of attorney–client privilege, which we will consider in detail in Workshop 19 (Ethics in Litigation). For now, the lesson you should take away is this: Do not contact an opposing party, or employees of an opposing party, without checking with your supervising attorney first.*

*Another issue that has great potential to get opponents into a high state of excitement is that of tape recording statements without the witness's knowl-edge. This is another minefield into which no paralegal should set foot without advance permission. If you are not a participant in a conversation, it is almost certainly illegal for you to record it. Even if you are recording your own telephone conversation with someone else (a witness, for example) you may be committing a crime if the person you are recording does not know you are doing it; state laws vary on this issue. Suppose you secretly record a face-to-face interview with a witness. In most states, this would not be a crime, but issues of legal ethics can arise, and the witness is unlikely to be pleased if she finds out. Bottom line: Get your supervising attorney's approval before you get out your tape recorder.*

## S I D E B A R

# Witness Statements

*A witness **statement** is a record of what a witness has said about the facts in dispute. In civil litigation, a statement usually means an informal interview at which only the witness and the interviewer are present.*

*Ideally, we want two things from a statement: (1) We would like the content—what the witness has said—to be helpful to our case; and (2) we want to preserve that content in a way that allows us to use it later in court, if necessary. Getting the right content is a matter of interviewing skills, understanding of the issues, and preparation, and it depends on the facts of each case. We will have more to say about the art of "knowing what to ask" in Workshop 13 on Working with Witnesses.*

*One way of preserving a witness's testimony is to take a deposition. Why not do that? There may be several reasons. A deposition is a more formal (and expensive) proceeding and the opposing lawyer would have a right to be present (see Rule 30, FRCP). Another factor that you may find significant is that in a deposition, a lawyer must conduct the questioning; paralegals can take witness statements.*

*There are many ways to accomplish the goal of preserving what the witness has said, including simply taking notes. Where a witness statement becomes really useful, however, is when a witness tries to change his story later, perhaps after some coaching by your opponent. Then you would like to be able to use the witness statement as evidence of the witness's prior inconsistent statement.*

*Your own notes are not very useful for that purpose. You do not want to have to testify as to what the witness said, and even if you did so it would be a matter of your word against that of the witness.*

*Tape recording the interview is a better way if the witness will allow it (be sure to get the witness's consent on tape!). One drawback is that tape recorders tend to make people careful, so the witness may not speak freely. Another negative is the fact that a tape recording preserves everything, the bad as well as the good, so you may be creating ammunition to be used against you.*

*Still another option is to take a written statement. To do this, you first interview the witness, taking careful notes. Then, on a fresh sheet of paper, write or type out the specific testimony that you wish to preserve; this can be in narrative form, or in a series of short numbered paragraphs. Ideally, if you are a notary public or have one available, write the statement in the form of a notarized affidavit. If you are not a notary, be sure to include a sentence saying that the entire statement is a true account to the best of the witness's knowledge and belief. After you interview the witness, it is usually best to write out the statement, go over it with the witness to correct any inaccuracies, and get it signed (and, ideally, notarized) then and there, before the witness has a chance to think up excuses for refusing to sign.*

assembling the documents that you know must exist (based on your client interview or based on your experience in similar cases).

## Step 11    *Interview Main Witnesses*

Once suit is filed, your freedom to contact potentially unfriendly witnesses will be much reduced. Obviously, we would not want opposing lawyers talking to our clients behind our back, and the rules of ethics restrict us from contacting a party or witness whom we know is represented by another lawyer. As a practical matter, once we sue someone, their first act will be to hire a lawyer; from then on, anything we get from them will be carefully sanitized.

What about nonparty witnesses—people whom we are not suing, but who have information about the dispute? In practice, we will find that there are two kinds: (1) the impartial witness, someone who is not a part of the dispute and does not side with either party; and (2) the involved witness—perhaps a friend or business associate of one of the parties— someone who can be expected to take sides. Whether we represent the plaintiff or the defendant, it is to our advantage to interview and take statements from as many of the impartial witnesses as we can find, as early as possible.

It can matter a great deal which side gets to these witnesses first. Ideally, the first side to talk to a witness will obtain (with the witness's permission) a tape-recorded or signed statement, locking the witness into one version of the facts for all time. A single answer to a single question can, at times, make or break a lawsuit, and a clever questioner can find many ways to cast questions so that a simple yes or no answer will carry vast implications that the witness may not have intended.

It goes without saying that we will contact all of the involved witnesses who sympathize with our side, find out what they have to say, and caution them of the dangers of speaking to our opponent without the benefit of our presence!

## SETTLEMENT DEMAND STEPS

Legal disputes can be settled—resolved by agreement—at any stage. The winner's prize in a civil lawsuit is money damages, so most settlements consist of the defendant paying an agreed amount of money to the plaintiff in exchange for plaintiff giving up the suit.

It costs money to file a lawsuit—at times, quite a lot of it—money which might be better used to pay

plaintiff and settle the case. Therefore, a pre-suit settlement proposal is usually worth considering.

The time-honored way of getting negotiations going is for plaintiff's attorney to send a demand letter to defendant (or defendant's insurance company or lawyer). In certain areas of practice—accident litigation, for example—many plaintiff's lawyers send pre-suit demand letters routinely in every case. Because the preparation of settlement demands is a job often assigned to paralegals, we include it as a part of this workshop.

Whether to make a pre-suit settlement demand in a given case is a matter of strategy. Some plaintiff's lawyers, even in garden-variety accident cases, make it a practice always to file suit first, believing that this will show determination and cause their demands to be taken seriously. There are also some opponents, usually large corporations or insurance companies, that deliberately cultivate a reputation of being tough litigants and of fighting every claim to the bitter end. In disputes involving them, settlement overtures may be futile, a waste of time and money.

Steps 12 through 16 describe the process of preparing a pre-suit settlement demand letter.

## Step 12    *Determine to Whom Demand Should Be Directed*

The purpose of a settlement demand letter is to get negotiations going. To do that, we need to be in contact with the person who has the authority to make a decision and pay money.

As a practical matter, the target in most lawsuits is a "deep pocket" of some kind—an insurance company, a large corporation, or a government agency. This fact simply reflects the reality that the vast majority of individuals are judgment proof, or close to it; they do not have enough nonexempt assets to satisfy a typical judgment. Therefore, in suits against individuals (i.e., accident cases), plaintiff's first task is to discover who will be paying the judgment if plaintiff wins (usually, an insurance company).

If we know that our opponent already has a lawyer, the settlement demand letter must be addressed to the lawyer (remember, we cannot ethically contact someone whom we know is represented, except through their lawyer). Otherwise, we will most likely send the demand to the insurance company covering the person we will be suing.

Sometimes, we will already have insurance information, perhaps from the police investigator's report. If not, a common way to proceed is to send a short letter to the person we are about to sue, along the lines of:

Dear Ms. Sideswipe:

This firm represents Irene Innocent in connection with the automobile accident of August 13, 2000. Would you please have your insurance company contact us.

## Step 13 Describe Facts of Dispute

The settlement demand letter should begin with an explanation of what the dispute is about. Be accurate in your facts, and write clearly and professionally! First impressions are important, and your opponent will be trying to decide how seriously to take your claims. Include pertinent names, dates, times, and locations.

## Step 14 Estimate Probability of Prevailing

Next, give an analysis of the liability issue. Your purpose here is to convince your opponent that your chances of winning the suit, if one is filed, are very high. This is your chance to argue the merits of your client's case. Emphasize the facts that are in your favor; if appropriate, discuss how the facts fit into your legal analysis of the case. Remember, all litigation is advocacy—your goal is to persuade.

## Step 15 Calculate Damages

Your opponent will use your settlement demand letter to try to decide how much the claim is worth. (See Step 3 earlier and the sidebar on the value of a claim.) Information about plaintiff's damages is therefore crucial. Your demand letter should lay out the damages elements of your claim in as much detail as possible. No defendant is going to pay out large sums of money without verifying plaintiff's damages, so it is best to enclose with your letter copies of whatever documents you will be relying on to prove damages. Bills, receipts, physicians' reports, repair estimates, employer's verification of time lost from work—the particulars depend on the case, but in general, the greater the amount of loss that you can document, the larger will be the settlement value of the case.

## Step 16 Make a Specific Demand

The demand letter concludes by demanding a specific sum of money in return for a release of plaintiff's claims. You are making an **offer**—a communication that, if accepted, becomes an enforceable contract—so be specific and precise. You do not want to trade the dispute you already have for another dispute over the interpretation of the settlement!

## SIDEBAR

### Releases

A **release** is an agreement whereby plaintiff relinquishes her claims against defendant, agreeing, in effect, not to sue on those claims. A release should always be reduced to writing and signed by the person whose claims are being released.

In complicated settlements, releases are custom written (with generous borrowing from the forms file, of course), and often done in the form of a contract signed by both sides. The drafting of such agreements is not a job for paralegals or even for inexperienced attorneys.

In routine insurance cases, the release is usually a printed form provided by the insurance company that is paying the settlement. Once the amount of the settlement has been agreed on, the insurance company sends a release, and a check or draft for the agreed sum of money, made out to the attorney and the plaintiff jointly. This procedure is called a **conditional delivery**. The check is not to be deposited until the release has been signed and placed in the return mail to the insurance company. Usually, the attorney has the client sign the release and endorse the check at the same time; then, after the release has been sent back to the insurance company, the attorney deposits the check in the law firm's trust account, waits for the check to clear, and then writes a check to the client after deducting the attorney's fees and expenses.

Often, paralegals are given responsibility for all or part of this process. You should be aware of a potential hazard: It is possible for the boilerplate in the insurance company release form to contain provisions that the client should not agree to. As long as the language of the release is limited to the relinquishment of claims, it is probably acceptable. But some release forms also include agreements to **indemnify** or **hold harmless**. Both terms mean to pay someone else's losses—in this case, the losses that the insurance company may incur if it turns out that someone else has a right to sue on the claim being settled. Although the risk is usually remote, releases that contain indemnification or hold harmless provisions should be reviewed by an attorney.

It is best to set a time limit, by specifying a deadline after which the offer to settle will terminate. Otherwise, your opponent will be tempted to play a delaying game, letting you "twist in the wind" waiting for the phone to ring—a weak negotiating position.

## Case Workup: Learning by Example

Now we will consider how these principles might be applied in Shannon's hypothetical case against Banbury Park Hotel.

### CLIENT INTERVIEWING STEPS

In our hypo, we left to the imagination most of the details of Allen Porter's initial interview with Shannon. We now know that his first questions must have been directed at identifying the other parties involved in the dispute. Once satisfied that there was no potential conflict of interest with other clients, Shannon would have been encouraged to tell her story. When she finished, Porter would have zeroed in with specific questions to fill any gaps: When, exactly, did this happen? What was the date? What was the name and telephone number of the police investigator? Did she give Shannon a card? Porter would take extensive notes, taking down any names and addresses that Shannon can provide, and any ideas about where to obtain additional information.

Estimating the settlement value of a claim of this kind is difficult, mainly because it is difficult to place a dollar value on how traumatic Shannon's experience was. Nevertheless, Porter would want some idea of the severity of Shannon's damages, so as to be able to decide whether the potential claim is large enough to justify the cost of litigating it. How much are the doctor bills so far? What additional treatment did the doctor tell Shannon she would need? What is the likely outcome of her job situation?

Before Shannon leaves, she will undoubtedly want to know what Porter thinks of her claim. Every client wants to know how much money the attorney thinks they can win, and nearly every client already has some amount, often unrealistically high, in mind. Because Porter is the attorney in charge of the case, he may decide to estimate upper and lower limits. If he does, these will be widely spread, deliberately calculated to err on the low side, and accompanied by strong warnings about the unreliability of such estimates. More likely, he may defer answering until more investigation has been done. (As a paralegal, you should never, ever, offer opinions to clients about the possible value of a claim unless you are looking for a one-way ticket to some other line of work.)

Porter will undoubtedly have a standard form contingent fee agreement for use in injury cases. In modern law offices, a secretary or word-processing clerk can likely fill in any blanks and print the agreement quickly, so that Porter can go over the agreement with Shannon, have her sign it, and give her a copy before she leaves.

### INVESTIGATION STEPS

A good first step in investigating a claim like Shannon's is to take advantage of the investigation already done by the police. Telephoning the detective, as Porter did, would be worth a try in an unusual case like this one; in a routine accident case, it would be more common to obtain the written police report before attempting to speak to the investigating officer.

Chuck's trip to Las Vegas to scout out the scene raises several knotty ethical issues, which we can assume Porter discussed thoroughly with Chuck before giving his approval. Was it proper, for example, for Chuck to conduct an investigation on premises owned by an adverse party without the knowledge of Park Hotels or its attorneys? We will revisit this and other issues in Workshop 19, Ethics in Litigation.

Our narrative did not dwell on all of the investigative work which, in a real lawsuit, would be going on behind the scenes. Immediately after Porter accepted the case, letters would be sent requesting any and all documents that might bear on the claims. Chuck would likely be directed to call the Las Vegas Police Department to find out what reports are available and how to obtain them; he would then send out the necessary request and follow up to be sure the reports arrived. The police reports would reveal the names and addresses of any witnesses interviewed by the police; part of Chuck's follow-up might consist of contacting these witnesses and taking statements from them.

Chuck might also be asked to assemble the documentation for the damages aspects of the claim. He would begin by requesting complete copies of medical records from each medical provider (physicians, surgeons, hospitals) involved in Shannon's treatment. Later, when Shannon's condition has become stable, he would request updates of the medical records, and perhaps also order narrative reports from one or more of Shannon's physicians (see sidebar).

## SIDEBAR

# Narrative Reports

*A high percentage of all lawsuits involve injuries of some kind. How can you place a dollar value on an injury? You could start by adding up the medical bills, but most people would agree that merely paying someone's medical bills would not be enough to compensate them for the pain and impairment of a serious injury. In practice, the way in which injuries are valued is that the jurors listen to all pertinent facts, deliberate, and vote on a number.*

*Because jury decisions are not arrived at in any scientific way, there is no formula to use to compute the value of an injury. The best you can do is try to assemble the same facts that the jurors would be asked to consider and, guided by experience, make some judgment about what a typical jury would likely award. (There are resources such as Jury Verdict Research that compile data about the amounts of jury verdicts in various types of cases; consult your law library.)*

*In addition to the actual medical costs as reflected by the bills, the jury in an injury case typically considers such factors as the extent to which the injury affects plaintiff's ability to carry out normal activities; the pain suffered; the permanency of the impairment, if any; and the possible need for future medical treatment.*

*In trial, we establish these intangibles mainly through the expert testimony of physicians who have treated or examined the injured person. (Defendant has a right to have the plaintiff examined by doctors of defendant's choosing.) At the pre-suit settlement stage, however, we will not yet have any doctor testimony to present. What do we do?*

*Routinely in injury cases, we order a **narrative report** from the treating physician. Usually, this is done by sending the doctor a brief letter requesting the report. Doctors who treat injuries are familiar with narrative reports and usually do not need to be told how to prepare one, although it is perfectly appropriate to request that the doctor address particular issues that may be of concern in a given case. It takes time to dictate a report, so most doctors will bill you for the service (typically in the range of a few hundred dollars); a few even require payment in advance.*

*The narrative report will summarize the nature of the injuries; the treatment rendered and its cost; the prognosis; and the doctor's opinions regarding any other important medical issues. The doctor's narrative report is submitted with the settlement demand letter, thereby giving the opposing party a preview of the medical evidence that would be presented at trial.*

## SIDEBAR

# Obtaining a Client's Records

*One of the routine tasks in most lawsuits is to obtain records pertaining to our own client—medical records, employment records, and any other records that pertain to the dispute. Usually, our client has a right to obtain copies of these records, so no subpoena will be necessary. (Recall that a subpoena duces tecum is a court order requiring a witness to appear and produce documents.)*

*Begin with a telephone call to the company, doctor's office, hospital—whatever organization we believe is maintaining the records we want. Many of the organizations from which you will be requesting records are large, so you should get the name of the individual to whom the record request should be sent; otherwise, your request letter may spend weeks being shuffled from one department to another. At the same time, you need to find out how to handle copying charges. Different organizations have different poli-*

*cies; some require an advance deposit, some send records to an outside copying center with which arrangements have to be made, some simply send the attorney a bill when the copies are completed.*

*Your supervising attorney will have a **record release form** in her form file. Fill in the client's name, make a dozen or so copies, and obtain the client's signature on each one. In the record release form, the client authorizes the release of records to the attorney (keep in mind that these are confidential records, and the holder of the records could be sued for releasing them improperly). Often, release forms also include a provision revoking any prior authorization to release records, and an admonition to the holder of the records not to release copies to anyone else. This is done because it is possible that our client has signed record release forms in the past, particularly if insurance is involved.*

## SIDEBAR

### Obtaining a Client's Records *continued*

*Send a letter, addressed to the individual in charge of the records you wish to obtain. In the letter, request the records that you want, designating them as broadly as possible—at this stage, you want everything, and you do not want a records clerk making judgments about which documents are important. You should enclose a signed release form and confirm whatever payment arrangement is necessary. You then calendar the request a reasonable distance into the future, so that you will be reminded to follow up if you do not receive a prompt response.*

*Is your task completed once you receive the copies? No, not until you verify that the copies are complete.*

*Do the pages that you were given refer to other pages that are not there? From your knowledge of records of this type, are there items that should be present that are not? Are all the pages legible? Mass copying jobs are notorious for producing occasional unreadable pages. With records that may be crucial to the case— important medical records, for example—it is wise to schedule an appointment to go and physically compare the copies with the original file, page by page. Only then can you be sure that the copying clerk did not inadvertently skip a few pages. Lawsuits have been won and lost on such details.*

Shannon can also claim damages based on her loss of income as a result of her injuries. To do so, it will be necessary to assemble evidence proving how much Shannon would have earned had the injury not occurred. Chuck may contact Shannon's employer to obtain copies of payroll records verifying Shannon's income.

Typically, we obtain routine documents such as the medical records and payroll records of our own client simply by sending a brief letter requesting them. Most employers and medical providers will turn over copies voluntarily, as long as we provide a release signed by our client (see Figure W3–2 and sidebar) and agree to pay the copying costs. If we are seeking records that pertain to an opposing party, we will probably have to subpoena them, which we cannot do until the lawsuit is filed.

### SETTLEMENT DEMAND STEPS

Figure W3–3 is a hypothetical settlement demand letter that Allen Porter might send on Shannon's behalf. (In a real-life dispute of this kind, Dr. Collins would likely have liability insurance, and we would therefore send the letter to the insurance carrier.) Due to space considerations, the letter is somewhat abbreviated; a real demand letter might be several pages in length and go into considerably more detail, particularly as to damages.

## Case Workup: Learning by Doing

Your assignment for this workshop is to perform part of the pre-suit workup for Dr. Collins's claim against Shannon.

### EXERCISES

In carrying out this assignment, you should follow the step-by-step formula described in this workshop.

1. Find out how to order a police investigative report from the police department of your locality. Find out what forms are needed, if any; what fees will be charged and how they are to be paid; and where the request is to be sent.

2. Assume that Dr. Collins was treated for his injuries at a hospital in your locality (choose one). Prepare a request letter for medical records.

3. Look up the statutes of limitations for your state (in most states, they will be grouped together in one section of the statute books). Find out what the limitation periods are for claims for personal injury/negligence; for assault and battery; for breach of contract. List at least three circumstances, citing the applicable statute, in which the limitations period would be tolled (i.e., the clock stopped). (You may wish to consider making a photocopy of your local statutes of limitations for your own litigation notebook.)

---

**Figure W3–3    Sample Settlement Demand Letter**

Ms. Rene Goodall, Claims Representative
Faithful and Dependable Insurance Company
Dallas, Texas

Dear Ms. Goodall,

As you know, I represent Ms. Shannon Martin, who was seriously injured when your insured, Dr. Arthur Collins, entered her hotel room without permission and assaulted her, during the early morning hours of February 6, 1996. The pertinent facts are summarized in the Las Vegas Police Department's investigative report, a copy of which I have previously furnished to you.

It is undisputed that your insured, using a key which he obtained by means which remain unclear, entered Ms. Martin's hotel room well after midnight while she was sleeping, and undressed himself at the foot of her bed. Ms. Martin, acting out of reasonable fear for her own safety, attempted to defend herself using a revolver which she had legally purchased; she received multiple injuries, including a broken finger, when your insured then threw himself bodily on top of her as she lay in her bed.

In my judgment, Ms. Martin has a very high probability of prevailing on the liability issue. Whatever was the source of the key used by your insured, it is undisputed that Ms. Martin did not give it to him; in fact, he acknowledged to the police that he had never seen Ms. Martin prior to the assault. Dr. Collins's claim of self-defense is legally untenable, and in any case, I believe that a jury will find it obvious that Dr. Collins, not Ms. Martin, was the aggressor here.

Ms. Martin's damages are thoroughly documented in the separate summary enclosed, with backup documentation attached. Briefly, her medical and hospital bills to date total $18,394. She has already been absent from her work for two full months, and is not expected to be released by her physicians for return to full-time employment for another six months; based on her annual income, her loss of earnings is estimated at $62,000. Finally, there is the most important element of damages in a claim of this nature, involving as it does a physical assault of the most frightening kind that a woman can experience: general damages for pain and suffering and for the traumatic experience of the assault itself. Taking into account all of these elements, I believe that a verdict in the range of $500,000 to $700,000 is probable.

To avoid litigating this claim, Ms. Martin has authorized me to offer your insured a full release of all liability (appropriately structured so as not to impair Ms. Martin's claims against others, including the hotel) in return for the sum of $450,000. This offer will terminate if not accepted in writing within fifteen days from the date of this letter, whereupon suit will be filed immediately.

Sincerely,


Allen Porter

---

**4.** At your law library, find out what research tools are available for accessing jury verdict statistics. Browse through them and find out how they are organized and what kinds of information can be obtained from them. Using the available tools, prepare a one-page memorandum giving your analysis of the probable verdict range for Dr. Collins's claim against Shannon. Assume that Dr. Collins's medical and hospital bills total $50,000, and that he lost income of $90,000 as a result of his injuries. (Recall that in estimating the probable verdict range, we are not concerned about Dr. Collins's *chances* of winning; we are only concerned with what the amount of the verdict would likely be if he *did* win.) You may make reasonable assumptions about any other necessary facts.

**5.** Assume that you are employed as a paralegal by Roger Yarborough, attorney for Dr. Collins. He assigns you to draft a settlement demand letter on Dr. Collins's behalf, raising Dr. Collins's claims against Shannon, and to be addressed to Allen Porter.

# PRACTICE POINTERS
## *Interviewing*

Before an interview, set up the room and chairs so as to make the client feel as comfortable as possible. Avoid furniture configurations that intimidate or otherwise inhibit open communication (e.g., putting the client in a small-backed chair while you sit behind a desk in a high-backed chair). Offer refreshments and engage in friendly small talk to minimize the client's uneasiness. Inform the client up front that you are a legal assistant, not an attorney, and then assure her that all communications to you, as a member of the firm, are confidential.

Remembering that this initial contact not only provides you with a first impression of the client, but also provides the client with a first impression of you and the firm. Be conscious of your verbal and nonverbal language. By the same token, be aware of your reactions to the client and take notes regarding your impressions of her story, her body language, how she responds to questions, her apparent veracity, and her potential strengths and weaknesses as a witness. Trust your instincts; they are often accurate.

If you are conducting the interview rather than observing, allow the client to give a free-flowing narrative at the beginning of the interview and then follow up with directed questions to fill in any gaps or clarify any points of confusion. Although you may want to use prepared questions to structure the interview (to ensure you cover all the salient points), do not become so dependent on your notes that you fail to hear the client. Listen carefully to what is said and be flexible enough to allow the client to take you into areas you might not have thought to explore. Assert enough control over the course of the interview, however, to prevent the client from digressing or becoming inordinately absorbed in unnecessarily detailed descriptions. Be an empathic listener—sensitive to the emotional needs and psychological defenses of the client without getting caught up in those same emotions and defenses.

Ask for background information as well as details about the issue to be litigated. In a torts case, for example, find out about the plaintiff's medical history, her insurance coverage, her employment status, and personal information, such as date of birth, Social Security number, address, telephone number, names and relationships of family members, and so on. Gather up enough details about the incident or issue in question that you can clearly picture the events in your mind. Take note of inconsistent statements and weaknesses in the case; reference them in your notes as issues/facts requiring further investigation. At the end of this interview you should have enough information to begin the investigatory process and to be able to respond, if asked, about whether you think the firm should take the case.

## TECHNO TIP

Many states have private companies that keep track of jury verdicts, arbitration results, and settlements. The data compiled may be local, regional, or statewide. In using this valuable research source care should be taken to use case results from your locality. A rural area's evaluation of damages, and even liability, may differ substantially from an urban area.

Many of these resources also keep track of attorneys, judges, and expert witnesses. For the expert witness you can find out which cases they testified in and whether "their" side won or not. Many of these companies may also be able to provide you with a compendium of cases where the injuries were similar, for example, loss of an eye, visible scarring, torn rotor cuff, and so on. If an expert is needed, it is prudent to talk to the attorney that used the expert in another case to get his opinion on the expert's abilities and credibility. One Internet site to start with is the National Association of State Jury Verdict Publishers at www.juryverdicts.com. In addition to giving you information on each

of its members on a state-by-state basis, the site also has a list of more than 20,000 experts that have testified in cases reported in their members' publications. To obtain additional information on the expert it is necessary to contact the reporting company and pay a fee.

If you do not know the opposing counsel, you can also have the same company pull up cases she has tried to help determine her experience and success in the types of cases she has been involved in. Having obtained specific case information you can also call the attorneys who tried cases against your opposing counsel to obtain information on opposing counsel. You can find out, for example, her predilections at depositions, her attitude about discovery (Does she hide the ball or not?) and other useful information. Many of these companies publish annual compendiums of all cases they have reported. Typically these compendiums will list all attorneys and the cases they were on, the judges hearing the case, expert witnesses, a summary of the case, and so on.

## FORMS FILE

*Include samples of the following in your forms notebook:*
- *Interview checklist;*
- *Settlement demand letter;*
- *Letter requesting medical or employment records; and*
- *Record release forms.*

## KEY TERMS

| | | |
|---|---|---|
| **Conditional delivery** | **Narrative report** | **Release** |
| **Disability** | **Offer** | **Statement** |
| **Hold harmless** | **Probable verdict range** | **Statute of limitations** |
| **Indemnify** | **Record release form** | **Time-barred** |
| **Limitations period** | | |

## INTRODUCTION: CREATING A COURT PAPER THAT COMPLIES WITH FORMAT RULES

Most of the work that goes on in the months or years before a suit is ready for trial involves papers. Pleadings, motions, discovery requests, discovery responses, notices—all are normally in written form. Litigators need some way to keep track of these papers so that there can be no dispute about what has or has not happened in the lawsuit. This means of tracking documents is called the court file.

The court file is the official record of the case kept by the clerk of the court. The clerk keeps a separate file for each case, and every important event in the lawsuit must be recorded in the file. Judges are responsible for hundreds of lawsuits at a time, so they cannot possibly reconstruct the details of individual cases by relying on memory alone. Cases are transferred from one judge to another. Appellate courts are asked to review what was done at the trial level. The court file is the single permanent and complete record of everything that has happened in the case, the record that all participants rely on. From the judge's standpoint, the court file *is* the case—the judge will usually refuse to consider any papers that are not part of the court file.

You might think of a court paper as being made up of two things: (1) the *body,* that is, the actual contents of the paper, where you list your allegations or present your argument, and (2) the *formal part—*caption, signatures, mailing certificate, etc.—which takes care of the various clerical needs. *Formal,* in this context, means "pertaining to matters of form" and includes such things as type of paper, margins, type size, and arrangement of parts.

Beginning with Workshop 5 on complaint drafting, much of the remainder of this text is devoted to learning how to prepare the body of various kinds of court papers. But because the formal part is essentially the same for all court papers, it will be easier if we learn to construct the formal part first, and prepare a form for doing so. Then, whenever we need to prepare a court paper, all we have to do is write the

body and plug it into the form. This is what is typically done in a law office.

When we present a court paper for filing, the clerk of the court will examine it to ensure that the paper complies with the formal requirements of the local rules. If we have not followed the rules, the clerk is likely to refuse the paper. The clerk does not care what you write in the body of a court paper—the clerk is not concerned with content. However, court clerks often exhibit near zero tolerance for deviations from correct form.[1] Urban court clerks often handle millions of pages of paper each year, and seemingly minor mistakes may be enough to bring the clerk's automated processing to a standstill or, worse, cause your paper to disappear forever into the wrong file.

There is another motivation: We want our work to convey an impression of professionalism. Like it or not, other people, including opponents and judges, will form opinions about us and our case based on the appearance that we present. A court paper that does not comply with the formal rules, as well as local customs, sends a message that the preparer is an amateur, someone who need not be taken as a serious threat.

Figure W4–1 lists the steps we will cover for creating the formal part of a court paper.

## Creating a Court Paper: Step-by-Step Instructions

The step-by-step instructions that follow describe requirements that apply in all American courts. The details, however, vary considerably from one place to another and from one court to another. The formal requirements of your local courts will quickly become second nature to you, although questions occasionally come up that send even experienced lawyers back to the books to check the rules. Whenever you are called on to prepare a paper for filing in some unfamiliar court, you will have to find out the specific requirements and customs of that court.

---

[1]We recognize that FRCP, Rule 5(e), states that "The clerk shall not refuse to accept for filing any paper presented for that purpose solely because it is not presented in proper form as required by these rules or any local rules or practices." Rule or no rule, the authors have had filings rejected by federal court clerks for minor format infractions, and the clerks of some state courts (New York City comes to mind) are notorious for refusing improperly formatted filings.

---

**Figure W4–1    Creating a Court Paper**

*Step 1—Comply with Mechanical Requirements*
*Step 2—Compose a Caption*
*Step 3—Introductory Paragraph*
*Step 4—Body of Document*
*Step 5—Date and Signature*
*Step 6—Certificate of Service*

---

How do you go about doing this? First, check the rules. Which rules? All of them. Formal requirements can appear in local rules; in the rules of procedure for the particular court; in statewide or district-wide rules of practice—sometimes partly in one source, partly in another. Your instructor will inform you of which rules prescribe the formal requirements for the courts of your locality.

Once you have identified and read the applicable rules, we strongly recommend that you obtain a few samples of court papers filed by a competent law firm in the court with which you are concerned. Formal rules can be tricky, and many of the errors beginners commonly make will become obvious if you compare your work to a properly prepared form. Finally, when in doubt, do not hesitate to ask for help from an expert: An experienced legal secretary will usually know the formal rules inside and out.

## Step 1    *Comply with Mechanical Requirements*

Most courts specify a number of mechanical details that must be followed when preparing a court paper. We list some of the common considerations; we also include a chart at the end of the chapter (Figure W4–3) for you to fill in the specific requirements and customs of your local court. Your instructor may provide the details for you to fill in or may assign you to obtain them as an exercise.

1. *Size, weight, and type of paper.* The rules of most courts place limits on the types of paper that are acceptable. The clerk's jobs of segregating papers into the correct files and of microfilming or electronically imaging papers for archiving can be carried out more efficiently if the items being processed are uniform.

2. *Whether line-numbered paper should be used.* Traditionally, court papers were prepared on "pleading paper" that had line numbers preprinted along the left margin. Many courts no longer require it, although many law firms continue to use it even where it is not required.

As with other formal requirements, when in doubt, let local custom be your guide.

3. *Margins.* Again, uniformity is the goal. Court clerks tend to be particularly fussy about the top margin on the first page, which many courts require to be several inches wide to provide room for the clerk's stamps.

4. *Font, type size, line spacing, and length limits.* Many courts specify a minimum type size, and most require court papers to be double spaced. This is done mainly to ensure readability, especially after copies have been made. Some courts specify the font (the design of the individual letters) to be used. Even if the rules are silent, it is wise to stick with a widely used font such as Courier—this is not a good place to show off your computer's font-making versatility.

   It is also becoming quite common for courts to place limits on the overall length of court papers. For example, they may limit motions to no more than fifteen pages. We mention this here because, sooner or later, it will occur to you that you could get more words into the same number of pages by using different or smaller type or by "fudging" on the margins. Our advice is to resist the temptation.

5. *Backings.* Some courts require court papers to be prepared with a colored backing, which serves as a visible separator between papers in the file.

6. *Other details not covered by the rules.* There are many other formal details which, although not specifically covered by the rules, are the subject of such long-standing custom that failure to observe them will be instantly noticed. These include such minutiae as the wording of the name of the court; whether to use parentheses or colons to make the vertical line down the middle of the caption; whether various parts are indented or kept on the left margin; how many spaces to indent paragraphs; and many other such items of seeming trivia. Pay attention to these details and follow your sample forms.

*Your Local Notes*

_____

_____

## Step 2   *Compose a Caption*

All pleadings begin with a caption, which serves the same function as a title page in a book. A caption has several parts, as shown later in Figure W4–2.

1. *Name, address and telephone number of the attorney filing the paper.* In courts that require this information to be included in the caption (not all do), the rules typically require it to be placed at the extreme upper left. In some courts, the attorney's name and address appear below the signature line. Many law firms use preprinted (or laser-printed) paper in which the firm's name and address appears at the side, in the left margin. Your instructor will inform you of the preferred practice in your locality. You should identify which party you are representing.

2. *Name of court.* The caption begins with the name of the court in which the action is pending, typically in capital letters and centered between the left and right margins. In many localities, it is customary to write this in formal language—that is, "IN THE SUPERIOR COURT OF THE STATE OF X IN AND FOR THE COUNTY OF Y," rather than the (perhaps more sensible) "Y COUNTY SUPERIOR COURT." Whatever the custom is, follow it.

3. *Names of parties.* Below the name of the court, on the left-hand half of the page, appear the names of the parties. In the first pleading filed in the case (usually the complaint) every party on each side must be listed, including spouses. It is customary to list the individuals first, followed by the entities such as corporations, trusts, estates, etc., and finally the "John Doe" parties, if any.

   On papers filed after the first one in the case, it is common to shorten the caption by listing only the first plaintiff and defendant, and referring to any others as *et ux.* (and wife) or *et al.* (and others). For example, if the list of defendants is "Davy Jones and Amanda Jones, husband and wife; Arnold Smith and Barbara Smith; husband and wife; and Ajax Corporation, a Delaware corporation," it will be shortened to "Davy Jones, *et ux., et al.*" on subsequent papers. Why bother to abbreviate in the age of word processing when it takes no more effort to

print the entire list? At the risk of repetition, the purpose of legal writing is to convince the judge to rule in your favor—you do not want to waste valuable page-one "real estate" on long boring lists of names. By shortening the caption, you will be left with more space at the bottom of the first page in which you can say something eye-catching and convincing.

The layout of the names of the parties is standard. Details such as which parts are capitalized, whether and how much to indent the words "Plaintiffs," "Defendants," and "vs.," and how and where to make the vertical border to the right of the names vary according to local custom.

4. *Case number.* The clerk of the court assigns the case number when the complaint is filed, so the 'No.' field is left blank on the complaint. It *must* be included on subsequent papers, or the clerk will refuse the filing. Clerks will not look up case numbers for you.

5. *Title of the paper.* Below the case number appears the title of this paper such as "Complaint" or "Motion for Summary Judgment" or some other title indicating what this particular paper is supposed to be. A common beginner's misconception is to think that there must be some approved list of types of papers that you can file—there is not. The first paper filed must generally be called a complaint, but after that, the clerk will not reject a filing merely because of the title that you gave it. Titles should be short but descriptive. The title is likely to be the first thing the judge will read, so try to choose titles that convey a concise idea of what the paper is about.

6. *Other information.* Local rules in some jurisdictions may require inclusion of certain other information in the caption, usually immediately below the title. Examples include the name of the assigned judge, the type of case, whether or not oral argument is requested, and hearing date.

*Your Local Notes*

_____

_____

## Step 3   *Introductory Paragraph*

Below the caption, the content portion of the document begins. As you would expect, the specifics vary depending on what kind of court paper you are writing. Several of the workshops that follow offer detailed instructions on how to construct the common pleadings, motions, and discovery documents. In this workshop, we limit ourselves to mentioning a few guiding principles that apply to all or most court papers.

If you browse through the court file of a lawsuit (an activity we highly recommend), you will find that a great many of the court papers look superficially alike. It is customary to begin motions and many other kinds of court papers with an introductory paragraph or preamble telling the court who is filing the paper, what its purpose is, and what the main legal authority is supporting it.

Here is an example preamble of a typical court paper:

> Plaintiffs respectfully move for summary judgment pursuant to Rule 56, Federal Rules of Civil Procedure.

This simple, three-part sentence can be readily adapted to fit many situations: For "Plaintiffs," you can substitute "Defendants," or "Plaintiff John Doe," or "all defendants except Richard Roe," or whatever best tells the judge who is filing the paper. Instead of "respectfully move for summary judgment" you can write, for example, "hereby give notice that they have filed their disclosure statement," or "hereby propound the following written interrogatories." Then simply add "pursuant to [whichever rule or statute governs whatever paper you are filing]." We will practice writing preambles later in this workshop.

Depending in part on local practice, many lawyers add date and signature lines immediately after the preamble. (Even if this is done, date and signature lines are still necessary at the end of the document; see Step 5.) Others would omit the date and signature lines and launch directly from the preamble into the body of the document. Your instructor will inform you of the preferred practice in your locality.

Not all court papers need this preamble. With argumentative papers whose purpose is obvious from the title (such as responses to motions) and where local practice allows it, the preamble is skipped entirely and the actual memorandum begins immediately below the caption. Then the argument itself will begin on the first page, where we hope the judge will notice our gripping lead-in and be compelled to read on!

## Step 4    *Body of Document*

What follows the introductory paragraph depends on the type of court paper. For example, motions have a "Memorandum of Points and Authorities" in which argument is presented; discovery requests may have lists of questions or lists of categories of documents being requested. We will leave discussion of the content of the various types of court papers for later workshops; in this workshop we confine ourselves to matters of format.

With a few exceptions, the format and layout of the body of the document are up to you. You are free to innovate within reasonable bounds and to construct the document in whatever way you think will be most effective or persuasive. If you have ever written a term paper for an English class, you probably found that the format and layout requirements were quite exacting—footnotes laid out to conform with some incomprehensible formula, headings and subheadings numbered in exactly the prescribed way, and so on. You will be glad to learn that the practice for routine court papers allows much more freedom. (Appellate briefs are a special case; format rules for these may be much more exacting.)

This is not to suggest that you should use the format of court papers as a medium to express your artistic urges. Format should be inconspicuous, so as not to distract the judge from the substance of your argument. A good approach is to study court papers written by lawyers or law firms whose work you admire, and imitate their style and layout. Here are a few format suggestions:

1. *Margins and indentation.* The rules will specify minimum margins; you are free to use wider ones (within reason). Unless a specific rule says otherwise, you are free to decide how much to indent paragraphs and blocked quotations.

2. *Type size and style.* The rules will specify the minimum type size and sometimes the font. You are free to use bold type, italics, or underlining for emphasis (we would suggest sparingly). When doing so within quoted material (or when changing anything else in a quotation) you must disclose what you have done, usually in a parenthetical following the citation.

3. *Citation of authorities.* When you make a statement about the law in a court paper, you are expected to support the statement by citing the authority for it. The term *authority* means the source of the law supporting the statement you are making. This may be a **primary authority**—usually a statute or a reported appellate court decision that has the force of law—or a **secondary authority** such as the *Restatement* or a textbook written by a legal scholar. To **cite** authority means to specify the place where it can be found.

How do we cite legal authority, and what should the format of a citation be? It depends on the source. In theory, citations of cases, statutes, and other authorities in court papers should be formatted in accordance with the rules set out in the handbook *The Bluebook: A Uniform System of Citation,* published by the Harvard Law Review Association.

In practice, most attorneys use the *Bluebook* only as a general guide, and are quite apt to improvise when citing an unusual source rather than spend hours trying to figure out where the *Bluebook* says the punctuation should go. Citations to statutes of your home state are almost always reduced to three- or four-letter abbreviations rather than the longer abbreviations called for by the *Bluebook.*

Traditionally, cases are cited to both the volume and page in which the case appears in the state's official reporter, and to the volume and page in the West regional reporter system. Case citation customs are also in somewhat of a state of flux at present due to the increased use of searchable computerized case law databases such as Westlaw. Some jurisdictions are now implementing quite radical changes in which cases are cited by a case number and paragraph number rather than by the traditional volume and page. Your instructor will explain any local customs governing the citation of the court rules, statutes, and cases of your home state; if you add to that a basic knowledge of how to cite the federal rules, federal statutes, and cases from the *Federal Supplement* and the *Federal Reporter,* you will be well equipped to write routine court papers, since by far the majority of citations come from those few sources.

4.  *Quotations.* It is often necessary when writing court papers to include quotations from cases or statutes, from other court papers, or from depositions or other discovery documents. Be absolutely scrupulous in identifying the source of any quoted material and pointing out any changes you have made in it. (Sometimes it is necessary to change details such as verb tense or punctuation so that the quotation will make sense in the context in which you are using it; any changed or substituted words go in square brackets.) Needless to say, you *must* cite the source whenever you copy or paraphrase published writings of which you are not the author; to do otherwise is considered plagiarism and will subject you to great embarrassment, or worse, if caught.

Short (less than three lines long) quotations may be placed continuously with the text of a court paper, where appropriate. Longer quotations are blocked and indented; that is, set out in a separate paragraph or series of paragraphs, usually single-spaced (but check your local rules), with margins that are indented inward from the rest of the text. Only the quoted material is blocked and indented; the citation of the source of the quote belongs in unindented text before or after the quotation.

Quotation format is another subject best learned by reading and imitating the work of others. For those so inclined, however, the *Bluebook* gives detailed rules.

5.  *Footnotes.* In court papers (unlike term papers and academic journal articles), routine citations belong in the text immediately preceding or following the points they are intended to support, not in footnotes. Explanatory footnotes may be used, but sparingly so as not to disrupt the flow of the main text.

6.  *Organization and headings.* It will improve the persuasiveness of your presentation if you organize longer documents into short segments using descriptive headings and subheadings in an outline format. This allows the main thrust of your argument to get through, even if the judge merely skims the document. We also favor including in legal memoranda a short "Summary of Argument" section at the beginning, as another way of allowing the judge to absorb your position quickly.

There is no prescribed format for headings and subheadings, or for the way in which you number them; use whatever system best promotes readability and persuasiveness. Do, however, regard them as part of the document and not mere appendages, and use them to advance your case. Usually, you can do this best by constructing headings that are complete sentences, encapsulating the main point of the material that follows them. Make your headings argumentative. For example, instead of "Was Defendant Negligent?" (too general and not assertive enough), write "Defendant Was Negligent When He Failed to Have His Brakes Repaired after He Knew They Were Defective" (specific and takes sides).

*Your Local Notes*

_____

_____

## Step 5  *Date and Signature*

FRCP, Rule 11, requires all papers filed with the court to be signed by the attorney. Court papers are always dated and signed at the end. Immediately after the body, the date line should appear. For court papers directed to the judge (motions, responses) this should be in the form "RESPECTFULLY SUBMITTED this 4th day of February, 2000." For papers directed to an opposing party (complaint, answer, notices, etc.) this is reduced to "DATED this 4th day of February, 2000." (You do not have to respectfully submit things to an opponent.) Your instructor will inform you of any local variations.

Below the date line is the line for the attorney's signature. The format is somewhat variable, but typically consists of the name of the law firm, if the attorney is a member of one; below that, a horizontal line on which the attorney signs; and on succeeding lines, the attorney's name and perhaps address, and finally the words "Attorney(s) for [whoever it is that the attorney represents—plaintiff, defendant, defendant John Doe, etc.]." The customary format is illustrated later in Figure W4–2. Among other things, be aware that the way in which the attorney signature line is worded may carry subtle implications about whether the attorney is or is not a partner in the firm, a matter about which some attorneys have little sense of humor; therefore, when you work in a law office, obtain a sample of the way your employer wants his or her signature line to read and follow it verbatim.

---

**Your Local Notes**

_____

_____

---

## Step 6  *Certificate of Service*

What do you do with a court paper once you have prepared it? Two things: (1) serve it and (2) file it with the clerk of the court. Why? Here is what FRCP, Rules 5(a) and 5(d), provide:

> 5(a) Service; When Required. Except as otherwise provided in these rules, every order required by its terms to be served, every pleading subsequent to the original complaint unless the court otherwise orders because of numerous defendants, every paper relating to discovery required to be served upon a party unless the court otherwise orders, every written motion other than

one which may be heard ex parte, and every written notice, appearance, demand, offer of judgment, designation of record on appeal, and similar paper shall be served upon each of the parties.

> 5(d) Filing; Certificate of Service. All papers after the complaint required to be served upon a party, together with a certificate of service, shall be filed with the court within a reasonable time after service, but the court may on motion of a party or on its own initiative order that depositions upon oral examination and interrogatories, requests for documents, requests for admission, and answers and responses thereto not be filed unless on order of the court or for use in the proceeding.

To satisfy the requirement of serving a court paper, you must (1) deliver it in the right way, (2) to the right people, and (3) be able to prove you did it. The right way is easy—all (well, almost all) court papers after the complaint are delivered either by mailing them or hand delivering them to the person who is to receive them. Determining who the right people are is usually also straightforward. Unless the judge orders otherwise (sometimes done in complex cases involving many parties), you serve every court paper on every other party to the suit. Under local rules in many courts, if the paper is a motion or a response or reply to a motion, you must also serve a copy on the judge. As with most issues in litigation, there are rules governing the minutiae of how and on whom papers are served; the details are the subject of another workshop (see Workshop 7 on service, docketing, and deadlines).

The proof that you served a court paper consists of a statement that appears at the end, following the attorney signature, reflecting the fact that the paper was mailed (or hand delivered), recording the date of mailing, and listing the names and addresses of each recipient. FRCP, Rule 5(d), calls this a **certificate of service;** be aware, however, that the terminology, layout, and content vary considerably by locality. The certificate of service shown later in Figure W4–2 is one of the common styles; your instructor will inform you of the preferred layout in your locality. The mailing certificate must be separately signed; in theory, by someone with personal knowledge of the fact that the paper was actually placed in the mail to the people listed. In practice, mailing certificates are routinely signed by the attorney or by a secretary, either of whom is likely relying on a messenger or clerk to do the actual mailing.

Although it might seem logical to do so, the mailing certificate does not always include the clerk of the court as one of the recipients. The proof that you filed a paper with the clerk lies in the fact that, if the paper found its way into the court file with the clerk's intake stamp on it, you must have filed it. What happens if a paper gets lost after you file it? This does occasionally happen; papers mailed to opponents also sometimes get lost in the mail. In many ways, litigation operates on the honor system; attorneys and judges usually accept the word of a fellow attorney who avows that a paper really was filed, or that a document was never received, and some reasonable agreement is worked out. (There is a potential trap, here, however: There are cases holding that it is the responsibility of each attorney to stay informed of the status of a case. Therefore, it is wise to anticipate what papers and communications you should be receiving from the court and opposing counsel at any given stage of a case, and to make reasonable inquiry if you do not receive them. We will have more to say on this in Workshop 7 when we take up the subject of docketing and deadlines.) If you have computer access to the court docketing system, you should check the status of filings on a regular basis.

Traditionally, rules of procedure required *all* court papers in a case to be filed with the clerk of the court. In many jurisdictions, this is no longer true. Once the use of discovery as an offensive weapon became widespread, discovery papers comprising thousands of pages became commonplace, overwhelming the capacity of court clerks' filing systems. The response of many courts was to change the rules so that certain types of court papers (mainly discovery requests and responses), although still served on opposing parties, are not filed with the clerk. FRCP, Rule 5(d), reproduced earlier, authorizes federal district courts to dispense with the filing of discovery papers by order in a particular case; many courts do so in all cases by local rule. What is filed instead is a one-page **notice of service,** a court paper reciting that the document in question was served. This creates a record in the court file establishing the fact that the paper exists and was served. (When a party later needs part of an unfiled discovery document to be in the record for some reason, such as to support a motion, the pertinent pages can then be filed.)

## Creating a Court Paper: Learning by Example

We now have all of the information needed to prepare a form that will include the caption, date and signature lines, and certificate of service, to be kept in a word processing file that we can reuse each time we need to prepare a court paper. Then, whenever we write a court paper, all we need to do is plug in the body of the paper in the space between the

caption and the date and signature lines, insert the title of the document into the caption, and our paper is ready to be signed, served, and filed.

Figure W4–2 is a sample form for our hypothetical lawsuit by Shannon Martin against Dr. Collins and the hotel.

## Creating a Court Paper: Learning by Doing

In this workshop, you will prepare a reusable version of the caption, preamble, date and signature lines, and certificate of mailing, for a hypothetical lawsuit by Dr. Collins against Shannon and the hotel. Assume the following facts:

> You are a paralegal in the law office of Roger Yarborough, attorney for Dr. Arthur Collins. Dr. Collins is a resident of your city, and Roger Yarborough practices in your city. Banbury Park Hotel is located in another city in your state. Shannon Martin resides in Arizona, and Park Hotels Group, Inc., is incorporated in Delaware.

> Roger Yarborough tells you that he intends to file suit on Dr. Collins's behalf against Shannon Martin and Park Hotels Group in the state superior court or county trial court having jurisdiction in your locality. In preparation for filing that suit, he assigns you to create a suitable formal part to be used in preparing the complaint and other future court papers.

### EXERCISES

In carrying out this assignment, you should follow the step-by-step formula described in this workshop.

*1.* Identify, locate, read, analyze, and (we would suggest) make copies for your notes of all of the rules of procedure that pertain to the formal requirements for court papers for use in (a) your local county superior court or trial court; (b) the federal district court in your locality.

*2.* (Instructor's opinion) Obtain one or two sample federal and state court filings to use as a guide.

*3.* From your notes, and using the rules you identified in Exercise 1, fill in Figure W4–3, which will provide you with a handy reference source for the common formal rules in your locality.

*4.* (Step 1) Obtain the correct type of paper. Set the correct margin, line spacing, font, and type size settings on your word processor.

*5.* (Step 2) Prepare the caption.

6.  (Step 5)  Add date and signature lines.

7.  (Step 6)  Prepare a form certificate of mailing.

8.  (Step 3)  Write suitable preambles for the following: (a) a motion for summary judgment; (b) a set of interrogatories; (c) a notice of filing answers to interrogatories. Your instructor may give you the rules citations to be used or may prefer to have you determine them on your own.

---

**Figure W4–2   A Court Paper for** *Martin v. Collins*

SIMON & PORTER
Allen Porter
1000 North Central Avenue, Suite 2800
Phoenix, Arizona 85004
(602) 555-4321
State Bar No. 00000
Attorneys for plaintiff

**IN THE UNITED STATES DISTRICT COURT**
**DISTRICT OF ARIZONA**

| | | |
|---|---|---|
| SHANNON MARTIN, a single woman, | ) ) ) | NO. _____ |
| Plaintiff, | ) ) | [TITLE GOES HERE] |
| vs. | ) | |
| ARTHUR COLLINS and JANE DOE COLLINS, husband and wife; PARK HOTELS GROUP, INC., a Delaware corporation; | ) ) ) ) ) | |
| Defendants. | ) ) | |
| _____ | ) | |

[BODY GOES HERE]

DATED this _____ day of _____, 20 __.

SIMONS & PORTER

_____
Allen Porter
Attorneys for plaintiff

---

**Figure W4–2  A Court Paper for _Martin v. Collins_,** _continued_

### CERTIFICATE OF SERVICE

The undersigned certifies that the foregoing was served in accordance with the requirements of FRCP, Rule 5, by mailing/hand-delivering a copy thereof this _____ day of _____, 20__ to:

Gail Stoddard, Esq.
CRANDALL, ELKINS & MAJOR
2000 North Central Avenue, Suite 2900
Phoenix, Arizona 85004
Attorneys for defendant Park Hotels Group, Inc.

Roger Yarborough, Esq.
500 Main Street
Dallas, Texas
Attorney for defendants Collins

(You may want to show that the original of the document was sent to the clerk's office and how it got there.)

_____

[signature goes here]

---

**Figure W4–3  Formal and Mechanical Requirements in Your Local Courts**

| ITEM | STATE COURT | FEDERAL COURT |
|---|---|---|
| Location of format rules (citation) | | |
| Paper type | | |
| How/where is attorney name and address shown? | | |
| How is name of court worded in caption? | | |
| Required top margin above caption | | |
| Top and bottom margins | | |
| Side margins | | |
| Line spacing | | |
| Page limit and citation of rule governing it | | |
| Preferred format for mailing certificate | | |
| What discovery documents are filed with court? | | |
| Where is the clerk's office for filing papers? | | |
| Where can court files be viewed? | | |
| Other local preferences | | |

## PRACTICE POINTERS
### *Public Records*

Court case files, unless they have been sealed by the courts, are matters of public record. Therefore, you can determine the litigation history of anyone (and you will be most interested in the litigation history of opponents) by accessing the records in the court clerk's office. Begin by checking with the court clerk's office to establish whether you must review the court files in person or whether the files are computerized. Typically these files are organized as plaintiffs' and defendants' logs in alphabetical order. Consulting these logs will provide you with case numbers and filing dates that will permit you to obtain and then review court records.

Other documents that are a matter of public record include:

- Property deeds
- Tax liens
- Marriage licenses
- Death certificates
- Driver's licenses
- Business certificates
- Partnership filings
- Professional licenses

State and local records are usually easily accessible; individuals can walk in and request copies of documents. At the federal level, however, requests for information often require going through the Freedom of Information Act (FOIA). To initiate a FOIA request first check with the *Code of Federal Regulations* (CFR) and ascertain the appropriate federal regulations governing record requests for the federal agency from which you are soliciting records. The CFR regulations set forth the content requirements of written requests for records, fee schedules, and other procedural requirements. These requests should be sufficiently narrow in scope that the agency can readily identify the nature of the records being sought; requests that are too broad are likely to be returned by the agency with a demand for a narrower description.

## TECHNO TIP

Many public records are now available on the Internet. County recorders' offices often have an index to all recorded documents—liens, deeds, assignments, etc.—available at no cost. Some, like the Maricopa County Recorder's office at http://recorder.maricopa.gov/recorder /imaging, have name data available back to 1983. Copies of recorded documents, however, are only available back to September 1991. If you need a document marked "Official Copy" you will have to set up an account (at least at the Maricopa County Recorder's office) and pay a fee for a computer printout of the official document. In a like manner the secretary of state's office usually maintains UCC filings, trade name registrations, and the like. It is now possible, in many states, to do your UCC searches on-line. The Arizona Secretary of State's web page is at www.sosaz.com. Copies of UCC filings are available for those filed after May 1994.

If you need to find out the assessed value of a party's real estate (people with expensive properties generally carry more insurance coverage than those of lesser means), you should check your county assessor's database. Unlike the county recorder, the assessor's office maintains records showing the assessed value of a person's property. Other information, such as the date of construction, number of rooms, square footage of the residence, type of garage, etc., is often also available. Check the Maricopa County Assessor's page at www.maricopa.gov/assessor_ query_ form.asp for an example of the type of information available from an assessor's office.

In many cases you will need to find out information about a corporation, a limited liability company (LLC), or a general or limited partnership. While states vary on the depository for these documents they can often be found at the state's corporation commission or at the secretary of state's office. Information that is generally accessible (even if digital images of the underlying documents such as the articles of incorporation, partnership agreement, or the articles of organization for a LLC are not available) includes the date of incorporation or filing of the formation documents; the name and address of the organization's partners or incorporators, and officers and directors or members and managers. The name and address of the organization's statutory agent are generally available. The database may also contain information on whether the organization is in good standing.

You can also check to see if a foreign entity has registered to do business in your state and, if so, who the statutory agent is (this may be valuable information if you need to know if a foreign entity can be sued in your state's courts). In Arizona, the corporation commission has a database that is accessible for a fee. The costs are, however, minimal when you consider you are charged only for the time you are on-line; the rates are quite reasonable and you are saving the expense of sending a paralegal to the main repository (or hiring a third party) to do a manual search.

---

### FORMS FILE

*Summarize the mechanical, caption, and signature requirements of court papers for the courts in your locality. Underline those requirements that are unique or particularly important (especially those that are likely to result in a rejection of your filings if they do not comply with local custom or requirements).*

*Include a sample copy of a certificate of service in your forms notebook.*

---

## KEY TERMS

| | | |
|---|---|---|
| **Certificate of service** | **Notice of service** | **Secondary authority** |
| **Cite** | **Primary authority** | |

## INTRODUCTION: COMPLAINT DRAFTING

The complaint is the first "official" document in a lawsuit. The filing of the complaint with the clerk of the court is the event that marks the beginning of the lawsuit. FRCP, Rule 3, provides, "A civil action is commenced by filing a complaint with the court."

In the "how to" part of this workshop, we present a cookbook approach to complaint drafting—that is, a series of step-by-step instructions for you to follow when drafting a complaint, together with an explanation of the reasons underlying each step.

In the second part, we demonstrate how to use our step-by-step instructions to prepare a complaint on behalf of our hypothetical plaintiff, Shannon Martin.

The final, and most important, part consists of practical, hands-on exercises. You will be asked to prepare a complaint on your own, using an assumed hypothetical fact situation and to explain the various choices you make as you do so.

The question uppermost in your mind as you begin any task in litigation should be "What purposes am I trying to accomplish with this task?" Complaint drafting is no exception. We will mention some of the important goals of complaint drafting in sidebars as we go along.

---

### SIDEBAR

### Dealing with Local Variability

*Complaint drafting is a detail-intensive task, and many of the details vary from state to state and from court to court. At each step in the discussion of this chapter, your instructor will tell you how to tailor your drafting to the courts of your locality.*

*We provide a checklist (see Figure W5–3 at end of workshop) for you to write down these points of local procedure. Filling in the details in the blanks provided in the checklist will be your first task in the "hands-on" segment of this workshop. You may want to read Figure W5–3 now and keep it in mind as your instructor explains the step-by-step instructions.*

---

## Complaint Drafting: Step-by-Step Instructions

There are many ways to draft a complaint, and given the same client and the same facts, it is unlikely that any two litigators would produce exactly identical complaints. Our instructions describe one way that will lead to an acceptable completed product.

Local variations are common. Your instructor will point out any changes that need to be made for the courts of your locality. You should always consult the local rules. You may also find it helpful to read, and perhaps copy and add to your form file, complaints filed by others in your area. Court files are public records, and if you do not have access to a law firm and its forms file, you can go to the courthouse and read complaints from the files of actual cases.

The preparation of pleadings is governed by FRCP, Rules 7 through 11. These rules answer many of the questions that will arise as you attempt to draft a complaint. We suggest that you peruse them now, even though you may not understand them completely, and then read them again carefully after you have finished reading the step-by-step instructions.

---

*Your Local Notes*

_____

_____

---

### PREPARATORY STEPS

The first two steps involve assembling the information that you will need to have ready as you begin drafting.

| **Step 1** | *Assemble the Basic Factual Information* |

Before you can begin to draft, you need to have some basic knowledge of the facts of the case. These facts are obtained by interviewing your client, and by obtaining pertinent facts and documents, such as police reports, from other sources. Obviously, we cannot give you a checklist of the facts you will need for every conceivable type of complaint because the facts needed will vary depending on what you are suing about. (Law firms that concentrate in specialized areas, such as automobile accidents, often do use printed client interview questionnaires that have been carefully designed to obtain the necessary facts.)

Certain facts, however, are necessary in every case. Here are some of them:

1. The names of the parties you are suing.

2. The state and county of residence of the parties you are suing. In the case of corporations and other entities, you need to know at least the state in which the entity is incorporated or created and may also need to know the county and state in which the entity has its principal place of business.

3. The main facts that led to the injury for which your client is suing.

4. The place where the injury to your client occurred, and the date on which it occurred.

### Step 2   *Determine the Elements of the Claims You Intend to Raise*

As we will see, the complaint must allege each element of each legal theory or cause of action on which you intend to base the suit.

In many lawsuits, the facts will support more than one possible cause of action. It is a matter of strategy whether to include all of the possible causes of action in the complaint (the "shotgun" approach) or whether to rely on one or a few of the strongest ones.

To be able to make this strategic decision, you first need to identify all of the causes of action that are possible under the facts given, and to determine and list the elements of each one. For commonplace causes of action, this may be very simple; you probably already know, for example, that the elements of negligence are duty, breach of duty, causation, and damages, without having to do any legal research. If your suit involves more complicated legal theories—securities fraud, say—you will need to spend some time doing legal research before you will be ready to start drafting.

Outlining the possible causes of action and their elements is a task of sufficient importance that we addressed it separately in Workshop 1. In this complaint drafting workshop, we will use the issues outline that we prepared in Workshop 1 as the basis for drafting our complaint.

*Your Local Notes*

_____

_____

## DRAFTING STEPS

Next, we begin drafting the complaint. For convenience, we will break the complaint up into smaller parts and take each in the order in which it appears in the complaint itself. You may find it helpful to refer to the sample complaint (see Figure W5–2 in a later section).

Because matters of style and format are essentially the same for all court papers, we will not repeat the material covered in the workshop on court papers (Workshop 4) except to note those few special requirements that apply to complaints.

Remember, one of the main jobs of the complaint is to begin the lawsuit. "A civil action is commenced by filing a complaint with the court"; see FRCP, Rule 3. Notice that drafting a complaint is not enough—you also have to file it. To do that, you must, at a minimum, prepare a complaint that the clerk will accept for filing. When you (or, more likely, your messenger or process server) present the complaint to the clerk for filing, the clerk will check to be sure you have followed various rules.

What things does the clerk check for at the time of filing, and what kinds of mistakes may prompt the clerk to reject the filing? First and foremost, the format must conform to the requirements in the court's local rules. Caption, paper size, type size, line spacing, margins, backing sheets if required—all must be correct. Be especially attentive to obvious rules such as the upper margin on the first page; many courts require a large margin to accommodate the stamps to be applied by the clerk. Another common reason for rejection of a filing is failure to present other required items, such as the filing fee and any information sheet, arbitration statement, or other papers required by local rule.

### Step 3   *Prepare the Caption*

The caption is in most respects the same as for all court papers. Again, you should refer to the workshop on court papers for the details. One important difference is that the caption of the complaint should list all parties to the suit. In court papers other than the complaint, it is commonplace to list only the first plaintiff and the first defendant. Instead of listing all additional plaintiffs and defendants, abbreviations like *et al.* (Latin for "and others") and *et ux.* (Latin for "and wife") are used. This is not done in the caption of the complaint because the complaint will be the first document in the file, and its caption needs to be complete.

The space for the case number is left blank in the caption of the complaint. The clerk of the court will assign a number when the complaint is filed.

Be aware that local rules sometimes specify additional bits of information to be included in the caption of the complaint, such as the type of case, whether it is subject to arbitration, or whether a jury trial is demanded. Your instructor will provide you with the details for the courts in your locality.

## Step 4  *The Preamble and Numbering Systems*

A complaint begins with a preamble, or introductory paragraph or phrase. Here we enter into the stylistic aspects of complaint drafting (see sidebar). Individual preferences and local customs vary from the simple and direct to the flowery and arcane. We favor the former, and believe that the modern trend is away from pleadings couched in archaic legalese.

As a preamble, we recommend the phrase "Plaintiff alleges:" or, if there is more than one plaintiff, "Plaintiffs allege:."

The individual paragraphs of the body of the complaint are numbered, so that the answer to the complaint can refer to each paragraph by number. Customarily, the complaint is also divided into separate sections, or *counts,* for each separate cause of action being asserted.

It is traditional, and still commonplace, to number the paragraphs of a complaint using centered, capitalized, Roman numerals above each paragraph. This method is perfectly acceptable, although our preferred method is to number the paragraphs at the side using ordinary numbers because large Roman numerals are confusing to many people. Some practitioners also number the paragraphs within each count separately, starting over with Roman numeral one in each new count; we recommend against this practice because having several paragraphs with the same number can lead to ambiguity and confusion.

---

**Your Local Notes**

_____

_____

---

## Step 5  *Jurisdiction and Parties*

FRCP, Rule 8, requires that the complaint include "a short and plain statement of the grounds upon which the court's jurisdiction depends." Although state court rules do not necessarily impose this requirement, it is customary (and a sensible precaution against future problems) to include jurisdictional allegations in all complaints. This practice also has the virtue of forcing the drafter to think about the issue of jurisdiction. Many defenses are lost if the defendant does not assert them early in the case, but the defense of lack of jurisdiction can be raised at any time—even after trial! So if there are any lurking jurisdictional defects, they need to be found and dealt with. Otherwise, you risk having your case suddenly dismissed out from under you after you have spent months of your time and thousands of dollars of your client's money getting ready for trial.

It is also necessary, somewhere in the complaint, to identify the parties. Since the court's jurisdiction often depends on the residence of the parties, it is convenient to group the pertinent allegations together at the beginning of the complaint.

In identifying the parties, the information to be included is the following:

1. The party's full name, if known. (What if you do not know a party's name? See sidebar on unidentified parties.)

2. If the party is an entity, such as a corporation or partnership, you should say what the party is and what state's laws it is organized under. If the entity does business in the state in which suit is being filed, that should be mentioned as well.

3. If the party is a natural person—a human being—give his or her county and state of residence. (Why the county rather than the city? Because the venue rules of most states are applied by county.)

4. If the party has some relationship with another party in the suit—husband, wife, employer, etc.—the relationship should be stated.

Paragraph 1, then, will identify and give the residences of the plaintiffs. For example: "Plaintiffs Ronald Albert Carson and Mary Jane Carson, his wife, are residents of Los Angeles County, California." (If there are more plaintiffs than will conveniently fit into one paragraph, then continue identifying plaintiffs in as many additional paragraphs as needed.)

After all the plaintiffs have been identified and their residences and relationships given, it is time to identify the defendants. This is done in identical fashion. For example: "Defendant Elite Fastener Corporation is a corporation organized and existing under the laws of Delaware, whose principal place of business is in Denver, Colorado."

We have seen (see Chapter 2) that we must be concerned with two kinds of jurisdiction: jurisdiction of the subject matter and jurisdiction of the person of each defendant. In the simple cases in state courts, the allegations giving the residence of the parties are enough to establish both. State courts are courts of "general subject matter jurisdiction"; that is, they are empowered to hear all types of cases, with few, if any, limits. (We are referring, of course, to the state superior courts or other original trial courts, whatever they may be called in your state. Some state courts, such as small claims courts, do have limits on their subject matter jurisdiction, and it is then necessary to show in the complaint that your case falls within those limits.) If the defendants are residents of the state in which suit is being filed, then the court automatically has jurisdiction of their persons—state courts always have jurisdiction over the persons of residents of the state. Thus, in suits in state court against state residents, it is sufficient to allege the identity and residence of each defendant.

Federal courts are courts of "limited subject matter jurisdiction"; that is, they are empowered to hear only those types of cases for which Congress has granted them power. Where does this power come from? Federal statutes. In your federal court complaint, you must state on which federal statute the court's jurisdiction will be based. The two most commonly seen are 28 U.S.C.§1332, giving federal courts the power to decide disputes between citizens of two different states where the amount in dispute is more than $75,000; and 28 U.S.C.§1331, granting jurisdiction over all civil actions arising under federal law. See the sample complaint later in this workshop for an example of how these allegations are worded.

Jurisdiction of the person can become more complicated when you file suit in state court against defendants who are not residents of the state in which the court sits. Then, it becomes necessary to rely on long-arm statutes to drag the defendant back into your state. We will not repeat the discussion of long-arm jurisdiction here (see Chapter 2). As a practical matter, however, most long-arm jurisdiction derives from the fact that the defendant did something in the state that caused the dispute. If so, when you identify that defendant, the allegation should mention defendant's connection with the forum state. There is standard language for this: "Defendant Roger Anderson is a resident of Michigan who caused an act or event to occur in Arizona out of which plaintiff's cause of action arises." (If the style seems inelegant, it is because the language follows that typically used in long-arm statutes.)

Obviously, jurisdictional issues can arise in a given case that raise complexities that go beyond what we have covered here. In such cases, you will need to research the issues and draft allegations tailored to your situation, sufficient to explain why the court has jurisdiction of the subject matter and the parties. Remember, the rules call for a "short and plain" explanation, not an essay!

## Step 6   *Relationships among Parties*

In all but the simplest cases, some of the defendants you are including in the suit are named not because they did anything to your client, but because they are responsible in some way for the actions of the person who did injure your client. There are many examples of this derivative liability. One of the most common is the tort doctrine of *respondeat superior,* which makes an employer liable for torts committed by an employee. Another, in community property states, is the liability of one spouse for acts of the other.

Relationships giving rise to liability must, of course, be alleged; otherwise, there would be nothing in the complaint to show why the innocent employer or spouse is being sued, and the judge would dismiss them from the suit.

> At all times material hereto, defendant John Raymond O'Hara was employed by defendant Purple Taxicab Company and acted within the course and scope of that employment. Defendant Purple Taxicab Company is liable for the acts and omissions of defendant John Raymond O'Hara complained of herein under the doctrine of respondeat superior.

> Defendant Anne Marie Brown is the wife of defendant Gerald Joseph Brown. At all times material hereto, defendant Anne Marie Brown acted both individually and on behalf of the marital community consisting of defendant Anne Marie Brown and Gerald Joseph Brown.

## Step 7   *General Allegations*

In the remainder of the body of the complaint, you must give "a short and plain statement of the claim showing that [plaintiff] is entitled to relief"; see FRCP, Rule 8(a). To do this, you must accomplish two main goals: (1) Give a short summary of the facts of your case—that is, tell what happened to your client; and (2) state the particular facts necessary to establish each of the elements of each cause of action.

We suggest that this is best done by dividing the task into two parts: First, tell what happened, in a section we will call "General Allegations"; then, in separate counts, one for each cause of action, establish the elements of the claims. This may entail some repetition, but there are good reasons for doing it this way.

Chief among these is the fact that this approach allows you to create a persuasive and compelling narrative of your client's story, free of the distraction of worrying about the legal minutiae. This is important, and goes to the heart of what litigation is all about. How do you convince a judge or jury to rule in your favor? By creating the impression that ruling in your favor is the *right thing to do, not* by showing that you have proven all the elements of your cause of action. You need to do that too, of course, but it will not be enough by itself to ensure success. *First,* persuade the judge or jury that justice is on the side of your client, that it is only fair and right for your client to win. *Then* provide enough law to support a decision in your favor. Remember, "a man convinced against his will is of the same opinion still."

In the General Allegations section, simply tell your client's story in the most convincing way you can. Properly told, your client's story may be the most persuasive argument you can make. Gerry Spence, one of today's premier trial lawyers, in his book *How to Argue and Win Every Time,* recommends that *all* legal arguments be cast in the form of stories. This part of the complaint represents a golden opportunity for you to begin persuading the judge of the rightness of your cause; in deciding motions, judges often scan the complaint to see what the suit is about.

How much detail should you include?: Obviously, some judgment is required. The General Allegations section should typically be a page or two (double-spaced, typewritten on standard paper) and should

---

## SIDEBAR

## Pleading Damages

*Can you guess what single thing is an element of every cause of action? Damages.*

*Lawsuits are about damages. You sue because you have suffered some loss as a result of defendant's conduct. What should you say about your losses in the complaint?*

*At a minimum, you must allege that "plaintiff has been damaged." Should you specify the kinds of losses or injuries plaintiff has suffered? Should you attach a dollar value?*

*In general, the General Allegations section should describe at least the general types of damages plaintiff has suffered. If plaintiff was physically injured, describe the type of injury; if plaintiff lost income or had property damaged or destroyed, say how, in a sentence or two. If plaintiff was (or still is) in pain, or if plaintiff has suffered some permanent injury or disability, these things should be mentioned. If plaintiff has incurred financial losses or specific expenses, it is important to allege at least the general categories, such as, "plaintiff incurred substantial hospital, physician, and related charges. . . ."*

*FCRP, Rule 9(g) requires that "items of special damage . . . be specifically stated." General damages are the losses that would naturally be expected to occur in every case based on the same theory of liability (for example, pain and suffering in a case of assault and battery). Special damages are the particular losses that your client has suffered, above and beyond the general damages (for example, a medical bill for setting your client's broken arm). The distinction between general and special damages can be rather technical and esoteric, and this is not the place for an extended essay on the subject; as a practical matter, the lesson of Rule 9(g) is that you should al-ways give a summary of the various ways in which your client has been injured or lost money as a result of defendant's conduct.*

*Having described plaintiff's injuries and losses in the General Allegations section, it is unnecessary to re-peat the description in each of the counts. Each count should simply conclude with the following boilerplate: "As a proximate result of the acts and omissions of de-fendant(s) complained of herein, plaintiff has been damaged in an amount which plaintiff will prove." This satisfies the requirement of pleading the causa-tion and damages elements, for this count.*

*Should you specify dollar amounts? It depends. If your client's medical bills are in six figures, that is a persuasive indication of the gravity of the injuries, and is well worth including in your narrative. Never pin yourself down exactly unless you are absolutely sure— opt for "medical bills in excess of $105,000," not "in-curred medical bills of $105,128.24," because you will invariably discover later that some item has been omitted. If in doubt, it is acceptable in many jurisdic-tions to plead more generally—say, "plaintiff incurred medical bills in a substantial amount"—without at-taching a number. Your instructor will tell you whether this is permitted in your locality.*

*A final caveat: The foregoing discussion deals with the question of whether to state the amount of money plaintiff claims to have lost. Whether to ask the court to award a specific amount of money is another question, which we will address in connection with the prayer for relief. The amount plaintiff has lost is not the same as the amount you are asking the court to award. In most cases plaintiff is entitled to be com-pensated for such things as pain and suffering that go beyond plaintiff's actual losses.*

not exceed four or five pages except in the most complicated, multiparty cases. This suggestion is based on consideration of what is desirable in order to create the most persuasive narrative. Too short, and there will not be enough detail to understand what the case is about. Too long, and the reader will lose interest.

Some facts should always be included in your narrative. The dates on which the main events happened are important, to make it clear that the suit is not barred by the statute of limitations. You should specify the places where events happened and make it clear "who did what to whom." Be sure to include the main "bad acts" of defendant. This is a lawsuit, and you are asking the court to take money away from the defendant and give it to your client, so you need to tell your client's story in a way that will make a judge or juror feel justified in doing so. For the same reason, always give a description of how your client has suffered losses, and tell how these losses were caused by defendant's conduct. (See sidebar on pleading damages.) After reading your narrative, the reader should be left with a clear sense that defendant's wrongful act, whatever it was, had a serious and harmful effect on your client.

The narrative should be in chronological order—do not resort to flashbacks, imagery, and other such literary devices. Just tell what happened in the order in which it happened. Try to include enough factual detail to make the sequence of events easy to follow—to make a readable and compelling story—but keep it short. Writing in litigation always involves a trade-off: On one hand, you would like to include all of your most persuasive arguments, but on the other hand, the reader likely will not have time to read more than some small number of pages. The solution is to make your writing clean, tight, and interesting, and to position the most important matters near the beginning.

At the time the complaint is prepared, you will often find that you simply do not have all of the facts. What then? Can you speculate as to what you think probably happened? In fact, to an extent, you can, if you follow the rules. See the sidebars "Truth or Consequences" and "Alternative Pleading."

---

### Step 8   *Causes of Action*

Having told your client's story, the task that remains is to allege each element of each cause of action. Our purpose now shifts from that of persuasively telling our client's story to that of forestalling

---

## SIDEBAR

### Truth or Consequences

*Do you have to tell the truth in a complaint? What happens if you do not? What do you do if you are not sure what really happened?*

*FRCP, Rule 11, is a very important rule, one that you should read, understand, and take to heart. It sets the boundaries between permissible advocacy and improper twisting of the facts. Rule 11(b) says that when an attorney files any court paper with the court, he or she is certifying that, to the best of his or her knowledge, information, and belief, "the allegations and other factual contentions have evidentiary support, or, if specifically so identified, are likely to have evidentiary support after a reasonable opportunity for further investigation or discovery. . . . "*

*Therefore, if you state in your complaint that "defendant John Doe was intoxicated at the time of the collision," you are certifying to the court that you have evidence that defendant was, in fact, intoxicated. The penalties allowed by Rule 11 for making bold factual statements that you cannot support can be quite severe, up to and including dismissal of your case and imposition of fines. The unstated penalty is perhaps even more severe: Attorneys who play fast and loose with the truth quickly lose their credibility with the court.*

*What if you are pretty sure that defendant was intoxicated, and you think that you will be able to prove it after you obtain discovery of defendant's blood alcohol test? Rule 11 offers the solution: You specifically identify that fact as one that is likely to have evidentiary support after a reasonable opportunity for discovery. How? The standard shorthand consists of the phrase, "upon information and belief." For example, "Upon information and belief, defendant John Doe was intoxicated. . . . "*

---

*Your Local Notes*

_____

_____

---

a motion to dismiss for failure to state a cause of action. Our exhortations about avoiding "legalese" and technical language do not apply here. Indeed, it is often better to recite the elements of the causes of action in the exact language of the cases or statutes from which they are derived, since doing so will make it harder for defendant to argue later that we have omitted some element.

## SIDEBAR

### Alternative Pleading

*Suppose Doug Ryder is a bouncer at the Rowdy Bar and Grille, and in the course of breaking up an altercation between other patrons, Doug hit your client with a pool cue. You are not sure whether Doug deliberately hit your client or was merely careless. If Doug acted deliberately, your client has a claim for battery, which is an intentional tort. If Doug was just careless, the claim should be for negligence. What should you do?*

*Plead in the alternative. FRCP, Rule 8(e)(2), allows you to "set forth two or more statements of a claim or defense alternately or hypothetically." In the General Allegations section, you allege: "On information and belief, defendant Doug Ryder intentionally struck plaintiff with a pool cue. In the alternative, in striking plaintiff with a pool cue, defendant Doug Ryder acted in a careless and negligent manner."*

*Then, in the Causes of Action section of the complaint, you include both a count of battery and a count of negligence against defendant Doug Ryder. These two counts are, of course, inconsistent—Doug's act of striking plaintiff with a pool cue cannot have been both intentional and unintentional. Does this matter? Not as long as you have a reasonable basis to believe that the evidence, once discovered, may support either version.*

*A final word of caution: Pleading in the alternative does not absolve you of the responsibility to obey Rule 11. You must still have a reasonable belief that evidentiary support is likely to exist for each of the factual statements you make.*

## SIDEBAR

### Notice Pleading

*Is it really necessary to recite laboriously the elements of each of your causes of action?*

*To answer that question, we must review a bit of history. In the early part of this century, pleading had evolved into a complex and arcane game in which trivial missteps could lead to sudden dismissal. The federal rules, first adopted in 1938, were intended to do away with this emphasis on form over substance by adopting what was termed notice pleading. In theory, the complaint is merely required to give notice to the defendant that suit has been filed, with at least some reasonable indication of the subject matter. For example, in theory, a complaint with only one allegation—*

*"Defendant owes me money"—is sufficient to state a claim in a suit on a debt. The idea is that, once given notice of the general nature of the suit, defendant can find out the details through discovery.*

*There is an important exception to the principle of notice pleading. FRCP, Rule 9(b), states that "In all averments of fraud or mistake, the circumstances constituting fraud or mistake shall be stated with particularity." Thus where fraud is alleged, the rules specifically require that you give a higher degree of detail, and cases decided under Rule 9(b) hold that you must specifically plead each element of the cause of action for fraud.*

Is this laborious enumeration of each element of each theory of liability necessary? In theory, except in fraud cases, probably not (see sidebar on notice pleading). It is, however, customary, and if you neglect to allege all the elements of your claims (or worse, attempt to allege them and inadvertently leave out an element), you invite a motion to dismiss, which will take time and cost money to respond to even if you ultimately prevail.

There is one potential downside to listing all of your causes of action and their elements: If

there is some other theory of liability that would have fit your facts, but which you did not think of, your opponent will argue that you cannot use it because you did not plead it. This argument is probably incorrect, since there is case law holding that a plaintiff is entitled to recover under any theory of liability supported by the facts alleged in the complaint, but such disputes are best anticipated and avoided. We recommend beginning the "Causes of Action" section with the following boilerplate allegation:

Plaintiff(s) are entitled to recover damages from defendants and each of them based on the theories of liability hereinafter enumerated in Counts I through ___, and under such other theories of liability as may be appropriate based upon the facts as alleged herein or as revealed during discovery.

Next should follow the causes of action themselves, set out in counts, one count for each separate theory of liability or cause of action. Each count begins with a centered heading, with the counts numbered in sequence. (In very simple cases, where there is only one theory of liability and it applies equally to all defendants, there will be only one count. In that case, it is unnecessary to set it off separately with its own heading.) To make the complaint easier to read, we suggest that the heading also state on what theory of liability this count is based, and indicate to which defendants it pertains. For example,

COUNT I—Negligence

(All defendants)

or,

COUNT XIV—Breach of Contract

(Against defendants Rogers and Acme Foundry Corporation)

After the heading, the elements of the pertinent theory of liability are alleged in a very summary fashion in a few short paragraphs. Paragraph numbering continues in sequence from the General Allegations section. A great deal of factual detail is unnecessary; include enough facts to tie the elements to your own fact situation, then stop. For example, if you have already described how the auto accident occurred in the General Allegations section, you need not repeat the description in the negligence count. Indeed, the negligence count may consist of a single paragraph:

Defendant Sue Johnson had a duty to operate her motor vehicle with due care, and breached said duty by failing to obey the red traffic signal. As a proximate result of the negligence of defendant Sue Johnson, plaintiff was damaged in an amount which plaintiff will prove.

This short paragraph alleges the four elements of the tort of negligence, which are duty, breach of duty, causation, and damages, and is sufficient to state a cause of action for negligence. (Some practitioners may prefer more factual detail in the counts; there is no great harm in erring on the side of too much detail as long as you can prove what you are alleging and as long as the allegations in the counts do not contradict what you already said in the General Allegations section.)

In garden-variety suits for damages, after alleging the elements of each theory of liability, you are finished with the "counts" and ready to move on to the prayer for relief (see Step 9). In more complex cases, however, where you are asking for more than just ordinary damage, you may need to include some additional counts to cover the particular kinds of relief you are seeking.

For example, to receive punitive damages—damages intended to punish the defendant—you must show that defendant acted in an unusually reprehensible manner deserving of punishment. Exactly what you must allege and prove to receive punitive damages depends on the substantive law on which your suit is based. Whatever the elements are that you must prove, allege them in a separate count for punitive damages. (In the sample complaint later in this workshop, Figure W5–2, we have used the standard for Arizona. Cases potentially involving punitive damages arise often enough that you should find out what the standards are in your state, either from your instructor or as a research exercise.)

Likewise, there are additional allegations that must be included if you are asking the court for an injunction or for a declaratory judgment. You can treat such requests simply as additional counts, making sure to include all of the elements required under whatever law applies to your case.

## Step 9 *Prayer for Relief*

The final section of the body of the complaint is the prayer for relief. It is here that you say what you are asking the court to do. The prayer for relief is worded in standard language, usually copied from a form complaint. In a typical lawsuit, plaintiff is asking for money damages. If local custom in your locality calls for a particular wording or layout, your instructor will inform you, or you can get an idea of local practice by reading complaints that others have filed. The following stock prayer for relief, with the appropriate dollar amount inserted, should be at least adequate in any American court:

Wherefore, plaintiff requests that the Court enter judgment in favor of plaintiff and against defendants and each of them as follows:

1. For general and special damages in the amount of $100,000.00.
2. For plaintiff's reasonable costs and attorney's fees incurred herein.
3. For such other and further relief as to the Court seems just in the premises.

The request for general and special damages is standard and should appear in every complaint. Should you specify a dollar amount? It depends on the court and the type of case. In some courts, the rules require you to ask for a specific amount. In others, it is permissible to substitute a request for "general and special damages in an amount which plaintiff will prove." Why would you want to be so vague about the amount you are asking for? Because deciding exactly how much to ask for is difficult, especially at the time of filing the complaint, when you are unlikely to have all the facts. If your complaint specifies a low amount and you later find that the evidence would support a higher demand, you will have to ask the court for permission to amend the complaint, and you may not get it. If you err on the high side—which is about the only way to avoid erring on the low side—you can be sure that your unreasonable demand will come flying back at you in front of the jury as your opponent tries to paint you and your client as greedy opportunists. For these reasons, we generally prefer not to specify a dollar amount in the complaint unless the court requires it. There is one exception: cases in which it appears that a defendant is likely to default. The court has no power to grant a default judgment exceeding the amount demanded in the complaint, so if a default is likely, a specific amount must be specified.

The party who wins a lawsuit is entitled to judgment for his or her court costs; see FRCP, Rule 54(d). The request for costs should be included in every complaint. The costs that can be awarded are limited to certain allowable categories of expenses. In federal court, the allowed categories are listed in 28 U.S.C. 1920 and include such things as filing fees, court reporter fees, witness fees, and process server fees. For the types of costs allowable in state court, it is necessary to consult state statutes or court rules.

Costs do not include attorney's fees. The winner of a lawsuit may or may not be entitled to judgment for attorney's fees; it depends on the type of case (awards of attorney's fees are common in breach of contract actions, uncommon in tort cases) and on the substantive law on which the claims are based. Since there is no penalty for asking, we suggest including the request for attorney's fees in every complaint unless it is completely clear that there is no basis for doing so.

The request for "other and further relief" is traditional, and probably accomplishes little or nothing in modern practice. Nevertheless, if practitioners in your locality customarily include it, you should do likewise.

Our stock prayer for relief serves as a starting point. In each new case, you will need to consider whether there is anything you are asking the court for that is not covered. If so, add one or more paragraphs. For example, if you are seeking an injunction, you must include the request in the prayer for relief—write exactly what you want the court to order defendant to do. If you are seeking a declaratory judgment, write the exact wording of the declaration you are seeking and include it in the prayer. If your lawsuit involves categories of damages other than general and special damages—punitive damages, treble damages under various statutes, etc.—these must be requested.

---

*Your Local Notes*

_____

_____

---

## Step 10 — Date, Signature, and Verification

The complaint concludes with the standard date and signature lines used in all court papers (see Workshop 4, Court Papers). There is no mailing certificate, since the complaint cannot be served by mail.

Notice that it is the attorney, not the client, who signs the complaint. FRCP, Rule 11(a), requires that "Every pleading . . . shall be signed by at least one attorney . . . " (except, of course, when the party has no attorney). Why the attorney instead of the plaintiff? Recall that FRCP, Rule 11(b), provides that when an attorney signs a complaint, he or she is certifying to the court that he or she has made a reasonable inquiry and believes that the allegations are supportable and proper. In other words, the attorney's signature on the complaint gives the court a weapon with which to enforce the ethical requirements of Rule 11.

In times past, there was often a requirement that, in addition to the attorney's signature, the client furnish a sworn affidavit attesting to the truth of the allegations of the complaint. This is called "verifying" the complaint, and is accomplished by following the signature line for the attorney with a "verification." The verification is pure boilerplate, and typically looks like that shown in Figure W5–1. The verification is signed by the plaintiff and notarized; it is the notarization that makes the verification "sworn."

The federal rules have abolished verification "except when otherwise provided by rule or statute." In ordinary suits for damages, verification is not required; if any of your theories of liability are derived from statute, consult the statute to be sure. State court verification requirements vary from one state to another. Your instructor will let you know about any important categories of cases for which verification is required in your locality.

Never verify a pleading if it is not required. (More generally, never let a client sign any paper in

---

**Figure W5–1    Verification of a Complaint**

### VERIFICATION

Plaintiff [put in name], being first duly sworn, upon his [her] oath deposes and says: That he [she] is the plaintiff in the above-entitled action; that he [she] has read the foregoing complaint and the allegations thereof are true of plaintiff's own knowledge, except such allegations as are made upon information and belief, and these plaintiff believes to be true.

_____
                                                             Plaintiff

SUBSCRIBED AND SWORN to this ___ day of _____, 20___, before me, the undersigned Notary Public.

_____
                                                      Notary Public

---

a lawsuit unless it is required.) A complaint is a technical document, much of which (in particular, the counts alleging the theories of liability) is incomprehensible to clients who lack legal training. A verified complaint is potential ammunition for your opponent to use to create an appearance that your client was untruthful when he or she swore to having "read and understood" the complaint; you can be sure that your client's understanding will be tested when your client's deposition is taken.

## CONCLUDING STEPS

**Step 11**    *Prepare Accompanying Papers*

For the clerk of the court to accept your complaint for filing, you must present, in addition to the complaint itself (including any exhibits that you have incorporated by reference), at least the following:

1.  A number of copies of the complaint at least equal to the number of defendants upon whom you will be serving process, plus one for your own file. The clerk will retain the original complaint for the court's file and "conform" the other copies by stamping them with the case number (assigned at the time of filing) and with the clerk's stamp or seal.

2.  An original summons for each defendant to be served, and a copy for your file. The clerk will issue these summonses by affixing the appropriate stamps or seals. Summonses are commonly either printed forms (available from a legal forms printer) or word processor forms; the only drafting necessary will be to fill in the caption and the names of the defendants to be served.

3.  A check for the required filing fee.

Many courts also require a completed information sheet for the use of the clerk or court administrator, giving summary information about the case, the parties, and the lawyers. Your instructor will apprise you of any such requirements in your locality, and of any other local requirements for filing a complaint in your jurisdiction. Whenever you are preparing a suit for filing in a court whose procedures are not familiar to you, it is essential to consult the local rules for any requirements beyond the summons and complaint.

You will also need an instruction sheet for the process server, indicating how, where, and on whom you want the summons and complaint served. This may be as simple as a handwritten note, or your law firm or process server may have printed forms. Any information you can give the process server about where defendants can be found will help reduce the need for expensive tracing procedures, and lower service costs.

It is often a good strategy (if the rules of your locality allow it) to serve discovery requests with the complaint. Because of the recent wave of experimentation with limitations on discovery, there is great variability from one locality to another in the kinds of discovery that are permitted in the early stages of a lawsuit. Your instructor will provide the details for your locality, or you can consult the local rules.

**Step 12**    *Check Accuracy and Make Revisions*

When you have completed your draft, read it carefully and make a systematic check for errors. This should include at least the following:

1. *A literacy check.* Success in litigation depends in great measure on projecting a competent and professional image; a complaint full of misspelled words and grammatical errors sends a powerful message that the drafter need not be taken as a serious threat. Use your word processor's spell checker. Rewrite awkward passages. Watch for ambiguous use of personal pronouns.

2. *A facts check.* Be sure you have alleged your facts accurately. Have your client read the complaint, and verify the facts with your client. If the complaint includes factual allegations that you cannot yet back up with solid evidence, be sure that you have made those allegations "on information and belief."

3. *An elements check.* Review your research notes and verify that you have included a count for each theory of liability and that no element of any of your theories of liability has been inadvertently omitted.

## Step 13    *File and Serve*

If you have followed Steps 1 through 12 carefully, you should now have a package ready for filing. It is commonplace for the actual filing to be done by a messenger or by the process server who will serve the complaint on the defendants, although anyone, including you, can go to the court and file the complaint. After filing, the process server will deliver the issued summonses and the conformed copies of the complaint to the various defendants.

---

**Your Local Notes**

_____

_____

---

**Some General Guidelines**—Here are some general rules that may assist you when drafting pleadings.

1. *Parties should be labeled as such throughout the complaint wherever their names appear.* You would write "defendant Ronald Carson," not merely "Ronald Carson" (fails to apprise the reader that Ronald Carson is a party) or "defendant" (ambiguous if there is more than one defendant). Some practitioners write the names of parties in capitals (i.e., "defendant RONALD CARSON") to make it easier to pick out the allegations involving a particular person. We suggest that you let local custom be your guide.

2. *Use shortened titles to avoid having to repeat cumbersome phrases.* For example: "Plaintiff Alpha Corporation and defendant Omega Company entered into a written agreement dated April 1, 1995, entitled "Agreement for the Lease of Certain Manufacturing Equipment" (hereinafter referred to as the "Alpha-Omega Agreement"). In subsequent paragraphs, you can simply refer to the agreement as the "Alpha-Omega Agreement" without having to repeat the lengthy title and date.

3. *Incorporate important documents by reference.* If the lawsuit is based on a contract, for example, you can avoid much of the need for quoting or paraphrasing the terms of the contract by simply attaching the document to the complaint as an exhibit and incorporating it in the complaint by reference. When you incorporate a document by reference, you make it, in effect a part of the complaint itself. Typical language: "Plaintiff Alpha Corporation and defendant Omega Company entered into a written agreement dated April 1, 1995, entitled "Agreement for the Lease of Certain Manufacturing Equipment" (hereinafter referred to as the "Alpha-Omega Agreement," a copy of which is attached hereto as Exhibit 1 and incorporated herein by reference)." Don't forget to attach the copy and label it as Exhibit 1. In general, only documents that are actually a part of the dispute (contracts, deeds, etc.) should be incorporated by reference; do not attach documents that are merely evidentiary (police reports, doctor bills).

4. *Do not overcapitalize.* You are writing a complaint, not the Declaration of Independence. The words "plaintiff" and "defendant" are not capitalized unless they occur at the beginning of a sentence. The same applies to words like "petitioner," "respondent," "appellant," "moving party," and other similar designations. The word "court" is capitalized only if you are referring to the particular court to which the pleading is addressed.

5. *Always be polite.* Write in an educated tone; avoid slang. Avoid statements about the character of opposing parties. Tempting as it may be to refer to your opponent as a scurrilous, unprincipled, lying scoundrel, it is far better and more persuasive to tell your client's story convincingly and let the facts speak for themselves.

6. *Avoid imagery and metaphor.* You may be called on to prove each statement in the complaint, so stick to the facts.

7. *Write pleadings in the third person.* Avoid the use of personal pronouns, because they tend to create ambiguity—refer to your client as "plaintiff John Doe," or perhaps simply "plaintiff" if there is only one, but not as "he" or "she."

8. *Write clearly and say exactly what you mean.* Never use words whose meanings you do not fully understand. Avoid using big words in the General Allegations section; your purpose is to communicate and persuade, not to show off your vocabulary.

> **Your Local Notes**
> 
> _____
> 
> _____

**Pleading Vocabulary**—In general, a simple, direct writing style is best. There are, however, a few phrases of "legalese" that are necessary when drafting pleadings because, either through long custom and usage or by virtue of being included in the wording of the rules of procedure, they have come to have precise meanings that cannot be expressed so exactly in ordinary language. Here are a few of the common ones:

***Upon information and belief:*** The party and the party's attorney have reasonable grounds to believe a statement is true and do believe it is true, but cannot prove it at this point. Example: "Upon information and belief, defendant John Doe is a resident of Dade County, Florida."

***At all times material hereto:*** The matter alleged was true during the entire time period that is involved in the lawsuit. Example: "At all times material hereto, defendant Jane Doe was employed by defendant Ajax Widget Corporation."

***Defendants and each of them:*** The fact alleged is true for each defendant taken separately *and* with respect to all the defendants taken together.

***Incorporated by reference:*** The document referred to (typically a contract or other similar document that is attached as an exhibit) is intended to be treated as a part of the complaint, just as if its contents had been copied word for word into the complaint itself.

## SIDEBAR

## Unidentified Parties

*You are about to sue Arnold Lush, the negligent driver that backed his delivery truck into your client's new Porsche, when you suddenly realize that you are in a community property state, you think Arnold is probably married, but you are not sure, and you certainly have no convenient way of finding out his wife's name. Furthermore, you are pretty sure that Arnold was on the job when the accident happened, but you do not know who Arnold's employer is.*

*What do you do?*

*It depends on the court. Obviously, you need to get the complaint filed against Arnold so you can take some discovery and find out the identities of Mrs. Lush and Arnold's employer. One option would be to leave out all mention of Mrs. Lush and the employer, file the complaint against Arnold, take discovery, and then amend the complaint to add the new parties. One drawback to this approach is that if Mrs. Lush and the employer can claim that they did not become aware of the suit until after the statute of limitations ran, you may not be allowed to add them as parties. Another is that, because of the delay in completing the pleadings, it may take longer to get the case scheduled for trial.*

*Some (but by no means all—check the rules) courts allow the designation of parties by fictitious names. Then the solution to the problem of Mrs. Lush is simple—you name Arnold Lush and Jane Doe Lush, husband and wife, as defendants. The process server finds Mrs. Lush and serves the complaint on her. Since the complaint describes her as the wife of Arnold Lush, she has adequate notice of the suit and will have to defend.*

*A similar tactic can be used on the employer: "Defendant Black Corporation was, at all times material hereto, the employer of Arnold Lush. . . . " The process server will probably not be able to serve the complaint on the employer without knowing its name, so it will still be necessary to take discovery and amend the complaint. But the amendment will consist merely of substituting the right name, rather than adding new allegations. The original complaint can be made to tell the complete story, instead of having to leave out some of the major players.*

*For the specific language used in suing fictitiously named defendants, see the sample complaint shown in Figure W5–2 later in this workshop.*

## SIDEBAR

### Precision in Drafting

*One way in which complaint drafting is different from other kinds of writing is the need for a high degree of precision. It is not enough to write allegations that can be interpreted to imply a cause of action; the complaint must actually state a cause of action in unambiguous terms. When you draft a sentence in a complaint, ask yourself if it is capable of any interpretation other than the one you intend. If so, rewrite it.*

*As you read the following allegation, try to identify the ambiguities:*

*Defendant William Bernstein and his supervisor, defendant Roger Gordon, were employees of defendant Haulrite Trucking Company. Defendant was not trained as a truck driver and was not qualified to drive large commercial trucks.*

*Answer: (1) The allegation does not say when defendants William Bernstein and Roger Gordon were employees. Haulrite can be held liable only if they were employees at the time of the accident. Obviously, this is what the drafter meant, but it is not enough to mean it—you have to say it. (2) The second sentence is ambiguous: Which defendant was not trained? William? Roger? Both? Also, the allegation needs to say that defendant was not trained at the time that is in question in the lawsuit. This is a good place for the phrase "at all times material hereto." See the text discussion of pleading vocabulary.*

## SIDEBAR

### Drafting Style

*You will occasionally see complaints that begin with such quaint phraseology as "Comes now the plaintiff, by and through his undersigned attorney, and for his first cause of action against defendants, alleges as follows. . . . " Often, this grandiloquent style is continued into the body of the complaint. Instead of simply "defendant drove his car into the side of mine," we read, "defendant did then and there operate his motor vehicle in such manner. . . . "*

*Such pretentious prose is likely to impress no one and makes the complaint hard to read. It will often be necessary for the judge to refer back to the complaint in deciding motions; it is better to focus the judge's time and attention on your most persuasive arguments, rather than waste it slogging through superfluous verbiage. Pleadings can also be read to the jury during trial, by either side, so it is advisable not to couch allegations in ways that will sound pompous.*

*As with most writing in litigation, an important goal of complaint drafting is to convince the reader of the rightness of your cause. This is best done by writing in a style that focuses the reader's attention on the message, not on the words used.*

**Allegation:** A statement in a pleading of some fact or conclusion that the pleader claims is true; an assertion.

**Including without limitation:** Used when giving a few examples, without raising an inference that the examples given are the only ones that exist. If you merely allege, "Plaintiff received injuries, including a broken arm and a concussion," there may be an inference that these are the only injuries plaintiff received. If you substitute "including without limitation" (or the equivalent, "including but not limited to") for the word "including," this makes clear that there may be other injuries as well.

**The Goals of Complaint Drafting**—What, then, are the purposes of drafting a complaint? Here are some of the most important ones; you can probably think of others. When you begin drafting, use this list of purposes and goals as a kind of checklist to guide your work, and try to make sure that you have accomplished each one.

1. Commencing the lawsuit.

2. Stating your claims in a way sufficient to avoid dismissal.

3. Forcing your opponent to admit or deny key facts.

4. Telling your client's story in a way that is persuasive to the reader.

5. Leaving sufficient flexibility that you have not painted yourself into a corner if the facts develop in unexpected ways, and you are not locked in on particular legal theories.

6. Including the correct parties, and leaving flexibility to add any other parties that you become aware of later.

*Your Local Notes*

_____

_____

## Complaint Drafting: Learning By Example

We now use our step-by-step instructions to draft a complaint on behalf of Shannon Martin.

### PREPARATORY STEPS

**Step 1**   *Assemble the Basic Factual Information*

We will base our complaint on the facts described in our hypo, Shannon's Ordeal, from Chapters 3 through 8. Referring back to those chapters, we first list the possible defendants. Obvious possible targets are Dr. Collins, the hotel, the Las Vegas Police Department (for false arrest), and Shannon's employer (for wrongfully suspending Shannon from her job). We will eliminate the last two, because the claims that Shannon may have against the police department or her employer mainly involve facts that are distinct from the incident in the hotel—it is better to sue them separately, if at all.

If we sue Dr. Collins, we will want to include his wife, assuming he has one, since Texas is a community property state. If we sue Dr. Collins without including his wife, we risk ending up with a judgment that might not be valid against the Collins's community property, which probably comprises most of the Collins's assets.

To sue the hotel, we need to know what entity is responsible for operating it. This information is often rather tricky to obtain. We begin by checking whatever materials we have available; hotel brochures, advertisements, or stationary may tell us what we need to know. Failing that, we try government agencies: Is there a state agency that regulates hotels? What do county real estate records show about the ownership of the land that the hotel occupies? Do the records of the state department of corporations show any corporation with a name similar to that of the hotel? It may take considerable investigative effort to determine whom to sue in a dispute that involves a large business concern, and sometimes it is necessary to employ an investigator who has access to a variety of information databases.

After investigating, we find that Banbury Park Hotel is owned and operated by Park Hotels Group, a Delaware corporation, with its main office in New Jersey and hotels in a number of other states. We will sue the corporation; should we also sue any of its employees? Its stockholders? Its officers or directors? In general, we probably would

include in the suit any employees who themselves engaged in actionable conduct. Arnie Trevayne would be a defendant, except that at the time of filing suit, his role has not yet come to light. Shareholders are not liable for the acts of a corporation (with a few exceptions, as always)—in fact, one of the main reasons for incorporating a business is to shield the shareholders from personal liability. Officers and directors can be liable if they participated in the wrongful conduct; in some situations, they can also be held liable for negligence in performing their supervisory duties. The potential liability of all of these peripheral players involves questions of substantive law. As a rule, when a suit involves a corporate setting, you should sue the corporation and the specific employee(s) whose conduct led to the suit, if known. You should not sue other employees, officers, directors, or shareholders, unless you have done the research and verified that a cause of action exists against them under substantive law.

For the moment, we will sue Park Hotels Group and Dr. and Mrs. Collins. In a jurisdiction that allows fictitious defendants, we might include several "John Doe" defendants to cover the negligent hotel employees that we expect to find during discovery.

**Step 2**   *Determine the Elements of the Claims You Intend to Raise*

What causes of action shall we assert against the hotel and Dr. Collins? The obvious ones are negligence against the hotel and assault and/or battery against Dr. Collins. To keep the example simple, we will confine our example complaint to these. There are, of course, a number of other possibilities, which we should by now have listed in our Issues Outline (see Workshop 1), researched, and considered.

We see from our Issues Outline that the elements of assault, as applied to our hypo, are (1) an act by Dr. Collins; (2) intent by Dr. Collins to cause harmful or offensive contact, or imminent apprehension (that is, fear) of harmful or offensive contact; and (3) causing Shannon to feel imminent apprehension of harmful or offensive contact. To this we add (4) damages proximately caused by Dr. Collins's wrongful conduct. The elements of battery are the same as those of assault, except that the third element is now "actual harmful contact" instead of "apprehension of harmful contact."

Since we have some doubt whether we will be able to prove that Dr. Collins's acts were intended to harm Shannon, and since Dr. Collins may have a valid defense (self-defense), we will leave ourselves some additional maneuvering room by also including a negligence count against Dr. Collins. We will also, of course, sue the hotel for negligence. We see from our issues outline that the elements of negligence are (1) duty, (2) breach of that duty, (3) causation, and (4) damages.

## DRAFTING STEPS

We now begin drafting, using Steps 3 through 10. The finished product is shown in Figure W5–2.

## CONCLUDING STEPS

### Step 11 *Prepare Accompanying Papers*

We will need three original summonses, one each for Arthur Collins, Mrs. Collins, and Park Hotels Group. We will need a copy of the complaint for each, plus one for our file and one for our client; the clerk will keep the original. We need a check for the filing fee, and, checking the local rules for the federal district court for the District of Arizona, an information sheet

---

**Figure W5–2   Sample Complaint**

**IN THE UNITED STATES DISTRICT COURT
DISTRICT OF ARIZONA**

| | |
|---|---|
| SHANNON MARTIN, a single woman, )<br>)<br>)     Plaintiff, )<br>)<br>v. )<br>)<br>ARTHUR COLLINS and JANE DOE )<br>COLLINS, husband and wife; PARK )<br>HOTELS GROUP, INC., a Delaware )<br>   corporation; )<br>)<br>    Defendants. )<br>)<br>_____ ) | NO. _____<br><br>COMPLAINT |

Plaintiff alleges:

**JURISDICTION AND PARTIES**

1. Plaintiff Shannon Martin is a resident of Maricopa County, Arizona.
2. Defendants Arthur Collins and Jane Doe Collins are residents of Dallas County, Texas. Defendant Jane Doe Collins is the wife of defendant Arthur Collins. At all times material hereto, defendant Arthur Collins acted both individually and on behalf of the marital community consisting of defendants Arthur Collins and Jane Doe Collins. Plaintiff does not know the true identity of defendant Jane Doe Collins, and will seek leave to amend her complaint to reflect such true identity after ascertaining it. Defendant Arthur Collins caused an act or event to occur in the state of Nevada out of which plaintiff's claims arose.
3. Defendant Park Hotels Group (hereinafter "Hotel") is a corporation organized and existing under the laws of the state of Delaware, and doing business in the state of Nevada out of which plaintiff's claim arose.
4. This Court has jurisdiction of this matter under the provisions of 28 U.S.C.§1332. The amount in controversy is greater than $75,000.

**Figure W5–2   Sample Complaint,** *continued*

## GENERAL ALLEGATIONS

**5.**   On the night of February 5, 1996, plaintiff Shannon Martin was a paying guest at the Banbury Park Hotel in Las Vegas, Nevada. The Banbury Park Hotel is owned and operated by defendant Park Hotels Group.

**6.**   At approximately 1:15 A.M. on the morning of February 6, 1996, plaintiff Shannon Martin was asleep in her hotel room at the Banbury Park Hotel. Prior to retiring, plaintiff closed and locked the door of her room. Defendant Arthur Collins, a stranger to plaintiff, using a key provided by defendant Banbury Park Hotel, entered plaintiff's room, stood at the foot of plaintiff's bed, and began removing his clothes.

**7.**   Plaintiff reasonably believed that defendant Arthur Collins was attacking her. Using a .22 caliber revolver which was lawfully in her possession, and acting in self-defense, plaintiff shot defendant Arthur Collins. Defendant Arthur Collins then threw himself on top of plaintiff, incapacitating plaintiff, and forcibly wrenched plaintiff's revolver from her, breaking her finger.

**8.**   Plaintiff suffered other physical injuries, including bruises and contusions, in addition to the broken finger. Plaintiff experienced extreme fear and anxiety and continues to have nightmares and panic attacks, requiring psychiatric care and medication. Plaintiff suffered the humiliation of being arrested and held by the police for her act in defending herself. Due to her repeated panic attacks, plaintiff was placed on extended leave from her employment as a sales representative for a computer software company, causing plaintiff to lose income and jeopardizing the client base which she had worked several years to build. Plaintiff incurred significant medical and psychiatric expenses for the treatment of her injuries. Plaintiff suffered these and other damages as a result of defendant Arthur Collins's illegal entry into plaintiff's hotel room and his attack upon her.

**9.**   Upon information and belief, defendant Hotel failed to act with reasonable care and was negligent in providing defendant Arthur Collins with a key to plaintiff's hotel room. Defendant Hotel failed to act with reasonable care and was negligent in maintaining the lock on the door of plaintiff's hotel room. Defendant Hotel's negligence was a proximate cause of the attack on plaintiff by defendant Arthur Collins and of the injuries suffered by plaintiff.

## CAUSES OF ACTION

**10.**   Plaintiff is entitled to recover damages from defendants and each of them based on the theories of liability hereinafter enumerated in Counts I through V, and under such other theories of liability as may be appropriate based upon the facts as alleged herein or as revealed during discovery.

### COUNT I—ASSAULT
(Against defendants Collins)

**11.**   In committing the acts alleged herein, defendant Arthur Collins intended to cause plaintiff imminent apprehension of harmful or offensive contact.

**12.**   The acts of defendant Arthur Collins alleged herein caused plaintiff to feel imminent apprehension of harmful and offensive contact, and caused plaintiff reasonably to apprehend that defendant Arthur Collins was about to attack plaintiff sexually.

**13.**   As a proximate result of the conduct of defendant Arthur Collins alleged herein, plaintiff has been damaged in an amount which plaintiff will prove.

### COUNT II—BATTERY
(Against defendants Collins)

**14.**   In committing the acts alleged herein, defendant Arthur Collins contacted plaintiff's person in a harmful and offensive manner, including without limitation throwing himself on plaintiff after removing his clothing and breaking plaintiff's finger.

**15.**   As a proximate result of the conduct of defendant Arthur Collins alleged herein, plaintiff has been damaged in an amount which plaintiff will prove.

### COUNT III—NEGLIGENCE
(Against defendants Collins)

**16.**   Defendant Collins had a duty to plaintiff to act with reasonable care in confining his movements to his own room and to the public areas of the hotel, and in behaving reasonably and with due

---

**Figure W5–2  Sample Complaint,** *continued*

care for other guests while on hotel premises. In engaging in the conduct alleged herein, defendant Collins breached such duty and failed to act with reasonable care.

    **17.**  As a proximate result of the conduct of defendant Arthur Collins alleged herein, plaintiff has been damaged in an amount which plaintiff will prove.

### COUNT IV—NEGLIGENCE
#### (Against defendant Hotel)

    **18.**  Defendant Hotel had a duty to plaintiff to act with reasonable care in providing reasonably safe lodging and in maintaining such lodging, and particularly the doors and locks thereof, in a reasonable manner. Defendant Hotel failed to act with reasonable care toward plaintiff, and breached such duty by, among other things, failing to maintain the door and lock of plaintiff's room in a reasonable manner so as to prevent unauthorized entry, and, upon information and belief, allowing defendant Collins to gain possession of a key capable of operating the lock of plaintiff's room.

    **19.**  As a proximate result of the conduct of defendant Arthur Collins alleged herein, plaintiff has been damaged in an amount which plaintiff will prove.

### COUNT V—PUNITIVE DAMAGES
#### (All defendants)

    **20.**  The conduct, acts, and omissions of defendants alleged herein were in part intentional and in part evinced a reckless and callous disregard for plaintiff's safety, were consciously malicious, and displayed a conscious disregard for the unjustifiable substantial risk of significant harm to plaintiff.

    **21.**  Plaintiff is entitled to receive punitive damages.

    WHEREFORE, plaintiff requests that the Court enter judgment in favor of plaintiff and against defendants and each of them as follows:

    **1.**  For general and special damages in the amount of $750,000.00.
    **2.**  For punitive damages in an amount which plaintiff will prove.
    **3.**  For plaintiff's reasonable costs incurred herein.
    **4.**  For such other and further relief as to the Court seems just in the premises.

    DATED this _____ day of _____, 2000.

                             SIMON & PORTER

                              _____

                              Allen Porter
                              Attorneys for plaintiff

---

and arbitration certificate. The attorney for plaintiff (here, Allen Porter) signs the complaint; the clerk of the court will sign and stamp the summonses.

### Step 12 — *Check Accuracy and Make Revisions*

Having written our draft, we check it for errors, then ask Shannon Martin to read it and point out any allegations that may be factually inaccurate. This is also a good opportunity to see whether our drafting is easily read and understood. If our own client has trouble understanding a passage, we can be certain that the average juror will find it incomprehensible. Reviewing our notes from Step 2, we double-check that we have alleged all the elements of each of our theories of liability.

### Step 13 — *File and Serve*

In a typical law office, after a litigation paralegal drafts a complaint, he or she checks it carefully, then passes it to the responsible attorney for review and signature. When the attorney has signed, the paralegal assembles (or assigns a secretary to assemble) a package having the required number of copies of the complaint, summonses, and other documents, in a form ready to give to the process server or messenger for filing.

## Complaint Drafting: Learning by Doing

Your main task for this workshop is to draft a complaint yourself. To do this, you need a fact situation. For most students, we suggest the following assignment:

> You are a paralegal in the law office of Roger Yarborough, attorney for Dr. Arthur Collins. Assume that Dr. Collins is a resident of your city, that Banbury Park Hotel is located in another city in your state, and that Roger Yarborough practices in your city. Shannon Martin resides in Arizona, and Park Hotels Group, Inc., is incorporated in Delaware.
>
> After discussing the case with Allen Porter, Roger Yarborough realizes that Porter is about to file suit on Shannon's behalf, naming Dr. Collins as one of the defendants. Yarborough decides that he would prefer to seize the initiative and file the suit himself. He assigns you to draft a complaint on behalf of Dr. Collins, for filing in the state superior court (or county trial court) having jurisdiction in your locality.

### EXERCISES

In carrying out this assignment, you should follow the step-by-step formula described in this workshop.

1. Review your notes, assemble the information about the local requirements in your jurisdiction, and fill in the Figure W5–3 checklist.

2. (Step 1)　Decide who Dr. Collins should sue. Assume that Shannon Martin's marital status is unknown. Consider, with your instructor's guidance, whether your complaint should include fictitiously named parties.

3. (Step 2)　Decide what theories of liability to assert and determine what their elements are. If you have completed Workshop 1, Claims and Their Elements, you should be able to obtain most of the information that you will need from the exercises in that workshop. If not, your instructor may wish to assign you to research one or more of the theories of liability.

4. (Step 2, optional)　If you completed Exercise 1 from Workshop 1 and made a list of possible causes of action, now list all of the causes of action on that list that you have decided *not* to in-

---

| Figure W5–3　Checklist |
| --- |

| | |
| --- | --- |
| I. | Assemble basic factual information |
| II. | Determine elements of claims |
| III. | Prepare caption |
| IV. | Prepare preamble and set up numbering systems |
| V. | Establish jurisdiction and identify parties |
| VI. | Identify relationships among parties giving rise to liability |
| VII. | State general allegations |
| VIII. | Allege each element of cause of action |
| IX. | Prepare prayer for relief |
| X. | Prepare date and signature lines and verification |
| XI. | Prepare accompanying papers |
| XII. | Check accuracy and make revisions |
| XIII. | File and serve complaint |

clude in your complaint, and briefly state why you decided not to include each. (Usually, the reason will be that some element is contradicted or impossible to prove.)

5. (Steps 3 and 4)　Prepare the caption and preamble. If you have completed the workshop on court papers, you can modify the caption you prepared there as necessary to comply with your local requirements for the caption of a complaint.

6. (Steps 5 and 6)　Draft the Jurisdiction and Parties section. Be sure to include jurisdictional allegations sufficient for the court in which the complaint is to be filed.

7. (Step 7)　Draft the General Allegations section.

8. (Steps 8, 9, and 10)　Draft the Causes of Action section and prayer for relief, and add appropriate date and signature lines.

9. (Step 11)　List exactly what accompanying papers will be needed, and how many copies of each. At your instructor's option, obtain forms for and prepare summonses and information sheets if required in your jurisdiction.

10. (Step 12)　Check your draft for accuracy. At your instructor's option, exchange your draft with another student who will assume the role of Dr. Collins and review your draft from the client's point of view.

**11.** (Step 13)  At your instructor's option, visit the office of the clerk of the court and observe how a deputy clerk handles a newly filed complaint. While there, obtain a copy of the clerk's fee schedule and any other informational brochures or material that the clerk may have available.

> **Your Local Notes**
>
> _____
>
> _____

## SIDEBAR

### Local Details Complaint Form and Filing Requirements

*Form and Format: (see also Workshop 4, Court Papers)*

*Paper size, line spacing, and margins*

*Caption—special requirements*

*Layout and paragraph numbering*

*Prayer for relief*

*Date and signature line format*

*Other local customs*

*Verification requirements, if any*

*Other papers required with complaint for filing*

   *Summons—local form*

*Filing fee amount, acceptable modes of payment*

*Other required papers*

*Discovery permitted with complaint*

*Particular pleading matters*

   *Spouses of defendants*

   *Fictitiously named parties*

   *Preferred practice re:*

   *Specifying dollar amounts in damages allegations*

     *Specifying dollar amounts in prayer for relief*

   *Form allegation for punitive damages*

   *Procedure for jury trial demand*

# PRACTICE POINTERS
## *Locating Attorneys and Court Files*

Sometimes you may find it helpful when drafting a complaint or when preparing other documents to have a model on which to base your work. Suppose you read about a case that is very similar to yours. How could you locate the attorney who litigated the case, assuming the article or case decision you read included his name?

You could begin by contacting the attorney's law office and talk to the attorney or his staff about the case. But how would you get the telephone number? If the article or decision you were reading gave the name of the city and state in which the attorney was practicing, you could look in *Martindale-Hubbell,* which provides a compilation of the names of attorneys, their areas of practice, and personal data, including phone number, fax number, address, e-mail address, and web site.

Alternatively, if you knew the trial court in which the litigation occurred, you could use the court's indexing system to pull the court file. Going to the court clerk's office, you could ask for the plaintiff or defendant's index and look under the plaintiff's or defendant's name. In this file you might find, in addition to information about the disposition of the matter, a gold mine of information, including pleadings, copies of interrogatories, requests for production, and various motions that might be well researched and well written. If the case were recent enough, you might even be able to use the jury instructions to assist in drafting jury instructions for your case. After reviewing the file, you could make copies of exemplary documents. If the case were particularly instructive, you would want to ask the attorneys or their staff questions or ask to see their files. Remember that "imitation is the sincerest form of flattery."

If the case had been appealed but the decision was not published, you could contact the appellate court and find out how to get a copy of the decision. At the clerk of the appellate court's office you would look in an index similar to that used by the trial courts. In addition to reviewing the documents listed above, you might want to look at briefs to take advantage of the research done in preparing them. You might also look for transcripts of oral arguments, which might, on request of the clerk's office, be available on audio tape.

## TECHNO TIP

Many students have problems setting up the caption due to the general use of right-hand parentheses that set the party's name apart from the case number and title of the document. While the use of parentheses is almost universal, most court rules make no mention of the need for them.

If you set up your new form using a template rather than a blank file that you later recopy you can avoid many problems. You should also make sure not to use the tab key to set the right-hand boundary of the caption for the party's names. If you use the tab key, when you input the names, the parentheses will move to the right. If you use the space bar to set the boundary, and input the party's name with the over-strike (insert) function on, the boundary will not move as you type in the data. More sophisticated users can set up forms that automatically ask for, and insert, the party's names.

## FORMS FILE

*In your forms file, include as many samples of complaints as you can find that your instructor or legal mentor believes exemplify good complaints. Try to get copies of complaints that represent a number of different areas of the law, for example, personal injury, contract, workers' compensation, domestic relations, real estate, criminal, probate, and bankruptcy. Include samples that show spouses of defendants, fictitiously named defendants, allegations of punitive damages, and requests for a jury trial.*

*Also, print a list of the format requirements for complaints as dictated by your local rules, including paper size, line spacing, margins, special caption requirements, date and signature line format, the preferred practices for pleading damages, layout, and paragraph numbering. Include also the appropriate filing fees and any other required items, such as information sheets or arbitration statements.*

## KEY TERMS

General damages                Special damages

## INTRODUCTION: RATIONALE BEHIND SERVICE OF COMPLAINTS

Lawsuits are made mostly of paper. A paper (the complaint) starts the lawsuit; the opposing litigants fire numerous other papers at each other as the suit progresses. As we will see in Workshop 7, most of these papers are delivered informally, either by ordinary mail or by messenger. They are delivered not to the *party,* but to the *attorney of record* for the party; see FRCP, Rule 5.

The summons and complaint are a different matter, and covered by a separate rule; see FRCP, Rule 4. Ordinary mail does not suffice for serving the summons and complaint; the requirements of Rule 4 are much more demanding than that, and there are good reasons for insisting on formality: When we serve a summons and complaint on someone, we want to be sure we get their undivided attention—we do not want our lawsuit mistaken for junk mail! The U.S. Supreme Court has ruled that a person being sued is entitled to be notified of that fact by the best means possible under the circumstances. It would be fundamentally unfair to allow a lawsuit to proceed and judgment to be taken against someone who has not even been made aware that there *is* a suit. Therefore, as we saw in Workshop 2, proper service of the complaint is a jurisdictional requirement, without which the court has no power to enter a binding judgment.

Because the defendant has no attorney of record in the suit at the time the complaint is filed, the summons and complaint must be served on the defendant himself, rather than on the attorney representing defendant. You might suppose that serving a complaint would be a simple enough task, and if the defendant is an individual who resides locally, often it is. But in many lawsuits, at least some of the defendants are entities—defendant X may be a corporation, or a partnership, trust, estate, government agency, or any of a number of other kinds of artificial targets. Or defendant may be located in some other state or country. Then what? As we will see, FRCP, Rule 4 provides a variety of options.

In this workshop, we explore the details of formal service—the type used for summonses and complaints, as prescribed by FRCP, Rule 4. Then, in Workshop 7, we will learn about routine service of other court papers under FRCP, Rule 5, and address the important subject of deadlines and how to compute them.

---

## HOW TO SERVE A SUMMONS AND COMPLAINT

A lawsuit begins at the instant that plaintiff files a complaint with the clerk of the court; see FRCP, Rule 3. As a practical matter, however, merely *filing* the complaint does not, by itself, set the wheels of the lawsuit in motion. If you file a complaint and do nothing else, the lawsuit will likely sit unnoticed in the clerk's file for some period of time [120 days in federal court; see FRCP, Rule 4(m)], and eventually be dismissed automatically for failure to prosecute. Nothing will happen unless you make it happen.

The lawsuit begins in earnest only when the complaint is *served.* A defendant's obligation to respond to the suit begins only when plaintiff has properly served the complaint on that defendant. Until then, defendant is unlikely to be aware that suit has even been filed (and would be perfectly free to ignore it even if she has become aware of the lawsuit in some other way).

How must we deliver the summons and complaint? What, specifically, do we have to do? The answer depends on the circumstances. The traditional, and most common, way of serving a summons and complaint is personal service. Personal service means having someone (usually a process server; see sidebar) locate each defendant, approach them in person, and physically hand the papers to them.

As simple as this may seem in theory, it is not always simple in practice. What if defendant is a corporation, for example? How do you physically hand papers to a corporation? (Can you suggest some ways in which you might do this?) What if you are suing the United States government—would you have to deliver papers to the president? What if defendant is a juvenile or someone who is mentally incapacitated? What if defendant is living in another state or, worse, a foreign country? What if defendant, anticipating your lawsuit, has gone into hiding? These are only a few of the problems that can arise. (Can you think of others?)

In most courts, therefore, you will find that there are a number of approved ways to serve the summons and complaint, each designed for some specific situation. Usually, you will have to look in more than one place to find them all. In federal court, the place to begin is FRCP, Rule 4, which offers a menu of alternatives for most of the commonplace situations. Rule 4 then refers you to other sources. When serving individual defendants (live human beings), for example, Rule 4 allows you to serve the summons and complaint in any way that would be allowed in the state courts of the state in which the district court sits or the state in which the service is to take place. Therefore, even in federal court, you must also consider the state court rule corresponding to Rule 4 (your instructor will tell you where to find it).

---

**Your Local Notes**

_____

_____

---

A number of statutes, both federal and state, also provide for service of the summons and complaint in particular types of cases. Most states, for example, have adopted statutes giving procedures for serving a lawsuit on an out-of-state motorist who causes an accident within the state. Statutes regulating various specialty fields (securities, taxes, etc.) also often include provisions allowing process to be served in a particular way. You cannot expect to be aware of all such enactments, so whenever you find yourself in a situation for which FRCP, Rule 4, and its state law counterparts do not give adequate guidance, researching the statutes may prove worthwhile.

Our objective in serving the summons and complaint is simple: we want to force defendant to file an answer to the suit. If defendant does not file an answer (or other allowed pleading) after being properly served, we can carry out other procedures to obtain a judgment by default. In other words, we will (barring other problems) win the lawsuit then and there because of defendant's failure to respond.

What happens if we make a mistake in serving the summons and complaint? There are several possibilities. First, suppose we simply drop the ball and fail to have one of the defendants served. In federal court, after 120 days, the court, "upon motion or on its own initiative after notice to the plaintiff, shall dismiss the action without prejudice as to that defendant"; see FRCP, Rule 4(m). In practice, what happens is this: The clerk of the court keeps track of which defendants have been served in each pending lawsuit. (The clerk can easily do this because, as we will see, a court paper called a *return of service* must be filed each time a defendant is served.) Once 120 days have passed from the filing of the complaint, the clerk will check to see whether returns of service

have been filed for each defendant named in the lawsuit. If any are missing, a notice will be sent to plaintiff's attorney, stating that the suit will be dismissed as to the defendants not served unless plaintiff shows good cause for the failure. If plaintiff's attorney convinces the court that there is a good reason why more time is needed (i.e., defendant is hiding) the court will extend the deadline. If plaintiff's attorney does nothing, or fails to persuade the judge that more time is warranted, the court will order the unserved defendants dismissed from the suit.

The dismissal, if any, is without prejudice. This means that plaintiff is free to refile the complaint and try again. In practice, however, refiling does not usually repair all of the damage. First, the lawsuit is now fragmented—instead of a single lawsuit against all defendants, you have two lawsuits: the original one against the defendants whom you did succeed in serving, and a new one against the defendant whom you are still trying to serve. Perhaps you can find some way to combine them back into a single lawsuit before trial, and perhaps not; either way, the procedural complexity of the situation has multiplied considerably and you will not get the whole case to trial or judgment as soon as you otherwise would have. Second, and most important, statutes of limitations may have expired in the time since the lawsuit was first filed; some or all of your causes of action against the dismissed defendant may now be time barred.

The validity of service is measured one defendant at a time. Service on defendant A does *not* obligate defendant B to appear and defend, even if defendant B is (for example) married to defendant A and hears all about the suit that evening at dinner. What happens, then, if we are simply unable to serve one of the defendants? Usually, we are free to proceed against all of the other defendants whom we have succeeded in serving (unless the judge determines the missing defendant to be an "indispensable party" under FRCP, Rule 19, which involves complexities beyond the scope of this text). Whether the suit will still be worth pursuing with defendants missing is a more complex question and depends on the circumstances. Certainly, we will have fewer targets from which to collect the judgment if we win. Nor will we be able to obtain discovery from the unserved defendants. (If we cannot serve the summons and complaint, it is unlikely we would be able to serve a subpoena.) Worse, in some states, if two defendants are jointly liable for an injury, and we are able to serve only one of them, we will not be able to recover full damages because the defendant whom we have served is required to pay only his fair share of the damages, not the share attributable to the other defendant. (Your instructor will inform you whether your state has a "joint and several liability" statute.)

Suppose, instead of a clear-cut failure to serve defendant X, there is something about the *way* in which you served the summons and complaint that gives defendant X an argument that the service did not comply with the rules. Then what? Defendant has several options.

First, if defendant is extremely confident that the service was defective, she can ignore the suit and do nothing. Without proper service, the court has no jurisdiction over the person of defendant (see Workshop 2) and any judgment would be void. The problem with this option—and the reason why no lawyer is likely to recommend it—is that if defendant does nothing, the court is likely to issue a default judgment, void or not. Plaintiff will then try to use the void judgment to seize defendant's property. To prevent that, defendant will have to convince a court that she was never properly served with the suit that led to the judgment. If the court is not persuaded, defendant has lost her property, without any opportunity to defend the suit on the merits.

A less hazardous option is to file a motion to dismiss or to quash service; see FRCP, Rule 12(b)(5). If the judge agrees that the method of service used was improper in some way, the most likely result will be an order quashing, or nullifying, the service. The parties are left in the same position they would have been in had service not been made at all on the defendant in question. Then what? Plaintiff will simply send out the process server and try again. Therefore, there is usually little for defendants to gain by attacking service of process, except in unusual circumstances. (Can you think of any circumstances in which defendant would benefit by forcing plaintiff to reserve?)

This brings us to the final option, which is to ignore the defect in service and simply file an answer. A defendant is always free to appear voluntarily in a lawsuit—defects in service can always be waived. (A defendant cannot cure a defect in subject matter jurisdiction, if there is one, by appearing or waiving service, but that is a separate issue; see Workshop 2.) If defendant concludes that a lawsuit is inevitable, and plaintiff's choice of forum is acceptable, and especially if it is obvious that plaintiff will be able to serve process on defendant sooner or later, there may be little attraction to the prospect of spending time and money arguing about service.

# Serving the Complaint: Step-by-Step Instructions

We analyze the problem of serving the summons and complaint in our usual step-by-step fashion. As before, the steps we suggest are not the only possible ones; they are intended to provide a systematic framework to help you make practical choices among the various options. In the discussion to follow, we have tried to describe the task of serving the summons and complaint in terms of the way a paralegal in a litigation office would actually deal with it, rather than in abstract terms suitable for a treatise on procedure. In a law office, the goal is not to serve process in the most elegant way; it is to get the job done quickly, efficiently, and with the least expenditure of lawyer and paralegal time. This dictates our overall strategy:

> Begin with the simplest and easiest ways of accomplishing service, apply them to as many defendants as possible, then proceed to the next easiest, and so on, until all defendants have been served.

**Step 1** *Obtain Necessary Copies of the Papers to Be Served*

Service of process is a formal way of delivering papers; to accomplish it, you must have the right papers to deliver. What, exactly, has to be delivered? Two things are required in every case: (1) a summons and (2) a copy of the complaint; see FRCP, Rule 4(c)(1).

Any other court papers that are filed at the same time as the complaint are served with it. This is necessary because FRCP, Rule 5(a) requires all filed court papers subsequent to the complaint to be served on every party. Because no defendants have appeared or filed answers yet, service on the attorneys by mail under FRCP, Rule 5(b), is not an option; therefore, any papers filed with the complaint must be served in accordance with Rule 4.

What other papers might be filed and served with the complaint? For one example, local rules in some jurisdictions require the filing of a separate paper stating whether or not the case is subject to compulsory arbitration. For another, it is permissible in some state courts to issue discovery requests, such as interrogatories and requests for production of documents, at the time the complaint is filed. [In federal court, discovery requests are generally not permitted until the time for filing disclosure statements has expired; see FRCP, Rules 30(a)(2)(c), 33(a), and 34(b).]

---

**Your Local Notes**

_____

_____

---

The summons is a court order directing each defendant to "appear and defend" the lawsuit. As usual in litigation, the court does not supply the summons; it is up to plaintiff's lawyer to prepare it. Most of the boilerplate language of a summons is the same from case to case, so summonses are usually prepared using preprinted or word-processor forms, to which it is necessary to add only the caption of the case and the name(s) of the defendant(s) being served. The summons is not official until it is signed and stamped by the clerk of the court; see FRCP, Rule 4(a).

In practice, the usual sequence of events is this: Someone in the office of plaintiff's attorney (often a paralegal) prepares a summons listing each of the defendants by name. (Another way is to prepare separate summonses, each listing one defendant; let local custom be your guide.) A sufficient number of photocopies of both the summons and the complaint are made to provide one for each defendant, plus copies for the client and the case file. To this stack of copies is added the original complaint for filing, the check for the filing fee, a memo providing information to the process server on how to locate the various defendants (many process servers have forms for this), and any other papers (see Step 11 of Workshop 5) to be filed with the complaint. The entire package is then taken to the clerk's office and presented for filing.

Who presents the complaint for filing? Usually _not_ a lawyer or paralegal—no need to waste expensive legal talent on what is essentially a clerical task. Some law firms use a messenger, who takes the papers to the clerk's office, waits for the clerk to accept and stamp them, and then turns them over to the process server. Other firms have regular accounts with process serving firms that make regular daily pickups at each law office and perform the filing tasks at the clerk's office as a part of their service.

Assuming all is in order, the clerk accepts and files the complaint, stamps and signs the summonses, stamps the case number on the copies of the complaint and any other papers to be served,

and gives the stack of copies back to the messenger or process server. The process server should now have one copy of the complaint, one original summons, and one copy of each other paper being served for each defendant. (Even though the summonses are photocopies, each is considered an original because each has been signed and stamped by the clerk of the court.)

As we will see shortly, in certain situations (i.e., registered mail service) the delivery of the summons and complaint to a given defendant will be arranged by plaintiff's attorney, rather than made by a process server. The messenger or process server will obtain the clerk's stamp and signature on the copies of the summons and complaint corresponding to any such defendants and return them to plaintiff's attorney.

---

**Your Local Notes**

_____

_____

---

Step 1 is complete when there is a properly issued summons and a copy of the complaint for each defendant to be served.

**Step 2**  *For Each Defendant, Decide Whether a Waiver of Service Should Be Sought*

The absolutely easiest way to accomplish service is to avoid having to do it at all. There is an alternative to formal service of process: The defendant can voluntarily accept service of the summons and complaint or, equivalently, waive service. To **waive** a right means to voluntarily and knowingly give up that right. Every defendant in a lawsuit has a right to insist that the summons and complaint be served in accordance with the rules; any defendant is free to waive the right, relieving plaintiff of the necessity of making formal service.

The federal rules seek to encourage waivers of service by providing an incentive. Under FRCP, Rule 4(d), plaintiff may make a written request to any defendant for a waiver of service. [FRCP, Rule 4(d), prescribes in detail how the request is to be made.] Defendants who accept are rewarded with additional time in which to answer the complaint; those who refuse are charged with the expenses incurred by plaintiff in making formal service on them. State courts may not have specific rules governing acceptance of service, but parties are nonetheless free to do it if they can agree.

In some situations, waiver of service makes good sense for both sides. Most commonly, these involve disputes in which the parties are already represented by lawyers and have attempted to negotiate a solution, but failed. The inevitability of a lawsuit is obvious to all concerned, and it is in everyone's interest simply to get on with it. (Divorce cases often fall in this category.) By waiving service, defendant avoids the potential embarrassment of being served at work or in public; plaintiff avoids having to pay a process server; and both parties may avoid whatever delay formal service would entail.

In more adversarial situations, however, plaintiff may well conclude that the disadvantages of seeking a waiver of service outweigh the benefits. By asking for a waiver, plaintiff gives up any possibility of surprise, giving a defendant who is inclined to avoid service plenty of time to hide. Furthermore, if defendant's attorney does agree to waive service, the necessary paperwork may be returned only after days or weeks of "telephone tag" and at a cost of additional concessions such as extended time in which to file an answer. Compared to the real costs of litigating (the attorney's fees), the cost of service is trivial, and, when in doubt, most plaintiff's attorneys would choose simply to send out a process server.

The procedure for waiving service begins with a request by plaintiff's attorney to defendant or, more commonly, to defendant's attorney. In federal court, the request may be a formal one under FRCP, Rule 4(d), in which case it must be made in strict compliance with the requirements of FRCP, Rule 4(d)(2). Or the request may be an informal one, often beginning with a telephone call by plaintiff's attorney to defendant's attorney asking whether the latter would like to accept service on his client's behalf. If agreed to, the acceptance or waiver of service is typically a court paper with the usual caption and formal parts, with a body consisting of a sentence or two reciting that "defendant X waives formal service of the summons and complaint and accepts service thereof," or words to that effect. The paper must be signed by defendant or defendant's attorney, and is filed with the court. The effect is exactly the same as if the summons and complaint had been formally served. The due date of the answer is computed from the date of the waiver, unless otherwise agreed (an extension of the deadline for answering is a common *quid pro quo* for agreeing to accept service).

Your supervising attorney will decide which, if any, defendants should be asked to waive service, and may make the initial contact to request it. As a paralegal, you may be assigned to complete the paperwork. An important part of this task is to keep track of the status of the request, making sure that the waiver is actually signed, returned, and filed within a reasonable time, so that formal service can be ordered if it appears that defendant is stalling.

---

*Your Local Notes*

_____

_____

---

### Step 3 — Assign Local Individual Defendants and Corporations to a Process Server for Routine Personal Service

If a waiver is not feasible, the next easiest way to accomplish service is to assign a process server to make personal service—"easiest" because the process server does most of the work, so very little input from expensive lawyers or paralegals is required.

Our purpose in this step is to weed out the defendants who can readily be served in this way. Individual defendants who reside locally fall into this category. So do corporations with a local presence, that is, those which are either incorporated in your state or have done the required paperwork to qualify to do business in your state.

These are not, of course, the only categories of defendants for which personal service by a process server is appropriate. In general, however, once we move beyond local individuals and corporations, we will be confronting additional complications, such as uncertainties in determining which human being to deliver the papers to, difficulties in locating the defendant, and legal complexities requiring additional paperwork. We address some of these more challenging situations in Step 4.

**Personal Service on Individuals**—You probably already have a mental image of what personal service entails: An anonymous stranger rings defendant John Smith's doorbell at six in the morning (most people are home at six in the morning), intones the time-honored phrase "Mr. John Smith? I have some papers for you," and hands the summons and complaint to the rudely awakened defendant (or drops them on the ground if he refuses to take them).

That is personal service, in its most basic form. FRCP, Rule 4(e)(2), authorizes you to serve individual defendants in this way. To use it, you need a live human being to hand the papers to, and the process server must be able to find him.

**Abode Service**—Suppose you are trying to serve an individual defendant (a live human being) who seems to be impossible to find at home. Must you pay your process server to stake out the place in the hope of catching defendant sneaking out to walk Fido at three in the morning?

One option, of course, is to serve the summons somewhere else. You are not restricted to serving defendants at home—you are perfectly free to catch them at work, while shopping, or even while delivering an important speech to a gathering of visiting dignitaries. Nevertheless, it is usually easier to find people at their residential addresses than it is to find them at work, where they may be closeted deep in some large complex that requires a security pass to enter.

Bowing to the practicalities, nearly all courts allow what is called abode service. **Abode service** is accomplished by leaving a copy of the summons and complaint at defendant's "usual place of abode with some person of suitable age and discretion then residing therein"; see FRCP, Rule 4(e)(2). In other words, instead of being required to hand the papers to defendant herself, the process server can hand them to whoever answers the door at defendant's house, assuming that person is "of suitable age and discretion" and "then residing therein."

As you might imagine, abode service provides fertile ground for disputes. "Of suitable age and discretion"—what age is *that?* (A fact question depending on the circumstances; older teenagers are usually safe, but small children do not qualify.) What does "then living therein" mean? Does a live-in maid qualify? (Yes, but a maid who works in defendant's residence every day but lives elsewhere does not, and it may not be easy for a process server to tell the difference.) What about a teenage daughter who lives with defendant every other week under a joint custody arrangement? (Could go either way.)

We have already said that serving process on defendant A does not obligate defendant B to appear and defend. Is abode service an exception to this? No, and herein lies an important distinction. Suppose you have sued John Doe and Jane Doe, husband and wife. The process server shows up at the Doe residence and rings the doorbell, and Jane Doe answers. John Doe is away on a business trip. If the process server hands the summons and complaint to Jane, does that not also constitute abode service on John?

Not necessarily. Certainly, the process server *can* serve both John and Jane at once, but to do so he would hand Jane *two* summonses—one addressed to John and one addressed to Jane—and *two* copies of the complaint. The return of service would reflect personal service of one copy on Jane and abode service of another copy on John. A return of service showing only personal service on Jane would not obligate John to file an answer. This may seem an overly picky distinction, but keep in mind that if the issue of the sufficiency of service on John should have to be decided by the judge, the only thing the judge will be interested in is whether the record—the return of service—reflects that John was properly served.

A final point: In federal court, and under most state court formulations, abode service can be made only on *individual* defendants; see FRCP, Rule 4(e)(2). As we will see shortly, when we serve process on corporations and other entities, we are usually delivering the papers to some human being who acts as an agent or representative of the entity. Can we take the next step and serve the corporation by delivering the summons and complaint to "a person of suitable age and discretion" at the representative's abode? No, the representative is not the defendant, and the corporation is not an individual.

---

*Your Local Notes*

_____

_____

---

**Personal Service on an Agent**—An **agent** is a person who has the legal authority to act for someone else. (The person for whom the agent is acting is called the **principal**.) Here is a simple example: Suppose you are going on a long trip in a foreign country, and you want your trusted friend Joe to be able to access your bank account in case you run short and need some money wired to you. You sign a "special power of attorney," a paper authorizing Joe to enter transactions on your behalf at the bank. By doing so, you have made Joe your agent, thereby conferring on Joe the legal authority to act in your place. Joe's acts will be legally binding on you just as if you had done them yourself. If Joe withdraws your money and loses it in Las Vegas, you will have no complaint coming against the bank, because, legally, Joe's act in withdrawing the money was your act.

Authority means the power of an agent to act in the name of the principal. An agent can be given very broad authority, and authorized to do virtually anything that the principal could do (as with a general power of attorney); or, the agent's power can be expressly limited, giving the agent authority to do only certain things (such as, in the preceding example, access a single bank account). The sum total of all the powers given to the agent by the principal is referred to as the agent's scope of authority. We will not delve into the details of how agents are appointed or the paperwork and other formalities involved; those are subjects for another course. However, keep in mind that there will often be no formal written appointment, nor are such documents necessarily made public even when they exist.

An agency can be created for almost any conceivable purpose, including receiving service of process. You can appoint someone else as your agent with authority to receive service of a summons and complaint on your behalf. If you do so, then a process server could serve a lawsuit on you by delivering the summons and complaint to your agent.

Why, you may be wondering, would you *want* to appoint an agent and make it easier for someone else to sue you? One reason may be that you are entering into a contract with someone who wants to be sure they can get you into court if a dispute arises, so they insist on appointment of an agent as part of the deal. Or the appointment may be required by law, as we are about to see.

---

*Your Local Notes*

_____

_____

---

**Serving Process on Corporations**—Personal service requires physical delivery of the summons and complaint to defendant in person. How would you physically deliver papers to an entity such as, say, General Motors Corporation? "Who" exactly is General Motors anyway? Is it the buildings? The factories? The workers? The board of directors? The stockholders?

Although General Motors may be all of those things and more, it is not practical to serve process on a building. The purpose of serving process is to give notice, and simply leaving the summons and complaint somewhere in a building or factory is not very likely to bring the lawsuit to the attention of anyone who would be in a position to respond to it. Therefore, the law takes the view that *a corporation acts only through its agents* (and employees, who are a specialized kind of agent). If you want to serve a summons and complaint on a corporation, you must deliver the papers to an agent of the corporation who has authority to receive them.

In general, the law assumes that an agent who is appointed to do a specific thing has the **implied authority** to act for the principal in whatever ways are reasonably necessary to accomplish what the agent was appointed for. The president of a corporation is appointed to run the business of the corporation; therefore, he has the authority, as an agent of the corporation, to do all the things reasonably necessary in running a business, including defending lawsuits. The president of a corporation is considered to have implied authority to receive service of the summons and complaint when the corporation is sued. Certain other officers of the corporation are also deemed to have implied authority to receive service of process. That is why, under the federal rules as well as the rules of most state courts, service of the summons and complaint can be made on a corporation by delivering the papers to "an officer, a managing or general agent, or to any other agent authorized by appointment or by law to receive service of process . . . ," FRCP, Rule 4(h).

It is not necessarily easy to be sure who qualifies as an officer or a managing or general agent for purposes of FRCP, Rule 4, and the equivalent state court rules. High officers such as the president, CEO, the secretary of the corporation (a corporate office, not the kind of secretary who types and files), and the treasurer clearly have authority to receive service. Determining whether a given lower level officer qualifies may require some legal research. Fortunately, it is usually not necessary to chase down corporate presidents, because there is an easier way to serve process on corporations.

One of the usual requirements that a corporation must meet when filing incorporation papers is to appoint an agent to receive service of process. Most states also require out-of-state corporations to appoint an agent to receive service before doing business in the state. You can easily get the name and address of a corporation's appointed agent by calling the state agency that regulates corporations. (Your instructor will tell you what the agency is called in your state; Corporations Commission and Department of Corporations are two of the common names.) Therefore, serving process on a corporation is usually as simple as making one phone call to get the name and address of the agent and instructing your process server to deliver the papers there.

---

*Your Local Notes*

_____

_____

---

**Your Role as Paralegal**—Your task as a paralegal will be to give instructions to the process server; to assist the process server with more information if difficulties arise when serving any of the defendants; and to keep track of which defendants have and have not been served so that problem situations are recognized and dealt with.

An established litigation office will already have an account with a process server or process server firm. Either the process server firm or your own law firm will likely have a printed form for you to fill out with your instructions for service. For individual defendants, it is usually sufficient to provide a name and residence address; nevertheless, it is best to include whatever information you have about defendant's identity and whereabouts. Work locations are helpful, as are telephone numbers. Social Security numbers are particularly useful in tracking down individual defendants; a process server with access to the usual array of computerized information sources can generally locate anyone from a Social Security number as long as the person is present somewhere in the United States. A physical description or some other means of identification may also be needed, especially if the defendant has a common name—otherwise you may find that you served the wrong "John Smith."

For corporation defendants, you must tell the process server where and to whom to deliver the summons and complaint. The process server may be able to assist you in obtaining the name and address of the corporation's designated agent for service of process, but it is up to you (with guidance from your supervising attorney) to decide to whom the papers should be delivered, and instruct the process server accordingly.

## Step 4 | Decide How to Serve Nonroutine Defendants

At this point, we have obtained whatever waivers we could, and sent the process server out to serve all of the defendants who are either locally resident individuals or corporations that have appointed local agents to receive service. In many lawsuits, we will find that we have now accounted for all defendants and we can proceed directly to Step 5.

Not all defendants in all lawsuits are so accommodating, however. We must be prepared to deal with some of the more challenging situations. These include individual defendants who are geographically distant or hard to find, corporations that have no local designated agent, entities other than corporations, and governmental agencies and officers.

**Serving Individuals the Hard Way**—Sooner or later, you will find yourself looking for an individual defendant for whom you can find no local address. Here is one common scenario: Your client was injured in an automobile accident. Your only information regarding the identity of the other driver is what appears on the police investigative report: Joe Schmoe, 333 Main Street. One small problem—the

address in question is an apartment building, and the manager has never heard of Joe Schmoe. Joe was, of course, driving a borrowed car.

Now you will have to do some detective work. Perhaps you can locate Joe by contacting the owner of the car he was driving or by contacting Joe's insurance company if he had insurance and the police took down the information. Or perhaps you can find an address for Joe in a telephone book or city directory, or in a computerized telephone directory covering the entire United States (available in many libraries), or by searching the Internet. Failing that, you will probably have to hire a private investigator or a process server who is experienced in skip-tracing to locate Joe.

Suppose you eventually discover that Joe moved out of his apartment at 333 Main Street a year before the accident and took up residence in another state; he was on vacation visiting friends when the accident occurred. How can you serve the summons and complaint on him? There are several options:

***Personal or abode service in another state:*** In federal court, as long as Joe is within a judicial district of the United States (i.e., located in one of the fifty states or in the District of Columbia, Guam, Puerto Rico, or the U.S. Virgin Islands), FRCP, Rule 4(e)(2), allows you to serve the summons and complaint by "delivering . . . to the individual personally" or by abode service. State court rules also typically allow personal service on defendants located in other states. (This assumes, of course, that there is a basis for personal jurisdiction over the out-of-state defendant; here, Joe has caused an act or event to occur in the forum state. See Workshop 2.)

How do you arrange for out-of-state personal service? Many process server firms have offices in other states or correspondent arrangements with process servers in other states. One of these full-service process server firms can usually arrange for personal service in any state. Or, you can make arrangements directly with a process server in the other state. In federal court, because there are no special licensing requirements for process servers [see FRCP, Rule 4(c)(2)], you can, if necessary, send someone to Joe's home state to make service. Another option is to contact the sheriff's office for the county in which defendant is to be served (usually a last resort because of the paperwork and delay involved).

***Service by mail:*** State court rules typically allow service of the summons and complaint on out-of-state defendants by registered or certified mail. In federal court, service on individuals [FRCP, Rule 4(e)(1)] may be made by any means allowable under the laws of either the state in which the suit is filed or the state in which service is to be made. Therefore, you can serve the summons and complaint by mail in either federal or state court, following the procedures prescribed in your state court rules.

To serve a summons and complaint by mail, you first mail the papers to defendant using the class of mail prescribed by your state court rules—usually registered or certified, with a return receipt. The return receipt is a postcard with your return address on it, which is attached to your envelope. The post office will deliver the letter only after the addressee signs the return receipt; the return receipt is then mailed back to you, furnishing proof that the letter was actually received. After you receive the return receipt, you prepare and file an affidavit reciting the circumstances making mail service appropriate (i.e., defendant is located in another state); that you mailed the summons and complaint addressed to the defendant as prescribed by the rule; and that you received the return receipt back with defendant's signature on it. The affidavit serves as a return of service; that is, it provides a record in the court's file showing that service was made.

As a practical matter, mail service is essentially useless against a defendant who is determined to resist. The reason lies in the requirement that the return receipt be signed by defendant. Defendant can easily defeat service simply by refusing to sign, in which case the post office will return the envelope to you undelivered.

***Nonresident motorist statutes:*** Motor vehicle accidents involving vacationing tourists and out-of-state truckers are a sufficiently common occurrence that state legislatures have adopted statutes to facilitate service of process. Typically, these provide that any nonresident, by the act of operating a motor vehicle in the state, automatically appoints some designated state official as an agent to receive service of process in any lawsuit arising from that act. So, in accident lawsuits against out-of-state drivers, one option is to serve the summons and complaint on the designated state official. (Your instructor will give you the citation for the nonresident motorist statute in your state.)

For such service to be valid, you must follow the procedure set out in the statute *exactly*—"close" does not count. The drawbacks are the same as with registered mail service: The statutory procedure typically requires you to send copies to defendant by registered or certified mail and to produce a return receipt signed by defendant.

In a modern litigation office, by far the preferred way of serving process on out-of-state defendants is to employ a process server firm with connections in the target state. Alternatives such as county sheriffs and registered mail service may seem to offer some slight cost savings, but the money saved, if any, is usually far outweighed by the attorney and paralegal time wasted on the additional paperwork. Moreover, as we will see, the number of days within which defendant must respond to the complaint depends on the manner in which the summons and complaint were served. If you use methods of service other than personal service, defendant will have a longer period in which to file an answer.

---

*Your Local Notes*

_____

_____

---

### Serving Corporations with No Local Agent—

Sometimes it is necessary to sue a corporation that is neither incorporated in your state nor has filed the necessary papers to qualify to do business in your state. When you call your state's department of corporations to obtain the name and address of XYZ Corporation's designated agent for service of process, you are told that they have no record on XYZ Corporation.

When this happens, your first impulse should be to review carefully whether the courts located in your state would have personal jurisdiction over XYZ Corporation. If it is true that XYZ Corporation does not do any business in your state, it may be difficult to convince a judge that it caused an act or event to occur there. Recall that, for the court to have jurisdiction of the person of a defendant, there must be both proper service of process *and* minimum contacts with the forum state (see Workshop 2). At a minimum, some legal research is probably in order.

If you conclude that the court would have personal jurisdiction, the easiest way to obtain service is usually to find out what state XYZ Corporation is incorporated in, telephone the department of corporations of that state, and obtain the name and address of the corporation's agent for service of process as shown in their records. The agent will, of course, be located in the state of incorporation, but you can arrange for the summons and complaint to be served there in the same way as you would with an out-of-state individual.

This is not the only possible way to obtain service on XYZ Corporation. If XYZ has qualified to do business in any states other than its state of incorporation, you can likely serve a designated agent in one of those states, if more convenient. If you can locate one of XYZ's officers or managing agents, you can serve the summons and complaint on them. In practice, however, your goal is to accomplish service quickly, by a method whose validity cannot be disputed, and with a minimum expenditure of attorney or paralegal time, and serving a designated agent is usually the method of choice.

---

**Your Local Notes**

_____

_____

---

**Serving Other Entities**—A corporation is one example of an entity type of defendant. (Recall that an *entity* is an artificial person or organization which the law treats as having its own existence.) You can undoubtedly think of many other kinds of entities, and you may even find it necessary to sue one. Here are a few of the more common entities:

***Partnerships:*** A partnership is an association of two or more persons who join together in some common business endeavor. As a business entity, the operation of a partnership is generally similar to that of a corporation; the income tax treatment of a partnership, however, is quite different.

Suing a partnership is inherently more complicated than suing a corporation. If you win a lawsuit against a corporation, you get a judgment against the corporation, which you can collect only from the corporation's assets. A judgment against a corporation does not entitle you to collect from the corporation's shareholders. This insulation of the owners (the shareholders) from liability is one of the main reasons for forming a corporation.

General partners of a partnership, on the other hand, are personally liable for the obligations of the partnership. Therefore, when suing a partnership, you can potentially get judgment not only against the partnership itself as an entity, but also against each of the general partners. To do so, of course, you must name each partner as a defendant and serve the summons and complaint on each one. It may sometimes require considerable research and detective work just to arrive at a list of all the partners.

Furthermore, it is possible to create a partnership without leaving much of a paper trail. Unlike corporations, which cannot exist unless the proper papers are filed with the proper state agency, any two or more people can create a partnership without filing anything anywhere. And even if an agent to receive service of process has been appointed, you will not be able to find out about it with one phone call.

As a practical matter, therefore, the usual way to serve process in a suit against a partnership is this: First, to bring the partnership *as an entity* into the suit, serve the copy of the summons addressed to the partnership, with a copy of the complaint, on any general partner. [Although FRCP, Rule 4(h),

does not specifically authorize serving a partner, it does allow service "in the manner prescribed by [FRCP, Rule 4(e)(1)]," which allows service in accordance with applicable state court rules; state court rules typically do allow service on a partner.]

Second, to be sure that you will be able to reach the assets of the individual partners if you win the suit, name each partner as a defendant and serve each in the usual way.

***Limited partnerships and limited liability companies:*** Limited partnerships and limited liability companies (LLCs) are both legislative creations that are designed to combine the advantages of a corporation (the shareholders cannot be sued for the corporation's sins) with the tax planning flexibility of a partnership. LLCs are (to oversimplify a bit) corporations that are taxed like partnerships; you serve process on an LLC in the same way as for a partnership. Limited partnerships are partnerships in which some of the partners (called *limited partners*) cannot be sued for the partnership's liabilities. You serve process on a limited partnership in the same way as for an ordinary partnership, except that you do not name the limited partners as defendants or serve process on them.

***Estates and trusts:*** A **probate estate** is an artificial entity that the law creates to receive and dispose of the assets of someone who dies. The person who died is called the **decedent.** The person in charge of a probate estate is variously called the **executor,** the **administrator,** or the **personal representative**—all three terms mean essentially the same thing (we use the latter). Sometimes it is necessary to sue a probate estate. Perhaps, for example, the decedent (before dying, of course) caused an accident in which others were injured. Or perhaps the assets of the estate include a business that has become involved in some dispute. Whenever you are preparing a suit against someone and you discover that the defendant has died, you will have to sue the defendant's estate.

The manner in which a probate estate can sue and be sued is dictated by the probate laws of each state. Commonly, to bring suit against an estate, you sue—and serve process on—the personal representative. However, extra restrictions may exist on suits against a personal representative; check the probate statutes for your locality. In particular, the probate laws are designed to allow the affairs of the decedent to be wrapped up quickly, so statutes of limitation and other time limits may be shortened.

To sue a decedent's estate, you need a properly appointed personal representative to name as defendant. A personal representative must be appointed by the probate court; even if decedent's last will names someone as personal representative, that person does not actually become one until the probate court appoints him or her (or "it"— corporations such as banks are often appointed as personal representatives). You can find out whether probate has been filed and a personal representative appointed by checking the court records at the office of the clerk of whatever court handles probate matters.

What if there is no properly appointed personal representative? What if no probate has been filed? Here, the situation gets more complicated, and you will have to research your options. Most likely, you will have to apply in probate court and ask for a personal representative to be appointed.

A trust is an entity in which one person (called the **grantor** or **trustor**) transfers property to another person (called the **trustee**) with instructions to use the property for some specified purpose. Trusts are often used in estate planning as a tool for keeping property under professional management (by the trustee), particularly when the heirs are too young to be entrusted with it. Any kind of property can be conveyed into trust, including real estate and going businesses, so it is sometimes necessary to be able to sue a trust. This is done by naming the trustee as a defendant; the summons and complaint are served on the trustee.

---

**Your Local Notes**

_____

_____

---

**Governmental Officers and Agencies**—To begin a suit against a government agency or officer, whether federal, state, or local, there are often a number of hoops to be jumped through, of which serving process correctly is only one. Often there are statutes requiring you to make written demand or give written notice of the amount and nature of the claim before filing suit. Special, shorter statutes of limitations may apply. Individual government officers are usually immune from personal liability for their acts while on duty, and can be named as defendants only in their official capacity. Suits against state governments in federal court are severely restricted by the 11th Amendment to the U.S. Constitution.

FRCP, Rule 4, gives directions for serving the summons and complaint on federal agencies and officers [FRCP, Rule 4(i)] and on foreign, state, or local governments [FRCP, Rule 4(j)]. The procedure for serving federal agencies illustrates the kind of procedural hurdles that are commonplace in litigation against the government: You must serve a copy of the summons and complaint on the U.S. attorney's office for the district in which the action is filed, *and* send a copy by certified or registered mail to the U.S. attorney general in Washington, D.C., *and* another to the agency being sued, *and* another to any other agency or officer whose order is being challenged in the suit.

Whenever you are handling a suit in which there appear to be potential claims against governmental defendants, you should research thoroughly the procedural requirements for doing so, or consult with a colleague who has experience in similar suits, or both.

---

**Your Local Notes**

_____

_____

---

**Step 5**  *Track Status of Pending Service Assignments*

Having arranged for service on all defendants, your next job—and it is an important one—is to make sure that service is completed as planned. FRCP, Rule 4(m), requires you to serve all defendants within 120 days after filing the complaint. If you fail to do so, the court must dismiss the suit (albeit without prejudice) unless you can show good cause for the failure.

Excuses like "the process server lost the file" or "I forgot to check whether the return receipt came back" are unlikely to be deemed "good cause." The only way to avoid such lapses is to approach the problem systematically: Keep a calendar, and whenever you initiate the steps to have someone served, post a reminder a week or so in the future to check whether the service was actually completed.

---

**Step 6**  *Check That Service was Completed Correctly*

As service is completed on each defendant, review the manner in which it was accomplished to verify that your instructions were followed and that service was validly made.

---

**Step 7**  *File Appropriate Return of Service*

It is not enough merely to serve each defendant— the judge must be able to look in the court file and verify that service was completed. Therefore, you must file a return of service (also sometimes called a proof of service or affidavit of service); see FRCP, Rule 4(l). A return of service is a court paper reflecting the time and manner in which service was made.

When service is assigned to a process server, the process server provides the return of service. For modes of service that involve registered mail delivery, it is up to the attorney or paralegal to prepare a suitable affidavit, reciting the specific matters required by the rule. As usual, the easiest way to prepare such affidavits is to begin with a form, either a preprinted or word-processor form, or an affidavit submitted in some other case.

Returns of service are filed with the clerk of the court. Unlike most other documents filed with the clerk, returns of service are typically not mailed to the opposing attorneys (you will usually not know who the opposing attorneys are until each defendant files an answer).

*Your Local Notes*

_____

_____

## Step 8    *Docket Answer Due Date*

The rules require each defendant to file either an answer or a motion to dismiss within a specified number of days after service of the complaint. Any defendant who fails to do so is in default, and plaintiff can begin procedures to obtain a default judgment. (Recall that a default judgment is not automatic; plaintiff must take the required steps.)

The normal time allowed for responding to a complaint in federal court is 20 days from the date of service; see FRCP, Rule 12(a). Other time periods may apply in suits against the government [see FRCP, Rule 12(a)(3)] and in certain other situations. Check the particular rule or statute for the mode of service used to see if a different response time is specified.

When you file each return of service, you compute the date on which the answer will be due and docket it on the office calendar. How? As usual, there are rules governing the computation of due dates, and, as usual, it is not always obvious how the rules should be applied. We will study the art and science of computing and calendaring due dates in much more detail in Workshop 7. For our present purposes, the point is that whenever you serve any court paper to which an opposing party must respond, you compute and calendar the due date for the response so that you can take appropriate action if it does not appear when due.

*Your Local Notes*

_____

_____

## Serving the Complaint: Learning by Example

We now apply our step-by-step instructions to the problem of serving the summons and complaint by Shannon against Dr. Collins, Mrs. Collins, and Park Hotels Group, Inc.

## Step 1    *Obtain Necessary Copies of the Papers to Be Served*

We have the complaint which we prepared in Workshop 5. We will need the following:

- Two original summonses, one directed to Dr. and Mrs. Collins, and another directed to Park Hotels Group, Inc.;
- Original and five copies of the complaint in addition to the original (original to be filed, one copy to be served on each defendant, one copy for our file, and one copy for our client)
- Copies of the summonses for our file, and for our client;
- A check for the filing fee; and
- A cover sheet and any other papers required by the rules of the court in which we are filing.

All of these papers must be taken to the filing window at the office of the clerk of the court and presented for filing. None of the defendants we will be serving are local. If our firm has an arrangement for regular pickups by a process server, we may leave the papers with the process server with instructions to file the complaint and bring back the issued summonses and copies. Or we may instruct a secretary or messenger to take the papers to the clerk's office for filing and return with the summonses and copies of the complaint.

<table>
<tr><td>**Step 2**</td><td>*For Each Defendant, Decide Whether a Waiver of Service Should Be Sought*</td></tr>
</table>

Our hypo highlights still another potential drawback to seeking a waiver of service: When we contact the defendants to request the waiver, we are both signaling our intent regarding choice of forum *and* giving them a chance to win the race to the courthouse by filing suit in some other court. In our hypo, Allen Porter decided to contact Dr. Collins's attorney, Roger Yarborough, who consented to suit in Arizona federal court; in doing so, Porter risked that Yarborough might have responded with the time-honored response "I'll think about it and get back to you" and, having thought about it for several seconds, immediately filed suit against Shannon in Nevada.

Yarborough's waiver having been already agreed to via an informal telephone contact, it is not necessary to follow the procedures specified in FRCP, Rule 4(d). A simple court paper, acknowledging the waiver and signed by Dr. Collins, is sufficient. (Ordinarily, it is also sufficient if defendant's attorney signs the waiver.) Here, however, the question would arise whether Yarborough has been admitted to practice before the U.S. District Court for the District of Arizona; if not, he could not validly sign a filed pleading. All U.S. district courts have established procedures in their local rules whereby out-of-state attorneys can be admitted to practice before them, and Yarborough will have to comply with these procedures before he can act for Dr. Collins in this lawsuit. Meanwhile, he may retain an Arizona attorney to act as local counsel so as to have someone available who can sign pleadings.

As for Park Hotels, there is little to be gained by requesting a waiver, from Shannon's standpoint. A corporation that has large fixed assets in the state (such as a hotel) is almost certain to have registered with the Corporation Commission and designated an agent for service of process, and so will not be difficult or expensive to serve. Requesting a waiver may actually be more expensive than serving process, taking into account the attorney and paralegal time required to make the contacts and handle the paperwork.

<table>
<tr><td>**Step 3**</td><td>*Assign Local Individual Defendants and Corporations to a Process Server for Routine Personal Service*</td></tr>
</table>

Since Park Hotels Group, Inc., operates a hotel in Arizona, our first step is to telephone the Arizona Corporation Commission to find out whether Park Hotels has appointed an agent to receive service of process in Arizona. If so, we can obtain the name and address of the agent over the telephone and instruct a process server to serve the agent.

<table>
<tr><td>**Step 4**</td><td>*Decide How to Serve Nonroutine Defendants*</td></tr>
</table>

In our hypo, we would arrive at this step only if we discover that Park Hotels has not appointed an agent to receive service of process in Arizona. In that case, we would have several options.

One would be to send a process server to Park Hotels Group's Arizona hotel with instructions to find and serve a director or managing agent. The drawback to this option is that we have no assurance that such a person could readily be found. Worse, if the process server did find someone to serve, we would likely be left with at least some uncertainty about whether the person really was a director or managing agent.

Better, instead, to telephone the department of corporations in Delaware, the state of incorporation of Park Hotels Group, Inc. and obtain the name and address of the corporation's agent in Delaware. Our local process server firm can probably arrange for service to be made on the agent in Delaware; if not, we can look up a Delaware process server in the Delaware Yellow Pages and make service arrangements by telephone.

<table>
<tr><td>**Step 5**</td><td>*Track Status of Pending Service Assignments*</td></tr>
</table>

In a litigation practice, all verbal understandings with opposing lawyers should be confirmed in writing immediately. When Roger Yarborough, Dr. Collins's attorney, agrees to waive service of process, Allen Porter immediately sends a confirming letter reciting the agreement and enclosing the necessary waiver forms. Such letters are a common part of litigation office routine; see Figure W6–1 for an example.

When the letter is sent, a calendar notation should be made to check in a week or two and be sure the signed waiver has been received. If it has not, a follow-up letter will be sent reminding Roger Yarborough to sign and return the waiver.

Similarly, a calendar notation should be made when the process server is instructed to serve Park Hotels. If the process server has not sent back a return of service within a reasonable time—a few days, if local, or a week or two if out of state—then

**Figure W6–1    Confirmation of Waiver Letter**

*SIMON & PORTER*
1000 North Central Avenue, Suite 2800
Phoenix, Arizona 85004
(602) 555-4321

September 9, 2000

Roger Yarborough, Esq.
500 Main Street
Dallas, Texas

Re: Martin v. Collins

Dear Roger:

This will confirm our telephone conversation of this afternoon, in which you have agreed to appear on behalf of your client, Dr. Arthur Collins, in the above-referenced lawsuit and to waive formal service of the summons and complaint. We have agreed that the due date for Dr. Collins to file a responsive pleading will be October 18, 2000. Thank you for your professional courtesy in this regard.

A copy of the summons and complaint are enclosed, together with a waiver of service. Please sign and return the latter to me for filing.

Sincerely,

_____

Allen Porter

we will follow up with a telephone call to the process server to determine whether there is some problem that needs our attention. We will continue to monitor the status of all pending service tasks and check on them every few days until they are completed.

**Step 6**    *Check that Service was Completed Correctly*

Review the return of service form for Park Hotels Group, Inc. to ensure that your instructions were followed and that the form is dated appropriately.

**Step 7**    *File Appropriate Return of Service*

In the case of Dr. Collins, we will not need to file a return of service; we will file the waiver instead. For the service on Park Hotels Group, Inc., the process server will provide the return of service after service has been completed. The process server may file the original with the court and send us a copy for our file, or may send us the original, in which case we would keep a copy and send the original to the clerk's office for filing.

**Step 8**    *Docket Answer Due Date*

Under FRCP, Rule 12, Dr. Collins' answer would be due when? The answer is not entirely predictable. Technically, the waiver request was not made pursuant to FRCP, Rule 4(d), so the time allowed for answering should be 20 days after service is complete. However, FRCP, Rule 12, provides a longer period of time (60 or 90 days) if the waiver is deemed to be a FRCP, Rule 4(d), waiver—an interpretation that, though unlikely and probably wrong, is not impossible. Moreover, when is service complete? Is it complete on the date when Roger Yarborough signs the waiver? The date when Allen Porter files it with the court?

Allen Porter and Roger Yarborough, both experienced litigators, have better things to do than get into disputes over such trivia. Therefore, when Yarborough agrees to waive service, they simply agree on an answer due date, and include it in the filed waiver. This due date *must* be docketed in the office calendars of both firms—in Yarborough's, so that he will not forget to file the answer on time (or seek another extension, if necessary); in Porter's, so that steps can be taken to enter a default if no answer

## Professional Courtesy

*It is sometimes physically impossible for defendant's attorney to file an answer within 20 days after the complaint is served, especially if the client waits until the nineteenth day before seeing an attorney! What then?*

*One thing that defendant's attorney (or paralegal) must never do is to ignore the problem and hope that plaintiff's attorney will not notice if the answer is a few days late—to do so is to invite a malpractice suit. Instead, the usual practice is to ask plaintiff's attorney for an extension.*

*In most localities, there are well-developed customs governing the asking and granting of extensions and other favors between opposing attorneys. These customs, known as **professional courtesy**, harken back to the days when lawyers were expected to be gentlemen and behave accordingly. If an attorney were asked for a reasonable accommodation by a brother lawyer, it would be granted as a matter of course—to refuse would be "ungentlemanly."*

*Extensions of deadlines are still routinely granted in most localities, out of pure self-interest if for no other reason. An attorney who refuses a reasonable extension request can expect to have his own "feet held to the fire" the first time he needs an extension. What is reasonable? Local custom dictates—your instructor will inform you of the usual practice in your locality.*

*One way in which modern practice differs from the days of "gentleman lawyers" is in the documenting of extensions when they are given. No longer is it acceptable simply to rely on another lawyer's word without confirming the extension in writing. In some courts, the rules require any extension to be reduced to a written stipulation, signed by both attorneys and filed with the court. In others, it is sufficient for one of the lawyers to send the other a confirming letter. Again, your instructor will inform you of the practice in your locality.*

*What if plaintiff's attorney refuses to grant an extension? Must defendant's attorney refuse the representation or risk a default? No; the alternative is to ask the court for an order extending the deadline. The judge has the authority to extend most of the deadlines provided for in the rules. Never assume that the judge will do so, however—the deadline is the deadline until the judge has actually ordered it extended.*

is filed. (As a matter of legal etiquette, however, where counsel have already conferred and agreed to one extension, Porter would not enter a default without first speaking to Yarborough again and verifying that the failure to answer was deliberate. If the failure were merely an oversight on Yarborough's part, Porter would give him additional time to file.)

Park Hotels Group, Inc., must file an answer within 20 days after service is made; see FRCP, Rule 12(a). The 20 days are counted from the day on which the papers are delivered, not the day on which the return of service is filed. In this, as in many such situations, Porter has no idea who will be representing this defendant, so he has no way of getting in contact with defendant's attorney. As a practical matter, what will most likely happen is that Porter will receive a telephone call from Park Hotels' attorney sometime before the 20 days are up, and an extended answer due date will be agreed on (in which case the new due date will be docketed on the office calendar). If Porter does not hear from some other lawyer representing Park Hotels by the time the 20 days are up, he will immediately enter the default.

## Serving the Complaint: Learning By Doing

### EXERCISES

In carrying out this assignment, you should follow the step-by-step formula described in this workshop.

1. (Step 1) Obtain a form for summons as used in a federal or state court in your locality (your instructor will specify which one). Use the form to prepare a summons to be used with the complaint that you drafted in Workshop 5. Take your summons and complaint to the office of the clerk of the court; at the deputy clerk's desk, explain that you are a paralegal student and ask the deputy clerk to walk you through the steps that the clerk would follow in filing the complaint and issuing the summons. Ask the deputy clerk to tell you about any common mistakes that she sees in lawsuit filings. Take notes on what you are told, and prepare a one-page summary of your experience to be turned in for credit.

2. [Step 2 and FRCP, Rule 4(d)] Assume that you are a paralegal in the office of Roger Yarborough, who has just filed suit on behalf of Dr. Arthur Collins against Shannon Martin in the U.S. District Court for the district that encompasses your locality. You are assigned

to prepare an FRCP, Rule 4(d), request for waiver of service by Shannon Martin, and a suitable cover letter addressed to Allen Porter, for Mr. Yarborough's signature.

3. (Step 3)   At random from the telephone directory, choose one individual living in your locality and one corporation that you know does business in your locality. (Optionally, your instructor may provide this information.) Contact a process server and explain that you are a paralegal student, and obtain copies of the service instructions form preferred by that process server. (*Hint:* A great way to contact a process server is to go to the office of the clerk of the court toward the end of the day. Usually there will be a number of process servers standing in line waiting to file papers, and since they are stuck standing in line anyway, they won't mind talking to you and giving you the benefit of their advice and experience.) Pretend that you are suing the individual and the corporation that you chose in your local state court, and obtain the information necessary to complete the service instructions form.

Find out what agency regulates corporations in your state, and telephone that agency to obtain the name and address of the agent appointed to receive service of process by the corporation that you are "suing." Prepare a service instructions form for the process server using the information that you obtained.

4. (Step 6)   Prepare a suitable return of service for the pretend service you prepared in the preceding exercise. Assume that the individual was served at the address that you gave in the service instructions, and that the corporation was served by delivering a copy of the summons and complaint to the agent whose name and address you obtained. You may invent the date and time of service and other necessary facts.

5. (Step 4)   Do research at the law library to find out the procedure for registered mail service under the rules of your local state court. Make a list of the required steps. Obtain or prepare a sample form for the return of service.

# PRACTICE POINTERS
## *Client Communications*

The primary culprit behind many malpractice claims is a breakdown in communication between client and attorney. Poor client relations is probably the single most important factor contributing to these claims. In fact, the most common complaint registered against attorneys, according to most state bar organizations, is lack of communication. The failure of lawyers to communicate with their clients has resulted in so many disciplinary and civil complaints that the American Bar Association's Model Rules of Professional Conduct now include Rule 1.4, which requires clients to be kept "reasonably informed about the status" of their case.

One simple way attorneys can keep clients informed is to send them copies of everything that is done in their case. When the complaint is filed, a conformed copy should be sent to the client; when summonses are mailed to defendants, copies of those summonses should be delivered to the client; when responses are received from the opposition, copies of those responses should be mailed to the client. In this way clients are immediately aware of the shifts and turns their case is taking and they have an ongoing sense of the status of their case. They are then less resistant to observations and suggestions made by counsel and they feel more connected to their cause of action. Without such efforts at communication, clients have a tendency to feel they have lost "ownership" of their case and begin to feel as if the attorney/firm is working against them instead of on their behalf.

Therefore, the simple act of keeping clients apprised as to the current status of their case and making them aware of the strengths and weaknesses of their case can minimize exposure to malpractice claims. Additionally, regular communication helps create realistic expectations on the part of the client and reassures the client that his case is important to the firm.

## TECHNO TIP

As you have seen, a licensed process server is not required to serve process in federal court. Most states do require that process be served by approved or licensed individuals. Sheriff's deputies are often given the right to serve process by virtue of their office. Costs can occur when you do not have a current address for the person or entity to be served. The process server, although not usually the sheriff's deputy, will attempt to locate the person to be served, for an additional fee. The procedure, often referred to as skip-tracing, can be expensive. Before you send process out for service, check to make sure the address is correct. If it is not use the Internet for a quick check on a person's current address before paying someone else to do so. If the person to be served is a statutory agent, check your corporation commission's database to see if a change of address has been filed. If access is possible, a good place to start is the driver's license bureau of your state. Privacy concerns often result in not being able to obtain an individual's driver's license data, including an address, without a written request being filed. You can still check the telephone company's database for new information. Reverse telephone books can be accessed so that if you know the telephone number of someone you can find the person's name and address. The county recorder's office and the secretary of state's database can also help find "missing" persons.

## FORMS FILE

*Make a list of the papers that must be included when filing a complaint in your jurisdiction. Write down the process that must be followed in serving process on a corporation as well as the method of identifying the agent appointed to receive service. Also, write out the process you must follow in serving an out-of-state defendant either personally or by mail and in serving a government agency.*

## KEY TERMS

| | | |
|---|---|---|
| Abode service | Grantor | Professional courtesy |
| Administrator | Implied authority | Trustee |
| Agent | Personal representative | Trustor |
| Decedent | Principal | Waive |
| Executor | Probate estate | |

# Paper Flow in a Litigation Office: Service, Docketing, and Deadlines

## INTRODUCTION: THE DEVIL IS IN THE DETAILS

In this workshop, you will learn about the rules that govern the flow of lawsuit paperwork: how incoming papers are received, how outgoing papers are delivered, how deadlines are computed, and how proper office systems can be used to prevent costly mistakes. These subjects may seem trivial, but they are not: Many a lawsuit has been lost over what amounts to paper-handling errors.

When plaintiff serves a complaint on defendant to begin a lawsuit, a clock starts running. Defendant has a fixed number of days in which to file and serve an answer. Defendant's attorney must do several things: (1) Consult the rules of procedure and determine exactly how many days defendant has (the answer depends on the circumstances); (2) compute the **deadline** date, which is the last day on which the answer can be filed and still be considered "on time"; (3) record the deadline in the office calendaring system so that appropriate reminders will be generated; (4) prepare the answer before the deadline; and (5) file the answer and serve it on the opposing party in the correct manner. A mistake anywhere along the way may cause a default to be entered against defendant, leading to a series of other consequences—none of which is likely to be career enhancing.

This sequence is repeated over and over in the course of a lawsuit. One party files something (a motion, a notice, a discovery paper) and serves it on the opposing party; the rules of procedure allow the opposing party a fixed time in which to respond. The response may itself trigger some action, setting up an entire chain of actions and responses.

Each step in the sequence must be carried out correctly. A complaint that is not served exactly in accordance with the rules may be treated as if it were not served at all—*even if the opposing party clearly received it.* If the judge is about to rule on a motion, and your response has not been filed, it does not matter whether you were only a day late or an entire month late—the result is likely to be the same. When you are dealing with the paper-processing requirements of the rules, "approximately correct" and "nearly on time" are not good enough.

Office procedures in a litigation law office are specifically designed to facilitate this process of time-sensitive moves and countermoves. Court papers of various kinds flow into the office in the morning mail (and throughout the day by messenger and fax). These are processed, often by paralegals, to determine what kind of response is required, deadlines are computed, they are calendared appropriately, and then each incoming paper is passed to the attorney or paralegal responsible for the case to which it pertains. The smooth operation of all this paper processing is absolutely critical to a successful litigation practice. Any law office, large or small, that fails to approach the task carefully and systematically will sooner or later have some important paper fall through a crack, and find itself on the receiving end of a malpractice suit.

Usually, the event that sets the clock running and triggers the need for action is the *service* of some paper. Many different papers are generated in the course of a lawsuit, and most require a response of some kind within a specified number of days after service. Recall that service means the delivery of a court paper in the manner prescribed by the rules.

What kinds of papers have to be served on opposing parties? How is this delivery accomplished? To whom is the paper delivered? In what manner is it delivered? For most papers generated after the lawsuit is under way, the answers to these questions are simple: Every paper filed with the court must be served on all parties, and this is done by sending a copy of the paper to the attorney for each party, by ordinary mail; see FRCP, Rule 5.

---

*Your Local Notes*

_____

_____

---

## HOW TO SERVE COURT PAPERS AFTER THE COMPLAINT

A great deal of paperwork is generated in the course of a typical lawsuit. As a general rule, every piece of paper must be served on every opposing party and (except for voluminous discovery papers in some courts) must also be filed with the clerk of the court. By requiring that papers be served on all parties, the system ensures that all of the attorneys are kept informed of what is going on in the suit. By requiring papers to be filed, the rules ensure that the court's file will contain an accurate record of everything that has happened in the suit.

Fortunately, the rules do *not* require formal service—the kind required for the summons and complaint—for all of these papers. Once served with the summons and complaint, each defendant is aware of the lawsuit and has an obligation to keep informed about what is going on. Therefore, papers subsequent to the complaint may be served in a much less formal manner.

**What Papers Must Be Served?**—The short answer is that all papers generated under the rules of procedure must be served on all opposing parties. Specifically, FRCP, Rule 6, requires service of the following types of court papers:

- Court orders,
- Pleadings subsequent to the complaint,
- Discovery papers,
- Written motions except those that may be heard *ex parte,* and
- Every written notice, appearance, demand, offer of judgment, designation of record on appeal, and similar paper.

This list covers essentially every type of court paper there is, so the general rule of thumb is that if a paper is in the form of a court paper (i.e., it has a caption and the other formal parts described in Workshop 4), it must be served on all opposing parties.

Note that this does *not* mean that all papers generated in the course of a lawsuit are served on your opponents. Many papers are confidential, and care must be taken that they do *not* fall into your opponents' hands. These include such things as letters to and from your client; research and other memos between attorneys or paralegals within your own office; private communications with witnesses, and especially those with expert witnesses hired by your firm to work on the case; private documents provided by your client or gathered through investigation; and other similarly confidential documents. (Some of these may eventually have to be turned over to opposing parties as part of the discovery process, but they are not court papers and you do not serve them under FRCP, Rule 5.) If you are in doubt about whether a particular paper is required to be served, never guess—consult your supervising attorney.

There is an exception to the general rule of serving every court paper on every party. It arises in the context of large, complex cases, in which there may be a hundred or more plaintiffs and defendants, each of which may have his or her own attorney. If two parties are each serving a paper on two other parties, four copies are needed in total; but if a hundred parties are each serving a paper on a hundred other parties, *ten thousand copies* (100 times 100) would be needed. You can easily see that if every paper in such a lawsuit were to be served on every party, entire forests would be required to supply enough paper to do the job. In such cases, however, the judge has the authority to short-circuit the general requirements of FRCP, Rule 5, by a specific court order; see FRCP, Rules 5(c) and 16.

---

*Your Local Notes*

_____

_____

---

**How Must Papers Be Served, and on Whom?**—FRCP, Rule 5(b), provides for two main ways of serving court papers other than the complaint: mailing and hand delivery. To whom? If an attorney has appeared for a party, service is always on the attorney, not on the party. (In fact, it is a violation of the rules of lawyer ethics to send *any* communication to an opposing party in a lawsuit whom you know to be represented by an attorney; all communications must be with the attorney.) Papers to be served on parties who are not represented by attorneys must be mailed or delivered to the party himself (or herself, or itself).

To serve a paper by mail, it is merely necessary to place a copy in an envelope addressed to the last known address of the attorney or party to whom it is being sent, affix first-class postage, and deposit the envelope in the U.S. Mail. At that point, the job is done and service is complete, regardless of whether the envelope actually arrives. (In practice, papers rarely disappear in the mail, and when they do, the attorneys and/or the judge can usually work out some reasonable way to get the case back on track.)

The alternative is to serve by hand delivery. Unlike formal service under FRCP, Rule 4, this does *not* require handing the paper directly to the attorney or party, nor is it necessary to employ a process server. It is sufficient to have a messenger leave the paper at the attorney's (or party's) office "with a clerk or other person in charge thereof, or if there is no one in charge, leaving it in a conspicuous place therein" [FRCP, Rule 5(b)]. If the office is closed, or if the person has no office, Rule 5 allows a paper to be delivered to the person's "dwelling or usual place of abode." In the unlikely event that the person to be served has no known address, service can be made by leaving the paper with the clerk of the court.

In practice, these options usually can be reduced to two: A paper is served either by mailing it to the office of the party's attorney, or by sending a messenger who will hand the paper to the receptionist in the attorney's office.

---

### SIDEBAR

## Is The Process Server Out of Work?

*Even though FRCP, Rule 5, allows most papers after the complaint to be served informally by mail or delivery to the attorneys' offices, a few situations still arise in which papers are usually served the hard way, by a process server. These situations typically involve the service of court orders of various kinds—subpoenas (recall that a subpoena is a court order requiring a witness to appear), orders to show cause, and injunctions are a few examples.*

*The reason for using formal service in these situations is not that the rules necessarily require it—in fact, FRCP, Rule 5, specifically includes orders among the categories of papers for which informal service is allowed. Rather, the reason has to do with the way in which court orders are enforced. What happens if someone violates a court order? The usual remedy is for the judge to hold the person in contempt of court; jail time and fines can be imposed as punishment for such disobedience. There is, however, a catch: Before the judge can hold someone in contempt, he must have proof that the person was aware of the court order—in other words, the disobedience has to be deliberate. As a practical matter, it would be impossible to prove that the party—the client—was aware of a court order if all you did was mail it to the attorney.*

*So, when you have a court order that you want to be able to enforce by having the judge punish disobedience with jail or a fine, you need to have a process server make personal service on the person to whom the order is directed. Such situations are commonplace in, for example, divorce cases.*

---

What about more modern methods of communication, such as faxing or electronic mail? Unfortunately, current court rules have not, on the whole, kept up with the explosion of technological advances. You are perfectly free to send a paper to an opposing attorney by fax or e-mail. Modern law offices use these technologies routinely. Faxing and e-mailing do not constitute valid service under FRCP, Rule 5, however, so you would still have to mail or deliver the paper to the opposing attorney, even if you have already faxed or e-mailed it. (This temporarily backward state of affairs is likely to change quickly, however. Some courts are already experimenting with electronic filing systems, in which papers could be filed with the court directly by e-mail, thereby potentially relieving the clerk's office of the necessity of physically handling and storing thousands of tons of paper. Once the practicability of such systems has been demonstrated, you can be sure that courts everywhere will be quick to jump on the bandwagon because of the potential for huge cost savings.)

If the alternatives are mailing and hand delivering, and service by mail is complete on mailing, why would anyone ever go to the extra bother and expense of hand delivering? One common reason is to force the opposing party to respond sooner. Why would the opposing party have to respond sooner to a paper that is hand delivered? As we will see shortly, the rules allow a longer response time for papers served by mail.

---

*Your Local Notes*

_____

_____

---

**If We Serve It, We File It**—The official record of everything that has happened in a case is the court file. Serving papers on opposing attorneys is important, but if we want there to be a record of what we did, we must file something with the clerk of the court.

Normally, what we file is the original of the paper itself (photocopies are served on the opposing attorneys). FRCP, Rule 5(d), states "All papers after the complaint required to be served upon a party . . . shall be filed with the court within a reasonable time after service." Thus, the general rule is that any paper that is in the form of a court paper (i.e., has a caption and the other formal parts) and that is served on opposing attorneys is also filed with the clerk.

There are, as always, a few exceptions. Discovery papers and responses to discovery present a special problem because they are often many pages long. It is not at all unheard of for a set of answers to interrogatories, or a response to a request for production of documents, with attachments, to run to many hundreds of pages. Formerly, rules of procedure in most courts required all such papers to be filed, and clerks' filing systems were becoming clogged with reams and reams of routine discovery papers, most of which the judge was unlikely ever to see.

To solve this problem, many courts no longer allow routine discovery papers to be filed with the clerk. FRCP, Rule 5(d), specifically authorizes U.S. district courts to adopt local rules providing that discovery papers should not be filed with the clerk, and many districts have done so. Your instructor will inform you of the practice in your locality regarding filing of discovery papers.

In jurisdictions where discovery papers are not filed, how is the court record made to reflect that the papers were ever served? A notice of service is filed. Thus, for example, when defendant Smith wishes to submit interrogatories to plaintiff Jones, the interrogatories themselves are served on Jones, but what is filed with the court is a one-page "Notice of Service of Interrogatories" reciting the date and the fact that the originals were served on Jones. Filing a notice is a handy technique any time you want to make a record of something that you have done in a lawsuit (see sidebar).

---

## SIDEBAR

### Notices

*Very often during the course of a lawsuit, a party needs to be sure that some event has been brought to the attention of other parties and/or made a part of the court record. This is routinely done via a court paper called a notice.*

*Suppose, for one example, that the court has ordered Park Hotels Group to turn over Banbury Park Hotel's telephone record for the night of Shannon's stay. The hotel's attorney, Gail Stoddard, complies with the court's order, but wants to be sure that she can prove that she did so. How? She files a notice (and, of course, serves copies of the notice on all the opposing attorneys).*

[Caption]

Notice is hereby given that defendant Park Hotels Group has delivered to plaintiff Shannon Martin the telephone records specified in the Court's order dated January 2, 2000.

[Date, signature lines, mailing certificate]

---

**How Do We Prove What We Served?**—Suppose we serve a paper by mailing or delivering it to our opponent's attorney, and she later denies having received it—how can we prove that we served it?

FRCP, Rule 5(d), provides the necessary mechanism. We attach a certificate of service (also often called a mailing certificate) to the paper. We have al-

ready seen, in Workshop 4, how to include a certificate of service in the formal skeleton of a court paper. Now, when we file the paper, with the certificate of service attached, there will be something in the court file to show when and how we served the paper.[1]

---

*Your Local Notes*

_____

_____

---

## HOW TO COMPUTE DEADLINES

There are few opportunities to win a lawsuit at a single stroke, but plenty of opportunities to lose one. Missing an important deadline ranks high in the latter category. The care and handling of deadlines in a lawsuit is not always simple, in part because it is often necessary for you to compute a deadline, rather than simply having the date given to you.

**Mail Handling**—Good management of deadlines in a law firm begins with proper mail handling practices. (We define *mail handling* broadly, to include the handling of all of the papers delivered by messenger throughout the day as well as those received in the morning mail.) Most of the deadlines you will be dealing with in litigation arise either from the need to respond to papers sent by opponents, or from court orders and minute entries ordering you to complete some task by a particular date.

Even relatively small litigation law firms may receive several mailbags full of documents each day. It is easy to see that if each paper in this daily river of documents were to be routed directly to the person it is addressed to, at least some of them would be overlooked. The attorney to whom a paper is addressed may be out of town, and it may sit unread on his desk for a week; a secretary may accidentally put an incoming motion in the case file instead of giving it to the attorney to respond to. The potential for oversights is enormous.

---

[1]A skeptic might object that the 'certificate' does not prove that we served the paper, it merely proves that we said we did! And, in fact, though clearly unethical, it is not unheard of for an attorney to "back date" a certificate of service so that a paper appears to have been mailed before some deadline. Fortunately, the system works well enough most of the time, and no one has thought of a better way. One may hope that such opportunities for cheating will disappear once electronic filing becomes universal, because electronic mail systems can automatically keep an accurate record of what was sent to whom and when.

Therefore, most law firms follow a strict policy whereby all incoming mail and deliveries *must* go first to some employee who is assigned the responsibility for checking each paper for potential deadlines, computing the dates if necessary, and making appropriate notations on the office calendar. This process is referred to as *docketing.* The **docket** is the office calendar, and may be kept in a regular (paper) calendar book or, increasingly, on a computer system of some kind. Typically, a central docket is kept containing all deadlines for all attorneys in the office; each attorney may also keep her own calendar or, in a computerized system, may simply access her portion of the central docket.

In a properly run system, no one—not even the senior partner of the firm—is allowed to touch an item of mail before the docketing clerk has processed it.

The docketing clerk stamps each incoming paper with a "Received" stamp that automatically imprints the date. This is important in case of a later dispute about when the paper was actually received. The docketing clerk also makes a notation on the paper, again using a rubber stamp, indicating any deadlines that are being docketed.

After a paper has been docketed, the docketing clerk determines which attorney is responsible for the case to which the paper pertains, and routes the paper to that attorney (or perhaps to his secretary) for the actual preparation of the required response.

At this point, you may be wondering, "What does any of this have to do with me as a paralegal? If the docketing clerk is responsible for calendaring deadlines, why do I need to know about this?"

One reason is that paralegals are sometimes assigned to do docketing. Another is that, even with the most carefully planned docketing system, mistakes will occasionally be made. Therefore, in a first-rate litigation firm, it is considered the responsibility of everyone—partners, associates, paralegals, down to the lowliest clerical employee—to worry continually about deadlines. We recommend that every attorney and paralegal should cultivate the following habit: Every time you see or come in contact with a new court paper in a case, give it a quick deadline check. If it has already been stamped with a response date, double check the deadline by recomputing it in your head; if not, consider whether a response requirement may have been overlooked. In the long run, this is a habit that will pay rich dividends in terms of avoiding malpractice claims.

More specifically, we note that as a litigation paralegal, you will often be assigned to draft responses of various kinds. Typically, your supervising attorney will hand you a motion, or a discovery request, and assign you to "deal with it." If the firm's

docketing system is working properly, the paper given you will already be stamped with the deadline date for the response. Your first reaction should be to verify that the deadline is correct. The step-by-step instructions to follow will tell you how.

> **Your Local Notes**
>
> _____
>
> _____

## Setting Deadlines: Step-by-Step Instructions

Deadlines arise in two main ways: (1) The court expressly orders you to do something by a certain date or (2) an opposing party serves a paper on you and the rules of procedure require you to respond to it within a certain amount of time. Determining the first kind of deadline is easy because no computation is required, the deadline date is set by the court. Our step-by-step instructions, therefore, are concerned only with the second kind.

You might suppose that response deadlines would also be easy to compute. All you have to do is count some number of days—surely this is not rocket science?

In fact, computing deadlines should not be difficult if you approach it in a systematic way—but, never forget, litigation is a contest among adversaries, and if a mistake can be taken advantage of, it will be. And yes, computing a deadline is a matter of counting days, but how many days, exactly? What day do you start counting from? Do you count weekends? What if the deadline falls on, say, Christmas? Some of these questions are answered by the rules of procedure; the answers to others depend on local rules, case law, and sometimes merely local custom.

### Step 1 | Determine What (If Any) Response Is Required

The deadline analysis process begins when your law firm receives a court paper—any court paper. The first decision that must be made is whether this paper is one that requires a response of some kind.

You might suppose that the answer would be obvious from the title of the paper, and often it is. If the caption contains the word *motion* or *petition,* you can usually be sure that a response date needs to be calendared. Other routine types of court papers requiring responses include discovery requests: interrogatories, requests for production of documents, and requests for admissions.

An opponent's response to a motion of yours also triggers a deadline—for the filing of a reply to the response. In general, if the title to an incoming paper begins with the word *response,* a reply to the response is usually needed.

The situation is not always so simple. For example, suppose you receive in the mail an answer to a complaint that you have filed and served. Does an answer to a complaint trigger any deadlines? Generally not, but what if it includes a counterclaim or a cross-claim? Then a reply is required; see FRCP, Rule 7(a). Moreover, under the rules of some courts, the filing of an answer sets other clocks in motion; for example, the rules may require the filing of a disclosure statement within a certain number of days after the answer is filed, or may require that discovery be completed within some number of months after issue is joined. In deciding whether nonroutine papers require responses, there is no substitute for experience and thorough familiarity with the rules. When in doubt, consult your supervising attorney.

---

**Your Local Notes**

_____

_____

---

**Step 2**  *Determine the Applicable Time Period*

Having decided that a particular court paper requires a response, the next step is to determine how much time is allowed. For certain types of responses (especially discovery responses) the response times are prescribed by the rules of procedure. For others, however (e.g., responses to motions) local practice, as set forth in the local rules or as dictated by local custom or by a particular judge's preferences, is usually controlling.

Here are some typical time limits for common types of responses (your instructor will inform you of the corresponding time periods for the courts of your locality):

- *Pleadings.* FRCP, Rule 12(a), governs the time that a defendant has to file an answer to a complaint or a reply to a counterclaim or cross-claim. The general rule is that answers are due 20 days after service of the complaint, but there are exceptions as set forth in the rule. State court time periods are quite variable and may be considerably lengthened if service was made out of state, or by some method other than personal service, or if the defendant is a government agency.

- *Routine motions.* The Federal Rules of Civil Procedure do not expressly prescribe a response time for motions. FRCP, Rule 6(d), requires motions to be served at least 5 days before the hearing on the motion, unless the court orders otherwise, which implies that the responding party would have no more than 5 days to respond; in practice, no federal court that the authors are aware of imposes such a short response time. Most U.S. district courts have a local rule specifying the procedure for filing motions and responses to them. Typical time periods under U.S. district court local rules are 10 days for a response and 5 days for a reply.

- *Motions for summary judgment.* Usually, much more work is required to respond to a motion for summary judgment than is required for a routine procedural motion. Motions for summary judgment carry the potential to decide all or part of the lawsuit in the moving party's favor, and often raise issues that are legally and factually complex. Recognizing this, most court rules allow a longer response time than for other motions. As with the routine motions just discussed, the Federal Rules of Civil Procedure imply an impossibly short response time [10 days; see FRCP, Rule 56(c)], which is invariably lengthened by local rule or custom. Typical time periods are 30 days for a response to a motion for summary judgment and 15 days for a reply to the response.

- *Discovery requests.* Answers to written interrogatories [see FRCP, Rule 33(b)(3)], responses to requests for admissions [see FRCP, Rule 36(a)], and responses to requests for production of documents [see FRCP, Rule 34(b)] are all due 30 days after the service of the discovery request on the answering party.

---

**Your Local Notes**

_____

_____

---

**Step 3**  *Determine Date from Which to Begin Counting*

By the time we get to this point in our analysis, we know that some opposing party has served a court paper on us that requires a response, and we know how many days are allowed for that type of response. Now we must compute the deadline. To do that, we need a starting point from which to count the required number of days.

The starting point is the date on which the opposing party served the paper on us that we are responding to. What date is that? It depends on the mode of service:

- *Papers personally served by a process server.* For papers served by a process server, the date of service is the date that the process server actually delivered the paper to the person being served. Therefore, if you are computing the due date for an answer to a complaint, you will need to know the exact date on which your client was served. Clients' recollections of such things are notoriously untrustworthy; when in doubt, the best course is to verify the service date via a call by your supervising attorney to the attorney who served the complaint. (You might suppose that it would be easier to check the court file for the return of service, but, in practice, it may take several weeks before a filed paper actually wends its way through the clerk's processing and into the actual file.)

- *Hand-delivered papers.* For a paper that was hand delivered to your law office, the date of service is the date on which the paper was actually delivered. No surprises here.

- *Papers served by mail.* For a paper that was mailed to your law office, the date of service is the date on which the paper was *deposited in the mail.* This is because FRCP, Rule 5(b), states that "service by mail is complete upon mailing." (As we will see in Step 4, service by mail also extends the response time.)

- *Other kinds of service.* The three methods of service just mentioned—personal service by a process server, hand delivery, and mail service—account for the great majority of papers that you will be called on to respond to in a litigation practice. Occasionally, however, a client will show up with a complaint or other paper that has been served by registered mail, or via the nonresident motorist statute, or by some other unusual means. Be warned that the statutes providing for such alternative means of service typically also specify how to determine when service is deemed to be complete. Therefore, to compute a response date, you must consult whatever statute or rule governs the particular method of service that was used.

<table>
<tr><td>*Your Local Notes*<br><br>_____<br><br>_____</td></tr>
</table>

## Step 4    *Compute the Deadline Date*

Now we have a starting date and we know the allowed time period. Surely, now, all that remains is a simple matter of counting days, right? The answer is "it depends." FRCP, Rule 6, sets out the rules for counting the days, and it adds a few complexities of its own. Here are the main rules:

- *The first day does not count.* We begin counting on the day *after* the date of service. FRCP, Rule 6(a), tells us that "the day of the act . . . from which the designated period of time begins to run"—here, the date that the paper we are responding to was served—"shall not be included."

  *Example:* A complaint is served on March 1, and the rules allow us 20 days in which to file an answer. In counting the 20 days, March 1 is day 0 in our count, day 1 is March 2, day 2 is March 3, etc.

- *The last day does count.* The last day of the period we are counting is included; see FRCP, Rule 6(a).

  *Example:* We are counting a 20-day period beginning on March 1. As before, day 1 is March 2, day 2 is March 3 (we will let you count days 3 through 19 on your own), and day 20 is March 21. Because the last day *does* count, the deadline falls on March 21.

- *We get 3 extra days if we were served by mail.* We have already seen that when a paper is served by mailing it to a party's attorney, service is complete when the paper is placed in the mail. Obviously, mail delivery is not yet instantaneous, so to make up for the several days of response time that the responding party is being deprived of while the paper floats through the mail system, the rules give the responding party an extra 3 days to respond to papers served by mail; see FRCP, Rule 6(e). (In state courts the problem of mail delay may be handled differently, or the number of extra days may be different. Your instructor will inform you of the practice in your locality.)

  *Example:* A motion is served on your client on March 1 by mailing it to your office. The response time is 15 days. Because the motion was served by mail, 3 days are added, so the response time becomes 18 days. March 1 is day 0 . . . March 19 is day 18, so the response is due on March 19.

- *For response times under 11 days, holidays and weekends do not count.* It stands to reason that if a party has, say, only 3 days to respond to some paper, and she received it on Friday, it would be a bit unfair to count Saturday and Sunday as part of the 3 days. To provide some relief in the case of short response times, FRCP, Rule 6(a), provides that "when the period of time prescribed or allowed is less than 11 days, intermediate Saturdays, Sundays, and legal holidays shall be excluded in the computation." [FRCP, Rule 6(a) specifies which holidays qualify.]

  *Example:* A motion is hand delivered to your office on March 1, a Thursday, and the response time is 5 days. March 1 is day 0; March 2, Friday, is day 1; March 3 and 4 are Saturday and Sunday and do not count; March 5, Monday, is day 2; March 6, Tuesday, is day 3; March 7, Wednesday, is day 4; and March 8, Thursday, is day 5. The response is due on March 8. (We assume that no federal or state holidays fell on March 2, 5, 6, 7, or 8.)

- *A deadline may not fall on a weekend or holiday.* It would be meaningless to make responses due on days when the clerk's office is not open. Therefore, FRCP, Rule 6(a), provides that if the last day of our count falls on a Saturday, Sunday, or legal holiday, the deadline shifts to the next day that is *not* a Saturday, Sunday, or legal holiday.

  *Example:* A complaint is served on our client on June 12, a Sunday. The rules allow us 20 days in which to file an answer. July 2, a Saturday, is day 20 (you should by now have no trouble verifying this for yourself). Because day 20 is a Saturday, the deadline shifts. The deadline cannot fall on the next day, July 3, because it is a Sunday. Nor can it fall on the next day, Monday, July 4, because July 4 is a national holiday. Therefore, the answer must be filed by Tuesday, July 5, which is the first day following the computed deadline that is not a Saturday, Sunday, or legal holiday.

With these rules, we should have no difficulty computing deadline dates in most situations. In the rare situation for which FRCP, Rule 6, gives no clear answer, do not guess—consult your supervising attorney.

---

**Your Local Notes**

_____

_____

---

| **Step 5** | *Consider Whether the Deadline Is Workable* |

Deadlines are a routine part of the landscape in a litigation practice, and every litigator or litigation paralegal must learn to cope with them. Some are easy to meet, some difficult, and a few are impossible. Sometimes, a given task will present the uneasy choice between doing a rushed, imperfect job or taking the time to do it right but missing the deadline.

There are essentially three options for dealing with an unworkable deadline: (1) Prepare the best response you can in the time allotted, working nights and weekends if necessary, file it on time, and live with its flaws, whatever they may be; (2) ask the opposing lawyer for an extension of the deadline; or (3) file a motion asking the court to extend the deadline.

Each of these options has a cost associated with it. For choice 1, the drawback is the risk that rushing will cause mistakes. For choice 2, the cost is that, having received an extension, you will be expected to reciprocate when the opposing lawyer needs one, perhaps in a situation in which it would have been to your client's advantage to refuse. Choice 3 entails preparing and filing a motion, which takes time and costs money, and risks annoying the judge (judges hate refereeing trivial scheduling disputes).

The point that we wish to emphasize is that the cost of choices 2 and 3 goes up as the deadline gets closer. If we decide that we need an extension and we act early, we can always fall back on choice 1 if opposing counsel is too demanding, and we can file a motion for an extension if opposing counsel refuses our request. If we wait until the day before the response is due, we are at opposing counsel's mercy; as a practical matter, it is very difficult or impossible to prepare, file, and get a ruling on a motion for extension if we only have one day in which to do it.

Therefore, we include as one of the steps in evaluating the deadline for a given response that you should quickly outline the work that will be required. Make a list of the major tasks and subtasks, and be sure to list all of the items—signatures, documents, affidavits, attachments—that you will need to obtain from others. Make a tentative schedule and consider carefully whether it is workable. If you conclude that more time will be needed, now is the time to tell your supervising attorney, so that he can contact opposing counsel for an extension and, if necessary, file a motion asking the court for an extension.

A contact with opposing counsel is also warranted if you conclude that the deadline date is uncertain or ambiguous for some reason. It is better to agree on a response date with opposing counsel than to guess at it and be found wrong. Again, your role as a paralegal is to point out the uncertainty to your supervising attorney; as a paralegal you should never contact opposing attorneys directly unless your supervising attorney has instructed you to do so.

If it does become necessary to contact opposing counsel, any extension agreed to should always be documented in writing. At a minimum, a confirming letter is sent by the attorney requesting the extension to the attorney granting it. In some courts, by local rule or custom, extensions should be documented in a stipulation signed by both attorneys and filed with the clerk.

---

**SIDEBAR**

## Stipulations

*A **stipulation** is an agreement between attorneys. When reduced to writing, it takes the form of a court paper, with appropriate caption and formal parts (see Workshop 4), which is filed with the clerk. In some courts, it is sufficient merely to file the stipulation; in others, a court order approving the terms of the stipulation is submitted. Figure W7–1 shows a sample of a stipulation.*

---

| Your Local Notes |
| --- |
| _____ |
| _____ |

---

**Step 6**  *Calendar the Deadline*

Ordinarily, by the time you as a paralegal are assigned a court paper to respond to, any deadlines will already have been entered in the central calendar for

---

**Figure W7–1   What a Stipulation Looks Like**

### IN THE UNITED STATES DISTRICT COURT
### DISTRICT OF ARIZONA

| | |
| --- | --- |
| SHANNON MARTIN, a single woman, ) | |
| ) | NO. 95-770 PHX-JML |
| Plaintiff, ) | |
| ) | STIPULATION FOR |
| v. ) | EXTENSION OF TIME |
| ) | |
| ARTHUR COLLINS and JANE DOE COLLINS, ) | |
| husband and wife; PARK HOTELS GROUP, ) | |
| INC., a Delaware corporation; ) | |
| ) | |
| Defendants. ) | |

Plaintiff and Defendant Park Hotels Group, Inc. hereby stipulate that Plaintiff shall have until August 19, 2000, to file a response to Defendant's motion for Summary Judgment and that Defendant shall have until September 19, 2000, to file a reply.

RESPECTFULLY SUBMITTED this _____ day of July, 2000.

CRANDALL, ELKINS & MAJOR                                    SIMON & PORTER

_____                    _____
Gail Stoddard                                                          Allen Porter
Attorney for Defendant                                            Attorneys for plaintiff
Park Hotels Group, Inc.

(Certificate of Mailing)

the office. If not, you must take steps to see that they are entered. All response deadlines, deadlines for filing papers with the court, and other court-related deadlines *must* get into the central calendar—even ones that you have entered in your own calendar and feel that you have well under control.

Why? One of the things that a proper central calendaring system does is generate daily reports for each attorney and paralegal in the office, showing the upcoming deadlines for all matters for which she is responsible, including projects assigned to subordinates. This provides a fail-safe mechanism in case an attorney or paralegal becomes ill or incapacitated, or simply drops the ball. In such case, the next person up the ladder of authority will automatically be made aware of any pending deadlines.

It is also imperative that every litigation paralegal keep a personal calendar. There are simply too many time-critical events in litigation to allow reliance on memory alone, and some of these events will be of a type (appointments with witnesses, progress checks for assigned tasks, etc.) not appropriate for the central office calendar. It goes without saying that all deadlines for projects assigned to you should be entered in your own calendar, even though they are already entered in the office calendar.

---

*Your Local Notes*

_____

_____

---

## Setting Deadlines: Learning by Example

To see how FRCP, Rules 5 and 6, work in practice, let us consider the situation that arises when Gail Stoddard files her motion for summary judgment on behalf of Park Hotels Group.

Even though the motion is really aimed at plaintiff (Shannon), Ms. Stoddard must serve it on all parties; see FRCP, Rule 5 (" . . . every written motion . . . shall be served on each of the parties. . . ."). She could do this either by having a messenger hand deliver a copy to the offices of each of the opposing attorneys or by mailing copies to each attorney. Since Dr. Collins's attorney is in another state, she would likely serve Dr. Collins's copy by mailing it to Roger Yarborough. Allen Porter's office is nearby, so she might consider having the motion hand delivered to him.

We will assume that Gail Stoddard files the motion for summary judgment with the clerk of the court on July 1, a Monday, and mails it to Allen Porter and Roger Yarborough the same day. When Allen Porter receives

it the following Wednesday, he hands the motion to Chuck Fletcher, the paralegal, with instructions to draft up a response. Chuck notes that the motion has the firm's docketing stamp, with a notation that the response is due on August 5. Well-trained paralegal that he is, Chuck's first reaction is to double-check the response date. We will do the same:

**Step 1** *Determine What (If Any) Response Is Required*

When a party moves for summary judgment, it is up to the opposing party to convince the court that the facts on her side are sufficiently strong to warrant the expense of a trial; see FRCP, Rule 56(c).

Because our hypothetical lawsuit is proceeding in the U.S. District Court for the District of Arizona, whose rules are not untypical of those in other district courts, we might ask ourselves whether the local rules have anything to say about what happens if we fail to respond to a motion for summary judgment. Indeed they do! Rule 1.10(i) states ". . . if the opposing party does not serve and file the required answering memoranda . . . such non-compliance may be deemed a consent to the . . . granting of the motion. . . ."

In fact, as a practical rule of thumb, if you do not file a response to a motion—any motion—the court is likely to assume that you do not object and rule accordingly. Therefore, we would not dream of letting any motion go by without a response, unless the motion is one that we do not mind having the court grant (and even then the civilized thing to do is to file a response stating that we have no objection).

### Step 2 — Determine the Applicable Time Period

The procedure for scheduling responses, replies, and hearings on motions for summary judgment varies considerably from one court to another. Again referring to the local rules for the U.S. District of Arizona, Rule 1.10(l) provides that the party opposing a motion for summary judgment "shall, unless otherwise ordered by the Court, have thirty (30) days after service within which to serve and file a responsive memorandum in opposition. . . ."

### Step 3 — Determine Date from Which to Begin Counting

Our hypothetical assumes that Gail Stoddard's motion was served by mail on Monday, July 1. FRCP, Rule 5(b), provides that "service by mail is complete upon mailing." Because the rule quoted in Step 2 requires us to respond within "30 days after service," and FRCP, Rule 6(a), provides that we do not count the day from which the time period begins to run (here, July 1), our count begins with day 1 on Tuesday, July 2.

### Step 4 — Compute the Deadline Date

Applying the rules described under Step 4, Wednesday, July 3, is day 2. Thursday, July 4, is a federal holiday; however, the time period we are counting (30 days) is longer than 11 days, so intermediate holidays and weekends are counted. Therefore, Thursday, July 4, is day 3. If we continue counting in this fashion, we will find that day 30 is July 31, a Wednesday. However, FRCP, Rule 6(e), gives us 3 additional days because the motion was served on us by mail. Three more days takes us to Saturday, August 3. Under FRCP, Rule 6(a), the deadline may not fall on a weekend, so our response is due the following Monday, August 5.

### Step 5 — Consider Whether the Deadline Is Workable

Is four and a half weeks (Wednesday, July 3, when Porter receives the motion in the mail to Monday, August 5, when the response is due) enough time to prepare a response to a motion for summary judgment? It depends.

Responding to a motion for summary judgment involves two main tasks:

1. You must write a legal argument sufficient to convince the judge that the substantive rules of law governing the issues raised by the motion come out the way you say they do.
2. You must assemble the necessary factual materials to convince the judge that you have at least some evidence to prove your client's version of the facts.

The first task will likely entail long hours spent hitting the books in the law library, or surfing your favorite on-line legal research tool. How many long hours? That, unfortunately, is unpredictable. In our hypo, Chuck will need at least to look for factually similar negligence cases in which, hopefully, the court ruled for plaintiff under similar circumstances. Negligence is a very broad area of the law, with many thousands of reported cases. Chuck may get lucky early, or he may spend a week in the library with nothing to show for it except a few legal pads full of dead ends.

The factual support for a response to a motion for summary judgment usually consists of affidavits, excerpts from deposition transcripts, and answers to interrogatories. In our hypo, Gail Stoddard is arguing that there is no evidence that the hotel was negligent because the key found by the police did not fit Shannon's lock; Allen Porter is arguing that Shannon's and Dr. Collins's testimony constitute evidence that Shannon's door was locked and that the key given to Dr. Collins opened it. Therefore, the main factual support that Chuck will need for the response will consist of Shannon's and Dr. Collins's testimony.

Providing Shannon's is easy—he can simply prepare an affidavit for her signature reciting that she locked the door. Dr. Collins's is another matter. If his deposition has been taken, and if he gave the needed testimony in the deposition, then a copy of the relevant portion of the transcript can be attached to the response. If not, then Allen Porter may try to convince Roger Yarborough to get Dr. Collins to provide an affidavit stating that the key he was given turned in the lock; failing that, it would be necessary either to send interrogatories to Dr. Collins or to take his deposition. Neither procedure could likely be completed in 30 days.

As a general rule, 30 days usually is enough time to prepare a response to a motion for summary judgment—*if* you have done your homework in terms of researching the claims in the suit early on (see Workshop 1), and *if* discovery is reasonably well along, and *if* the motion you are responding to is relatively straightforward and uncomplicated, and *if* your calendar is light enough to allow you to actually use the 30 days to work on the response. Any glitch, however, will put you squarely behind the eight ball.

Chuck Fletcher, having been around this track a few times, wisely concludes that an extension should be requested. Allen Porter telephones Gail Stoddard, who grudgingly extends the due date for the response to August 19—and, in return, gets an agreement that she will have until September 19 to file a reply. Under the local rules of the U.S. District Court for the District of Arizona [see Rules 2.7(d) and 1.10(n)], extensions of time are valid only if reduced to a written stipulation, signed by both attorneys, filed, and approved by the court. Chuck therefore prepares a stipulation, which Allen Porter signs, setting forth the extension agreement. Chuck then sends the stipulation, with a suitable cover letter, to Gail Stoddard for her signature. She will sign the stipulation and return it to Allen Porter's office for filing with the court.

## Step 6    *Calendar the Deadline*

Now the firm's central calendar needs to be updated to reflect the extended deadline date. Because the extension is not effective until the court approves the stipulation, the central calendar entry will not be changed until that has occurred. Then it is the docketing clerk who will make the change, not Chuck himself—in most law firms, authority to make changes to the central calendar is tightly restricted, for obvious reasons.

## Setting Deadlines: Learning by Doing

### EXERCISES

In completing these exercises, you should following the step-by-step formula described in this workshop.

1.  Obtain a copy of the local rules for the U.S district court having jurisdiction over your locality. Review them and note any rules that affect filing and service of court papers, allowed response times, extensions, and stipulations.

2.  Obtain a copy of the local rules for the superior court or other state court in which civil lawsuits would be filed in your locality. Review them and note any rules that affect filing and service of court papers, allowed response times, extensions, and stipulations.

3.  Assume that Shannon's complaint is filed in the U.S. district court having jurisdiction over your locality. Her summons and complaint are served on defendant Park Hotels Group, Inc., on February 1, a Tuesday, by delivering a copy to Park Hotels Group's designated agent, at its office in your city. What is the deadline for Park Hotels Group to file an answer or other responsive pleading?

4.  Same facts as Exercise 3, except that Shannon's complaint is filed in the superior court or other state court in which civil lawsuits would be filed in your locality. What is the deadline for Park Hotels Group to file an answer or other responsive pleading? Does it differ from your answer to Exercise 3? If so, how and why?

5.  Assume that Shannon's lawsuit is pending in the U.S. district court having jurisdiction over your locality. Allen Porter files a motion to compel asking the judge to order Park Hotels Group to answer certain interrogatories that Park Hotels Group has refused to answer. The motion is filed on November 1, a Thursday, and a copy is hand delivered by messenger to the office of Gail Stoddard, attorney for defendant Park Hotels Group, on Friday, November 2. What is the deadline for Park Hotels Group's response to the motion?

6.  Same facts as Exercise 5, except that Shannon's lawsuit is pending in the superior court or other state court in which civil lawsuits would be filed in your locality. What is the deadline for Park Hotels Group's response? Does it differ from your answer to Exercise 5? If so, how and why?

7.  Assume that Shannon's lawsuit is pending in the U.S. district court having jurisdiction over your locality. On behalf of defendant Dr. Collins, Roger Yarborough submits written interrogatories to be answered by Shannon Martin. He serves the interrogatories by mailing them to Allen Porter, whose office is in your locality. He deposits them in the mail on April 5, a Saturday, and Allen Porter's office receives them in the morning mail on Tuesday, April 8. What is the

deadline for Porter to serve answers to the interrogatories on Shannon's behalf?

8. Same facts as Exercise 7, except that Shannon's lawsuit is pending in the superior court or other state court in which civil lawsuits would be filed in your locality. What is the deadline for Porter to serve answers to the interrogatories on Shannon's behalf? Does it differ from your answer to Exercise 7? If so, how and why?

9. Assume that Shannon's lawsuit is pending in the U.S. district court having jurisdiction over your locality. On behalf of defendant Dr. Collins, Roger Yarborough files a motion for summary judgment asking the court to find as a matter of law that Shannon's claim against Dr. Collins for battery is invalid. The motion is filed on February 25, a Thursday, and Yarborough's secretary mails a copy of the motion to Allen Porter on the same day. She inadvertently fails to put Park Hotels Group's copy in the mail that day, but does so the next day, Friday, February 26. What is the deadline for Allen Porter to file a response on behalf of Shannon Martin? What

is the deadline for Gail Stoddard to file a response on behalf of Park Hotels Group if she decides to do so?

10. Same facts as Exercise 9, except that Shannon's lawsuit is pending in the superior court or other state court in which civil lawsuits would be filed in your locality. What is the deadline for Allen Porter to file a response on behalf of Shannon Martin? What is the deadline for Gail Stoddard to file a response on behalf of Park Hotels Group if she decides to do so?

11. In Exercise 9, Porter finds that he needs more time in which to prepare a response, so he calls Roger Yarborough to ask for an extension. Roger Yarborough agrees that Porter may have an additional 21 days in which to respond, and that Yarborough will then have 30 days in which to file and serve a reply. Porter assigns you to prepare the necessary paperwork to document the extension, which you should do in accordance with the local rules of your U.S. district court and in accordance with customary practice in your locality.

# PRACTICE POINTERS
## *Tickler Systems*

The importance of adhering to court dates and deadlines established by the procedural rules cannot be overestimated. Failure to meet these deadlines can potentially result in the dismissal of a case or a loss of a claim, thereby causing, at best, a serious breach of confidence with the client and, at worst, a malpractice claim. Therefore, attorneys and legal assistants must devise effective ways of ensuring that no deadline is overlooked.

Attorneys have developed various types of tickler systems that either manually or electronically alert members of the legal team to upcoming deadlines. One simple manual form requires you to note the client's name, the file number, the action to be completed, and the date it is to be completed on a tickler form. You then choose at least three dates on which you want to be reminded about this task and on each of those dates, the employee in charge of the tickler system gives you the reminder. This gives you three distinct opportunities to begin working on the required task.

Scheduling reminders well in advance of the deadline helps ensure that you have ample time to complete the necessary work and accommodates for emergencies that arise that preclude the initial completion of a task. In other words, tickler systems can prevent crisis management and can encourage the avoidance of last minute scrambling to meet court deadlines. Computerized systems can also be set up to give multiple warnings and can even be programmed to flash upcoming deadlines on your computer screen.

## TECHNO TIP

Commercial calendaring programs are now available that seem to do it all. Reminders (ticklers) can be set at a variety of dates prior to the deadline to remind you of the upcoming response. Be very careful when using any piece of software. Never leave it to the program to determine a deadline. Do the computing yourself, without guidance from the program, and make sure the software got it right as well.

Many of today's personal information managers (PIMs) appear to have the capability to calculate due dates. Be aware! They may not use the same algorithm as set forth in your state's court rules. They may consider a holiday that is not recognized by your rules or not consider one that is a holiday in your state. PIMs also have reminders that can be set for a fixed number of days prior to the deadline. Do not rely on them either!

## FORMS FILE

*Summarize the rules pertaining to the computation of deadlines for responses to parties served on you by opponents. Include the time period that applies, what day to begin counting from, and what days to exclude.*

## KEY TERMS

**Deadline**                **Docket**                **Stipulation**

## INTRODUCTION: THE ROLE OF THE ANSWER

We now shift our point of view and examine the beginning stages of a lawsuit from the standpoint of the defendant. If you are named as a defendant in a lawsuit, you will quite likely first become aware of it when the summons and complaint are served on you. You are going about your normal daily business one day, and suddenly some stranger walks up to you and hands you a stack of papers. Congratulations! You're a defendant! Now what?

One next step would be to file an answer, in preparation to defend the suit "on the merits," and that is what you will learn to do in this workshop. When we refer to the **merits** of plaintiff's case, we are concerned with whether (1) the acts and events plaintiff as alleged in the complaint are *legally sufficient* to entitle plaintiff to win a judgment against you, and (2) whether plaintiff can produce *evidence sufficient* to prove that those acts and events actually happened.

## ALTERNATIVES TO FILING AN ANSWER

Filing an answer is not, however, the only option. Before we immerse ourselves in the details of answer drafting, let us acquaint ourselves with some of the other possibilities, so that you can better understand the thought process that a litigator must go through when a client is sued. Here are some of your other options as a defendant:

1. *Do nothing, default.* You could decide to do nothing—simply ignore the suit. But if you fail to file an answer or other responsive pleading, sooner or later the person suing you will almost certainly obtain a judgment by default for the full amount he is suing for.

    Would that be a bad outcome? Not necessarily. Remember that judgments are not self-executing (see Chapter 5). Suppose you have no assets from which a judgment could be collected. Are there people in that situation? Yes, many more than you might suppose. The laws of most states do not allow the winner of a judgment to grab everything the loser owns, leaving her destitute. The judgment debtor—the loser of the suit—is entitled by law to keep certain assets that are exempt from execution. **Exempt property** means an asset that the law does not allow to be seized to pay a judgment. In most states, the loser of a lawsuit is allowed to keep her house, a car or two, some books, clothing, and tools, and perhaps some cash, up to some limited (but usually generous) amount. If everything that you own falls into one of the exempt categories (or can be sold or traded for something that does), then quite possibly the only adverse effects of having a judgment against you is that your credit rating will be ruined, and that if you should later find yourself with more money, you may then be forced to pay (but see option 2 next).

    On the other hand, if you decide to defend the suit, you will have to hire a lawyer, which will probably cost a great deal of money—at least thousands of dollars, perhaps tens of thousands. Faced with a choice between doing nothing and keeping your assets, or hiring a lawyer to defend you and having to take out a second mortgage on your house to pay him, what would you do? As you can see, the choice is not an easy one.

2. *File for bankruptcy.* If you qualify to file for bankruptcy, you can not only keep all of your exempt property, you can get a **discharge in bankruptcy,** which is a court order by the bankruptcy court wiping out all of your debts. Not only that, when you first file the bankruptcy proceeding, all lawsuits against you are immediately and automatically stayed. (An **automatic stay** is an order by the bankruptcy court ordering anyone suing you to refrain from proceeding further with their suit.) Filing for bankruptcy is not free (the cost of a typical consumer bankruptcy is in the ballpark of $1,000 including lawyer fees and court filing fees) but it is a good deal less expensive than defending a lawsuit.

    The bottom line is that unless the person being sued is either wealthier than the average middle-class American wage earner or is covered by insurance, there may be little to be gained and much to be lost by filing an answer and defending.

3. *Seek a Different Forum.* If plaintiff's attorney is doing a good job, you may assume that the court in which the suit is filed is the one that is best for plaintiff and worst for you. (See the discussion of choice of forum in Workshop 2.) Are you stuck with the choice? Not necessarily. If

plaintiff has filed in state court, and the case qualifies for federal jurisdiction, you may be able to remove the case to the U.S. district court sitting in the same state. See Chapter 2 for a discussion of removal. If plaintiff has filed in U.S. District Court in State X, it may be possible to get the case transferred to the U.S. District Court for State Y, if the case can be more conveniently litigated there. And in a suit that could have been brought in more than one state, there may be ways (beyond the scope of this text) to force the suit into the courts of a different state.

4. *Move to Dismiss for Lack of Jurisdiction, Improper Service, Etc.* If you file an answer to the complaint, you are, by definition, addressing the merits of plaintiff's case. But before the court can adjudicate the merits of the case, plaintiff must cross a number of procedural hurdles. The court must have jurisdiction of the subject matter, jurisdiction of defendant's person, venue must be proper, process must have been correctly served, any indispensable parties must be included, and any other procedural prerequisites must have been satisfied.

If procedural defects of this kind occur, defendant may prefer not to file an answer. There is a tendency for judges to interpret the filing of an answer as, in effect, consent by defendant to proceed on the merits. Whether filing an answer constitutes a waiver of jurisdictional and venue defenses depends on the situation, but why take the chance if there is some other way to raise these defenses? And there is: a motion to dismiss under FRCP, Rule 12.

FRCP, Rule 12(b), authorizes a defendant to file a motion to dismiss instead of an answer, to raise defenses involving jurisdiction, venue, service of process, and failure to join an indispensable party. We will study motions to dismiss in greater detail in Workshop 16, and we mention them now merely as a part of our discussion of the various options that a defendant has other than filing an answer.

A defendant who files a motion to dismiss under FRCP, Rule 12(b), does not have to file an answer until 10 days after the court rules on the motion to dismiss (obviously, there is no point to dealing with the merits if the whole lawsuit might be dismissed); see FRCP, Rule 12(a)(4). And, of course, if the court grants the motion to dismiss, the lawsuit is over and defendant does not have to answer at all, ever!

5. *Negotiate a Settlement.* In most lawsuits, one of the first things that defendant's attorney does after receiving the complaint is to contact plaintiff's attorney and explore whether there is some way to make the suit go away. (Experience teaches that most lawsuit settlements occur either soon after the complaint is filed, or not until the case is about to go to trial. Can you see why?)

A settlement may simply involve defendant paying plaintiff some money to drop the case, or it may require some much more complicated deal between plaintiff and defendant. Either way, the parties avoid the risk, expense, and aggravation of litigating on the merits.

6. *Move to Dismiss for Failure to State a Claim.* Suppose plaintiff sues defendant for doing something that is not actionable, something that the law simply does not regard as illegal. An example will make this clearer: Wanda Walker is out taking her daily stroll one day, accompanied by her best friend Betty. When they finish their walk, Wanda continues down the sidewalk toward her home, while Betty starts across the street in another direction. Suddenly, a pickup truck, driven by Dave Drinker, careens through a red light, striking Betty and killing her in full view of Wanda. Wanda is understandably distraught and depressed, and would like to sue. But, according to the law of torts in every state of which the authors are aware, the law does not make someone who causes an accident liable to others who merely witness the accident, if they are not physically injured in some way, or at least threatened with injury.

Suppose Wanda does sue. Must the case go all the way through a trial? No. FRCP, Rule 12(b)(6), allows Dave's attorney to file a motion to dismiss for failure to state a claim on which relief can be granted. In effect, Dave's attorney is saying to the court, "Even if everything happened exactly the way it says in Wanda's complaint, Wanda is still not entitled to judgment. The allegations of Wanda's complaint, even if every one of them is true, do not describe something that the law regards as actionable."

Motions to dismiss of this kind bear a close relationship to motions for summary judgment. We will take up both in much more detail in Workshop 14. For our present purposes, it suffices merely to be aware that the option exists to ask the court to decide, *before the answer is filed,* whether the allegations of the complaint, if taken as true, describe conduct that the law allows people to sue for.

Must defendant move to dismiss in order to raise the defense of failure to state a claim? No, defendant is free to include the defense in her answer (and should always do so, as we will shortly see).

If defendant does decide to move to dismiss under FRCP, Rule 12(b)(6), for failure to state a claim, and the court rules in favor of plaintiff, then, as with other motions to dismiss, defendant has until 10 days after the court's ruling in which to file an answer.

**7.** *Move for a More Definite Statement.* FRCP, Rule 12(e), offers still another possible countermove to someone who has just been sued. If plaintiff's complaint is so "vague or ambiguous" that defendant cannot reasonably be required to respond to it, then, instead of filing an answer, defendant can ask the court to order plaintiff to rewrite the complaint! We will revisit the subject of motions for more definite statement in Workshop 16.

---

**Your Local Notes**

_____

_____

---

## STRATEGIC CONSIDERATIONS AND THE ROLE OF THE PARALEGAL

Defendant's objectives in a lawsuit are (usually) several:

**1.** To avoid having to pay money to plaintiff, if possible;

**2.** If it is necessary to pay, to delay payment as long as possible; and

**3.** To keep the costs of the suit (legal fees, discovery costs, etc.) to a minimum.

Of the options we have discussed, which best achieves those goals depends on the circumstances.

If defendant has no insurance, and has no assets that could be seized to satisfy a judgment, then, as we have seen, bankruptcy or simply defaulting may offer defendant the best outcome. Suits against uninsured individuals often follow this path.

If defendant has a weak case, and the amount of money at stake is large compared to the legal costs, defendant may prefer simply to delay the day of reckoning for as long as possible, and will do anything that makes the suit take longer. [In theory, it is against the rules and unethical for an attorney to make moves in a lawsuit whose only purpose is to cause delay, see FRCP, Rule 11(b). In practice, litigation attorneys can always think of some "legitimate" reason for taking any action, and if delay is caused,

that is purely a side effect, of course! We will consider the ethical implications of delaying tactics, as well as other ethical issues that arise in litigation, in Workshop 19. The delaying game—the litigation equivalent of the four-corner offense—is a tactic most commonly used by large corporate or government defendants.]

If there are legal issues that, if resolved in defendant's favor, would end the case, then a pre-answer motion under FRCP, Rule 12(b), may be the strategy of choice.

Finally, if the decision is to seize the bull by the horns and get on with defending the suit on the merits, the choice will likely be to prepare and file an answer.

Advising a client on the strategy to follow in defending a lawsuit obviously requires legal judgment and experience of the highest order, and strategic decisions of this kind must ultimately be made by the responsible attorney. This does not, of course, prevent paralegals from participating in such decisions, and most supervising attorneys will willingly explain the reasons behind a given strategic choice to a paralegal who demonstrates a desire to learn and understand.

Paralegals are often assigned to draft the papers to implement the choices made by the supervising attorney. Highly complex answer drafting of the kind needed in, for example, commercial litigation, is usually a task for attorneys, but answer preparation in cases that do not require a deep understanding of some specialty area of the law (routine auto accident cases, for example) is very definitely a suitable assignment for paralegals. The depth with which you understand the purposes of and reasons behind the tasks that you are assigned will have a strong influence on how well you do them.

---

**Your Local Notes**

_____

_____

---

## *Answer Drafting: Step-by-Step Instructions*

Just as the complaint is the document that defines the issues that plaintiff intends to present to the court, the answer is the document that defines the issues from defendant's standpoint. An answer is, first and foremost, a point-by-point response to the allegations of the complaint. FRCP, Rule 8(b), requires the answer to "admit or deny the averments" of the complaint. In the drafting steps discussed later, we will see how this is done.

As with complaint drafting, however, we have some homework to do before we can start writing. We have seen that to draft a proper complaint, plaintiff must first research the claims that he intends to assert, so as to be sure of correctly alleging all of the required elements of each cause of action. To draft a proper answer, defendant must of course investigate each of the facts alleged in plaintiff's complaint, since FRCP, Rule 8(b) requires defendant to admit or deny each one. More than this, however, defendant must be able to correctly allege all of the required elements of each affirmative defense to be raised, and to identify any missing elements in plaintiff's causes of action. The legal and factual research required in order to prepare an answer is not, therefore, very different from that required to draft a complaint.

**The Objectives of Answer Drafting**—As we proceed to draft an answer, it is important for us to keep in mind the objectives that we are trying to accomplish when we do so. Let us try to list some of them:

1. We wish to avoid a default. Therefore, we must file an answer at least minimally satisfying FRCP, Rule 8, before the deadline for doing so has passed.

2. We wish to avoid setting ourselves up for a quick summary judgment in plaintiff's favor. Therefore, we must take care to offer defenses of some kind to each of plaintiff's causes of action.

3. We wish to comply with our ethical obligations. Therefore, we must be sure that we have a reasonable basis for believing in the truth of whatever we assert in the answer.

4. We wish to produce a document that, when the judge reads it, will quickly and concisely convey defendant's side of the dispute and enable the judge to discern exactly what are the issues on which plaintiff and defendant disagree.

5. We wish to avoid losing any potential defenses by accidentally leaving them out. Therefore we must do careful legal research and factual investigation to be sure that we have identified all of the possible defenses.

**Your Local Notes**

_____

_____

## PREPARATORY STEPS

**Step 1** *Determine When Responsive Pleading Is Due*

We do not repeat here the details of deadline computation, a subject on which, after completing Workshop 7, you should now be an expert!

It is worth pointing out, however, that complaints needing to be answered typically arrive on a defense attorney's desk only after being brought in by some prospective client—sometimes with only a day or two left before the answer deadline. The deadline for filing an answer depends on when and how the complaint was served, facts of which the defense attorney has no direct knowledge and about which clients are notoriously imprecise. The defense attorney's first job, therefore—and the first job of an intake paralegal given responsibility for screening prospective clients—is to nail down the answer deadline. The importance of doing so cannot be overstated.

Often, the easiest way to solve the deadline problem is simply to make an agreement with plaintiff's attorney that the answer will be due on an agreed date. In many jurisdictions, extensions of time to file answers are requested and given routinely. The attorneys involved must, of course, take care to satisfy any formalities required by local rules in documenting the extension. A caveat: A paralegal should not initiate calls to opposing attorneys unless her supervising attorney has specifically authorized it.

Needless to say, once the deadline date has been established, it must be entered in the firm's central calendar and in the calendars of the responsible attorney and paralegal.

**Step 2** *Assemble the Basic Factual Information*

It is actually possible to draft a reasonably workable answer to the typical complaint even with relatively little knowledge of the facts of the case. Plaintiff has the burden of telling a complete and consistent story with sufficient detail to establish a legally recognized cause of action. Defendant is not required to provide a counterstory, and is free to file an answer simply denying everything in the complaint and alleging a generic set of affirmative defenses. This is obviously the easiest way to prepare an answer, and avoids the hazard of accidentally admitting some fact that will later turn out to be damaging.

We do not recommend this approach. In a lawsuit, the attorney who is first to fully grasp the facts of the case and the elements of each cause of action will have numerous opportunities to "steal the ball" from an opponent who is operating in the dark. This is especially true in the growing number of jurisdictions that have adopted rules requiring each side to file disclosure statements early in the case.

How should a defense attorney or paralegal approach the problem of factual investigation? The first step, of course, is to obtain as much information as possible from the client. Here are some examples of the kinds of things the defense attorney or paralegal should obtain from the client:

- A complete narrative of what happened;

- A clear understanding of whom you are being asked to represent (see sidebar);

- Names, addresses, and phone numbers of everyone involved;

- Names, addresses, and phone numbers of any possible witnesses; and

- A list of all documents that may bear on the case (with copies, if possible, and leads to follow in obtaining copies, if not).

Obviously, much more information than this will be needed, depending on the facts and the type of case. As with plaintiff's attorneys, defense firms that specialize in a particular type of case (such as insurance defense) often use a standard client questionnaire to be sure that basic facts are not overlooked.

In addition to understanding the factual background of the case—the "story"—the defense attorney or paralegal has another, more specific task: that of checking each and every fact alleged in plaintiff's complaint. There is a temptation, in answering the more mundane allegations in a complaint, to simply admit the unimportant-seeming ones without checking. We recommend that you resist the temptation. It is amazing how often some seemingly trivial and insignificant fact later turns out to be the very one that blows a huge hole in your case! (We will have a good deal more to say about the art of admitting and denying facts when we study Step 8.)

---

*Your Local Notes*

_____

_____

_____

---

## SIDEBAR

## Multiple Parties: Who Are You Answering For?

*One of the questions that a defense attorney or paralegal must address at the outset is "Who would I be representing?" It is very common for a lawsuit to name more than one defendant, and for the needs of various defendants to conflict with each other. Accordingly, it is essential that the attorney not only run the usual new-client conflict check to ensure that the representation does not create a conflict of interest with existing clients of the firm, the attorney must also ensure that he does not create a conflict by agreeing to represent defendants who will potentially need to make cross-claims against each other. Multiple-defendant lawsuits can pose knotty ethical problems, which we will visit in Workshop 19.*

*Often, your firm may decide to represent defendants A and B, whereas defendants C through Z are represented by other attorneys. Then who files the answer? Typically, each attorney files a separate answer for the defendants she is representing. Instead of being titled simply "Answer" in the caption, the document will be titled "Separate Answer of Defendants A and B." In writing the answer, the phrase "these answering defendants" will be used instead of simply "defendants" (which would imply all defendants). Example: "These answering defendants deny the allegations of paragraph 5," instead of "defendants deny the allegations of paragraph 5."*

---

| **Step 3** | *Decide Whether Anyone Else Needs to Be in the Suit* |

One of the decisions that a defense attorney must make before answering the complaint is whether there are any claims that should be made against others who are not parties to the lawsuit. A simple example will help clarify the problem: Your cousin Al is trying to buy a car, but, Al's credit history being what it is, the dealer will not write the loan without a cosigner. You agree to cosign, the loan is made, and off goes Al with the car. Later (as inevitably seems to happen to cosigners) Al falls on bad times and is unable to make the payments. The lender sues you for the money. Your reaction, quite correctly, is "Wait a minute—if I have to pay this, Al has to pay *me*." But Al is not named as a defendant in the lawsuit. Now what do you do?

You bring Al into the suit yourself, via a third-party claim. A third-party claim is a claim that you make in your answer against someone who is not already named as a plaintiff or defendant in the complaint.

As to the third-party claim, you are the third-party plaintiff, and the person you are bringing into the suit—Cousin Al, in this case—is the third-party defendant. The third-party claim must, of course, be served on the third-party defendant in the same way that a complaint would be served, and the third-party defendant must file an answer to it.

The form of a third-party claim is similar to that of a claim in a complaint. It must allege all of the required elements of some cause of action, and include an appropriate prayer for relief. Typically, the third-party claim is tacked on at the end of the answer. We have purposely omitted any third-party claim from the example answer provided later in this workshop, so as to avoid overly complicating our introduction to answer drafting. At this stage of your paralegal education, we simply want you to be aware that mechanisms do exist for adding new parties to the suit—you are not stuck with plaintiff's choice of defendants.

---

**Your Local Notes**

_____

_____

---

# SIDEBAR

## Indispensable Parties

*Sometimes a claim needs to be made against someone who is not named in the complaint, but it is impossible to bring that person into the suit. What if, for example, Cousin Al is now living somewhere in Brazil, address unknown, and you have no way to serve process on him. In such situations, the judge must decide whether the person to be added is an **indispensable party**; that is, whether, "in equity and good conscience," a just result cannot be achieved without (in our example) Al's presence in the suit.*

*If the judge deems Cousin Al an indispensable party, the suit is dismissed; otherwise, the suit simply continues against you, without benefit of Cousin Al's presence. (How the judge decides this is outlined in FRCP, Rule 19, as supplemented by a good deal of case law. In our example, Al would not be considered an indispensable party. Sorry, but a trained paralegal such as yourself should know better than to act as a cosigner!)*

---

| Step 4 | *Research the Elements of the Claims to Which You Are Responding* |

We have spent considerable time, in Workshop 1 (Claims and Their Elements) and again in Workshop 5 (Drafting Pleadings: Complaints), learning to analyze a cause of action or defense in terms of its elements. Rightly so; claims and elements of claims are the basic building blocks with which litigators work, and almost every task in a lawsuit requires that you understand how to use and analyze them.

As we have seen, plaintiff must draft the complaint in such a way as to allege each element of each cause of action being asserted. If plaintiff is suing for negligence, for example, then the complaint must allege facts establishing each of the elements of negligence.

The answer is constructed somewhat differently. There are essentially three ways in which defendant can defeat a cause of action asserted by plaintiff in the complaint:

1. If plaintiff's complaint leaves out a required element;

2. If plaintiff is unable to prove the facts supporting a required element; and

3. If defendant establishes an affirmative defense.

An example will make this clearer. In our hypo, Shannon is suing Dr. Collins for battery. In Workshop 1, we found that the elements of the tort of battery are (1) an act; (2) which is intended to cause harmful or offensive contact; (3) harmful or offensive contact does in fact occur; and (4) damages are proximately caused by the act.

Suppose Shannon, in her complaint, alleged that Dr. Collins committed an act by throwing himself on top of her; that in doing so he caused harmful or offensive contact; and that his act proximately caused Shannon to be injured. Is there a problem? Yes, indeed; element (2) is missing. Intent has not been alleged. Result? The complaint fails to state a claim on which relief can be granted, and unless the defect is fixed (typically, by amending the complaint), defendant wins.

Now suppose that Shannon properly alleges all four elements of the tort of battery in her complaint, but, at trial, is unable to *prove* that Dr. Collins intended to make physical contact. Suppose, for example, that Dr. Collins testifies that he simply fell on top of Shannon because he was unable to stand up after being shot, and produces an expert witness who testifies that Shannon's finger was broken by the recoil of the gun. If the jury believes defendant's evidence, then, again, defendant wins because plaintiff has failed to *prove* all of the elements of the tort of battery.

Obviously, to know whether plaintiff has missed any required elements of a given cause of action, the attorney or paralegal representing defendant must know what the required elements are. If the suit involves routine causes of action (i.e., automobile negligence) that are already very familiar and well understood, no actual research may be required. In more complicated cases (i.e., commercial cases), the wise defense attorney or paralegal completes the analysis we learned about in Workshop 1 before starting to draft an answer.

### Step 5 — Determine the Elements of the Affirmative Defenses You Intend To Raise

To continue our examination of the three ways in which defendant can win, let us suppose that Shannon properly alleges all four elements of battery in her complaint, and convinces the jury that all four have been proved. Now does she win? Not necessarily. Defendant has one more way of defeating plaintiff's claim: Defendant can prove an affirmative defense. An affirmative defense is a defense that relies on factual issues not raised in the complaint. Instead of contesting plaintiff's facts, it adds some new ones. Dr. Collins might, for example, allege and prove that he acted in self-defense. Self-defense is an affirmative defense to the tort of battery. If Dr. Collins persuades the jury that he acted in self-defense, he wins, even though Shannon has proved that he committed battery.

For purposes of drafting an answer, affirmative defenses work much the same way that causes of action do in the complaint. Affirmative defenses have elements, and defendant must allege facts supporting each element in the answer. To do so, it is necessary to know what the required elements are for each affirmative defense being asserted. Again, the analysis described in Workshop 1 is necessary.

> *Your Local Notes*
> _____
> _____

## DRAFTING STEPS

### Step 6 — Prepare the Caption

In Workshop 4, we learned how to prepare the formal parts of a court paper: the caption, date and signature lines, and certificate of service. Our answer will use what we prepared. The caption will be copied from plaintiff's complaint, except that the title will now be "Answer," or, if we represent only Smith and Jones and there are other defendants as well, "Separate Answer of Defendants Smith and Jones."

### Step 7 — The Preamble and Numbering Systems

Immediately below the caption, we begin the body of the answer. First comes the preamble. Common phraseology is "Defendant(s), for his (her, its, their) answer to plaintiff's complaint, admits, denies, and alleges as follows:" (If we represent less than all defendants, then we would write: "Defendants Smith and Jones, for their answer to plaintiff's complaint, admit, deny, and allege as follows:") Your instructor will advise you if some other language is preferred under the customs of your locality.

Like complaints, answers are organized in numbered paragraphs. In numbering the paragraphs of the answer, you are not required to use the same numbering system as used by plaintiff in the complaint—you are free to use your own system. Our preference, for the reasons given in Step 4 of Workshop 5, is to use ordinary Arabic numerals at the beginning (side) of each paragraph.

Note that the numbers of the paragraphs of the answer have nothing to do with the numbers of the paragraphs of the complaint. The paragraphs of the answer are numbered sequentially; the answer will *refer* to the paragraphs of the complaint by number, but its own paragraphs are numbered in their own sequence.

> *Your Local Notes*
> _____
> _____

### Step 8 — Respond to Allegations of Complaint

Now we come—at last!—to the part of the answer in which we get to respond to all of the unpleasant things that plaintiff has said about our client! FRCP, Rule 8(b), requires us to answer each of the allegations of the complaint. FRCP, Rule 8, gives us essentially five tools to use in responding to a paragraph of the complaint:

1. We can deny the whole paragraph.

2. We can admit the whole paragraph.

3. We can admit part and deny part.

4. We can state that we are "without knowledge or information sufficient to form a belief as to the

truth" of the paragraph, which, under FRCP, Rule 8(b), has the same effect as a denial.

5. We can, after admitting or denying, allege something new if we need to in order to get an important point across.

Now let us try a few examples and see how we might use these tools.

**Example 1: A Simple Admission**—In the example complaint that we presented in Workshop 5 (see Figure W5–1), paragraph 1 alleged:

> 1. Plaintiff Shannon Martin is a resident of Maricopa County, Arizona.

Suppose we represent defendant Park Hotels Group, Inc. How would we answer this paragraph?

First, if we are doing our job properly, we would find out whether Shannon Martin is indeed a resident of Maricopa County, Arizona. (Why? For one thing, if she turned out not to be an Arizona resident, the U.S. district court's jurisdiction might be affected. We reiterate the importance of *checking every fact.*) Suppose we conclude that, yes, paragraph 1 is true, and we decide to admit it. (Should we? See sidebar.) What language do we use to express our admission? The following is customary:

> 1. Answering paragraph 1, admits the allegations thereof.

*Who* admits the allegations thereof? The preamble supplies the subject of the sentence: defendant Park Hotels Group. Where appropriate (see Example 3) we will specify.

**Example 2: A Simple Denial**—Now suppose that, instead, we decided to deny paragraph 1. What would we write?

> 1. Answering paragraph 1, denies the allegations thereof.

No surprises here.

**Example 3: A Denial for Lack of Information**—Having disposed of paragraph 1, let us attack paragraph 2 of the example complaint from Workshop 5. It alleges:

> 2. Defendants Arthur Collins and Jane Doe Collins are residents of Dallas County, Texas. Defendant Jane Doe Collins is the wife of defendant Arthur Collins. At all times material hereto, defendant Arthur Collins acted both individually and on behalf of the marital community consisting of defendants Arthur Collins and Jane Doe Collins. Plaintiff does not know the true identity of defendant Jane Doe Collins, and will seek leave to amend her complaint to reflect such true identity after

ascertaining it. Defendant Arthur Collins caused an act or event to occur in the state of Nevada out of which plaintiff's claims arose.

Remember, we represent Park Hotels Group, Inc. Our client does not have a clue about whether Dr. Collins is married, and if so to whom. As for whether Dr. Collins did something in Nevada out of which plaintiff's claim arose—that is what the whole lawsuit is about, so we certainly aren't about to admit that! On the other hand, we really have no factual basis to deny these things, either. What do we do? This is a perfect opportunity to use the tool that FRCP, Rule 8(b), gives us, which allows us to deny on account of lack of knowledge. (Notice that we use the exact language of Rule 8 in phrasing the reason for our denial.)

> 2. Answering paragraph 2, defendant Park Hotels Group is without knowledge or information sufficient to form a belief as to the truth of the allegations of said paragraph, and therefore denies them.

(Some drafters would say "this answering defendant" instead of "defendant Park Hotels Group"; we prefer to avoid depersonalizing our own client whenever possible.)

---

### SIDEBAR

## To Deny or Not to Deny?: That Is the Question

*What do we do with facts that we are sure plaintiff can prove?*

*This question brings up one of the ways in which the styles of litigators differ. Some litigators prefer an aggressive style—deny everything! Make plaintiff prove it! Defendant has (in theory) the right to make plaintiff prove every single fact, however obvious, and some litigators would say "Why give anything away?" After all, if we make plaintiff spend energy and money proving the obvious, plaintiff will have that much less energy and money to spend proving facts that might really hurt our case!*

*Other litigators would prefer to concede the facts that the opponent will clearly be able to prove anyway, and save their ammunition for the truly contested issues. Our own preference tends toward the latter view, in part because excessive contentiousness over trivia has a way of annoying judges and juries.*

*Deciding where along the scale of provability the line should be drawn is a judgment call, and not always an easy one. Most litigators would choose to err on the side of caution—if there is any doubt, and especially if the fact is harmful, deny.*

## Example 4: Answering Several Paragraphs at Once

—We are not restricted to answering plaintiff's complaint one paragraph at a time. Where convenient, we may lump several paragraphs together. Here is another way that we might have answered paragraphs 1 and 2:

> 1. Answering paragraphs 1 and 2, defendant Park Hotels Group is without knowledge or information sufficient to form a belief as to the truth of the allegations of said paragraphs, and therefore denies them.

Why would we want to do this?: At the risk of repetition, the main purpose of *every* written submission to the court is to advocate our client's cause to the reader. Space wasted on endless single-paragraph denials is space that we cannot use to say something that might advance our own case.

Notice that, since we answered paragraphs 1 and 2 of the complaint in paragraph 1 of the answer, the next paragraph of the answer will be paragraph 2, even though we will use it to answer paragraph 3 of the complaint.

## Example 5: Admit in Part, Deny in Part

—The third paragraph of our example complaint alleges:

> 3. Defendant Park Hotels Group (hereinafter "Hotel") is a corporation organized and existing under the laws of the state of Delaware, and doing business in the state of Nevada out of which plaintiff's claim arose.

We (representing Park Hotels Group) agree that we are a Delaware corporation and that we do business in Nevada, but we are certainly not going to admit that plaintiff's claim arose from anything we did. (The problem is not that the legal issues would be affected by our doing so—they would not—the problem is that pleadings can be read to the jury and we do not want to give plaintiff any opening to imply that we admitted fault.) Therefore, we respond:

> 2. Answering paragraph 3, defendant Park Hotels Group admits that it is a corporation organized and existing under the laws of the state of Delaware, admits that it does business in the state of Nevada, and denies that plaintiff's claim arose from the business done by it.

## Example 6: Admit/Deny Plus Add New Allegations

—Now let us try a more challenging example, using paragraph 6 of the example complaint from Workshop 5. The paragraph we are answering alleges:

> 6. At approximately 1:15 A.M. on the morning of February 6, 1996, plaintiff Shannon Martin was asleep in her hotel room at the Banbury Park Hotel. Prior to retiring, plaintiff closed and locked the door of her room. Defendant Arthur Collins, a stranger to plaintiff, using a key provided by defendant Banbury Park Hotel, entered plaintiff's room, stood at the foot of plaintiff's bed, and began removing his clothes.

Obviously, if we represent Park Hotels, we will deny everything in this paragraph, but we would also like to get across the idea that we gave Dr. Collins the key to his own room, not the key to Shannon's room. Here is one way:

> 5. (or whatever number we are up to) Answering paragraph 6, defendant Park Hotels Group denies that defendant Arthur Collins used a key provided by Banbury Park Hotel to enter plaintiff's hotel room, and alleges that the only key provided by Banbury Park Hotel to defendant Arthur Collins was the key to his own room, and that said key was not capable of being used to unlock the door to plaintiff's hotel room. Defendant Park Hotels Group is without knowledge or information sufficient to form a belief as to the truth of the remaining allegations of said paragraph, and therefore denies them.

Notice how, by including an allegation of our own, we begin educating the reader about our own version of the facts (see sidebar).

**SIDEBAR**

## Getting Our Own Story Told

*You may be wondering where, exactly, is the part of the answer where we get to tell defendant's side of the story? Unfortunately, the rules, as usually interpreted, do not allow us a General Allegations section of the kind that we used in the complaint (unless we assert counterclaims, in which case we would write the counterclaim section in much the same way as if we were writing a complaint). In the answer proper, we are limited to responding to the allegations made by plaintiff.*

*How, then, do we communicate our client's version of the facts?: Mainly, by including explanatory allegations of the kind used in Example 6. One word of caution: An answer is supposed to give our client's version of the facts, not present evidence. We might be tempted, for example, to mention that the police investigation showed that the key in Dr. Collins's possession was the key to his own room. Should we? How far one should go down this road is a judgment call, and varies with local custom. Your instructor will advise you on the level of advocacy considered proper in your locality.*

Using the techniques you have just learned, we go through the complaint paragraph by paragraph, responding to each one, until we reach the end. At the end of the complaint, we come to the prayer for relief—do we admit or deny it, too? No, we will present our own prayer for relief at the end of our answer. Before doing so, however, we have a few other details to take care of.

## Step 9  *Include the Boilerplate Defenses*

We have now responded to every allegation of the complaint. Or did we? We responded to every *paragraph,* but what if, while we were doing all of this admitting, denying, and alleging, we accidentally overlooked some phrase somewhere? FRCP, Rule 8(d), says that allegations are deemed "admitted when not denied in the responsive pleading." We don't want to risk that, so we protect ourselves with the following, which should be included in every answer:

10. (or whatever number we are up to) Defendant Park Hotels Group denies each and every allegation of plaintiff's complaint not expressly admitted herein.

## Step 10  *Include Specific Affirmative Defenses*

At this point, we have taken care of the elements of the causes of action alleged by plaintiff; now we need to allege our affirmative defenses. We have already done our research to determine what the elements are of each affirmative defense that we intend to raise, if any. This is the place in the complaint at which we do so. Depending on local custom, we may begin with a new section heading, Affirmative Defenses, or we may use a new heading for each affirmative defense; paragraph numbering, however, continues in sequence.

**Example**—Here are two paragraphs alleging self-defense as they might appear in Dr. Collins's answer. (See Workshop 1 for the elements of the affirmative defense of self-defense.) Notice how we begin by taking the opportunity to tell part of our story, so that anyone (i.e., the judge) skimming our answer will immediately understand why we are claiming self-defense, without having to look elsewhere in the file for the facts:

13. (or whatever the next number is) Plaintiff aimed her pistol in the direction of defendant Dr. Arthur Collins and fired, striking him in the abdomen and critically injuring him. Only then, confronted by plaintiff's evident intention to continue firing her pistol at him, did defendant Dr. Arthur Collins attempt to take plaintiff's pistol from her.

14. In using physical force against plaintiff, defendant Dr. Arthur Collins acted for the purpose of defending himself against plaintiff, who was at the time brandishing and repeatedly firing a pistol with the evident intention of injuring or killing him. The acts of plaintiff in doing so were not privileged. Defendant Dr. Arthur Collins did not intend to cause death or serious bodily harm to plaintiff, and used force which was reasonable in the circumstances and was not likely to cause death or serious bodily harm.

If we have other affirmative defenses, we include them in sequence.

## Step 11  *Include a Boilerplate Defense*

There is one defense that we include in every answer: failure to state a claim. Why? Actually, it is not necessary to do so for legal reasons—the defense is not waived if we leave it out; see FRCP, Rule 12(h)(2). It is, however, customary. A standard boilerplate paragraph suffices:

15. Plaintiff's complaint fails to state a claim upon which relief can be granted.

There are other defenses that *can be* lost if omitted from the answer. FRCP, Rule 8(c), requires an answer to "set forth affirmatively" any of the defenses listed in the rule.

It is wise to use FRCP, Rule 8(c), as a checklist of common defenses when deciding which defenses to raise in the answer; any Rule 8(c) defenses that have particular applicability to our case should be alleged separately, with enough facts to explain how they apply. What about those defenses that do not seem germane? Most litigators, probably out of an excess of caution, include a boilerplate paragraph listing them, so as to avoid any possible waiver. Whether the tactic works is debatable (we would be skeptical) but it is, again, commonplace. Here is a typical Rule 8(c) paragraph (do not be surprised if you have never heard of most of these defenses):

> 16. At this early stage of the case, defendant Park Hotels Group is unable to determine the applicability of the defenses enumerated in FRCP, Rule 8(c), but intends to preserve those defenses to the extent they should be deemed pertinent, and therefore affirmatively alleges the defenses of accord and satisfaction, arbitration and award, assumption of risk, contributory negligence, discharge in bankruptcy, duress, estoppel, failure of consideration, fraud, illegality, injury by fellow servant, laches, license, payment, release, res judicata, statute of frauds, statute of limitations, and waiver.

(We would suggest removing from the list any defenses that you are alleging separately in another paragraph, and any that obviously could have no possible bearing on your case.)

What about jurisdictional defenses? Are we forgetting something?: No, if we intend to claim that the court does not have jurisdiction, we can best do so via a motion to dismiss, which we would file and have heard before filing the answer.

---

*Your Local Notes*

_____

_____

---

## Step 12    *Prayer for Relief*

We have now finished the main part of the answer. Next comes the prayer for relief. Here is typical verbiage (consult your instructor for any local preferences):

> WHEREFORE, having fully defended, defendant Park Hotels Group, Inc. prays that plaintiff's complaint be dismissed, that plaintiff take nothing thereby, for defendant's costs and attorney's fees incurred herein, and for such other and further relief as to the Court seems just in the premises.

(Yes, we know; it is a bit flowery for our tastes, too. But—all together, now—*it's customary!*)

---

*Your Local Notes*

_____

_____

---

## Step 13    *Plead Counterclaims and Cross-Claims*

So, we're done, right?

Not so fast. Remember, the best defense is often a good offense. Why settle for dodging the other guy's bullets when you could be shooting a few back?

This is the point in our thought process where we consider what claims of our own we might have against the plaintiff, or other defendants. If we have any claims that we could bring against plaintiff in a separate suit, we can assert them here and now (and must do so if they are transactional; see sidebar). Likewise, if we have transactional causes of action against other defendants, we can (but are not required to) assert them as cross-claims.

From the drafter's standpoint, counterclaims and cross-claims are written and organized exactly as a complaint would be written (but without undue belaboring of facts already alleged in the complaint or in the first part of the answer). Counterclaims and cross-claims are tacked on at the end of the answer, rather than put into a separate filing. (In the caption, we title the document "Answer and Counterclaim" or "Answer and Cross-claim" instead of merely "Answer.") But in general, to write a counterclaim, we write exactly what we would write if we were drafting the body of complaint on behalf of the defendant and against plaintiff—including prayer for relief—and we copy-type it on to the end of the answer (after the answer's prayer for relief but before the signature lines).

The only problem that arises in approaching the problem this way is that, technically, the parties are referred to differently when we are talking about a counterclaim or cross-claim. In a counterclaim, if we wish to be excruciatingly proper, defendant—the person who is asserting the counterclaim—becomes the **counterclaimant,** and the plaintiff is referred to as the **counterdefendant.** Similarly, in a cross-claim, the defendant who is asserting the claim is the **cross-claimant** and the other defendant against whom it is asserted is the **cross-defendant.** All of this properness has the unfortunate side effect of making it nearly impossible for someone reading the answer to figure out who is doing what to whom, and our preference would therefore be to refer to the parties as before, always including their names, for instance, "defendant Arthur Collins" and "plaintiff Shannon Martin" rather than "counter-claimant" and "counterdefendant"—even at the risk of being slightly improper. (Local custom may dictate a different conclusion.)

No special effort is required to serve a counterclaim; plaintiff is already a party to the suit, the counterclaim is part of the answer, so simply mailing or delivering the answer to plaintiff's attorney suffices. The same principle applies to cross-claims; merely serving the answer on the other parties is all that is required.

---

*Your Local Notes*

_____

_____

---

**Step 14** | *Date, Signature, Certificate of Service, Verification*

Now we are, at last, done. The finishing touches—date, signature line, and certificate of service—are the same as for any other court paper (see Workshop 4).

---

## SIDEBAR

### Compulsory Counterclaims

*What if Dr. Collins prefers to press his cause of action against Shannon for battery by filing a separate suit against Shannon, instead of using it as a counterclaim in her suit? May he do so?*

*FRCP, Rule 13, is the rule that governs counterclaims and cross-claims. If plaintiff's cause of action against defendant and defendant's cause of action against plaintiff both arise from the same factual setting, they are said to be **transactional**; that is, in the words of FRCP, Rule 13, they arise from the same "transaction or occurrence."*

*Any transactional claims that defendant has are considered **compulsory counterclaims**, and will be lost if not raised in the existing lawsuit. Dr. Collins's battery claim is, of course, transactional because it arises from the same fact background as Shannon's claims. Therefore, it is a compulsory counterclaim, and Dr. Collins must litigate it as a counterclaim in this lawsuit. If he fails to do so his claim will be barred forever when this lawsuit is over.*

---

Answers are always signed by the *attorney* for defendant (see FRCP, Rule 11), *never* by the actual defendant unless some specific statute or rule requires it. (Nowadays, in most jurisdictions, requirements for defendant to sign or "verify" are rare.)

---

*Your Local Notes*

_____

_____

---

## CONCLUDING STEPS

Our drafting complete, we print our answer (or send it to word processing to be typed). When it is ready, we begin preparing to send it to the opposing parties.

---

## SIDEBAR

### Replies to Counterclaims

*If there are no counterclaims or cross-claims, then the pleading process is over when the answer is filed. Even if plaintiff disagrees with the things defendant says in the answer (as most plaintiffs do), plaintiff does not get to file a rebuttal. According to FRCP, Rule 7(a), "there shall be a complaint and an answer," and that's all—no other pleading is allowed.*

*If, however, defendant has asserted a counterclaim, FRCP, Rule 7(a), requires plaintiff to file a reply to it. The reply is like a "mini-answer" directed at the counterclaim. It is written in exactly the same way that an answer would be written, admitting and denying the paragraphs of the counterclaim. (Only the counterclaim—the reply does not attack the rest of the answer.)*

*Drafting a counterclaim is like drafting a complaint by the defendant against the plaintiff; drafting a reply is like drafting an answer to it. If you know how to draft an answer, you know how to draft a reply to a counterclaim!*

---

*Your Local Notes*

_____

_____

---

## Step 15    *Accuracy Check and Revisions*

First, we give it a careful read for accuracy. Have we spelled the names—especially our client's name—correctly? (We used a spell-checker, of course, but proper names may still be spelled incorrectly.) Have we double-checked every factual statement for accuracy? Made sure we have included all of the defenses that we intended to? Read every sentence to be sure each is grammatically correct and, more importantly, easy to follow and understand?

Next, we have our client read the draft, with instructions to call our attention to any inaccuracies. Clients are sometimes reluctant to give this task the time and attention it requires; if necessary, we must insist, or read the answer with them.

When we are sure that we have produced a high-quality product, we have our answer reprinted in final form and pass it to the supervising attorney for her signature. Then it is ready for filing and service.

## Step 16    *File and Serve*

Usually, we will have a process server or messenger take the original answer to the clerk of the court for filing. Many courts charge a filing fee for filing an answer, and the firm's check in the required amount accompanies the filing.

Answers are served in the same way as other court papers subsequent to the complaint (see Workshop 7). Typically, a copy will be mailed or hand delivered to plaintiff's attorney, and to each attorney representing any of the other defendants.

# Answer Drafting: Learning by Example

We will now use what we have learned to draft an answer on behalf of our hypothetical defendant, Park Hotels Group, Inc.

## PREPARATORY STEPS

## Step 1    *Determine When Responsive Pleading Is Due*

In the circumstances of our hypo, Park Hotels Group, Inc., will likely learn of the suit when its designated agent is served and forwards the complaint to the corporation's management. If Park Hotels has liability insurance, its next step will be to contact the insurance carrier. The insurance carrier will be obligated to defend the suit on behalf of Park Hotels and will choose an attorney. Most insurance companies have ongoing relationships with defense attorneys in each city, and work with the same attorneys almost exclusively. (For a defense attorney in need of cases to defend, insurance companies are the mother lode, so to speak, and slots in a major insurance company's stable of attorneys are highly coveted.) If Park Hotels does not have liability insurance (some companies self-insure) management will find and hire an attorney to defend the suit, probably with advice from their regular attorneys.

In our hypo, Park Hotels hires Gail Stoddard. She could probably determine the exact date of service by checking with the designated agent on whom the complaint was served. More likely, however, she will simply telephone Allen Porter, and an answer date will be agreed on.

## Step 2    *Assemble the Basic Factual Information*

Gail Stoddard (and her paralegals) must now inform themselves of the facts of the suit. They will assemble as much documentation as is available by obtaining police reports and any records kept at the hotel, and will schedule interviews with the key Park Hotels employees.

## Step 3    *Decide Whether Anyone Else Needs to Be in the Suit*

Who else might Park Hotels Group consider bringing into the lawsuit? Certainly, they want Dr. Collins present, but plaintiff has already named him as a party. Who else? Investigation will be required. Possibilities include the manufacturer of the door lock (it might be defective; remember, Park Hotels likely does not know about Arnie Trevayne switching the keys); perhaps the contractor who installed it (it might have been installed wrong); conceivably the desk clerk, Arnie Trevayne (but not very likely, since Park Hotels will not want to risk losing control of him by having him represented by some other attorney). Unfortunately for Park Hotels, the chances of finding someone else to blame Shannon's injuries on seem scarce in the circumstances of this hypo.

## Step 4    *Research the Elements of the Claims to Which You Are Responding*

| **Step 5** | *Determine the Elements of the Affirmative Defenses You Intend To Raise* |

In a typical insurance defense firm, research assignments are given to new attorneys in their first year or two of practice. One of Crandall, Elkins associate attorneys will be assigned to research plaintiff's claims and any defenses that suggest themselves, and will write a memorandum summarizing his findings.

## DRAFTING STEPS

The finished product is shown in Figure W8–1. Park Hotels Group, Inc., has no obvious counterclaim to assert. A cross-claim for indemnification against Dr. Collins might be included, claiming, in effect, that if Park Hotels Group is found liable to plaintiff, then Dr. Collins is liable to reimburse Park Hotels Group since he is the one who actually injured plaintiff. In the interest of not overly complicating this introductory discussion, we elect not to include such a cross-claim.

---

**Figure W8–1   A Sample Answer**

### IN THE UNITED STATES DISTRICT COURT
### DISTRICT OF ARIZONA

| | |
|---|---|
| SHANNON MARTIN, a single woman, | ) |
| | ) |
| | ) NO. CV98 -01456 PHX RGS |
| Plaintiff, | ) |
| | ) |
| | ) SEPARATE ANSWER OF |
| vs. | ) DEFENDANT PARK |
| | ) HOTELS |
| | ) GROUP, INC. AND |
| | ) CROSS-CLAIM |
| | ) |
| ARTHUR COLLINS and JANE DOE | ) |
| COLLINS, husband and wife; PARK | ) |
| HOTELS GROUP, INC., a Delaware | ) |
| corporation; | ) |
| | ) |
| Defendants. | ) |
| _____ | ) |

Defendant Park Hotels Group, Inc., for its separate answer to plaintiff's complaint, admits, denies, and alleges as follows:

1.   Answering paragraphs 1 and 2, defendant Park Hotels Group, Inc. is without knowledge or information sufficient to form a belief as to the truth of the allegations of said paragraphs, and therefore denies them.

2.   Answering paragraph 3, admits that it is a corporation organized and existing under the laws of the state of Delaware, admits that it does business in the state of Nevada, and denies that plaintiff's claim arose from the business done by it.

3.   Answering paragraph 4, defendant Park Hotels Group, Inc. is without knowledge or information sufficient to form a belief as to the truth of the allegations of said paragraph, and therefore denies them.

4.   Answering paragraph 5, admits the allegations thereof.

5.   Answering paragraph 6, denies that defendant Arthur Collins used a key provided by Banbury Park Hotel to enter plaintiff's hotel room, and alleges that the only key provided by Banbury Park Hotel to defendant Arthur Collins was the key to his own room, and that said key was not capable of being used to unlock the door to plaintiff's hotel room. Defendant Park Hotels Group, Inc. is without knowledge or information sufficient to form a belief as to the truth of the remaining allegations of said paragraph, and therefore denies them.

**Figure W8–1   A Sample Answer,** *continued*

6.   Answering paragraphs 7 and 8, defendant Park Hotels Group, Inc. is without knowledge or information sufficient to form a belief as to the truth of the allegations of said paragraphs, and therefore denies them.

7.   Answering paragraphs 9 through 17, inclusive, denies the allegations thereof.

8.   Answering paragraph 18, defendant Park Hotels Group, Inc. admits that it had a duty of reasonable care toward plaintiff as it does to all hotel guests, and alleges that it fully complied with said duty. Defendant Park Hotels Group, Inc. denies the remaining allegations of paragraph 18, denies that it breached any duty toward plaintiff, specifically denies that it in any way allowed defendant Collins to gain possession of a key capable of operating the lock of plaintiff's room, and alleges that it at all material times acted properly and with due care.

9.   Answering paragraphs 19 through 21, inclusive, denies the allegations thereof.

10.   Defendant Park Hotels Group, Inc. denies each and every allegation of plaintiff's complaint not expressly admitted herein.

### AFFIRMATIVE DEFENSES

11.   Plaintiff's complaint fails to state a claim upon which relief can be granted

12.   At this early stage of the case, defendant Park Hotels Group, Inc. is unable to determine the applicability of the defenses enumerated in FRCP, Rule 8(c), but intends to preserve those defenses to the extent they should be deemed pertinent, and therefore affirmatively alleges the defenses of accord and satisfaction, arbitration and award, assumption of risk, contributory negligence, discharge in bankruptcy, duress, estoppel, failure of consideration, fraud, illegality, injury by fellow servant, laches, license, payment, release, res judicata, statute of frauds, statute of limitations, and waiver.

WHEREFORE, having fully defended, defendant Park Hotels Group, Inc. prays that plaintiff's complaint be dismissed, that plaintiff take nothing thereby, for defendant's costs and attorney's fees incurred herein, and for such other and further relief as to the Court seems just in the premises

DATED this _____ day of _____, 2000.

CRANDALL, ELKINS & MAJOR

_____

Gail Stoddard
Attorney for defendant
Park Hotels Group, Inc.

(Certificate of service goes here—see Workshop 4 for details.)

## CONCLUDING STEPS

The answer now complete, Gail Stoddard checks it for accuracy and faxes it to Park Hotels Group management for their review. When any necessary corrections have been completed, she signs the answer and turns it over to her legal secretary, who arranges for filing and delivery to the opposing attorneys.

## *Answer Drafting: Learning by Doing*

You have seen how Park Hotels Group might answer Shannon's complaint; now it is your turn. Assume that you are a paralegal in the office of Roger Yarborough, who represents defendant Collins. He hands you a copy of Shannon's complaint (see Workshop 5) and assigns you to draft an answer on behalf of Dr. Collins.

## EXERCISE

In carrying out this assignment, you should follow the step-by-step formula described in this workshop. You may skip Step 1 because we covered deadline problems separately in Workshop 7. For steps 2 through 5, make use of the work that you did in completing Workshops 1 and 3. For steps 6 and 14, use the form you prepared in Workshop 4.

## PRACTICE POINTERS
### *Working with Clients*

Not infrequently, clients become very distraught during the litigation process. One of the greatest assets a legal assistant can bring to a law firm is an ability to manage difficult or emotionally volatile clients. Attorneys often have neither the time, desire, nor ability to handle such clients and gladly defer to someone with superior human relations skills.

Particularly in a defense practice where attorneys have less control over the litigation process than do their plaintiff counterparts, attorneys often have all they can manage to adhere to deadlines and complete their legal work in a timely basis. They do not have time as well to wrestle with the emotional ups and downs of their clients. Some attorneys find client relations one of the most trying and frustrating of their responsibilities and will do everything possible to insulate themselves from clients. Additionally, clients who find themselves to be defendants are frustrated and angry at having been sued and expect the law firm not only to represent them but to be available to answer their concerns and to listen to them as they vent their feelings.

Since the attorney is more often than not unavailable to fulfill this role, the legal assistant often finds herself serving as the caretaker of the client. Good client relations often involve going beyond simply answering questions. It is being there to listen as the clients explain (yet one more time) why they feel a particular way, why they think they have been wronged, and why they believe the legal system is unjust. It means cultivating the patience that allows you to take the time to bolster client morale and encourage their perseverance when you would really like to spend that time meeting your own deadlines and tending to other tasks that demand your attention. It means answering client calls promptly even when you know what awaits you on the other end of that line.

This nonglamorous aspect of being a legal assistant is rarely addressed by legal textbooks but is an issue of which every practitioner is aware. Mastery of the art and science of client management is what separates the mediocre legal assistants from the really great ones and what makes some legal assistants such invaluable assets to their firms. To include yourself among this rarefied category of legal assistants, consider taking human relations and communications courses to begin developing these skills now. As importantly, seek out those who have a reputation for dealing effectively with others and find out their secrets. Then begin practicing now—with family members, friends, customers, or anyone who challenges your ability to remain calm and focused. Remember that you are developing a lifelong skill that will serve you no matter what your profession.

## TECHNO TIP

Setting up a pleadings page for use with line numbers is a difficult task. Prior to the use of computers the law firm's name was set out in the left-hand margin in portrait format on a preprinted page. Often two thin lines would appear to the right of the law firm's name to separate the name and address from the body of the pleading. In many forms, line numbers, double spaced, would appear just to the left of the two thin lines. When the information was typed on the form, the typist lined up the line numbers with the typed information.

With the advent of computers and word processors the use of preprinted forms waned. Printers were designed that could print in portrait and landscape mode on the same page, at the same time. Traditionalists wanted to keep the same look and wanted to print the pleading on plain paper and end up with the same format as when using preprinted paper. Using your word processor's line number function, and most popular word processors have them, is quite complicated. The caption is usually single spaced, the body of the pleading, except for quotes is usually double spaced. Charts, graphs, and other graphics are often not defined in line space terms. To generate a pleading page with line numbers in other than double-spaced text is beyond the capabilities of most students, legal secretaries, and all but the most knowledgeable users (of which group the authors are not).

The authors are not aware of any court that requires line numbers on pleadings. Most require only a certain minimum font size, predefined margins, and a page limitation. If line numbers are absolutely required by your firm, ask if you can use preprinted pleading pages. Hopefully line numbering will not be required.

## FORMS FILE

*Include samples of the following in your forms notebook:*

- An answer, including affirmative defenses
- An answer with counterclaims and cross-claims
- An answer with third-party claims
- A reply to a counterclaim

## KEY TERMS

| | | |
|---|---|---|
| **Automatic stay** | **Cross-claimant** | **Indispensable party** |
| **Compulsory counterclaims** | **Cross-defendant** | **Merits** |
| **Counterclaimant** | **Discharge in bankruptcy** | **Transactional** |
| **Counterdefendant** | **Exempt property** | |

# Introduction to the Discovery Workshops

*Discovery* refers to a set of procedural tools that we can use to extract information from unwilling or reluctant sources, including our opponent. What kinds of information?

- We can use discovery to gather the items of evidence that we will need to prove our case, or to disprove our opponent's case.

- We can use discovery to obtain other information that might help us *find* the evidence that we need.

- We can use discovery to find out about our opponent's case, and what our opponent plans to present at trial, so that we can better prepare to rebut it.

What, exactly, are these tools? As we will see, discovery in American courts has traditionally been "request centered"—when a party wants some piece of information, he or she must request it. The procedural tools most frequently used for doing so are these:

- The request for production of documents (FRCP, Rule, 34) allows us to obtain documents that are in the possession of an opposing party. The subpoena *duces tecum* allows us to obtain documents from persons that are not parties to our lawsuit.

- Interrogatories (FRCP, Rule 33) are written questions that we can submit to an opposing party, who must then provide written answers to them. Requests for admissions (FRCP, Rule 36) allow us to try to extract admissions from an opposing party.

- Depositions (FRCP, Rule 30) provide a means of taking and recording testimony from potential witnesses.

- Independent medical examinations (FRCP, Rule 35) allow us to have a physician of our choice examine an opposing party (commonly used by defendants in injury cases as a way of verifying the extent of plaintiff's injuries).

Although there is some local variation, the mechanics and procedural paperwork involved in using these discovery tools is essentially the same in most American jurisdictions.

## DISCOVERY REFORM AND MANDATORY DISCLOSURE

The last decade has seen the emergence of a reform movement advocating "disclosure-centered" discovery, in which parties are required to disclose information voluntarily without waiting for a request. The traditional discovery tools are still made available, but their use is greatly restricted so as to reduce costs. To understand what is going on, we need to understand what the reformers are trying to accomplish; for that, we need some background.

When the Federal Rules of Civil Procedure were adopted in 1938, the discovery rules that they embodied were seen as a radical change from prior practice. Before the federal rules, a party needing information or evidence from an opposing party could generally get it only by filing a motion and obtaining a court order. This state of affairs was wasteful and inefficient and—perhaps most importantly in terms of getting the rules changed—tedious for judges.

With the adoption of the federal rules, the pendulum swung hard in the opposite direction. Now litigants could, in effect, write their own tickets. Instead of needing a motion and a court order to make an opponent cough up a document or answer a question, all that would be needed was a written request, signed by the requesting attorney, which would be enforceable as though it *were* a court order!

The federal rules contemplated "open" discovery. Litigants could ask for—and opponents would be required to turn over—not only evidence, but, in the words of FRCP, Rule 26, anything "reasonably calculated to *lead* to admissible evidence." Open discovery, however, brought with it its own set of problems.

In the first place, it could easily be used as a tactical weapon. Litigators became adept at creating discovery requests whose real purpose was not to obtain useful information, but rather to force an opponent to expend huge quantities of money and legal talent compiling the data requested. Another problem was that lawyers were almost forced to carry open discovery to its limits. If the rules *allow* us to fish through every single record that an opponent has ever committed to paper in the last decade, can we safely stop short of doing so? Or would it be malpractice to leave any stone unturned?

By the 1970s and 1980s, in the view of many judges, the discovery tail was clearly wagging the dog. The cost of discovery in a typical lawsuit was all out of proportion to its contribution to the justness of the outcome. What could be done, short of requiring judges to micromanage the discovery in each lawsuit?

A few progressive courts experimented with tentative, and usually minor, changes. A typical one consisted of limiting the number of interrogatories allowed. Where, before, any party could send out long sets of written questions to be answered by an opposing party, with no limits on how many sets or how many questions in each set, henceforth each party would be limited to, say, 25 questions for the entire lawsuit. Such measures did little to contain the rising cost of litigation, but did serve to improve the skill of litigators in writing single questions that would take enormous work to answer! (Example, only slightly exaggerated: "State the substance of each and every communication had by any employee of defendant General Motors Corp. with any other person during the last 10 years, the subject matter of which involved any customer complaint regarding the quality or safety of any General Motors vehicle.")

In the 1990s, judicial dissatisfaction with perceived abuses came to a full boil, and, in jurisdiction after jurisdiction, the decision was made to shift to a different system of discovery, based on mandatory disclosure. The idea on which mandatory disclosure is based is this: Under the old system, if you wanted information, you had to ask for it—and describe what you wanted in clear enough terms that your opponent could not get away with hiding some crucial bit of evidence by claiming that your request was ambiguous. That process is inherently inefficient. Since the requesting party has no knowledge of what information is there to be discovered, he or she has no option but to ask to see everything there is. In some ways, traditional discovery is like the game "Battleship," in which each player tries to guess where the other player's ships are on a grid of squares.

Instead of putting the requesting party to the impossible task of firing requests off in the dark, why not simply *require* each party to disclose—without being asked—every bit of information in his possession that is relevant to any of the issues being litigated? Would not such an approach eliminate a great deal of the gamesmanship that had come to characterize the discovery process, and much of the paperwork as well? The old discovery tools might still be needed to flesh out the information voluntarily provided, but their use could now be greatly limited.

After some early experimentation in state courts (the authors' home state, Arizona, was at the forefront of the move to disclosure-based discovery), sweeping amendments were made in 1993 to the discovery provisions of the Federal Rules of Civil Procedure. Under the 1993 amendments:

- Each party to a lawsuit would be required, prior to a deadline set within a few months of the beginning of the suit, to make initial disclosures of several categories of information, including "all documents . . . in the possession, custody, or control of the party that are relevant to disputed facts alleged with particularity in the pleadings" [FRCP, Rule 26 (a)(1)(B)].

- At approximately the same time, the attorneys for all parties to the suit would be required to meet to discuss the case and develop a proposed discovery plan, setting forth the subjects on which additional discovery might be needed, proposed deadlines for accomplishing it, and indicating the extent to which the traditional discovery tools would be needed; see FRCP, Rule 26(f).

- The judge would review the proposed discovery plan, and perhaps hold a scheduling conference with the attorneys to discuss it. The judge would then enter a scheduling order, setting deadlines and specifying what discovery would be required or allowed; see FRCP, Rule 16(b).

Problem solved! Well, sort of. Of course, there were, and are, a few spoilsports who would argue that all we have done is create still another procedure for lawyers to argue about. The new rules do raise some difficult issues (see sidebar).

## LOCAL VARIATIONS

We have said that the mix of allowed discovery procedures varies greatly by locality. Why would that be? Surely, at least, the Federal Rules of Civil Procedure make discovery procedure uniform for all U.S. district courts?

Quite the contrary. When the U.S. Supreme Court adopted the 1993 amendments, it made them optional! Each U.S. district court was free to decide for itself whether to follow all of the changes, some of them, or none of them. At about the same time, Congress added to the confusion by passing legislation authorizing District Courts to look for ways to improve efficiency by experimenting with changes in their own local rules—an invitation enthusiastically taken up by many district courts. The net result has been that, today, almost no two U.S. District Courts follow exactly the same discovery rules. Some have adhered to the old system; others have completely embraced the new; and a great many operate with some unholy mixture of the two.

## SIDEBAR

### Mandatory Disclosure Rules: Blessing or Curse?

*Not every litigator is a fan of disclosure-based discovery, and the detractors do have some valid points to make. Here are a few of the common criticisms:*

*1. Litigants are naturally tempted to try to hide evidence that they think will hurt their case. By severely restricting the use of the old discovery tools, the new rules make it harder to detect such cheating, and the punishment for parties who are caught "hiding the ball" is neither certain enough nor severe enough to have much deterrent effect. In short, mandatory disclosure rules—or more accurately the limitations on traditional discovery that accompany them—make the outcome of litigation depend overly much on the ethics and honesty of one's opponents.*

*2. Mandatory disclosure rules put lawyers in the uncomfortable position of having to, in effect, build an opponent's case for her. Disclosure rules may require a diligent lawyer to reveal evidence that will lead to new claims or defenses that a lazy opponent would otherwise never have thought of. This seems unfair to the client of the diligent lawyer, who is paying for work that undercuts his own case.*

*3. Disclosure rules undermine the attorney–client privilege. If a client discusses some damaging bit of evidence with his lawyer, the lawyer has no choice but to reveal it to the opposing party under the disclosure rules. A client who understands the system will be motivated not to tell his lawyer about the bad bits of evidence.*

*Are mandatory disclosure rules an improvement, or a mistake? What is your opinion?*

State courts have not, on the whole, rushed to a wholesale adoption of the federal, disclosure-based system of discovery, and many states continue to experiment with their own solutions to the problems of discovery abuse and excessive cost. It is impossible, therefore, to offer a single, consistent tutorial on discovery that will be accurate for every jurisdiction.

Nevertheless, there is a great deal about discovery that is relatively uniform, regardless of place. The raw materials on which the discovery process operates—mainly paper records and testimony of live witnesses—are the same everywhere. A great deal of the work of discovery consists of analyzing the information obtained (a fertile source of work for paralegals); disclosure rules change only the way in which information is gathered, not what is done with it thereafter. The goals and motivations of the litigants are largely unchanged, regardless of the system used. Even the tools of traditional discovery—interrogatories, depositions, requests for production of documents—are by no means eliminated in mandatory disclosure systems; they merely take on a different purpose, that of filling in the inevitable gaps in the required disclosure.

Our intended focus in these workshops is on the hands-on skills needed by litigation paralegals. The knowledge required to prepare a disclosure statement is essential in jurisdictions where disclosure rules are in force. We begin with a workshop on that subject, which instructors in nondisclosure jurisdictions may wish to skip. The remaining discovery workshops should be valid and relevant for all students. Litigation paralegals in all localities need the basic skills involved in working with requests for production of documents, subpoenas, interrogatories, and depositions. Those in disclosure jurisdictions will use these tools to supplement disclosure; for those in traditional discovery jurisdictions, they comprise the principal means for obtaining information. Likewise, paralegals in all jurisdictions must learn to respond to discovery requests, to analyze discovery responses, and to prepare and respond to discovery motions.

## DISCOVERY—SEEING THE BIG PICTURE

In the workshops to follow, we will be zeroing in on the minutiae of various common discovery tasks. Before doing so, it is worth reminding ourselves that our goal in conducting discovery is to improve our chances of winning the lawsuit. Individual discovery tasks should continually be evaluated on the basis of their contribution to that ultimate goal.

Getting maximum advantage from discovery requires planning. Successful litigators do not simply start shooting out a random stream of discovery requests—they take the trouble to map out in advance the information that will be needed and the steps that can be taken in pursuing it. In Workshop 1, we advocated the preparation of an issues outline as a way of organizing your understanding of the claims and the facts needed to support them. A good place to start in planning discovery is to go through your issues outline, element by element, issue by issue, and decide how you can best prove each required fact. List all of the facts for which you need more evidence, and decide which discovery procedures

**Figure I–1 Discovery Flow Chart**

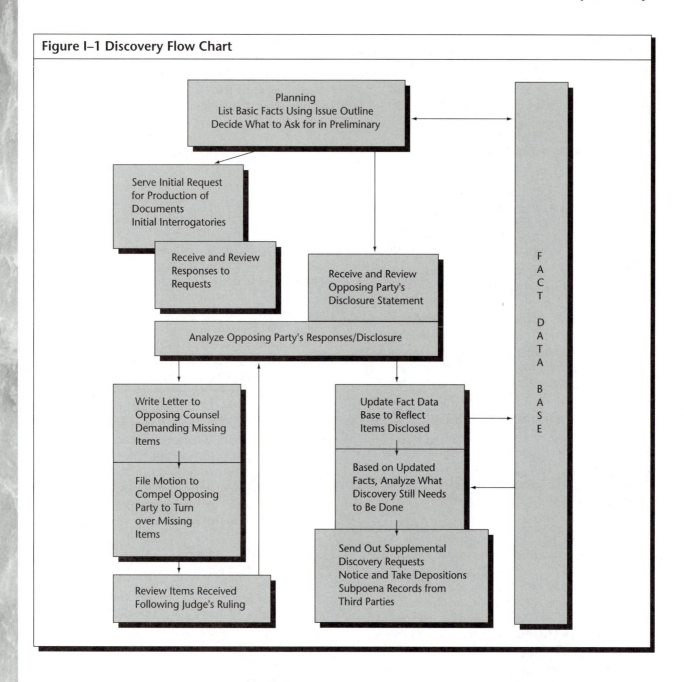

should be used to obtain each one. Keep track of the status of each required fact as discovery progresses, so that you can fill in any gaps.

The chart shown in Figure I–1 illustrates the way in which discovery begins with a plan, elicits preliminary responses, and uses the information gained to tailor subsequent requests, while at the same time resolving the gaps in the responses received.

Discovery planning is, of course, ultimately the job of the responsible attorney, but you will be more effective as a litigation paralegal if you understand what your supervising attorney is trying to accomplish. The main motivations are fairly obvious: One party is trying to pry loose some piece of evidence or information, the opposing party is try-

ing to keep it hidden if possible. (Disclosure rules do not make litigation any less an adversary process; they merely change the tactics by which litigants try to shape the factual development of a case to their own advantage.)

What are some of the tactics used? Some litigators use a "scorched earth" strategy, in which nothing useful will be disclosed without a fight. Discovery requests are met first with incomplete responses and responses that claim to disclose everything but in fact do not. If the opponent presses, claims of privilege and other objections will be tried, forcing the requesting party to file motions and jump through additional procedural hoops. If a damaging bit of information cannot be suppressed, misdirection may be used—disclose the information, but do it in a way that makes it seem unimportant, or bury it in a mass of other disclosure. By making every step as difficult, time consuming, and expensive for the requesting party as possible, he or she will be induced to cut corners on account of sheer exhaustion.

Although such tactics may seem improper, the discovery process poses ethical issues that are not simple to resolve. You have an obligation under the rules to comply with discovery requests, but you have an obligation to your own client to fight for her cause. These competing obligations sometimes require us to draw lines that are not easy to draw. We visit the subject of ethics in discovery in Workshop 19, Ethics in Litigation.

## ROLE OF THE PARALEGAL

Discovery probably consumes more paralegal hours than any other activity in litigation. Discovery in modern civil litigation is so time consuming that having it done exclusively by lawyers would be prohibitively expensive. Yet good legal judgment is often required, so leaving all but the most routine tasks to untrained clerks or secretaries risks costly mistakes. Paralegals are positioned perfectly by their training to carry out much of this vital work.

Much of the effort in discovery involves analyzing the responses received, which can amount to literally tens of thousands of pages in a complex case.

This task is well suited for paralegals under proper supervision, and, routine though it may seem, there is often plenty of opportunity for an ambitious paralegal to show off his talent by discovering some case-winning piece of evidence among the piles of seemingly mundane documents.

Another critically important but endlessly time-consuming task is that of making disclosure to opposing parties and responding to their discovery requests. Reliable judgment here is indispensable, because this is the place in a lawsuit where we most risk accidentally revealing to an opponent some damaging fact that should not have been disclosed.

While attorneys are usually responsible for a number of lawsuits at any given time, and cannot hope to keep the factual details of each one in memory, a paralegal can be assigned to become expertly familiar with the facts of one or two cases. Such a person is then in a unique position to be able to pull together quickly the facts needed to respond to a discovery request. Such an ability is especially useful in courts using disclosure-based discovery, since the time allotted for making initial disclosure is usually short.

In short, for paralegals, discovery is a growth industry.

## INTRODUCTION: THE OBJECTIVES OF DOCUMENT DISCOVERY

In this workshop, we focus on **document discovery**—that is, discovery procedures whose purpose is to obtain documents. We can use two main procedural tools for this purpose; which one we choose depends on *who* has the document that we are trying to obtain. To get documents from another party (usually an opponent), we use a request for production of documents under FRCP, Rule 34. If the documents we are seeking are in the hands of someone who is not a party to the lawsuit—medical records from a hospital, say—then we use a subpoena *duces tecum*. We will learn to use both in this workshop.

Document discovery is, in many ways, a natural place to start our overview of the discovery process, although certainly not the only possible one. Preferred discovery strategies vary greatly from one litigator to another, and often depend on the needs of a given case. However, one common way to begin the discovery process is to assemble and analyze as much of the pertinent documentation as possible, with the idea that the documents will contain the identities of important witnesses and leads to other evidence.

## DOCUMENT DISCOVERY STRATEGY AND GOALS

Ideally, the goal of each party—plaintiff or defendant—in document discovery is to assemble a complete set containing every single piece of paper that could conceivably bear on the case, whether helpful or harmful to our case. We want "good" documents so that we can use them as evidence to support our case; we want the documents that are harmful to our case, as well, because if they are "bad" for us, they are probably "good" for our opponent, and we need to be ready to counter them.

Our goal goes far beyond that of merely gathering documents to use as evidence. In fact, many of the documents we are gathering will never see the light of day in a courtroom. Our main purpose in gathering documents is to provide a body of data that we can use in tracking down other evidence. Every document was written by someone—someone who is a potential witness, if the document seems to indicate that the author knows something about the facts at issue in the lawsuit. Documents often refer to other documents, so even if the document in front of us is not helpful, the one it refers to may be.

Often, another goal of document discovery is to establish that given documents do *not* exist. If we properly request a particular category of documents from defendant X, and none are produced, then for practical purposes we have proved that defendant X does not have any documents of the type requested. (It is important to frame document requests clearly and concisely, so that opposing parties do not have room to hedge by later claiming that the request was ambiguous.)

Real discovery, of course, falls short of the ideal of gathering every pertinent document. Like everything in litigation, discovery is an adversary process. Our opponent is not about to turn over willingly some document that is likely to cement his undoing. Resistance is a given, sometimes within the bounds of the rules, and sometimes, unfortunately, extending to unethical tactics such as hiding and destroying evidence. Another problem is that we live in an age of record proliferation. It is not at all unusual in complex cases to be confronted with, literally, rooms full of potentially relevant documents and computer disks full of data; analyzing every page may not be cost effective.

Finally, the time allowed by the court for completing discovery is not unlimited. Discovery consists of chasing the facts from lead to lead, and the process must end somewhere. The goal is to find all the information that exists, but usually one settles for finding enough to prove one's case.

## THE DOCUMENT DISCOVERY PROCESS IN A NUTSHELL

How do we accomplish all of this document gathering? Here is the basic overall strategy that we will use. First, we serve a very broad request for production of documents on each opponent. We try to ask for every document and category of documents that we can think of that could conceivably be useful to us. (In a court that requires disclosure statements, this step is unnecessary and probably not allowed; instead, we will simply wait for our opponent's initial disclosure package.)

Eventually, we will receive a written response to our request, stating which items are being provided and which are being objected to, and accompanied by a stack of papers. (In courts using disclosure-based discovery, the stack of papers will accompany the opposing party's initial disclosure statement.) Invariably, the pile of papers contains some, but not all, of the documents to which we are entitled. We read and analyze the papers that were provided and use them to improve our understanding of the facts of the case. We also use any information available from other sources, such as deposition testimony, answers to interrogatories, and informal interviews of witnesses. All of this information will no doubt point to other documents or categories of documents that we did not know about, so we expand our list of documents and send new requests and subpoenas asking for the new additions to the list.

Meanwhile, we take steps to pursue the documents that are missing from the responses (or disclosure packages) that we received. First, we send opposing counsel a letter politely asking for the missing items; if they are not forthcoming promptly, we file a motion asking the court to order our opponent to produce them. You may wonder why we mention this as a routine part of document discovery—surely having to chase after documents that should have been provided in the first place is a rare event? Unfortunately, no; as we will see, discovery responses are almost always at least partially incomplete. Sometimes, papers that we ask for are not turned over simply because the party asked for them does not have them. Other times, it is because someone is being careless, lazy, or deliberately obstructive. We will revisit the important task of forcing opponents to turn over everything that they are required to when we take up the topic of Discovery Motions in Workshops 10 and 15.

Opposing parties will not be able to provide some types of documents, so we instead seek them from sources that are not directly involved in the lawsuit. (A common example: medical records of a plaintiff suing for injuries, which both sides need to obtain from the hospital or treating physician.) We begin early in the case—as early as court rules permit—to prepare and send subpoenas for all such documents that we can think of.

As the documents flow in, we begin organizing them using a suitable filing and indexing system. In small cases, this is likely to be done by hand; in big cases, a computerized litigation support database is almost certainly necessary. Either way, we must ensure that we can ascertain, if necessary, where each document came from, how we obtained it, where the original is, and who might be called as a witness to testify that it is authentic if necessary. In all but the smallest cases, we will also devise some way of indexing documents by subject, so that we can locate important papers quickly when we need them. We have more to say later regarding the fine art of organizing documents.

By the time we have received the second or third set of documents from our opponent, and have received subpoenaed records from other sources, we should be well on our way toward assembling a complete set of documents. When we analyze them, if we find that gaps still exist, we continue to send requests for production, issue subpoenas, and file motions where necessary, until either we are satisfied that we have everything needed or the discovery completion deadline prevents us from continuing.

In following this basic plan, we make each move as early as reasonably possible. Most American courts today set a **discovery cutoff date** in each case. This is a date set by court order after which no further discovery is permitted. A party who is resisting disclosure will often try to stall until the cutoff arrives; therefore, we must react immediately when an opposing party tries to get away with an incomplete response. Moreover, the documents that we are assembling will reveal leads to other kinds of evidence—names of witnesses, facts of which we were unaware—and we need time to locate and depose witnesses and follow up on new facts.

---

*Your Local Notes*

_____

_____

_____

---

## THE TOOLS OF DOCUMENT DISCOVERY

Our overall approach, then, is to generate a list of documents that we would like to examine and then follow some procedure that will lead to the possessors of those documents giving them to us. The procedure chosen depends on who has the documents we require.

**Request for Production of Documents**—In general, to obtain documents from someone who is a party to the lawsuit, we use a request for production of documents as provided for by FRCP, Rule 34. (In some jurisdictions it is also permissible to use a subpoena *duces tecum* to obtain documents from a party, but this will often provoke opposition because a subpoena typically provides less time for response than the 30 days allowed for a request for production under FRCP, Rule 34.) As we will see shortly, a Rule 34 request for production is prepared in the form of a court paper, with the usual caption and formal parts. The body of the request lists the documents that we are requesting.

A request for production of documents is signed by the attorney for the requesting party and served on the party from whom the documents are requested. Service is usually of the informal kind under FRCP, Rule 5—that is, by mail or hand delivery to the attorney.

In addition to producing the requested documents, a party who receives a request for production must also file and serve a written response to the request; see FRCP, Rule 34(b). We will look more closely at the response requirement in Workshop 11.

**Subpoena *Duces Tecum*—**To obtain documents from someone who is not a party to the lawsuit, we use a subpoena. A subpoena is the modern descendant of what was, at common law, a formal court order commanding a witness to appear and testify. Under traditional subpoena practice (and even today in some state courts), there were two types of subpoenas—subpoenas *ad testificandum,* which ordered a witness to appear at a specified time and place to give testimony, and subpoenas *duces tecum* (Latin for "bring with you"), which also ordered a witness to appear and give testimony, with the added requirement that the witness bring along specified documents or things to be examined.

Modern courts have streamlined subpoena procedures considerably over the years in an effort to eliminate unnecessary burden on the clerk's office. Originally, subpoenas had to be signed by judges; all modern courts long ago abandoned that time-wasting practice in favor of authorizing the clerk of the court to issue subpoenas. In many courts, the clerks eventually began issuing stacks of subpoenas to attorneys "in blank"—already stamped, sealed, and ready for the attorney to fill in the name of the witness and other information, and thus eliminating the burden on the clerk's office of having to issue subpoenas one at a time. Finally, in 1991, the federal courts took the logical next step of authorizing attorneys to sign subpoenas, thereby taking the clerk's office completely out of the loop. A subpoena signed by an attorney under FRCP, Rule 45, still has the force and effect of a court order.

The 1991 amendments to the federal rules also solved another vexing problem with subpoena practice: Formerly (and even today in some state courts), by definition, a subpoena was an order commanding a witness to appear and give testimony. The witness could be commanded to bring documents, but there was no procedure for getting documents without making a witness show up too. This dilemma was routinely solved in practice (and still is in some state courts) by sending a letter with the subpoena advising the witness that her presence, though commanded by the subpoena, was not really desired. (Predictably, some witnesses, nervous about disobeying a court order, show up in person anyway.) The current version of FRCP, Rule

45, solves the problem by specifically authorizing a subpoena for documents only. In this workshop, we emphasize the procedure under the federal rules; your instructor will inform you of the customary procedure for obtaining documents by subpoena in the state courts of your locality.

> *Your Local Notes*
> _____
> _____

**Informal Requests—**We can also sometimes obtain documents in other ways, such as by Freedom of Information Act requests, by perusing public records, or simply by asking people for the documents we want. There is an advantage to be gained by employing such informal methods when possible: We avoid the involvement of opposing lawyers. Any records we obtain via a FRCP, Rule 34, request for production will have been thoroughly reviewed by our opponent's attorney before we see them. We can be sure that no "smoking guns" will be disclosed without a fight. Furthermore, a formal Rule 34 request, by spelling out exactly what documents we want to review, inevitably provides opposing counsel with clues about how our own factual development is progressing.

We must, however, think carefully about how and from whom we obtain documents by informal methods. If the document that we seek is a public record, we are always free to obtain and use it. We are usually not, however, free to obtain documents in the possession of an opponent by informal means. For example, if we are suing a large corporation, the idea might occur to us to go to one of the company's offices and try to get documents or information from some helpful employee. Rules of legal ethics, however, prohibit lawyers—and paralegals working for lawyers—from communicating about matters related to the lawsuit with an opposing party who is represented by another lawyer. Depending on the circumstances and on the ethics rules of the locality, this prohibition may also extend to communications with *employees* of an opposing party. Therefore, a paralegal should never contact offices or employees of an opposing party without first getting the approval of a supervising attorney.

An attorney may freely contact third-party witnesses as long as they do not have some protected confidential relationship with an opposing party. Suppose, for example, we represent the defendant in an auto accident case and we learn that one of the witnesses to the accident took photographs of the scene. We are perfectly free to contact that witness and attempt to obtain copies of the photographs, and we have no obligation to tell opposing counsel that we are doing so. We may not, however, contact plaintiff's doctor on the sly and try to obtain medical records without opposing counsel's knowledge, since the doctor–patient relationship is a confidential one and medical records are privileged. To obtain medical records, we must subpoena them.

Deciding which witnesses may be contacted and which may not often involves drawing fine legal and ethical lines, and may also involve strategy questions best left up to the attorney in charge of the case. As a paralegal, you should never contact third-party witnesses unless your supervising attorney has expressly authorized you to do so.

---

**SIDEBAR**

## The Virtue of Viewing the Original File

*Even though FRCP, Rule 34, requests and subpoenas duces tecum specify a time and place at which documents are to be produced, it is quite common to respond simply by mailing photocopies of the documents to the requesting attorney, prior to the date specified. Should we, as representatives of the requesting party, be satisfied with photocopies?*

*On a preliminary basis, yes. Photocopies are admissible in evidence as "duplicate originals" under Rule 1003 of the Federal Rules of Evidence, so we do not have to have originals in order to use the documents in court. Nevertheless, the requesting party has a right to inspect the original documents, and should always insist on viewing the originals of any files containing documents that are crucial to the issues of the case. Why? The copies that we receive in response to a Rule 34 request or subpoena are likely to have been made by some overworked clerical employee, who is given boxes of files with the instruction "Copy these by 5:00 P.M." Inevitably, pages will get stuck together and be skipped; the backs of pages may be missed; sticky notes attached to pages may be omitted; the file folders themselves may have notes written on them but will not be copied. In short, you cannot be sure that you have seen everything there is to see unless you have gone through the original file yourself and looked at every page.*

---

# Document Requests: Step-by-Step Instructions

## PREPARATORY STEPS

Our first goal is to prepare an initial set of FRCP, Rule 34, document requests and subpoenas *duces tecum* that will bring in the main body of documents that we need to review when we begin preparing our case and assembling the evidence for trial. To do this, we must determine two things: (1) *What* documents do we need? (2) *From whom* can we obtain them?

**Step 1** | *Plan Your Request and List the Documents Requested*

Our objective in this step is to make a master list of all documents we can think of that might exist and might conceivably be useful to us. At this stage, we do not care where the documents are or who has possession of them. We simply try to list every kind of document we can think of, regardless of where or in whose hands it may be.

We may list:

■ *Specific* documents, if we are aware of any. For example, "invoice for mechanical work done on the brakes of defendant's car on March 5, 1999 at Al's Brake Shop."

■ *Categories* of documents. For example, "Each and every document pertaining to any mechanical work done on the brakes of defendant's car during the one-year period preceding the accident."

In deciding what documents to request, we wish to cast our nets wide, so that we can decide for ourselves what is useful and what is not after seeing everything that there is. FRCP, Rule 26(b), sets the standard for deciding which documents we can get and which we cannot:

> Parties may obtain discovery regarding any matter, not privileged, which is relevant to the subject matter involved in the pending action, whether it relates to the claim or defense of the party seeking discovery or to the claim or defense of any other party, including the existence, description, nature, custody, condition, and location of any books, documents, or other tangible things and the identity and location of persons having knowledge of any discoverable matter. The information sought need not be admissible at the trial if the information sought appears

reasonably calculated to lead to the discovery of admissible evidence.

If a document or other item of information is "not privileged" and is "reasonably calculated to lead to" admissible evidence, we say that it is **discoverable** and we are entitled to ask for it and get it. FRCP, Rule 26(b), is broad enough that it allows us to ask for essentially anything we can think of that might conceivably be useful.

In writing discovery requests, we do not (within reasonable limits) worry about whether some document that we want is discoverable. We assume that it is, and let the opposing party object if he disagrees.

### Figuring Out What to Ask For

—Obviously, we want our master list to be as complete as possible. Is there any systematic approach that we can use to be sure we have included all of the possible target documents? It will be helpful if we approach the problem from two different angles. We begin with the specific, and try to guess what kinds of documents should exist in the situation involved in the current lawsuit. Then we protect ourselves with generic, "boilerplate" requests, which are general categories of documents that we will want to request in every lawsuit, regardless of the subject matter, to be sure we have not left any gaps in the coverage of our specific requests.

### Documents Specific to the Current Lawsuit

—First, we consider the specifics of the current lawsuit, and try to generate a custom list that will capture all of the documents that we expect might exist in the situation involved in the suit. Here are a few ways to get started:

- Use your issue outline (see Workshop 1) as a checklist, and consider which categories of documents might be pertinent to each of the issues on the outline.

- Obtain copies of document requests used in other lawsuits similar to yours. Your supervising attorney will usually be able to suggest other files in the office from which you can obtain sample requests.

- Carefully read the opposing party's complaint or answer and think about each of the factual allegations. Ask yourself what documents might exist that would tend to prove or disprove each allegation.

- Examine the documents that you already have (such as those provided by your client) for clues about what other documents may exist.

If you have a working background in a particular business or profession, you may have opportunities to put your experience to good use in document discovery, because record keeping is becoming increasingly specialized. For example, in a medical malpractice case, it is necessary to gather and interpret medical and hospital records. The keeping of medical records is practically a profession unto itself; medical record technicians undergo an entire curriculum of study to learn what kinds of records there are and how to administer them. A suit against a real estate broker would involve an entirely different type of records. In either case, a number of different kinds of records are routinely kept in the business in question, and it takes experience with that business to know what they are. (That is why experienced nurses who are trained as paralegals are eagerly sought by law firms specializing in personal injury and medical malpractice cases.)

### Generic Document Categories to Be Requested

—Most litigators have a standard set of boilerplate document categories that they automatically include in their first FRCP, Rule 34, request for production to each opposing party. Here are examples of a few of the categories typically included:

- Documents that an opponent will use as an exhibit at trial (see sidebar on supplementation).

- Documents (like receipts or bills) that evidence expenditures included in the amounts for which an opposing party is suing.

- Insurance policies covering any of the damages involved in the suit.

- Correspondence between any of the parties to the suit.

- Reports of expert witnesses retained by an opposing party.

- Documents supporting the allegations made by the opposing party in its pleadings.

(The foregoing list is intended to give a general idea of some of the categories of documents that we may want to request; it is by no means exhaustive. Nor are the items in the foregoing list worded in the way that they would be in an actual document request. For proper wording, see the examples under Step 1 in the Learning by Example section later, and see the sidebars on redundancy and discovery legalese.)

Where can you go for ideas about what other categories of documents to include? If you work as a litigation paralegal, your supervising attorney will undoubtedly have sample document requests from which you can work. Also consider the court rules of other jurisdictions that have adopted mandatory disclosure—mandatory disclosure rules are intended to embrace the kinds of documents that a competent litigator would request in every case. As you gain experience and have occasion to see the work of others, you should compile your own generic list of documents to be requested.

Our master list will inevitably grow and evolve as the discovery process continues. As we review documents in the case and familiarize ourselves with the facts, we will get ideas about additional documents to request.

| *Your Local Notes* |
| --- |
| _____ |
| _____ |

**How to Compose "Bulletproof" Requests —** Because we will be block-copying items from our master list directly into the individual lists of documents to be requested or subpoenaed, we need to write each item in the form in which it will appear in the actual request or subpoena. We have already

had much to say about adapting one's writing to the goals sought to be achieved, especially in the context of writing for the purpose of persuasion. Discovery requests typify a different type of legal writing; here, the purpose is not to persuade, but rather to describe something so comprehensively that there is *no* possibility that someone can credibly claim to have misunderstood what was asked for. Elegance of phrasing here is worth nothing; better to come at our descriptions from as many different angles as possible, using as much repetition as needed. Otherwise, we will find ourselves on the receiving end of arguments like President Clinton's contention that "sexual relations" does not include "oral sex" (see sidebar on redundancy).

As you gain experience with discovery requests, you will find that certain language patterns are used over and over. There is a reason for this: Many of these cumbersome phrases have been interpreted by judges often enough that it is nearly impossible for anyone to argue about their meaning. Here, literary inventiveness is not a virtue; better to stick with tried and tested phrasing (see sidebar on discovery legalese).

## SIDEBAR

## Supplementation of Responses

*When we send out a FRCP, Rule 34, request for production, we hope to receive a response based on the documents that the opposing party has—at the time of the response. What if the opposing party turns over everything available at the time of our request, but later obtains additional documents of the kinds that we asked for? Does she have to turn them over?*

*Parties responding to discovery requests do have some duty to supplement responses. FRCP, Rule 26(e)(2), provides that "a party is under a duty seasonably to amend a prior response to an interrogatory, request for production, or request for admission if the party learns that the response is in some material respect incomplete or incorrect and if the additional or corrective information has not otherwise been made known to the other parties during the discovery process or in writing."*

*Can we, then, assume that our opponent will voluntarily turn over additional documents as he or she obtains them? Sorry—not a safe assumption. It is too easy for the opposing party to argue that the additional documents were not "material" or that the original response was complete and correct when made.*

*What can we do, then? One tactic commonly seen is to serve a formal request for supplementation of prior responses. This can take the form of a one-paragraph court paper requesting that the opposing party supplement responses to specified prior discovery requests. This is intended to obligate the opposing party to bring the previous responses up to date. Does this have the desired effect? Most judges would probably enforce requests for supplementation. Unfortunately, though, the federal rules do not expressly provide for this procedure; therefore, it is probably safer to serve a complete new request for production, at least with regards critical categories of documents. And with subpoenas, there is no other choice—if you think that a third-party witness may have acquired some new documents, you will need another subpoena.*

*The rules of most courts require parties to exchange all trial exhibits at some time before trial, so at least we will eventually get to see any after-acquired documents that our opponent intends to use as exhibits. Of course, these are unlikely to include any documents that will help our case.*

## SIDEBAR

# The Virtue of Redundancy

The goal of an opposing party responding to our discovery request will be to turn over to us as many tons of useless paper as possible, while withholding any documents that would really help us win our case. Opposing parties will attempt to withhold documents—that is a given. Our goal is to write our requests in such a way that if our opponent does withhold the documents we want, we will be able to show the judge very clearly that we did ask for them.

How can we write requests that accurately describe documents that we have not yet seen? This is a little like trying to hunt blackbirds at 2:00 A.M. on a moonless night. Overly specific descriptions are like shooting with a rifle—unless we are exactly on the mark, our opponent will point to all of the words in our description that do not match document X, and use the differences as an excuse not to give it to us. On the other hand, if our descriptions are too broad—the "shotgun" approach—our opponent will point to all of the details of document X that are not included in our description, and claim that our description was too vague.

One strategy that we can use to good effect is to do both. An example based on our hypo will help make this clear: In taking Arnie Trevayne's deposition, Allen Porter gets the impression that Arnie is a shady character and suspects that Arnie may have been involved in other misconduct in the past. It would be reasonable to suppose that documentation of previous misconduct would be in Arnie's personnel file, so we will include in our request to the hotel a specific item asking for that:

All documents, including without limitation personnel records, pertaining to the employment of Arnold Trevayne by Park Hotels Group.

However, it is also possible that, for example, some hotel customer wrote a letter complaining about something that Arnie did, and the letter was filed in a general hotel guest complaint file and not in Arnie's personnel file. In that case, Park Hotels Group could comply with our document request without ever telling us about the complaint. So, we will add a second "shotgun" item:

All documents comprising, reflecting, or pertaining to any communication made by any person at any time, the subject matter of which related to any conduct by Arnold Trevayne.

One caveat: some courts impose limits on the number of items that can be included in document requests. Such limitations add another dimension to the problem of writing watertight document descriptions, because they restrict our ability to shotgun using multiple items to describe the same documents.

## SIDEBAR

# Discovery Legalese

In writing FRCP, Rule 34, requests for production and subpoenas, we want to make our document descriptions as all-encompassing as possible, so as to avoid giving the opposing party an excuse to withhold documents. Here are a few ideas that will help you do this:

- Use general words like communication rather than specific words like letter, memo, contract, and the like.

- Use phrases like "all documents evidencing, reflecting, comprising, or pertaining to" to broaden the scope of your requests. "All contracts between X and Y" will get you only documents that are clearly contracts. "All documents evidencing, reflecting, comprising, or pertaining to any contract between X and Y" should fairly entitle you to the contracts, plus any notes or letters about the contracts, addenda or amendments to the contracts, prior drafts of the contracts, etc.

- Use the phrase "including without limitation" or "including but not limited to" as a way of including the specific and the general in the same description. For example, write "all communications between X and Y, including without limitation the letter from Y to X dated March 15, 2000."

As you gain experience responding to discovery requests, keep your eyes open for other useful additions to your vocabulary of discovery jargon.

*Decide from Whom to Request Each Document or Category of Documents*

After completing Step 1, we now have a master list of all documents that we can think of that might be pertinent to our suit. Now we must decide which documents should be requested from which sources. For each source, we will generate a separate list of documents to be produced; we can do this easily by cutting and pasting from our master list. The separate lists will be used in creating the individual document requests and subpoenas: lists of documents to be obtained from sources who are parties to the suit will be attached to FRCP, Rule 34, requests for production of documents, and lists directed to nonparties will be attached to FRCP, Rule 45, subpoenas.

How do we decide from whom to request each category of document? Do we choose the most likely source for each one? No. Document discovery is done with a shotgun, not a rifle. There is nothing wrong with requesting or subpoenaing the same document from more than one source; in fact, doing so may help us protect ourselves against opposing parties who deliberately hide or alter evidence.

When we finish this step, we should have a stack of document lists, one list for each person from whom we will be seeking documents. Some of the lists will be short, perhaps listing only a single document. Others will be as long as the master list itself. Generally, we attach our *entire* list—all documents and categories of documents that we can think of— to the Rule 34 requests directed to each opposing party. When we request documents from an opposing party, we include even those documents (such as medical records, police reports, etc.) that we know we can obtain elsewhere or that we may think the opposing party is unlikely to have. Copies of documents can be anywhere, and we want to know exactly what our opponent—and our opponent's lawyer—has. If our opponent does not have the documents we request, let him file a response saying so.

## DRAFTING STEPS: REQUESTS FOR PRODUCTION

Now we separate our stack of document lists into two groups—one consisting of lists to be requested from parties to the suit, and the other of lists to be requested from nonparties. To request documents from a party, we will prepare a Rule 34 request for production of documents and incorporate our list in it. Steps 3, 4, 5, and 6 explain how to do this. To request documents from a nonparty, we will use a subpoena. Steps 7, 8, and 9 explain how to prepare and issue a subpoena.

Our initial requests for production are usually directed to all opposing parties in the suit. Often, we may be requesting the same documents from each opposing party, so each of the requests may appear identical. Nevertheless, we prepare a separate request to be sent to each opposing party. Each request names the party who is to respond (usually in the preamble; see Step 4 later). We do this so as to be able to require individual responses from each party. If we send out a blanket request to "all defendants," the response we receive is likely to be a blanket response by all defendants, and we will have no way to prove that any given defendant did or did not produce what she was supposed to. Ideally, we will repeat Steps 3 through 7 separately for each opposing party, and produce individualized requests for each.

*Formal Parts: Caption, Date and Signature Lines, Certificate of Service*

A FRCP, Rule 34, request for production is a court paper, with the usual caption and other formal parts. As usual, we will begin with the form caption and mailing certificate that we prepared in Workshop 4. Then all we need to do is plug in the main body and put an appropriate title in the caption. The title will usually be simply "Request for Production of Documents." In a complex case in which there will be many such requests, some litigators prefer to use more specific titles, such as "Plaintiffs' First Request for Production of Documents to Defendants Smith." Let local custom be your guide.

> **Your Local Notes**
> _____
> _____

*Preamble, Instructions, and Definitions*

The main body of the request begins immediately after the caption. As usual, the body should begin with a preamble telling the reader what the document is. A typical preamble might be written as follows:

> Plaintiff requests, pursuant to the provisions of Rule 34, Federal Rules of Civil Procedure, that defendant Park Hotels Group produce the documents and things listed herein for inspection and copying at 10:00 A.M. on January 14, 2000, at the law offices of Simon &

Porter, 1000 North Central Avenue, Suite 2800, Phoenix, Arizona 85004.

Notice that the preamble specifies a time and place for production. The literal provisions of FRCP, Rule 34, require us to do this, even though in actual practice the response will nearly always consist of mailing photocopies rather than someone showing up in person with originals (see Step 11 below). FRCP, Rule 34(b), allows us to "specify a reasonable time, place, and manner of making the inspection," but it does not give us the power to require the responding party to make copies for us. (Rule 34 is to some extent a relic of prehistoric times when dinosaurs ruled the Earth and law offices did not have copying machines.)

The time we specify must be at least 30 days after the date on which we serve the request. Rule 34 does not specifically say this, but it follows from the fact that the opposing party's written response is not due until 30 days have elapsed. In practice, the documents requested and the written response to the request usually arrive together.

Following the preamble, it is quite common to include a section of instructions and definitions. For example, we might include a paragraph defining the term *document* to include such things as tape recordings, computer disks, and other forms of electronic storage. A typical sample of instructions and definitions appears in our example request for production in the Learning by Example section later. (We do not include a complete set. Sets of instructions and definitions that run to five or more pages are not uncommon.) Instructions and definitions are not required by Rule 34, but many litigators like to use them, feeling that they close off some of the loopholes that a responding party might otherwise be tempted to use to avoid disclosure. If your supervising attorney is one of those who prefers to include instructions and definitions, he will undoubtedly have a boilerplate set from which you can cut and paste into any requests that you are preparing.

## Step 5 — Insert List of Documents Requested

After the preamble and the instructions and definitions, if any, the list of documents to be produced appears. Here, you simply block-copy the list that you generated in Step 2. The format, within reason, is up to you; as always, we would suggest that you follow a suitable sample form reflecting local practice in the court in which the suit is pending. Each item in the list should be numbered, so that the responding party can refer to the numbered items in the written response.

## Step 6 — File and Serve

Requests for production are served as provided by FRCP, Rule 5, in the same way as any other court paper subsequent to the complaint. (There is one exception. Some jurisdictions allow plaintiff to have the process server serve a request for production with the complaint.) Should you also file the request with the clerk of the court? The answer depends on the rules in effect in your jurisdiction. Some courts require the entire request to be filed; others, seeking to minimize storage of voluminous discovery documents, require that you file a notice reciting that the request for production has been served, and prohibit the filing of the actual request. When in doubt, consult the rules of procedure and local rules for the court in which the suit is pending. Your instructor will inform you of the practice in your locality.

| Your Local Notes |
| --- |
|  |
|  |

## DRAFTING STEPS: SUBPOENAS

We cannot obtain documents from nonparties using Rule 34 requests for production of documents, so we use subpoenas instead. Again, we use a separate subpoena for each person from whom we wish to obtain documents. The issuance of subpoenas is governed by FRCP, Rule 45. As we have seen, a traditional subpoena is a court order requiring someone to appear and testify at a designated time and place and, optionally, to bring along documents or things for inspection at the time of their appearance. FRCP, Rule 45(c), provides that a subpoena may

> command each person to whom it is directed to attend and give testimony or to produce and permit inspection and copying of designated books, documents or tangible things in the possession, custody or control of that person, or to permit inspection of premises, at a time and place therein specified. . . .

Current FRCP, Rule 45(d), expressly allows us to dispense with hauling in the witness when all we want are the documents:

> A command to produce evidence or to permit inspection may be joined with a command to appear at trial or hearing or at deposition, or may be issued separately.

What if we want documents from a corporation or other business entity? How can a corporation be ordered to appear and testify? For that matter, suppose we are seeking medical records from a doctor's office—must we subpoena the doctor in order to obtain her files?

No. In such situations we direct the subpoena to the **custodian of records** of the corporation or business whose records we are seeking. The custodian of records is the person having responsibility for the files and records of the entity. The subpoena is served on the entity and the entity decides which individual is the custodian of the records requested.

## Step 7    *Prepare Subpoena Form*

Subpoenas are usually one-page preprinted or word processor forms in which there are blanks for you to fill in the caption of the lawsuit, the name and address of the person or entity being subpoenaed, and the date on which appearance or production of documents is required, if any. There is also a blank for listing the documents that the person is to bring; in that blank, we write "see attached list" and simply staple our list of documents to the form.

FRCP, Rule 45, requires that a subpoena also set forth a copy of the provisions of subsections (c) and (d) of the rule. These give instructions to the party receiving the subpoena regarding his right to object.

How do we determine the appearance or production date? How much time must we allow? The answer varies with the locality—your instructor will inform you of the customary practice in the courts of your area. In federal court, in theory, there is nothing stopping an attorney from issuing a subpoena today requiring a witness to appear tomorrow; as a practical matter, however, witnesses are likely to ignore unreasonable deadlines, and judges are unlikely to punish them for doing so. FRCP, Rule 45, gives the person to whom the subpoena is directed 14 days in which to file an objection, so, as a practical matter, document subpoenas should normally allow at least 14 days for the witness to produce the requested documents.

*Your Local Notes*

_____

_____

## Step 8    *Issue Subpoena*

Procedures for issuing subpoenas vary considerably from one court to another. Although a subpoena is technically a court order, subpoenas are almost never signed by judges—judges are far too busy to waste time on such mundane tasks. The clerk of the court is authorized to issue certain kinds of routine court orders without having to consult a judge first, and subpoenas fall into this category. Therefore, in many courts (including, at your option, in federal court) when you want a subpoena, you prepare the subpoena form and take it (or send it with the process server) to the clerk of the court, who will sign it, seal it, stamp it, or do whatever else is necessary in your jurisdiction to make the subpoena official. The clerk may require you to provide another form (again, typically a one-page preprinted form on which you fill in the blanks) called a *praecipe*. A praecipe is a written request for the clerk to issue a subpoena or other routine paper. The praecipe goes into the court's file and serves as a record that a subpoena was issued.

In federal court under current Rule 45, we may dispense with the need to involve the clerk of the court in subpoena issuance. FRCP, Rule 45(a)(3), provides that "An attorney as officer of the court may also issue and sign a subpoena. . . ."

## Step 9    *Serve Subpoena, File Proof of Service, Notify Opposing Parties*

Because we are using the subpoena to obtain documents from a nonparty, the rules do not authorize us to serve the subpoena informally under FRCP, Rule 5. Instead, in federal court, FRCP, Rule 45(b)(1), governs: "Service of a subpoena upon a person named therein shall be made by delivering a copy thereof to such person."

Formal service is necessary if we want to be able to enforce the subpoena as a court order. If the subpoena has been properly issued and served, and the person subpoenaed fails to appear or produce documents as ordered, we can (in theory) get the judge to have her arrested and brought before the court for a good scolding or worse. As with any court order, the judge has the power (albeit rarely used) to punish someone who defies a subpoena by jailing her for contempt of court.

Before we can ask the judge to enforce a subpoena, we must be able to prove that we served it properly. For lawsuits in federal court, FRCP, Rule 45(b)(3), provides that "Proof of service when necessary shall be made by filing with the clerk of the court by which the subpoena is issued a statement of the date and manner of service and of the names of the persons served, certified by the person who made the service."

State court procedures for serving subpoenas and filing proof of service are typically similar to those provided under FRCP, Rule 45. Your instructor will inform you of the usual practice in the state courts of your locality and tell you where to find the governing rules.

---

**Your Local Notes**

_____

_____

---

As a practical matter, of course, we may not always care whether a subpoena is technically enforceable. Often, we will be making routine document requests addressed to sources who are willing to cooperate and merely want a subpoena as protection in case someone later claims that they gave out information improperly. In situations of this kind—obtaining medical records from a hospital, for example—we may often dispense with the expense of formal service and send the subpoena by mail, relying on the fact that we can always serve the subpoena properly later if cooperation is not forthcoming.

When we subpoena documents from nonparties, do we have to let our opponents in the lawsuit know what we are doing? In federal court, yes. FRCP, Rule 45(b)(1), requires that "prior notice of any commanded production of documents . . . shall be served on each party in the manner prescribed by FRCP, Rule 5(b)." State court rules vary, but professional courtesy and ethics will usually dictate that we both notify opposing parties when we send out a subpoena, and that we furnish opposing parties with copies of any documents we receive in response to the subpoena. Of course, we have a right to insist on similar courtesy from our opponents.

---

**Your Local Notes**

_____

_____

---

## CONCLUDING STEPS

Merely issuing discovery requests does not make the documents we need magically show up in our in-box. Opposing parties will resist, and third-party witnesses will procrastinate; it is up to us to make sure that we get what we have asked for. One of the most important activities in discovery is that of scheduling and keeping track of the status of all of the document requests, subpoenas, and other discovery procedures that we have set in motion. (As it happens, this is a task that is tailor-made for paralegals. If you want to impress your supervising attorney with your competence and value to the firm, this is a great place to demonstrate your initiative and talent.)

**Step 10** *Docket Response Due Date and Follow-Up*

The first step in tracking the status of document requests is to enter the due date for the response on the office docket. You should do this automatically as you send out the requests and subpoenas. You may also wish to keep a separate calendar for yourself, in which you enter response deadline dates for the cases to which you are assigned.

Often, you will check your calendar and find that a response that was due did not arrive. What then? We will study the various ways in which we can enforce compliance with our discovery requests in Workshop 15, but our first step is always to send out a letter demanding compliance. When? Usually, we allow a few days leeway in case the response is in the mail, but ideally we want to send the demand letter no more than a week or so after a deadline has passed. In the letter, we demand a full and complete response to our document request by some nearby date that we specify (10 days or so in the future) and note that date on our calendar. If that date passes without a response, we send another, stronger demand.

You may be wondering what good it will do to send a letter demanding documents if a formal request did not get the job done. Why bother? Here is the reason: Ultimately, if we do not get the documents we requested, we will file a motion to compel discovery asking the judge to order our opponent to comply. Most judges dislike discovery disputes and consider them a waste of time, feeling that parties ought to be able to resolve such minutiae on their own. Before we go to the judge for an order, we need to be able to show very clearly that we left no stone unturned in trying to solve the problem without bothering the court, and were unable to do so only because our opponent obstructed us at every turn. In that way, the judge's irritation at having to waste time on a discovery dispute will, we hope, be aimed at our opponent instead of at us.

**Step 11** *Catalog the Incoming Documents*

With either a request for production or a subpoena, our eventual goal is of course for our opponent to give us access to the actual documents we requested. Recall that a FRCP, Rule 34, request for production instructs the opposing party to produce documents for inspection and copying at a specified date and time, usually at the office of the requesting party's attorney (see Step 4 earlier). In other words, the procedure as contemplated by Rule 34 is for the opposing party to show up at our office with original documents, which we could then review and copy.

In today's world of expensive attorneys and cheap copies, document production is almost never done in the manner prescribed by Rule 34. Instead, if the documents requested are not too voluminous, we are likely to receive a stack of photocopies in the mail, probably with a bill for the copies. (Recall that under the literal provisions of Rule 34, we, as the requesting party, are supposed to make the copies. The responding party is not required to pay for them.)

If we have requested quantities of documents amounting to more than a few hundred to a few thousand pages, we may be invited to come to wherever the documents are to inspect them and make whatever copies we desire. Usually, counsel will be able to come to some agreement on how, when, and where documents will be inspected and copied. It is not uncommon in big document cases for several attorneys and/or paralegals to spend many days or weeks closeted in a conference room at opposing counsel's offices examining scores of boxes of files, one page at a time, and photocopying the pages deemed important. (Needless to say, this is a fertile source of paralegal employment.) In very complex lawsuits, which can involve literally hundreds of thousands of pages of documents, the court will often order the creation of a central document depository—a neutral location is obtained, clerical personnel hired, copying machines installed, and all of the original documents are kept there for the duration of the lawsuit so that all parties can access them as desired.

As we receive incoming documents, we must keep in mind that the goal of discovery is to develop evidence that we can use to prove our case. To accomplish that goal, we need to have some way of proving where documents came from. There are a variety of ways to accomplish this. In routine cases (i.e., those not involving many thousands of pages of documents), our preferred approach is to stamp each page of each document that we obtain, using a sequential numbering stamp. We start with number 000001 on the first page of the first document that we receive in the lawsuit, and continue in sequence as we receive new ones. In this way, each page of each document has a unique number. We then keep a log in which, at a minimum, each time we receive a new bundle of documents from someone, we enter the beginning and ending page numbers, together with information about when and from

whom we received each set. We can also use litigation support software tools to catalog documents; these allow us to record detailed information about each document and to locate documents via computerized searches. However we choose to do it, we must employ some systematic method of organizing and cataloging the documents that we receive.

**Step 12**　*Analyze Response and Take Any Needed Further Action*

In processing the responses that we receive to our document requests, we have several purposes:

- To check that we received all of the documents that we asked for, so that we can take further steps to pursue any that our opponent withheld.

- To organize and file the documents in such a way that we can later locate the items we need.

- To identify any documents that we want to use as evidence, and begin building the proof that we will need at trial.

- To improve our understanding of the facts so that we can frame additional discovery requests and find more evidence.

**Following Up on Incomplete Responses**—Our first task is to determine whether we have received a complete response to our request. This effort requires us to analyze the documents produced in an effort to determine whether anything is missing. You will find that responses to document requests are often woefully incomplete. You then have two options:

1. Bring pressure to bear via the court's power to impose sanctions under FRCP, Rule 37. We will study the steps that we can take to force opposing parties to provide discovery in Workshop 15.

2. Try to get the documents in some other way. Try other sources or try other discovery methods (such as a deposition of the person whom you believe has custody of the document that you want).

Which option should you choose? The answer depends on a great many factors. We nearly always begin with a letter to opposing counsel demanding that any missing documents be supplied. To that end, one of our first tasks in analyzing documents produced in response to a Rule 34 request for production or subpoena is to go through the request or subpoena item by item, compare each item with the documents we actually received, and make a list of all of the ways in which the opposing party's response failed to comply with our request or subpoena. Then when we send our demand letters, or later, if we file motions asking the court to intervene, we can simply attach our list and save ourselves the work of having to re-analyze the documents each time.

We will leave the task of analyzing a response for completeness and preparing a list of deficiencies, along with other tasks related to enforcing our rights under the discovery rules, for more detailed examination in Workshop 11.

**Organizing and Filing Documents**—We have already mentioned the need to keep a record of the source of each document that we obtain in the course of discovery. It will come as no surprise that good document management in complex lawsuits can involve far more than that. In cases involving large quantities of documents, it is a daunting task to maintain a filing and indexing system that allows us to access the documents we need in a useful way.

Here is an example of the kind of assignment you can expect to receive as a paralegal in charge of the documents in a lawsuit: Your supervising attorney is about to take the deposition of a key witness, so he asks you to assemble every document in which the witness's name is mentioned. In a case involving only a few hundred pages of documents, you can probably accomplish this task in a short time by skimming through the file. But if there are thousands of pages of documents, you will need an indexing system of some kind.

There are many possible ways of organizing document filing systems, and choices are made based on individual preferences and the needs of a given case. In most situations, a simple chronological organization is best; that is, we simply file the documents in the order in which we received them. If we have number-stamped the pages (see Step 11 earlier), this system allows us to find any document easily by its page number. We can then create indices by topic if we wish, listing the page numbers of all documents that pertain to a particular issue or person. In our list of facts to be proved (see preceding chapter, "Introduction To The Discovery Workshops"), we can note the page numbers of documents that bear on each of the facts we have listed. Tempting as it may be to try to organize the documents themselves by topic or in some other way that groups related documents together, experience teaches that the complexity of such schemes usually outweighs their usefulness. It is better, in most situations, to leave the documents in their original order and use separate tools to organize them such as our list of facts to be proved, a topic index, or document retrieval software of the kind discussed in the next paragraph. Using these tools, we can always locate all

of the documents on a given topic, and we can make copies of them to assemble into a file or binder for that topic if needed.

Software tools are available that support document retrieval systems versatile enough for cases of nearly any level of complexity. These tend to be expensive to install and operate, and considerable training of law firm personnel may be required to make them useful. Furthermore, no litigation support software has yet been invented that can exercise good legal judgment and make decisions about which facts are important and which are not—the computer industry adage "garbage in, garbage out" is as apt as ever. Litigation support software can automate a great deal of the tedious job of keeping track of which documents are where and what each one's content is, but it still takes competent people with legal training (often paralegals) to read each document, identify the important points, and enter them into the system.

**Identifying and Developing Evidence to Be Used as Exhibits**—Not all of the documents you gather during discovery will be used as evidence—far from it. Many a good case has been lost at trial by presenting such voluminous and complicated evidence that the main themes become lost in the noise.

One of your tasks, as you sift through documents, is to make judgments about which documents are important enough to be used in trial, and to begin taking the steps necessary to ensure that you will be able to use them. In general, you will need to be able to prove the authenticity of each document and to overcome any objections that opposing parties may make. The easiest way to establish the authenticity of documents is to get opposing parties to admit that they are authentic; FRCP, Rule 36, provides a procedure that we can use for this purpose (see discussion of requests for admissions in Workshop 10). To anticipate objections that our opponents may make to the introduction of particular documents, we need to know in advance what the objections are. FRCP, Rule 33, gives us a useful tool, written interrogatories, for prying this kind of information from opposing parties (see Workshop 10).

**Setting Up Further Discovery**—As we saw in the Introduction To The Discovery Workshops, discovery is an ongoing process of requesting, analyzing responses, filling in gaps, and making new requests. As we review and analyze the documents that flow in response to our requests for production and subpoenas, one of our tasks is to identify leads to other documents that we did not think of the first time around. Often, the documents we receive mention other documents that we do not yet have; we add these to our master list. Even when the documents produced do not make specific reference to other documents, reading them may trigger ideas that will lead us to other evidence. In this process, the quality of your results will depend on your creativity and judgment—still another reason why trained paralegals are in demand.

---

**Your Local Notes**

_____

_____

---

## Document Requests: Learning by Example

We now use what we have learned to prepare a Rule 34 request for production seeking documents from defendant Park Hotels Group on behalf of Shannon Martin. We also prepare a subpoena to obtain the records of Dr. Collins's hospitalization in Las Vegas.

## PREPARATORY STEPS

**Step 1**  *Plan Your Request and List the Documents Requested*

We begin by making a list of all specific documents and categories of documents that we can think of that might help us prove our case. This is largely a creative process; no mechanical formula exists that guarantees we will think of every possible document that should be requested. We prime our mental pumps by reviewing our research and notes, examining our issues outline, and making notes as ideas occur to us. Here are some of the categories of documents we might include on our master list, accompanied by comments in italics. See the earlier sidebars on redundancy and discovery legalese for additional guidance on composition, style, and wording. (For brevity, we limit ourselves to a few examples—the list in a real lawsuit would be much longer.)

1.  All documents reflecting or pertaining to any maintenance performed on any guest room doors or locks at Banbury Park Hotel after January 1, 1995.

    *(Notice that we are being very general. We have purposely not specified by whom the maintenance might have been performed, for example. That way, if the hotel had some of its maintenance done by an outside contractor, it would still be required to furnish us with the records.)*

2.  All documents or records evidencing, reflecting, recording, or pertaining to any telephone calls made from the front desk of the Banbury Park Hotel from 6:00 P.M. on February 5, 1996, to 6:00 A.M. on February 6, 1996.

    *(Here, we limit ourselves to the specific time period that we are interested in so that our request will not appear overbroad if challenged.)*

3.  All documents, including without limitation personnel records, pertaining to the employment of Arnold Trevayne by Park Hotels Group.

    *(What we are really after is Arnie's personnel record, but we word the request this way to prevent the hotel from withholding part of its records on Arnie by claiming that they are not part of his personnel record.)*

4.  All documents comprising, reflecting, or pertaining to any complaint made by any person at any time, the subject matter of which related to any conduct by Arnold Trevayne.

    *(This illustrates the use of redundancy in discovery requests; see sidebar. Anything covered by this item should also be covered by the preceding one, but we want to approach important categories from several different angles so as to allow as little hedging as possible. Also notice that we asked for complaints by "any person," not just hotel guests.)*

5.  All documents comprising, reflecting, or pertaining to any complaint made by any hotel guest at any time after January 1, 1995, the subject matter of which related to any defect or claimed defect in any guest room door or lock.

    *(You will sometimes see requests that ask for, i.e., "any complaint made during the three years preceding this lawsuit." We prefer to use specific dates whenever possible—doing so makes it much harder for a responding party to "accidentally" misremember the date on which the lawsuit started.)*

6.  All documents, including without limitation registration cards, reflecting the identities of all hotel guests occupying or registered in Rooms 400 through 447 of the Banbury Park Hotel on the night of February 5, 1996.

    *(We want the identities of other guests on Shannon's floor so that we can contact them and find out whether they may have witnessed anything useful to us.)*

7.  All documents, including without limitation medical records and bills of the hospital and other medical service providers, arising from or pertaining to the hospitalization and treatment of defendant Arthur Collins for the in-

juries alleged in defendant Arthur Collins's counterclaim against plaintiff.

*(This version is for our Rule 34 request for production to defendant Collins. We put the burden on defendant to decide what hospitalization and treatments he is claiming compensation for.)*

8. All documents, including without limitation medical records and bills of the hospital and other medical service providers, arising from or pertaining to the hospitalization and treatment of defendant Arthur Collins at Las Vegas Municipal Hospital on or after February 6, 1996.

*(This version is for the subpoena to the hospital—here we must be more specific since the hospital has no way of knowing what Dr. Collins is counterclaiming for.)*

We will also have a number of generic categories of documents to ask for, but most of these will be plugged in or adapted from forms developed in previous cases. By covering more general territory, these generic categories will help plug any gaps that may remain in our specific list. Here are a few sample generic requests (again, highly abridged due to space limitations):

9. All documents that defendant Park Hotels Group will seek to introduce as an exhibit at the trial of this matter.

*(But wait—will not Park Hotels easily weasel out of this one by responding that they have not yet decided what exhibits they will use? Almost certainly that will be defendant's initial response, but under FRCP, Rule 26(e)(2), defendant has a continuing duty to supplement the response when it does decide. See sidebar.)*

10. All documents that Park Hotels Group will use in any court proceeding in this matter, including without limitation demonstrative evidence, documents used for the purpose of refreshing a witness's recollection, and exhibits to motions or affidavits.

*(Again, note the redundancy. We want to be sure that there will be no surprises in documents submitted to the court, so we ask for them in several different ways.)*

11. All documents reflecting, comprising, or pertaining to any statement obtained by any person of any witness in connection with any matters relating to this lawsuit.

*(First, we ask for witness statements specifically. . . .)*

12. All documents reflecting, comprising, or pertaining to any communication between any party to this suit or any representative of any party, and any other person concerning the facts or subject matter of this suit.

*(. . . then we ask in a more general way, so that defendant cannot withhold information by, for example, claiming that "this isn't a witness statement, it's just a letter from the witness.")*

13. All documents reflecting, comprising, or pertaining to any report of any expert witness who will testify at the trial of this matter or whose opinion is otherwise subject to disclosure under the provisions of FRCP, Rule 26.

*(Expert witnesses often prepare reports summarizing their conclusions for their clients; the expert's report will be indispensable in preparing to take a deposition. Not only that. . .)*

14. All documents provided by or on behalf of Park Hotels Group at any time to any expert witness.

*(. . . we can also learn a great deal about what to expect from an opposing party's expert witness by finding out what evidence the expert was given to review.)*

The numbering and sequence in our master list does not matter, since we will be block-copying parts of the list to the specific requests. Modern word processors will renumber the items automatically after they are copied.

**Step 2**    *Decide from Whom to Request Each Document or Category of Documents*

In Shannon's suit, Allen Porter will sooner or later be requesting or subpoenaing documents from a number of sources. These will certainly include the opposing parties in the suit—Park Hotels Group, Inc., and Dr. Collins—and will likely include other sources such as the Las Vegas Police Department, Arnie Trevayne, the hospital where Dr. Collins was treated, any physicians who treated Dr. Collins, any outside contractors who worked on the hotel room door or lock, perhaps the hotel's telephone service provider, the company that provides hotel security services to Banbury Park Hotel, if any, and any others that Shannon's attorney can think of who may have documents that would be helpful in preparing Shannon's case.

We will review the master list of documents that we want item by item and ask ourselves who might have each one. Often, we request the same items from multiple sources. Continuing with the example of looking for documents about Arnie Trevayne's background and prior conduct, we include items 3 and 4 from our list in our Rule 34 request for production to defendant Park Hotels Group, Inc. We also subpoena the same items from Arnie.

# DRAFTING STEPS: REQUESTS FOR PRODUCTION

**Step 3**    *Formal Parts: Caption, Date and Signature Lines, Certificate of Service*

**Step 4**    *Preamble, Instructions, and Definitions*

**Step 5**    *Insert List of Documents Requested*

We first copy the caption and formal parts from the form that we created in Workshop 4. Then we write a suitable preamble and add any instructions and definitions that we want to include. For brevity, we have only included three of the more commonplace ones. Your instructor or supervising attorney probably has a preferred set of instructions and definitions that you can copy. (We should note that the third of our instructions is commonplace in another way, in that it probably goes well beyond what Rule 34 actually authorizes us to ask for. You will often see such "overreaching" instructions, and we will show you how to respond to them in Workshop 11.)

After the instructions and definitions, if any, we insert our list. The resulting Rule 34 request for production is shown in Figure W9–1.

---

**Figure W9–1    Request for Production**

SIMON & PORTER
Allen Porter
1000 North Central Avenue, Suite 2800
Phoenix, Arizona 85004
(602)555-4321
Attorneys for plaintiff

**IN THE UNITED STATES DISTRICT COURT**
**DISTRICT OF ARIZONA**

| | |
|---|---|
| SHANNON MARTIN, a single woman,     ) | |
|                ) | NO. CIV 98-01456 PHX RGS |
|          Plaintiff,     ) | |
|                ) | REQUEST FOR PRODUCTION |
|          v.        ) | OF DOCUMENTS |
|                ) | |
| ARTHUR COLLINS and JANE DOE   ) | |
| COLLINS, husband and wife; PARK   ) | |
| HOTELS GROUP, INC., a Delaware    ) | |
| corporation;             ) | |
|                ) | |
|          Defendants.   ) | |
| ——————————————— ) | |

Plaintiff requests, pursuant to the provisions of Rule 34, Federal Rules of Civil Procedure, that defendant Park Hotels Group produce the documents and things listed herein for inspection and copying at 10:00 A.M. on January 14, 2000, at the law offices of Simon & Porter, 1000 North Central Avenue, Suite 2800 Phoenix, Arizona 85004.

**INSTRUCTIONS AND DEFINITIONS**

1.   "Document" means and includes writings, letters, memoranda, contracts, agreements, conveyances, drawings, graphs, charts, photographs, computer printouts, electronic mail messages, phone records, computer disks and/or disk files, audio, video, or data tape recordings, and any other data compilations from which information can be obtained.

**Figure W9–1,** *continued*

2.   You are required to produce all documents of the kinds described herein that are in your possession or control, including without limitation all documents that are now or at any time during the pendency of this lawsuit in your own possession or that of your attorneys, partners, officers, employees, agents, or other representatives or which you have the power or ability to obtain from others.

3.   In the event that you claim that any document requested herein is not subject to production by reason of any privilege, you are required to state the basis for your claim of privilege in your written response hereto, which statement shall include a description stating, for each and every document as to which you claim privilege, the general nature or type of document, the name of the author of the document, the date of the document, the specific privilege claimed, and the legal and factual basis for the claim of privilege as to that document.

## DOCUMENTS TO BE PRODUCED

1.   All documents reflecting or pertaining to any maintenance performed on any guest room doors or locks at Banbury Park Hotel after January 1, 1995.

2.   All documents or records evidencing, reflecting, recording, or pertaining to any telephone calls made from the front desk of the Banbury Park Hotel from 6:00 p.m. on February 5, 1996, to 6:00 a.m. on February 6, 1996.

3.   All documents, including without limitation personnel records, pertaining to the employment of Arnold Trevayne by Park Hotels Group.

4.   All documents comprising, reflecting, or pertaining to any complaint made by any person at any time, the subject matter of which related to any conduct by Arnold Trevayne.

5.   All documents, including without limitation registration cards, reflecting the identities of all hotel guests occupying or registered in Rooms 400 through 447 of the Banbury Park Hotel on the night of February 5, 1996.

6.   All documents comprising, reflecting, or pertaining to any complaint made by any hotel guest at any time after January 1, 1995, the subject matter of which related to any defect or claimed defect in any guest room door or lock.

7.   All documents, including without limitation medical records and bills of the hospital and other medical service providers, arising from or pertaining to the hospitalization and treatment of defendant Arthur Collins at Las Vegas Municipal Hospital on or after February 6, 1996.

8.   All documents that defendant Park Hotels Group will seek to introduce as an exhibit at the trial of this matter.

9.   All documents that Park Hotels Group will use in any court proceeding in this matter, including without limitation demonstrative evidence, documents used for the purpose of refreshing a witness's recollection, and exhibits to motions or affidavits.

10.   All documents reflecting, comprising, or pertaining to any statement obtained by any person of any witness in connection with any matters relating to this lawsuit.

11.   All documents reflecting, comprising, or pertaining to any communication between any party to this suit or any representative of any party, and any other person concerning the facts or subject matter of this suit.

12.   All documents reflecting, comprising, or pertaining to any report of any expert witness who will testify at the trial of this matter or whose opinion is otherwise subject to disclosure under the provisions of FRCP, Rule 26.

13.   All documents provided by or on behalf of Park Hotels Group at any time to any expert witness.

DATED this ___ day of _____, 2000.

SIMON & PORTER

_____
Allen Porter
Attorney for plaintiff

*continued*

**Figure W9–1,** *continued*

## CERTIFICATE OF SERVICE

The undersigned certifies that the foregoing was served in accordance with the requirements of FRCP, Rule 5, by mailing / hand-delivering a copy thereof this ____ day of _____, 2000 to:

Gail Stoddard, Esq.
CRANDALL, ELKINS & MAJOR
2000 North Central Avenue, Suite 2900
Phoenix, Arizona 85004
Attorneys for defendant Park Hotels Group, Inc.
Roger Yarborough, Esq.
500 Main Street
Dallas, Texas
Attorney for defendants Collins

[signature goes here]
_____

### Step 6   *File and Serve*

After Allen Porter reviews the request for production and signs it, we serve copies by mail on defendants (see Workshop 7). Which defendants? Both of them. We serve it on Park Hotels Group's attorney because Rule 34 requires us to serve the request on the party to whom we are making it; we serve it on Dr. Collins's attorney because FRCP, Rule 5, requires us to serve all court papers on all opposing parties.

If we are in a jurisdiction that has restricted the filing of discovery papers [see Workshop 7 and FRCP, Rule 5(d)], we prepare a notice reflecting the fact that we have served a request for production on defendant Park Hotels Group. We serve a copy of the notice on each defendant with the request itself, and we file the original notice with the clerk of the court. If we are in a jurisdiction that still requires the filing of discovery papers, we file the original request for production with the clerk of the court.

## DRAFTING STEPS: SUBPOENAS

### Step 7   *Prepare Subpoena Form*

### Step 8   *Issue Subpoena*

Preparation of the subpoena form is easy; we simply pull out a printed form (or word processor form) and fill in the blanks. Because Shannon's lawsuit is in federal court, Allen Porter, as an attorney admitted to practice before the U.S. district court, can issue the subpoena himself simply by signing it.[1] (In other courts, depending on local practice, it might be necessary to take the completed subpoena to the clerk's office to be stamped, or to obtain from the clerk blank, prestamped forms to fill out in the first place.)

The completed subpoena is shown in Figure W9–2.

### Step 9   *Serve Subpoena, File Proof of Service, Notify Opposing Parties*

Because Shannon's lawsuit is in federal district court, FRCP, Rule 45(b)(1), allows the subpoena to be served by "any person who is not a party and is not less than 18 years of age." As a practical matter, we would usually have a process server do the job.[2] The process server provides the necessary proof of service, which we file with the clerk of the court, keeping a copy for our own file. Rule 45's requirement that we notify opposing parties of the subpoena is most easily satisfied simply by mailing a copy to each defendant.

[1] Allen Porter can sign even though the person being subpoenaed—the custodian of records of Las Vegas Municipal Hospital—is outside the District of Arizona, because the subpoena pertains to a lawsuit that is in the District of Arizona. See Rule 45(a)(3)(B).

[2] Since we would have to find a process server in another state, however, and since this is a routine subpoena for medical records, we may decide to deliver the subpoena by mail and see whether the hospital will comply voluntarily.

---

**Figure W9–2   A Sample Subpoena**

### IN THE UNITED STATES DISTRICT COURT
### DISTRICT OF ARIZONA

| | |
|---|---|
| SHANNON MARTIN, a single woman ) | |
| ) | NO. CIV 98-01456 PHX RGS |
| Plaintiff, ) | |
| v. ) | |
| ) | SUBPOENA |
| ARTHUR COLLINS and JANE DOE ) | IN A CIVIL CASE |
| COLLINS, husband and wife; ) | |
| PARK HOTELS GROUP, INC., a ) | |
| Delaware corporation; ) | |
| ) | |
| Defendants. ) | |
| _____ ) | |

TO: Custodian of Records, Las Vegas Municipal Hospital, 233 B Street, Las Vegas, Nevada

YOU ARE COMMANDED to appear in the United States District Court at the place, date and time specified below to testify in the above case.

PLACE OF TESTIMONY COURTROOM:

TIME AND DATE:

YOU ARE COMMANDED to appear at the place, date, and time specified below to testify at the taking of a deposition in the above case.

PLACE OF DEPOSITION:

TIME AND DATE:

YOU ARE COMMANDED to produce and permit inspection and copying of the following documents or objects at the place, date and time specified below:

1.   PLACE: Law offices of Allen Porter, SIMON & PORTER, 1000 North Central Avenue, Suite 2800, Phoenix, Arizona 85004

TIME AND DATE: January 14, 2000

DOCUMENTS TO BE PRODUCED:

1.   All documents and records relating to the care and treatment of Dr. Arthur Collins, SSN aaa-bb-cccc, since February of 1996 including, without limitation, intake records and notes, medical tests and test results, progress notes, any diagnosis or diagnostic tests, medications, therapies, billing statements, surgical and follow-up notes and all discharge documents.

YOU ARE COMMANDED to permit inspection of the following premises at the date and time specified below:

PREMISES:

TIME AND DATE:

Any organization not a party to this suit that is subpoenaed for the taking of a deposition shall designate one or more officers, director, or managing agents, or other persons who consent to testify on its behalf, and may set forth, for each person designated, the matters on which the person will testify. FRCP, Rule 30(b) (6).

_____
Allen Porter
Issuing Officer Signature and Title
(Indicate if Attorney for Plaintiff or Defendant)

*continued*

**Figure W9–2  A Sample Subpoena,** *continued*

SIMON & PORTER
Allen Porter
1000 North Central Avenue, Suite 2800
Phoenix, Arizona 85004
(602) 555-4321
Attorneys for plaintiff

Rule 45, Federal Rules of Civil Procedure, Parts C & D

**(c)      Protection of Persons Subject to Subpoenas.**

(1)      A party or an attorney responsible for the issuance and service of a subpoena shall take reasonable steps to avoid imposing undue burden or expense on a person subject to that subpoena. The court on behalf of which the subpoena was issued shall enforce this duty and impose upon the party or attorney in breach of his duty an appropriate sanction, which may include, but is not limited to, lost earnings and a reasonable attorney's fee.

(2)(A)    Subject to paragraph (d)(2) of this Rule, a person commenced to produce and permit inspection and copying may, within 14 days after service of the subpoena or before the time specified for compliance if such time is less than 14 days after service, serve upon the party or attorney designated in the subpoena written objection to inspection or copying of any or all of the designated materials or of the premises. If objection is made, the party serving the subpoena shall not be entitled to inspect and copy the materials or inspect the premises except pursuant to an order of the court by which the subpoena was issued. If objection has been made, the party serving the subpoena may, upon notice to the person commanded to produce, move at any time for an order to compel the production. Such an order to compel production shall protect any person who is not a party or an officer of a party from significant expense resulting from the inspection and copying commanded.

(3)(A)    On timely motion, the court by which a subpoena was issued shall quash or modify the subpoena if it:
    (i)      fails to allow reasonable time for compliance;
    (ii)     requires a person who is not a party or an officer of a party to travel to a place more than 100 miles from the place where that person resides, is employed or regularly transacts business in person, except that, subject to the provisions of clause (c)(3)(B)(iii) of this Rule, such a person may in order to attend trial be commanded to travel from any such place within the State in which the trial is held; or
    (iii)    requires disclosure of privileged or other protected matter and no exception or waiver applies; or
    (iv)     subjects a person to undue burden.
  (B)    If a subpoena:
    (i)      requires disclosure of a trade secret or other confidential research, development or commercial information, or
    (ii)     requires disclosure of an unretained expert's opinion or information not describing specific events or occurrences in dispute and resulting from the expert's study made not at the request of any party, or
    (iii)    requires a person who is not a party or an officer of a party to incur substantial expense to travel more than 100 miles to attend trial, the court may, to protect a person subject to or affected by the subpoena, quash or modify the subpoena or, if the party in whose behalf the subpoena is issued shows a substantial need for the testimony or material that cannot be otherwise met without undue hardship and assures that the person to whom the subpoena is addressed will be reasonably compensated, the court may order appearance or production only upon specified conditions.

**(d)      Duties in Responding to Subpoena.**

(1)      A person responding to a subpoena to produce documents shall produce them as they are kept in the usual course of business or shall organize and label them to correspond with the categories in the demand.

(2)      When information subject to a subpoena is withheld on a claim that it is privileged or subject to protection as trial preparation materials, the claim shall be made expressly and shall be supported by a description of the nature of the documents, communications or things not produced that is sufficient to enable the demanding party to contest the claim.

## CONCLUDING STEPS

### Step 10 — *Docket Response Due Date and Follow-Up*

We make a notation on the office's central calendar that Park Hotels Group's response to the request for production of documents in *Martin vs. Collins* is due on January 14, 2000. Similarly, we note the due date for the documents called for by the subpoena to Las Vegas Municipal Hospital. When the indicated dates arrive, the calendaring system will remind us to check whether we have received the documents and to follow up with demand letters if necessary.

### Step 11 — *Catalog the Incoming Documents*

When we receive the requested documents, we number stamp the pages in sequence and file the documents in our office filing system in the order in which we received them. We make a record in the file of the page numbers, where they came from, and when we received them.

### Step 12 — *Analyze Response and Take Any Needed Further Action*

Now we review the documents, page by page. We compare them to our request and make a list of any items that seem to be missing or incomplete. As we read the documents, we make notes of any ideas that occur to us concerning other discovery that we may need to take or other documents that we may wish to obtain. We make note of any documents that are likely to be important in proving our case (adding notations to our issue outline is one way to do this).

A case like *Martin vs. Collins,* arising from a physical injury rather than from some dispute over paperwork, is unlikely to involve huge volumes of documents, so we will not need a sophisticated document indexing scheme; careful note taking by hand will probably suffice. If this were a case involving large quantities of complex documents, we would use appropriate document retrieval software, and we would enter data into the system as we reviewed the documents.

## Document Requests: Learning by Doing

### PROJECT 1

Your task for this workshop is as follows: You are a paralegal in the office of Roger Yarborough, and you are assigned to prepare (1) an initial Rule 34 request for production of documents on behalf of Dr. Collins to be served on Shannon, and (2) a subpoena for the records pertaining to Shannon's follow-up treatment for her broken finger by her physician, Dr. Roland Carter.

For simplicity, assume that the lawsuit is pending in the federal district court having jurisdiction in your locality (or, at your instructor's option, in the state court of your locality), and that all parties and attorneys are present in your locality. You may invent suitable local addresses for the parties, attorneys, and others as necessary.

### EXERCISES

1. (Step 1)  Make a master list of all specific documents and categories of documents that you might want to obtain on behalf of Dr. Collins.

2. (Step 1)  Obtain one or more document requests from actual lawsuits and make your own list of generic document categories to be requested. Add the appropriate ones to your master list.

3. (Step 2)  From your master list, choose the items that you will include in the document request to Shannon Martin and in the subpoena to Shannon's physician, and make separate lists for each of these.

4. (Step 4)  Obtain one or more document requests from actual lawsuits having an Instructions and Definitions section. Read the instructions and definitions and make up your own set for use in your own discovery requests. (In doing this, it is perfectly proper to plagiarize shamelessly. Do not feel that you have to change wording that works well the way it is.)

5. (Steps 3, 4, and 5)  Prepare the document request to Shannon Martin.

6. (Step 6)  Find out whether the rules of the court in which *Martin vs. Collins* is assumed to

be pending allow discovery papers to be filed with the clerk of the court or not. If not, prepare a notice suitable for filing, reciting the service of your request for production on Allen Porter.

7. (Steps 7 and 8)   Obtain a subpoena form of the kind used in the court in which *Martin vs. Collins* is assumed to be pending. Fill in the blanks appropriately and insert or attach the list of documents to be produced. Find out, under the rules of the court in which *Martin vs. Collins* is assumed to be pending, whether Roger Yarborough can issue the subpoena or whether it must be issued by the clerk.

8. Find out whether, under the rules of the court in which *Martin vs. Collins* is assumed to be pending, it is possible to issue a subpoena for production of documents without requiring a witness to appear and give testimony at the same time. If not, find out what the customary local practice is for obtaining documents from nonparty witness(es) and prepare the necessary documents to accompany your subpoena.

9. Find out, under the rules of the court in which *Martin vs. Collins* is assumed to be pending, how to have a subpoena served on a nonparty witness. Must it be done by a process server?

What is the governing rule? Write a paragraph summarizing what you found.

## PROJECT 2

This project consists of a game intended to be played by two competing teams. (In a large class, it may be desirable to break the class into several pairs of teams.)

**Instructions for Team A**—Assume that you represent a wealthy client who has just lost a lawsuit and had judgment entered against him for a large sum of money. Write a list of all the documents that you can think of that your client might have which would contain information about any of his assets. Try to list as many specific documents as you can.

**Instructions for Team B**—Assume that you represent someone who has won a large judgment against Team A's wealthy client, and you are assigned to prepare a request for production of documents that will require Team A to give you as many of the documents on their list as possible.

When both teams have completed their work, compare Team B's request for production with the documents on Team A's list and see how many of Team A's documents "escaped."

# PRACTICE POINTERS
## *Numbering Documents*

---

Document organization requires that each page of every document received from the opposing parties be numbered. The mechanics of this vary depending on the size of the case, that is, how many documents are involved, and the litigation software invested in by the firm. The reason for marking each page remains the same, however, regardless of the mechanics of the numbering process. Only by marking each page (both front and back) and by then carefully indexing those documents can a legal assistant have any hope of quickly and efficiently locating any document at any time when an attorney requests it. After you have reviewed hundreds or thousands of documents, they all begin to blur in your memory until the request to single out a particular document becomes an ordeal of virtually Herculean proportions. The lesson you can glean from hearing tales related by more experienced legal assistants is to number and index documents as soon as they come into your possession.

Most legal assistants prefer numbering documents in the order in which they are produced. Reorganizing them before they are numbered makes it difficult later to determine which documents were produced in response to which request. Keeping documents in the order in which a client provides them is also generally appreciated by clients.

The actual numbering process varies depending on the level of technical sophistication of the law firm. Traditionally, documents were "Bate-stamped" using a machine by the same name. This resulted in an inked, 6- to 10-digit number on the page; the number of the Bates stamping machine automatically

# PRACTICE POINTERS
## *Numbering Documents* continued

advanced to the next sequential number as the numbering machine was used. Today Bates numbering is often done using a computerized process that obviates the need for any number to actually be affixed to the page.

In small cases an alphanumeric system can be used with the first one or two letters designating the source of the documents and the following numbers identifying each page of the document. Alternatively, if a numbering machine is equipped with only numbers, all numbers can be used. In such a case the first two numbers represent the source of the documents and the following numbers represent the page numbers of each document.

Once the numbering process is complete, you must then index the documents. In the absence of any litigation support software, you can use a word processing program to create a simple index. Minimally, you must indicate the number the document begins with, the date the document was prepared, and a description of the document. A separate index should be prepared for each individual or entity that produces records.

## TECHNO TIP

Programs are available to assist in handling document-laden cases. Litigation support software can scan documents, label and organize them, and coordinate them with deposition testimony, which it also organizes. A concordance of all words or phrases used in a deposition can be created for instant retrieval. These programs, such as Utility Support Services, Inc's. SUMMATION and inData Corporation's trio of TrialDirector, DocumentDirector, and DepositionDirector, can be invaluable in coordinating a case for trial. Even without the "bells and whistles" often found in trial presentation software, the ability to have all relevant documents, depositions, and research files readily available is critical for pretrial motion practice. These types of software packages can bring up a portion of a person's deposition testimony (on video if you had a videotaped deposition) and cross-reference it to answers to interrogatories, requests for admissions, other documents, and other depositions. You can cut and paste to your word processor as the document is being created from the real documents contained in your database, without having to take up two conference tables!

## FORMS FILE

*Include samples of the following in your forms file:*
- Request for production of documents
- Subpoena *duces tecum*

## KEY TERMS

Custodian of records  Discoverable  Discovery cutoff date

## INTRODUCTION: INTERROGATORIES AND REQUESTS FOR ADMISSIONS

In this workshop, we begin examining procedures that allow us to make our adversary answer questions. FRCP, Rule 33, allows us to submit written questions, called interrogatories, to an opposing party, and requires the opposing party to answer them within 30 days. FRCP, Rule 36, provides a formal way of establishing uncontested facts in advance of trial, so that court time will not be wasted on trivial issues that are not really in dispute in the first place. This is done by submitting a request for admissions, requiring the opposing party to furnish written admission or denial of the facts stated in the request. Both of these procedures involve written questions and answers, and both can be used to ask questions only of a *party*.

We can also question either a party or a non-party verbally, face to face. Rule 30 allows us to do this by taking a deposition. We will examine the procedures for taking depositions in Workshop 13.

## USES OF INTERROGATORIES AND REQUESTS FOR ADMISSIONS

Strategically, written discovery serves a fundamentally different purpose than does deposition discovery. Answers to interrogatories and responses to requests for admissions are not very well suited for ferreting out the proof that we will need to establish the elements of our own case. Here are a few of the disadvantages of written discovery:

- Answers to interrogatories and responses to requests for admissions are invariably written by the opposing party's lawyer, not by the opposing party himself. Therefore, they are likely to be carefully drafted to give away as little as possible.

- The answering party has at least 30 days to think about the questions and hone the answers. The responses will be thoroughly edited.

- There is no immediate opportunity to follow up evasive or ambiguous answers with additional questions, as there would be in a deposition.

- When we send out interrogatories, our questions may reveal to our opponent information about the strengths and weaknesses of our own case.

- To answer interrogatories and requests for admissions, the opposing attorney will have

to research factual issues and think about the claims and defenses involved in the case. In effect, we are prodding our opponent into action when it might be preferable to let her drift along in a state of complacency.

What is written discovery good for, then? Perhaps we would be better off to just skip it, and rely entirely on depositions? No; although written discovery is very unlikely to pry loose any "smoking guns," it does have several important uses, each of which we consider in detail in this workshop. These uses fall into three general categories:

1. *Getting background facts.* We can find out names, addresses, locations of documents, and similar information that will enable us to track down the specific evidence that we need.

2. *Placing limits on our opponent's case.* We do this by framing open-ended questions that ask our opponent to disclose *all* evidence that he has on a given issue. Here, opposing counsel's natural tendency to disclose as little as possible works in our favor: Within reasonable limits, evidence not disclosed in response to a proper interrogatory will not be allowed at trial.

3. *Pinning down known facts.* There is a difference between knowing a fact and being able to prove it. Interrogatories and requests for production give us a simple and inexpensive way of establishing the noncontroversial details of our case, by getting our opponent to admit them.

With these strategic considerations in mind, we now examine the procedure governing interrogatories and requests for admissions.

## PROCEDURE FOR INTERROGATORIES AND REQUESTS FOR ADMISSIONS

An interrogatory is simply a written question that we submit (or, in common legalese, "propound") to our opponent. We submit interrogatories in sets containing a series of numbered questions. To get an idea of what an interrogatory looks like, consider this example, which was taken at random from a larger set:

*Interrogatory No. 3*

State the name, address, and telephone number of each and every person who witnessed the automobile collision described in plaintiff's complaint.

A request for admission looks nearly the same as an interrogatory, except that instead of being worded as a question, it begins with the words "Admit that . . . ," followed by a statement expressing the fact to be admitted. Here is an example of a typical request for admission, again taken at random from a larger set:

*Request For Admission No. 7*

Admit that the Real Estate Purchase Agreement dated March 15, 2000, attached as Exhibit 1 to plaintiff's complaint bears the genuine signature of defendant John Smith as seller.

The procedure governing interrogatories appears in FRCP, Rule 33. The procedure governing requests for admissions appears in FRCP, Rule 36. State court procedures in most states are similar to those under the federal rules; your instructor will inform you of the applicable rules or statutes for the state courts in your locality, and apprise you of any important differences.

---

**Your Local Notes**

_____

_____

---

Rules 33 and 36 are similar in many respects: Both interrogatories and requests for admissions can be submitted only to a party, in both cases a written response is expected, and under both rules the responding party is given 30 days to respond unless a shorter or longer response time is ordered by the court or agreed to by the parties.

Sets of interrogatories and sets of requests for admissions are also nearly identical in form and appearance. Both take the form of a court paper, with the usual caption, date and signature lines, and certificate of mailing. Following the caption is a preamble, then perhaps a list of instructions and definitions. The numbered questions or requests for admissions comprise the body of the document. We serve a copy of the set of interrogatories or requests for admissions on the party who is to respond to them. In courts that do not restrict the filing of discovery papers, we file the original set of interrogatories or requests for admissions with the clerk of the court. In courts that do restrict the filing of discovery papers, we file a notice reciting that we served them.

As we will see in more detail in Workshop 11, Responding to Discovery Requests, answers to interrogatories are prepared by taking the set of interrogatories itself and adding the answers to it. Before word processing became commonplace

(and even today in some courts), sets of interrogatories were prepared with blank spaces for the answers. Using a photocopy (or, earlier, a carbon copy) of the set of interrogatories, the responding party typed the answers into the blanks, typed the words "and answers thereto" onto the title in the caption, and added a signature page and mailing certificate. Nowadays, it may be more convenient for the responding party to obtain an electronic copy of the interrogatories, add the answers to each, and print the whole document. Either way, the end result is a document in the form of a court paper, with a caption, an appropriate title, a series of questions each followed by its answer, date and signature lines for the answering party and the answering party's attorney, and a certificate of mailing.

Responses to requests for admissions are essentially identical in form and appearance; the only difference is the title, and the fact that the answers merely say either "admitted" or "denied," or set forth an objection, if any.

**Requests for Admissions: Why Not Just Say "No"?**—We have seen that FRCP, Rule 36, offers a procedure whereby an opposing party can ask us to admit facts. But why would we ever want to help out someone who is suing us by admitting facts at their request? Why not refuse to admit *anything,* and force our opponent to prove each and every detail of his case?

In fact, we have every right to do just that if we want to, but if we refuse to admit facts that are not really in dispute we may find ourselves paying for our lack of cooperativeness. If we refuse our opponent's request for admission of a fact, and the judge later determines that we did not have reasonable grounds for our refusal, FRCP, Rule 37, requires the judge to make us pay the cost incurred by our opponent in proving the fact, including attorney's fees. FRCP, Rule 37(c)(2), provides in part:

If a party fails to admit the genuineness of any document or the truth of any matter as requested under Rule 36, and if the party requesting the admissions thereafter proves the genuineness of the document or the truth of the matter, the requesting party may apply to the court for an order requiring the other party to pay the reasonable expenses incurred in making that proof, including reasonable attorney's fees. The court shall make the order unless it finds that . . . the party failing to admit had reasonable ground to believe that the party might prevail on the matter, or . . . there was other good reason for the failure to admit.

There is also a practical reason for being reasonably cooperative in admitting minor facts that are not seriously in dispute: Judges are quite apt to become annoyed with litigants who make trials take longer by forcing others to put on formal proof of facts that are not really in doubt. Judges who are annoyed have plenty of subtle ways of getting even with the offending party. Excessive obstructiveness in admitting facts may also provoke our opponent into being equally obstructive in responding to our own requests for admissions, making our own case more expensive and time consuming to prove.

The question of whether and how much to admit in response to requests for admissions is an interesting one that we will examine in more detail in Workshop 11.

> **Your Local Notes**
> _____
> _____

## Combining Interrogatories and Requests for Admissions in the Same Court Paper

Given the fact that interrogatories and requests for admissions are so similar in form and purpose, it might occur to us to wonder why we don't just combine both in the same document and title it "Interrogatories and Requests for Admission"? In fact, many litigators favor this practice. Even though the federal rules do not specifically authorize us to combine the two in this way, neither do they prohibit it. A responding attorney is unlikely to find it strategically advantageous to waste a judge's time arguing that interrogatories and requests for admissions should have been in two separate documents, and if such a dispute should arise, we could always separate them out and resubmit them if necessary. Therefore, there is usually relatively little risk in combining the two, unless doing so is clearly contrary to preferred practice in a given court.

As we will see, it is often quite useful to send one's opponent both a request for admission and an interrogatory covering the same topic. For example, we might request an admission that document X is authentic and bears a genuine signature; then add an interrogatory to be answered if the request is denied, asking for the facts on which the denial is based. We can, of course, do this even if the requests for admissions and the interrogatories are not in the same physical document, but it is more convenient and logical to group related requests together.

In this workshop, we will follow the approach of combining requests for admission and interrogatories in the one document. Your instructor will inform you of whether this practice is appropriate under the customs of your locality. If not, we would suggest that it is still best to think of the drafting task as a single undertaking, and write interrogatories and any related requests for admissions at the same time, rather than to think of interrogatories as one project and requests for admissions as another. Our focus should be on our discovery goals and on the information we are trying to discover, rather than on the mechanics and paperwork involved in discovering it. Our approach should be first to decide what information or evidence we are trying to obtain, and then to choose whichever discovery tool—or combination of tools—is best suited for the job.

> **Your Local Notes**
> _____
> _____

## When Do We Use Interrogatories and Requests for Admissions?

Under the federal rules, and in many state courts, discovery is permitted only after the suit has gotten well under way. The discovery process as contemplated by FRCP, Rule 26, begins with a meeting between the opposing attorneys to plan out the discovery that needs to be accomplished, schedule it, and set deadlines. After this meeting, there is a scheduling conference with the judge in which the discovery plan is reduced to an order and signed; see FRCP, Rule 26(f).

FRCP, Rule 26(d), provides that neither side may engage in discovery at all until they have met and conferred as required by Rule 26(f), unless all parties agree to allow earlier discovery or permission is obtained from the judge. (The judge always has power to alter schedules and deadlines in an appropriate situation; for example, to allow the early taking of the deposition of a witness who is about to move to another country.)

Once discovery has begun, anyone can use any discovery procedure at any time unless the scheduling order says otherwise. FRCP, Rule 26(d), provides that "unless the court . . . orders otherwise, methods of discovery may be used in any sequence, and the fact that a party is conducting discovery, whether by deposition or otherwise, shall not operate to delay any other party's discovery." In other words, discovery is not like a well-ordered tennis match, where each side takes turns hitting

## SIDEBAR

### Limitations on the Number of Interrogatories

*Interrogatories lend themselves very readily to use as an offensive tool. In all but the simplest of cases, with the help of the block-copy features of modern word processing, a competent paralegal could easily generate a set of hundreds or even thousands of interrogatories in an hour or two. Answering them would require months of full-time work for an entire team of paralegals working for the opposing party—perhaps not entirely a bad thing from the standpoint of paralegal employment, but an expensive burden for the litigant who has to pay for it.*

*By the 1970s, the use of massive sets of interrogatories as a weapon for running up opponents' costs was becoming widespread. Sets of interrogatories several inches thick were becoming commonplace, to the point where litigators worried that it might be considered malpractice not to try to carpet-bomb one's opponents into the Stone Age using 10-pound stacks of paper.*

*Various solutions to the problem were proposed. One obvious response was to have judges look over and approve discovery requests for reasonableness before requiring answers, but, as a practical matter, judges have neither the time nor much enthusiasm for micromanaging the discovery process in each of the several hundred lawsuits that may be pending before them at any given time.*

*Another proposal was to place a limit—say, 25—on the number of interrogatories that a party could submit in one case. This was an inherently ter-*

*rible idea, for several reasons. First of all, how much is "one" interrogatory? If we ask, "State your name," pretty clearly we could call that one interrogatory. But what if we ask "State the names, addresses, and telephone numbers of each person employed by you in the last ten years," and our opponent is General Motors Corporation? Is that still "one" interrogatory? Second, is it reasonable to impose a limit of 25 interrogatories in a simple lawsuit to collect a debt and also in a complex antitrust case involving hundreds of witnesses and rooms full of documents?*

*Nevertheless, the idea of limiting the number of interrogatories caught on and gained broad acceptance, mainly because no one could think of any other way to impose reasonable bounds without making judges into full-time discovery referees. FRCP, Rule 33(a), allows interrogatories "not exceeding 25 in number including all discrete subparts." A number of state courts have adopted similar rules. Your instructor will inform you of what, if any, limitations there are on the use of interrogatories in the state courts of your locality.*

*Even in jurisdictions in which numerical limits are imposed, the judge retains the power to authorize parties to exceed the limits in appropriate situations; see FRCP, Rule 33(a). In courts that have adopted mandatory disclosure rules, of course, the need for interrogatories is, at least theoretically, reduced.*

the ball; rather, it is a free-for-all, with both parties serving and receiving at the same time.

Therefore, the sequence and timing of discovery becomes largely a matter of strategy, and depends considerably on the rules in force in the court in which the case is being litigated. In a federal court that has adopted mandatory disclosure rules, interrogatories are used mainly for pinning down important factual issues and hardly at all for "fishing" for evidence. Both interrogatories and requests for admissions are most likely to be used late in the discovery process, after the mandatory disclosures have been made and the factual issues of the case are well defined. In "old-fashioned" courts, where there is no mandatory disclosure and no limits on written discovery, interrogatories may be used much earlier, to try to obtain all of the background information that would flow in auto-

matically as a result of the disclosure rules in a jurisdiction that has adopted them. Your instructor will inform you of the usual practice in the courts of your locality.

```
Your Local Notes
_____
_____
```

## Drafting Interrogatories: Step-by-step Instructions

We now review the steps for taking discovery via interrogatories and requests for admissions, including drafting the interrogatories and requests, serving and filing them, obtaining and analyzing responses, and performing needed follow-up. We reiterate that it is not our intent to imply that the steps that follow embody the only way to conduct written discovery. Rather, we present one formula that works and that you can use as a starting point.

## PREPARATORY STEPS

### Step 1 Define Your Objectives

Keeping in mind the strengths and weaknesses of written discovery, here is a list of some of the specific objectives for which interrogatories and requests for admissions are well suited. At this point, we merely summarize the objectives; we will translate them into actual interrogatories and requests for admissions in the Learning By Example section later.

### Getting Background Facts

1. *Mapping out the totality of the document landscape.* To complete our document discovery effectively, we need to have an accurate picture of what kinds of documents our opponent has or knows about, how they are organized, in whose custody they are kept, and what kinds of information they contain. FRCP, Rule 26(b)(1), allows us to obtain discovery of "the existence, description, nature, custody, condition, and location of any books, documents, or other tangible things. . . . " We can use interrogatories to begin assembling this background information, keeping in mind that the answers we get will probably not tell us everything that there is to know.

2. *Identifying potential witnesses.* We can use interrogatories to make our opponent tell us the names and addresses of all individuals known to have information concerning the matters in dispute. FRCP, Rule 26(b)(1), allows us to inquire about "the identity and location of persons having knowledge of any discoverable matter. . . . "

3. *Obtaining information about expert witnesses and their opinions.* Using interrogatories, we can find out how our opponent is approaching the technical or scientific issues in the case, if any. We can find out the identities of our opponent's trial experts, and we can get background information about them that will be useful in planning how to deal with their testi-

mony at trial. For example, we can find out what other cases they have testified in, what publications they have authored, and other similar information that will let us track down any opinions they have expressed in the past. Interrogatories are particularly useful here; we could get the same information by deposing the expert, but there are compelling reasons not to do it that way. When we depose an opponent's expert witness, we will be billed for her time. For medical experts and other highly compensated professionals, the expert's fee for a few hours of deposition testimony can be thousands of dollars. The court may not allow us to depose the same expert more than once, even if we are willing to pay again. We want to make every minute of deposition count, so we need to be as well prepared and as well armed with background information as possible before we confront an expert across the deposition table.

### Placing Limits On Our Opponent's Case

1. *Limiting our opponent's legal theories.* We have seen in previous workshops that the pleadings—the complaint and answer—do not necessarily dictate what causes of action or defenses an opposing party can assert.

Ideally, all causes of action should be alleged in the complaint and all defenses should be alleged in the answer, but, especially in federal court where the rules call for "notice pleading," a party is entitled to assert any cause of action or defense that is reasonably supported by the facts alleged in the complaint or answer. Moreover, complaints and answers can be amended to add new causes of action or defenses. Obviously, we do not want to be ambushed with surprise legal theories at trial, so what can we do?

Here, interrogatories provide a solution that we could not achieve in any other way. We would not be permitted to ask an opposing party about legal theories in a deposition—such a question would be objectionable as calling for opinion or speculation. FRCP, Rule 33, however, provides that "An interrogatory otherwise proper is not necessarily objectionable merely because an answer to the interrogatory involves an opinion or contention that relates to fact or the application of law to fact. . . . " This provision has been interpreted by the federal courts as authorizing an interrogatory that asks an opposing party to state (for example) all of the legal theories that he relies on in support of each claim or defense. Interrogatories of this kind are very helpful in avoiding surprises, since the court will be unlikely to allow new legal theories that a party has failed to disclose when asked for them in interrogatories.

2. *Limiting the facts that can be used to prove claims and defenses.* Complaints and answers are often not very informative documents, their main purpose being merely to give notice of the overall claims and defenses. The complaint may allege in general terms what defendant did that plaintiff is suing about. But to prepare for trial, defendant's attorney needs to pin down the details of exactly what plaintiff says happened. Similarly, plaintiff's attorney needs more than just defendant's denial of plaintiff's version of the dispute—plaintiff's attorney needs to know the specific facts underlying defendant's story.

In jurisdictions that have not adopted mandatory disclosure rules, it is commonplace for defendant's attorney to send out a set of interrogatories soon after answering the complaint. Among other things, this initial set of interrogatories will typically go through the complaint, allegation by allegation and ask plaintiff to state the facts underlying each one. Plaintiff's attorney, upon receiving defendant's answer, will send out a similar set of interrogatories asking for the details supporting each denial or allegation in the answer. (In mandatory disclosure jurisdictions, the disclosure rules typically require the parties to include this information in their disclosure statements, so interrogatories of this kind may not be necessary.)

This technique can be used defensively as well. We can, for example, send interrogatories that ask, item by item, what facts our opponent has that would tend to *disprove* each of the elements of our own claims or defenses. This will help us avoid those pesky embarrassing moments where an opponent blows a hole in one of the main elements of our case at trial, using facts that we never thought of looking for. (Again, in mandatory disclosure jurisdictions, nasty surprises of this kind should not happen because all evidence will have been disclosed.)

3. *Limiting witnesses and exhibits.* The evidence each side will offer at trial will consist primarily of testimony by witnesses, and exhibits (mainly documents). Here the discovery needs of the opposing parties are in direct conflict. Each party would prefer to make the other specify, as far in advance as possible, exactly which witnesses and documents the other intends to offer at trial. On the other hand, each party would prefer to preserve for herself as much flexibility as possible, waiting until the last possible moment to make final decisions about which witnesses to call and which exhibits to offer.

As a practical matter, developing a witness and exhibit list in a case is an evolutionary process. We start, early in the case, by gathering all of the names of potential witnesses and all of the copies of documents that we can, and we then begin refining the lists and removing the unnecessary items. Every witness and every document that we offer must advance our cause enough to justify taking up valuable trial time. By the time the trial date arrives, we should have quite definite ideas about what we will present at trial and how.

We can—and should—send out an interrogatory that asks what witnesses our opponent may call at trial and what documents he will introduce as exhibits. The response will invariably be that our opponent has not yet decided, so what does this interrogatory buy us? Quite a lot, actually: FRCP, Rule 26(e)(2), states that "A party is under a duty seasonably to amend a prior response to an interrogatory . . . if the party learns that the response is in some material respect incomplete or incorrect. . . ." If the judge concludes that a party has deliberately "hidden the ball" by failing to disclose a witness or exhibit, there is a good chance that the offending party will be prohibited from using that witness or exhibit at trial. Therefore, if it becomes obvious that a particular witness will be called or that a particular document will be used, it is foolhardy not to supplement the prior answers to interrogatories. Again, as is typical of the discovery process, interrogatories asking for disclosure of trial witnesses and exhibits will not provide us with perfect information about our opponent's case, but they will help us keep the uncertainties and surprises within manageable bounds.

4. *Establishing the computation of damages.* The issue of damages is present in nearly every lawsuit, regardless of what the dispute is about. If plaintiff wins, how much money will be awarded? How will that amount be computed? What losses or expenses will plaintiff be entitled to include in the total, and what proof is there to verify that these are real? If we represent the defendant, one of our main objectives will be to place an upper limit on the amount that we can lose if the trial goes badly. Our

client will not appreciate it if we go to trial thinking that the most we can lose is $50,000, and we get hit with a million dollar verdict. And if we represent the plaintiff, we want to know how defendant claims the damages should be calculated, so that we will be ready to counter defendant's arguments.

Interrogatories are perfectly suited for forcing an opponent to be candid about the calculation of damages. For example, if we represent defendant, we will always, in every case, send out an interrogatory requiring plaintiff to state exactly how much money she is asking for and how the amount is calculated, and to tell us about every bit of supporting documentation (receipts, bills, etc.) that plaintiff has. This practically forces plaintiff to give us a reasonable number. If plaintiff claims an unsupportably high amount, we will simply read plaintiff's answer to this interrogatory to the jurors so that they can see for themselves how greedy plaintiff is. Similarly, if we represent plaintiff, we will ask defendant what he contends is the correct amount of damages in the event that plaintiff should win; again, if the response is too stingy, we will use it to paint defendant as a Scrooge in front of the jury.

When representing defendants, interrogatories also offer a useful way of getting the background information supporting plaintiff's damage claims. Using interrogatories and FRCP, Rule 34, requests for production of documents, defendant's attorney can obtain an itemization of the expenses and losses that comprise plaintiff's damages, and copies of the receipts, invoices, and other documents that underlie them. This information will allow defendant's attorney to verify the items claimed by plaintiff, and may provide leads that will help in the search for evidence to disprove plaintiff's damage claims.

## Pinning Down Known Facts

1. *Establishing the genuineness of documents.* Before we are allowed to introduce documents in evidence at trial, we are first required to authenticate them. We must prove that each document is what we say it is (i.e., not a forgery or an altered copy) and that any signatures are genuine. Authentication is required for every document introduced in evidence. In a simple case involving few documents, it may be easiest to authenticate them the old-fashioned way, by showing each document to a witness and having the witness testify that it is genuine. In cases where numerous documents will be introduced, however, it is

far preferable to authenticate documents in advance. Requests for admissions are perfect for this task: We simply serve requests asking the opposing party to admit the genuineness of each document that we intend to use as an exhibit.

In doing this we must be careful to create a clear record showing exactly which documents our requests for admissions are referring to—we do not want to leave room for an opponent to claim that the exhibit we are trying to introduce at trial is not the same one that she admitted was genuine. Often, by the time we get to the stage of the case where we need to think about authenticating trial exhibits, we will already have given our opponent copies of our exhibits in a numbered set; then we can simply refer to the exhibits in our requests for admissions by an exhibit number and a short description. If we want to be even more careful, we can always nail down what documents we are referring to by attaching copies of them to the requests for admissions.

In the vast majority of cases, there will be little serious question about the authenticity of the documents involved in the case, and admissions concerning the genuineness of documents are routinely given with little hesitation. Once in a while, however, a litigant may have a legitimate issue to raise—what then? Obviously, he will deny the request for admission that the document is genuine, but this leaves the requesting party in the dark about what the problem is. The solution is for the requesting party to serve, with the request for admission, an interrogatory asking for the reasons behind any denials. For example:

*Request for Admission No. 5*

Admit that the document attached to plaintiff's complaint as Exhibit 1 is a true and correct copy of a contract entered into between plaintiff and defendant on or about March 15, 2000, and that said contract bears the genuine signatures of plaintiff and defendant.

*Interrogatory No. 5*

In the event that you deny the foregoing request for admission, state each and every fact tending to show that the document attached to plaintiff's complaint as Exhibit 1 is not a true and correct copy of a contract entered into between plaintiff and defendant on or about March 15, 2000, or that said contract does not bear the genuine signatures of plaintiff and defendant.

(If we are in a court that limits the number of interrogatories, we will not want to waste an entire interrogatory on each request for admission, of which there may be hundreds if we have many documents to authenticate. In that case, we may use a single interrogatory, for example: "With respect to each and every request for admission in this set which you have denied in whole or in part, state each and every fact supporting such denial." However, by using a blanket question of this kind, we leave an evasive opponent more room to give us a smokescreen of extraneous detail that omits the facts that we really wanted.)

2. *Establishing facts that are not seriously contested.* In most lawsuits, there are some facts that we are required to prove but that no one seriously disputes. In our hypo, for example, it is unlikely that either defendant intends to waste energy contesting the fact that Shannon was a paying guest in Room 409 on the night in question. We are free to use requests for admissions to establish facts of this kind, and to use interrogatories to obtain the facts underlying any denials. The procedure is identical to the one we just reviewed for obtaining admissions of the genuineness of documents.

Do we gain much from such admissions? The answer depends on the situation, but usually not. In the example just given, we can just as easily bring out the facts of Shannon's stay at Banbury Park Hotel as part of the direct testimony in which she tells her story, so there is little need to establish such facts in advance. An opposing party is unlikely to admit any facts that she does not think we can easily prove anyway.

Not all of these uses for written discovery fit the needs of every lawsuit. We offer them as a kind of checklist for you to use in analyzing the particular discovery demands of the case before you. When you sit down to draft interrogatories and requests for admissions, we recommend that you begin by spending some time carefully mapping out what you are trying to accomplish in the case at hand. Make a list of topics that you want to cover. Keep your goals squarely in view as you begin to draft.

## DRAFTING STEPS

Now we begin the task of putting together the actual court paper that we will serve on our opponent. As usual, much will be boilerplate block-copied from discovery requests that we have used in other lawsuits, or from forms. We do not suggest that this is a purely mechanical process; it takes trained legal judgment to decide what things to copy, and which bits of boilerplate will advance our discovery goals. By the time we have put together what we can by

adapting discovery requests that we or someone else has already written in some other case, a good deal of our work may be done. In Step 5, we add whatever needs to be written from scratch.

### Step 2    *Caption and Preamble*

As with all court papers, we begin with the caption, date and signature lines, and certificate of mailing that we prepared in Workshop 4. Next comes the preamble; as usual, we recite who we are, what authority we are acting under, and what the document is all about. Here is a sample (but, as always, you should modify your preamble to conform to local custom):

> Plaintiff Shannon Martin, pursuant to Rules 33 and 36, Federal Rules of Civil Procedure, propounds the following interrogatories and requests for admissions to defendant Park Hotels Group to be answered in writing and under oath within 30 days.

*Your Local Notes*

_____

_____

### Step 3    *Instructions and Definitions*

As we saw with FRCP, Rule 34, requests for production of documents, many litigators like to include an Instructions and Definitions section with a set of interrogatories or requests for admission. See Workshop 9 for discussion and examples. If your instructor or your supervising attorney is one of those who favors this practice, he will undoubtedly have a form set of instructions and definitions that you will use, and you will block-copy it into your document immediately after the preamble.

One caveat: In many of the situations in which an answer to an interrogatory will be used—arguing to the judge or jury, for example—having to flip back through pages of interrogatories to find the right definition in the definition section is a distraction best avoided. It is better to make each interrogatory self-contained to the extent possible. Therefore, we would include in the definition section only definitions of words that will be used over and over, like "document" or "person." Words that are used only in one or a few interrogatories should be defined in each interrogatory in which they are used.

---

**Your Local Notes**

_____

_____

---

### Step 4 — Include the Standard Interrogatories

No lawsuit is entirely unique, and many vary surprisingly little from one to the next. Given two lawsuits based on the same cause of action, it is axiomatic that the elements of the claims must be the same. For example, physical contact is an element of every suit for battery. Some elements, like causation and damages, are present in nearly all lawsuits. Other litigators have spent much time and talent honing and perfecting discovery requests in all kinds of cases, and it would be senseless not to take advantage of what has already been done. Not only senseless, but perhaps an invitation to malpractice—if we try to reinvent everything from scratch, we may well leave out something important that we would never have missed had we used the discovery requests from some similar case as a guide.

When you are assigned to write interrogatories or requests for admissions in a case, your first step should be to try to find a case involving similar claims and defenses, and to obtain copies of the discovery requests used in that case. In a litigation office, your supervising attorney will certainly be able to suggest other files in the office for you to examine; failing that, try your local law library, where you can often find sample discovery requests in practice manuals or in books about the various litigation specialties.

If you are working in a jurisdiction that does not have mandatory disclosure, do not overlook the mandatory disclosure rules of other courts as a source for ideas. These rules have been drafted by highly experienced litigators and judges with the intention of requiring disclosure of everything that ought to be important in any lawsuit. At a minimum, your interrogatories need to cover all of the factual territory that typical mandatory disclosure rules cover.

---

**Your Local Notes**

_____

_____

---

## Numbering Interrogatories

_It is customary for interrogatories to be numbered; this makes it easier to refer to a particular interrogatory in some other court paper. The Federal Rules do not specify the details of how interrogatories are to be numbered. The numbering system shown in the examples in this Workshop—in which each interrogatory has an underlined sidehead in the form "Interrogatory No. X"—is commonplace, but local customs vary and should usually be followed._

_The numbering sequence is another matter not covered by the Federal Rules. We recommend that the numbering sequence begun in the first set of interrogatories in the lawsuit be continued through successive sets, so that each interrogatory has a unique number. In other words, if plaintiff's first set of interrogatories to defendant has 15 interrogatories numbered 1 through 15, the second set would start at number 16. This practice will avoid a great deal of confusion and ambiguity when referring to specific interrogatories in motions or in argument before the judge or jury._

---

### Step 5 — Write the Individualized Interrogatories

Writing interrogatories involves two main skills: (1) figuring out what questions to ask and (2) figuring out how to word the individual questions in as "watertight" a manner as possible. Both are important—obviously, if we fail to ask the right questions, we will not get the information that we want, but we can also miss important facts by asking questions in such a sloppy and imprecise way that our opponent is able to evade them.

**Knowing What Questions to Ask**—After we have pieced together and organized all of the questions that we have been able to borrow from forms, discovery requests in other cases, textbooks, practice manuals, and other similar sources, we should have covered most of the routine issues that we need to cover. Now we need to write the customized interrogatories and requests for admissions necessary to fill in any gaps and to deal with any unusual or unique aspects of our case.[1] Is there some systematic way in

---

[1] In a jurisdiction with mandatory disclosure rules, the routine issues should be covered by the disclosure statement, so the customized interrogatories may be the only ones that we will need.

which we can do this, so as to ensure ourselves that nothing important will be overlooked?

Yes and no. There is no "formula" approach that will guarantee that we have not missed anything, but certainly there are things that we can do that will make our task easier and less error prone. It will help if we make a checklist of the topics that we want to be sure to cover. A good place to begin in making such a checklist is with the issues outline; we can go through the outline issue by issue and fact by fact, noting the ideas that occur to us with respect to each one. This does not mean that we will draft an interrogatory addressing every issue and every fact; as we have seen, interrogatories are not the discovery weapon of choice in many situations. But by reviewing the issues systematically, one at a time, we can make an intelligent judgment about each one in turn, think about how best to obtain the needed proof, and be reasonably confident that we have not overlooked any important issues.

Ideally, this review of the issues should be done before we begin drafting. As we draft our interrogatories and requests for admissions, if we have prepared our minds by going through the issues outline and thinking about the case, additional ideas will occur to us, and we can add them to our list of topics. (A good habit to cultivate is to make our list of topics on a separate legal pad that we keep continually at hand as we are drafting, so that whenever an idea strikes, we can write it down immediately.)

**Writing the Questions**—When we write discovery requests, our goal is not so much to write convincingly or elegantly as it is to write precisely. As we will see in Workshop 11 on responding to discovery, the responding party will be analyzing each interrogatory or request for admissions word by word, with the goal of answering the question in whatever way provides the *smallest* quantity of useful information. If it is possible to interpret a question in such a way as to avoid revealing damaging facts, that is how the responding party will interpret it.

The responding party's only obligation is to answer the questions that we have asked. Volunteering information that we have not clearly asked for is something that our opponent is neither required to do nor likely to do. Suppose our opponent withholds information that we feel we have asked for—what happens then? There is, of course, a good possibility that we will never find out that the information exists, in which case our opponent will gain an advantage and escape with impunity. If we are lucky enough to get the information from another source, FRCP, Rule 37, allows us to ask the judge to punish the party who withheld the information. To succeed in this, however, we must be able to convince the judge that our interrogatory fairly covered the information withheld.

It is up to us to word our questions in such a way that they leave no room for evasion. A question can provide an excuse for the responding party to withhold facts in two main ways:

*1.* By using vague or ambiguous language, a question may fail to describe the desired information precisely enough. Example: "State the names and addresses of all persons who witnessed the industrial accident described in plaintiff's complaint." What does "witnessed" mean? Would it include someone who, for example, heard a loud noise and came running over just after the accident occurred? If there were such persons, and the responding party did not want their identities known, this interrogatory would not obtain their names. Better: "State the names and addresses of each and every person who was present in the building in which the industrial accident described in plaintiff's complaint occurred, at any time within one hour before or after said accident occurred." The moral: Use words about whose meanings there can be no reasonable difference of opinion. Whether or not people are "present" at a particular place and time is not debatable; whether or not they "witnessed" an event can be a matter of opinion.

*2.* By using wording that is overly specific, we could inadvertently exclude possible variations of the expected facts. Example: "State the names and addresses of all employees of defendant City Hospital who were present in the operating room at the time of the operation described in plaintiff's complaint." The word "employees" here is too specific. There could easily have been doctors, nurses, anesthetists, even medical students present, none of whom were "employees" of the defendant hospital. Better: "State the names and addresses of all persons who were present in the operating room at the time of the operation described in plaintiff's complaint." The moral: Avoid using words that unnecessarily restrict the scope of the question.

To see what happens when we are not careful enough in our drafting, see the sidebar on "leaky" interrogatories.

**Step 6**    *Write the Requests for Admissions, If Any*

We have said that we would follow the practice of combining interrogatories and requests for admissions in the same physical document, unless local rules require us to do otherwise. This does not necessarily mean that every set must have both; the ac-

## SIDEBAR

### "Leaky" Interrogatories: An Example

*Here is an example that illustrates how poor wording can result in an interrogatory that fails to obtain the desired information.*

*Assume the following facts: Two years prior to the incident in which Shannon was injured, John Smith, the assistant maintenance supervisor at Banbury Park Hotel, wrote a memo to Ron Jones, a company vice-president at Park Hotels Group corporate headquarters. In the memo, Smith informed Jones that the door closers on the entrance doors of many of the rooms on the fourth floor were badly worn and preventing the doors from closing properly, and recommended replacing all the door closers on the fourth floor. (The door closer is the arm at the top of the door that pushes the door closed.)*

*Suppose Shannon's attorney serves the following interrogatory on defendant Park Hotels Group: "Identify and describe the contents of all letters written by any management-level employee of defendant pertaining to the maintenance of the guest room door locks at Banbury Park Hotel."*

*Is this interrogatory as watertight as it can be? Will it force Park Hotels Group to cough up Smith's memo?*

*Not likely—remember, the responding party is not obligated to volunteer information beyond what is clearly asked for, and there are several good arguments to be made that Smith's memo is not within the scope of what the interrogatory asked for. (Before you read on, see if you can think of at least three arguments that Park Hotels Group's attorney could make.)*

*Here are a few possibilities: (1) The interrogatory refers to "letters"—a memo is not a letter. (2) The interrogatory refers to letters written by any "management-level employee." Smith, as an assistant maintenance supervisor, is arguably not one. (3) The interrogatory refers to letters "pertaining to the maintenance of the room door locks." A door closer is not a door lock.*

*How could we fix the leaks in this interrogatory? Use words that are broader in scope and delete unnecessary restrictive adjectives like "management-level." For example: "Identify and describe the contents of each and every communication by any employee of defendant pertaining to the maintenance of the guest room doors, door locks, and/or other hardware associated with guest room doors at Banbury Park Hotel."*

tual contents of each submission will be dictated by the discovery needs of the case. In the early stages of discovery, the emphasis is likely to be on interrogatories, since we will be concerned more with finding out what the facts are than with proving them. As the trial date nears, requests for admissions take on greater importance for tasks such as authenticating documents. We had better not need to submit general, fact-gathering interrogatories at this stage, because the trial will be upon us before we can get the answers and put them to use. The only interrogatories we are likely to include in these late-stage discovery requests are those designed to follow up on any of our requests for admissions that the responding party denies.

The suggestions that we have made regarding the drafting of interrogatories apply equally here.

**Early-Stage Requests for Admissions**—The main use of requests for admissions in the early stages of a lawsuit is to help separate the factual issues that are genuinely in dispute from those that are not. You may be wondering why we would need to do this; surely, the complaint and answer are supposed to define the issues?

It is true that the defendant has an opportunity to admit undisputed facts in the answer. As a practical matter, however, the pleading process is inadequate as a way of zeroing in on the factual issues that are seriously contested, for a number of reasons:

- The answer is filed at a time when defendant's attorney has probably not yet had much chance to investigate the facts.

- If there is any doubt about whether the answer should admit or deny an allegation, it will be denied. In fact, FRCP, Rule 8(b), expressly allows a defendant to deny allegations of the complaint if she is without sufficient information to decide whether they are true.

- There is no incentive for a defendant to make admissions in the answer. FRCP, Rule 37(c)(2), imposes penalties on parties who deny requests for admissions without having reasonable grounds for doing so, but there is no similar penalty for making "unreasonable" denials in an answer.

- There is usually no opportunity for *defendant* to obtain admissions from *plaintiff* during the pleading process, since there are no pleadings

# SIDEBAR

## The Top Ten List for Learning to Draft Interrogatories

*Avoiding the problems of vagueness, ambiguity, and overspecificity requires us to write interrogatories and requests for admissions in a style that, in any other kind of writing, would be considered ugly and redundant. This kind of writing does not come naturally to most people—it is a learned skill that comes with practice. Nevertheless, a few pointers can be given. Here is our Top 10 list:*

1. *Wherever possible, describe the information you want with the most general words possible. Here are a few examples of this technique:*

   | Too specific: | Better: |
   | --- | --- |
   | *"all memos"* | *"each and every communication"* |
   | *"every employee"* | *"every person"* |
   | *"all receipts"* | *"each and every document evidencing or reflecting any expenditure"* |
   | *"all sales"* | *"each and every transaction"* |

2. *Scrutinize the adjectives in a question carefully. Eliminate unnecessary limiting words. Avoid using adjectives whose meaning is debatable.*

3. *Consider defining words whose meaning is uncertain, either in a separate Definitions section or (we would prefer) in the interrogatory itself. There is no rule that requires an interrogatory to be a single sentence. For example, we could write: "State the name and address of each and every person who has performed maintenance or other services with respect to guest room door locks or door hardware at Banbury Park Hotel at any time since January 1, 1996. For purposes of this interrogatory, "maintenance or other services" shall mean any services of whatsoever nature involving repair, adjustment, rekeying, removal, replacement, alteration, inspection, or other activities involving any door lock, door closer, strike plate, safety latch or chain, or other door hardware installed or to be installed on any guest room door at Banbury Park Hotel."*

4. *Each interrogatory should, as far as possible, be self-contained and stand on its own.*

*When you are arguing about an interrogatory before the judge, or reading an interrogatory to the jury, you do not need the distraction of having to flip through a stack of papers looking for some external reference. Although it is permissible to refer specifically to other interrogatories in the same set (i.e., "State the address of each person identified in your response to Interrogatory No. 5"), this should be avoided where possible. Similarly, it is preferable to include any important definitions in each interrogatory rather than in a separate Definitions section.*

5. *Specify a date range where necessary to avoid ambiguity. For example, write "Describe each and every communication between defendant Brown and defendant Green from January 1, 1998, to the present." If you do not specify the date range, the responding party will take the opportunity to decide how far back in time the response will cover. Where possible, use a specific date—i.e., "January 1, 1998, to the present"—in preference to an event that requires the reader to look up a date, i.e., "during the five years preceding the filing of plaintiff's complaint."*

6. *Keep interrogatories short where possible. Long, run-on sentences make it too easy for the responding party to claim that he or she did not understand what was being asked. If necessary, break the interrogatory up into two or more sentences (see the example in item 3 above).*

7. *In jurisdictions that do not impose limits on the number of interrogatories, clarity can often be improved by breaking one interrogatory into two or more separate ones.*

8. *Approach the process of writing interrogatories as one of making successive improvements to a first draft. Write a first draft of the question; then try to think of all the ways in which the information you want could exist that would not be covered by the interrogatory as you wrote it. Then rewrite the question and repeat the analysis, as many times as it takes, until you are sure that you have closed off every loophole in your wording that an opponent could use as an excuse not to give you the information that you want. As with most kinds of writing, there is no such thing as good writing of interrogatories—there is only good rewriting.*

9. *Study interrogatories written by skilled litigators and copy shamelessly. Try to match your writing style, choice of words, and format to theirs.*

10. *Practice, practice, practice.*

after defendant's answer unless defendant asserts counterclaims.

■ Because allegations in pleadings are usually quite general, it is difficult for a responsive pleading to admit narrow undisputed facts without also potentially giving away issues that are genuinely disputed.

Requests for admissions, however, are well suited for the purpose of making an opposing party fish or cut bait on peripheral issues. It is often useful in the early stages of a lawsuit to go through the complaint and answer carefully, analyze them issue by issue against your issues outline, and make a list of the facts and issues that seem unlikely to be in genuine dispute. From this list, you can then prepare requests for admissions, backed up by interrogatories to be answered whenever a request for admission is denied.

Here is an example: In our hypo, Shannon's attorney alleged in paragraph 4 of plaintiff's complaint that the "Court has jurisdiction of this matter under the provisions of 28 U.S.C. §1332." (28 U.S.C. §1332 gives federal courts subject matter jurisdiction over cases in which the plaintiffs and defendants are from different states. See Workshop 2.) In its answer, defendant Park Hotels Group responded that it was "without knowledge or information sufficient to form a belief as to the truth of the allegations of said paragraphs, and therefore denies them."

If we are representing Shannon, we do not want to leave the issue of subject matter jurisdiction in a state of uncertainty. If a defect of subject matter jurisdiction arises, even at the late stages of the lawsuit, the court will have no choice but to dismiss, so if there is any problem, we want to know about it immediately. A request for admission, backed up by a follow-up interrogatory, is a good tool to use for this purpose:

*Request for Admission No. 1*

Admit that this court has valid subject matter jurisdiction of this matter under the provisions of 28 U.S.C. §1332.

*Interrogatory No. 1*

In the event that you deny the foregoing Request for Admission No. 1, state each and every fact upon which such denial is based, and state each and every respect in which you contend that the jurisdictional requirements of 28 U.S.C. §1332 are not met in this action.

Why stop at issues that seem unlikely to be disputed? Could we not use the same technique to flush out the facts of issues that *are* in dispute? We could, but, as we have seen in the introduction to this workshop, written discovery is not very well suited for establishing disputed facts. In the first place, opposing parties are usually not a good source of evidence on

disputed facts—disputed facts in a lawsuit are established (usually) by evidence that we already have, or obtain from friendly or neutral sources. And if we are going to seek evidence about disputed facts from an opponent, written discovery is a poor way to do it because the responding party has too much opportunity to think about and edit the response. Depositions are preferable for such tasks.

---

*Your Local Notes*

_____

_____

---

**Late-Stage Requests for Admissions**—When discovery has progressed to the point where we have a reasonably clear idea of what documents will be used as exhibits at trial, it is time to review our exhibit list carefully and make sure that we have the evidence we need to establish the admissibility of each exhibit. Requests for admissions are a useful tool for this purpose. Precisely what needs to be established depends on the document and the circumstances. We will need to analyze the evidence rules as they apply to each document in order to determine exactly what must be proved to make each one admissible. There are, however, two situations that occur often and are worth a closer look:

1. *Establishing genuineness.* Some documents in a lawsuit are themselves evidence of some event that needs to be proved. In our hypo, for example, Shannon's attorney will no doubt offer copies of Shannon's medical bills and the checks written to pay them as proof of the amount of Shannon's medical expenses. Here, it is merely necessary to prove that the receipts and checks are authentic—that is, that the document really is what it appears to be, and is not a forgery or altered copy:

   *Request for Admission No. 10*

   Admit that the documents attached hereto as Exhibits 14 through 33 are true and correct copies of receipts for amounts actually expended by plaintiff in payment of medical expenses incurred as a result of the injuries described in plaintiff's complaint.

   *Interrogatory No. 39*

   In the event that you deny the Request for Admission No. 10 in whole or in part, state which of Exhibits 14 through 33 you contend are not true and correct copies of receipts for amounts actually expended by plaintiff in payment of medical expenses incurred as a result of the injuries described in plaintiff's complaint, and, for each such Exhibit, state each and every fact upon which your denial is based.

2. *Establishing admissibility of regularly kept records.* Another very common use of documents as exhibits in a lawsuit is to establish facts that are recorded in the documents. In our hypo, for example, Shannon might want to introduce some of the notes kept by her doctor, to help show the extent and severity of her injuries.

It is still necessary to prove that a record of this kind is genuine, but there is a further problem: the physician's records are hearsay. The written record is really nothing but a factual statement by the physician—at a time when he was not under oath and could not be cross-examined. In principle, letting the report "testify" about what the doctor concluded is no different from letting some third person do so.

Records of this kind that are kept in accordance with some regular procedure are, however, inherently more reliable than, say, the testimony of, say, a nurse who happened to overhear the doctor talking about the case. Recognizing this, the rules of evidence make an exception to the hearsay rule for "regularly kept records"; Rule 803(6), Federal Rules of Evidence, tells us exactly what we must show to make a record admissible:

> A memorandum, report, record, or data compilation, in any form, of acts, events, conditions, opinions, or diagnoses, made at or near the time by, or from information transmitted by, a person with knowledge, if kept in the course of a regularly conducted business activity, and if it was the regular practice of that business activity to make the memorandum, report, record, or data compilation, all as shown by the testimony of the custodian or other qualified witness, unless the source of information or the method or circumstances of preparation indicate lack of trustworthiness. The term "business" as used in this paragraph includes business, institution, association, profession, occupation, and calling of every kind, whether or not conducted for profit.

To establish the admissibility of Shannon's medical record, Shannon's attorney might use the following request for admission and interrogatory:

### Request for Admission No. 7

Admit that the document attached hereto as Exhibit 4 is a true and correct copy of the medical record pertaining to the treatment of plaintiff by Dr. Ronald M. Green,

M.D., and that said document is entitled to be admitted in evidence herein pursuant to Rule 803(6), Federal Rules of Evidence.

### Interrogatory No. 19

In the event that you deny Request for Admission No. 7 in whole or in part, state each and every fact upon which such denial is based, and state each and every respect in which you contend that such document does not meet the requirements of Rule 803(6) for admissibility.

Of course, many other legal issues can arise that affect the admissibility of documents, most of which are best left for a course on evidence law. (You can get an idea of the rules that apply to many of the common document types by perusing the rest of Rule 803 of the Federal Rules of Evidence.) Our purpose here is merely to indicate how to use requests for admissions as a procedural tool for establishing admissibility of a document.

```
Your Local Notes
_____
_____
```

## CONCLUDING STEPS

When we have completed our drafting, proofread our work, and produced the document in final form, it must be reviewed and signed by an attorney. Then it is ready to be served on the responding party.

**Step 7** *Serve and Comply with Filing Requirements*

Interrogatories and requests for admissions are served informally, by mail or hand delivery in compliance with FRCP, Rule 5, on the attorney for the party to whom they are directed. Naturally, we keep a copy for our own file.

As discussed in detail in Workshop 7, some courts still require us to file discovery papers with the clerk of the court, while others prohibit us from doing so. In courts that no longer allow filing of interrogatories, we prepare a notice reciting that we have served them, and we file the notice and mail or deliver the notice to the attorneys for all parties.

```
Your Local Notes
_____
_____
```

**Step 8** *Docket Response Due Date and Follow-Up*

Answers to interrogatories and responses to requests for admissions are nominally due 30 days after service. FRCP, Rule 33(b)(3), provides:

> The party upon whom the interrogatories have been served shall serve a copy of the answers, and objections if any, within 30 days after the service of the interrogatories. A shorter or longer time may be directed by the court or, in the absence of such an order, agreed to in writing by the parties. . . .

If we have served the responding party by mail, FRCP, Rule 6(e), adds three extra days to the response time. (See Workshop 7 for details on computing deadlines.)

We enter the response due date in the office docketing system and also in our personal calendar. If the response does not arrive within a reasonable time after the due date, we follow up with a reminder letter or two, and then a motion to compel, if necessary. (Remember, though, that the response is deemed served when the opposing attorney mails it, so we have to allow time for it to arrive in the mail before we can conclude that it is late.)

---

**Your Local Notes**

_____

_____

---

**Step 9** *Analyze Response and Take Any Needed Further Action*

When the response arrives, we first check to see that it is signed by the party to whom it is directed. FRCP, Rule 33(b)(2), states "The answers are to be signed by the person making them, and the objections signed by the attorney making them." If we need to use any of the answers when cross-examining the responding party, we do not want to leave any room for her to squirm out of them by claiming that it was the attorney who prepared and signed them. We have the right to insist that answers to interrogatories be signed by the party—not just the attorney—and we should always do so.

We next go through the response carefully, question by question, and analyze the answers given. It is rare for a set of answers to interrogatories to be complete when we receive it—nearly always, the answers will fall short of what we are entitled to, and we will have to follow up with a demand letter. In Workshop 15 on discovery en-

forcement, we will examine in detail the procedures for forcing an opposing party to provide the information we have requested. To make our follow-up task easier, we will keep a list as we analyze our opponent's answers, and note any matters that require further attention.

We have several purposes in mind as we review the answers:

1. We want to verify that each interrogatory has been answered. Although it may seem surprising, it is not at all unusual to receive a set of answers to interrogatories in which some of the questions are not answered at all, or are answered with a vague promise to answer them some time in the future. We note any such "non-answers" on our follow-up list.

2. We want to verify that each answer is reasonably complete. A common tactic used by a party who is reluctant to divulge some damaging fact is to write an answer that seems to be responsive but, on closer scrutiny, is not. For a simplistic example, if the question is "Did you beat up your wife?", the answer "I love my wife very much" is not responsive—it does not actually answer the question. It often takes a degree of legal judgment, as well as a meticulous reading of the response, to detect such evasions. When detected, they must be followed up with a demand for a responsive answer.

3. We want to note any objections that the responding party has made. As we will see in detail in Workshop 11 on responding to discovery requests, the responding party is entitled to object to questions that are improper. If any of our questions have been objected to, we will need to analyze the legal basis given for each objection and decide whether valid grounds exist. If not, we will briefly set out in our demand letter the reasons why the objection is invalid.

4. We want to organize and catalog whatever new information the answers provided, and plan any additional discovery needed to fill in any gaps.

**Step 10** *Request Supplementation as Appropriate*

Some kinds of interrogatories elicit answers that are inherently unlikely to be complete and final. For example, we will nearly always send an interrogatory asking for the identities of any witnesses. The problem is that, even if the answer is complete when given, our opponent will probably become aware of additional witnesses as the case progresses.

In theory, our opponent should make a supplemental response disclosing new information as it is obtained. FRCP, Rule 26(e)(2), provides: " A party is under a duty reasonably to amend a prior response to an interrogatory, request for production, or request for admission if the party learns that the response is in some material respect incomplete or incorrect and if the additional or corrective information has not otherwise been made known to the other parties during the discovery process or in writing."

As a practical matter, however, we cannot depend on opposing parties to supplement answers voluntarily. If an opposing party fails to supplement, we will have already missed out on the information we need, and will be left arguing about whether the unsupplemented facts were material.

Far better, therefore, to make a formal request for supplementation. This can be a simple, one-page court paper entitled "Request for Supplementation" and reciting a request that the responding party supplement his answers to particular numbered interrogatories. For example:

> Plaintiff requests pursuant to the provisions of FRCP, Rule 26, that defendant supplement its answers to plaintiffs interrogatories numbered 5, 6, 9, and 24 dated June 1, 2000.

We can make such requests as often as reasonably needed. By making it impossible for the responding party to claim that the need to supplement was somehow forgotten or overlooked, appropriate use of requests for supplementation will make it much more likely that we will actually get updated information.

We will note on our list any interrogatories whose answers may change as the case develops, and make an entry on our personal calendar to remind us to prepare requests for supplementation at the appropriate time.

---

**Your Local Notes**

_____

_____

---

## Drafting Interrogatories: Learning by Example

We will now put the interrogatory drafting principles that we have learned into practice by drafting a set of interrogatories and requests for admissions for use in our hypothetical lawsuit, *Martin v. Collins.* We will prepare a partial set of interrogatories typical of the kind that plaintiff might serve on defendant shortly after the defendant's answer is filed. We will assume that we are in a jurisdiction that does not have mandatory disclosure rules, and that there is no numerical limit on the number of interrogatories we are allowed to submit.

Obviously, space limitations do not permit us to reproduce a complete set of interrogatories here. Moreover, as we have seen, the content of a set of interrogatories varies considerably depending on how close the case is to trial, whether it is the plaintiff or defendant who is submitting them, and other factors. Therefore, the set of interrogatories and requests for admissions that we present here should be taken as an illustration of what written discovery papers look like, not as a definitive model for all cases and all situations.

## PREPARATORY STEPS

### Step 1 — *Define Your Objectives*

Since this is an early-stage discovery request made by a plaintiff, we choose the following objectives:

1. *To obtain more information about what kinds of maintenance records Banbury Park Hotel maintains concerning the guest room doors and door locks.* We want to explore any such records to see whether we might discover evidence of some defect that could have made the lock ineffective. We have, of course, also asked for such records in our Rule 34 request for production, but that, by itself, is not enough—we also want to find out enough detail about what records are kept and what information they contain to be able to judge whether the documents we get in response to the request for production are complete. This is typical of discovery; we use the various discovery tools in combination to ensure that we obtain a complete picture of the facts.

2. *To obtain the identities of any witnesses that Park Hotels Group knows about and that we do not know about.* Under the facts of our hypo, the hotel defendant is in a far better position than is plaintiff to investigate the events leading to Shannon's injury. It is entirely possible that other hotel guests or employees were in a position to observe all or part of what happened.

3. *To place some limits on the affirmative defenses raised in Park Hotels Group's answer.* Paragraph 12 of Park Hotels Group's answer is a boilerplate paragraph alleging a number of affirmative defenses:

12. At this early stage of the case, defendant Park Hotels Group, Inc., is unable to determine the applicability of the defenses enumerated in FRCP, Rule 8(c), but intends to preserve those defenses to the extent they should be deemed pertinent, and therefore affirmatively alleges the defenses of accord and satisfaction, arbitration and award, assumption of risk, contributory negligence, discharge in bankruptcy, duress, estoppel, failure of consideration, fraud, illegality, injury by fellow servant, laches, license, payment, release, res judicata, statute of frauds, statute of limitations, and waiver.

We might assume that Park Hotels has no real evidence to back up any of these affirmative defenses and is merely trying to preserve them in case some evidence turns up later. We cannot be sure, however, so we will draft an interrogatory asking defendant to tell us what evidence it has on any of these issues, and thereby prevent any nasty surprises.

4. *To get defendant's version of what happened.* Defendant's answer, as is typical, denies plaintiff's version of what happened, but does not tell us what defendant says happened. An interrogatory will not get us a deep and probing factual account of the kind that we could elicit in a deposition, but at least it will force defendant to go on the record with some version of the facts as defendant contends they occurred.

5. *To force defendant to keep us informed about what witnesses and exhibits defendant is plan-* ning to use at trial. (This will usually be a boilerplate interrogatory that we copy from our standard set to be used in all cases.) Because we are submitting this interrogatory early in the lawsuit, the answer we get will undoubtedly be incomplete. That does not matter—we will ask for the answer to be supplemented later. The earlier and more often we ask for this information, the harder it will be for defendant to get away with incomplete disclosure later on.

We will draft one interrogatory for each of these objectives. Obviously, in a real lawsuit, this set of interrogatories would be much larger. We reiterate that our choice of objectives and example interrogatories is arbitrary, and dictated by space limitations rather than by good litigation strategy.

We will also include the request for admission that we discussed earlier in Step 6, which is intended to help lay the subject matter jurisdiction issue to rest.

## DRAFTING STEPS

Figure W10–1 shows the finished set of interrogatories and requests for admissions, which is put together using Steps 2 through 6 as a guide. The instructions/definitions section is from Appendix A of the local rules of the United States District Court for the District of Arizona. They are designed for an automobile accident case. A more detailed (and perhaps objectionable) set of instructions and definitions that could be used is shown in Figure W10–2.

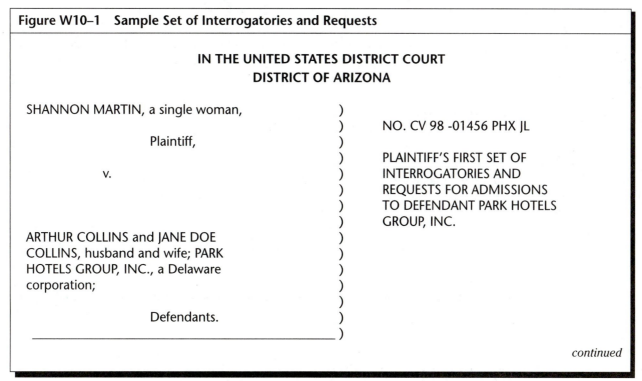

**Figure W10–1    Sample Set of Interrogatories and Requests**

**IN THE UNITED STATES DISTRICT COURT**
**DISTRICT OF ARIZONA**

| | |
|---|---|
| SHANNON MARTIN, a single woman, | ) ) NO. CV 98 -01456 PHX JL |
| Plaintiff, | ) ) |
| v. | ) PLAINTIFF'S FIRST SET OF ) INTERROGATORIES AND ) REQUESTS FOR ADMISSIONS ) TO DEFENDANT PARK HOTELS ) GROUP, INC. |
| ARTHUR COLLINS and JANE DOE COLLINS, husband and wife; PARK HOTELS GROUP, INC., a Delaware corporation; | ) ) ) ) ) |
| Defendants. | ) ) |
| _____ | ) |

*continued*

**Figure W10–1    Sample Set of Interrogatories and Requests,** *continued*

Plaintiff hereby submits interrogatories and requests for admission to defendant Park Hotels Group, pursuant to the provisions of Rules 33 and 36, Federal Rules of Civil Procedure, to be answered in writing and under oath within 30 days from the date of service hereof.

### *INSTRUCTIONS AND DEFINITIONS*

A.    All information is to be divulged which is in the possession of the individual or corporate party, his attorney, investigators, agents, employees, or other representatives of the named party and his attorney.

B.    A "medical practitioner" as used in these interrogatories is meant to include any medical doctor, osteopathic physician, podiatrist, doctor of chiropractic, naturopathic physician, or other person who performs any form of healing art.

C.    Where an individual interrogatory calls for an answer which involves more than one part, each part of the answer should be clearly set out so that it is understandable.

D.    Where the terms "you," "plaintiff," or "defendant" are used, they are meant to include every individual part and separate answers should be given for each person named as a party, if requested.

E.    Where the terms "accident" or "the accident" are used, they are meant to mean the incident which is the basis of the lawsuit, unless otherwise specified.

F.    A space has been provided on the Form of Interrogatories for your answer. _____ [four (4)] copies are served herewith. Complete all copies and serve a copy upon each separate counsel representation, retaining a copy in your file. Attach a verification and certificate of mailing.

*Interrogatory No. 1*

Identify and describe all documents recording or memorializing any repairs, maintenance, or installation or replacement of parts or components, relating to the entrance door of any guest room at Banbury Park Hotel or to any lock, strike, hinge, door closer, or other hardware attached to or associated with any such door, at any time after January 1, 1995.

*Interrogatory No. 2*

With respect to each and every person who witnessed or was present in the vicinity of the events described in plaintiff's complaint occurring at Banbury Park Hotel on the night of _____, state the name, address, and telephone number of each such person, state the substance of what such person observed, and identify each and every written or recorded statement given by such person.

*Interrogatory No. 3*

Separately with respect to each affirmative defense enumerated in paragraph 12 of defendant Park Hotels Group's answer herein, state the basis of each such defense and state each and every fact upon which each such defense is based.

*Interrogatory No. 4*

Describe in detail what you contend were the true facts surrounding the events of the night of _____ at Banbury Park Hotel leading up to plaintiff's injury.

*Interrogatory No. 5*

With respect to each witness, including expert witnesses, that you will or may call to testify at the trial of this matter, state the name, address, and telephone number of each such witness, and, separately for each such witness, state the substance of what you anticipate the testimony of each such witness to be.

*Request for Admission No. 1*

Admit that this court has valid subject matter jurisdiction of this matter under the provisions of 28 U.S.C. §1332.

*continued*

---

**Figure W10–1  Sample Set of Interrogatories and Requests,** *continued*

---

*Interrogatory No. 6*
In the event that you deny the foregoing Request for Admission No. 1, state each and every fact upon which such denial is based, and state each and every respect in which you contend that the jurisdictional requirements of 28 U.S.C. §1332 are not met in this action.

DATED this _____ day of _____, 20___.

SIMON & PORTER

_____

Allen Porter
Attorney for plaintiff

(Certificate of service goes here—see Workshop 4 for details.)

---

**Figure W10–2  More Detailed Instruction/Definition Set**

---

*DEFINITIONS*

Unless otherwise indicated, the following definitions are applicable to all Interrogatories contained herein.

1.  Any pronoun shall be deemed to designate the masculine, feminine, or neuter gender, and singular or plural, as in each case may be appropriate.

2.  "Any," "each," and "all" shall be read to be all-inclusive, and to require the enumeration of each and every item of information or document responsive to the Interrogatory in which such term appears.

3.  "And" and "or" and any other conjunctions or disjunctions used herein, shall be read both conjunctively and disjunctively so as to require the enumeration of all information responsive to all or any part of each Interrogatory in which any conjunction or disjunction appears.

4.  The word "person" means an individual, firm, corporation, association, organization, partnership, joint venture, trust, estate, public agency, department, bureau, board, or other entity.

5.  "You" or "your" means each defendant, and all persons acting or purporting to act on your behalf, including your attorney and his associates and partners and, if applicable, your former attorneys and their associates and partners.

6.  "Document" means any physical thing containing information, including (without limiting the generality of the foregoing) any book, paper, warrant, affidavit, appraisal, evaluation, bulletin, card, ticket, log, pamphlet, memorandum, invoice, instrument, agreement, correspondence (sent or received), telegram (sent or received), minutes, prospectus, note, receipt, voucher, book of account, ledger sheet, inventory list, canceled check, check stub, photograph, map, blueprint, drawing, computer input or output material, computer storage device, writing, graph, chart, scroll, notebook, register, appointment calendar, diploma, recording of any kind (whether or not transcribed), working paper, audit paper, report, study, statement, application, diary, any notes or summarization of any conversation, telephone call, meeting or other communication or other data compilation from which information can be obtained or translated through detection devices into reasonably usable form when translation is practically necessary and includes all copies (with or without notes or changes thereon) and drafts of any of the foregoing.

*continued*

**Figure W10–2　More Detailed Instruction/Definition Set,** *continued*

7.　"Identify" as used herein with respect to a document shall be read to require a statement of all of the following information relative to such document: (1) title; (2) nature and subject matter; (3) date; and (4) author.

8.　"Identify" as used herein with respect to any individual shall be read to require a statement of all of the following information pertaining to such individuals: (1) present or last-known home address; (2) present home telephone number; (3) employer; (4) present or last-known business address; and (5) business telephone number.

9.　"Identify" as used herein with respect to any conversation (including any telephone communication) or meeting shall be read to require a statement of all the following information relating to such conversation or meeting: (1) the date on which it occurred; (2) the identity of each and every person who was present or who participated; (3) the place at which it occurred or, in the case of a telephone communication, the location of each party; and (4) a detailed statement of the substance of what was discussed or what actions were taken.

10.　"This litigation" means Cause No. CV _____ now pending in the Superior Court of the State of _____ in and for the County of _____ bearing the heading set forth above.

### INSTRUCTIONS

A.　All information is to be divulged which is in the possession, custody, or control of the named party or parties, their attorneys, investigators, agents, employees or other representatives of the named parties and their attorneys.

B.　The Interrogatories shall be deemed continuing so as to require supplemental answers if the named parties obtain further information after the Answers to Interrogatories are made.

C.　A space has been provided on the form of Interrogatories for your Answer. In the event the space provided is not sufficient for your Answer to any of the Interrogatories, attach a separate sheet of paper with the additional information.

D.　In the event you cannot answer any Interrogatory in full, after exercising due diligence to secure the information, so state and answer to the fullest extent possible, specifying your inability to answer the remainder and stating whatever information or knowledge you have concerning the unanswered portion.

E.　In the event an Answer or portion thereof is based upon information and belief, rather than actual knowledge, the Answer should so state, and the source or sources upon which such information and belief are based should be specifically described and identified.

## CONCLUDING STEPS

**Step 7**　*Serve and Comply with Filing Requirements*

Since our hypothetical lawsuit is proceeding in the U.S. District Court for the District of Arizona, we will process our paperwork in accordance with the local rules of that court. Local rule 1.9 sets forth the forms of papers (i.e., attorney and court identification, case numbering, spacing and the like). Local rule 2.5 deals specifically with interrogatories and requests for admissions. Both rules are set forth in Figures W10–3 and W10–4.

**Step 8**　*Docket Response Due Date and Follow-Up*

We compute the due date for the answers to our interrogatories (see Workshop 7 for details on how to do this) and make a notation in the office docket and in our personal calendar. If the answers do not arrive within a few days after the due date, we begin taking the steps described in Workshop 12, starting with a demand letter.

**Step 9**　*Analyze Response and Take Any Needed Further Action*

When we have received the answers, we first verify that they are properly signed. Then we look through them to note any missing or incomplete answers and any objections that have been made.

---

**Figure W10–3    Arizona's Local Rule 1.9**

---

Rule 1.9

## FORMS OF PAPERS—CIVIL AND CRIMINAL

(a)    Title Page. The following information shall be stated upon the first page of every document and may be presented for filing single-spaced:

(1)    The name, address, State Bar Attorney number, and telephone number of the attorney appearing for the party in the action or proceeding and whether the attorney appears for the plaintiff, defendant, or other party—in propria persona—shall be typewritten or printed in the space to the left of the center of the page and beginning at line one (1) on the first page. The space to the right of the center shall be reserved for the filing marks of the Clerk.

(2)    The title of the Court shall commence on or below line six (6) of the first page.

(3)    Below the title of the Court, there shall be inserted in the space to the left of the center of the paper the title of the action or proceeding. If the parties are too numerous for all to be named on the first page, the names of the parties only may be continued on the second or successive pages. In the space to the right of the center there shall be inserted (A) the number of the action or proceeding; (B) a brief description of the nature of the document, including demand for trial by jury if made in the document; and (C) mention of any notice of motion or affidavits or memorandum in support.

(b)    Case Numbering. The number to be assigned to each case shall initially be placed thereon by the Clerk. Such number shall also include the designation "CR" for criminal cases and "CV" for civil cases, followed by the last two digits of the calendar year in which each case is filed; the number of the case in the order filed during each calendar year, followed by the designation of the division where filed, and ending with the initials of the District Judge to whom the case is assigned. Phoenix and Prescott cases shall be numbered together, differentiated only by the designation "PHX" for Phoenix cases and "PCT" for Prescott cases. Tucson cases shall be designated "TUC" for Tucson cases.

       CV-94-1-PHX-RCB        CR-94-1-PCT-EHC
       CV-94-2-TUC-ACM       CR-94-2-PHX-WPC
       CV-94-3-PCT-CAM       CR-94-3-TUC-RMB

(c)    Pleadings and Other Papers.

(1)    All pleadings and other papers shall be submitted on unglazed paper 8 1/2 inches by 11 inches, and shall be signed as provided in Rule 11 of the Federal Rules of Civil Procedure. Documents intended for filing shall be presented to the Clerk's Office without being folded or rolled and shall be kept in flat files. The body of all documents shall be typed space-and-a-half or double-spaced; they shall not be single-spaced except for (A) footnotes which may be single-spaced, and (B) quotations which may be single-spaced and indented. All typewritten pleadings, motions and other original papers filed with the Clerk shall be in a type size no smaller than ten (10) pitch (10 letters per inch). Those that are printed or otherwise produced with proportional type shall be in a size no smaller than 11 point.

(2)    Proposed orders prepared for the signature of a United States District Judge or a Magistrate Judge will be prepared on a separate document containing the heading data required by subparagraphs (a) (2) and (3) above as appropriate, and shall not be included as an integral part of stipulations, motions, or other pleadings. The following uniform signature block will be contained in the proposed order as indicated below: (Magistrate Judges would be adapted accordingly.)

                    DATED this _____ day of _____, 20_____

                   _____

                   (Judge's Name)
                   United States District Judge

(d)    Fictitious Parties. Unless otherwise ordered by the Court in a particular case, the Clerk shall refuse to accept for filing in any civil action or proceeding originally commenced in this Court any complaint wherein any party is designated and sought to be joined under a fictitious name. (See *Molnar v. National Broadcasting Company,* 231 F.2d 684, 687 (9th Cir. 1956).)

(e)    Amended Pleadings. Any party filing an amended pleading shall retype the entire pleading and may not incorporate any part of the preceding pleading, including the exhibits, by reference.

*continued*

**Figure W10–3   Arizona's Local Rule 1.9,** *continued*

(f)   Attachments to Pleadings and Memoranda.

(1)   Attachments. No copy of a pleading, exhibit or minute entry which has been filed in a case shall be attached to the original of a subsequent pleading, motion or memorandum of points and authorities.

(2)   Incorporation by Reference. If a party desires to call the Court's attention to anything contained in a previous pleading, motion or minute entry, the party shall do so by incorporation by reference.

(3)   Authorities Cited in Memoranda. Copies of authorities cited in memoranda shall not be attached to the original of any motion or memorandum of authorities.

(4)   Attachments to Judge. Nothing herein shall be construed as prohibiting a party from attaching copies of pleadings, motions, exhibits, minute entries or texts of authorities to a copy of a motion or memorandum of points and authorities delivered to the District Judge or Magistrate Judge to whom the case has been assigned. Any such attachments or authorities provided to the District Judge or Magistrate Judge must also be provided to all other attorneys.

(5)   Sanctions. For violation of this Rule, the Court may order the removal of the offending document and charge the offending party or counsel such costs or fees as may be necessary to cover the Clerk's costs of filing, preservation, or storage.

(g)   Copy for Judge. A clear, legible copy of every pleading or other document filed shall accompany each original pleading or other document filed with the Clerk for use by the District Judge or Magistrate Judge to whom the case is assigned and additional copies for each Judge in three-judge cases.

(h)   Civil Cover Sheet.

(1)   The Clerk is authorized and instructed to require a complete and executed AO form JS-44a, Civil Cover Sheet, which shall accompany each civil case to be filed.

(2)   Persons filing civil cases who are at the time of such filing in custody of Civil, State, or Federal institutions, and persons filing civil cases *pro se,* are exempted from the foregoing requirements.

---

**Figure W10–4   Arizona's Local Rule 2.5**

Rule 2.5

### INTERROGATORIES AND REQUESTS FOR ADMISSIONS

(a)   Form

(1)   When serving interrogatories and requests for admission the propounding party shall serve upon the responding party a number of sets equal to the total number of separate counsel representations in the action, plus one (1).

(2)   The propounding party shall prepare interrogatories and requests for admission so that the responding party can provide his or her response in an adequate blank space.

(3)   The responding party shall complete all copies of the set served upon him or her, attach a verification and certificate of mailing, and serve one (1) of such sets upon each separate counsel representation in the action.

(4)   All responses to interrogatories and requests for admission which are not completed in accordance with subparagraphs (1), (2), and (3) above, shall restate the interrogatory or request for admission immediately before stating the responses.

(b)   Uniform Interrogatories

(1)   The interrogatories set forth in Appendix A to these Rules are denominated as Uniform Interrogatories and are approved for use in accordance with Rule 33 of the Federal Rules of Civil Procedure, the instructions for use set forth in the Appendix, and this Rule.

(2)   The annexed Uniform Interrogatories are not to be used as a standard set of interrogatories for submission in all cases. Each interrogatory should be used only if it is appropriate in the particular case. Objections will be sustained to Uniform Interrogatories as a whole set or as to a particular interrogatory if the provisions of this subparagraph are violated or the interrogatory requires a response not within the scope of permissible discovery in the particular action.

We analyze the facts disclosed in the answers, making a note in our issues outline of any disclosures that may be useful in proving any of the elements of our case, and keeping a list of any factual trails that need to be explored further.

### Step 10 — Request Supplementation as Appropriate

When we compute and docket the due date for the answers, we make another notation in our personal calendar for a date a few months into the future to remind ourselves to file a request for supplementation.

## Drafting Interrogatories: Learning by Doing

Now it is your turn to try your hand at drafting interrogatories and requests for admissions. Assume that you are a paralegal in the office of Gail Stoddard, attorney for Park Hotels Group. Plaintiff's complaint (in the form appearing in Workshop 5) has been received and an answer (in the form appearing in Workshop 8) has just been prepared and filed. Assume that the lawsuit is pending in the state court having general civil jurisdiction in your locality. You have been assigned to prepare a set of interrogatories and requests for admissions.

### EXERCISES

In carrying out this assignment, you should follow the step-by-step formula for Steps 1 through 7 described in this workshop.

1. In formulating your goals in Step 1, consider that some of the allegations of the complaint are quite unspecific and lacking in detail, and consider how you might use interrogatories to flesh out the allegations of the complaint. Be sure to take into account whether the court in your locality limits the number of interrogatories that can be submitted.

2. In Step 2, use the caption that you prepared in Workshop 4, and write a preamble appropriate for the court of your locality. Be sure to refer to the correct rules, and try to imitate as closely as possible the style and language customary in your locality.

3. In Step 3, ask your instructor for advice regarding the inclusion of an Instructions and Definitions section. If you are to do so, your instructor will provide a form for you to follow.

4. In Step 4, go through your set of boilerplate interrogatories, choose which ones are appropriate for this situation, and modify them as necessary.

5. In Steps 5 and 6, write the individualized interrogatories and requests for admissions as appropriate to carry out the goals you set in Step 1.

6. In Step 7, consult the rules of procedure applicable in your court and determine how your set of interrogatories should be filed and served. If your court does not allow filing of discovery papers, prepare an appropriate notice reciting service of the interrogatories and requests for admissions.

## PRACTICE POINTERS
### Finding Samples

If you are asked to draft interrogatories or requests for admissions, consider consulting other court and case files. Begin by looking at your own firm's case files for similar cases as well as any general interrogatories and requests for admissions form files. If you are aware of a reported case with similar issues that was tried outside of your firm (especially one that was tried to completion), obtain the trial court case number. Go to the clerk of the court that tried the case and ask the clerk to pull those files. In many courts interrogatories, answers to interrogatories, and requests for admission are not filed with the clerk as a matter of course. In those courts these discovery documents are available in the court's file only when they have been submitted as exhibits at trial.

If these documents are not in the file and the case appears pertinent enough, you may want to contact the attorney who prepared the interrogatories or requests for admission and ask if you can review the file. Such a request

# PRACTICE POINTERS
## *Finding Samples* continued

should be made only with the permission of your supervising attorney. Also keep in mind that no substantial use should be made of such documents without the express permission of the attorney who prepared them.

You can also find sample interrogatories in publications prepared by trial lawyers associations. A list of available resources can be identified by consulting the web page for the American Trial Lawyers Association (atlanet.org). Keep in mind, however, that some of these services are available only at cost. Litigation books typically contain sample interrogatories. When looking for any book remember amazon.com, the web address for the world's biggest bookstore, as well as the web page of any legal publisher, such as West, Prentice Hall, Lexus, and others. Also consider publications prepared by state and local bar associations. They often have books and pamphlets that are used as part of continuing legal education courses containing samples that have been prepared by leading law firms, many of which have withstood court scrutiny.

## TECHNO TIP

If you are using the internet to assist in the preparation of interrogatories you may find it helpful to visit the Lois® web site at www.pita.com. If you use the "Classic" button you can find your way to various legal sites that are linked to that web page. In addition, various legal search engines are available there to assist you in focusing on the area you want to research. The site can also take you to numerous CLE (continuing legal education) pages where the legal specialty or subject matter you are looking for might be found. Other places to visit are the web sites of legal publishers such as those mentioned in the practice pointers. Summaries and reviews of books, treatises, practice pamphlets, and the like are often accessible.

If you are sufficiently proficient you may be able to phrase your search requests so as to be able to search the various state and federal case databases to pull up any interesting interrogatories. Gleaning court-reviewed interrogatories from cases involving the legal issues you are dealing with is not an easy task.

## FORMS FILE

*Include samples of the following in your forms file:*

* *Nonuniform interrogatories*

* *Requests for admission*

*If possible obtain samples from different types of cases (e.g., personal injury, commercial litigation, criminal).*

## INTRODUCTION: PURPOSE OF PREPARING DISCOVERY RESPONSE

In this workshop, we shift our point of view to that of the party who must respond to a discovery request. Usually, this is not a task that the responding attorney approaches with great relish—the responding party has nothing to gain and everything to lose by engaging in this forced disclosure of information to an opponent. Preparing a discovery response is a task requiring trained legal judgment, meticulous attention to detail, and, often, enormous quantities of time. In other words, it is a task for which trained litigation paralegals are perfectly suited and routinely employed.

Our main goal in preparing a discovery response is to comply with the rules without giving away anything that will unnecessarily benefit our opponent. Modern discovery rules place lawyers and paralegals responding to discovery in somewhat of an ethical bind. We have an ethical obligation to represent our clients zealously and do our best to win, but the discovery rules may require us to turn over to our adversary information that will be used as ammunition against us. Under the circumstances, it is perfectly appropriate that we look for every possible way—within the bounds of the rules—to avoid handing our opponent any more bullets than necessary.

## PROCEDURE FOR RESPONDING TO DISCOVERY REQUESTS

The discovery rules provide a procedure for responding to discovery requests that fulfills two main functions: (1) turning over the requested information to the requesting party and (2) making a record of what information has been turned over. With interrogatories and requests for admissions, both of these functions are accomplished by a document in the form of a court paper, having the usual caption, signature line, and mailing certificate, in which each of the questions is reproduced and answered. This document is served on all other parties to the lawsuit, not just the requesting party, and a record is made by filing the document itself with the clerk of the court in jurisdictions where this is allowed, or, in jurisdictions that prohibit filing of discovery papers, by filing a notice reflecting that answers have been served.

When we respond to an FRCP, Rule 34, request for production of documents, we must turn over to the requesting party the actual documents requested or copies of them. It is not unusual for the documents assembled in response to a Rule 34 request for production to comprise many thousands of pages, so it would obviously be impractical to file copies of the actual documents with the clerk of the court. Therefore, the rules require us to make the requested documents available directly to the requesting party. To make our record, we then prepare a written response to the Rule 34 request for production, which we file with the clerk and serve on all parties to the suit.

To arrive at the desired end product—appropriate responses that we can file and serve—will require a good deal of preparation and thought. The necessary preparatory work may include these steps:

- Assembling the factual information and documents called for by the request. Usually, the attorneys and paralegals do not have the degree of detailed knowledge of the facts of the case required. Often, even the client will not have the required information readily at hand, and will have to gather it from a variety of sources. When the client is a corporation or other entity, it is often necessary for someone to conduct an investigation in order to determine which individuals in the organization have the needed information and to obtain it from them (an important task often assigned to paralegals).

- Making strategic decisions about what information must be disclosed and what may be withheld.

- Analyzing the requests themselves to identify any that are improper and should be objected to.

- Deciding how to organize, express, and present the information to be disclosed in such a way as to minimize its usefulness as ammunition against us.

Because of space limitations, the remainder of this workshop concentrates mainly on the procedure for answering interrogatories. This will provide an overview and understanding of the general process involved in responding to discovery requests, which you will easily be able to extend to other kinds of discovery requests. To assist you in this, after we have covered our suggested step-by-step system for answering interrogatories, we will take a brief look at the procedures for responding to

FRCP, Rule 34, requests for production of documents and to requests for admissions, and try to point out some of the special concerns that these may present.

# Answering Interrogatories: Step-by-step Instructions

A set of interrogatories arrives in the morning mail; answers need to be prepared. How do we get from a stack of questions with blank spaces for the answers to a proper response that we can serve on the responding party within the time allowed by the rules? As usual, we advocate a methodical, step-by-step approach as the best way of ensuring that no details are overlooked and that all the requirements of the rules are met.

## PREPARATORY STEPS

As we will see, a good deal needs to be done before we can begin drafting answers. First we must plan our work, analyze the questions, and gather the necessary factual information.

### Step 1  Docket Response Due Date

Most incoming court papers trigger fixed-response deadlines, and interrogatories are no exception. If your office has a proper central docketing and mail handling system in place, the tentative due date for answers to interrogatories will already have been computed and entered into the office's central calendar before you ever receive the interrogatories to work on.

Nevertheless, it is vitally important that you make your own computation of the due date for the response and keep track of it in your own calendar. Docketing clerks occasionally make mistakes; if you are assigned the task of preparing answers to interrogatories, it is *your* responsibility—not that of the docketing clerk—to see that the response is ready on time.

The usual time allowed for answering interrogatories is 30 days from the date of service. FRCP, Rule 33(a)(3), provides:

> The party upon whom the interrogatories have been served shall serve a copy of the answers, and objections if any, within 30 days after the service of the interrogatories. A shorter or longer time may be directed by the court or, in the absence of such an order, agreed to in writing by the parties. . . .

See Workshop 7 for details about how to compute due dates.

As Rule 33(a)(3) implies, the court has the power to lengthen or shorten the response time. Often, when you receive a set of interrogatories and look over the questions, it immediately becomes obvious that it will take much longer than 30 days to prepare complete answers. The usual solution is to ask opposing counsel to agree to an extension of the response date. Such extensions are routinely given, up to a point. The opposing attorney has a strong motivation to be reasonable, because she knows that if you ask the judge for an extension, you will probably get one, and the judge will be annoyed that it was not given voluntarily. How long an extension should you ask for? Enough to give you time to prepare complete answers. It is a mistake to let opposing counsel bully you into an extension that is not long enough to allow you to get the job done. If you have already agreed to one extension, it may be hard to convince the judge that you need another one.

Extensions should *always* be confirmed in writing. In some jurisdictions, it is enough for you to write a confirming letter to the party who is granting the extension; in others, a stipulation signed by both parties and filed with the court is required. Your instructor will inform you of the practice in your locality.

What happens if your response is late? As a practical matter in most jurisdictions, opposing counsel will have to send you a demand letter before he can ask the court to order you to file a response, so it is not uncommon to see answers to interrogatories served a few days late. There is, however, a hazard to doing this, even apart from the lack of professionalism that it implies: There is case law holding that objections not served within the prescribed response period are waived. Therefore, a party who files answers to interrogatories late runs the risk that the judge may later summarily overrule any objections appearing in the answers.

If you approach the due date for answers and it is obvious that you need a few more days, *never* ignore the due date; make your supervising attorney aware of the situation. She may ask the opposing attorney for the time needed, or may decide that it is better to serve answers that are not complete, and serve supplemental answers when the complete answers are ready.

*Your Local Notes*

_____

_____

## Step 2 — *Analyze the Entire Request Question by Question*

In answering interrogatories, careful planning is essential. Only in the simplest cases will you have enough information in the file to allow you to prepare competent answers without obtaining information from other sources. You cannot possibly pull together the information required to write answers to a complex set of interrogatories in 30 days unless you approach the task in an organized way.

When you receive a set of interrogatories to answer, your first task after calendaring the due date is to read the set carefully, question by question, and make a list of what work you will need to do in order to be able to answer each one. As you go through the questions for the first time, we suggest making notations under each one, classifying them into categories as follows:

■ *Questions that can be answered with information that you already have in the file.* These are the easy ones—questions like "State plaintiff's full name and address." On these questions, if you have the answer readily at hand, you may wish to jot it down immediately; if not, make a notation indicating that the required information is in the file.

■ *Questions that will obviously be objected to.* Questions calling for information that is privileged or that involve attorney work product fall into this category. Make a notation indicating the nature of the objection.

■ *Questions that require legal research.* Sometimes a question may seem improper or objectionable, but you cannot be sure without doing some legal research. Make a notation indicating what it is that needs to be researched.

■ *Questions that require legal judgment about case strategy.* For example, an interrogatory may ask what witnesses you intend to call at trial or what exhibits you intend to offer. Deciding on the preferred strategy for answering this kind of question involves judgment calls best left to your supervising attorney; unless you know how he wants such questions answered, make a note to ask for instructions.

■ *Questions that call for information that you will need to obtain from other sources.* As a practical matter, most interrogatories fall into this category. Note what additional information will be needed, and what steps you can take to obtain it. Sometimes you will know exactly where to go to obtain the needed information; more often, you will have to track it down.

## Step 3 — *Request Information from Client and Others as Necessary*

When you finish Step 2, you should easily be able to go through your notes and assemble a list of the information that you need to obtain from others. Usually, it is worthwhile to sit down with your client at this point and review the list with her.

If your client is a corporation or other entity, it may not be clear at first whom you should speak to. There will almost always be a contact person within the client organization who is mainly responsible for dealing with the organization's lawyers; that person can likely put you in touch with anyone else whom you need to contact. Since answers to interrogatories are to be signed by the client, you will also need to find out who within the organization will sign. It goes without saying, of course, that you should never make direct contacts with clients, or with anyone in a client organization, without advance permission from your supervising attorney.

Your client, or, in the case of a corporation, your client's representative, is likely to be able to provide the information to answer some of the questions at once. You should write this information down immediately in your notes for those questions.

On other questions, your client will not have the required information immediately available, but can obtain it and give it to you. As you go through the questions with your client, make a separate checklist of all the items that your client is undertaking to obtain. Find out how long it will take your client to obtain each item and get it to you, and indicate in your notes the expected time frame. Before you end the session, give your client a copy of your checklist so that there will be no confusion about what she is expected to provide.

Still other questions will require investigation that your client is not equipped to carry out. Nevertheless, in many such situations, your client will be able to suggest where to go to find the needed information. Perhaps there are records that you can go through, or perhaps your client can tell you who to contact. Record any such suggestions in your notes.

Sometimes, the answer to a question can most easily be obtained by ordering records from outside sources. In an accident case, for example, the police investigative report is often a good source of facts. In a medical malpractice case, much information can be obtained from hospital records. The kinds of records that exist, and the usefulness of the information contained in them, depend on the circumstances of the case.

Usually, after going through the questions with your client and taking advantage of all the record sources available to you, some questions will remain that simply require investigation. Keep in mind that there are limits to the amount of investigation that you are required to do in answering interrogatories, as discussed in the sidebar.

## DRAFTING STEPS

As we obtain the necessary information, we can begin putting together the pieces of the response.

If we have been keeping our notes using a word processing document containing an electronic copy of the original interrogatories, we can do this by editing our notes for each question into a proper answer. We may do this a few questions at a time as information becomes available, or all at once when we have gathered all of the necessary information.

---

### SIDEBAR

## The Duty of Inquiry—How Much Investigation Must You Do?

*You will often see interrogatories that call for information that is broader in scope or deeper in detail that you can readily obtain. In our hypo, for example, Shannon's attorney might reasonably send Park Hotels Group an interrogatory asking Park Hotels Group to itemize and describe all maintenance on all Banbury Park Hotel guest room doors during the last year. It may be that Park Hotels Group does not keep detailed records of all such maintenance. In theory, an accurate and detailed answer could be constructed, but it might require an all-out investigation—tracking down and interviewing former employees, contacting outside service contractors and materials suppliers, digging records out of archives, etc. To what lengths are we required to go to answer this kind of interrogatory?*

*The textbook answer is that we are required to disclose any information that is in the possession or control of our client. In general, this means that if the answer is obtainable from records that belong to our client, or known by any employees of our client, we are required to track down the information and include it*

*in our answers. Moreover, if someone within the client's control—for example, a lawyer working for the client—has the information, it must be provided. We are not, however, required to extend our investigation to purely outside sources. (If we do obtain information from outside sources, however—say, as a part of our own investigation of the case—that information is now within the possession and control of our client because we have it, and we cannot hold it back unless it qualifies under the work product doctrine discussed later in this workshop.)*

*At times, it is not clear whether information called for by an interrogatory is within the possession and control of our client. If our client is General Motors, must we check with each of its hundreds of thousands of employees to see if anyone has the facts called for? No, in such situations a reasonable in-house investigation is probably enough. When in doubt, some quality time spent doing legal research will likely result in a clearer idea of what is the range of knowledge with which your client is chargeable.*

---

### SIDEBAR

## Keep Your Deadlines in View

*We hate to keep harping about deadlines, but experience teaches that one of the pitfalls for new paralegals assigned to answer interrogatories is the potential conflict that can arise between a looming due date on one hand and a procrastinating client on the other. To answer interrogatories, you need information, part of which must usually come from your client. You cannot prepare proper answers until you get that information. Paralegals who wait until the*

*day answers are due and then, unable to produce a response ready to serve, offer excuses about the client not cooperating, should expect a short career path. Keep close track of your deadlines. Stay in contact with your client—do not make a pest of yourself, but stay in contact—and if a problem seems to be developing, alert your supervising attorney well in advance of the deadline.*

### Step 4 — *Caption and Preamble*

As with any court paper, answers to interrogatories begin with the usual caption and end with date and signature lines and a certificate of mailing. The document to be served is, however, typically assembled in a way that is somewhat different from the way in which we have prepared other court documents. Traditionally, interrogatories were served in multiple copies, and the answers were typed into blank spaces provided for the purpose on the original document. (Under the rules of most courts, it is also permissible, though usually viewed as somewhat tacky, to hand write answers into the blanks.) A signature page was added, the words "AND ANSWERS THERETO" were added after the title "INTERROGATORIES" to the right of the caption, and the resulting document was served as the response.

Since we are, by preference, working with an electronic copy of the original interrogatories, our easiest choice will be to insert our answers into the word processing document containing the questions. We will change the title in the caption as necessary, add our own signature page and certificate of mailing, and print the finished response.

---

**Your Local Notes**

_____

_____

---

### Dealing with Overreaching Instructions and Misleading Definitions

We have seen in previous workshops that many practitioners routinely include a boilerplate section entitled Instructions and Definitions at the beginning of a set of interrogatories, requests for admissions, or requests for production. Often, these include instructions or definitions that purport to place burdens and obligations on the answering party that go beyond the requirements of the discovery rules.

For example, there may be an instruction purporting to require investigation to obtain information beyond that in the possession or control of the answering party. Or there may be a definition that takes a word with a commonly understood meaning and attempts to redefine it in some way more advantageous to the propounding party.

As we have seen, answers to interrogatories can be used for a number of purposes at trial, and blowups of salient passages can be paraded in front of the jury. We must therefore go over the Instructions and Definitions section carefully, if one is present, looking for any improper or misleading material. When misleading definitions are found, an objection should be inserted immediately after the offending paragraph (see Step 5 for instructions on how to express an objection). Overreaching instructions can easily be dealt with by a blanket objection, which, in the spirit of answering boilerplate with boilerplate, can be inserted after the Instructions and Definitions section as a matter of routine:

> To the extent that the foregoing Instructions and Definitions purport to impose burdens or obligations beyond those imposed by the applicable rules of civil procedure, they are objected to, and will not be complied with.

### Step 5 — *Object to Each Objectionable Question If It Is Strategically Beneficial to Do So*

We now turn to the important subject of objections. To use objections intelligently and advantageously, we first need to know what kinds of questions are objectionable. Then, we need to learn when to object and when not to; that is, how to tell when an objection will advance our case and when we are better off just answering the question.

**When and Why to Object**—Perhaps the most important thing to keep in mind about interrogatories is that every single answer that we give carries the potential to blow a gaping hole in our case. Our opponent can—and will, if it seems advantageous to do so—present any interrogatory and our answer to it as a part of his evidence at trial. In some ways, a large blowup of a bad interrogatory answer sitting on an easel in front of the jury is worse than a bad answer given by our client while testifying because with the interrogatory, there is no opportunity to elaborate, the answer is just there and we are stuck with it.

This is not to suggest tampering with the truth in our answers. Answers to interrogatories are sworn testimony. Never yield to the temptation to give a false answer—to do so is unethical, and, even leaving aside the moral issues, it is not worth risking your career and your future over one client and one case.

On the other hand, neither do we volunteer damaging information if we have some legal way to avoid doing so. If a question is legally objectionable, we have every right to object. But should we?

**When Not to Object**—Sometimes, an objection may harm our case more than the answer to the question would have. How can this happen? Remember, our opponent is a litigator too and may not be accustomed to taking "no" for an answer. Our objection to a question may merely serve to plant a red flag on whatever subject the question is asking about, and provoke our opponent to dig more deeply than ever in precisely that spot.

Excessive objection can also alienate the judge. We can be sure that no judge will ever agree with 100 percent of our objections, however well founded they may be. Add to this the fact that most judges hate wasting their time on discovery disputes, and it is easy to see why litigators who insist on making a war out of every discovery question may find the weather inside the courtroom turning chilly.

Here are a few suggestions about the proper use of objections:

- Use objections purely as a tool to advance your case. If you gain nothing by making an objection, do not make it.

- Make appropriate use of the "object, then answer anyway" technique. See sidebar.

- Never make frivolous objections. If you make an objection, be sure that you can cite a rule or case law to back it up.

- Keep in mind that objecting to a question may serve merely to increase your opponent's determination. Before deciding to object, interpret the question carefully and try drafting sample answers. It may be that you can find a way to answer the question truthfully but harmlessly.

**Types of Objectionable Questions**—What are the common grounds for objection to an interrogatory? What things in an interrogatory should alert us to object? Although a complete treatment of the subject is best left for a course on evidence, we can easily make a checklist of the most common objections. Some of these are based on rules of evidence, such as objections to the form of a question and objections based on privilege. Others are based on the discovery rules, which impose their own limits on the kinds of questions that can be asked. Here is a summary of the grounds for objection most useful in answering interrogatories, together with example objections:

*Questions exceeding the scope of discovery:* Not all of the rules of evidence apply to interrogatories and other discovery questions; the range of permissible questions is broader in discovery than it is in the courtroom. In particular, a discovery question is not objectionable merely because it is irrelevant by evidentiary standards or because it calls for hearsay. The standard for discovery questions is Rule 26(b)(1), which provides:

> Parties may obtain discovery regarding any matter, not privileged, which is relevant to the subject matter involved in the pending

action. . . . The information sought need not be admissible at the trial if the information sought appears reasonably calculated to lead to the discovery of admissible evidence.

Even though the requirement of relevancy is relaxed—a question need only be relevant to the subject matter of the action, rather than strictly relevant to the issues raised by the pleadings—there are limits to how far a party can go in asking about matters not directly pertinent to the lawsuit. Any discovery question must, at a minimum, be reasonably calculated to *lead to* admissible evidence. We are free to object to any question that fails this test.

**Example interrogatory:** Suppose Park Hotels Group's attorney sends Shannon an interrogatory asking "State the names of all clubs, organizations, or associations of which you have been a member at any time since January 1, 1998."

**Analysis:** Could this information be useful to Park Hotels Group's attorney? Conceivably—any information about a witness's likes, dislikes, and biases can be useful in preparing for cross-examination. But is it reasonably calculated to lead to admissible evidence? Few judges would think so. This kind of overreaching question should usually be objected to as a matter of principle, if for no other reason than to send the opposing attorney a message that we will not be patsies.

**Example objection:** "This interrogatory is objected to as irrelevant to the subject matter of the action and not reasonably calculated to lead to admissible evidence."

*Ambiguous questions:* In general, the rules of evidence governing the form in which questions are stated apply to interrogatories. This is only reasonable, since these rules are designed to ensure that the question is clear enough so that the answering party knows what is being asked. An ambiguous question—a question capable of more than one meaning—is objectionable.

**Example interrogatory:** Suppose Shannon's attorney sends Park Hotels Group an interrogatory asking "Describe all maintenance performed on the room door since January 1, 1995."

**Analysis:** *Which* room door? The interrogatory is probably intended to refer to the door to the room occupied by Shannon, but it does not say so. Usually, ambiguous interrogatories are the result of poor drafting rather than an intention to set a trap of some kind. It is often easiest to note the objection, then reinterpret the question and go ahead and answer it—if we stand on ceremony, the opposing party will resubmit the question in better form, and all we will have bought ourselves is another response to write. See sidebar on the "object, then answer anyway" technique.

**Example objection and response:** "This interrogatory is objected to as ambiguous, in that it does not indicate the specific door to which it refers. Assuming that the door of Room 409 at Banbury Park Hotel is intended, for plaintiff's information, the maintenance performed on that room door since January 1, 1995, included replacement of the door closer spring on May 24, 1998; rekeying the door lock on February 3, 1998, September 17, 1998, and May 2, 1999; and periodic preventive maintenance inspections and lubrication performed approximately on a monthly basis."

*Misleading questions:* Misleading questions are another category of questions that are improper because of their form. The subject matter of the question may be perfectly appropriate, but the question is asked in such a way that the answer is likely to be misinterpreted. The classic example of a misleading question is "Have you stopped beating your wife?"

**Example interrogatory:** Suppose Park Hotels Group's attorney sends Shannon the following interrogatory: "Describe the events that occurred after you admitted defendant Collins to your room."

**Analysis:** Regardless of how Shannon answers this interrogatory, her answer will give the impression that she is admitting that she voluntarily allowed Dr. Collins into her room. Misleading questions should always be objected to. Whether to use the "object, then answer anyway" technique here is a judgment call.

**Example objection and response:** "This interrogatory is objected to as misleading, in that plaintiff at no time admitted defendant Collins to her room, and defendant Collins entered the room without plaintiff's knowledge or consent."

*Questions calling for privileged communications:* Evidentiary privileges arise from laws that allow certain types of communications to be kept private. Which privileges exist, and what their limits are, depends on the state; each state has its own laws governing evidentiary privilege. Even in federal court, evidentiary privileges are mainly determined by the laws of the state in which the court sits.

Common evidentiary privileges include the following:

- *Physician–patient privilege.* Communications between a doctor and patient involving medical treatment are usually privileged and cannot be inquired into.

- *Husband–wife privilege.* A wife cannot be compelled to testify about private communications with her husband, or vice versa. A question inquiring into such communications is objectionable.

- *Attorney–client privilege.* An attorney is not permitted to answer questions about what a client has said to the attorney in confidence while seeking legal advice. Under the laws of most states, this privilege extends to communications made through paralegals and others in the employ of the attorney.

- *Priest–penitent privilege.* Under the laws of most states, a statement made privately to a member of the clergy in the course of confession or counseling is privileged.

- *Privilege against self-incrimination.* The Fifth Amendment of the U.S. Constitution gives each person the right to refuse to answer a question if the answer would tend to incriminate her.

- *Other privileges.* Some states also grant privileged status to communications with accountants, journalists, social workers, and others. Your instructor will inform you of what privileges are available in your state, and tell you where to locate the legal authority for them.

Exactly what kinds of communications qualify for these and other privileges depends on the specific provisions of the state laws prescribing each privilege. Usually, a communication is not privileged if a third person is present when it occurs; for this reason, lawyers (and paralegals) must be careful not to allow anyone other than the client to be present when discussing the case with the client. In theory, if you allow, say, your client's girl friend to be present in the room while interviewing the client, the attorney–client privilege does not attach and you could be compelled to testify about what was said.

**Example interrogatory:** Suppose, in our hypo, that Shannon's attorney sent the following interrogatory to Dr. Collins's wife (recall that she was included in the suit because Texas is a community property state): "Relate the substance of each and every communication between you and defendant Arthur Collins the subject matter of which concerned the nature of the injuries received by defendant Arthur Collins."

**Analysis:** Some—but not necessarily all—of the communications called for by this interrogatory are privileged. Communications made in the presence of people other than

Dr. Collins and his wife would likely not be privileged. With this kind of question, we must be very careful, because of the potential problem of waiver (see sidebar). We are free to refuse to answer the entire interrogatory, since, by its terms, it is not limited to unprivileged communications. Most litigators would strongly resist discovery aimed at communications between client spouses, privileged or otherwise.

**Example objection and response:** "This interrogatory calls for communications between defendants Collins that are privileged by reason of defendants' status as husband and wife; defendants object on the basis of marital privilege and decline to answer."

---

## SIDEBAR

### The Problem of Waiver

*One hazard to answering a question that is objectionable is that doing so usually constitutes a waiver of the objection. So what? If we are answering the question anyway, surely we did not mind waiving our objection?*

*Not necessarily. Unfortunately, sometimes the waiver can extend to other things beside the question that we answered. Questions delving into areas that are privileged are a particular source of concern. Consider, for example, the example interrogatory to Dr. Collins's wife, "Relate the substance of each and every communication between you and defendant Arthur Collins the subject matter of which concerned the nature of the injuries received by defendant Arthur Collins."*

*Clearly, this interrogatory calls for a communication that is privileged—a wife cannot be compelled to testify about communications with a spouse. However, the subject matter of the question seems harmless, and there could also be nonprivileged communications between Dr. Collins and his wife—perhaps this would be a good candidate for the "object, then answer anyway" strategy?*

*Not a good idea with privilege objections. If we answer the question, we run the risk that by doing so, we will be deemed to have waived the husband–wife privilege—not only for this question, but for all questions, present and future. When a question appears to invade an area covered by an evidentiary privilege, we will always object and decline to answer, unless we are sure that we are willing to waive the privilege entirely.*

---

---

***Work product:*** If the rules allow interrogatories about any subject relevant to the subject matter of the action, can a party ask for, say, an opposing attorney's recollection or notes of an interview with a witness? Or suppose a paralegal—maybe you!—has spent weeks going through a roomful of business records and prepared a summary of their contents—can the opposing party ask for your conclusions in an interrogatory?

Here a difficult issue arises. Clearly, these questions address relevant subject matter, yet there is something disturbing about the idea of requiring an attorney to turn over the fruits of his legal work for a client.

The courts grappled with the problem for years, and the resulting legal principles now appear in FRCP, Rules 26(b)(3) and 26(b)(4). These rules embody what is usually referred to as the *work product doctrine.*

What is attorney work product, and under what circumstances is it discoverable? Rule 26(b)(3) expressly applies to any "documents . . . prepared in anticipation of litigation or for trial by or for another party or by or for that other party's. . . attorney. . . ." Such materials can be obtained only upon a showing that the requesting party has a "substantial need" for the information they contain and has no other practical way to get it.

Although Rule 26(b)(3) refers only to "documents and tangible things"—not to interrogatories— it is logical that if a party is not entitled to obtain a document because it is attorney work product, neither would an interrogatory asking about the contents of the document be proper, absent the showing of need required by the rule.

Work product issues most commonly arise in connection with statements taken by an attorney or paralegal from a nonparty witness and reports obtained from expert witnesses. In general, witness statements are work product and not discoverable as long as the witness is available so that the party seeking the information can take her own statement. However, a witness has the right to a copy of his own statement. The discoverability of reports and other information submitted by expert witnesses raises issues that are beyond the scope of this introductory text; the general principles can be found in FRCP, Rule 26(b)(4).

**Example interrogatory:** "Identify each and every person from whom you have obtained information or statements in connection with this matter, and, separately for each such person, state the substance of the information so obtained."

**Analysis:** This interrogatory is asking for work product. We will object and decline to answer.

**Example objection:** "This interrogatory is objected to as calling for attorney work product."

***Burdensome questions:*** Any competent litigator in a case of any complexity can dictate in an hour a set of interrogatories that will take a team of paralegals months of full time work to answer. Must we really sit still for discovery tactics of this kind?

Traditionally, the answer was "yes." If an interrogatory was otherwise proper, it had to be answered, regardless of how much work would be required to do so. If you peruse the case annotations under the federal discovery rules, you will find cases in which federal courts have required parties to answer interrogatories requiring review of hundreds of thousands of pages of records to answer.

In the last decade or so, however, many courts have become much less tolerant of discovery requests that seem designed mainly to make the responding party spend time and money. Although there is considerable variability from one jurisdiction to another and even from one judge to another, many judges nowadays refuse to require answers to discovery requests deemed unreasonably burdensome in relation to the importance of the information sought to be obtained. In theory, when confronted with an unreasonably burdensome interrogatory, it is up to the responding party to file a motion for a protective order under FRCP, Rule 26(c). In practice, however, many litigators would simply object to such questions and leave it up to the opposing party to raise the issue with the judge if desired.

**Example interrogatory:** Suppose you represent a large corporation with 250,000 employees that is being sued by a former employee for an alleged sexual harassment. The plaintiff's attorney submits the following interrogatory to be answered by your client: "State the name, address, and telephone number of each and every person who has made any allegation of sexual harassment or other employment-related misconduct against defendant corporation at any time during the five years preceding this lawsuit, and, with respect to each such allegation, describe the conduct alleged to have occurred and identify all persons involved therein."

**Analysis:** Relevant to the subject matter of the lawsuit? Probably. Calculated to lead to admissible evidence? Possibly. Reasonable in terms of the work required to compile the information necessary to give a complete answer? Most judges would probably say "no." We would object to this kind of question, and throw in a scope of discovery objection for good measure.

**Example objection:** "Defendant objects to this interrogatory as burdensome and oppressive and not reasonably calculated to lead to admissible evidence."

---

## SIDEBAR

### The "Object, Then Answer Anyway" Technique

*As we have seen, some interrogatories are objectionable, but only because of some defect that is easily corrected. This is often the case with poorly worded questions. If we object to such questions and provide no response, the opposing party is likely to reword the question and send it to us again. Then we will have another set of interrogatories to keep track of and more work to do, and since the opposing party will now have been forced to think about the question, it will no doubt be framed in a way that is better for our opponent. One useful response tactic is to set out our objection to the question, thereby preserving the objection, then reword the question to our liking and answer it.*

*Example interrogatory: Suppose Dr. Collins's attorney submits the following interrogatory to be answered by Shannon. "With regard to the hand gun with which plaintiff shot defendant, state the date on which plaintiff purchased said hand gun and the name and address of the seller."*

*Analysis: This interrogatory is technically misleading and lacking in foundation in that it assumes that Shannon acquired her hand gun by purchasing it. Let us assume that, in fact, it was given to her by her father. Theoretically, her attorney could object to the form of the interrogatory and not answer it, but there is really nothing to be gained by doing so. Better to note the objection, and give defendant the information.*

*Example response: "Plaintiff objects to the form of this interrogatory in that it assumes that plaintiff was the owner of the hand gun and acquired it by purchase. For defendant's information, and without waiving said objection, the hand gun was a gift to plaintiff from her father."*

If you are to become truly expert at responding to written discovery, you need to evolve your own check-list of all of the things that can provide a basis for objecting to an interrogatory. A good way to do this is to go through the annotations to FRCP, Rules 26 and 33, in one of the annotated sets of federal statutes such as U.S. Code Annotated. The annotations—paragraph-sized summaries of the holdings of federal cases—are organized by topic, making it easy to list the various grounds on which federal courts have held interrogatories objectionable, and to get an idea of what kinds of facts are needed to sustain each kind of objection. If you do this, it is useful to include in your checklist or notes the citations to a few key cases in each category; including a case citation or two in an objection can be a useful way to make the objection look well thought out and serious.

---

**Your Local Notes**

_____

_____

---

| **Step 6** | *Answer Each Question That Should Be Answered* |

Let us assume that we have carefully analyzed our set of interrogatories, culled out all of the objectionable questions, and done enough research and fact gathering to locate the information necessary to answer the rest. Now we can begin drafting answers.

As we write a discovery response, we are always mindful of the fact that, under many circumstances, the opposing attorney can use the questions and answers in cross-examining our witnesses and read them to the jury during argument. Therefore, our approach will include these tasks:

1.  Draft an answer.

2.  Check the draft answer against the question to be sure that we have addressed everything that the question requires and that we have not included anything in the answer that the question does not specifically ask for.

3.  Imagine the ways in which our answer could be used to imply things that we did not intend. Imagine the answer being read to the jury, or used to contradict a statement made by our client on the witness stand. Imagine yourself in the position of the opposing attorney—how could she best use this answer against our client?

4.  Redraft the answer.

We repeat this process of drafting, analysis, and re-drafting as many times as necessary, until we are sure that we have sanitized our answer, eliminating every unnecessary word or fact, and that nothing unexpected can be made of what remains.

The discussion to follow will offer specific advice about how to write answers, with examples to illustrate the concepts.

**Style and Wording of Answers**—We do not write interrogatory answers in a conversational style or, for that matter, in a style that an English composition teacher would approve of. The style that we use is chosen to advance our goals, which are to provide our opponent with the least useful answer that satisfies the requirements of the discovery rules. As you carry out work assignments involving discovery, you will quickly develop an ear for the required style. Meanwhile, we can offer a few suggestions about style and wording, using the following example interrogatory as a basis for discussion:

> **Example interrogatory:** "State whether defendant Arthur Collins had consumed any alcohol or other intoxicating substances in the twelve-hour period prior to his entering plaintiff's hotel room " Assume that Dr. Collins had had a few glasses of wine with dinner, but that he had drunk no alcohol since dinner time and was not intoxicated at the time he returned to the hotel.

The suggestions:

■ Answers should be couched in simple declaratory sentences and be limited to statements of fact. Never resort to imagery, metaphor, or comparisons.

> **Example of how not to answer:** "Dr. Collins was sober as a judge when he returned to the hotel after dinner."
> **Analysis:** The opposing party will easily find witnesses who will testify that Dr. Collins had wine with dinner, and the "sober as a judge" comment will be used to make him look ridiculous. Worse yet, it is the kind of catchy phrase that the jury will remember forever. Better to limit ourselves to provable facts.

■ Answers should include no unnecessary words. This is not literature—we do not need or want lead-in paragraphs, long narratives, or other verbiage whose only purpose is to make the answer more readable or interesting.

> **Example of how not to answer:** "While enjoying his dinner at the MGM Grand Hotel, Dr. Collins, an expert oenophile, shared with his companions an excellent California Cabernet Sauvignon."

**Analysis:** We are writing a discovery response, not a novel. This answer would easily be used to make Dr. Collins appear snobbish and superior, and would alienate many jurors.

■ Discovery answers are not the place for humor, ridicule, sarcasm, anger, cheap shots at the opposing party, or other appeals to emotion. The opposing attorney will read your humorous jibe to the jury in a such a way that no one will laugh—guaranteed. Avoid the temptation.

**Example of how not to answer:** "Dr. Collins, unlike plaintiff, is not in the habit of indulging in escapes from reality, chemical-induced or otherwise."

**Analysis:** Remember, interrogatory answers are in writing. Your opponent will have plenty of time—months and months—to think of exactly the best way to use this response against your client in the most embarrassing way possible.

■ Avoid volunteering information that is not asked for. Your job is not to enlighten your opponent—it is to comply with the discovery rules, period.

**Example of how not to answer:** "Dr. Collins drank two glasses of wine with his dinner at approximately 8:00 P.M. and had no other alcohol in the twelve hours preceding the incident. Dr. Collins does not use "other intoxicating substances.""

**Analysis:** Want to bet that plaintiff's attorney will not be able to find a waiter, another diner at the restaurant, or someone else who will testify that Dr. Collins actually consumed at least four glasses of wine at dinner? That is the bet you are making if you give this answer, and if you lose it, your client will look like a liar in front of the jury. Worse yet, the answer volunteers the claim that Dr. Collins does not use other intoxicating substances—practically an engraved invitation to check out his personal life to see whether anyone can be found who will say that he smoked some marijuana once.

■ Use words and phrases like "approximately" and "to the best of defendant's present knowledge" to leave yourself some wiggle room in case the facts turn out to be different than you are supposing.

**Example of how not to answer:** "Dr. Collins drank two glasses of wine between 8:00 and 9:00 P.M. and had no other alcohol in the twelve hours preceding the incident."

**Analysis:** Leaving aside the problem that this answer volunteers information that the question does not ask for, it is stated in terms that are far too precise. Better to write, "To the best of Dr. Collins's present recollection and belief, he had two glasses of wine between the hours of approximately 8:00 and 9:00 P.M." Then when it turns out that he actually had half a bottle of wine with dinner and two cocktails at the show later that night, it will be harder for plaintiff to make him look like a deliberate liar.

■ However, do not get carried away with the "weasel words" to the point that the answer can be made to seem evasive, as though your client is hiding something.

**Example of how not to answer:** "It is possible that Dr. Collins may have consumed some wine during the period referred to, but he does not recall at this time."

**Analysis:** Although "I don't recall" is a perfectly appropriate answer if it is true, judges and jurors tend to be skeptical of litigants whose memory always seems to fail whenever a tough question is asked. Avoid using the "I don't recall" excuse except where the answering party genuinely does not recall.

**And now, how we *would* answer the question:**

**Example Interrogatory:** "State whether defendant Arthur Collins had consumed any alcohol or other intoxicating substances in the twelve-hour period prior to his entering plaintiff's hotel room "

**Example Answer:** "Any alcohol: yes. Other intoxicating substances: No."

## Dealing with Some Commonplace Situations—

We now move from the general to the specific. We have just offered some general suggestions that are valid regardless of the type of question; now, let us examine some of the specific situations that come up frequently in civil discovery.

***Answering questions when all of the facts are not yet in:*** The response date is fast approaching. You have tried to assemble the information required to answer the question and you have part of the information in hand—but not all. This situation arises all the time in civil lawsuits. Precisely how best to deal with it depends somewhat on local custom and on the strictness of your local judiciary; your instructor will advise you what is expected in your locality.

---

*Your Local Notes*

_____

_____

---

**Example interrogatory** (To plaintiff Shannon Martin): "With respect to each medical expense that you claim to have incurred as a result of the incident related in plaintiff's complaint, state the name of the medical provider, the amount of the expense, and the nature of the service or other benefit for which the expense was paid, and identify each invoice or other document reflecting or evidencing each expense."

(Assume that at the time the interrogatory is received, Shannon is still undergoing medical treatment. She has received final bills for some of the medical expenses already incurred, but the paperwork for others is still wending its way through the insurance system.)

Here are examples illustrating some of the strategies commonly seen for answering an interrogatory of this kind:

**Example answer 1:** "Investigation continuing."

**Analysis:** This kind of answer is technically improper, but often seen because many judges do not enforce the rules rigorously. In theory, the responding party must answer as completely as possible within the 30 days allowed by the rules; as a practical matter, it will take the requesting party at least a month or two, and often more, to set up and file a motion to compel answers and have it heard and decided—by which time the responding party may be in a position to give a complete answer, or may respond to the motion by arguing that the facts are still not available. It appears that the judiciary, at least at the federal level, is becoming less tolerant of this kind of rule bending.

**Example answer 2:** "Plaintiff does not have the information necessary to give a complete answer to this interrogatory at this time. Plaintiff will supplement this response at such time as the information becomes available."

**Analysis:** Not recommended. We would never voluntarily take on an obligation to supplement beyond that imposed by Rule 26. If we should forget to send out the supplemental answer, we might find ourselves in trouble. Better to leave the burden on the requesting party to ask for supplementation.

**Example answer 3:** "Dr. John Smith, orthopedic surgeon, for setting plaintiff's broken finger, $500; Dr. Bill Jones, emergency physician assisting, $150; Clark County Hospital, emergency room treatment of broken finger, $410;. . . . (etc.)."

**Analysis:** We regard this kind of answer as risky. It does comply with the rules by disclosing the information that plaintiff now has. But it does not make clear that these are not the only expenses claimed.

**Example answer 4:** "The medical expenses for which plaintiff has received final bills to date are: [list them]. Plaintiff has incurred some medical expenses for which she has not yet received final bills. Plaintiff continues to undergo medical treatment and to incur expenses of such ongoing treatment."

**Analysis:** Our preferred response would be along these lines. We have carried out our obligation to disclose all information that we have; and we have made it clear that we do not yet have all the information requested. Notice that we have *not* offered to supplement the answer when we get the information.

***Answering questions that call for extensive research:*** It is not difficult to draft an interrogatory that will require a great deal of time and work to answer. Suppose, in our hypo, that Banbury Park Hotel's usual way of keeping records of general maintenance and repairs is to issue work orders, with any notes by the maintenance technician being made on copies of the work orders. Work orders are filed in chronological order, not in order by subject or location.

Now plaintiff's attorney serves the following interrogatory:

**Example Interrogatory:** "For each occasion since January 1, 1995, on which maintenance or repairs were performed on any guest room door, door lock, or door hardware, state the date, the name of the person performing the maintenance or repair, the nature of the maintenance or repair, and the number of the room where the maintenance or repair was performed."

The work orders in question fill several large filing cabinets. The only way to distill the information called for is for someone to go through the work orders, one by one, and pull out those that involved doors, locks, or door hardware, a task that will take days. Must the hotel really pay for a high-priced paralegal to spend days sifting through reams of boring work orders?

Rule 33(d), FRCP, offers an alternative way to respond:

(d) *Option to Produce Business Records.* Where the answer to an interrogatory may be derived or ascertained from the business records of the party upon whom the interrogatory has been served or from an examination, audit or inspection of such business records, including a compilation, abstract or summary thereof, and the burden of deriving or ascertaining the answer is substantially the same for the party serving the interrogatory as for the party served, it is a sufficient answer to such interrogatory to specify the records from which the answer may be derived or ascertained and to afford to the party serving the interrogatory reasonable opportunity to examine, audit or inspect such records and to make copies, compilations, abstracts or summaries. A specification shall be in sufficient detail to permit the interrogating party to locate and to identify, as readily as can the party served, the records from which the answer may be ascertained.

Park Hotels Group could therefore respond along the following lines:

> **Example response:** "The answer to this interrogatory may be derived or ascertained from business records of Park Hotels Group, specifically maintenance work order files for Banbury Park Hotel. These records are located in the main file storage room at Banbury Park Hotel, Las Vegas, Nevada. Plaintiff will be afforded a reasonable opportunity to examine, audit, or inspect such records and to make copies, compilations, abstracts, or summaries thereof upon reasonable request by plaintiff, at a time and place to be agreed upon between plaintiff and defendant.

Problem solved! Well, not entirely. There is always a risk involved with turning an opposing party loose among a client's records. You can be sure that if there exists, anywhere on earth, a piece of paper capable of destroying Park Hotels Group's case, Mr. Murphy (of Murphy's law fame) will have misfiled it somewhere in those filing cabinets full of work orders!

We do not mean to imply that the voluminous records response should never be used—merely that reasonable care should be taken. Certainly, a lawyer or paralegal for Park Hotels Group should look through any records before the opposing party is allowed access. It goes without saying that an opposing party should never be left alone in a client's file room. It is best to move the records to another location. We would also discuss the pros and cons of the voluminous record response with our client and get our client's approval before responding in this way.

***Handling "bad" facts:*** As we have learned in this workshop, the mechanics of writing a discovery response are quite straightforward. If we were not working in the context of an adversary process, the task would be easy. Any reasonably literate person can learn the skills necessary to research and write answers to questions. The real challenge lies in the fact that *every word we put into a discovery response has the potential to come flying back at us and blow a hole in our case.* How, then, should we approach the problem of answering questions that call for "bad" facts? Here are a few suggestions:

- As a general rule, volunteer nothing without a compelling reason to do so. When you are writing a discovery response, you have no idea what future directions the case may take. A bit of information that now seems utterly innocent may turn out to be the torpedo that sinks your case later on. Answer what the question asks, and *only* what the question asks—then stop.

- Use objections appropriately. If you have a valid objection to a question that would otherwise require you to disclose a bad fact, assert the objection and be prepared to go to the mat over it. But do not assert objections that you know are unfounded, and try to avoid provoking battles over trivial questions that are objectionable as worded but that you will have to answer as soon as your opponent rewords them. (See sidebar on the "object, then answer anyway" technique.)

- If a question clearly asks for information that you know is bad for your case, disclose the bad fact openly and forthrightly. Never yield to the temptation to tone down a bad fact or to bury it in the middle of some unrelated disclosure in the hope it will not be noticed. Attempts to camouflage or downplay bad facts merely serve to call attention to them and make them look worse—no one is fooled.

- Most especially, never hide, destroy, or alter evidence. Such tactics are unethical, can destroy your reputation and career, and almost never work. Bad facts have a way of coming out eventually, however hard you try to hide them.

***Interrogatories calling for disclosure of exhibits and witnesses:*** As we saw in Workshop 10, each party in every lawsuit should nearly always submit interrogatories to all opposing parties asking for disclosure of witnesses and exhibits.

> **Example interrogatory** (Submitted by Shannon's attorney to defendant Park Hotels Group): "State the name, address, and telephone number of each and every person whom you will or may call as a witness at the trial of this matter or whose testimony you will or may offer, whether in person, by deposition or affidavit, or otherwise, in connection with any proceeding herein."

We must take particular care with interrogatories of this kind. Judges can, and sometimes do, prohibit a party from offering an exhibit or calling a witness if proper disclosure has not been made. The problem is, of course, that witness and exhibit interrogatories are usually served in the early stages of the case, at a time when we are still investigating and have no idea of even who all the witnesses are and what documents exist, much less which ones we will want to use at trial.

The key to responding to witness and exhibit interrogatories is to have a clear understanding of when and how often interrogatory answers must be supplemented. Unfortunately, supplementation rules vary considerably from one jurisdiction to another, and depend in part on judges' attitudes and local customs. Your instructor will inform you of the accepted practice in your locality.

The general strategy is this:

1. We answer the interrogatories as best we can when the answer is due, making it clear that the answer is not complete or final.

2. We determine a reasonable interval at which we will review the answers for supplementation. In the absence of a specific rule, we will do this at least every 2 months.

3. We will docket the dates for reviewing the answers on the office calendar so that we do not forget to do it.

4. At the intervals chosen, we will analyze our answers in light of what we now know about the case, and file supplemental answers to disclose any witnesses or exhibits in addition to those already disclosed.

**Example response:** "At this early stage, plaintiff cannot make a final determination of which witnesses she will call at trial or of the persons whose testimony will be used herein. As best plaintiff can determine at present, plaintiff will likely call the following witnesses: plaintiff Shannon Martin; defendant Arthur Collins; Arnold Trevayne; Detective Sgt. Marnell, Las Vegas Police Dept. Plaintiff's address and telephone number are [list them]; plaintiff does not have the addresses and telephone numbers of the other individuals named. Plaintiff will call other witnesses at trial as appropriate, based on the outcome of investigation and discovery."

*Interrogatories calling for the factual basis of allegations:* Many litigators routinely submit a series of interrogatories asking for the factual basis of each allegation of the complaint or answer.

**Example interrogatory** (By defendant Park Hotels Group to Shannon): "With respect to the allegation made in paragraph 6 of plaintiff's complaint that defendant Arthur Collins entered plaintiff's hotel room using a key provided by Banbury Park Hotel, state each and every fact and identify each and every document supporting such allegation."

"Factual basis" allegations are potentially troublesome because the opposing party can use a care-

less answer to support a motion for summary judgment. Consider the following response:

**Example of how not to respond:** "Defendant Collins's key was found in plaintiff's room."

**Analysis:** This response is a time bomb waiting to explode. As soon as defendant becomes aware of the fact that the key found in plaintiff's room did not fit the door, defendant will file a motion for summary judgment, using plaintiff's response as the centerpiece. This response establishes, in effect, that *plaintiff has no other facts* to support the allegation about the key—the interrogatory asks for "each and every" fact, and this is all that plaintiff has disclosed.

**Example of a better response:** "Plaintiff made sure the hotel room door was locked the last time that she entered the room before retiring, and checked again that the door was locked before she went to bed. Dr. Collins stated to police investigating officers that he used the key provided by the desk clerk to enter the room."

*Interrogatories calling for disclosure of rebuttal evidence:* One of the most exciting and satisfying experiences in litigation is to catch an opposing witness telling a lie and have just the right piece of evidence to prove it. Unfortunately, modern discovery rules make such moments uncommon. All too often, we are required to disclose that right piece of evidence, and the opposing attorney will have plenty of opportunity to coach the witness in advance. When we have evidence that we think has great "ambush potential," is there anything we can do to hold it back?

The discovery rules in some jurisdictions provide a procedure whereby evidence intended only for rebuttal can be filed with the court in a sealed envelope and not disclosed until it is used. Your instructor will inform you of whether any such rules apply in the courts of your locality.

Usually, the best strategy is to try to schedule your discovery in such a way that you can take a deposition or statement from the witness whom you expect to lie *before* answers are due to any interrogatories that would require you to turn over the evidence that you intend to use against the witness.

## Step 7 — *Date, Signature, and Verification*

Answers to interrogatories are not just a court paper—they are also the equivalent of testimony by a witness. You might expect that something more than an attorney's signature would be required, and you would be right.

According to FRCP, Rule 33(b)(2), "The answers are to be signed by the person making them, and the objections signed by the attorney making them." In those simple words, however, lurk a few complications.

First of all, who *is* the "person making" the answers? Does this rule mean that, for example, a paralegal who researches and drafts answers to interrogatories should sign them? What if the answers are on behalf of a corporation, and a number of people contribute information—must they all sign?

In general, the "person making" the answers is the party to whom the questions were directed. We know this because FRCP, Rule 33(a), states that interrogatories are to be "answered by the party served." (Recall that interrogatories can be served only on someone who is a party to the suit.) Therefore, if your client is an individual, he or she must sign the answers, even if, as is usually the case, the answers have actually been drafted by someone else (such as you).

Not only that, the answers must be given "under oath"; see FRCP, Rule 33(b)(1). This makes the answers subject to the penalties for perjury. In practice, the oath consists of a paragraph reciting that the answers are given under oath; the signer's signature is then notarized. Mechanically, where and how the oath paragraph appears in the document varies considerably with locality; when in doubt, use answers prepared by other local practitioners as a guide. The fact that answers to interrogatories are given "under oath" raises some strategic issues (see sidebar).

> **Your Local Notes**
> _____
> _____

What if your client is a corporation or other entity—then who signs? FRCP, Rule 33(a), offers some guidance: "If the party served is a public or private corporation or a partnership or association or governmental agency," the answers are to be signed "by an officer or agent, who shall furnish such information as is available to the party."

Usually, when you represent a corporation, a contact person within the organization is given the responsibility of acting for the entity in dealings with

---

### SIDEBAR

## Be Careful What You Let Your Client Swear To

Because your client has signed them "under oath," answers to interrogatories make great ammunition for cross-examining your client when he or she takes the witness stand to testify at trial. Let your client say one word that contradicts anything in the answers to interrogatories, and you may be sure that your opponent will confront him with the conflicting answer—and the sworn signature. This may seem unfair, since everyone knows that it is the lawyers and paralegals, not the clients, who write answers to interrogatories, but it is the reality.

It is absolutely essential, therefore, that your client read every word of the answers before signing; better yet, if possible, the lawyer or paralegal should go through the answers sentence by sentence with the client before signing. Answers to interrogatories are not one of those documents that the client can safely skim or sign without reading.

Also consider carefully the wording of the oath that your client is signing—in federal court, no particular form of oath is required, so instead of the traditional, flowery oath, we would prefer one that accurately reflects the way in which answers to interrogatories are prepared in the real world:

Example of how not to "answer under oath": "John Doe, being first duly sworn, upon his oath deposes and says: That he has read the foregoing answers to interrogatories and the same are true and correct and made on the basis of his personal knowledge."

Analysis: This oath leaves no wiggle room. These are John Doe's answers and he is stuck with them.

Example of a better oath paragraph: "John Doe, being first duly sworn, upon his oath deposes and says: That the foregoing answers to interrogatories have been prepared by his attorney based upon information provided by him and others from sources that he believes to be trustworthy, and are true to the best of his present knowledge, recollection, information, and belief."

the corporation's lawyers. Sometimes, that person is the one who provides the information needed for answering interrogatories; other times, the corporation's contact person will put you in touch with others in the organization who are more familiar with the facts needed. So who signs? The rule requires the signer to "furnish such information as is available" to the corporate party, but it does not prevent the signer from assembling that information from other sources, which will often be necessary, since no single person may have all the information required. We would prefer the signer not be someone that our opponent can paint as an important witness; generally, therefore, the signer should not be a high officer of the corporation, nor someone who was directly involved in the dispute that gave rise to the lawsuit.

What about the attorney? Must the attorney also sign? In practice, it has long been customary for attorneys to sign answers to interrogatories in the same way as they would sign any other court paper. In federal court, after the 1993 amendment to Rule 11 [see FRCP, Rule 11(d)], there is no express requirement that the attorney sign answers to interrogatories [although the attorney must sign any objections, see FRCP, Rule 33(b)(1)]. Many state courts still have rules patterned after the former practice under Rule 11, and require attorneys to sign all court papers. Your instructor will inform you of the preferred practice in your locality.

> **Your Local Notes**
> _____
> _____

## CONCLUDING STEPS

After we have drafted answers or objections to each question, and have rewritten and revised them until we are satisfied with our work, we are ready to send them out.

**Step 8**  *Filing and Service*

As we have seen, many courts have joined a growing trend and adopted rules prohibiting parties from filing routine discovery papers with the clerk of the court. Your instructor will inform you of the applicable rules for the courts of your locality. If you are in a traditional type jurisdiction, you file and serve answers to interrogatories in the same way that you would file and serve any other court paper. See Workshop 6 for details. If your court does not allow filing of discovery papers, you should prepare a no-

tice reciting that you have served answers to interrogatories and then file and serve the notice.

> **Your Local Notes**
> _____
> _____

**Step 9**  *Review and Supplement as Required*

When we have filed and served the answers to interrogatories, is our job over? Not quite. Answers that seem correct today may look wrong tomorrow. It is wise to docket the answers for periodic review to consider whether they should be supplemented.

In federal court, FRCP, Rule 26(e)(2), provides:

> A party is under a duty seasonally to amend a prior response to an interrogatory . . . if the party learns that the response is in some material respect incomplete or incorrect and if the additional or corrective information has not otherwise been made known to the other parties during the discovery process or in writing.

Therefore, if we obtain additional information later, we *must* amend or supplement our answers. We may also decide to supplement voluntarily, even when we are not technically required to. Keeping in mind that our opponent can read our answers to the jury, amending or supplementing gives us a way to "fix" answers that, in the light of subsequent developments, we wish that we had worded differently. Facts and perceptions change as a lawsuit moves forward, and it is worthwhile to revisit past discovery responses periodically and fine-tune them if necessary.

> **Your Local Notes**
> _____
> _____

## Answering Interrogatories: Learning by Example

Now we will put into practice the ideas that we have just explored, by drafting answers to the interrogatories that we prepared in Workshop 10. We will assume that Shannon's attorney, Allen Porter, served the interrogatories on defendant Park Hotels Group by mailing them to Gail Stoddard, attorney for Park

## SIDEBAR

### Requests for Production of Documents

The task of responding to an FRCP, Rule 34, request for production of documents is in most ways similar to that of preparing answers to interrogatories. We begin by docketing the response date, reviewing and analyzing each request, and making the necessary inquiries to find out where the requested documents are kept.

#### The Formal Response

The response itself is somewhat different from a set of answers to interrogatories. As with all discovery responses, it is in the form of a court paper, with caption, signature lines, and certificate of service. The body of the response, however, takes the numbered requests one by one, with a separate paragraph for each item. For each numbered item in the request, the response either states an objection or states that the documents will be provided. Responses to requests for production are therefore usually fairly short.

#### Producing the Documents

Note that the documents requested do not form a part of the response itself—they are produced separately. FRCP, Rule 34(b), states that "The request shall specify a reasonable time, place, and manner of making the inspection. . . . " In practice, documents are almost never produced in the manner specified in the request.

If the quantity of documents is small, the responding attorney simply sends photocopies with the written response. In complex cases, however, the documents necessary to respond to a document request may comprise many file boxes of paper. The cost of copying would be prohibitive, and even if we could turn over copies, we would prefer not to give our opponent unlimited time in which to review them. The usual solution is that we first go through the boxes of documents carefully ourselves, to make sure no surprises are lurking, and then we put them in an empty conference room or other neutral location and let opposing counsel examine them there and make whatever copies are desired. Either the responding attorney can provide access to a copying machine, or the reviewing attorney can rent a copying machine and have it temporarily installed at the place where the documents are being reviewed. Usually, attorneys are able to agree on reasonable procedures for reviewing and copying documents; if not, the judge can enter appropriate orders.

#### Making a Record of What Was Produced

A problem arises when the documents produced are voluminous—how do you prove exactly what you produced? If we have turned over photocopies, we can keep a set of copies for ourselves, but if we have turned our opponent loose in a room with a hundred boxes of files, how do we prove what we turned over? We use the response itself to make a record. Instead of responding merely "Item 4: Produced," we will respond, "Item 4: Produced six boxes of records comprising all maintenance department work orders for January 1, 1998, through March 15, 2000."

## SIDEBAR

### Responding to Requests for Admissions

In form and appearance, the response to a set of requests for admissions is nearly identical to a set of answers to interrogatories (and may even be part of the same document if the interrogatories and requests for admissions have been combined in one document). Responding to a request for admission is much like answering an interrogatory except that the answer must admit or deny the assertion made in the request.

#### The Form of Admissions and Denials

In a request for admissions, the individual items to be admitted or denied are set out in numbered paragraphs. As with interrogatories, the response is entered in the space below each request. Usually, the answer to a request for admission should be a single word: "admit" or "deny." Occasionally, more is required: FRCP, Rule 36, provides that "when good faith requires that a party qualify an answer or deny only a part of the matter of which an admission is requested, the party shall specify so much of it as is true and qualify or deny the remainder." Usually, however, long-winded responses should be avoided. We should never admit anything unless we are reasonably certain that the admission cannot harm our case; if we are in doubt, it is best to deny.

#### If in Doubt, Deny

You might wonder why anyone would ever respond to a request for admission with anything but a

## SIDEBAR

### Responding to Requests for Admissions, *continued*

*denial—why not make the opposing party prove everything the hard way? The answer is that if we deny a request for admission and force our opponent to prove the point, FRCP, Rule 37(c)(2), allows the judge to make us pay the costs incurred by our opponent in doing so. In theory, the judge is required to do so unless we had "reasonable grounds" for our denial. In practice, however, awards of costs are uncommon, and anyway we would rather risk having to pay a few of our opponent's costs than risk losing the whole case. We do not mean to suggest that you deny requests when you have no basis for doing so; but never give away an admission on an important issue unless you are sure that the issue cannot be won.*

#### Objecting to Requests for Admission

*As with interrogatories, we should always be on the lookout for requests for admissions that are objec-*

*tionable. In general, requests for admissions are subject to the same kinds of objections as are interrogatories. As with answers to interrogatories, our opponent can read our admissions to the jury, so we must be especially watchful for admissions that are misleading or could be misinterpreted.*

#### A Timely Response Is Critical

*One important way in which requests for admissions differ from interrogatories is that requests for admissions are automatically deemed admitted if not denied within the 30-day response time provided by FRCP, Rule 36. In other words, if you are late with your response, you have just admitted every request in the set. In practice, judges can sometimes be persuaded to give you another chance to respond, but—trust us—you do not want to bet your career that the judge will be feeling lenient. File on time—always.*

---

Hotels Group, on May 2, 2000. Since we are dealing with a hypothetical fact situation, we will simply invent the facts needed for our answers as we go along.

## PREPARATORY STEPS

### Step 1    *Docket Response Due Date*

When Gail Stoddard receives the interrogatories in the morning mail on Thursday, May 4, 2000, she notes that, according to the attached certificate of service, Allen Porter mailed them to her on May 2. The firm's docketing clerk has already computed and docketed the due date for answers—June 5— and entered it in the firm's central calendar, as Gail can tell from the docketing stamp on the first page of the document.

Gail assigns us the task of preparing draft answers. Careful paralegals that we are, we begin by double-checking the computation of the due date. Consulting FRCP, Rule 33(b)(3), we see that we are required to serve answers within 30 days. Applying the principles that we learned in Workshop 7, we add 3 days because the interrogatories were served on us by mail [see FRCP, Rule 6(e)], giving us a total of 33 days. We do not count the day of service, May 2 [see FRCP, Rule 6(a)]; we start counting on May 3 and continue counting until we reach the

33rd day, which is June 4. June 4, 2000, is a Sunday, so the answers are due on the following Monday, June 5 [see FRCP, Rule 6(a)]. We note the due date in our personal calendar.

### Step 2    *Analyze the Entire Request Question by Question*

Next we sit down with the interrogatories and our laptop computer (or a legal pad) and start reading, analyzing, and taking notes. Here is an example of what our notes might look like when we are done:

*Int. No. 1:* Documents only. Call Banbury Park maintenance supervisor and find out how records are kept. Find out if any maintenance done by outside contractors, if so by whom. Interrogatory seems overbroad in that it asks about all guest room doors, not just the one in issue. Review records first, if harmless turn them over, otherwise consider objecting.

*Int. No. 2:* Witnesses to incident, statements. Check police report, review case file for any references to witnesses. Docket for supplementation check. Statements—object, work product. "Vicinity" is vague; consider objecting.

*Int. No. 3:* Affirmative defenses. Check issues outline for factual basis. Can flesh out contributory negligence now, rest are probably inapplicable but note investigation not complete.

*Int. No. 4:* Facts of incident. Review notes of interview with desk clerk, review police report. Note investigation not complete, docket for supplementation check.

*Int. No. 5:* Trial witnesses. Assemble from police report and issues outline, note not complete, docket for supplementation check.

*RFA No. 1:* Subject matter jurisdiction. Based on earlier research, appears no viable issue. Will probably admit; check with Gail.

*Int. No. 6:* Facts re RFA No. 1. No need to answer assuming we admit RFA 1.

| Step 3 | *Request Information from Client and Others as Necessary* |
|--------|----------------------------------------------------------|

When we have gone through the entire set of interrogatories and analyzed each question, we can then easily determine from our notes what further information we need and whom we need to contact to get it. Usually, a paralegal's first step after reading and analyzing the interrogatories should be to consult with the supervising attorney. Some questions will raise issues on which we need guidance; others will require information from the client, and we do not contact the client without prior permission.

Because we analyzed and took notes on the entire set of interrogatories before trying to gather information, we will not need to keep interrupting our supervising attorney with repeated questions; instead, we can meet with her once to go over our notes. We will, of course, add to our notes any suggestions that our supervising attorney may offer. Assuming she approves, we can then begin contacting the appropriate hotel employees to gather the information that we need.

It is important to do this in an organized and professional way. When we interact with employees of our client, we are acting as a representative of our law firm, and everything we do reflects on the reputation of the firm. We prepare thoroughly before any client contact. Often, we may find that the person to whom we are speaking does not have the information that we need, but can suggest someone else to try. We pursue each lead as necessary, taking notes all along the way.

As we gather information, we begin incorporating it into draft answers. By the time the due date nears, we should be well on our way to a final draft.

## DRAFTING STEPS

We use Steps 4 through 7 to prepare the document, which is shown in Figure W11–1.

---

**Figure W11–1    Sample Answers**

### IN THE UNITED STATES DISTRICT COURT
### DISTRICT OF ARIZONA

| | |
|---|---|
| SHANNON MARTIN, a single woman,<br>　　　　　　　Plaintiff,<br>　　　v.<br><br><br><br><br><br>ARTHUR COLLINS and JANE DOE<br>COLLINS, husband and wife;<br>PARK HOTELS GROUP, INC.,<br>a Delaware corporation;<br>　　　　　　　Defendants. | )<br>)<br>)<br>)<br>)<br>)<br>)<br>)<br>)<br>)<br>)<br>)<br>)<br>) | NO. CV98 -01456 PHX JL<br>PLAINTIFF'S FIRST SET OF<br>INTERROGATORIES AND REQUESTS<br>FOR ADMISSIONS TO<br>DEFENDANT PARK HOTELS<br>GROUP, INC. AND ANSWERS THERETO |

Plaintiff hereby submits interrogatories and requests for admission to defendant Park Hotels Group, pursuant to the provisions of Rules 33 and 36, Federal Rules of Civil Procedure, to be answered in writing and under oath within 30 days from the date of service hereof.

*continued*

**Figure W11–1  Sample Answers,** *continued*

### INSTRUCTIONS AND DEFINITIONS

A.   All information is to be divulged which is in the possession of the individual or corporate party, his attorney, investigators, agents, employees, or other representatives of the named party and his attorney.

B.   A "medical practitioner" as used in these interrogatories is meant to include any medical doctor, osteopathic physician, podiatrist, doctor of chiropractic, naturopathic physician, or other person who performs any form of healing art.

C.   Where an individual interrogatory calls for an answer which involves more than one part, each part of the answer should be clearly set out so that it is understandable.

D.   Where the term "you," "plaintiff," or "defendant" are used, they are meant to include every individual part and separate answers should be given for each person named as a party, if requested.

E.   Where the terms "accident" or "the accident" are used, they are meant to mean the incident which is the basis of the lawsuit, unless otherwise specified.

F.   A space has been provided on the Form of Interrogatories for your answer. Four (4) copies are served herewith. Complete all copies and serve a copy upon each separate counsel representation, retaining a copy in your file. Attach a verification and certificate of mailing.

To the extent that the foregoing "Instructions and Definitions" purport to impose burdens or obligations beyond those imposed by the applicable rules of civil procedure, they are objected to, and will not be complied with.

*Interrogatory No. 1*
Identify and describe all documents recording or memorializing and repairs, maintenance, or installation or replacement of parts or components, relating to the entrance door of any guest room at Banbury Park Hotel or to any lock, strike, hinge, door closer, or other hardware attached to or associated with any such door, at any time after January 1, 1997.

> The answer to this interrogatory may be derived or ascertained from business records of Park Hotels Group, specifically maintenance work order files for Banbury Park Hotel. These records are located in the main file storage room at Banbury Park Hotel, Las Vegas, Nevada. Plaintiff will be afforded a reasonable opportunity to examine, audit, or inspect such records and to make copies, compilations, abstracts, or summaries thereof upon reasonable request by plaintiff, at a time and place to be agreed upon between plaintiff and defendant.

*Interrogatory No. 2*
With respect to each and every person who witnessed or was present in the vicinity of the events described in plaintiff's complaint occurring at Banbury Park Hotel on the night of February 5, 1996, state the name, address, and telephone number of each such person, state the substance of what such person observed, and identify each and every written or recorded statement given by such person.

> Defendant objects to this interrogatory in that the word "vicinity" is vague, and in that it purports to call for statements of witnesses that would constitute work product of defendant's attorneys.
> For plaintiff's information, and interpreting "vicinity" as referring to Room 407 and the hall area immediately adjacent to it, to the best of defendant's present information and belief, the persons present were plaintiff and defendant Arthur Collins. Defendant has not taken statements from either.

*Interrogatory No. 3*
Separately with respect to each affirmative defense enumerated in paragraph 12 of defendant Park Hotels Group's answer herein, state the basis of each such defense and state each and every fact upon which each such defense is based.

> As noted therein, the purpose of paragraph 12 of defendant's answer was to preserve the listed affirmative defenses pending a full investigation of the facts. Such investigation is not yet complete.

*continued*

**Figure W11–1   Sample Answers,** *continued*

To the best of defendant's present information and belief, the basis of the defense of contributory negligence is that plaintiff negligently failed to lock the door to Room 407 and/or negligently admitted defendant Collins to her room; plaintiff also negligently failed to secure the locking chain. These omissions on plaintiff's part were a contributing cause of the events leading to her injury.

*Interrogatory No. 4*

Describe in detail what you contend were the true facts surrounding the events of the night of February 5, 1996, at Banbury Park Hotel leading up to plaintiff's injury.

To the best of defendant's present information and belief, and keeping in mind that investigation is far from complete at this early stage of this lawsuit, the facts were as follows: Plaintiff, who was staying in room 407, either failed to lock the room door or unlocked and opened the room door. Defendant Collins entered the room. Subsequently, plaintiff shot Collins and Collins broke plaintiff's finger.

*Interrogatory No. 5*

With respect to each witness, including expert witnesses, that you will or may call to testify at the trial of this matter, state the name, address, and telephone number of each such witness, and, separately for each such witness, state the substance of what you anticipate the testimony of each such witness to be.

At this early stage, defendant cannot make a final determination of which witnesses will be called at trial. As best defendant can determine at present, defendant's witnesses and the substance of their testimony will include: Plaintiff Shannon Martin, address and telephone number unknown. Ms. Martin will be called to testify concerning the events described in plaintiff's complaint. Defendant Arthur Collins, address and telephone number unknown. Dr. Collins will be called to testify concerning the events in room 407 and specifically the manner by which he gained entry to said room. Detective Sgt. Janet Marnell, Las Vegas Police Department, address and telephone number unknown. Detective Marnell will be called to testify concerning the results of the police investigation into the events in room 407. Arnold Trevayne, Banbury Park Hotel, Las Vegas, Nevada. Mr. Trevayne will be called to testify concerning his observations relating to defendant Collins picking up his room key, his observations of plaintiff following the incident, and his acts in summoning emergency assistance. Donald Armstrong, maintenance supervisor, Banbury Park Hotel, Las Vegas, Nevada. Mr. Armstrong will testify concerning the condition and operability of the room 407 door lock. Defendant anticipates retaining one or more medical experts to examine plaintiff and render an opinion regarding her injuries, but has not yet done so. Defendant anticipates retaining one or more experts to testify concerning the condition and operation of the room 407 door lock, but has not yet done so. Defendant will call other witnesses whose identities are revealed as discovery proceeds.

*Request for Admission No. 1*

Admit that this court has valid subject matter jurisdiction of this matter under the provisions of 28 U.S.C. §1332.

Admit.

*Interrogatory No. 6*

In the event that you deny the foregoing Request For Admission No. 1, state each and every fact upon which such denial is based, and state each and every respect in which you contend that the jurisdictional requirements of 28 U.S.C. §1332 are not met in this action.

Not applicable.

DATED this _____ day of _____, 20 ___.

CRANDALL, ELKINS & MAJOR

_____

Gail Stoddard
Attorneys for defendant Park
Hotels Group

*continued*

---

**Figure W11–1    Sample Answers,** *continued*

STATE OF ARIZONA          )

                                        )    ss.

County of Maricopa         )

The undersigned, being first duly sworn, upon his oath deposes and says: "That he is an officer or agent of defendant Park Hotels Group, Inc. designated by said corporation to answer the foregoing interrogatories; that the foregoing answers to interrogatories have been prepared by defendant's attorney based upon information provided by him and others from sources that he believes to be trustworthy, and are true to the best of his present knowledge, recollection, information, and belief."

_____

Ronald M. Jansen

SUBSCRIBED AND SWORN to before me, the undersigned Notary Public, this 5th day of June, 2000.

_____

Notary Public

(Certificate of service goes here—see Workshop 4 for details.)

---

## CONCLUDING STEPS

### Step 8    *Filing and Service*

We consult the local rules of the U.S. District Court for the District of Arizona and find that Rule 1.2(a)(2) provides that "Unless ordered by the Court . . . interrogatories and answers thereto . . . shall not be filed with the Court, except that a 'Notice of Service' of the foregoing papers on opposing counsel shall be filed with the Court. . . ." Therefore, we mail a copy of the answers to each opposing attorney but do not file the answers with the clerk of the court. We prepare a notice of service reciting that we have served the answers by mail, and we include a copy of the notice in the mailing to each opposing attorney. We file a copy of the notice of service with the clerk of the court.

### Step 9    *Review and Supplement as Required*

When we first read and analyzed the interrogatories, we noted that several of the answers would need to be reviewed later to see whether supplementation would be required. We make a notation in our personal calendar for August 15, 2000—approximately two months in the future—to remind ourselves to do so. At that time, we will calendar a reminder to do another review a few months later, and continue to check our answers for accuracy at 2- or 3-month intervals until the case goes to trial.

## Answering Interrogatories: Learning by Doing

Your task for this workshop is to answer a set of interrogatories served on Park Hotels Group by Dr. Arthur Collins's attorney. Assume that Dr. Collins has made a cross-claim against Park Hotels Group alleging that the hotel was negligent and is liable for his injuries. Assume that the interrogatories shown in Figure W11–2 arrived by mail on the second Wednesday of February of the current year, and assume that the action is pending in the U.S. District Court having jurisdiction in your locality.

## EXERCISES

In carrying out this assignment, you should follow the step-by-step formula described in this workshop.

*1.* Determine the last day on which the answers can be filed and still comply with the rules, and date your answers for that day.

---

**Figure W11–2  Sample Interrogatories**

## IN THE UNITED STATES DISTRICT COURT
## DISTRICT OF ARIZONA

| | | |
|---|---|---|
| SHANNON MARTIN, a single woman,<br>　　　　　　Plaintiff,<br>　　v.<br><br><br>ARTHUR COLLINS and JANE DOE<br>COLLINS, husband and wife;<br>PARK HOTELS GROUP, INC., a Delaware<br>corporation;<br>　　　　　　Defendants. | )<br>)<br>)<br>)<br>)<br>)<br>)<br>)<br>)<br>)<br>)<br>)<br>)<br>) | NO. CV98-01456 PHX JL<br><br>INTERROGATORIES AND<br>REQUESTS FOR ADMISSIONS<br>TO DEFENDANT PARK HOTELS<br>GROUP, INC. |

　　Defendant Arthur Collins hereby submits interrogatories and requests for admission to defendant Park Hotels Group, pursuant to the provisions of Rules 33 and 36, Federal Rules of Civil Procedure, to be answered in writing and under oath within 30 days from the date of service hereof.

### INSTRUCTIONS AND DEFINITIONS

[insert instructions and definitions]

*Interrogatory No. 1*
With respect to each and every employee of Park Hotels Group, Inc. or Banbury Park Hotel who had, at the time of the incident described in plaintiff's complaint, any responsibilities involving maintenance, repair, record keeping, or key issuance or changing with respect to any guest room door, door hardware or lock, state the name, address, and telephone number of each such person and the nature of each such person's duties.

*Interrogatory No. 2*
With respect to each and every person having information concerning the events described in plaintiff's complaint occurring at Banbury Park Hotel on the night of February 5, 1996, state the name, address, and telephone number of each such person, state the substance of the information possessed by each such person, and identify each and every written or recorded statement given by such person.

*Interrogatory No. 3*
State how you contend that, immediately prior to the incident described in plaintiff's complaint, the door of Room 407 was able to be opened using the key provided by the desk clerk.

*Request for Admission No. 1*
Admit that the desk clerk employed by defendant Park Hotels Group, Inc. issued a room key to defendant Arthur Collins immediately prior to the incident described in plaintiff's complaint, and that said room key was able to operate the door lock of Room 407.

*Interrogatory No. 4*
In the event that you deny the foregoing Request for Admission No. 1, state each and every fact upon which such denial is based.

DATED this _____ day of _____, 20 ___.

_____
Roger Yarborough, Esq.
Attorney for defendants Collins

**2.** In answering the interrogatories, you will need to gather facts. Your sources of facts are as follows:

    a. The facts related in the Shannon's Ordeal hypothetical;

    b. The facts related in the Learning by Doing exercises in Workshop 12;

    c. Your contact person at Park Hotels Group, Inc., Mr. Leonard Shapiro, vice president. His home address and phone are: 1429 Rustic Dr., Asbury Park, NJ 07712, phone: 732-555-3983. The address and telephone of Mr. Shapiro's office (the Park Hotels Group, Inc. main office) is 3 Municipal Plaza, Asbury Park, NJ 07712, phone: 732-555-2929, extension 903.

(At your instructor's option, your instructor may take the role of Mr. Shapiro, or may assign that role to a student; then you can write memos to the fictitious Mr. Shapiro with your requests, if any, for additional facts, and the fictitious Mr. Shapiro can respond with additional hypothetical facts as appropriate.)

**3.** When you have completed the answers to interrogatories, determine whether, under the rules of the U.S. District having jurisdiction in your locality, the answers would be filed with the clerk of the court. If so, prepare them as appropriate for filing; if not, prepare a suitable notice for filing.

# PRACTICE POINTERS
## *Copying Documents*

When responding to a request for production of documents, the attorney must decide whether to produce the originals or copies. Although producing originals saves the cost of making copies, most attorneys choose to provide copies to prevent alterations from being made, to ensure that an original document is not lost, and to avoid the confusion that results when documents get out of order.

Before copies are made, each document should be stamped to show that they have been produced by your law firm. Such stamping helps avoid confusion when multiple parties are involved. Documents that are confidential should be clearly marked "Confidential." If large numbers of copies are to be made, they should be organized in cardboard boxes and clearly labeled showing the range of numbers of documents contained in each box. Once the copies are made, the originals should be placed back in the box in the same order in which they were removed.

Some legal assistants complain that copywork is "busy work" and find ways to delegate this task to others. Consider this: Failure to produce readable copies can create problems later on at trial or can lead to unnecessary misunderstandings and strained relations with opposing counsel. If the person doing the copying is unfamiliar with the case and the documents being copied, she can easily overlook two pieces of paper sticking together so that one of them does not get copied or she can fail to notice that a paper is improperly seated in the feeder so that only part of the page is copied or she can inadvertently make multiple sets of copies, some of which are missing a page. These errors not only create the appearance of unprofessionalism but they can result in confusion and tension at later stages in the litigation process.

If you want your attorney to learn she can rely on you, make sure you carry out every task you are assigned diligently and conscientiously. The job of copying documents may be tedious but it is certainly not trivial. Rather than looking for ways to avoid time before the copy machine, consider ways you can more efficiently and accurately carry out this important responsibility.

## TECHNO TIP

Answering a set of interrogatories is not a task that lends itself easily to the "normal" way of writing, in which you start at the beginning and keep writing until you get to the end. One question may require only a phone call to your client to get the necessary information; the next may require you to search through a roomful of files located in another state.

The easiest way to handle the job, therefore, is to have some means by which you can add information to individual answers as you obtain it. Before personal computers arrived on the law office scene, this usually meant setting up a notebook, cutting and pasting one interrogatory on each page, and keeping notes on each question. With a computer—preferably a notebook or laptop so that you can take it with you on out-of-the-office information-gathering excursions—the task is much easier. You should be able to obtain the interrogatories in the form of a word processor file, either by asking opposing counsel for an electronic copy or, if necessary, by scanning the interrogatories using a scanner and converting the resulting image to a word processing file using optical character recognition software.

With the interrogatories in a word processing file, it becomes a simple matter to make notes, record contacts, and eventually draft answers, simply by typing the pertinent information in after the question to which it pertains. In this way, you will always have a current and complete record of the status of your work on each question.

## FORMS FILE

*Include samples of the following in your forms file:*
* *Answers to the sample interrogatories you collected for your forms file from Workshop 10*
* *Answers to the sample requests for admissions you collected for your forms file from Workshop 10*
* *Checklist of possible objections to interrogatories*

## INTRODUCTION: REENGINEERING THE DISCOVERY PROCESS

Many judges and legal scholars today would say that traditional discovery mechanisms are seriously flawed. The discovery tools that we have been studying up to now are request-based, that is, a litigant need not—and should not—tell an opponent anything unless the opponent specifically requests it. The duty of the responding party to provide information depends mainly on whether the requesting party asked the right questions in the right way.

Traditional discovery is expensive. Interrogatories, depositions, and requests for production are deliberately used to inundate one's opponent with paperwork and drive up costs. (If you have completed Workshops 9, 10, and 11, it should be obvious to you that the discovery process offers plenty of opportunity for procedural gamesmanship.) Judges find themselves spending too much time refereeing arguments about discovery and not enough deciding cases.

## MANDATORY DISCLOSURE

Therefore, many courts are gradually moving away from the traditional discovery mechanisms and looking for ways to force litigants to be more cooperative in conducting discovery. Each of the opposing attorneys certainly knows which facts are likely to be of greatest interest to his opponent. So, instead of making attorneys try to guess the right questions to ask, why not simply order both sides to disclose *everything,* and skip the tedious and expensive procedural games?

You may doubt that the solution could be that easy, and you would be right. Changing the discovery rules does not suddenly change opposing attorneys from tenacious adversaries into helpful allies in the Quest for Truth (and if it did, the clients would look for new attorneys!). Skeptics would say that mandating disclosure does not eliminate the game—it merely adds a few new plays. Instead of skirmishing over the interpretation of an opponent's questions, litigators argue over the interpretation of the disclosure rules.

Whatever your philosophical view is about how the discovery process might best be made to function, if you practice in a jurisdiction that has adopted disclosure-based discovery, you need to learn to use the tools of that system. The centerpiece of disclosure-based discovery systems is the **disclosure statement.** The disclosure statement is a document that each party is required to prepare and serve on opposing parties shortly after the lawsuit commences. The rules require each party's disclosure statement to contain certain specific categories of information about that party's case. Litigants are required to update and supplement their disclosure statements periodically as new information becomes available. The main focus of this workshop is the task of preparing a disclosure statement. To understand where the disclosure statement fits in the overall scheme of things, see the sidebar.

As we have pointed out in detail elsewhere (see Introduction to the Discovery Workshops), disclosure rules vary greatly from one jurisdiction to another. Some jurisdictions have embraced the disclosure paradigm almost completely, and require disclosure of everything about each side's case, including legal theories and detailed factual descriptions. Others, including the federal courts, have taken a more tentative approach, requiring disclosure of the identities of witnesses and exhibits, computations of damages, and reports of expert witnesses, but leaving the parties to flesh out the details using the traditional discovery tools. Even given two jurisdictions with identical disclosure rules, judges may have different ideas about how much disclosure is required. Disclosure rules describe the subject matter for disclosure in broad categories; the level of detail expected depends on the judge and on local customs.

In this workshop, we base our discussion on the disclosure rules that were added to the Federal Rules of Civil Procedure by the 1993 amendments. Even in the federal courts, adherence to these rules is far from uniform, because it is up to each district to decide whether to adopt the disclosure amendments in whole, in part, or not at all. In state court, the variation is even greater; you would be hard pressed to find any two states with identical disclosure rules. Your instructor will tell you where to find the disclosure rules, if any, for the courts of your locality, and point out any important variations from the federal scheme.

---

*Your Local Notes*

_____

_____

_____

## SIDEBAR

# How the Disclosure Statement Fits into the Trial Preparation Process

*In federal district court, the disclosure statement comprises one step in a larger process designed to ensure that every case is fully ready for trial by the time the scheduled trial date arrives. Here are the main steps in that process, as outlined by FRCP, Rules 26(f) and 16(b):*

*1. Order setting scheduling conference. As a practical matter, the event that triggers the disclosure process to begin is the issuance of an order by the court setting a date for a scheduling conference (see item 4). In most federal courts, this order issues automatically and, typically, but depending on the court's backlog, the initial scheduling conference is set at some point 3 to 6 months after issue is joined (i.e., the complaint and answer are filed).*

*2. Meeting of attorneys. FRCP, Rule 26(f), requires the attorneys for all parties to the lawsuit to meet and confer for the purpose of agreeing on a discovery plan. This meeting is to take place no later than 14 days before the scheduling conference date set by the court. (This meeting is not the scheduling conference. The scheduling conference takes place in court with the judge present. This meeting is to prepare for the scheduling conference.) Ideally, the opposing attorneys will reach agreement on issues such as these:*

- *What limits will be placed on the use of interrogatories and other discovery devices.*

- *What documents need to be reviewed, and when and where this will be done.*

- *Which witnesses will need to be deposed, and when and where the depositions will take place.*

- *Setting deadlines for the completion of the various phases of discovery.*

- *Setting deadlines for various required disclosures.*

- *Setting deadlines for filing motions, amending pleadings, and other procedural matters; see FRCP, Rule 16(b).*

*3. Report on discovery plan. After the meeting, the attorneys for all parties are to jointly prepare a report to the court outlining the proposed discovery plan, and submit it to the court within 10 days after the meeting of attorneys; see FRCP, Rule 26(f).*

*4. FRCP, Rule 26(a)(1), disclosure statements. Each side's disclosure statement is due 10 days after the discovery planning meeting. Since the planning meeting is to be held no later than 14 days before the scheduling conference, this means that the disclosure statements will be due a few days before the scheduling conference. The intent of the rules is to require both sides to disclose at the same time, so as not to give one side the advantage of seeing the other's disclosure statement first. What is the disclosure statement supposed to look like? FRCP, Rule 26, is not very specific, preferring to leave the details to each individual court or judge. Rule 26(a) (4) merely requires that the disclosure statement be in writing, signed in accordance with Rule 26(g), and filed with the court.*

*5. FRCP, Rule 16(b), scheduling conference. At the scheduling conference, the judge reviews the proposed schedule submitted by the attorneys, and hears argument about any issues on which the attorneys do not agree. After the scheduling conference, the judge enters an order. If the process works as intended, the order that the judge enters will closely follow the discovery plan submitted by the attorneys. (If not, the judge may send the attorneys back for another try!)*

*6. FRCP, Rule 26(a)(2), disclosure of expert witnesses. At some point after the Rule 26(a)(1) disclosure statement, at times usually set by the judge in the scheduling order, each side must disclose detailed information about any expert witnesses who are expected to testify at the trial. Discovery relating to expert witnesses is a somewhat complex topic that is beyond the scope of this introductory text. For the basic requirements, see generally FRCP, Rules 26(a)(2), 26(b)(4), and 26(e)(1).*

*7. Supplementation of disclosure. The initial FRCP, Rule 26(a)(1), disclosure takes place early in the case, usually before any other discovery is taken, so it is expected that neither side's disclosure will be complete. The intended thrust of Rule 26 is that each party will supplement the initial disclosure "at appropriate intervals." (What intervals? Every 60 days is a common requirement. Check the scheduling order and/or local rules.) In this way,*

## SIDEBAR

## How the Disclosure Statement Fits into the Trial Preparation Process *continued*

*each side's disclosure is brought up to date periodically as the case wends its way toward trial.*

*8. Pretrial disclosure. Shortly before trial, FRCP, Rule 26(a)(3), requires each side to make some specific additional disclosure about the witnesses and exhibits to be used at trial. How do we know when to do this? Often, the scheduling order specifies a deadline for Rule 26(a)(3) disclosure; if not, then the deadline is 30 days before trial; see FRCP, Rule 26(a)(3). The matters to be disclosed are listed in Rule 26(a)(3):*

- *Names, addresses, and telephone numbers of each expected trial witness;*

- *Designation of any deposition testimony that each party expects to present at trial in lieu of live testimony by a witness; and*

- *Identification of each document or exhibit.*

*9. Disclosure of objections. Within 14 days after the FRCP, Rule 26(3), pretrial disclosure, each side must file a list disclosing any known objections to deposition testimony or exhibits. This is intended to give each side a chance to anticipate the other's objections and do any legal research necessary to answer them. It is important to be thorough when disclosing objections, because any objections not disclosed are waived.*

*10. Pretrial order. At some point shortly before trial, nearly all federal judges require the attorneys for both sides to get together and prepare a document, often called a pretrial order (terminology may vary), that will be used as a kind of script for the conduct of the trial. The pretrial order typically names the witnesses that each side will call, describes the testimony to be given by each, lists the exhibits that each side will be allowed to introduce, specifies any known objections by each side, and describes the legal theories that each side is advancing. You will not be able to find much information about pretrial orders in the rules. FRCP, Rule 16, grants federal judges broad power to enter pretrial orders, but does not specify the contents of a pretrial order nor the exact procedure for preparing one. Nor are local rules usually very informative on this topic. The specifics of pretrial order procedure are usually left up to individual judges. Some judges publish information about their required procedures on the Internet or elsewhere; others issue a standard minute entry in each case describing their requirements. Your instructor will tell you what the usual pretrial order practice is in the courts of your locality.*

---

*Your Local Notes*

_____

_____

## OTHER DISCOVERY REFORM

Even in courts whose disclosure rules are all encompassing, disclosure statements do not eliminate the need for the traditional discovery tools. A disclosure statement is much like a set of answers to certain specific interrogatories. The disclosure rules, in effect, amount to a series of questions that each party has to answer without being asked. In the context of each individual case, there will usually be other questions that also need asking. Written disclosure is not a very good substitute for a deposition of a witness, because it gives no opportunity to ask follow-up questions or to observe demeanor. Nor is a disclosure statement a substitute for reviewing files of documents in their original form. Nevertheless, one of the main goals of disclosure-based discovery is to reduce the need for interrogatories and depositions. Therefore, the discovery rules in disclosure jurisdictions typically place strict limits on the use of other discovery tools (see sidebar).

*Your Local Notes*

_____

_____

## SIDEBAR

# Rules Limiting Discovery

*With or without disclosure rules, more and more courts are adopting rules seeking to rein in the overuse or abuse of traditional discovery tools like interrogatories and depositions. Some of the measures commonly seen are discussed here.*

- *Increased Planning and Judicial Oversight. One of the common aims of discovery reform is to introduce a greater degree of planning into the discovery process. Instead of allowing litigants to decide what discovery they need as they go along—practically guaranteeing procrastination and delay—why not figure out in advance what discovery will be needed and make a schedule that will get it done?*

*The federal rules attempt to involve the attorneys for both sides and also the judge in this planning process. First, the attorneys are to meet, and "make or arrange for the disclosures required by [FRCP, Rule 26(a)(1)] and to develop a proposed discovery plan" [FRCP, Rule 26(f)]. Within 10 days after the meeting, the attorneys are to submit to the court a "written report outlining the plan" [FRCP, Rule 26(f)].*

- *Court-Imposed Time Limits and Deadlines. Under the federal rules, after the discovery plan is submitted, the judge then holds a scheduling conference with the attorneys present, and enters a scheduling order that sets deadlines for the completion of discovery. The order may also set or modify the deadlines for disclosure statements and prescribe what discovery will be conducted and when; see FRCP, Rule 16(b).*
- *Limitations on Written Discovery. Many courts now place strict limits on the number of inter-*

*rogatories that a party may submit. FRCP, Rule 33(a), is typical: "Without leave of court or written stipulation, any party may serve upon any other party written interrogatories, not exceeding 25 in number including all discrete subparts. . . ."*

- *Limitations on Deposition Discovery. Under the traditional open discovery rules, litigants could, and often did, take depositions of every witness who could conceivably have information about any aspect of the case. Every time one party takes a deposition, the opposing party is put to the expense of paying a lawyer to attend and, usually, paying hundreds of dollars for a transcript. Deposition costs alone could run to tens of thousands of dollars even in routine cases. Courts have experimented with various ways of imposing some limits. Under the federal rules, each side is allowed 10 depositions "for free"—to take more than 10, court permission is required; see FRCP, Rule 30(a)(2). Some state courts impose stricter limits, and also limit each deposition to a specified number of hours.*
- *Discretion and Flexibility. Obviously, limitations on discovery that are appropriate in a garden-variety lawsuit may be far too restrictive in a large, complex case. Is there any way to adjust the rules to the needs of the case? Yes. In general, the opposing attorneys can modify the limits if they can agree. If not, either side can ask the judge to allow additional discovery. The court always retains the power to regulate the cases before it.*

## SIDEBAR

# Other Kinds of Required Disclosure

*Even in courts that do not require disclosure statements, some kinds of voluntary disclosure are often required. It has, for example, long been a common practice of judges to require parties to exchange witness and exhibit lists at some point before trial. [In federal court, such a requirement may be found in Rule 26(a) (3).] Discovery rules often require that litigants voluntarily supplement discovery responses, es-*

*pecially if the responses previously given would be misleading when viewed in the light of information that later becomes available.*

*There can be situations in which the rules of ethics raise disclosure issues. Consider the following hypothetical: Suppose you are defending a lawsuit in a jurisdiction that has no specific disclosure rules. Your client is an art dealer who sold an expensive painting, supposedly a*

## SIDEBAR

## Other Kinds of Required Disclosure *continued*

*Braque, that the purchaser now claims was a forgery. The purchaser's lawsuit is well under way. Art experts have examined the painting and disagree about its authenticity. Predictably, your expert says the painting is genuine and your opponent's expert says it is a forgery.*

*You are assigned to do some investigation, and you begin tracing the history of the painting. While in France conducting your investigation (every paralegal should get assignments like this!), in the musty basement of a small library, you discover a document that proves beyond question that the painting sold by your client is a fake.*

*Must the document be disclosed? What do you think? (Read Rule 3.4 of the ABA Model Code Of Professional Responsibility and the official comments to the rule, reproduced in Figure W12–1).*

---

### Figure W12–1   Rule 34 and Its Official Comments

A lawyer shall not:

   (a)   unlawfully obstruct another party's access to evidence or unlawfully alter, destroy or conceal a document or other material having potential evidentiary value. A lawyer shall not counsel or assist another person to do any such act;

   (b)   falsify evidence, counsel or assist a witness to testify falsely, or offer an inducement to a witness that is prohibited by law;

   (c)   knowingly disobey an obligation under the rules of a tribunal except for an open refusal based on an assertion that no valid obligation exists;

   (d)   in pretrial procedure, make a frivolous discovery request or fail to make reasonably diligent effort to comply with a legally proper discovery request by an opposing party;

   (e)   in trial, allude to any matter that the lawyer does not reasonably believe is relevant or that will not be supported by admissible evidence, assert personal knowledge of facts in issue except when testifying as a witness, or state a personal opinion as to the justness of a cause, the credibility of a witness, the culpability of a civil litigant or the guilt or innocence of an accused; or

   (f)   request a person other than a client to refrain from voluntarily giving relevant information to another party unless:

      (1)   the person is a relative or an employee or other agent of a client; and

      (2)   the lawyer reasonably believes that the person's interests will not be adversely affected by refraining from giving such information.

Comment

   [1]   The procedure of the adversary system contemplates that the evidence in a case is to be marshalled competitively by the contending parties. Fair competition in the adversary system is secured by prohibitions against destruction or concealment of evidence, improperly influencing witnesses, obstructive tactics in discovery procedure, and the like.

   [2]   Documents and other items of evidence are often essential to establish a claim or defense. Subject to evidentiary privileges, the right of an opposing party, including the government, to obtain evidence through discovery or subpoena is an important procedural right. The exercise of that right can be frustrated if relevant material is altered, concealed or destroyed. Applicable law in many jurisdictions makes it an offense to destroy material for purposes of impairing its availability in a pending proceeding or one whose commencement can be foreseen. Falsifying evidence is also generally a criminal offense. Paragraph (a) applies to evidentiary material generally, including computerized information.

   [3]   With regard to paragraph (b), it is not improper to pay a witness's expenses or to compensate an expert witness on terms permitted by law. The common law rule in most jurisdictions is that it is improper to pay an occurrence witness any fee for testifying and that it is improper to pay an expert witness a contingent fee.

   [4]   Paragraph (f) permits a lawyer to advise employees of a client to refrain from giving information to another party, for the employees may identify their interests with those of the client. See also Rule 4.2.

*Your Local Notes*

_____

_____

## Disclosure Statements: Step-by-Step Instructions

If we are handling a lawsuit in a jurisdiction that has adopted disclosure-based discovery, then we will have to prepare a disclosure statement. Our first task must be to find out exactly what disclosure is required in the court in which our lawsuit is pending.

### PREPARATORY STEPS

**Step 1** — *Determine the Disclosure Requirements of Our Court*

As we have seen, even in disclosure jurisdictions, the required disclosure varies quite a lot from one court to another, because courts have adopted different rules and because judges do not interpret and enforce the rules uniformly even when the rules are the same.

In this workshop, we will assume that FRCP, Rule 26(a), is in force. (For state court cases, consult the appropriate state court rules; your instructor will tell you where to find them.) As we have seen, however, federal district courts are free to follow Rule 26(a) in whole, in part, or not at all. Before we can prepare a disclosure statement, we must find out what rules apply. Rule 26(a) provides that each party must make the disclosure described in the rule "except to the extent otherwise stipulated or directed by order or local rule." Therefore, if a district court has opted not to follow Rule 26(a), the local rules of that court will so provide.

One easy place to get information about the local rules and procedures in any federal district court is the U.S. courts site on the World Wide Web at www. uscourts.gov. Search the site for your state or district and see what resources are available. Most districts have their local rules posted, and in some districts each judge has posted procedures for his or her own court. (For an example of individual judge postings, see, e.g., the link to "Judges' Individual Practices and Procedures" for the Southern District Of New York at www.nysd.uscourts.gov. For a complete compilation showing, for the federal courts of every district, which parts of Rule 26(a) each court has chosen to follow, see the section entitled "Local Discovery Practices" in the *Federal Civil Rules Handbook* published annually by West Publishing, St. Paul, MN.)

*Your Local Notes*

_____

_____

### SIDEBAR

## Current Status of Federal Disclosure Rules

*The flexibility of individual U.S. district courts to "opt out" of or modify the disclosure requirements of Rule 26(a) may be about to end. The Judicial Conference Advisory Committee responsible for proposing changes to the Federal Rules of Civil Procedure has proposed making Rule 26(a) mandatory in all U.S. district courts. Many federal judges have expressed their strong opposition to the proposal, but, in the end, it is up to the U.S. Supreme Court to decide (unless the Congress decides to enter the debate, which is possible). At this writing, the outcome of the proposal is impossible to predict. For the latest on the changes to the discovery rules currently under consideration, see the official web site of the U.S. federal courts at www.uscourts.gov.*

**Step 2** — *Determine When Disclosure Is Due and Docket It*

Nailing down the deadline for the FRCP, Rule 26(a)(1), disclosure statement is not always easy, because it depends on an unpredictable event: the judge's order setting the scheduling conference. It goes without saying, of course, that when we receive the judge's order, we will immediately verify that the firm's docketing clerk has correctly noted the deadline dates for the discovery planning meeting and the Rule 26(a)(1) disclosure statement in the office's central calendar. We also note the dates in our personal calendar.

What happens, though, if 5 months have passed since we filed the suit and we have heard nothing from the court? Has the court simply not issued the order setting the scheduling conference, or did it somehow get by us or get lost in the mail? Constant worry about this sort of thing is one of the traits that distinguishes great paralegals from merely good ones. Working as a litigation paralegal, you will soon develop a feel for how much time should pass between events in a lawsuit, and if your sixth sense tells you that something should have happened by now, call the clerk's office or the judge's secretary and find out.

---

**Your Local Notes**

_____

_____

---

**Step 3**    *Update the Issues Outline*

Preparing a proper disclosure statement in a complex case is a time-consuming task that cannot be accomplished in a few days or weeks without proper preparation. If you wait until the last minute, you will not be able to lay hands on the documents and information that you need. Therefore, it is wise to begin early to assemble and organize your case.

There are many ways to do this; one that works well is to use your issues outline as a kind of checklist. Begin by going through the issues outline point by point, making notes of any documents pertinent to each point, and jotting down the names of any witnesses who might be in a position to shed light on each point. As you review the issues outline, make a checklist of items for follow-up: documents to obtain, witnesses to interview, etc.

Then set about gathering the required information and noting the information obtained in your issues outline as you complete each item on your checklist. As you gather information, read the documents and listen to the witnesses for clues about other evidence of which you were not aware, and add to your checklist.

If you follow this strategy, by the time the due date for disclosure arrives you will be able to write the disclosure statement from the information recorded in your issues outline.

One alternative strategy is, of course, to wait until the last minute, then scramble around trying to fill in the needed disclosure an item at a time. Procrastination about disclosure is hazardous, because the judge can exclude an item of evidence if it turns out that you had it all along, missed it because you were in a hurry, and failed to disclose it when required.

A final caveat about the issues outline: By the time the FRCP, Rule 26(a) (1), disclosure statement is due, the legal issues in the case are usually beginning to gel. At the scheduling conference, the judge will want to know what the legal issues are, and the scheduling order will likely limit discovery in ways that will make it harder (not impossible, but harder) to introduce new issues thereafter. It is therefore quite important to deal with any loose ends in your research of the legal theories of the case well before you begin preparing a disclosure statement. Update your issues outline accordingly.

## DRAFTING STEPS

What, exactly, is a disclosure statement supposed to look like? The federal rules give only a very general answer. FRCP, Rule 26(a) (4), provides that unless the court directs otherwise by order or local rule, all disclosures are to be "in writing, signed, served, and promptly filed with the court."

Since the disclosure must be filed with the court, it must take the form of a court paper, with caption and other formal parts, complying with any local rules governing the form of filed papers. The body of the disclosure statement must address the four areas of subject matter described in subparagraphs (A) through (D) of Rule 26(a) (1). Beyond that, the organization and format of the disclosure is up to you; if possible, obtain sample disclosures filed by other practitioners in the courts of your locality, and imitate them.

**Step 4**    *Caption and Preamble*

The caption is the same as for any filed court paper, and can be block-copied from the word processor form we prepared in Workshop 4. In federal court, an appropriate title is "Plaintiff's (or Defendant's) Rule 26(a) (1) Disclosure"; state court terminology will vary. The preamble should, as always, describe in concise terms the nature of the paper being filed. For example: "Pursuant to Rule 26(a) (1), Federal Rules of Civil Procedure, plaintiff (defendant) makes the following disclosures."

**Step 5**    *List Persons with Discoverable Information*

The first category of required disclosure is:

> [T]he name and, if known, the address and telephone number of each individual likely to have discoverable information relevant to disputed facts alleged with particularity in the pleadings, identifying the subjects of the information. [FRCP, Rule 26(a) (1) (A)]

Notice that FRCP, Rule 26(a) (1) (A), is not asking us to specify what witnesses we will call at trial. Its reach is much broader than that. It requires us to identify any person we know of who is likely to have information about disputed facts, whether or not we might call that person to testify.

Superficially, FRCP, Rule 26(a) (1) (A), ought to be simple to comply with—just list anyone who may have information about the case. Keep in mind, however, that the Rule 26(a) disclosure occurs early in the case, at a time when our own investigation may not be very far along. Worse yet, Rule 26(a) (1) (A) requires us to guess at whether an individual is "likely" to have discoverable information.

Consider the way in which we would typically identify the individuals likely to have discoverable information. Our initial information usually comes from our client, who can likely suggest others who can provide information. Documents furnish another source of information; as we review documents, we will often come across names of people who might be contacted for additional information. Factual development is an ongoing process, and at any given moment we will usually be aware of at least a few individuals who may be able to supply pertinent information but whom we have not yet contacted. Must we disclose their identities?

The answer is yes—we must disclose. FRCP, Rule 26(a) (1), provides:

> A party shall make its initial disclosures based on the information then reasonably available to it and is not excused from making its disclosures because it has not fully completed its investigation of the case. . . .

What about individuals whom we know have information that is adverse to our case? Must we disclose their identities, in effect giving our opponent ammunition to use against us? Again, yes; we must disclose the identities of everyone we know of, and there is no exception for witnesses whose testimony we do not like.

Usually, the best course of action here is to err on the side of overdisclosure. We systematically review our notes and any available documents, and we disclose any names that we find there. We hold back a name only if there are compelling reasons for doing so, and then only after doing careful research and assuring ourselves that there is a valid legal argument for not disclosing it. Among other things, we always list:

- All individual parties to the suit;
- For any corporate party, the employees of the corporation whom we believe to have been involved in the events out of which the lawsuit arises;

- All individuals from whom statements have been taken;
- All individuals listed as witnesses in any police investigative report or similar document;
- All individuals having custody of documents that might be relevant to the suit;
- All individuals whom we expect to call as witnesses; and
- All individuals associated with our client who may be in possession of discoverable information.

We list the names of each person in the body of the disclosure statement itself, together with each person's address and telephone number, if known. We must also specify the "subjects of the information" expected from each person. This should be short and to the point. We are not required to *describe* the information expected, or to disclose what we think each person's testimony will be—we must merely identify the subject.

**Example of how not to do it** (Park Hotels Group's disclosure statement): "Arnold Trevayne, Banbury Park Hotel, Las Vegas, Nevada, telephone 555-8765; will testify that he gave defendant Collins the key to room 409 at approximately 1:00 A.M., and at plaintiff's request called the police at approximately 1:15 A.M.

**Analysis:** This disclosure is more specific than the rule requires. Only the subject matter is needed, not the specific facts. Best not to commit ourselves to a particular version of the facts until we have done more investigation. Also, the fact that Arnie called the police at Shannon's request is not in dispute, and does not need to be addressed in disclosure.

**Example of how to do it:** "Arnold Trevayne, Banbury Park Hotel, Las Vegas, Nevada, telephone 555-8765. Subject matter: his observations as desk clerk at Banbury Park Hotel on the night in question."

---

*Your Local Notes*

_____

_____

---

**Step 6**     *List All Discoverable Documents*

FRCP, Rule 26(a) (1) (B) requires us to disclose

> [A] copy of, or a description by category and location of, all documents, data compilations, and tangible things in the

# SIDEBAR

## Inadequate Disclosure: The Consequences

*Disclosure statements, like discovery responses, provide information—potential ammunition—to our opponent. Obviously, we would rather not give away any more of it than necessary. Suppose we file a disclosure statement that is not complete, either because we deliberately held back information, or because we were less than diligent in gathering the facts to be disclosed. Is there a downside to this kind of behavior?*

*Yes. In the first place, some judges are apt to react to blatant and deliberate infractions of the disclosure rules by making an ethics complaint against the offending attorney, resulting in bar disciplinary proceedings and possible censure, suspension, or disbarment. Such severe measures are uncommon, however, and imposed only in extreme cases. What about more subtle omissions? In our hypo, assume that another hotel guest saw Arnie Trevayne enter Shannon's room when he went there to switch the keys. Park Hotels Group's attorney knows of the other guest and what she observed. Suppose Park Hotels Group's attorney decides to "accidentally" forget to mention the other guest in the disclosure statement—is there any hazard to doing so?*

*FRCP, Rule 37(c) (1), gives the judge a veritable arsenal of weapons with which to punish a party who, "without substantial justification," fails to disclose required information. Among other sanctions, the judge has the power to:*

- *Prohibit the offending party from using the witness or document that was not disclosed. (This threat alone is usually not much of a deterrent. If the other guest's testimony is adverse enough to tempt Park Hotels' attorney to withhold disclosure, calling her as a witness at trial is likely the last thing that Park Hotels would want to do.)*

- *Order the offending party to pay the opposing party's expenses, including attorney's fees, caused by the failure to disclose. Suppose Shannon's attorney hires an investigator to locate and interview everyone who was a guest on the fourth floor on the night in question. This investigation cost $20,000 but did ultimately turn up the guest who saw Arnie enter the room. The judge could order the hotel to pay the $20,000.*

- *Order that those particular facts are deemed established. Here, for example, the judge could enter an order finding as a fact that Arnie Tre-*

*vayne entered Shannon's room and switched the keys. When the case goes to the jury, the judge would instruct the jury to assume that fact. Had they disclosed the witness, Park Hotels' attorneys could have put on other evidence to refute her testimony, or to show that Arnie had some legitimate purpose in entering the room. Now, however, they are stuck with the worst possible interpretation.*

- *Inform the jury of the nondisclosure. In our example, the judge might simply instruct the jury that Park Hotels knew about the other guest and what she saw, was required to disclose that information, and deliberately covered it up. Jurors tend to be unforgiving when lied to, and many people view concealing evidence as the equivalent of lying.*

- *Prohibit the offending party from introducing particular evidence. The judge has the power to level the playing field by taking away some of the evidence that would have favored the nondisclosing party.*

- *Strike claims or defenses from the pleadings, dismissing claims, or rendering judgment by default against the offending party. If the nondisclosure is sufficiently compelling, FRCP, Rule 37(b) (2) (C), gives the judge the power to end the lawsuit then and there and enter judgment in favor of the other party.*

*Are these weapons enough, as a practical matter, to deter litigants and attorneys from engineering their disclosure statements so as to avoid giving away bad facts? Unfortunately, it is hard to prove that an opposing party willfully violated the rules. Even if you do ultimately discover the facts that your opponent withheld, how do you prove that your opponent knew about them? Anyway, judges are often not very inclined to impose severe punishment for discovery infractions even when the offender is caught redhanded. So we must always be alert to the possibility that an opponent may not be disclosing all that the rules require.*

*In preparing our own disclosures, however, we must take into account the very real possibility that, if we are caught hiding the ball, the consequences may be severe. Punishment or no punishment, there is no excuse for deliberately violating the rules, and you should never yield to the temptation to conceal evidence.*

possession, custody, or control of the party that are relevant to disputed facts alleged with particularity in the pleadings.

Some lawsuits are document intensive; some are not. In a simple automobile accident case, aside from perhaps a police report, there may not be *any* documents relevant to the issue of liability. [There will be documents establishing the amount of damages, but those are disclosed separately under FRCP, Rule 26(a) (1) (C).] At the other extreme, in some kinds of commercial litigation—antitrust lawsuits and securities fraud cases come to mind—the relevant documents may literally fill many rooms.

### Identifying the Documents to be Disclosed—

Whatever the size of the problem, our first task is to determine exactly what documents exist. At this point, we are concerned only with documents that are in our client's "possession, custody, or control." That description includes any documents in our own file, and any that are "reasonably available" to our client [see the last sentence of FRCP, Rule 26(a) (1)]. Court decisions have found that documents are within a party's "possession, custody, or control" if they are in the possession of:

- The party's attorney;
- The party's insurance company or agent; or
- A corporate party's subsidiary or branch office, even if in another state.

Even if documents are owned by someone else, they must be disclosed if they are in the party's possession, custody, or control.

Obviously, what documents might exist that would be relevant in a given lawsuit depends greatly on the facts. Usually, the documents that need to be disclosed fall into one of three main categories:

1. *Documents that, in and of themselves, form part of the dispute.* For example, if the lawsuit involves a claim of breach of a written contract, the contract is a document that would be disclosed. So would any other documents relating to it: prior drafts, notes, correspondence, etc.

2. *Documents comprising communications about the subject matter of the suit.* These may include letters, memos, telephone messages—and do not overlook electronic mail messages, which are fast becoming an important source of evidence in lawsuits. Such communications again comprise three categories:

   (a) Those between your client (or an employee of your client) and the opposing party (or an employee of the opposing party). In general, all such communications must be disclosed if relevant to a disputed issue.
   (b) Those between your client and a third party. Again, such communications must usually be disclosed (unless, of course, the third party is your client's lawyer!).
   (c) Internal communications between one employee of your client and another: internal memoranda, internal electronic mail messages, and the like. Deciding whether to disclose this kind of communication can pose difficult issues, since work product and other privileges may apply.

3. *Business records relating to factual matters that are at issue in the suit.* In our hypo, the records relating to door and lock maintenance would be one example of this kind of record. In preparing your disclosure, it is wise to read through the complaint and answer, line by line, and ask yourself what records your client might have that might bear on each allegation.

If we have properly done our homework in Step 3, we have already consulted with our client and made careful notes (or, if feasible, copies) of any documents of which our client is aware. If our client is a corporation, we have consulted with the corporate representative who is coordinating our work in the lawsuit, obtained the names of other employees who are in a position to know what records exist, and followed up any leads. Our objective here is to put ourselves in a position where we can be confident that we know exactly what documents our client has. Particularly when representing corporate clients in document-intensive cases, merely identifying all of the documents can be a daunting task, and it is one that needs to be performed with considerable care. If, through careless investigation, we fail to disclose some important category of documents that was in our client's possession, the judge has the power to impose severe punishment on us or on our client. (See the sidebar on Inadequate Disclosure: The Consequences.)

---

*Your Local Notes*

_____

_____

**Relevant to Disputed Facts Alleged with Particularity**—Assume that we have already gathered all the documents that we can find that could conceivably have anything to do with the case. Which ones must be disclosed? According to FRCP, Rule 26(a) (1) (B), any that are "relevant to disputed facts alleged with particularity in the pleadings."

> **Example:** In paragraph 3 of Shannon's complaint, she alleged that "Defendant Park Hotels Group (hereinafter "Hotel") is a corporation organized and existing under the laws of the state of Delaware, and doing business in the state of Nevada. . . . " You represent Park Hotels Group. Obviously, your client has a number of documents that would be relevant to its corporate status—incorporation papers of various kinds, for example. Must you include these in Park Hotels' disclosure statement?
>
> **Analysis:** Park Hotels' corporate existence is not a disputed fact. Paragraph 2 of Park Hotels' answer admits that Park Hotels Group is a Delaware corporation doing business in Nevada. Therefore, there is no need to disclose the incorporation papers.

> **Example:** In paragraph 18 of Shannon's complaint, she alleged that Park Hotels "failed to maintain the door and lock of plaintiff's room in a reasonable manner so as to prevent unauthorized entry. . . . " You represent Park Hotels Group. The hotel maintains maintenance records on all maintenance done in the hotel, including maintenance done on doors and locks of all guest rooms. Must these records be disclosed?
>
> **Analysis:** Paragraph 8 of Park Hotels' answer denies the allegation that Park Hotels failed to maintain the door and lock of plaintiff's room, making that alleged fact a disputed one. Notice, however, that the allegation referred only to *plaintiff's* room, not to all the rooms in the hotel. Therefore, Park Hotels need only disclose the maintenance records pertaining to the door and lock of that one room, and need not disclose the others.

**The Manner of Disclosure**—In lawsuits where the documents are few, the mechanics of the disclosure task are easy. We gather up all the disclosable documents that we have, make copies of them, and attach the copies to the disclosure statement. That way, there is no room for argument later on about what we disclosed.

Where documents are voluminous, it is usually not practical to attach copies. Then FRCP, Rule 26(a) (1) (B), requires us to give a "description by category and location." How detailed should this description be and how broad are the categories? The rules do not say, and judges' expectations vary. As a rule of thumb, if you find yourself trying to decide whether your document descriptions need to be broken down into more categories or levels of detail, try this: Pick a single document at random from the category that you are concerned about and ask yourself the following question: "If the opposing party claimed that I did not adequately disclose this document, would the judge agree that my description in this disclosure statement covered this document?" If the answer is no, then you need a more detailed breakdown.

In big-document cases, where there may be rooms full of relevant documents, the task of disclosure, even by categories and locations, may be dauntingly large. An alternative in such cases is for the attorneys on both sides to reach some agreement about document access. Often, this involves setting up a central document depository, to which both sides will have access. Within reasonable limits, the attorneys are free to work out their own document disclosure scheme in lieu of the listing by categories and locations called for by FRCP, Rule 26(a) (1) (B). By its terms, Rule 26(a) (1) applies "except to the extent otherwise stipulated or directed by order. . . . "

**Step 7** *Show Computation Of Damages*

The next subject of required disclosure is the computation of damages. FRCP, Rule 26(a) (1) (C), requires the disclosure statement to include:

> a computation of any category of damages claimed by the disclosing party, making available for inspection and copying as under Rule 34 the documents or other evidentiary material, not privileged or protected from disclosure, on which such computation is based, including materials bearing on the nature and extent of injuries suffered. . . .

**Which Parties Must Disclose Computation of Damages**—Notice that the rule refers to damages "claimed by the disclosing party." There is no requirement that we disclose how we contend that another party's damages should be computed. In our hypo, for example, Shannon is claiming damages, so she must disclose how much money she is asking for and how the amount was computed. Park Hotels does not need to disclose how it thinks Shannon's damages, if any, should be computed. In fact, since Park Hotels has not claimed any damages (there is no counterclaim) it can skip this item of disclosure completely. Similarly, Dr. Collins need not disclose his views on the computation of Shannon's damages, but if he has asserted a counterclaim or cross-claim asking for damages for his own injuries, he must of course disclose how he thinks the amount should be computed.

In practice, plaintiff's attorney will certainly want to find out what arguments defendant will be making about the computation of plaintiff's damages, so as to avoid any nasty surprises at trial. In our hypo, Shannon's attorney will undoubtedly send Park Hotels an interrogatory asking how it contends Shannon's damages should be computed.

### Mechanics of Disclosing Damage Computations—FRCP, Rule 26(a) (1) (C), requires two things: (1) a computation of damages and (2) disclosure of the documents underlying the computation. The computation of damages is a part of the body of the disclosure statement itself. It is usually best presented in tabular form, listing each item for which a claim is being made, giving the dollar amount of each, and indicating what documents support each. The suggested format is shown later in Figure W12–2 in the Learning by Example section. (But keep in mind that, absent a local rule or court order to the contrary, you are free to adjust the style and format of the disclosure to fit the needs of the situation.)

Care should be taken to avoid casting the damage calculation in concrete. As with most factual issues in lawsuits, our perception of how best to present our case on damages will usually evolve as the lawsuit progresses. A tight, well-organized presentation of damages may seem impressive—and we will need one when we are ready to argue to the jury—but at the disclosure statement stage we are better off leaving some flexibility for change. One way to do this is to make it clear that the dollar figures in our damage claim are preliminary and subject to change, and to clearly label items as estimates if that is what they are. It is also not a bad idea to include some "weasel words" to the effect that the damage computation is preliminary and subject to change. (Of course, when the computation does change we will have to supplement our disclosure.)

As usual, one question that arises is "How much detail?" In disclosing damages, the answer is "The more detail, the better." This does not mean that we need to list every 89-cent bottle of aspirin separately in our damage computation—instead, we would most likely show a general category for "medications" and a total of all expenditures for such items. In general, though, we do not want to run the risk that the judge might exclude some item

of damages because we did not mention it in our disclosure. There is usually no way in which information about our damages can hurt our case, so we will err on the side of overdisclosure.

The items comprising a party's damage claims usually fall into one of three categories:

1. Items involving concrete, provable expenses that are easy to establish. Example: a doctor's bill for treatment of injuries. For such items, all we need to do is list a description and amount, separately or by categories, and attach copies of the bills.

2. Items such as damages for pain and suffering that are difficult or impossible to quantify. There is no way to compute the amount to be claimed for pain and suffering; instead, it will be up to the jury to decide how much to award after hearing evidence about how much pain plaintiff has suffered. At trial, plaintiff will want to put on as much evidence as possible to be sure the jury gets the full impact of how badly defendant's conduct has affected plaintiff's life. In a case involving severe physical injuries, plaintiff's attorney may even have videos made showing plaintiff in everyday situations, so that the jury can see just how wretched plaintiff's life is as a result of her condition. Often, treating physicians or physician experts will be called as witnesses to describe how the injury in question affects the sufferer. Medical records may be introduced to show the nature of plaintiff's injuries. Plaintiff's attorney does not want to risk having any of this evidence excluded because of nondisclosure, so the disclosure statement should list the main factors comprising such claims, and all supporting documents should be disclosed.

3. Items that are based on provable quantities, but nevertheless require estimates or computations. *Example:* A claim for future income lost due to an injury. The amount of the claim is not mere guesswork—it can be computed if we know what salary the injured person would have received and how long a period of time will elapse before she can return to work. It may be necessary to estimate some of the quantities needed to make the calculation, but this is something that an expert witness can do if necessary. *Another example:* A claim for damages for breach of contract often involves estimating how much it would cost to go into the open market and replace whatever it was that the breaching party had contracted to provide. Again, given the necessary market data, an ex-

pert witness can compute the amount of money necessary to make the nonbreaching party whole. For items of this kind, the damages disclosure must include all of the data on which the computation will be based, and also must show how the computation is to be carried out. [Of course, FRCP, Rule 26(a) (2) requires us to disclose all reports of any expert witnesses who will testify, so we may be able to kill two birds with one stone here, by simply turning over the reports of our damages experts.]

---

**Your Local Notes**

_____

_____

---

**Disclosing the Backup Documentation**—In addition to the computation of damages, FRCP, Rule 26(a) (1) (C), requires disclosure of the documents supporting the damage claims. This can be done either by accompanying the disclosure statement with copies of the documents, or, as the rule suggests, by making the documents available for inspection and copying as would be done with an FRCP, Rule 34, request for production of documents. The virtue of attaching copies is that doing so makes it easy to prove exactly what documents were disclosed. However, particularly with claims requiring evidence of the extent and severity of personal injuries, the universe of possibly relevant documents may be quite large, extending to such voluminous records as hospital charts and physician's notes. Therefore, except in the simplest cases where our position on damages is unlikely to change, attaching copies of all relevant documents may be impracticable.

**Step 8**    *Disclose Insurance Coverage*

The final category of information to be included in a FRCP, Rule 26(a) (1), disclosure is:

> any insurance agreement under which any person carrying on an insurance business may be liable to satisfy part or all of a judgment which may be entered in the action or to indemnify or reimburse for payments made to satisfy the judgment.

In other words, any insurance policy covering the defendant for the liabilities claimed in the suit must be disclosed.

The disclosure rules, and before them the discovery rules, have long allowed litigants to find out how much insurance coverage the opposing party has. This may seem surprising, since, as everyone knows, not only is evidence of insurance coverage inadmissible at trial, mere mention of the word "insurance" in front of the jury is apt to result in an instant mistrial. The reason why insurance coverage is discoverable and, in disclosure jurisdictions, a required item of disclosure is because judges want to encourage litigants to settle, and the availability of insurance is usually an important factor in settlement decisions. Like it or not, the settlement value of a claim often depends greatly on whether a judgment, if won, could be collected. If a defendant has no insurance coverage and no other assets from which a judgment could be collected, plaintiff will be much more likely to accept a low cash payment rather than spend several years and tens of thousands of dollars obtaining an uncollectable judgment.

FRCP, Rule 26(a) (1) (D), calls for the disclosing party to provide any insurance policies to the other parties "for inspection and copying as under FRCP, Rule 34." In the usual case, this is accomplished by attaching a copy of the insurance policy to the disclosure statement.

---

**Your Local Notes**

_____

_____

---

**Step 9**    *Date, Signature, and Verification*

Disclosure statements are signed by the party's attorney in the same manner as any other court paper. You are already aware that an attorney's signature on a court paper carries with it certain implied representations, as provided by FRCP, Rule 11(b). In the case of disclosure statements, FRCP, Rule 26(g) (1), adds an additional avowal of completeness and correctness:

> Every disclosure made pursuant to [Rule 26(a) (1) or 26(a) (3)] shall be signed by at least one attorney of record in the attorney's individual name, whose address shall be stated. . . . The signature of the attorney . . . constitutes a certification that to the best of the signer's knowledge, information, and belief, formed after a reasonable inquiry, the disclosure is complete and correct as of the time it is made.

## SIDEBAR

### Taking the Next Step

*As we have seen, the federal rules do not carry the disclosure philosophy to its logical limit. The disclosure of potential witnesses, documents, damage calculations, insurance, and expert witnesses required by FRCP, Rule 26(a), is enough to provide litigants with a good start to their factual development, but the intent of Rule 26 is that interrogatories, depositions, and other traditional discovery tools will still be needed to fill in the gaps. Rule 26 aims to provide the litigants with the sources of information—potential witnesses and documents—but it is up to each party to extract the desired information from those sources using other discovery methods.*

*Some judges and scholars favor much more comprehensive disclosure schemes. In some state courts, the rules require more detailed disclosure encompassing not only the sources of information, but the information itself. In the authors' home state, Arizona, for*

*example, state court rules require a disclosure statement to include, in addition to the categories covered by federal FRCP, Rule 26(a), the following:*

- *The factual basis of each claim or defense. (Not just the subject matter—the rule requires a party to state in detail the facts underlying each claim or defense.)*

- *The legal theory underlying each claim or defense, including citation of authorities where necessary.*

*Disclosure rules are still in an experimental stage. If you practice in a disclosure jurisdiction, you will have to inform yourself of the precise requirements of your courts. Your instructor will tell you whether the disclosure rules of the courts of your locality go beyond the requirements of federal Rule 26.*

---

Your Local Notes

_____

_____

## CONCLUDING STEPS

### Step 10  *File and Serve*

FRCP, Rule 26(a) (4), provides that "Unless otherwise directed by order or local rule, all disclosures shall be . . . signed, served, and promptly filed with the court." Served on whom? All other parties, whether adverse or not.

We have seen that many courts, seeking to avoid clogging the clerk's office with unnecessary paper, do not allow filing of discovery papers. Disclosure statements, however, are filed with the clerk unless there is a specific local rule or order providing otherwise.

Your Local Notes

_____

_____

### Step 11  *Docket Supplementation Checks*

The initial FRCP, Rule 26(a) (1), disclosure occurs in the early stages of the lawsuit, before other discovery has even commenced. To make disclosure-based discovery work effectively, it is obviously necessary for the parties to update their disclosures as new information becomes available. The rules expressly require supplementation. FRCP, Rule 26(e) (1), provides:

A party is under a duty to supplement at appropriate intervals its disclosures under [Rule 26(a)] if the party learns that in some material respect the information disclosed is incomplete or incorrect and if the additional or corrective information has not otherwise been made known to the other parties during the discovery process or in writing. . . .

We have already seen that the judge has the authority to impose quite severe punishment on parties who fail to comply with the disclosure rules (see sidebar on Inadequate Disclosure: The Consequences). The sanctions for failure to disclose apply equally to failure to supplement; see FRCP, Rule 37(c) (1). Forgetting to file a supplemental disclosure to reveal some newly discovered witness or document is just as hazardous as leaving a witness or document out of the original disclosure statement—the obligation is the same.

FRCP, Rule 26(e) (1), requires supplementation "at appropriate intervals." What is an appropriate interval? The answer depends on the court and the situation. At a minimum, disclosures should be reviewed for supplementation no less often than every 60 days. Other time periods may be imposed by local rule or by court order in a particular case. The circumstances of a given case may also require more rapid supplementation. If for example, you discover some important new witness a few weeks before the date when discovery is supposed to be completed, and you nevertheless wait 60 days before disclosing the information, the judge is likely to be seriously annoyed.

We will check the applicable rules for the court in which our lawsuit is pending for any specific time limits on supplementation. We will make notations in the office docket, and in our personal calendar, to remind us to review the disclosure statement for needed supplementation at the indicated intervals, and again a week or so before the final discovery cutoff.

## Disclosure Statements: Learning by Example

We now apply what we have learned by preparing an initial FRCP, Rule 26(a) (1), disclosure statement to be filed on behalf of Shannon. In a real lawsuit, of course, we would be able to obtain documents and names of witnesses from our client, and, by studying these and following up any leads, obtain still more. For purposes of this hypothetical exercise, we will have to resign ourselves to inventing a typical set of documents and witnesses.

### PREPARATORY STEPS

**Step 1** *Determine the Disclosure Requirements of Our Court*

Since our hypothetical action is pending in the U.S. District Court for the District of Arizona, we will consult that court's local rules to determine what, if any, disclosure is required. When we do so, we find that the District of Arizona local rules are silent concerning adoption of FRCP, Rule 26(a). What does this mean? Rule 26(a), by its own terms, applies in all federal civil actions "except to the extent otherwise . . . directed by order or local rule. Since there is no order or local rule directing otherwise, full FRCP, Rule 26(a), disclosure is required.

Out of an excess of caution, we consult the "Local Discovery Practices" section of the current is-

sue of West's *Federal Civil Rules Handbook,* and verify that, in the District of Arizona, Rules 26(a) (1)–(3) apply.

**Step 2** *Determine When Disclosure Is Due and Docket It*

We will imagine for purposes of our hypo that we have just received a minute entry from the U.S. District Court setting the FRCP, Rule 26(f), initial scheduling conference for February 8. The last day for the discovery planning meeting between counsel is therefore 14 days earlier, or January 25. The initial FRCP, Rule 26(a) (1), disclosure statement is due no later than 10 days after the discovery planning meeting, so the last possible day is February 4.

The actual deadline could, however, be earlier, because the discovery planning meeting could be held earlier. As a practical matter, we will docket the scheduling conference for February 8 , docket February 4 as the final due date for the FRCP, Rule 26(a) (1), disclosure statement, docket January 25 as the last day for the discovery planning meeting, and, finally, make a docket notation for a date in mid-January to review the other deadline dates and adjust them if the discovery planning meeting has been scheduled for an earlier date.

Usually, what will happen is that, sometime shortly after receiving the minute entry, one of the attorneys will begin contacting the others to schedule the discover planning meeting. Often, the attorneys will at the same time try to agree on a date for disclosure statements. Naturally, when dates have been agreed on, the entries in the office calendar are modified accordingly.

**Step 3** *Update the Issues Outline*

Before we can write a disclosure statement, we must first assemble all of the required information. We begin by reviewing our issues outline. Since FRCP, Rule 26(a), is worded in terms of "disputed facts alleged with particularity in the pleadings," we go through the complaint and answer one phrase at a time, and verify that every disputed allegation in the complaint appears in our issues outline.

Then we go through our issues outline, point by point, and try to assess what work needs to be done to pull together a reasonably complete list of witnesses and documents pertinent to each issue. We make a list of the items needing further investigation or follow-up.

Once we have a reasonably clear grasp of what additional information we need, we begin contacting the people who can provide the missing items. For purposes of our hypo, this would likely include:

- Contacting any witnesses listed in the police investigating officer's report to determine what each observed;

- Contacting each medical provider who has treated Shannon for her injuries and obtaining copies of medical records and billing statements; and

- Contacting Shannon's employer to determine what documentation can be obtained to establish Shannon's earnings. (To establish her claim for lost earnings, we will need information about how much she has earned in the past.)

## DRAFTING STEPS

We use steps 4 through 9 to create Shannon's disclosure statement. It is shown in figure W12–2.

## CONCLUDING STEPS

### Step 4      *File and Serve*

We check the local rules of the District of Arizona and find that Rule 1.2 provides that interrogatories and depositions should not be filed with the court, but does not mention disclosure statements. Therefore, FRCP, Rule 26(a) (4), controls, and we file the original disclosure statement with the clerk. We serve copies by mail on counsel for each other party.

### Step 5      *Docket Supplementation Checks*

The local rules for the District of Arizona do not specify at what intervals FRCP, Rule 26(a) (1), disclosures are to be supplemented. Therefore, our obligation is to supplement at "appropriate intervals" as provided in FRCP, Rule 26(e) (1). We make entries on the office central calendar and on our personal calendar to remind us to review the disclosure for supplementation in approximately 60 days, on April 7.

## Disclosure Statements: Learning by Doing

Your task for this workshop is to prepare a Rule 26(a) (1) disclosure statement on behalf of Park Hotels Group, Inc. In doing so you will use hypothetical facts, some of which appear below, some of which will be supplied by your instructor, and some of which you will generate on your own. It is up to you to decide which of them should be disclosed, and to prepare the disclosure statement in the proper format.

## EXERCISES

In carrying out this assignment, you should follow the step-by-step formula described in this workshop.

1.  Following Step 1, determine the disclosure requirements in effect in the U.S. district courts having jurisdiction in your locality. Your instructor will tell you whether to prepare your disclosure statement in accordance with Rule 26(a) or in accordance with the rules in effect in your local U.S. district court.

2.  Your contact person in Park Hotels Group, Inc., is Mr. Leonard Shapiro, vice president. His home address and phone are 1429 Rustic Dr., Asbury Park, NJ 07712, phone: 732-555-3983. The address and telephone of Mr. Shapiro's office (the Park Hotels Group, Inc. main office) is 3 Municipal Plaza, Asbury Park, NJ 07712, Phone: 732-555-2929, extension 903. (At your instructor's option, your instructor may take the role of Mr. Shapiro, or may assign that role to a student; then you can write memos to the fictitious Mr. Shapiro with your requests, if any, for additional facts, and the fictitious Mr. Shapiro can respond with additional hypothetical facts as appropriate.)

3.  You are given the following hypothetical facts. It is up to you to decide which of them should be disclosed.

*Hotel guests:* From the room registrations, the names, addresses, and telephone numbers of the guests in Rooms 405 through 412 on the night of the incident were as follows: Mrs. Helen Barnes, 3816 Kansas Ave, Omaha, NE 68111, phone: 402-555-6303 (room 405, next door to Shannon's room to the south); Mr. and Mrs. Gerald Monson, 1514 Mills Ave, Gulfport, MS 39501, phone: 228-555-1539 (room 406, across the hall and one door to the south from Shannon's room); Ms. Shannon Martin,

---

**Figure W12–2   Disclosure Statement**

**IN THE UNITED STATES DISTRICT COURT**
**DISTRICT OF ARIZONA**

| | |
|---|---|
| SHANNON MARTIN, a single woman, | ) |
| | ) |
| | )   NO. CV98-01456 PHX JL |
| Plaintiff, | ) |
| | )   PLAINTIFF'S RULE 26(a) (1) |
| | )   DISCLOSURE |
| v. | ) |
| | ) |
| ARTHUR COLLINS and JANE DOE COLLINS, | ) |
| husband and wife; PARK | ) |
| HOTELS GROUP, INC., a Delaware | ) |
| corporation; | ) |
| | ) |
| Defendants. | ) |
| | ) |

Pursuant to Rule 26(a) (1), Federal Rules of Civil Procedure, plaintiff (defendant) makes the following disclosures:

1. *Persons Having Discoverable Information.* The names and, if known, the addresses and telephone numbers of each individual likely to have discoverable information relevant to disputed facts alleged with particularity in the pleadings, to the extent known to plaintiff at this time, are:

Plaintiff Shannon Martin
8000 East Chaparral Road #422
Scottsdale, AZ
(602) 555-3857

Subject: Events at Banbury Park Hotel leading to her injury; nature and extent of her injuries; loss of employment/earnings.

Defendant Arthur Collins
Address and telephone number
unknown.

Subject: Events at Banbury Park Hotel leading to plaintiff's injury; manner of his entry to plaintiff's hotel room.

Detective Sgt. Janet Marnell
Officer Edward Flanigan
Officer Barbara Goldberg
Las Vegas Police Department
400 Stewart Ave
Las Vegas, NV 89101
(702) 555-3513

Subject: Police response and investigation into events at Banbury Park Hotel leading to plaintiff's injury and observations made and information obtained in connection therewith.

Arnold Trevayne
Address and telephone number
unknown

Subject: Events at Banbury Park Hotel leading to plaintiff's injury.
Circumstances surrounding delivery of room key to defendant Collins.

Mr. and Mrs. Carl Mitchell
295 E. Shelbourne
Las Vegas, NV 89123
Telephone: 702-555-4578

Subject: Police report indicates that Mr. and Mrs. Mitchell shared an elevator with Defendant Collins while ascending to 4th floor of hotel immediately prior to incident, and may have information concerning his condition and demeanor at that time.

*continued*

**Figure W12–2, Disclosure Statement,** *continued*

Mr. Andrew Garrison
905 E. Desert Inn Road #313
Las Vegas, NV 89109
Phone: 702-555-9059

Mr. Manuel Rivera
7327 Cherry Valley Circle
Las Vegas, NV 89117
Phone: 702-555-6831

Subject: Police report indicates that Mr. Garrison and Mr. Rivera were paramedics who responded to the scene and treated defendant Collins. They are believed to have made observations of plaintiff's hotel room and persons and objects therein, and condition of defendant Collins immediately after the incident.

Ellen Sayers, M.D.
Desert Lake Hospital
1825 E Flamingo Rd.
Las Vegas, NV 89119
(702) 555-6600

Subject: Nature and severity of, emergency treatment for, and prognosis of plaintiff's injuries.

Paul Norling, M.D.
1350 East McDowell Road
Phoenix, AZ
(602) 555-3651

Subject: Nature and severity of, ongoing treatment for, and prognosis of plaintiff's injuries and expected cost of treatment.

Robin Carter, M.D.
Scottsdale Medical Center
7480 East Osborne Rd.
Scottsdale, AZ

Subject: Plaintiff's hand surgery, prognosis, cost of treatment

Gordon McCormick, P.T.
5210 N Scottsdale Rd #101,
Scottsdale, AZ 85250
(602) 555-2922

Subject: Rehabilitation services for plaintiff's hand injury

Anne Resnick, M.D.
Scottsdale Medical Center
7480 East Osborne Rd.
Scottsdale, Az

Subject: Anaesthesiology during plaintiff's hand surgery; cost of treatment

Dennis Tang, M.D.
350 West Thomas Road
Phoenix, AZ
(602) 555-9287

Subject: Nature and extent of psychological trauma suffered by plaintiff, treatment therefor, prognosis, and expected cost of treatment.

Bruce DeAngelo
Network Software Solutions, Inc.
6366 N. 76th St.
Scottsdale, AZ
(602) 555-7230

Subject: Plaintiff's employment, compensation therefore, compensation and opportunities lost due to injuries

*2. Documents Relevant to Disputed Issues Other Than Damages.* Documents, data compilations, and tangible things in the possession, custody, or control of plaintiff that are relevant to disputed facts alleged with particularity in the pleadings, to the extent known to plaintiff at this time are:

| | |
|---|---|
| Police investigating officer's report | Copy attached, see attachment 2-1. |
| Copy of plaintiff's room registration and receipt | Copy attached, see attachment 2-2. |

**Figure W12–2, Disclosure Statement,** *continued*

3. *Computation of Damages.* Following is a computation of damages claimed by plaintiff to the extent they can be computed and/or estimated at this early stage. This computation of damages is preliminary and subject to change as investigation continues and additional information becomes available. Supporting documents are either attached or will be made available for inspection and copying upon reasonable request.

*Summary of Damage Computation:* Plaintiff's damage claim totals the sum of $643,827.03. The computation of this amount is summarized below, followed by more detailed enumerations of each category of damages.

Medical treatment through January 15, _____         28,667.24

| | |
|---|---|
| Other out-of-pocket expenses | 838.79 |
| Loss of employment/earnings | 114,321.00 |
| General damages for pain and suffering | 500,000.00 |
| TOTAL | 643,827.03 |

*Medical treatment through January 15, ____.* Plaintiff has incurred medical expenses in the amount of $28,667.24, as summarized below, for which bills have been received as of January 15, _____.

| | |
|---|---|
| Desert Lake Hospital, emergency treatment for broken finger (statement, attachment 3-1) | $588.35 |
| Dr. Ellen Sayers, emergency treatment for broken finger (statement, attachment 3-2) | $467.00 |
| Paul Norling, M.D., ongoing treatment of plaintiff's broken finger (statement, attachment 3-3) | $2,089.38 |
| Robin Carter, M.D., hand surgery (statement, attachment 3-4) | $9,350.00 |
| Anne Resnick, M.D., anaesthesiology during hand surgery (statement, attachment 3-5) | $1,650.00 |
| Gordon McCormick, P.T., rehabilitation therapy following hand surgery (statement, attachment 3-6) | $922.65 |
| Scottsdale General Hospital hospitalization in connection with hand surgery (statement, attachment 3-7) | $6,313.00 |
| Dennis Tang, M.D., psychiatric treatment (statement, attachment 3-8) | $6,018 |
| Misc. medications and supplies (receipts, attachment 3-9) | $1,268.86 |
| TOTAL | $28,667.24 |

*Other Out-of-Pocket Expenses.* Plaintiff has incurred other expenses in the amount of $838.79, as summarized below, for which bills have been received as of January 15, _____.

| | |
|---|---|
| Mileage for trips to doctors, etc., (mileage log, attachment 3-10) | $513.79 |
| Housekeeper during plaintiff's convalescence after surgery (cancelled check, attachment 3-11) | $325.00 |
| TOTAL | $838.79 |

*continued*

**Figure W12–2,   Disclosure Statement,** *continued*

*Future Medical Treatment.* It is anticipated that plaintiff will incur future medical expenses in the estimated amount of $5,200.00 as follows:

| | |
|---|---|
| Ongoing treatment and physical therapy for hand injury (letter from Dr. Norling, attachment 3-12) | $1,800.00 |
| Ongoing psychiatric treatment (letter from Dr. Tang, attachment 3-13) | $3,400.00 |
| TOTAL | $5,200.00 |

*Loss Of Employment/Earnings.* Plaintiff's loss of employment/earnings claim is computed as follows:

| | |
|---|---|
| Loss of earnings for 17-week period from date of injury until plaintiff was released by her physicians to return to work, at $2,317 per week (based on plaintiff's average weekly earnings for preceding six months, see paycheck checkfoils, attachment 3-14) | $39,321.00 |
| Value of plaintiff's client list lost when she was terminated from her employment, based on estimated present value of expected future commissions (amount approximate; correct amount to be established by expert testimony of expert economist, report will be furnished when available) | $75,000.00 |
| TOTAL | $114,321.00 |

*General Damages.* Plaintiff claims general damages for pain and suffering in the amount of $500,000. This claim is based in part upon documents establishing the nature and severity of plaintiff's injury and the mental trauma which she suffered.

| | |
|---|---|
| Medical records, Desert Lake Hospital | Copy attached, see attachment 3-15 |
| Medical records, Dr. Sayers | Copy attached, see attachment 3-16 |
| Medical records, Dr. Norling | Copy attached, see attachment 3-17 |
| Medical records, Dr. Carter | Not yet received |
| Medical records, Dr. Tang | Copy attached, see attachment 3-18 |
| Photographs of plaintiff's hand | Copies attached, see attachment 3-19 |

4. *Insurance.* Rule 26(a) (1) (D) does not apply since there are no claims made against plaintiff herein. DATED this _____ day of _____, 20__

SIMON & PORTER

_____

Allen Porter
Attorneys for plaintiff

(Certificate of service goes here—See Workshop 4 for details.)

8000 East Chaparral Road #422, Scottsdale, AZ, phone: 602-555-3857 (room 407); Mr. Chris Jansen, 2326 E. Empire, Spokane, WA 99207, phone: 509-555-6947 (room 408, directly across the hall from Shannon's room); Dr. Arthur Collins, M.D., 1154 Waterford Dr., Dallas, TX 75218, phone: 214-555-6888 (room 409, next door to Shannon's room to the north); Mr. and Mrs. Barry Levine, 1518 N Shore Dr., Moline, IL 61265, phone: 309-555-1445 (room 410, directly across the hall from Dr. Collins's room); Dr. Donald Gellman, D.D.S., 1005 Buhne Street, Eureka, CA 95501, phone: 707-555-8525 (room 411, next door to Dr. Collins's room to the north); Bruce Brown, 3844 West 4990 South, Salt Lake City, UT 84118, phone: 801-555-8879 (room 412, across the hall from Dr. Collins's room and one door to the north). You have not interviewed any of these people and you do not know whether any of them saw or heard anything.

*Police report:* The police investigating officer's report reflects that Detective Sgt. Janet Marnell, Officer Edward Flanigan, and Officer Barbara Goldberg, all of Las Vegas Police Department, 400 Stewart Ave, Las Vegas, NV 89101, phone: 702-555-3513, responded to the scene. The report states that Mr. and Mrs. Carl Mitchell, 295 E. Shelbourne, Las Vegas, NV 89123, phone: 702-555-4578, rode to the fourth floor in the same elevator as Dr. Collins immediately before the incident. It does not indicate what, if any, information they gave to the police. Paramedics responding were Mr. Andrew Garrison, 905 E. Desert Inn Road, #313, Las Vegas, NV 89109, phone: 702-555-9059; and Mr. Manuel Rivera, 7327 Cherry Valley Circle, Las Vegas, NV 89117, phone: 702-555-6831.

*Hotel employees:* The following individuals are hotel employees: Arnold Trevayne, 8354 W. Sahara Ave., #238, Las Vegas, NV 89117, phone: 702-555-0867 (desk clerk on the night of the incident); Corby Jamison, 4656 Monument Valley Rd., Las Vegas, NV 89129, phone: 702-658-3254 (hotel manager, Banbury Park Hotel); Marcos Davila, 1594 E. Viking Rd., Las Vegas, NV 89119, phone: 702-555-5254 (head of maintenance department, Banbury Park Hotel); Carolyn Zale, 8815 Smokey Dr., Las Vegas, NV 89134, phone: 702-555-6233 (chief of housekeeping, Banbury Park Hotel); Charles O'Meary, 1516 Mancha Dr., Boulder City, NV 89005, phone: 702-555-6549 (head of bookkeeping department, Banbury Park Hotel); Ron Kanne, 5626 Alfred Dr., Las Vegas, NV 89108, phone: 702-555-2645 (chief of security, Banbury Park Hotel); Donald McLane, 4712 Arid Ave., Las Vegas, NV 89115, phone: 702-555-2874 (night housekeeping crew supervisor). You have not yet interviewed any of these except Trevayne. Of these,

only Trevayne and McLane's were present in the hotel on the night of the incident. McLane's housekeeping crew was also present; you have asked Mr. Shapiro for the names and addresses of the workers on the housekeeping crew but have not yet received them.

*Hotel records:* The hotel keeps the following records, among others: registration cards for each guest; credit card slips for each guest bill charged to a credit card; (computerized) ledger sheets reflecting each guest's itemized bill; computerized reservation system reflecting all hotel reservations; computer files generated by the telephone system reflecting, for all outgoing calls, the room number placing the call, the number dialed, time of call, and duration, and for incoming calls, the room number receiving the call, time, and duration; maintenance work order files reflecting all maintenance performed in the hotel; books of account reflecting the financial operations of the hotel; purchase orders reflecting all purchases by the hotel; payroll records and, for hourly employees, time cards; personnel files for all employees of the hotel; housekeeping logs reflecting the work done by each housekeeping crew on each shift; files on each contract entered into with outside contractors for maintenance or construction work in the hotel; and correspondence files containing all letters or memos written by management employees, including memos between Banbury Park Hotel employees and headquarters employees discussing the incident and the hotel's liability exposure. Also, the hotel manager, Mr. Jamison, interviewed Arnold Trevayne and Donald McLane and took notes of the interviews, and also did some investigation about the condition of the door lock on Room 407, about which he kept notes.

*Insurance:* At your instructor's option, do one of the following:

*Option 1:* Assume that Park Hotels Group has the following insurance: a vehicle liability policy covering all vehicles owned by the company, issued by Associated Risks Insurance Co., Trenton, NJ; a premises liability policy for the Banbury Park Hotel, covering liability involving injuries to persons on the premises of the hotel, issued by Bonded Liability Insurance Co., Omaha, NE; a director's liability policy covering acts of the corporate board of directors, issued by Old Faithful Insurance Co., New York, NY; a group medical policy covering employees of Park Hotels Group, issued by Health Providers Corporation, Wilmington, DE; and a general liability umbrella policy issued by Affiliated Reinsurance Company, New York, NY.

*Option 2:* Find out what kinds of insurance a chain hotel corporation operating in your locality would be likely to have, and from what companies. Places to consult to obtain this information include your library, insurance company sites on the World Wide Web, and a local insurance agent or hotel manager. (Contacting strangers to get information is good practice for the work you will be asked to do as a litigation paralegal! If you are assigned option 2, be honest with those whom you contact, and tell them that you are a student working on an assignment.

You may be surprised at how helpful people are willing to be.)

4. Assume that you have just received the U.S. district court's order setting a scheduling conference for the third Friday in April of the current year. Assume that the attorney's conference to prepare a discovery plan takes place on the last possible day. Date your Rule 26(a) disclosure for the last day on which the disclosure can be filed and still comply with the rules.

# PRACTICE POINTERS
## *Taking the Initiative*

Lawyers are responsible for crafting legal theories and designing case strategies but legal assistants are responsible for managing cases. They are the ones that ensure that cases keep on track, that deadlines can and will be met, that the necessary arrangements are made to secure documentation, that clients are kept informed, and that a myriad of other details are attended to. Consequently, legal assistants quickly discover that the more they are kept informed about the status of a case and the more they are involved as the case develops, the easier it is for them to manage the case.

Not all attorneys, however, are diligent about keeping their legal assistants "in the loop." Therefore, it behooves conscientious legal assistants to take the initiative in asking questions and volunteering to assume responsibilities that were not assigned them. Those who sit back and wait to be told what to do next are unlikely to experience rapid advances in their profession. They will always be adequate but never outstanding legal assistants. Those who want to be granted greater responsibilities and allowed to assume a more creative role will have to prove their capabilities. One of the best ways to become irreplaceable to an attorney is to be the individual on whom they can rely to see that cases progress in accordance with all court mandates and procedural rules and to prevent them from being surprised or unprepared at any stage of litigation. To actualize this kind of role in a law firm, legal assistants must assert themselves as professional members of a legal team.

## TECHNO TIP

We have talked about using the World Wide Web portion of the Internet without speaking much about it. The web is that part of the Internet that allows users to publish and post their own web pages (the home page). Remember that e-mail and other Internet uses do not require either party to have their own web page.

Older browsers required that the complete address of the site you wanted to get to be entered, such as **http://www.abanet.org** (the home page of the American Bar Association). Today most updated browsers can take you where you want to go with just **www.abanet. org** being entered. Some sites can be found without the **www** prefix.

The address of the web page is called a uniform resource locator (URL). The **http://** portion of the address represents Hypertext Transfer Protocol. If you go to an ftp site (such as **ftp.isoc.org**) you are using the File Transfer Protocol.

## FORMS FILE

*Include a sample disclosure statement for your forms file. If possible obtain at least two samples prepared by different firms so that you have examples of different types of formats.*

*Summarize the applicable rules in your jurisdiction that govern the substance and procedures surrounding the preparation, submission, and response to disclosure statements.*

## KEY TERM

**Disclosure statement**

## INTRODUCTION: FINDING OUT WHAT WITNESSES WILL SAY AND HOW THEY WILL SAY IT

At trial, the litigants tell their stories to the jury mainly through the testimony of witnesses. The discovery tools we have studied so far—interrogatories, document requests, requests for admissions, and disclosure statements—are certainly useful, but they fall short in one important respect: They do not allow us to evaluate how witnesses will perform while actually testifying. We can use interrogatories to discover the general shape of a witness's testimony, but the impact that the witness has on the jury depends greatly on the witness's demeanor, manner of speech, body language, and a host of other intangible factors that we can never assess without actually seeing the witness in action.

The mainstay of witness discovery is the deposition. A deposition is a proceeding in which the attorneys ask questions and a witness, also referred to as the deponent, answers them. In the vernacular of litigation, if the witness's name is John Doe, we may speak of "taking John Doe's deposition," or we may say that we are "**deposing** John Doe."

Usually, a deposition is conducted at the office of one of the attorneys. The witness is placed under oath, usually by a court reporter who is authorized to administer oaths. The judge is not present. The attorneys' questions and the deponent's answers are recorded, either electronically or in shorthand by a court reporter. Later, the court reporter uses the recording or shorthand notes to produce a written transcript of the testimony—that is, a typed or printed booklet in which the questions and answers are reproduced, word for word. The attorney who scheduled the deposition questions the witness first; then the opposing attorney may take a turn if desired.

When we schedule a deposition, we must notify all other parties so that they can attend. This is done by serving a **notice of deposition.** Lawyers and paralegals often use the shorthand phrase **noticing a deposition** to refer to the process of scheduling a deposition and preparing and serving the required paperwork. Depending on the circumstances, we may also issue a subpoena to the witness to ensure her attendance.

In this workshop, we study the basic procedural tools and concepts that you need in order to be able to use deposition discovery effectively as a paralegal. We base our discussion on deposition discovery procedure as practiced in the federal district courts under FRCP, Rule 30. State court procedure is generally similar or identical; your instructor will apprise you of any important differences in the practice followed in the state courts of your locality.

---

*Your Local Notes*

_____

_____

---

## ADVANTAGES OF DEPOSITIONS OVER WRITTEN DISCOVERY

Why take a deposition? Depositions can be used for a number of important purposes that we cannot achieve with written discovery:

- Depositions allow us to find out exactly what the *witness* will say in response to specific questions. (As we have seen, answers to interrogatories give us the opposing *lawyer's* carefully edited answer to our questions, not the witness's answer.)

- We can use depositions to take discovery from nonparty witnesses. Usually, written discovery can be directed only to someone who is a party to the suit.

- Depositions allow us not only to hear the witness's answers to our questions but also to observe the witness's demeanor, body language, and attitude.

- If a witness gives an evasive answer in a deposition, we can follow up immediately with additional questions.

- In a deposition, we can follow the thread of the witness's story wherever it may lead, since we can continue asking questions.

- The deposition transcript is a particularly effective tool for cross-examination at trial, because it reflects the witness's own words. If the witness gives an answer at trial that contradicts the answer given to the same question in the deposition, we can read the witness's earlier answer from the deposition transcript and show the jury that the witness is not being truthful.

- We can use depositions as a substitute for trial testimony in situations where the witness cannot testify in person. For example, a witness may be dying and not expected to be available when the trial takes place or may be at some distant location. Then we can go to the witness, take a deposition, and read the deposition (or, in an increasing number of courts, show a video recording of the deposition) at trial as a substitute for live testimony.

## PROCEDURAL GOALS

The goals that we seek to achieve through deposition discovery are several, and worth reviewing before we begin exploring the procedural details:

- We want to obtain information. Two of the main purposes of a deposition are to find out what facts the witness can provide and to get leads to other sources of information.

- We want to pin down the witness's story. Our questions need to cover the subject matter thoroughly, excluding all possible alternate versions of the facts, so that the witness has no room to tell a different story at trial.

- We want to finish with a usable transcript. This means avoiding procedural errors that would render the deposition or the transcript invalid; it also means making sure that the deposition covers the right questions and answers, asked in the right way.

- We want to come away from the deposition with a clear idea of how to handle this witness at trial. What is the witness's personality like? Are there particular kinds of questions that he has trouble with? Is he easily led? Prone to blurt out poorly thought-out answers? Easily provoked to anger?

- We want to lay the groundwork for cross-examination at trial. A deposition is a perfect place to get a witness to commit to essential facts that will prevent her from deviating from the story we want told at trial.

- We want to avoid using good ammunition that is better saved for trial. Remember that there is no judge or jury at a deposition. It may feel good to "score points" on a witness in a deposition and catch him lying, but doing so merely gives him plenty of time to think up a better story before trial.

A deposition is not, of course, the only tool available for accomplishing these goals. In fact, many litigators would depose a witness only if the witness is adverse or uncooperative, or if the witness may not be able to attend the trial. See the sidebar on Alternatives to Taking a Deposition.

---

*Your Local Notes*

_____

_____

---

## Depositions: Step-by-Step Instructions

In this workshop, we will be concerned with three main aspects of deposition discovery procedure:

1.  *The procedures to schedule a deposition, compel the witness to attend, and produce a valid and usable transcript.* This aspect of deposition taking is essentially clerical, but nevertheless important. For a deposition to take place, a number of people—court reporter, witness, attorneys—have to show up at the same place and the same time ready to proceed. Some of them may be eager to seize any excuse not to appear. If all of the elements do not come together as required, the usual result is a gaggle of angry attorneys sitting around, clocks running, with nothing to do to pass the time except to berate the unfortunate paralegal who dropped the ball.

2.  *Planning and supporting the questioning.* Paralegals do not conduct depositions—a licensed attorney must examine the witness—but paralegals can still have a role in the deposition itself. Paralegals are routinely assigned to prepare an outline of the subjects to be covered in the questioning. Paralegals often attend depositions with their supervising attorneys and help the attorneys locate facts and documents needed during the questioning. Therefore, even though they will not be the ones asking the questions, paralegals need to understand what the attorney is trying to accomplish, and, to do so, must grasp the strategic considerations underlying deposition questioning.

3.  *Using the deposition to best advantage after it has been completed.* In even a moderately complex lawsuit, it is not unusual to have thousands of pages of deposition testimony. To make effective use of the transcripts at trial, someone—often a paralegal—must organize, summarize, and index the transcripts so that important passages can be found quickly.

## PREPARATORY STEPS

Before we can begin doing the paperwork necessary to arrange depositions, we must first deter-

## SIDEBAR

# Alternatives to Taking a Deposition

*Depositions offer a useful way of discovering what a witness will say, but they also have a few drawbacks. One is that the opposing attorney must be notified of a deposition in advance and will certainly attend. Everything that we learn from the witness, our opponent also learns. Worse, the opposing attorney will have the opportunity to contact the witness in advance of the deposition and possibly provide some coaching. Also, the opposing attorney will get a chance to watch us in action as we question the witness, and she is likely to come away with a good sense of the strengths and weaknesses of our examination.*

### When a Statement Is Preferable to a Deposition

*When dealing with a friendly witness, therefore, we are often best advised not to take a deposition. (Our opponent may, of course, decide to depose the witness anyway, but in that case we are likely to refrain from asking any questions.) If a witness is cooperating, we do not need a deposition to set up later cross-examination.*

*Even with a cooperative witness, however, there is always the risk of an unexpected change in story. We can easily guard against this hazard by taking a statement from the witness. A **witness statement** is a written or electronically recorded reproduction of a witness's version of the facts. It may be a word-for-word reproduction of questions and the witness's answers, or it may be a paraphrased summary of main points. Our goal in obtaining a statement from a witness is to have a piece of paper with the witness's signature, or a recording with the witness's voice, which we could use in court to prove what the witness told us if necessary. The advantage of taking a statement is that we can do so without having to inform our opponent.*

### How to Take a Witness Statement

*In terms of the mechanics, there are two main ways of taking a witness statement. Each has its advantages and disadvantages. The first is to tape record the interview with the witness; the second is to write or type the main points of the witness's testimony and have the witness sign. A tape recording captures every word and produces maximum jury impact; however, some witnesses "clam up" instantly at the sight of a tape recorder, and if the witness blurts something that we would rather not have in our statement, there is no good way to get rid of it. With a written statement, we can edit, paraphrase, and leave out extraneous comments.*

*To take a tape-recorded statement, we begin by asking the witness's permission to tape record (usually after talking to the witness informally so as to obtain a general idea of what he will say). If the witness agrees, we then turn on the tape recorder and ask the witness to confirm his willingness to be recorded. Then we proceed with the interview, taking the witness through his story in much the same way that we would in a deposition. At the end of the interview, we again ask the witness to confirm on tape that he is aware the interview has been taped and has consented to the taping.*

*To take a written statement, we first interview the witness, taking careful notes. We then use our notes to prepare a summary of what the witness has said, being careful to capture the important points in simple declarative sentences. It is not necessary for the statement to be typed—given the choice between hand writing a statement and getting a signature then and there, or going back to the office to have it typed and hoping that the witness will still be willing to sign when we return, we would opt for hand writing. When the statement is ready, we ask the witness to read and sign it. If the witness does not agree with a particular wording, we change it by interlineation and have the witness initial the change. The statement should end with a recital that the signer has read its contents and that its contents are true on the basis of the witness's personal knowledge. If we have access to a notary, we may have the witness's signature notarized. Doing so is not necessary, but it adds an element of seriousness that may help make the witness think twice before changing his testimony. We also have the witness sign or initial each page, so that no one can later argue that we replaced a page.*

### Uncooperative Witnesses: The Temptation to Tape

*Suppose you are interviewing a witness who has important testimony to give, but seems unlikely to consent to taping or to sign a written statement. Can you tape the interview without telling the witness? There are two main kinds of surreptitious taping:*

- *Taping your own conversation with someone—for example, using a concealed tape recorder to record your own interview with a witness.*

- *Third-party taping—eavesdropping on a conversation between other people when you are not a participant in the conversation. For example, tapping a witness's telephone line.*

**SIDEBAR**

### Alternatives to Taking a Deposition *continued*

*Third-party taping without the consent of all participants to the conversation is a criminal offense under federal law and under the laws of most states. Under certain circumstances law enforcement officers can obtain court permission to eavesdrop on the conversations of suspected criminals, but "bugging" is not an appropriate tool in civil litigation.*

*Taping your own telephone conversation without the other party's consent is legal under current federal law, but illegal under the laws of some states. Taping your own in-person, face-to-face conversation with someone is usually legal, so in most states it would not be a criminal*

*offense to tape a face-to-face witness interview without the witness's knowledge. The fact that it is legal, however, does not make it a good idea. Many people—including jurors—tend to react quite negatively to the idea of secretly tape recording someone. Surreptitious taping may also violate the rules of attorney ethics, depending on how your state's bar association interprets them. All in all, great though the temptation may sometimes be, the risks involved in secretly taping conversations with witnesses usually outweigh the rewards. As a paralegal, do not even consider doing it without your supervising attorney's express approval.*

mine which witnesses we need to depose and when and where the depositions will take place. This seemingly easy task is more complicated than it appears. Some of the participants may prefer that there be no deposition, and will do everything possible to resist and delay. The order in which depositions are taken, and the timing of depositions in relation to other discovery, can give one side or the other an advantage in the lawsuit. Typically, each side would like to depose the other side's witnesses first. We would prefer to know exactly what our opponent's witnesses will say, and get their stories on the record, before having our own witnesses testify.

**Limitations on Deposition Scheduling under the Federal Rules**—Traditionally, in federal court and in state courts having procedures based on the federal rules, deposition scheduling was somewhat of a free-for-all. The old federal rules allowed any party to schedule depositions of any witness for any desired date, beginning immediately upon filing the complaint. The rules did not give either party the right to be first in taking depositions, and the process tended to degenerate into petty scheduling feuds. Another problem was that it was becoming standard practice for attorneys to depose every person who could conceivably have anything to say about the case, and to spend hours or even days on each deposition. The cost of deposition discovery was eclipsing even the cost of the trial itself, and making litigation prohibitively expensive.

The current federal rules place some limits on the freedom of the attorneys to schedule depositions and give judges a more active role in the man-

agement of deposition discovery. Here are the main points to consider in deciding how to schedule depositions under the federal rules:

- Ordinarily, no party may schedule any depositions until after the initial discovery planning meeting required by FRCP, Rule 26(f); see FRCP, Rule 26(d). [However, depositions can be taken earlier if all parties agree to do so, see FRCP, Rule 30(a)(2), or if the person to be deposed is about to leave the country, see FRCP, Rule 30(a)(2)(C).]

- Each side may schedule depositions of up to ten witnesses without court permission. All the plaintiffs together make up one side and all the defendants together make up the other. To depose any more witnesses after the tenth, a party must file a motion and ask the court for permission [see FRCP, Rule 30(a)(2)(A)] or get the opposing party to agree.

- Unless the judge orders otherwise [and some judges do incorporate quite specific deposition schedules into the scheduling order under FRCP, Rule 16(b)], after the discovery planning meeting, each side is free to schedule its ten depositions at any time and in any order desired; see FRCP, Rule 26(d).

- Scheduling orders commonly include a discovery cutoff date after which neither side is allowed to conduct further discovery. To take a deposition after the discovery cutoff date, it is necessary to ask the judge for permission. The answer will almost certainly be "no" unless there are unusually compelling reasons why the deposition could not have been completed earlier. All routine depositions should be scheduled well in advance of the discovery cutoff, so as to allow some time for maneuvering if something goes wrong (i.e., the witness does not show up).

■ In general, no party has any inherent right to have depositions take place in any particular sequence. If there is some important reason why defendant ought to be allowed to depose witness X before plaintiff deposes witness Y, the judge may order accordingly. Absent such an order, however, depositions may be noticed "in any sequence, and the fact that a party is conducting discovery, whether by deposition or otherwise, shall not operate to delay any other party's discovery" [FRCP, Rule 26(d)].

■ Judges always have the power to intervene in deposition scheduling, and also to dictate what subject matter may be inquired about in a deposition. Both the opposing party and the witness to be deposed are free to move for a protective order under FRCP, Rule 26(c), to ask the judge to order that a deposition be scheduled for a different date or that it not be held at all. Of course, the judge will not grant the motion unless the moving party presents good reasons for doing so.

Some state court rules impose much stricter limitations on the parties' freedom to take depositions, and call for correspondingly greater involvement by the judge in deposition scheduling. Your instructor will point out any important differences between the federal rules and the rules governing the state courts of your locality.

---

**Your Local Notes**

_____

_____

---

**Step 1** | *Decide Which Witnesses Should Be Deposed*

As we will see in Step 3, for each witness whom we intend to depose, we must give notice to the other parties specifying the witness's name and the date, time, and place of the deposition. Our first objective, therefore, is to produce a list of the witnesses whom we want to depose. Then, in Step 2, we will decide when and in what order to conduct the depositions. The list that we will produce is, of course, subject to modification—we will undoubtedly add and delete names as our understanding of the facts increases.

**Listing the Possible Witnesses**—How can we decide who should be deposed? Our objective is to select the optimal list of deposition witnesses from all of the people whom we might conceivably depose.

Who can be a deposition witness? There are very few limitations. According to FRCP, Rule 30(a)(1), "A party may take the deposition of *any person.* . . ." Certainly, anyone who could testify at trial can be deposed. Unlike interrogatories and FRCP, Rule 34, requests for production, we can use depositions to take discovery from witnesses who are not parties to the suit. If we attempt to depose a small child or a person who is medically unstable, special arrangements may be required (such as a psychologist or doctor in attendance). To depose a witness who resides in another state or country, we may have to travel to the witness's location. Additional procedural steps are required to depose someone who is currently in prison. But, in general, the rules allow us to depose whomever we wish, including corporations and other entities (see sidebar).

Given the fact that there is a limit to the number of depositions we can take, how can we decide which witnesses are the most important to depose? You will sometimes see litigators simply start writing down names (shooting from the hip is an occupational hazard in litigation), but we can do better if we attack the problem systematically. Instead of relying on memory, we will prepare a list, as complete as we can make it, of every potential witness we can think of. Then we can select the best names from the list, and be reasonably confident that we have not overlooked anyone. Our general strategy is as follows:

*1.* We begin by listing everyone whose name appears in the case file and in our notes. We list each witness named in our opponent's disclosure statement or answers to interrogatories. We question our client carefully to identify any other potential witnesses. As best we can, we list anyone who may be in a position to help either our case or, more importantly, our opponent's case. If there are potential witnesses whose names we do not know, we list them according to their role (i.e., "scrub nurse who assisted operation"). We can always get names later via discovery or through investigation.

*2.* We add to the list any corporations or other entities that we think may have useful information.

the rules of the court in which the case is pending (in federal court, the ten-deposition limit).

**6.** From the highest priority names, we make a final list of the witnesses whom we will actually try to depose.

The most difficult aspect of this analysis is, of course, assigning priorities and deciding which witnesses are the most important to depose. It is important to keep our goals clearly in mind. Our objective is not simply to gather a lot of information, it is to gather the information that will best help us win the lawsuit. Therefore, as we consider each potential witness, we ask ourselves, "How would a deposition of this person advance our case?" In particular, we are concerned with the likely role of each potential witness at trial. We can usually predict which individuals our opponent is likely to call as witnesses at trial to testify about the main issues in the case. These are the witnesses who have the potential to win the case for our opponent, and the more we can pin down in advance what they are going to say, the better prepared we will be to deal with them at trial.

There are certain categories of witness whom we will almost always depose unless the amount of money at stake in the lawsuit is too small to justify the expense. These include:

■ *The opposing party.* We need to find out whether the opposing party has any relevant factual information of which we are not yet aware. Of equal importance, we need to pin down exactly what our opponent claims the facts are, in minute detail; otherwise, we leave her free to concoct a new story after seeing what the rest of the evidence shows.

■ *Any expert witnesses designated to testify for the opposing party, and any expert witnesses appointed by the court.* Litigants typically hire expert witnesses to testify about highly specialized and often complicated technical or scientific issues that require a level of knowledge and experience that most people—including lawyers and paralegals—do not have. To cross-examine an expert effectively, the lawyer must acquire at least a basic understanding of the subject matter about which the expert will testify. Therefore, it is essential to know well in advance of trial exactly what the expert's testimony will be.

■ *Eyewitnesses to the events at issue in the suit.* For example, in an auto accident case, we would usually depose anyone who saw the accident happen, unless the facts of the accident are not seriously in dispute. In a medical

---

## SIDEBAR

### Deposing a Corporation or Other Entity

*A deposition is a live proceeding in which the lawyers ask questions and the witness answers them. Therefore, obviously, there must be a natural person—a live human being—to answer the questions. But suppose we are suing (or defending a suit by) a corporation. Have we lost the ability to make our opponent answer deposition questions?*

*No. FRCP, Rule 30(b)(6), expressly allows us to issue a notice of deposition and subpoena to "a public or private corporation or a partnership or association or governmental agency. . . ." How can a corporation testify? In the same way that it does everything else—through human agents who are empowered to act on its behalf.*

*When we issue a notice of deposition to a corporation or other entity, we must "describe with reasonable particularity the matters on which examination is requested." The entity must then "designate one or more officers, directors, or managing agents, or other persons who consent to testify on its behalf" concerning the topics specified. The designated spokesperson is to testify "as to matters known or reasonably available to the organization" [FRCP, Rule 30(b)(6)].*

---

**3.** We revisit our issues outline and review each of the factual matters that we will be required to prove. With each one, we ask ourselves whether there are any witnesses not yet on our list who could help us with the required proof. We add them to the list.

**4.** Next, we go through the list carefully, considering each name in turn, and ranking the potential witnesses in order of importance.

**5.** We decide how far down the scale of "importance" we need to go to prepare our case adequately. This is to some extent a judgment call, but usually there will be a few witnesses at the top of the list who clearly must be deposed, and others near the bottom who clearly need not be. The point at which we draw the line will depend in part on what is at stake in the case. We are willing to spend more money taking depositions in a $50 million commercial case than in a $5,000 fender-bender. We will also have to consider the restrictions, if any, imposed by

malpractice case involving a botched surgical operation, we would depose any nurses, anesthetists, and others present in the operating room.

- *Individuals directly involved in a disputed transaction.* In lawsuits arising not from physical events like accidents but from business or financial disputes, there are not necessarily any eyewitnesses as such, but there are individuals who participated directly in the transactions that led to the lawsuit. These are prime candidates for depositions. Suppose, for example, that you represent a client who bought a used car from a dealership, only to find out later that the car's odometer had been rolled back to show much less than the true mileage. In your fraud suit against the dealer, it would be natural to depose the salesperson who dealt directly with your client.

Beyond these "key" witnesses, the decision of whom to depose is a judgment call mainly involving a trade-off between the amount of money we can afford to spend on discovery and the expected value of the information to be obtained. One common motivation for additional deposition-taking is to look for documents. See the sidebar on Deposing Custodians of Records.

> *Your Local Notes*
>
> _____
>
> _____

**Step 2** | *Decide Where, When, and in What Order to Schedule the Depositions*

Once we have arrived at a final list of names of persons to be deposed, we must then decide where, when, and in what order to depose them. These decisions depend on the circumstances of each individual case, but we can offer a few general guidelines, as discussed next.

**Location**—The preferred site for a deposition is usually a conference room at our own law office. We want to create an atmosphere of formality and control, in which the witness will feel psychological pressure to take the proceeding seriously and opposing counsel will find it more difficult to distract us from our purpose. This is why we would usually avoid conducting any important deposition at the office of the opposing attorney, where our opponent's witnesses are likely to feel more at ease and the opposing attorney can easily engineer interruptions any time the witness encounters difficulty with our questioning. There is also the question of cost. If we schedule our depositions for our own office, we avoid the time and expense of travel. We and our supervising attorney can do other work until all other participants are ready to proceed, instead of sitting around in some other lawyer's reception area waiting for the court reporter to show up.

In a few situations, we may decide that it is better to go to the witness than make the witness come to us. If we are deposing our opponent's star medical expert, for example—for whose time we will be billed at rates sometimes in excess of $1,000 per hour—we would rather not pay for the witness to sit around in traffic. And with out-of-town witnesses, we may have no choice but to travel to the witness; the rules do not allow us to force a witness to travel more than 100 miles to attend a deposition; see FRCP, Rule 45(b)(2) and (c)(3)(A). As a practical matter, for out-of-town depositions we will usually borrow the office of some obliging local attorney.

> *Your Local Notes*
>
> _____
>
> _____

**Order and Timing**—When should we schedule each deposition? Should we aim for early depositions, so as to pin down facts before our opponent has a chance to manipulate them too much? Or should we wait until later, when our written discovery is further along and we are factually better prepared? Which witnesses should we depose first?

As a general rule, we may depose each witness only once. To depose the same witness more than once, we must first obtain the judge's permission [see FRCP, Rule 30(a)(2)(B)] and the opposing attorney will surely resist. Therefore, we must sequence our depositions carefully, so that information needed for later depositions can be obtained in the earlier ones.

As a matter of personal style and preference, we would generally depose the opposing party as early as possible. When we depose an opposing party, the most important objectives are to find out exactly what our opponent is claiming and make him go on the record with as much factual detail as possible. There is no compelling need to depose others first.

Document-gathering depositions and custodian of records depositions are also taken early in the case. We need to build a full set of documents as

# SIDEBAR

## Deposing Custodians of Records

*We have learned how to use subpoenas and Rule 34 requests for production of documents to obtain needed records from others. These tools, useful as they are, have two major inadequacies: (1) They do not give us any way of verifying that we are really getting all of the documents we asked for, and (2) to use them, we must already know what documents or categories of documents to ask for.*

*Fortunately, we have at our disposal another tool that can help us overcome both of these limitations: the custodian of records deposition. As we have learned, we can issue a subpoena to a business or entity, specifying the subject matter of the desired testimony, and the rules require the business or entity to designate an individual to testify about that subject. Here, we issue a subpoena in which the specified subject matter is the nature and contents of the records kept by the business or entity. Often, this is done in a kind of shorthand way by issuing the subpoena in the name of, for example, "Custodian of records of Ajax Widget Corporation," and serving it on Ajax Widget Corporation. Everyone understands that Ajax Widget Corporation is to designate someone who knows about its filing system and records to respond to the subpoena. Your instructor will inform you of the customary way of noticing a custodian of records deposition in your locality.*

*Our purpose at the deposition is to find out everything we can about the way in which the entity keeps its records. You may be wondering why we would want to do this—after all, could we not simply issue a document request for "all documents" containing the type of information that we want, and put the onus on the opposing party to find them?*

*This question illustrates an important principle about discovery in litigation. In seeking information, we can adopt a passive strategy, in which we depend on our opponent to obey the rules and respond diligently to our discovery requests. Or, we can take a "proactive" stance, in which we assume our opponent will probably try to hide or withhold information that might help our case, and we insist on checking every possible detail ourselves. Cynical though it may seem, the latter approach wins more lawsuits.*

*Another reason for using a deposition to find out what records exist is that many records today are kept electronically rather than on paper. This allows companies to keep much more complex and detailed records than was possible in the days of paper files. Twenty years ago, it might have been possible for an experienced lawyer to make an accurate guess about what kinds of records a company might have; today, with the explosion of computerized record keeping, it would be foolhardy to try.*

*Once we have determined in detail exactly what records the entity has, we can then zero in using document subpoenas and Rule 34 requests to obtain the specific information we want, and be reasonably confident that we have found everything there is to find.*

---

early as possible, to use as a basis for other factual development.

Expert witness depositions are usually left for later in the discovery cycle. Expert witnesses typically offer opinions based on the facts they are given, and the facts they are given often come in part from depositions of other witnesses. In any case, we certainly want to receive and digest the expert's written report before taking her deposition, and probably go over it in detail with our own expert.

In the end, timing and sequence of depositions is a matter of judgment, usually involving choices between imperfect alternatives. After you have gained some experience as a litigation paralegal, you will develop a feel for deposition scheduling and sequencing; meanwhile, when in doubt, consult your supervising attorney.

**Creating a Tentative Schedule**—At this point, we have decided, at least on a preliminary basis, which witnesses to depose, in what order to depose them, and at approximately what stage in the case we would like to conduct each deposition. Now we come face to face with the realities of litigation scheduling: A deposition requires a number of very busy people—two or more attorneys, a court reporter, and a witness—to coordinate their busy calendars so as to be at the same place at the same time. At least some of them—the opposing attorney and the witness—may not be very inclined to cooperate. How can we select specific dates and times that will satisfy all of these people?

The process varies somewhat depending on local custom. Some attorneys in some jurisdictions routinely notice depositions without regard to anyone's calendar but their own. If one of the other participants has a conflict with the date and time selected, too bad! He can ask the judge to order a different one. There is nothing specific in the federal rules that prohibits us from scheduling depositions for whatever reasonable dates and times we choose, however inconvenient they may be for other attorneys or for the witness.

As a practical matter, however, if we notice a deposition for a date when, say, the opposing attorney is in trial on another case, she will probably not bother asking the judge for a different date. Instead, we will receive a letter politely informing us that no one is going to show up on the date we selected. Then it will be up to us to ask the judge to order that the deposition proceed, which the judge cannot very well do if opposing counsel has to be somewhere else that day. In the end, we will have wasted a lot of time, annoyed the judge, and, most important, will not be any closer to getting the deposition taken than when we started. Therefore, it usually makes sense to try to coordinate deposition scheduling with the opposing attorney. Often, we can get what we need by simply telephoning her secretary and asking for open dates.

Must we also coordinate with the witness? Unless the witness is someone "important" such as a doctor or government official, courts tend to display surprisingly little consideration for the witness's schedule. Testifying is seen as a civic duty, and the inconvenience of testifying is simply the price of good citizenship! It is not unusual for lawyers to serve a subpoena on a witness and expect him to drop everything and show up for a deposition or trial appearance 2 or 3 days later. Nevertheless, there is nothing to prevent us from contacting the witness (as long as the witness is not a party represented by an attorney) and trying to accommodate his schedule. The witness's testimony may turn out to be friendlier to our client if we act with courtesy rather than arrogance.

The court reporter's schedule usually presents little problem as long as we are able to give reasonable advance notice. For depositions that we schedule, we select and pay the court reporter, and if our chosen court reporter cannot accommodate us we can always select a different one.

## CLERICAL STEPS

Suppose we have decided to depose a particular witness, and we have selected a date, time, and place for the deposition. Let us now review the procedural steps that are necessary to make the deposition happen. These include giving the required notice to other parties (Step 3) and ensuring that the witness will attend (Step 4). We may also want the witness to produce documents at the deposition (Step 5).

### Step 3 — Notice the Deposition

FRCP, Rule 30(b)(1), states that "A party desiring to take the deposition of any person . . . shall give reasonable notice in writing to every other party to the action." The notice is to state "the time and place for taking the deposition and the name and address of each person to be examined. . . ." The purpose of the notice of deposition is to let the other litigants know of the deposition so that they can attend, participate, and make objections.

In practice, notices of deposition are usually one-page printed or word processor forms. They have the usual caption, signature line for the attorney, and certificate of service. The body of the notice typically contains blanks in which the name and address of the witness and the date, time, and place of the deposition can be filled in. See Figure W13–2 later in this workshop for a sample notice of deposition.

FRCP, Rule 30, requires us to serve a copy of the notice of deposition on the attorney for each other party to the suit. We do this by mailing or hand delivering a copy to each attorney's office in accordance with FRCP, Rule 5(b). We file the original notice with the clerk of the court.

> **Your Local Notes**
> _____
> _____

**Court Reporters and the Alternatives**—FRCP, Rule 30(b)(2), also requires us to state in the notice "the method by which the testimony shall be recorded." Most often, depositions are recorded stenographically by a court reporter using a shorthand machine. The machine operates in a manner similar to a typewriter, but it types in a special shorthand code onto a paper strip and/or computer disk. Its keys are designed for fast input, so that an experienced court reporter can take down testimony faster than a witness can talk. The court reporter later uses a computerized transcription device to "read" the shorthand code and produce a printed booklet containing a word-for-word transcript of everything said at the deposition.

It is up to the party noticing the deposition to arrange for a court reporter to be present. Sometimes, if a law firm has an ongoing relationship with a firm of court reporters, this is done by sending a copy of the notice of deposition to the court reporter firm. Or we may make arrangements with the court reporter by telephone.

Court reporter fees comprise a significant part of the cost of deposition discovery. The party noticing the deposition pays for the court reporter's services, and for the original transcript to be filed with the court. Court reporters typically bill at a fixed rate per page of transcript; at this writing, customary West Coast metropolitan area court reporter fees are upwards of $5 per double-spaced typed page. A typical 2- or 3-hour deposition can easily run well in excess of 100 pages.

You may be wondering why the practice of taking down deposition testimony in shorthand continues, in an age of tape recorders, video cameras, and even computers with voice recognition capabilities. In fact, the current federal rules allow us to choose between "sound, sound-and-visual, or stenographic" recording. Why not get out our video camera, save hundreds of dollars, and, as a bonus, finish up with a recording that reflects not just the words spoken but also gestures, tone of voice, and body language?

There are several reasons why court reporters are unlikely to be rendered extinct by video cameras. One is that a deposition must be taken in the presence of "an officer authorized to administer oaths by the laws of the United States or of the place where the examination is held . . ." [FRCP, Rule 28(a)]. Court reporters are authorized to administer oaths, and typically act as the FRCP, Rule 28, officer in addition to taking down the testimony. Certainly, we could find someone else authorized to administer oaths—appointment as a notary public suffices—but FRCP, Rule 28(c), prohibits anyone who is an employee of any party's attorney from presiding over a deposition, so we could not use any of our own employees.

There are also certain advantages to stenographic recording over video. Experienced court reporters are able to distinguish and correctly transcribe words under conditions that would render an electronic recording unintelligible, such as when the witness is mumbling or facing away from the microphone, or when two people speak at the same time. And video recordings record *everything,* warts and all. If the attorney doing the questioning seems to be struggling, pausing frequently, or saying "umm" a lot, the resulting video may be rather unflattering.

As a practical matter, even when using sound or video recording to take a deposition, most attorneys hire a court reporter to operate the recording equipment. Most court reporting firms now offer video recording as an option. Better to pay a court reporter and be sure of a usable record than to try to save a few dollars and risk losing some crucial bit of testimony because someone forgot to turn over the tape! Also, even if we record the deposition electronically, we will still need a written transcript to work from, and if we hire a court reporter to make the recording, we will get one.

---

*Your Local Notes*

_____

_____

---

**Consequences of Not Giving Notice**—Suppose a clerical error occurs and the notice of deposition is never sent out to one or more of the attorneys for the other parties. Then what? According to federal case law, the deposition cannot be used against the party who was not given notice—*even if the party or his attorney knew about the deposition from other sources.* In small, routine lawsuits, this issue is unlikely to arise, because there is only one party on each side and the mistake will be obvious when his attorney does not show up at the deposition. In complex cases, however, where there may be many plaintiffs and defendants, and attorneys pick and choose which depositions to attend, failure to serve notices properly can lead to a nasty surprise later when the judge excludes important deposition testimony.

**Step 4**    *Take Steps Necessary to Secure Attendance of Witness*

Having satisfied the notice requirement of Rule 30(b), let us now consider what must be done to ensure that the deponent will appear for the deposition at the designated time and place. Is serving the notice of deposition enough or must we do something else?

The answer depends on whether or not the deponent is a party. Although the rules do not expressly say so, serving a notice of deposition designating a party as the witness is sufficient to compel the party to attend. If the witness is not a party, then the correct procedure is to serve a subpoena.

FRCP, Rule 45, spells out the procedure for issuing and serving a subpoena and describes the required contents. We have already explored subpoena procedure in detail in Workshop 9 on document discovery. The procedure for issuing and serving a deposition subpoena is identical to that described in Workshop 9, except that a deposition subpoena includes the date, time, and place of the required appearance.

The sole purpose of serving a subpoena is to force the witness to attend (and, perhaps, to produce documents). Failure to issue a subpoena does not render the deposition invalid, assuming the witness shows up and testifies voluntarily. As a general rule, however, we recommend issuing a subpoena, even to a witness who is willing to appear without one. If we do not subpoena the witness, the witness is under no legal obligation to appear. If the witness has a last minute change of heart, or decides to move to another state the day before the deposition, we have no recourse other than to reschedule the deposition and try again with a subpoena—which, depending on the discovery schedule and deadlines, we may not have time to do. Better to do the job right the first time.

---

*Your Local Notes*

_____

_____

---

### Step 5   *Take Steps Necessary to Ensure Availability of Documents*

Deposition testimony often involves documents. If, for example, we are deposing the doctor who treated the injuries for which plaintiff is suing, we will certainly want to see plaintiff's medical records and ask the doctor questions about what is recorded in them. Some of the documents that we use in a deposition will already be in our possession as a result of FRCP, Rule 34, document requests and other discovery. Quite commonly, however, we want to see documents that are in the possession of the witness and that we do not yet have.

If the witness is not a party, the solution is simple: Subpoena the documents with the witness. FRCP, Rule 45, allows us to include both a command to appear and testify and a command to produce evidence in the same subpoena. FRCP, Rule 45(a)(1), provides, "A command to produce evidence . . . may be joined with a command to appear . . . at deposition, or may be issued separately." There is one additional procedural hoop to jump through: If we subpoena documents from a nonparty witness, our notice of deposition must say so. "If a subpoena duces tecum is to be served on the person to be examined, the designation of the materials to be produced as set forth in the subpoena shall be attached to, or included in, the notice [of deposition]" [FRCP, Rule 30(b)(1)].

To obtain documents from a witness who is also a party, a FRCP, Rule 34, request for production of documents is the obvious choice. FRCP, Rule 30(b)(5) provides "The notice to a party deponent may be accompanied by a request made in compliance with Rule 34 for the production of documents . . . at the taking of the deposition. The procedure of Rule 34 shall apply to the request." There is a significant disadvantage to a FRCP, Rule 34, request compared to a subpoena. The responding party has 30 days to respond to a FRCP, Rule 34, request for production of documents. In the context of deposition scheduling, 30 days is a relatively long time; subpoenas are routinely issued with much shorter response times. Could we skip the FRCP, Rule 34, request and use a subpoena to obtain documents from a party, thereby circumventing the 30-day response time? Federal case law says no, but litigators still occasionally try this tactic.

One drawback of using either a FRCP, Rule 34, request or a subpoena to make a witness bring documents to a deposition is that we will have little time to digest the documents. Usually, when a witness brings documents to the deposition, the lawyer conducting the deposition asks to see the documents and spends a few moments perusing them before beginning the questioning. But it is hard to conduct a thorough review with the witness, the court reporter, the client, and one or more opposing attorneys all sitting there staring into space waiting for the deposition to begin. Therefore, if the discovery schedule allows enough time, and unless the expected documents are few and simple, it is better to obtain documents beforehand.

---

*Your Local Notes*

_____

_____

---

## PLANNING AND TAKING THE TESTIMONY

We now turn our attention from the clerical aspects of scheduling a deposition to the content of the testimony to be taken. Obviously, the specific subject matter areas to be covered in a deposition depend greatly on the facts of the case and the relationship of the witness to them. There are, however, some guiding principles that apply in most situations. We explore these principles in Steps 6 and 7.

## Step 6 — *Prepare a Topic Outline for Use by the Attorney Who Will Conduct the Deposition*

Our goal in this step is to assemble the information that our supervising attorney will need in preparing for the deposition. This will consist of an outline setting forth suggested topics and questions, accompanied by copies of all discovery documents that may be pertinent. The documents that the attorney decides to use in the deposition will be marked and designated as exhibits (see the Using Exhibits section in Step 8). As we add topics and questions to our outline, we also note which documents relate to each. The attorney will use our outline and documents as a starting point from which to plan the questioning.

**The Paralegal's Job in Preparing for a Deposition**—Our role as paralegals is to review thoroughly all available sources of information, to address every possible point on which the witness may have information to contribute. Ideally, our outline and the accompanying package of selected discovery documents should together comprise every bit of information that the attorney needs to consult in preparing for the deposition. There should be no need for the attorney to dig through the file looking for additional facts if we have done our job well.

How do we produce the desired outline? As with most planning tasks in litigation, we will do better if we look for topics in a systematic way rather than relying on memory and trying to pick topics out of the air. The issues outline is a good place to start; we can review the issues point by point, asking ourselves whether this witness is likely to contribute anything on each issue. We may also skim through the file, or at least the main pleadings, looking for ideas. As questions or topics of inquiry occur to us, we jot them down.

One of the most important sources of deposition subject matter is the set of documents gathered in discovery. Any documents in which the witness's name appears—especially any authored by the witness—should be set aside, copied, and considered as possible material to ask about in the deposition. Any documents describing events that the witness observed or transactions in which the witness participated should be set aside, as should any documents needing authentication by this witness. In a smaller case where the quantity of documents is manageable, we may go through the documents by hand looking for potential deposition documents. In a complex case where the discovery documents may comprise many thousands of pages, it is impractical to review every document for every deposition; better to set up a computerized document retrieval database and enter all of the document information into it as the documents are received. Then we can query the database for a list of all the documents in which the witness's name appears.

After we have reviewed the issues outline, the case file, the discovery documents, and any other likely sources of ideas, we pull our notes together into a final outline for use by the attorney who will conduct the questioning. We assemble copies of all the pertinent documents and check to be sure that we have included all relevant documents.

**The Attorney's Role**—Helpful though the paralegal's outline is, it is not a substitute for proper preparation by the attorney who will conduct the deposition. The paralegal's job is to make sure that no important subject matter is overlooked; it is the attorney who must make the strategic decisions about what questions to ask, what subjects to avoid, how to phrase the questions, and in what order to cover the topics. The attorney's final plan for the deposition, whether expressed in the form of an outline, scribbled notes on a legal pad, on index cards (our own preference) or in some other way, may bear rather little resemblance to the paralegal's outline.

From the attorney's standpoint, a successful deposition is the result of thorough preparation combined with a willingness to be flexible. As a litigation paralegal, you will see many different styles of deposition questioning. New lawyers sometimes make the mistake of trying to "script" a deposition as though it were a stage production, writing out each question verbatim. Others "shoot from the hip" with little preparation. Neither extreme works very well. Fail to prepare thoroughly enough, and we will forget to cover some important topic. Plan in too much detail, and instead of following the witness's answers wherever they lead, we will be trying to force the testimony to fit our planned questions.

Our own preferred way of preparing for a deposition consists of writing broad topics on index cards, one topic per card. On each card, we write a short reminder of what it is we want to cover. Usually, we avoid writing out specific questions, but if there are particular questions about a topic that we want to be sure to word in a particular way, we may write them on the card too, or write them on a separate card. We also note on each card any documents that we may want to refer to in connection with the card's topic.

The advantages are several:

- It is easy to add topics.
- Because of their size, index cards inherently discourage the inclusion of too much detail.
- It is easy to change the order of topics, both before and during the deposition. In a depo-

sition, it is undesirable to adhere slavishly to the logical sequence of an outline. Often, particularly with adverse witnesses, it is desirable to jump around, change topics in midstream, and return to topics already covered to make the questioning unpredictable and keep the witness off balance. The use of index cards facilitates this.

- As we will see, there are certain questions and areas of inquiry that we will pursue in almost every deposition. We can reuse the index cards pertaining to these standard topics in deposition after deposition, honing our technique and noting ideas and improvements on the cards.

- Before adjourning the deposition, we can quickly run through the cards, and check that we have covered every issue we intended to cover.

## Step 7  *Assist at the Deposition*

Although paralegals do not conduct the questioning in a deposition, they do commonly attend and assist. Here are some functions commonly assigned to paralegals at a deposition:

- *Keeping track of documents and exhibits.* When an exhibit is marked, it is customary to provide copies for each opposing attorney. Particularly in a deposition involving a large number of documents, it is very helpful to have a paralegal present to locate exhibits and distribute the copies.

- *Helping keep track of what topics have been covered and what loose ends remain.* Deposition questioning often jumps from topic to topic in an unpredictable way as the attorney follows new threads raised by the witness's answers. The paralegal can help by keeping notes of the extent to which each topic has been fully explored, and sharing this information with the attorney during breaks in the questioning.

- *Observing the witness and making notes of the witness's demeanor and reactions to questions.* A good deal of the attorney's attention in a deposition is occupied with the mechanics of phrasing questions. The paralegal is in a position to pay closer attention to the witness's body language and behavior.

- *Helping detect evasive or unresponsive answers.* As absorbed in the questioning as the

attorney often is, she will sometimes fail to notice when the witness gives an answer that does not fully answer the question asked.

**Using Exhibits**—Often, while questioning a witness in a deposition, we will want to refer to documents. These may be documents that we have already obtained through discovery or investigation or from our client, or documents brought to the deposition by the witness.

We are free to refer to documents by naming or describing them (i.e., "the construction contract" or "your divorce decree"), but if we do that, it may be hard to prove later on which document the witness was talking about. What we need is a way to put a document into the deposition record so that anyone referring to the transcript can see the same document that the witness was looking at when she testified. We do this by marking documents as exhibits.

To use an exhibit in a deposition, we first hand the document to the court reporter to be marked. The court reporter will stamp the document with an exhibit stamp, write an exhibit number on it, and note in the shorthand record a brief description of the document. As a matter of courtesy, it is customary to provide copies of the document to the attorneys for other parties who are attending the deposition. We use the stamped copy to show to the witness.

What sort of a numbering system is used for exhibits? The answer is up to the attorney, and varies according to personal preference and local custom. The question deserves some thought, however, particularly in cases involving large volumes of documents. If, for example, we let the court reporter start numbering from "Exhibit 1" in each deposition, and we take ten depositions, we will wind up with ten "Exhibit 1's." If we have to refer to deposition testimony involving several of these "Exhibit 1's" at trial, we may confuse the jury—and possibly ourselves. Our preferred solution is to assign numbers to the most important documents in a case sequentially, starting from one, before ever taking depositions, then use the same numbers for the same documents in all the depositions, and, if the judge will allow it, at trial. When we mark additional documents on the fly at a deposition, we start with whatever number we left off with in our global numbering system. This means that, in a given deposition, the numbers may not start with "1" or run in sequence, but we avoid having more than one document with the same exhibit number. This system offers the added advantage of allowing us to refer to documents by their global exhibit number while preparing and taking notes.

*Your Local Notes*

_____

_____

_____

**What to Expect at a Deposition**—Let us now describe the sequence of events at a typical deposition. We will assume that the deposition we are describing is one that we ourselves have noticed, and that it will be held at the offices of our own law firm.

As the time for the deposition nears, we check to be sure that the conference room we have reserved is in order and that our copies of documents are ready to go. When the court reporter arrives, the firm's receptionist shows him to the conference room to set up whatever recording equipment will be used, typically a shorthand machine.

If the witness is an opposing party or someone who is cooperating with the opposing party, she will often arrive in the company of the opposing attorney. The receptionist will wait until the witness and all of the attorneys expected to attend have arrived, then notify the attorney who will conduct the deposition that all is in readiness.

Customarily, the court reporter sits at the head of the conference table, so as to have the best vantage point from which to hear all participants. The witness sits at one side of the table adjacent to the court reporter. The attorney who will conduct the questioning sits at the opposite side of the table, facing the witness, and the assisting paralegal sits next to the attorney. Usually, the opposing attorney sits next to the witness.

After introductions and, perhaps, a few moments of polite interchange of pleasantries, the proceeding begins by the court reporter swearing in the witness. This is done in exactly the same manner as in court, with the witness raising her right hand and swearing to tell the truth. Then the questioning begins.

The attorney begins by asking the witness to state her name for the record. We would usually also ask for the witness's current address and telephone number, to make it easier to contact the witness in the future should the need arise. After these identification questions, many attorneys ask whether the witness has ever been deposed before, and then describe the ground rules for the proceeding to the witness. Here is a typical introductory speech by an attorney taking a deposition:

Attorney:   Have you ever had your deposition taken before?

Witness:   No.

Attorney:   Let me begin by explaining a few ground rules. I will be asking you a number of questions, which you are required to answer. The court reporter, whom you see seated here on your right, will take down my questions and your answers, and everything else that is said here today, word for word, and prepare a printed transcript. The testimony you give here today will appear verbatim in the transcript, and can be used or quoted at the trial or in other proceedings in this lawsuit. Do you understand all that?

Witness:   Yes.

Attorney:   Your testimony here is under oath, the same as if you were testifying in court in front of the judge. Do you understand that?

Witness:   Yes.

Attorney:   Please take care to answer questions audibly, because the court reporter cannot interpret nods and shakes of the head, okay?

Witness:   Okay.

Attorney:   Mr./Ms. _____ [the opposing attorney] may object to one of my questions from time to time. If that happens, the court reporter will record the objection so that the judge can consider it later, but you will go ahead and answer the question. Do you understand that?

Witness:   Yes.

Attorney:   If you do not understand any of my questions, it is important that you tell me so that I can rephrase the question until you do understand it. Will you do that?

Witness:   Yes.

You may sometimes see attorneys follow the last question with another along the following lines: "So if you do go ahead and answer a question, we will assume that you did understand it, okay?" The intent is to prevent the witness from later weaseling out of an answer by claiming to have misunderstood the question. However, to ask the witness to agree, in advance, to having understood questions that have not yet been asked is misleading, and should be objected to—after all, it is possible for a witness to misunderstand a question without realizing it.

Once the preliminaries are attended to, the questioning gets under way in earnest. Absent unusual circumstances, the first phase of questioning should be aimed at getting the witness to tell her story in her own words. Suppose, for example, we are deposing someone who witnessed an auto accident; a good first question would be "I understand that you witnessed the accident that led to this lawsuit—please tell me what you saw." The next question, and the next one after that, for as long as it takes to get the whole story, should be "What happened next?" We are much more likely to get testimony that we can use if we let the witness narrate as much as possible, than if we try to force the testimony into our preconceived factual theories via narrow questions.

In this respect, deposition questioning is much different from cross-examination in court. You may have heard or read the adage that, in cross-examining an adverse witness, a wise attorney never asks a question unless the answer is known in advance. To violate this rule is to invite the witness to drop some unexpected bombshell that may leave an otherwise effective cross-examination in tatters. In a deposition, however, we *want* bombshells—if there is anything that the witness can say that can hurt our case, we want to know about it here and now.

After the witness has been given ample opportunity to relate her story, we then back up to fill in gaps and pin down details. While narrating, witnesses are often imprecise about times and locations; it is important to go back and ask the witness when and where each event took place and who else, if anyone, was present. The witness may have referred to documents while telling her story; if so, we need to mark them as exhibits and have the witness identify them on the record (see the Using Exhibits section in Step 8). Another useful technique is to ask the witness to make a rough drawing or map as an aid in clarifying where people and objects were situated during the events that the witness is describing; the drawing can be marked as an exhibit and included in the record.

Notice that, so far, we have not even needed to glance at our topic outline or notes—we are simply following the witness's narration wherever it leads. Only after having the witness narrate her story in as much depth and detail as possible, do we get out our index cards or notepad and start asking specific questions. Even then, our questions will likely have to be reshaped to fit what the witness has already told us. As we go through our notes, we are likely to find that some topics have already been fully or partially covered in the witness's narration. As we ask questions to fill in the gaps, we may jump around from topic to topic rather than proceed in a predictable order. If there are facts that the witness is trying to keep from us, they are more likely to slip out if the order of questioning is unpredictable, so that the witness has less time to anticipate questions and engineer evasive answers.

While we are doing all this, the opposing attorney is not, of course, sitting quietly and letting us do whatever we want. The opposing attorney has an important role to play at a deposition, one that we explore in the following sidebar.

> *Your Local Notes*
>
> _____
>
> _____

## SIDEBAR

## Depositions: The Opposing Attorney's Role

*The purpose of a deposition is to gather information—information that the opposing attorney may not want brought to light. The opposing party can use several weapons to prevent us from obtaining the information we need.*

### Resisting Attendance

*The opposing party's first line of defense is to try to find some way to prevent the deposition from occurring at all. This will succeed only if there are valid legal grounds for opposing the deposition, such as procedural errors by the party who notices the deposition. If, for example, the notice of deposition fails to conform to the limitations of FRCP, Rule 30(a)(2), or the subpoena violates the geographic restrictions of FRCP, Rule 45, or the deposition is not allowed under the court's scheduling order, then the opposing party may have grounds to avoid it altogether.*

*What should the opposing party do in that case? The answer depends on the circumstances. If the infraction is clear, it may be sufficient to send the noticing attorney a letter reciting the problem and simply not attend. A safer course, however, is to file a motion for a protective order under Rule 26(c). Rule 26(c) gives the judge broad power to enter orders regulating discovery matters, and a motion for protective order is the correct procedural move when another party attempts to engage in improper discovery.*

### Avoiding Damaging Testimony

*If nothing can be done to prevent the deposition proceeding, the opposing party will next try to weaken*

## SIDEBAR

## Depositions: The Opposing Attorney's Role *continued*

*the damaging testimony. Among other things, the opposing attorney may try these ploys:*

■ *Make objections. Since there is no judge present, the normal procedure at a deposition [see FRCP, Rule 30(c)] is for the court reporter to note the objection on the record. The witness then answers the question despite the objection (otherwise the deposition would have to be taken again if the judge overruled the objection). One problem with objections at depositions is that attorneys are tempted to make so-called "speaking objections" when a witness is getting into trouble—objections that, in effect, tell the witness how to answer. The federal rules prohibit this. FRCP, Rule 30(d)(1), states "Any objection to evidence during a deposition shall be stated concisely and in a non-argumentative and non-suggestive manner." Nevertheless, faced with a choice between the possibility of a scolding from the judge for a suggestive objection and the certainty that a witness is about to torpedo the case with a bad answer, many litigators will opt to bend FRCP, Rule 30(d)(1).*

■ *Confer with the witness if the witness is the attorney's client. A witness is free to confer with his attorney during a deposition. A recess may be taken, or the witness and attorney may engage in a whispered conference during questioning. This is, in fact, the proper tactic to use when one's client is obviously having trouble with a question. However, the attorney conducting the questioning can, and usually should, note the conference on the record (i.e., "Let the record show that the witness is conferring with his attorney before answering the question.").*

■ *Instruct the witness not to answer a question. This is a proper tactic only if the witness is the attorney's client, and then only if the question calls for privileged information, violates a court-ordered limitation on discovery, or is so unreasonable that the attorney is prepared to stop the deposition and go track down the judge for an order then and there (not a recommended move except under the most compelling of circumstances).*

## CONCLUDING STEP

### Step 8    *Analyze and Digest Transcript*

After the deposition is over, we will, in due course, receive a transcript from the court reporter. (How soon depends on how much we are willing to pay. Standard processing typically takes a week or two; we can order expedited or even next-day transcripts, at additional cost.) What do we do with the transcripts once we have them? What can we use them for, and what, as a practical matter, must we do to make the information in them readily accessible?

**Rule 32 and the Uses of Depositions**—Deposition transcripts have a variety of uses in litigation, so many that an entire rule (FRCP, Rule 32) is devoted to the subject. Here are some common uses:

■ We can use deposition testimony for impeachment when we cross-examine a witness at trial. FRCP, Rule 32(a)(1), provides: "Any deposition may be used by any party for the purpose of contradicting or impeaching the

testimony of deponent as a witness. . . ." In other words, if the witness makes some statement while testifying at trial that differs from what the witness said in deposition, we can confront the witness with the inconsistent questions and answers from the deposition. ("Isn't it a fact that, at your deposition, you gave the following answer to the following question. . . ?")

■ We can use the deposition as a substitute for live testimony in circumstances where it is impracticable for the witness to testify in person (i.e., the witness is dead, aged, sick, hiding, in prison, or lives more than 100 miles away); see FRCP, Rule 32(a)(3). Traditionally, when offering a deposition in lieu of a live witness, it was customary to have some volunteer (perhaps a paralegal!) take the stand and pretend to be the witness, reading answers from the transcript as the attorney read the questions. Today, most litigators would prefer to use a videotaped deposition in such circumstances.

■ We can use the deposition of an opposing party (including the individual designated to testify for a corporate party) for any purpose.

- We can quote from deposition testimony to establish facts in support of or in opposition to a motion for summary judgment; see FRCP, Rule 56(e). Typically, we do this by attaching photocopies of the pertinent transcript pages to the supporting affidavit, and quoting the testimony in the body of the motion. See Workshop 16 for more detail.

- We can use the information that we obtain in a deposition to help us find other evidence.

It is sometimes tempting, particularly to beginning lawyers, to set traps and confront deposition witnesses with inconsistencies, much as we might do in cross-examination at trial. Except in unusual circumstances, experienced litigators resist the temptation. Our purpose at a deposition is to *gather* ammunition to be used at trial—not to waste it. The idea is for us to find out what the witness will do at trial, not for the witness to find out what we will do.

After covering all of our planned topics, it is time to wrap up. Here, a break may be in order so that the attorney can consult with the paralegal and both can consider whether any important subject matter has been overlooked. Then the attorney will ask some concluding questions, designed to make a clear record that the witness has told us everything there is to tell. Examples:

- "Have you now told me everything you can remember that has anything to do with the accident that you witnessed?"

- "Is there anything else you are aware of that you feel is pertinent to this lawsuit?"

- "Have you now told us about every conversation you have had with anyone, at anytime, in which the subject matter of this lawsuit was mentioned?"

We would usually then add a few more questions, this time intended to make a record that we can use later if the witness tries to weasel out of any of his or her answers:

- "Do you feel that you have understood all of my questions?"

- "As you think back over this deposition, is there anything that you want to clarify?"

- "Have you answered each of my questions truthfully and completely to the best of your ability?"

Then we thank the witness and state on the record that we have no more questions. At this point, it is the opposing attorney's turn to ask questions if desired. If the witness is cooperating with the opposing attorney, the opposing attorney is unlikely to ask questions unless the witness has said something in response to our questions that the opposing attorney wants to clarify or "reengineer." If the opposing attorney has no questions, then the deposition is over.

At the conclusion of the deposition, the court reporter has a few clerical matters to attend to, including these:

- Gather all of the original marked exhibits (which, by the end of a deposition, are likely to be scattered over the conference table). Copies may be substituted if desired [see FRCP, Rule 30(f)(1)]. The exhibits will be bound with the transcript.

- Ask which attorneys are ordering copies of the transcript. If the deposition is deemed unimportant, and/or if the case is likely to settle before trial, attorneys may sometimes delay ordering a transcript to avoid the additional expense.

- Check with the witness to verify spelling of any unusual words or names.

- Ask whether the witness is to read and sign the deposition. See sidebar.

## SIDEBAR

### Read and Sign?

FRCP, Rule 30(e), provides that the witness shall have 30 days in which to review the transcript and make a list of any corrections. The rule is not intended to allow the witness to change an answer that, in retrospect, the witness does not like (although witnesses have been known to try); rather, the purpose is to allow for correction of errors by the court reporter. If the witness does have changes, the witness lists them on a form provided by the court reporter and signs the form. The court reporter does not change the transcript, but does attach the list of changes at the end.

Under the rules of some state courts, the witness is to sign the deposition itself after reading it. The federal rules no longer require signature. Under current federal rules, it is up to the witness whether to read the transcript or not. In state courts where the rules require the witness to read and sign the deposition, the attorneys often stipulate to waive reading and signing, trusting the court reporter to transcribe accurately. (Some attorneys, however, insist that the witness read and sign, to prevent the opposing party from later claiming that a troublesome answer was the result of a court reporter mistake.)

---

*Your Local Notes*

_____

_____

---

### Organizing Deposition Testimony

**Organizing Deposition Testimony**—In a lawsuit of average complexity, the transcripts of the depositions taken by both sides may amount to several thousand pages. Taking into account that the case load of the average litigator or litigation paralegal may include a number of such lawsuits at any given time, obviously we cannot expect to locate important deposition testimony on command by memory alone. Neither is it practical to search through reams of transcripts whenever we need to find some particular bit of testimony. We need a systematic way of cataloging and indexing our deposition transcripts.

The traditional deposition transcript is simply a verbatim, typed or printed record of questions, answers, objections, and anything else said on the record during the deposition. These are customarily double spaced, and often on smaller-than-letter-sized paper, so not very many questions and answers fit on one page, and not indexed in any way. To make the testimony accessible by subject matter, someone (often a paralegal) had to go through the transcript question by question and prepare an outline or index.

In the last decade or so, as court reporters have embraced computerized note taking and transcription, several innovations have been introduced that make organizing deposition testimony easier:

- *Computer-generated indexes.* A modern, computer-generated transcript comes with a word index that lists *every single word* in the deposition (except words like "a" and "the"), and gives page and line numbers of every place where each word appears in the transcript.

- *Transcripts on disk.* Most court reporters can provide, for an extra charge, a diskette with a word processing file containing the entire transcript. This allows us to do word searching and other processing using word processing software (and also saves typing when we want to quote long passages in another document).

- *"Min-u-script" transcripts.* In addition to the usual transcript, we can get a transcript in which the questions and answers appear in single-spaced fine print, several columns per letter-sized page. This allows us to see, at a glance on a single page, testimony that occupies ten or more pages in the standard transcript.

### Deposition Outlining

**Deposition Outlining**—With word-for-word indices and searchable disk files available, you might suppose that there would no longer be any need for paralegals to wade through transcripts laboriously making outlines. Isn't modern technology wonderful!

Sorry. Computerized indexing is not a substitute for trained legal judgment. The computer can locate words, but it cannot decide which ones are important, nor can it assess meaning and relevance. Someone who is properly trained and familiar with the facts and issues of the case must read the transcripts, analyze the testimony, identify the questions and answers that may prove useful or need follow-up, and preserve the analysis in such a way as to allow the attorney to find needed testimony quickly.

A common solution is to have a paralegal summarize or outline each deposition. In a typical deposition, even though the questioning may jump around from topic to topic, we can identify "blocks," or short sequences of questions and answers, that together add up to one main point. When we summarize a deposition, we try to express the main point of each block in a few, well-chosen words. If possible without sacrificing brevity, we use the same words as the witness used, rather than paraphrasing.

There is no correct format for a deposition outline. We are preparing a tool for our own use and that of our supervising attorney, and we are free to tailor it to fit our needs. A certain customary layout is often used, but there is considerable local variation. Commonly, a deposition outline has a narrow column on the left for the page and line number of each entry, with the summary of the main point of each chunk to the right. No effort is made to rearrange the order—we simply summarize the chunks in the sequence in which they appear in the deposition. (See the Practice Pointers section at the end of this workshop for some samples.)

The trick to identifying the main point of each segment is to focus not on the words, but on the relationship of the testimony to the issues in the case. We ignore extraneous detail and facts that are not in doubt. The main point that we would like to capture in each segment is the tendency of the testimony to prove or disprove some disputed issue.

Outlines of all the depositions in the case will go into the attorney's trial notebook. Then, when it is necessary to find the page where a witness talked about a particular subject, the attorney can easily skim through the deposition outlines. In a case where the deposition testimony is extensive, it may be desirable to prepare additional outlines where the main points are organized by subject matter. Obviously, the ways in which the standard layout can be improved are limited only by our imagination and the amount of time available.

## Depositions: Learning by Example

We will now apply the principles we have learned by setting up deposition discovery in our hypothetical lawsuit, *Martin v. Collins,* on behalf of defendant Park Hotels Group. We will assume that the Rule 16 scheduling conference has just occurred, and that the discovery cutoff date is 6 months from now. We have already received plaintiff's disclosure statement as it appears in the Learning by Example section of Workshop 12, and we are also aware of the information described in the Learning by Doing section of Workshop 12.

## PREPARATORY STEPS

**Step 1**  *Decide Which Witnesses Should Be Deposed*

Our first task is to assemble a comprehensive list of possible witnesses. For brevity, we will leave out those who are employed by or under the control of our client, since, as you now know, we normally do not depose our own witnesses. The list would look something like the one shown in Figure W13–1.

Next, we decide how important it is that each of these be deposed. Here are our conclusions:

*1.* It goes without saying that Park Hotels' attorney must depose Shannon Martin. She is both the principal opposing party and one of only two eyewitnesses to the incident that led to the lawsuit.

---

**Figure W13–1  Sample List of Possible Witnesses**

| Person | Role |
|---|---|
| Shannon Martin | Plaintiff |
| Arthur Collins | Co-defendant, witness to incident |
| Detective Sgt. Janet Marnell | In charge of police investigation |
| Officer Edward Flanigan | Assisted in police investigation |
| Officer Barbara Goldberg | Assisted in police investigation |
| Mr. and Mrs. Carl Mitchell | Shared an elevator with defendant Collins immediately prior to incident |
| Mr. Andrew Garrison<br>Mr. Manuel Rivera | Paramedics who responded to the scene and treated defendant Collins; may have made observations of plaintiff's hotel room and persons and objects therein, and condition of defendant Collins immediately after the incident. |
| Ellen Sayers, M.D. | Emergency room doctor, treated plaintiff |
| Paul Norling, M.D. | Plaintiff's primary care physician |
| Robin Carter, M.D. | Plaintiff's hand surgeon |
| Gordon McCormick, P.T. | Plaintiff's physical therapist |
| Anne Resnick, M.D. | Anaesthesiologist during plaintiff's hand surgery |
| Dennis Tang, M.D. | Plaintiff's psychiatrist |
| Network Software Solutions, Inc. | Plaintiff's employer |
| Bruce DeAngelo | Plaintiff's supervisor |
| Mrs. Helen Barnes | Hotel guests in nearby rooms |
| Mr. and Mrs. Gerald Monson | |
| Mr. Chris Jansen | |
| Mr. and Mrs. Barry Levine | |
| Dr. Donald Gellman, D.D.S. | |
| Bruce Brown | |

2.  Whether Park Hotels would depose Dr. Collins or not would depend on whether Park Hotels and Dr. Collins were cooperating in the defense or asserting claims against each other. If the former, there would be no need to depose him; if the latter, it would be essential to do so.

3.  There are a number of individuals who may have varying degrees of light to shed on the events surrounding Shannon's injury: three police officers, two paramedics, two people who shared an elevator with Dr. Collins, and eight hotel guests from surrounding rooms. Det. Sgt. Marnell, as the police officer in charge of the scene, is a relatively high priority. The other two officers and the paramedics may or may not have anything useful to add to what Sgt. Marnell can tell us. The people in the elevator with Dr. Collins and the other hotel guests are unknown quantities. We would certainly depose Sgt. Marnell; we would probably contact the other officers, paramedics, and hotel guests informally and try to find out what, if anything, they observed, then take statements or depositions as appropriate.

4.  Since Shannon's damage claim includes amounts relating to her loss of income from employment, and since those amounts are large and, in the case of the lost clients, debatable, we assign a relatively high priority to deposing Shannon's employer. We would probably notice the deposition of the corporation and specify the subject matter rather than depose the supervisor and hope that he can tell us everything we need to know.

5.  The remaining names on our list are medical providers: doctors, hand surgeon, physical therapist, psychiatrist, etc. Certainly, we will depose any of these who are designated to testify at trial. We will, of course, have to wait until we receive the written reports.

At this point, our list of deponents appears to be Shannon, Dr. Collins, Sgt. Marnell, and Network Software Solutions, Inc. We may add hotel guests or others to the list later after we contact them informally. We will add to the list any medical experts designated to testify at trial.

| **Step 2** | *Decide Where, When, and in What Order to Schedule the Depositions* |

Scheduling the depositions in this case is somewhat complicated because the participants are not all located in one city. Obviously, Park Hotels' attorney, whose office is in Phoenix, would prefer to hold depositions at her own office to the extent possible. However, she cannot force out-of-state witnesses to come to Phoenix.

Shannon's deposition would certainly be noticed for Phoenix.

Even though Dr. Collins lives in another state, most judges will require a party to the suit to submit to deposition at least once in the state where the lawsuit is pending. In ordinary circumstances, Park Hotels' attorney would simply notice the deposition for Phoenix. However, Dr. Collins was severely injured and may not be in a condition to travel anytime soon. Therefore, if it is considered important to take the deposition immediately, it may be necessary to conduct it in Dallas.

Network Software Solutions, Inc., since it is based in the Phoenix area, is within the geographical area that is subject to the subpoena power of the District Court; see FRCP, Rules 45(b)(2) and (c)(3)(b)(3).

Sgt. Marnell is not subject to subpoena in the District of Arizona since she cannot be served within the district and Las Vegas is more than 100 miles from the place of the deposition (Phoenix); see FRCP, Rule 45(b)(2). She presents the typical out-of-state witness situation, one that occurs frequently in litigation. There are several possible solutions:

1.  Subpoena can issue from the District of Nevada and the deposition can be taken in Nevada. Of course, all of the attorneys would then need to travel to Nevada to conduct the deposition, an expensive proposition, taking into account the cost of travel and the attorney time spent sitting around in airplanes (for which attorneys routinely bill the client). Nevertheless, having the attorneys go to the witness may be the only way to get the deposition taken if the witness will not cooperate.

2.  The witness may be willing to come to the attorneys, especially if the attorneys are willing to pay the witness's expenses (as well they should be, since it is far cheaper to transport one witness than three attorneys).

3.  The deposition can be conducted telephonically if all parties agree. At present, telephonic depositions are not in widespread use, in part because of the difficulty of showing documents to the witness and in part because of the inability to see the witness and observe demeanor and body language. However, as teleconferencing technology improves, we can expect that more and more depositions will be taken in this way.

What about the order and timing of the depositions? Our own preference is usually to depose the principal opposing party first and as early as possible; we would notice Shannon's deposition immediately, for a date about 10 days in the future. Ideally, Dr. Collins would be next. As a matter of courtesy, since Dr. Collins's health is in question, we would try to cooperate with Dr. Collins's attorney in arranging his deposition. We would take Sgt. Marnell's deposition as early as it could conveniently be arranged, probably after consultation with the Las Vegas Police Department and the other attorneys in an effort to find a mutually acceptable time and place. The deposition of Network Software Solutions, Inc., can be left for later, since it relates only to the issue of damages.

## CLERICAL STEPS

In Steps 3, 4, and 5, we prepare a notice of deposition and subpoena *duces tecum*. We have selected the deposition of Network Software Solutions, Inc., for this example, since it allows us to illustrate the procedure for deposing a corporation.

### Step 3  *Notice the Deposition*

Figure W13–2 shows the notice of deposition we would prepare for our hypothetical situation.

---

**Figure W13–2   Sample Notice of Deposition**

CRANDALL, ELKINS & MAJOR
Gail Stoddard, Esq.
2000 North Central Avenue, Suite 2900
Phoenix, Arizona 85004
(602) 555-1234
Attorneys for defendant Park Hotels Group, Inc.

### IN THE UNITED STATES DISTRICT COURT
### DISTRICT OF ARIZONA

| | |
|---|---|
| SHANNON MARTIN, a single woman, ) | |
| ) | |
| ) | NO. CV98 -01456 PHX JL |
| Plaintiff, ) | |
| ) | NOTICE OF DEPOSITION |
| v. ) | |
| ) | |
| ARTHUR COLLINS and JANE DOE ) | |
| COLLINS, husband and wife; PARK ) | |
| HOTELS GROUP, INC., a Delaware corporation; ) | |
| ) | |
| Defendants. ) | |
| _____ ) | |

Notice is hereby given pursuant to Rule 30, Federal Rules of Civil Procedure, that the deposition upon oral examination of the person whose name and address appear below will be taken at date, time and place indicated.

Name of Deponent:  Network Software Solutions, Inc., by and through one or more officers, directors, or managing agents, or other persons who consent to testify on behalf of said corporation, concerning the following matters:
Terms of employment, duties, and compensation of Shannon Martin; pecuniary loss, if any, suffered by Shannon Martin as a result of suspension/termination of her employment; rights and obligations of Shannon Martin with respect to commission clients and accounts; qualifications and performance of employment duties by Shannon Martin; any communications with or from Shannon Martin from February 5, 1996, onward.

*continued*

---

**Figure W13–2   Sample Notice of Deposition,** *continued*

| | |
|---|---|
| Address of Deponent: | 6366 N. 76th St. |
| | Scottsdale, AZ |
| Date and Time: | 9:00 a.m., July 14, 2000 |
| Location: | Law Offices of Crandall, Elkins & Major |
| | 2000 North Central Avenue, Suite 2900 |
| | Phoenix, Arizona 85004 |

A subpoena *duces tecum* is being served on the person to be examined. A copy of the designation of the materials to be produced as set forth in the subpoena is attached hereto.

DATED this 21st day of June, 2000.

CRANDALL, ELKINS & MAJOR

_____

Gail Stoddard
Attorneys for defendant Park Hotels Group, Inc.

(Certificate of service goes here—see Workshop 4 for details.)

---

As required by FRCP, Rule 30(b)(1), we attach to the notice of deposition a copy of the same schedule of documents to be produced that we attach to the subpoena (see Step 5 later). The notice of deposition is served by mail or hand delivery to the offices of each of the other attorneys; see FRCP, Rule 5(b).

**Step 4**   *Take Steps Necessary to Secure Attendance of Witness*

**Step 5**   *Take Steps Necessary to Ensure Availability of Documents*

The deponent, Network Software Solutions, Inc., is not a party to the lawsuit, so the notice of deposition alone is not sufficient to compel it to attend (indeed, since it is not a party, it does not even receive a copy of the notice of deposition). We need a subpoena. The federal district courts have an approved printed-form subpoena that we can use (obtainable on many U.S. district court web sites; for instance, you can download one from the District of New Mexico web site, **www.nmcourt.fed.us/dcdocs/ courtfrms.html).** The subpoena also accomplishes Step 5. We check the third box, and attach a list of the documents to be produced.

## PLANNING AND TAKING THE TESTIMONY

**Step 6**   *Prepare a Topic Outline for Use by the Attorney Who Will Conduct the Deposition*

The deposition we have chosen for our example has a quite narrow focus: assigning a dollar amount to the losses Shannon incurred as a result of the interruption of her career. The topic outline is therefore relatively simple, much shorter than the one we would prepare for, say, Shannon's deposition.

**Outline of Topics to Cover in Deposition of Network Software Solutions, Inc.**
Preliminary questions
General description of Shannon's position and duties

> Were duties such that a broken finger would prevent her performing them
> Job performance, company's satisfaction with her work
> Expectations of continued employment/ advancement
> When, based on nature of injuries, should she have been able to return to work

Nature of Shannon's compensation arrangement

> Salary (objective: establish amount of monthly income at time of injury)
> Base amount at time of injury

Overtime
Average monthly compensation in months
   leading up to injury
Fringe benefits
   Amount/value
   Were they cut off after injury
Identify and review pay records
Commissions (objective: establish how much
   commission income she could reasonably
   expect in the time period following the injury)
   How computed
   Average amount in months leading up to
      injury
   Number of clients on which based
   Company policy re rights to retain clients
   Expected commissions in period following
      injury
   Any changes in client base or other condi-
      tions affecting commissions
   Identify and describe any documents per-
      taining to commissions

Nature/substance of any communications between
Shannon and company after injury, especially concerning:

   Circumstances of her injury (what description
   of the incident did she give her employer?)

   Her ability to perform her duties/return to
   work

Concluding questions

## Step 7   *Assist at the Deposition*

We have already described a variety of ways in
which a paralegal can assist at a deposition: keeping the documents organized, helping make sure
all topics are covered, observing witness demeanor, and watching for evasive or unresponsive
answers.

## CONCLUDING STEP

## Step 8   *Analyze and Digest Transcript*

Obviously, space does not permit us reproduce an
entire deposition transcript and summary here. We
will have to settle for a short excerpt, enough for a
single entry in the summary:

Q: As of February 1996, how long had Ms. Martin worked for Network Software Solutions?
A: About three years, give or take.
Q: As of February 1996, what was Ms. Martin's monthly income?

A: Just the base salary, you mean, or every-
   thing, including commissions?
Q: Did Ms. Martin have a base salary?
A: Yes.
Q: How much was it?
A: Sixteen hundred.
Q: Per month?
A: Right.
Q: Did she also receive commission income?
A: Yes.
Q: In addition to the base salary, or was the
   base salary like a minimum commission?
A: The commissions were in addition to the
   base salary.
Q: As of February 1996, how much was Ms.
   Martin making in commissions?
A: It varied. Around fifteen hundred, two
   thousand.
Q: How much was her commission income
   for January 1996?
A: Can I see those papers? It was $1,388.
Q: How about the months before that, say,
   October through December?
A: October, $1,732. November, $1,934. Decem-
   ber, $1,671.
Q: Did Ms. Martin receive any other income
   from the company beside base salary and
   commission?
A: No.
Q: Did she get paid for overtime?
A: No.
Q: Did she receive bonuses?
A: Christmas bonus, but those are just $100.
Q: Did Ms. Martin's duties involve any physi-
   cal labor or exertion?
A: Not really.
Q: Was there anything about Ms. Martin's du-
   ties such that a broken finger would inter-
   fere with her performing them?

Here is an excerpt from the deposition
summary:

   . . . .

p. 17, lines 4-29   Pl's income at time of incident
   was approx. $3,300 per month,
   base salary $1,600,
   commissions $1,388 to $1,934
   in four months preceding.

   . . . .

## Depositions: Learning by Doing

For this workshop, assume you are a paralegal
working under the supervision of Roger Yarborough, attorney for defendant Collins. Assume the

lawsuit, *Martin v. Collins,* is pending in the U.S. district court having jurisdiction in your locality, and that Mr. Yarborough practices in your city. Assume Shannon lives and is employed in your city, and all other witnesses are located as indicated in the workshops where they appear. Mr. Yarborough assigns you to do the following exercises.

## EXERCISES

In carrying out this assignment, you should follow the step-by-step formula described in this workshop.

1. Following the instructions in Step 1,
   a. Make a comprehensive list of the names of every person who might conceivably be deposed, showing the role or relationship of each in the case. As sources of names, refer to the factual information about the Shannon's Ordeal hypo described elsewhere in this text, in particular, that contained in the example disclosure statement and in the Learning by Doing exercises from Workshop 12.
   b. Draft a short memo to your supervising attorney stating which witnesses you would depose and why. In the memo, also indicate

for each of the remaining names (or groups of names, where they have similar roles) why you chose not to depose them.

2. Assume that the FRCP, Rule 16(b), scheduling conference was held on the Friday immediately preceding your receiving this assignment. Following the instructions given in Step 2, add to your memo the dates, times, and places at which you propose that the depositions you are calling for should be held.

3. Your instructor will choose one deposition for which you are to do the following:
   a. Following the instructions in Step 3, prepare a notice of deposition.
   b. Following the instructions in Steps 4 and 5, prepare a subpoena *duces tecum.*
   c. Following the instructions in Step 6, prepare an outline of topics to be covered.

4. If possible, at your instructor's option, arrange to sit in on and observe a deposition.

5. Obtain a transcript of a deposition (or, at your instructor's option, he or she will provide one) and prepare a deposition summary following the instructions given in Step 8.

# PRACTICE POINTERS
## *Summarizing Depositions*

A number of different formats can be used for summarizing depositions. Because only one of those formats is discussed in this workshop, some alternative formats are presented here in Figures W13–3 through W13–7. Most importantly, however, remember that you should consult with your supervising attorney to find out which format to use. Format preference in not only a matter of personal choice but is dependent on the purpose for which the summary is being prepared. Therefore, you should be familiar with a variety of formats so that you have the flexibility necessary to work with different attorneys under different conditions.

A narrative summary (Figure W13–3) is merely a summation of the testimony but cannot be used as a reference tool because it does not refer to specific pages and line numbers in the deposition. It is used to summarize the testimony of minor witnesses or as an adjunct to other more complete summations.

Testimony can also be summarized by subject matter (Figures W13–4 and W13–5). This method requires more time to complete and is especially helpful when the deposition is lengthy and complex. The beauty of this approach is that it can greatly assist an attorney attempting to impeach a witness at trial because the attorney can zoom into a specific subject very efficiently.

In complex cases it is helpful to prepare an index, listing the main subjects by page number (Figure W13–6). This index can also be used by itself as a summary or to assist in accessing the more detailed summaries described earlier.

# PRACTICE POINTERS
## *Summarizing Depositions* continued

To help track the deposition process, consider preparing a deposition table (Figure W13–7). This table records the names of the deponents, the time and location of their deposition, the names and phone numbers of the court reporters, whether a transcript was received, and the status of the deposition summary. Such a table enables you to see at a glance the status of each deposition and allows you to easily contact the appropriate reporter without going through the files.

---

**Figure W13–3    Deposition of Arresting Officer Flanigan**

3/24/99

Circumstances of Arrest: Flanigan arrived at the hotel in response to call from Pl. No one from Hotel called police.

Observations at Scene: Immediately saw that Pl. was highly agitated, dressed in pajamas, and insisting that officer arrest D2. Observed no signs on injury except to finger.

Actions Taken: After talking with Pl., D2, and rep. from Hotel, decided to arrest Pl. on weapons and assault charges. Took Pl. to station for booking.

---

**Figure W13–4    Deposition of Treating Physician Sayers**

4/1/99

| ASSESSMENT OF MENTAL CONDITION: | PAGE | LINES |
|---|---|---|
| Initial exam: Pl. was highly reactive and Dr. found it difficult to talk with her. She pieced together story of assault but found it hard to keep Pl. focused on chronology. | 4 | 1–19 |
| Tests ordered: Ordered std. battery of psy. tests to be done immediately. Also arranged to have blood drawn. | 9 | 10–22 |
| Follow-up exam one week later: Found Pl. calmer and easier to relate to. Still had difficulty relating story of assault. Having insomnia and panic attacks. | 6<br>14 | 6–15<br>2–20 |
| Prescriptions ordered: Zoloft during day; Xanax when needed for insomnia. | 8 | 16–24 |

---

**Figure W13–5    Deposition of Examining Physician Sayers**

4/1/99

| PAGE | TESTIMONY |
|---|---|
| 2 | Witness: Ellen Sayers resides at 2020 E. Central, Tempe. Explanation of depo procedure. |

**Figure W13–5    Deposition of Examining Physician Sayers,** *continued*

| PAGE | TESTIMONY |
|---|---|
| 3 | Educational Background: B.S. Chemistry—1973 from ASU; M.D.—1980 from UofA; residency at Good Samaritan Hosp. in Tucson |
| 4 | Initial exam of Pl. showed Pl. was highly agitated and difficult to talk to. Pieced together story of assault but had hard time focusing Pl. on chronology of events. Did cursory physical exam and observed no external signs of injury. |
| 5 | Dr's initial assessment of Pl. was that she was suffering from type of post-traumatic stress disorder. Defined this disorder. |
| 6 | Conducted follow-up exam of Pl. one week later. Found Pl. to be calmer and easier to relate to. Described sequence of events in this exam. |

(Alternatively, this summary can be further defined using line numbers as well.)

| PAGE | LINES | TESTIMONY |
|---|---|---|
| 4 | 1–10 | Initial exam of Pl. showed Pl. was highly agitated and difficult to talk to. |
|  | 11–16 | Pieced together story of assault but had hard time focusing Pl. on chronology of events. |
|  | 17–21 | Did cursory physical exam and observed no external signs of injury. |

**Figure W13–6    Index to Deposition of Plaintiff**

| SUBJECT | PAGES |
|---|---|
| Assault | |
|     At moment of entry | 17, 19–20 |
|     Before entry | 16, 18 |
|     Contact with Collins | 17, 21–23 |
|     During Collins's undressing | 24–29 |
| Injuries | |
|     Finger | 4, 7, 31, 36, 40 |
|     Head | 4, 8, 32 |
|     Insomnia | 5, 7, 32–33 |
|     Panic disorder | 31, 34–36 |
|     Shock | 4, 22, 36–37 |
| Treatment | |
|     Emergency room | 40–41, 44 |
|     General physician | 44, 46 |
|     Psychiatrist | 45, 47, 48–50 |
| Work History | |
|     Sales manager | 9, 12, 15 |
|     Sales rep | 4, 6, 20, 28 |
|     Training | 10, 12 |

**Figure W13–7  Deposition Table**

| DEPONENT | TIME | PLACE | COURT REPORTER | TRANS REC'D | SUMMARIZED |
|---|---|---|---|---|---|
| Dr. Sayers | 4/1/99 1:00 pm | St. Luke's Hospital | Ginny Bush 945-6670 | no | no |
| Dr. Collins | 2/2/99 8:00 am | Our office | Sammy Smith 966-4312 | yes | yes |
| Officer Flanigan | 3/24/99 9:00 am | DPS Office | Craig Monroe 465-9911 | yes | no |
| Det. Marnell | 3/27/99 3:00 pm | DPS Office | Craig Monroe 465-9911 | yes | yes |

## TECHNO TIP

In many firms that do a lot of litigation, specialized software is used to help manage documents and data obtained in discovery, including depositions. One company that has won widespread acceptance of its product is Summation Legal Technologies, Inc. If you visit its site at www.summation. com you can obtain a CD providing an extensive demonstration of its database manipulation skills. Information on its various products, including deposition summaries, is available online along with demonstrations of some of its products.

## FORMS FILE

*Include samples of the following in your forms file:*
• *Notice of deposition*
• *Subpoena duces tecum*
• *Deposition summary (try to get several different types)*

## KEY TERMS

Deposing
Notice of deposition

Noticing a deposition

Witness statement

# Introduction to the Motion Practice Workshops

In a typical lawsuit, the judge must make a number of decisions as the case progresses. As a general rule, the judge is *not* the one who determines *which* decisions need to be made—it is up to the attorneys to select the appropriate issues and submit them to the judge for decision.

The attorneys do this by presenting motions. A *motion* is a formal request to the court for an order. An *order* is an official pronouncement by the judge. It may, as the word *order* implies, require someone to do something. More commonly, an order may merely recite a decision that the judge has made.

To be effective in using motions to advance our cases, we need to develop three main skills:

*1.* We must know how to present our motion in a manner that complies with the rules.

*2.* We must be able to identify the right things to ask for. That is, we must be able to recognize the situations in which a particular motion may advance our case.

*3.* We must be able to construct logically compelling arguments, backed by citation of legal authority, sufficient to convince the judge to rule in our favor.

We begin our study of motions with Workshop 14, on how to construct and present a generic motion. With motions, most of the challenge involves the content, not the packaging. In general, the mechanics of motion procedure are not particularly complicated, and, subject to minor variations, are the same for motions of all kinds. Once we have mastered the basic step-by-step process for writing and presenting a simple motion as outlined in Workshop 14, it will be easy to adapt it to more complex situations.

We introduce the more difficult subject of what motions to make and when to make them in Workshops 15 and 16. This is not an easy subject to encapsulate into a few short chapters. The universe of possible motions to make is a large one (see the table that follows), and the strategic decisions required call for a level of judgment that comes only with experience.

Rather than attempt to cover the entire spectrum of motion practice, which we could do only superficially, if at all, we have chosen to focus on two specific subject areas that together account for per-

haps a majority of the motions filed: discovery motions and early-stage defensive motions.

Discovery enforcement, the subject of Workshop 15, provides a convenient point of departure because it allows us to explore motions procedure and strategy in the context of a subject—discovery—whose rules are already familiar. Also, the situations calling for discovery motions are relatively easy to identify, making this a good area in which to begin developing the skill of recognizing when a particular motion is called for.

The theme of Workshop 16 is the process of refinement that takes place as a lawsuit moves from the pleading stage toward trial. Some of the claims and defenses asserted in the complaint and answer will turn out to be incorrectly stated, unprovable, or otherwise flawed. The procedural posture of the case may be incorrect, due to errors or unforeseen circumstances. There may be disputes over admissibility of evidence, scheduling, procedural requirements, or other administrative matters. By the time the trial date arrives, all of the defective claims and defenses need to be weeded out, and all of the disputed issues that can be decided beforehand need to be decided, so that the trial can proceed smoothly and efficiently. It is by the use of motions of various kinds that we accomplish these things.

So as to keep the discussion within manageable bounds, and to illustrate the thought process underlying motion strategy, we have chosen to focus our main attention in Workshop 16 on the motions available to a defense attorney in the early stages of a lawsuit. We will also bring in via sidebars a few other common motion types that do not fit perfectly within that main theme but that are important enough to deserve some mention.

## WHAT KINDS OF MOTIONS ARE THERE, ANYWAY?

Suppose we decided to spend an afternoon in the records room at the courthouse, going through case files and jotting down the titles of all the motions. What would we find? Which motions would we find most often? Here is our take on a Top Ten list (well, okay, a few more than ten), not in any particular order, although motions to compel and motions for summary judgment probably deserve the No. 1 and

No. 2 positions.[1] Please note that the descriptions are greatly oversimplified due to space limitations—see the workshops for details. Note also that the table by no means encompasses all of the motions that can be made in civil cases—only those seen most frequently.

| MOTION TYPE | DESCRIPTION | BASIS |
|---|---|---|
| **Discovery Motions** | | |
| Motion to compel | Asks the judge to order another party to respond to a discovery request. Made when a party refuses to respond or, more often, makes a response that is evasive or incomplete. (Covered in Workshop 15.) | Rule 37 |
| Motion for sanctions | Asks the judge to punish a party who has failed to comply with an order to respond to discovery. Typically, the party seeking discovery first files a motion to compel; if the responding party still does not respond properly to the discovery request even after losing a motion to compel, the next step is a motion for sanctions. (Covered in Workshop 15.) | Rule 37 |
| Motion for protective order | Asks the judge to rule that a discovery request is improper, and that the responding party or witness need not comply with it. Made when a party is attempting to obtain discovery to which he is not entitled. (Discussed in Workshop 15.) | Rule 26(c) |
| **Substantive Motions Addressed to the Claims and Defenses** | | |
| Motion to dismiss | Asks the judge to dismiss one or more claims (or the entire lawsuit). Usually made when a required element of a claim is left out of the complaint. Can also be made when there are certain procedural defects in plaintiff's case (i.e., lack of jurisdiction). (Covered in Workshop 16.) | Rule 12(b) |
| Motion to strike | Asks the judge to strike a defense from the defendant's answer. Can be thought of as like motion to dismiss, except that it challenges defendant's defenses instead of plaintiff's claims. Sometimes made when defendant has failed to plead a defense correctly. (Discussed in Workshop 16.) | Rule 12(f) |
| Motion for summary judgment | Asks the judge to enter judgment for or against one or more claims, without a trial. To succeed, the moving party must persuade the judge that the evidence is so clear that there is no genuine issue of material fact. (Covered in Workshop 16.) | Rule 56 |
| **Other Miscellaneous Motions** | | |
| Motion for leave to amend complaint or answer | Asks for permission to file an amended complaint or answer. Under FRCP, Rule 15, judges are to be liberal in allowing amendments. Made when a party becomes aware | Rule 15 |

[1]The list is based strictly on the authors' experience. The authors are not aware of any available sources of statistics on the frequency of motions by type in federal civil cases. But see *teddy.law.cornell.edu:8090/questata.htm* for a searchable database of general statistics on lawsuits, from which are derived some of the conclusions stated in the table.

| MOTION TYPE | DESCRIPTION | BASIS |
|---|---|---|
| | of a mistake in a pleading, or wishes to add a party or a claim or defense. (Discussed in Workshop 14.) | Rule 12(e) |
| Motion for a more definite statement | Asks the judge to order the plaintiff to make the allegations of the complaint more specific. Usually made in cases involving fraud claims, which, under Rule 9(b), must be "stated with particularity" in the complaint. | |
| Motion in limine | Asks the judge to make an advance ruling about admissibility of evidence. Made when it appears that an opposing party will try to put a particular piece of evidence before the jury that is inadmissible, and even the attempt to do so may plant improper ideas in the minds of the jurors. | Judge's inherent power to make evidentiary rulings |
| Motion to continue (and similar scheduling motions) | Asks the judge to postpone the trial date or some other deadline. | Rule 40 and local rules |
| Motion for pretrial conference | Asks the judge to schedule a pretrial conference, usually for the purpose of making a ruling on some disputed procedural issue or for scheduling and setting deadlines. Of declining usefulness in federal court, since most federal judges schedule status conferences frequently without being asked. | Rule 16 |
| Motion to set attorneys' fees | Asks the judge to set the amount of attorneys' fees to be awarded to the successful party in lawsuits where allowed (class actions, contract cases, certain cases involving statutory claims such as securities fraud). | Local rules |
| Motion for new trial | Asks the judge to set aside a jury verdict and order a new trial. Made routinely by the losing party at trial; granted if the judge believes that an error has occurred that will cause the appellate court to remand for a new trial anyway. | Rule 59 |
| Motion for judgment notwithstanding the verdict | Asks the judge not only to set aside the jury verdict but also to enter judgment in favor of the losing party. To grant, judge must find that the jury verdict was clearly wrong. | Rule 50 |
| Motion for relief from judgment | Asks the judge to set aside a judgment after it has already been entered. Granted only in situations where it would be seriously unjust to let the judgment stand (i.e., when a judgment is obtained by defrauding the court). | Rule 60 |

*Other Miscellaneous Motions* continued

## INTRODUCTION: SIGNIFICANCE OF MOTION PRACTICE

Motions comprise a significant part of the workload of a litigator or litigation paralegal. According to a study of the approximately 250,000 civil cases filed in federal courts in one recent year, barely 7,000—roughly 3 percent—actually went to trial. Approximately 40,000, nearly six times as many, were disposed of by motions of various kinds. Add in the unsuccessful motions to dismiss and motions for summary judgment made in all the other cases, and all of the discovery motions and procedural motions, and it is easy to see why a litigation paralegal can expect to spend plenty of time writing and responding to motions.

The skills you will learn in this workshop are enough, if mastered, to allow you to carry out the motion-related assignments typically given to beginning litigation paralegals. No one expects a new paralegal—or for that matter, a beginning attorney—to be able to analyze a case file and develop a motion strategy without assistance from someone with more experience. If you are given a motion-writing assignment, your supervising attorney will tell you what kind of motion is called for and, in general terms, what the supporting argument is to be. Your task will consist of gathering the necessary information and supporting documents, pulling them together into a finished set of motion papers that complies with the rules of procedure, and, perhaps, taking the clerical steps necessary to put the motion before the court to be decided. That is the task that this workshop addresses.

## WHAT IS A MOTION PRACTICE?

Before we begin exploring the fine points of motions procedure, it will be helpful to have a general picture of what is involved. For purposes of this workshop, a motion is a written request for an order or ruling by the judge. We will not concern ourselves with motions made during trial, which may not always be in writing. The motion is a court paper, having a caption and complying with the other applicable format rules. (In some courts, the written filing is called a **notice of motion.**) The party making the motion is called the **moving party,** or the **movant;** the party who is opposing the motion is called the **responding party,** or **respondent.** Included in the motion, or accompanying it, is a *memorandum* (also

sometimes called a brief) expounding in detail the moving party's argument. The moving party files the motion, memorandum, and any other required supporting documents with the clerk of the court, and serves a copy on each of the other parties to the suit. Within a prescribed time period, the responding party may file and serve a written response. It, too, is accompanied by a memorandum presenting the responding party's reasons why the judge should deny the motion, and countering the arguments made in the moving party's memorandum. The moving party is then given a short time in which to file and serve a written reply, with a memorandum answering the arguments made in the response. The documents filed by a party in connection with a motion are sometimes referred to generically as the party's motion papers.

After the motion, response, and reply have all been filed, there may be a hearing at which the judge hears oral argument—oral presentations by the attorneys in which they debate their positions before the judge. In many courts, however, the judge may decide the motion based on the memoranda alone, without a hearing. After considering the arguments on both sides, the judge may take the matter under advisement—that is, think about it for a period before rendering a decision. When the judge does decide, the parties are notified of the decision by minute entry.

> *Your Local Notes*
>
> _____
>
> _____

## WHAT RULES GOVERN MOTION WRITING?

It goes without saying that, when we present a motion, we must follow the prescribed procedure. But what *is* the prescribed procedure, and where can we find it? In federal court, the starting point is FRCP, Rule 7(b), which provides:

> (1) An application to the court for an order shall be by motion which, unless made during a hearing or trial, shall be made in writing, shall state with particularity the grounds therefor, and shall set forth the relief or order sought. . . .

(2) The rules applicable to captions and other matter of form of pleadings apply to all motions. . . .

(3) All motions shall be signed in accordance with Rule 11.

Somewhat cryptic though it may seem, FRCP, Rule 7(b), gives us several clues to the required format and content of a motion. A motion must:

- Be in writing;
- Have a caption and, by implication, follow the other format rules for filed court papers (see Workshop 4);
- Be signed by the attorney making the motion;
- State what it is that we are asking the judge to do ("set forth the relief or order sought"); and
- State why the judge should do it ("state with particularity the grounds therefor").

Obviously, there must be more to the formalities of motion writing than that—where are the *rest* of the instructions? Some come from local rules, which often specify format, layout, organization, page limitations, and the like. Others arise from rules governing specific motion types. For example, FRCP, Rule 56, expands on the procedure for motions for summary judgment. Many of the established conventions of motion practice have never been reduced to written rules at all. Instead, they have arisen from custom and usage. And, of course, we have already studied the rules that dictate the format and layout of court papers in general (see Workshop 4); these apply to motions just as they do to any other filed court paper.

## THE DETAILS ARE IN THE LOCAL RULES

A number of technical issues arise in connection with the filing and presentation of a motion, about which FRCP, Rule 7(b), is utterly silent (or at least awfully quiet). Each U.S. district court specifies the details of its motions procedure via local rules. (Most U.S. district courts have web sites on which current local rules are posted; links to the various districts may be found at the main federal judiciary web site, **www.uscourts.gov/allinks.html**.) In most districts, the local rules add to the barebones requirements of FRCP, Rule 7(b), in at least the following ways:

- *By requiring a memorandum of points and authorities.* FRCP, Rule 7(b), tells us that we must "state the grounds" for the motion, but does not specify how or where to do so. Local rules provide more specific guidance.

**Example:** "[A]ll motions and oppositions thereto shall be supported by a memorandum of law, setting forth the points and authorities relied upon in support of or in opposition to the motion, and divided, under appropriate headings, into as many parts as there are points to be determined." (*Source:* Local Rule 7.1, Southern District of New York.)

- *By specifying how the motion is to be heard and decided.* Some courts schedule hearings automatically when motions are filed, and notify all parties by minute entry or otherwise. Others require the moving party to obtain a hearing date, or to select a schedule "law and motions day" from the court's public calendar, and serve a notice of hearing or notice of motion on other parties. And an increasing number of district courts decide motions on the basis of the memoranda alone; there is no hearing unless the judge asks for one.

**Example:** "Motions in civil cases shall be submitted and determined upon the memoranda without oral argument. The court may in its discretion order oral argument on any motion." (*Source:* Local Rule 78-40.2, Eastern District of Missouri.)

- *By specifying time limits for response and reply.* In some districts, a response is due a mere 5 days after the motion is served; others allow as much as 30 days. Many judges enforce time limits strictly, and rule on motions summarily (usually in favor of the moving party) if the response date arrives and no response has been filed.

**Example:** "A response and brief to an opposed motion must be filed within twenty days from the date the motion is filed. . . . Unless otherwise directed by the presiding judge, a party who has filed an opposed motion may file a reply brief within fifteen days from the date the response is filed." (*Source:* Local Rule 7.1, Northern District of Texas.)

- *By specifying page limits.* Most district courts disallow memoranda exceeding a specified number of pages. Pay close attention to these limits. In some courts, the clerk will not even accept for filing a motion that exceeds the allowed number of pages.

**Example:** "Except upon good cause shown and leave given by the court, all briefs in support of a motion or in response to a motion are limited in length to 20 pages; the movant's reply brief may not exceed 10 pages." (*Source:* Local Rule 7.4, Middle District of Georgia.)

Other local rules provisions less widely embraced include these:

- Requiring a moving party to confer with the opposing party and attempt to reach an agreement before filing a motion [see, e.g., Local Rule 7.1(d), Western District of Michigan];

- Requiring both the moving party and the responding party to submit a proposed order for the judge to sign when the motion is decided, reflecting the desired outcome [see, e.g., Local Rule 7.1(c), Northern District of Texas];

- Allowing the clerk to grant short extensions, giving additional time in which to file a response or reply (see, e.g., Local Rule 6.2, Middle District of Georgia); and

- Requiring submission of supporting documents, especially any evidentiary documents with which the motion is concerned [see, e.g., Local Rule 7.1(d), Northern District of Iowa].

*Your Local Notes*

_____

_____

## Writing a Motion: Step-by-Step Instructions

Now that we have covered the basic ground rules, let us see how to put together a simple motion filing. In this workshop, we do not concern ourselves with the strategic questions of *whether* to make a motion or of *what* motion to make. (We leave those questions for Workshops 15 and 16.) We instead assume that our supervising attorney has given us a specific assignment and our job is to write the assigned motion and get it filed.

### DRAFTING STEPS

It is convenient to think of a motion filing as comprising three pieces: (1) the motion proper, a short, formal statement of what we are asking for; (2) the memorandum, typically a longer document in which we lay out our argument; and (3) the attachments, consisting of any supporting papers that we are required to submit with the motion.

The exact way in which these pieces are assembled varies somewhat from one jurisdiction to another, and it is worthwhile to respect local cus-

tom unless there is some good reason to deviate from it. The layout and organization portrayed in Steps 1 through 3 is typical of that used in many courts; we will point out common variations as appropriate. Your instructor will help you unravel the particular rules and customs of your locality; as always, it is worthwhile to obtain sample motions written by local practitioners and imitate them.

*Your Local Notes*

_____

_____

**Step 1**    *Draft the Motion*

The motion proper is a document in the form of a court paper; it has a caption, a title, and complies with the format rules. In its most common form, the motion is a separate document from the memorandum, although some practitioners in some jurisdictions combine the two into a single document. The purpose of the motion is to tell the judge *what* we are asking for; the purpose of the memorandum is to tell the judge *why* he should grant our request.

The title appearing in the caption should begin with the word "Motion" and encapsulate in a few words the general type of ruling that we are asking for. Most of the motions that we file will fall into one of the recognized categories (see the table in the Introduction to the Motion Practice Workshops); if so, we do not make up our own title, but stick to the accepted wording (i.e., "Motion to Compel," not "Motion for Order Requiring Defendant to Answer Interrogatories").

The body of the motion (the motion, not the memorandum) consists of two paragraphs stating who is making the motion, what the motion is asking for, what rule the motion arises under, and what other documents support the motion.

> **Example:**
> [caption]
> Defendant respectfully moves pursuant to Rule 12(b)(6), Federal Rules of Civil Procedure, for an order of the Court dismissing Count II of plaintiff's complaint.
> This motion is based upon the accompanying memorandum of points and authorities.
> [date and signature lines]

(In a jurisdiction in which the filed document is a notice of motion instead of the motion itself, the wording is slightly different. Also, some district courts require a recitation that counsel have attempted to resolve the issue raised by the motion—see sidebar on Confer before Filing. Your instructor will inform you of the motion boilerplate customarily used in the courts of your locality.)

---

*Your Local Notes*

_____

_____

---

How the motion body and the memorandum relate to each other varies considerably according to the customs of each jurisdiction. In what is perhaps the most common permutation (and the one we will follow), the motion and memorandum are each complete, separate, self-contained court papers, each with its own caption, signature line, and certificate of mailing. In some jurisdictions, the preferred practice is to combine the motion and memorandum in a single document, with a single caption and certificate of mailing (but perhaps with separate signature lines for the motion and memorandum). In still others, the motion and memorandum are combined but a separate notice of motion is required. Unfortunately, local rules rarely cover layout details of this kind—other practitioners' motions are the best source of guidance.

### Step 2    *Draft the Memorandum*

In federal court, the memorandum is the key to a successful motion. Even in districts that routinely allow oral argument on motions—which are becoming fewer and fewer—most federal judges do read the motion papers, and often have their law clerks analyze the memoranda and recommend a ruling, all in advance of the hearing. By the time the hearing is held, the judge's mind is made up, or nearly so. (State court practice may differ, and oral argument may take on much greater relative importance. State court judges often have punishingly large caseloads, rarely have law clerks, and do not always have time to read motions in advance of oral argument.)

**Writing to Persuade**—Our goal in writing a memorandum is to convince the judge to do something—usually something that our opponent will not like. Everything about a memorandum—style, layout, format, choice of words, and especially organization and content of argument—must be de-

## SIDEBAR

## Confer before Filing

*A growing number of federal district courts have adopted local rules requiring a litigant to confer with her opponent before filing a motion. District of Oregon Local Rule 7.1 is typical:*

*(1)  The first paragraph of every motion must certify that: (A) The parties made a good faith effort through personal or telephone conferences to resolve the dispute, and have been unable to do so; or (B) The opposing party willfully refused to confer.*

*(2)  The court may deny any motion that fails to meet this certification requirement.*

*Confer before filing rules originated as a mechanism for reducing the glut of discovery motions clogging the courts. The theory is that the attorneys ought to be able to reach reasonable compromises on many issues instead of involving the judge in routine procedural disputes. Skeptics may doubt whether many motions are avoided by such rules; more often than not, in the authors' experience, their effect is merely to add another hoop for the moving party to jump through, delaying resolution. Nevertheless, the trend is in the direction of broader adoption of confer before filing rules, so we as litigators and litigation paralegals must take care to comply with them.*

signed around the central goal of persuading the judge to rule our way.

How can we make our motions more persuasive? Here are a few tips:

■ Concentrate mainly on fairness, not legalities. Arguments citing endless legal authorities, aimed at showing through laborious logical gymnastics that "the law" requires the result that we want, are rarely enough. The opposing party can always (well, almost always) find legal authorities contrary to ours. If we can convince the judge that ruling our way is the *right* thing to do, and provide at least enough legal authority on which to hang a decision in our favor, we will win. If the judge concludes that ruling the way we want would be the wrong thing to do, we will lose, regardless of how logically compelling our arguments may be.

■ Nevertheless, research the law thoroughly. If our opponent is able to cite controlling case law or statutes contrary to our position, and we have not discussed them or explained why they do not entitle our opponent to win, we suffer a serious loss of credibility. Further, if the judge concludes that considerations of fairness favor neither side, the winner is likely to be the party with the weight of legal authority on his side.

■ Concentrate on advancing our own argument, not on responding to the opposing party's argument. This does not mean that we ignore the opposing party's arguments—of course, we must respond to them and explain why they do not prevent the judge from doing what we want. But our main focus should be on the positives of our own position, not the negatives of our opponent's.

■ Organize the argument in such a way that the judge can find and grasp our main points quickly. The amount of time that a judge can spend reading each motion or response is limited. We do not want the judge to spend that time trying to figure out what we meant to say. A short, accurate summary of the main points at the beginning, and descriptive, well-organized headings and subheadings will help the judge zero in on the issues quickly.

■ Write in a style that is clear, direct, professional, and to the point. As a rule, avoid literary writing, colloquialisms, and any other stylistic mannerisms that may divert the reader's attention from the argument being made.

■ Keep it short. A motion is not a textbook on whatever branch of the law the motion is concerned with. A single citation of a controlling case that is directly on point is more persuasive than pages of string cites (successive chain of case citations).

■ Be meticulous about supporting every assertion with evidence and legal authority. Take nothing for granted. See sidebar on Backing Up What We Say.

■ Never engage in personal attacks on opponents. Tempting though it may sometimes be to portray opposing counsel as an unprincipled villain, doing so will, at a minimum, distract attention from our real arguments, and may also annoy the judge.

**Organizing the Memorandum**—In most courts, the rules do not specify how a motion or memorandum is to be organized. The sequence of argument, the division into sections, the use and layout of headings and subheadings—all of these are left to

the discretion of the writer. Therefore, there is no such thing as the "right" way to organize a memorandum; there are many acceptable styles. In the discussion to follow, we present our own preferred layout; in your class discussion, your instructor may disagree with some of our preferences, or suggest modifications based on local custom.

---

*Your Local Notes*

_____

_____

---

Whatever the style and organization chosen, the argument should be broken into logical subtopics under appropriate headings. (In some courts, the local rules specifically require this.) Each heading should express a complete idea and encapsulate the point of the section they accompany. The goal is not merely to convey the topic of the section, but, if possible, the desired conclusion and the reason for it. To accomplish this, of course, our headings will need to be sentence length, not merely one or two words. Ideally, a reader should be able to understand the thrust of our argument by reading the headings alone.

Here are a few examples to clarify what we mean. Assume we represent defendant Park Hotels Group in our hypothetical lawsuit *Martin v. Collins,* and we have just written a section of a memorandum in which we attack the causation issue, arguing that the hotel did not cause Shannon's injuries. What would be a suitable heading?

| | |
|---|---|
| **How not to do it:** | B. *Causation* |
| **Better:** | B. *Defendant Did Not Cause Plaintiff's Injuries* |
| **Better yet:** | B. *It Was Defendant Collins, Not Park Hotels, Who Broke Plaintiff's Finger* |

**Parts of a Memorandum**—Our suggested basic memorandum format comprises four main parts as follows:

*1. Summary of Argument.* If the judge sees only one thing in our memorandum, it will likely be whatever is on the first page below the caption—that is the prime real estate in a memorandum. Therefore, our preferred layout begins with a section entitled "Summary of Argument" in which we lay out the main points of our argument in a few short, simple, easy-to-grasp sentences. Ideally, the judge should be able to skim our Summary of Argument section in less than a minute, and come away with a reasonable understanding of the argument we are making in the memorandum. (Although it begins the memorandum, we usually prefer to write this section last, when we have the details of our argument more clearly in mind.)

2. *Factual background.* Never assume that the judge is familiar with the facts of the case. Judges are often responsible for hundreds of cases, and cannot possibly remember even the broad outlines of each one, let alone the details. If there are any facts about our case that the judge needs to know in order to understand our motion, it is up to us to supply them. Usually, this should be done in a separate section at the beginning of the memorandum, before we get into the legal arguments.

The factual background section should begin with a heading that conveys the main factual point we are trying to make. If the required facts are not simple enough to be expressed in a page or less, the factual background section should be broken up into subsections each with its own heading.

Factual statements must be supported by evidence; this is done by quoting from deposition transcripts and/or by attaching affidavits and other supporting documents (see Step 3 later and also the sidebar on Backing Up What We Say).

In some jurisdictions, local rules also require a separate statement of facts to accompany some motions (such as motions for summary judgment). The separate statement of facts is typically a separate document, with its own caption. It lists the factual assertions on which the motion depends in a series of short, numbered paragraphs, citing the source or support for each. The separate statement of facts is not the same as the factual background section of the memorandum, and the memorandum still needs to have its own discussion of factual background. The separate statement of facts merely lists each fact in a sterile fashion, without attempting to relate one fact to another or to draw conclusions or inferences from them. In the factual background section of the memorandum, we try to weave the facts into a compelling story, one that will help sway the judge to rule our way.

3. *Argument.* The argument section is the main part of the memorandum and usually the largest. Its organization depends on the issues being addressed; we organize the argument in whatever way expresses our point most convincingly. Absent good reasons to choose some other strategy, we would usually follow a loose outline format. We begin with a short section in which we state the conclusion and summarize the main points supporting it in a few sentences. Then follow a series of subsections, one for each main point, in which we explain each of the main points in detail. If any of the main points is complex, we may apply the same outline strategy again. That is, we begin the subsection with a short summary of the arguments supporting the main point, and follow with subsubsections detailing each one.

4. *Conclusion.* We end the memorandum with a short conclusion, in which we again state the main proposition that we are arguing for, and again briefly summarize the main points supporting it. You may reasonably wonder, are we not repeating ourselves overly much?

Repeating ourselves, yes; overly much, no. It is true that by the time we get to the end of the memorandum we will have stated our conclusion and main points at least three times. In part, this follows a well-known truism of advocacy: "Tell them what you're going to tell them; then tell them what you're telling them; then tell them what you told them." In part, the repetition merely concedes the reality: we can never assume that the judge will read the entire memorandum, so we must do everything possible to improve the odds that at least the main points will get across.

**Rechecking, Revising, Rewriting**—Having written the memorandum, are we done? By no means. Advocative writing in litigation is unlike any other kind of writing, in that there is an opposing party who is highly motivated to take apart what we wrote and call attention to every flaw. Therefore, before declaring the job done, we attack our own memorandum in the same way that our opponent will, looking for weaknesses and mistakes.

We double-check every fact. We proofread all quotes for accuracy. We check the citations, and Shepardize, KeyCite, or otherwise verify that none of the cases we have cited has been overruled. We check the Summary of Argument section with a fresh eye, to be sure that it is clear, logical, and as short and concise as possible. We go through the entire memorandum editing, revising, rewriting, eliminating unnecessary verbiage, and rewording awkward passages. There is no such thing as good writing—only good rewriting.

## SIDEBAR

### Backing Up What We Say

*An argument consists of a series of statements that we hope leads to a logical conclusion. For the conclusion to be believable, all of the statements on which it is based must be true.*

*A memorandum in support of a motion is a written argument. The validity of the conclusion—that the judge should make the ruling that we are asking for—depends on the reliability of the statements or assertions leading to it. In a legal argument, the supporting assertions are of two main kinds: (1) statements of fact—that is, statements describing some situation or event; and (2) statements of legal principles—statements whose purpose is to establish the legal rules applicable to the situation.*

*The judge will not take our word for it that the statements we make in an argument are true. It is up to us to back up everything we say. Each factual assertion we make in our memorandum must be supported with evidence. Testimony of a witness (an affidavit or excerpt from a deposition) is evidence; documents can be evidence (but we will still need testimony of a witness to establish the genuineness and admissibility of the documents). Usually, we submit copies of the evidence needed to support our factual*

*assertions as attachments to the memorandum. (See Step 3 of this workshop.) Suppose, for example, we are arguing that Dr. Collins committed battery against Shannon and we want to establish the element of "harmful or offensive contact" by referring to Shannon's broken finger. It is not enough merely to state in our argument that Dr. Collins broke Shannon's finger; we must provide evidence that he did so. An affidavit signed by Shannon stating that he did so would suffice.*

*Whenever we assert a legal rule, we must include a citation to authority; that is, we must tell the reader where to go to verify that the rule is what we say it is. For example, if we argue that a cause of action for battery requires proof of "harmful or offensive contact," we must tell the reader where to find some authoritative source that says so. We might give the citation of a case decided by an appellate court in which the elements of battery are stated, or, if our jurisdiction accepts the Restatement as authority, we might cite Section 21 of the Restatement 2d, Torts. (For a full exploration of the various sources that can be used as authority in a legal argument, consult a course or textbook on legal research and writing.)*

---

### Step 3    *Assemble the Attachments*

Whether a motion requires attachments, and what attachments are required, depends on the type of motion and, to some extent, on the local rules. It is also sometimes advantageous to attach documents to a motion even if the applicable rules do not require it—if there is some document that will make our presentation more convincing, certainly we should attach a copy.

What kinds of documents might we consider including as attachments to a motion? What kinds of attachments are required? Here is a typical local rule (from Local Rule CV-7, Eastern District of Texas):

> When allegations of fact not appearing in the record are relied upon in support of a motion, all affidavits and other pertinent documents shall be served and filed with the motion.
> . . . When discovery or disclosure documents or portions thereof are needed in

support of a motion, those portions of the discovery or disclosure which are relevant to the motion shall be submitted with the motion and attached thereto as exhibits.

Here are some examples of documents that may be submitted as attachments to motions where appropriate:

- *Copies of answers to interrogatories, responses to requests for admissions, and deposition transcripts.* When we make factual statements in the memorandum, we must back them up with evidence. To use an example from our *Martin v. Collins* hypo, suppose, in a memorandum supporting a motion, we needed to base some argument on the fact that Dr. Collins obtained the key that he used to enter Shannon's room from Arnie Trevayne. Merely stating the fact is not enough; we must support it with evidence. One way to do this might be to cite Dr. Collins's deposition testimony. Better yet, if our opponent has admitted whatever fact it is that we want to establish—perhaps in answers to interrogatories or responses to requests for admissions—we can use our opponent's own words to make our point.

When we refer to a discovery document to support a factual assertion, must we attach the document? In some courts (such as the Eastern District of Texas, whose local rule we quoted earlier), clearly we must. In some other jurisdictions, citing the source document is enough.

- *Copies of documents that play a central role in the case.* For example, if we are preparing a motion in a breach of contract suit, and we need to refer to the provisions of the contract in the motion, it may be desirable to attach a copy. Technically speaking, a document of this kind is not evidence until there has been testimony to identify and authenticate it. Therefore, it is usually necessary also to attach an affidavit or quote an excerpt from deposition testimony in which a witness testifies to the facts needed to make the document admissible. What facts? The answer depends on the document and the situation—consult a textbook on the law of evidence, or see the Federal Rules of Evidence, especially Rules 901 through 1008.

- *Copies of cases, statutes, or other legal authorities.* In general, when we cite a legal authority such as an appellate case or statute, it is sufficient to give the citation; that is, a reference to the source where the case or statute may be found. We do not attach copies of cases or statutes to our memorandum unless there are special reasons for doing so. When might we decide to attach a copy of a case or statute? If the source is unusually difficult to find—a statute from a foreign country, for example—we would attach a copy. Our personal preference would be to also provide a copy of a case or statute if it is important enough in our argument that we want to encourage the judge to read it, and it comes from a source that the judge is not likely to have readily available in her office.

As a general rule, when we attach documents to a motion or memorandum, we attach only the relevant pages. If, for example, we are quoting one paragraph of testimony from a 200-page deposition, we attach only the page on which the testimony appears, not the whole deposition. We recommend using a highlighter to mark the exact passage referred

to, so that the judge can find it with the least possible expenditure of time and effort.

Where there are multiple attachments, they should be separated using colored or tabbed dividers, and referred to by number or other suitable designation. A common way to do this is to number the attachments sequentially, and refer to them by number in the body of the argument. Consider, for example, the following excerpt from a hypothetical memorandum:

> . . . Defendant Collins then threw himself on top of plaintiff, wrenching the pistol from her hand and breaking her finger. See Affidavit of Shannon Martin dated November 19, 2000, Attachment 4 hereto, at paragraph 14. . . .

Now if the judge wants to see exactly what the affidavit says, he or she can easily locate the tab or divider for Attachment 4 and find the cited passage.

The person whom we are targeting with our attachments is, of course, the judge. It is improper, however, to submit documents in support of a motion without providing copies to the other litigants. Whatever package of attachments we provide for the judge, we must include the same package when we serve the motion on the other parties. If, in the judge's copy, we included tabbed dividers or highlighted certain passages, we must do the same in the copies served on other parties.

Whether we include the attachments in the package we file with the clerk of the court depends on local practice. In some courts, to reduce the volume of paper flowing through the clerks' offices, attachments to motions are included with the judge's copy of a motion, but not with the copy filed with the clerk. The judge will discard his copy of the motion papers as soon as the motion is decided, and thereafter only the motion and memorandum will appear in the clerk's file.

---

**Your Local Notes**

_____

_____

_____

---

## CONCLUDING STEPS

When we have assembled our motion papers—motion, memorandum, and attachments—into a complete package, it is time to submit the motion to the court for a decision. In all courts, this entails at least filing the motion papers with the clerk and serving copies on the other parties to the suit (see

## SIDEBAR

## Responding to a Motion

*Writing a response to a motion is a good deal like writing a motion. You might suppose that a response memorandum would be devoted mainly to answering the arguments made in the motion you are responding to, but such is not the case. To write a good response to a motion, imagine that you are writing a new and separate motion, asking the court to do the opposite of what is asked for by the motion to which you are responding. It is appropriate to challenge the moving party's arguments if doing so will help advance your own argument. But the purpose of a response is not to offer a point-by-point refutation of the moving party's memorandum. The purpose of a response is to present an argument that will persuade the court to deny the motion.*

*The Mechanics of Response Writing*

*The format and layout of a response is similar to that of a motion, except that we would not include a part corresponding to what we have called the motion proper—the boilerplate preamble that recites what the motion is asking for. Unless local rules or customs require otherwise, a response should consist of the response memorandum and attachments to it, if any. Everything that we have said about writing the memorandum in support of a motion applies equally to a memorandum opposing a motion, and the organization is similar: a summary of argument, a section on factual background, an argument with headings and subheadings, and a conclusion.*

*Arguing the Facts in a Response*

*With some motions, the main disagreement may be over a legal issue—both sides may agree on what the facts are. If so, there is no need to repeat them in detail in the response. Nevertheless, if the motion is written well, the presentation of factual background will be slanted in subtle ways to favor the moving party's argument. Therefore, a response should almost always include its own version of the facts deemed important, reshaped to favor the responding party.*

*The Importance of Docketing and Deadlines*

*Attention to deadlines is always important in litigation, and nowhere more so than in responding to motions. In federal district court, the local rules establish the formula for computing the response deadline; your instructor will tell you how to find the rules that apply in the state courts of your locality. In many courts, if the response has not been filed by the applicable deadline, the motion is presented to the judge for ruling immediately and, usually, is summarily granted.*

*How to Research a Response*

*How do we research a response? From scratch. The legal argument in a motion can be thought of as a series of statements of claimed legal rules, each supported by citation of case law or statute. That argument may be flawed in three main ways: (1) The cases or statutes cited may not really support the legal rules claimed; (2) there may be other, better cases or statutes that support a different legal rule; or (3) there may be other legal rules which, if applied, would undercut the moving party's entire chain of argument. If all that we do is research the issues argued by our opponent, we will never become aware of other possible lines of argument that might easily allow us to win.*

*A helpful technique is to pretend that there is no memorandum supporting our opponent's motion. There is only the motion itself, stating only the ruling that our opponent is seeking. We pretend that the judge has expressed an inclination to grant the motion unless we can show why not. In that way, we approach the problem with a fresh point of view. After we have thoroughly explored all of the possible arguments, only then do we begin dissecting our opponent's memorandum, reading the cases cited, Shepardizing or KeyCiting, and verifying that our opponent's citations really support the points for which they are cited.*

Step 4). What else is required depends on local practice, as we will see in Step 5. The opposing party has an opportunity to respond to the motion and present argument against it (see sidebar); then we may reply to our opponent's response (Steps 6 and 7). Finally, if there is to be a hearing on the motion, both sides must prepare and present argument (Step 8). There may also be things that we need to do to follow up on the ruling (Step 9).

## Step 4  *File and Serve*

As with any other filed court paper, we serve copies of the motion, memorandum, and attachment on all other parties. FRCP, Rule 5(a), provides, ". . . every written motion other than one which may be heard ex parte . . . shall be served on each of the parties. . . ." FRCP, Rule 5(a), requires us to serve *all* other parties, not only the opposing parties. If, for example, we represent one defendant out of several, we must serve copies of our motion papers not only on plaintiff but on the other defendants as well.

We file the original motion and memorandum with the clerk of the court. FRCP, Rule 5(d), provides "All papers after the complaint required to be served upon a party, together with a certificate of service, shall be filed with the court within a reasonable time after service. . . ." Whether or not we include the attachments, if any, in the materials filed with the clerk depends on local practice.

In some jurisdictions, we also serve a copy of the motion papers on the judge who will decide the motion. See Step 5.

---

*Your Local Notes*

_____

_____

---

### Step 5 — Do What Is Necessary to Put the Motion before the Judge for Decision

Merely filing a motion may or may not be enough to start the machinery moving to get the motion decided. A judge, not the clerk's office, must rule on the motion, so someone must do something to make the motion come to the judge's attention. *Who* must do *what* depends on the local rules and customs.

**Decision Without Oral Argument**—The trend in federal district courts is to decide most motions on the filed motion papers alone, without hearing oral argument. After one party files a motion, the opposing party is given a fixed period of time in which to file a response. If a response is filed within the allowed time, the moving party has a fixed number of days in which to file a reply. After the reply time has expired, or earlier if the response is not filed within the allotted time, the judge makes a decision based on each sides' motion papers. The judge then announces the decision in a minute entry (or, in some cases, a published opinion) which is sent to the attorneys in due course.

How are the motion papers routed to the judge for decision? In many courts, the rules require us to file two copies of the motion papers with the clerk (the original plus a copy). The clerk places the original in the court file and transmits the copy to the judge's office. (A common variation is to provide for only the original to be filed, but require the parties to deliver copies of their motion papers to the as-

signed judge's office.) Each judge's own clerical staff keeps track of the status of all pending motions assigned to that judge. In a federal district court, the judge has one or more law clerks, usually recent law school graduates who take a one-year clerkship appointment to gain experience. Often, motions are assigned first to one of the law clerks, who writes a memorandum for the judge summarizing each side's position and perhaps recommending an outcome. When the motion is ready for decision—either the motion, response, and reply are all present and accounted for, or the deadlines for filing them have passed—the judge's staff places the motion papers, any necessary parts of the court file, and the law clerk's memo, if any, in the judge's "in basket." The judge reads whatever parts of these she deems necessary and makes a decision.

---

*Your Local Notes*

_____

_____

---

**Decision After Hearing**—Traditionally—as recently as a decade or so ago in federal court, and even today in some state courts—it has been the normal practice for attorneys to present oral argument before the judge rules on a motion. Motions would routinely be scheduled for a hearing, either in the courtroom or in the judge's chambers. At the hearing, the judge would hear argument, ask questions, and perhaps announce a decision then and there.

The reason for courts' increasing reluctance to hear argument on motions is that motion hearings are time consuming and expensive. On motion day in a busy federal district court, it is not unusual to see fifty lawyers sitting around for several hours, collectively charging their clients thousands of dollars per hour, with nothing to do but wait for the judge to finish the cases ahead of them. Many federal judges have little enthusiasm for listening to attorneys talk about arguments that could just as well have been made in the motion papers. (On the other hand, many attorneys feel that oral argument allows them to focus the judge's attention on the points they consider most important, in a way that written argument does not.)

Nowadays, most federal courts will schedule a hearing on a routine motion only if one of the parties makes a formal, written request. Even then, it is up to the judge whether to allow a hearing—federal judges often refuse. Other courts allow hearings on *dispositive motions*—motions that have the potential to end the lawsuit if granted, such as motions for summary judgment and motions to dismiss—but not on other routine motions. In some state courts, and a dwindling number of federal courts, judges still decide most motions after hearing oral argument.

When courts do hold hearings on motions, how are they scheduled? In courts that require a formal request for oral argument, the judge's staff typically schedules the hearing and notifies the parties of the date and time. Courts that routinely hear argument on motions may also schedule the hearings and notify the parties, or may put the onus on the moving party to obtain a hearing date from the judge's staff and notify the other parties.

As you can see, each court has its own procedure for getting motions decided. Unfortunately, local rules sometimes do not spell out everything that a moving party is expected to do. To be effective as a litigation paralegal, it is important for you to know how to find out about a court's unwritten procedures and customs. How can you do it? If necessary, you can contact the clerk's office and ask one of the deputy clerks to explain the procedure to you.

> **Your Local Notes**
> _____
> _____

### Step 6 — Docket Response, Reply, and Hearing Dates

When we file a motion, we immediately compute the due date of the opposing party's response, and enter a notation in the office's central calendar and in our personal calendar. Why? The docket entry will remind us to look for the response and to make appropriate inquiry if we do not see it. Of course, if the court does not receive the response to a motion by the due date, many judges will summarily grant the motion, which is fine with us if we represent the moving party. The problem, however, is that it may only be *our copy* of the response that got lost. Now, the tables are turned—our reply to the response will be late because we are not aware the response has been filed, and the judge may rule based on the motion and response without our having an opportunity to reply.

How do we compute the response and reply dates? How much time is allowed? The Federal Rules of Civil Procedure do not answer this question. Time limits pertaining to motions are left to each court to determine by local rule, and they vary widely. Here is an example of a typical rule:

> Unless otherwise ordered by the Court, all memoranda in opposition to a motion shall be filed within fourteen days of the service of the motion and any reply memoranda within eleven days after service of the opposition memoranda. . . . Where service is made by mail, the provisions of Fed. R. Civ. P. 6(e) apply.
> [*Source:* District of Maryland Local Rule 105(2).]

Notice that the due date for the reply depends on when the response is served; therefore we cannot docket the reply date until we receive the response.

Needless to say, if the court schedules a hearing on our motion, we immediately docket the hearing date in the office's central calendar.

> **Your Local Notes**
> _____
> _____

### Step 7 — Analyze Response and Prepare Reply

After we have filed our motion and docketed the response date and hearing date, if any, there is nothing to do until the response arrives. When it does, we analyze it carefully to assess how best to reply.

A reply memorandum should do more than merely counter the arguments made in the response. If we devote the entire reply to the points raised by our opponent, we are simply focusing the judge's attention on our opponent's arguments. To prepare a reply, we begin by reviewing our own motion. We note how our opponent has responded to each of our arguments, with special attention to the points that our opponent has *failed* to answer.

The reply should first briefly reiterate the reasons why the court should grant our motion. We review the main points made in our motion, one by one. If our opponent has failed to answer any of our arguments, we call attention to that fact, and take the opportunity to reemphasize the now undisputed point. As for the arguments that our opponent's response does address, we first restate concisely our own position and summarize the reasons supporting it; then we show why our opponent's counterargument is invalid; then we reiterate our own position, which we have now shown to be superior to that of our opponent. In this way, we recast the debate in terms that favor our position, instead of letting our opponent set the focus.

The format of a reply, like that of a response, is not usually specified precisely in the local rules. Unless local rules or customs dictate otherwise, our preference is to launch into the argument immediately below the caption, rather than take up valuable first-page real estate reciting that we "hereby reply to plaintiff's response to defendant's motion for," etc.— a fact that is obvious from the title of the document.

A reply memorandum should be short, as befits its purpose, which is to allow the moving party to address any new issues raised by the response. You may sometimes see someone deliberately save the best argument for the reply, so that the opposing party has no opportunity to respond to it. This tactic—known in the vernacular as "sandbagging"—is a breach of litigation etiquette, and risks a good scolding by the judge. A well-written reply should address any damaging points made in the response, but do so in the context of reemphasizing the high points of the moving party's argument and recasting the focus of the debate on the moving party's terms.

## Step 8          *Prepare and Assist at Argument*

If the court hears oral argument on a motion, an attorney must make the presentation. Paralegals can, however, attend motion hearings to observe and assist. Paralegals can also assist the attorney with the preparation of the argument.

Good preparation for a motion hearing entails becoming as familiar as possible with every detail of every issue addressed by the motion or response. Motion hearings are very unpredictable; an attorney arguing a motion must be prepared for anything.

Sometimes, the judge will have read the motion papers thoroughly and understood the issues perfectly, and will begin the argument by asking if either attorney has anything to add to what is in the written filings. If either attorney stands up and begins repeating what is already in the motion papers, the judge is likely to interrupt, sometimes not too politely.

At other times, the judge may not have even looked at the motion papers before the hearing, and will be surreptitiously skimming them as the attorneys present argument. Then it is essential for the attorney to cover the main points in oral argument.

The rules governing who speaks when are also often unpredictable. In theory, the moving party speaks first; then the responding party responds; then the moving party has the last word. However, real-life oral arguments seldom follow the prescribed pattern. For one thing, many judges interrupt with questions during argument. Skilled attorneys welcome the judge's questions, because they reveal which arguments the judge is finding most persuasive or unpersuasive. More troublesome, however, are interruptions by the opposing attorney. Some judges allow attorneys to get away with

frequent interruptions of their opponent's arguments, to the point that it becomes necessary to retaliate in kind to avoid having the argument dominated by one's opponent.

The attorney presenting oral argument must be prepared not only to lead the judge through the main points of the motion, but to answer probing questions about any detail, perhaps while fending off interruptions by opposing counsel. It goes without saying that the arguer must be thoroughly familiar with his own motion papers, and those of the opposing party, but that, alone, is not enough. Judges' questions may also delve into the specific facts of the cases cited in either the motion or the response; into the wording of statutes or rules whose interpretation may be at issue; into the pleadings or other papers in the court file; and into the factual particulars of the documents, if any, attached as evidentiary support for the motion.

The paralegal's main role in this preparation is to assemble all of the necessary materials—motion papers, attachments, copies of cases and statutes, and any other documents that may be helpful—and to package them in such a way as to facilitate the attorney's review. Some attorneys find it helpful to have these materials organized in a three-ring binder, so that all of the pertinent papers are at hand in one place.

At the motion hearing, the paralegal can be most helpful by standing ready to retrieve needed items quickly. If, for example, the judge asks a question about one of the cases cited, the paralegal should be able to produce a copy of the opinion, preferably with the important passages highlighted. The paralegal should not, however, interrupt the attorney while the argument is under way, even while the opposing attorney is speaking.

## Step 9          *Follow Up and Deal with Ruling*

If a hearing is held on a motion, the judge may announce a decision at the conclusion of the hearing. Often, however, the judge will take the decision under advisement—that is, defer the ruling until later, perhaps to allow time for further reflection, or perhaps merely to avoid the awkwardness of having to give the losing party the bad news in person. In that case, or if the court does not hear oral argument, the court must notify the attorneys of the ruling after the judge has decided. Usually this is done by issuing a minute entry.

Herein lies a potential dilemma for the litigants. A motion ruling, particularly on a dispositive motion such as a motion for summary judgment, can have a huge impact on our case. We do not want to waste time conducting discovery and preparing for trial on some issue that may be foreclosed by the judge's ruling on a motion. However, judges sometimes take a very long time to rule on a motion, and it is considered bad form (and, by some attorneys, bad luck!) to badger the judge's secretary with repeated inquiries. Suppose a month passes, and we do not receive a ruling. Is it because the judge has still not ruled or is it because the ruling got lost in the mail? Most litigators let a reasonable period of time go by—a few weeks or a month, depending somewhat on the particular judge's reputation for promptness—then check to see if opposing counsel has heard anything and, if not, perhaps contact the court.

Suppose the judge's ruling is not to our liking. Is there anything that we can do about it? Can we appeal?

One option is to file a motion for reconsideration of the judge's ruling. As a practical matter, however, such motions are almost never granted unless the judge's ruling reflects some obvious mistake. Motions for reconsideration that merely reargue the points made in the original motion papers are overwhelmingly unlikely to succeed at anything other than annoying the judge. Many federal district courts have adopted local rules governing motions for reconsideration. Often, these provide that no response need be filed unless the judge asks for one, the assumption being that the judge will usually deny the motion for reconsideration without needing to see a response.

As for appellate remedies, the general rule is that an appeal may be taken only from a final judgment that disposes of the entire case. Judges make many rulings during the course of a lawsuit; if there were to be a multi-year detour through the court of appeals every time the judge rules on a motion, lawsuits might well go on forever! Nevertheless, there are procedures whereby, under extraordinary circumstances, the court of appeals may hear an appeal of an interlocutory decision—a decision that does not result in a final judgment. Generally, interlocutory review is an option only if the judge's ruling is one that, if wrong, could cause extreme and unusual prejudice—situations in which the potential for harm from an erroneous ruling clearly outweighs the inefficiency of piecemeal appellate review.

For routine motions, therefore, as a practical matter, the judge's ruling is best regarded as final, at least until the lawsuit is over and the case is on appeal.

# Writing a Motion: Learning by Example

We now apply the principles we have been discussing by preparing a motion to amend a pleading. In this section, we rough out the skeleton of the motion; then in the Learning by Doing section, you will adapt the motion to conform to the rules of your local court, and flesh out the memorandum and attachments.

Here is the hypothetical assignment: Assume that we represent Park Hotels Group, Inc. Diligent paralegals that we are, while working on our issues outline, we decide to do a Westlaw search to see whether there were any statutes that might be useful in building a defense. Our search turns up section 651.15 of the Nevada Revised Statutes, which provides as follows:

**651.15 Civil liability of innkeepers for death or injury of person on premises caused by person who is not employee.**

1. An owner or keeper of any hotel, inn, motel, motor court, boardinghouse or lodginghouse is not civilly liable for the death or injury of a patron or other person on the premises caused by another person who is not an employee under the control or supervision of the owner or keeper unless:

(a) The wrongful act which caused the death or injury was foreseeable; and

(b) There is a preponderance of evidence that the owner or keeper did not exercise due care for the safety of the patron or other person on the premises.

2. An owner or keeper of any hotel, inn, motel, motor court, boardinghouse or lodginghouse is civilly liable for the death or injury of a patron or other person on the premises caused by another person who is not an employee under the control or supervision of the owner or keeper if:

(a) The wrongful act which caused the death or injury was foreseeable; and

(b) The owner or keeper failed to take reasonable precautions against the foreseeable wrongful act.

The court shall determine as a matter of law whether the wrongful act was foreseeable and whether the owner or keeper had a duty to take reasonable precautions against the foreseeable wrongful act of the person who caused the death or injury.

3. For the purposes of this section, a wrongful act is not foreseeable unless:

(a) The owner or keeper failed to exercise due care for the safety of the patron or other person on the premises; or

(b) Prior incidents of similar wrongful acts occurred on the premises and the owner or keeper had notice or knowledge of those incidents.

Naturally, we are overjoyed at this find, our optimism clouded only by the fact that the answer has already been filed. But, no matter—we can file a motion to amend the answer, and add an affirmative defense based on the statute.

We have seen that motion procedure is in large part governed by local rules and customs. The examples that follow assume that the lawsuit is pending in the U.S. District Court for the District of Arizona; the local rules for that court can be found on the internet at **www.azd.uscourts.gov.** In the Learning by Doing section, we will modify our motion to conform to the rules of the courts of your locality.

## DRAFTING STEPS

**Step 1**    *Draft the Motion*

Motions procedure in the U.S. District Court for the District of Arizona is governed by Local Rule 1.10. Checking that rule, we find that there is a confer before filing provision [Local Rule 1.10(j)], but it applies only to discovery motions.

Even though the rule does not require it, some attorneys would telephone opposing counsel to inquire whether consent to the amendment might be given, before going to the trouble of filing a motion. The drawback to doing so is that opposing counsel will likely want time to confer with her client before giving an answer, and the process will deteriorate into a game of stalling and telephone tag. Also, if opposing counsel consents, we will owe a favor. For these reasons, we would usually file first, get the clock running on the response, and let opposing counsel offer to consent to the amendment if she wants to.

Our motion is shown in Figure W14–1.

**Step 2**    *Draft the Memorandum*

As you can see, the motion itself was not difficult to draft. The memorandum will require more effort.

---

**Figure W14–1    Sample Motion**

CRANDALL, ELKINS & MAJOR
Gail Stoddard, Esq.
2000 North Central Avenue, Suite 2900
Phoenix, Arizona 85004
(602) 555-1234
Attorneys for defendant Park Hotels Group, Inc.

### IN THE UNITED STATES DISTRICT COURT
### DISTRICT OF ARIZONA

| | |
|---|---|
| SHANNON MARTIN, a single woman, ) | |
| ) | NO. CV98 -01456 PHX JL |
| Plaintiff, ) | |
| ) | MOTION FOR LEAVE TO |
| v. ) | AMEND ANSWER |
| ) | |
| ARTHUR COLLINS, et ux., et al., ) | |
| ) | |
| Defendants. ) | |
| _____ ) | |

   Defendant Park Hotels Group, Inc. respectfully moves pursuant to Rule 15(a), FRCP, for an order of the court granting leave to file an amended answer in the form accompanying this motion.
   This motion is based upon the accompanying memorandum of points and authorities.
   RESPECTFULLY SUBMITTED this 25th day of April, 2000.

                                        CRANDALL, ELKINS & MAJOR

                                        _____
                                        Gail Stoddard
                                        Attorneys for defendant Park Hotels
                                        Group, Inc.

(Certificate of mailing goes here—see Workshop 4.)

**Figure W14–2  Sample Memorandum**

CRANDALL, ELKINS & MAJOR
Gail Stoddard, Esq.
2000 North Central Avenue, Suite 2900
Phoenix, Arizona 85004
(602) 555-1234
Attorneys for defendant Park Hotels Group, Inc.

### IN THE UNITED STATES DISTRICT COURT DISTRICT OF ARIZONA

| | |
|---|---|
| SHANNON MARTIN, a single woman, ) | |
| ) | NO. CV98 -01456 PHX JL |
| Plaintiff, ) | |
| v. ) | MEMORANDUM OF POINTS AND AUTHORITIES IN SUPPORT OF MOTION FOR LEAVE TO AMEND ANSWER |
| ARTHUR COLLINS, et ux., et al., ) | |
| Defendants. ) | |

#### Summary of Argument

1. Nevada statute provides that a hotel is not liable when a guest is injured by a third person not employed by the hotel, unless the injury is foreseeable. Nev. Rev. Stat. Ann. §651.15.

2. Nevada has the most "significant relationship" to plaintiff's claims which arise from events at a Nevada hotel. Defendant's liability is to be determined according to Nevada law.

3. Defendant seeks leave to amend its answer to add this statutory affirmative defense. FRCP, Rule 15(a), provides that such leave should be freely given.

#### Argument

1. *Factual Background: Plaintiff Was Injured By Another Hotel Guest: The Circumstances Were Unforeseeable.*

Plaintiff, while a guest at the Las Vegas hotel operated by defendant Park Hotels Group, had her finger broken by another hotel guest, defendant Collins. The incident occurred in plaintiff's room; the evidence is conflicting as to how defendant Collins came to be there. There is, however, no evidence whatever that defendant Park Hotels Group. . .

II. *Nev. Rev. Stat. Ann. §651.15 Provides A Valid Affirmative Defense To Plaintiff's Claims Against Defendant Park Hotels Group*

Defendant Park Hotels Group seeks to amend its answer to assert a statutory affirmative defense arising under Nevada statute. See Nev. Rev. Stat. Ann. §651.15, discussed in detail *infra*.

A. *Nevada Law Determines The Rights And Liabilities Arising From These Injuries Occurring At A Nevada Hotel.*

The liability of defendant Park Hotels Group is to be determined by Nevada law. Plaintiff's injury occurred in Nevada, while plaintiff was a guest in a Nevada hotel, and was inflicted by another hotel guest.

Arizona courts apply the "most significant relationship" test to determine which state's law should be applied in a tort action . *E.g., Bill Alexander Ford, Lincoln Mercury, Inc. v. Casa Ford, Inc.,* 187 Ariz. 616, 931 P.2d 1126 (Ariz.App. 1996). Clearly, Nevada is the state with the most significant relationship—

*continued*

Due to space limitations, we present in Figure W14–2 only enough of the memorandum to allow you to see its general structure and appearance.

Checking the local rules, the only provision affecting the writing of the memorandum is Local Rule 1.10(e), which limits size of the memorandum to "fifteen (15) pages, exclusive of attachments and any required statement of facts." This is a simple motion; the memorandum should not exceed 3 or 4 pages.

---

**Figure W14–2  Sample Memorandum,** *continued*

indeed, the only relationship—to this lawsuit. No events pertinent to this suit occurred in any state other than Nevada, and . . .

B. *In Nevada By Statute, Hotels Are Not Liable To Guests For Unforeseeable Injuries Received From Other Guests.*

Under applicable Nevada law, hotels are not liable to guests for personal injuries inflicted by third persons who are neither hotel employees nor under the hotel's control. The only exception to this rule is for foreseeable injuries, which the governing statute defines in narrow terms. Nev. Rev. Stat. Ann. §651.15 provides as follows:

An owner or keeper of any hotel, inn, motel, motor court, boardinghouse or lodginghouse is not civilly liable for the death or injury of a patron or other person on the premises caused by another person who is not an employee under the control or supervision of the _____

III. *Leave to Amend An Answer Is To Be Freely Given Where The Purpose Is To Add A Valid Affirmative Defense.*

The Federal Rules of Civil Procedure contemplate a liberal policy toward amendments of pleadings. FRCP, Rule 15(a), provides in pertinent part:

[A] party may amend the party's pleading only by leave of court or by written consent of the adverse party; and leave shall be freely given when justice so requires. . . .

The Court of Appeals for the Ninth Circuit has held that where the purpose of an . . .

IV. *Conclusion: This Court Should Grant Defendant Park Hotels Group Leave To Amend Its Answer To Add Its Statutory Defense Under Nev. Rev. Stat. Ann. §651.15*

The Nevada statute governing hotel liability to guests for injuries by other guests, Nev. Rev. Stat. Ann. §651.15, provides what is potentially a complete defense to the liability asserted against defendant Park Hotels Group in this lawsuit. All of the events relevant to this lawsuit occurred in Nevada, and it would in any case be unfair to judge the conduct of a Nevada hotel by the laws of some state other than Nevada. Taking into account the liberal policy of federal courts toward the amendment of pleadings, this Court should grant defendant Park Hotels Group leave to file the amended answer submitted herewith, asserting its defense under the Nevada statute. Defendant's motion for leave to amend its answer should be granted.

RESPECTFULLY SUBMITTED this 25th day of April, 2000.

CRANDALL, ELKINS & MAJOR

_____

Gail Stoddard
Attorneys for defendant Park Hotels
Group, Inc.

(Certificate of mailing goes here—see Workshop 4.)

---

## Step 3    *Assemble the Attachments*

This being a simple motion, only two attachments are needed. The first is the amended answer that we are asking leave to file. When moving for leave to amend a pleading, it is customary to attach the amended pleading that we are asking to file, so that the judge can see exactly what the proposed changes are. The amended answer comprises the entire answer, not just the changed or added portions. We redo the original answer, retaining everything that was already present, and adding the new material. In some courts, the answer that

we attach to the motion for leave to amend is deemed filed if the court grants the motion; in other courts, it is necessary to file the amended answer as a separate document after the motion is granted. Either way, the amended answer does not *add* to the existing answer, it *replaces* the existing answer.

We would also attach a photocopy of the Nevada statute, since we assume that a federal judge sitting in Arizona probably does not have a set of Nevada statutes handy. There is no need to attach copies of Arizona or federal cases. All of the cases we are citing stand for well-known legal principles, so the judge is unlikely to want to read them.

The proposed amended answer would be included in all sets of the motion papers, including the original to be filed. The copy of the Nevada statute would be included in the set of attachments accompanying the judge's copy of the motion, and those served on other parties, but not the set filed with the clerk. The District of Arizona has a local rule prohibiting the filing of such attachments; see District of Arizona Local Rule 1.9(f)(4).

## CONCLUDING STEPS

### Step 4 — File and Serve

District of Arizona Local Rule 1.9(g) provides:

(g) Copy for Judge. A clear, legible copy of every pleading or other document filed shall accompany each original pleading or other document filed with the Clerk for use by the District Judge or Magistrate Judge to whom the case is assigned. . . .

Therefore, we file the original motion papers with the clerk, together with a copy for the judge. We serve a copy on each of the other parties by mailing one copy to Shannon's attorney and one copy to Dr. Collins's attorney, as required by FRCP, Rule 5.

### Step 5 — Do What Is Necessary to Put the Motion before the Judge for Decision

District of Arizona Local Rule 1.10(h) provides:

(h) Submitted Motions. It is presumed that motions, other than motions filed pursuant to Rule 12(b) or Rule 56 of the Federal Rules of Civil Procedure, will be considered and decided without oral argument, unless otherwise requested and permitted by the Court.

Local Rule 1.10(f)(2) does offer the option of requesting oral argument. For a simple motion to amend, however, there is no need to do so, and such requests are rarely granted in any event.

Although the local rules do not explicitly say so, we can infer—from the presumption of no oral argument and from the requirement of filing an extra copy for the judge—that the clerk's office will route the motion to the judge for decision, and that we will be notified of the outcome by minute entry. (If we were filing in an unfamiliar district, we would nonetheless verify this inference via a phone call to the clerk's office.)

### Step 6 — Docket Response, Reply, and Hearing Dates

District of Arizona Local Rule 1.10(c) provides:

(c) Responsive Memorandum. The opposing party shall, unless otherwise ordered by the Court and except as otherwise provided by Rule 56 of the Federal Rules of Civil Procedure and paragraph (1) of this Rule, have ten (10) days after service in a civil or criminal case within which to serve and file a responsive memorandum.

Because we are serving the motion by mail, we add 3 days as provided by FRCP, Rule 6(e), making the response due 13 days later. We make a notation of the due date in the office central calendar and in our personal calendar. We cannot compute the reply date until we receive the response, and there is no hearing date to docket since the motion will be decided without oral argument.

### Step 7 — Analyze Response and Prepare Reply

District of Arizona Local Rules 1.10(c) and (d) provide for the party responding to a motion to file and serve a "responsive memorandum," after which the moving party may file a "reply memorandum." Except for the title, these memoranda are identical in format and appearance to the memorandum in support of the motion shown under Step 2 earlier. Under District of Arizona Local Rule 1.10(e), a reply memorandum is subject to a shorter page limit (10 pages).

### Step 8 — Prepare and Assist at Argument

Because nondispositive motions are decided without oral argument under District of Arizona practice, no preparation is necessary.

### Step 9 — Follow Up and Deal with Ruling

The court will notify us of the judge's ruling by minute entry. The practice in the District of Arizona is that if the motion for leave to amend is granted, the order granting the motion will direct the clerk to file the amended answer that was submitted with the motion. (This is another example of a procedural detail not specified by the local rules, verifiable only by inquiring of the clerk's office or by searching the case law for a sample order.)

# Writing a Motion: Learning by Doing

Now it is your turn. Your assignment for this workshop is to begin with the excerpts from the motion for leave to amend as shown in the preceding Learning by Example section of this workshop, and produce a finished set of motion papers conforming to the rules and customs of the U.S. district court of your locality. (At your instructor's option, the state court of your locality may be substituted.) Assume the following:

> You are a paralegal in the office of Gail Stoddard, who represents Park Hotels Group, Inc. The firm's office is in your city (make up a suitable address). The lawsuit, *Martin v. Collins,* is pending in the U.S. district court having jurisdiction in your locality. The other facts of the hypothetical are unchanged. You have discovered Nev. Rev. Stat. Ann. §651.15 (reproduced in full in the preceding Learning by Example section), and Ms. Stoddard has assigned to you the task of preparing a motion for leave to amend Park Hotels' answer to add the statutory defense.

## EXERCISES

In carrying out this assignment, you should follow the step-by-step formula described in this workshop.

1.  Locate the local rules of your U.S. district court pertaining to (a) motions practice and (b) filing of documents with the clerk. (For many districts, the local rules can be accessed from the U.S. Courts Internet site, **www.uscourts.gov;** if the rules for your court are not available there, they can be obtained from the clerk's office.)

2.  Determine the following from your local rules, from your instructor, or by calling the clerk's office:

    a.  Any page limits applicable to motions and responses;

    b.  Whether the court holds hearings on motions, and, if so, how they are scheduled;

    c.  How many copies are filed with the clerk;

    d.  The time periods allowed for response and reply;

    e.  Any restrictions on the inclusion of attachments in the original motion papers filed with the clerk;

    f.  How decisions on motions are communicated to the participants;

    g.  When a motion for leave to amend a pleading is granted, is it necessary for the moving party to then file the amended pleading with the clerk, or does the attachment of the amended pleading to the motion suffice?; and

    h.  Any other requirements or customs that you need to take into account in preparing a motion for leave to amend an answer.

3.  Review, and if possible obtain copies for your forms file, of a motion, response, and reply filed in the U.S. district court of your locality to use as a guide on matters of format, layout, and organization. Your instructor may be able to provide these or suggest how to obtain them. Failing that, you can access the court files of pending lawsuits at the clerk's office (but in that case be prepared to take notes— copies are expensive). Find out exactly what papers need to be filed in connection with a motion in your court, and what each one needs to contain. Find out whether a notice of motion is required.

4.  Prepare, in final form suitable for filing in the U.S. district court of your locality, the motion papers needed to amend Park Hotels' answer, including the following:

    a.  The motion proper, notice of motion, and/or other paper required under the rules and customs of your U.S. District Court; and

    b.  The memorandum in support of the motion. You may use the excerpts shown in Step 2 of the Learning by Example section as a guide, but (i) be sure to follow any suggestions of your instructor as necessary to make the format and organization conform to local practice; and (ii) at your instructor's option, replace the case citation and related discussion in section II(A) of the memorandum with an appropriate case decided by the appellate courts of your state.

    c. At your instructor's option, the amended answer is to be attached. Use the answer of Park Hotels Group, Inc. appearing in the Learning by Example section of Workshop 8, and add the necessary paragraph.

# PRACTICE POINTERS
## *Writing Tips: Using Transitions and Providing Clear Explanations*

The preparation of effective motions requires clear, concise writing. Such writing is effortless to follow and assists the reader in connecting one thought with the next. Although this sounds obvious, it is all too easy to assume that the reader will understand why you shifted from one idea to the next. After all, by the time you commit your thoughts to writing, your thought process is so self-evident to you that explanation seems unnecessary. Remember that readers have not been privy to your analytical maneuvering. They need direction every step of the way.

Use transitional words and phrases to provide that direction. Imagine that you are laying a footpath for the reader to follow. Every step should be clearly set so that all the reader has to do is to follow your verbal signs. Examples of such verbal signs are:

| | |
|---|---|
| Additionally | Moreover |
| Although | Next |
| Because | On the other hand |
| Even though | Therefore |
| First (second, third, etc.) | To illustrate |
| For example | To the contrary |
| Furthermore | Whereas |
| However | While |
| In spite of | |

Incorporate these words into your writing. Use them at the beginning of paragraphs and to transition from one thought to the next within a paragraph. Ask yourself as you go from one paragraph to the next what the connection between the two paragraphs is. Then use the appropriate word or phrase to indicate that connection.

You can also assist readers in moving from one idea to the next by summarizing what you have just said. This summary gives readers some closure and allows them to assimilate what has been discussed in capsule form. Frequent summaries assist in "teaching" readers the material previously presented before confronting them with new information.

Similarly, you may anticipate what you are going to discuss by offering readers a brief preview. Such a preview allows readers to glean the essence of what is to be discussed in detail. This technique allows them to transition into new territory with less trepidation because they have been prepared in advance. They also know specifically what to look for as they read.

Although transitional phrases provide road signs for your reader to follow, you still must consciously focus on explaining your thought process every step of the way. Lack of explanation is one of the primary flaws in legal writing. Once writers have thoroughly researched and pondered an issue, they tend to forget the cognitive steps taken in reaching the conclusion and assume that anyone would necessarily follow the same steps.

Good writing is just like any other art. It should appear simple to the observer. Figure skaters, dancers, gymnasts, and other athletes and performers who are highly skilled are a joy to watch because what they do looks deceptively easy. Good writing shares that deception. Because readers find the reasoning simple to follow, they conclude that the subject matter is simple and that the conclusions are inescapable.

One of the purposes of preparing motions is to educate the judge. You can best do that by explaining each step so carefully that the judge cannot possibly go astray. You do not want the judge wondering how you went from Step A to B. Rather you want to lay out your thinking so clearly and plainly that even a novice to the law could understand your reasoning. Remember that judges cannot honor requests they do not understand and will not honor requests for which they can find no legal basis.

## TECHNO TIP

When you are on the Internet you may notice that the speed at which you communicate varies. Somedays large files are downloaded with ease. On other days it seems that it takes forever to download a small file. Communication speeds are constrained by two factors: the speed of your modem and how fast the site you are looking at can respond to you.

In the late 1990s, the standard modem operated at a maximum of 56,000 bits per second (bps). Since ASCII characters are sent in 8-bit blocks, such a modem can send 7,000 characters per second. If your modem operates at 9,600, 14,400 or 28,800 bps it is inherently limited to a fraction of the speed of the 56k bps (k equaling 1,000) modem. If the site you are at is busy, it may be communicating with you at a speed of substantially less than 56k bps, even if it has the capability of transmitting at that rate. Because the number of lines to a site is limited, the site manager can either opt to communicate with a few "visitors" at the site's maximum rate or to share its information with more visitors at a slower rate (multiplexing). Even if the site is not busy if your Internet service provider is maxed out, it cannot pass the site's information along to you as fast as the site itself can.

## FORMS FILE

*Summarize the local rules and customs in your jurisdiction governing the submission and preparation of motions. Make sure this summary is complete enough that when you are called on to draft a motion, you can refer to it without having to reference each specific rule.*

## KEY TERMS

Movant

Notice of motion

Responding party

Moving party

Respondent

## INTRODUCTION: HOW DISCOVERY CAN BECOME ABUSIVE

People who are suing each other do not always respond fully and properly to discovery requests. This should not come as any surprise. It is almost axiomatic that whatever information one party most earnestly desires is precisely that which the opposing party is least eager to turn over. Disputes over discovery are inevitable and frequent, and the system could not function without mechanisms to resolve them.

■ You serve interrogatories on your opponent. Thirty days go by, then 40—no response. You make a phone call to inquire. The answers are "almost ready," you are told; they should be in the mail tomorrow. Another week goes by; you call again. After still another week the answers finally arrive in the mail. You flip through the inch-thick stack of paper. At least a third of the questions are either objected to or not answered at all.

■ Your supervising attorney is taking the deposition of the opposing party. Each time the questioning begins to probe a sensitive area, the opposing attorney objects and instructs the witness not to answer.

■ You are assigned to review a number of file boxes full of documents that were produced in response to an FRCP, Rule 34, request for production of documents. As you begin cataloging them, you find that each box contains a mixture of documents from a variety of sources. Obviously the documents have been deliberately scrambled.

We do not mean to imply that the fault always lies with the responding party. Litigants also sometimes attempt to obtain discovery to which they are not entitled:

■ Among the interrogatories that your opponent has just served are several that call for information that is only marginally relevant, and will require hundreds of hours of work to compile.

■ Your client is being sued by a neighbor whose child claims to have been bitten by your client's dog. The opposing attorney has just served a subpoena on your client's accoun-

tant, calling for production of your client's personal income tax returns.[1]

■ You represent a plaintiff who was injured while riding as a passenger in someone else's car. While taking your client's deposition, the other driver's attorney is insisting on asking questions about a misdemeanor citation for drunk driving that your client received 2 years ago.

## THE ADVERSARIAL SIDE OF DISCOVERY

As the foregoing examples make clear, discovery is often a tug of war between the requesting party, who might like to obtain more than the discovery rules allow, and the responding party, who might prefer to disclose less than the rules require. Let us consider the problem from each of these competing points of view, beginning with that of the responding party.

**The Responding Party's Weapons**—When a discovery request asks for too much, what are the responding party's options? Here are the main ones:

***Not responding:*** The party who receives an improper discovery request could simply ignore it. We mention this by way of pointing out that it is a poor choice. The rules require us to respond to all discovery requests, however flawed or improper they may seem. Furthermore, a party who fails to serve any response to a discovery request within the response time allowed by the rules may be held to have waived any objections. Then the judge may order the party to respond to the request, even though an objection might otherwise have succeeded.

***Objecting:*** The best strategy for dealing with garden-variety overreaching in a written discovery request is to serve a response objecting to the offending item and stating the reasons why the request is improper. By objecting, we avoid turning over the disputed information to our opponent. This leaves our opponent with the option of abandoning

---

[1]There can be circumstances in which a party's tax returns would be discoverable; tax returns are not, however, routinely subject to discovery in a tort suit.

the request, or filing a motion to compel asking the judge to order us to comply with it. In other words, objecting puts the ball back in our opponent's court, and costs us essentially nothing. (We should clarify that there *is* a potential cost to objecting *improperly,* which is that the judge can make us reimburse the attorney's fees that our opponent spends contesting the groundless objection.)

***Filing a motion for a protective order:*** When our opponent attempts to obtain information improperly via a deposition or a subpoena for documents, objecting does not necessarily solve our problem. If the opposing attorney is deposing our client, we can object and instruct our client not to answer, but what if the witness is a third party? Then the court reporter will note our objection, the witness will go ahead and answer the objectionable question, and the cat will be out of the bag. Even if the judge eventually sustains our objection, our opponent will have obtained the information that he was seeking. Similarly, if our opponent serves a document subpoena on a third party, merely expressing our objection will not prevent the third party from turning over the subpoenaed documents.

In situations of this kind, the weapon of choice is a motion for protective order. FRCP, Rule 26(c), gives the judge broad power to issue an order blocking or limiting proposed discovery in advance:

(c) Upon motion by a party or by the person from whom discovery is sought . . . the court . . . may make any order which justice requires . . . including one or more of the following:

    (1)    that the disclosure or discovery not be had;

    (2)    that the disclosure or discovery may be had only on specified terms and conditions, including a designation of the time or place;

    (3)    that the discovery may be had only by a method of discovery other than that selected by the party seeking discovery;

    (4)    that certain matters not be inquired into, or that the scope of the disclosure or discovery be limited to certain matters;

    (5)    that discovery be conducted with no one present except persons designated by the court;

    (6)    that a deposition, after being sealed, be opened only by order of the court;

    (7)    that a trade secret or other confidential research, development, or commercial information not be revealed or be revealed only in a designated way; and

    (8)    that the parties simultaneously file specified documents or information enclosed in sealed envelopes to be opened as directed by the court.

**The Propounding Party's Weapons**—The goal of a discovery request is to obtain evidence or information. There are essentially three ways in which an opposing party can try to avoid giving us what we ask for: (1) fail to respond; (2) object or move for a protective order; and (3) provide a response that purports to be complete but is not. Incomplete responses pose a particular challenge. When an important detail is missing from an otherwise complete response, the omission may be hard to detect and even harder to prove.

Suppose we decide that an opposing party's response is not adequate. What can we do about it? Here are the main options, which are discussed in order of escalating aggressiveness.

***Getting the information in some other way (or not at all):*** One alternative is to seek the information elsewhere. Unsatisfying though it may seem to let our opponent get away with breaking the rules, there are situations in which this is, in fact, the right choice. Waging a motion battle to force a proper response will be time consuming, expensive, and divert our attention from the more important job of preparing our case for trial. Even if we win it, there is no guarantee that we will get the information we want. On the other hand, if we let our opponent's response stand, and find out the true facts in some other way (i.e., investigation or discovery from others), we have our opponent on the record with an answer that we can prove is false or at least misleading—good jury ammunition.

We may also decide, on reflection, that the information in question is simply not worth the effort required to get it. In a typical real-life lawsuit, we are likely to see inadequate responses to many of our discovery requests, and we cannot afford to do battle over all of them. Our time and our client's money are not unlimited, and we want to spend them on the things that will best help us win the lawsuit. We must therefore prioritize, and have the discipline to walk away from minor discovery offenses that do not really affect our prospects of winning.

***Seeking voluntary compliance:*** There are, of course, situations in which we have a vital need for the evidence or information that we have requested and cannot get it anywhere except from our opponent. Then, there is no choice but to try to get our opponent to comply with the rules, either by persuasion or by force.

**SIDEBAR**

## A Federal Judge's Point of View on Discovery Disputes

*To the federal judiciary, discovery motions are a source of considerable frustration. Consider what Judge Wayne D. Brazil had to say in In re Convergent Technologies Securities Litigation, 108 F.R.D. 328 (N.D.Cal. 1985):*

> *The courts, sorely pressed by demands to try cases promptly and to rule thoughtfully on potentially case-dispositive motions, simply do not have the resources to police closely the operation of the discovery process. The whole system of civil adjudication would be ground to a virtual halt if the courts were forced to intervene in even a modest percentage of discovery transactions. That fact should impose on counsel an acute sense of responsibility about how they handle discovery matters. They should strive to be co-operative, practical and sensible, and should turn to the courts (or take positions that force others to turn to the courts) only in extraordinary situations that implicate truly significant interests.*

*Noble sentiments, if not, in our view, terribly realistic. As an indication of how the litigants view the notion of cooperating on discovery, consider this: Judge Brazil made the foregoing observations while ruling on a dispute over when plaintiff would have to answer certain interrogatories—both sides agreed that plaintiff had to answer, the only dispute was over the timing of the answers. And the two sides had, at that point spent $4,000,000 in attorney's fees and costs—not on the entire lawsuit, but on that one discovery motion!*

---

You might guess that persuasion is unlikely to work, and most of the time, in our experience, you would be right. Nevertheless, the federal rules (and those of many state courts) require us to try to resolve discovery disputes on our own before asking the judge to intervene, so we must at least go through the motions. For a federal judge's perspective on the need for voluntary cooperation, see the sidebar.

How best to do this depends on the specific requirements of the local rules, and on the expectations of the local judges. A phone call may suffice; a demand letter followed by a phone call is another option. We will have more to say about this subject later under Step 2.

***Filing a motion to compel:*** The word *compel* means to force someone to do something. A motion to compel asks the judge to order an opposing party to respond to a discovery request. For example:

- If our opponent has failed to answer some of the interrogatories in a set, we can file a motion to compel asking the judge to order her to file answers by a certain date.

- If our opponent has objected to one of our document requests, we can file a motion to compel asking the judge to overrule the objection and order our opponent to turn over the requested documents.

- If our opponent has answered one of our interrogatories in an evasive manner, we can file

a motion to compel asking the judge to order her to answer the question properly.

The rule governing motions to compel is FRCP, Rule 37(a). Much of this workshop is devoted to learning how to construct a motion to compel.

***Filing a motion for sanctions:*** A motion for sanctions asks the judge to impose a sanction—in effect, a punishment—on a party who is willfully disobeying the rules. A motion for sanctions represents a level of escalation that is a step above a motion to compel. With a motion to compel, the worst that can happen to the disobedient party is that the judge may order him to make a proper response, and possibly pay some attorney's fees. With a motion for sanctions, the disobedient party could conceivably lose the entire lawsuit, and then be thrown in jail for contempt of court. (Judges rarely impose such severe sanctions; the threat is usually enough to induce obedience.)

A motion for sanctions is allowed in two main situations:

*1.* We can ask for sanctions if an opposing party has completely failed to respond to a discovery request. If, for example, we serve a set of interrogatories and our opponent simply ignores them, we can move for sanctions. If, on the other hand, our opponent serves a set of answers, but does not answer all the questions or answers some of them evasively, then we can move to compel but we cannot ask for sanctions. The underlying idea is that sanctions are possible only if the responding party has made *no* response. If there has been some response, even if it is incomplete or inadequate, a motion for sanctions is not the remedy.

2. We can ask for sanctions if we have already moved to compel, gotten an order compelling our opponent to provide the discovery that we asked for, and our opponent has not obeyed the order. This is the usual situation in which a motion for sanctions is called for. For example, suppose we serve interrogatories; our opponent serves an incomplete set of answers; we move to compel and the judge orders our opponent to serve complete answers by a certain date; and our opponent does nothing or again serves incomplete answers. Now, we can move for sanctions.

FRCP, Rule 37(b), gives the judge a variety of punishment options, ranging in severity from a mild "slap on the wrist" to the litigation equivalent of nuclear annihilation. These will be easier to understand in the context of an example; consider the following scenario:

In our hypo, recall that Shannon is claiming damages not only for the injury to her finger but also for psychological trauma. She must, of course, present evidence showing the nature and extent of that psychological trauma. Suppose Park Hotels serves interrogatories asking for the name and address of all psychiatrists who treated Shannon after her injury, and Shannon's attorney leaves that interrogatory unanswered. (Why might he do that? Perhaps because he does not like the testimony that the treating psychiatrist might offer, and prefers to hire some other psychiatrist to testify.) Park Hotels then moves to compel and obtains an order requiring Shannon to answer.

Shannon's attorney now answers the interrogatory, and discloses the name of the new psychiatrist he has hired to testify, but leaves out any mention of the psychiatrist who treated Shannon after the injury. (Of course, a response of this kind is unethical and the deception is almost guaranteed to be discovered, so obviously a fine attorney of Allen Porter's caliber would never do such a thing—but for the sake of our hypothetical we will assume that he suffered an attack of temporary insanity.)

Park Hotels eventually finds out about the original psychiatrist, and files a motion for sanctions.

What are the judge's punishment options? Here are some of the things that the judge could do in this situation, singly or in combination [see FRCP, Rule 37(b) for the complete list]:

- *Assess attorney's fees.* Park Hotels' attorneys spent time and money filing a motion to compel, filing a motion for sanctions, and conducting the discovery and investigation by which they discovered the identity of the original psychiatrist. Naturally, they billed Park Hotels for the time and expenses. The judge can make Shannon pay for these fees and costs [and, indeed, is probably required to do so under these hypothetical facts—see FRCP, Rule 37(b)(2), last paragraph].

- *Make factual rulings.* Here, for example, the judge could enter an order finding as a fact that Shannon did not suffer any psychological trauma; see FRCP, Rule 37(b)(2)(A). The idea here is to deter parties from hiding adverse facts via the threat that, if the deception is caught, the facts will be made even more adverse.

- *Disallowing designated evidence.* The judge could, for example, enter an order prohibiting Shannon's attorney from calling any psychiatric witness *other than* the one whose identity he attempted to conceal; see FRCP, Rule 37(b)(2)(B).

- *Prohibiting any evidence on particular claims or defenses.* The judge could enter an order prohibiting Shannon from introducing any evidence to support her claim of psychological trauma; see FRCP, Rule 37(b)(2)(B).

- *Striking claims or defenses.* The judge could enter an order completely striking Shannon's claim for damages for psychological trauma from the complaint.

- *Rendering judgment.* The judge could dismiss the lawsuit and render judgment for Park Hotels. (This is a relatively severe punishment, typically imposed only in unusually compelling situations.)

- *Holding the offending party or attorney in contempt of court.* The judge could hold Shannon's attorney (and Shannon too, if the judge found that she deliberately participated in the decision to disobey the court's order) in contempt of court. Although it rarely happens in civil lawsuits, the judge can also, in theory, impose jail time as part of the punishment for contempt.

# Motions to Compel: Step-by-Step Instructions

As our project for this workshop, we have chosen to concentrate on a single task: dealing with an incomplete response to a set of interrogatories or other written discovery. We begin by analyzing the response to determine exactly in what respects it falls short; then we take the necessary steps to prepare and file a motion to compel.

## PREPARATORY STEPS

The answers to the interrogatories that we sent out 6 weeks ago just arrived in the mail. Quickly skimming through the pages, we can already see that we did not get all of the information we were expecting. A few of the answer spaces have been left entirely blank; other interrogatories have been answered in a sentence or two where we were expecting at least a few paragraphs. Several of the answers merely say "investigation continuing, will supplement." Where do we go from here?

We need to complete several preparatory tasks before we will be ready to prepare and file a motion to compel. First, we must analyze the offending response carefully and identify each instance where it fails to provide all of the information requested. Second, if we are going to move to compel, FRCP, Rule 37(a), requires us to certify that we made a good faith effort to work out the problem with our opponent. Finally, when we tell the judge in our motion that a given answer is inadequate, we must be able to explain *why* it is inadequate, and to cite some case law or other authority to back up our assertion.

### Step 1 — Analyze the Response and Make a List of Items Not Fully Responded To

In a motion to compel, we must tell the judge exactly what is wrong with the response that we are complaining about. We do not want the judge to enter an order merely telling our opponent to file a better response. It would be too easy for our opponent to send us another response, still incomplete but worded differently, and tell the judge that everything is now fixed. We want an order that tells our opponent exactly what must be disclosed, in detail. The judge will not analyze the facts for us; it is up to us to say exactly what we want the opposing party to do.

In principle, there is nothing complicated about analyzing a discovery response. We asked for a series of items, and the response has either provided them, or not. We want to know which of our questions, document requests, or requests for admissions have not been fully and completely responded to. There are many ways in which we could approach the task; in this workshop, we explain our own preferred method, which involves preparing a detailed list of the inadequate responses, in a specified format that we will describe. Our method may seem rather obsessive-compulsive—and certainly, it is possible to put together the necessary backup for a motion to compel without being so finicky. Our goal is to use a routine that is easy to follow and that avoids having to do the same things twice. We also want to produce an unambiguous paper trail from which the judge can clearly see that it is our opponent, not us, who is being unreasonable.

**Making the List**—Before we can say what is wrong with a discovery response, we must analyze the entire response item by item. Is this really necessary? What if we receive set of answers to interrogatories and, skimming through them, we can see that some questions are left unanswered, others are answered in a few words with little or no real information provided. Must we really waste our time laboriously analyzing each answer?

Sorry, but yes. By the time our motion to compel is placed before the judge for decision, our opponent will have done everything possible to create an impression of cooperation and compliance. Quite likely, after we contact our opponent to try to resolve the dispute, as required by FRCP, Rule 37, our opponent will serve an "improved" response, so as to be able to tell the judge that she has bent over backward to comply with our request. It is therefore useful to create, from the outset, a detailed paper trail reflecting every single problem with the response. That way, we are in a position to show the judge that we told our opponent exactly what needed to be done, and we can point to the things that remain undone from our original list.

Our suggested formula for conducting this item-by-item analysis involves making a detailed list of all of the ways in which the response fails to comply with the rules. We do this in such a way that we will be able to incorporate our list, wholesale, in the eventual motion to compel. We go through the discovery response that we are analyzing, one item at a time, and determine whether each answer fully and properly responds to the request. Each defect that we find in the response becomes a separate item in our list. Each item in the list will have four subparts, with uniform headings, along the following lines:

> [Type of request] No. _____
> **Calls for:** [Here we briefly quote or paraphrase enough of our request to make clear what we asked for. Note that the local rules in some districts require that a motion to compel quote the pertinent request item and the response to it verbatim.]
> **Response:** [Here we quote the response that we are complaining about.]
> **Insufficient because:** [Here we describe what is wrong with the response. If it is easy to find a case or two to cite (from our discovery citations notebook, for example; see sidebar) we do so. We do not necessarily spend time doing extensive legal research at this stage—we save that for Step 3.]
> **Action required:** [Here we say exactly what we want the judge to order the opposing party to do. We will block-copy this subpart when we prepare the part of our motion that sets forth the ruling that we are requesting.]

As we check each item in the response, what can we expect to find? Here are the main possibilities, illustrated by examples:

1. *The response to the item appears to provide what we asked for.* If so, we move on to the next one.

> **Example:**
> *Interrogatory No. 1*
> State the make and model number of the lock(s) installed on the door of Room 407 of the Banbury Park Hotel on the night of February 5, 1996.
> **Analysis:** Nothing to do here. The response appears complete.

2. *The response is left blank.* Although contrary to the rules, it is not unusual to see a few unanswered items in a discovery response. Sometimes this is done as a stalling tactic. Our opponent knows that it will take us at least several weeks to send out a demand letter, wait for a response, and prepare a motion to compel. If the missing answers are supplied within that time, there is little that we can do as a practical matter—we are not going to file a motion to compel over a few late answers that we have now received.

> **Example:**
> *Interrogatory No. 2*
> State the name, address, and telephone number of each employee of Banbury Park Hotel who was present at the hotel or on duty at any time between 6:00 p.m. on February 5, 1996, and 6:00 a.m. on February 6, 1996.
> [answer left blank]
> **Analysis:** We add this interrogatory to our list of deficiencies:
> Interrogatory No. 2
> **Calls for:** Identity of each employee of Banbury Park Hotel who was present or on duty on the night of plaintiff's injury.
> **Response:** Left blank
> **Insufficient because:** No response
> **Action required:** Serve a complete answer to Interrogatory No. 2.

3. *The item is objected to.* We must then analyze the objection to determine whether it has any validity. If we conclude that it does not, we include the item in our list. If we can do so without an inordinate amount of research, we may also want to cite some legal authority supporting our contention that the objection is improper. (In the sidebar, we suggest keeping a notebook of discovery case citations; if you do this, you will eventually have at hand the citations that you will need in most of the common situations.)

> **Example:**
> *Interrogatory No. 3*
> State the name, address, and telephone number of each person who was a registered guest on the fourth floor of Banbury Park Hotel on the night of February 5, 1996.
> Objection. Not calculated to lead to admissible evidence. Disclosure of identities of other hotel guests violates their right to privacy.
> **Analysis:** After doing some legal research, we conclude that the right of privacy objection is not valid. Notice that we copy the language of the request verbatim in the "Action required" subpart of our list entry. We could have said, simply, "comply with Request For Production No. 5." But we will be block-copying from our list to create the order that we will ask the judge to enter. We would prefer to have the order specify exactly what our opponent must produce, so that if compliance is still not forthcoming, the record will be very clear and there can be no debate about what our opponent was ordered to do.
> Interrogatory No. 3:
> **Calls for:** Name, address, and telephone number of hotel guests on the same floor on the night of the events at issue.
> **Response:** Objected to as not calculated to lead to admissible evidence and violating guests' right to privacy.
> **Insufficient because:** Persons in the immediate vicinity of a disputed event are potential witnesses, and their identities are discoverable. Right of hotel guests to privacy is not a recognized privilege preventing discovery

of their identities. See *Davis v. Leal,*— F.Supp.2d—, 1999 WL 183643 (E.D.Cal. 1999) [an objection based on privacy is inappropriate]; *Pagano v. Oroville Hosp.,* 145 F.R.D. 683 (E.D.Cal 1993) [privacy objection inappropriate where none of the recognized privileges applies].

**Action required:** Produce all documents, including without limitation registration cards, reflecting the identities of all hotel guests occupying or registered in Rooms 400 through 447 of the Banbury Park Hotel on the night of February 5, 1996.

**4.** The item is answered without objection, but the answer is evasive or incomplete.

**Example:**
Interrogatory No. 4
State the name, address, and telephone number of each individual who at any time from January 1, 1995, to the present performed any repair or maintenance on the door lock or door hardware of Room 407 at the Banbury Park Hotel.

Marcos Davila, head of maintenance department, Banbury Park Hotel, 1594 E. Viking Rd., Las Vegas, NV 89119 Phone: 702-555-5254. Maintenance was performed by various employees of the hotel's maintenance department; defendant's investigation is continuing.

**Analysis:** It is clear from the response itself that the information provided is incomplete. "Various employees" is not adequate; we asked for names and addresses, and we are entitled to get them.

Interrogatory No. 4
**Calls for:** Identities of all persons who performed maintenance on Room 407 door lock or door hardware.

**Response:** Discloses identity of hotel maintenance supervisor, then states: "Maintenance was performed by various employees of the hotel's maintenance department; defendant's investigation is continuing."

**Insufficient because:** Defendant is required to disclose all information in its possession or control. "Investigation continuing" is not an excuse for failing to answer an interrogatory. *Williams v. Chicago Bd. of Educ.,* 155 F.3d 853, 41 Fed.R.Serv.3d 433 (7th Cir.1998)

**Action required:** Disclose the name, address, and telephone number of each person who performed maintenance on Room 407 door lock or door hardware during the period specified in Interrogatory No. 4.

**5.** The item is answered without objection and is not obviously evasive or incomplete, but you suspect that not all of the information called for has been provided.

**Example:**
Interrogatory No. 4
State the name, address, and telephone number of each individual who at any time from January 1, 1995, to the present performed any repair or maintenance on the door lock or door hardware of Room 407 at the Banbury Park Hotel.

Marcos Davila, head of maintenance department, Banbury Park Hotel, 1594 E Viking Rd., Las Vegas, NV 89119 Phone: 702-555-5254.

**Analysis:** This is the same interrogatory as in the preceding example, but now the answer leaves out the disclosure that there were others beside Marcos Davila who performed repairs or maintenance on Shannon's door lock. It seems intuitively unlikely that the head of the maintenance department would be the only one to work on the door locks, so we suspect that the answer is incomplete. We have two options: (1) We can wait until we have a chance to follow up in a deposition and find out whether there were others who worked on the locks (see sidebar on follow-up depositions); or (2) we can state in our demand letter that we surmise that there were others and ask our opponent to supplement the answer. Since we may want to depose anyone who worked on the door, and we want to know whom to depose, we will choose the latter alternative. (Of course, if our opponent continues to insist that the answer is complete as written, we will not be able to include this item in our motion to compel until we come up with some proof that some names were left out.)

Interrogatory No. 4
**Calls for:** Identities of all persons who performed maintenance on Room 407 door lock or door hardware.

**Response:** Discloses identity only of hotel maintenance supervisor.

**Insufficient because:** Defendant is required to disclose all information in its possession or control. Plaintiff believes there were others in addition to maintenance supervisor who performed maintenance or repairs on Room 407 door lock or door hardware.

**Action required:** Disclose the name, address, and telephone number of each person who performed maintenance on Room 407 door lock or door hardware during the period specified in Interrogatory No. 4.

**Step 2**     *Make a Record of Seeking Voluntary Compliance*

FRCP, Rule 37(a)(2)(B), provides that when a litigant moves to compel,

[t]he motion must include a certification that the movant has in good faith conferred or

---

# SIDEBAR

## Follow-Up Depositions

*For our overall discovery plan to succeed, it is important to get the right information early. To be able to plan our depositions, we need complete and accurate information from our opponent's disclosure statement and responses to our initial interrogatories and request for production of documents. It is from these sources that we will obtain the identities of witnesses and leads to other information.*

*Of course, our opponent would be happy if our discovery did not succeed very well, so we should expect that our opponent's initial disclosure and discovery responses may be somewhat incomplete. How incomplete depends on such things as the opposing attorney's sense of ethics; the judge's reputation for enforcing or not enforcing the rules; our own vigor in verifying compliance; and our opponent's perception of what can be gotten away with.*

*Occasionally we will receive early-stage discovery responses that seem very incomplete. There may not be anything that we can prove is missing, but common sense tells us that there must be some additional witnesses here, some other documents there. We cannot base a motion to compel on mere suspicions; yet, if we wait, we place ourselves at a serious disadvantage.*

*In such situations it is often useful to take a deposition for the purpose of verifying the discovery responses. Deposition of whom? If the opposing party is an individual, then that is whom we need to depose. (We would probably want to depose the opposing party as early as possible anyway, so we can just plan to verify the discovery responses while we are doing it.)*

*If the opposing party is a corporation or other entity, then, using FRCP, Rule 30(b)(6), we require our opponent to designate someone to testify about the subject we specify, which would be the discovery responses whose completeness is in question.*

*In the deposition, we can ask questions to probe each of the suspect items. Take, for example our interrogatory asking for the identities of everyone who worked on Shannon's door lock; assume that the response discloses only the name of the maintenance chief. We can ask questions such as these: "How did you determine that no one but the maintenance chief worked on the door lock?" "Does the hotel keep records of door lock maintenance?" "Did you ask the maintenance chief if anyone else worked on the door lock?"*

*The technique works equally well for incomplete responses to document requests. Suppose our opponent responds to our initial document request with a suspiciously small stack of documents. As usual, we number stamp each page when we log them in. When we take our deposition, we can mark the entire stack as an exhibit, then ask questions such as these: "Request No. 1 calls for 'all documents reflecting or pertaining to any maintenance performed on any guest room doors or locks at Banbury Park Hotel after January 1, 1995.' Show me which pages of Exhibit 1 comprise the response to that request." "How many guest room doors are there at Banbury Park Hotel?" "How often does a door lock typically require maintenance?" "When you perform maintenance on a door lock, what paperwork is involved?" "Is there a work order?"*

---

attempted to confer with the person or party failing to make the discovery in an effort to secure the information or material without court action.

When we have finished analyzing the response and making a list of all the deficiencies we find, we are ready to contact opposing counsel, and make the required "good faith effort" to resolve our differences and avoid a motion to compel. The exact requirements for doing this vary from one jurisdiction to another; we consult the applicable local rule. Local Rule 37.1 of the U.S. District Court for the Northern District of Iowa will serve as an example:

[N]o motion relating to depositions or other discovery shall be filed by the Clerk unless

counsel for the moving party files a separate affidavit stating that counsel has conferred personally with counsel for the opposing party in good faith to resolve or narrow by agreement the issues raised by the motion without the intervention of the court, has been unable to reach such agreement and that the resulting motion is therefore contested. In the alternative, counsel must certify such a conference was impossible and the efforts made.

Notice that the rule—as is typical of federal district court rules on this subject—does not ask us to send a demand letter, but it does ask us to "confer personally" with opposing counsel. Several practical problems arise:

## SIDEBAR

# A Notebook of Discovery Citations

*Discovery disputes are inherently factual in nature, and the judge's decision on a motion to compel is usually driven mainly by the judge's commonsense analysis of what facts are relevant to the circumstances of the lawsuit. Deep legal analysis is typically not required.*

*Nevertheless, as you gain experience analyzing discovery responses, you will find that the same issues and objections come up over and over. Courts have ruled over and over on many of these common issues and distilled many general principles, which are expressed in reported cases.*

*In a motion to compel, we are expected to cite authority to support the legal principles that we argue for. It is, of course, possible to obtain the necessary citations by researching each issue each time we write a discovery motion. There is, however, a more efficient way.*

*Go to annotations following Rules 26 through 37 in U.S. Code Annotated, U.S. Code Service, or any other source containing annotations for the Federal Rules of Civil Procedure. Following each rule, you will find annotations, one-paragraph summaries of the holdings of reported decisions that interpret the rule. The annotations are organized into a large number of subtopics, in an outline form by subject.*

*Skimming through the annotations, you will often find that a large number of the cases under one*

*subtopic seem to say the same thing. That means two things: the cases involve an issue that comes up often, and the courts have evolved a case law principle to deal with it.*

*In a relatively short time you can peruse all of the subtopics annotated under the discovery rules. Keep a notebook. Whenever you find a large number of cases saying the same thing, take a fresh page of your notebook and write down the discovery issue that they are addressing, the rule or principle that they are applying, and the citations of two or three of the cases. Choose at least one case from your local U.S. district court or from the court of appeals for your circuit; also choose one of the most recent cases. With a small investment of time (a few days, tops—trust us), you will enormously broaden your grasp of what is and is not allowed in discovery. As an added bonus, you will have created a tool that will allow you, on an instant's notice and without having to spend hours doing research, to produce citations of cases covering many common discovery situations. A tool that can grow— when you do have to research a discovery issue, you can add another page summarizing your findings. With time, you will be able to write most discovery motions without needing to do legal research.*

*A great way to spend a long weekend! Highly recommended! Give it a try—you'll be glad you did!*

■ We have no control over the opposing attorney; we cannot force him to confer with us. The rule quoted above—again, as is typical—anticipates the problem of the uncooperative opponent by allowing us, in lieu of certifying that we conferred, to certify that we tried to and a "conference was impossible." Problem solved? Not quite. Our opponent is not so inept as to refuse to confer because that might annoy the judge. What he may do, however, is cite a busy trial calendar, agree to confer with us a week from next Friday, and then have a last minute emergency and ask us to reschedule the appointment.

■ To confer in any meaningful way, there has to be an agenda. Both attorneys need to have

some idea, in advance, of what the issues are so that they can prepare properly. Otherwise, when we do confer, the opposing attorney will have a legitimate reason to ask for time to look into the issues that we raise.

■ When we confer, our opponent may promise to send us more information—information that, if it really lives up to our opponent's representations, would resolve all or part of the dispute. Naturally, the opposing attorney will need some time to check with his client, assemble the information, prepare the amended response, review it for accuracy—and before we know it, another month will have gone by and we will still not have our information.

Keep in mind that the reason there is a discovery dispute is because we are insisting on getting information that our opponent does not want to give us—otherwise, the information would have been in the response. It is only to be expected that our opponent will stall, offer arguments and excuses, and try to make the situation confusing so that the judge will find it hard to rule.

Our best defense against such tactics is a clear record. Therefore, even though most district court local rules do not require it, our first move would usually be to send the opposing attorney a letter. The letter will be easy to write because we have already done the hard part, which is going through the response and listing all of the problems. We simply enclose a copy of our list with the letter, and ask for a telephone call within some reasonably short period of time for the purpose of conferring as required by the rule. (Most local rules require "counsel" to confer, so the letter should be prepared for our supervising attorney's signature, and an attorney would need to handle the phone call when it comes. See Figure W15–1 in the Learning by Example section for a sample letter.)

Since we have enclosed our list, the opposing attorney cannot claim to be unprepared; we have informed him or her in advance, in writing, of what we want to talk about. If the opposing attorney does not call within the prescribed time, we can credibly certify to the court that we tried to confer. If the opposing attorney does call, and promises us more information, we immediately send a confirming letter reciting exactly what was promised and which of our list of items the promised information relates to. That way, we maintain a clear paper trail showing what we asked for and what we have been given.

### Step 3   *Do Legal Research and Assemble Authorities*

The final task that we need to accomplish before we can write a motion to compel is to obtain the case citations and other legal authorities to support the arguments that we will be making. There are basically two kinds of cases that we will need.

First, there will be places in our argument where we will want to recite some well-established general principle, such as "the identities of eyewitnesses to a

---

## SIDEBAR

## Other Ways of Dealing with Discovery Disputes

*In recent years, judges and legal scholars have devoted considerable energy to the question of how to reduce the costs, delays, and consumption of court time occasioned by discovery disputes. We have already seen one of the resulting reforms: mandatory disclosure rules. Discovery disputes still occur, however, and the courts continue to look for innovative ways to resolve them.*

*One of the perceived drawbacks of the present, motion-based system is that there is no mechanism for resolving small problems quickly, before they escalate into a full-blown motion battle. In this context, even the requirement for counsel to confer before filing a motion, well intentioned though it may be, merely serves to interpose still another hoop to be jumped through on the way to a decision by the judge. What is needed is a more streamlined procedure, but one that still results in a binding ruling. Here are a few of the ideas that some districts are experimenting with:*

■ *A number of districts delegate the adjudication of discovery motions to magistrates, special masters, or other officers who are not judges. These officials are generally able*

*to devote more time to a given matter than a judge could.*

■ *The U.S. District Court for the Eastern District of Texas has instituted a "discovery hotline." Local Rule 26 provides:*

*The court shall provide a judicial officer on call during business hours to rule on discovery disputes and to enforce provisions of these rules. Counsel may contact the judicial officer by dialing the hotline number listed above for any case in the district and get an immediate hearing on the record and ruling on the discovery dispute or request to enforce or modify provisions of the rules as they relate to a particular case.*

■ *Local Rule 37.2 of the U.S. District Court for the Southern District of New York does not allow a discovery motion to be heard unless "counsel for the moving party has first requested an informal conference with the court and such has either been denied or the discovery dispute has not been resolved as a consequence of such a conference."*

disputed event are generally discoverable." Any such statements need to be supported by citation of authorities, such as citations to reported appellate cases, statutes, or rules. The easiest way to find cases that can be cited for general principles is to consult a digest under the civil procedure/discovery headings, or check the annotations under Rules 26–37 in a set of annotated federal statutes. This kind of research is most easily done in the library, with books—computerized research aids do not lend themselves very well to skimming and browsing. Of course, if you follow our suggestion about a notebook of discovery case citations (see sidebar), you may be able to find much of what you need in your own notebook.

Second, we would like to be able to cite cases that apply the general principles to fact situations similar to our own, and reach conclusions similar to the ones that we are arguing for. If we want to argue, for example, that we are entitled to see the maintenance records on the door locks for all the rooms in the hotel, we had better be prepared to tell the judge why those records are "reasonably calculated to lead to admissible evidence"; see FRCP, Rule 26(b)(1). If possible, we would like to be able to cite a case or two in which similar records were held discoverable under similar circumstances. For finding cases with similar facts, computerized research aids such as Westlaw and Lexis are ideal.

A motion to compel lends itself easily to researching the legal issues in advance. For each item on our list there is really only one issue: Are we entitled to the discovery that we requested; that is, is the requested information discoverable? We already have a list of all of the things that we think are wrong with our opponent's response; now all we need to do is go through the list, item by item, and try to find cases or other authorities to support our contentions.

## DRAFTING STEPS

If we have done the preparatory work well, writing the motion will be easy. We already have the necessary ingredients—all we need to do is pull them together into a written filing.

A motion to compel follows the same basic layout and format as any other motion (see Workshop 14). We will need the motion itself, the supporting memorandum, and, depending on the content of the motion and the requirements of the local rules, attachments. In this workshop, we will rearrange the steps a bit and write the memorandum first; we do this because our decisions about which issues to include in the memorandum will determine what specific orders we ask for in the motion.

It goes without saying that we must check the local rules carefully before we start writing. Many courts have adopted special rules for discovery motions. Here is a sampling:

- Some courts require the moving party to reproduce each disputed request item and the response to it, verbatim. Some require this to be in the body of the memorandum supporting the motion (see, e.g., Local Rule 37.2, Northern District of Ohio), others in an attachment [see, e.g., Local Rule CV-7(b)(1), Eastern District of Texas]. Don't forget to check **www.uscourts.gov/links** for most of the district court local rules.

- Some courts require the title of the motion to reflect the identities of the parties involved. In other words, not "Motion to Compel" but "Plaintiff John Doe's Motion to Compel Answers to Interrogatories by Defendant ABC Corp." (see, e.g., District of Oregon Local Rule 7.3).

- Some courts require the motion itself to recite that counsel have conferred in an effort to resolve the dispute (see Local Rule 37, Middle District of Georgia). Others require a separate affidavit or certificate containing the recital attachment [see, e.g., Local Rule CV-7(h), Eastern District of Texas]. Some require the recital to include details, such as the date and time when counsel conferred, the names of the attorneys who conferred, and the manner in which they conferred (i.e., in person or by telephone) (see Local Rule 37–3.04(B), Eastern District of Missouri).

## Step 4 | Draft the Memorandum

Before we start writing, some planning is in order. We need to decide exactly which issues to present in our motion to compel and how best to organize the presentation.

The motion to compel does not necessarily have to include every item in our list of deficiencies. Based on our research and review of legal authorities, we evaluate the strength of our position on each disputed item. We also consider the importance of each item on our list in the context of the overall lawsuit. The judge's attention is a limited resource, and we will get only so much of it so it is better to concentrate on the items that really matter. In short, we save our ammunition for battles that we can win, over issues that will make a difference to the outcome of the lawsuit. We prune our list accordingly.

After deciding which issues to include, we must decide how best to present them. There are several possible ways to organize the memorandum supporting a motion to compel:

1. We can simply take the issues in the order in which they appear in our list of deficiencies (which is presumably in the numerical sequence of the original request). This makes the writing task easy—begin with the list as it is, add headings, argument, and a conclusion, and we have a memorandum.

2. Sometimes, the problem areas in a discovery response reduce to one or two important items that we badly need (and perhaps a larger number of minor omissions which, though aggravating, involve facts that we can establish in other ways if necessary). In such situations, we may decide to address our motion to the few important issues and abandon the others entirely because, as mentioned, it is better to keep the judge's focus on the things that we most want. We prune the less important items from our list, and create our memorandum from the remaining ones, adding argument as necessary.

3. It may also happen that the overall depth and quality of the disclosure is poor. Many items are answered incompletely or evasively. There is no single item that stands out—the problems affect the entire response. Then we may need to organize our motion differently. Instead of addressing each item individually, we may decide to group related items. We might, for example, have one section in our motion in which we present legal argument that a particular type of objection is invalid, then list all of the items involving that objection.

In the Summary of Argument section of the memorandum, we try to convey an accurate general impression of the kinds of information we are trying to obtain, and briefly summarize the principal arguments supporting their discoverability. The main body of the memorandum is derived from the list that we prepared in Step 2.

## Step 5    *Draft the Motion*

We block-copy the caption from our form (see Workshop 4) and enter an appropriate title. The preamble begins in the usual way, but rather than a generic statement that the moving party "moves to compel discovery," we recommend a very specific enumeration of exactly what the moving party is asking the court to order the responding party to do.

**Example of how not to do it:**
Plaintiff respectfully moves to compel discovery pursuant to FRCP, Rule 37(a).

**Example of a better preamble:**
Plaintiff respectfully moves pursuant to FRCP, Rule 37(a), for an order of the court compelling defendant Park Hotels Group, Inc., to serve, on or before August 7, 2000, answers to plaintiff's interrogatories to said defendant dated April 24, 2000, in accordance with the following:

1. Disclose the name, address, and telephone number of each person who performed maintenance on Room 407 door lock or door hardware during the period specified in Interrogatory No. 4.

. . . .
Etc.

The preamble in the first example is too general. If the court grants our motion and takes the trouble to dictate an order specifying what the opposing party is to do, well and good. But if, as sometimes happens, the court simply issues a minute entry saying "motion granted," all we will have is an order telling the opposing party, in effect, to do a better job. When the opposing party serves another response that still does not measure up, there will be plenty of room for her to argue about whether the new response now complies with the discovery rules.

In the second example, we specify exactly what we want the court to order our opponent to do. Now, if the minute entry merely says "motion granted," what the court has granted is a motion asking for an order whose terms we have already specified in the motion. In effect, the language of the motion becomes the order. If our opponent serves another response that fails to disclose everything that we specified in the motion, we should have no trouble moving for sanctions, because we can point to the specific terms that were not complied with.

If we were careful in writing the Action Required paragraphs of our list of deficiencies, we can block-copy them for the numbered subparts of the requested order. Of course, the requested order should match the argument in the memorandum—if we have decided to leave out any items, or if we have grouped the items in some particular way, we do the same in the requested order.

The motion ends with the usual reference to the memorandum and other supporting attachments, if any (see Workshop 14, Step 1), and appropriate date and signature lines.

## Step 6    *Attachments*

Attachments commonly submitted with motions to compel include the following:

- The required certificate stating that the attorneys have conferred in an effort to resolve the dispute. Whether this should be submitted as an attachment or included as a part of the motion itself depends on the local rules and customs of each district.

- Copies of the pertinent discovery papers. In some jurisdictions, the local rules require attachment of copies of the discovery request and response to which the motion pertains. (Typically, these would be included only with the copy intended for the judge.)

- Copies of important legal authorities cited in the memorandum. As discussed more fully in Workshop 14, Step 3, it may be appropriate to attach a copy of a case or statute to the judge's copy of a motion if the case or statute is important to our argument and not likely to be readily accessible by the judge.

## CONCLUDING STEPS

Most U.S. district courts handle discovery motions in the same way that they do any other motion. Therefore, the follow-up steps—filing, serving, docketing, getting the motion placed before the judge for decision—are generally as described in Workshop 14, Steps 4 through 6. Be sure to consult your local rules for any specific provisions affecting discovery motions.

## *Motions to Compel: Learning by Example*

We will now apply our skills to the task of analyzing a hypothetical response and taking the steps to prepare and file a motion to compel. As in Workshop 14, we will demonstrate the basic principles and present a partially completed motion to compel; you will complete the motion and modify it as necessary to conform to customary practice in your district.

We will assume that Shannon's attorney has served on Park Hotels Group a set of interrogatories consisting of the first four that we used as examples in Step 1 earlier, plus two more that we will leave for you to practice on in the Learning by Doing section. (Real-world sets of interrogatories are often larger, but we are limited by space considerations.) Here are the interrogatories and answers:

*Interrogatory No. 1*
State the make and model number of the lock(s) installed on the door of Room 407 of the Banbury Park Hotel on the night of February 5, 1996.
Schlage AL85PD F93

*Interrogatory No. 2*
State the name, address, and telephone number of each employee of Banbury Park Hotel who was present at the hotel or on duty at any time between 6:00 p.m. on February 5, 1996, and 6:00 a.m. on February 6, 1996.
**[answer left blank]**

*Interrogatory No. 3*
State the name, address, and telephone number of each person who was a registered guest on the fourth floor of Banbury Park Hotel on the night of February 5, 1996.
Objection. Not calculated to lead to admissible evidence. Disclosure of identities of other hotel guests violates their right to privacy.

*Interrogatory No. 4*
State the name, address, and telephone number of each individual who at any time from January 1, 1995, to the present performed any repair or maintenance on the door lock or door hardware of Room 407 at the Banbury Park Hotel.
Marcos Davila, head of maintenance department, Banbury Park Hotel, 1594 E Viking Rd., Las Vegas, NV 89119 Phone: 702-555-5254. Maintenance was performed by various employees of the hotel's maintenance department; defendant's investigation is continuing.

*Interrogatory No. 5*
With respect to each civil lawsuit brought against any person arising from any injury or claimed injury occurring on the premises of Banbury Park Hotel at any time from January 1, 1994, to the present, state the names and addresses of all parties to each such lawsuit, state in what court each such lawsuit was brought, and state the cause number of each such lawsuit.
Objected to as irrelevant and not calculated to lead to admissible evidence.

*Interrogatory No. 6*
Is it your contention that the key furnished to defendant Collins by your employee was incapable of opening the door lock of Room 407? _____ If yes, state in detail each and every fact upon which you base such contention.
Objected to on the grounds that "contention" interrogatories are improper in the early stages of discovery. See, e.g., *In re Convergent Technologies Securities Litigation*, 108 F.R.D. 328 (N.D.Cal. 1985).

# SIDEBAR

## Responding to Motions to Compel

*So far, we have been viewing discovery motion procedure from the standpoint of the moving party—the party who served a discovery request and is dissatisfied with the response. Now let us shift our focus and consider the responding party's position. When we find ourselves on the receiving end of a threatened motion to compel, it is usually because of one or more of the following:*

### Our Response Was Inadequate

*We would not, of course, deliberately serve a response that did not comply with the discovery rules. Nevertheless, mistakes are sometimes made and, sometimes, we find it necessary to serve an incomplete response because of circumstances beyond our control. Perhaps our client was unable to assemble the information that we needed in time, or perhaps we were depending on someone else (say, an expert witness) who did not meet agreed deadlines. In theory, if it is obvious that we cannot serve a complete response on time, we should contact the opposing attorney and try to agree on an extension, or, failing that, file a motion and ask the court for an extension. But opposing attorneys do not always cooperate in such matters, and there may not be time to have a motion for an extension decided.*

*Our best strategy in this situation is to try to get our response into compliance with the rules as quickly as possible. We will have at least a few days or weeks before our opponent can comply with the requirement to confer and prepare and file a motion to compel, and then we will have some period of time before our response to the motion to compel is due. If we turn over whatever information is missing by the time we file our response to the motion to compel, our opponent will most likely withdraw the motion; if not, we will have little to fear as long as our response makes it clear that we are doing the best that we can to comply.*

### There Is a Genuine Dispute over Discoverability

*Another reason why our opponent may be threatening a motion to compel is because we have objected to one or more of our opponent's questions or requests. Our goal here should be to avoid disclosing anything that will harm our case to the extent that we have legitimate legal grounds to support our objection. At the same time, we would like, if possible, to avoid the expense and distraction of having to respond to a motion to compel. Therefore, when the opposing attorney contacts us to confer about the dispute, we will do our best to sell him on the validity of our objection. Often, it may be helpful to try to reach some compromise—perhaps by offering to disclose part of the requested information, if we can do so without handing our opponent ammunition that will seriously jeopardize our case.*

*Failing that, we will have no choice but to respond to the motion to compel. We will research and prepare a response memorandum that presents the reasons for our objection and cites appropriate cases, statutes, or rules to support our position.*

### The Opposing Party Believes Our Response Is Incomplete

*If our response actually is incomplete, we should fix it. But our opponent may believe that we are holding out when we are not, and threaten a motion to compel. Unlike disputes over objections, where the outcome depends on how the judge applies the applicable legal rules, disputes over the completeness of answers are inherently factual. It is up to the moving party to convince the judge that we have more information than we disclosed. Here again, we will do our best to convince the opposing attorney that we have disclosed everything, so as to avoid a distracting motion battle if possible. If our opponent insists on filing a motion to compel, we will need to present a response memorandum showing what information exists and what we disclosed.*

## PREPARATORY STEPS

**Step 1** *Analyze the Response and Make a List of Items Not Fully Responded To*

Here is our list, based on the first four interrogatories. The last two are left for you—see the Learning by Doing section later in this workshop.

> *Interrogatory No. 2*
> **Calls for:** Identity of each employee of Banbury Park Hotel who was present or on duty on the night of plaintiff's injury.
> **Response:** Left blank
> **Insufficient because:** No response
> **Action required:** Serve a complete answer to Interrogatory No. 2.

> *Interrogatory No. 3*
> **Calls for:** Name, address, and telephone number of hotel guests on the same floor on the night of the events at issue.
> **Response:** Objected to as not calculated to lead to admissible evidence and violating guests' right to privacy.
> **Insufficient because:** Persons in the immediate vicinity of a disputed event are potential witnesses, and their identities are discoverable. Right of hotel guests to privacy is not a recognized privilege preventing discovery of their identities. See *Davis v. Leal,*—F.Supp.2d—, 1999 WL 183643 (E.D.Cal. 1999) [an objection based on privacy is inappropriate]; *Pagano v. Oroville Hosp.,* 145 F.R.D. 683 (E.D.Cal 1993) [privacy objection inappropriate where none of the recognized privileges applies].
> **Action required:** Produce all documents, including without limitation registration cards, reflecting the identities of all hotel guests occupying or registered in Rooms 400 through 447 of the Banbury Park Hotel on the night of February 5, 1996.

> *Interrogatory No. 4*
> **Calls for:** Identities of all persons who performed maintenance on Room 407 door lock or door hardware.
> **Response:** Discloses identity of hotel maintenance supervisor, then states: "Maintenance was performed by various employees of the hotel's maintenance department; defendant's investigation is continuing."
> **Insufficient Because:** Defendant is required to disclose all information in its possession or control. "Investigation continuing" is not an excuse for failing to answer an interrogatory. *Williams v. Chicago Bd. of Educ.,* 155 F.3d 853, 41 Fed.R.Serv.3d 433 (7th Cir.1998)

> **Action required:** Disclose the name, address, and telephone number of each person who performed maintenance on Room 407 door lock or door hardware during the period specified in Interrogatory No. 4.

**Step 2** *Make a Record of Seeking Voluntary Compliance*

We check the local rules for the U.S. District Court for the District of Arizona, and find that Local Rule 1.10(j) provides:

> No discovery motion filed in a civil case and no motion filed in a criminal case will be considered or decided unless a statement of moving counsel is attached thereto certifying that after personal consultation and sincere efforts to do so, counsel have been unable to satisfactorily resolve the matter. Any civil discovery or criminal motion brought before the Court without prior personal consultation with the other party and a sincere effort to resolve the matter, may result in sanctions.

Although the local rule does not require a written demand, we choose to initiate contact with opposing counsel by letter, so that when we do confer directly, our opponent cannot claim lack of opportunity to prepare. The letter is shown in Figure W15–1.

We hope Gail Stoddard will telephone Allen Porter as requested. If not, Porter will attempt to telephone her. If he does so, and she does not return the calls within a few days, he will be free to file the motion to compel because he can certify that he made reasonable efforts to confer, and recite that he sent a letter and attempted telephone contact.

**Step 3** *Do Legal Research and Assemble Authorities*

Legal research entails two quite distinct skills: (1) knowing what kinds of cases or other authorities to look for and (2) knowing how to use the right legal research techniques to find them. Research techniques are properly the subject of another course. Knowing what to look for is another matter—when we do legal research to support a motion, we usually have at least a general idea of what it is that we are trying to establish.

What kinds of cases should we look for to support plaintiff's position on Interrogatories 2, 3, and 4? Let us try to list the main points that we might want to make in our motion. We would like to be able to cite case law or other authority supporting each one, if possible.

---

**Figure W15–1   Letter Seeking Voluntary Compliance**

**SIMON & PORTER**
Attorneys
1000 North Central Avenue, Suite 2800
Phoenix, Arizona 85004
(602) 555-4321

June 7, 2000

Gail Stoddard, Esq.
Crandall, Elkins & Major
2000 North Central Avenue, Suite 2900
Phoenix, Arizona 85004

Re: Martin v. Collins

Dear Ms. Stoddard:

   This concerns the answers to interrogatories dated May 29, 2000, which you served on behalf of defendant Park Hotels Group, Inc. in the above referenced action. Plaintiff's position is that defendant's answers to Interrogatories Nos. 2, 3, and 4 are insufficient, for the reasons specified in the analysis enclosed.

   In keeping with the requirements of Local Rule 1.10(j), I would like to speak to you at your convenience, but in any case no later than June 21, 2000, in an effort to arrive at a satisfactory resolution.

Sincerely,

Allen Porter

---

1. An order compelling answers is appropriate where some answers have been left blank.

2. Persons in the vicinity of a disputed event are potential witnesses; information about their identities is "reasonably calculated to lead to admissible evidence."

3. When information meets the discoverability test of Rule 26 ("reasonably calculated to lead to admissible evidence"), it must be provided unless an applicable privilege applies.

4. There is no privilege covering the identity of hotel guests.

5. "Right to privacy" is not a recognized basis for withholding the identities of potential witnesses in federal court.

6. In factually similar cases, courts have granted discovery of the identities of persons who were physically in the same vicinity as a disputed event.

7. The fact that a party has not completed her investigation is not an excuse for failing to answer an interrogatory.

8. A party must disclose in answer to an interrogatory all information available to the party.

Using the legal research techniques that we have learned in our legal research course, we try to find cases supporting each of these points. Inevitably, we will find that the cases do not say exactly what we anticipated, and we will have to modify our arguments accordingly. After we have spent a few hours in the library or on the computer, we should be able to modify our list of main points to argue, based on what we have read in the cases. When we have a viable list of main points and case, statute, or rule citations to support each one, we arrange them in logical order and outline our argument. Then we are ready to start writing the motion papers.

## DRAFTING STEPS

**Step 4**   *Draft the Memorandum*

As we did in Workshop 14, we sketch in the broad outlines of the memorandum, as shown in Figure W15–2. In the Learning by Doing section later you will be assigned to fill in the gaps.

**Figure W15–2  Sample Memorandum in Support of Plaintiff's Motion to Compel**

SIMON & PORTER
Allen Porter
1000 North Central Avenue, Suite 2800
Phoenix, Arizona 85004
(602) 555-4321
Attorneys for plaintiff

**IN THE UNITED STATES DISTRICT COURT**

**DISTRICT OF ARIZONA**

| | |
|---|---|
| SHANNON MARTIN, a single woman, )<br>)<br>)<br>Plaintiff, )<br>)<br>v. )<br>)<br>ARTHUR COLLINS, et ux., et al., )<br>)<br>Defendants. )<br>_____ ) | NO._____<br><br>MEMORANDUM IN SUPPORT OF<br>PLAINTIFF'S MOTION TO COMPEL<br>ANSWERS TO INTERROGATORIES<br>BY DEFENDANT PARK HOTELS<br>GROUP, INC. |

<u>Summary of Argument</u>

1. Defendant has made *no* answer to Interrogatory No. 2, and should be ordered to do so.

2. Other hotel guests may have witnessed the events from which this lawsuit arises; their identities are not privileged and should be disclosed.

3. Plaintiff is entitled to discover the identities of persons who performed maintenance on the door lock by which plaintiff's assailant gained entrance. That defendant's investigation is incomplete is not an excuse for withholding whatever information is now in defendant's possession or control.

*Argument*

*I. Factual Background: The Manner of Defendant Collins's Entry Into Plaintiff's Room Is The Main Factual Issue In This Lawsuit: Evidence Thereon Is Discoverable.*

The injuries for which plaintiff is suing occurred when defendant Collins, using a key given him by defendant Hotel, entered plaintiff's hotel room while she was sleeping. How this could have happened is the central factual issue in this lawsuit. Plaintiff served interrogatories for the purpose of identifying the individuals who were in a position to have information about the events surrounding plaintiff's injury, or about the operation and condition of the door lock by which defendant Collins gained admittance to plaintiff's room.

*II. Defendant Has Made No Response To Plaintiff's Interrogatory Asking For The Identities Of Hotel Employees Present On The Night Of Plaintiff's Injury.*

Interrogatory No. 2 seeks to discover the identities of hotel employees present on the night of plaintiff's injury:

*Interrogatory No. 2*

State the name, address, and telephone number of each employee of Banbury Park Hotel who was present at the hotel or on duty at any time between 6:00 p.m. on February 5, 1996, and 6:00 a.m. on February 6, 1996.

*III. Other Hotel Guests On The Floor Where Plaintiff's Injury Occurred May Have Witnessed Relevant Events: Their Identities Are Discoverable.*

*continued*

**Figure W15–2    Sample Memorandum in Support of Plaintiff's Motion to Compel,** *continued*

Interrogatory No. 3 seeks to discover the identities of other hotel guests registered on plaintiff's floor on the night of the plaintiff's injury. Any of these may have had the opportunity to observe or hear all or part of the events at issue. Plaintiff seeks their names and addresses so that plaintiff can contact each one to determine what, if anything, each observed. Defendant has refused to disclose the information requested.

*Interrogatory No. 3*

State the name, address, and telephone number of each person who was a registered guest on the fourth floor of Banbury Park Hotel on the night of February 5, 1996.

Objection. Not calculated to lead to admissible evidence. Disclosure of identities of other hotel guests violates their right to privacy.

*V. Conclusion: The Court Should Order Defendant To Disclose The Identities Of Potential Witnesses As Called For By Plaintiff's Interrogatories.*

Each of the three interrogatories here at issue seeks to identify potential witnesses, a legitimate, indeed essential, goal of discovery. Defendant has withheld the information requested—in the case of Interrogatories Nos. 2 and 4 with no excuse offered, and in the case of Interrogatory No. 3 on the basis of a 'right of privacy' having no basis under federal law.

    Plaintiff's motion to compel should be granted.

    RESPECTFULLY SUBMITTED this 12th day of June, 2000.

                                 SIMON & PORTER

                              ————————————

                              Allen Porter

                              Attorneys for plaintiff

(Certificate of mailing goes here—see Workshop 4.)

---

### Step 5    *Draft the Motion*

Now we prepare the motion (see Figure W15–3). We have elected to wait until the memorandum is complete before writing the motion—that way, we know exactly what kind of order our argument will support.

### Step 6    *Attachments*

To the set of motion papers for the judge, we attach a copy of the interrogatories and answers, since they are not voluminous. With all copies, we attach a certification that we have complied with Local Rule 1.10(j), as shown in Figure W15–4.

## Motions to Compel: Learning by Doing

Your assignment for this workshop is to expand the skeleton motion to compel shown in Figure W15–2

into a complete memorandum and modify it as necessary to conform to the local rules and customs of the U.S. district court having jurisdiction in your locality. (At your instructor's option, the state court of your locality may be substituted.) Assume the following hypothetical facts:

> You are a paralegal in the office of Allen Porter, attorney for Shannon Martin. The firm's office is in your city (make up a suitable address). The lawsuit, *Martin v. Collins,* is pending in the U.S. district court having jurisdiction in your locality. The other facts of the hypothetical are unchanged. You have received the answers to the six interrogatories shown at the beginning of the Learning by Example section. Allen Porter has assigned you to analyze the answers and, to the extent that you find them to be insufficient, take appropriate steps to obtain proper answers.

## EXERCISES

In carrying out this assignment, you should follow the step-by-step formula described in this workshop.

*1.*  Locate the local rules of your U.S. district court pertaining to discovery motions. (For

---

**Figure W15–3 Sample Motion to Compel**

SIMON & PORTER
Allen Porter
1000 North Central Avenue, Suite 2800
Phoenix, Arizona 85004
(602) 555-4321
Attorneys for plaintiff

### IN THE UNITED STATES DISTRICT COURT

### DISTRICT OF ARIZONA

| | |
|---|---|
| SHANNON MARTIN, a single woman, ) ) ) Plaintiff, ) ) v. ) ) ARTHUR COLLINS, et ux., et al., ) ) Defendants. ) ) | NO._____ PLAINTIFF'S MOTION TO COMPEL ANSWERS TO INTERROGATORIES BY DEFENDANT PARK HOTELS GROUP, INC. |

Plaintiff respectfully moves pursuant to Rule 37(a), FRCP, for an order of the court compelling defendant Park Hotels Group, Inc., to serve, on or before August 7, 2000, full and complete answers to plaintiff's interrogatories to said defendant dated April 24, 2000, and ordering that said answers shall:
1. Disclose the name, address, and telephone number of each employee of Banbury Park Hotel who was present at the hotel or on duty at any time between 6:00 p.m. on February 5, 1996, and 6:00 a.m. on February 6, 1996.
2. Disclose the name, address, and telephone number of each person who was a registered guest on the fourth floor of Banbury Park Hotel on the night of February 5, 1996.
3. Disclose the name, address, and telephone number of each individual who at any time from January 1, 1995, to the present performed any repair or maintenance on the door lock or door hardware of Room 407 at the Banbury Park Hotel.
This motion is based upon the accompanying memorandum of law.
RESPECTFULLY SUBMITTED this 12th day of June, 2000.

SIMON & PORTER

_____
Allen Porter
Attorneys for plaintiff

(Certificate of mailing goes here—see Workshop 4.)

---

many districts, the local rules can be accessed from the U.S. Courts Internet site, **www.uscourts.gov;** if the rules for your court are not available there, they can be obtained from the clerk's office.) Also, while carrying out this assignment, comply with the local rules governing motions in general which you found while carrying out your assignment in Workshop 14.

2. Review and if possible obtain copies for your forms file of a motion to compel, response, and reply filed in the U.S. district court of your locality to use as a guide on matters of format, layout, and organization. Your instructor may be able to provide these or suggest how to obtain them. Failing that, you can access the court files of pending lawsuits at the clerk's office (but in that case be prepared to take

**Figure W15–4   Sample Certification**

SIMON & PORTER
Allen Porter
1000 North Central Avenue, Suite 2800
Phoenix, Arizona 85004
(602) 555-4321
Attorneys for plaintiff

### IN THE UNITED STATES DISTRICT COURT

### DISTRICT OF ARIZONA

| | |
|---|---|
| SHANNON MARTIN, a single woman, ) | |
| ) | |
| ) | NO.\_\_\_\_\_ |
| Plaintiff, ) | |
| ) | LOCAL RULE 1.10(J) CERTIFICATE |
| v. ) | OF CONFERENCE IN SUPPORT OF |
| ) | PLAINTIFF'S MOTION TO COMPEL |
| ARTHUR COLLINS, et ux., et al., ) | ANSWERS TO INTERROGATORIES |
| ) | BY DEFENDANT PARK HOTELS |
| Defendants. ) | GROUP, INC |
| _____) | |

The undersigned attorney hereby certifies that he has personally consulted with Gail Stoddard, Esq., attorney for defendant Park Hotels Group, Inc. in a sincere effort to resolve the issues presented by the discovery motion that this certificate accompanies, and that counsel have been unable to resolve the matter.

RESPECTFULLY SUBMITTED this 12th day of June, 2000.

SIMON & PORTER

\_\_\_\_\_
Allen Porter
Attorneys for plaintiff

(Certificate of mailing goes here—see Workshop 4.)

---

notes—copies are expensive). Find out exactly what papers need to be filed in connection with a motion to compel in your court, and what each one needs to contain.

3. Following the instructions under Step 1, complete the list of deficiencies begun under Step 1 in the Learning by Example section by analyzing Interrogatories Nos. 5 and 6 and writing appropriate list entries.

4. At your instructor's option, modify the letter appearing in Figure W15–1 to conform to local practice as specified by your instructor.

5. Following the instructions under Step 3, perform the research necessary to complete the drafting of the memorandum. At your instructor's option, either:

a. (Minimum research option) Research the objection made to Interrogatory No. 6 by reading the case cited in the objection, In re Convergent Technologies Securities Litigation, 108 F.R.D. 328 (N.D.Cal. 1985). Do not forget to Shepardize or KeyCite to determine whether the holding of the case has been overruled or modified.

b. (Full research option)  Research each of the points listed under Step 3 in the Learning by Example section. List the issues that you think should be researched that arise from Interrogatories Nos. 5 and 6 and research those issues. On each issue, try to find at least one case decided by a U.S. district court or U.S. Court of Appeals in the circuit having appellate jurisdiction over the federal courts of your locality. Take notes of the citations and holdings of the cases that you find.

6. Taking as a starting point the memorandum excerpted in Figure W15–2, and, at your instructor's option, either:
   a. (Minimum research option) Prepare a complete memorandum supporting a motion to compel addressed only to Interrogatory No. 6.
   b. (Full research option) Prepare a complete memorandum supporting a motion to compel addressed to whatever issues you deem appropriate to assert, arising from all six interrogatories.

In drafting the memorandum, conform to the local rules and customs of your local court.

7. Following the instructions under Step 5, prepare the motion to compel, conforming to the local rules and customs of your local court. The motion should be addressed either to Interrogatory No. 6 only, or to the entire set, depending on which option your instructor has assigned.

8. Following the instructions under Step 6 and applicable local rules and customs, prepare a certificate complying with the requirement to certify that counsel have attempted to resolve the issues.

# PRACTICE POINTERS
## *Writing Tips: Brevity and Simplicity*

In motion writing one of the aims is to educate the reader as effortlessly as possible. Therefore, brevity must be your motto. Keep your paragraphs as short as possible. Paragraphs that run on for pages are intimidating to readers. Long paragraphs tend to have too many ideas, which makes it difficult for readers to assimilate even if you provide wonderful transitions and lead them through every step of the analysis.

Legal concepts tend to be abstract and sometimes complex. Long paragraphs add to that complexity. If you are expressing difficult concepts you want to express them in as concise and succinct a manner as possible. Turn to your own experience for verification. When you are learning a foreign concept do you appreciate short paragraphs with brief, to-the-point explanations? Or do you enjoy sifting through lengthy paragraphs with ponderous explanations? Write as you prefer to be written to.

Sentences too should be as short as possible without sacrificing content. Sometimes you will find it necessary to write relatively long sentences, because to break up the thought into separate sentences would interfere with your explanation. Just remember that long sentences are not a sign of superior intellect. More often they are a sign of laziness—of a writer who failed to take the time to rewrite. Keep in mind as well that your most powerful sentences will probably be your shortest sentences. When you really want to make a lasting impression use a short sentence.

To reinforce this concept of brevity think for a moment of some of the most powerful oratorical statements: "I have a dream," "Physician, heal thyself," "The unexamined life is not worth living." What made these statements so memorable? In part because they were so short and yet so meaningful. Advertising slogans are another prime example of the power of brevity. Effective communicators are masters of verbal efficiency.

You can, however, take brevity to an extreme and make every sentence short. To make your writing more interesting and powerful, vary your sentence length. Short sentences are not powerful if every sentence is short. They gain power because they stand apart from the other sentences. In a nutshell, avoid writing interminably long, convoluted sentences that have to be read several times before they can be understood. And when you have an important point to make, make it using a short sentence.

In keeping with the theme of brevity, simplicity is another goal toward which to strive. Nothing is served if you write short paragraphs and sentences and use convoluted language in the process. Choose your words carefully and selectively, opting for words that effectively and simply convey ideas. The ideas you are presenting are often complex enough. Do not complicate the matter by using complex terminology.

Simplicity does not require weak words, however. To the contrary, powerful words that conjure up vivid images are preferred. Such words are efficient and accurate. They are efficient in that they create mental image pictures with a minimal use of words. They are accurate in that they are likely to create the same mental image in the reader's mind that exists in the writer's mind. For example, describing a man as "ambling" creates a clearer mental image than describing him as "walking slowly and aimlessly." The image is not only clearer but requires fewer words.

Choose your words, especially your verbs and adjectives, as carefully as you do your wardrobe. You select clothes to convey an image of professionalism or casualness or elegance, etc. Your vocabulary creates an image as well. If you want to bore your reader you say over and over "The court held" but if you want to create a stronger image in the reader's mind you choose your verbs more carefully. You might say that the "The court articulated" or the "The court explained" or "The court pontificated" or "The court bemoaned" or "The court accentuated." If you want to create a vague mental image picture you say "It was hot that day." But if you want to create a vivid mental image picture you say "The searing sun blistered their skin in a few minutes." The client isn't merely "upset," the client is "tormented" or "agitated." Your opposition doesn't just "argue" it "strains to argue" or it "lamely argues." The words you choose must accurately portray what you are describing but they should be vivid. Accurate but vivid words are more powerful than bland, generic words.

Another aspect of simplicity is the avoidance of extraneous words, words that take up space but whose absence will not affect the meaning of what you are conveying. Legalisms abound in extraneous words: heretofore, aforesaid, herein, thereunto, etc. Eliminate these words from your vocabulary. Do not operate under the delusion that you are more "lawyerly" if you adopt such archaic jargon. When you consider incorporating such a phrase as "in excess of" ask yourself if you couldn't as easily say "more than." Isn't "annually" just as good as "per annum"? Isn't "for" just as effective as "for the purpose of," "by" more concise than "on or before," and "use" more succinct than "utilize"? Must you tell someone you are giving them your "honest opinion"? Can't we assume that any opinion you give will be honest? Why say "In the case of *X. v. Y.*" when you can simply say "In *X. v. Y.*"?

When reviewing your writing, take on the role of an efficiency expert. Imagine that each word costs you money. Then eliminate every word that is duplicative, archaic, or otherwise unnecessary. Be tough with yourself in this process but fair. Do not eliminate important words in the name of efficiency and do not change the meaning in the process.

## TECHNO TIP

Most of us use the copper wire telephone line to connect with the Internet. Current technology limits the transmission rates on these lines to 56k bps. If you are connected to a fiber optics line the potential for data transmission greatly increases. Currently fiber optic lines can transmit at over 10,000k bps (10,000,000 bps). Transmission rates of 1,000,000k bps are possible because fiber optic cables transmit with light rather than electrical impulses. Currently the cost of such a connection is out of reach for the individual. Satellite communication is, however, available. In satellite systems the data is downloaded at extremely high data rates (approximately 1,000k bps) but the user communicates with the site at her modem rate, generally a maximum of 56k bps.

Special lines now being offered by the communication industry, such as the T-1 connection can transmit at over 1,000k bps. These lines are becoming more economically feasible but only for the serious (and financially benefited) user. Technology in this area is constantly evolving. Wireless solutions currently exist that allow you to use your cellular phone to receive and transmit data. A modem is still required but many have interfaces that allow connection to the cellular phone.

## FORMS FILE

*In your forms file, include a copy of a motion to compel, a motion for sanctions, or a motion for a protective order as well as a response and a reply. Make sure each motion includes a memorandum of points and authorities. Have an attorney or faculty member review each motion to make sure that it is well researched, argued, and written.*

# Motions for Summary Judgment and Other Tactical Motions

## INTRODUCTION: WHAT MOTIONS CAN ACHIEVE

The right motion at the right time can often win a lawsuit, or at least gain such an advantage that the opposing party has no choice but to offer favorable settlement terms. A motion to dismiss, if successful, may terminate the lawsuit in defendant's favor; a motion for summary judgment can be used by either party to obtain judgment without a trial when the evidence disproportionately favors one side. In this workshop, we learn how to analyze a case to determine what motions of this kind, if any, should be filed. We also examine in detail the procedure for filing a motion for summary judgment.

## THE DECISION TO FILE A MOTION

Most of the motions that we have considered in the preceding workshops are reactive in nature; that is, an event occurs that makes the need for a motion obvious. For example:

- Your supervising attorney represents clients in two different lawsuits that are scheduled for trial on the same date. Obviously, a motion for a continuance is in order in one or the other.

- An opposing party has not answered your interrogatories. The 30-day period for answering is long past, and your demand letters have been ignored. Obviously, you need to file a motion asking the judge to order your opponent to serve answers.

- Your client has just been sued over an automobile accident that happened several years ago, beyond the time period allowed by the applicable statute of limitations. Obviously, a motion to dismiss is called for.

At the beginning stages of a lawsuit, however, motion opportunities often exist that we may fail to notice unless we are looking for them. For example:

- You are defending a suit in which the opposing party's complaint fails to include one of the required elements of one of the causes of action alleged. Unless the cause of action in question is one with which you are very familiar, it is unlikely that you will notice the omission unless you are looking for it.

- Someone is suing your client on a claim arising from a statute, but has not complied with the statutory prerequisites for suing. You may never discover the defect unless you research the statute, find out what the prerequisites are, and check specifically to see whether they have been met.

To deal with situations of the kind to which this workshop is addressed, we need a systematic way of dissecting a case to ensure that we have not overlooked any important issues. The best way to ensure that nothing is missed is to make a checklist of the possible motions, determine what circumstances would support each one, and ask ourselves whether those circumstances exist in our case.

## CHECKLIST OF EARLY-STAGE TACTICAL MOTIONS

In the discussion to follow, we review a number of common types of motions and learn how to recognize the situations in which each can be used to advantage. We do this in the context of the analysis that an attorney would perform in the beginning stages of a lawsuit—defendant's attorney after receiving the complaint, plaintiff's attorney after receiving defendant's answer. We begin with motions that address the claims and defenses raised by the pleadings, then proceed to motions involving technical or procedural issues.

Most, but not all, of the motions we discuss here are inherently defense oriented; they are aimed at various defects that may exist in plaintiff's case. Does this mean that the kind of analysis that we are describing is of interest only to defendants? Most emphatically not; to succeed in litigation, we must always be on the lookout not only for opportunities to attack the opposing party's case, but also for opportunities for the opposing party to attack *our* case. When we represent a plaintiff, we want to anticipate—and correct—any problems that might otherwise give the defendant an opportunity to move against us.

We include for each type of motion a highlighted summary description giving a brief example, citing the governing federal rule, and providing space for you to write in the corresponding rule for the state courts of your locality. Since part of our purpose is to suggest a systematic way of analyzing a case, we also offer what we have called an "analysis question" encapsulating the thought process that you would follow to decide whether each motion is warranted in a given situation. We summarize this material in a chart (Figure W16–1) at the end of this section.

### Motions Relating to the Claims and Defenses

We begin with the workhorse motions of civil litigation, those used for testing and refining the claims and defenses asserted in the complaint and answer. These are the motion to dismiss for failure to state a claim; the motion to strike; and the motion for summary judgment. The purpose of each is to try to defuse one or more of the opposing party's claims or defenses.

#### Motion to Dismiss for Failure to State a Claim

**Analysis question:** For each claim being asserted in the complaint, (1) does the law recognize a cause of action and (2) are all elements of that cause of action properly alleged?

**Authority:** FRCP, Rule 12(b)(6).

**When permitted:** Before answer is filed.

**Example:** The complaint alleges a cause of action for the tort of battery, but fails to include any allegation that defendant made a harmful or offensive physical contact with plaintiff. Since "harmful or offensive touching" is an element of the tort of battery (see Workshop 1), the complaint, on its face, fails to state a valid cause of action for battery. Defendant can move to dismiss the cause of action for battery.

---

**Your Local Notes**

_____

_____

---

There are two basic ways in which a claim or defense can be subject to attack by motion:

1. There can be an inherent defect in the way that the claim or defense has been pleaded—that is, one or more of the elements of the claim or defense can be incorrectly stated or missing; or

2. The claim or defense can be correctly pleaded, with all of its elements correctly alleged, but the evidence supporting one or more elements is not sufficient to create a "genuine issue of material fact."

The first type of defect may be attacked via a motion to dismiss (claims) or motion to strike (defenses). The second type requires a motion for summary judgment.

A motion to dismiss for failure to state a claim—often referred to in federal court as an "FRCP, Rule 12(b)(6) motion," and in older case law sometimes called a "demurrer"—provides a way for defendant to seek dismissal of improperly pleaded claims. Under the federal rules, a motion to dismiss must be made, if at all, before the answer is filed.

In deciding a motion to dismiss, the issue is whether, if all of the allegations of plaintiff's complaint are taken as true, there would be a basis for a judgment in plaintiff's favor. If plaintiff has included in the complaint any cause of action that is not recognized as legally valid, or has omitted required elements of an otherwise valid cause of action, the court has the power to dismiss the invalid claim or claims.

Obviously, to analyze whether plaintiff's complaint correctly alleges each element of each cause of action, we would first need to ascertain what *are* the elements of each of the causes of action. A good way to do this is to research and prepare an issues outline, following the instructions given in Workshop 1, then compare the outline with the complaint to see whether each required element is present.

A motion to dismiss may be directed to one claim, several claims, or the entire complaint. Where plaintiff has "shotgunned" the case, accompanying some arguably meritorious causes of action with others of improbable validity, a motion to dismiss can sometimes be a useful tool for weeding out the shakier claims.

As a weapon for killing off badly pleaded claims, however, motions to dismiss suffer from one serious drawback: The claims they attack tend not to stay dead. When granting motions to dismiss for failure to state a claim, judges routinely grant plaintiff leave to amend the complaint and restate the defective claim. In effect, by moving to dismiss, defendant is merely giving plaintiff a free education and a chance to correct pleading defects before they do any real damage to plaintiff's case. For this reason, experienced litigators prefer to avoid motions to dismiss for failure to state a claim. It is better to include some argument about the lack of evidence, call the motion a motion for summary judgment, and get a ruling that will stick.

#### Motion to Strike

**Analysis question:** For each affirmative defense alleged in the answer, (1) does the law recognize the defense as valid and (2) is the defense correctly pleaded?

**Authority:** FRCP, Rule 12(f).

**When permitted:** Within 20 days after answer is filed.

**Example:** The complaint alleges a valid cause of action for the tort of battery. The answer alleges "contributory negligence" as an affirmative defense. "Contributory negligence" is not a valid defense to a claim for battery. Plaintiff could make a motion to strike the "contributory negligence" defense.

---

*Your Local Notes*

_____

_____

---

A motion to strike is plaintiff's counterpart to the motion to dismiss. Plaintiff can use a motion to strike to ask the court to eliminate invalid or improperly pleaded defenses from defendant's answer. A motion to strike an invalid defense must be made within 20 days after the answer is filed; see FRCP, Rule 12(f). (Motions to strike can also be used for other purposes, such as to remove "redundant, immaterial, impertinent, or scandalous matter" from either the complaint or the answer. However, motions to strike used for such purposes rarely accomplish anything very useful strategically, and are therefore seldom seen.)

As with the motion to dismiss, the practical utility of motions to strike is questionable. If a defense is invalid now, it will still be invalid later. There is usually little point in educating the opposing party about the problems with his pleadings any earlier than necessary.

### Motion for Summary Judgment (by Defendant)

**Analysis question:** On any element of any of the causes of action alleged in the complaint, is plaintiff's evidence so weak as not to raise a genuine issue of material fact?

**Authority:** FRCP, Rule 56(b).

**When permitted:** At any time after the filing of the complaint; no later than the cutoff date, if any, set by the scheduling order.

**Example:** The complaint alleges a cause of action for the tort of battery, and properly alleges that defendant "touched" plaintiff in a harmful or offensive way. In fact, however, plaintiff has no evidence that any touching occurred. The complaint is not defective, because the correct elements of the tort of battery have been alleged. Defendant could, however, file a motion for summary judgment, accompanied by proof that no touching occurred, asking the judge to throw out the plaintiff's battery claim.

---

*Your Local Notes*

_____

_____

---

The purpose of a motion for summary judgment is to weed out claims or defenses that are so weakly supported by the evidence that it would be a waste of time to submit them to the jury for decision. If the facts on which a claim depends are clear, and there is no dispute about what happened, then the judge can, and should, decide the claim immediately.

To understand how motions for summary judgment work, think about how claims are proved in a lawsuit. Take a simple example: a suit in which the complaint makes only one claim, for battery, and the answer raises no affirmative defense. The elements of the tort of battery (see Workshop 1) are (1) an act by defendant, (2) intent, (3) harmful or offensive contact, and (4) damages. Suppose plaintiff presents her evidence, and defendant presents no evidence at all—could a jury reasonably find each of the four elements to be established? If so, then defendant is not entitled to summary judgment, regardless of how strong defendant's evidence may be. If, however, plaintiff's evidence on any of the elements is not sufficient to allow a reasonable jury to consider that element established, then defendant is entitled to summary judgment.

How does the judge determine whether a party has presented enough evidence to establish a fact? Since the trial has not yet begun, what evidence is there for the judge to base the decision on? A defendant's motion for summary judgment is said to "put the plaintiff to her proof"—when defendant files a motion for summary judgment, it is up to plaintiff to put forward whatever evidence there is to support the claim being attacked. Plaintiff can do this by submitting copies of discovery responses or deposition transcripts and by submitting affidavits of witnesses stating what their testimony would be. FRCP, Rule 56(c), states:

> [Summary judgment] shall be rendered forthwith if the pleadings, depositions, answers to interrogatories, and admissions on file, together with the affidavits, if any, show that there is no genuine issue as to any material fact and that the moving party is entitled to judgment as a matter of law.

It is possible for defendant to obtain summary judgment on a claim by "knocking out" any required element of the claim. It is also possible for defendant to obtain summary judgment by establishing a valid affirmative defense. If defendant presents evidence (discovery responses and affidavits) sufficient to support each required element of an affirmative defense, and plaintiff is unable to produce enough contrary evidence to create a genuine factual issue, defendant is entitled to summary judgment.

A motion for summary judgment may seek to dispose of all the claims in a case—in effect, ending the entire lawsuit—or may be aimed at only certain claims. A party may also, in appropriate circumstances, move for "partial summary judgment" on particular issues; see FRCP, Rule 56(d).

The procedural details involved in submitting a motion for summary judgment—paperwork required, time limits, and the like—are governed partly by FRCP, Rule 56, and partly by local rule. We explore summary judgment procedure in detail later in this workshop.

### Motion for Summary Judgment (by Plaintiff)

**Analysis question:** For each of plaintiff's causes of action, can plaintiff produce enough evidence to establish a *prima facie* case on each element? If so, is defendant unable to produce sufficient evidence to raise a genuine issue of material fact on any element?

**Authority:** FRCP, Rule 56(a).

**When permitted:** At least 20 days after complaint is filed or after service of motion for summary judgment by defendant; no later than the cutoff date, if any, set by the scheduling order.

**Example:** The complaint alleges a cause of action to collect a debt for which defendant has given a promissory note. Plaintiff can produce evidence that the loan was made and that it remains unpaid. Defendant is unable to produce any evidence to counter any of the elements of plaintiff's claim or to establish any valid defense. Plaintiff can move for summary judgment, asking the court to enter judgment against defendant for the amount owed.

---

*Your Local Notes*

_____

_____

---

If plaintiff presents evidence in support of each element of a claim, and defendant is unable to present evidence to negate any element, then plaintiff is entitled to move for—and win—summary judgment. The procedure for presenting and deciding the motion is the same as that for a motion for summary judgment by defendant.

## Motions Asserting Defects Unrelated to the Merits

—Sometimes the flaws in a case have to do with jurisdictional or procedural problems, rather than with the elements of the claims themselves. The rules of procedure provide an array of options for attacking such "nonmerits" defects. We examine several of the most important here; others, such as motions addressing the capacity of the parties, joinder of indispensable parties, and other similar technical issues, are beyond the scope of this introductory text.

### Motion to Dismiss for Lack of Subject Matter Jurisdiction

**Analysis question:** Does the court have jurisdiction of the subject matter of the action?

**Authority:** FRCP, Rule 12(b)(1).

**When permitted:** Although Rule 12(b) purports to require that a motion to dismiss be made before the answer is filed, the cases hold that lack of subject matter jurisdiction may be raised at any time, including on appeal.

**Example:** Defendant injures plaintiff in a motor vehicle accident. Plaintiff and defendant are both residents of the same state. Plaintiff sues in federal district court. Motor vehicle negligence does not arise from federal law, and there is no "diversity of citizenship" jurisdiction because plaintiff and defendant are residents of the same state. The federal district court has no subject matter jurisdiction. Defendant may move to dismiss under Rule 12(b)(1), FRCP.

---

*Your Local Notes*

_____

_____

---

Courts of limited subject matter jurisdiction have no power to adjudicate any cases other than those for which authority has been granted by statute. Federal courts are courts of limited subject matter jurisdiction, so in federal court lawsuits, it is very important for both parties to verify carefully that the court has jurisdiction. The main trial courts in each state typically have subject matter jurisdiction to hear any kind of case, so subject matter jurisdiction is usually not an issue in state court (although in rare circumstances it can be). If defendant believes that the court does not have subject matter jurisdiction, a motion to dismiss under FRCP, Rule 12(b)(1), is appropriate. See Workshop 2 for detailed coverage of jurisdiction of the subject matter.

### Motion to Dismiss for Lack of Personal Jurisdiction

**Analysis question:** Does the court have jurisdiction of the person of each defendant?

**Authority:** FRCP, Rule 12(b)(2).

**When permitted:** Before the answer is filed; filing an answer waives the defense.

**Example:** Plaintiff, a resident of Vermont, is vacationing in New York City. He is injured when defendant, a New York resident, runs the wheel of her taxicab over his foot. Plaintiff files suit in Vermont. Defendant has no "minimum contacts" with that state, so a Vermont court cannot assert personal jurisdiction over her. Defendant may move to dismiss under Rule 12(B)(2).

> *Your Local Notes*
>
> _____
>
> _____

The court has no power to render a binding judgment against a person over whom the court does not have personal jurisdiction. We explored the intricacies of personal jurisdiction in Workshop 2. If the court does not have jurisdiction over the person of a given defendant, that defendant may, if desired, nonetheless consent to jurisdiction, explicitly or by the act of filing an answer. If defendant wishes to contest the court's jurisdiction of her person, a motion to dismiss under FRCP, Rule 12(b)(3), is the proper choice.

### Motion to Dismiss for Improper Venue

**Analysis question:** Was the action brought in a place that is permitted under the applicable venue statutes?

**Authority:** FRCP, Rule 12(b)(3).

**When permitted:** Before the answer is filed.

**Example:** Same facts as the previous example: Plaintiff, a resident of Vermont, is vacationing in New York City and is injured when defendant, a New York City resident, runs the wheel of her taxicab over his foot. This time, plaintiff files suit in the Northern District of New York. Defendant is a resident of New York so the court has personal jurisdiction over her. However, New York City is in the Southern District of New York, not the Northern District, so plaintiff's choice of forum does not comply with the federal venue statute, 28 U.S.C. §1391. Defendant may move to dismiss under Rule 12(B)(3).

> *Your Local Notes*
>
> _____
>
> _____

Venue, as we explained in detail in Workshop 2, involves statutory limits on the place of filing suit. If plaintiff's choice of venue does not comply with

the applicable venue statute, defendant may move to dismiss under FRCP, Rule 12(b)(3), before filing an answer; if defendant fails to do so, any venue defects are waived; see FRCP, Rule 12(h).

### Motion to Dismiss or Motion for Summary Judgment Based on Statute of Limitations

**Analysis question:** Was the action filed within the time period allowed under the applicable statute of limitations?

**Authority:** FRCP, Rule 12(b)(6) and Rule 56.

**When permitted:** Motion to dismiss: before the answer is filed. Motion for summary judgment: any time after the filing of the complaint and before the cutoff, if any, stated in the scheduling order.

**Example (Motion to Dismiss):** Plaintiff sues defendant, a surgeon, for medical malpractice. Under the applicable state statute of limitations, the limitation period for actions based on medical negligence is 1 year. The complaint alleges that the defendant doctor negligently left a surgical instrument inside plaintiff during an operation on February 1, 2001. The complaint is filed on February 2, 2002. Defendant can move to dismiss for failure to state a claim since the facts alleged in the complaint, if taken as true, are not sufficient to establish a valid cause of action.

**Example (Motion for Summary Judgment):** Same facts, except that the complaint does not say when the negligent act was committed. Defendant can, however, move for summary judgment, supporting the motion with an affidavit establishing the date on which the surgery took place. Assuming plaintiff cannot produce contrary evidence of a different date, summary judgment would be granted.

> *Your Local Notes*
>
> _____
>
> _____

Plaintiff's claims should always be scrutinized for statute of limitations defenses. As the examples indicate, sometimes a statute of limitations defense is apparent by reference to the complaint alone; in other cases, it is necessary to obtain the dates through discovery or from other sources. Remember, however, that in many cases the "triggering of the statute of limitations does not begin until the plaintiff knew, or should have known, of the conduct giving rise to the claim." See Workshop 3 for more detail on statutes of limitations.

**A Checklist of Tactical Motions**—We conclude our discussion of tactical motions with the chart

**Figure W16–1    Checklist of Tactical Motions**

| Analysis question | Motion | When Made | Authority |
|---|---|---|---|
| For each claim being asserted in the complaint, (1) does the law recognize a cause of action and (2) are all elements of that cause of action properly alleged? | Motion to Dismiss for Failure to State a Claim | Before answer is filed | FRCP, Rule 12(b)(6) |
| For each affirmative defense alleged in the answer, (1) does the law recognize the defense as valid and (2) is the defense correctly pleaded? | Motion to Strike | Within 20 days after answer is filed | FRCP, Rule 12(f) |
| On any element of any of the causes of action alleged in the complaint, is plaintiff's evidence so weak as not to raise a genuine issue of material fact? | Motion for Summary Judgment (by Defendant) | At any time after the filing of the complaint; no later than the cutoff date, if any, set by the scheduling order | FRCP, Rule 56(b) |
| For each of plaintiff's causes of action, can plaintiff produce enough evidence to establish a *prima facie* case on each element? If so, is defendant unable to produce sufficient evidence to raise a genuine issue of material fact on any element? | Motion for Summary Judgment (by Plaintiff) | At least 20 days after complaint is filed or after service of motion for summary judgment by defendant; no later than the cutoff date, if any, set by the scheduling order | FRCP, Rule 56(a) |
| Does the court have jurisdiction of the subject matter of the action? | Motion to Dismiss for Lack of Subject Matter Jurisdiction | At any time, including on appeal | FRCP, Rule 12(b)(1) |
| Does the court have jurisdiction of the person of each defendant? | Motion to Dismiss for Lack of Personal Jurisdiction | Before the answer is filed—filing an answer waives the defense | FRCP, Rule 12(b)(2) |
| Was the action brought in a place that is permitted under the applicable venue statutes? | Motion to Dismiss for Improper Venue | Before the answer is filed | FRCP, Rule 12(b)(3) |
| Was the action filed within the time period allowed under the applicable statute of limitations? | Motion to Dismiss or Motion for Summary Judgment Based on Statute of Limitations | Motion to dismiss before the answer is filed. Motion for summary judgment: any time after the filing of the complaint and before the cutoff, if any, stated in the scheduling order. | FRCP, Rule 12(b)(6); Rule 56(b) |

shown in Figure W16–1, which summarizes the main points and illustrates the thought process that we would follow in analyzing a case for possible motions to be filed. (We reiterate that the list that we have presented is not exhaustive; it does not include motions under FRCP, Rules 17, 19, and 21, for example. Our intent is merely to provide the student with a starting point for understanding how motions are used.)

# Motions for Summary Judgment by Defendant: Step-by-Step Instructions

The remainder of this workshop is devoted to examining one particular type of motion, the defense motion for summary judgment. We have chosen this particular motion because it is made in almost every case of any complexity, often repeatedly as defendant attempts to pick off one of plaintiff's claims, then another, and because it provides a good vehicle for illustrating some of the details of federal court motion procedure.

Here are the basic steps that a defendant might follow to prepare a motion for summary judgment. For brevity, we describe only the preparation and drafting steps. The follow-up steps (filing, getting the motion before the judge for decision, docketing the response date, etc.) are essentially the same as for any other motion—see Steps 4 through 9 of Workshop 14.

### Step 1  Analyze Complaint and Identify Issues to Attack

To grant a motion for summary judgment, the judge must find that (1) there is no genuine issue of material fact and (2) the moving party is entitled to judgment as a matter of law; see FRCP, Rule 56(c). For a defense motion for summary judgment to succeed, defendant must establish to the judge's satisfaction both that the elements of plaintiff's claims are what defendant says they are (i.e., establish what the law is), and that, at least as to one element, plaintiff lacks enough evidence to even create a genuine debate. (Defendant may also, of course, succeed by establishing an affirmative defense.)

Before we can prepare a motion for summary judgment, we must first identify the points where the plaintiff's claims are vulnerable to attack. This requires a systematic review of the claims and defenses, along the following lines:

1. Read the complaint carefully and make a list of each legal theory or cause of action being asserted.

2. Research each cause of action on the list and determine exactly what elements plaintiff must prove to establish it.

3. Element by element, for each element of each cause of action, list the evidence, if any, that plaintiff is likely to be able to produce.

4. Identify the gaps in plaintiff's evidence—any elements for which there seems to be no supporting evidence. Any causes of action requiring proof of any of those elements are good candidates for a motion for summary judgment.

5. Also research each cause of action to determine what, if any, affirmative defenses apply.

6. List the elements of each affirmative defense.

7. List the evidence available to establish each element of each affirmative defense, and the counterevidence that plaintiff will likely offer to rebut each one.

8. If there is a legally recognized affirmative defense to a given cause of action, and if we can produce evidence to establish each element of that affirmative defense, and if plaintiff is unable to produce significant counterevidence on any of the elements, we can move for summary judgment based on the affirmative defense.

Plaintiffs' attorneys are usually not so inept as to file complaints alleging causes of action for which they have no evidence. Usually, the opportunity for defendant to move for summary judgment arises from a disagreement about what the law requires in terms of the elements of plaintiff's claims. According to plaintiff's theory of the case, plaintiff need only prove elements A, B, and C to succeed, but under defendant's legal analysis plaintiff must prove elements A, B, C, and D—and plaintiff has no evidence to prove D.

Most of the argument in a motion for summary judgment is aimed at trying to convince the judge of the moving party's formulation of the legal theories. Factual arguments are generally useless; if the evidence is conflicting as to what the facts are, then there is, almost by definition, a "genuine issue of material fact" and summary judgment is not appropriate.

Therefore, what we are really looking for as we analyze the claims is authorities that will allow us to argue that plaintiff's legal theories have some additional elements that plaintiff has overlooked, and/or authorities supporting affirmative defenses that plaintiff cannot rebut.

### Step 2  Draft the Motion

A motion for summary judgment is a filed court paper of the usual kind, constructed with the usual caption, title, preamble, date and signature lines, and certificate of service. All of these parts should be familiar; if not, see Workshops 4 and 14.

The exact wording of the preamble and the way in which the motion, memorandum, statement of facts, and supporting evidence are divided up among separately captioned documents depend on local rules and customs.

## Step 3 — Memorandum of Points and Authorities

The heart of a motion for summary judgment is the memorandum. This is where we present the argument that will succeed or fail at convincing the judge that the law applicable to plaintiff's claims is what we say it is. We have examined the fine points of memorandum writing elsewhere (see Step 2 of Workshop 14) and the same principles apply here.

## Step 4 — Statement of Facts

To make it easier for the judge to determine exactly what each party's factual contentions are, many federal district courts have adopted local rules requiring each party to submit a formal "statement of facts" with any motion for summary judgment or response. The idea is to force the parties to specify the precise facts claimed to be in dispute. The moving party submits list of the facts she deems pertinent to the motion, each fact set forth separately and numbered. Then the responding party submits a similar list, indicating which of the moving party's facts are disputed. Both lists must support each fact with citations to the record (i.e., indicate which affidavit or discovery response establishes the fact and give the page and paragraph or line number where it appears). The judge can then compare the two statements of facts, item by item, to determine for which facts the evidence is conflicting. Local Rule CV-56 of the U.S. District Court for the Eastern District of Texas is typical:

> Any party moving for summary judgment should identify both the legal and factual basis for its motion. The text of the motion or an appendix thereto must include a "Statement of Material Facts." If the movant relies upon evidence to support its motion, the motion should include appropriate citations to proper summary judgment evidence as to which the moving party contends there is no genuine issue of material fact for trial. Proper summary judgment evidence should be attached to the motion in accordance with section (d) of this rule.

(What is "proper summary judgment evidence"? See Step 5 next.)

Some districts require the parties to submit the statements of facts as separately captioned documents; others provide for the statement of facts to be included as part of the memorandum. Consult your local rules for the procedure followed in the federal district court of your locality. As for state courts, some now require a separate statement of facts and some do not; your instructor will inform you of the practice in the state courts of your locality, and tell you where to find the applicable rules, if any.

| Your Local Notes |
| --- |
| |
| |
| |

## Step 5 — Supporting Evidence and Affidavits

Motions for summary judgment differ from many other kinds of routine motions in the need for establishing facts.

If the motion seeks to win by asserting an affirmative defense, defendant, as moving party, must submit with the motion *prima facie* evidence of the facts needed to establish each element of the defense. (*Prima facie* evidence of a fact means enough evidence to support a finding that the fact is true, if neither side presented any other evidence about the fact.) To overcome the motion and avoid summary judgment, plaintiff would then need to accompany the response with at least some credible evidence to rebut at least one of the elements of the affirmative defense.

If the motion is based on plaintiff's inability to produce *prima facie* evidence supporting all of the elements of plaintiff's causes of action, it is still advisable for defendant to submit evidence that one or more of the elements of plaintiff's claims could *not* be true. Defendant can, by moving for summary judgment, force plaintiff to "put up or shut up"—either show evidence supporting the claims, or see them dismissed. FRCP, Rule 56(e) provides:

> When a motion for summary judgment is made and supported as provided in this rule, an adverse party may not rest upon the mere allegations or denials of the adverse party's pleading, but the adverse party's response [to the motion for summary judgment], by affidavits or as otherwise provided in this rule, must set forth specific facts showing that there is a genuine issue for trial. If the adverse party

does not so respond, summary judgment, if appropriate, shall be entered against the adverse party.

In practice, the motion is more likely to succeed if defendant takes the initiative and produces evidence of what the real facts are, rather than passively relying on plaintiff's inability to establish his version of the facts.

A basic principle of summary judgment procedure is that the judge does not decide factual disputes. In fact, one good way to defeat a motion for summary judgment is to convince the judge that the evidence is genuinely conflicting—then the judge *must* let the jury sort out the evidence and decide what the facts are.

There are several ways in which we can present evidence to the judge in connection with a motion for summary judgment:

- We can submit affidavits. In summary judgment practice, affidavits are routinely used as a kind of substitute for live testimony, to show what a witness's testimony would be. FRCP, Rule 56(e), provides that the affidavits must "be made on personal knowledge," must "set forth such facts as would be admissible in evidence," and must "show affirmatively that the affiant is competent to testify to the matters stated." (The **affiant** is the person signing the affidavit.) In effect, the affidavit may say only those things that the affiant would be allowed to testify to on the witness stand—hearsay is not allowed, and proper foundation must be laid.

- We can attach document exhibits to the affidavits. Just as in court, the documents must be admissible in evidence and submitted in a form complying with FRCP, Rule 56(e) (that is, sworn or certified copies).

- We can submit copies of discovery responses and/or excerpts from deposition transcripts. FRCP, Rule 56(c), directs the judge to consider "the pleadings, depositions, answers to interrogatories, and admissions on file, together with the affidavits, if any. . . ." As a practical matter, the judge will usually consider only what the parties submit. Judges do not have time to browse through all of the pleadings and discovery in the case file, and, anyway, in most federal courts today the depositions and discovery responses are never filed so the judge has no way to consider them unless the parties submit them.

Some federal district courts have adopted local rules specifying the manner in which the evidentiary materials are to be presented. Here is how Local Rule CV-56(d) of the U.S. District Court for the Eastern District of Texas defines "proper summary judgment evidence"—its instructions are good advice, even in districts that lack such a rule:

> "[P]roper summary judgment evidence" means excerpted copies of pleadings, depositions, answers to interrogatories, admissions, affidavits, and other admissible evidence cited in the motion for summary judgment or the response thereto. The phrase "appropriate citations" means that any excerpted evidentiary materials that are attached to the motion or the response should be referred to by page and, if possible, by line. Any attached evidentiary materials should have the cited portions highlighted in the copy provided to the court, unless the citation encompasses the entire page. The page preceding and following a highlighted page may be submitted if necessary to place the highlighted material in its proper context. Only relevant, cited-to excerpts of evidentiary materials should be attached to the motion or the response.

*Your Local Notes*

_____

_____

## Motions for Summary Judgment by Defendant: Learning by Example

We now illustrate the ideas just presented by applying them to the facts of our *Martin vs. Collins* hypo and preparing a motion for summary judgment on behalf of defendant Park Hotels Group, Inc.

**Step 1**    *Analyze Complaint and Identify Issues to Attack*

Plaintiff's complaint (see Workshop 5) asserts only one cause of action against defendant Park Hotels Group, Inc. Counts I, II, and III of the complaint are against defendant Collins only; Count IV is against the hotel, for negligence. Count V is not strictly a "cause of action"—it sets forth the claim that plaintiff is entitled to punitive damages against all defendants.

There are two possible ways of attacking the negligence cause of action. One is to convince the court that plaintiff has no evidence to support one of the elements of the claim; the other is to establish an affirmative defense based on facts that plaintiff cannot dispute.

The elements of the tort of negligence are (1) a duty, (2) its breach, (3) causation, and (4) damages. The damages element is not promising: clearly Shannon can produce evidence showing that she was injured. Causation has possibilities—the question is whether Shannon's damages were caused *by the negligence of the hotel.* From our knowledge of tort law, we are aware that there is a body of case law dealing with the concept of "intervening cause." We might be able to find case law support for the argument that even if the hotel was negligent, the real cause of plaintiff's damages was the actions of Dr. Collins; this issue is worth researching.

We will assume (but in a real case we would research it) that a hotel has a duty not to give strangers access to a guest's hotel room. The question, of course, is whether the hotel breached that duty. The hotel could argue (as Gail Stoddard does in the story on which our hypo is based, see Chapter 5, that the evidence is undisputed that the key found in Shannon's room could not have opened her door). However, plaintiff could properly argue (as Allen Porter does in our story) that Shannon testified that she locked the door, and Dr. Collins testified that the key he was given did open the door. Therefore (as the judge properly found in our story), what we have is a classic question of fact—part of the evidence (the key) suggests that hotel could not have been responsible for Dr. Collins gaining entry to Shannon's room, and part of the evidence (Shannon's and Dr. Collins's testimony) suggest the contrary.

What about affirmative defenses? The obvious affirmative defense to negligence is the defense of contributory negligence (or, in some states, comparative negligence). Shannon's failure to secure the chain lock on her door lends some support; this defense also bears researching.

There is another affirmative defense, however, that has considerable potential: section 651.15 of the Nevada Revised Statutes. This is the statute limiting the liability of a hotel for death or injury to a guest caused by someone who is not an employee of the hotel. We reproduce the salient provisions here:

### 651.15 Civil liability of innkeepers for death or injury of person on premises caused by person who is not employee.

1. An owner or keeper of any hotel, inn, motel, motor court, boardinghouse or lodginghouse is not civilly liable for the death or injury of a patron or other person on the premises caused by another person who is not an employee under the control or supervision of the owner or keeper unless:

(a) The wrongful act which caused the death or injury was foreseeable; and

(b) There is a preponderance of evidence that the owner or keeper did not exercise due care for the safety of the patron or other person on the premises.

. . . .

The court shall determine as a matter of law whether the wrongful act was foreseeable. . . .

3. For the purposes of this section, a wrongful act is not foreseeable unless:

(a) The owner or keeper failed to exercise due care for the safety of the patron or other person on the premises; or

(b) Prior incidents of similar wrongful acts occurred on the premises and the owner or keeper had notice or knowledge of those incidents.

This statute furnishes a nearly ideal basis for a motion for summary judgment—it could hardly be more favorable if we had written it ourselves (and, in fact, it probably *was* written by lawyers for the Nevada hotel industry).

We analyze section 651.15 to distill the elements of the affirmative defense that it creates. Figure W16–2 lists our breakdown, together with our tentative conclusions concerning the evidence on each element:

## Step 2     Draft the Motion

After conducting the necessary research, we proceed to draft the motion and supporting papers. Since our hypothetical lawsuit is pending in the U.S. District Court for the District of Arizona, we will follow that court's local rules regarding format, layout, and required parts. The draft motion is shown in Figure W16–3.

## Step 3     Memorandum of Points and Authorities

The memorandum is, of course, the heart of the motion (Figure W16–4). Memoranda in support of motions for summary judgment are necessarily lengthy in order to allow presentation of the legal argument and discussion of the supporting authorities. Not too lengthy, however; we must be mindful of the page limit set by local rules. In this case, the limit set by Local Rule 1.10(e) of the U.S. District Court for the District of Arizona is "fifteen (15) pages, exclusive of attachments and any required statement of facts."

| Figure W16–2 Elements of Affirmative Defense under Nevada Revised Statute §651.15 | |
| --- | --- |
| Element | Evidence |
| 1. Defendant is the owner of a hotel. | Undisputed; plaintiff will not be able to produce evidence to the contrary. |
| 2. Plaintiff was injured while a "patron or other person on the premises." | Again, undisputed; plaintiff's own complaint establishes this element. |
| 3. Plaintiff's injury was "caused by another person who is not an employee under the control or supervision of the owner." | Plaintiff will be unable to dispute that Dr. Collins is not a hotel employee. Plaintiff will try to argue that it was the hotel's negligence, not Dr. Collins, that "caused" her injury. This issue is probably plaintiff's best chance to avoid summary judgment, and will have to be researched. |
| 4. The wrongful act which caused the death or injury was not foreseeable; to establish this we must show both: | (To evaluate foreseeability element, we must break it down into its subelements in accordance with subsection 3 of the statute.) |
| 4(a). Defendant did not fail to exercise due care for plaintiff's safety; and | This is another element that leaves plaintiff some opening; to support motion for summary judgment, we can submit hotel manager's affidavit that the hotel exercised due care. |
| 4(b). No prior incidents of similar wrongful acts had occurred on the premises | We can establish this element by the hotel manager's affidavit; assuming no prior incidents occurred, plaintiff will be unable to rebut. We will, of course, carefully investigate to verify that no prior incidents occurred. |

## Step 4 *Statement of Facts*

Looking up the local rules for the U.S. District Court for the District of Arizona, we find that Local Rule 1.10(1)(1) requires that a motion for summary judgment be accompanied by a separate statement of facts:

> Any party filing a motion for summary judgment shall set forth separately from the memorandum of law, and in full, the specific facts on which that party relies in support of the motion. The specific facts shall be set forth in serial fashion and not in narrative form. As to each fact, the statement shall refer to a specific portion of the record where the fact may be found (i.e., affidavit, deposition, etc.).

Figure W16–5 shows our statement of facts for *Martin v. Collins.*

You may be wondering why, given our usual distaste for archaic phraseology, we keep using the word "herein" (i.e., "complaint herein"). The word "herein" in this context is simply a shorthand way of saying "filed in this lawsuit."

You may also be wondering how we can get away with citing the complaint as a source of evidence in the statement of facts. If we were representing plaintiff, we could not; but since we are representing defendant, we can assume that if plaintiff alleged a fact in the complaint, and we agree with it, it must be undisputed.

In paragraph 5 of the statement of facts we state that the hotel uses due care for the safety of its guests. Obviously, we do that because, under the Nevada statute, we need to show that the hotel used due care in order to establish that the injury was not foreseeable. The statement seems quite conclusory; surely the court is not just going to take the hotel manager's word for it that we use due care—isn't that what the lawsuit is all about? In fact, in a real lawsuit, where we would not be limited by space constraints, we would certainly want to "beef up" this point, probably by getting affidavits from the hotel security chief and other similarly placed employees detailing all the measures that the hotel takes to ensure the safety of its guests.

---

**Figure W16–3   Sample Motion for Summary Judgment**

CRANDALL, ELKINS & MAJOR
Gail Stoddard, Esq.
2000 North Central Avenue, Suite 2900
Phoenix, Arizona 85004
(602) 555-1234
Attorneys for defendant Park Hotels Group, Inc.

## IN THE UNITED STATES DISTRICT COURT

## DISTRICT OF ARIZONA

| | | |
|---|---|---|
| SHANNON MARTIN, a single woman, | ) | |
| | ) | |
| | ) | NO. CV98 -01456 PHX JL |
| Plaintiff, | ) | |
| | ) | MOTION FOR SUMMARY |
| v. | ) | JUDGMENT OF DEFENDANT |
| | ) | PARK HOTELS GROUP, INC. |
| ARTHUR COLLINS, et ux., et al., | ) | |
| | ) | |
| Defendants. | ) | |
| | ) | |

Defendant Park Hotels Group, Inc. respectfully moves pursuant to Rule 56, Federal Rules of Civil Procedure, for summary judgment dismissing plaintiff's claims against said defendant.

This motion is based upon the accompanying memorandum of points and authorities and affidavit of Corby Jamison.

RESPECTFULLY SUBMITTED this 25th day of June, 2000.

CRANDALL, ELKINS & MAJOR

_____
Gail Stoddard
Attorneys for defendant Park Hotels
Group, Inc.

(Certificate of mailing goes here—see Workshop 4.)

---

**Step 5**   *Supporting Evidence and Affidavits*

Along with our motion for summary judgment and supporting memorandum, we need to submit any supporting evidence and affidavits. Figure W16–6 shows the affidavit of Corby Jamison, which is referenced extensively in our statement of facts (see Figure W16–5).

## Motions for Summary Judgment by Defendant: Learning by Doing

Your assignment for this workshop is to begin with the excerpts from the motion for summary judgment as shown in the Learning by Example section

of this workshop, and produce a finished set of motion papers conforming to the rules and customs of the court selected by your instructor. This may be the U.S. district court having jurisdiction in your locality or, at your instructor's option, the state trial court for your county. Assume the following:

You are a paralegal in the office of Gail Stoddard, who represents Park Hotels Group, Inc. The firm's office is in your city (make up a suitable address). The lawsuit, *Martin v. Collins*, is pending in the court selected by your instructor. The other facts of the hypothetical are unchanged. Ms. Stoddard has assigned to you the task of preparing a motion for summary judgment asserting the statutory defense under Nev. Rev. Stat. Ann. §651.15 (reproduced in full in Workshop 14).

**Figure W16–4    Sample Memorandum in Support of Motion for Summary Judgment**

CRANDALL, ELKINS & MAJOR
Gail Stoddard, Esq.
2000 North Central Avenue, Suite 2900
Phoenix, Arizona 85004
(602) 555-1234
Attorneys for defendant Park Hotels Group, Inc.

### IN THE UNITED STATES DISTRICT COURT

### DISTRICT OF ARIZONA

| | |
|---|---|
| SHANNON MARTIN, a single woman, ) | |
| ) | |
| ) | NO. CV98 -01456 PHX JL |
| Plaintiff,        ) | |
| ) | MEMORANDUM IN SUPPORT OF |
| v.        ) | MOTION FOR SUMMARY |
| ) | JUDGMENT OF DEFENDANT |
| ARTHUR COLLINS, et ux., et al.,        ) | PARK HOTELS GROUP, INC |
| ) | |
| Defendants.        ) | |
| _____ ) | |

*Summary of Argument*

1. By Nevada statute, a hotel is not liable to a guest for injuries inflicted by another guest unless the wrongful act causing the injury was foreseeable. Nev. Rev. Stat. Ann. §651.15.

2. Also by Nevada statute, an injury to a hotel guest by another guest is not foreseeable as a matter of law unless either the hotel owner failed to exercise due care for the safety of the guest, or was placed on notice by prior incidents involving similar wrongful acts. As established by the accompanying affidavit of Corby Jamison, the hotel owner at all times exercised due care and no similar prior incidents have occurred.

3. Nevada has the most "significant relationship" to plaintiff's claims which arise from events at a Nevada hotel. Defendant's liability is to be determined according to Nevada law.

*Argument*

I.    *Factual Background: Plaintiff Was Injured*
      *by Another Hotel Guest: The Circumstances Were Unforeseeable.*

While staying at the Las Vegas hotel operated by defendant Park Hotels Group, plaintiff was injured in her room by another hotel guest, defendant Collins. The

.......

II.    *Nevada Hotels Are Not Liable to Guests*
       *for Acts Committed by Other Guests Where Hotel Used Due Care and No Previous Similar Incidents*
*Had Occurred*

In Nevada by statute, a hotel owner is not liable for injuries inflicted by one hotel guest on another unless the injuries are "foreseeable" as that term is defined by the statute. Nev. Rev. Stat. Ann. §651.15 provides:

.......

V.    *Conclusion: Nev. Rev. Stat. Ann. §651.15*
      *Provides a Valid and Complete Affirmative*
      *Defense to Plaintiff's Claim against Defendant*
      *Park Hotels Group*

*continued*

---

**Figure W16–4   Sample Memorandum in Support of Motion for Summary Judgment,** *continued*

Under Nevada law by statute, hotels are not liable for injuries inflicted by one hotel guest on another unless either the hotel owner failed to exercise due care for the safety of the injured guest, or had notice of similar previous incidents.

Defendant Park Hotels Group not only exercised due care, it took extraordinary precautions for the safety of its guests, including providing each room with a chain lock, which, had plaintiff used it, would clearly have prevented the incident for which she is suing. There has never been any report of any other incident in which a guest at Banbury Park Hotel entered the room of another guest and committed an assault.

The Court should grant summary judgment dismissing plaintiff's claims against defendant Park Hotels Group, Inc.

RESPECTFULLY SUBMITTED this 25th day of June, 2000.

CRANDALL, ELKINS & MAJOR

_____

Gail Stoddard
Attorneys for defendant Park Hotels
Group, Inc.

(Certificate of mailing goes here)

---

## EXERCISES

In carrying out this assignment, you should follow the step-by-step formula described in this workshop.

1.  Locate the local rule(s) of the court selected by your instructor, if any, pertaining to motions for summary judgment. (For many federal district courts, the local rules can be accessed from the U.S. Courts Internet site, www. uscourts.gov.)

2.  Determine from your local rules, from your instructor, or by calling the clerk's office:
    a. Any page limits applicable to motions for summary judgment and responses;
    b. The time periods allowed for response and reply (these are often longer for motions for summary judgment than for other motions);
    c. Any requirements for a statement of facts or other similar required accompanying papers;
    d. Whether the court routinely hears argument on motions for summary judgment and, if so, how the argument is scheduled and noticed;
    e. Any other provisions specifically applicable to motions for summary judgment.

Write a short memo to your supervising attorney summarizing your findings.

3.  Review and if possible obtain copies for your forms file of a motion for summary judgment, response, and reply filed in the U.S. district court of your locality, together with supporting papers, to use as a guide on matters of format, layout, and organization. Your instructor may be able to provide these or suggest how to obtain them. Failing that, you can access the court files of pending lawsuits at the clerk's office (but in that case be prepared to take notes—copies are expensive). Find out exactly what papers need to be filed in connection with a motion for summary judgment in your court, and what each one needs to contain.

4.  Prepare, in final form suitable for filing in the U.S. district court of your locality, a motion for summary judgment on behalf of Park Hotels Group, Inc., asserting the defense of Nev. Rev. Stat. Ann. §651.15, together with all required supporting papers. Prepare:
    a. The affidavit of Corby Jamison. Do not change the facts stated, but redo the affidavit to make it suitable for filing in the court selected by your instructor.
    b. An affidavit for signature by Ron Kanne, who is the chief of security for Banbury Park Hotel. Your main purpose in submitting this affidavit is to establish that the hotel does, in the words of the Nevada statute, "exercise due care for the safety" of its guests. To prepare the affidavit you will need to interview Ron Kanne to find out in detail what measures Banbury Park Hotel takes to ensure the safety of its guests. This will be accomplished by students in pairs as follows: One student in each pair will play the role of Ron

---

**Figure W16–5   Sample Statement of Facts**

CRANDALL, ELKINS & MAJOR
Gail Stoddard, Esq.
2000 North Central Avenue, Suite 2900
Phoenix, Arizona 85004
(602) 555-1234
Attorneys for defendant Park Hotels Group, Inc.

### IN THE UNITED STATES DISTRICT COURT

### DISTRICT OF ARIZONA

| | | |
|---|---|---|
| SHANNON MARTIN, a single woman, | ) | |
| | ) | |
| | ) | NO. CV98 -01456 PHX JL |
| Plaintiff, | ) | |
| | ) | STATEMENT OF FACTS IN |
| v. | ) | SUPPORT OF MOTION FOR |
| | ) | SUMMARY JUDGMENT OF |
| ARTHUR COLLINS, et ux., et al., | ) | DEFENDANT PARK HOTELS |
| | ) | GROUP, INC. |
| Defendants. | ) | |
| | ) | |

Defendant Park Hotels Group, Inc., pursuant to Local Rule 1.10(1) of the U.S. District Court for the District of Arizona, submits the following statement of facts in support of its motion for summary judgment:

1. Plaintiff was a guest at the Banbury Park Hotel, Las Vegas, Nevada, on the night of February 5, 1996. (Complaint herein at paragraph 5; answer herein at paragraph 4; affidavit of Corby Jamison dated June 22, 2000, at paragraph 2.)

2. Banbury Park Hotel was at all material times owned and operated by defendant Park Hotels Group, Inc. (Affidavit of Corby Jamison dated June 22, 2000, at paragraph 3.)

3. Plaintiff's injuries were inflicted by defendant Arthur Collins. (Complaint herein at paragraph 7.)

4. Defendant Arthur Collins has never been an employee of defendant Park Hotels Group, Inc. (Affidavit of Corby Jamison dated June 22, 2000, at paragraph 4.)

5. Banbury Park Hotel exercises due care for the safety of its guests. (Affidavit of Corby Jamison dated June 22, 2000, at paragraphs 5, 6, and 7.)

6. Banbury Park Hotel complies with all applicable building safety regulations, including provision of interior safety chain locks on all guest room doors, and including the posting of safety notices urging guests to fasten the safety chain locks while occupying their rooms. (Affidavit of Corby Jamison dated June 22, 2000, at paragraph 6.)

7. There has at no time been any reported previous incident at Banbury Park Hotel in which any person has entered the room of a hotel guest and assaulted the guest therein. (Affidavit of Corby Jamison dated June 22, 2000, at paragraph 7.)

RESPECTFULLY SUBMITTED this 25th day of June, 2000.

CRANDALL, ELKINS & MAJOR

_____

Gail Stoddard
Attorneys for defendant Park Hotels
Group, Inc.

(Certificate of mailing goes here)

**Figure W16–6   Sample Affidavit**

CRANDALL, ELKINS & MAJOR
Gail Stoddard, Esq.
2000 North Central Avenue, Suite 2900
Phoenix, Arizona 85004
(602) 555-1234
Attorneys for defendant Park Hotels Group, Inc.

**IN THE UNITED STATES DISTRICT COURT**

**DISTRICT OF ARIZONA**

| | | |
|---|---|---|
| SHANNON MARTIN, a single woman, ) | | |
| | ) | |
| | ) | NO. CV98 -01456 PHX JL |
| Plaintiff, ) | | |
| | ) | AFFIDAVIT OF CORBY JAMISON |
| v. | ) | IN SUPPORT OF MOTION FOR |
| | ) | SUMMARY JUDGMENT OF |
| ARTHUR COLLINS, et ux., et al., ) | ) | DEFENDANT PARK HOTELS |
| | ) | GROUP, INC. |
| Defendants. ) | | |
| _____ ) | | |

STATE OF NEVADA          )
                                           )
County of Clark          )

Corby Jamison, being first duly sworn, upon his oath deposes and says:

1. I have been the general manager of Banbury Park Hotel, Las Vegas, Nevada, at all times since the hotel opened on January 22, 1992. I make this affidavit on the basis of personal knowledge.

2. According to the records of the hotel, Plaintiff was a guest at the Banbury Park Hotel, Las Vegas, Nevada, on the night of February 5, 1996.

3. Banbury Park Hotel was on that date, and at all times since, owned and operated by defendant Park Hotels Group, Inc.

4. Defendant Arthur Collins has never been an employee of defendant Park Hotels Group, Inc.

5. Banbury Park Hotel at all times exercises the highest care for the safety of its guests.

6. Banbury Park Hotel complies with all applicable building safety regulations, including provision of interior safety chain locks on all guest room doors, and including the posting of safety notices urging guests to fasten the safety chain locks while occupying their rooms.

7. There has at no time been any reported previous incident at Banbury Park Hotel in which any person has entered the room of a hotel guest and assaulted the guest therein.

DATED this 22nd day of June, 2000.

_____
Corby Jamison

SUBSCRIBED AND SWORN to before me, the undersigned Notary Public, this 22nd day of June, 2000.

_____
Notary Public

(Certificate of mailing goes here—see Workshop 4.)

Kanne; the other will play the role of the paralegal and conduct the interview. The student playing the role of Ron Kanne will try to answer the interviewer's questions in the most helpful way possible, and is free to make up the answers to the interviewers questions as the interview proceeds. The objective of the student playing the role of Ron Kanne is to "invent" the best (reasonable) security arrangements for guest safety that he or she can imagine. The objective of the student playing the role of the interviewer is to produce the strongest possible affidavit to support the motion for summary judgment. After the interview, the pair will together prepare an affidavit for signature by Ron Kanne in a form suitable for submission to the court selected by your instructor in support of the motion for summary judgment.

c. The statement of facts, if required under the rules or customary practice of the court selected by your instructor. You may refer to the affidavit of Corby Jamison and the affi-

davit of Ron Kanne. You may also refer to the complaint and answer.

d. The memorandum in support of the motion. You may use the excerpts shown in Step 3 of the Learning by Example section as a guide, or you may completely rewrite the memorandum in your own way. You may assume that the court will follow Nevada law, and omit the part of the argument showing that Nevada has the most "significant relationship" with the facts of the case. In writing the memorandum, be sure to follow any suggestions of your instructor as necessary to make the format and organization conform to local practice. At your instructor's option, do additional legal research and obtain case citations as appropriate to support the arguments made in your motion.

e. The motion for summary judgment itself and any notice of motion and/or other paper required under the rules and customs of the court selected by your instructor.

# PRACTICE POINTERS
## *Writing Tips*
## *Refining Your Writing Skills*

**Say What Is Important First**—Reserve the beginning of sentences for the most important part of your message. Do not stash the subject of the sentence away in the middle or leave it to the end. Say it up front. Consider the following example:

> Whether or not subject matter jurisdiction existed was the matter to be resolved by the court.

The writer is trying to convey the nature of the issue the court had to resolve. Why not let the reader know in the first few words that this sentence reveals what the court resolved?

> The court had to resolve the issue of subject matter jurisdiction.

**Avoid Long Quotations**—When you are reading, do you have a tendency to skip over extensive quotations, hoping they are not crucial to your understanding? Follow the "golden" rule of good writing. Do not inflict on others what you would not have inflicted on yourself. Few people have the discipline required to read through lengthy quotations. Therefore, if you feel you must quote, pick out the essential phrases or words and express the remainder in your own words. If you absolutely cannot forgo the quote (on the grounds that the court or legal commentator said it so much better than you could) then either before or after the quote explain what they said in your own words. Such paraphrasing will discourage you from too easily succumbing to the temptation to quote. You will find that there are few expressions that are so eloquent that they must be quoted.

On the other hand, in some cases quoting is necessary. If you are discussing a statute, ordinance, or regulation you must quote the relevant parts. Similarly, if you are discussing a contract you should quote the sections at issue. Also, if you need to convey a court's or party's exact words, especially if legal terms of art are being used, then you should quote. The latter is a judgment call. If you are not sure that you can accurately paraphrase what is being said, first quote and then paraphrase. The reader can then decide if you have paraphrased accurately.

**Avoiding the "in *X. v. Y.*" Construction**—Tempting as it may be to begin each sentence "In *U.S. v. White* the court held . . . while in *U.S. v. Black* the court held. . . ," avoid this configuration as much as possible. A preferable way to discuss case law is to set forth the holding of the court in terms that make its relevance to the case at hand clear. Then identify the court using a citation at the end of the sentence.

> When a court is faced with an equal protection claim it must use one of three levels of review. *City of Cleburne v. Cleburne Living Center,* 473 U.S. 432 (1985). To determine the appropriate level of review the court must first decide whether the statute affects a suspect class. *Id.* at 439. A suspect class is one that has endured a history of purposeful and invidious discrimination and lacks the political power to obtain redress from the political branches of government. *Watkins v. U.S. Army,* 875 F.2d 699 (9th Cir. 1989).

Notice how much more fluently this paragraph reads than the following paragraph.

> In *City of Cleburne v. Cleburne Living Center,* 473 U.S. 432 (1985), the Court held equal protection claims require the use of one of three levels of review. The Court also held that before determining the appropriate level of review a court must first decide whether the statute affects a suspect class. In *Watkins v. U.S. Army,* 875 F.2d 699 (9th Cir. 1989), the court held that a suspect class is one that has endured a history of purposeful and invidious discrimination and that lacks the political power to obtain redress from the political branches of government.

Citations at the beginning of sentences tend to interfere with the legal concepts being presented. They grab the reader's attention and divert it away from the more important concepts presented within the sentence.

You will find it tempting to use the "In *A. v. B.* the court held . . ." construction because it relieves you of the responsibility of connecting one case to another. Transitions tend to disappear and your memo becomes a string of cases discussed one after one another with no mention of how they are all related. You can avoid this trap by incorporating transitional words into your writing and always asking "Why am I discussing this case" and "How does this case relate to the previous case and the next case?"

## TECHNO TIP

Being able to communicate and transfer information cheaply and instantaneously on the Internet carries with it a price often overlooked—lack of security. As you will see in Workshop 19 (and which you probably already know) a client's confidences must be maintained "inviolate." How can we be sure that the information we are transmitting remains confidential? How can we ensure that our data is not compromised or received by someone other than the person we are directing it to?

Various encryption programs that scramble data so that it is unintelligible to anyone who does not have the decoding program, are now available. Some of the programs are very sophisticated and so difficult to "break" that the federal government has put restrictions on their exportation. One of the problems with these programs is that they can be used only when the recipient has access to the same program.

## FORMS FILE

*Include a sample motion for summary judgment and a response and a reply in your forms file. You may also want to include samples of other types of tactical motions as well. Make sure to get copies of the supporting papers (such as affidavits) as well.*

## KEY TERM

**affiant**

## INTRODUCTION: THE ORDEAL OF TRIAL

Modern civil jury trials are, above all, expensive. If all of the costs are included—lawyer's fees, expert witness fees, jury fees, cost of the facilities, salaries of judge, court reporter, bailiff, and clerk—all but the simplest trials can generate costs running to many thousands of dollars per trial day.

As these costs rise, so does the determination of courts and judges to try each case as efficiently as possible. Lengthy arguments over objections, lines of questioning that turn out to lead nowhere, testimony proving facts that no one seriously disputes—in short, any activities that take up time and do not contribute directly to the presentation of the main case—are seen as costly wastes of time.

A trial is made up of a great many details, all of which must come together at a single time and place. Witnesses must be scheduled and prepared. Exhibits must be copied, marked, and organized. Jury instructions must be researched and submitted. Disputes over legal and evidentiary issues must be anticipated, any necessary research completed, and memoranda prepared. Rather than take the chance that trials will be interrupted or delayed because some item has been overlooked, courts are increasingly adopting procedures designed to force the lawyers to attend to all of the required preparation tasks well before the trial begins.

In this workshop, we study the procedures that relate directly to trial preparation. We begin with a brief look at the steps required to obtain a trial date. Then we will present a checklist of typical trial preparation tasks, and examine each of the procedures that must be completed before trial. Finally, we will assemble a **trial notebook,** a loose-leaf binder used to organize the papers that the trial attorney may need to locate quickly during the trial.

## HOW TO OBTAIN A TRIAL SETTING

Before there can be a trial, the court must assign a trial date. You might suppose that getting a trial date would be simple—how hard can it be for a secretary to check the judge's calendar for an open date?—but there are several reasons why this is not so.

**Why Trial Scheduling Is Complicated**—First of all, like everything in litigation, trial setting often becomes a tactical battleground between the litigants.

To win any money from defendant, plaintiff must get the case to judgment. Absent a successful motion for summary judgment or other similar maneuver, plaintiff cannot win without a trial. Defendant, on the other hand, already has the money that plaintiff is trying to win, and would usually like to keep it as long as possible. As long as there is no trial, there can be no judgment ordering defendant to pay plaintiff. Therefore, unless defendant is fairly sure of winning, defendant may have a strong incentive to delay going to trial, and will do everything possible to convince the judge that the case is not ready for trial.

There is also the problem of overbooking. Judges know that the majority of trials do not actually proceed as scheduled. Many cases are settled on the eve of trial—there is nothing more effective than the pressure of a looming trial date to bring litigants to the bargaining table. Trials may also be postponed at the last minute due to unexpected procedural glitches or scheduling conflicts. Postponements also occur when a trial takes longer than expected—sometimes weeks longer—preventing the next trial from starting. The result is that courts must schedule as many as half a dozen trials for each available time slot, so as to be sure of having at least one that will actually proceed. Of course, there is no reliable way to predict which cases will settle or need to be postponed, so there is a high risk of having two or more active trials set at the same time before the same judge.

Because of these problems, in many courts a case often goes through a series of trial settings. Priority for trial is often based on the age of the case. If several cases are ready to proceed on the same trial date, the case that was filed earliest goes to trial and the rest are postponed. In a system of this kind, the likelihood of actually going to trial on the first trial setting tends to be low, and increases with each postponement as the case gets older. The attorneys can never be absolutely sure that a case will or will not proceed as scheduled, so they must prepare for each trial setting as though certain of going forward. The costs spiral upward, as attorneys are forced to prepare for trial several times on each case.

*Your Local Notes*

_____

_____

**The Virtue of Firm Trial Dates**—In 1990, the Congress enacted legislation requiring each U.S. district court to appoint an advisory group of lawyers and citizens to study the problem of rising expense and delay in civil litigation, and to recommend plans designed to process civil cases more efficiently; see 28 U.S.C. § 471 *et seq.* As we have seen, one major target for reform has been the discovery process. Trial scheduling procedure is another important focus. According to the Civil Justice Expense and Delay Reduction Plan adopted by the U.S. District Court for the Northern District of Texas, "A credible, firm trial date is the *sine qua non* of reducing excessive costs and delay." When a court grants a **firm trial date,** the parties are assured that, barring some extraordinary event, the case *will* go to trial on that date—no excuses accepted. Much duplication of effort is eliminated since the attorneys need only prepare for trial once.

How can a court grant firm trial dates when there is no way to predict which cases will settle before trial? Must we schedule only one case per time slot, leaving the judge sitting around with nothing to do every time a case settles? What about the problem of trials that take longer than expected?

There are no easy solutions to these problems, but many U.S. district courts have found ways of coping with them, to the point that trial settings can be made reasonably firm:

■ If two cases are ready to begin trial at the same time, another judge can be brought in to try one of them. Perhaps another judge's cases have all settled, leaving him free to help with the overflow. In appropriate circumstances, cases can be tried before magistrate judges or *pro tem* judges. (A **judge *pro tem*** is usually an experienced attorney who volunteers to act as a judge in a particular case. Many courts have programs to recruit and qualify *pro tem* judges, so as to have help available when needed.)

■ The court can require the parties to substantially complete their discovery and other preparation before asking for a trial date. Many U.S. district courts issue a trial setting only after the parties appear at a pretrial conference and convince the judge that all is in readiness. That way, neither party can credibly ask for a postponement by claiming that more discovery or pretrial work remains to be done.

■ Mandatory settlement conferences can be held, well in advance of trial, so that some of the cases that are destined to settle will settle earlier.

**Trial Setting Procedure in U.S. District Courts**—Each U.S. district court establishes its own procedures for setting trial dates. You cannot find out how to obtain a trial setting in a given court by consulting the Federal Rules of Civil Procedure; trial setting procedure is found in local rules and in orders issued by individual judges. Rule 40, FRCP, provides:

> The district courts shall provide by rule for the placing of actions upon the trial calendar (1) without request of the parties or (2) upon request of a party and notice to the other parties or (3) in such other manner as the courts deem expedient.

The first two options specified reflect traditional practice, still followed in some state courts but largely abandoned in U.S. district courts. Courts that calendar trials "without request of the parties" typically issue minute entries setting a trial date. This is done automatically when each case reaches a designated stage. In courts that set trial dates "upon request of a party," the usual procedure allows either party to file a motion to set. The rules may require the moving party to certify that the case is ready for trial; that is, issue is joined, discovery is complete, all necessary parties are present. If the opposing party disputes the motion to set, the judge decides when and if the case should go to trial; if the motion is unopposed, the court sets a trial date and notifies the parties by minute entry.

In most federal district courts, pretrial procedure has been substantially overhauled in response to Congress's 1990 mandate for each district to adopt a plan for reducing expense and delay in civil lawsuits. No two districts' procedures are identical, but many include some or all of the following features:

■ *Greater judicial supervision.* Instead of allowing the attorneys a completely free hand in case preparation, the judge takes an active role. Attorneys are required to appear in court for scheduling conferences and status conferences, at which the judge asks for detailed information about what each side is doing to prepare for trial. The judge makes specific decisions about what discovery and other preparation tasks the attorneys need to complete, and sets deadlines.

■ *Active verification of trial readiness.* Since the judge is keeping informed about the status of the case, she is in a position to make an informed decision about the parties' readiness for trial before setting a trial date.

- *Case tracking.* Cases are assigned to different "tracks" according to their complexity and other factors. Routine cases (such as collection of student loans) are segregated in separate tracks. Tracking helps make the court's trial load more predictable by identifying the cases that will need extended trial time and providing alternate pathways for those that do not.

- *Formal articulation of preparation tasks.* Instead of leaving it to the attorneys to figure out what tasks need to be completed prior to trial, the local rules spell out a number of specific requirements, with completion deadlines for each.

The exact procedure by which a trial date is obtained varies considerably from district to district. (Your instructor will inform you of the procedure followed in the U.S. district court having jurisdiction in your locality, or you can check the local rules.) By way of example, here are the broad outlines of the trial setting procedure under current Local Rule 16 of the U.S. District Court for the Northern District of California. It is fairly typical of the relatively complex case management schemes commonly seen in busy metropolitan districts. (We do not reproduce the entire rule because it is some ten pages long; you can find it on the Internet by going to www.cand.uscourts.gov and following the links.)

1. *Case management schedule (Local Rule 16-2).* When plaintiff files the complaint, the clerk automatically issues an initial "case management schedule" setting various deadlines. Trial counsel for both sides must meet and confer by the 90th day after the filing of the complaint. The litigants must make their initial disclosures by the 100th day, file a "case management statement" by the 110th day, and appear before the court for a case management conference by the 120th day.

2. *Case management statement (Local Rule 16-13).* The case management statement, prepared jointly by the attorneys for both parties and filed by the 110th day, is to inform the court about the factual and legal issues and propose a detailed schedule for completing all anticipated discovery, disclosure, motions, and other pretrial tasks. The clerk issues instructions for preparing the statement, and a list of its required contents, when the suit is filed. In the case management statement, the attorneys request a trial date and indicate how long the trial is expected to take.

3. *Initial case management conference [Rules 16-14(a) and (b)].* By the 120th day, the attorneys must appear for an initial case management conference, which may be conducted by the assigned district judge or by a magistrate judge. This is basically a Rule 16(b) scheduling conference of the kind we discussed in Workshop 14, but with an extended agenda. The judge reviews the case management statement filed by the parties, discusses any problems with the attorneys, and enters an "initial case management order."

4. *Case management order [Rule 16-14(b)].* The goal of the conference is to produce a case management order. The order must "identify the principal issues of the case, review the parties' disclosure and document production, review motions to be filed, establish a discovery plan, set appropriate limits on discovery and consider the propriety of referring the case to ADR." Rule 16-14(b) lists fifteen different items that the order may address. Among other things, the order may set a trial date and schedule.

5. *Subsequent case management statements and case management conferences [Rules 16-14(c) and (d)].* The court may require the attorneys to appear periodically for additional case management conferences, so that the judge can monitor their progress in completing the assigned tasks. Prior to each conference, the attorneys must file an updated joint case management statement reflecting the current status of the case. If no trial date was set at the initial case management conference, the judge may do so at a subsequent conference.

6. *Joint pretrial conference (Rule 16-15).* At the time that the judge sets a trial date, he or she also sets a date for a final pretrial conference. At least 30 days before the conference, the lead attorneys who will try the case must meet and confer to prepare the "pretrial conference statement." The pretrial conference statement is to contain detailed descriptions of the factual and legal issues, lists of witnesses and exhibits, and other information to be used in planning for the trial. (We will have more to say about pretrial statements and pretrial orders later.) The orders that the judge makes at the pretrial conference "control the subsequent course of the action"; see FRCP, Rule 16.

Trial setting procedure in state court ranges over the entire spectrum of possibilities, from simple systems in which the court issues trial dates more or less automatically, to complex ones that are as demanding as those of the busiest federal district courts. State court procedures are not always spelled out very clearly in published local rules, so you may need to consult your instructor or speak to a judge's secretary or someone in the clerk's office to find out exactly how the trial-setting system works in the state courts of your locality.

---

*Your Local Notes*

_____

_____

---

## TRIAL PREPARATION TASKS

We have obtained a trial date, and it is fast approaching. Now what? What must we do to ensure that all is in readiness when the trial begins?

Every trial is different—and every trial is the same. The parties and issues change, but every jury case involves the same basic sequence of events. A jury trial is like a stage production: We have actors (the witnesses), a script (good attorneys plan the questioning in advance), and props (exhibits and demonstrative evidence). Behind the scenes, other activities are going on: motions, scheduling, settling of jury instructions and voir dire questions. All of these details require careful advance preparation.

The preparation tasks that we discuss here are not necessarily carried out in any particular order. Many of the deadlines are compressed into the space of a few weeks immediately prior to the beginning of trial, so we will usually be working feverishly on a number of items at the same time. (During the week or so preceding a major trial, the trial attorneys and litigation paralegals assigned to the case are often running on pure adrenaline, putting in 16-hour days, going home only to shower and change, if at all.)

Because there is no prescribed sequence, we will deviate from our usual step-by-step presentation, and instead merely list the tasks that must typically be done during the last stages of preparing for a jury trial.

## Trial Preparation: A Task-Oriented Checklist

The following discussion describes and illustrates the trial preparation tasks called for in a typical federal district court. As usual, the details vary somewhat according to the rules and customs of each jurisdiction. To determine how your local courts handle each task, begin by consulting the local rules. Next, look for published general orders and

"judge-specific" rules and orders. You may not succeed in finding all of the information that you need. Many of the details—the way in which *voir dire* is conducted, the procedure for submitting jury instructions, how exhibits are to be marked—are often left up to the individual judge's discretion. Some judges issue standard minute entries in each case, describing their preferences and expectations. Others offer little or no guidance beyond a few verbal instructions in pretrial conferences. Sometimes, a judge's particular requirements can be nailed down in advance only by consulting another attorney who has tried cases before the same judge (not a bad idea, in any case) or by asking the judge's secretary or clerk.

Your instructor will apprise you of the pertinent rules and practices of the courts of your locality.

---

*Your Local Notes*

_____

_____

---

**Task 1** — *Final Discovery Supplementation and Disclosure*

By the time trial preparation gets under way in earnest, discovery should usually be complete or nearly so. In most federal district courts, the initial scheduling order imposes a discovery cutoff date, usually several months in advance of the expected trial date.

There is, however, one part of discovery that is necessarily left until the final pretrial preparation stage: the designation of trial witnesses and exhibits. In the early stages of the lawsuit, we disclose the identities of people who have information relating to the case and turn over pertinent documents, but it is usually impossible to say at that point exactly which of those people will actually be called as witnesses at the trial, and which documents will actually be offered as exhibits.

In districts that do not opt out of Rule 26(a) disclosure, the final "wave" of required disclosure is due 30 days before trial. At that time, each party must disclose the name, address, and telephone number of each witness to be called at trial, and a list identifying each document and exhibit to be offered. Each party must also designate which, if any, deposition testimony will be used at trial in lieu of live witnesses; see FRCP, Rule 26(a)(3). The opposing party must then, no later than 14 days before trial, specify any objections to exhibits.

In courts that adhere to traditional discovery methods, similar disclosure is usually required, not because the rules mandate it, but because the opposing party will almost certainly have served discovery requests asking for the identities of witnesses and copies of exhibits. If that information has not been provided already, Rule 26(e) requires a supplemental response disclosing it.

---

*Your Local Notes*

_____

_____

---

## Task 2    *Pretrial Statement or Order*

Faced with punishing caseloads, most federal judges today keep a tight rein on the proceedings in their courtrooms. Trial time is a scarce commodity, and not to be wasted on unprepared attorneys who flounder around trying to figure out which witness to call next. Before beginning a trial, judges want to be assured that the attorneys know exactly what they are going to present and, to the extent possible, have prepared everything that they will need in advance.

One procedural tool that judges use to accomplish this is the pretrial statement or pretrial order. A pretrial order is a document, in the form of a filed court paper typically prepared jointly by the attorneys and signed by the judge, that specifies exactly what the attorneys may present at the trial. Some courts provide instead for the attorneys to jointly prepare and file a document, often called a pretrial statement or pretrial conference statement; the contents are the same, but instead of signing the document itself the judge enters an order approving it. Either way, the end result is a filed document that controls the course of the trial. (To avoid repetition, we will use the term *pretrial order* to encompass all of the various permutations.)

In some federal district courts, the local rules spell out clearly the items to be included in a pretrial order and specify the procedure to be followed. In others, pretrial order procedure is left up to individual judges. Whether the procedure calls for a pretrial order or a pretrial statement, it is the attorneys, not the judge, who write it—the judge's role is to review, order changes if necessary, and approve. Usually, each attorney writes a rough draft setting forth proposed wording for the items that he wants included in the final pretrial order. Then the attorneys meet and combine the drafts into a single document. For items that all attorneys agree should be included, it is usually possible to agree on wording that all can accept. Items that the attorneys cannot agree on are included with a brief explanation of each side's position.

A pretrial order typically includes all or most of the following categories, which appear in separate numbered or lettered sections[1]:

- *Names, addresses, and telephone numbers* of the attorneys for all parties.

- *A statement of the court's jurisdiction.* Usually, by the time the case is nearing readiness for trial, any serious jurisdictional disputes should already have been raised by motion and decided. In many cases, the parties do not dispute the court's jurisdiction, and the pretrial order merely recites the agreed basis for it.

- *A description of the nature of the action.* A short (a paragraph or less) statement of what the lawsuit is about.

- *Contentions of the parties.* A short description of what each side claims happened. The statement of contentions does not delve into evidentiary details. It is a short and conclusory statement of what each side intends to prove, suitable for telling someone unfamiliar with the case—such as a prospective juror—what each side's position is.

- *Stipulations and uncontested facts.* Recall from Workshop 1 that plaintiff's job in a lawsuit is to prove one or more causes of action; each cause of action has elements that plaintiff must establish by proving specific facts. Defendant can defeat a given cause of action either by preventing plaintiff from proving one of its required elements, or by proving facts establishing each of the elements of a recognized affirmative defense. The purpose of a trial is to decide which facts each side has proved. There is, of course, no point wasting trial time proving facts that both sides agree are true. This section of the pretrial order is intended to force the attorneys to think about and discuss their factual contentions, and to articulate the facts on which they agree.

---

[1] These are generic categories distilled from Eastern District of Texas Local Rule CV-16 and Eastern District of Nebraska Local Rule 16.2. For a sample form pretrial order, see Appendix D of the Eastern District of Texas Local Rules, which may be found on the Internet at www.txed.uscourts.gov.

■ *Contested issues of fact.* By the same token, the trial can proceed most efficiently if the attorneys have clearly specified exactly what facts are in dispute. The pretrial order provides an incentive for the attorneys to do so, since the judge may refuse to allow presentation of evidence on issues not specified in the pretrial order.

■ *Contested and uncontested issues of law.* Here, the parties list any legal issues that have not yet been resolved. Normally, if the attorneys have done their jobs, any important issues relating to the claims and defenses should already have been raised by motion long before trial. Often, however, the intensity of trial preparation smokes out issues that have gone unnoticed. If the attorneys are able to agree on how to resolve an issue, it is listed as uncontested; otherwise, it is contested and the judge will sooner or later have to decide which side is right.

■ *Status of parties.* Some courts require the pretrial order to indicate whether there are any parties who have been named as defendants or third-party defendants who have not been served, and whether there are any unnamed parties who need to be included in the suit. (Under some circumstances, failure to include a necessary party can result in a judgment that is unenforceable. Including information about party status in the pretrial order allows the judge to spot joinder-related problems before everyone spends tens or hundreds of thousands of dollars on a useless trial.)

■ *List of witnesses.* In modern civil litigation, there are no surprise witnesses. We have already seen that Rule 26(a)(3) requires disclosure of the names and addresses of all witnesses at least 30 days before trial. The pretrial order sets forth each side's final witness list; witnesses not listed in the pretrial order cannot be called—period—unless the judge can be persuaded that the omission was somehow justified (don't bet on it).

■ *List of exhibits.* A great deal of trial time can be wasted if the questioning has to be stopped every few minutes while attorneys look for exhibits or argue about their admissibility. Therefore, most courts have engineered their rules so as to ensure that all possible exhibit-related tasks are done before trial (see Task 6). In the pretrial order, each litigant is typically required to include a formal list showing each exhibit to be offered, and the opposing party is to state what, if any, objections will be made to each. Pretrial order rules usually provide that ex-

hibits not listed in the pretrial order will not be admitted absent compelling reasons to allow them, and objections not stated in the pretrial order are deemed waived.

■ *Designation of deposition testimony.* Recall that when a witness cannot testify in person, it is sometimes permissible to read the person's deposition testimony at trial; see FRCP, Rule 32(a)(3). Discovery depositions often cover a great deal of ground beyond the testimony to be used at trial. We do not read entire depositions to the jury, only the parts that are pertinent to issues being tried. It is common to require parties who intend to offer deposition testimony at trial to specify in the pretrial order which pages of which depositions they intend to read. As with exhibits, the opposing party is often required to designate any objections to the testimony specified.

■ *Pending motions.* The pretrial order may include a list of all motions that have been made and are not yet decided. This allows the judge to be sure that all necessary rulings have been made by the time the trial begins.

■ *Trial schedule and limitations.* Often, the pretrial order will recite the estimated length of the trial, and any limitations that the judge has imposed or that the attorneys have agreed to. By long-standing tradition, trials in the American system have been allowed to continue for as long as the parties could find admissible evidence to put on (which could sometimes be a very long time indeed). Increasingly, judges are setting limits by allowing only a specified number of days for each side's case, limiting the number of experts allowed to testify, and disallowing repetitive testimony.

The importance of careful attention to detail in drafting a pretrial order cannot be overstated. The pretrial order literally dictates the issues to be tried [see FRCP Rule 16(e)], in effect taking the place of the complaint and answer. Claims left out of the pretrial order are likely to be gone forever, so it is natural to err on the side of completeness. It is no wonder that trial attorneys sometimes spend days writing drafts and negotiating language, or that pretrial orders in complex cases are sometimes hundreds of pages long.

*Your Local Notes*

_____

_____

| Task 3 | *Preparing the Closing Argument and Opening Statement* |
|---|---|

Only a licensed attorney may present a case to the jury, and attorneys usually compose their own jury arguments. A paralegal who is assisting in trial preparation may be able to make helpful suggestions about points to be included in jury arguments, and to serve as a sounding board for rehearsals, but is unlikely to be asked to write an argument.

Why, then, are we taking up space talking about jury arguments in a textbook for paralegals? Because many attorneys consider that the best way to prepare a case for trial is to begin with the closing argument. That is, we *first* decide what we want to say to the jury in closing argument, *then* we organize the witnesses and exhibits so as to provide evidence to support that argument. It is important to keep this perspective in mind when we prepare the rest of the presentation for trial. In the end, what matters is persuading the jury that rendering a verdict for our client is the *fair* thing to do. We can best do that by stressing a few simple and compelling themes, not by getting bogged down in a morass of technical detail (unless, of course, we have a poor case on the merits, and prefer to leave the jury confused).

No doubt there are as many opinions about how best to prepare and deliver a closing argument as there are trial attorneys. One of our favorite sources for guidance on the subject, and a book that we highly recommend, is *How to Argue and Win Every Time,* written by Gerry Spence, an attorney who has achieved spectacular successes in a series of highly publicized trials, criminal and civil. Our other recommendation for anyone who wants to learn what distinguishes an effective argument from an ineffective one is to go to the courthouse and watch some trial attorneys in action.

In the closing argument, we are free (mostly) to say anything that we think will persuade the jury to arrive at the desired verdict. We can talk about what the evidence has shown, of course, but we can also tell stories, we can argue by analogy, we can draw logical inferences from the evidence, we can appeal to the jurors' common sense and general knowledge about life. There are some limits, of course: Usually, we cannot state or imply that the defendant has insurance. We cannot state our own opinions or beliefs (we can say "Mr. X lied to you," but not "I know Mr. X lied to you"). And, in most courts, the judge will not allow us to ask the jurors to put themselves in the place of the plaintiff or victim (i.e., "How much would someone have to pay you to give up the use of your legs for the rest of your life?").

Opening statements, by contrast, are much more limited in permissible scope. In an opening statement, we are not supposed to *argue* (although we would not be very good trial lawyers if we didn't use the opening statement as a persuasive tool to the extent possible). The opening statement is (theoretically) confined to telling the jury what we expect the evidence to be. How far we can go beyond the sterile confines of the evidence depends on the judge. Most attorneys would write the opening statement last, after thoroughly mapping out the presentation of witnesses and exhibits. One thing that we want to avoid at all costs is promising evidence in the opening statement that we then never deliver.

| Task 4 | *Task 4 "Voir Dire" Questions* |
|---|---|

The jury selection process begins with a roomful of prospective jurors (also called the venire members) and, by a process of elimination, we arrive at a jury panel of (typically, in a federal civil case) between six and twelve jurors and one or more alternates. The exact procedure by which this is accomplished is up to the individual judge, but always involves some kind of *voir dire* questioning. FRCP, Rule 47(a), provides:

> **Examination of Jurors.** The court may permit the parties or their attorneys to conduct the examination of prospective jurors or may itself conduct the examination. In the latter event, the court shall permit the parties or their attorneys to supplement the examination by such further inquiry as it deems proper or shall itself submit to the prospective jurors such additional questions of the parties or their attorneys as it deems proper.

*Voir dire* questioning is aimed at getting information about each juror. This information has several purposes:

- *Identifying prospective jurors who should be removed for cause.* Prospective jurors who have a conflict of interest, or who admit to being biased against one of the litigants, or who because of strongly held beliefs are unable to follow the judge's instructions are not qualified to serve and will be excused. *Voir dire* questioning helps identify those prospective jurors.

- *Allowing the litigants to use their peremptory challenges effectively.* Plaintiff and defendant will each be allotted a specified number of "strikes" or peremptory challenges, which can be used to remove jurors deemed unfavorable (as long as racial motivations are not involved). Obviously, to assess which jurors are least likely to favor our case, we need information about each juror's background and views—information that comes from *voir dire* questioning.

■ *Helping the attorneys to focus their trial presentation.* To tailor our presentation and make it as persuasive as possible to the audience that we have—the jurors—we need as much information as we can get about each juror's likely opinions and biases.

Traditionally, the attorneys were allowed to question the jurors individually, one on one, about nearly any subject matter that could conceivably have a bearing on the juror's qualifications. In courts that allow open *voir dire*—some state courts still do—attorneys have developed into an art form the practice of asking *voir dire* questions that are really thinly veiled arguments on the merits (i.e., "If the evidence showed that defendant was falling down drunk when he ran over my client in a crosswalk while running a red light, do you have any beliefs that would prevent you from awarding punitive damages against him?").

Most federal judges today place tight limits on the kinds of questions that can be asked in *voir dire,* and usually it is the judge, not the attorneys, who asks the questions. Attorneys submit their proposed *voir dire* questions in advance, and the judge decides which, if any, will be asked. Needless to say, argumentative or slanted *voir dire* questions are unlikely to pass muster.

Each judge sets her own procedure for submitting *voir dire* questions and for conducting *voir dire* questioning. Some federal judges publish their procedures in "judge-specific" rules or orders; you can find examples on the Internet sites of the busier metropolitan districts such as the Southern District of New York or the Northern District of California (see www.uscourts.gov and follow links). The following provision, taken from the Standing Order for Pre-Trial Preparation of Judge Charles R. Breyer of the U.S. District Court for the Northern District of California, is typical (see www.cand.uscourts.gov and follow links):

> The attached *voir dire* questionnaire will be given to the venire members, and copies of the responses will be made available to counsel at the beginning of *voir dire.* Counsel should submit a set of additional requested *voir dire,* to be posed by the Court, to which they have agreed at the pretrial meeting. Any *voir dire* questions on which counsel cannot agree shall be submitted separately. Counsel will be allowed brief follow-up *voir dire* after the Court's questioning.

What kinds of questions should we submit? The answer depends on the case, and on the judge. In general, we would like to know as much about each juror as the judge will allow us to find out. There are basically four possible sources of information about jurors:

1. *The jury questionnaire.* As the order just quoted implies, most courts today require each prospective juror to fill out a questionnaire. A few typical questions:

   ■ What is your occupation?

   ■ Are you married? Do you have children? What does your wife/husband do? What do your children do?

   ■ What is your educational background?

   ■ Do you have any legal training?

   ■ Do you or any of your family members work in law enforcement?

   ■ Have you ever sued anyone or been sued yourself? What was the case about and how did it turn out?

   ■ Have you ever sat on a jury before? What was the case about and how did it turn out?

2. *The judge's general* voir dire *questions.* Usually, the jurors fill out the jury questionnaire before they are assigned to a particular case. After they are in the assigned courtroom and the attorneys and parties are present, the judge usually asks a series of general *voir dire* questions that are used in every case and directed to the panel as a whole. These are mainly aimed at discovering any reasons why a juror might need to be disqualified or excused, and typically include questions such as these:

   ■ Are any of you acquainted with any of the parties or attorneys?

   ■ Do any of you have any disabilities or medical problems that would prevent you from serving?

   ■ Do you have any financial interest in the suit (for example, a juror might be a shareholder in a corporation that is a party to the suit)?

   ■ Do any of you have any moral or philosophical beliefs that would prevent you from rendering a fair and impartial verdict?

3. *Specific* voir dire *questions submitted or asked by the attorneys.* Most of the general information that we need about each juror will come from the questionnaire. Therefore, our main purpose in submitting our own *voir dire* questions is to try to get specific information that is useful in the context of our particular case. For ex-

ample, in our *Martin v. Collins* hypo, we might submit questions such as these:

- Do you own a hand gun?

- Have you ever been assaulted?

- Do you believe it is possible for someone to be so traumatized by an assault that psychiatric treatment would be needed?

- Have you ever worked in a hotel?

4. *Outside sources.* The three sources of information we have mentioned so far are part of the formal jury selection process provided by the court system. What about going outside that system for information? Where the importance of the case justifies the expense, there is always the possibility of enlisting the assistance of investigators or jury consultants. Direct out-of-court contact with jurors or their families is, of course, a serious ethical breach. However, there is nothing to prevent gathering information that is in the public domain. Often, a simple Internet search will turn up an amazing amount of information about a person. Another tactic that some jury consultants recommend is to have an investigator do "drive-bys" of jurors' homes, to note the type of neighborhood, presence of toys, and other clues to the jurors' personality. Investigating jurors can raise prickly ethical issues and also has the potential to alienate jurors should they become aware of it, so activities of this kind should never be undertaken without the express approval of your supervising attorney.

How are proposed *voir dire* questions to be submitted? The procedure depends on the rules and customs of the court. Sometimes, the pretrial statement or order includes a section for proposed *voir dire* questions. In many courts, it is up to the individual judge to decide how he wants *voir dire* questions submitted.

---

**Your Local Notes**

_____

_____

---

## Task 5   *Jury Instructions*

We have seen in previous workshops (see especially Workshop 1) that for plaintiff to win a lawsuit, plaintiff must offer evidence establishing each of the elements of one or more causes of action. We saw, for

example, that the cause of action for battery has four elements: (1) an act by defendant, that is (2) intentional, (3) causing harmful or offensive contact with plaintiff and (4) damages proximately caused by the act. The question now is, how does the jury know whether plaintiff has established all of the elements of a cause of action? How does a juror know what the elements of battery are, for example?

It is up to the judge to instruct the jury on the law. Among other things, that includes, in a battery case, telling the jury what are the elements of the tort of battery. The judge gives the instructions verbally, usually after the attorneys have made their closing arguments.

How does the judge know what to say? Does the judge think up the instructions as the need arises, drawing on her own knowledge of the law? No. As you might imagine, small differences in the wording of jury instructions can have a big impact on the outcome of the case. A wrong word or two, and the losing party will appeal, and win the appeal. The rules therefore place the burden on the litigants to submit any desired instructions in writing. The judge merely passes on each proposed instruction and decides to give it, not give it, or give it after first modifying the wording. Then, when the time comes to instruct the jury, the judge simply reads the instructions that she has approved.

The procedure for submitting proposed jury instructions depends on the rules and customs of each court. FRCP, Rule 51, merely provides:

> At the close of the evidence or at such earlier time during the trial as the court reasonably directs, any party may file written requests that the court instruct the jury on the law as set forth in the requests. The court shall inform counsel of its proposed action upon the requests prior to their arguments to the jury. . . .

To prepare and submit proposed jury instructions for a given case, we need to determine (1) what subjects we need instructions on, (2) what each instruction should say, and (3) what the procedure is for submitting them.

**Deciding What Instructions Are Needed**—Getting the jury instructions right is important, not so much because of the effect that the instructions will have on the jury's decision (debatable, in the view of many trial lawyers), but because a correct set of jury instructions is essential for the verdict to be sustained on appeal. Suppose, for example, plaintiff is asserting a cause of action for battery, and the judge gives a jury instruction that leaves out one of the four required elements. Plaintiff wins a verdict. The likely result? Defendant appeals, and the court of appeals automatically reverses. It does not matter that jury might have found for plaintiff even if the instruction had been correct (there is no way to know, of course)—the case will have to be retried from the beginning.

In principle, if we represent a plaintiff, we need a jury instruction on each cause of action that we intend to submit to the jury. If, as in our hypo, we are suing for assault, battery, and negligence, we need instructions covering the elements of each of those causes of action. If we represent a defendant, we need a jury instruction covering each affirmative defense that we intend to present. We may also need instructions on other legal principles, such as burden of proof, and the weight to be given certain types of evidence. The judge will also routinely give a series of instructions laying out ground rules for the jury deliberations and telling the jury how to evaluate the evidence.

To make a list of the jury instructions that we may need in a given case, we recommend a two-step process: (1) Begin with your issues outline, and decide what instructions will be needed to support the causes of action and/or defenses that you are asserting and then (2) consult one or more sets of model or recommended jury instructions for additional ideas of topics to be covered.

**Content of Instructions**—Ideally, we would like the court's jury instructions to express the law accurately—to avoid reversal on appeal—but be phrased in a way that favors our case as much as possible. The problem, of course, is that our opponent would also like the wording slanted in his favor, and the resulting tug-of-war over seemingly inconsequential differences in phraseology takes up valuable trial time.

One solution widely embraced by the courts is to adopt model or recommended instructions covering all of the commonly litigated issues. These instructions are typically written by committees of judges and legal scholars and are designed to be accurate, impartial, and worded in everyday language that the average juror can understand. For example, the U.S. Court of Appeals for the Ninth Circuit publishes a *Manual of Model Civil Jury Instructions* (also available online at www.ce9.us-courts.gov). In any lawsuit pending in any U.S. district court located within the Ninth Circuit, if the *Manual of Model Civil Jury Instructions* includes an instruction on a given topic, that is the instruction the judge will use, absent compelling reasons to do otherwise. Your instructor will inform you of whether there are any sets of model or recommended jury instructions for use in the courts of your locality.

---

> *Your Local Notes*
>
> _____
>
> _____

---

Even if there are no model jury instructions designed for use in the courts of your locality, the model instructions from other jurisdictions provide a good place to start when drafting your own instructions. Often, when you need an instruction on a given point, you can find a model instruction from another court on the same issue and modify it as appropriate to fit your circumstances. Another place to look for guidance is the appellate case law; if you do a Westlaw search for your topic issue and use the phrase "jury instruction" you will often find reported decisions in which jury instructions used in the trial court are quoted and analyzed. If you simply cannot find an instruction on the topic that you need, the only remaining alternative is to draft one yourself, based on your research and knowledge of the law on the issue that the instruction addresses. Try to imitate the style and tone of the approved instructions, and try to word the instructions succinctly and impartially. As the Trial Court Guidelines for the U.S. District Court for the District of Oregon wisely suggest (see www.uscourts.gov/guidelin.html): "Remember less is better than more and 'advocacy' instructions will be rejected."

---

> *Your Local Notes*
>
> _____
>
> _____

---

**Procedure for Submitting Jury Instructions**—Considerable local variation is seen in the procedure for submitting proposed jury instructions. Some courts require submission of proposed instructions as early as 10 days or more before trial; others accept them even after both sides have put on their evidence. In some courts, proposed jury instructions are filed; in others, they are given to the judge. Your instructor will apprise you of the preferred procedure in the courts of your locality, and provide citations to the applicable local rules, if any. By way of example, many U.S. district courts follow procedures similar to those described in Local Rule 51.1 of the U.S. District Court for the District of Alaska:

> Except as the court may otherwise direct, the parties shall file their requested jury

instructions 10 days before trial. The requested instructions shall be numbered consecutively, shall indicate which party requests them, and shall embrace but one subject. The principle of law embraced in any requested instruction shall not be repeated in subsequent requests. Each request shall state what form it copies or on what authorities it relies. Requests that do not comply with the terms of this rule will not be considered by the court. Each side may also submit a set of instructions on a computer disk in a computer language compatible with the court's computer system.

---

*Your Local Notes*

_____

_____

---

## Task 6  *Marking and Preparing Exhibits*

Many lawsuits arise directly from disputes over documents—contracts, wills, patents, tax returns, corporate securities registrations, conveyances of property. Many other cases involve events—accidents, hospital stays, construction projects—that generate records. And all but the most trivial lawsuits require the use of documents to prove damages (receipts and records of expenditures). It is inevitable that documents play an important role in modern trials.

We have already seen that the discovery rules, disclosure rules, and pretrial order procedure in federal court work together to force each litigant to list, in advance of trial, the specific documents to be used as exhibits, and to disclose the list, and copies of the documents, to the opposing party. In most federal courts, each party is also required to specify any objections to the opposing party's exhibits.

The task that remains is the physical document handling for the trial (a task often delegated to paralegals): the marking, indexing, and organizing of the exhibits and copies. When an attorney wishes to have a witness refer to a document while testifying, it is necessary for the document to be marked with an exhibit number. Exhibits are marked in order to create an unambiguous record. If a witness refers to a document by its exhibit number, and the marked exhibit is included in the record, an appellate judge reading a transcript of the trial can be sure that she is looking at the same document.

Traditionally, exhibits were marked by the judge's clerk at the time of their use. To use an exhibit, the attorney would first ask the clerk to mark the document, then show the document to the witness and ask the witness to identify it, then ask any required foundation questions, then offer the document in evidence. The opposing attorney would voice any objections, and the judge would decide whether to admit the document in evidence. Only after being admitted by the judge could the document be used as evidence.

Today, with copying machines and computers spewing out documents in ever greater volume, most courts have abandoned the traditional procedure as too time consuming. By requiring advance disclosure of exhibits and advance assertion of objections, there is rarely any need for the trial to be delayed over issues of admissibility. Such issues are decided in advance, and some judges enter a ruling receiving all of the approved exhibits into evidence at once in advance, avoiding the need to waste time asking for admission in evidence exhibit by exhibit. And to facilitate the listing of exhibits and objections and avoid taking up trial time, most courts now place the burden on the litigants to mark their own exhibits before the trial begins. The exact means by which this is done depends on the judge's individual preferences. Some courts provide labels that contain blank spaces for the exhibit number and for the clerk's notation of whether the exhibit was admitted into evidence or not.

The numbering system used is also up to the individual judge. Many courts cling to the tradition of using numbers for plaintiff's exhibits and letters of the alphabet for defendant's exhibits. Where appropriate, the parties can stipulate (or, if necessary, file a motion) to use some other numbering system. In complex cases involving large quantities of documents and numerous depositions (each with exhibits), it is usually preferable to agree on a unified numbering system in the early stages of discovery and stick to it at trial.

Your instructor will inform you of the preferences of the courts of your locality regarding the premarking of exhibits, and direct you to any applicable local rules. It is usually also worth checking with the judge's secretary or clerk to see if the judge has any particular requirements of his own. By way of example, here is Local Rule 39.1(b) of the U.S. District Court for the Northern District of Ohio, which follows the typical pattern:

(b) Marking of Exhibits. All exhibits must bear the official case number and shall be marked before trial with official exhibit stickers which are available upon request from the Clerk. The plaintiff shall mark exhibits with numbers and the defendant shall mark exhibits with letters, unless otherwise ordered by the Court. Joint exhibits shall be marked with numbers. If there are multiple defendants, letters shall be used followed by the party's last name. If the defendant has more than 26 exhibits, double letters shall be used.

What happens to the exhibits after they are marked? During trial, the judge's clerk (who sits at a table below the bench in the courtroom) keeps them. In most federal courts, when an attorney wants a witness to refer to an exhibit, she directs the request to the judge (i.e., "Your honor, may the witness be shown Exhibit A?"). The bailiff then gets the exhibit from the clerk and hands it to the witness; the attorney is required to remain at the lectern and may not approach the witness without the judge's permission.

Which brings up the question of what does the attorney use, if the witness has the original exhibit? Obviously, there must be a complete and well-indexed set of copies of all exhibits—our own, and our opponent's—for the attorney to refer to while questioning the witness. Keeping these in order, locating particular passages on a second's notice, and anticipating which exhibits will be needed next are all important jobs for paralegals who assist at trial.

It may also be necessary to make extra copies of exhibits for the jury. Court rules regarding what materials may be given to the jury during trial and during deliberations vary greatly. At a minimum, the marked exhibits will be made available to the jury during deliberations. Some courts go much further and allow the attorneys to furnish each juror with a notebook containing copies of important exhibits, to be used during trial. Within reasonable limits, the degree of latitude permitted is up to the individual judge.

---

*Your Local Notes*

_____

_____

---

| **Task 7** | *Arranging for Demonstrative Evidence, Visual Aids, and Other Props* |

The exhibits that we have been discussing so far are paper documents that comprise part of the formal evidence in the lawsuit. Most successful trial attorneys also make heavy use of a variety of visual aids. Here is a list of some of the items used, together with brief discussion of the preparatory work required:

- *Blowups of exhibits.* An important passage in a document will make a much greater impression on jurors if they can see it and read it for themselves while the witness is reading

it aloud. To facilitate this, most trial attorneys have blowups made, which are placed on an easel before the jury during the pertinent testimony. It is up to each attorney to bring to court any desired blowups. Blowups can be made professionally by a graphics company, or, increasingly as computer publishing technology improves, in house.

- *Drawing tablet.* Most courts provide a drawing pad on an easel for use by attorneys during argument and for use by witnesses to illustrate points made while testifying. Many also provide a blackboard or whiteboard. (It is sometimes desirable to preserve a record of what was displayed, a purpose for which a blackboard or whiteboard is not adequate.)

- *Television and display equipment for video recordings.* Videos have become an essential presentation tool in many lawsuits. Particularly in cases involving serious injury, videos depicting a "day in the life" of the victim are often very effective. Animated reconstructions of accidents are growing in popularity as a way of letting an expert witness "show" the jury the reconstructed events instead of merely describing them. A growing number of depositions are being recorded on video, and some cases involve evidence in the form of video recordings (i.e., surveillance tapes). Most courts provide equipment with which to display standard VHS videocassettes (but do not assume equipment will be available without checking).

- *Sound recording and playback equipment.* Some cases involve tape-recorded evidence or depositions. Not all courts provide playback equipment, so check in advance or plan to bring your own.

- *Specialized viewing equipment.* If specialized equipment will be needed (e.g., x-ray viewing box, special projectors, etc.), it is up to the party to supply it and to obtain the judge's permission to bring it in to the courtroom.

- *Computer equipment.* There are many potential uses for computer technology in the courtroom, and a few courts have already implemented "high-tech" courtrooms on an experimental basis; see the sidebar for a description of one such initiative. In most courts, a litigant desiring computer equipment in the courtroom must still, today, provide the equipment *and* obtain the judge's permission to bring it in and use it. Since most court systems have already embraced computerized record keeping, and judges are

## SIDEBAR

## The Computerized Courtroom of the Future

*The potential benefits of computer technology in the courtroom can perhaps be best appreciated by seeing a computerized courtroom in action. One U.S. district court, the District of Arizona, has implemented a "computer-integrated courtroom" demonstration project, an actual working courtroom equipped with state-of-the-art technology. The courtroom has its own computer system, with display terminals on the judge's bench and the attorney tables, and monitors for viewing by the jury. Here are a few of the services that the system provides:*

- *Real-time court reporting. The court reporter's stenographic machine is linked directly to the courtroom computer system. The trial transcript is available continuously and instantaneously. There is never a need to ask the court reporter to read back a question or answer—all testimony in the case is instantly accessible. When an attorney objects to a question, the judge has the benefit of being able to see the exact wording of the question on the screen before making a ruling. When an attorney is examining a witness and needs to refer to earlier testimony, the desired passages can readily be brought up on the screen—no need to flip through stacks of transcripts looking for the right question and answer.*

- *Litigation support in the courtroom. We have already seen that computerized litigation support databases are extensively used to organize and index discovery documents and depositions in cases involving large quantities of documents. In the computer-integrated courtroom, the attorneys' litigation support databases can be tied directly into the courtroom computer system so that they can be used during trial. The system also allows the attorneys (or their trial paralegals) to key in codes for particular issues on the fly—if a witness makes a statement that is pertinent to a given issue, the tes-*timony can immediately be flagged with an issue code. Then if the attorney needs to see everything that any witness has said about a particular point, it is a simple matter to search for the appropriate issue code. The system also supports real-time note taking—the attorneys and paralegals can enter notes about testimony as the testimony is being given.*

- *Evidence presentation system. The computer-integrated courtroom includes a versatile display system that is linked to the courtroom computer system. The display system accommodates a variety of inputs—regular videotape, paper documents, photographs, overhead transparencies, slides—and displays them on monitors so that the judge, the attorneys, and each juror can all view exhibits clearly and simultaneously. (The judge can, of course, turn off the jury's view.) This system makes testimony about document exhibits much easier for the jury to follow, since jurors can see the document while the witness is talking about it instead of having to wait until the witness finishes and the paper document is circulated to the jury. The system also facilitates presentation of videos, animations, and other multimedia presentations that can often communicate ideas to the jury more effectively than dry testimony.*

- *Availability of other computer resources. Since the computer-integrated courtroom includes computer terminals on each attorney table, the attorneys can take advantage of the other familiar software tools that have become so important in the modern law practice: computerized legal research through Westlaw, Internet access, electronic mail, word processing, and scheduling.*

*For more details about the computer-integrated courtroom, see the District of Arizona's web site at www.azd.uscourts.gov/cic.*

becoming increasingly comfortable with technology through their own use of computers for word processing, legal research, and scheduling, it will not be long before computer technology becomes as commonplace in the courtroom as it is everywhere else.

*Your Local Notes*

_____

_____

## Task 8    *Motions "in Limine"*

Through discovery, disclosure, and the process of preparing a pretrial statement or order, we can usually foresee with reasonable accuracy the main themes that our opponent will use to try to make points with the jury. As long as those themes are based on proper evidence, our opponent has a right to assert them, but it often happens that some of a party's best ammunition involves evidence that is technically inadmissible.

The fact that the answer to a question is inadmissible does not, of course, stop our opponent from asking the question in the first place—it is up to us to object. Unfortunately, in many situations, the opposing attorney can get an inadmissible idea across to the jury merely by asking the right question. We can object, and the judge can sustain the objection, but the damage is done, and there is no way to "*un*-ring the bell." An example will make the problem clearer.

>    **Example.** Suppose, in our hypo, that Shannon's attorney assigns Chuck, the paralegal, to run a background check on Arnie Trevayne. Chuck discovers that 5 years ago Arnie, while still a juvenile, was caught selling illegal drugs and was confined in a juvenile correctional institution for 14 months. Naturally, Shannon's attorney would love to make the jury aware of this fact because the jury is likely to mistrust any testimony by a convicted drug dealer. However, in federal court, juvenile offenses are generally not admissible to impeach a witness [see Rule 609(d), Federal Rules of Evidence].
>    Now suppose that, while cross-examining Arnie, Shannon's attorney asks the question, "Isn't it a fact that before you worked for Banbury Park Hotel you spent fourteen months in a correctional institution for dealing illegal drugs?" Park Hotels' attorney objects, the judge sustains the objection—and the jurors understand perfectly well that Arnie is a convicted drug dealer but because of some legal technicality they are not supposed to know about it.

What can Park Hotels' attorney do to prevent this outcome? She can file a motion *in limine*. *In limine* means "preliminarily" or "at the beginning." A motion *in limine* is a motion made (usually) before the trial begins in anticipation of an issue that is expected to come up during trial. The usual purpose of a motion *in limine* is to get an advance ruling to prevent an opposing party from bringing up some inadmissible matter. In the example, Park Hotels' attorney could file a motion *in limine* asking the judge to rule in advance that Arnie's juvenile offense is inad-

missible, and—this is the important part—to prohibit Shannon's attorney from asking any questions about it or otherwise mentioning it. Then, assuming the judge grants the motion, if Shannon's attorney should be foolish enough to ask the question anyway (Allen Porter, being a reputable attorney, would not do so) he risks a mistrial and a fine for contempt.

Motions *in limine* are a routine part of trial preparation in the average federal trial. First, an effort should be made to outline, in as much detail as possible, the opposing party's expected trial presentation. Then, identify any subject matter that is both objectionable and sufficiently damaging that we cannot willingly allow the jury to hear about it. (The judge's attention is a limited resource, and we do not waste it filing motions to exclude evidence that is technically inadmissible but does not really hurt us.) Once we have identified each issue requiring a motion *in limine,* we prepare the motions and file them.

Deadlines and other procedural requirements for motions in limine in federal district court are typically left up to the individual judge, and set forth in "judge-specific" rules, standing orders, or in the trial setting minute entry. Many federal district judges require the parties to exchange motions *in limine* before filing them and to attempt to reach agreement. The deadline for filing motions *in limine* is typically 7 or 15 days before the start of trial, and the judge usually rules on the motions immediately before the trial begins.

---

*Your Local Notes*

_____

_____

---

## Task 9    *Preparing the Presentation of Testimony*

Most of the time in a trial is spent questioning witnesses. The presentation and questioning may seem spontaneous, but it is not. Effective trial presentations are usually scripted, rehearsed, and choreographed in fine detail. Some of the typical preparation steps are discussed next.

**Planning Which Witnesses to Call and in What Order**—The goal of a jury trial is to sell our client's case to the jurors. To do that, we need to present the facts in such a way that the jurors can follow and understand the main themes of our case without becoming bored, offended, or confused. The standard format of a trial makes this quite difficult—we must present one witness at a time, and finish with each witness before moving to the next. We cannot question several witnesses at the same time, or question a witness on one topic and have them come back later when we are ready for another topic. Worse yet, each time we finish with a witness, before we can get on with the next one we will have to wait hours or days while our opponent cross-examines. This leads to an inherently disjointed presentation. Trial attorneys often describe a trial as being like putting together a jigsaw puzzle: Each witness contributes one or more pieces, but a clear picture emerges only at the end. It is easy to see why the choice of witnesses and the sequence of testimony can be critical.

Formulating the overall plan is, of course, the job of the lead trial attorney (but paralegals, who have often had much more direct contact with the witnesses, often have valuable input to contribute).

**Scheduling the Witnesses**—Making sure that witnesses are present and ready to testify at the right times is another critically important behind-the-scenes task that is often assigned to paralegals, one often requiring considerable skill, judgment, and diplomacy. It is rarely possible to predict exactly when a witness will be needed, because there is no way to know how long examination of preceding witnesses will take. Yet some of the most important witnesses—medical experts are a notable example—will insist on knowing, perhaps weeks in advance, exactly when they will be called to testify. Then there is the problem of whether we can depend on a witness's promise to show up in court at the appointed time. If we protect ourselves with a subpoena, the witness may be offended (and testify accordingly), but if we do not and the witness fails to appear, we may be left with a gaping hole in our case. And, there is the matter of waiting. In most trials, the judge excludes all witnesses from the courtroom except the witness who is testifying. (This is done so that witnesses are not influenced by each other's testimony.) This means that witnesses waiting to testify must usually remain out in the hall, with nowhere comfortable to sit, nothing to do, and no clear indication of how long the wait will be—a situation well calculated to make witnesses cranky and, in the case of expert witnesses (especially doctors), prompt a bill for hundreds of dollars per hour for waiting time.

There is no perfect formula that will guarantee happy witnesses present when needed with no waiting time, but there are a few general principles that will help. The first is to explain the uncertainties to the witnesses and keep them informed. Before the trial begins, the best we may be able to do is give each witness an estimate of the date he is likely to be needed. As the trial progresses, we should be able to provide better and better guesses. To accommodate the schedules of doctors and other expert witnesses, judges will often allow examination of another witness to be interrupted so that the expert can be taken out of order at a prearranged time. As for the risk of nonattendance, if there is any doubt about the witness's reliability, we would always issue a subpoena, but alert the witness to expect it and explain that it is a technicality required of us by the rules.

**Preparing the Testimony**—To what extent should we script a witness's testimony in advance? On this question, trial lawyers' views differ. Some would go so far as to write out the questions and expected answers verbatim; others use at most a list of topics to be covered, and make up the questions as they go along. There is a trade-off here: On one hand, testimony that is *too* well planned may come across as insincere, staged rather than genuine. There is also the risk that the overprepared trial lawyer may become too attached to her game plan and fail to notice opportunities to take the testimony in unplanned directions. At the other extreme is the trial lawyer who "shoots from the hip" entirely. Here, the risk is that he will forget to cover some important point, or that the witness will blurt some damaging answer that could have been avoided had the attorney planned better.

Our experience suggests that a compromise between the two extremes is best. In preparing the direct examination of a friendly witness, we would do the following:

1. Prepare an outline or topic list, taking care to include all of the main facts that we need to establish through this witness's testimony. On most points, the outline should not be too detailed; its main function is to serve as a checklist, not a verbatim script.

2. In the outline, we may write out verbatim any questions that need to be worded in a certain way. Sometimes, for example, the law or rules governing one of the issues in our case may be worded in terms of a particular catch phrase like "record of a regularly conducted activity" (see Rule 803(6), Federal Rules of Evidence), and we want to be sure to use the exact phrase in our question. In such a situation, we would write out the question in advance.

3. In the outline, we include references (by both number and brief description) to each exhibit that will be shown to the witness in connection with each main point. Again, the purpose is to provide a checklist with which the trial

attorney can rapidly verify that she has covered all of the exhibits on each point.

4. With at least the most important witnesses, we would conduct a rehearsal of the testimony. That is, we would put the witness "on the stand" in a quiet conference room and go through our entire examination as if we were in court. This has several benefits: It allows the trial attorney to work the kinks out of the questioning. It lets the witness know what questions to expect. Most important, poorly considered answers can be discussed and, if appropriate, reworded (but see the sidebar on the ethics of coaching witnesses).

Preparing to cross-examine an adverse witness is fundamentally different from preparing direct examination of a friendly witness. Obviously, there will be no opportunity to rehearse with the witness, although it is sometimes useful to rehearse by having someone else act the part of the witness. More importantly, in direct examination, we want the witness to do most of the talking, while in cross examination we must maintain tight control, usually limiting the witness to saying "yes" or "no." This makes it possible—and usually necessary—to plan cross-examination in detail, listing the sequence of questions or topics and the exhibits to be used in connection with each.

### Designating the Deposition Testimony—We have seen that, when a witness cannot conveniently be brought in to testify at trial, it is sometimes permissible to use the witness's deposition in lieu of live testimony. The local rules of most U.S. district courts require the parties to designate the testimony to be used in advance. For example, Local Rule 16.2 of the U.S. District Court for the District of Nebraska requires the parties to include a section in the pretrial order listing "All depositions, answers to interrogatories, and requests for admissions or portions thereof which are expected to be offered in evidence by the plaintiff as part of the plaintiff's case-in-chief. . . ."

To do this, we identify which testimony we will use, and list the beginning and ending page and line numbers of the selected passages. This requirement applies only to testimony to be used as a substitute for live testimony; we are not required to designate testimony that we may use during cross-examination to impeach a witness. Often, the rules do require us, upon receiving our opponent's designation, to indicate any objections that we may make to the designated testimony. We do this by listing the page and line numbers of each objectionable passage, together with the nature of the objection.

---

## SIDEBAR

### Ethics of Coaching Witnesses

*Is it proper to suggest how a witness should answer a question? How far can an attorney or paralegal go in scripting a witness's testimony? The issue comes up routinely in preparing clients for their appearances as witnesses, and opportunities also arise to give friendly nonparty witnesses advice on how to testify. There are two important considerations, one ethical and one practical, both leading to approximately the same conclusion.*

*From an ethical standpoint, it is never appropriate to suggest that a witness testify in a manner that the witness does not believe to be true. Apart from being morally reprehensible, that sort of coaching has a high probability of exposure (all it takes is for the witness to become unhappy with the lawyer for some reason), and potentially leads to unpleasant consequences like disbarment or, in an extreme case, criminal prosecution for suborning perjury.*

*On the other hand, a lawyer or paralegal has an ethical obligation to present the best case possible within the bounds of the law. Seen in that light, it would be unethical not to help a client or friendly witness deliver his testimony in a more persuasive way, as long as the testimony remains truthful.*

*As a practical matter, the problem with excessive or inept coaching is that it often makes the witness's testimony seem insincere. If the witness uses words that seem not to fit the witness's personality, or answers questions in an unnatural way, the jury will distrust the testimony.*

*Trial attorneys differ in their views and preferences. Our own stems from a general philosophical view that our clients have the right to know everything about their cases that we can tell them. We have already said that, with important friendly witnesses and especially with clients, we would conduct a dry run of the examination. If an answer has harmful implications of which the witness is not aware, we think it is appropriate and useful to point them out. We would not suggest the wording of an answer, however; we would let the witness rephrase the answer in his own words.*

---

*Your Local Notes*

_____

_____

## Task 10 *Trial Brief/Trial Memoranda*

Although most of the legal issues should be resolved by motion before the trial begins, it often happens that a few issues are left to be decided during the trial. This may be because problems have been overlooked, or because a party delays raising an issue for strategic reasons. Increasingly, U.S. district courts are adopting rules calling for the parties to prepare memoranda in advance of trial arguing their positions on any issues that they anticipate arising. Local Rule 16.1(f)(10) of the U.S. District Court for the Southern District of California is typical:

> Unless otherwise ordered, the parties shall, not less than seven (7) calendar days prior to the date on which the trial is scheduled to commence . . . [s]erve and file briefs of all significant disputed issues of law, including foreseeable procedural and evidentiary issues, setting forth briefly the party's position and the supporting arguments and authorities. . . .

Rules requiring submission of memoranda for trial are less common in state court; your instructor will apprise you of any such provisions applicable to your local courts. Even if not required by rule, however, it is often advantageous to prepare short memoranda on anticipated issues. That way, we are in a position to present a reasoned argument, backed up by authority, should the occasion arise.

There is another kind of trial brief or memoranda that is typically submitted only in nonjury trials. In trials to the court, the judge may allow or require each party to submit a brief summarizing the evidence and relating it to the causes of action and defenses raised by the pleadings. Sometimes briefs of this kind are submitted in lieu of oral closing arguments. Trial briefs of this kind are typically written after the evidence has been presented, since it is difficult to summarize the evidence before the witnesses have testified.

---

*Your Local Notes*

_____

_____

---

## Task 11 *The Trial Notebook*

A trial attorney putting on a typical federal civil trial needs access—sometimes instantaneous access—to a huge variety of papers. One of the most important ways in which paralegals can be useful in trial is by anticipating what papers may be needed at any point, and having them ready to hand.

As a way of locating the most important papers quickly, most trial lawyers use a trial notebook. Traditionally, this consists of a loose-leaf binder with tabbed separators and an index. As computer technology becomes more and more widespread, we are likely to see increasing substitution of laptop computers, which can hold many more documents and also facilitate searching.

What goes into the trial notebook is partly a matter of personal preference, and partly determined by the document requirements of the particular case. Here are some of the items that many trial lawyers would usually include:

- *An index or outline of the notebook's contents.* The purpose of a trial notebook is to facilitate rapid access to the most important papers. An index allows us to locate specific documents quickly.

- *An outline and schedule of the trial.* Here we list what is to happen on each trial day. Among other things, the list should indicate which witnesses are expected to testify each day, in what order, and at what times, to the extent that we can estimate these things.

- *The pleadings.* It is sometimes necessary to refer to the complaint or answer to determine exactly what causes of action and defenses are framed by the pleadings. (However, in most U.S. district courts, there is a pretrial statement or order that sets forth the issues to be tried, and that takes precedence over the pleadings in controlling the course of the trial. Therefore, the pleadings themselves take on lesser importance in most federal trials.)

- *The issues outline.* The pretrial statement or order is worded and organized to carry out strategic objectives rather than to provide a complete and concise listing of the causes of action and defenses and their elements. We would always include in the trial notebook a current, updated copy of our issues outline (see Workshop 1).

- *The pretrial statement or order.* Since it is the pretrial order that determines which issues are fair game during the trial, it will be consulted often and needs to be ready to hand.

- *A procedural history of the suit.* By the time a lawsuit goes to trial in federal court, the judge will typically have made a number of rulings on motions and in status conferences. When procedural disputes arise during trial, it is important to be able to analyze them in the context of what has already been decided. It is therefore useful to include in the trial book a summary of all of the procedural events in the case, giving the date of each and a short description.

- *Minute entries.* In this section, in chronological order, we include copies of any significant minute entries, so that we are in a position to establish exactly what the judge's ruling was on a particular point should the need arise.

- Voir dire *questions and jury selection notes.* Jury selection procedures vary greatly, so the materials to be included in the trial notebook depend on the situation and the lawyer's preferred approach. If, as is common in federal district courts, the judge will be conducting *voir dire,* then we need to have available our and our opponent's proposed questions, together with any argument notes and citations of authorities, so that we will be prepared when the judge is ready to decide which *voir dire* questions to use. To the extent that the court allows attorney-conducted *voir dire,* we will need an outline or draft of the questions we want to cover. We may also want to include other notes, checklists, or forms to use for keeping track of prospective jurors' background information and answers to *voir dire* questions.

- *Jury instructions and supporting notes.* We will need both parties' proposed jury instructions, together with argument notes and supporting authorities, when the judge hears argument to decide which instructions to give. Once the judge has settled the instructions, we will replace this section with the set of instructions that will actually be given. We will want these accessible, especially when we prepare for closing argument because we may want to quote from the instructions while arguing to the jury.

- *Notes, memoranda, and copies of important case law pertaining to legal issues expected to arise during trial.* To the extent that we can anticipate disputes over the interpretation of procedural rules or over the admission of particular evidence, we will try to research the pertinent legal issues in advance. When issues come up during trial, the judge will usually want to decide them immediately so as not to delay the trial. Obviously, if we have done our research in advance and can access it quickly, we will be in an advantageous position compared to an opponent who has not researched her side of the issue and is forced to improvise.

- *Outline or draft of opening statement.* Most trial lawyers would consider it poor technique to read from notes when delivering an opening statement or closing argument. Nevertheless, good opening statements are prepared in advance, and it is helpful to be able to review an outline or notes to fix the main points firmly in mind before beginning.

- *Outline of direct examinations of favorable witnesses.* Here we insert our outlines for the testimony of our own witnesses. See Task 9.

- *Outline of cross-examinations of opposing party's witnesses.* Here we place our notes and outlines for cross-examination. See Task 9.

- *Copies of principal exhibits.* In most lawsuits, there are a few documents that bear directly on the claims and defenses and that we will need to refer to frequently (for example, the contract in a breach of contract case). Except in the simplest of cases, we cannot include all of the exhibits in our trial notebook, but we can include a few of the most important.

- *Outline or draft of closing argument.* Here we include the notes for the closing argument, together with some blank sheets on which to jot ideas for points to be included in the argument as they occur to us during trial.

Obviously, in a complex case, there is no way in which we can fit all of the papers we have just described into a single notebook. One solution is to use several notebooks; another is to keep the materials pertaining to each witness—outline of examination, exhibits, etc.—in a separate file folder. The point is that there is a host of materials that needs to be available for nearly instantaneous retrieval during trial, and it is essential to have some practical system for managing them. Especially where the required materials are voluminous, the most important component of this system may be a competent trial paralegal who is intimately familiar with all of the documents and who has the judgment and training to anticipate which ones will be needed at each point in the trial.

## Trial Preparation: Learning by Example

We now consider each of these eleven tasks in the context of our *Martin v. Collins* hypo, from the standpoint of an attorney representing Shannon Martin. The lawsuit in our hypo was filed in the U.S.

District Court for the District of Arizona, so we begin by reviewing the local rules of that court (available on the Internet at www.azd.uscourts.gov). As is typical, we find that the local rules do not give us very specific guidance on most of these tasks because the usual practice is for each judge to designate his own requirements in each case.

### Task 1 — Final Discovery Supplementation and Disclosure

The District of Arizona has not opted out of any of the requirements of FRCP, Rules 26(a)(1)–(3). Rule 26(a)(3) therefore requires each side to disclose its witnesses and exhibits at least 30 days before trial. The judge may, of course, impose different deadlines.

### Task 2 — Pretrial Statement or Order

The District of Arizona's system for case tracking appears in Local Rule 2.12. We will assume that *Martin v. Collins* has been assigned to the standard track. Local Rule 2.12(b)(4)(B) calls for a scheduling conference within 180 days after the filing of the complaint, at which, among other things, the judge is to set "dates for filing a joint proposed pretrial order and conducting a pretrial conference." The rule does not specify the contents of the pretrial order—it is up to the judge to do that—but most judges require some combination of the items discussed under Task 2 earlier.

### Task 3 — Preparing the Closing Argument and Opening Statement

We begin by checking the local rules to see if there are any provisions governing opening statements or jury arguments. We find that District of Arizona Local Rule 2.14 provides that the "opening statement to the jury shall be confined to a concise and brief statement of the facts which the parties propose to establish by evidence on the trial," and, incidentally, allows the defendant to defer making an opening statement until the close of plaintiff's evidence if desired. The local rules have nothing specific to say about closing arguments.

Due to space limitations, and because the writing of arguments is normally a job for the trial attorney rather than the paralegal, we will not present sample arguments here.

### Task 4 — "Voir Dire" Questions

The local rules of the District of Arizona are silent on the subject of *voir dire,* leaving jury selection procedure up to each judge. We will assume that our assigned judge follows the prevalent practice of requiring advance submission of *voir dire* questions, and that the judge, not the attorneys, will conduct the questioning. We have already given a few sample *voir dire* questions in the instructions given earlier.

### Task 5 — Jury Instructions

Local Rule 2.16 governs the submission of proposed jury instructions. It provides:

> (a) Proposed instructions for the jury shall be presented to the Court at the opening of the trial unless otherwise directed by the Court; but the Court, in its discretion, may at any time prior to the opening of the argument, receive additional requests for instructions on matters arising during the trial. The requested instructions shall be properly entitled in the cause, distinctly state by which party presented, and shall be prepared in all capital letters of even type size. They shall be numbered consecutively and contain not more than one (1) instruction per page. Each requested instruction shall be understandable, brief, impartial, free from argument, and shall embrace but one (1) subject, and the principle therein stated shall not be repeated in subsequent requests.
>
> . . . .
>
> (c) All instructions requested of the Court shall be accompanied by citations of authorities supporting the proposition of law stated in such instructions.
>
> (d) At the time of presenting the instructions to the Court, a copy shall be served upon the other parties.

From Local Rule 2.16(a), we see that the proposed jury instructions are to be in the form of a court paper with caption (that is what "properly entitled in the cause" means); the title is to make it clear which party's they are (i.e., "Defendant's proposed jury instructions," not "Proposed jury instructions"); and the proposed instructions themselves are to be one to a page in capital letters (easier for the judge to read to the jury). We can assume that the other formal rules applicable to filed court papers apply as well such as margins, paper size, and spacing.

As for the contents of the instructions, we see from our issues outline that we will need instructions on at least assault, battery, negligence, and punitive damages (those being the claims pleaded in the complaint). We will also need jury instructions on whatever defenses are being asserted, and perhaps on other issues (for example, the weight to be given certain kinds of evidence). Notice that *all* parties will usually submit proposed instructions on all issues—you might suppose, for example, that only defendant would need to submit instructions on affirmative defenses, but plaintiff will not want to let defendant dictate the wording of the instruction, and so will have to submit her own proposal.

Where do we get these instructions? First, we look for instructions that we can modify or copy. Since the District of Arizona is part of the Ninth Circuit, we will first consult the Ninth Circuit Model Civil Jury Instructions (available on the Internet at the Ninth Circuit web site, www.ce9.uscourts.gov and follow the "documents" link). We go through the model instructions and select those applicable to our case. For example, under "damages," if we represent plaintiff, we would select instructions 7.1 (proof of damages), 7.2 (measures of types of damages), and 7.5 (punitive damages).

There are no Ninth Circuit model instructions covering the elements of the causes of action for assault, battery, or negligence. We will have to find these elsewhere or write our own. Since these are causes of action arising under state law, we would first consult the Arizona state court recommended jury instructions; for any causes of action that we could not find there, we would probably try the California state court jury instructions. (Books of approved jury instructions from other states can usually be found in a comprehensive county law library or law school library. The California Civil Jury Instructions are particularly useful because they cover a huge variety of issues. They can be found on the Internet at www.net-lawlibraries.com/jurinst/ji_toc.html.)

Figure W17–1 shows what an excerpt from Shannon's proposed jury instructions might look like (due to space limitations, we include only two instructions; the real submission would have many more).

**Task 6**     *Marking and Preparing Exhibits*

Since the U.S. District Court for the District of Arizona does not opt out of FRCP, Rule 26(a)(3), the parties are required to exchange copies of their exhibits. By checking the District of Arizona local rules, we find that no rule specifies how exhibits are to be marked. Therefore, the procedure is up to each judge; we will call the judge's secretary for instructions.

**Task 7**     *Arranging for Demonstrative Evidence, Visual Aids, and Other Props*

The visual aids needed in a trial very much depend on the style and preferences of the attorney trying the case. Here are a few examples of items that Shannon's attorney might use:

- A blowup showing the layout of Shannon's hotel room and the adjoining hall area, to help the jury visualize the scene.

- A blowup of the hotel's telephone printout showing that Arnie Trevayne did not answer the phone at the front desk immediately after his call to 911, even though he testified that he remained at the front desk until the police arrived.

- A blowup summarizing the main items of Shannon's damage claim.

Why blowups rather than overhead transparencies or PowerPoint slides? Because blowups are easily visible without dimming the lights, require no special equipment that may malfunction, and can often be left in a position where the jury can see them even when they are not in use.

**Task 8**     *Motions "in Limine"*

The District of Arizona local rules do not specify a deadline for filing motions *in limine;* presumably the judge would set a deadline in the initial scheduling order. We have already given a detailed example of a typical situation calling for a motion *in limine* in our earlier discussion of Task 8.

**Task 9**     *Preparing the Presentation of Testimony*

The first step in planning the presentation of testimony is to make a tentative decision about which witnesses to call and in what order to call them. How? It is helpful to divide the testimony into two main categories: liability and damages.

On the liability issue, our goal is to present testimony establishing the elements of each cause of action. Obviously, Shannon will need to testify; we may also want to call Dr. Collins and Arnie Trevayne. What about others such as police investigators, other hotel guests, other hotel employees, paramedics—how do we decide how many witnesses to call? Our general approach is to first choose the witnesses who can best tell our client's story; then add others as necessary to be sure that we have presented evidence supporting

**Figure W17–1**

SIMON & PORTER
Allen Porter
1000 North Central Avenue, Suite 2800
Phoenix, Arizona 85004
(602) 555-4321
Attorneys for plaintiff

## IN THE UNITED STATES DISTRICT COURT
## DISTRICT OF ARIZONA

| | | |
|---|---|---|
| SHANNON MARTIN, a single woman, | ) | |
| | ) | |
| | ) | NO. ____ |
| Plaintiff, | ) | |
| | ) | PLAINTIFF'S PROPOSED JURY |
| v. | ) | INSTRUCTIONS |
| | ) | |
| ARTHUR COLLINS and JANE DOE | ) | |
| COLLINS, husband and wife: PARK | ) | |
| HOTELS GROUP, INC., a Delaware cor- | ) | |
| poration; | ) | |
| | ) | |
| Defendants. | ) | |

Pursuant to Rule 2.16, Local Rules of Practice of the U. S. District Court for the District of Arizona, plaintiff hereby submits the proposed jury instructions appearing on the following pages.
RESPECTFULLY SUBMITTED this _____ day of _____th, 20 ___.

SIMON & PORTER

_____
Allen Porter
Attorneys for Plaintiff

---------------------------------------------------------------------------------------------------------

THE PLAINTIFF, SHANNON MARTIN, ALSO SEEKS TO RECOVER DAMAGES BASED UPON A CLAIM OF BATTERY.
THE ESSENTIAL ELEMENTS OF A CLAIM FOR BATTERY ARE:
1. DEFENDANT INTENTIONALLY DID AN ACT WHICH RESULTED IN A HARMFUL OR OFFENSIVE CONTACT WITH THE PLAINTIFF'S PERSON;
2. PLAINTIFF DID NOT CONSENT TO THE CONTACT;
3. THE HARMFUL OR OFFENSIVE CONTACT CAUSED INJURY, DAMAGE, LOSS OR HARM TO THE PLAINTIFF.

Source: California Civil Jury Instructions No. 7.50; see Restatement (2d) of the Law, Torts, Section 13.

---------------------------------------------------------------------------------------------------------

A CONTACT WITH THE PLAINTIFF'S PERSON IS OFFENSIVE IF IT OFFENDS A REASONABLE SENSE OF PERSONAL DIGNITY.
TO BE OFFENSIVE, THE CONTACT MUST BE OF A CHARACTER THAT WOULD OFFEND A PERSON OF ORDINARY SENSITIVITY, AND BE UNWARRANTED BY THE SOCIAL USAGES PREVALENT AT THE TIME AND PLACE AT WHICH THE CONTACT IS MADE.
Source: California Civil Jury Instructions No. 7.51; see Restatement (2d) of the Law, Torts, Section 13.

(Certificate of service goes here on a separate page—see Workshop 4.)

each element of each cause of action, so that the judge cannot dismiss any of our claims for lack of evidence.

To establish damages, we will need, in addition to Shannon's testimony about the expenses she has incurred, at least one physician expert to testify about the cost and appropriateness of the treatment already rendered, the prognosis, and the expected cost of any needed future treatment. We will also need a witness who can speak for Shannon's employer concerning her income, terms of employment, and future prospects. And, in an injury case of this kind, we would probably retain an expert economist to take the raw data, compute a single number representing the present value of the damages, and present a summary of the claimed damages.

The order in which witnesses are called is a strategic decision about which trial lawyers do not always agree. Given the facts of our hypo, we will call Shannon first, then call Dr. Collins to hammer home the fact that the key Arnie gave him opened Shannon's door. We will call the "damage" witnesses last. We will pass on calling Arnie Trevayne ourselves—better to let defendant call him, then cross-examine.

To put the finishing touches on our trial schedule, we need to estimate how much time we will spend examining each witness. We can best do this after outlining the questions to be asked of each witness. Due to space limitations, we cannot include a complete outline, but a short excerpt appears below. Notice that our outline is essentially a checklist of the facts that we want to establish; we will make up the questions as we conduct the examination so that they will seem natural and spontaneous.

Direct Examination—Shannon Martin
(estimated time—four hours)
1. Circumstances of presence in Las Vegas and at Banbury Park Hotel.
   a. Employed by Network Software Solutions, Inc., as marketing representative.
   b. In Las Vegas for sales presentation.
   c. Checked in to Banbury Park Hotel; date and time.
   d. What room.
2. Events leading up to injury.
   a. Was asleep.
   b. Awoke to find intruder standing at foot of bed.
   c. Intruder disrobed.
   d. Believed an attack was imminent.
   e. Did not recognize intruder; had never seen intruder before.

. . . .

## Task 10    *Trial Brief/Trial Memoranda*

The District of Arizona local rules do not call for a trial brief. We may wish to research and prepare memoranda on any legal, procedural, or evidentiary issues that are likely to arise during trial.

## Task 11    *The Trial Notebook*

Our hypothetical lawsuit is simple and straightforward enough that we should be able to prepare a trial notebook encompassing all of the documents that need to be immediately accessible. We will include the following, each under its own tabbed divider:

- List of the notebook's contents
- Schedule or list showing which witnesses will be called in what order
- Issues outline
- Complaint and answer
- Pretrial order
- Copies of significant minute entries—any rulings on motions for summary judgment, any scheduling orders, any minute entries requiring the parties to carry out particular preparation tasks
- *Voir dire* questions; jury selection worksheets
- Outline of opening statement
- Outline of examinations of plaintiff's witnesses
- Outline of cross-examinations of defendant's witnesses
- Copies of principal exhibits
- Draft of closing argument

## Trial Preparation: Learning by Doing

Now it is your turn to try your hand at some of the trial preparation tasks that we have described.

Assume that you are a paralegal in the law firm Crandall, Elkins & Major, representing Park Hotels Group, Inc. Your supervising attorney is Gail Stoddard. Crandall, Elkins' office is in your city. For this workshop, your instructor will designate either the U.S. district court having jurisdiction over your locality or the county trial court of your county. In the exercises that follow, "your local court" refers to the court specified by your instructor. Assume that the hypothetical lawsuit, *Martin v. Collins,* is pending in the court specified by your instructor.

## EXERCISES

In carrying out this assignment, you should refer to the tasks described in this workshop.

1. Find out what the procedure is for getting a trial date in your local court. In doing so, find out (a) how much time elapses in a typical case between filing of the complaint and trial; (b) whether the trial dates are "firm" or not; and (c) whether the court schedules more than one trial on the same day, and, if so, how it handles any scheduling conflicts that result. Write a short memo to your supervising attorney describing the procedure, citing the applicable rules of procedure and local rules and any other sources you consulted.

2. (Task 1)  Determine whether there are any applicable late-stage disclosure requirements. If your instructor has chosen the U.S. district court for this exercise, determine whether Rule 26(a)(1)–(3) is in effect. Identify any other requirements imposed by the applicable rules of procedure or local rules involving the exchange or disclosure of witness lists and exhibits. Write a short memo to your supervising attorney describing your findings.

3. (Task 2)  Determine whether the rules of procedure and/or local rules of your local court provide for a pretrial order, pretrial statement, or other document of similar purpose. Write a short memo to your supervising attorney (a) describing the procedure by which the pretrial order or statement is to be created; (b) citing the rule or rules governing the procedure; and (c) listing the types of information required to be included. If possible, obtain and attach a form pretrial order or statement suitable for use in your local court.

4. (Task 2)  Prepare a draft pretrial order or statement conforming to the rules of your local court, on behalf of defendant Park Hotels Group, Inc.

5. (Task 3)  Your supervising attorney, who appreciates all of your work on the case and values your insight, has asked you what you think would be the most persuasive themes to emphasize in closing argument. She asks you to write a draft of the argument that you would deliver on Park Hotels Groups' behalf if you were the trial attorney. (Of course, plaintiff's attor-

ney gets to argue first, and you do not know what he will say, but that is a problem that defense attorneys confront in every case, so you will simply have to try to anticipate the arguments that plaintiff's attorney is likely to make and do your best.)

6. (Task 4)  Determine what procedure your local court uses for *voir dire.* If the procedure varies from one judge to another, choose one judge and determine what procedure he uses. Write a short memo to your supervising attorney describing the procedure and citing the applicable rules, if any.

7. (Task 4)  Imagine that you will be allowed ten specific *voir dire* questions to be asked of the entire panel, in addition to the judge's general *voir dire* questions. What questions would you ask on behalf of defendant Park Hotels Group, Inc.? You may write the questions yourself or obtain them from other sources; if you obtain them from other sources, cite the sources. The questions should be written in a way reasonably calculated to be approved by the judge; that is, they should not be argumentative and not addressed to inappropriate subject matter.

8. (Task 5)  Determine what procedure your local court uses for submitting and settling jury instructions. Write a short memo to your supervising attorney describing the procedure and citing the applicable rules. In your memo, address (a) the deadline or time limit, if any, for submitting instructions; and (b) the format in which proposed instructions are to be submitted.

9. (Task 5)  Determine whether there are any model or approved sets of jury instructions favored by your local court, and find out how to access them.

10. (Task 5)  Prepare a proposed jury instruction or instructions to be submitted on behalf of defendant Park Hotels Group, Inc., to be used in instructing the jury on what plaintiff must prove to establish her negligence claim. The instruction is to be in a form complying with the rules of your local court. In carrying out this assignment, you may borrow from any appropriate model instructions or instructions from other sources, but you must cite each source used.

11. (Task 6)  Determine the procedure followed by one judge of your local court concerning the pre-marking of exhibits. Write a short memo to your supervising attorney describing the procedure.

12. (Task 7)  Describe three blowups or other visual aids that you think would be useful in

presenting the case on behalf of Park Hotels Group, Inc.

**13.** (Task 9)  Prepare an outline of the direct examination of Arnie Trevayne on behalf of Park Hotels Group, Inc.

**14.** (Task 9)  Prepare an outline of the cross-examination of Shannon Martin on behalf of Park Hotels Group, Inc.

**15.** (Task 11)  Prepare a trial notebook for use by your supervising attorney. To the extent that the items included consist of papers that you have prepared in other workshops, use copies of the actual papers; for each of the other items, use a single sheet of paper describing the item. Be sure to include a table of contents or list showing all of the items contained in the notebook.

# PRACTICE POINTERS
## *Courtroom Testimony*

Being a witness is not as simple as being willing to tell what you know and remembering the details of what you have come to testify about. Most litigators have learned how to manipulate adverse witnesses to minimize the damage they do to their client's case. Therefore, witnesses must be able to anticipate the kinds of questions they will receive during cross-examination and the types of cross-examination techniques to which they will be exposed.

The following observations serve as an introduction to the preparation for courtroom testimony. Testifying is more of an art than a science, an art that expert witnesses often spend months learning about before they appear in court. Nevertheless, an understanding of some basic concepts can make the courtroom experience more productive and pleasant. If you become a litigation paralegal, you would be well advised to attend a number of jury trials as well as any seminars or workshops that are offered dealing with courtroom testimony so that you can assist in preparing your witnesses for their courtroom experience.

**Always Talk to the Jury**—This is one of the most important attributes of an effective witness. Good communication requires eye contact. Witnesses who talk to the attorney who is questioning them lose the attention of the jury. Remember that it is the jurors who render the ultimate decision and who must assess the testimony they hear. For that reason witnesses must focus on convincing the jury (not the attorneys and not the judge, unless the judge is the trier of the fact) of the truthfulness and accuracy of their testimony.

**Never Volunteer Any Information**—Those who volunteer information usually discover, much to their chagrin, that they have subjected themselves to additional cross-examination. The wise witness answers only what is asked of him and nothing more. The more information a witness offers, the more ammunition he provides the attorney for cross-examination.

**Feel Free to Say You Do Not Know**—Witnesses who admit they do not know cannot be cross-examined in any depth about their lack of knowledge and their willingness to admit their limitations bolsters jurors' confidence in their expertise. Those who speculate open themselves to additional questions and lose credibility when they cannot provide the answers.

**Never Lose Your Temper**—Attorneys are delighted when witnesses lose their temper on the witness stand because they know they will automatically lose some credibility with the jury. Some attorneys deliberately provoke witnesses to anger, especially when they have no substantive grounds for impeaching the witness. Masters of this technique will probe until they find the witness's vulnerabilities. Putting the witness on the defensive then becomes a simple matter of verbally jabbing until the witness explodes. An angry witness is an irrational witness and is easily incited into making comments that the attorney can use to his advantage.

**Do Not Try to Verbally Spar with an Attorney**—You will lose. Most litigators are accustomed to verbal repartee and excel at quick responses. Attempts at one-upmanship usually backfire and result in the witness appearing foolish.

**Dress Conservatively**—First impressions are very important, especially in the courtroom, where jurors often have only one opportunity to see a witness. Avoid dressing in such a manner that might be offensive or distracting to anyone. Surveys of jurors indicate that jurors are very influenced by the dress and mannerisms of attorneys and witnesses and sometimes form opinions based on those reactions rather than more objective assessments of the evidence.

**Speak Clearly and Use Language That Those with Minimal Education Can Understand**—Witnesses who testify to the jury can quickly assess whether they are being understood. Jurors who cannot hear or who are confused by what is being said will usually telegraph their lack of understanding with their body language. Be aware that juries in some states have an educational level that averages around the fifth grade. While witnesses should never "talk down" to jurors, they should avoid using terminology that interferes with their ability to communicate. If witnesses must use specialized terms, they should define those terms, either directly or parenthetically.

## TECHNO TIP

Preparing for trial often involves the need to find an expert in a particular field to give testimony in support of your client's position. Oftentimes the expert may also be a fact witness (such as a treating physician in a tort case). In other cases it may be necessary to find an expert (such as in medical malpractice and product liability cases). Numerous organizations exist that provide help with finding experts. Some are paid by the expert for listing his or her name and providing a link to those seeking the service of an expert witness. Other groups, such as TASA (Technical Advisory Service for Attorneys), are brokers who provide assistance in selecting the right witness, introduce the witness to the prospective client, and bill the client for services rendered. TASA's web site and an explanation of the services it provides can be viewed at www.tasanet.com. Other "listing" services are, for example, expertwitness.com, lawinfo.com, and experts.com. You may also want to refer to the Techno Tip for Workshop 3. By the way, if you are just now looking for an expert, you are way too late!

---

**FORMS FILE**

*In your forms file, include:*

- *Summaries of the trial setting procedures for the courts in your jurisdiction*
- *A sample pretrial statement or order*
- *Sample jury instructions and a summary of the format and procedure required for submitting jury instructions*
- *A sample motion in limine*
- *The table of contents from a sample trial notebook*

---

## KEY TERMS

**Firm trial date**                **Judge *pro tem***                **Trial notebook**

## INTRODUCTION: WHAT IS A JUDGMENT AND WHY DO WE NEED ONE?

The judgment is the piece of paper that declares who won the lawsuit. In this workshop, we learn how to get the court to issue a judgment. You might suppose that, after a party has won the suit, it would be trivially simple to obtain a judgment reflecting the fact. As we will see, however, there are still a few hoops to be jumped through.

Plaintiff's purpose in filing a lawsuit is to force defendant to pay plaintiff money. Winning at trial does not automatically put any money in plaintiff's pocket, so there must be procedures by which plaintiff can force defendant to pay up. How? Several procedural tools are available to plaintiff for trying to collect what he has won, including attachment, garnishment, sale on execution, and foreclosure. In essence, all of these collection procedures involve using the police power of the government to seize defendant's assets and use them to pay plaintiff.

To take advantage of any of these collection procedures, plaintiff must have a judgment. The clerk will not issue a writ of execution, attachment, or garnishment unless a valid judgment has first been entered. It is not enough to win at trial—when plaintiff wins at trial, the jury renders a *verdict,* and a verdict is not the same as a judgment. The outcome of the case is not "official" until the court enters a judgment.

Suppose defendant wins. Does a judgment still need to be entered? Yes. In the first place, defendant will usually be entitled to make plaintiff reimburse the costs of suit. To collect, defendant needs a judgment. Also, it is the judgment—whether for plaintiff or defendant—that makes the court's decision final, and prevents the losing party from filing another suit involving the same subject matter. Once the court has entered judgment in a case, the principle of **res judicata** (a Latin phrase meaning "thing decided") applies, and neither party can relitigate any of the issues embraced by the judgment.

The entry of judgment is also the event that triggers the losing party's right to appeal. In general, American appellate courts will not entertain an appeal until the case in the trial court is completely over. If litigants were allowed to appeal every time the trial judge made an unfavorable ruling, lawsuits would drag on for decades. Therefore, the statutes and rules governing civil appeals invariably allow appeals only after a final judgment has been entered at the trial court level. In fact, FRCP, Rule 54(a), de-

fines a judgment (somewhat circularly) as "any order from which an appeal lies."

What, exactly, *is* a judgment, then? It is a document in the form of a filed court paper, with the case caption, signed by the judge (or in some situations by the clerk). If the judgment is in favor of plaintiff, the body of the document recites the amount that plaintiff has won; if in favor of defendant, the body of the document recites that plaintiff's claims are dismissed. We discuss the exact language and format in more detail later in this workshop.

A judgment becomes valid only when it is entered; until then, it has no effect. Under the federal rules, a judgment is considered entered only when it is both (1) set forth in a separate written document and properly signed by the judge or the clerk and (2) recorded in the clerk's docket (an index-like record kept by the clerk in which all judgments are recorded). State court procedural rules vary; your instructor will inform you of what steps are required for a judgment to be considered as "entered" under the rules of the state courts of your locality.

---

*Your Local Notes*

_____

_____

---

## PROCEDURE FOR OBTAINING A JUDGMENT

Before we can obtain a judgment, we must first establish that we are entitled to one. As we will see, the exact procedural steps for obtaining a judgment vary depending on the manner in which the prevailing party won the case. Here are some of the ways in which a party can become entitled to a judgment:

- *Win a jury verdict at trial.* Of course, the losing party can move for a new trial (FRCP, Rule 59) or for judgment notwithstanding the verdict [FRCP, Rule 50(b)], but if the judge does not set aside the verdict, the winner of the trial is entitled to a judgment.

- *Win a motion for judgment as a matter of law during trial.* Under traditional trial practice, if, after plaintiff rested, the judge concluded that plaintiff had not produced enough evidence to establish all the elements of plaintiff's cause of action, the judge could grant a motion to dismiss. If, after defendant rested, defendant had not produced enough evidence to justify a reasonable juror in finding for defendant, the judge could grant a motion for a directed verdict in favor of plaintiff. In effect, these motions allow the judge to save time by taking the decision away from the jury in cases where the evidence so disproportionately favors one party that only one reasonable outcome is possible.

Some state courts still follow the traditional terminology. The federal rules, however, provide for a single motion—the motion for judgment as a matter of law—in place of the motion to dismiss at the conclusion of plaintiff's evidence and the motion for directed verdict at the conclusion of defendant's evidence. FRCP, Rule 50(a), allows the court to grant judgment as a matter of law if, at any time during trial, "a party has been fully heard . . . and there is no legally sufficient evidentiary basis for a reasonable jury to find for that party. . . ."

■ *Win a renewed motion for judgment as a matter of law after trial.* Traditionally, the losing party at trial could file a motion for judgment notwithstanding the verdict (also called a "motion for judgment n.o.v.," for *non obiter verdictum,* which means the same thing). If the judge were persuaded that the jury's verdict was wrong as a matter of law—that there was no way in which reasonable jurors following the instructions given could properly have reached the verdict based on the evidence presented—the judge could set aside the verdict and enter judgment for the party who lost at trial!

Again, the procedure in some state courts still allows for motions for judgment notwithstanding the verdict. In federal court, the corresponding procedure is a renewed motion for judgment as a matter of law made under FRCP, Rule 50(b). The moving party must first make a motion for judgment as a matter of law under FRCP, Rule 50(a), at the close of all the evidence (i.e., immediately before the case is submitted to the jury). If the court denies the motion, the moving party may renew it—in effect, make the same motion again—after the verdict is in.

---

*Your Local Notes*

_____

_____

---

■ *Win a trial to the court.* Not all trials are jury trials. There is no right to a jury trial for some kinds of cases, and in cases where the parties do have a right to a jury trial they can waive the jury by agreement. The alternative is to conduct a **trial to the court** in which the judge performs the functions of both judge and jury. In a trial to the court, there is no jury verdict; it is the judge who decides the outcome. Since there is typically no urgent need to hurry—there are no jurors being kept away from their jobs and families—the judge often announces the decision by minute entry after taking the case under advisement for some period of time. The winning party is, of course, entitled to judgment.

■ *Win a motion for summary judgment.* As we have seen elsewhere (see, e.g., Workshop 16), the rules offer a procedure for dealing with situations in which one party's case is so weak that the outcome of the lawsuit is a foregone conclusion, making it a waste of time to conduct a trial. FRCP, Rule 56, allows either party to file a motion for summary judgment, asking the judge to end the lawsuit and grant immediate judgment. To succeed, the moving party must convince the judge that there are no genuine issues of material fact; in other words, there is *no* credible evidence on the opposing party's side. Motions for summary judgment can be made at any time after the complaint is filed (subject to any restrictions or deadlines imposed in scheduling orders).

■ *Win a motion to dismiss.* When plaintiff's case is procedurally defective in some way—for example, if plaintiff has failed to allege in the complaint facts sufficient to establish a valid cause of action, or if the court does not have jurisdiction, or if the complaint has not been properly served—defendant has the option of moving to dismiss under FRCP, Rule 12(b). If the judge grants the motion, then defendant is entitled to a judgment reflecting the dismissal.

■ *Win by default.* If defendant fails to appear and respond to plaintiff's complaint within the time period allowed by FRCP, Rule 12, plaintiff may take steps to obtain judgment by default.

■ *Settlement or stipulation.* When litigants settle a lawsuit, the defendant wants to be assured that plaintiff cannot take the settlement money and then sue again. Therefore, it is customary for settlement agreements to provide for the entry of a stipulated judgment. If the defendant is paying cash or otherwise carrying out the settlement terms immediately, the quid pro quo is usually a stipulated judgment of dismissal. If the defendant is agreeing to pay in the future, plaintiff may insist on a stipulated judgment for the amount defendant is agreeing to pay, so that if defendant fails to pay as agreed, plaintiff can immediately start collection proceedings. Subject to the judge's approval (which is rarely withheld—if the parties want to settle, the judge is unlikely to object!) the parties are free to enter into a stipulation calling for entry of judgment on whatever terms they can agree on.

Notice that in all of these situations, the *entry* of the judgment is a separate event from the *ruling* entitling a party to judgment. For example, if the judge grants a motion for judgment as a matter of law, the ruling granting the motion is not a judgment. If the judge grants a motion for summary judgment, the minute entry granting the motion is not a judgment—a minute entry is never (well, almost never) a judgment. A judgment is a separate, self-contained document, and the appropriate procedural steps must be taken to prepare it, get it signed, and have it entered.

In this workshop, we study the steps required to obtain a judgment. Our main focus, and the subject of our step-by-step instructions, will be the procedure for obtaining a default judgment when defendant fails to file an answer or other responsive pleading. We have chosen default judgment procedure as our main topic because obtaining a default judgment involves most of the same steps as are required to obtain other kinds of judgments (plus a few additional ones), and because obtaining a default judgment is a task often assigned to paralegals. Before we begin our exploration of default judgment procedure, however, we will briefly explain what is entailed in getting the court to enter judgment when we have won the case at trial or by motion.

---

**Your Local Notes**

_____

_____

---

## JUDGMENT AFTER ADJUDICATION

In most U.S. district courts, entry of judgment happens more or less automatically after an adjudication by the court. (By "adjudication by the court" we mean a jury verdict, a decision by the judge following a trial to the court, or a ruling granting a motion for judgment as a matter of law, motion for summary judgment, motion to dismiss, or other motion entitling a party to judgment.)

**Judgments Entered by the Clerk**—The rules make a distinction between simple situations, in which the clerk of the court is empowered to pre-

pare and sign the judgment, and more complicated situations in which the judge will need to review and approve the judgment. FRCP, Rule 58(1), provides:

> [U]pon a general verdict of a jury, or upon a decision by the court that a party shall recover only a sum certain or costs or that all relief shall be denied, the clerk, unless the court otherwise orders, shall forthwith prepare, sign, and enter the judgment without awaiting any direction by the court. . . .

A "sum certain" means a specified dollar amount. If the jury returns a general verdict for plaintiff for a specified amount of money, or if the jury returns a verdict for defendant, or if the judge grants a motion that disposes of the case in such a way that no calculation of the amount of the judgment is required, then the rule places on the clerk of the court the duty to "prepare, sign, and enter" the judgment. Of course, judgments of the kind that the clerk can enter are simple documents, and the clerk can simply use a printed or word processor form, fill in the dollar amount, sign the judgment, and enter it in the docket. No involvement by the judge is needed, because there are no decisions to make. Figure W18–1 is an example of a simple judgment for a sum certain, of the kind that would be entered after, in our hypo, the jury renders a verdict for Shannon in the amount of $375,000. (In this example, we are assuming that Shannon's claims against Dr. Collins have previously been settled and dismissed, so that the claims against Park Hotels Group, Inc., are the only remaining claims in the lawsuit. When judgment is rendered as to some but not all parties or claims, the court must decide whether the partial judgment is to be final or not; see sidebar on FRCP, Rule 54(b), findings.) Notice that our example judgment provides for interest. The right to interest on the judgment arises from a federal statute; see sidebar.

---

**Your Local Notes**

_____

_____

---

**Judgments Requiring the Judge's Approval**—Sometimes, however, the judgment is for relief other than or in addition to money damages. Perhaps plaintiff is asking for an injunction, a judgment ordering defendant not to take some specified action. Now, the wording of the judgment takes on greater importance. Or perhaps the judge has granted plaintiff's motion for summary judgment, but it is not clear from the ruling exactly what amount of damages plaintiff is entitled to. In such

| Figure W18–1   Sample Judgment |
| --- |

**IN THE UNITED STATES DISTRICT COURT**
**DISTRICT OF ARIZONA**

SHANNON MARTIN, a single woman,   )
　　　　　　　　　　　　　　　　　　)
　　　　　　　　　　　　　　　　　　)    NO. CV98 -01456 PHX JL
　　　　　　　　　Plaintiff,　　　　　)
　　　　　　　　　　　　　　　　　　)    JUDGMENT
　　　v.　　　　　　　　　　　　　　)
　　　　　　　　　　　　　　　　　　)
ARTHUR COLLINS and JANE DOE　　　)
COLLINS, husband and wife; PARK　　)
HOTELS GROUP, INC., a Delaware　　 )
corporation;　　　　　　　　　　　 )
　　　　　　　　　　　　　　　　　　)
　　　　　　　　　Defendants.　　　　)
_____)

　　This action came on for trial before the Court and a jury, Honorable Jerome Lewis, District Judge, presiding, and the issues having been duly tried and the jury having duly rendered its verdict,
IT IS ORDERED AND ADJUDGED that the plaintiff Shannon Martin recover of the defendant Park Hotels Group, Inc. the sum of Three Hundred Seventy-Five Thousand and no/100 Dollars ($375,000.00), with interest thereon at the rate of 6.5 percent as provided by law, and her costs of action;
Dated at Phoenix, Arizona this _____ day of _____, 20 ___.

　　　　　　　　　　　　　　　　　　　　　　　_____
　　　　　　　　　　　　　　　　　　　　　　　　　　　　Clerk of Court

## SIDEBAR

## Interest on Judgments

*The winner of a lawsuit is entitled to interest on the money owed from the time the judgment is entered until it is paid. In federal court, the right to interest comes from 28 U.S.C. § 1961(a), which provides:*

> *Interest shall be allowed on any money judgment in a civil case recovered in a district court. . . . Such interest shall be calculated from the date of the entry of the judgment, at a rate equal to the coupon issue yield equivalent (as determined by the Secretary of the Treasury) of the average accepted auction price for the last auction of fifty-two week United States Treasury bills settled immediately prior to the date of judgment.*

*In plain English, the judgment is to include interest at the current rate for one-year Treasury bills, which rate you can find in any financial newspaper.*

*Since federal court judgments are (usually) prepared by the court, the court will insert the correct rate.*

*In state court, the interest rate applied to civil judgments depends on state law. Your instructor will inform you of the applicable rates in the state courts of your locality.*

*What about interest before the date of the judgment? Lawsuits sometimes take years to resolve. Does plaintiff lose the interest on her money for however long the defendant can drag out the suit? Yes and no. If the damages claimed are a "liquidated sum"—a term approximately equivalent in meaning to "sum certain"—plaintiff is entitled to interest from the date the obligation sued on was incurred, and the interest will be included in the judgment as part of the damages. If the damages are not liquidated, prejudgment interest is not awarded.*

## SIDEBAR

## Rule 54(b) Findings

*Sometimes the court enters a judgment that does not dispose of all the issues in the case. This can happen in two main ways:*

*1. The judge makes a ruling that ends the case as to one or more but not all defendants. Suppose, in our hypothetical lawsuit, that Dr. Collins moves for summary judgment and the judge grants the motion. The lawsuit is over as far as Dr. Collins is concerned, but continues against Park Hotels Group, Inc.*

*2. The judge makes a ruling that disposes of one or more causes of action, but not all. For example, in our hypothetical lawsuit, suppose the judge dismisses Shannon's negligence claim against Dr. Collins, but not her assault and battery claims.*

*When a ruling by the judge disposes of part but not all of the claims in the lawsuit, it is necessary for the judge to decide whether the judgment is to be final. Why do we care? Several reasons: (1) The judgment cannot be appealed until it is final; (2) if the judgment is for plaintiff, plaintiff cannot begin proceedings to collect the judgment until it is final; and*

*(3) the judge retains the power to revise a ruling that is not final.*

*Rule 54(b) gives the judge the authority to make a judgment final even if it does not dispose of all claims against all parties, but to do so the judge must make an express finding:*

*When more than one claim for relief is presented in an action . . . or when multiple parties are involved, the court may direct the entry of a final judgment as to one or more but fewer than all of the claims or parties only upon an express determination that there is no just reason for delay and upon an express direction for the entry of judgment.*

*Typically, this is done by including "Rule 54(b) language" in the judgment—a recital that the court has determined that there is no just reason for delay and expressly directs immediate entry of the judgment. Rule 54(b) determinations are not granted routinely, however, because they lead to different parts of the case being appealed at different times. The party seeking the determination must show good reasons why the partial judgment should be made final.*

situations, the judge must approve and sign the judgment, then transmit it to the clerk of the court to be entered in the docket.

When a judgment requires the judge's approval, who prepares it? In many federal district courts, the judge's law clerk is assigned that duty. The alternative is for the winning party to prepare and submit the proposed judgment. In theory, under the federal rules, the court, not the winning party, is responsible for preparing the judgment. FRCP, Rule 58, provides that "Attorneys shall not submit forms of judgment except upon direction of the court, and these directions shall not be given as a matter of course." Nevertheless, some federal district courts provide by local rule that it is up to the attorney for the winning party to submit the proposed judgment to the court.

**State Court Procedure**—In state court, it is uncommon for either the clerk of the court or the judge to prepare judgments. Both are far too busy, and state court judges rarely have law clerks to help them. The usual procedure in state court is for the attorney for the winning party to submit a proposed judgment, that is, the actual paper that the judge will

sign. If the judgment involves anything more complicated than money damages in a "sum certain," the winning party must send a copy of the proposed judgment to the losing party, who is then given a short period of time in which to file any objection to the form of the judgment. If necessary, the judge may hold a hearing to settle the exact wording of the judgment. After the judge approves the judgment, he signs it and transmits it to the clerk for filing and docketing. The precise steps that constitute "entry" of the judgment in state court depend on the rules in effect in that state. Your instructor will inform you of the procedure by which a judgment is prepared and entered under the rules of the state courts having jurisdiction in your locality.

*Your Local Notes*

_____

_____

**Taxation of Costs**—We have seen that in federal district court, either the judge or the clerk prepares and signs the judgment. Is there, then, nothing that the attorneys need do? In fact, there is one thing: establish the amount of costs that the winning party is entitled to recover. In federal district court, this is done by submitting a bill of costs. The procedure for doing this is the same whether the judgment is on the merits or by default, and we describe it in detail under Step 6.

---

**Your Local Notes**

_____

_____

---

## Obtaining a Default Judgment: Step-by-Step Instructions

We now examine the steps required to obtain a default judgment in the not uncommon situation where a defendant has failed to respond to plaintiff's complaint. First, we must take the required steps to establish that a default has, in fact, occurred. Then we can request entry of judgment, but, depending on the circumstances, notice to the defaulting party may be required, and a hearing may be necessary. Once the judgment is entered, we need to take steps to have our court costs added to the judgment.

The procedure that we describe here is that dictated by the Federal Rules of Civil Procedure for use in federal district courts. State court default procedure often differs from that under the federal rules (even in states whose civil procedure otherwise follows the federal rules) and varies considerably from one state to another. There is also some variability in the federal system, with some district courts adopting local rules governing some aspects of judgment procedure. We will point out the respects in which state court procedure commonly differs from the federal as we go along, and your instructor will inform you of the exact procedure to be followed in the state courts of your locality and give you citations for the pertinent state court rules.

A final caveat before we begin: If the defaulting party is an agency of the government, additional complications arise that are beyond the scope of this introductory text. Suits against the government are fraught with many procedural pitfalls, and default judgments are usually difficult or even impossible to obtain. Should the need arise, plan on spending a few days of quality time at the law library researching your options.

**Step 1**    *Determine That a Default Has Occurred*

For plaintiff to be entitled to a default judgment, defendant must first default. [It is, of course, possible for someone other than plaintiff to seek a default—for example, there can be a failure to respond to a counterclaim, cross-claim, or third party claim; see FRCP, Rule 55(d). In the vast majority of cases, however, the default consists of one or more defendants failing to file an answer, and it is plaintiff who is seeking the default judgment, so it will be easier if we cast our discussion accordingly.]

In general, for a defendant to be in default, four things must be true:

1. The complaint has been properly served on that defendant;

2. The court has jurisdiction of the subject matter of the action and of the person of defendant (see Workshop 2);

3. The time period allowed by FRCP, Rule 12(a), for filing a responsive pleading has expired; and

4. Defendant has not filed and served *either* an answer to the complaint *or* a motion to dismiss or other motion permitted under FRCP, Rule 12. (Of course, if a motion to dismiss has already been denied, then only an answer will do.)

If we represent the plaintiff, we computed and docketed the due date for the answer as soon as the complaint was served, so we know when the FRCP, Rule 12(a), time period expires. As a practical matter, however, it is not always easy to determine whether a given defendant has filed and served an answer. Recall that FRCP, Rule 5(b), allows defendant to serve the answer by mailing it to plaintiff's attorney, and service is complete when defendant places the answer in the mail. Mail sometimes takes a week or more to arrive or is lost entirely. Nor can we necessarily find out whether an answer has been filed at the clerk's office. It takes time for the clerk to process incoming papers, and meanwhile they may not be accessible. Because of these uncertainties, we would usually wait at least a week after the due date for the answer before beginning the steps to obtain a default judgment.

Notice that defendant does not necessarily have to file an answer to avoid default. FRCP, Rule 12(a)(4), provides that any motion under Rule 12—a motion to dismiss, motion for judgment on the pleadings, motion for a more definite statement, or motion to strike—suspends the need to file an answer until (typically) 10 days after the court rules on the motion. Therefore, as a practical matter, defendant can avoid default either by filing an answer or by filing a motion to dismiss or other motion under FRCP, Rule 12.

---

**Your Local Notes**

_____

_____

---

## Step 2   Provide the Clerk with the Necessary Paperwork to Enter the Default

Before plaintiff can apply for judgment by default, the clerk must first enter the default; see FRCP, Rule 58(a). The terminology is somewhat confusing—"entering default" under FRCP, Rule 58(a), is *not the same* as "entering judgment by default" under FRCP, Rule 58(b). "Entry of default" refers to an action taken by the clerk to take official recognition of the fact that defendant has defaulted. As we will see in Steps 3 and 4, the clerk enters the default by signing and filing an entry of default, a court paper that plaintiff's attorney provides. This establishes the fact of default on the record.

The clerk is authorized to enter a default only after determining that defendant has, in fact, failed to file a responsive pleading. How? FRCP, Rule 58(a) provides:

> When a party against whom a judgment for affirmative relief is sought has failed to plead or otherwise defend as provided by these rules and that fact is made to appear by affidavit or otherwise, the clerk shall enter the party's default.

As this rule indicates, the usual procedure by which the default is established is for plaintiff's attorney to file with the clerk an affidavit verifying that defendant has not responded to the complaint. Plaintiff's attorney also provides the entry of default for the clerk to sign, and may be required to submit a written request asking the clerk to enter default. To see what an affidavit of default and an entry of default look like, see Step 2 in the Learning by Example section later in this workshop.

---

**Your Local Notes**

_____

_____

---

## Step 3   Apply for Judgment by Default

After the clerk has entered default, plaintiff may apply for a default judgment. The procedure for obtaining the actual judgment may be simple, or not so simple, depending on the type of relief that plaintiff is asking for.

To understand why the rules make the distinctions that they do, you must first realize that defendant still has some rights even after defaulting. By defaulting, defendant gives up the right to contest liability. The default automatically makes plaintiff the winner of the lawsuit, regardless of what the evidence might show if the case went to trial. However, even after defaulting, defendant still has the right to insist that the amount of the judgment not exceed the amount of plaintiff's actual, provable damages. Plaintiff is not free simply to pull a number out of the air.

Likewise, defendant is entitled to rely on the amount plaintiff has demanded in the complaint as an upper limit on the amount of the judgment. FRCP, Rule 54(c), states that "A judgment by default shall not be different in kind from or exceed in amount that prayed for the demand for judgment." If plaintiff asks for $100,000 in the complaint, and defendant defaults, plaintiff cannot then obtain a judgment for $200,000, even if the evidence would support the higher figure.

Therefore, whether it is simple or complicated to obtain a default judgment depends mainly on how difficult it is to nail down the amount of the damages. We will take the easy case first.

---

**Your Local Notes**

_____

_____

---

**Judgments That Can Be Issued by the Clerk—** The clerk of the court is empowered to enter a default judgment, without any need for approval from the judge, if each of the following three things is true:

1. *The default is because a defendant has failed to appear.* But wait—do not *all* defaults involve a failure to appear? Not necessarily. For example, the judge has the power to default a party as a sanction for certain discovery infractions; see FRCP, Rule 37(b)(2)(C). Also, it is possible to *appear* in a case without filing an answer. One way is to file a notice of appearance; an-

other is to file a motion under Rule 12. Suppose, for example, defendant files a motion to dismiss under FRCP, Rule 12(b)(6), the motion is denied, and defendant then fails to file an answer. Defendant has appeared in the action by filing the motion, but is in default for not filing an answer. In such a situation, the clerk cannot issue the default judgment (but the judge can, see below).

2. *The defendant has capacity to be sued.* If defendant is below the age of adulthood, or is insane, or is otherwise incompetent to defend a lawsuit, the clerk cannot enter a default judgment; see FRCP, Rule 55(b)(1). [Again, the judge may be able to, but only if the person's guardian or conservator has appeared in the action to represent the person; see FRCP, Rule 55(b)(2).]

3. *The amount of damages is either a sum certain or an amount that "can be made certain by computation."* Plaintiff must establish the amount of damages by submitting an affidavit. If the affidavit does not state that the amount claimed is a sum certain or a sum that can be made certain by computation, the clerk cannot issue a default judgment (but, again, the judge can).

In the normal, routine default situation, the default has occurred because defendant has simply ignored the complaint and done nothing. (Why would a defendant do that? Often, when the suit is to collect a debt, defendant has no real defense, and it would be a waste of money to hire a lawyer. Better and cheaper to file for bankruptcy than to spend money defending a lawsuit that cannot be won.) In practice, suits against minors and insane people do not happen very often. Therefore, the issue that usually determines whether the clerk can issue a default is the question of whether plaintiff's claim is for a sum certain.

---

**Your Local Notes**

_____

_____

---

**When is a sum certain?:** What kinds of damages qualify as a sum certain? As with most issues in litigation, there is no bright line distinguishing sums that are "certain" from those that are not. At one extreme, a lawsuit to collect a debt, where the debtor has signed a promissory note for a specific amount of money, clearly involves a sum certain—it is clear from the complaint exactly how much plaintiff is asking for. Even if the promissory note provides for interest on the debt, the interest is an amount that "can by computation be made certain" so the clerk can still issue the judgment.

At the other extreme, a personal injury lawsuit seeking damages for pain and suffering, where it is normally up to the jury to attach a dollar figure to plaintiff's pain, clearly involves damages that are not a sum certain. The clerk is not equipped to decide how much the damages should be in such cases.

What about a suit for breach of a construction contract, in which the damages are calculable in principle, but doing so may require a good deal of bookkeeping, adding up receipts, and making decisions about which expenses are properly chargeable? Sum certain or not? In borderline situations of this kind, it may be necessary to do some legal research to determine whether the damages qualify as a sum certain. Or, perhaps, simply state in the affidavit that the damages are a sum certain, since the clerk has no way of checking? Not a good idea—see the sidebar on Consequences of Guessing Wrong.

***Default judgments issued by the clerk—documents required:*** If the case qualifies for issuance of a default judgment by the clerk, what paperwork is required of plaintiff? FRCP, Rule 55(b)(1), directs the clerk to enter judgment "upon request of the plaintiff and upon affidavit of the amount due." Therefore, plaintiff must submit two documents: a request for entry of judgment and an affidavit establishing the amount of damages. We will also need a judgment. In some district courts, the clerk prepares the judgment, using a printed form. In other courts, plaintiff's attorney prepares and submits the form of judgment for the clerk to sign.

There is one additional paperwork requirement, arising from the federal Soldiers and Sailors Relief Act, 50 App.U.S.C. § 520. This statute provides:

> In any action or proceeding commenced in any court, if there shall be a default of any appearance by the defendant, the plaintiff, before entering judgment shall file in the court an affidavit setting forth facts showing that the defendant is not in military service. . . .

If the defendant *is* a member of the military, no default judgment is allowed unless the court first appoints an attorney to represent the defendant (in which case, the appointed attorney will of course immediately file an answer and eliminate the default). The practical effect of the act for our purposes is that we will also need to file an affidavit stating that defendant is not in the military service (or add such a statement to the affidavit on damages).

## SIDEBAR

### Consequences of Guessing Wrong

*Default procedure is unique in that defendant is usually not around to contest plaintiff's assertions. All plaintiff need do to get the clerk to issue a default judgment is submit the right documents. The clerk takes plaintiff's word for it that the requirements of FRCP, Rule 55(a), are met. If plaintiff submits an affidavit stating that defendant has not appeared in the action or that the amount claimed is a sum certain, the clerk assumes that the affidavit is true and issues the judgment. As a practical matter, therefore, there is nothing to stop plaintiff from getting the clerk to issue a default judgment even in cases that do not qualify.*

*A reputable attorney would, of course, never deliberately lie in an affidavit. To do so would be unethical and could conceivably lead to bar disciplinary proceedings or worse. The real problem is that the case law is quite inconsistent and unpredictable on issues like what a sum certain is and what an appearance is. Suppose, for example, we do some legal research to try*

*to determine whether the damages in our case are a sum certain or not, and we find cases going both ways. Could we not go ahead and file our affidavit claiming that our damages are a sum certain, since there is no one who can contest our conclusion anyway?*

*The problem is that defendant has the right to appeal from a default judgment. Defendant cannot reopen the merits of the case on appeal, but she can attack the validity of the process by which the default judgment was issued. If the court of appeals decides that the amount claimed was not a sum certain, it will order the default judgment set aside and we will be back to square one. Similarly, if we did not give notice to defendant and the court of appeals decides that defendant had appeared, the court will set aside our judgment. Better to follow the rules carefully in the first place, and err on the side of caution, than to spend years in the court of appeals trying to defend an invalid judgment.*

For examples of the motion for judgment, affidavit, and judgment see Step 3 in the Learning by Example section later in this workshop.

```
Your Local Notes
_____
_____
```

**Judgments That Require the Judge's Involvement**—If the case does not qualify for issuance of a judgment by the clerk, the alternative is to apply to the judge. The basic procedure is the same as that for obtaining judgment from the clerk, except that the motion for judgment by default is directed to the court instead of to the clerk. There are, however, a few additional complications, as we will see in Steps 4 and 5.

**Step 4**   *Give Notice If Defendant Has Appeared*

We have already seen that if defendant has appeared in the action, the clerk cannot issue a default judgment and our motion for default judgment will have to go to the judge. Additionally, if defendant has appeared, FRCP, Rule 55(b), requires us to give defendant notice of our application for default judg-

ment, at least 3 days before any hearing on our application takes place. (For more about default hearings, see Step 5.)

You may be wondering why the rules would require giving notice to a defendant who is in default. If defendant cannot be bothered to comply with the rules and file an answer, why should we have to give him notice of anything? One reason is that if a defendant has taken enough action to constitute an appearance, it is less likely that he intended to default. Misunderstandings sometimes arise. For example, it may be that defendant did not file an answer due to a belief, mistaken or otherwise, that plaintiff had granted an extension of time. If the case were allowed to proceed to judgment with no notice to the defendant, it is likely that defendant would move to set aside the default judgment (see sidebar). The court would spend time holding a default hearing and then hearing the motion to set aside the default judgment. The end result most of the time would be that the court would allow defendant to file an answer and the case would proceed. Better to require notice, and give defendant a chance to contest the default before the situation degenerates.

What does it take for defendant to make enough of an appearance to require us to give notice of default? Clearly, filing a notice of appearance would suffice, as would filing any other paper such as a motion to dismiss, motion for more definite statement, or motion to strike. But some appellate

# SIDEBAR

## Setting Aside a Default

*Some defaults happen because the defendant decides to ignore the lawsuit, skip town, or file bankruptcy. Sometimes, however, defendant's attorney fails to file an answer because of a mistake or misunderstanding: an extension is misunderstood (a good reason for always confirming extensions in writing); the office's docketing clerk miscalculates the due date for the answer and no one catches the mistake; the responsible attorney goes home sick at the wrong time and the task of filing the answer falls through a crack.*

*Fortunately, all is not lost (although—trust us—having to explain this kind of mishap to a client is punishment enough). Consistent with the federal courts' general preference for deciding cases on the merits where possible, FRCP, Rule 55(c), allows the judge to set aside a default, or even a default judgment, in an appropriate case: "For good cause shown, the court may set aside an entry of default and, if a judgment by default has been entered, may likewise set it aside in accordance with Rule 60(b)." FRCP, Rule 60(b)(1), allows the court to relieve a party from the effect of a judgment upon a showing of "mistake, inadvertence, surprise, or excusable neglect."*

*What sort of showing must the defaulting party make to convince the judge to set aside the default?*

*What constitutes the "good cause" required by FRCP, Rule 55(c)? To answer these questions, it is necessary to research the case law interpreting FRCP, Rule 55(c). Here are some of the factors that judges typically take into account.*

- *Whether the default was intentional or inadvertent;*
- *Whether the defaulting party acted promptly to correct the default;*
- *Whether it appears that the defaulting party has valid defenses to raise if the case is allowed to go forward on the merits;*
- *Whether plaintiff would be prejudiced in some way if the default is set aside; and*
- *Whether the mistake, if any, causing the default was excusable—in other words, not the result of incompetence or gross negligence.*

*The procedure for seeking relief from a default is to file a motion to set aside the default under FRCP, Rule 55(c), if judgment has not yet been entered. If judgment has been entered, a motion for relief from judgment under FRCP, Rule 60(b)(1), is required. If the judge grants either motion, the defaulting party will be given leave to file her answer, and the case will proceed as if the default never happened.*

---

courts have gone much further, even deeming a letter from defendant to plaintiff's attorney an appearance for purposes of FRCP, Rule 55. When in doubt, we would give the notice; see the sidebar on Consequences of Guessing Wrong.

The notice, if required, can be of the kind that we have seen repeatedly in these workshops: a filed court paper, with caption and certificate of service, stating the date and time of the default hearing. See Step 4 of the Learning by example section for an example. FRCP, Rule 55(b)(2), requires the notice to be "served." Service may be by mail as provided by FRCP, Rule 5(b), or, if defendant's address is unknown, Rule 5(b) allows plaintiff to serve the notice on defendant by leaving it with the clerk of the court.

*Your Local Notes*

_____

_____

**Step 5**  *Hold Default Hearing If the Amount Claimed Is Not a "Sum Certain"*

If the damages that plaintiff is claiming do not qualify as a sum certain, then the court will need to hear evidence to determine the amount of the default judgment. FRCP, Rule 55(b), provides:

> If, in order to enable the court to enter judgment . . . it is necessary to . . . determine the amount of damages or to establish the truth of any averment by evidence . . . the court may conduct such hearings . . . as it deems necessary and proper and shall accord a right of trial by jury to the parties when and as required by any statute of the United States.

As a practical matter, the court will schedule a number of default hearings for the same time period, usually before a magistrate judge or other judicial officer (not a district judge; federal district judges are too busy to spend time on routine default hearings). At the hearing, the cases will be called one at a time. When a case is called, plaintiff (or some other witness who is competent to testify about plaintiff's damages) takes the stand, and is examined briefly—no more than a few minutes—to establish the amount of damages. Obviously, the plaintiff's testimony does not get into any of the details of how damages were computed; plaintiff merely states the conclusions. As soon as plaintiff has testified, the officer conducting the hearing will sign the judgment.

Rarely, a defendant will show up at the default hearing to dispute plaintiff's computation of the damages. By defaulting, defendant gives up the right to dispute the facts alleged in the complaint, but still has the right to challenge the amount of damages claimed. Default hearings are usually run as a production line operation, with a large number of cases scheduled to be heard in a 2- or 3-hour session, so if it is necessary to conduct an adversary hearing on damages, it will be necessary to reschedule it and allow more time. If necessary, the court will conduct an actual trial, before a judge or in some cases, a jury, in order to decide the amount of damages to be included in the default judgment.

---

**Your Local Notes**

_____

_____

---

## Step 6    *Tax the Costs*

It is common knowledge that, in a lawsuit, the loser pays the court costs. As a lawsuit progresses, each party is paying out money for expenses—filing fees, process server fees, witness fees, and a host of other charges. So far, however, we have not seen any mechanism that would allow the winner to recover the money spent for these items.

The rules provide for the winning party's costs to be included as part of the judgment against the losing party. The process of establishing the amount for which the winning party is entitled to be reimbursed is referred to as **taxation of costs.** The procedure is the same, whether the judgment is by default or on the merits. FRCP, Rule 54(d)(1), provides:

> Except when express provision therefor is made either in a statute of the United States or in these rules, costs other than attorneys' fees shall be allowed as of course to the prevailing party unless the court otherwise directs. . . . Such costs may be taxed by the clerk on one

day's notice. On motion served within 5 days thereafter, the action of the clerk may be reviewed by the court.

Traditionally, the losing party is not required to pay the winning party's attorneys' fees. Increasingly, however, when the Congress or state legislatures create new statutory causes of action, the statutes give the winning party the right to collect attorneys' fees from the losing party. Many contracts also provide for the winning party to receive attorneys' fees in the event of a dispute leading to a lawsuit, so attorneys' fees are often awarded in breach of contract cases. And in class actions and shareholder derivative suits, where the recovery, if any, is a fund that will be distributed to a large number of claimants, courts usually pay the winning plaintiff's attorney from the fund. As a practical matter, therefore, there are many cases in which the winning party is entitled to be reimbursed for attorneys' fees.

In establishing the procedure for taxing costs, FRCP, Rule 54(d), makes a distinction between attorneys' fees and other costs. Attorneys' fees are often large in amount—sometimes amounting to more than the amount sued for—and the charges are often disputed. Ordinary costs are usually small compared to the amount of the underlying judgment, and disputes over the amounts charged are infrequent. Therefore, it is reasonable to handle ordinary costs via a routine filing with the clerk, while attorneys' fees claims require deeper scrutiny.

---

**Your Local Notes**

_____

_____

---

**Taxation of Costs Other Than Attorneys' Fees**—We will address first the taxation of costs other than attorneys' fees. Three main questions arise: (1) What kinds of costs may the winning party recover from the losing party? (2) What procedural steps must we take to have them included in the judgment? (3) How can we determine which party is the "winner" for purposes of awarding costs?

***What kinds of costs are taxable?:*** The Federal Rules of Civil Procedure do not say what kinds of expenses are taxable as costs. There is, however, a federal statute, 28 U.S.C. § 1920, which provides:

> A judge or clerk of any court of the United States may tax as costs the following:
> (1) Fees of the clerk and marshal;
> (2) Fees of the court reporter for all or any part of the stenographic transcript necessarily obtained for use in the case;

(3) Fees and disbursements for printing and witnesses;

(4) Fees for exemplification and copies of papers necessarily obtained for use in the case;

(5) Docket fees under section 1923 of this title;

(6) Compensation of court appointed experts, compensation of interpreters, and salaries, fees, expenses, and costs of special interpretation services under section 1828 of this title.

A bill of costs shall be filed in the case and, upon allowance, included in the judgment or decree.

Obviously, this statute fails to mention a great many of the kinds of expenses, many of them quite large in amount, that are commonly incurred in a lawsuit. What about the fees of expert witnesses who are *not* court appointed? What about court reporter fees for depositions? What about the attorneys' travel and lodging expenses for attending out-of-town depositions? Each of these items can easily run to thousands or even tens of thousands of dollars in a routine federal civil lawsuit.

District court judges have discretion to award costs other than those listed in 28 U.S.C. § 1920 in appropriate situations (although the U.S. Supreme Court has held that this discretion should be used sparingly). In practice, the way in which many district courts handle the problem is by adopting a local rule prescribing in great detail which expenses may be taxed as costs. See, for example, Local Rule 54-3 of the U.S. District Court for the Northern District of California, which answers each of the questions that we posed:

(c) Depositions.

(1) The cost of an original and one copy of any deposition (including video taped depositions) taken for any purpose in connection with the case is allowable.

(2) The expenses of counsel for attending depositions are not allowable.

. . . .

(e) Witness Expenses. Per diem, subsistence and mileage payments for witnesses are allowable to the extent reasonably necessary and provided for by 28 U.S.C. § 1821 [a statute requiring a party who subpoenas a witness in a federal case to pay the witness per diem and other expenses]. No other witness expenses, including fees for expert witnesses, are allowable.

Consult the local rules of the U.S. district court in your locality to see what, if any, provisions have been adopted dealing with taxation of costs. As for the state courts of your locality, your instructor will tell you where to find the applicable rules and/or statutes.

*Procedure for taxing costs:* The procedure for taxing costs in federal district court is not very well spelled out in the Federal Rules of Civil Procedure. FRCP, Rule 54(d), does not tell us what the party seeking costs is supposed to do, or when he is supposed to do it. FRCP, Rule 54(d)(1), states: "Such costs may be taxed by the clerk on one day's notice. On motion served within 5 days thereafter, the action of the clerk may be reviewed by the court."

In practice, the party entitled to costs prepares and files a **bill of costs** itemizing the expenses sought to be taxed. See 28 U.S.C. § 1920, which provides that "a bill of costs shall be filed in the case. . . . " The bill of costs is typically a printed form with blanks in which the totals for each category can be listed. (The standard bill of costs form is available by download from many U.S. district court Internet sites; go to www.uscourts.gov, follow the links to the district court of interest, and look for "forms" links.) Copies of receipts and itemizations of each expense category are attached to the bill of costs. The printed form bill of costs also includes a declaration for signature by the prevailing party's attorney, affirming that the costs listed are correct and properly taxable. (For a sample bill of costs, see Step 6 in the Learning by Example section later.)

Many federal district courts have adopted local rules filling in some of the gaps left by FRCP, Rule 54(d), and specifying the procedure for taxing costs in more detail. For example, Local Rule 54-8.03 of the U.S. District Court for the Eastern District of Missouri states:

A party seeking an award of costs shall file a verified bill of costs, upon a form provided by the Clerk, no later than twenty (20) days after entry of final judgment pursuant to Fed.R.Civ.P. 58. Failure to file a bill of costs within the time provided may constitute a waiver of taxable costs. Each party objecting to a bill of costs shall file, within fourteen (14) days of being served, a memorandum stating specific objections. Within five (5) days after being served with the memorandum, the moving party may file a reply memorandum. The Clerk shall tax costs as claimed in the bill if no timely objection is filed.

We can summarize the usual sequence of procedural steps for taxing costs as follows:

***1.*** The prevailing party, within the time specified by local rule after the judgment is entered, files a bill of costs using the court approved form. (In the case of a default judgment, plaintiff will usually file the bill of costs together with the other papers required for the default, all at once.) The bill of costs form includes the required declaration. Notice that taxation of costs and entry of judgment are separate events. FRCP, Rule 58, states that "entry of the judgment shall not be delayed, nor the time for appeal extended, in order to tax costs or award fees."

***2.*** Notice is given to the party against whom the costs are to be assessed. This is done by mailing a copy of the bill of costs. The form has blanks in which the party submitting it can certify that a copy was mailed to the opposing attorney.

***3.*** The opposing party is given a short period of time in which to object to the bill of costs. This is done by filing a court paper setting forth the objections and the reasons for them. For example, if the bill of costs includes items that are not properly chargeable as costs, or for which the charges are excessive, objection is appropriate. (Checking over an opponent's bill of costs is a task often assigned to paralegals.)

***4.*** If objections are filed, a hearing is held to decide which costs are properly taxable. Once the total amount of taxable costs is established (or immediately, if no objection is filed) the clerk taxes the costs. The clerk does this by noting the amount of costs taxed on the bill of costs form, and signing and dating it. The bill of costs is filed in the case file and becomes part of the record.

You may be wondering how the costs get included when the judgment is collected. After all, the judgment is typically entered before the costs are taxed, and usually does not specify the dollar amount of the costs. The answer is that, if a dispute arises and it is necessary to establish the exact amount, the clerk will provide a certificate showing the amount of costs that were taxed. The judgment, by including the words "and costs" or some similar language, serves as notice to the world that there are some costs to be paid—anyone who wants to know the amount can find out from the clerk.

***Who is entitled to costs?:*** FRCP, Rule 54(d), calls for costs to be allowed to the "prevailing party." The prevailing party is the party who has won the lawsuit. In many situations, it is obvious who the **prevailing party** is. If plaintiff takes a default judgment against defendant, plaintiff is clearly the prevailing party. If plaintiff wins at trial, plaintiff is the prevailing party. If defendant wins a motion to dismiss, or wins at trial, then defendant is the prevailing party—defendant gets a judgment for costs against plaintiff.

Sometimes, however, it is not so clear which party has prevailed. Suppose, for example, plaintiff sues defendant, defendant counterclaims against plaintiff, and both sets of claims are ultimately dismissed—who has won? In such situations, the court has discretion to decide how costs should be awarded, if at all.

### Assessment of Attorneys' Fees—FRCP, Rule 54(d), also provides for awards of attorneys' fees in appropriate cases. A party claiming attorneys' fees must file a motion asking for them, within 14 days after entry of judgment; see FRCP, Rule 54(d)(2)(A) and (B). The motion is to state the amount of the fees requested, and also cite the "statute, rule, or other grounds entitling the moving party to the award."

The opposing party is entitled to contest the motion, and usually should. Attorneys' fees claims in federal lawsuits often amount to hundreds of thousands of dollars, and not uncommonly include time that is excessive or not properly attributable to the lawsuit. Ethical lawyers do not overbill, but not all lawyers are as scrupulous as they should be, and our client has a right to expect us to scrutinize an opponent's attorneys' fees claim carefully.

The judge has a variety of options at his disposal for adjudicating the attorneys' fees claim. The court can hold a hearing, if appropriate; appoint a special master to investigate and make recommendations; or, by local rule, invent other procedures for resolving claims without a need for evidentiary hearings.

Once the attorneys' fees claim is decided, FRCP, Rule 54(d)(2)(C), directs the court to award them via a separate judgment entered, like any other judgment, in the manner provided by FRCP, Rule 58. FRCP, Rule 58, provides that entry of judgment in the lawsuit is not to be delayed in order to award fees; FRCP, Rule 54(d)(2)(C), accomplishes this by relegating the attorneys' fees award to a separate judgment, entered later.

---

*Your Local Notes*

_____

_____

---

*Your Local Notes*

_____

_____

## Obtaining a Default Judgment: Learning by Example

Now we put our knowledge of default judgment procedure into practice, using an example drawn from our *Martin v. Collins* hypo. Assume the following: Shannon's lawsuit has been filed and properly served on Park Hotels Group, Inc. Roger Yarborough (Dr. Collins's attorney) has agreed to waive service of the summons and complaint, and the required waiver has been filed. Before the answer is due, Yarborough files a motion to dismiss under FRCP, Rule 12(b)(6). The court denies the motion. Unfortunately, when the court's minute entry denying the motion arrives, the regular mail clerk in Yarborough's firm is out sick. The secretary who is filling in does not realize that a denial of a motion to dismiss starts the clock running on the deadline for filing an answer, and so does not docket the answer deadline in the office calendar. Yarborough, who is in the midst of a 4-week trial at the time, glances at the minute entry, feels momentarily annoyed that the court has denied his motion, and does not notice the absence of the docketing stamp. By the time the deadline arrives, Yarborough is busy with another trial, and the answer is never filed.

The deadline has passed a week ago, and Allen Porter (Shannon's attorney) assigns us to analyze the situation and do what is appropriate.

### Step 1 — Determine That a Default Has Occurred

We analyze whether Dr. Collins is in default by applying our four-point test:

1. A valid waiver of service has been filed, so the complaint is deemed served.

2. The court has "diversity of citizenship" jurisdiction of the subject matter of the action, as we concluded in Workshop 2.

3. Defendant has initially avoided default by filing a motion to dismiss, but once the court denied the motion, defendant was required to file an answer within 10 days. FRCP, Rule 12(a)(4), provides:

> Unless a different time is fixed by court order, the service of a motion permitted under this rule alters these periods of time as follows:
>
> (A) if the court denies the motion . . . the responsive pleading shall be served within 10 days after notice of the court's action. . . .

Therefore, the time period for filing an answer has expired.

4. Defendant has apparently not filed an answer.

But wait—you may be wondering—how can we be so sure that defendant has not filed an answer? After all, the answer could have been filed, and the copy sent to us could be lost in the mail. Perhaps we should find out for sure whether the answer was filed before we apply for default judgment?

Herein lies a dilemma. We can check with the clerk of the court, but even if the clerk cannot find a record of the answer it is still possible that the answer was filed and has not yet been processed. The only way in which we can find out for certain is to call Dr. Collins's attorney and ask. If we do that, and it turns out that Dr. Collins's attorney dropped the ball, we will have alerted him to correct the problem and possibly thrown away an opportunity to gain an advantage for our client. On the other hand, if we file default papers, we will likely alienate Dr. Collins' attorney. Forgetting to file an answer is the sort of thing that gets attorneys sued for malpractice, so attorneys tend to take default judgments personally. If the default is set aside for any reason, we should not plan on getting any favors or concessions from Dr. Collins's attorney.

Certainly we, as paralegals, should not make the decision whether to go ahead with the default. This is a decision best made by the client, with the benefit of the attorney's explanation of the alternatives. So that we can continue our hypothetical, we will assume that the decision is to press ahead with the default. (In a real-life situation of this kind, however, we might well recommend checking with Dr. Collins's attorney first. Our recommendation would depend on our assessment of the likelihood of making the default stick.)

### Step 2 — Provide the Clerk with the Necessary Paperwork to Enter the Default

We need an affidavit of default (Figure W18–2) and a request for entry of default (Figure W18–3). In some jurisdictions, it is customary to combine the affidavit and request into a single document. We will also need an entry of default for the clerk to sign.

All of the papers in this workshop are essentially form file items. Any litigation firm will have word processing files with forms suitable for the local courts. Failing that, a good source of forms of this kind is Am.Jur. Pleading and Practice Forms. This is an encyclopedia-like set of books containing sample forms for every conceivable situation. It is available in most law libraries and on Westlaw.

---

**Figure W18–2   Sample Affidavit of Default**

---

SIMON & PORTER
Allen Porter
1000 North Central Avenue, Suite 2800
Phoenix, Arizona 85004
(602) 555-4321
Attorneys for plaintiff

### IN THE UNITED STATES DISTRICT COURT
### DISTRICT OF ARIZONA

| | | |
|---|---|---|
| SHANNON MARTIN, a single woman, | ) | |
| | ) | |
| | ) | NO. CV98-01456 PHX JL |
| Plaintiff, | ) | |
| | ) | AFFIDAVIT OF DEFAULT |
| v. | ) | |
| | ) | |
| ARTHUR COLLINS and JANE DOE | ) | |
| COLLINS, husband and wife; PARK | ) | |
| HOTELS GROUP, INC., a Delaware | ) | |
| corporation; | ) | |
| | ) | |
| Defendants. | ) | |

STATE OF ARIZONA     )
County of Maricopa            )
Allen Porter, being first duly sworn, upon his oath states:

1. I am the attorney for plaintiff in the above-entitled action.
2. A waiver of service of the summons and complaint on behalf of defendants Arthur Collins and Jane Doe Collins, whose real name is Anne R. Collins, was filed pursuant to Rule 4(d), Federal Rules of Civil Procedure, on [date].
3. Defendants Collins filed a Motion to Dismiss pursuant to Rule 12(b)(6), Federal Rules of Civil Procedure, on [date]. The court denied the motion on [date] and notified the parties by minute entry dated [date]. The time allowed for defendants Collins to answer plaintiff's complaint has expired, and defendants Collins have not answered plaintiff's complaint.

DATED this _____ day of _____, 20 ___.

_____
                     Allen Porter

Dated at Phoenix, Arizona this ___ day of _____, 20 ___.

_____
                     Clerk of Court

    SUBSCRIBED AND SWORN to before me, the undersigned Notary Public, this _____ day of _____, 20 ___.

_____
                     Notary Public

---

**Figure W18–3   Sample Request to Enter Default**

SIMON & PORTER
Allen Porter
1000 North Central Avenue, Suite 2800
Phoenix, Arizona 85004
(602) 555-4321
Attorneys for plaintiff

### IN THE UNITED STATES DISTRICT COURT
### DISTRICT OF ARIZONA

| | |
|---|---|
| SHANNON MARTIN, a single woman,    ) <br>    ) <br>    ) <br> Plaintiff,    ) <br>    ) <br> v.    ) <br>    ) <br> ARTHUR COLLINS and JANE DOE <br> COLLINS, husband and wife; PARK <br> HOTELS GROUP, INC., a Delaware <br>   corporation; <br>    ) <br> Defendants.    ) | NO. CV98-01456 PHX JL <br><br> REQUEST TO ENTER DEFAULT |

To: Clerk of the U.S. District Court for the District of Arizona

    Defendants Arthur Collins and Jane Doe Collins, whose real name is Anne R. Collins, having failed to answer plaintiff's complaint herein following the denial by the Court of said defendants' Motion to Dismiss pursuant to Rule 12(b)(6), and the time for answering having expired, you are requested to enter their default pursuant to Rule 55(a), Federal Rules of Civil Procedure.

    DATED this _____ day of _____, 20 ___.

SIMON & PORTER

_____

Allen Porter
Attorneys for plaintiff

---

### Step 3   *Apply for Judgment by Default*

After the clerk has entered the default (Figure W18–4) we must apply for entry of judgment by default (Figure W18–5). For the clerk to enter the judgment, three things must be true: the default is for failure to appear, defendant has capacity to be sued, and the amount sought is a sum certain. Our situation fails on two of the three points: defendants *have* appeared (filing the motion to dismiss constitutes appearance), and the amount we are seeking is not a sum certain. Therefore, the clerk cannot enter the judgment and our motion will have to be directed to the court.

If this were entirely a paperwork default, the motion would be accompanied by an affidavit establishing the amount of damages and confirming that defendants are not in the military service. Under the facts of our hypothetical, however, a hearing will be required (see Step 5), so these facts will instead be established via testimony at the hearing.

### Step 4   *Give Notice If Defendant Has Appeared*

The motion to dismiss filed on behalf of Dr. and Mrs. Collins constitutes an appearance, so, according to FRCP, Rule 55(b), we must give at least 3 days notice of the default hearing, as is done in Figure W18–6.

---

**Figure W18–4    Sample Entry of Default**

**IN THE UNITED STATES DISTRICT COURT**
**DISTRICT OF ARIZONA**

SHANNON MARTIN, a single woman,          )
                                         )
                                         )          NO. CV98-01456 PHX JL
                  Plaintiff,             )
                                         )          ENTRY OF DEFAULT
        v.                               )
                                         )
ARTHUR COLLINS and JANE DOE              )
COLLINS, husband and wife; PARK          )
HOTELS GROUP, INC., a Delaware           )
   corporation;                          )
                                         )
                  Defendants.            )
_____      )

Defendant having waived service of the summons and complaint pursuant to Rule 4(d), Federal Rules of Civil Procedure, and having failed to answer plaintiff's complaint, and the time allowed by law for answering having expired, the default of defendant is hereby entered.

DATED this _____ day of _____, 20 ___.

_____
Clerk of the United States
District Court for the
District of Arizona

---

**Figure W18–5    Sample Entry of Judgment by Default**

SIMON & PORTER
Allen Porter
1000 North Central Avenue, Suite 2800
Phoenix, Arizona 85004
(602) 555-4321
Attorneys for plaintiff

**IN THE UNITED STATES DISTRICT COURT**
**DISTRICT OF ARIZONA**

SHANNON MARTIN, a single woman,          )
                                         )
                                         )          NO. CV98-01456 PHX JL
                  Plaintiff,             )
                                         )          APPLICATION TO COURT
        v.                               )          FOR ENTRY OF FINAL
                                         )          JUDGMENT BY DEFAULT
ARTHUR COLLINS and JANE DOE              )
COLLINS, husband and wife; PARK          )
HOTELS GROUP, INC., a Delaware           )
   corporation;                          )

---

**Figure W18–5    Sample Entry of Judgment by Default,** *continued*

                                         )

              Defendants.       )

_____ )

    Plaintiff applies to the Court pursuant to Rules 55(b)(2) and 54(b), Federal Rules of Civil Procedure, for entry of final judgment by default, after notice and hearing, in favor of plaintiff and against defendants Arthur Collins and Jane Doe Collins, whose real name is Anne R. Collins, and awarding damages in favor of plaintiffs and against said defendants in an amount to be determined after hearing.

    This application is made upon the ground that said defendants have failed to file an answer to plaintiff's complaint following the Court's denial of said defendants' Motion to Dismiss dated [date], that the time for filing said defendants' answer has expired, and that said defendants' default was entered on [date].

    DATED this _____ day of _____, 20 ___.

                                       SIMON & PORTER

                                      _____

                                      Allen Porter
                                      Attorneys for plaintiff

---

**Figure W18–6    Notice of Application to Court for Entry of Final Judgment by Default**

SIMON & PORTER
Allen Porter
1000 North Central Avenue, Suite 2800
Phoenix, Arizona 85004
(602) 555-4321
Attorneys for plaintiff

**IN THE UNITED STATES DISTRICT COURT**
**DISTRICT OF ARIZONA**

| | | |
|---|---|---|
| SHANNON MARTIN, a single woman, | ) | |
| | ) | |
| | ) | NO. CV98-01456 PHX JL |
| Plaintiff, | ) | |
| | ) | NOTICE OF PLAINTIFF'S |
| v. | ) | APPLICATION TO COURT |
| | ) | FOR ENTRY OF FINAL |
| | ) | JUDGMENT BY DEFAULT |
| ARTHUR COLLINS and JANE DOE | ) | |
| COLLINS, husband and wife; PARK | ) | |
| HOTELS GROUP, INC., a Delaware | ) | |
|   corporation; | ) | |
| | ) | |
| Defendants. | ) | |
| _____ ) | | |

    Notice is hereby given that on [date], at [time], or as soon thereafter as counsel may be heard, at the U.S. District Court for the District of Arizona, 230 North First Avenue, Phoenix, Arizona, Room 305, the undersigned will make application to the court for final judgment by default against defendants Arthur Collins and Jane Doe Collins, whose real name is Anne R. Collins. A copy of plaintiff's Application to Court for Entry of Final Judgment by Default accompanies this notice.

    DATED this _____ day of _____, 20 ___.

                                          SIMON & PORTER

                                      _____

                                      Allen Porter
                                      Attorneys for plaintiff

**Step 5** | *Hold Default Hearing If the Amount Claimed Is Not a "Sum Certain"*

Shannon is suing for damages for a personal injury. Personal injury damages do not qualify as a sum certain. The value of Shannon's claim cannot be determined by computation from a contract or receipts or other objective sources. A judge or jury will have to determine the amount to be awarded after hearing evidence.

The procedure for setting a hearing and obtaining a hearing date depends on the practices and customs of each court. Your instructor will inform you of the procedures used in the courts of your locality.

---

**Your Local Notes**

_____

_____

---

At the hearing, Shannon must present sufficient evidence to allow the judicial officer conducting the hearing to fix the amount of the judgment. How much evidence and in how much detail? If the hearing were to proceed without opposition by defendants—if Dr. Collins's attorney did not file any opposition or attend the hearing—Shannon's evidence could be quite perfunctory. It would probably be sufficient for Shannon herself to take the stand and relate the total amount of her medical expenses and other quantifiable losses, briefly describe her injuries, and state on the record her belief that the total amount claimed is reasonable and appropriate compensation for the pain and suffering that she experienced. The judicial officer presiding over the hearing would then state her findings on the record, and sign the judgment.

Under the facts of our hypothetical, however, it is a virtual certainty that Dr. Collins's attorney would take steps to oppose the default. He would doubtless begin by moving to set aside the entry of default. If he failed to get the entry of default set aside and could not avoid a default hearing, he would file an opposition to plaintiff's application for judgment by default and would litigate the issue of damages. In that case, the default hearing would become the equivalent of an actual trial—perhaps even a jury trial—for the purposes of assessing the amount of plaintiff's damages. The court would, of course, reset the hearing to another date and time since a full-blown trial on damages would require much more time than a routine default hearing.

**Step 6** | *Tax the Costs*

Once the judgment has been entered, the local rules give us 10 days in which to file a bill of costs. Local Rule 2.19 of the U.S. District Court for the District of Arizona states:

> Costs shall be taxed as provided in Rule 54(d), Federal Rules of Civil Procedure. A party entitled to costs shall, within ten (10) days after the entry of final judgment . . . file with the Clerk of Court and serve upon all parties, a bill of costs on a form provided by the Clerk, together with a notice of application to have the costs taxed. The notice of application to have the costs taxed shall contain a date for taxation (normally three (3) weeks after the date of filing the bill of costs), which shall be secured from the Clerk. This bill of costs shall include a memorandum of the costs and necessary disbursements, so itemized that the nature of each can be readily understood, and, where available, documentation of requested costs in all categories must be attached. The bill of costs shall be verified by a person acquainted therewith.

In a default situation, the costs to be taxed are relatively few, since little has happened in the lawsuit to generate any costs. A sample form is shown in Figure W18–7. You should fill out this form as an exercise.

## Obtaining a Default Judgment: Learning by Doing

In this assignment, you will prepare the paperwork to obtain a default judgment. Assume the following hypothetical facts:

> You are a paralegal in the office of Allen Porter, attorney for plaintiff Shannon Martin. Allen Porter's firm has its offices in your city. For this workshop, your instructor will designate either the U.S. district court having jurisdiction over your locality or the county trial court of your county. In the exercises that follow, "your local court" refers to the court specified by your instructor. Assume that the hypothetical lawsuit, *Martin v. Collins,* is pending in the court specified by your instructor.

Shannon's complaint was served on defendant Park Hotels Group, Inc., on April 17 of the current year. Service was accomplished by having a process server deliver a copy of the summons and complaint to Park Hotels' designated statutory

**Figure W18–7    Sample Bill of Costs**

AO 133 (Rev. 9/89) Bill of Costs ⊕

# United States District Court

_____ **DISTRICT OF** _____

**BILL OF COSTS**

**V.**

Case Number: _____

_____

Judgment having been entered in the above entitled action on _____ against _____,

*Date*

the Clerk is requested to tax the following as costs:

| | |
|---|---|
| Fees of the Clerk . . . . . . . . . . . . . . . . . . . . . . . . . . . . . . . . . . . . . . | $ _____ |
| Fees for service of summons and subpoena . . . . . . . . . . . . . . . . . . . . . . . . . . . | _____ |
| Fees of the court reporter for all or any part of the transcript necessarily obtained for use in the case | _____ |
| Fees and disbursements for printing . . . . . . . . . . . . . . . . . . . . . . . . . . . | _____ |
| Fees for witnesses (itemize on reverse side) . . . . . . . . . . . . . . . . . . . . . . . | _____ |
| Fees for exemplification and copies of papers necessarily obtained for use in the case . . . . . . . . . | _____ |
| Docket fees under 28 U.S.C. 1923 . . . . . . . . . . . . . . . . . . . . . . . . . | _____ |
| Costs as shown on Mandate of Court of Appeals . . . . . . . . . . . . . . . . . . . . . | _____ |
| Compensation of court-appointed experts . . . . . . . . . . . . . . . . . . . . . . . . | _____ |
| Compensation of interpreters and costs of special interpretation services under 28 U.S.C. 1828 . . . | _____ |
| Other costs (please itemize) . . . . . . . . . . . . . . . . . . . . . . . . . . . . | _____ |
| TOTAL    $ | _____ |

SPECIAL NOTE: Attach to your bill an itemization and documentation for requested costs in all categories.

## DECLARATION

I declare under penalty of perjury that the foregoing costs are correct and were necessarily incurred in this action and that the services for which fees have been charged were actually and necessarily performed. A copy of this bill was mailed today with postage prepaid to:

_____ .

Signature of Attorney: _____

Name of Attorney: _____

For: _____    Date: _____

*Name of Claiming Party*

Costs are taxed in the amount of _____ and included in the judgment.

_____    By: _____    _____
*Clerk of Court*                        *Deputy Clerk*                        *Date*

| WITNESS FEES (computation, cf. 28 U.S.C. 1821 for statutory fees) | | | | | | | |
|---|---|---|---|---|---|---|---|
| NAME AND RESIDENCE | ATTENDANCE | | SUBSISTENCE | | MILEAGE | | Total Cost Each Witness |
| | Days | Total Cost | Days | Total Cost | Miles | Total Cost | |
| | | | | | | | |
| | | | | | | TOTAL | |

## NOTICE

**Section 1924, Title 28, U.S. Code (effective September 1, 1948) provides:**
"Sec. 1924. Verification of bill of costs."

"Before any bill of costs is taxed, the party claiming any item of cost or disbursement shall attach thereto an affidavit, made by himself or by his duly authorized attorney or agent having knowledge of the facts, that such item is correct and has been necessarily incurred in the case and that the services for which fees have been charged were actually and necessarily performed."

**See also Section 1920 of Title 28, which reads in part as follows:**
"A bill of costs shall be filed in the case and, upon allowance, included in the judgment or decree."

**The Federal Rules of Civil Procedure contain the following provisions:**
Rule 54 (d)

"Except when express provision therefor is made either in a statute of the United States or in these rules, costs shall be allowed as of course to the prevailing party unless the court otherwise directs, but costs against the United States, its officers, and agencies shall be imposed only to the extent permitted by law. Costs may be taxed by the clerk on one day's notice. On motion served within 5 days thereafter, the action of the clerk may be reviewed by the court."

Rule 6 (e)

"Whenever a party has the right or is required to do some act or take some proceedings within a prescribed period after the service of a notice or other paper upon him and the notice or paper is served upon him by mail, 3 days shall be added to the prescribed period."

Rule 58 (In Part)

"Entry of the judgment shall not be delayed for the taxing of costs."

agent in Delaware. It is now the first Monday in June, and no answer has been received. Allen Porter assigns you to analyze the situation and, if appropriate, prepare default papers.

## EXERCISES

In carrying out this assignment, you should follow the step-by-step formula described in this workshop.

*1.* If your instructor has chosen your local state court as the court for this assignment, identify the state court rules governing default procedure.

*2.* Look for any local rules affecting entry of default, entry of default judgment, or taxation of costs. Write a short memo to your supervising attorney summarizing your findings.

*3.* (Step 1) Determine the due date for the answer. Apply the appropriate tests to analyze whether Park Hotels is in default. Write a short memo to your supervising attorney describing your findings and recommending what should be done next. Include citations to applicable rules.

*4.* (Step 2) Assume that Allen Porter has read your memo from the preceding step and has discussed your findings with Shannon. The decision has been made to seek a default judgment. Prepare the filings necessary to have the clerk of the court enter the default.

*5.* (Step 3) Assume that the clerk has now entered the default. Prepare the application for judgment by default.

*6.* (Step 4) Decide whether notice to defendant is required and, if so, prepare the notice. Write a short memo to the file stating whether you are giving notice and why. Include citations to applicable rules.

*7.* (Step 5) Decide whether a hearing will be required. Write a short memo to the file summarizing your conclusions. Include citations to applicable rules. If you conclude that a hearing is required, briefly state in your memo what evidence should be presented at the hearing.

*8.* Prepare a judgment suitable for signature by the judge at the completion of the default hearing. Consider whether "FRCP, Rule 54(b), language" is required; draft the judgment accordingly and write a short memo to the file stating what you concluded and why.

*9.* (Step 6) Obtain a bill of costs form suitable for use in the court designated by your instructor. (At your instructor's option, you may use the standard bill of costs form for use in federal district courts. This may be found on the Internet on the "forms" page of the U.S. District Court for the Northern District of Texas. Go to www.txnd. uscourts.gov and follow the "forms" link.) Fill in the form as appropriate, using dollar figures for filing fees that are accurate for the court designated by your instructor.

## PRACTICE POINTERS
### *Wrapping Up after Trial*

However tempting it might be to simply pack up the files, the trial notebooks, and the boxes of documents and put them in storage after the trial is over, your work is not yet done. The case is not necessarily over—the opposing party may file post-trial motions or an appeal—and what you thought was behind you may come back to haunt you again. Therefore, it is imperative that you reorganize everything, returning it to pretrial order. Doing this now, while the case is still fresh in your mind, will save you and your attorney time if you have to reopen the files to prepare an appellate brief or do whatever else might need to be done.

In this process be sure you locate copies of all the exhibits introduced by all parties during the trial, collect all of the trial notes and organize them in a folder, find any research done before or during the trial and place it in a separate folder, and make sure you have copies of all the deposition transcripts you relied on during the trial. Download all the computer files and mark each tape or floppy disk with the case name.

Once this reorganization is complete, prepare a memo for the file. In it include the name and phone number of the court reporter who prepared the trial transcript (in case you need to order a transcript), the results of any polling of the jury, and an inventory of what is contained in each newly packed box (including the location of the most important documents and the computer tapes or disks as well as the information they contain).

## TECHNO TIP

If you have already done the asset search referred to in the Techno Tip for Chapter 8 you already have some of the information necessary to begin collection on the judgment. Since there is no national depository for judgments (other than child support orders), it is necessary to record your judgment in each county where you believe the judgment debtor has property if you wish to impose a judgment lien on the debtor's real property. You must check your state rules regarding authentication of an out-of-state judgment before it can be recorded. Most states consider the judgments entered in any other jurisdiction as a "foreign" judgment and require certain procedures to be accomplished prior to recognizing their validity.

## FORMS FILE

*Summarize the rules in your jurisdiction regarding the entry of a judgment, the obtaining of a default judgment, and the taxing of costs. Include copies of a bill of costs form and all the affidavits and other forms associated with obtaining a default judgment in your forms file.*

## KEY TERMS

| | | |
|---|---|---|
| **Bill of costs** | *Res judicata* | **Trial to the court** |
| **Prevailing party** | **Taxation of costs** | |

## INTRODUCTION: IMPORTANCE OF ETHICS

In the preceding eighteen workshops, we have examined most of the procedural weapons available to litigators and litigation paralegals, and we have considered how and when each might best be used to help us win a lawsuit. Along the way, we have attempted to point out some of the ethical dilemmas that arise in litigation, but our main focus has been on questions of "how to" rather than "whether to."

In this final workshop we turn our attention explicitly to the ethical side of litigation. We dispense with our usual step-by-step formula and instead examine, through the use of discussion hypos, several situations that arise often in litigation and that raise difficult ethical issues. We make no pretense of comprehensive coverage of the law of ethics; that is a task best left for an ethics text. We cannot become experts on the law of ethics in one workshop, but we *can* begin developing an ethical "sense of smell"— an instinct for recognizing when we are about to enter ethically questionable territory.

In our view, there is no more important skill for a litigation paralegal.

## WHAT IS ETHICS AND HOW DOES IT CONNECT TO LITIGATION?

*Ethics* is another of those words whose meaning as a legal term is different from its meaning in everyday speech. In ordinary usage, ethics and morality are closely related concepts. Legal ethics, on the other hand, is a subject having essentially nothing to do with morality. The law judges the conduct of lawyers and paralegals, not by any moral standards, but by an explicit set of rules of professional responsibility. For example, many people would consider it immoral to foreclose on widows and orphans, seize their homes, and throw them into the street, but bank lawyers do such things routinely, and without violating the rules of ethics. On the other hand, it is hard to see anything immoral about, say, a lawyer sharing a fee with a paralegal who helps with the case, but doing so clearly violates the rules of ethics in most jurisdictions (there is a rule against fee splitting with a nonlawyer).

## WHERE DO ETHICAL STANDARDS COME FROM?

What are these rules that determine whether a lawyer's conduct is ethical or not? Each state has its own set of rules, but all follow an established pattern. The American Bar Association publishes the *Model Rules of Professional Conduct,* a set of suggested ethical rules that was approved by the ABA House of Delegates after exhaustive study by a committee of eminent legal scholars. The ABA rules have no official status in and of themselves, but many states have adopted rules of professional conduct closely patterned after the ABA model rules. Our discussion in this workshop will be based on the ABA model rules. Your instructor will inform you of any important differences between the ABA model rules and the rules governing the professional conduct of lawyers and paralegals in your state, and will tell you where to find the rules for your state.

*Your Local Notes*

_____

_____

## CONSEQUENCES OF BREAKING THE RULES

Each state has a system for enforcing its ethical rules. Typically, the primary mechanism for enforcement is a **disciplinary proceeding** against the attorney who is accused of violating the rules of ethics, administered (at least in the initial phases) by the state's bar association. Each state has its own rules and procedures for investigating complaints against attorneys and, if appropriate, administering punishment.

The punishment meted out to an attorney who is found to have violated the rules of ethics can range from mere censure—in effect, an official scolding—to disbarment and permanent loss of the license to practice law. Another option is suspension—prohibition from practicing law for a specified period of time.

You may be wondering, what do bar association rules of ethics have to do with you as a paralegal?

Paralegals are not members of the bar, and the bar has no direct power to administer discipline against a paralegal. Although a few states have studied the idea of licensing paralegals through the state bar association, in the same way that attorneys are licensed, such proposals have so far not succeeded.

This does not mean, however, that paralegals are exempt from ethical standards. It simply means that current ethical rules place the responsibility for a paralegal's conduct on the supervising attorney and, to some extent, on the partners of the employing law firm. ABA Model Rule 5.3 states:

> With respect to a nonlawyer employed or retained by or associated with a lawyer:
>
> (a) a partner in a law firm shall make reasonable efforts to ensure that the firm has in effect measures giving reasonable assurance that the person's conduct is compatible with the professional obligations of the lawyer;
>
> (b) a lawyer having direct supervisory authority over the nonlawyer shall make reasonable efforts to ensure that the person's conduct is compatible with the professional obligations of the lawyer; and
>
> (c) a lawyer shall be responsible for conduct of such a person that would be a violation of the Rules of Professional Conduct if engaged in by a lawyer if:
>
> (1) the lawyer orders or, with the knowledge of the specific conduct ratifies the conduct involved; or
>
> (2) the lawyer is a partner in the law firm in which the person is employed, or has direct supervisory authority over the person, and knows of the conduct at a time when its consequences can be avoided or mitigated but fails to take reasonable remedial action.

Therefore, in a roundabout way, paralegals are subject to the same ethical rules as attorneys. As ABA Model Rule 5.3(c) indicates, if a paralegal engages in conduct that would be a violation for an attorney, the potential exists for the paralegal's supervising attorney, as well as the partners of the firm, to be held responsible. Moreover, disciplinary proceedings are not the only threat; certain kinds of misconduct by paralegals may lead to malpractice suits against the law firm. It is easy to see that lawyers and law firms have a strong incentive to ensure that paralegals in their employ comply with the rules of ethics. In reputable firms, a knowing ethical violation by a paralegal leads to exactly the same consequences as a knowing ethical violation by an attorney: instant unemployment.

In some ways, paralegals are subject to even more ethical regulation than attorneys. In addition to their obligation to comply with the rules of attorney ethics, paralegals must also concern themselves with state law restrictions on unauthorized practice of law. Also, paralegals who belong to the National Association of Legal Assistants, the organization that administers the popular Certified Legal Assistant credential, are subject to the NALA code of ethics for paralegals, and can have their CLA certification revoked for violating it. (You can access the NALA code of ethics on the Internet at NALA's web site, www.nala.org by following the "standards" link.)

---

*Your Local Notes*

_____

_____

---

## ETHICAL RULES FOR LITIGATORS AND LITIGATION PARALEGALS

Our project for this workshop consists of analyzing several hypothetical fact situations and making recommendations. To analyze the hypotheticals, we will need a basic familiarity with the pertinent ABA model rules (or the corresponding rules regulating the conduct of lawyers and paralegals in your state). The ABA model rules cover a variety of topics. Many of the model rules regulate matters that are not specific to litigation, such as lawyer advertising or fee setting. We, however, will limit ourselves to the rules that we regard as most pertinent to the situations typically confronted by litigation paralegals.

Not all of the ethical principles that we are concerned with come from the rules of ethics. The Federal Rules of Civil Procedure also contain provisions that have ethical implications, and perhaps the most important source of ethical guidance is not in any book—it is your own instinct for discerning what is reasonable and what is not. Working litigators and litigation paralegals do not have time to research ethics opinions continually as they go about their duties—staying out of ethical trouble is mainly a matter of good habits and common sense. In that vein, we begin our discussion of the ethics rules by offering our own Top Ten list of ethical do's and don'ts for litigation paralegals, after which we will examine some specific rules limiting the tactics that we can use against an opposing party.

Here are the ten ethical commandments for litigation paralegals.

**Commandment 1: Never Talk about Client Business**—Consulting a lawyer is in some ways like confessing to a priest: The expectation exists that whatever is said will go no further. ABA Model Rule 1.6 states:

> (a) A lawyer shall not reveal information relating to representation of a client unless the client consents after consultation except for disclosures that are impliedly authorized in order to carry out the representation, and except as stated in paragraph (b).

[The exception covered by paragraph (b), deals with situations in which it *is* proper for a lawyer to divulge client confidences—for example, to prevent a client from committing a serious crime. Although interesting to ethicists, such situations are exceedingly rare in practice. In more than 50 combined years of litigating, none of the authors has yet had occasion to "blow the whistle" on a client.]

On the other hand, we *have* seen paralegals fired for talking about client business. Notice that ABA Model Rule 1.6 goes further than merely prohibiting us from divulging information given us by the client—it prohibits us from revealing *any* information about the representation. What does this mean? It means that we do not talk about *any aspect* of the client's legal business—even information that is public knowledge—except as necessary to carry out the tasks assigned to us. We do not talk about the client's business to our spouse, to our friends, to other paralegals. We do not swap interesting anecdotes about our cases, even without mentioning names.

## Commandment 2: Never Overpromise (Especially to Clients)

—ABA Model Rule 1.3 states: "A lawyer shall act with reasonable diligence and promptness in representing a client." Although we have no statistics to offer, in our experience "diligence" and "promptness" issues lead to more bar complaints than any other cause. *Diligence* means making sure that everything that needs to be done in a case is being done and done on time. It also means keeping promises made to clients and others, especially promises to complete a task by a specified time.

Most people are not late completing tasks because they are lazy; they are late because they have promised to do more than they are able to do. Good litigators and paralegals are always under pressure to accept more work and to commit to unrealistic deadlines. It is easy to find oneself constantly working in disaster avoidance mode, going from crisis to crisis, and letting less important tasks slide until they, too, reach crisis proportions.

Lawyers and paralegals have an ethical responsibility to avoid promising more than they can deliver. According to the ABA comment to Model Rule 1.3: "A lawyer's workload should be controlled so that each matter can be handled adequately."

Learn to say "no." Be scrupulous about not allowing yourself to be pressured into promising the impossible. And if you do find yourself unable to meet a promised completion date, immediately contact the person to whom you made the promise and let them know that you will be late—and set a new completion date that you are sure you can meet.

## Commandment 3: Keep the Client Informed

—Another common cause of bar complaints is lack of communication. Clients are paying substantial fees for our services, and they expect to be kept abreast of what is going on in their cases. ABA Rule 1.4 makes this mandatory: "A lawyer shall keep a client reasonably informed about the status of a matter and promptly comply with reasonable requests for information."

Apart from being ethically required, good client communication is simply good business. One easy way to keep clients informed of what is going on—and one that pays rich dividends in terms of client satisfaction—is to make it a habit to copy the client on everything (after getting your supervising attorney's approval, of course). When you write a letter, file a paper with the court, receive a paper from opposing counsel, send the client a copy. This habit will also improve the spirit in which bills are received because it gives clients a tangible sample of what they are paying for.

## Commandment 4: Paper the File

—By "paper the file" we mean get in the habit of writing confirming letters, case notes, and memos to the file. Litigation files have a section for attorney notes. Whenever you do something relating to a case, make notes of what you did and date them. When you speak to the client, make a note of what you said. If your duties include contact with the opposing lawyer or paralegals concerning anything involving extensions, deadlines, or other promises by either side, send confirming letters. We cannot cite an ABA model rule requiring you to do these things—this commandment is based on painful experience (gained, fortunately, as the attorney, not the person accused). Losing a lawsuit is often a wrenching experience for clients, and they sometimes react by looking for someone to blame. If someone ever does accuse you of ethical impropriety, you will need to be able to prove exactly what happened. You will be in a far better position if you can point to documentation in the file to back up your version of the facts.

## Commandment 5: If It Does Not Pass the Smell Test, Think Again

—Sometimes a course of action presents itself that, upon analysis, does not seem to violate any rule of ethics or other law that we can think of, yet an inner voice tells us that there is something wrong. Wise litigators learn to heed these subliminal warnings. When the alarm bells are going off in your head, it is often because you have subconsciously remembered a case or made a connection that has escaped your conscious awareness. Either back away or research the issue until you can put your finger on whatever it is that is bothering you.

## Commandment 6: Know Your Limitations

—It may surprise you that the very first of the ABA model rules, ABA Model Rule 1.1, states that "A lawyer shall provide competent representation to a client." Surely that goes without saying? In fact, lawyers can be, and often are, disbarred for incompetent representation of a client, and often the aggrieved client then follows up by suing the lawyer for malpractice. What this rule means to you as a paralegal is, above all, *know your limitations*. When lawyers—and paralegals—get into trouble over competence issues, the reason, almost by definition, is that they have involved themselves in work for which their training and skills are not adequate. When in doubt about how to handle a task, do not wing it; consult your supervising attorney for guidance.

## Commandment 7: Be Zealous on Behalf of Your Client and Do Your Best to Win

—As the ABA comment to Model Rule 1.3 makes clear, we have an ethical obligation to "go to the mat" for our clients:

> A lawyer should pursue a matter on behalf of a client despite opposition, obstruction or personal inconvenience to the lawyer, and may *take whatever lawful and ethical measures are required* to vindicate a client's cause or endeavor. A lawyer should act with commitment and dedication to the interests of the client and with zeal in advocacy upon the client's behalf. [Emphasis added].

There are, of course, limits—see Commandment 8.

## Commandment 8: Never Knowingly Bend the Rules or the Law for a Client

—You may sometimes find yourself under pressure from a client, or even—sadly—an attorney, to take some action that you know is a violation of the rules of procedure or, worse, a criminal infraction. For example, you may be asked to make what you know to be an untrue statement in a discovery response or an affidavit, which is a violation of FRCP, Rule 11, an act of criminal perjury. You might also feel the temptation to bend the rules on your own. Say, for example, you dropped the ball and missed a response deadline, but you could cover up your mistake by back-dating the certificate of mailing to make it appear that the paper was timely served. Or you may be assigned to take an action in a lawsuit that you know is prohibited by the rules of ethics (see the Ethical Limits on Litigation Tactics section later in this workshop).

Never yield to the temptation to cheat, even in seemingly minor ways. Your reputation will follow you forever.

## Commandment 9: Do Not Give Legal Advice

—In addition to complying with all of the ethical rules governing the conduct of lawyers, paralegals must also take care not to run afoul of the prohibitions against unauthorized practice of law. Each state has its own laws on the subject; your instructor will inform you about whether your state has any provisions specifically regulating what paralegals may do in litigation. The National Association of Legal Assistants publishes guidelines outlining the kinds of tasks that paralegals should, and should not, be assigned (available on the Internet at www.nala.org; follow the "standards" link).

Of the listed acts, the one that most often gets paralegals in trouble is giving legal opinions or advice. Why? In a well-managed firm, paralegals are not put in positions where there is any opportunity to establish attorney–client relationships, set fees, or represent clients in court. They are, however, necessarily in contact with clients, and clients inevitably have questions and want advice. Giving a client advice that turns out to be wrong—especially if the wrong advice is perceived to harm the client's case—is a sure ticket to a stern reprimand or worse. The ability to distinguish between questions that can be legitimately answered (i.e., factual questions such as "Has the answer been filed yet?") and questions that call for legal advice or opinion (i.e., questions like "How should I testify about X?") is a skill that comes with experience. Meanwhile, if in doubt, pass the buck to your supervising attorney when a client asks you to offer an opinion about some aspect of the case.

*Your Local Notes*

_____

_____

**Commandment 10: If in Doubt, Consult Your Supervising Attorney**—In the end, if there are difficult ethical decisions to make, it is the supervising attorney who should make them, not the paralegal. This does not mean that you are free to engage in behavior that you know is unethical or improper simply because a supervising attorney has authorized it. The "I was just following orders" defense rarely succeeds. However, your supervising attorney is likely at least as eager as you are to stay out of ethical trouble and is your first and best source of advice when you are unsure of the ethical implications of a proposed action.

## ETHICAL LIMITS ON LITIGATION TACTICS

The hypotheticals that we present later in this workshop are intended to explore the ethical limits on the kinds of tactics that we can use against opposing parties. We are, of course, ethically bound to do our best to win our clients' cases. We have already seen that the ABA comment to Model Rule 1.3 encourages us to take "whatever lawful and ethical measures are required to vindicate a client's cause or endeavor."

As the foregoing comment implies, however, there are limits beyond which we cannot go in advocating our clients' causes, even if the fate of the lawsuit hangs in the balance: We may not act in ways that are not "lawful and ethical." These limits are not always easy to apply. We do not want to win by cheating, but neither do we want to lose through excessive caution. It is therefore crucial for litigators and litigation paralegals to know exactly where the ethical lines are (and, of course, to stay within them).

We will now try to list some of the things that we may not do in litigation. Many of the prohibitions are unsurprising and involve conduct that you would, we hope, reject on the basis of common sense alone. Others, such as the restrictions on contacting witnesses who are employed by a corporate opposing party, are less obvious and more technical in nature.

The sources for the ethical restrictions that we discuss are the ABA model rules and the Federal Rules of Civil Procedure. You will notice that the ABA model rules often begin with the phrase, "A lawyer shall not. . . ." It will come as no surprise that what lawyers cannot do themselves, they cannot do indirectly by having a paralegal perform the prohibited act. ABA Model Rule 5.3 makes a lawyer responsible for known conduct of a paralegal that "would be a violation of the Rules of Professional Conduct if engaged in by a lawyer. . . ."

The ethical principles that we will draw from the Federal Rules of Civil Procedure arise from the certification provisions of FRCP, Rules 11 and 26(g). FRCP, Rule 11, provides that, by presenting a pleading, motion, or similar paper to the court, an attorney is automatically certifying that it meets the standards set forth in Rule 11(b). FRCP, Rule 26(g), provides for a similar "implied certification" with respect to discovery requests, responses, and objections. We discuss the specific standards imposed by FRCP, Rules 11 and 26(g), under the appropriate topics later. Because only an attorney can sign a pleading or present a paper to the court, these provisions, and the punishments for violating them, apply only to attorneys. However, a paralegal who carelessly or improperly prepares a paper that the attorney later signs, and thereby subjects the attorney to sanctions under FRCP, Rule 11 or 26(g), should expect to share in the unpleasantness that will surely follow.

**Lying to the Court**—It goes without saying, we hope, that reputable lawyers and paralegals do not deliberately lie to judges. If this is not obvious, ABA Model Rule 3.3(a)(1) makes it explicit: "A lawyer shall not knowingly . . . make a false statement of material fact or law to a tribunal." (**Tribunal** is the word that the ABA model rules use to refer to the court or to any other adjudicative officer such as an administrative law judge.)

**Presenting False Evidence**—Similarly, it is unethical for a lawyer to knowingly present false evidence to the court. ABA Model Rule 3.3(a)(4) states: "A lawyer shall not knowingly . . . offer evidence that the lawyer knows to be false." Furthermore, "If a lawyer has offered material evidence and comes to know of its falsity, the lawyer shall take reasonable remedial measures." Id.

In real life, of course, it is rare that we "know" any fact with absolute certainty. As a practical matter, the situation that most commonly raises concerns about false evidence issues is the one that arises when a client tells the lawyer one version of the facts, and later wants to testify to a materially different version. If, upon close questioning, the client insists that the revised version is the truth, the lawyer cannot know that it is false simply because the client told a different story at another time. Unless the amended story is so preposterous as to be unbelievable, most trial lawyers would probably let the witness testify.

Even though the lawyer is not *required* to refuse to present evidence when he reasonably suspects that it is false, but does not know of a certainty, ABA Model Rule 3.3(c) gives the lawyer the option of refusing: "A lawyer may refuse to offer evidence that the lawyer reasonably believes is false."

**Asserting Unmeritorious Claims and Contentions**—Not only do the rules of ethics prohibit us from knowingly presenting false evidence, they also prohibit us from asserting claims or defenses that we know are unsupportable. ABA Model Rule 3.1 states:

> A lawyer shall not bring or defend a proceeding, or assert or controvert an issue therein, unless there is a basis for doing so that is not frivolous, which includes a good faith argument for an extension, modification or reversal of existing law. . . .

FRCP, Rule 11(b)(2), further provides that by presenting a pleading, motion, or other paper, a lawyer certifies to the court that "the claims, defenses, and other legal contentions therein are warranted by existing law or by a nonfrivolous argument for the extension, modification, or reversal or existing law or the establishment of new law." Rule 26(g) provides similarly with respect to discovery papers. (Why is it necessary to say essentially the same thing twice, once in the rules of ethics and again in FRCP, Rule 11? Because rules of ethics are enforced via bar discipline, which is often glacially slow and unevenly applied, while FRCP, Rule 11, allows the judge to impose immediate punishment if appropriate.)

FRCP, Rule 11, also implies a certification that any claims presented to the court have a reasonable basis in fact. By filing a pleading, the attorney certifies that "the allegations and other factual contentions have evidentiary support or, if specifically so identified, are likely to have evidentiary support after a reasonable opportunity for further investigation or discovery . . ."; see FRCP, Rule 11(b)(3).

If plaintiff's attorney is ethically bound to ensure that the complaint alleges only meritorious legal theories and facts supportable by evidence, what about defendant's attorney? Is not defendant's attorney free to deny everything and make plaintiff prove every point? At least in theory, no. ABA Model Rule 3.1 allows a defense attorney in a criminal proceeding to make the prosecutor dot every *i* and cross every *t:* "A lawyer for the defendant in a criminal proceeding . . . may nevertheless so defend the proceeding as to require that every element of the case be established."

In a civil lawsuit, however, defendant's answer is subject to FRCP, Rule 11, and the Rule 11 certification extends even to denials made in defendant's answer. The defense attorney filing an answer certifies that "the denials of factual contentions are warranted on the evidence or, if specifically so identified, are reasonably based on a lack of information or belief"; see FRCP, Rule 11(b)(4). FRCP, Rule 11(b), requires the attorney to make "an inquiry reasonable under the circumstances. . . ." Therefore, if plaintiff alleges a fact in the complaint, and defen-

dant does not know whether or not the fact is true, defendant is free to deny it. But if defendant's attorney, after the reasonable inquiry required by FRCP, Rule 11, does know that the fact alleged by plaintiff is true, the answer must admit it.

**Citing Controlling Authority**—"Legal argument based on a knowingly false representation of law constitutes dishonesty toward the tribunal. A lawyer is not required to make a disinterested exposition of the law, but must recognize the existence of pertinent legal authorities," so states the ABA comment to ABA Model Rule 3.3(a)(3).

Normally, in legal arguments in a lawsuit, each side aggressively asserts its own position. If the opposing attorney has overlooked case law that could have been used to attack our position, well and good—surely it is not up to us to straighten him or her out? True in general, but not if the overlooked authority is both (1) in the controlling jurisdiction and (2) directly adverse to our position. ABA Model Rule 3.3(a)(3) states: "A lawyer shall not knowingly . . . fail to disclose to the tribunal legal authority in the controlling jurisdiction known to the lawyer to be directly adverse to the position of the client and not disclosed by opposing counsel. . . ."

The "controlling jurisdiction" means a source of authority that our court regards as binding. If our lawsuit is pending in state court, "controlling jurisdiction" includes the appellate courts of the same state, but not the federal courts or the courts of other states. If our lawsuit is in federal district court, "controlling jurisdiction" includes the U.S. Court of Appeals for the circuit in which our district court is located, the U.S. Supreme Court, and possibly the state appellate courts of the state in which the district court sits, to the extent the suit involves claims based on state law.

**Duty to Respond Properly to Discovery**—Both in traditional discovery and in discovery based on mandatory disclosure, there is an ethical duty to disclose the facts completely and accurately. ABA Model Rule 3.4(d) states: "A lawyer shall not . . . fail to make reasonably diligent effort to comply with a legally proper discovery request by an opposing party. . . ." FRCP, Rule 26(g)(1), provides that by signing a disclosure statement, an attorney certifies to the court that "to the best of the signer's knowledge, information, and belief, formed after a reasonable inquiry, the disclosure is complete and correct as of the time it is made."

**Tampering with Evidence**—It will come as no surprise that the rules of ethics prohibit evidence tampering. ABA Model Rule 3.4(a) states:

A lawyer shall not . . . unlawfully obstruct another party's access to evidence or unlawfully alter, destroy or conceal a document or other material having potential evidentiary value. A lawyer shall not counsel or assist another person to do any such act. . . .

### Improper Communications with an Opposing Party

We are not permitted to communicate directly with the opposing attorney's client. The lawyer for one party must channel all communications about the case through the other party's attorney. ABA Model Rule 4.2 states:

> In representing a client, a lawyer shall not communicate about the subject of the representation with a party the lawyer knows to be represented by another lawyer in the matter, unless the lawyer has the consent of the other lawyer or is authorized by law to do so.

(Model Rule 4.2 does make an exception where the "consent of the other lawyer" is given; however, no competent litigator would ever willingly allow a client to communicate with the opposing attorney outside her presence.)

For litigators, the main significance of the prohibition against direct contact with the opposing party is that it limits the kinds of investigation that we can do when we are litigating against a corporation or other entity. The comment to ABA Model Rule 4.2 states:

> In the case of an organization, this Rule prohibits communications by a lawyer for one party concerning the matter in representation with persons having a managerial responsibility on behalf of the organization, and with any other person whose act or omission in connection with that matter may be imputed to the organization for purposes of civil or criminal liability or whose statement may constitute an admission on the part of the organization.

In other words, if the opposing party is, say, a corporation, we must be careful not to attempt to interview anyone having "managerial responsibility" or anyone who was directly involved in the events giving rise to the lawsuit. In effect, as a practical matter, the rule prohibits us from speaking to anyone in the corporation who would be likely to have any information of interest to us. State law varies somewhat as to how far down the corporate hierarchy the prohibition extends, so, in a case in which it is important to investigate a corporate opponent thoroughly, it will be necessary to conduct some research to establish the boundaries clearly.

### Witness Tampering and Dealings with Third-Party Witnesses

If we were unscrupulous, an obvious way to improve our chances of winning would be to engineer the testimony of nonparty witnesses. Several of the rules of ethics seek to forestall such tactics, and, of course, serious witness tampering is a crime.

Needless to say, it is unethical to attempt to induce a witness to lie. ABA Model Rule 3.4(b) states: "A lawyer shall not . . . falsify evidence, counsel or assist a witness to testify falsely, or offer an inducement to a witness that is prohibited by law. . . ."

It is also a federal crime—subornation of perjury—to attempt to influence a witness to lie under oath in a proceeding in federal court. 18 U.S.C. § 1622 provides:

> Whoever procures another to commit any perjury is guilty of subornation of perjury, and shall be fined under this title or imprisoned not more than five years, or both.

Subornation of perjury is also a crime under the laws of each state.

Bribing a witness is, of course, also a crime; see 18 U.S.C. § 210(b)(4). And 18 U.S.C. § 1512(b) imposes criminal penalties on most other kinds of witness tampering:

> Whoever knowingly uses intimidation or physical force, threatens, or corruptly persuades another person, or attempts to do so, or engages in misleading conduct toward another person, with intent to . . . influence, delay, or prevent the testimony of any person in an official proceeding . . . shall be fined under this title or imprisoned not more than ten years, or both.

It is unethical for a lawyer to attempt to persuade a nonparty witness not to testify, or to withhold information from the opposing party, unless the witness is a relative or employee of the lawyer's client. ABA Model Rule 3.4(f) states:

> A lawyer shall not . . . request a person other than a client to refrain from voluntarily giving relevant information to another party unless:
>
> (1) the person is a relative or an employee or other agent of a client; and
>
> (2) the lawyer reasonably believes that the person's interests will not be adversely affected by refraining from giving such information.

When contacting a nonparty witness, the lawyer may not try to mislead the witness into thinking that the lawyer is in a nonadvocative role. ABA Model Rule 4.3 states:

In dealing on behalf of a client with a person who is not represented by counsel, a lawyer shall not state or imply that the lawyer is disinterested. When the lawyer knows or reasonably should know that the unrepresented person misunderstands the lawyer's role in the matter, the lawyer shall make reasonable efforts to correct the misunderstanding.

In general, when interviewing nonparty witnesses, the lawyer should forthrightly disclose his identity and status. And if, as often happens, the witness asks questions of the lawyer, the lawyer should refrain from giving any legal advice, other than for the witness to consult her own attorney.

Attorneys are ethically bound to respect the rights of nonparty witnesses. ABA Model Rule 4.4 states:

In representing a client, a lawyer shall not use means that have no substantial purpose other than to embarrass, delay, or burden a third person, or use methods of obtaining evidence that violate the legal rights of such a person.

What are the "methods of obtaining evidence that violate the legal rights of" a witness? One practice which, though undeniably tempting at times, is improper under the ethics rules of many states is that of secretly tape recording a conversation or interview with a witness. Although surreptitious taping is not illegal under the laws of many states, especially if done in person rather than over the telephone, a number of states have disciplined attorneys for engaging in the practice. For a comprehensive survey of various states' ethics rules on the subject, see Annot., Propriety of Attorney's Surreptitious Sound Recording Of Statements By Others Who Are Or May Become Involved In Litigation, 32 A.L.R.5th 715 (1995), also available on Westlaw.

## Delaying Tactics and Escalation of Costs—

Many more lawsuits are settled than tried, and the high cost of litigation provides a strong motivation to compromise. Obviously, one way to intensify the pressure on the opposing party to settle is to make continued litigation as expensive as possible. And one way to make litigation more expensive is to drag it out because, typically, the longer a lawsuit takes, the more it costs. For defendants, there is a further motivation to delay: As long as the lawsuit is still pending, defendant keeps the money that plaintiff is suing for.

Nevertheless, the rules of ethics, as well as the rules of procedure, clearly prohibit tactics whose sole purpose is to cause delay or drive up costs. According to ABA Model Rule 3.2, "A lawyer shall make reasonable efforts to expedite litigation consistent with the interests of the client." By presenting a pleading, motion, or other paper, an attorney certifies to the court that "it is not being presented for any improper purpose, such as to harass or to cause unnecessary delay or needless increase in the costs of litigation"; see FRCP, Rules 11(b)(1) and 26(g)(2)(B).

Under FRCP, Rule 26(g), when an attorney submits a discovery request, he also certifies that the request is "not unreasonable or unduly burdensome or expensive, given the needs of the case, the discovery already had in the case, the amount in controversy, and the importance of the issues at stake in the litigation." ABA Model Rule 3.4(d) provides similarly:

A lawyer shall not . . . in pretrial procedure, make a frivolous discovery request or fail to make reasonably diligent effort to comply with a legally proper discovery request by an opposing party. . . .

## Improperly Influencing the Judge or Jurors—

All courts have strict rules governing communications between attorneys and jurors. Contacting a juror before or during trial, whether by a lawyer or by a paralegal employed by the lawyer, is a serious ethical breach that will likely cause a mistrial and result in serious sanctions against the offender. Many federal district courts also have local rules restricting contacts by attorneys with jurors after the case is concluded.

Attempting to influence a juror improperly is, of course, unethical as well as criminally punishable in most jurisdictions. Similarly, lawyers are prohibited from influencing judges by means other than proper argument in court. In particular, except in limited circumstances specified in the rules of procedure, it is improper for a lawyer to communicate *ex parte* with the judge about a pending lawsuit, that is, to communicate with the judge without the opposing lawyer being present.

ABA Model Rule 3.5 states:

A lawyer shall not:
(a) seek to influence a judge, juror, prospective juror or other official by means prohibited by law; [or]
(b) communicate *ex parte* with such a person except as permitted by law. . . .

As you would expect, attempting to improperly influence a federal court jury is also a federal crime. Naturally, threatening or bribing a juror is an extremely serious offense; but you can get 6 months in a federal prison for merely "writing or sending to [a juror] a written communication" relating to the case; 18 U.S.C. §1503-04.

**Improper Statements to the Press**—The ethical rules regulating communications with members of the press reflect an uneasy balance between the free speech rights of the litigants and lawyers on the one hand, and the repugnance with which most judges regard trial publicity. The basic standard is expressed in ABA Model Rule 3.6:

> (a) A lawyer shall not make an extrajudicial statement that a reasonable person would expect to be disseminated by means of public communication if the lawyer knows or reasonably should know that it will have a substantial likelihood of materially prejudicing an adjudicative proceeding.

Press contact is a minefield for litigators. The ethical rules governing it are complex and exacting. (If you doubt this, read the rest of ABA Model Rule 3.6, which takes up two pages.) Press reports are unpredictable and sometimes inaccurate, and judges tend to be congenitally hostile to the idea of lawyers talking to reporters about pending cases under any circumstances. It is essential that any contact with members of the press be carefully thought out, and it goes without saying that it is not the job of the paralegal (or for that matter junior attorneys assisting with the case) to make decisions of this kind. There are no conceivable circumstances in which a paralegal should communicate with the press on any subject remotely connected to pending litigation. If you are ever contacted by a reporter concerning one of your cases, our advice is to refer her to your supervising attorney, then politely excuse yourself.

---

*Your Local Notes*

_____

_____

---

## ETHICS IN LITIGATION: TOPICS FOR DISCUSSION

As you read the foregoing summary of ethics rules, you may have been struck by the impression that many of these standards seem at odds with the real world of litigation. Many of the rules seem to conflict with each other, and especially with the lawyer's duty under ABA Model Rule 1.3 to take all appropriate measures to win the case for the client.

We now give you an opportunity to explore the application of ethics rules to several commonplace situations that we regard as the most ethically troublesome from a practical standpoint. The hypotheticals that follow are intended primarily for class discussion; but, of course, to participate effectively, you will need to analyze them in advance. In doing so, try to identify the ethical rules that apply in each situation (there will often be more than one), and also take into account your knowledge and experience with real litigation and litigators. To the extent that the rules do not seem to square with real life, try to discover why.

**Hypo 1: The Lawsuit as a License to Fish**—The federal Age Discrimination in Employment Act, 14 U.S.C. §621 *et seq.,* makes it unlawful for an employer to discriminate against employees or prospective employees on the basis of age if they are between the ages of 40 and 70. An employee or prospective employee who is discriminated against in violation of the act has the right to sue the employer for damages (after first complying with some administrative prerequisites). It is possible to base an age discrimination case on direct proof that a particular employment decision was motivated by improper consideration of the employee's age. It is also possible to prove age discrimination via statistics showing that employees in the 40 to 70 age group are treated less favorably than younger employees.

Ann Anderson, age 48, recently graduated from a top-ten law school. Although she ranked second in her class, she has had difficulty finding employment with a law firm. She has interviewed with all of the top firms in her city, but has received no offers. Her latest interview was with the prestigious 100-lawyer firm of Baker & Canfield; although the interview seemed to go well, the firm's offer went to one of Ann's classmates, a 26-year-old student whose academic credentials were clearly inferior to Ann's.

In desperation, Ann asked the advice of one of her favorite law school professors, Dave Dawkins. Dawkins candidly explained to Ann (off the record, of course) that large law firms all follow a policy of hiring young lawyers directly out of law school. The reason is that older beginning lawyers would be perceived by their younger peers as having an unfair advantage, which would create dissension and resentment. Also, the cost of training a new lawyer is enormous, and law firms want their trainees to have long careers ahead of them so as to justify the expense. Dawkins suggests to Ann that she would be best advised to apply for a position with a government agency.

Ann instead retains prominent employment rights lawyer Ed Epstein to sue Baker & Canfield for age discrimination. Ann makes it clear to Ed that she has no proof that Baker & Canfield discriminated against her. Ed tells her not to worry, that he will take discovery regarding Baker & Canfield's employment policies and hiring statistics. If discovery does not turn up enough evidence to go forward, Ed is sure that Baker & Canfield will agree to a voluntary dismissal, or perhaps even pay a small amount to make the suit go away.

Is Ed's proposed strategy ethically permissible?

### Hypo 2: The Lawsuit as an Interest-Free Loan—

Frank Forrester is seriously injured in a motor vehicle accident. The accident was witnessed by a group of eight Catholic priests who happened to be standing at the intersection waiting for the light to change so that they could cross the street, all of whom saw the other driver, George Granger, run the red light at high speed while driving in the oncoming traffic lane. George's blood alcohol was measured at 0.28 percent, nearly three times the legal limit.

Frank retains personal injury attorney Harriet Harris to represent him. Harriet is able to verify that George has a $500,000 liability policy with Inland Indelible Insurance Company. Frank's medical bills amount to $40,000, and Harriet tells Frank that, in her opinion, his claim is worth about $250,000.

Harriet makes a settlement demand on Inland Indelible for $260,000 (to leave some negotiating room), which Inland Indelible turns down cold. Harriet files suit on Frank's behalf.

Jim Jernigan is a recent law school graduate hired by Inland Indelible to defend insurance cases. Frank's lawsuit is routed to Jim. Jim reviews the file and writes a memo to Kathy Kowalski, the Inland Indelible claims manager to whom he reports, estimating the value of the claim at $250,000 and recommending that Inland Indelible offer to settle for that amount.

Kathy rejects the recommendation and instructs Jim to file an answer. When Jim asks her why, she explains: Inland Indelible's preference in cases of this kind is to wait to settle until the suit has progressed further. Inland Indelible earns an average 15% return on its investment portfolio, she explains. The earnings on $250,000 would amount to $37,500 over the course of a year. It will easily take at least a year for Frank's lawsuit to get on the calendar for trial, and the cost of keeping the suit going for that long will be far less than $37,500—merely the cost of having Jim file an answer and respond to a few discovery requests. It is a simple matter of economics, Kathy explains to Jim. She tells Jim to file the answer, do the minimum amount of work necessary, and keep her posted—she will decide when it makes sense to settle.

What should Jim do? Can he ethically follow Kathy's instructions?

### Hypo 3: The Ethics of Damages Engineering—

Larry Larsen is on his way home from work when he is rear-ended while stopped at a traffic light. Larry is shaken up, but suffers no obvious injury.

The next day, one of Larry's coworkers tells Larry that he should go see an injury lawyer. The coworker recommends the law office of Montague and Nichols, an accident injury firm whose advertisements appear frequently on the local television station. Larry makes an appointment for that afternoon.

Larry is interviewed by paralegal Oscar O'Malley. Oscar has Larry sign the firm's standard retainer agreement. Oscar tells Larry that Larry ought to see a doctor. Larry asks why—his neck is slightly stiff, but otherwise he feels fine. Oscar explains that soft tissue "whiplash" injuries sometimes do not manifest themselves fully until several days after the accident. Also, Oscar explains, the settlement value that an insurance company assigns to an injury claim depends in large part on the total amount of the medical bills, so it is in Larry's interest to receive as much medical treatment as can be reasonably justified.

Oscar makes an appointment for Larry to see Dr. Peter Potter, M.D., a physician who specializes in accident rehabilitation cases. Dr. Potter examines Larry, orders x-rays, and prescribes a 7-week course of physical therapy. Larry's medical bills eventually total $2,300, and the other driver's insurance company settles Larry's injury claim for $7,000.

Have any ethical rules been violated?

### Hypo 4: The Ethics of Hiding the Ball—Quincy
Medical Devices Corp. manufactures an electronic heart pacemaker. Implanted surgically, the pacemaker administers a periodic electrical pulse to the patient's heart, stimulating it to beat at the proper rate. Quincy's pacemaker has been approved by the FDA and is in wide use.

Recently, claims have been made that Quincy's pacemaker is susceptible to malfunction if exposed to a radio-frequency signal of a type emitted by certain cellular telephones under the right conditions. A class action lawsuit has been brought on behalf of all persons with Quincy pacemakers, claiming that the company was negligent in the design of its pacemaker, and that its management knew or should have known about the claimed defect. An independent testing laboratory has tested the pacemaker and has confirmed that it can be made to malfunction under certain unusual conditions.

Richard Roberts is a paralegal in the firm defending the suit on behalf of Quincy. Quincy has denied any knowledge of any defect of the kind claimed. Richard is assigned to prepare answers to interrogatories, one of which asks specifically for

Quincy to "identify each and every memo, letter, or other communication whose subject matter concerns any occurrences of malfunctions in the Quincy pacemaker during clinical testing."

Quincy has delivered all of its records pertaining to the clinical trials of the pacemaker; these comprise some fifty boxes of documents. Going through the records, Richard finds a memo from one of the junior design engineers, addressed to Quincy's chief engineer, expressing the opinion that a malfunction observed in that day's testing was caused by the patient's use of a cellular telephone, and suggesting a design change to correct the problem. With the memo is the chief engineer's response, rejecting the cellular telephone hypothesis as unlikely and the design change as too costly.

When Richard found them, the memo and response were in a file marked "Atlanta Convention—Travel Expenses." In addition to the memo and response, the file contained approximately fifty pages of travel vouchers and hotel receipts.

Richard replaces the memo and response in the file, placing them in the middle of a stack of receipts. He replaces the file in its box, which contains other files of expense records pertaining to the development of the pacemaker. He answers the interrogatory (as permitted by Rule 33, FRCP) as follows: "The answer to this interrogatory may be derived or ascertained from the business records of defendant, specifically fifty boxes of records pertaining to the development and clinical testing of the Quincy pacemaker marked boxes D-1 through D-50, which will be produced for plaintiffs' review upon request."

Has Richard acted unethically?

### Hypo 5: The Ethics of Mandatory Disclosure—

Sally Sullivan has been sued as a result of an auto accident which occurred when the brakes on Sally's car suddenly failed. In the weeks before the accident, Sally had noticed that her brakes did not seem to be working as well as they usually did, and took the car to Tom's Auto Service to have the brakes checked. Tom Turner, the mechanic, diagnosed the problem and recommended replacement of an expensive pump. Not wanting to spend the money, Sally procrastinated.

Ursula Ulrich is a paralegal working for the attorney who is defending Sally in the lawsuit. The complaint alleges that "defendant had a duty to maintain her vehicle in a safe condition" and that "plaintiff has been damaged as a proximate result of defendant's failure to maintain her vehicle in a safe condition." Ursula has been assigned to interview Sally and prepare a Rule 26(a) disclosure statement. FRCP, Rule 26(a)(1)(A), requires each litigant to disclose "the name and, if known, the address and telephone number of each individual likely to have discoverable information relevant to disputed facts alleged with particularity in the pleadings, identifying the subjects of the information."

Ursula explains the disclosure process to Sally and tells her that Rule 26(a)(1)(A) requires disclosure of the names of anyone having any information pertinent to the allegations made in the complaint. Ursula then tells Sally to be careful what she says, because if there are any witnesses who would be bad for Sally's case, if she (Ursula) knows about them, she will be obligated to disclose them.

Sally therefore elects not to mention Tom Turner and his advice to replace the brake pump, and Ursula prepares the disclosure statement accordingly.

Has Ursula acted appropriately?

# PRACTICE POINTERS
## *Professionalism*

The ethical canons and considerations are the legal profession's attempt to encapsulate the most critical rules of professionalism. As with any codified law, however, these rules tend to represent the bottom line for the profession. Mere adherence to them does not ensure that a member of the legal profession has attained a high standard of practice any more than an individual's adherence to the law of the state indicates that he is a model citizen. Professionalism requires more than avoiding a violation of the ethical code. It is a way of conducting yourself that brings honor to the profession, that enhances your sense of integrity, and that creates a sense of trust with all with whom you come into contact.

*continued*

## PRACTICE POINTERS
### *Professionalism* continued

What kind of actions and behaviors does professional conduct entail? It means being someone who does what you say you are going to do when you say you are going to do it. If you say you are going to call on a certain day, you do. If you promise to deliver something by a particular date, you do. If you commit to taking on a project, you do it.

Legal professionals are civil at all times, no matter what the circumstances. They do not belittle or ridicule others and they do not harass their opponents. They cooperate as much as possible in scheduling meetings and court dates and are courteous about granting time extensions and continuances when circumstances dictate their necessity. They actively seek ways to ease the negotiation and litigation processes by trying to resolve matters as expeditiously and fairly as possible. At the very least, they do nothing to further antagonize their opposition. They advocate vigorously for their clients but remain impeccably honest with the court and their opponents. In short, they practice the Golden Rule of litigation and never do to another what they would not want done to them.

Being a professional does not imply being a workaholic. The law is often depicted as a "jealous mistress" and many a lawyer and paralegal have been seduced by its never-ending demands. The healthy professional, however, has a balanced life that denies neither family, friends, nor personal development. Such a person also contributes to the well-being of the community by doing pro bono (volunteer legal work) and public interest work. They also support the profession as a whole by serving on committees, attending professional meetings, and volunteering to organize and participate in workshops, conferences, and seminars.

As paralegals strive to shape their place in the legal community, they would be well advised to avoid the traps lawyers have fallen into. Seeds of discontent permeate the legal profession. They can be seen in the disproportionate numbers of lawyers experiencing problems with substance abuse, marital crises, emotional instability, and other problems that reflect the burnout and stress that has become characteristic of their profession. As paralegals mold their professional image, they would do well to create a model that reflects balance and integrity for their profession as well as competence and skill.

## TECHNO TIP

Although the rules have not yet been written, ethics and the Internet (and intranets for that matter) need to be considered prior to use of the Internet. Issues abound about lawyer advertising and which state's ethical rules apply to a lawyer's or law firm's web site. Since the site is accessible from anywhere in the country could New York rules apply to a California-based web site? If a major firm has lawyers that are licensed in a total of twenty different states, must its web site conform to the rules of each of those states? Can a web site be constructed in such a way as to be considered an attempt to solicit clients (often forbidden) rather than provide information about the firm's personnel and available services?

The American Bar Association (ABA) Commission on Advertising is looking at these issues. Check the ABA web site for updates and policies regarding Internet advertising.

## FORMS FILE

*Include a copy of the code of professional conduct prepared by NALA, NFPA, and your local paralegal organization (if they have one) in your forms file. You might also consider including copies of any significant legal opinions (or summaries of those opinions) relating to paralegals.*

## KEY TERMS

**Disciplinary proceeding**          **Tribunal**

# APPENDIX A

## Answers to Practice Exams and Litigation Lingo and Litigation Logistics Features

### CHAPTER 1

**Practice Exam**

1. D
2. E
3. B
4. D
5. D
6. B
7. D
8. C
9. D
10. civil procedures
11. substantive law
12. civil action
13. injunction
14. judgment
15. jurisdiction
16. venue
17. arbitrator
18. service
19. pleadings
20. issue
21. documentary; testimonial
22. trial, verdict
23. pleadings
24. discovery
25. alternative dispute resolution
26. arbitrator; mediator
27. F
28. F
29. F
30. F
31. F
32. T
33. T
34. T
35. F
36. F
37. F
38. T
39. T
40. F
41. F
42. T
43. F
44. T
45. T

**Litigation Lingo**
**DOWN**
1. litigate
3. venue
4. court
5. evidence
8. jurisdiction
9. arbitrator
10. injunction

**ACROSS**
2. service
6. issue
7. pleading
8. judgment
9. adjudicate
11. procedural
12. motion
13. mediator
14. ADR
15. concurrent

## Litigation Logistics

1. Elements of negligence
2. Time periods for filing complaint, answer, doing discovery, etc.
3. Which courts have jurisdiction; venue
4. File complaint
5. Extent of damages to vehicle
6. Does insurance company have legal obligation to pay
7. Copy of defendant's insurance policy
8. Insurance company refuses to provide discovery materials you request
9. Locate assets of defendant, foreclose liens, and seize assets; defendant may appeal
10. Arbitration

# CHAPTER 2

## Practice Exam

1. B
2. D
3. C
4. E
5. A
6. D
7. E
8. E
9. A
10. D
11. Constitution
12. separation of powers
13. U.S. Supreme
14. trial; appellate
15. district; U.S. Court of Appeals
16. circuit
17. appellant; brief; appellee
18. reversed; overturned
19. court clerk
20. presiding judge
21. secretary
22. *ex parte*
23. forum; forum shopping

24. *Federal Practice and Procedure* by Wright and Miller; U.S. Code Annotated; pocket parts
25. annotations; citations
26. local
27. T
28. T
29. F
30. F
31. T
32. T
33. F
34. T
35. F
36. F
37. F
38. F
39. T
40. F
41. T
42. T
43. T
44. F
45. F
46. T
47. F
48. T
49. F
50. T
51. F

## Litigation Lingo

1. citation
2. district court
3. brief
4. appellee
5. annotations
6. forum
7. presiding judge
8. court clerk
9. small claims court or justice of the peace court or city court
10. circuit
11. reverses
12. local rule
13. discretionary
14. court administrator
15. judge's secretary
16. *Federal Practice and Procedure* by Wright and Miller
17. pocket parts

## Litigation Logistics

1. State court, federal court, small claims court. You would have to know the amount of damages, what the provisions of the Federal

Tort Claims Act are, which court could lead to the most favorable outcome.

2. Where do I find copies of the local rules? What are the steps I must follow in filing a court paper? What are the business hours of the office? Who in the office has the most experience and who would be the best person to consult if I have an obscure question? How do I get a subpoena or summons drawn up? How do I get a paper filed after closing hours? Are the court's files computerized? What can I access from my office and how do I do so?

3. Begin with the Federal Rules of Civil Procedure. For more information consult *Federal Practice and Procedure* by Wright and Miller and the U.S.C.A. and update these resources using the pocket parts. Use the citations in these references to find cases in the law reporters.

# CHAPTER 3

## Practice Exam

1. A
2. D
3. D
4. C
5. D
6. B
7. A
8. D
9. C
10. sovereign immunity
11. demand
12. pleadings; complaint; answer
13. allegations; caption; prayer for relief
14. cover or information sheet
15. summons
16. process server; affidavit of service
17. affidavit
18. appear; answer
19. affirmative defense
20. counterclaims; cross-claims
21. third-party; severing
22. default judgment
23. reply
24. forum; removal
25. issue has been joined
26. F
27. F
28. F
29. T
30. T
31. F
32. T
33. T
34. T
35. T
36. F
37. T
38. T
39. T
40. F
41. F
42. T
43. F
44. F
45. F
46. F
47. F
48. F
49. T
50. T
51. F
52. F
53. F
54. T
55. T
56. T
57. F

## Litigation Lingo

1. complaint
2. default
3. reply
4. allegations
5. caption
6. service
7. removal
8. affidavit
9. sovereign
10. demand
11. joined
12. cross
13. affirmative
14. forum
15. prayer
16. elements
17. answer
18. appear
19. counterclaim
20. summons

## Litigation Logistics

1. You would need to check to see if there was jurisdiction, both of subject matter and of the person. If no federal questions were involved you would have to meet the diversity

requirements of 28 USC §332, currently $75,000. As plaintiff you might want to stay in state court but you should always consider the benefits of federal court.

a. They would need to meet the requirements of 28 USC §1441 (but see also 28 USC §1445).

b. Each state has its own requirements but in Arizona, for example, each county has its own local rules. In Maricopa County, Local Rules 2.16 and 2.17 set the format and font size requirements.

Each state has its own requirements but in Arizona, for example, each county has its own local rules. In Maricopa County, Local Rule 3.1 requires a cover sheet and 3.10(b) requires that a certificate of compulsory arbitration be filed with the complaint. The certificate is also required by Arizona Rules of Civil Procedure (ARCP), Rule 5(i).

c. Careful review of the Federal Tort Claims Act and cases interpreting the act.

d. Your imagination is the only limitation. Practically speaking the courts can only award money. Asking for other relief in settlement is generally not fruitful.

2. Analyze your case as suggested in this chapter including all possible claims (don't forget intentional torts).

a. Each state has its own requirements but in Arizona, for example, ARCP, Rule 4(d), sets forth the requirements of who may serve the complaint. ARCP, Rules 4.1 and 4.2, define how service may be made. ARCP, Rule 4(i), requires service to be complete in 120 days. See also FRCP, Rules 4(c) and (m).

b. Check your rules for service by publication and service by mail. In Arizona, for example, ARCP, Rules 4.1(n) and 4.2(c) and (f).

c. Obtain and file a waiver of service (usually required to be notarized).

d. She must file a return of service as required by state rule. Usually it is an affidavit stating the time, place, and manner of service and upon whom it was made. In Arizona see ARCP, Rules 4(g), 4.1(n) and (o), and 4.2(b) and (c).

3. Most states allow 20 days for an answer to be filed if served within the state and 30 days if served outside of the state. See ARCP, Rules 12(a), 4.2(d) and (l). See also FRCP, Rule 12(a).

a. Yes. See FRCP, Rule 12(a), and ARCP, 12(a).

b. If a timely answer has not been filed a default may be sought. Note that if personal service was not used additional requirements may be required for service by mail and/or service by publication. Defaults in federal court are governed by FRCP, Rule 55, and applicable local rule. Some states require additional notice be given before a default is entered. See ARCP, Rule 55, for additional notice and time requirements.

c. First check your state's forcible detainer (eviction statutes). A nonhabitable residence, lack of heating/cooling, sanitation facilities, and the like might be a defense to a claim for unpaid rent. Then check your state's rules for affirmative defenses and when they must be made. See FRCP, Rule 8(c), and ARCP, Rule 8(c).

d. First check your state's forcible detainer (eviction statutes). Oftentimes defenses to a claim (such as a nonhabitable residence) may give rise to claim for damages by the tenant.

Generally counterclaims must follow the same requirements for other pleadings, such as the complaint. Check your local rules to see if the caption requires a reference that the document is a counterclaim. See FRCP and ARCP, Rules 7 and 13.

e. Generally within 20 days. See FRCP and ARCP, Rule 12(a)(2).

4. Against his subcontractors for indemnity for their shoddy work.

a. No, if filed within 10 days of his answer. See FRCP and ARCP, Rules 14.

b. Yes. See FRCP and ARCP, Rules 14.

c. The same amount of time as when filing an answer after service (we now have a new plaintiff and a new defendant). See FRCP and ARCP, Rules 12.

d. He would probably file a cross-claim against the subcontractors. See FRCP and ARCP, Rules 12 and 13.

5. If it were determined that the error was not in good faith or represented a failure to conduct a reasonable inquiry into the facts prior to filing suit, sanctions could be entered against the party or the attorney. Rule 11 has been changed by many of the states that have their rules based on the federal rules. Always carefully review the rule itself and court interpretations of it.

In Arizona, a comparable procedural rule is, for example, ARCP, Rule 11.

# CHAPTER 4

## Practice Exam

1. D
2. B

3. C
4. D
5. D
6. C
7. D
8. A
9. D
10. motion
11. testimonial; documentary
12. excluded; admissible
13. mandatory
14. deposition
15. transcripts
16. subpoena
17. 10
18. expert
19. interrogatories; propounding; responding
20. request for production of documents;
   subpoena duces tecum
21. request for entry upon land
   for inspection
22. independent medical examination
23. F
24. T
25. T
26. F
27. F
28. F
29. T
30. F
31. T
32. T
33. F
34. T
35. T
36. T
37. F
38. F
39. F
40. F
41. T
42. T
43. T
44. T

## Litigation Lingo

1. deposition
2. transcript
3. impeach
4. duces tecum
5. examine
6. propound
7. expert
8. interrogatory
9. production
10. notice of IME

11. disclosure
12. exclude
13. admit
14. admission
15. deponent
16. discovery
17. subpoena
18. inspection

## Litigation Logistics

1. a. Yes. Parties can always be deposed. See
      FRCP and ARCP, Rules 30. Rules for out-of-
      state deponents vary. You may have to go
      to the defendant's home state for the
      deposition or pay to have him come to
      your state.
   b. Give appropriate notice. If a nonparty, a
      subpoena is required. The federal rules
      require reasonable notice. Many states
      have a set time period such as 10 days
      notice.
   c. He should seek a stipulation to continue
      the deposition date, which normally will
      be granted by opposing counsel. If a
      stipulation cannot be agreed to, he would
      need to seek a protective order. See FRCP
      and ARCP, Rules 14. See also FRCP and
      ARCP, Rules 26(c).
   d. FRCP, Rule 30, does not limit who may be
      deposed although Rule 30(a)(2)(A)
      requires leave of the court to conduct more
      than 10 depositions. Many states restrict
      depositions of nonparties. See, for
      example, ARCP, Rule 30.
   e. You may have to wait for his report to be
      prepared although all jurisdictions allow
      for the deposition of an expert witness.
      See FRCP and ARCP, Rules 26(b)(4).
2. a. Most states limit the number of
      interrogatories. Many states, however,
      with court-approved uniform inter-
      rogatories do not count them (or
      sometimes their subparts) against the
      total. Additional interrogatories may be
      served with leave of the court. The
      federal rules limit the number to 25. See
      FRCP, Rules 25 and 26(b)(2), and ARCP,
      Rule 33.1 (40 interrogatory limit).
   b. No. See FRCP, Rule 25, and ARCP, Rule 33.1.
   c. The same number. It is based on who is the
      party, not how many partners there are.
      The interrogatories are served on the
      partnership's attorney.
   d. For nonuniform interrogatories you
      generally have to leave enough space for
      the answer.

e. Any applicable ground will support an objection. Objections must be made with specificity. See FRCP, Rule 33, and ARCP, Rule 33.

f. Usually 30 or 40 days, unless served with the complaint. See FRCP, Rule 33 (30 days), and ARCP, Rule 33(a) (40 days).

3. a. File a request for production of documents. They may, however, be required to be disclosed pursuant to mandatory disclosure rules. See FRCP, Rules 34 and 45, and ARCP, Rule 34 and 45.

b. You would need a subpoena duces tecum. The party is usually under an obligation to obtain documents within the party's control to respond to a Rule 34 request. See FRCP, Rule 34, and ARCP, Rule 34.

c. You do not usually need court permission. If inspection of the premises is relevant to the lawsuit, a Rule 34 request is all that is needed. You do need to give reasonable notice and, generally, the time period for documents applies to inspection of property. See FRCP, Rule 34, and ARCP, Rule 34.

d. After researching the issue, and coming to the conclusion that the papers are relevant—and discoverable—attempts to negotiate disclosure of the papers with opposing counsel should be made. If negotiation is futile, a motion to compel discovery could be filed. Most courts require an affidavit of the attempts to resolve the discovery issue before a motion to compel is filed. See FRCP, Rule 37, and ARCP, Rule 37. If an order is obtained and not complied with, a motion for sanctions would be in order. See FRCP, Rule 34, and ARCP, Rule 37.

4. a. Many state courts and the federal courts have mandatory disclosure requirements. The information that must be disclosed, the timing of the disclosure, and the effect of failing to disclose vary. See FRCP, Rule 26, and ARCP, Rule 26.1.

b. Yes. You may also have a duty to disclose the expert's qualifications and opinions without being asked to do so. Most states allow, in addition to the party's deposition, that the deposition of experts be allowed without leave of the court. See FRCP, Rules 26(a)(2) and (b)(4), and ARCP, Rules 26.1(a)(6) and 26(b)(4).

c. Generally yes. The federal rules do not limit the number of requests for admission that can be made although local rules may

do so. The state courts vary widely. See FRCP, Rule 36, and ARCP, Rule 36.

# CHAPTER 5

## Practice Exam

1. C
2. A
3. D
4. D
5. C
6. A
7. D
8. B
9. D
10. memorandum of points and authorities
11. response; reply
12. motion papers
13. oral arguments
14. under advisement
15. minute entry
16. matter of law
17. motion to strike
18. summary judgment; partial motion for summary judgment
19. for leave to amend
20. for a more definite statement; to dismiss
21. to compel discovery
22. for protective order
23. for sanctions
24. for a pretrial conference
25. T
26. F
27. T
28. F
29. F
30. T
31. F
32. F
33. T
34. F
35. T
36. F
37. F
38. F
39. T
40. T
41. T
42. T
43. F
44. F
45. F
46. T
47. F

48. T
49. T
50. T

## Litigation Lingo

### DOWN
1. propound
2. amend
3. pretrial
4. scheduling
5. entry
6. sanctions
7. FRCP
8. response
9. summary
10. disclosure
11. advisement
12. claim
13. trial

### ACROSS
1. definite
2. compel
3. transcript
4. strike
5. admit
6. dismiss
8. reply
9. order
10. duces tecum
11. expert
12. production
13. minute
14. points
15. depose
16. motion
17. IME

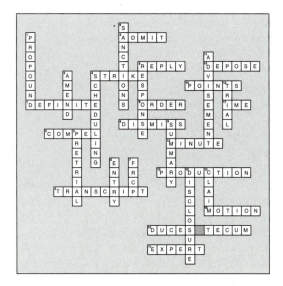

## Litigation Logistics

1. File a motion for partial summary judgment on the issue of immunity. See FRCP, Rule 56, and ARCP, Rule 56.

    In federal court you normally obtain the hearing date from the court's staff and serve notice of the hearing with the motion. Local rules modify how (and if) a hearing can be had. If no request for oral argument is made the court will enter its ruling based on the pleadings submitted. In Arizona, for example, you have 15 days after service of the motion to file your response. See FRCP, Rules 56 and 78, and ARCP, Rule 56.

2. If the answer is responsive it is not objectionable (not everybody has a detailed answer for every question). If you believe that it is obvious that the interrogatory should be able to be answered, you should consider a motion to compel (see answers to Litigation Logistics for Chapter 4).

    Motions might be made to dismiss for failure to state a claim; a motion for more definite statement (preferred) could be filed or a motion to strike could be considered. A careful reading (and proper research) might preclude the motion to strike option. See FRCP, Rule 12, and ARCP, Rule 12. The first two motions do not generally have a fixed time period for filing. If, however, you engage in discovery and otherwise move the case along, it may be difficult to later say you did not know what the counterclaim was about. See FRCP and ARCP, Rules 12 and 12(b)(6).

3. a. You could be ordered to appear for the I.M.E. if the opposing side filed a motion to compel and be required to pay the attorney's fees for the motion. If you refused to obey then really bad things can happen—including having your complaint dismissed! See FRCP and ARCP, Rule 37.

    b. It depends on when you discovered the school was part of a franchise. If a responsive pleading has not yet been filed leave of the court is not required and an amended complaint could be filed and served (but why didn't you know it was a franchise before the original complaint was filed?). If no responsive pleading is required, you may have a time limit to file an amended pleading. If a responsive pleading has been filed you normally require leave of the court. See FRCP and ARCP, Rule 15.

4. You would file a motion for partial summary judgment on the issue of negligence (often no easy task). States vary about whether oral argument is by right or at the discretion of the court. Federal courts are not obliged to grant oral argument. In Arizona, however, the rule states the court shall grant a hearing if a timely request is made. See FRCP and ARCP, Rule 56.

Most states allow for a scheduling conference to be held. Some are mandatory and others are set only at the request of a party or on the court's discretion. If you are having a problem with scheduling you could request a conference even if your rules do not specifically provide for one. See FRCP and ARCP, Rule 16. You could also file a motion for an order setting a discovery schedule. You should include the basis for why the motion is being filed and a proposed schedule for the court to consider.

# CHAPTER 6

## Practice Exam

1. D
2. B
3. C
4. A
5. D
6. B
7. C
8. A
9. B
10. C
11. B
12. D
13. A
14. D
15. C
16. B
17. D
18. A
19. D
20. B
21. mediation
22. arbitration; mini-trials
23. med-arb
24. summary jury trial
25. binding; nonbinding; *de novo*
26. mandatory
27. court-annexed; private
28. American Arbitration Association
29. voluntary
30. community; transformative
31. med-arb
32. summary jury trial
33. mini-trials
34. private judging; neutral expert fact-finding
35. ombudsmen
36. F
37. T
38. T
39. F
40. T
41. F
42. T
43. F
44. F
45. T
46. T
47. T
48. F
49. T
50. F
51. T
52. F
53. F
54. T
55. F
56. F
57. F
58. T
59. F
60. T
61. F
62. T
63. F
64. F
65. T
66. T
67. F
68. T
69. F
70. F
71. F
72. T
73. F
74. T
75. T
76. F
77. F
78. F
79. F
80. T
81. T
82. F
83. T
84. F
85. F
86. F
87. T

88. F
89. F
90. T
91. T
92. F
93. F
94. T
95. T
96. F
97. T
98. T
99. F
100. T
101. T
102. T
103. F
104. F
105. T
106. T
107. F

## Litigation Lingo

1. *de novo*
2. ombudsman
3. med-arb
4. transformative
5. binding
6. mediator
7. mini-trial
8. summary jury
9. arbitrator
10. annexed

## Litigation Logistics

1. a. If punitive damages can be sought, ADR would not appear appropriate. If only monetary damages are sought (and it would appear only the amount could be contested), ADR (arbitration) would be a viable alternative.
   b. Yes. Depending on what issues are being contested (i.e., is liability admitted?) all forms of ADR could be used. If only the amount of damages is contested either mediation or arbitration would be viable.
   c. Yes. Mediation would be best for this family dispute.
   d. Yes. Often construction contracts have mandatory arbitration clauses for disputes. Arbitration would be most appropriate.
   e. No. To be able to evict the tenant, you must have a court order.

2. a. In the Maricopa County Superior Court of Arizona all cases involving monetary damages of $50,000 or less are subject to mandatory arbitration. If nonmonetary damages are sought the case is not subject to mandatory arbitration.

   All cases with monetary damages of less than $50,000 damages are subject to mandatory arbitration.
   b. In the Maricopa County Superior Court of Arizona all court-annexed arbitrations require that an attorney (selected from a list of all Maricopa County attorneys) be the arbitrator.
   c. In the Maricopa County Superior Court of Arizona attorneys are selected at random irrespective of their specialty or experience (but they must have been an attorney for 5 years).
   d. In the Maricopa County Superior Court of Arizona the arbitrator selects the location for the hearing.
   e. In the Maricopa County Superior Court of Arizona, yes.

      Good cause accepted by the arbitrator.
   f. In the Maricopa County Superior Court of Arizona the Arizona Rules of Evidence apply.
   g. In the Maricopa County Superior Court of Arizona, yes.
   h. In the Maricopa County Superior Court of Arizona no court reporter is provided unless requested. A deposit is required to be made before the arbitrator selects a reporter.
   i. In the Maricopa County Superior Court of Arizona the award is to be made within 10 days from the conclusion of the hearing.
   j. In the Maricopa County Superior Court of Arizona an appeal must be made within 20 days after the filing of the award or the award becomes final.
   k. In the Maricopa County Superior Court of Arizona all appeals from arbitration are *de novo*.
   l. In the Maricopa County Superior Court of Arizona, no.
   m. In the Maricopa County Superior Court of Arizona if the appellant does not do at least 10 percent better at trial she is liable for taxable costs and attorney's fees to be determined by the trial judge.

# CHAPTER 7

## Practice Exam

1. D
2. B

3. C
4. B
5. C
6. A
7. D
8. D
9. B
10. A
11. B
12. B
13. D
14. C
15. A
16. C
17. C
18. trial setting
19. pretrial order
20. set and certificate of readiness
21. *in limine*
22. jury instructions
23. demonstrative
24. *voir dire*
25. peremptory challenge
26. findings of facts and conclusions of law
27. opening statements
28. *prima facie;* directed verdict
29. direct; cross
30. hostile
31. under the rule
32. leading
33. preponderance of the evidence
34. sandbagging
35. closing arguments
36. general; special
37. general verdict with written interrogatories
38. hung jury
39. poll the jury
40. new trial; judgment notwithstanding the verdict
41. remittitur
42. entry of judgment
43. lodge
44. statement of costs
45. F
46. F
47. T
48. T
49. T
50. F
51. F
52. T
53. F
54. T
55. T
56. F
57. T
58. T
59. T

60. F
61. T
62. F
63. T
64. T
65. F
66. F
67. F
68. F
69. T
70. T
71. F
72. F
73. F
74. T
75. T
76. T
77. F
78. T
79. F
80. T
81. F
82. T
83. T
84. F
85. T
86. F
87. F
88. F
89. T
90. T
91. T
92. F
93. F
94. F
95. T
96. T
97. T
98. F
99. F
100. T
101. T
102. T
103. F
104. T
105. F
106. F
107. T
108. T
109. T
110. F
111. F

## Litigation Lingo

1. affirmative defense
2. demonstrative evidence
3. opening statements

4. pretrial order
5. motion to set and certificate of readiness
6. rebuttal
7. motion *in limine*
8. *voir dire*
9. entry of judgment
10. motion for directed verdict
11. peremptory challenge
12. closing argument
13. findings of fact and conclusions of law
14. taxable costs
15. cross-examination
16. hostile witness
17. form of judgment
18. *prima facie* case
19. special verdict
20. hung jury
21. leading question
22. preponderance of the evidence
23. motion for judgment notwithstanding the verdict
24. general verdict with written interrogatories
25. remittitur
26. polls the jury

## Litigation Logistics

1. Although states vary in their requirements, most provide a mechanism to notify the court that one side, at least, thinks it is ready for trial. A list of witnesses and exhibits might be required along with a certificate of readiness for trial. In federal court the trial date is usually set at, or shortly after, the pretrial conference. See FRCP and ARCP, Rule 16.
   a. Normally yes. Although they may be called by different names most courts enter orders, or sometimes minute entries, setting the various dates for completing pretrial matters including the dates for motions *in limine,* jury instructions, the latest date for dispositive motions to be filed, exhibits to be marked, etc.
      1. When ordered by the court.
      2. Pretrial statements generally differ from pretrial orders. Check your state and local rules carefully.
   b. General jury instructions regarding juror conduct, burden of proof, credibility, stipulations and the like.
      Specific instructions regarding the legal obligations of each party, defenses, mode and manner of calculating damages, etc.
      1. When required by the pretrial order or minute entry setting the respective dates, generally a week or so prior to trial.

2. Many states have standard jury instructions that have been approved by the courts or created by the state or local bar associations. If standard instructions are court approved getting a "custom" instruction for an area covered by the standard could be difficult. In Arizona, for example, we have what are called RAJIs (Recommended Arizona Jury Instructions) that cover negligence, fault, medical malpractice, product liability, bad faith, premises liability, contracts, eminent domain, employment law, and commercial torts. Many books have been written that provide sample jury instructions covering the whole gambit of jury trials, including criminal trials.

c. Yes.
   1. All exhibits should have been exchanged if there are mandatory disclosure requirements. In any event the court normally sets a date for the exhibits to be brought to the court and marked by the clerk, at least a day or more before trial is to begin. Always check with the court's staff to see if the judge wants his own copy of the exhibits to refer to at trial. In many states it is possible to provide the jurors with selected exhibits—check your local rules and the judge's preferences.
   2. You can often get the other party to stipulate to the authenticity and admissibility of many exhibits. The rules of evidence have been codified in federal court, see the Federal Rules of Evidence for United States Courts. Many states pattern their rules of evidence after the federal rules, just as many do their rules of procedure.
   3. Almost always.

2. a. Someone predisposed to your client's position, a conservative, elderly, non- or very moderate drinker, for example.
   b. Each state varies. For a jury of eight, each side may have two or four preemptory challenges. In federal court each party has three preemptory challenges. No reason need be given to challenge a juror but race cannot be a factor. See FRCP and ARCP, Rule 47. Criminal rules generally allow for more preemptory challenges (often a jury of twelve is required).
   c. Most states allow the judge to determine how *voir dire* will be conducted. Some

judges will ask accepted proposed questions from counsel; others allow counsel to conduct all *voir dire* except background questions. Many judges allow *voir dire* by counsel but set time limits or limit the areas of inquiry. See FRCP and ARCP, Rule 47.

d. Only those questions reasonably expected to uncover bias or prejudice.

e. Depends. If you know the judge, and your case, a court trial may be the best way to go. If costs, including attorney's fees, represent a true hardship on the client, some savings may be had with a trial to the court. If your case is more "legal" than factual or you have an "unattractive" case you may want a judge to decide rather than a jury. In most instances a trial to the court can only occur by stipulation or when a jury trial is not allowed.

Findings of fact and conclusions of law are required only in a trial to the court. Even then, in many states, they are not required if no request for them is made by counsel. The federal rules require findings of fact and law without the request of a party. See FRCP and ARCP, Rule 52.

f. Special verdicts are not often used in the average jury trial. In complex cases or those where the law is unsettled they are more common. Using a special verdict is solely within the discretion of the trial judge. See FRCP and ARCP, Rule 49.

3. A motion for a directed verdict by the defendant is usually made at the close of the plaintiff's case. A motion by the plaintiff is made at the close of defendant's case. Such a motion must be made before the case is submitted to the jury. Motions for a directed verdict are now generally referred to as a motion for judgment as a matter of law. See FRCP and ARCP, Rule 50.

a. There is no legally sufficient evidentiary basis for the jury to find in favor of the other party. See FRCP and ARCP, Rule 50.

b. Move for a new trial. See FRCP and ARCP, Rule 59.

The time period varies but is usually 10 to 20 days after entry of judgment (which can take a substantial period of time if all procedural avenues are followed). See FRCP and ARCP, Rule 50 (10 days in federal court; 15 days in Arizona).

c. Move for a judgment as a matter of law after the verdict is returned (also known as a judgment notwithstanding the verdict or

judgment n.o.v.). This motion is often combined with a motion for a new trial. See FRCP and ARCP, Rule 50.

Usually the same as for a motion for a new trial. Care should be taken if both motions are not made simultaneously—filing one may not extend the time to file the other. See FRCP and ARCP, Rules 50 and 59.

d. File a motion to amend the judgment (a remittitur decreases the award; an additur increases the award). Now generally filed as part of a motion for a new trial. If the party against whom remittitur is sought refuses to accept the judge's proposed decrease in the award, the motion for a new trial is granted. See FRCP, Rule 59, and ARCP, Rule 59(i).

4. a. Have the judgment signed and filed with the clerk of the court. Some states require the judge to sign the judgment, others allow the clerk to do so. When the judgment is signed and properly docketed in the clerk of court's office it is said to be entered. Time periods for post-trial motions usually run from the date of entry of judgment. See FRCP, Rules 58 and 79, and ARCP, Rules 54, 58, and 77.

b. Within the prescribed period of time after entry of judgment, generally 20 or 30 days. The filing of various post-trial motions may extend the appeal period until those motions are resolved. Most states and the various federal circuits have appellate rules setting the time period for appeal of a final judgment. Always check the appellate court rules for the proper time period.

c. By court rule. See FRCP and ARCP, Rule 54. An objection to the form of judgment submitted to the court by the opposing party is generally available. Having the parties submit forms of judgment is frowned on in federal court and objections to the form prepared by the judge are not normally well received unless to correct clerical errors. See FRCP and ARCP, Rule 58(d).

d. Each state defines what are taxable costs, often by statute, sometimes by rule. Filing fees, service of process costs, fees for subpoenas, witness fees (generally minimal with some mileage provision; not expert witness fees), necessary copy costs, and the like are often allowed to the prevailing party as taxable costs. In some states, although not federal court, the judgment is not entered until costs (and sometimes attorney's fees) are determined. See FRCP and ARCP, Rule 58.

e. It depends. In most cases attorney's fees are allowed only when provided for by statute or by written agreement (a contractual provision, for example). An application for attorney's fees must be filed, the requirements for which vary greatly. An opportunity for the opposing party to object and/or question the amount of the fee request is allowed.

5. a. Cross-examination is usually limited to the subject matter brought out on direct examination as well as matters relating to the witness's credibility. The court may allow additional, relevant questions. Check your rules and statutes carefully! See Federal Rules of Evidence, Rule 611.

b. Redirect examination is generally limited to clarifying any responses developed in cross-examination. The judge has considerable discretion in controlling the mode and manner of examination of witnesses.

c. Questions can be asked on any relevant matter. Certain matters can be excluded if the court determines its disclosure would be unduly prejudicial or if it is merely repetitive. Some relevant matters, such as subsequent remedial matters, are excluded on public policy grounds. See Federal Rules of Evidence, Rules 401 through 415.

# CHAPTER 8

## Practice Exam

1. A
2. B
3. C
4. A
5. D
6. D
7. A
8. C
9. B
10. D
11. D
12. judgment
13. judgment creditor; judgment debtor
14. stay; supersedes
15. execution
16. debtor's exam
17. lien; judgment lien
18. writ of execution
19. writ of garnishment
20. fraudulent conveyance
21. reversible; harmless
22. cross-appeal
23. interlocutory
24. appellant; notice of appeal; appellee
25. opening; authorities; responding; reply
26. mandate
27. T
28. F
29. T
30. T
31. T
32. T
33. F
34. T
35. F
36. F
37. T
38. T
39. F
40. T
41. T
42. T
43. F
44. F
45. F
46. T
47. T
48. T
49. F
50. T
51. F
52. F
53. T
54. F
55. T
56. F
57. T
58. F
59. F
60. F
61. F
62. T
63. T
64. T
65. F
66. F
67. F
68. T
69. T
70. F
71. F
72. T
73. F
74. F
75. T
76. T

## Litigation Lingo

1. interlocutory
2. stay
3. supersedes bond
4. garnish
5. fraudulent conveyance
6. reversible
7. appellee
8. reply
9. mandate
10. execution
11. proof
12. examination
13. lien
14. authorities

## Litigation Logistics

1. If the driver had insurance. If not you would want to check to see that he had nonexempt assets. If there was insurance you would want to know if it indemnified for punitive damages (most do not).

   If uninsured, get a judgment. You would have to review the applicable garnishment laws and follow the procedures to the letter.

2. After any mandatory waiting periods the corporation would need to file a supersedes bond.
   a. File a notice of appeal
   b. Check the applicable rules of appellate procedure—often 30 days after the appeal is at issue (all fees paid).
   c. Check the applicable rules of appellate procedure—often 25 to 30 pages.
   d. Check the applicable rules of appellate procedure—usually the rules are very specific.
   e. Check the applicable rules of appellate procedure—many times one or three.

3. You could schedule a debtor's exam, record the judgment as a lien against the debtor's real property in the county where the judgment was recorded, begin execution on the judgment.

   You would get a writ of execution to have the sheriff seize and sell the property.
   1. Normally an automobile may be claimed as exempt up to a certain equity value, often only $1,500 to $2,500.
   2. As required by state law.
   3. Usually yes if the property was transferred without valuable consideration.

4. Perhaps.
   a. The procedures of the federal bankruptcy court. All actions are initially automatically stayed by the filing of a bankruptcy petition.
   b. Do the debtor's examination according to bankruptcy rules.
   c. Record the judgment with the county recorder in the county where the building is located.

      Obtain a writ of execution for the sale of real property.

5. File an interlocutory appeal (in some states a "special action").

   Your options would be the same as the above.

# APPENDIX B

## *Federal Rules of Civil Procedure for the United States District Courts*

**As Amended through December 1, 1997**

**I.  Scope of Rules—One Form of Action.**

### Rule 1. Scope and Purpose of Rules.

These Rules govern the procedure in the United States district courts in all suits of a civil nature whether cognizable as cases at law or in equity or in admiralty, with the exceptions stated in Rule 81. They shall be construed and administered to secure the just, speedy, and inexpensive determination of every action.

### Rule 2. One Form of Action.

There shall be one form of action to be known as "civil action."

**II.  Commencement of Action; Service of Process, Pleadings, Motions and Orders.**

### Rule 3. Commencement of Action.

A civil action is commenced by filing a complaint with the court.

### Rule 4. Summons.

**(a) Form.** The summons shall be signed by the clerk, bear the seal of the court, identify the court and the parties, be directed to the defendant, and state the name and address of the plaintiff's attorney, or, if unrepresented, of the plaintiff. It shall also state the time within which the defendant must appear and defend, and notify the defendant that failure to do so will result in a judgment by default against the defendant for the relief demanded in the complaint. The court may allow a summons to be amended.

**(b) Issuance.** Upon or after filing the complaint, the plaintiff may present a summons to the clerk for signature and seal. If the summons is in proper form, the clerk shall sign, seal, and issue it to the plaintiff for service on the defendant. A summons, or a copy of the summons if addressed to multiple defendants, shall be issued for each defendant to be served.

**(c) Service with Complaint; by Whom Made.**

(1) A summons shall be served together with a copy of the complaint. The plaintiff is responsible for service of a summons and complaint within the time allowed under subdivision (m) and shall furnish the person effecting service with the necessary copies of the summons and complaint.

(2) Service may be effected by any person who is not a party and who is at least 18 years of age. At the request of the plaintiff, however, the court may direct that service be effected by a United States marshal, deputy

United States marshal, or other person or officer specially appointed by the court for that purpose. Such an appointment must be made when the plaintiff is authorized to proceed in forma pauperis pursuant to 19 U.S.C. §1915 or is authorized to proceed as a seaman under 18 U.S.C. §1916.

**(d) Waiver of Service; Duty to Save Costs of Service; Request to Waive.**

(1) A defendant who waives service of a summons does not thereby waive any objection to the venue or to the jurisdiction of the court over the person of the defendant.

(2) An individual, corporation, or association that is subject to service under subdivision (e), (f), or (h) and that receives notice of an action in the manner provided in this paragraph has a duty to avoid unnecessary costs of serving the summons. To avoid costs, the plaintiff may notify such a defendant of the commencement of the action and request that the defendant waive service of a summons.

The notice and request

(A) shall be in writing and shall be addressed directly to the defendant, if an individual, or else to an office or managing or general agent (or other agent authorized by appointment or law to receive service of process) of a defendant subject to service under subdivision (h);

(B) shall be dispatched through first-class mail or other reliable means;

(C) shall be accompanied by a copy of the complaint and shall identify the court in which it has been filed;

(D) shall inform the defendant, by means of a text prescribed in an official form promulgated pursuant to Rule 84, of the consequences of compliance and of a failure to comply with the request;

(E) shall set forth the date on which the request is sent;

(F) shall allow the defendant a reasonable time to return the waiver, which shall be at least 30 days from the date on which the request is sent, or 60 days from that date if the defendant is addressed outside any judicial district of the United States; and

(G) shall provide the defendant with an extra copy of the notice and request, as well as a prepaid means of compliance in writing.

If a defendant located within the United States fails to comply with a request for waiver made by a plaintiff located within the United States, the court shall impose the costs subsequently incurred in effecting service on the defendant unless good cause for the failure be shown.

(3) A defendant that, before being served with process, timely returns a waiver so requested is not required to serve an answer to the complaint until 60 days after the date on which the request for waiver of service was sent, or 90 days after that date if the defendant was addressed outside any judicial district of the United States.

(4) When the plaintiff files a waiver of service with the court, the action shall proceed, except as provided in paragraph (3), as if a summons and complaint had been served at the time of filing the waiver, and no proof of service shall be required.

(5) The costs to be imposed on a defendant under paragraph (2) for failure to comply with a request to waiver service of a summons shall include the costs subsequently incurred in effecting service under subdivision (e), (f) or (h), together with the costs, including a reasonable attorney's fee, of any motion required to collect the costs of service.

**(e) Service Upon Individuals Within a Judicial District of the United States.** Unless otherwise provided by federal law, service upon an individual from whom a waiver has not been obtained and filed, other than an infant or an incompetent person, may be effected in any judicial district of the United States:

(1) pursuant to the law of the state in which the district court is located, or in which service is effected, for the service of a summons upon the defendant in an action brought in the courts of general jurisdiction of the State; or

(2) by delivering a copy of the summons and of the complaint to the individual personally or by leaving copies thereof at the individual's dwelling house or usual place of abode with some person of suitable age and discretion then residing therein or by delivering a copy of the summons and of the complaint to an agent authorized by appointment or by law to receive service of process.

**(f) Service Upon Individuals in a Foreign Country.** Unless otherwise provided by federal law, service upon an individual from whom a waiver has not been obtained and filed, other than an infant or an incompetent person, may be effected in a place not within any judicial district of the United States:

(1) by an internationally agreed means reasonably calculated to give notice, such as those means authorized by the Hague Con-

vention on the Service Abroad of Judicial and Extrajudicial Documents; or

(2) if there is no internationally agreed means of service or the applicable international agreement allows other means of service, provided that service is reasonably calculated to give notice:

(A) in the manner prescribed by the law of the foreign country for service in that country in an action in any of its courts of general jurisdiction; or

(B) as directed by the foreign authority in response to a letter rogatory or letter of request; or

(C) unless prohibited by the law of the foreign country, by

(i) delivery to the individual personally of a copy of the summons and the complaint; or

(ii) any form of mail requiring a signed receipt, to be addressed and dispatched by the clerk of the court to the party to be served; or

(3) by other means not prohibited by international agreement as may be directed by the court.

**(g) Service Upon Infants and Incompetent Persons.** Service upon an infant or an incompetent person in a judicial district of the United States shall be effected in the manner prescribed by the law of the state in which the service is made for the service of summons or other like process upon any such defendant in an action brought in the courts of general jurisdiction of that state. Service upon an infant or an incompetent person in a place not within any judicial district of the United States shall be effected in the manner prescribed by paragraph (2)(A) or (2)(B) of subdivision (f) or by such means as the court may direct.

**(h) Service Upon Corporations and Associations.** Unless otherwise provided by federal law, service upon a domestic or foreign corporation or upon a partnership or other incorporated association that is subject to suit under a common name, and from which a waiver of service has not been obtained and filed, shall be effected:

(1) in a judicial district of the United States in the manner prescribed for individuals by subdivision (e)(1), or by delivering a copy of the summons and of the complaint to an officer, a managing or general agent, or to any other agent authorized by appointment or by law to receive service of process and, if the agent is one authorized by statute to receive

service and the statute so requires, by also mailing a copy to the defendant, or

(2) in a place not within any judicial district of the United States in any manner prescribed for individuals by subdivision (f) except personal delivery as provided in paragraph (2)(C)(i) thereof.

**(i) Service Upon the United States and Its Agencies, Corporations or Officers.**

(1) Service upon the United States shall be effected

(A) by delivering a copy of the summons and complaint to the United States attorney for the district in which the action is brought or to an assistant United States attorney or clerical employee designated by the United States attorney in a writing filed with the clerk of the court or by sending a copy of the summons and of the complaint by registered or certified mail addressed to the civil process clerk at the office of the United States Attorney and

(B) by also sending a copy of the summons and complaint by registered or certified mail to the Attorney General of the United States at Washington, District of Columbia, and

(C) in any action attacking the validity of an order of an officer or agency of the United States not made a party, by also sending a copy of the summons and complaint by registered or certified mail to the officer or agency.

(2) Service upon an officer, agency or corporation of the United States shall be effected by serving the United States in the manner prescribed by paragraph (1) of this subdivision and also by sending a copy of the summons and of the complaint by registered or certified mail to the officer, agency or corporation.

(3) The court shall allow a reasonable time for service of process under this subdivision for the purpose of curing the failure to serve multiple officers, agencies or corporations of the United States if the plaintiff has effected service on either the United States Attorney or the Attorney General of the United States.

**(j) Service Upon Foreign, State or Local Governments.**

(1) Service upon a foreign state or a political subdivision, agency or instrumentality thereof shall be effected pursuant to 28 U.S.C. §1608.

(2) Service upon a state, municipal corporation or other governmental organization

subject to suit shall be effected by delivering a copy of the summons and of the complaint to its chief executive officer or by serving the summons and complaint in the manner prescribed by the law of that state for the service of summons or other like process upon any such defendant.

**(k) Territorial Limits of Effective Service.**

(1) Service of a summons or filing a waiver of service is effective to establish jurisdiction over the person of a defendant

(A) who could be subjected to the jurisdiction of a court of general jurisdiction in the state in which the district court is located, or

(B) who is a party joined under Rule 14 or rule 19 and is served at a place within a judicial district of the United States and not more than 100 miles from the place from which the summons issues, or

(C) who is subject to the federal interpleader jurisdiction under 28 U.S.C. §1335, or

(D) when authorized by a statute of the United States.

(2) If the exercise of jurisdiction is consistent with the Constitution and laws of the United States, serving a summons or filing a waiver of service is also effective, with respect to claims arising under federal law, to establish personal jurisdiction over the person of any defendant who is not subject to the jurisdiction of the courts of general jurisdiction of any state.

**(l) Proof of Service.** If service is not waived, the person effecting service shall make proof thereof to the court. If service is made by a person other than a United States marshal or deputy United States marshal, the person shall make affidavit thereof. Proof of service in a place not within any judicial district of the United States shall, if effected under paragraph (1) of subdivision (f), be made pursuant to the applicable treaty or convention, and shall, if effected under paragraph (2) or (3) thereof, include a receipt signed by the addressee or other evidence of delivery to the addressee satisfactory to the court. Failure to make proof of service does not affect the validity of the service. The court may allow proof of service to be amended.

**(m) Time Limit for Service.** If service of the summons and complaint is not made upon a defendant within 120 days after the filing of the complaint, the court, upon motion or on its own initiative after notice to the plaintiff, shall dismiss the action without prejudice as to that defendant or direct that service be ef-

fected within a specified time; provided that if the plaintiff shows good cause for the failure, the court shall extend the time for service for an appropriate period. This subdivision does not apply to service in a foreign country pursuant to subdivision (f) or (j)(1).

**(n) Seizure of Property; Service of Summons Not Feasible.**

(1) If a statute of the United States so provides, the court may assert jurisdiction over property. Notice to claimants of the property shall then be sent in the manner provided by the statute or by service of a summons under this Rule.

(2) Upon a showing that personal jurisdiction over a defendant cannot, in the district where the action is brought, be obtained with reasonable efforts by service of summons in any manner authorized by this Rule, the court may assert jurisdiction over any of the defendant's assets found within the district by seizing the assets under the circumstances and in the manner provided by the law of the State in which the district court is located.

### Rule 4.1. Service of Other Process.

**(a) Generally.** Process other than a summons as provided in Rule 4 or subpoena as provided in Rule 45 shall be served by a United States marshal, a deputy United States marshal or a person specially appointed for that purpose, who shall make proof of service as provided in Rule 4(l). The process may be served anywhere within the territorial limits of the State in which the district court is located, and, when authorized by a statute of the United States, beyond the territorial limits of that State.

**(b) Enforcement of Orders; Commitment for Civil Contempt.** An order of civil commitment of a person held to be in contempt of a decree or injunction issued to enforce the laws of the United States may be served and enforced in any district. Other orders in civil contempt proceedings shall be served in the State in which the court issuing the order to be enforced is located or elsewhere within the United States if not more than 100 miles from the place at which the order to be enforced was issued.

### Rule 5. Service and Filing of Pleadings and Other Papers.

**(a) Service: When Required.** Except as otherwise provided in these rules, every order required by its terms to be served, every pleading subsequent to the original complaint unless the court otherwise orders because of numerous defendants, every paper relating to discovery required to be served upon a party unless the court otherwise orders, every written motion other than one which may be heard ex parte, and every written notice, appearance, demand, offer of judgment, designation of record on appeal, and similar paper shall be served upon each of the parties. No service need be made on parties in default for failure to appear except that pleadings asserting new or additional claims for relief against them shall be served upon them in the manner provided for service of summons in Rule 4.

In an action begun by seizure of property, in which no person need be or is named as defendant, any service required to be made prior to the filing of an answer, claim, or appearance shall be made upon the person having custody or possession of the property at the time of its seizure.

**(b) Same: How Made.** Whenever under these rules service is required or permitted to be made upon a party represented by an attorney, the service shall be made upon the attorney unless service upon the party is ordered by the court. Service upon the attorney or upon a party shall be made by delivering a copy to the attorney or party or by mailing it to the attorney or party at the attorney's or party's last-known address or, if no address is known, by leaving it with the clerk of the court. Delivery of a copy within this rule means: handing it to the attorney or to the party; or leaving it at the attorney's or party's office with a clerk or other person in charge thereof; or, if there is no one in charge, leaving it in a conspicuous place therein; or, if the office is closed or the person to be served has no office, leaving it at the person's dwelling house or usual place of abode with some person of suitable age and discretion then residing therein. Service by mail is complete upon mailing.

**(c) Same: Numerous Defendants.** In any action in which there are unusually large numbers of defendants, the court, upon motion or of its own initiative, may order that service of the pleadings of the defendants and replies thereto need not be made as between the defendants and that any cross-claim, counterclaim or matter constituting an avoidance or affirmative defense contained therein shall be deemed to be denied or avoided by all other parties and that the filing of any such plead-

ing and service thereof upon the plaintiff constitutes due notice of it to the parties. A copy of every such order shall be served upon the parties in such manner and form as the court directs.

**(d) Filing; Certificate of Service.** All papers after the complaint required to be served upon a party, together with a certificate of service, shall be filed with the court within a reasonable time after service, but the court may on motion of a party or on its own initiative order that depositions upon oral examination and interrogatories, requests for documents, requests for admission, and answers and responses thereto not be filed unless on order of the court or for use in the proceeding.

**(e) Filing with the Court Defined.** The filing of papers with the court as required by these Rules shall be made by filing them with the clerk of the court, except that the judge may permit the papers to be filed with the judge, in which event the judge shall note thereon the filing date and forthwith transmit them to the office of the clerk. A court may by local rule permit papers to be filed, signed or verified by electronic means that are consistent with technical standards, if any, which establishes the Judicial Conference of the United States. A paper filed by electronic means in compliance with a local rule constitutes a written paper for the purpose of applying these Rules. The clerk shall not refuse to accept for filing any paper presented for that purpose solely because it is not presented in proper form as required by these Rules or by any local rules or practices.

### Rule 6. Time.

**(a) Computation.** In computing any period of time prescribed or allowed by these Rules, by the local rules of any district court, by order of court, or by any applicable statute, the day of the act, event or default from which the designated period of time begins to run shall not be included. The last day of the period so computed shall be included. The last day of the period so computed shall be included, unless it is a Saturday, a Sunday or a legal holiday or, when the act to be done is the filing of a paper in court, a day on which weather or other conditions have made the office of the clerk of the district court inaccessible, in which event the period runs until the end of the next day which is not one of the aforementioned days. When the period of time prescribed or allowed is less than 11 days, intermediate Saturdays, Sundays and legal holidays shall be excluded in the computation. As used in this Rule and in Rule 77(c), "legal holiday" includes New Year's Day, Birthday of Martin Luther King, Jr., Washington's Birthday, Memorial Day, Independence Day, Labor Day, Columbus Day, Veterans Day, Thanksgiving Day, Christmas Day and any other day appointed as a holiday by the President or the Congress of the United States or by the state in which the district court is held.

**(b) Enlargement.** When by these Rules or by a notice given thereunder or by order of court an act is required or allowed to be done at or within a specified time, the court for cause shown may at any time in its discretion (1) with or without notice or notice order the period enlarged if request therefor is made before the expiration of the period originally prescribed or as extended by a previous order, or (2) upon motion made after the expiration of the specified period permit the act to be done where the failure to act was the result of excusable neglect; but it may not extend the time for taking any action under Rules 50(b) and (c)(2), 52(b), 59(b), (d) and (e), 60(b) and 74(a), except to the extent and under the conditions stated in them.

**(c) Unaffected by Expiration of Term.** Rescinded Feb. 28, 1966, eff. July 1, 1966.

**(d) For Motions - Affidavits.** A written motion, other than one which may be heard ex parte, and notice of the hearing thereof shall be served not later than 5 days before the time specified for the hearing, unless a different period is fixed by these Rules or by order of the court. Such an order may for cause shown be made on ex parte application. When a motion is supported by affidavit, the affidavit shall be served with the motion; and, except as otherwise provided in Rule 59(c), opposing affidavits may be served not later than 1 day before the hearing, unless the court permits them to be served at some other time.

**(e) Additional Time After Service by Mail.** Whenever a party has the right or is required to do some act or take some proceedings within a prescribed period after the service of a notice or other paper upon the party and the notice or paper is served upon the party by mail, 3 days shall be added to the prescribed period.

**III.** **Pleadings and Motions.**

### Rule 7. Pleadings Allowed; Form of Motions.

**(a) Pleadings.** There shall be a complaint and an answer; a reply to a counterclaim denominated as such; an answer to a cross-claim, if the answer contains a cross-claim; a third-party complaint, if a person who was not an original party is summoned under the provisions of Rule 14; and a third-party answer, if a third-party complaint is served. No other pleading shall be allowed, except that the court may order a reply to an answer or a third-party answer.

**(b) Motion and Other Papers.**

(1) An application to the court for an order shall be by motion which, unless made during a hearing or trial, shall be made in writing, shall state with particularity the grounds therefor, and shall set forth the relief or order sought. The requirement of writing is fulfilled if the motion is stated in a written notice of the hearing of the motion.

(2) The Rules applicable to captions and other matters of form of pleadings apply to all motions and other papers provided for by these Rules.

(3) All motions shall be signed in accordance with Rule 11.

**(c) Demurrers, Pleas, Etc., Abolished.** Demurrers, pleas and exceptions for insufficiency of a pleading shall not be used.

### Rule 8. General Rules of Pleading.

**(a) Claims for Relief.** A pleading which sets forth a claim for relief, whether an original claim, counterclaim, cross-claim or third-party claim, shall contain (1) a short and plain statement of the grounds upon which the court's jurisdiction depends, unless the court already has jurisdiction and the claim needs no new grounds of jurisdiction to support it, (2) a short and plain statement of the claim showing that the pleader is entitled to relief, and (3) a demand for judgment for the relief the pleader seeks. Relief in the alternative or of several different types may be demanded.

**(b) Defenses; Forms of Denials.** A party shall state in short and plain terms the party's defenses to each claim asserted and shall admit or deny the averments upon which the adverse party relies. If a party is without knowledge or information sufficient to form a belief as to the truth of an averment, a party shall so state and this has the effect of a denial.

Denials shall fairly meet the substance of the averments denied. When a pleader intends in good faith to deny only a part or a qualification of an averment, the pleader shall specify so much of it as is true and material and shall deny only the remainder. Unless the pleader intends in good faith to controvert all the averments of the preceding pleading, the pleader may make denials as specific denials of designated averments or paragraphs or may generally deny all of the averments except such designated averments or paragraphs as the pleader expressly admits; but, when the pleader does so intend to controvert all of its averments, including averments of the grounds upon which the court's jurisdiction depends, the pleader may do so by general denial subject to the obligations set forth in Rule 11.

**(c) Affirmative Defenses.** In pleading to a preceding pleading, a party shall set forth affirmatively accord and satisfaction, arbitration and award, assumption of risk, contributory negligence, discharge in bankruptcy, duress, estoppel, failure of consideration, fraud, illegality, injury by fellow servant, laches, license, payment, release, res judicata, statute of frauds, statute of limitations, waiver and any other matter constituting an avoidance or affirmative defense. When a party has mistakenly designated a defense as a counterclaim or a counterclaim as a defense, the court on terms, if justice so requires, shall treat the pleading as if there had been a proper designation.

**(d) Effect of Failure to Deny.** Averments in a pleading to which a responsive pleading is required, other than those as to the amount of damage, are admitted when not denied in the responsive pleading. Averments in a pleading to which no responsive pleading is required or permitted shall be taken as denied or avoided.

**(e) Pleading to Be Concise and Direct; Consistency.**

(1) Each averment of a pleading shall be simple, concise and direct. No technical forms of pleadings or motions are required.

(2) A party may set forth two or more statements of a claim or defense alternately or hypothetically, either in one court or defense or in separate counts or defenses. When two or more statements are made in the alternative and one of them if made independently would be sufficient, the pleading is not made insufficient by the sufficiency of one or more of the alternative statements. A party may also state as many separate claims or defenses as the party has regardless of consistency and whether based on legal, equitable or maritime grounds. All statements shall be made subject to the obligations set forth in Rule 11.

**(f) Construction of Pleadings.** All pleadings shall be so construed as to do substantial justice.

## Rule 9. Pleading Special Matters.

**(a) Capacity.** It is not necessary to aver the capacity of a party to sue or be sued or the authority of a party to sue or be sued in a representative capacity or the legal existence of an organized association of persons that is made a party, except to the extent required to show the jurisdiction of the court. When a party desires to raise an issue as to the legal existence of any party or the capacity of any party to sue or be sued or the authority of a party to sue or be sued in a representative capacity, the party desiring to raise the issue shall do so by specific negative averment, which shall include such supporting particulars as are peculiarly within the pleader's knowledge.

**(b) Fraud, Mistake, Condition of the Mind.** In all averments of fraud or mistake, the circumstances constituting fraud or mistake shall be stated with particularity. Malice, intent, knowledge and other condition of mind of a person may be averred generally.

**(c) Conditions Precedent.** In pleading the performance or occurrence of conditions precedent, it is sufficient to aver generally that all conditions precedent have been performed or have occurred. A denial of performance or occurrence shall be made specifically and with particularity.

**(d) Official Document or Act.** In pleading an official document or official act, it is sufficient to aver that the document was issued or the act done in compliance with law.

**(e) Judgment.** In pleading a judgment or decision of a domestic or foreign court, judicial or quasi-judicial tribunal, or of a board or officer, it is sufficient to aver the judgment or decision without setting forth matter showing jurisdiction to render it.

**(f) Time and Place.** For the purpose of testing the sufficiency of a pleading, averments of time and place are material and shall be considered like all other averments of material matter.

**(g) Special Damage.** When items of special damage are claimed, they shall be specifically stated.

**(h) Admiralty and Maritime Claims.** A pleading or count setting forth a claim for relief within the admiralty and maritime jurisdiction that is also within the jurisdiction of the district court on some other ground may contain a statement identifying the claim as an admiralty or maritime claim for the purposes of Rules 14(c), 38(e), 82, and the Supplemental Rules for Certain Admiralty and Maritime Claims. If the claim is cognizable only in admiralty, it is an admiralty or maritime claim for those purposes whether so identified or not. The amendment of a pleading to add or withdraw an identifying statement is governed by the principles of Rule 15. A case that includes an admiralty or maritime claim within this subdivision is an admiralty case within 28 U.S.C. §1292(a)(3).

## Rule 10.  Form of Pleadings.

**(a) Caption; Names of Parties.** Every pleading shall contain a caption setting forth the name of the court, the title of the action, the file number and a designation as in Rule 7(a). In the complaint the title of the action shall include the names of all parties, but in other pleadings it is sufficient to state the name of the first party on each side with an appropriate indication of other parties.

**(b) Paragraphs; Separate Statements.** All averments of claim or defense shall be made in numbered paragraphs, the contents of each of which shall be limited as far as practicable to a statement of a single set of circumstances; and a paragraph may be referred to by number in all succeeding pleadings. Each claim founded upon a separate transaction or occurrence and each defense other than denials shall be stated in a separate count or defense whenever a separation facilitates the clear presentation of the matters set forth.

**(c) Adoption by Reference; Exhibits.** Statements in a pleading may be adopted by reference in a different part of the same pleading or in another pleading or in any motion. A copy of any written instrument which is an exhibit to a pleading is a part thereof for all purposes.

## Rule 11. Signing of Pleadings, Motions and Other Papers; Representations to Court; Sanctions.

**(a) Signature.** Every pleading, written motion and other paper shall be signed by at least one attorney of record in the attorney's individual name, or if the party is not represented by an attorney, shall be signed by the party. Each paper shall state the signer's address and telephone number, if any. Except when otherwise specifically provided by rule or statute, pleadings need not be verified or accompanied by affidavit. An unsigned paper shall be stricken unless omission of the signature is corrected promptly after being called to the attention of the attorney or party.

**(b) Representations to Court.** By presenting to the court (whether by signing, filing, submitting or later advocating) a pleading, written motion or other paper, an attorney or unrepresented party is certifying that to the best of the person's knowledge, information and belief, formed after an inquiry reasonable under the circumstances,

(1) it is not being presented for any improper purpose, such as to harass or to cause unnecessary delay or needless increase in the cost of litigation;

(2) the claims, defenses and other legal contentions therein are warranted by existing law or by a non-frivolous argument for the extension, modification or reversal of existing law or the establishment of new law;

(3) the allegations and other factual contentions have evidentiary support or, if specifically so identified, are likely to have evidentiary support after a reasonable opportunity for further investigation or discovery; and

(4) the denials of factual contentions are warranted on the evidence or, if specifically so identified, are reasonably based on a lack of information or belief.

**(c) Sanctions.** If, after notice and a reasonable opportunity to respond, the court determines that subdivision (b) has been violated, the court may, subject to the conditions stated below, impose an appropriate sanction upon the attorneys, law firms or parties that have violated subdivision (b) or are responsible for the violation.

(1) *How Initiated.*

(A) *By Motion.* A motion for sanctions under this Rule shall be made separately from other motions or requests and shall describe the specific conduct alleged to violate subdivision (b). It shall be served as provided in Rule 5, but shall not be filed with or presented to the court unless, within 21 days after service of the motion (or such other period as the court may prescribe), the challenged paper, claim, defense, contention, allegation or denial is not withdrawn or appropriately corrected. If warranted, the court may award to the party prevailing on the motion the reasonable expenses and attorney's fees incurred in presenting or opposing the motion. Absent exceptional circumstances, a law firm shall be held jointly responsible for violations committed by its partners, associates and employees.

(B) *On Court's Initiative.* On its own initiative, the court may enter an order describing the specific conduct that appears to violate subdivision (b) and directing an attorney, law firm, or party to show cause why it has not violated subdivision (b) with respect thereto.

(2) *Nature of Sanctions; Limitations.* A sanction imposed for violation of this Rule shall be limited to what is sufficient to deter repetition of such conduct or comparable conduct by others similarly situated. Subject to the limitations in subparagraphs (A) and (B), the sanction may consist of, or include, directives of a nonmonetary nature, an order to pay a penalty into court, or, if imposed on motion and warranted for effective deterrence, an order directing payment to the movant of some or all of the reasonable attorneys' fees and other expenses incurred as a direct result of the violation.

(A) Monetary sanctions may not be awarded against a represented party for a violation of subdivision (b)(2).

(B) Monetary sanctions may not be awarded on the court's initiative unless the court issues its order to show cause before a voluntary dismissal or settlement of the claims made by or against the party which is, or whose attorneys are, to be sanctioned.

(3) *Order.* When imposing sanctions, the court shall describe the conduct determined to constitute a violation of this Rule and explain the basis for the sanction imposed.

**(d) Inapplicability to Discovery.** Subdivisions (a) through (c) of this Rule do not apply to disclosures and discovery requests, responses, objections and motions that are subject to the provisions of Rules 26 through 37.

### Rule 12. Defenses and Objections— When and How Presented—by Pleading or Motion—Motion for Judgment on the Pleadings.

**(a) When Presented.**

(1) Unless a different time is prescribed in a statute of the United States, a defendant shall serve an answer

(A) within 20 days after being served with the summons and complaint, or

(B) if service of the summons has been timely waived on request under Rule 4(d), within 60 days after the date when the request for waiver was sent, or within 90 days after that date if the defendant was addressed outside any judicial district of the United States.

(2) A party served with a pleading stating a cross-claim against that party shall serve an answer thereto within 30 days after being served. The plaintiff shall serve a reply to a counterclaim in the answer within 20 days after service of the answer, or, if a reply is ordered by the court, within 20 days after service of the order, unless the order otherwise directs.

(3) The United States or an officer or agency thereof shall serve an answer to the complaint or to a cross-claim, or a reply to a counterclaim, within 60 days after the service upon the United States Attorney of the pleading in which the claim is asserted.

(4) Unless a different time is fixed by court order, the service of a motion permitted under this Rule alters these periods of time as follows:

(A) if the court denies the motion or postpones its disposition until the trial on the merits, the responsive pleading shall be served within 10 days after notice of the court's action; or

(B) if the court grants a motion for a more definite statement, the responsive pleading shall be served within 10 days after the service of the more definite statement.

**(b) How Presented.** Every defense, in law or fact, to a claim for relief in any pleading, whether a claim, counterclaim, cross-claim or third-party claim, shall be asserted in the responsive pleading thereto if one is required, except that the following defenses may at the option of the pleader be made by motion: (1) lack of jurisdiction over the subject matter, (2) lack of jurisdiction over the person, (3) improper venue, (4) insufficiency of process, (5) insufficiency of service of process, (6) failure to state a claim upon which relief can be granted, (7) failure to join a party under Rule 19. A motion making any of these defenses shall be made before pleading if a further pleading is permitted. No defense or objection is waived by being joined with one or more other defenses or objections in a responsive pleading or motion. If a pleading sets forth a claim for relief to which the adverse party is not required to serve a responsive pleading, the adverse party may assert at the trial any defenses in law or fact to that claim for relief.

If, on a motion asserting the defense numbered (6) to dismiss for failure of the pleading to state a claim upon which relief can be granted, matters outside the pleading are presented to and not excluded by the court, the motion shall be treated as one for summary judgment and disposed of as provided in Rule 56, and all parties shall be given reasonable opportunity to present all material made pertinent to such a motion by Rule 56.

**(c) Motion for Judgment on the Pleadings.** After the pleadings are closed but within such time as not to delay the trial, any party may move for judgment on the pleadings. If, on a motion for judgment on the pleadings, matters outside the pleadings are presented to and not excluded by the court, the motion shall be treated as one for summary judgment and disposed of as provided in Rule 56, and all parties shall be given reasonable opportunity to present all material made pertinent to such a motion by Rule 56.

**(d) Preliminary Hearings.** The defenses specifically enumerated (1)-(7) in subdivision (b) of this Rule, whether made in a pleading or by motion, and the motion for judgment mentioned in subdivision (c) of this Rule shall be heard and determined before trial on application of any party, unless the court orders that the hearing and determination thereof be deferred until the trial.

**(e) Motion for More Definite Statement.** If a pleading to which a responsive pleading is permitted is so vague or ambiguous that a party cannot reasonably be required to frame a responsive pleading, the party may move for a more definite statement before interposing a responsive pleading. The motion shall point out the defects complained of and the details desired. If the motion is granted and the order of the court is not obeyed within 10 days after notice of the order or within such other time as the court may fix, the court may strike the pleading to which the motion was directed or make such order as it deems just.

**(f) Motion to Strike.** Upon motion made by a party before responding to a pleading or, if no responsive pleading is permitted by these Rules, upon motion made by a party within 20 days after the service of the pleading upon the party or upon the court's own initiative at any time, the court may order stricken from any pleading any insufficient defense or any redundant, immaterial, impertinent or scandalous matter.

**(g) Consolidation of Defenses in Motion.** A party who makes a motion under this Rule may join with it any other motions herein provided for and then available to the party. If a party makes a motion under this Rule but omits therefrom any defense or objection then available to the party which this Rule permits to be raised by motion, the party shall not thereafter make a motion based on the defense or objection so omitted, except a motion as provided in subdivision (h)(2) hereof on any of the grounds there stated.

**(h) Waiver or Preservation of Certain Defenses.**

(1) A defense of lack of jurisdiction over the person, improper venue, insufficiency of process or insufficiency of service of process is waived (A) if omitted from a motion in the circumstances described in subdivision (g), or (B) if it is neither made by motion under this Rule nor included in a responsive pleading or an amendment thereof permitted by Rule 15(a) to be made as a matter of course.

(2) A defense of failure to state a claim upon which relief can be granted, a defense of failure to join a party indispensable under Rule 19, and an objection of failure to state a legal defense to a claim may be made in any pleading permitted or ordered under Rule 7(a), or by motion for judgment on the pleadings, or at the trial on the merits.

(3) Whenever it appears by suggestion of the parties or otherwise that the court lacks jurisdiction of the subject matter, the court shall dismiss the action.

### Rule 13. Counterclaim and Cross-Claim.

**(a) Compulsory Counterclaims.** A pleading shall state as a counterclaim any claim which at the time of serving the pleading the pleader has against any opposing party, if it arises out of the transaction or occurrence that is the subject matter of the opposing party's claim and does not require for its adjudication the presence of third parties of whom the court cannot acquire jurisdiction. But the pleader need not state the claim if (1) at the time the action was commenced the claim was the subject of another pending action, or (2) the opposing party brought suit upon the claim by attachment or other process by which the court did not acquire jurisdiction to render a personal judgment on that claim, and the pleader is not stating any counterclaim under this Rule 13.

**(b) Permissive Counterclaims.** A pleading may state as a counterclaim any claim against an opposing party not arising out of the transaction or occurrence that is the subject matter of the opposing party's claim.

**(c) Counterclaim Exceeding Opposing Claim.** A counterclaim may or may not diminish or defeat the recovery sought by the opposing party. It may claim relief exceeding in amount or different in kind from that sought in the pleading of the opposing party.

**(d) Counterclaim Against the United States.** These Rules shall not be construed to enlarge beyond the limits now fixed by law the right to assert counterclaims or to claim credits against the United States or an officer or agency thereof.

**(e) Counterclaim Maturing or Acquired after Pleading.** A claim which either matured or was acquired by the pleader after serving a pleading may, with the permission of the court, be presented as a counterclaim by supplemental pleading.

**(f) Omitted Counterclaim.** When a pleader fails to set up a counterclaim through oversight, inadvertence or excusable neglect, or when justice requires, the pleader may by leave of court set up the counterclaim by amendment.

**(g) Cross-Claim Against Co-Party.** A pleading may state as a cross-claim any claim by one party against a co-party arising out of the transaction or occurrence that is the subject matter either of the original action or of a counterclaim therein or relating to any property that is the subject matter of the original action. Such cross-claim may include a claim that the party against whom it is asserted is or may be liable to the cross-claimant for all or part of a claim asserted in the action against the cross-claimant.

**(h) Joinder of Additional Parties.** Persons other than those made parties to the original action may be made parties to a counterclaim or cross-claim in accordance with the provisions of Rules 19 and 20.

**(i) Separate Trials; Separate Judgments.** If the court orders separate trials as provided in Rule 42(b), judgment on a counterclaim or cross-claim may be rendered in accordance with the terms of Rule 54(b) when the court has jurisdiction so to do, even if the claims of the opposing party have been dismissed or otherwise disposed of.

## Rule 14. Third-Party Practice.

**(a) When Defendant May Bring in Third Party.** At any time after commencement of the action a defending party, as a third-party plaintiff, may cause a summons and complaint to be served upon a person not a party to the action who is or may be liable to the third-party plaintiff for all or part of the plaintiff's claim against the third-party plaintiff. The third-party plaintiff need not obtain leave to make the service if the third-party plaintiff files the third-party complaint not later than 10 days after serving the original answer. Otherwise the third-party plaintiff must obtain leave on motion upon notice to all parties to the action. The person served with the summons and third-party complaint, hereinafter called the third-party defendant, shall make any defenses to the third-party plaintiff's claim as provided in Rule 12 and any counterclaims against the third-party plaintiff and cross-claims against other third-party defendants as provided in Rule 13. The third-party defendant may assert against the plaintiff any defenses which the third-party plaintiff has to the plaintiff's claim. The third-party defendant may also assert any claim against the plaintiff arising out of the transaction or occurrence that is the subject matter of the plaintiff's claim against the third-party plaintiff. The plaintiff may assert any claim against the third-party defendant arising out of the transaction or occurrence that is the subject matter of the plaintiff's claim against the third-party plaintiff, and the third-party defendant thereupon shall assert any defenses as provided in Rule 12 and any counterclaims and cross-claims as provided in Rule 13. Any party may move to strike the third-party claim, or for its severance or separate trial. A third-party defendant may proceed under this Rule against any person not a party to the action who is or may be liable to the third-party defendant for all or part of the claim made in the action against the third-party defendant. The third-party complaint, if within the admiralty and maritime jurisdiction, may be in rem against a vessel, cargo or other property subject to admiralty or maritime process in rem, in which case references in this Rule to the summons include the warrant of arrest and references to the third-party plaintiff or defendant include, where appropriate, the claimant of the property arrested.

**(b) When Plaintiff May Bring in Third Party.** When a counterclaim is asserted against a plaintiff, the plaintiff may cause a third party to be brought in under circumstances which under this Rule would entitle a defendant to do so.

**(c) Admiralty and Maritime Claims.** When a plaintiff asserts an admiralty or maritime claim within the meaning of Rule 9(h), the defendant or claimant, as a third-party plaintiff, may bring in a third-party defendant who may be wholly or partly liable, either to the plaintiff or to the third-party plaintiff, by way of remedy over, contribution or otherwise on account of the same transaction, occurrence or series of transactions or occurrences. In such a case, the third-party plaintiff may also demand judgment against the third-party defendant in favor of the plaintiff, in which event the third-party defendant shall make any defenses to the claim of the plaintiff as well as to that of the third-party plaintiff in the manner provided in Rule 12 and the action shall proceed as if the plaintiff had commenced it against the third-party defendant as well as the third-party plaintiff.

### Rule 15. Amended and Supplemental Pleadings.

**(a) Amendments.** A party may amend the party's pleading once as a matter of course at any time before a responsive pleading is served or, if the pleading is one to which no responsive pleading is permitted and the action has not been placed upon the trial calendar, the party may so amend it at any time within 20 days after it is served. Otherwise, a party may amend the party's pleading only by leave of court or by written consent of the adverse party; and leave shall be freely given when justice so requires. A party shall plead in response to an amended pleading within the time remaining for response to the original pleading or within 10 days after service of the amended pleading, whichever period may be the longer, unless the court otherwise orders.

**(b) Amendments to Conform to the Evidence.** When issues not raised by the pleadings are tried by express or implied consent of the parties, they shall be treated in all respects as if they had been raised in the pleadings. Such amendment of the pleadings as may be necessary to cause them to conform to the evidence and to raise these issues may be made upon motion of any party at any time, even after judgment; but failure so to amend does not affect the result of the trial of these issues. If evidence is objected to at the trial on the ground that it is not within the issues made by the pleadings, the court may allow the pleadings to be amended and shall do so freely when the presentation of the merits of the action will be subserved thereby and the objecting party fails to satisfy the court

that the admission of such evidence would prejudice the party in maintaining the party's action or defense upon the merits. The court may grant a continuance to enable the objecting party to meet such evidence.

**(c) Relation Back of Amendments.** An amendment of a pleading relates back to the date of the original pleading when:

(1) relation back is permitted by the law that provides the statute of limitations applicable to the action, or

(2) the claim or defense asserted in the amended pleading arose out of the conduct, transaction or occurrence set forth or attempted to be set forth in the original pleading; or

(3) the amendment changes the party or the naming of the party against whom a claim is asserted if the foregoing provision (2) is satisfied and, within the period provided by Rule 4(m) for service of the summons and complaint, the party to be brought in by amendment (A) has received such notice of the institution of the action that the party will not be prejudiced in maintaining a defense on the merits, and (B) knew or should have known that, but for a mistake concerning the identity of the proper party, the action would have been brought against the party.

The delivery or mailing of process to the United States Attorney or United States Attorney's designee or the Attorney General of the United States, or an agency or officer who would have been a proper defendant if named, satisfies the requirement of subparagraphs (A) and (B) of this paragraph (3) with respect to the United States or any agency or officer thereof to be brought into the action as a defendant.

**(d) Supplemental Pleadings.** Upon motion of a party the court may, upon reasonable notice and upon such terms as are just, permit the party to serve a supplemental pleading setting forth transactions or occurrences or events which have happened since the date of the pleading sought to be supplemented. Permission may be granted even though the original pleading is defective in its statement of a claim for relief or defense. If the court deems it advisable that the adverse party plead to the supplemental pleading, it shall so order, specifying the time therefor.

### Rule 16. Pretrial Conferences; Scheduling; Management.

**(a) Pretrial Conferences; Objectives.** In any action, the court may in its discretion, direct the attorneys for the parties and any unrepresented parties to appear before it for a conference or conferences before trial for such purposes as:

(1) expediting the disposition of the action;

(2) establishing early and continuing control so that the case will not be protracted because of lack of management;

(3) discouraging wasteful pretrial activities;

(4) improving the quality of the trial through more thorough preparation, and;

(5) facilitating the settlement of the case.

**(b) Scheduling and Planning.** Except in categories of actions exempted by district court rule as inappropriate, the district judge, or a magistrate judge when authorized by district court rule, shall, after receiving the report from the parties under Rule 26(f) or after consulting with the attorneys for the parties and any unrepresented parties by a scheduling conference, telephone, mail or other suitable means, enter a scheduling order that limits the time:

(1) to join other parties and to amend the pleadings;

(2) to file motions; and

(3) to complete discovery.

The scheduling order also may include:

(4) modification of the time for disclosures under Rules 26(a) and 26(e)(1) and of the extent of discovery to be permitted;

(5) the date or dates for conferences before trial, a final pretrial conference, and trial; and

(6) any other matters appropriate in the circumstances of the case.

The order shall issue as soon as practicable but in any event within 90 days after the appearance of a defendant and within 120 days after the complaint has been served on a defendant. A schedule shall not be modified except upon a showing of good cause and by leave of the district judge or, when authorized by local rule, by a magistrate judge.

**(c) Subjects for Consideration at Pretrial Conferences.** At any conference under this Rule consideration may be given, and the court may take appropriate action with respect to:

(1) the formulation and simplification of the issues, including the elimination of frivolous claims or defenses;

(2) the necessity or desirability of amendments to the pleadings;

(3) the possibility of obtaining admissions of fact and of documents which will avoid

unnecessary proof, stipulations regarding the authenticity of documents and advance rulings from the court on the admissibility of evidence;

(4) the avoidance of unnecessary proof and of cumulative evidence and limitations or restrictions on the use of testimony under Rule 702 of the Federal Rules of Evidence;

(5) the appropriateness and timing of summary adjudication under Rule 56;

(6) the control and scheduling of discovery, including orders affecting disclosures and discovery pursuant to Rule 26 and Rules 29 through 37;

(7) the identification of witnesses and documents, the need and schedule for filing and exchanging pretrial briefs, and the date or dates for further conferences and for trial;

(8) the advisability or referring matters to a magistrate judge or master;

(9) settlement and the use of special procedures to assist in resolving the dispute when authorized by statute or local rule;

(10) the form and substance of the pretrial order;

(11) the disposition of pending motions;

(12) the need for adopting special procedures for managing potentially difficult or protracted actions that may involve complex issues, multiple parties, difficult legal questions or unusual proof problems; and

(13) an order for a separate trial pursuant to Rule 42(b) with respect to a claim, counterclaim, cross-claim or third-party claim, or with respect to any particular issue in the case;

(14) an order directing a part or parties to present evidence early in the trial with respect to a manageable issue that could, on the evidence, be the basis for a judgment as a matter of law under Rule 50(a) or a judgment on partial findings under Rule 52(c);

(15) an order establishing a reasonable limit on the time allowed for presenting evidence; and

(16) such other matters as may facilitate the just, speedy and inexpensive disposition of the action.

At least one of the attorneys for each party participating in any conference before trial shall have authority to enter into stipulations and to make admissions regarding all matters that the participants may reasonably anticipate may be discussed. If appropriate, the court may require that a party or its representative be present or reasonably available by telephone in order to consider possible settlement of the dispute.

**(d) Final Pretrial Conference.** Any final pretrial conference shall be held as close to the time of trial as reasonable under the circumstances. The participants at any such conference shall formulate a plan for trial, including a program for facilitating the admission of evidence. The conference shall be attended by at least one of the attorneys who will conduct the trial for each of the parties and by any unrepresented parties.

**(e) Pretrial Orders.** After any conference held pursuant to this Rule, an order shall be entered reciting the action taken. This order shall control the subsequent course of the action unless modified by a subsequent order. The order following a final pretrial conference shall be modified only to prevent manifest injustice.

**(f) Sanctions.** If a party or party's attorney fails to obey a scheduling or pretrial order, or if no appearance is made on behalf of a party at a scheduling or pretrial conference, or if a party or party's attorney is substantially unprepared to participate in the conference, or if a party or party's attorney fails to participate in good faith, the judge, upon motion or the judge's own initiative, may make such orders with regard thereto as are just, and among others any of the orders provided in Rule 37(b)(2)(B), (C), (D). In lieu of or in addition to any other sanction, the judge shall require the party or the attorney representing the party or both to pay the reasonable expenses incurred because of any noncompliance with this Rule, including attorney's fees, unless the judge finds that the noncompliance was substantially justified or that other circumstances make an award of expenses unjust.

IV. **Parties.**

### Rule 17. Parties Plaintiff and Defendant; Capacity.

**(a) Real Party in Interest.** Every action shall be prosecuted in the name of the real party in interest. An executor, administrator, guardian, bailee, trustee of an express trust, a party with whom or in whose name a contract has been made for the benefit of another, or a party authorized by statute may sue in that person's own name without joining the party for whose benefit the action is brought; and when a statute of the United States so provides, an action for the use or benefit of another shall be brought in the name of the United States. No action shall be dismissed on the ground that it is not prosecuted in the name of the real party in interest until a reasonable time has been allowed after objection for ratification of commencement of the action by, or joinder or substitution of, the real party in interest; and such ratification, joinder or substitution shall have the same effect as if the action had been commenced in the name of the real party in interest.

**(b) Capacity to Sue or Be Sued.** The capacity of an individual, other than one acting in a representative capacity, to sue or be sued shall be determined by the law of the individual's domicile. The capacity of a corporation to sue or be sued shall be determined by the law under which it was organized. In all other cases capacity to sue or be sued shall be determined by the law of the state in which the district court is held, except (1) that a partnership or other unincorporated association, which has no such capacity by the law of such state, may sue or be sued in its common name for the purpose of enforcing for or against it a substantive right existing under the Constitution or laws of the United States, and (2) that the capacity of a receiver appointed by a court of the United States to sue or be sued in a court of the United States is governed by Title 28, U.S.C. §§754 and 959(a).

**(c) Infants or Incompetent Persons.** Whenever an infant or incompetent person has a representative, such as a general guardian, committee, conservator or other like fiduciary, the representative may sue or defend on behalf of the infant or incompetent person. An infant or incompetent person who does not have a duly appointed representative may sue by a next friend or by a guardian ad litem. The court shall appoint a guardian ad litem for an infant or incompetent person not otherwise represented in an action or shall make such other order as it deems proper for the protection of the infant or incompetent person.

### Rule 18. Joinder of Claims and Remedies.

**(a) Joinder of Claims.** A party asserting a claim to relief as an original claim, counterclaim, cross-claim or third-party claim, may join, either as independent or as alternate claims, as many claims, legal, equitable or maritime, as the party has against an opposing party.

**(b) Joinder of Remedies; Fraudulent Conveyances.** Whenever a claim is one heretofore cognizable only after another claim has been prosecuted to a conclusion, the two claims may be joined in a single action; but the court shall grant relief in that action only in accordance with the relative substantive rights of the parties. In particular, a plaintiff may state a claim for money and a claim to have set aside a conveyance fraudulent as to that plaintiff, without first having obtained a judgment establishing the claim for money.

### Rule 19. Joinder of Persons Needed for Just Adjudication.

**(a) Persons to Be Joined if Feasible.** A person who is subject to service of process and whose joinder will not deprive the court of jurisdiction over the subject matter of the action shall be joined as a party in the action if (1) in the person's absence complete relief cannot be accorded among those already parties, or (2) the person claims an interest relating to the subject of the action and is so situated that the disposition of the action in the person's absence may (i) as a practical matter impair or impede the person's ability to protect that interest or (ii) leave any of the persons already parties subject to a substantial risk of incurring double, multiple or otherwise inconsistent obligations by reason of the claimed interest. If the person has not been so joined, the court shall order that the person be made a party. If the person should join as a plaintiff but refuses to do so, the person may be made a defendant, or, in a proper case, an involuntary plaintiff. If the joined party objects to venue and joinder of that party would render the venue of the action improper, that party shall be dismissed from the action.

**(b) Determination by Court Whenever Joinder Not Feasible.** If a person as described in subdivision (a)(1) - (2) hereof cannot be made a party, the court shall determine whether in equity and good conscience the action should proceed among the parties before it, or should be dismissed, the absent person being thus regarded as indispensable. The factors to be considered by the court include: first, to what extent a judgment rendered in the person's absence might be prejudicial to the person or those already parties; second, the extent to which, by protective provisions in the judgment, by the shaping of relief, or other measures, the prejudice can be lessened or avoided; third, whether a judgment rendered in the person's absence will be adequate; fourth, whether the plaintiff will have an adequate remedy if the action is dismissed for nonjoinder.

**(c) Pleading Reasons for Nonjoinder.** A pleading asserting a claim for relief shall state the names, if known to the pleader, of any persons as described in subdivision (a)(1) - (2) hereof who are not joined, and the reasons why they are not joined.

**(d) Exception of Class Actions.** This Rule is subject to the provisions of Rule 23.

### Rule 20. Permissive Joinder of Parties.

**(a) Permissive Joinder.** All persons may join in one action as plaintiffs if they assert any right to relief jointly, severally or in the alternative in respect of or arising out of the same transaction, occurrence or series of transactions or occurrences and if any question of law or fact common to all these persons will arise in the action. All persons (and any vessel, cargo or other property subject to admiralty process in rem) may be joined in one action as defendants if there is asserted against them jointly, severally or in the alternative, any right to relief in respect of or arising out of the same transaction, occurrence or series of transactions or occurrences and if any question of law or fact common to all defendants will arise in the action. A plaintiff or defendant need not be interested in obtaining or defending against all the relief demanded. Judgment may be given for one or more of the plaintiffs according to their respective rights to relief, and against one or more defendants according to their respective liabilities.

**(b) Separate Trials.** The court may make such orders as will prevent a party from being embarrassed, delayed or put to expense by the inclusion of a party against whom the party asserts no claim and who asserts no claim against the party, and may order separate trials or make other orders to prevent delay or prejudice.

### Rule 21. Misjoinder and Nonjoinder of Parties.

Misjoinder of parties is not ground for dismissal of an action. Parties may be dropped or added by order of the court on motion of any party or of its own initiative at any stage of the action and on such terms as are just. Any claim against a party may be severed and proceeded with separately.

### Rule 22. Interpleader.

(1) Persons having claims against the plaintiff may be joined as defendants and required to interplead when their claims are such that the plaintiff is or may be exposed

to double or multiple liability. It is not ground for objection to the joinder that the claims of the several claimants or the titles on which their claims depend do not have a common origin or are not identical but are adverse to and independent of one another, or that the plaintiff avers that the plaintiff is not liable in whole or in part to any or all of the claimants. A defendant exposed to similar liability may obtain such interpleader by way of cross-claim or counterclaim. The provisions of this Rule supplement and do not in any way limit the rejoinder of parties permitted in Rule 20.

(2) The remedy herein provided is in addition to and in no way supersedes or limits the remedy provided by Title 28, U.S.C. §§1335, 1397 and 2361. Actions under those provisions shall be conducted in accordance with these Rules.

## Rule 23. Class Actions.

**(a) Prerequisites to a Class Action.** One or more members of a class may sue or be sued as representative parties on behalf of all only if (1) the class is so numerous that joinder of all members is impracticable, (2) there are questions of law or fact common to the class, (3) the claims or defenses of the representative parties are typical of the claims or defenses of the class, and (4) the representative parties will fairly and adequately protect the interest of the class.

**(b) Class Actions Maintainable.** An action may be maintained as a class action if the prerequisites of subdivision (a) are satisfied, and in addition:

(1) the prosecution of separate actions by or against individual members of the class would create a risk of:

(A) inconsistent or varying adjudications with respect to individual members of the class which would establish incompatible standards of conduct for the party opposing the class, or

(B) adjudications with respect to individual members of the class which would as a practical matter be dispositive of the interests of the other members not parties to the adjudications or substantially impair or impede their ability to protect their interest; or

(2) the party opposing the class has acted or refused to act on grounds generally applicable to the class, thereby making appropriate final injunctive relief or corresponding declaratory relief with respect to the class as a whole; or

(3) the court finds that the questions of law or fact common to the members of the class predominate over any questions affecting only individual members, and that a class action is superior to other available methods for the fair and efficient adjudication of the controversy. The matters pertinent to the findings include: (A) the interest of members of the class in individually controlling the prosecution or defense of separate actions; (B) the extent and nature of any litigation concerning the controversy already commenced by or against members of the class; (C) the desirability or undesirability of concentrating the litigation of the claims in the particular forum; (D) the difficulties likely to be encountered in the management of a class action.

**(c) Determination by Order Whether Class Action to Be Maintained; Notice; Judgment; Actions Conducted Partially as Class Actions.**

(1) As soon as practicable after the commencement of an action brought as a class action, the court shall determine by order whether it is to be so maintained. An order under this subdivision may be conditional, and may be altered or amended before the decision on the merits.

(2) In any class action maintained under subdivision (b)(3), the court shall direct to the members of the class the best notice practicable under the circumstances, including individual notice to all members who can be identified through reasonable effort. The notice shall advise each member that (A) the court will exclude the member from the class if the member so requests by a specified date; (B) the judgment, whether favorable or not, will include all members who do not request exclusion; and (C) any member who does not request exclusion may, if the member desires, enter an appearance through his counsel.

(3) The judgment in an action maintained as a class action under subdivision (b)(1) or (b) (2), whether or not favorable to the class, shall include and describe those whom the court finds to be members of the class. The judgment in an action maintained as a class action under subdivision (b)(3), whether or not favorable to the class, shall include and specify or describe those to whom the notice provided in subdivision (c)(2) was directed, and who have not requested exclusion, and whom the court finds to be members of the class.

(4) When appropriate (A) an action may be brought or maintained as a class action with respect to particular issues, or (B) a class may be divided into subclasses and

each subclass treated as a class, and the provisions of this Rule shall then be construed and applied accordingly.

**(d) Orders in Conduct of Actions.** In the conduct of actions to which this Rule applies, the court may make appropriate orders: (1) determining the course of proceedings or prescribing measures to prevent undue repetition or complication in the presentation of evidence or argument; (2) requiring, for the protection of the members of the class or otherwise for the fair conduct of the action, that notice be given in such manner as the court may direct to some or all of the members of any step in the action, or of the proposed extent of the judgment, or of the opportunity of members to signify whether they consider the representation fair and adequate, to intervene and present claims or defenses, or otherwise to come into the action; (3) imposing conditions on the representative parties or on intervenors; (4) requiring that the pleadings be amended to eliminate therefrom allegations as to representation of absent persons, and that the action proceed accordingly; (5) dealing with similar procedural matters. The orders may be combined with an order under Rule 16, and may be altered or amended as may be desirable from time to time.

**(e) Dismissal or Compromise.** A class action shall not be dismissed or compromised without the approval of the court, and notice of the proposed dismissal or compromise shall be given to all members of the class in such manner as the court directs.

### Rule 23.1. Derivative Actions by Shareholders.

In a derivative action brought by one or more shareholders or members to enforce a right of a corporation or of an unincorporated association, the corporation or association having failed to enforce a right which may properly be asserted by it, the complaint shall be verified and shall allege (1) that the plaintiff was a shareholder or member at the time of the transaction of which the plaintiff complains or that the plaintiff's share or membership thereafter devolved on the plaintiff by operation of law, and (2) that the action is not a collusive one to confer jurisdiction on a court of the United States which it would not otherwise have. The complaint shall also allege with particularity the efforts, if any, made by the plaintiff to obtain the action the plaintiff desires from the directors or comparable authority and, if necessary, from the shareholders or members, and the reasons for the plaintiff's failure to obtain the action or for not making the effort. The derivative action may not be maintained if it appears that the plaintiff does not fairly and adequately represent the interests of the shareholders or members similarly situated in enforcing the right of the corporation or association. The action shall not be dismissed or compromised without the approval of the court, and notice of the proposed dismissal or compromise shall be given to shareholders or members in such manner as the court directs.

### Rule 23.2. Actions Relating to Unincorporated Associations.

An action brought by or against the members of an unincorporated association as a class by naming certain members as representative parties may be maintained only if it appears that the representative parties will fairly and adequately protect the interests of the association and its members. In the conduct of the action, the court may make appropriate orders corresponding with those described in Rule 23(d), and the procedure for dismissal or compromise of the action shall correspond with that provided in Rule 23(e).

### Rule 24. Intervention.

**(a) Intervention of Right.** Upon timely application anyone shall be permitted to intervene in an action: (1) when a statute of the United States confers an unconditional right to intervene; or (2) when the applicant claims an interest relating to the property or transaction which is the subject of the action and the applicant is so situated that the disposition of the action may as a practical matter impair or impede the applicant's ability to protect that interest, unless the applicant's interest is adequately represented by existing parties.

**(b) Permissive Intervention.** Upon timely application anyone may be permitted to intervene in an action: (1) when a statute of the United States confers a conditional right to intervene; or (2) when an applicant's claim or defense and the main action have a question of law or fact in common. When a party to an action relies for ground of claim or defense upon any statute or executive order administered by a federal or state governmental officer and agency or upon any regulation, order, requirement or agreement issued or made pursuant to the statute or executive order, the officer or agency upon timely application may be permitted to intervene in the action. In exercising its discretion, the court shall consider whether the intervention will unduly delay or prejudice the adjudication of the rights of the original parties.

**(c) Procedure.** A person desiring to intervene shall serve a motion to intervene upon the parties as provided in Rule 5. The motion shall state the grounds therefor and shall be accompanied by a pleading setting forth the claim or defense for which intervention is sought. The same procedure shall be followed when a statute of the United States gives a right to intervene. When the constitutionality of an act of Congress affecting the public interest is drawn in question in any action to which the United States or an officer, agency or employee thereof is not a party, the court shall notify the Attorney General of the United States as provided in Title 28, U.S.C. §2403. When the constitutionality of any statute of a State affecting the public interest is drawn in question in any action in which that State or any agency, officer or employee thereof is not a party, the court shall notify the attorney general of the State as provided in Title 28, U.S.C. §2403. A party challenging the constitutionality of legislation should call the attention of the court to its consequential duty, but failure to do so is not a waiver of any constitutional right otherwise timely asserted.

### Rule 25. Substitution of Parties.

**(a) Death.**

(1) If a party dies and the claim is not thereby extinguished, the court may order substitution of the proper parties. The motion for substitution may be made by any party or by the successors or representatives of the deceased party and, together with the notice of hearing, shall be served on the parties as provided in Rule 5 and upon persons not parties in the manner provided in Rule 4 for the service of a summons, and may be served in any judicial district. Unless the motion for substitution is made not later than 90 days after the death is suggested upon the record by service of a statement of the fact of the death as provided herein for the service of the motion, the action shall be dismissed as to the deceased party.

(2) In the event of the death of one or more of the plaintiffs or of one or more of the defendants in an action in which the right sought to be enforced survives only to the surviving plaintiffs or only against the surviving defendants, the action does not abate. The death shall be suggested upon the record and the action shall proceed in favor of or against the surviving parties.

**(b) Incompetence.** If a party becomes incompetent, the court upon motion served as provided in subdivision (a) of this rule may allow the action to be continued by or against the party's representative.

**(c) Transfer of Interest.** In case of any transfer of interest, the action may be continued by or against the original party, unless the court upon motion directs the person to whom the interest is transferred to be substituted in the action or joined with the original party. Service of the motion shall be made as provided in subdivision (a) of this Rule.

**(d) Public Officers; Death or Separation from Office.**

(1) When a public officer is a party to an action in an official capacity and during its pendency dies, resigns or otherwise ceases to hold office, the action does not abate and the officer's successor is automatically substituted as a party. Proceedings following the substitution shall be in the name of the substituted party, but any misnomer not affecting the substantial rights of the parties shall be disregarded. An order of substitution may be entered at any time, but the omission to enter such an order shall not affect the substitution.

(2) A public officer who sues or is sued in an official capacity may be described as a party by the officer's official title rather than by name; but the court may require the officer's name to be added.

V.    **Depositions and Discovery.**

### Rule 26. General Provisions Governing Discovery; Duty of Disclosure.

**(a) Required Disclosures; Methods to Discover Additional Matter.**

(1) *Initial Disclosures.* Except to the extent otherwise stipulated or directed by order or local rule, a party shall, without awaiting a discovery request, provide to other parties:

(A) the name and, if known, the address and telephone number of each individual likely to have discoverable information relevant to disputed facts alleged with particularity in the pleadings, identifying the subjects of the information;

(B) a copy of, or a description by category and location of, all documents, data compilations, and tangible things in the possession, custody or control of the party that are relevant to disputed facts alleged with particularity in the pleadings;

(C) a computation of any category of damages claimed by the disclosing party, making available for inspection and copying as under Rule 34 the documents or other evidentiary material, not privileged or protected from disclosure, on which such computation is based, including materials bearing on the nature and extent of injuries suffered; and

(D) for inspection and copying as under Rule 34 any insurance agreement under which any person carrying on an insurance business may be liable to satisfy part or all of a judgment which may be entered in the action or to indemnify or reimburse for payments made to satisfy the judgment.

Unless otherwise stipulated or directed by the court, these disclosures shall be made at or within 10 days after the meeting of the parties under subdivision (f). A party shall make its initial disclosures based on the information then reasonably available to it and is not excused from making its disclosures because it has not fully completed its investigation of the case or because it challenges the sufficiency of another party's disclosures or because another party has not made its disclosures.

(2) *Disclosure of Expert Testimony.*

(A) In addition to the disclosures required by paragraph (1), a party shall disclose to other parties the identity of any person who may be used at trial to present evidence under Rules 702, 703 or 705 of the Federal Rules of Evidence.

(B) Except as otherwise stipulated or directed by the court, this disclosure shall, with respect to a witness who is retained or specially employed to provide expert testimony in the case or whose duties as an employee of the party regularly involve giving expert testimony, be accompanied by a written report prepared and signed by the witness. The report shall contain a complete statement of all opinions to be expressed and the basis and reasons therefor; the data or other information considered by the witness in forming the opinions; any exhibits to be used as a summary of or support for the opinions; the qualifications of the witness, including a list of all publications authored by the witness within the preceding ten years; the compensation to

be paid for the study and testimony; and a listing of any other cases in which the witness has testified as an expert at trial or by deposition within the preceding four years.

(C) These disclosures shall be made at the times and in the sequence directed by the court. In the absence of other directions from the court or stipulation by the parties, the disclosures shall be made at least 90 days before the trial date or the date the case is to be ready for trial, or, if the evidence is intended solely to contradict or rebut evidence on the same subject matter identified by another party under paragraph (2)(B), within 30 days after the disclosure made by the other party. The parties shall supplement these disclosures when required under subdivision (e)(1).

(3) *Pretrial Disclosures.* In addition to the disclosures required in the preceding paragraphs, a party shall provide to other parties the following information regarding the evidence that it may present at trial other than solely for impeachment purposes:

(A) the name and, if not previously provided, the address and telephone number of each witness, separately identifying those whom the party expects to present and those whom the party may call if the need arises;

(B) the designation of those witnesses whose testimony is expected to be presented by means of a deposition and, if not taken stenographically, a transcript of the pertinent portions of the deposition testimony; and

(C) an appropriate identification of each document or other exhibit, including summaries of other evidence, separately identifying those which the party expects to offer and those which the party may offer if the need arises.

Unless otherwise directed by the court, these disclosures shall be made at least 30 days before trial. Within 14 days thereafter, unless a different time is specified by the court, a party may serve and file a list disclosing (i) any objections to the use under Rule 32(a) of a deposition designated by another party under subparagraph (B) and (ii) any objection, together with the grounds therefor, that may be made to the admissibility of materials identified under subparagraph (C). Objections not so disclosed, other than objections under Rules 402 and 403 of the Federal Rules of Evidence, shall be deemed waived unless excused by the court for good cause shown.

(4) *Form of Disclosures; Filing.* Unless otherwise directed by order or local rule, all dis-

closures under paragraphs (1) through (3) shall be made in writing, signed, served and promptly filed with the court.

(5) *Methods to Discover Additional Matter.* Parties may obtain discovery by one or more of the following methods: depositions upon oral examination or written questions; written interrogatories; production of documents or things or permission to enter upon land or other property under Rule 34 or 45(a)(1)(C), for inspection and other purposes; physical and mental examinations; and requests for admission.

**(b) Discovery Scope and Limits.** Unless otherwise limited by order of the court in accordance with these Rules, the scope of discovery is as follows:

(1) *In General.* Parties may obtain discovery regarding any matter, not privileged, which is relevant to the subject matter involved in the pending action, whether it relates to the claim or defense of the party seeking discovery or to the claim or defense of any other party, including the existence, description, nature, custody, condition and location of any books, documents or other tangible things and the identity and location of persons having knowledge of any discoverable matter. The information sought need not be admissible at the trial if the information sought appears reasonably calculated to lead to the discovery of admissible evidence.

(2) *Limitations.* By order or by local rule, the court may alter the limits in these Rules on the number of depositions and interrogatories and may also limit the length of depositions under Rule 30 and the number of requests under Rule 36. The frequency or extent of use of the discovery methods otherwise permitted under these Rules and by any local rule shall be limited by the court if it determines that: (i) the discovery sought is unreasonably cumulative or duplicative, or is obtainable from some other source that is more convenient, less burdensome or less expensive; (ii) the party seeking discovery has had ample opportunity by discovery in the action to obtain the information sought; or (iii) the burden or expense of the proposed discovery outweighs its likely benefit, taking into account the needs of the case, the amount in controversy, the parties' resources, the importance of the issues at stake in the litigation and the importance of the proposed discovery in resolving the issues. The court may act upon its own initiative after reasonable notice or pursuant to a motion under subdivision (c).

(3) *Trial Preparation: Materials.* Subject to the provisions of subdivision (b)(4) of this Rule, a party may obtain discovery of documents and tangible things otherwise discoverable under subdivision (b)(1) of this Rule and prepared in anticipation of litigation or for trial by or for another party or by or for that other party's representative (including the other party's attorney, consultant, surety, indemnitor, insurer or agent) only upon showing that the party seeking discovery has substantial need of the materials in the preparation of the party's case and that the party is unable without undue hardship to obtain the substantial equivalent of the materials by other means. In ordering discovery of such materials when the required showing has been made, the court shall protect against disclosure of the mental impressions, conclusions, opinions or legal theories of an attorney or other representative of a party concerning the litigation.

A party may obtain without the required showing a statement concerning the action or its subject matter previously made by that party. Upon request, a person not a party may obtain without the required showing a statement concerning the action or its subject matter previously made by that person. If the request is refused, the person may move for a court order. The provisions of Rule 37(a)(4) apply to the award of expenses incurred in relation to the motion. For purposes of this paragraph, a statement previously made is (A) a written statement signed or otherwise adopted or approved by the person making it, or (B) a stenographic, mechanical, electrical or other recording, or a transcription thereof, which is a substantially verbatim recital of an oral statement by the person making it and contemporaneously recorded.

(4) *Trial Preparation: Experts.*

(A) A party may depose any person who has been identified as an expert whose opinions may be presented at trial. If a report from the expert is required under subdivision (a)(2)(B), the deposition shall not be conducted until after the report is provided.

(B) A party may, through interrogatories or by deposition, discover facts known or opinions held by an expert who has been retained or specially employed by another party in anticipation of litigation or preparation for trial and who is not expected to be called as a witness at trial, only as provided in

Rule 35(b) or upon a showing of exceptional circumstances under which it is impracticable for the party seeking discovery to obtain facts or opinions on the same subject by other means.

(C) Unless manifest injustice would result, (i) the court shall require that the party seeking discovery pay the expert a reasonable fee for time spent in responding to discovery under this subdivision; and (ii) with respect to discovery obtained under subdivision (b)(4)(B) of this Rule the court may require the party seeking discovery to pay the other party a fair portion of the fees and expenses reasonably incurred by the latter party in obtaining facts and opinions from the expert.

(5) *Claims of Privilege or Protection of Trial Preparation Materials.* When a party withholds information otherwise discoverable under these Rules by claiming that it is privileged or subject to protection as trial preparation material, the party shall make the claim expressly and shall describe the nature of the documents, communications or things not produced or disclosed in a manner that, without revealing information itself privileged or protected, will enable other parties to assess the applicability of the privilege or protection.

**(c) Protective Orders.** Upon motion by a party or by the person from whom discovery is sought, accompanied by a certification that the movant has in good faith conferred or attempted to confer with other affected parties in an effort to resolve the dispute without court action, and for good cause shown, the court in which the action is pending or alternatively, on matters relating to a deposition, the court in the district where the deposition is to be taken may make any order which justice requires to protect a party or person from annoyance, embarrassment, oppression or undue burden or expense, including one or more of the following:

(1) that the disclosure or discovery not be had;

(2) that the disclosure or discovery may be had only on specified terms and conditions, including a designation of the time or place;

(3) that the disclosure or discovery may be had only by a method of discovery other than that selected by the party seeking discovery;

(4) that certain matters not be inquired into, or that the scope of the disclosure or discovery be limited to certain matters;

(5) that discovery be conducted with no one present except persons designated by the court;

(6) that a deposition, after being sealed, be opened only by order of the court;

(7) that a trade secret or other confidential research, development or commercial information not be revealed or be revealed only in a designated way; and

(8) that the parties simultaneously file specified documents or information enclosed in sealed envelopes to be opened as directed by the court.

If the motion for a protective order is denied in whole or in part, the court may, on such terms and conditions as are just, order that any party or other person provide or permit discovery. The provisions of Rule 37(a)(4) apply to the award of expenses incurred in relation to the motion.

**(d) Timing and Sequence of Discovery.** Except when authorized under these Rules or by local rule, order or agreement of the parties, a party may not seek discovery from any source before the parties have met and conferred as required by subdivision (f). Unless the court upon motion, for the convenience of parties and witnesses and in the interests of justice, orders otherwise, methods of discovery may be used in any sequence and the fact that a party is conducting discovery, whether by deposition or otherwise, shall not operate to delay any other party's discovery.

**(e) Supplementation of Disclosures and Responses.** A party who has made a disclosure under subdivision (a) or responded to a request for discovery with a disclosure or response is under a duty to supplement or correct the disclosure or response to include information thereafter acquired if ordered by the court or in the following circumstances:

(1) A party is under a duty to supplement at appropriate intervals its disclosures under subdivision (a) if the party learns that in some material respect the information disclosed is incomplete or incorrect and if the additional or corrective information has not otherwise been made known to the other parties during the discovery process or in writing. With respect to testimony of an expert from whom a report is required under subdivision (a)(2)(B) the duty extends both to information contained in the report and to information provided through a deposition of the expert, and any additions or other

changes to this information shall be disclosed by the time the party's disclosures under Rule 26(a)(3) are due.

(2) A party is under a duty seasonably to amend a prior response to an interrogatory, request for production or request for admission if the party learns that the response is in some material respect incomplete or incorrect and if the additional or corrective information has not otherwise been made known to the other parties during the discovery process or in writing.

**(f) Meeting of Parties; Planning for Discovery.** Except in actions exempted by local rule or when otherwise ordered, the parties shall, as soon as practicable and in any event at least 14 days before a scheduling conference is held or a scheduling order is due under Rule 16(b), meet to discuss the nature and basis of their claims and defenses and the possibilities for a prompt settlement or resolution of the case, to make or arrange for the disclosures required by subdivision (a)(1), and to develop a proposed discovery plan. The plan shall indicate the parties' views and proposals concerning:

(1) what changes should be made in the timing, form or requirement for disclosures under subdivision (a) or local rule, including a statement as to when disclosures under subdivision (a)(1) were made or will be made;

(2) the subjects on which discovery may be needed, when discovery should be completed, and whether discovery should be conducted in phases or be limited to or focused upon particular issues;

(3) what changes should be made in the limitations on discovery imposed under these Rules or by local rule, and what other limitations should be imposed; and

(4) any other orders that should be entered by the court under subdivision (c) or under Rule 16(b) and (c).

The attorneys of record and all unrepresented parties that have appeared in the case are jointly responsible for arranging and being present or represented at the meeting, for attempting in good faith to agree on the proposed discovery plan, and for submitting to the court within 10 days after the meeting a written report outlining the plan.

**(g) Signing of Disclosures, Discovery Requests, Responses and Objections.**

(1) Every disclosure made pursuant to subdivision (a)(1) or subdivision (a)(3) shall be signed by at least one attorney of record in the attorney's individual name, whose address shall be stated. An unrepresented party shall sign the disclosure and state the party's address. The signature of the attorney or party constitutes a certification that to the best of the signer's knowledge, information and belief, formed after a reasonable inquiry, the disclosure is complete and correct as of the time it is made.

(2) Every discovery request or response or objection made by a party represented by an attorney shall be signed by at least one attorney of record in the attorney's individual name, whose address shall be stated. An unrepresented party shall sign the request, response or objection and state the party's address. The signature of the attorney or party constitutes a certification that to the best of the signer's knowledge, information and belief, formed after a reasonable inquiry, the request, response or objection is:

(A) consistent with these Rules and warranted by existing law or a good-faith argument for the extension, modification or reversal of existing law;

(B) not interposed for any improper purpose, such as to harass or to cause unnecessary delay or needless increase in the cost of litigation; and

(C) not unreasonable or unduly burdensome or expensive, given the needs of the case, the discovery already had in the case, the amount in controversy and the importance of the issues at stake in the litigation.

If a request, response or objection is not signed, it shall be stricken unless it is signed promptly after the omission is called to the attention of the party making the request, response or objection and a party shall not be obligated to take any action with respect to it until it is signed.

(3) If without substantial justification a certification is made in violation of the Rule, the court, upon motion or upon its own initiative, shall impose upon the person who made the certification, the party on whose behalf the disclosure, request, response or objection is made, or both, an appropriate sanction, which may include an order to pay the amount of the reasonable expenses incurred because of the violation, including a reasonable attorney's fee.

### Rule 27. Depositions Before Action or Pending Appeal.

**(a) Before Action.**

(1) *Petition.* A person who desires to perpetuate testimony regarding any matter that

may be cognizable in any court of the United States may file a verified petition in the United States district court in the district of the residence of any expected adverse party. The petition shall be entitled in the name of the petitioner and shall show: 1, that the petitioner expects to be a party to an action cognizable in a court of the United States but is presently unable to bring it or cause it to be brought, 2, the subject matter of the expected action and the petitioner's interest therein, 3, the facts which the petitioner desires to establish by the proposed testimony and the reasons for desiring to perpetuate it, 4, the names or a description of the persons the petitioner expects will be adverse parties and their addresses so far as known, and 5, the names and addresses of the persons to be examined and the substance of the testimony which the petitioner expects to elicit from each, and shall ask for an order authorizing the petitioner to take the depositions of the persons to be examined named in the petition, for the purpose of perpetuating their testimony.

(2) *Notice and Service.* The petitioner shall thereafter serve a notice upon each person named in the petition as an expected adverse party, together with a copy of the petition, stating that the petitioner will apply to the court, at a time and place named therein, for the order described in the petition. At least 20 days before the date of hearing the notice shall be served either within or without the district or state in the manner provided in Rule 4(d) for service of summons; but if such service cannot with due diligence be made upon any expected adverse party named in the petition, the court may make such order as is just for service by publication or otherwise, and shall appoint, for persons not served in the manner provided in Rule 4(d), an attorney who shall represent them, and in case they are not otherwise represented, shall cross-examine the deponent. If any expected adverse party is a minor or incompetent the provisions of Rule 17(c) apply.

(3) *Order and Examination.* If the court is satisfied that the perpetuation of the testimony may prevent a failure or delay of justice, it shall make an order designating or describing the persons whose depositions may be taken and specifying the subject matter of the examination and whether the depositions shall be taken upon oral examination or written interrogatories. The depositions may then be taken in accordance with these Rules;

and the court may make orders of the character provided for by Rules 34 and 35. For the purpose of applying these Rules to depositions for perpetuating testimony, each reference therein to the court in which the action is pending, shall be deemed to refer to the court in which the petition for such deposition was filed.

(4) *Use of Deposition.* If a deposition to perpetuate testimony is taken under these Rules or if, although not so taken, it would be admissible in evidence in the courts of the state in which it is taken, it may be used in any action involving the same subject matter subsequently brought in a United States district court, in accordance with the provisions of Rule 32(a).

**(b) Pending Appeal.** If an appeal has been taken from a judgment of a district court or before the taking of an appeal if the time therefor has not expired, the district court in which the judgment was rendered may allow the taking of the depositions of witnesses to perpetuate their testimony for use in the event of further proceedings in the district court. In such case the party who desires to perpetuate the testimony may make a motion in the district court for leave to take the depositions, upon the same notice and service thereof as if the action was pending in the district court. The motion shall show (1) the names and addresses of persons to be examined and the substance of the testimony which the party expects to elicit from each; (2) the reasons for perpetuating their testimony. If the court finds that the perpetuation of the testimony is proper to avoid a failure or delay of justice, it may make an order allowing the depositions to be taken and may make orders of the character provided for by Rules 34 and 35, and thereupon the depositions may be taken and used in the same manner and under the same conditions as are prescribed in these Rules for depositions taken in actions pending in the district court.

**(c) Perpetuation by Action.** This Rule does not limit the power of a court to entertain an action to perpetuate testimony.

### Rule 28. Persons Before Whom Depositions May Be Taken.

**(a) Within the United States.** Within the United States or within a territory or insular possession subject to the jurisdiction of the United States, depositions shall be taken before an officer authorized to administer oaths by the laws of the United States or of the place where the examination is held, or before a person appointed by the court in which the action is pending. A person so appointed has power to administer oaths and take testimony. The term officer as used in Rules 30, 31, and 32 includes a person appointed by the court or designated by the parties under Rule 29.

**(b) In Foreign Countries.** Depositions may be taken in a foreign country (1) pursuant to any applicable treaty or convention, or (2) pursuant to a letter of request (whether or not captioned a letter rogatory), or (3) on notice before a person authorized to administer oaths in the place where the examination is held, either by the law thereof or by the law of the United States, or (4) before a person commissioned by the court and a person so commissioned shall have the power by virtue of the commission to administer any necessary oath and take testimony. A commission or a request shall be issued on application and notice and on terms that are just and appropriate. It is not requisite to the issuance of a commission or a letter of request that the taking of the deposition in any other manner is impracticable or inconvenient; and both a commission and a letter of request may be issued in proper cases. A notice or commission may designate the person before whom the deposition is to be taken either by name or descriptive title. A letter of request may be addressed "To the Appropriate Authority in [here name the country:]." When a letter of request or any other device is used pursuant to any applicable treaty or convention, it shall be captioned in the form prescribed by that treaty or convention. Evidence obtained in response to a letter of request need not be excluded merely because it is not a verbatim transcript, because the testimony was not taken under oath or because of any similar departure from the requirements for depositions taken within the United States under these Rules.

**(c) Disqualification for Interest.** No deposition shall be taken before a person who is a relative or employee or attorney or counsel of any of the parties, or is a relative or employee of such attorney or counsel, or is financially interested in the action.

### Rule 29. Stipulations Regarding Discovery Procedure.

Unless otherwise directed by the court, the parties may by written stipulation (1) provide that depositions may be taken before any person, at any time or place, upon any notice, and in any manner and when so taken may be used like other depositions, and (2) modify other procedures governing or limitations placed upon discovery, except that stipulations extending the time provided in Rules 33, 34 and 36 for responses to discovery may, if they would interfere with any time set for completion of discovery, for hearing of a motion, or for trial, be made only with the approval of the court.

### Rule 30. Depositions Upon Oral Examination.

**(a) When Depositions May Be Taken; When Leave Required.**

(1) A party may take the testimony of any person, including a party, by deposition upon oral examination without leave of court except as provided in paragraph (2). The attendance of witnesses may be compelled by subpoena as provided in Rule 45.

(2) A party must obtain leave of the court, which shall be granted to the extent consistent with the principles stated in Rule 26(b)(2), if the person to be examined is confined in prison or if, without the written stipulation of the parties.

(A) a proposed deposition would result in more than ten depositions being taken under this Rule or Rule 31 by the plaintiffs, or by the defendants, or by third-party defendants;

(B) the person to be examined already has been deposed in the case; or

(C) a party seeks to take a deposition before the time specified in Rule 26(d) unless the notice contains a certification, with supporting facts, that the person to be examined is expected to leave the United States and be unavailable for examination in this country unless deposed before that time.

**(b) Notice of Examination: General Requirements; Recording; Production of Documents and Things; Deposition of Organization; Deposition by Telephone.**

(1) A party desiring to take the deposition of any person upon oral examination shall give reasonable notice in writing to every other party to the action. The notice shall state the time and place for taking the deposition and the name and address of each person to be examined, if known, and, if the name is not known, a general description sufficient to identify the person or the particular class or group to which the person belongs. If a subpoena *duces tecum* is to be served on the person to be examined, the designation of the

materials to be produced as set forth in the subpoena shall be attached to, or included in, the notice.

(2) The party taking the deposition shall state in the notice the method by which the testimony shall be recorded. Unless the court orders otherwise, it may be recorded by sound, sound-and-visual, or stenographic means, and the party taking the deposition shall bear the cost of the recording. Any party may arrange for a transcription to be made from the recording of a deposition taken by non-stenographic means.

(3) With prior notice to the deponent and other parties, any party may designate another method to record the deponent's testimony in addition to the method specified by the person taking the deposition. The additional record or transcript shall be made at that party's expense unless the court otherwise orders.

(4) Unless otherwise agreed by the parties, a deposition shall be conducted before an officer appointed or designated under Rule 28 and shall begin with a statement on the record by the officer that includes (A) the officer's name and business address; (B) the date, time, and place of the deposition; (C) the name of the deponent; (D) the administration of the oath or affirmation to the deponent; and (E) an identification of all persons present. If the deposition is recorded other than stenographically, the officer shall repeat items (A) through (C) at the beginning of each unit of recorded tape or other recording medium. The appearance or demeanor of deponents or attorneys shall not be distorted through camera or sound-recording techniques. At the end of the deposition, the officer shall state on the record that the deposition is complete and shall set forth any stipulations made by counsel concerning the custody of the transcript or recording and the exhibits, or concerning other pertinent matters.

(5) The notice to a party deponent may be accompanied by a request made in compliance with Rule 34 for the production of documents and tangible things at the taking of the deposition. The procedure of Rule 34 shall apply to the request.

(6) A party may in the party's notice and in a subpoena name as the deponent a public or private corporation or a partnership or association or governmental agency and describe with reasonable particularity the matters on which examination is requested. In that event, the organization so named shall designate one or more officers, directors or managing agents, or other persons who consent to testify on its behalf, and may set forth, for each person designated, the matters on which the person will testify. A subpoena shall advise a non-party organization of its duty to make such a designation. The persons so designated shall testify as to matters known or reasonably available to the organization. This subdivision (b)(6) does not preclude taking a deposition by any other procedure authorized in these Rules.

(7) The parties may stipulate in writing or the court may upon motion order that a deposition be taken by telephone or other remote electronic means. For the purposes of this Rule and Rules 28(a), 37(a)(1) and 37(b)(1), a deposition taken by such means is taken in the district and at the place where the deponent is to answer questions.

**(c) Examination and Cross-Examination; Record of Examination; Oath; Objections.** Examination and cross-examination of witnesses may proceed as permitted at the trial under the provisions of the Federal Rules of Evidence except Rules 103 and 615. The officer before whom the deposition is to be taken shall put the witness on oath or affirmation and shall personally, or by someone acting under the officer's direction and in the officer's presence, record the testimony of the witness. The testimony shall be taken stenographically or recorded by any other method authorized by subdivision (b)(2) of this Rule. All objections made at time of the examination to the qualifications of the officer taking the deposition, to the manner of taking it, to the evidence presented, to the conduct of any party, or to any other aspect of the proceedings, shall be noted by the officer upon the record of the deposition but the examination shall proceed, with the testimony being taken subject to the objections. In lieu of participating in the oral examination, parties may serve written questions in a sealed envelope on the party taking the deposition and the party taking the deposition shall transmit them to the officer, who shall propound them to the witness and record the answers verbatim.

**(d) Schedule and Duration; Motion to Terminate or Limit Examination.**

(1) Any objection to evidence during a deposition shall be stated concisely and in a non-argumentative and non-suggestive manner. A party may instruct a deponent not to answer only when necessary to preserve a privilege, to enforce a limitation on evidence

directed by the court, or to present a motion under paragraph (3).

(2) By order or local rule, the court may limit the time permitted for the conduct of a deposition, but shall allow additional time consistent with Rule 26(b)(2) if needed for a fair examination of the deponent or if the deponent or another party impedes or delays the examination. If the court finds such an impediment, delay or other conduct that has frustrated the fair examination of the deponent, it may impose upon the persons responsible an appropriate sanction, including the reasonable costs and attorney's fees incurred by any parties as a result thereof.

(3) At any time during a deposition, on motion of a party or of the deponent and upon a showing that the examination is being conducted in bad faith or in such manner as unreasonably to annoy, embarrass or oppress the deponent or party, the court in which the action is pending or the court in the district where the deposition is being taken may order the officer conducting the examination to cease forthwith from taking the deposition, or may limit the scope and manner of the taking of the deposition as provided in Rule 26(c). If the order made terminates the examination, it shall be resumed thereafter only upon the order of the court in which the action is pending. Upon demand of the objecting party or deponent, the taking of the deposition shall be suspended for the time necessary to make a motion for an order. The provisions of Rule 37(a)(4) apply to the award of expenses incurred in relation to the motion.

**(e) Review by Witness; Changes; Signing.** If requested by the deponent or a party before completion of the deposition, the deponent shall have 30 days after being notified by the officer that the transcript or recording is available in which to review the transcript or recording and, if there are changes in form or substance, to sign a statement reciting such changes and the reasons given by the deponent for making them. The officer shall indicate in the certificate prescribed by subdivision (f)(1) whether any review was requested and, if so, shall append any changes made by the deponent during the period allowed.

**(f) Certification and Filing by Officer; Exhibits; Copies; Notice of Filing.**

(1) The officer shall certify that the witness was duly sworn by the officer and that the deposition is a true record of the testimony given by the witness. This certificate shall be in writing and accompany the record

of the deposition. Unless otherwise ordered by the court, the officer shall securely seal the deposition in an envelope or package indorsed with the title of the action and marked "Deposition of [here insert name of witness]" and shall promptly file it with the court in which the action is pending or send it to the attorney who arranged for the transcript or recording, who shall store it under conditions that will protect it against loss, destruction, tampering or deterioration. Documents and things produced for inspection during the examination of the witness, shall, upon the request of a party, be marked for identification and annexed to the deposition and may be inspected and copied by any party, except that if the person producing the materials desires to retain them the person may (A) offer copies to be marked for identification and annexed to the deposition and to serve thereafter as originals if the person affords to all parties fair opportunity to verify the copies by comparison with the originals, or (B) offer the originals to be marked for identification, after giving to each party an opportunity to inspect and copy them, in which event the materials may then be used in the same manner as if annexed to the deposition. Any party may move for an order that the original be annexed to and returned with the deposition to the court, pending final disposition of the case.

(2) Unless otherwise ordered by the court or agreed by the parties, the officer shall retain stenographic notes of any deposition taken stenographically or a copy of the recording of any deposition taken by another method. Upon payment of reasonable charges therefor, the officer shall furnish a copy of the transcript or other recording of the deposition to any party or to the deponent.

(3) The party taking the deposition shall give prompt notice of its filing to all other parties.

**(g) Failure to Attend or to Serve Subpoena; Expenses.**

(1) If the party giving the notice of the taking of a deposition fails to attend and proceed therewith and another party attends in person or by attorney pursuant to the notice, the court may order the party giving the notice to pay to such other party the reasonable expenses incurred by that party and that party's attorney in attending, including reasonable attorney's fees.

(2) If the party giving the notice of the taking of a deposition of a witness fails to

serve a subpoena upon the witness and the witness because of such failure does not attend, and if another party attends in person or by attorney because that party expects the deposition of that witness to be taken, the court may order the party giving the notice to pay to such other party the reasonable expenses incurred by that party and that party's attorney in attending, including reasonable attorney's fees.

### Rule 31. Depositions Upon Written Questions.

**(a) Serving Questions; Notice.**

(1) Any party may take the testimony of any person, including a party, by deposition upon written questions without leave of court except as provided in paragraph (2). The attendance of witnesses may be compelled by the use of subpoena as provided in Rule 45.

(2) A party must obtain leave of court, which shall be granted to the extent consistent with the principles stated in Rule 26(b)(2), if the person to be examined is confined in prison or if, without the written stipulation of the parties,

(A) a proposed deposition would result in more than ten depositions being taken under this Rule or Rule 30 by the plaintiffs, or by the defendants, or by third-party defendants;

(B) the person to be examined has already been deposed in the case; or

(C) a party seeks to take a deposition before the time specified in Rule 26(d).

(3) A party desiring to take a deposition upon written questions shall serve them upon every other party with a notice stating (1) the name and address of the person who is to answer them, if known, and if the name is not known, a general description sufficient to identify the person or the particular class or group to which the person belongs, and (2) the name or descriptive title and address of the officer before whom the deposition is to be taken. A deposition upon written questions may be taken of a public or private corporation or a partnership or association or governmental agency in accordance with the provisions of Rule 30(b)(6).

(4) Within 14 days after the notice and written questions are served, a party may serve cross questions upon all other parties. Within 10 days after being served with cross questions, a party may serve redirect questions upon all other parties. Within 10 days after being served with redirect questions, a

party may serve recross questions upon all other parties. The court may for cause shown enlarge or shorten the time.

**(b) Officer to Take Responses and Prepare Record.** A copy of the notice and copies of all questions served shall be delivered by the party taking the deposition to the officer designated in the notice, who shall proceed promptly, in the manner provided by Rule 30(c), (e) and (f), to take the testimony of the witness in response to the questions and to prepare, certify and file or mail the deposition, attaching thereto the copy of the notice and the questions received by the officer.

**(c) Notice of Filing.** When the deposition is filed, the party taking it shall promptly give notice thereof to all other parties.

### Rule 32. Use of Depositions in Court Proceedings.

**(a) Use of Depositions.** At the trial or upon the hearing of a motion or an interlocutory proceeding, any part or all of a deposition, so far as admissible under the rules of evidence applied as though the witness were then present and testifying, may be used against any party who was present or represented at the taking of the deposition or who had reasonable notice thereof, in accordance with any of the following provisions:

(1) Any deposition may be used by any party for the purpose of contracting or impeaching the testimony of deponent as a witness or for any other purpose permitted by the Federal Rules of Evidence.

(2) The deposition of a party or of anyone who at the time of taking the deposition was an officer, director or managing agent or a person designated under Rule 30(b)(6) or 31(a) to testify on behalf of a public or private corporation, partnership or association or governmental agency which is a party may be used by an adverse party for any purpose.

(3) The deposition of a witness, whether or not a party, may be used by any party for any purpose if the court finds:

(A) that the witness is dead; or

(B) that the witness is at a greater distance than 100 miles from the place of trial or hearing, or is out of the United States, unless it appears that the absence of the witness was procured by the party offering the deposition; or

(C) that the witness is unable to attend or testify because of age, illness, infirmity or imprisonment; or

(D) that the party offering the deposition has been unable to procure the attendance of the witness by subpoena; or

(E) upon application and notice, that such exceptional circumstances exist as to make it desirable, in the interest of justice and with due regard to the importance of presenting the testimony of witnesses orally in open court, to allow the deposition to be used.

A deposition taken without leave of court pursuant to a notice under Rule 30(a)(2)(C) shall not be used against a party who demonstrates that, when served with the notice, it was unable through the exercise of diligence to obtain counsel to represent it at the taking of the deposition; nor shall a deposition be used against a party who, having received less than 11 days notice of a deposition, has promptly upon receiving such notice filed a motion for a protective order under Rule 26(c)(2) requesting that the deposition not be held or be held at a different time or place and such motion is pending at the time the deposition is held.

(4) If only part of a deposition is offered in evidence by a party, an adverse party may require the offeror to introduce any other part which ought in fairness to be considered with the part introduced, and any party may introduce any other parts.

Substitution of parties pursuant to Rule 25 does not affect the right to use depositions previously taken; and when an action has been brought in any court of the United States or of any State and another action involving the same subject matter is afterward brought between the same parties or their representatives or successor in interest, all depositions lawfully taken and duly filed in the former action may be used in the latter as if originally taken therefor. A deposition previously taken may also be used as permitted by the Federal Rules of Evidence.

**(b) Objections to Admissibility.** Subject to the provisions of Rule 28(b) and subdivision (d)(3) of this Rule, objection may be made at the trial or hearing to receiving in evidence any deposition or part thereof for any reason which would require the exclusion of the evidence if the witness were then present and testifying.

**(c) Form of Presentation.** Except as otherwise directed by the court, a party offering deposition testimony pursuant to this Rule may offer it in stenographic or non-stenographic form, but, if in non-stenographic form, the party shall also provide the court with a transcript of the portions so offered. On request of any party in a case tried before a jury, deposition testimony offered other than for impeachment purposes shall be presented in non-stenographic form, if available, unless the court for good cause orders otherwise.

**(d) Effect of Errors and Irregularities in Depositions.**

(1) *As to Notice.* All errors and irregularities in the notice for taking a deposition are waived unless written objection is promptly served upon the party giving the notice.

(2) *As to Disqualification of Officer.* Objection to taking a deposition because of disqualification of the officer before whom it is to be taken is waived unless made before the taking of the deposition begins or as soon thereafter as the disqualification becomes known or could be discovered with reasonable diligence.

(3) *As to Taking of Deposition.*

(A) Objections to the competency of a witness or to the competency, relevancy or materiality of testimony are not waived by failure to make them before or during the taking of the deposition, unless the ground of the objection is one which might have been obviated or removed if presented at that time.

(B) Errors and irregularities occurring at the oral examination in the manner of taking the deposition, in the form of the questions or answers, in the oath or affirmation, or in the conduct of parties, and errors of any kind which might be obviated, removed or cured if promptly presented, are waived unless seasonable objection thereto is made to the taking of the deposition.

(C) Objections to the form of written questions submitted under Rule 31 are waived unless served in writing upon the party propounded them within the time allowed for serving the succeeding cross or other questions and within 5 days after service of the last questions authorized.

(4) *As to Completion and Return of Deposition.* Errors and irregularities in the manner in which the testimony is transcribed or the deposition is prepared, signed, certified, sealed, endorsed, transmitted, filed or otherwise dealt with by the officer under Rules 30 and 31 are waived unless a motion to suppress the deposition or some part thereof is made with reasonable promptness after such defect is, or with due diligence might have been, ascertained.

## Rule 33. Interrogatories to Parties.

**(a) Availability.** Without leave of court or written stipulation, any party may serve upon any other party written interrogatories, not to exceed 25 in number including all discrete subparts, to be answered by the party served or, if the party served is a public or private corporation or a partnership or association or governmental agency, by any officer or agent, who shall furnish such information as is available to the party. Leave to serve additional interrogatories shall be granted to the extent consistent with the principles of Rule 26(b)(2). Without leave of court or written stipulation, interrogatories may not be served before the time specified in Rule 26(d).

**(b) Answers and Objections.**

(1)  Each interrogatory shall be answered separately and fully in writing under oath, unless it is objected to, in which event the objecting party shall state the reasons for objection and shall answer to the extent the interrogatory is not objectionable.

(2)  The answers are to be signed by the person making them, and the objections signed by the attorney making them.

(3)  The party upon whom the interrogatories have been served shall serve a copy of the answers, and objections if any, within 30 days after the service of the interrogatories. A shorter or longer time may be directed by the court or, in the absence of such an order, agreed to in writing by the parties subject to Rule 29.

(4)  All grounds for an objection to an interrogatory shall be stated with specificity. Any ground not stated in a timely objection is waived unless the party's failure to object is excused by the court for good cause shown.

(5)  The party submitting the interrogatories may move for an order under Rule 37(a) with respect to any objection to or other failure to answer an interrogatory.

**(c) Scope; Use at Trial.** Interrogatories may relate to any matters which can be inquired into under Rule 26(b), and the answers may be used to the extent permitted by the rules of evidence.

An interrogatory otherwise proper is not necessarily objectionable merely because an answer to the interrogatory involves an opinion or contention that relates to a fact or the application of law or fact, but the court may order that such an interrogatory need not be answered until after designated discovery has been completed or until a pretrial conference or other later time.

**(d) Option to Produce Business Records.** Where the answer to an interrogatory may be derived or ascertained from the business records of the party upon whom the interrogatory has been served or from an examination, audit or inspection of such business records, including a compilation, abstract or summary thereof, and the burden of deriving or ascertaining the answer is substantially the same for the party serving the interrogatory as for the party served, it is a sufficient answer to such interrogatory to specify the records from which the answer may be derived or ascertained and to afford to the party serving the interrogatory reasonable opportunity to examine, audit or inspect such records and to make copies, compilations, abstracts or summaries. A specification shall be in sufficient detail to permit the interrogating party to locate and to identify, as readily as can the party served, the records from which the answer may be ascertained.

## Rule 34. Production of Documents and Things and Entry Upon Land for Inspection and Other Purposes.

**(a) Scope.** Any party may serve on any other party a request (1) to produce and permit the party making the request, or someone acting on the requestor's behalf, to inspect and copy, any designated documents (including writings, drawings, graphs, charts, photographs, phono-records and other data compilations from which information can be obtained, translated, if necessary, by the respondent through detection devices into reasonably usable form), or to inspect and copy, test or sample any tangible things which constitute or contain matters within the scope of Rule 26(b) and which are in the possession, custody or control of the party upon whom the request is served; or (2) to permit entry upon designated land or other property in the possession or control of the party upon whom the request is served for the purpose of inspection and measuring, surveying, photographing, testing or sampling the property or any designated object or operation thereon, within the scope of Rule 26(b).

**(b) Procedure.** The request shall set forth, either by individual item or by category, the items to be inspected and describe each with reasonable particularity. The request shall specify a reasonable time, place and manner of making the inspection and performing the related acts. Without leave of court or written stipulation, a request may not be served before the time specified in Rule 26(d).

The party upon whom the request is served shall serve a written response within 30 days after the service of the request. A shorter or longer time may be directed by the court or, in the absence of such an order, agreed to in writing by the parties, subject to Rule 29. The response shall state, with respect to each item or category, that inspection and related activities will be permitted as requested, unless the request is objected to, in which event the reasons for objection shall be stated. If objection is made to part of an item or category, the part shall be specified and inspection permitted of the remaining parts. The party submitting the request may move for an order under Rule 37(a) with respect to any objection to or other failure to respond to the request or any part thereof, or any failure to permit inspection as requested.

A party who produces documents for inspection shall produce them as they are kept in the usual course of business or shall organize and label them to correspond with the categories in the request.

**(c) Persons Not Parties.** A person not a party to the action may be compelled to produce documents and things or to submit to an inspection as provided in Rule 45.

### Rule 35. Physical and Mental Examination of Persons.

**(a) Order for Examination.** When the mental or physical condition (including the blood group) of a party, or of a person in the custody or under the legal control of a party, is in controversy, the court in which the action is pending may order the party to submit to a physical examination by a physician or mental examination by a physician or psychologist or to produce for examination the person in the party's custody or legal control. The order may be made only on motion for good cause shown and upon notice to the person to be examined and to all parties and shall specify the time, place, manner, conditions and scope of the examination and the person or persons by whom it is to be made.

**(b) Report of Examining Physician.**

(1) If requested by the party against whom an order is made under Rule 35(a) or the person examined, the party causing the examination to be made shall deliver to the requestor a copy of a detailed written report of the examining physician setting out the physician's findings, including results of all tests made, diagnoses and conclusions, together with like reports of all earlier examinations of the same condition. After delivery the party causing the examination shall be entitled upon request to receive from the party against whom the order is made a like report of any examination, previously or thereafter made, of the same condition, unless, in the case of a report of examination of a person not a party, the party shows that such party is unable to obtain it. The court on motion may make an order against a party requiring delivery of a report on such terms as are just, and if a physician fails or refuses to make a report, the court may exclude the physician's testimony if offered at the trial.

(2) By requesting and obtaining a report of the examination so ordered or by taking the deposition of the examiner, the party examined waives any privilege the party may have in that action or any other involving the same controversy, regarding the testimony of every other person who has examined or may thereafter examine the party in respect of the same mental or physical condition.

(3) This subdivision applies to examinations made by agreement of the parties, unless the agreement expressly provides otherwise. This subdivision does not preclude discovery of a report of an examiner or the taking of a deposition of the examiner in accordance with the provisions of any other Rule.

### Rule 36. Requests for Admission.

**(a) Request for Admission.** A party may serve upon any other party a written request for the admission, for purposes of the pending action only, of the truth of any matters within the scope of Rule 26(b)(1) set forth in the request that relate to statements or opinions of fact or of the application of law to fact, including the genuineness of any documents described in the request. Copies of documents shall be served with the request unless they have been or are otherwise furnished or made available for inspection and copying. Without leave of court or written stipulation, requests for admission may not be served before the time specified in Rule 26(d).

Each matter of which an admission is requested shall be separately set forth. The matter is admitted unless, within 30 days after service of the request, or within such shorter or longer time as the court may allow or as the parties may agree to in writing, subject to Rule 29, the party to whom the request is directed serves upon the party requesting the admission a written answer or objection addressed to the matter, signed by the party or by the party's attorney. If objection is made, the reasons therefor shall be stated. The answer shall specifically deny the matter or set forth in detail the reasons why the answering party cannot truthfully admit or deny the matter. A denial shall fairly meet the substance of the requested admission, and when good faith requires that a party qualify an answer or deny only a part of the matter of which an admission is requested, the party shall specify so much of it as is true and qualify or deny the remainder. An answering party may not give lack of information or knowledge as a reason for failure to admit or deny unless the party states that the party has made reasonable inquiry and that the information known or readily obtainable by the party is insufficient to enable the party to admit or deny. A party who considers that a matter of which an admission has been requested presents a genuine issue for trial may not, on that ground alone, object to the request; the party may, subject to the provisions of Rule 37(c), deny the matter or set forth reasons why the party cannot admit or deny it.

The party who has requested the admissions may move to determine the sufficiency of the answers of objections. Unless the court determines that an objection is justified, it shall order that an answer be served. If the court determines that an answer does not comply with the requirements of this Rule, it may order either that the matter is admitted or that an amended answer be served. The court may, in lieu of these orders, determine that final disposition of the request be made at a pretrial conference or at a designated time prior to trial. The provisions of Rule 37(a)(4) apply to the award of expenses incurred in relation to the motion.

**(b) Effect of Admission.** Any matter admitted under this Rule is conclusively established unless the court on motion permits withdrawal or amendment of the admission. Subject to the provisions of Rule 15 governing amendment of a pretrial order, the court may permit withdrawal or amendment when the presentation of the merits of the action will be subserved thereby and the party who obtained the admission fails to satisfy the court that withdrawal or amendment will prejudice the party in maintaining the action or defense on the merits. Any admission made by a party under this Rule is for the purpose of the pending action only and is not an admission for any other purpose nor may it be used against the party in any other proceeding.

### Rule 37. Failure to Make or Cooperate in Discovery; Sanctions.

**(a) Motion for Order Compelling Discovery.** A party, upon reasonable notice to other parties and all persons affected thereby, may apply for an order compelling disclosure or discovery as follows:

(1) *Appropriate Court.* An application for an order to a party shall be made to the court in which the action is pending. An application for an order to a person who is not a party shall be made to the court in the district where the discovery is being, or is to be, taken.

(2) *Motion.*

(A) If a party fails to make a disclosure required by Rule 26(a), any other party may move to compel disclosure and for appropriate sanctions. The motion must include a certification that the movant has in good faith conferred or attempted to confer with the party not making the disclosure in an effort to secure the disclosure without court action.

(B) If a deponent fails to answer a question propounded or submitted under Rules 30 or 31, or a corporation or other entity fails to make a designation under Rule 30(b)(6) or 31(a), or a party fails to answer an interrogatory submitted under Rule 33, or if a party, in response to a request for inspection submitted under Rule 34, fails to respond, that inspection will be permitted as requested or fails to permit inspection as requested, the discovering party may move for an order compelling an answer, or a designation or an order compelling inspection in accordance with the request. The motion must include a certification that the movant has in good faith conferred or attempted to confer with the person or party failing to make the discovery in an effort to secure the information or material without court action. When taking a deposition on oral examination, the proponent of the question may complete or adjourn the examination before applying for an order.

(3) *Evasive or Incomplete Disclosure, Answer, or Response.* For purposes of this subdi-

vision an evasive or incomplete disclosure, answer or response is to be treated as a failure to disclose, answer or respond.

(4) *Expenses and Sanctions.*

(A) If the motion is granted or if the disclosure or requested discovery is provided after the motion was filed, the court shall, after affording an opportunity to be heard, require the party or deponent whose conduct necessitated the motion or the party or attorney advising such conduct or both of them to pay to the moving party the reasonable expenses incurred in making the motion, including attorney's fees, unless the court finds that the motion was filed without the movant's first making a good faith effort to obtain the disclosure or discovery without court action, or that the opposing party's nondisclosure, response or objection was substantially justified or that other circumstances make an award of expenses unjust.

(B) If the motion is denied, the court may enter any protective order authorized under Rule 26(c) and shall, after affording an opportunity to be heard, require the moving party or the attorney filing the motion or both of them to pay to the party or deponent who opposed the motion the reasonable expenses incurred in opposing the motion, including attorney's fees, unless the court finds that the making of the motion was substantially justified or that other circumstances make an award of expenses unjust.

(C) If the motion is granted in part and denied in part, the court may enter any protective order authorized under Rule 26(c) and may, after affording an opportunity to be heard, apportion the reasonable expenses incurred in relation to the motion among the parties and persons in a just manner.

**(b) Failure to Comply with Order.**

(1) *Sanctions by Court in District Where Deposition Is Taken.* If a deponent fails to be sworn or to answer a question after being directed to do so by the court in the district in which the deposition is being taken, the failure may be considered a contempt of that court.

(2) *Sanctions by Court in Which Action Is Pending.* If a party or officer, director or managing agent of a party or a person designated under Rule 30(b)(6) or 31(a) to testify on behalf of a party fails to obey an order to provide or permit discovery, including an order made under subdivision (a) of this Rule or Rule 35, or if a party fails to obey an order entered under Rule 26(f), the court in which the action is pending may make such orders in regard to the failure as are just, and among others the following:

(A) An order that the matters regarding which the order was made or any other designated facts shall be taken to be established for the purposes of the action in accordance with the claim of the party obtaining the order;

(B) An order refusing to allow the disobedient party to support or oppose designated claims or defenses, or prohibiting that party from introducing designated matters in evidence;

(C) An order striking out pleadings or parts thereof, or staying further proceedings until the order is obeyed or dismissing the action or proceeding or any part thereof, or rendering a judgment by default against the disobedient party;

(D) In lieu of any of the foregoing orders or in addition thereto, an order treating as a contempt of court the failure to obey any orders except an order to submit to a physical or mental examination;

(E) Where a party has failed to comply with an order under Rule 35(a) requiring that party to produce another for examination, such orders as are listed in paragraphs (A), (B) and (C) of this subdivision, unless the party failing to comply shows that party is unable to produce such person for examination.

In lieu of any of the foregoing orders or in addition thereto, the court shall require the party failing to obey the order or the attorney advising that party or both to pay the reasonable expenses, including attorney's fees, caused by the failure, unless the court finds that the failure was substantially justified or that other circumstances make an award of expenses unjust.

**(c) Failure to Disclose; False or Misleading Disclosure; Refusal to Admit.**

(1) A party that without substantial justification fails to disclose information required by Rule 26(a) or 26(e)(1) shall not, unless such failure is harmless, be permitted to use as evidence at a trial, at a hearing, or on a motion any witness or information not so disclosed. In addition to or in lieu of this sanction, the court, on motion and after affording an opportunity to be heard, may impose other appropriate sanctions. In addition to requiring payment of reasonable expenses, including attorney's fees, caused by the failure, these sanctions may include any of the actions authorized under subparagraphs (A),

(B) and (C) of subdivision (b)(2) of this Rule and may include informing the jury of the failure to make the disclosure.

(2) If a party fails to admit the genuineness of any document or the truth of any matter as requested under Rule 36, and if the party requesting the admissions thereafter proves the genuineness of the document or the truth of the matter, the requesting party may apply to the court for an order requiring the other party to pay the reasonable expenses incurred in making that proof, including reasonable attorney's fees. The court shall make the order unless it finds that (A) the request was held objectionable pursuant to Rule 36(a) or (B) the admission sought was of no substantial importance, or (C) the party failing to admit had reasonable ground to believe that the party might prevail on the matter, or (D) there was other good reason for the failure to admit.

**(d) Failure of Party to Attend at Own Deposition or Serve Answers to Interrogatories or Respond to Request for Inspection.** If a party or an officer, director or managing agent of a party or a person designated under Rule 30(b)(6) or 31(a) to testify on behalf of a party fails (1) to appear before the officer who is to take the deposition, after being served with a proper notice, or (2) to serve answers or objections to interrogatories submitted under Rule 33, after proper service of the interrogatories, or (3) to serve a written response to a request for inspection submitted under Rule 34, after proper service of the request, the court in which the action is pending on motion may make such orders in regard to the failure as are just, and among others it may take any action authorized under subparagraphs (A), (B) and (C) of subdivision (b)(2) of this Rule. Any motion specifying a failure under clause (2) or (3) of this subdivision shall include a certification that the movant has in good faith conferred or attempted to confer with the party failing to answer or respond in an effort to obtain such answer or response without court action. In lieu of any order or in addition thereto, the court shall require the party failing to act or the attorney advising that party or both to pay the reasonable expenses, including attorney's fees, caused by the failure, unless the court finds that the failure was substantially justified or that other circumstances make an award of expenses unjust.

The failure to act described in this subdivision may not be excused on the ground that the discovery sought is objectionable unless the party failing to act has a pending motion for a protective order as provided by Rule 26(c).

**(e) Subpoena of Person in Foreign Country.** Abrogated by amendment Apr. 29, 1980, eff. Aug. 1, 1980.

**(f) Expenses Against United States.** Repealed by P.L. 69-481, eff. Oct. 1, 1981.

**(g) Failure to Participate in the Framing of a Discovery Plan.** If a party or a party's attorney fails to participate in good faith in the development and submission of a proposed discovery plan as required by Rule 26(f), the court may, after opportunity for hearing, require such party or attorney to pay to any other party the reasonable expenses, including attorney's fees, caused by the failure.

**VI. Trials.**

### Rule 38. Jury Trial of Right.

**(a) Right Preserved.** The right of trial by jury as declared by the Seventh Amendment to the Constitution or as given by a statute of the United States shall be preserved to the parties inviolate.

**(b) Demand.** Any party may demand a trial by jury of any issue triable of right by a jury by (1) serving upon the other parties a demand therefor in writing at any time after the commencement of the action and not later than 10 days after the service of the last pleading directed to such issue, and (1) filing the demand as required by Rule 5(d). Such demand may be endorsed upon a pleading of the party.

**(c) Same: Specification of Issues.** In the demand, a party may specify the issues which the party wishes so tried; otherwise the party shall be deemed to have demanded trial by jury for all of the issues so triable. If the party has demanded trial by jury for only some of the issues, any other party within 10 days after service of the demand or such lesser time as the court may order, may serve a demand for trial by jury of any other or all of the issues of fact in the action.

**(d) Waiver.** The failure of a party to serve and file a demand as required by this Rule constitutes a waiver by the party of trial by jury. A demand for trial by jury made as herein provided may not be withdrawn without the consent of the parties.

**(e) Admiralty and Maritime Claims.** These Rules shall not be construed to create a right to trial by jury of the issues in an admiralty or maritime claim within the meaning of Rule 9(h).

## Rule 39. Trial by Jury or by the Court.

**(a) By Jury.** When trial by jury has been demanded as provided in Rule 38, the action shall be designated upon the docket as a jury action. The trial of all issues so demanded shall be by jury, unless (1) the parties or their attorneys of record, by written stipulation filed with the court or by an oral stipulation made in open court and entered in the record, consent to trial by the court sitting without a jury or (2) the court upon motion or of its own initiative finds that a right of trial by jury of some or all of those issues does not exist under the Constitution or statutes of the United States.

**(b) By the Court.** Issues not demanded for trial by jury as provided in Rule 38 shall be tried by the court; but, notwithstanding the failure of a party to demand a jury in an action in which such a demand might have been made of right, the court in its discretion upon motion may order a trial by a jury of any or all issues.

**(c) Advisory Jury and Trial by Consent.** In all actions not triable of right by a jury, the court upon motion or of its own initiative may try any issue with an advisory jury or, except in actions against the United States when a statute of the United States provides for trial without a jury, the court, with the consent of both parties, may order a trial with a jury whose verdict has the same effect as if trial by jury had been a matter of right.

## Rule 40. Assignment of Cases for Trial.

The district courts shall provide by rule for the placing of actions upon the trial calendar (1) without request of the parties or (2) upon request of a party and notice to the other parties or (3) in such other manner as the courts deem expedient. Precedence shall be given to actions entitled thereto by any statute of the United States.

## Rule 41. Dismissal of Actions.

**(a) Voluntary Dismissal: Effect Thereof.**

(1) *By Plaintiff; by Stipulation.* Subject to the provisions of Rule 23(e), of Rule 66, and of any statute of the United States, an action may be dismissed by the plaintiff without order of court (i) by filing a notice of dismissal at any time before service by the adverse party of an answer or of a motion for summary judgment, whichever first occurs, or (ii) by filing a stipulation of dismissal signed by all parties who have appeared in the action. Unless otherwise stated in the notice of dismissal or stipulation, the dismissal is without prejudice, except that a notice of dismissal operates as an adjudication upon the merits when filed by a plaintiff who has once dismissed in any court of the United States or of any state an action based on or including the same claim.

(2) *By Order of the Court.* Except as provided in paragraph (1) of this subdivision of this Rule, an action shall not be dismissed at the plaintiff's instance save upon order of the court and upon such terms and conditions as the court deems proper. If a counterclaim has been pleaded by a defendant prior to the service upon the defendant of the plaintiff's motion to dismiss, the action shall not be dismissed against the defendant's objection unless the counterclaim can remain pending for independent adjudication by the court. Unless otherwise specified in the order, a dismissal under this paragraph is without prejudice.

**(b) Involuntary Dismissal: Effect Thereof.** For failure of the plaintiff to prosecute or to comply with these Rules or any order of court, a defendant may move for dismissal of an action or of any claim against the defendant. Unless the court in its order for dismissal otherwise specifies, a dismissal under this subdivision and any dismissal not provided for in this Rule, other than a dismissal for lack of jurisdiction, for improper venue or for failure to join a party under Rule 19, operates as an adjudication upon the merits.

**(c) Dismissal of Counterclaim, Cross-Claim or Third-Party Claim.** The provisions of this Rule apply to the dismissal of any counterclaim, cross-claim or third-party claim. A voluntary dismissal by the claimant alone pursuant to paragraph (1) of subdivision (a) of this Rule shall be made before a responsive pleading is served or, if there is none, before the introduction of evidence at the trial or hearing.

**(d) Costs of Previously Dismissed Action.** If a plaintiff who has once dismissed an action in any court commences an action based upon or including the same claim against the same defendant, the court may make such order for the payment of costs of the action previously dismissed as it may deem proper and may stay the proceedings in the action until the plaintiff has complied with the order.

## Rule 42. Consolidation; Separate Trials.

**(a) Consolidation.** When actions involving a common question of law or fact are pending before the court, it may order a joint hearing or trial of any or all of the matters in issue in the actions; it may order all of the actions consolidated; and it may make such orders concerning proceedings therein as may tend to avoid unnecessary costs or delay.

**(b) Separate Trials.** The court, in furtherance of convenience or to avoid prejudice, or when separate trials will be conducive to expedition and economy, may order a separate trial of any claim, cross-claim, counterclaim or third-party claim, or of any separate issue or of any number of claims, cross-claims, counterclaims, third-party claims or issues, always preserving inviolate the right of trial by jury as declared by the Seventh Amendment to the Constitution or as given by a statute of the United States.

## Rule 43. Taking of Testimony.

**(a) Form.** In every trial, the testimony of witnesses shall be taken in open court, unless a federal law, these Rules, the Federal Rules of Evidence, or other rule adopted by the Supreme Court provide otherwise. The court may, for good cause shown in compelling circumstances and upon appropriate safeguards, permit presentation of testimony in open court by contemporaneous transmission from a different location.

**(b) Abrogated**

**(c) Abrogated**

**(d) Affirmation in Lieu of Oath.** Whenever under these rules an oath is required to be taken, a solemn affirmation may be accepted in lieu thereof.

**(e) Evidence on Motions.** When a motion is based on facts not appearing of record, the court may hear the matter on affidavits presented by the respective parties, but the court may direct that the matter be heard wholly or partly on oral testimony or deposition.

**(f) Interpreters.** The court may appoint an interpreter of its own selection and may fix the interpreter's reasonable compensation. The compensation shall be paid out of funds provided by law or by one or more of the parties as the court may direct, and may be taxed ultimately as costs, in the discretion of the court.

## Rule 44. Proof of Official Record.

**(a) Authentication.**

(1) *Domestic.* An official record kept within the United States, or any state, district, commonwealth, or within a territory subject to the administrative or judicial jurisdiction of the United States, or an entry therein, when admissible for any purpose, may be evidenced by an official publication thereof or by a copy attested by the officer having the legal custody of the record, or by the officer's deputy, and accompanied by a certificate that such officer has the custody. The certificate may be made by a judge of a court of record of the district or political subdivision in which the record is kept, authenticated by the seal of the court or may be made by any public officer having a seal of office and having official duties in the district or political subdivision in which the record is kept, authenticated by the seal of the officer's office.

(2) *Foreign.* A foreign official record, or an entry therein, when admissible for any purpose, may be evidenced by an official publication thereof; or a copy thereof, attested by a person authorized to make the attestation, and accompanied by a final certification as to the genuineness of the signature and official position (i) of the attesting person, or (ii) of any foreign official whose certificate of genuineness of signature and official position relates to the attestation or is in a chain of certificates of genuineness of signature and official position relating to the attestation. A final certification may be made by a secretary of embassy or legation, consul general, consul, vice consul or consular agent of the United States or a diplomatic or consular official of the foreign country assigned or accredited to the United States. If reasonable opportunity has been given to all parties to investigate the authenticity and accuracy of the documents, the court may, for good cause shown, (i) admit an attested copy without final certification or (ii) permit the foreign official record to be evidenced by an attested summary with or without a final certification.

**(b) Lack of Record.** A written statement that after diligent search no record or entry of a specified tenor is found to exist in the records designated by the statement, authenticated as provided in subdivision (a)(1) of this Rule in the case of a domestic record, or complying with the requirements of subdivision (a)(2) of this Rule for a summary in the case of a foreign record, is admissible as evidence that the records contain no such record or entry.

**(c) Other Proof.** This Rule does not prevent the proof of official records or of entry or lack of entry therein by any other method authorized by law.

## Rule 44.1. Determination of Foreign Law.

A party who intends to raise an issue concerning the law of a foreign country shall give notice by pleadings or other reasonable written notice. The court, in determining foreign law, may consider any relevant material or source, including testimony, whether or not submitted by a party or admissible under the Federal Rules of Evidence. The court's determination shall be treated as a ruling on a question of law.

## Rule 45. Subpoena.

**(a) Form; Issuance.**

(1) Every subpoena shall:

(A) state the name of the court from which it is issued; and

(B) state the title of the action, the name of the court in which it is pending, and its civil action number; and

(C) command each person to whom it is directed to attend and give testimony or to produce and permit inspection and copying of designated books, documents or tangible things in the possession, custody or control of that person, or to permit inspection of premises, at a time and place therein specified; and

(D) set forth the text of subdivisions (c) and (d) of this Rule.

A command to produce evidence or to permit inspection may be joined with a command to appear at trial or hearing or at deposition, or may be issued separately.

(2) A subpoena commanding attendance at a trial or hearing shall issue from the court for the district in which the hearing or trial is to be held. A subpoena for attendance at a deposition shall issue from the court for the district designated by the notice of deposition as the district in which the deposition is to be taken. If separate from a subpoena commanding the attendance of a person, a subpoena for production or inspection shall issue from the court for the district in which the production or inspection is to be made.

(3) The clerk shall issue a subpoena, signed but otherwise in blank, to a party requesting it, who shall complete it before service. An attorney as officer of the court may also issue and sign a subpoena on behalf of:

(A) a court in which the attorney is authorized to practice; or

(B) a court for a district in which a deposition or production is compelled by the subpoena, if the deposition or production pertains to an action pending in a court in which the attorney is authorized to practice.

**(b) Service.**

(1) A subpoena may be served by any person who is not a party and is not less than 18 years of age. Service of a subpoena upon a person named therein shall be made by delivering a copy thereof to such person and, if the person's attendance is commanded, by tendering to that person the fees for one day's attendance and the mileage allowed by law. When the subpoena is issued on behalf of the United States or an officer or agency thereof, fees and mileage need not be tendered. Prior notice of any commenced production of documents and things or inspection of premises before trial shall be served on each party in the manner prescribed by Rule 5(b).

(2) Subject to the provisions of clause (ii) of subparagraph (c)(3)(a) of this Rule, a subpoena may be served at any place within the district of the court by which it is issued, or at any place without the district that is within 100 miles of the place of the deposition, hearing, trial, production or inspection specified in the subpoena or at any place within the State where a State statute or rule of court permits service of a subpoena issued by a State court of general jurisdiction sitting in the place of the deposition, hearing, trial, production or inspection specified in the subpoena. When a statute of the United States provides therefor, the court upon proper application and cause shown may authorize the service of a subpoena at any other place. A subpoena directed to a witness in a foreign country who is a national or resident of the United States shall issue under the circumstances and in the manner and be served as provided in Title 28, U.S.C. §1783.

(3) Proof of service when necessary shall be made by filing with the clerk of the court by which the subpoena is issued a statement of the date and manner of service and of the names of the persons served, certified by the person who made the service. A subpoena may also command the person to whom it is directed to produce the books, papers, documents or tangible things designated therein;

but the court, upon motion made promptly and in any event at or before the time specified in the subpoena for compliance therewith, may (1) quash or modify the subpoena if it is unreasonable and oppressive or (2) condition denial of the motion upon the advancement by the person in whose behalf the subpoena is issued of the reasonable cost of producing the books, papers, documents or tangible things.

**(c) Protection of Persons Subject to Subpoenas.**

(1) A party or an attorney responsible for the issuance and service of a subpoena shall take reasonable steps to avoid imposing undue burden or expense on a person subject to that subpoena. The court on behalf of which the subpoena was issued shall enforce this duty and impose upon the party or attorney in breach of his duty an appropriate sanction, which may include, but is not limited to, lost earnings and a reasonable attorney's fee.

(2) (A) Subject to paragraph (d)(2) of this Rule, a person commenced to produce and permit inspection and copying may, within 14 days after service of the subpoena or before the time specified for compliance if such time is less than 14 days after service, serve upon the party or attorney designated in the subpoena written objection to inspection or copying of any or all of the designated materials or of the premises. If objection is made, the party serving the subpoena shall not be entitled to inspect and copy the materials or inspect the premises except pursuant to an order of the court by which the subpoena was issued. If objection has been made, the party serving the subpoena may, upon notice to the person commanded to produce, move at any time for an order to compel the production. Such an order to compel production shall protect any person who is not a party or an officer of a party from significant expense resulting from the inspection and copying commanded.

(3) (A) On timely motion, the court by which a subpoena was issued shall quash or modify the subpoena if it:

(i) fails to allow reasonable time for compliance;

(ii) requires a person who is not a party or an officer of a party to travel to a place more than 100 miles from the place where that person resides, is employed or regularly transacts business in person, except that, subject to the provisions of clause (c)(3)(B)(iii) of this Rule, such a person may in order to attend trial be commanded to travel from any such place within the State in which the trial is held; or

(iii) requires disclosure of privileged or other protected matter and no exception or waiver applies; or

(iv) subjects a person to undue burden.

(B) If a subpoena:

(i) requires disclosure of a trade secret or other confidential research, development or commercial information, or

(ii) requires disclosure of an unretained expert's opinion or information not describing specific events or occurrences in dispute and resulting from the expert's study made not at the request of any party, or

(iii) requires a person who is not a party or an officer of a party to incur substantial expense to travel more than 100 miles to attend trial, the court may, to protect a person subject to or affected by the subpoena, quash or modify the subpoena or, if the party in whose behalf the subpoena is issued shows a substantial need for the testimony or material that cannot be otherwise met without undue hardship and assures that the person to whom the subpoena is addressed will be reasonably compensated, the court may order appearance or production only upon specified conditions.

**(d) Duties in Responding to Subpoena.**

(1) A person responding to a subpoena to produce documents shall produce them as they are kept in the usual course of business or shall organize and label them to correspond with the categories in the demand.

(2) When information subject to a subpoena is withheld on a claim that it is privileged or subject to protection as trial preparation materials, the claim shall be made expressly and shall be supported by a description of the nature of the documents, communications or things not produced that is sufficient to enable the demanding party to contest the claim.

**(e) Contempt.** Failure by any person without adequate excuse to obey a subpoena served upon that person may be deemed a contempt of the court from which the subpoena issued. An adequate cause for failure to obey exists when a subpoena purports to require a nonparty to attend or produce at a place not within the limits provided by clause (ii) of subparagraph (c)(3)(A).

### Rule 46. Exceptions Unnecessary.

Formal exceptions to rulings or orders of the court are unnecessary; but for all purposes for which an exception has heretofore been necessary it is sufficient that a party, at the time the ruling or order of the court is made or sought, makes known to the court the action which the party desires the court to take or the party's objection to the action of the court and the grounds therefor; and, if a party has no opportunity to object to a ruling or order at the time it is made, the absence of an objection does not thereafter prejudice the party.

### Rule 47. Jurors.

**(a) Examination of Jurors.** The court may permit the parties or their attorneys to conduct the examination of prospective jurors or may itself conduct the examination. In the latter event, the court shall permit the parties or their attorneys to supplement the examination by such further inquiry as it deems proper or shall itself submit to the prospective jurors such additional questions of the parties or their attorneys as it deems proper.

**(b) Peremptory Challenges.** The court shall allow the number of peremptory challenges provided by 28 U.S.C. §1870.

**(c) Excuse.** The court may for good cause excuse a juror from service during trial or deliberation.

### Rule 48. Number of Jurors—Participation in Verdict.

The court shall seat a jury of not fewer than six and not more than twelve members and all jurors shall participate in the verdict unless excused from service by the court pursuant to Rule 47(c). Unless the parties otherwise stipulate, (1) the verdict shall be unanimous and (2) no verdict shall be taken from a jury reduced in size to fewer than six members.

### Rule 49. Special Verdicts and Interrogatories.

**(a) Special Verdicts.** The court may require a jury to return only a special verdict in the form of a special written finding upon each issue of fact. In that event the court may submit to the jury written questions susceptible of categorical or other brief answer or may submit written forms of the several special findings which might properly be made under the pleadings and evidence; or it may use such other method of submitting the issues and re-quiring the written findings thereon as it deems most appropriate. The court shall give to the jury such explanation and instruction concerning the matter thus submitted as may be necessary to enable the jury to make its findings upon each issue. If in so doing the court omits any issue of fact raised by the pleadings or by the evidence, each party waives the right to a trial by jury of the issue so omitted unless before the jury retires the party demands its submission to the jury. As to an issue omitted without such demand, the court may make a finding; or, if it fails to do so, it shall be deemed to have made a finding in accord with the judgment on the special verdict.

**(b) General Verdict Accompanied by Answer to Interrogatories.** The court may submit to the jury, together with appropriate forms for a general verdict, written interrogatories upon one or more issues of fact the decision of which is necessary to a verdict. The court shall give such explanation or instruction as may be necessary to enable the jury both to make answers to the interrogatories and to render a general verdict, and the court shall direct the jury both to make written answers and to render a general verdict. When the general verdict and the answers are harmonious, the appropriate judgment upon the verdict and answers shall be entered pursuant to Rule 58. When the answers are consistent with each other but one or more is inconsistent with the general verdict, judgment may be entered pursuant to Rule 58 in accordance with the answers, notwithstanding the general verdict, or the court may return the jury for further consideration of its answers and verdict or may order a new trial. When the answers are inconsistent with each other and one or more is likewise inconsistent with the general verdict, judgment shall not be entered, but the court shall return the jury for further consideration of its answers and verdict or shall order a new trial.

### Rule 50. Judgment as a Matter of Law in Jury Trials; Alternative Motion for New Trial; Conditional Rulings.

**(a) Judgment as a Matter of Law.**

(1) If during a trial by jury a party has been fully heard on an issue and there is no legally sufficient evidentiary basis for a reasonable jury to find for that party on that issue, the court may determine the issue

against that party and may grant a motion for judgment as a matter of law against that party with respect to a claim or defense that cannot under the controlling law be maintained or defeated without a favorable finding on that issue.

(2) Motions for judgment as a matter of law may be made at any time before submission of the case to the jury. Such a motion shall specify the judgment sought and the law and the facts on which the moving party is entitled to the judgment.

**(b) Renewing Motion for Judgment After Trial; Alternative Motion for New Trial; Conditional Rulings.** If, for any reason, the court does not grant a motion for judgment as a matter of law made at the close of all the evidence, the court is considered to have submitted the action to the jury subject to the court's later deciding the legal questions raised by the motion. The movant may renew its request for judgment as a matter of law by filing a motion no later than 10 days after entry of judgment—and may alternatively request a new trial or join a motion for a new trial under *Rule 59.* In ruling on a renewed motion, the court may:

(1) if a verdict was returned:

(A) allow the judgment to stand,

(B) order a new trial, or

(C) direct entry of judgment as a matter of law; or

(2) if no verdict was returned:

(A) order a new trial, or

(B) direct entry of judgment as a matter of law.

**(c) Granting Renewed Motion for Judgment as a Matter of Law; Conditional Rulings; New Trial Motion.**

(1) If the renewed motion for judgment as a matter of law is granted, the court shall also rule on the motion for a new trial, if any, by determining whether it should be granted if the judgment is thereafter vacated or reversed, and shall specify the grounds for granting or denying the motion for the new trial. If the motion for a new trial is thus conditionally granted, the order thereon does not affect the finality of the judgment. In case the motion for a new trial has been conditionally granted and the judgment is reversed on appeal, the new trial shall proceed unless the appellate court has otherwise ordered. In case the motion for a new trial has been conditionally denied, the appellee on appeal may assert error in that denial; and if

the judgment is reversed on appeal, subsequent proceedings shall be in accordance with the order of the appellate court.

(2) Any motion for a new trial under *Rule 59* by a party against whom judgment as a matter of law is rendered shall be filed no later than 10 days after entry of the judgment.

**(d) Same: Denial of Motion for.** If the motion for judgment as a matter of law is denied, the party who prevailed on that motion may, as appellee, assert grounds entitling the party to a new trial in the event the appellate court concludes that the trial court erred in denying the motion for judgment. If the appellate court reverses the judgment, nothing in this rule precludes it from determining that the appellee is entitled to a new trial, or from directing the trial court to determine whether a new trial shall be granted.

### Rule 51. Instructions to Jury: Objection.

At the close of the evidence or at such earlier time during the trial as the court reasonably directs, any party may file written requests that the court instruct the jury on the law as set forth in the requests. The court shall inform counsel of its proposed action upon the requests prior to their arguments to the jury. The court, at its election, may instruct the jury before or after argument, or both. No party may assign as error the giving or the failure to give an instruction unless that party objects thereto before the jury retires to consider its verdict, stating distinctly the matter objected to and the grounds of the objection. Opportunity shall be given to make the objection out of the hearing of the jury.

### Rule 52. Findings by the Court; Judgment on Partial Findings.

**(a) Effect.** In all actions tried upon the facts without a jury or with an advisory jury, the court shall find the facts specially and state separately its conclusions of law thereon, and judgment shall be entered pursuant to Rule 58; and in granting or refusing interlocutory injunctions the court shall similarly set forth the findings of fact and conclusions of law which constitute the grounds of its action. Requests for findings are not necessary for purposes of review. Findings of fact, whether based on oral or documentary evidence, shall not be set aside unless clearly erroneous, and due regard shall be given to the opportunity of the trial court to judge of the credibility of the witnesses. The findings of a master, to the extent that the court adopts them, shall be considered as the findings of the court. It will be sufficient if the findings of fact and conclusions of law are stated orally and recorded in open court following the close of the evidence or appear in an opinion or memorandum of decision filed by the court. Findings of fact and conclusions of law are unnecessary on decisions of motions under Rule 12 or 56 or any other motion except as provided in subdivision (c) of this rule.

**(b) Amendment.** On a party's motion filed no later than 10 days after entry of judgment, the court may amend its findings—or make additional findings—and may amend the judgment accordingly. The motion may accompany a motion for a new trial under Rule 59. When findings of fact are made in actions tried without a jury, the sufficiency of the evidence supporting the findings may be later questioned whether or not in the district court the party raising the question objected to the findings, moved to amend them, or moved for partial findings.

**(c) Judgment on Partial Findings.** If during a trial without a jury a party has been fully heard on an issue and the court finds against the party on that issue, the court may enter judgment as a matter of law against that party with respect to a claim or defense that cannot under the controlling law be maintained or defeated without a favorable finding on that issue, or the court may decline to render any judgment until the close of all the evidence. Such a judgment shall be supported by findings of fact and conclusions of law as required by subdivision (a) of this rule.

### Rule 53. Masters.

**(a) Appointment and Compensation.** The court in which any action is pending may appoint a special master therein. As used in these Rules the word "master" includes a referee, an auditor, an examiner and an assessor. The compensation to be allowed to a master shall be fixed by the court, and shall be charged upon such of the parties or paid out of any fund or subject matter of the action, which is in the custody and control of the court as the court may direct; provided that this provision for compensation shall not apply when a United States magistrate judge is designated to serve as a master. The master shall not retain the master's report as security for the master's compensation; but when the party ordered to pay the compensation al-

lowed by the court does not pay it after notice and within the time prescribed by the court, the master is entitled to a writ of execution against the delinquent party.

**(b) Reference.** A reference to a master shall be the exception and not the rule. In actions to be tried by a jury, a reference shall be made only when the issues are complicated; in actions to be tried without a jury, save in matters of account and of difficult computation of damages, a reference shall be made only upon a showing that some exceptional condition requires it. Upon the consent of the parties, a magistrate judge may be designated to serve as a special master without regard to the provisions of this subdivision.

**(c) Powers.** The order of reference to the master may specify or limit the master's powers and may direct the master to report only upon particular issues or to do or perform particular acts or to receive and report evidence only and may fix the time and place for beginning and closing the hearings and for the filing of the master's report. Subject to the specifications and limitations stated in the order, the master has and shall exercise the power to regulate all proceedings in every hearing before the master and to do all acts and take all measures necessary or proper for the efficient performance of the master's duties under the order. The master may require the production before the master of evidence upon all matters embraced in the reference, including the production of all books, papers, vouchers, documents and writings applicable thereto. The master may rule upon the admissibility of evidence unless otherwise directed by the order of reference and has the authority to put witnesses on oath and may examine them and may call the parties to the action and examine them upon oath. When a party so requests, the master shall make a record of the evidence offered and excluded in the same manner and subject to the same limitations as provided in the Federal Rules of Evidence for a court sitting without a jury.

**(d) Proceedings.**

(1) *Meetings.* When a reference is made, the clerk shall forthwith furnish the master with a copy of the order of reference. Upon receipt thereof unless the order of reference otherwise provides, the master shall forthwith set a time and place for the first meeting of the parties or their attorneys to be held within 20 days after the date of the order of reference and shall notify the parties or their attorneys. It is the duty of the master to proceed with all reasonable

diligence. Either party, on notice to the parties and master, may apply to the court for an order requiring the master to speed the proceedings and to make the report. If a party fails to appear at the time and place appointed, the master may proceed ex parte or, in the master's discretion, adjourn the proceeding to a future day, giving notice to the absent party of the adjournment.

(2) *Witnesses.* The parties may procure the attendance of witnesses before the master by the issuance and service of subpoenas as provided in Rule 45. If without adequate excuse a witness fails to appear or give evidence, the witness may be punished as for a contempt and be subjected to the consequences, penalties and remedies provided in Rules 37 and 45.

(3) *Statement of Accounts.* When matters of accounting are in issue before the master, the master may prescribe the form in which the accounts shall be submitted and in any proper case may require or receive in evidence a statement by a certified public accountant who is called as a witness. Upon objection of a party to any of the items thus submitted or upon a showing that the form of statement is insufficient, the master may require a different form of statement to be furnished, or the accounts or specific items thereof to be proved by oral examination of the accounting parties or upon written interrogatories or in such other manner as the master directs.

**(e) Report.**

(1) *Contents and Filing.* The master shall prepare a report upon the matters submitted to the master by the order of reference and, if required to make findings of fact and conclusions of law, the master shall set them forth in the report. The master shall file the report with the clerk of the court and in an action to be tried without a jury, unless otherwise directed by the order of reference, shall file with it a transcript of the proceedings and of the evidence and the original exhibits. The clerk shall forthwith mail to all parties notice of the filing.

(2) *In Non-Jury Actions.* In an action to be tried without a jury the court shall accept the master's findings of fact unless clearly erroneous. Within 10 days after being served with notice of the filing of the report, any party may serve written objections thereto upon the other parties. Application to the court for action upon the report and upon objections thereto shall be by motion and upon notice as prescribed in Rule 6(d). The court after hearing may adopt the report or may modify it or may reject in whole or in part or may receive further evidence or may recommit it with instructions.

(3) *In Jury Actions.* In an action to be tried by a jury, the master shall not be directed to report the evidence. The master's findings upon the issues submitted to the master are admissible as evidence of the matters found and may be read to the jury, subject to the ruling of the court upon any objections in point of law which may be made to the report.

(4) *Stipulation as to Findings.* The effect of a master's report is the same whether or not the parties have consented to the reference; but, when the parties stipulate that a master's findings of fact shall be final, only questions of law arising upon the report shall thereafter be considered.

(5) *Draft Report.* Before filing the master's report a master may submit a draft thereof to counsel for all parties for the purpose of receiving their suggestions.

**(f) Application to Magistrate Judge.** A magistrate judge is subject to this Rule only when the order referring a matter to the magistrate judge expressly provides that the reference is made under this Rule.

**VII. Judgment.**

### Rule 54. Judgments; Costs.

**(a) Definition; Form.** "Judgment" as used in these Rules includes a decree and any order from which an appeal lies. A judgment shall not contain a recital of pleadings, the report of a master or the record of prior proceedings.

**(b) Judgment Upon Multiple Claims or Involving Multiple Parties.** When more than one claim for relief is presented in an action, whether as a claim, counterclaim, cross-claim or third-party claim, or when multiple parties are involved, the court may direct the entry of a final judgment as to one or more but fewer than all of the claims or parties only upon an express determination that there is no just reason for delay and upon an express direction for the entry of judgment. In the absence of such determination and direction, any order or other form of decision, however designated, which adjudicates fewer than all of the claims or the rights and liabilities of fewer than all of the parties shall not terminate the action as to any of the claims or parties, and the order or other form of decision is subject to revision at any time before the entry of judgment adjudicating all of the claims and the rights and liabilities of all of the parties.

**(c) Demand for Judgment.** A judgment by default shall not be different in kind from or exceed in amount that prayed for in the demand for judgment. Except as to a party against whom a judgment is entered by default, every final judgment shall grant the relief to which the party in whose favor it is rendered is entitled, even if the party has not demanded such relief in the party's pleadings.

**(d) Costs; Attorney's Fees.**

(1) *Costs Other than Attorney's Fees.* Except when express provision therefor is made either in a statute of the United States or in these Rules, costs other than attorney's fees shall be allowed as of course to the prevailing party unless the court otherwise directs; but costs against the United States, its officers and agencies shall be imposed only to the extent permitted by law. Such costs may be taxed by the clerk on one day's notice. On motion served within 5 days thereafter, the action of the clerk may be reviewed by the court.

(2) *Attorney's Fees.*

(A) Claims for attorney's fees and related nontaxable expenses shall be made by motion unless the substantive law governing the action provides for the recovery of such fees as an element of damages to be proved at trial.

(B) Unless otherwise provided by statute or order of the court, the motion must be filed and served no later than 14 days after entry of judgment; must specify the judgment and the statute, rule or other grounds entitling the moving party to the award; and must state the amount or provide a fair estimate of the amount sought. If directed by the court, the motion shall also disclose the terms of any agreement with respect to fees to be paid for the services for which claim is made.

(C) On request of a party or class member, the court shall afford an opportunity for adversary submissions with respect to the motion in accordance with Rule 43(e) or Rule 78. The court may determine issues of liability for fees before receiving submissions bearing on issues of evaluation of services for which liability is imposed by the court. The court shall find the facts and state its conclusions of law as provided in Rule 52(a), and a judgment shall be set forth in a separate document as provided in Rule 58.

(D) By local rule the court may establish special procedures by which issues relating to such fees may be resolved without extensive evidentiary hearings. In addition, the court may refer issues relating to the value of services to a special master under Rule 53 without regard to the provisions of subdivision (b) thereof and may refer a motion for attorney's fees to a magistrate judge under Rule 72(b) as if it were a dispositive pretrial matter.

(E) The provisions of subparagraphs (A) through (D) do not apply to claims for fees and expenses as sanctions for violations of these Rules or under 28 U.S.C. §1927.

### Rule 55. Default.

**(a) Entry.** When a party against whom a judgment for affirmative relief is sought has failed to plead or otherwise defend as provided by these Rules and that fact is made to appear by affidavit or otherwise, the clerk shall enter the party's default.

**(b) Judgment.** Judgment by default may be entered as follows:

(1) *By the Clerk.* When the plaintiff's claim against a defendant is for a sum certain or for a sum which can by computation be made certain, the clerk upon request of the plaintiff and upon affidavit of the amount due shall enter judgment for that amount and costs against the defendant, if the defendant has been defaulted for failure to appear and is not an infant or incompetent person.

(2) *By the Court.* In all other cases the party entitled to a judgment by default shall apply to the court therefor; but no judgment by default shall be entered against an infant or incompetent person unless represented in the action by a general guardian, committee, conservator or other such representative who has appeared therein. If the party against whom judgment by default is sought has appeared in the action, the party (of, if appearing by representative, the party's representative) shall be served with written notice of the application for judgment at least 3 days prior to the hearing on such application. If, in order to enable the court to enter judgment or to carry it into effect, it is necessary to take an account or to determine the amount of damages or to establish the truth of any averment by evidence or to make an investigation of any other matter, the court may conduct such hearings or order such references as it deems necessary and proper

and shall accord a right of trial by jury to the parties when and as required by any statute of the United States.

**(c) Setting Aside Default.** For good cause shown, the court may set aside an entry of default and, if a judgment by default has been entered, may likewise set it aside in accordance with Rule 60(b).

**(d) Plaintiffs, Counterclaimants, Cross-Claimants.** The provisions of this Rule apply whether the party entitled to the judgment by default is a plaintiff, a third-party plaintiff or a party who has pleaded a cross-claim or counterclaim. In all cases a judgment by default is subject to the limitations of Rule 54(c).

**(e) Judgment Against the United States.** No judgment by default shall be entered against the United States or an officer or agency thereof unless the claimant establishes a claim or right to relief by evidence satisfactory to the court.

### Rule 56. Summary Judgment.

**(a) For Claimant.** A party seeking to recover upon a claim, counterclaim or cross-claim or to obtain a declaratory judgment may, at any time after the expiration of 20 days from the commencement of the action or after service of a motion for summary judgment by the adverse party, move with or without supporting affidavits for a summary judgment in the party's favor upon all or any part thereof.

**(b) For Defending Party.** A party against whom a claim, counterclaim or cross-claim is asserted or a declaratory judgment is sought may, at any time, move with or without supporting affidavits for a summary judgment in the party's favor as to all or any part thereof.

**(c) Motion and Proceedings Thereon.** The motion shall be served at least 10 days before the time fixed for the hearing. The adverse party prior to the day of hearing may serve opposing affidavits. The judgment sought shall be rendered forthwith if the pleadings, depositions, answers to interrogatories and admissions on file, together with the affidavits, if any, show that there is no genuine issue as to any material fact and that the moving party is entitled to a judgment as a matter of law. A summary judgment, interlocutory in character, may be rendered on the issue of liability alone although there is a genuine issue as to the amount of damages.

**(d) Case Not Fully Adjudicated on Motion.** If on motion under this Rule judgment is not rendered upon the whole case or for all of the relief asked and a trial is necessary, the court

at the hearing of the motion, by examining the pleadings and the evidence before it and by interrogating counsel, shall if practicable ascertain what material facts exist without substantial controversy and what material facts are actually and in good faith controverted. It shall thereupon make an order specifying the facts that appear without substantial controversy, including the extent to which the amount of damages or other relief is not in controversy, and directing such further proceedings in the action as are just. Upon the trial of the action the facts so specified shall be deemed established, and the trial shall be conducted accordingly.

**(e) Form of Affidavits; Further Testimony; Defense Required.** Supporting and opposing affidavits shall be made on personal knowledge, shall set forth such facts as would be admissible in evidence and shall show affirmatively that the affiant is competent to testify to the matters stated therein. Sworn or certified copies of all papers or parts thereof referred to in an affidavit shall be attached thereto or served therewith. The court may permit affidavits to be supplemented or opposed by depositions, answers to interrogatories or further affidavits. When a motion for summary judgment is made and supported as provided in this Rule, an adverse party may not rest upon the mere allegations or denials of the adverse party's pleading, but the adverse party's response, by affidavits or as otherwise provided in this Rule, must set forth specific facts showing that there is a genuine issue for trial. If the adverse party does not so respond, summary judgment, if appropriate, shall be entered against the adverse party.

**(f) When Affidavits Are Unavailable.** Should it appear from the affidavits of a party opposing the motion that the party cannot for reasons stated present by affidavit facts essential to justify the party's opposition, the court may refuse the application for judgment or may order a continuance to permit affidavits to be obtained or depositions to be taken or discovery to be had or may make such other order as is just.

**(g) Affidavits Made in Bad Faith.** Should it appear to the satisfaction of the court at any time that any of the affidavits presented pursuant to this Rule are presented in bad faith or solely for the purpose of delay, the court shall forthwith order the party employing them to pay to the other party the amount of the reasonable expenses which the filing of the affidavits caused the other party to incur, including reasonable attorney's fees and any offending party or attorney may be adjudged guilty of contempt.

### Rule 57. Declaratory Judgments.

The procedure for obtaining a declaratory judgment pursuant to Title 28 U.S.C. §2201, shall be in accordance with these Rules, and the right to trial by jury may be demanded under the circumstances and in the manner provided in Rules 38 and 39. The existence of another adequate remedy does not preclude a judgment for declaratory relief in cases where it is appropriate. The court may order a speeding hearing of an action for a declaratory judgment and may advance it on the calendar.

### Rule 58. Entry of Judgment.

Subject to the provisions of Rule 54(b): (1) upon a general verdict of a jury, or upon a decision by the court that a party shall recover only a sum certain or costs or that all relief shall be denied, the clerk, unless the court otherwise orders, shall forthwith prepare, sign and enter the judgment without awaiting any direction by the court; (2) upon a decision by the court granting other relief or upon a special verdict or a general verdict accompanied by answers to interrogatories, the court shall promptly approve the form of the judgment, and the clerk shall thereupon enter it. Every judgment shall be set forth on a separate document. A judgment is effective only when so set forth and when entered as provided in Rule 79(a). Entry of the judgment shall not be delayed nor the time for appeal extended, in order to tax costs or award fees, except that, when a timely motion for attorney's fees is made under Rule 54(d)(2), the court, before a notice of appeal has been filed and has become effective, may order that the motion have the same effect under Rule 4(a)(4) of the Federal Rules of Appellate Procedure as a timely motion under Rule 59. Attorneys shall not submit forms of judgment except upon direction of the court, and these directions shall not be given as a matter of course.

### Rule 59. New Trials; Amendment of Judgments.

**(a) Grounds.** A new trial may be granted to all or any of the parties and on all or part of the issues (1) in an action in which there has been a trial by jury, for any of the reasons for which new trials have heretofore been granted in ac-

tions at law in the courts of the United States; and (2) in an action tried without a jury, for any of the reasons for which rehearings have heretofore been granted in suits in equity in the courts of the United States. On a motion for a new trial in an action tried without a jury, the court may open the judgment if one has been entered, take additional testimony, amend findings of fact and conclusions of law or make new findings and conclusions, and direct the entry of a new judgment.

**(b) Time for Motion.** A motion for new trial shall be filed no later than 10 days after entry of the judgment.

**(c) Time for Serving Affidavits.** When a motion for new trial is based upon affidavits, they shall be filed with the motion. The opposing party has 10 days after service to file opposing affidavits, but that period may be extended for up to 20 days, either by the court for good cause shown or by the parties' written stipulation. The court may permit reply affidavits.

**(d) On Initiative of Court.** No later than 10 days after entry of judgment the court, on its own, may order a new trial for any reason that would justify granting one on a party's motion. After giving the parties notice and an opportunity to be heard, the court may grant a timely motion for a new trial for a reason not stated in the motion. When granting a new trial on its own initiative or for a reason not stated in a motion, the court shall specify the grounds in its order.

**(e) Motion to Alter or Amend a Judgment.** Any motion to alter or amend a judgment shall be filed no later than 10 days after entry of the judgment.

### Rule 60. Relief from Judgment or Order.

**(a) Clerical Mistakes.** Clerical mistakes in judgments, orders or parts of the record and errors therein arising from oversight or omission may be corrected by the court at any time of its own initiative or on the motion of any party and after such notice, if any, as the court orders. During the pendency of an appeal, such mistakes may be so corrected before the appeal is docketed in the appellate court, and thereafter while the appeal is pending may be so corrected with leave of the appellate court.

**(b) Mistakes; Inadvertence; Excusable Neglect; Newly Discovered Evidence; Fraud, etc.** On motion and upon such terms as are just, the court may relieve a party or a party's legal representative from a final judgment,

order or proceeding for the following reasons: (1) mistake, inadvertence, surprise or
excusable neglect; (2) newly discovered evidence which by due diligence could not have
been discovered in time to move for a new
trial under Rule 59(b); (3) fraud (whether
heretofore denominated intrinsic or extrin-
sic), misrepresentation or other misconduct
of an adverse party; (4) the judgment is void;
(5) the judgment has been satisfied, released
or discharged, or a prior judgment upon
which it is based has been reversed or otherwise vacated, or it is no longer equitable that
the judgment should have prospective application; or (6) any other reason justifying relief from the operation of the judgment. The
motion shall be made within a reasonable
time, and for reasons (1), (2) and (3) not
more than one year after the judgment, order
or proceeding was entered or taken. A motion under this subdivision (b) does not affect the finality of a judgment or suspend its
operation. This Rule does not limit the power
of a court to entertain an independent action
to relieve a party from a judgment, order or
proceeding, or to grant relief to a defendant
not actually personally notified as provided
in Title 28, U.S.C., §1655, or to set aside a
judgment for fraud upon the court. Writs of
coram nobis, coram vobis, audita querela
and bills of review and bills in the nature of a
bill of review, are abolished and the procedure for obtaining any relief from a judgment
shall be by motion as prescribed in these
Rules or by any independent action.

### Rule 61. Harmless Error.

No error in either the admission or the exclusion of evidence and no error or defect in any
ruling or order or in anything done or omitted
by the court or by any of the parties is ground
for granting a new trial or for setting aside a
verdict or for vacating, modifying or otherwise disturbing a judgment or order, unless
refusal to take such action appears to the
court inconsistent with substantial justice.
The court at every stage of the proceeding
must disregard any error or defect in the proceeding which does not affect the substantial
rights of the parties.

### Rule 62. Stay of Proceedings to Enforce a Judgment.

**(a) Automatic Stay; Exceptions - Injunctions, Receiverships and Patent Accountings.** Except as stated herein, no execution shall issue
upon a judgment nor shall proceedings be
taken for its enforcement until the expiration
of 10 days after its entry. Unless otherwise ordered by the court, an interlocutory or final
judgment in an action for an injunction or in a
receivership action, or a judgment or order
directing an accounting in an action for infringement of letters patent, shall not be
stayed during the period after its entry and
until an appeal is taken or during the pendency of an appeal. The provisions of subdivision (c) of this Rule govern the suspending,
modifying, restoring or granting of an injunction during the pendency of an appeal.

**(b) Stay on Motion for New Trial or for Judg-
ment.** In its discretion and on such conditions
for the security of the adverse party as are
proper, the court may stay the execution of or
any proceedings to enforce a judgment pending the disposition of a motion for a new trial
or to alter or amend a judgment made pursuant to Rule 59, or of a motion for relief from
a judgment or order made pursuant to Rule
60, or of a motion for judgment in accordance
with a motion for a directed verdict made pursuant to Rule 50, or of a motion for amendment to the findings or for additional findings
made pursuant to Rule 52(b).

**(c) Injunction Pending Appeal.** When an appeal is taken from an interlocutory or final
judgment granting, dissolving or denying an
injunction, the court in its discretion may suspend, modify, restore or grant an injunction
during the pendency of the appeal upon such
terms as to bond or otherwise as it considers
proper for the security of the rights of the adverse party. If the judgment appealed from is
rendered by a district court of three judges
specially constituted pursuant to a statute of
the United States, no such order shall be
made except (1) by such court sitting in open
court or (2) by the assent of all the judges of
such court evidenced by their signatures to
the order.

**(d) Stay Upon Appeal.** When an appeal is
taken, the appellant by giving a supersedes
bond may obtain a stay subject to the exceptions contained in subdivision (a) of this Rule.
The bond may be given at or after the time of
filing the notice of appeal or of procuring the
order allowing the appeal, as the case may be.
The stay is effective when the supersedes
bond is approved by the court.

**(e) Stay in Favor of the United States or
Agency Thereof.** When an appeal is taken by
the United States or an officer or agency

thereof or by direction of any department of the Government of the United States and the operation or enforcement of the judgment is stayed, no bond, obligation or other security shall be required from the appellant.

**(f) Stay According to State Law.** In any state in which a judgment is a lien upon the property of the judgment debtor and in which the judgment debtor is entitled to a stay of execution, a judgment debtor is entitled, in the district court held therein, to such stay as would be accorded the judgment debtor had the action been maintained in the courts of that state.

**(g) Power of Appellate Court Not Limited.** The provisions in this Rule do not limit any power of an appellate court or of a judge or justice thereof to stay proceedings during the pendency of an appeal or to suspend, modify, restore or grant an injunction during the pendency of an appeal or to make any order appropriate to preserve the status quo or the effectiveness of the judgment subsequently to be entered.

**(h) Stay of Judgment as to Multiple Claims or Multiple Parties.** When a court has ordered a final judgment under the conditions stated in Rule 54(b), the court may stay enforcement of that judgment until the entering of a subsequent judgment or judgments and may prescribe such conditions as are necessary to secure the benefit thereof to the party in whose favor the judgment is entered.

## Rule 63. Inability of a Judge to Proceed.

If a trial or hearing has been commenced and the judge is unable to proceed, any other judge may proceed with it upon certifying familiarity with the record and determining that the proceedings in the case may be completed without prejudice to the parties. In a hearing or trial without a jury, the successor judge shall at the request of a party recall any witness whose testimony is material and disputed and who is available to testify again without undue burden. The successor judge may also recall any other witness.

## VIII. Provisional and Final Remedies and Special Proceedings.

## Rule 64. Seizure of Person or Property.

At the commencement of and during the course of an action, all remedies providing for seizure of person or property for the purpose of securing satisfaction of the judgment ultimately to be entered in the action are available under the circumstances and in the manner provided by the law of the state in which the district court is held, existing at the time the remedy is sought, subject to the following qualifications: (1) any existing statute of the United States governs to the extent to which it is applicable; (2) the action in which any of the foregoing remedies is used shall be commenced and prosecuted or, if removed from a state court, shall be prosecuted after removal, pursuant to these Rules. The remedies thus available include arrest, attachment, garnishment, replevin, sequestration and other corresponding or equivalent remedies, however designated and regardless of whether by state procedure the remedy is ancillary to an action or must be obtained by an independent action.

## Rule 65. Injunctions.

**(a) Preliminary Injunction.**

(1) *Notice.* No preliminary injunction shall be issued without notice to the adverse party.

(2) *Consolidation of Hearing with Trial on Merits.* Before or after the commencement of the hearing of an application for a preliminary injunction, the court may order the trial of the action on the merits to be advanced and consolidated with the hearing of the application. Even when this consolidation is not ordered, any evidence received upon an application for a preliminary injunction which would be admissible upon the trial on the merits becomes part of the record on the trial and need not be repeated upon the trial. This subdivision (a)(2) shall be so construed and applied as to save to the parties any rights they may have to trial by jury.

**(b) Temporary Restraining Order; Notice; Hearing; Duration.** A temporary restraining order may be granted without written or oral notice to the adverse party or that party's attorney only if (1) it clearly appears from specific facts shown by affidavit or by the verified complaint that immediate and irreparable injury, loss or damage will result to the applicant before the adverse party or that party's attorney can be heard in opposition, and (2) the applicant's attorney certifies to the court in writing the efforts, if any, which have been made to give the notice and the reasons supporting the claim that notice should not be required. Every temporary restraining order granted without notice shall be indorsed with the date and hour of issuance; shall be filed forthwith in the clerk's office and entered of record; shall define the injury and state why it is irreparable and why the order was granted without notice; and shall expire by its terms within such time after entry, not to exceed 10 days, as the court fixes, unless within the time so fixed the order, for good cause shown, is extended for a like period or unless the party against whom the order is directed consents that it may be extended for a longer period. The reasons for the extension shall be entered of record. In case a temporary restraining order is granted without notice, the motion for a preliminary injunction shall be set down for hearing at the earliest possible time and takes precedence of all matters except older matters of the same character; and when the motion comes on for hearing, the party who obtained the temporary restraining order shall proceed with the application for a preliminary injunction and, if the party does not do so, the court shall dissolve the temporary restraining order. On 2 days' notice to the party who obtained the temporary restraining order without notice or on such notice to that party as the court may prescribe, the adverse party may appear and move its dissolution or modification and in that event the court shall proceed to hear and determine such motion as expeditiously as the ends of justice require.

**(c) Security.** No restraining order or preliminary injunction shall issue except upon the giving of security by the applicant, in such sum as the court deems proper, for the payment of such costs and damages as may be incurred or suffered by any party who is found to have been wrongfully enjoined or restrained. No such security shall be required of the United States or of an officer or agency thereof.

The provisions of Rule 65.1 apply to a surety upon a bond or undertaking under this Rule.

**(d) Form and Scope of Injunction or Restraining Order.** Every order granting an injunction and every restraining order shall set forth the reasons for its issuance; shall be specific in terms; shall describe in reasonable detail and not by reference to the complaint or other document, the act or acts sought to be restrained; and is binding only upon the parties to the action, their officers, agents, servants, employees and attorneys, and upon those persons in active concert or participation with them who receive actual notice of the order by personal service or otherwise.

**(e) Employer and Employee; Interpleader; Constitutional Cases.** These Rules do not modify any statute of the United States relating to temporary restraining orders and preliminary injunctions in actions affecting employer and employee; or the provisions of Title 28, U.S.C., §2361, relating to preliminary injunctions in actions of interpleader or in the nature of interpleader; or Title 28, U.S.C., §2284, relating to actions required by Act of Congress to be heard and determined by a district court of three judges.

### Rule 65.1. Security; Proceedings Against Sureties.

Whenever these Rules, including the Supplemental Rules for Certain Admiralty and Maritime Claims, require or permit the giving of security by a party, and security is given in the form of a bond or stipulation or other undertaking with one or more sureties, each surety submits to the jurisdiction of the court and irrevocably appoints the clerk of the court as the surety's agent upon whom any papers affecting the surety's liability on the bond or undertaking may be served. The surety's liability may be enforced on motion without the necessity of an independent action. The motion and such notice of the motion as the court prescribes may be served on the clerk of the court, who shall forthwith mail copies to the sureties if their addresses are known.

### Rule 66. Receivers Appointed by Federal Courts.

An action wherein a receiver has been appointed shall not be dismissed except by order of the court. The practice in the administration of estates by receivers or by other similar officers appointed by the court shall be in accordance with the practice heretofore followed in the courts of the United States or as provided in rules promulgated by the district courts. In all other respects the action in which the appointment of a receiver is sought or which is brought by or against a receiver is governed by these Rules.

### Rule 67. Deposit in Court.

In an action in which any part of the relief sought is a judgment for a sum of money or the disposition of a sum of money or the disposition of any other thing capable of delivery, a party, upon notice to every other party, and by leave of court, may deposit with the court all or any part of such sum or thing, whether or not that party claims all or any part of the sum or thing. The party making the deposit shall serve the order permitting deposit on the clerk of the court. Money paid into court under this Rule shall be deposited and withdrawn in accordance with the provisions of Title 28, U.S.C., §§2041 and 2042; the Act of June 26, 1934, c. 756, §23, as amended (48 Stat. 1236, 58 Stat. 845), U.S.C., Title 31, §725v; or any like statute. The fund shall be deposited in an interest-bearing account or invested in an interest-bearing instrument approved by the court.

### Rule 68. Offer of Judgment.

At any time more than 10 days before the trial begins, a party defending against a claim may serve upon the adverse party an offer to allow judgment to be taken against the defending party for the money or property or to the effect specified in the offer, with costs then accrued. If, within 10 days after the service of the offer, the adverse party serves written notice that the offer is accepted, either party may then file the offer and notice of acceptance together with proof of service thereof and thereupon the clerk shall enter judgment. An offer not accepted shall be deemed withdrawn and evidence thereof is not admissible except in a proceeding to determine costs. If the judgment finally obtained by the offeree is not more favorable than the offer, the offeree must pay the costs incurred after the making of the offer. The fact that an offer is made but not accepted does not preclude a subsequent offer. When the liability of one party to another has been determined by verdict or order or judgment, but the amount or extent of the liability remains to be determined by further proceedings, the party adjudged liable may make an offer of judgment, which shall have the same effect as an offer made before trial if it is served within a reasonable time not less than 10 days prior to the commencement of hearings to determine the amount or extent of liability.

### Rule 69. Execution.

**(a) In General.** Process to enforce a judgment for the payment of money shall be a writ of execution, unless the court directs otherwise. The procedure on execution, in proceedings supplementary to and in aid of a judgment, and in proceedings on and in aid of execution shall be in accordance with the practice and procedure of the state in which the district court is held, existing at the time the remedy is sought, except that any statute of the United States governs to the extent that it is applicable. In aid of the judgment or execu-tion, the judgment creditor or a successor in interest when that interest appears of record, may obtain discovery from any person, including the judgment debtor, in the manner provided in these Rules or in the manner provided by the practice of the state in which the district court is held.

**(b) Against Certain Public Officers.** When a judgment has been entered against a collector or other officer of revenue under the circumstances stated in Title 28, U.S.C., §2006, or against an officer of Congress in an action mentioned in the Act of March 3, 1875, c. 130, §8 (18 Stat. 401), U.S.C., Title 2, §118, and when the court has given the certificate of probable cause for the officer's act as provided in those statutes, execution shall not issue against the officer or the officer's property but the final judgment shall be satisfied as provided in such statutes.

### Rule 70. Judgment for Specific Acts; Vesting Title.

If a judgment directs a party to execute a conveyance of land or to deliver deeds or other documents or to perform any other specific act and the party fails to comply within the time specified, the court may direct the act to be done at the cost of the disobedient party by some other person appointed by the court and the act when so done has like effect as if done by the party. On application of the party entitled to performance, the clerk shall issue a writ of attachment or sequestration against the property of the disobedient party to compel obedience to the judgment. The court may also in proper cases adjudge the party in contempt. If real or personal property is within the district, the court in lieu of directing a conveyance thereof may enter a judgment divesting the title of any party and vesting it in others and such judgment has the effect of a conveyance executed in due form of law. When any order or judgment is for the delivery of possession, the party in whose favor it is entered is entitled to a writ of execution or assistance upon application to the clerk.

### Rule 71. Process in Behalf of and Against Persons Not Parties.

When an order is made in favor of a person who is not a party to the action, that person may enforce obedience to the order by the same process as if a party; and, when obedience to an order may be lawfully enforced against a person who is not a party, that person is liable to the same process for enforcing obedience to the order as if a party.

### Rule 71A. Condemnation of Property.

**(a) Applicability of Other Rules.** The Rules of Civil Procedure for the United States District Courts govern the procedure for the condemnation of real and personal property under the power of eminent domain, except as otherwise provided in this Rule.

**(b) Joinder of Properties.** The plaintiff may join in the same action one or more separate pieces of property, whether in the same or different ownership and whether or not sought for the same use.

**(c) Complaint.**

(1) *Caption.* The complaint shall contain a caption as provided in Rule 10(a), except that the plaintiff shall name as defendants the property, designated generally by kind, quantity and location, and at least one of the owners of some part or interest in the property.

(2) *Contents.* The complaint shall contain a short and plain statement of the authority for the taking, the use for which the property is to be taken, a description of the property sufficient for its identification, the interests to be acquired, and as to each separate piece of property a designation of the defendants who have been joined as owners thereof or of some interest therein. Upon the commencement of the action, the plaintiff need join as defendants only the persons having or claiming an interest in the property whose names are then known, but prior to any hearing involving the compensation to be paid for a piece of property, the plaintiff shall add as defendants all persons having or claiming an interest in that property whose names can be ascertained by a reasonably diligent search of the records, considering the character and value of the property involved and the interests to be acquired, and also those whose names have otherwise been learned. All others may be made defendants under the designation "Unknown Owners." Process shall be served as provided in subdivision (d) of this Rule upon all defendants, whether named as defendants at the time of the commencement of the action or subsequently added, and a defendant may answer as provided in subdivision (e) of this Rule. The court meanwhile may order such distribution of a deposit as the facts warrant.

(3) *Filing.* In addition to filing the complaint with the court, the plaintiff shall furnish to the clerk at least one copy thereof for the use of the defendants and additional copies at the request of the clerk or of a defendant.

**(d) Process.**

(1) *Notice; Delivery.* Upon the filing of the complaint, the plaintiff shall forthwith deliver to the clerk joint or several notices directed to the defendants named or designated in the complaint. Additional notices directed to defendant subsequently added shall be so delivered. The delivery of the notice and its service have the same effect as the delivery and service of the summons under Rule 4.

(2) *Same; Form.* Each notice shall state the court, the title of the action, the name of the defendant to whom it is directed, that the action is to condemn property, a description of the defendant's property sufficient for its identification, the interest to be taken, the authority for the taking, the uses for which the property is taken, that the defendant may serve upon the plaintiff's attorney an answer within 20 days after service of the notice, and that the failure so to serve an answer constitutes a consent to the taking and to the authority of the court to proceed to hear the action and to fix the compensation. The notice shall conclude with the name of the plaintiff's attorney and an address within the district in which action is brought where the attorney may be served. The notice need contain a description of no other property than that to be taken from the defendants to whom it is directed.

(3) *Service of Notice.*

(A) *Personal Service.* Personal service of the notice (but without copies of the complaint) shall be made in accordance with Rule 4 upon a defendant whose residence is known and who resides within the United States or a territory subject to the administrative or judicial jurisdiction of the United States.

(B) *Service by Publication.* Upon the filing of a certificate of the plaintiff's attorney stating that the attorney believes a defendant cannot be personally served, because after diligent inquiry within the state in which the complaint is filed the defendant's place of residence cannot be ascertained by the plaintiff or, if ascertained, that is beyond the territorial limits of personal service as provided in this Rule, service of the notice shall be made on this defendant by publication in a newspaper published in the county where the property is located, or if there is no such newspaper, then in a newspaper having a general circulation where the property is located, once a week for not less than three successive weeks. Prior to the last publication, a copy of the notice shall also be mailed to a defendant who cannot be personally served as provided in this Rule but whose place of residence is then known. Unknown owners may be served by publication in like manner by a notice addressed to "Unknown Owners."

Service by publication is complete upon the date of the last publication. Proof of publication and mailing shall be made by certificate of the plaintiff's attorney, to which shall be attached a printed copy of the published notice with the name and dates of the newspaper marked thereon.

(4) *Return; Amendment.* Proof of service of the notice shall be made and amendment of the notice or proof of its service allowed in the manner provided for the return and amendment of the summons under Rule 4.

**(e) Appearance or Answer.** If a defendant has no objection or defense to the taking of the defendant's property, the defendant may serve a notice of appearance designating the property in which the defendant claims to be interested. Thereafter the defendant shall receive notice of all proceedings affecting it. If a defendant has any objection or defense to the taking of the property, the defendant shall serve an answer within 20 days after the service of notice upon the defendant. The answer shall identify the property in which the defendant claims to have an interest, state the nature and extent of the interest claimed, and state all of the defendant's objections and defenses to the taking of the property. A defendant waives all defenses and objections not so presented, but at the trial of the issue of just compensation, whether or not the defendant has previously appeared or answered, the defendant may present evidence as to the amount of the compensation to be paid for the property, and the defendant may share in the distribution of the award. No other pleading or motion asserting any additional defense or objection shall be allowed.

**(f) Amendment of Pleadings.** Without leave of court, the plaintiff may amend the complaint at any time before the trial of the issue of compensation and as many times as desired, but no amendment shall be made which will result in a dismissal forbidden by subdivision (i) of this Rule. The plaintiff need not serve a copy of an amendment, but shall serve notice of the filing, as provided in Rule 5(b), upon any party affected thereby who has appeared and, in the manner provided in subdivision (d) of this Rule, upon any party affected thereby who has not appeared. The plaintiff shall furnish to the clerk of the court for the use of the defendants at least one copy of each amendment, and he shall furnish additional copies of the request of the clerk or of a defendant. Within the time allowed by subdivision (e) of this Rule a defendant may serve an answer to the amended pleading, in the form and manner and with the same effect as there provided.

**(g) Substitution of Parties.** If a defendant dies or becomes incompetent or transfers an interest after the defendant's joinder, the court may order substitution of the proper party upon motion and notice of hearing. If the motion and notice of hearing are to be served upon a person not already a party, service shall be made as provided in subdivision (d)(3) of this Rule.

**(h) Trial.** If the action involves the exercise of the power of eminent domain under the law of the United States, any tribunal specially constituted by an Act of Congress governing the case for the trial of the issue of just compensation shall be the tribunal for the determination of that issue; but if there is no such specially constituted tribunal any party may have a trial by jury of the issue of just compensation by filing a demand therefor within the time allowed for answer or within such further time as the court may fix, unless the court in its discretion orders that, because of the character, location or quantity of the property to be condemned, or for other reasons in the interest of justice, the issue of compensation shall be determined by a commission of three persons appointed by it.

In the event that a commission is appointed, the court may direct that not more than two additional persons serve as alternate commissioners to hear the case and replace commissioners who, prior to the time when a decision is filed, are found by the court to be unable or disqualified to perform their duties. An alternate who does not replace a regular commissioner shall be discharged after the commission renders its final decision. Before appointing the members of the commission and alternates the court shall advise the parties of the identity and qualifications of each prospective commissioner and alternate and may permit the parties to examine each such designee. The parties shall not be permitted or required by the court to suggest nominees. Each party shall have the right to object for valid cause to the appointment of any person as a commissioner or alternate. If a commission is appointed, it shall have the powers of a master provided in subdivision (c) of Rule 53 and proceedings before it shall be governed by the provisions of paragraphs (1) and (2) of subdivision (d) of Rule 53. Its action and report shall be determined by a majority and its findings and report shall have the effect, and be dealt with by the court in accordance with the practice, prescribed in paragraph (2) of subdivision (e) of Rule 53. Trial of all issues shall otherwise be by the court.

**(i) Dismissal of Action.**

(1) *As of Right.* If no hearing has begun to determine the compensation to be paid for a piece of property and the plaintiff has not acquired the title or a lesser interest in or taken possession, the plaintiff may dismiss the action as to that property, without an order of the court, by filing a notice of dismissal setting forth a brief description of the property as to which the action is dismissed.

(2) *By Stipulation.* Before the entry of any judgment vesting the plaintiff with title or a lesser interest in or possession of property, the action may be dismissed in whole or in part, without an order of the court, as to any property by filing a stipulation of dismissal by the plaintiff and the defendant affected thereby; and, if the parties so stipulate, the court may vacate any judgment that has been entered.

(3) *By Order of the Court.* At any time before compensation for a piece of property has been determined and paid and after motion and hearing, the court may dismiss the action as to that property, except that it shall not dismiss the action as to any part of the property of which the plaintiff has taken possession or in which the plaintiff has taken title or lesser interest, but shall award just compensation for the possession, title or lesser interest so taken. The court at any time may drop a defendant unnecessarily or improperly joined.

(4) *Effect.* Except as otherwise provided in the notice, or stipulation of dismissal, or order of the court, any dismissal is without prejudice.

**(j) Deposit and Its Distribution.** The plaintiff shall deposit with the court any money required by law as a condition to the exercise of the power of eminent domain; and, although not so required, may make a deposit when permitted by statute. In such cases the court and attorneys shall expedite the proceedings for the distribution of the money so deposited and for the ascertainment and payment of just compensation. If the compensation finally awarded to any defendant exceeds the amount which has been paid to the defendant or distribution of the deposit, the court shall enter judgment against the plaintiff and in favor of that defendant for the deficiency. If the compensation finally awarded to any defendant is less than the amount which has been paid to that defendant, the court shall enter judgment against that defendant and in favor of the plaintiff for the overpayment.

**(k) Condemnation Under a State's Power of Eminent Domain.** The practice as herein prescribed governs in actions involving the exercise of the power of eminent domain under the law of a state, provided that if the state law makes provision for trial of any issue by jury, or for trial of the issue of compensation by jury or commission or both, that provision shall be followed.

IX.  **Magistrates.**

*Rule 72. Magistrate Judges; Pretrial Matters.*

**(a) Nondispositive Matters.** A magistrate judge to whom a pretrial matter not dispositive of a claim or defense of a party is referred to hear and determine shall promptly conduct such proceedings as are required and when appropriate enter into the record a written order setting forth the disposition of the matter. Within 10 days after being served with a copy of the magistrate judge's order, a party may serve and file objections to the order; a party may not thereafter assign as error a defect in the magistrate judge's order to which objection was not timely made. The district judge to whom the case is assigned shall consider objections and shall modify or set aside any portion of the magistrate judge's order found to be clearly erroneous or contrary to law.

**(b) Dispositive Motions and Prisoner Petitions.** A magistrate judge assigned without consent of the parties to hear a pretrial matter dispositive of a claim or defense of a party or a prisoner petition challenging the conditions of a confinement shall promptly conduct such proceedings as are required. A record shall be made of all evidentiary proceedings before the magistrate judge and a record may be made of such other proceedings as the magistrate judge deems necessary. The magistrate judge shall enter into the record a recommendation for disposition of the matter, including proposed findings of fact when appropriate. The clerk shall forthwith mail copies to all parties.

A party objecting to the recommended disposition of the matter shall promptly arrange for the transcription of the record, or portions of it as all parties may agree upon or the magistrate judge deems sufficient, unless the district judge otherwise directs. Within 10 days after being served with a copy of the recommended disposition, a party may serve and file specific, written objections to the proposed findings and recommendations. A party may respond to another party's objections within 10 days after being served with a copy thereof. The district judge to whom the case is assigned shall make a de novo determination upon the record, or after additional evidence, of any portion of the magistrate judge's disposition to which specific written objection has been made in accordance with this Rule. The district judge may accept, reject or modify the recommended decision, receive further evidence or recommit the matter to the magistrate judge with instructions.

### Rule 73. Magistrate Judges; Trial by Consent and Appeal Options.

**(a) Powers; Procedure.** When specially designated to exercise such jurisdiction by local rule or order of the district court and when all parties consent thereto, a magistrate judge may exercise the authority provided by Title 28, U.S.C. §636(c), and may conduct any or all proceedings, including a jury or nonjury trial, in a civil case. A record of the proceedings shall be made in accordance with the requirements of Title 28, U.S.C. §636(c)(5).

**(b) Consent.** When a magistrate judge has been designated to exercise civil trial jurisdiction, the clerk shall give written notice to the parties of their opportunity to consent to the exercise by a magistrate of judge civil jurisdiction over the case, as authorized by Title 28, U.S.C. §636(c). If, within the period specified by local rule, the parties agree to a magistrate judge's exercise of such authority, they shall execute and file a joint form of consent or separate forms of consent setting forth such election.

A district judge, magistrate judge or other court official may again advise the parties of the availability of the magistrate judge, but, in so doing, shall also advise the parties that they are free to withhold consent without adverse substantive consequences. A district judge or magistrate judge shall not be informed of a party's response to the clerk's notification, unless all parties have consented to the referral of the matter to a magistrate judge.

The district judge, for good cause shown on the judge's own initiative or under extraordinary circumstances shown by a party, may vacate a reference of a civil matter to a magistrate judge under this subdivision.

**(c) Normal Appeal Route.** In accordance with Title 28, U.S.C. §636(c)(3), unless the parties otherwise agree to the optional appeal route provided for in subdivision (d) of this Rule, appeal from a judgment entered upon direction of a magistrate judge in proceedings under this Rule will lie to the court of appeals as it would from a judgment of the district court.

**(d) Optional Appeal Route.** In accordance with Title 28, U.S.C. §636(c)(4), at the time of reference to a magistrate judge, the parties may consent to appeal on the record to a district judge of the court and thereafter, by petition only, to the court of appeals.

### Rule 74. Abrogated

### Rule 75. Abrogated

### Rule 76. Abrogated

**X.    District Courts and Clerks.**

### Rule 77. District Courts and Clerks.

**(a) District Courts Always Open.** The district courts shall be deemed always open for the purpose of filing any pleading or other proper paper, of issuing and returning mesne and final process and of making and directing all interlocutory motions, order and rules.

**(b) Trials and Hearings; Orders in Chambers.** All trials upon the merits shall be conducted in open court and so far as convenient in a regular court room. All other acts or proceedings may be done or conducted by a judge in chambers, without the attendance of the clerk or other court officials and at any place either within or without the district; but no hearing, other than one ex parte, shall be conducted outside the district without the consent of all parties affected thereby.

**(c) Clerk's Office and Orders by Clerk.** The clerk's office with the clerk or a deputy in attendance shall be open during business hours on all days except Saturdays, Sundays and legal holidays, but a district court may provide by local rule or order that its clerk's office shall be open for specified hours on Saturdays or particular legal holidays other than New Year's Day, Birthday of Martin Luther King, Jr., Washington's Birthday, Memorial Day, Independence Day, Labor Day, Columbus Day, Veterans Day, Thanksgiving Day and Christmas Day. All motions and applications in the clerk's office for issuing mesne process, for issuing final process to enforce and execute judgments, for entering defaults or judgments by default, and for other proceedings which do not require allowance or order of the court are grantable of course by the clerk; but the clerk's action may be suspended or altered or rescinded by the court upon cause shown.

**(d) Notice of Orders or Judgments.** Immediately upon the entry of an order of judgment the clerk shall serve a notice of the entry by mail in the manner provided for in Rule 5 upon each party who is not in default for failure to appear, and shall make a note in the docket of the mailing. Any party may in addition serve a notice of such entry in the manner provided in Rule 5 for the service of papers. Lack of notice of the entry by the clerk does not affect the time to appeal or relieve or authorize the court to relieve a party for failure to appeal within the time allowed, except as permitted in Rule 4(a) of the Federal Rules of Appellate Procedure.

### Rule 78. Motion Day.

Unless local conditions make it impracticable, each district court shall establish regular times and places, at intervals sufficiently frequent for the prompt dispatch of business, at which motions requiring notice and hearing may be heard and disposed of; but the judge at any time or place and on such notice, if any, as the judge considers reasonable, may make orders for the advancement, conduct and hearing of actions.

To expedite its business, the court may make provision by rule or order for the submission and determination of motions without oral hearing upon brief written statements of reasons in support and opposition.

### Rule 79. Books and Records Kept by the Clerk and Entries Therein.

**(a) Civil Docket.** The clerk shall keep a book known as a "Civil Docket" of such form and style as may be prescribed by the Director of the Administrative Office of the United States Courts with the approval of the Judicial Conference of the United States, and shall enter therein each civil action to which these Rules are made applicable. Actions shall be assigned consecutive file numbers. The file number of each action shall be noted on the folio of the docket whereon the first entry of the action is made. All papers filed with the clerk, all process issued and returns made thereon, all appearances, orders, verdicts and judgments shall be entered chronologically in the civil docket on the folio assigned to the action and shall be marked with its file number. These entries shall be brief but shall show the nature of each paper filed or writ issued and the substance of each order or judgment of the court and of the returns showing execution of process. The entry of an order or judgment shall show the date the entry is made. When in an action trial by jury has been properly demanded or ordered, the clerk shall enter the word "jury" on the folio assigned to that action.

**(b) Indices; Calendars.** Suitable indices of the civil docket and of every civil judgment and order referred to in subdivision (b) of this Rule shall be kept by the clerk under the direction of the court. There shall be prepared under the direction of the court calendars of all actions ready for trial, which shall distinguish "jury actions" from "court actions."

### Rule 80. Stenographer; Stenographic Report or Transcript as Evidence.

**(a) Stenographer.** Abrogated Dec. 27, 1946, eff. Mar. 19, 1948.

**(b) Stenographic Report or Transcript of Evidence.** Whenever the testimony of a witness at a trial or hearing which was stenographically reported is admissible in evidence at a later trial, it may be proved by the transcript thereof duly certified by the person who reported the testimony.

**XI. General Provisions.**

### Rule 81. Applicability in General.

**(a) To What Proceedings Applicable.**

(1) These Rules do not apply to prize proceedings in admiralty governed by Title 10, U.S.C. §7651-7681. They do not apply to proceedings in bankruptcy or proceedings in copyright under Title 17, U.S.C., except insofar as they may be made applicable thereto by rules promulgated by the Supreme Court of the United States. They do not apply to mental

health proceedings in the United States District Court for the District of Columbia.

(2) These Rules are applicable to proceedings for admission to citizenship, habeas corpus and quo warranto, to the extent that the practice in such proceedings is not set forth in statutes of the United States and has heretofore conformed to the practice in civil actions. The writ of habeas corpus or order to show cause, shall be directed to the person having custody of the person detained. It shall be returned within 3 days unless for good cause shown additional time is allowed which in cases brought under 28 U.S.C. §2254 shall not exceed 40 days, and in all other cases shall not exceed 20 days.

(3) In proceedings under Title 9, U.S.C., relating to arbitration, or under the Act of May 20, 1926, ch. 347, §9 (44 stat. 585), U.S.C., Title 45, §159, relating to board of arbitration of railway labor disputes, these Rules apply only to the extent that matters of procedure are not provided for in those statutes. These Rules apply to proceedings to compel the giving of testimony or production of documents in accordance with a subpoena issued by an officer or agency of the United States under any statute of the United States except as otherwise provided by statute or by rules of the district court or by order of the court in the proceedings.

(4) These Rules do not alter the method prescribed by the Act of February, 18, 1922, c. 57, §2 (42 Stat. 388), U.S.C. Title 7, §292; or by the Act of June 10, 1930, c. 436, §7 (46 Stat. 534), as amended, U.S.C., Title 7, §499g(c), for instituting proceedings in the United States district courts to review orders of the Secretary of Agriculture; or prescribed by the Act of June 25, 1934, c. 742, §2 (48 Stat. 1214), U.S.C., Title 15, §522, for instituting proceedings to review orders of the Secretary of the Interior; or prescribed by the Act of February 22, 1935, c. 18, §5 (49 Stat. 31), U.S.C., Title 15, §715d(c), as extended, for instituting proceedings to review orders of petroleum control boards; but the conduct of such proceedings in the district courts shall be made to conform to these Rules as far as applicable.

(5) These Rules do not alter the practice in the United States district courts prescribed in the Act of July 5, 1935, c. 372, §§9 and 10 (49 Stat. 453), as amended, U.S.C., Title 29, §§159 and 160, for beginning and conducting proceedings to enforce orders of the National Labor Relations Board; and in respects not covered by those statutes, the practice in the district courts shall conform to these Rules so far as applicable.

(6) These Rules apply to proceedings for enforcement or review of compensation orders under the Longshoremen's and Harbor Workers' Compensation Act, Act of March 4, 1927, c. 509, §§18, 21 (44 Stat. 1434, 1436), as amended, U.S.C., Title 33, §§918, 921, except to the extent that matters of procedure are provided for in that Act. The provisions for service by publication and for answer in proceedings to cancel certificates of citizenship under the Act of June 27, 1952, c. 477, Title III, c. §340 (66 Stat. 260), U.S.C., Title 8, §1451, remain in effect.

**(b) Scire Facias and Mandamus.** The writs of scire facias and mandamus are abolished. Relief heretofore available by mandamus or scire facias may be obtained by appropriate action or by appropriate motion under the practice prescribed in these Rules.

**(c) Removed Actions.** These Rules apply to civil actions removed to the United States district courts from the state courts and govern procedure after removal. Repleading is not necessary unless the court so orders. In a removed action in which the defendant has not answered, the defendant shall answer or present the other defenses or objections available under these Rules within 20 days after the receipt through service or otherwise of a copy of the initial pleading setting forth the claim for relief upon which the action or proceeding is based, or within 20 days after the service of summons upon such initial pleading, then filed, or within 5 days after the filing of the petition for removal, whichever period is longest. If at the time of removal all necessary pleadings have been served, a party entitled to trial by jury under Rule 38 shall be accorded it, if the party's demand therefor is served within 10 days after the petition for removal is filed if the party is the petitioner, or if not the petitioner within 10 days after service on the party of the notice of filing the petition. A party who, prior to removal, has made an express demand for trial by jury in accordance with state law, need not make a demand after removal. If state law applicable in the court from which the case is removed does not require the parties to make express demands in order to claim trial by jury, they need not make demands after removal unless the court directs that they do so within a specified time if they desire to claim trial by jury. The court may make this direction on its own motion and shall do so as a matter of course at the request of any party. The failure of a party to make demand as directed constitutes a waiver by that party of trial by jury.

**(d) District of Columbia; Courts and Judges.** Abrogated Dec. 29, 1948, eff. Oct. 20, 1949.

**(e) Law Applicable.** Whenever in these Rules the law of the state in which the district court is held is made applicable, the law applied in the District of Columbia governs proceedings in the United States District Court for the District of Columbia. When the word "state" is used, it includes, if appropriate, the District of Columbia. When the term "statute of the United States" is used, it includes, so far as concerns proceedings in the United States District Court for the District of Columbia, any Act of Congress locally applicable to and in force in the District of Columbia. When the law of a state is referred to, the word "law" includes the statutes of that state and the state judicial decisions construing them.

**(f) References to Officer of the United States.** Under any Rule in which reference is made to an officer or agency of the United States, the term "officer" includes a district director of internal revenue, a former district director or collector of internal revenue or the personal representative of a deceased district director or collector of internal revenue.

### Rule 82. Jurisdiction and Venue Unaffected.

These Rules shall not be construed to extend or limit the jurisdiction of the United States district courts or the venue of actions therein. An admiralty or maritime claim within the meaning of Rule 9(h) shall not be treated as a civil action for the purposes of Title 28, U.S.C., §§1391-93.

### Rule 83. Rules by District Courts; Judge's Directives.

**(a) Local Rules.**

(1) Each district court, acting by a majority of its district judges, may, after giving appropriate public notice and an opportunity for comment, make and amend rules governing its practice. A local rule shall be consistent with—but not duplicative of—Acts of Congress and rules adopted under 28 U.S.C. §§2072 and 2075, and shall conform to any uniform numbering system prescribed by the Judicial Conference of the United States. A local rule takes effect on the date specified by the district court and remains in effect unless

amended by the court or abrogated by the judicial council of the circuit. Copies of rules and amendments shall, upon their promulgation, be furnished to the judicial council and the Administrative Office of the United States Courts and be made available to the public.

(2) A local rule imposing a requirement of form shall not be enforced in a manner that causes a party to lose rights because of a nonwillful failure to comply with the requirement.

**(b) Procedures When There Is No Controlling Law.** A judge may regulate practice in any manner consistent with federal law, rules adopted under 28 U.S.C. §§2072 and 2075, and local rules of the district. No sanction or other disadvantage may be imposed for noncompliance with any requirement not in federal law, federal rules, or the local district rules unless the alleged violator has been furnished in the particular case with actual notice of the requirement.

### Rule 84. Forms.

The forms contained in the Appendix of Forms are sufficient under the Rules and are intended to indicate the simplicity and brevity of statements which the Rules contemplate.

### Rule 85. Title.

These Rules may be known and cited as the Federal Rules of Civil Procedure.

### Rule 86. Effective Date.

**(a) Effective Date.** These Rules will take effect on the day which is 3 months subsequent to the adjournment of the second regular session of the 75th Congress, but if that day is prior to September 1, 1938, then these Rules will take effect on September 1, 1938. They govern all proceedings in actions brought after they take effect and also all further proceedings in actions then pending, except to the extent that in the opinion of the court their application in a particular action pending when the Rules take effect would not be feasible or would work injustice, in which event the former procedure applies.

**(b) Effective Date of Amendments.** The amendments adopted by the Supreme Court on December 27, 1946, and transmitted to the Attorney General on January 2, 1947, shall take effect on the day which is three months subsequent to the adjournment of the first regular session of the 80th Congress, but, if that day is prior to September 1, 1947, then these amendments shall take effect on September 1, 1947. They govern all proceedings in actions brought after they take effect and also all further proceedings in actions then pending, except to the extent that in the opinion of the court their application in a particular action pending when the amendments take effect would not be feasible or would work injustice, in which event the former procedure applies.

**(c) Effective Date of Amendments.** The amendments adopted by the Supreme Court on December 29, 1948, and transmitted to the Attorney General on December 31, 1948, shall take effect on the day following the adjournment of the first regular session of the 81st Congress.

**(d) Effective Date of Amendments.** The amendments adopted by the Supreme Court on April 17, 1961, and transmitted to the Congress on April 18, 1961, shall take effect on July 19, 1961. They govern all proceedings in actions brought after they take effect and also all further proceedings in actions then pending, except to the extent that in the opinion of the court their application in a particular action pending when the amendments take effect would not be feasible or would work injustice, in which event the former procedure applies.

**(e) Effective Date of Amendments.** The amendments adopted by the Supreme Court on January 21, 1963, and transmitted to the Congress on January 21, 1963, shall take effect on July 1, 1963. They govern all proceedings in actions brought after they take effect and also all further proceedings in actions then pending, except to the extent that in the opinion of the court their application in a particular action pending when the amendments take effect would not be feasible or would work injustice, in which event the former procedure applies. [The practice of amending Rule 86 to show effective times of amendments was discontinued after the 1963 amendments. Adoption and effective dates of subsequent amendments are shown after the relevant change in the Rule.]

# Appendix of Forms

## Appendix of Forms
## Introductory Statement

1. The following forms are intended for illustration only. They are limited in number. No attempt is made to furnish a manual of forms. Each form assumes the action to be brought in the Southern District of New York. If the district in which an action is brought has divisions, the division should be indicated in the caption.

2. Except where otherwise indicated, each pleading, motion and other paper should have a caption similar to that of the summons, with the designation of the particular paper substituted for the word "Summons". In the caption of the summons and in the caption of the complaint all parties must be named but in other pleadings and papers, it is sufficient to state the name of the first party on either side, with an appropriate indication of other parties. See Rules 4(b), 7(b)(2) and 10(a).

3. In Form 3 and the forms following, the words, "Allegation of jurisdiction", are used to indicate the appropriate allegation in Form 2.

4. Each pleading, motion and other paper is to be signed in his individual name by at least one attorney of record (Rule 11). The attorney's name is to be followed by his address as indicated in Form 3. In forms following Form 3 the signature and address are not indicated.

5. If a party is not represented by an attorney, the signature and address of the party are required in place of those of the attorney.

**Sample Caption of Case**

**IN THE UNITED STATES DISTRICT COURT**

**FOR THE DISTRICT OF NEW YORK**

| _____, | ) | |
|---|---|---|
| | ) | |
| Plaintiff, | ) | Civil Action, File No. _____ |
| | ) | |
| v. | ) | (TITLE OF PLEADING, MOTION, ETC.) |
| | ) | |
| _____, | ) | |
| | ) | |
| Defendant. | ) | |
| _____ | ) | |

---

**Sample Mailing Certificate**   (Placed at end of Pleading, Motion, etc.)

ORIGINAL and COPY of
the foregoing delivered/
mailed this _____ day of
_____, 20\_\_\_\_, for filing
to:

Clerk of the United States
District Court
District of Arizona
(Address of Court)

COPY of the foregoing
delivered/mailed this _____
day of _____, 20\_\_\_\_, to:

Attorney for Plaintiff
(Address)
(Designation of Attorney)

_____
Signature of Attorney
Mailing Pleading

---

**Form 1.    Summons**

CAPTION OF CASE

SUMMONS

To the above-named Defendant:

You are hereby summoned and required to serve upon _____, plaintiff's attorney, whose address is _____, an answer to the complaint which is herewith served upon you, within 20[1] days after service of this summons upon you, exclusive of the day of service. If you fail to do so, judgment by default will be taken against you for the relief demanded in the complaint.

<br>

_____
Clerk of Court

[Seal of the U.S. District Court]
Dated _____

(This summons is issued pursuant<br>to Rule 4 of the Federal Rules of<br>Civil Procedure)

---

[1.] If the United States or an officer or agency thereof is a defendant, the time to be inserted as to it is 60 days.

---

| **Form 1-A.** | **Notice of Lawsuit and Request for Waiver of Summons** |
|---|---|

TO: _____ (A) _____

[as _____ (B) _____ of _____ (C) _____ ]

    A lawsuit has been commenced against you (or the entity on whose behalf you are addressed). A copy of the complaint is attached to this notice. It has been filed in the United States District Court for the _____ (D) _____ and has been assigned docket number _____ (E) _____ .

    This is not a formal summons or notification from the court, but rather my request that you sign and return the enclosed waiver of service in order to save the cost of serving you with a judicial summons and an additional copy of the complaint. The cost of service will be avoided if I receive a signed copy of the waiver within _____ (F) _____ days after the date designated below as the date on which this Notice and Request is sent. I enclose a stamped and addressed envelope (or other means of cost-free return) for your use. An extra copy of the waiver is also attached for your records.

    If you comply with this request and return the signed waiver, it will be filed with the court and no summons will be served on you. The action will then proceed as if you had been served on the date the waiver is filed, except that you will not be obligated to answer the complaint before 60 days from the date designated below as the date on which this notice is sent (or before 90 days from that date if your address is not in any judicial district of the United States).

    If you do not return the signed waiver within the time indicated, I will take appropriate steps to effect formal service in a manner authorized by the Federal Rules of Civil Procedure and will then, to the extent authorized by those Rules, ask the court to require you (or the party on whose behalf you are addressed) to pay the full costs of such service. In that conclusion, please read the statement concerning the duty of parties to waive the service of the summons, which is set forth on the reverse side (or at the foot) of the waiver form.

I affirm that this request is being sent to you on behalf of the plaintiff, this _____ day of _____, _____.

_____
Signature of Plaintiff's Attorney
or Unrepresented Plaintiff

---

**Form 1-B.      Waiver of Service of Summons**

---

TO: _____ (name of plaintiff's attorney or unrepresented plaintiff) _____

    I acknowledge receipt of your request that I waive service of a summons in the action of _____ (caption of action) _____, which is case number _____ (docket number) _____ in the United States District Court for the _____ (district) _____. I have also received a copy of the complaint in the action, two copies of this instrument, and a means by which I can return the signed waiver to you without cost to me.

    I agree to save the cost of service of a summons and an additional copy of the complaint in this lawsuit by not requiring that I (or the entity on whose behalf I am acting) be served with judicial process in the manner provided by Rule 4.

    I (or the entity on whose behalf I am acting) will retain all defenses or objections to the lawsuit or to the jurisdiction or venue of the court except for objections based on a defect in the summons or in the service of the summons.

    I understand that a judgment may be entered against me (or the party on whose behalf I am acting) if an answer or motion under Rule 12 is not served upon you within 60 days after _____ (date request was sent) _____, or within 90 days after that date if the request was sent outside the United States.

_____
Date/Signature
Printed/typed name:

[as ] _____

[of ] _____

    To be printed on reverse side of the waiver form or set forth at the foot of the form:

Duty to Avoid Unnecessary Costs of Service of Summons

    Rule 4 of the Federal Rules of Civil Procedure requires certain parties to cooperate in saving unnecessary costs of service of the summons and complaint. A defendant located in the United States to waive service of a summons, fails to do so will be required to bear the cost of such service unless good cause be shown for its failure to sign and return the waiver.

    It is not good cause for a failure to waive service that a party believes that the complaint is unfounded, or that the action has been brought in an improper place or in a court that lacks jurisdiction over the subject matter of the action or over its person or property. A party who waives service of the summons retains all defenses and objections (except any relating to the summons or to the service of the summons), and may later object to the jurisdiction of the court or to the place where the action has been brought.

    A defendant who waives service must within the time specified on the waiver form serve on the plaintiff's attorney (or unrepresented plaintiff) a response to the complaint must also file a signed copy of the response with the court. If the answer or motion is not served within this time, a default judgment may be taken against that defendant. By waiving service, a defendant is allowed more time to answer than if the summons had been actually served when the request for waiver of service was received.

---

**Form 2. Allegation of Jurisdiction**

    (a)   Jurisdiction founded on diversity of citizenship and amount.

    Plaintiff is a [citizen of the State of Connecticut][2] [corporation incorporated under the laws of the State of Connecticut having its principal place of business in the State of Connecticut] and defendant is a corporation incorporated under the laws of the State of New York having its principal place of business in a State other than the State of Connecticut. The matter in controversy exceeds, exclusive of interest and costs, the sum of ten thousand dollars.

    (b)   Jurisdiction founded under [the Constitution of the United States, Article _____, §_____]; [the _____ Amendment to the Constitution of the United States, §_____]; [the Act of _____, _____ Stat. _____; U.S.C., Title _____, §_____]; [the Treaty of the United States (here describe the treaty)],[3] as hereinafter more fully appears. The matter in controversy exceeds, exclusive of interest and costs, the sum of ten thousand dollars.

    (c)   Jurisdiction founded on the existence of a question arising under particular statutes.
    The action arises under the Act of _____, _____ Stat. _____; U.S.C., Title _____, §_____, as hereinafter more fully appears.

    (d)   Jurisdiction founded on the admiralty or maritime character of the claim. This is a case of admiralty and maritime jurisdiction, as hereinafter more fully appears. [If the pleader wishes to invoke the distinctively maritime procedures referred to in Rule 9(h), add the following or its substantial equivalent: This is an admiralty or maritime claim within the meaning of Rule 9(h).]

---

[2] Form for natural person.
[3] Use the appropriate phrase or phrases. The general allegation of the existence of a Federal question is ineffective unless the matters constituting the claim for relief as set forth in the complaint raise a Federal question.

---

**Form 3. Complaint on a Promissory Note**

CAPTION OF CASE

COMPLAINT ON A
PROMISSORY NOTE

    1.   Allegation of jurisdiction.

    2.   Defendant on or about _____, 20____, executed and delivered to plaintiff a promissory note [in the following words and figures: (here set out the note verbatim)]; [a copy of which is hereto annexed as Exhibit A]; [whereby defendant promised to pay to plaintiff or order on _____, 19____ the sum of _____ dollars with interest thereon at the rate of _____ percent per annum].

    3.   Defendant owes plaintiff the amount of said note and interest.

Wherefore plaintiff demands judgment against defendant for the sum of _____ dollars, interest and costs.

Signed: _____
Attorney for Plaintiff
Address _____

**Form 4.    Complaint on an Account**

CAPTION OF CASE

COMPLAINT ON AN
ACCOUNT

1.    Allegation of jurisdiction.

2.    Defendant owes plaintiff _____ dollars according to the account hereto annexed as Exhibit A.

Wherefore (etc. as in Form 3).

---

**Form 5.    Complaint for Goods Sold and Delivered**

CAPTION OF CASE

COMPLAINT FOR GOODS
SOLD AND DELIVERED

1.    Allegation of jurisdiction.

2.    Defendant owes plaintiff _____ dollars for goods sold and delivered by plaintiff to defendant between _____, 20____ and _____, 20____.

Wherefore (etc. as in Form 3).

---

**Form 6.    Complaint for Money Lent**

CAPTION OF CASE

COMPLAINT FOR MONEY
LENT

1.    Allegation of jurisdiction.

2.    Defendant owes plaintiff _____ dollars for money lent by plaintiff to defendant on _____, 20____.

Wherefore (etc. as in Form 3).

**Form 7.  Complaint for Money Paid by Mistake**

CAPTION OF CASE

COMPLAINT FOR MONEY
PAID BY MISTAKE

1.  Allegation of jurisdiction.

2.  Defendant owes plaintiff _____ dollars for money paid by plaintiff to defendant by mistake on _____, 20____, under the following circumstances: [here state the circumstances with particularity - see Rule 9(b)].

Wherefore (etc., as in Form 3).

**Form 8.  Complaint for Money Had and Received**

CAPTION OF CASE

COMPLAINT FOR MONEY
HAD AND RECEIVED

1.  Allegation of jurisdiction.

2.  Defendant owes plaintiff _____ dollars for money had and received from one _____ on _____, 20____, to be paid by defendant to plaintiff.

Wherefore (etc., as in Form 3).

**Form 9.  Complaint for Negligence**

CAPTION OF CASE

COMPLAINT FOR
NEGLIGENCE

1.  Allegation of jurisdiction.

2.  On _____, 20____, in a public highway called _____ in _____, _____, defendant negligently drove a motor vehicle against plaintiff who was then crossing said highway.

3.  As a result, plaintiff was thrown down and had his leg broken and was otherwise injured, was prevented from transacting business, suffered great pain of body and mind, and incurred expenses for medical attention and hospitalization in the sum of _____ dollars.

Wherefore plaintiff demands judgment against defendant in the sum of _____ dollars and costs.

**Form 10.   Complaint for Negligence Where Plaintiff Is Unable to Determine Definitely Whether the Person Responsible Is C.D. or E. F. or Whether Both Are Responsible and Where His Evidence May Justify a Finding of Wilfulness or of Recklessness or of Negligence**

CAPTION OF CASE

COMPLAINT

1.   Allegation of jurisdiction.

2.   On _____, 20____, in a public highway called _____ in _____, _____, defendant C. D. or defendant E. F., or both defendants C. D. and E. F. wilfully or recklessly or negligently drove or caused to be driven a motor vehicle against plaintiff who was then crossing said highway.

3.   As a result, plaintiff was thrown down and had his leg broken and was otherwise injured, was prevented from transacting his business, suffered great pain of body and mind, and incurred expenses for medical attention and hospitalization in the sum of _____ dollars.

Wherefore plaintiff demands judgment against C. D. or against E. F., or against both in the sum of _____ dollars and costs.

---

**Form 11.   Complaint for Conversion**

CAPTION OF CASE

COMPLAINT FOR
CONVERSION

1.   Allegation of jurisdiction.

2.   On or about _____, 20____, defendant converted to his own use _____ of the _____ Company (here insert brief identification as by number and issue) of the value of _____ dollars, the property of plaintiff.

Wherefore plaintiff demands judgment against defendant in the sum of _____ dollars, interest and costs.

---

**Form 12.   Complaint for Specific Performance of Contract to Convey Land**

CAPTION OF CASE

COMPLAINT FOR SPECIFIC
PERFORMANCE OF CONTRACT
TO CONVEY LAND

1.   Allegation of jurisdiction.

2.   On or about _____, 20____, plaintiff and defendant entered into an agreement in writing a copy of which is hereto annexed as Exhibit A.

3.   In accord with the provisions of said agreement, plaintiff tendered to defendant the purchase price and requested a conveyance of the land, but defendant refused to accept the tender and refused to make the conveyance.

4.   Plaintiff now offers to pay the purchase price.

Wherefore plaintiff demands (1) that defendant be required specifically to perform said agreement, (2) damages in the sum of _____ dollars, and (3) that if specific performance is not granted to plaintiff, that plaintiff has judgment against defendant in the sum of _____ dollars.

---

**Form 13.   Complaint on Claim for Debt and to Set Aside Fraudulent Conveyance Under Rule 18(b)**

CAPTION OF CASE

COMPLAINT ON CLAIM
FOR DEBT AND TO SET
ASIDE FRAUDULENT
CONVEYANCE UNDER
RULE 18(b)

1.   Allegation of jurisdiction.

2.   Defendant C. D. on or about _____, 20____ executed and delivered to plaintiff a promissory note [in the following words and figures: (here set out the note verbatim)]; [a copy of which is hereto annexed as Exhibit A]; [whereby defendant C. D. promised to pay to plaintiff or order on _____, 20____ the sum of _____ Dollars with interest thereon at the rate of ____ percent per annum].

3.   Defendant C. D. owes to plaintiff the amount of said note and interest.

4.   Defendant C. D. on or about _____, 20____ conveyed all of his property, real and personal [or specify and describe] to defendant E. F. for the purpose of defrauding plaintiff and hindering and delaying the collection of the indebtedness evidenced by the note above referred to.

Wherefore plaintiff demands:

(1)   That plaintiff have judgment against defendant C. D. for _____ dollars and interest; (2) that the aforesaid conveyance to defendant E. F. be declared void and the judgment herein be declared a lien on said property; (3) that plaintiff have judgment against the defendants for costs.

---

**Form 14.   Complaint for Negligence Under Federal Employers' Liability Act**

CAPTION OF CASE

COMPLAINT FOR NEGLI-
GENCE UNDER FEDERAL
EMPLOYERS' LIABILITY ACT

1.   Allegation of jurisdiction.

2.   During all the times herein mentioned, defendant owned and operated in interstate commerce a railroad which passed through a tunnel located at _____ and known as Tunnel No. _____.

3.   On or about _____, 20____, defendant was repairing and enlarging the tunnel in order to protect interstate trains and passengers and freight from injury and in order to make the tunnel more conveniently usable for interstate commerce.

4.   In the course of thus repairing and enlarging the tunnel on said day defendant employed plaintiff as one of its workmen, and negligently put plaintiff to work in a portion of the tunnel which defendant had left unprotected and unsupported.

5.   By reason of defendant's negligence in thus putting plaintiff to work in that portion of the tunnel, plaintiff was, while so working pursuant to defendant's orders, struck and crushed by a rock, which fell from the unsupported portion of the tunnel, and was (here describe plaintiff's injuries).

6.   Prior to these injuries, plaintiff was a strong, able-bodied man, capable of earning and actually earning _____ dollars per day. By these injuries he has been made incapable of any gainful activity, has suffered great physical and mental pain, and has incurred expenses in the amount of _____ dollars for medicine, medical attendance and hospitalization.

Wherefore plaintiff demands judgment against defendant in the sum of _____ dollars and costs.

---

**Form 15.   Complaint for Damages Under Merchant Marine Act**

CAPTION OF CASE

COMPLAINT FOR DAMAGES
UNDER MERCHANT MARINE
ACT

1.    Allegation of jurisdiction. [If the pleader wishes to invoke the distinctively maritime procedures referred to in Rule 9(h), add the following or its substantial equivalent: This is an admiralty or maritime claim within the meaning of Rule 9(h).]

2.    During all the times herein mentioned defendant was the owner of the steamship _____ and used it in the transportation of freight for hire by water in interstate and foreign commerce.

3.    During the first part of (month and year) at _____ plaintiff entered the employ of defendant as an able seaman on said steamship under seamen's articles of customary form for a voyage from _____ ports to the Orient and return at a wage of _____ dollars per month and found, which is equal to a wage of _____ dollars per month as a shore worker.

4.    On _____, 20____, said steamship was about _____ day out of the port of _____ and was being navigated by the master and crew on the return voyage of _____ ports. (Here describe weather conditions and the condition of the ship and state as in an ordinary complaint for personal injuries the negligent conduct of defendant).

5.    By reason of defendant's negligence in this (brief statement of defendant's negligent conduct) and the unseaworthiness of said steamship, plaintiff was (here describe plaintiff's injuries).

6.    Prior to these injuries, plaintiff was a strong, able-bodied man, capable of earning and actually earning _____ dollars per day. By these injuries he has been made incapable of any gainful activity; has suffered great physical and mental pain and has incurred expenses in the amount of _____ dollars for medicine, medical attendance and hospitalization.

Wherefore plaintiff demands judgment against defendant in the sum of _____ dollars.

---

**Form 16.   Complaint for Infringement of Patent**

CAPTION OF CASE

COMPLAINT FOR
INFRINGEMENT OF PATENT

1.   Allegation of jurisdiction.

2.   On _____, 20____, United States Letters Patent No. _____ were duly and legally issued to plaintiff for an invention in an (here insert description of invention); and since that date plaintiff has been and still is the owner of those Letters Patent.

3.   Defendant has for a long time past been and still is infringing those Letters Patent by making, selling and using _____ embodying the patented invention, and will continue to do so unless enjoined by this court.

4.   Plaintiff has placed the required statutory notice on all _____ manufactured and sold by him under said Letters Patent and has given written notice to defendant of his said infringement.

Wherefore plaintiff demands a preliminary and final injunction against continued infringement, an accounting for damages and an assessment of interest and costs against defendant.

---

**Form 17.   Complaint for Infringement of Copyright and Unfair Competition**

CAPTION OF CASE

COMPLAINT FOR
INFRINGEMENT OF
COPYRIGHT AND UNFAIR
COMPETITION

1.   Allegation of jurisdiction.

2.   Prior to _____, 20____, plaintiff, who then was and ever since has been a citizen of the United States, created and wrote an original book, entitled _____.

3.   This book contains a large amount of material wholly original with plaintiff and is copyrightable subject matter under the laws of the United States.

4.   Between _____, 20____, and _____, 20____, plaintiff complied in all respects with the Act of (give citation) and all other laws governing copyright, and secured the exclusive rights and privileges in and to the copyright of said book, and received from the Register of Copyrights a certificate of registration, dated and identified as follows: "_____, 20____, Class _____, No. _____".

5.   Since _____, 20____, said book has been published by plaintiff and all copies of it made by plaintiff or under his authority or license have been printed, bound and published in strict conformity with the provisions of the Act of _____ and all other laws governing copyright.

---

**Form 17.   Complaint for Infringement of Copyright and Unfair Competition,** *continued*

6.   Since _____, 20____, plaintiff has been and still is the sole proprietor of all rights, title and interest in and to the copyright of said book.

7.   After _____, 20____, defendant infringed said copyright by publishing and placing upon the market a book entitled _____, which was copied largely from plaintiff's copyrighted book, entitled _____.

8.   A copy of plaintiff's copyrighted book is hereto attached as Exhibit "1"; and a copy of defendant's infringing book is hereto attached as Exhibit "2";

9.   Plaintiff has notified defendant that defendant has infringed the copyright of plaintiff, and defendant has continued to infringe the copyright.

10.   After _____, 20____, and continuously since about _____, 20____, defendant has been publishing, selling and otherwise marketing the book entitled _____, and has thereby been engaging in unfair trade practices and unfair competition against plaintiff to plaintiff's irreparable damage.

Wherefore plaintiff demands:

(1)   That defendant, his agents and servants be enjoined during the pendency of this action and permanently from infringing said copyright of said plaintiff in any manner, and from publishing, selling, marketing or otherwise disposing of any copies of the book entitled _____.

(2)   That defendant be required to pay to plaintiff such damages as plaintiff has sustained in consequence of defendant's infringement of said copyright and said unfair trade practices and unfair competition and to account for:

(a) all gains, profits and advantages derived by defendant by said trade practices and unfair competition and

(b) all gains, profits and advantages derived by defendant by his infringement of plaintiff's copyright or such damages as to the court shall appear proper within the provisions of the copyright statutes, but not less than _____ dollars.

(3)   That defendant be required to deliver up to be impounded during the pendency of this action all copies of said book entitled _____ in his possession or under his control and to deliver up for destruction all infringing copies and all plates, molds and other matter for making such infringing copies.

(4)   That defendant pay to plaintiff the costs of this action and reasonable attorney's fees to be allowed to the plaintiff by the court.

(5)   That plaintiff have such other and further relief as is just.

*continued*

---

**Form 18. Complaint for Interpleader and Declaratory Relief**

CAPTION OF CASE

COMPLAINT FOR INTER-
PLEADER AND DECLARA-
TORY RELIEF

1.  Allegation of jurisdiction.

2.  On or about _____, 20____, plaintiff issued to _____ a policy of life insurance whereby plaintiff promised to pay to _____ as beneficiary the sum of _____ dollars upon the death of _____. The policy required the payment by _____ of a stipulated premium on _____, 20____, and annually thereafter as a condition precedent to its continuance in force.

3.  No part of the premium due _____, 20__, was ever paid and the policy ceased to have any force or effect on _____, 20____.

4.  Thereafter, on _____, 20____, _____ and _____ died as the result of a collision between a locomotive and the automobile in which _____ and _____ were riding.

5.  Defendant _____ is the duly appointed and acting executor of the will of _____; defendant _____ is the duly appointed and acting executor of the will of _____; defendant _____ claims to have been duly designated as beneficiary of said policy in place of _____.

6.  Each of defendants, _____, _____ and _____ is claiming that the above-mentioned policy was in full force and effect at the time of the death of _____; each of them is claiming to be the only person entitled to receive payment of the amount of the policy and has made demand for payment thereof.

7.  By reason of these conflicting claims of the defendants, plaintiff is in great doubt as to which defendant is entitled to be paid the amount of the policy, if it was in force at the death of _____.

Wherefore Plaintiff demands that the court adjudge:

(1)  That none of the defendants is entitled to recover from plaintiff the amount of said policy or any part thereof.

(2)  That each of the defendants be restrained from instituting any action against plaintiff for the recovery of the amount of said policy or any part thereof.

(3)  That, if the court shall determine that said policy was in force at the death of _____, the defendants be required to interplead and settle between themselves their rights to the money due under said policy, and that plaintiff be discharged from all liability in the premises except to the person whom the court shall adjudge entitled to the amount of said policy.

(4)  That plaintiff recover its costs.

## Form 18-A. Notice and Acknowledgment for Service by Mail

CAPTION OF CASE

NOTICE AND ACKNOW-
LEDGMENT OF RECEIPT
OF SUMMONS AND
COMPLAINT

*Notice*

To: (Insert the name and address of the person to be served.)

The enclosed summons and complaint are served pursuant to Rule 4(c)(2)(C)(ii) of the Federal Rules of Civil Procedure.

You must complete the acknowledgment part of this form and return one copy of the completed form to the sender within 20 days.

You must sign and date the acknowledgment. If you are served on behalf of a corporation, unincorporated association (including a partnership), or other entity, you must indicate under your signature your relationship to that entity. If you are served on behalf of another person and you are authorized to receive process, you must indicate under your signature your authority.

If you do not complete and return the form to the sender within 20 days, you (or the party on whose behalf you are being served) may be required to pay any expenses incurred in serving a summons and complaint in any other manner permitted by law.

If you do complete and return this form, you (or the party on whose behalf you are being served) must answer the complaint within 20 days. If you fail to do so, judgment by default will be taken against you for the relief demanded in the complaint.

I declare, under penalty of perjury, that this Notice and Acknowledgment of Receipt of Summons and Complaint will have been mailed on (insert date).

_____

Signature

_____

Date of Signature

*Acknowledgment of Receipt of Summons and Complaint*

I declare, under penalty of perjury, that I received a copy of the summons and complaint in the above-captioned matter at (insert address).

_____

Signature

_____

Relationship to Entity/Authority to
Receive Service of Process

_____

Date of Signature

**Form 19.   Motion to Dismiss, Presenting Defenses of Failure to State a Claim, of Lack of Service of Process, of Improper Venue and of Lack of Jurisdiction Under Rule 12(b)**

CAPTION OF CASE

MOTION TO DISMISS

The defendant moves the court as follows:

    1.   To dismiss the action because the complaint fails to state a claim against defendant upon which relief can be granted.

    2.   To dismiss the action or in lieu thereof to quash the return of service of summons on the grounds (a) that the defendant is a corporation organized under the laws of _____ and was not and is not subject to service of process within the _____ District of _____, and (b) that the defendant has not been properly served with process in this action, all of which more clearly appears in the affidavits of _____ and _____ hereto annexed as Exhibits A and B, respectively.

    3.   To dismiss the action on the ground that it is in the wrong district because (a) the jurisdiction of this court is invoked solely on the ground that the action arises under the Constitution and laws of the United States and (b) the defendant is a corporation incorporated under the laws of the State of _____ and is not licensed to do or doing business in the _____ District of _____, all of which more clearly appears in the affidavits of _____ and _____ hereto annexed as Exhibits C and D, respectively.

    4.   To dismiss the action on the ground that the court lacks jurisdiction because the amount actually in controversy is less than _____ dollars.

_____

Attorney for Defendant

_____

Address of Attorney for Defendant

*Notice of Motion*

To: _____
     Attorney for Plaintiff

    Please take notice that the undersigned will bring the above motion on for hearing before this Court at Room _____, United States Courthouse, _____, _____, on the _____ day of _____, 20____, at _____ o'clock ___. M., in the forenoon of that day or as soon thereafter as counsel can be heard.

_____

Signature of Attorney for Defendant

Address: _____

**Form 20.   Answer Presenting Defenses under Rule 12(b)**

CAPTION OF CASE

ANSWER PRESENTING<br>DEFENSES UNDER RULE<br>12(b)

First Defense

The complaint fails to state a claim against defendant upon which relief can be granted.

Second Defense

If defendant is indebted to plaintiff for the goods mentioned in the complaint, he is indebted to them jointly with _____. _____ is alive; is a citizen of the State of _____ and a resident of this district, is subject to the jurisdiction of this court, as to both service of process and venue; can be made a party without depriving this court of jurisdiction of the present parties, and has not been made a party.

Third Defense

Defendant admits the allegation contained in paragraphs ____ and ____ of the complaint; alleges that he is without knowledge or information sufficient to form a belief as to the truth of the allegations contained in paragraph ____ of the complaint, and denies each and every other allegation contained in the complaint.

Fourth Defense

The right of action set forth in the complaint did not accrue within _____ years next before the commencement of this action.

Counterclaim

(Here set forth any claim as a counterclaim in the manner in which a claim is pleaded in a complaint. No statement of the grounds on which the court's jurisdiction depends need be made unless the counterclaim requires independent grounds of jurisdiction.)

Cross-Claim Against Defendant _____

(Here set forth the claim constituting a cross-claim against defendant _____ in the manner in which a claim is pleaded in a complaint. The statement of grounds upon which the court's jurisdiction depends need not be made unless the cross-claim requires independent grounds of jurisdiction.)

---

**Form 21.   Answer to Complaint Set Forth in Form 8, With Counterclaim for Interpleader**

CAPTION OF CASE

ANSWER TO COMPLAINT;
COUNTERCLAIM IN INTER-
PLEADER

Defense

Defendant admits the allegations stated in paragraph ____ of the complaint; and denies the allegations stated in paragraph ____ to the extent set forth in the counterclaim herein.

Counterclaim for Interpleader

1.   Defendant received the sum of _____ dollars as a deposit from _____.

2.   Plaintiff has demanded the payment of such deposit to him by virtue of an assignment of it which he claims to have received from _____.

3.   _____ has notified the defendant that he claims such deposit, that the purported assignment is not valid, and that he holds the defendant responsible for the deposit.

Wherefore defendant demands:

(1)   That the court order _____ to be made a party defendant to respond to the complaint and to this counterclaim.[4]

(2)   That the court order the plaintiff and _____ to interplead their respective claims.

(3)   That the court adjudge whether the plaintiff or _____ is entitled to the sum of money.

(4)   That the court discharge defendant from liability in the premises except to the person it shall adjudge entitled to the sum of money.

(5)   That the court award to the defendant its costs and attorney's fees.

---

[4] Rule 13(h) provides for the court ordering parties to a counterclaim, but who are not parties to the original action, to be brought in as defendants.

---

**Form 22-A.   Summons and Complaint Against Third-Party Defendant**

CAPTION OF CASE

SUMMONS

To the above-named Third-Party Defendant:

You are hereby summoned and required to serve upon _____, plaintiff's attorney, whose address is _____, and upon _____, who is the attorney for _____, defendant and third-party plaintiff, and whose address is _____, an answer to the third-party complaint which is herewith served upon you within 20 days after the service of this summons upon you exclusive of the day of service. If you fail to do so, judgment by default will be taken against you for the relief demanded in the third-party complaint. There is also served upon you herewith a copy of the complaint of the plaintiff which you may but are not required to answer.

_____

Clerk of the Court

[Seal of District Court]
Dated _____

CAPTION OF CASE

THIRD-PARTY COMPLAINT

1.   Plaintiff _____ has filed against defendant _____ a complaint, a copy of which is hereto attached as Exhibit "A".

2.   (Here state the grounds upon which _____ is entitled to recovery from _____, all or part of what _____ may recover from _____. The statement should be framed as in an original complaint.)

Wherefore _____ demands judgment against third-party defendant _____ for all sums[5] that may be adjudged against defendant _____ in favor of plaintiff _____.

_____

Attorney for Third-Party Plaintiff

Address _____

---

[5.] Make appropriate change where _____ is entitled to only partial recovery-over against _____.

**Form 22-B.   Motion to Bring in Third-Party Defendant**

CAPTION OF CASE

MOTION TO BRING IN
THIRD-PARTY DEFENDANT

Defendant moves for leave, as third-party plaintiff, to cause to be served upon _____ a summons and third-party complaint, copies of which are hereto attached as Exhibit "____".

_____

Attorney for Defendant _____

Address _____

Notice of Motion

(Contents the same as in Form 19. The notice should be addressed to all parties to the action.)

---

**Form 23.   Motion to Intervene as a Defendant Under Rule 24**

CAPTION OF CASE

MOTION TO INTERVENE
AS A DEFENDANT UNDER
RULE 24

_____ moves for leave to intervene as a defendant in this action, in order to assert the defenses set forth in his proposed answer, of which a copy is hereto attached, on the ground that he is the manufacturer and vendor to the defendant, as well as to others, of the articles alleged in the complaint to be an infringement of plaintiff's patent, and as such has a defense to plaintiff's claim presenting both questions of law and of fact which are common to the main action.[6]

_____
Attorney for _____, Applicant
for Intervention

Address _____

*Notice of Motion*
(Contents the same as in Form 19)
CAPTION OF CASE

INTERVENOR'S ANSWER

First Defense

Intervenor admits the allegations stated in paragraphs _____ and _____ of the complaint; denies the allegations in paragraph __, and denies the allegations in paragraph __ insofar as they assert the legality of the issuance of the Letters Patent to plaintiff.

Second Defense

Plaintiff is not the first inventor of the articles covered by the Letters Patent specified in his complaint, since articles substantially identical in character were previously patented in Letters Patent granted to intervenor on _____, 20____.

_____
Attorney for _____, Intervenor

Address _____

[6.] For other grounds of intervention, either of right or in the discretion of the court, see Rule 24(a) and (b).

---

**Form 24.   Request for Production of Documents, etc., Under Rule 34**

CAPTION OF CASE

REQUEST FOR PRODUCTION
OF DOCUMENTS, ETC.,
UNDER RULE 34

Plaintiff _____ requests Defendant _____ to respond within _____ days to the following requests:

(1)   That defendant produce and permit plaintiff to inspect and to copy each of the following documents:

(Here list the documents either individually or by category and describe each one of them.)

(Here state the time, place and manner of making the inspection and performance of any related acts.)

(2)   That defendant produce and permit plaintiff to inspect and to copy, test or sample each of the following objects:

(Here list the objects either individually or by category and describe each of them.)

(Here state the time, place and manner of making the inspection and performance of any related acts.)

(3)   That defendant permit plaintiff to enter (here describe property to be entered) and to inspect and to photograph, test or sample (here describe the portion of the real property and the objects to be inspected.)

(Here state the time, place and manner of making the inspection and performance of any related acts.)

_____
Attorney for Plaintiff

Address _____

**Form 25.    Request for Admission Under Rule 36**

CAPTION OF CASE

REQUEST FOR ADMISSION
UNDER RULE 36

Plaintiff _____ requests defendant _____ within _____ days after service of this request to make the following admissions for the purpose of this action only and subject to all pertinent objections to admissibility which may be interposed at the trial:

    1.   That each of the following documents, exhibited with this request, is genuine.

(Here list the documents and describe each document.)

    2.   That each of the following statements is true.

(Here list the statements.)

_____

Attorney for Plaintiff

Address _____

**Form 26.    Allegation of Reason for Omitting Party**

When it is necessary, under Rule 19(c), for the pleader to set forth in his pleading the names of persons who ought to be made parties, but who are not so made, there should be an allegation such as the one set out below:

John Doe named in this complaint is not made a party to this action [because he is not subject to the jurisdiction of this court]; [because he cannot be made a party to this action without depriving this court of jurisdiction].

**Form 27.    Abrogated**

---

**Form 28.   Notice: Condemnation**

IN THE UNITED STATES DISTRICT COURT
FOR THE SOUTHERN DISTRICT OF NEW YORK

UNITED STATES OF AMERICA,

|  |  |  |
|---|---|---|
| Plaintiff, | ) | Civil Action, File No. _____ |
|  | ) |  |
| v. | ) | NOTICE |
|  | ) |  |
| 1,000 ACRES OF LAND IN (here | ) |  |
| insert a general location as | ) |  |
| "City of _____" or "County | ) |  |
| of _____", JOHN DOE, et | ) |  |
| al., and UNKNOWN OWNERS, | ) |  |
|  | ) |  |
| Defendants. | ) |  |
|  | ) |  |

TO: (Here insert the names of the defendants to whom the notice is directed):

You are hereby notified that a complaint in condemnation has heretofore been filed in the office of the clerk of the United States District Court for the Southern District of New York, in the United States Courthouse in New York City, New York, for the taking (here state the interest to be acquired, as "an estate in fee simple") for use (here state briefly the use, "as a site for a post-office building") of the following described property in which you have or claim an interest.

(Here insert brief description of the property in which the defendants to whom the notice is directed, have or claim an interest.)

The authority for the taking is (here state briefly, as "the Act of _____, _____ Stat. _____, U.S.C., Title _____, §_____").[7]

You are further notified that if you desire to present any objection or defense to the taking of your property you are required to serve your answer on the plaintiff's attorney at the address herein designated within 20 days after _____.[8]

Your answer shall identify the property in which you claim to have an interest, state the nature and extent of the interest you claim, and state all of your objections and defenses to the taking of your property. All defenses and objections not so presented are waived. And in case of your failure so to answer the complaint, judgment of condemnation of that part of the above-described property in which you have or claim an interest will be rendered.

*continued*

[7] And where appropriate add a citation to any applicable Executive Order.
[8] Here insert the words "personal service of this notice upon you," if personal service is to be made pursuant to subdivision (d)(3)(i) of this rule [Rule 71A]; or, insert the date of the last publication of notice, if service by publication is to be made pursuant to subdivision (d)(3)(ii) of this rule.

---

**Form 28.   Notice: Condemnation,** *continued*

But without answering, you may serve on the plaintiff's attorney a notice of appearance designating the property in which you claim to be interested. Thereafter you will receive notice of all proceedings affecting it. At the trial of the issue of just compensation, whether or not you have previously appeared or answered, you may present evidence as to the amount of the compensation to be paid for your property, and you may share in the distribution of the award.

_____

United States Attorney

Address _____

(Here state an address within the district where the United States Attorney may be served, as "United States Courthouse, New York, N. Y.")

---

**Form 29.   Complaint: Condemnation**

CAPTION OF CASE (set forth above)

COMPLAINT IN
CONDEMNATION

1.   This is an action of a civil nature brought by the United States of America for the taking of property under the power of eminent domain and for the ascertainment and award of just compensation to the owners and parties in interest.[9]

2.   The authority for the taking is (here state briefly, as "the Act of _____, _____ Stat. _____, U.S.C., Title _____, §_____").[10]

3.   The use for which the property is to be taken is (here state briefly the use, "as a site for a post-office building").

4.   The interest to be acquired in the property is (here state the interest as "an estate in fee simple").

5.   The property so to be taken is (here set forth a description of the property sufficient for its identification) or (described in Exhibit A hereto attached and made a part hereof).

6.   The persons known to the plaintiff to have or claim an interest in the property[11] are:

(Here set forth the names of such persons and the interest claimed.)[12]

*continued*

[9] If the plaintiff is not the United States, but is, for example, a corporation invoking the power of eminent domain delegated to it by the state, then this paragraph 1 of the complaint should be appropriately modified and should be preceded by a paragraph appropriately alleging federal jurisdiction for the action, such as diversity. See Form 2.

[10] And where appropriate add a citation to any applicable Executive Order.

[11] At the commencement of the action the plaintiff need name as defendants only the persons having or claiming an interest in the property whose names are then known, but prior to any hearing involving the compensation to be paid for a particular piece of property the plaintiff must add as defendants all persons having or claiming an interest in that property whose names can be ascertained by an appropriate search of the records and also those whose names have otherwise been learned. See Rule 71A(c)(2).

[12] The plaintiff should designate, as to each separate piece of property, the defendants who have been joined as owners thereof or of some interest therein. See Rule 71A(c)(2).

---

**Form 29.  Complaint: Condemnation,** *continued*

7.   In addition to the persons named, there are or may be others who have or may claim some interest in the property to be taken, whose names are unknown to the plaintiff and on diligent inquiry have not been ascertained. They are made parties to the action under the designation "Unknown Owners."

Wherefore the plaintiff demands judgment that the property be condemned and that just compensation for the taking be ascertained and awarded and for such other relief as may be lawful and proper.

_____

United States Attorney

Address _____

(Here state an address within the district where the United States Attorney may be served, as "United States Courthouse, New York, N. Y.")

---

**Form 30.   Suggestion of Death Upon the Record Under Rule 25(a)(1)**

CAPTION OF CASE

SUGGESTION OF DEATH
UPON THE RECORD UNDER
RULE 25(a)(1)

_____ [describe as a party, or as executor, administrator or other representative or successor of _____, the deceased party] suggests upon the record, pursuant to Rule 25(a)(1), the death of _____ [describe as party] during the pendency of this action.

---

**Form 31.   Judgment on Jury Verdict**

CAPTION OF CASE

JUDGMENT

This action came on for trial before the court and a jury, Honorable _____, District Judge, presiding, and the issues having been duly tried and the jury having rendered its verdict,

It is Ordered and Adjudged

[that the plaintiff _____ recover of the defendant _____ the sum of _____ dollars with interest thereon at the rate of ____ percent as provided by law, and his costs of action.]

[that the plaintiff take nothing, that the action be dismissed on the merits, and that the defendant _____ recover of the plaintiff _____ his costs of action.]

DATED at New York, New York, this _____ day of _____, 20____.

_____

Clerk of the Court

---

**Form 32.   Judgment on Decision by the Court**

CAPTION OF CASE

JUDGMENT

This action came on for [trial] [hearing] before the Court, Honorable _____, District Judge, presiding, and the issues having been duly [tried] [heard] and a decision having been duly rendered,

It is Ordered and Adjudged

[that plaintiff _____ recover of the defendant _____ the sum of _____ dollars, with interest thereon at the rate of _____ percent as provided by law, and his costs of action.]

[that the plaintiff take nothing, that the action be dismissed on the merits, and that the defendant _____ recover of the plaintiff _____ his costs of action.]

Dated at New York, New York this _____ day of _____, 20____.

_____<br>Clerk of the Court

---

**Form 33.   Notice of Availability of a Magistrate Judge to Exercise Jurisdiction**

[Caption and Names of Parties]

In accordance with the provisions of Title 28, U.S.C. §636(c), you are hereby notified that a United States magistrate judge of this district court is available to exercise the court's jurisdiction and to conduct any or all proceedings in this case including a jury or nonjury trial, and entry of a final judgment. Exercise of this jurisdiction by a magistrate judge is, however, permitted only if all parties voluntarily consent.

You may, without adverse substantive consequences, withhold your consent, but this will prevent the court's jurisdiction from being exercised by a magistrate judge. If any party withholds consent, the identity of the parties consenting or withholding consent will not be communicated to any magistrate judge or to the district judge to whom the case has been assigned.

An appeal from a judgment entered by a magistrate judge may be taken directly to the United States court of appeals for this judicial circuit in the same manner as an appeal from any other judgment of a district court.

Copies of the Form for the "Consent to Jurisdiction by a United States Magistrate Judge" are available from the clerk of the court.

---

**Form 34.   Consent to Exercise of Jurisdiction by a United States Magistrate Judge**

[Caption and Names of Parties]

CONSENT TO JURISDICTION BY A UNITED
STATES MAGISTRATE JUDGE

In accordance with the provisions of Title 28, U.S.C. §636(c), the undersigned party or parties to the above-captioned civil matter hereby voluntarily consent to have a United States magistrate judge conduct any and all further proceedings in the case, including trial, and order the entry of a final judgment.

_____

*Date/Signature*

Note: Return this form to the Clerk of the Court if you consent to jurisdiction by a magistrate judge. Do not send a copy of this form to any district judge or magistrate judge.

---

**Form 34A.   Order of Reference**

[Caption and Names of Parties]

ORDER OF REFERENCE

IT IS HEREBY ORDERED that the above-captioned matter be referred to United States Magistrate Judge _____ for all further proceedings and entry of judgment in accordance with Title 28, U.S.C. §636(c) and the consent of the parties.

_____

*U.S. District Judge*

---

### Form 35.    Report of Parties' Planning Meeting

[Caption and Names of Parties]

   1.    Pursuant to *Fed. R. Civ. P. 26(f)* , a meeting was held on _____ (date) _____ at
_____ (place) _____ and was attended by:

_____ (name) _____ for plaintiff(s)

_____ (name) _____ for defendant(s) _____ (party name) _____

_____ (name) _____ for defendant(s) _____ (party name) _____

   2.    **Pre-Discovery Disclosures.** The parties [have exchanged] [will exchange by
_____(date)_____] the information required by [*Fed. R. Civ. P. 26(a)(1)* ] [local rule _____].

   3.    **Discovery Plan.** The parties jointly propose to the court the following discovery plan: [Use
separate paragraphs or subparagraphs as necessary if parties disagree.]

Discovery will be needed on the following subjects: _____ (brief description of subjects on
which discovery will be needed) _____.

All discovery commenced in time to be completed by _____ (date) _____. [Discovery on
_____ (issue for early discovery) _____ to be completed by _____(date)_____.]

Maximum of _____ interrogatories by each party to any other party. [Responses due _____
days after service.]

Maximum of _____ requests for admission by each party to any other party. [Responses due
_____ days after service.]

Maximum of _____ depositions by plaintiff(s) and _____ by defendant(s).

Each deposition [other than of _____ ] limited to maximum of _____ hours unless extended
by agreement of parties.

Reports from retained experts under Rule *26(a)(2)* due: from plaintiff(s) by _____ (date) _____
from defendant(s) by _____ (date) _____.

Supplementations under *Rule 26(e)* due _____ (time(s) or interval(s))_____.

   4.    **Other Items.** [Use separate paragraphs or subparagraphs as necessary if parties disagree.]

      The parties [request] [do not request] a conference with the court before entry of the scheduling
order. The parties request a pretrial conference in _____(month and year)_____.

Plaintiff(s) should be allowed until _____(date)_____ to join additional parties and until
_____(date)_____ to amend the pleadings.

Defendant(s) should be allowed until _____(date)_____ to join additional parties and until
_____(date)_____ to amend the pleadings.

All potentially dispositive motions should be filed by _____(date)_____.

Settlement [is likely] [is unlikely] [cannot be evaluated prior to _____(date)_____] [may be
enhanced by use of the following alternative dispute resolution procedure: _____ ].

Final lists of witnesses and exhibits under Rule 26(a)(3) should be due from plaintiff(s) by
_____(date)_____ from defendant(s) by _____(date)_____.

Parties should have _____ days after service of final lists of witnesses and exhibits to list objections
under *Rule 26(a)(3)* .

The case should be ready for trial by _____(date)_____ [and at this time is expected to take
approximately _____(length of time)_____].

[Other matters.]

Date: _____

# GLOSSARY

**Abode service** Leaving a copy of a summons and complaint at the defendant's usual place of abode with a person of suitable age and discretion residing there.

**Actionable wrong** Established category of offenses for which lawsuits are allowed.

**Adjudicate** Resolve a dispute.

**Administrator** Person in charge of a probate estate.

**Admit** Allow in the court record and as part of the evidence to be considered by the jury.

**ADR** *See* alternative dispute resolution.

**Affiant** Person signing an affidavit.

**Affidavit** Sworn testimony that is written down and notarized.

**Affidavit of service** Affidavit serving as proof that service of court papers was completed (also called return of service).

**Affirm** Let a lower court's decision stand.

**Affirmative defense** Reasons offered by the defendant as to why the defendant cannot be found liable even if the plaintiff establishes every element of her cause of action.

**Agent** Person who has the legal authority to act for someone else.

**Allegations** Statements in pleading laying out the party's version of what caused the dispute.

**Alternative dispute resolution (ADR)** Means of resolving disputes that are used as alternatives to litigation including arbitration, mediation, med-arb, summary jury trial, and mini-trial.

**Annotation** Summary of case.

**Answer** Pleading in which defendant gives his side of the story.

**Appeal** Formal request in which a party asks a higher court to review the decision of a lower court and change it in some way.

**Appear** Submit formally to jurisdiction of the court.

**Appellant** Party filing an appeal.

**Appellate court** Court that decides appeals.

**Appellate jurisdiction** Power of court to hear appeals.

**Appellee** Party responding to an appeal.

**Arbitration** Informal hearing held before a neutral third party who renders a decision and issues an award.

**Arbitrator** Disinterested third party chosen by the parties or appointed by the court to render a decision.

**As a matter of law** The law requires.

**Attorney** Any person who acts formally for another person.

**Authorities** Statutes and reported appellate cases.

**Automatic stay** Order by the bankruptcy court ordering creditors to refrain from proceeding further with their suit against a debtor.

**Bill of costs** Itemization of expenses a party is seeking to be taxed.

**Binding** Final and nonappealable.

**Brief** Formal written argument citing reasons why the trial court decision was or was not in error.

**Burden of proof** A party's burden of proving each element of a cause of action or of a defense.

**Caption** Title block of caption, which includes names of parties, the name of the court, and the case number.

**Cause of action** Type of offense that is considered an actionable wrong.

**Certificate of service** Statement appearing at the end of a court paper reflecting the fact that the paper was mailed (or hand-delivered), recording the date of mailing, and listing the names and addresses of each recipient.

**Chambers** Judge's private office.

**Choice of forum** Process by which parties decide which court will hear the case.

**Circuit** A geographical region into which the U.S. Court of Appeals is divided.

**Citation** Information giving the name of a case as well as the name, volume number, and page number of the reporter in which it can be found.

**Cite** Specify where legal authority can be found.

**Civil action** *See* civil lawsuit.

**Civil lawsuit** Process by which a person who believes he has been wronged can ask a court to order his adversary to repair the wrong.

**Civil procedure** Law that deals with the rules for conducting cases.

**Claim**   Assertion of liability based on a single cause of action.

**Closing argument**   Final statements made by an attorney to jury or court that summarizes evidence.

**Complaint**   Formal, written statement describing what a dispute is about and what plaintiff wants court to do.

**Compulsory counterclaims**   Transactional claims defendant has.

**Concurrent jurisdiction**   Shared jurisdiction.

**Conditional delivery**   Check made out to the plaintiff by the insurance company that is not to be deposited until the plaintiff has signed the release and returned it in the mail to the insurance company.

**Counterclaim**   Lawsuit by the defendant against the plaintiff, which is raised in the defendant's answer.

**Counterclaimant**   Person asserting a counterclaim.

**Counterdefendant**   Plaintiff in a counterclaim.

**Court**   A place where judges work.

**Court papers**   Papers generated in a lawsuit that must be filed with the court or delivered to the opposing party.

**Court reporter**   Person who takes down in shorthand everything that is said.

**Court-annexed arbitration**   Arbitration that takes place within the court system and that is governed by the local rules.

**Cross-claim**   Claim made by one defendant against another defendant.

**Cross-claimant**   Person asserting a cross-claim.

**Cross-defendant**   Defendant against whom a cross-claim has been filed.

**Cross-examination**   Examination by an attorney of a witness called by the opposing party.

**Custodian of records**   Person responsible for the files and records of an entity.

**Damages**   Money determined by court as remedy in civil action.

**Deadline**   Last day on which a response can be filed.

**Decedent**   Person who has died.

**Default judgment**   Judgment entered in plaintiff's name when defendant fails to respond to a complaint in a timely manner.

**Defendant**   Party being sued.

**Demonstrative evidence**   Visual aids used to prove the facts of a case.

**Deponent**   One who is deposed.

**Deposing**   Taking a person's deposition.

**Deposition**   Discovery procedure in which a person is required to appear at a specified place and time to answer questions.

**Direct examination**   Examination by the attorney that called the witness.

**Disability**   Situations recognized by statute that prevent plaintiffs from being able to sue.

**Discharge in bankruptcy**   Order by bankruptcy court wiping out all of a debtor's debts.

**Disciplinary proceeding**   Proceeding instituted against an attorney accused of violating the rules of ethics.

**Disclosure statement**   Document each party is required to prepare and serve on opposing parties shortly after the lawsuit commences.

**Discoverable**   Any document or information that is not privileged and that is reasonably calculated to lead to admissible evidence.

**Discovery**   Process by which parties can obtain information pertinent to their dispute.

**Discovery cutoff date**   Date set by court order after which no further discovery is permitted.

**Discretionary**   Within the discretion (choice) of the person making the decision; not mandatory.

**Dismiss**   Declare invalid.

**District court**   Trial court in the federal system.

**Diversity of citizenship jurisdiction**   Jurisdiction of federal courts over cases between residents of different states.

**Docket**   Put on office calendar.

**Documentary evidence**   Written or recorded information used to establish the facts and presented as evidence.

**Domicile**   Any state in which a party is physically present with the intent to remain indefinitely.

**Elements**   Specific things you must prove in order to win a lawsuit.

**Entity**   Artificial "person" or organization, such as corporation, partnership, or limited liability company.

**Entry of judgment**   Point of time when a judgment is entered.

**Evidence**   Factual information about a dispute that is presented to the trier of the fact.

*Ex parte*   Speaking to the judge without the opposing attorney having an opportunity to participate.

**Examine**   Question a witness.

**Exclude**   Reject (as in the rejection of evidence).

**Execution**   Process of seizing the judgment debtor's property and applying it to pay a judgment.

**Executor**   Person in charge of a probate estate.

**Exempt property**   Asset the law does not allow to be seized to pay a judgment.

**Expert witness**   Witness hired by a party to give an opinion about a topic around which they have received specialized training or education.

**Failure to state a claim**  Law does not allow such a claim.

**Federal courts**  Courts deriving their power from the federal government, including district and circuit courts.

**Federal question jurisdiction**  Subject matter jurisdiction of federal courts allowing them to hear all civil actions arising under the Constitution, laws, or treaties of the U.S.

**Federal Rules of Civil Procedure**  Rules that apply to the federal government's treatment of civil cases; have been adopted and/or amended by many of the states.

**Filed**  Delivery of court papers to the court clerk.

**Filing**  Submission of written materials to the court for inclusion in the permanent record of the case.

**Findings of fact and conclusions of law**  Judge's findings of facts and law on which the judge's decision is based.

**Firm trial date**  Date that case will definitely go to trial barring some extraordinary event.

**Form of judgment**  Exact wording of a judgment.

**Forum**  Court in which a case is being heard.

**Forum non conveniens**  Grounds for dismissal based on the argument that the forum is not convenient for the defendant.

**Forum shopping**  Looking for a court that will lead to the most favorable results for the plaintiff.

**Forum state**  State in which the court hearing the case is located.

**Fraudulent conveyance**  Any transfer made by a judgment debtor that leaves her without the assets to pay a judgment.

**Garnishment**  Obtaining a court order requiring someone who owes money to the judgment debtor to pay it to the judgment creditor.

**General damages**  Losses that would naturally be expected to occur in every case based on the same theory of liability.

**General subject matter jurisdiction**  Power to hear and decide all types of cases with certain exceptions.

**General verdict**  Finding by jury for either plaintiff or defendant.

**General verdict with written interrogatories**  General verdict accompanied by answers to specific factual questions on which the verdict depends.

**Grantor**  Person designated in a trust to transfer property to another person.

**Hearing**  Proceeding at which the judge listens to oral arguments by both parties and asks questions.

**Hold harmless**  Pay for someone else's losses; indemnify.

**Hostile witness**  Uncooperative witness.

**Hung jury**  Jury unable to reach a verdict.

**Impeach**  To discredit.

**Implied authority**  Authority of an agent to act for the principal.

**Indemnify**  Pay for someone else's losses; hold harmless.

**Independent medical examination**  Examination of a party whose medical condition is at issue by a doctor of the requesting party's choice.

**Indispensable party**  Party without whom a just result cannot be achieved.

**Injunction**  Court order to refrain from doing something.

**Interlocutory appeal**  Appeal taken before a case is over and judgment is entered.

**Interrogatories**  Written questions directed to an opposing party.

**Issue of fact**  Question relating to what happened resulting in dispute between litigants.

**Issue of law**  Question relating to what the law requires.

**Joinder**  Joinder of issue occurs when all the pleadings have been filed.

**Judge**  Person who runs a courtroom, makes all legal decisions, and can sometimes decide entire cases.

**Judge pro tem**  Experienced attorney who volunteers to act as a judge in a particular case.

**Judgment**  Court paper specifying what the plaintiff is awarded.

**Judgment**  Formal decision.

**Judgment creditor**  Party to whom money is awarded.

**Judgment debtor**  Party ordered to pay the money awarded the judgment creditor.

**Judgment debtor's examination**  Questioning of the judgment debtor about its assets.

**Judgment lien**  Lien that arises out of recording a judgment.

**Judgment proof**  Person or entity without assets that can be collected by a judgment creditor.

**Jurisdiction**  Power to adjudicate a particular kind of dispute.

**Jurisdiction of the person**  Power of the court to render a decision that will be binding on that party.

**Jurisdiction of the subject matter**  Power to hear and decide cases of a given type.

**Jurisdictional amount**  Amount in controversy in a federal case.

**Jury instructions** Rules of substantive law a jury must apply in rendering its decision.

**Leading question** Question that tells the witness the answer the attorney wants to hear.

**Lien** Security interest giving the lienholder the right to sell property to pay off a debt.

**Limitations period** Time during which a suit must be filed.

**Limited subject matter jurisdiction** Power to hear only certain categories of cases.

**Litigant** Party to a lawsuit.

**Litigate** Conduct or defend a lawsuit.

**Litigator** Attorney who specializes in handling lawsuits.

**Lodge** Prepare and deliver a court paper.

**Long-arm statute** Statutes that authorize suits against non-residents in certain situations.

**Mandate** Order telling the trial court what to do next.

**Mandatory arbitration** Arbitration that is required of parties before they can have a conventional trial.

**Mandatory disclosure rules** Rules that require a party to turn over information to the opposing party without being asked to do so.

**Med-arb** Mediation followed by an arbitration using the same neutral third party if the mediation fails to resolve the conflict.

**Mediation** Problem-solving process involving a neutral third party who facilitates the parties in reaching a resolution but who lacks authority to render a decision.

**Mediator** Disinterested third party who assists the parties in negotiating a compromise.

**Memorandum of points and authorities** Memorandum accompanying a motion; gives the detailed reasons of why the judge should do as the moving party is requesting.

**Merits** Whether acts and events alleged in plaintiff's complaint are legally sufficient to entitle plaintiff to win a judgment and whether plaintiff has sufficient evidence to prove those acts and events.

**Minimum contacts** Contacts a non-resident must have with a state before the court in that state can assert jurisdiction under its long-arm statutes in accord with constitutional due process requirements.

**Mini-trial** Settlement process in which the parties present their case to a neutral third party who issues an advisory opinion, which the parties use to negotiate a settlement.

**Minute entry** Formal written communication of a judge's decision.

**Motion** Formal request by the parties asking the court to resolve an issue of law about which the parties disagree.

**Motion for a directed verdict** Motion to direct verdict in favor of the party making the motion.

**Motion for a judgment notwithstanding the verdict** Motion to set aside the jury's verdict and enter a verdict in favor of the party filing the motion.

**Motion for a more definitive statement** Request that plaintiff be required to be more specific in the complaint.

**Motion for a new trial** Motion requesting a new trial due to an alleged error made by the judge during the trial.

**Motion for a pretrial conference** Request that the judge intervene to facilitate the "just, speedy, and inexpensive disposition of the action."

**Motion for leave to amend** Request to revise a complaint to correct a defect.

**Motion for protective order** Request that the judge rule that the opposing party's discovery request is improper and need not be complied with.

**Motion for sanctions** Request that the opposing party be punished for refusing to disclose after a motion to compel has been granted and the opposing party has been ordered to disclose.

**Motion for summary judgment** Request for judgment in favor of the moving party on the grounds that no genuine issue of material fact exists.

**Motion *in limine*** Motion requesting that a judge rule in advance on the admissibility of evidence.

**Motion papers** Motions, responses, replies, and the accompanying memoranda.

**Motion practice** Process by which the parties ask the judge to resolve questions of law.

**Motion to compel discovery** Request that the judge order the responding party to produce information that has been requested during discovery.

**Motion to dismiss** Request to invalidate a claim because there is something wrong with it.

**Motion to set and certificate of readiness** Motion that informs the court of how many trial days are needed, whether a jury is needed, and any other information the court clerk needs to schedule a trial.

**Motion to strike** Request to eliminate an insufficient defense.

**Movant** Moving party; party making a motion.

**Moving party** Party making a motion.

**Narrative report** Report prepared by a treating physician, summarizing the nature of the injuries, the treatment rendered, the cost of treatment, the prognosis, and the doctor's opinions regarding any important medical issues.

**Natural person**   Live human being.

**Neutral**   Neutral third party.

**Neutral expert fact finding**   Resolution process in which the parties present their case to a neutral third party with expertise in the matter at hand who makes recommendations to the parties.

**Nonbinding**   Appealable.

**Notice of appeal**   Court paper indicating that the filing party is appealing.

**Notice of deposition**   Document notifying other parties that a deposition has been scheduled.

**Notice of Independent Medical Examination**   Notice that the requesting party wants to conduct an examination of a party whose medical condition is at issue by a doctor of the requesting party's choice.

**Notice of motion**   Written filing of a motion.

**Notice of service**   A court paper indicating that the document in question was served.

**Noticing a deposition**   Process of scheduling a deposition and preparing and serving the appropriate paperwork.

**Offer**   Communication which, if accepted, creates an enforceable contract.

**Ombudsman**   Employee of an organization or institution who hears complaints and disputes and recommends how they might be resolved.

**Opening brief**   Appellant's brief stating the reasons why the appellate court should reverse the trial court's decision.

**Opening statements**   Opening speech by attorneys to jury in which they tell their client's version of the facts.

**Oral argument**   Verbal presentation by an attorney.

**Order**   Written decision either granting or denying a motion.

**Original jurisdiction**   Power of court to try a case.

**Overrule**   Appellate court's decision not to follow rules laid down in a previous decision.

**Parties**   People who are suing or being sued.

**Pendent jurisdiction**   Jurisdiction of federal courts over state law causes of action that are appended to a valid federal cause of action.

**Peremptory challenge**   Limited number of challenges attorneys can use to remove prospective jurors from a panel; no cause is needed.

**Personal representative**   Person in charge of a probate estate.

**Personal service**   Hand delivery of summons and complaint to defendant.

**Plaintiff**   Party bringing suit.

**Pleadings**   Formal process in lawsuit by which parties are compelled to specify in writing what the dispute is about; includes complaint, answer, and reply.

**Political subdivision**   City or county.

**Poll the jury**   Public questioning of the jury by the judge to make sure each juror agreed to the verdict.

**Praecipe**   Formal request for a court clerk to take some action.

**Prayer for relief**   Concluding section of complaint stating specifically what plaintiff wants court to do.

**Preponderance of the evidence**   Plaintiff's obligation to prove that each element of a cause of action more probably than not occurred.

**Pretrial order**   Court paper that specifies what attorneys can and cannot present at trial.

**Pretrial statement**   *See* pretrial order.

**Prevailing party**   Party who has won a lawsuit.

*Prima facie*   Credible evidence presented to support each element of a cause of action.

**Primary authority**   Source of law, such as a statute or case law.

**Principal**   Person for whom an agent is acting.

**Private arbitration**   Arbitration arising out of a contractual agreement.

**Private judging**   Resolution process in which the parties agree to have a neutral third party, usually a retired judge, hear and decide their case.

**Probable verdict range**   Maximum and minimum amounts a jury is likely to award if it decides in favor of the plaintiff.

**Probate estate**   Artificial entity created by the law to receive and dispose of the assets of the deceased.

**Procedural law**   Law of remedies.

**Process server**   Someone whose job is to locate parties and witnesses and serve court papers on them.

**Professional courtesy**   Customs governing the asking and granting of extensions and other favors between opposing attorneys.

**Propounding**   Preparing interrogatories and submitting them to the opposing party to be answered.

**Propounding party**   Party who prepares interrogatories or some other discovery document.

**Rebuttal**   Plaintiff's response to defendant's presentation.

**Record release form**   Form signed by a client authorizing records to be released to an attorney.

**Redirect examination**   Reexamination of a witness by the attorney who called him after the witness has been subjected to cross-examination.

**Release** Agreement in which a plaintiff relinquishes her claims against the defendant.

**Remittitur** Reduction of an unreasonably excessive award.

**Removal** Moving of a case from one court to another.

**Reply** Court paper prepared by the moving party in rebuttal to the response prepared by the party opposing the motion.

**Reply brief** Brief in which the appellant answers any questions raised in the appellee's responding brief.

**Request for admissions** Request that a party admit or deny specific factual statements.

**Request for entry upon land for inspection** Request to enter a location that is under another person's control for reasons of inspection.

**Request for production of documents and things** Court paper requesting documents from an opposing party.

**Res judicata** Prohibition against relitigating any issues around which a court has entered judgment.

**Respondent** Responding party; party opposing a motion.

**Responding brief** Appellee's brief stating the reasons why the appellate court should not reverse the trial court's decision.

**Responding party** Party required to answer interrogatories or some other discovery request.

**Response** Court paper prepared by the party opposing a motion.

**Rests** Party is finished presenting evidence.

**Return of service** Affidavit serving as proof that service of court papers was completed (also called affidavit of service).

**Reverse** Set aside a trial court's decision.

**Reversible error** Error that justifies an appellate court setting aside or modifying a trial court's decision.

**Scheduling conference** Conference involving the parties and the judge at which the judge issues a scheduling order, specifying what discovery will be allowed, what motions will be filed, and the deadlines for the completion of each task.

**Scope** Subject matter covered during examination.

**Secondary authority** Legal reference used to find primary authority, such as a treatise or Restatement.

**Service** Delivery of court papers via a formal process.

**Settle** Agreement to end a dispute.

**Sever** Split off a claim for a separate decision.

**Sovereign immunity** Immunity of government from suit.

**Special damages** Particular losses suffered by a plaintiff.

**Special verdict** Written findings prepared by jury on particular issues of fact.

**Specific performance** Court order requiring party to do something the party contracted to do.

**State a claim** Assert liability.

**State courts** Courts deriving their power from the states.

**Statement** Record of what a witness has said about the facts in dispute.

**Statement of costs** Winner's statement filed with the court listing the costs involved in litigating.

**Status conference** Conferences scheduled every few months at which the parties and judge discuss the status of the case.

**Statute of limitations** Statute that requires suit to be filed on a particular type of claim within a specified time after the claim occurs.

**Stay** Court order preventing the judgment creditor from collecting on the judgment for a period of time.

**Stipulate** To mutually agree so as to avoid the need for argument.

**Stipulation** Agreement between attorneys.

**Subpoena** Court order requiring a witness to appear at a specified time and place to give testimony.

**Subpoena duces tecum** Subpoena ordering a witness to provide specified documents.

**Substantive law** Law that relates to the regulation of human conduct.

**Summary jury trial** An abbreviated trial in which the parties present evidence in a summary fashion to a jury, allowing the attorneys to receive an evaluation of their case.

**Summons** Court order requiring the defendant to appear before the court and defend the suit.

**Supersedes bond** Bond posted by a judgment debtor in order to obtain a stay; this bond is a promise to pay the award once the appeal is decided and is usually accompanied by some form of security.

**Taxable costs** Those expenses related to a suit for which the winner is entitled to judgment.

**Taxation of costs** Process of establishing the amount for which a party is entitled to be reimbursed.

**Testify** Give evidence under oath.

**Testimonial evidence** Oral presentation of evidence used to establish the facts.

**Testimony** Responses by witnesses to questions put to them while they are on the witness stand.

**Theory of liability** Rationale offered by the plaintiff for why the court should hold the defendant liable.

**Third-party claim** Claim by the defendant against someone the plaintiff has not sued.

**Third-party complaint** Complaint brought by defendant in a lawsuit against someone not in the lawsuit.

**Time-barred** Cause of action can no longer be sued on because limitations period has run out.

**Transactional** When plaintiff's cause of action against defendant and defendant's cause of action against plaintiff both arise from the same factual setting.

**Transcript** Printed or typewritten booklet containing every word that was said at a deposition or trial.

**Transformative mediation** Form of mediation that is nondirective whose primary purpose is to allow the parties to speak until they have nothing left to say.

**Trial court** Court of general jurisdiction in which lawsuits generally begin.

**Trial *de novo*** New trial.

**Trial notebook** Loose-leaf binder used to organize papers that a trial attorney may need to access quickly during a trial.

**Trial setting** Minute entry specifying the date, time, and place for trial.

**Trial to the court** Trial in which a judge functions as both judge and jury.

**Tribunal** Court or any other adjudicative officer.

**Trier of fact** One who renders a verdict (judge or jury).

**Trustee** Person designated in a trust to whom property is transferred.

**Trustor** Person designated in a trust to transfer property to another person (trustee).

**Under advisement** Judge's decision to issue a decision about a matter before her at a later date.

**Venue** Rules requiring suit to be brought in place least inconvenient for parties and witnesses.

**Verdict** Formal written decision indicating how dispute was resolved.

***Voir dire*** Questioning of potential jurors.

**Voluntary arbitration** Arbitration used by the parties by choice.

**Waive** Voluntarily and knowingly give up a right.

**Witness statement** Written or electronically recorded reproduction of a witness's version of the facts.

**Writ of execution** Court order directing a law enforcement official to seize specific property and sell it at public auction.

# INDEX